www.wadsworth.com

www.wadsworth.com is the World Wide Web site for Thomson Wadsworth and is your direct source to dozens of online resources.

At *www.wadsworth.com* you can find out about supplements, demonstration software, and student resources. You can also send email to many of our authors and preview new publications and exciting new technologies.

www.wadsworth.com
Changing the way the world learns®

Law and the
Administrative Process

Law and the Administrative Process

JOHN M. SCHEB
Judge, Florida Court of Appeal, 2nd District (Ret.)
Distinguished Professorial Lecturer, Stetson University College of Law

JOHN M. SCHEB II
Professor of Political Science
University of Tennessee

THOMSON
WADSWORTH

Australia • Canada • Mexico • Singapore • Spain
United Kingdom • United States

THOMSON

™

WADSWORTH

Publisher: *Clark Baxter*
Executive Editor: *David Tatom*
Development Editor: *Drake Bush*
Assistant Editor: *Rebecca Green*
Editorial Assistant: *Reena Thomas*
Technology Project Manager: *Michelle Vardeman*
Marketing Manager: *Janise Fry*
Marketing Assistant: *Mary Ho*
Advertising Project Manager: *Kelley McAllister*

Project Manager, Editorial Production: *Jennifer Klos*
Print Buyer: *Doreen Suruki*
Permissions Editor: *Kiely Sexton*
Production Service: *Shepherd, Inc.*
Copy Editor: *Jean Ives*
Cover Designer: *Sue Hart*
Cover Image: *Digital Vision/Getty Images*
Text and Cover Printer: *Quebecor World/Kingsport*
Compositor: *Shepherd, Inc.*

Printed in United States of America
1 2 3 4 5 6 7 08 07 06 05 04

For more information about our products, contact us at:
Thomson Learning Academic Resource Center
1-800-423-0563
For permission to use material from this text or product, submit a request online at
http://www.thomsonrights.com
Any additional questions about permissions can be submitted by email to
thomsonrights@thomson.com.

Library of Congress Control Number: 2004103668

ISBN 0-534-17708-5

Thomson Wadsworth
10 Davis Drive
Belmont, CA 94002-3098
USA

Asia
Thomson Learning
5 Shenton Way #01-01
UIC Building
Singapore 068808

Australia/New Zealand
Thomson Learning
102 Dodds Street
Southbank, Victoria 3006
Australia

Canada
Nelson
1120 Birchmount Road
Toronto, Ontario M1K 5G4
Canada

Europe/Middle East/Africa
Thomson Learning
High Holborn House
50/51 Bedford Row
London WC1R 4LR
United Kingdom

Latin America
Thomson Learning
Seneca, 53
Colonia Polanco
11560 Mexico D.F.
Mexico

Spain/Portugal
Paraninfo
Calle/Magallanes, 25
28015 Madrid, Spain

This book is dedicated, with love to
Mary Burns Scheb and Sherilyn Claytor Scheb

Table of Contents

4 THE STATUTORY FRAMEWORK OF THE ADMINISTRATIVE PROCESS   116

5 INVESTIGATION AND ENFORCEMENT 164

7 ADJUDICATION   255

11 GOVERNMENTAL LIABILITY   437

Preface

We are pleased to present to students and instructors in political science, public administration, and legal studies this new textbook on administrative law. The text examines the essentials of administrative law, which include rulemaking, adjudication, and judicial review of agency action. Yet it goes beyond standard treatments of the subject by devoting considerable attention to the development of the administrative state, the constitutional foundations and statutory framework of the administrative process, agency investigation and enforcement, political control of the bureaucracy, the rights of public employees, and governmental liability. The final chapter discusses significant contemporary trends likely to affect the future of administrative law, including the rise of electronic government, the emergence of the neoadministrative state, and the increasing globalization of both politics and economic activity. We believe that a background in these areas will broaden the horizon of those seeking careers in industry and government.

Perhaps the most significant difference between this book and most competing texts is that it ventures beyond the federal context. Although our primary focus is on federal institutions, agencies, statutes, and decisions, every chapter contains significant coverage of the state and local aspects of administrative law. We hope that the inclusion of material on state and local administrative law will be useful to students who may be interested in careers in state or local government.

PEDAGOGICAL FEATURES

- To enhance student comprehension, each chapter contains a **chapter outline** delineating the major topics covered. To help students navigate through the chapters, we also make extensive use of subheadings.

- **Key terms** are identified in boldface type throughout each chapter and listed at the end of the chapter.

- Chapters 3-11 include boxes labeled **Case in Point**. These concise summaries of state and federal judicial decisions illustrate key concepts and serve as the basis for thought and discussion.

- Throughout the book shaded boxes labeled **Supreme Court Perspective** provide brief excerpts from important Supreme Court decisions pertaining to specific issues of administrative law and procedure.

- A number of boxed inserts furnish relevant information without disrupting the flow of the text.

- **Questions for Thought and Discussion** to test understanding and stimulate classroom discussion are included at the end of each chapter.

- For the student or instructor who wishes to delve more deeply into the decisional law we have included more than forty **Edited Cases**, which contain leading judicial opinions on significant issues in administrative law. Throughout the book are pointers indicating where one or more of these cases are relevant to the material.

- Appendices include the **United States Constitution**, the federal **Administrative Procedure Act,** which is the single most important statute ever enacted by Congress in the field of administrative law.

- For students and instructors who wish to venture into the realm of legal research, we offer an appendix covering **Basic Legal Research**.

- A **glossary** includes definitions of all key terms identified in the chapters as well as other law and political terminology relevant to the administrative process.

ACKNOWLEDGMENTS

We wish to express our appreciation to these four scholars, who reviewed the first draft of this manuscript and offered many valuable corrections, criticisms, and suggestions: Marcus E. Ethridge, University of Wisconsin—Milwaukee; Albert C. Price, University of Michigan—Flint; Stefanie A. Lindquist, University of Georgia; and Christopher P. Banks, University of Akron.

We appreciate the counsel of Philip H. Des Marais, a retired federal official and academician, who offered valuable suggestions on the chapter on political control of the bureaucracy. We also acknowledge the assistance of Sally G. Waters,

Esq., research librarian at Stetson University College of Law, St. Petersburg, Florida, who reviewed our appendix on legal research and added up-to-date information on computerized legal research and use of the Internet. Professors Martin Carcieri, Michael Fitzgerald, David Folz, and William Lyons of the University of Tennessee Political Science Department read various parts of the manuscript and made a number of valuable comments and suggestions, for which we are most grateful.

We also wish to thank Judy Ludowitz, project editor at Shepherd, Inc., and the team at Thomson Wadsworth—in particular, David Tatom, executive editor, Drake Bush, developmental editor, Jennifer Klos, production project manager, and Reena Thomas, editorial assistant—for their guidance and support throughout this project.

Finally, we thank our wives, Mary Burns Scheb and Sherilyn Claytor Scheb, for their patience and support, without which the project could not have been completed. This book is dedicated to them.

We have endeavored to make *Law and the Administrative Process* the most complete and up-to-date textbook in the administrative law field. Statutes, court rules, and agency regulations are frequently revised. Moreover, their application depends on specific factual situations, so the reader should regard our references as illustrative. Of course, this text is not intended to be a substitute for independent legal research or competent legal advice.

We welcome comments and suggestions from our readers so that a future edition may be improved. We assume responsibility for any errors that might be contained herein.

John M. Scheb

John M. Scheb II
May 31, 2004

Law and the
Administrative Process

1

Administrative Law in American Government

"... [A]dministrative law deals with the field of legal control exercised by law-administering agencies other than courts, and the field of control exercised by courts over such agencies."

FELIX FRANKFURTER
THE TASK OF ADMINISTRATIVE LAW, 75 U. PA. L. REV. 614 (1927).

INTRODUCTION

When terrorists struck the United States on September 11, 2001, Americans immediately looked to government to respond. Local, state, and federal agencies swung into action and officials from all levels of government were highly visible directing emergency response activities and communicating with an alarmed public. The immediate response to the crisis and the subsequent war on terrorism involved a host of government agencies responsible for such matters as national security, military intelligence, law enforcement, public transportation, civil defense, emergency management, airline safety, immigration, public health, and social welfare. Some of these agencies, such as the FBI, were already well known to the average American. Others were less well known. But before too long the American people had become much better acquainted with federal agencies like the Federal Emergency Management Agency (FEMA), the Federal Aviation Administration (FAA), and the National Transportation Safety Board (NTSB). These agencies, and hundreds more, are part of the **modern administrative state,** a conglomeration of agencies designed to meet the demands that modern American society makes on its government.[1] In Chapter 2, we discuss in some detail the evolution of the administrative state from the founding of the Republic to the present day.

What Is Administrative Law?

Administrative law is the body of law that governs the activities of the modern administrative state. Administrative law includes the **statutes** enacted by Congress and the state legislatures that establish, empower, and restrict agency actions. It includes the **executive orders** issued by presidents and governors that direct agencies to undertake certain activities or conduct their activities in certain ways. Administrative law also includes the myriad rules, regulations, and orders issued by agencies themselves under powers delegated to them by legislatures. Finally, and most importantly,

administrative law encompasses the decisions of the federal and state courts interpreting these statutes, orders, and rules as well as the relevant principles of the federal and state constitutions. Administrative law is thus a branch of **public law,** which is the body of law that deals with government. Accordingly, administrative law is closely related to **constitutional law,** which consists of judicial interpretations of the federal and state constitutions. Administrative law overlaps with constitutional law to the extent that courts rely on constitutional provisions in reviewing the actions of public agencies and the laws by which legislatures delegate power to agencies.

Why Is Administrative Law Important? As a constitutional republic, the United States is founded on the idea of the **rule of law.** The law accords administrative agencies considerable deference to enable them to accomplish their economic and social purposes. Although we all understand that government officials must have a reasonable degree of **discretion** in performing their duties, we are equally aware that power corrupts and that discretion is prone to abuse. Thus we demand that officials and agencies will operate within parameters established by law and that when they violate legal constraints, legal sanctions will be imposed on them. We expect that government agencies will demonstrate **procedural regularity** in making decisions, which means that lawfully established procedures are followed in good faith. We also expect that the substance of these policies and rulings will be fair, reasonable, and just. As citizens in a democracy, we believe that the people have a right to know what their government is up to, and so we demand that decisions are made in a way that is transparent and that information collected by the bureaucracy is accessible to the public. Finally, as residents of the information age, we understand the threats posed to our privacy when agencies collect data about our activities. Administrative law strives to make governmental bureaucracy conform to the rule of law and in so doing protect the values of freedom, equality, privacy, and democracy.

INSTITUTIONAL FOUNDATIONS OF ADMINISTRATIVE LAW

The first concept that one must understand in trying to comprehend administrative law or any branch of American law is **separation of powers,** which is the division of governmental functions among separate legislative, executive, and judicial branches. Legislatures are established to make laws; executive branches enforce those laws and administer government programs, and courts are responsible for resolving controversies about the meaning of the laws. The second basic concept is **federalism,** which is the division of authority and responsibility between the national government and each of the fifty states. Within our federal system, there are fifty-one distinctive sets of governmental machinery—fifty-one executive branches of government, fifty-one legislatures, and fifty-one court systems. Of course, the institutional boundaries between branches and levels of government are somewhat blurry and have changed considerably over the history of the Republic. The principles of administrative law are fashioned by legislation enacted by the United States Congress and the state legislatures, by decisions of the federal and state courts, and, to a lesser extent, by executive orders issued by presidents, governors, and mayors.

The Executive Branches

As government has taken on more and more responsibility for solving social and economic problems, it has found it necessary to create agencies to administer programs and promulgate and enforce regulations. These agencies are located within the executive branches of federal, state, and local governments. The president of the United States and the governors of the fifty states, in exercise of their constitutional responsibilities, are responsible for administering the respective executive branches.

Although we often refer to the sum total of these agencies as the "bureaucracy," a basic distinction can be made between **administrative agencies** and **regulatory agencies.**[2] Administrative agencies carry out government programs such as highway construction, education, or the delivery of social services. At the federal level, the Social Security Administration is a good example. Its function is not to regulate, but to administer this country's social insurance program for the elderly, widowed, and disabled. At the state and local levels, one finds agencies devoted to highway construction, education, public housing, social welfare, public health, and various other functions.

Regulatory agencies promulgate and enforce rules pursuant to authority delegated to them by Congress and state legislatures. For example, at the federal level, the Nuclear Regulatory Commission (NRC), the Federal Aviation Administration (FAA), and the Securities and Exchange Commission (SEC) are just a few of the many agencies created by Congress to regulate particular industries. States also have regulatory agencies that deal with everything from alcoholic beverages to the licensing of physicians. At the state level, agencies have long regulated professional and occupation licensing, adjudicated the need to issue bank charters, alcoholic beverage licenses, and insurance company licenses, and have regulated public utilities. In recent years the determination of eligibility for certificates of need for health-care facilities and environmental and natural resource permits have assumed an increasing role in state administrative proceedings.

While we normally associate the modern administrative state with the federal government in Washington, D.C., it is important to realize that government at all levels is highly bureaucratized. State and local governments have their own bureaucracies. To some extent, these bureaucracies exist to perform functions traditionally assigned to the states. To a very great extent today, state and local agencies work with federal agencies under the banner of **cooperative federalism.** Partnerships involving federal, state, and local agencies are now commonplace in law enforcement, welfare programs, and environmental regulation, to name but a few policy areas. A familiar example of cooperative federalism is the Medicaid program that provides medical care to the poor. An important element of President Lyndon Johnson's Great Society program, Medicaid was adopted by Congress in 1965. The program relies primarily on federal funding and is supervised by an agency located within the executive branch of the federal government. But it is actually administered by agencies within each of the fifty states. Citizens seeking Medicaid benefits thus deal with state employees who staff these agencies. States are free, within certain parameters, to adopt variations on the program. In recent years, some states have sought to extend their Medicaid programs to cover citizens who are above the poverty level but who are unable to obtain health insurance through the private sector.

The Legislative Branches

Legislative branches of the government are empowered to enact statutes—the laws that apply generally throughout the state or nation. In our republican form of government, bureaucratic agencies derive their authority principally from statutes enacted by legislatures. Federal agencies are created and empowered by Congress, which is the national legislature. State agencies are created and empowered by the legislatures of their respective states.

When an agency is vested with regulatory authority, the legislature has, in effect, delegated a measure of its lawmaking power to that agency. Of course, the legislature can rescind or modify this delegation of power at any time and retains other means of controlling agencies that operate in ways contrary to the prevailing views of legislators.

Congress The United States Congress is comprised of the 435 elected members of the House of Representatives and the one hundred elected members of the U.S. Senate. In addition to being the nation's lawmaking body, Congress exercises **oversight** of the administration of laws by the executive branch and its administrative and regulatory agencies. This function is extremely important in the modern era, as Congress has delegated a considerable degree of its lawmaking power to these agencies within the executive branch.

The process by which Congress makes law is highly complex. Bills introduced in either the House or the Senate must pass through a complicated maze of committees, subcommittees, and legislative calendars before they reach the floor of one chamber. Most bills never make it to the floor. If a bill passes on the floor, it must begin a similar process in the other house. Then differences between the House and Senate versions of the bill must be ironed out. Finally, the bill must pass the scrutiny of the president, who must either accept or veto the bill in its entirety. If the president exercises the veto, a two-thirds majority of each house of Congress is required to override that veto.

Once a bill has become a federal law, it is published in **United States Statutes at Large**, an annual publication in which federal statutes are arranged in order of their adoption. New statutes are then merged into legal codes that systematically arrange the statutes by subject. To find federal law as it currently stands, arranged by subject matter, one must consult the latest edition of the **United States Code**, which is broken down into fifty subjects, called "titles." It is indexed by subject matter and by statutes' popular names, making it relatively easy to find what the *United States Code* currently has to say on a given matter. Students can access the *United States Code* on the Web.[3] Throughout this text, we refer to the annotated version of the U.S. Code, published by the West Group and cited as U.S.C.A. Thus, for example, "28 U.S.C.A. § 1331" refers to Section 1331 of Title 28 of the **United States Code Annotated (U.S.C.A.).**

State Legislatures Under the United States Constitution, each state must have a democratically elected legislature because that is the most fundamental element of a "republican form of government." Like Congress, each of the state legislatures considers proposed legislation, enacts a budget, and exercises important oversight responsibilities. State legislatures for the most part resemble the United States Congress, each being composed of representatives chosen by the voters of their respective states. All states have bicameral (i.e., two-house) legislatures, except Nebraska, which has a unicameral legislature.

The processes by which the state legislatures consider and adopt legislation are similar to the procedures followed by Congress, though each state legislature is free to adopt its own procedural rules, and no two state legislatures operate in exactly the same way. Like the president of the United States, most state governors have the power to veto legislation, but in some states, legislatures can override vetoes with simple majorities.

After the American Revolution most states enacted reception statutes adopting the English common law, as it existed at the time of the Declaration of Independence, as their own state law. (Congress, on the other hand, never did.) Eventually, however, state legislatures codified much of the common law by enacting statutes, which in turn have been developed into comprehensive state codes. Periodically, states revise portions of their codes to make sure they retain relevance to a constantly changing society. Once state legislative enactments become law, they are published in volumes known as **session laws.** Periodically, the statutes are integrated into official state codes. Annotated versions of all fifty state codes, which include court interpretations and other editorial features, are available in law libraries. Unannotated versions of most state codes are now available on the Internet.

The Judicial Branches

The national government and each of the fifty states maintains its own system of courts, which play a pivotal role in administrative law. Courts interpret the constitutional provisions, statutes, ordinances, regulations, executive orders, treaties, and principles of common law that bear on the outcome of these cases. They also exercise the power of **judicial review**—the power to review the legal and factual determinations of administrative agencies and lower courts. The term judicial review also refers to the power of courts to determine the constitutionality of all governmental enactments and actions in administrative law cases.

Law evolves not only through the legislative process, but also through judicial interpretation in the context of particular cases. These cases arise in both federal and state courts. Although there is significant variance among the federal and state judicial systems, each is based on a constitution, which represents the fundamental and supreme law within the system, and each has many common features.

Every judicial system includes both **trial courts** and **appellate courts.** Trial courts conduct civil and criminal trials and various types of hearings; they make factual determinations, award judgments, and impose sanctions and punishments. In some instances trial courts hear lawsuits challenging actions of administrative agencies, although usually disputes with agencies are heard first by **administrative tribunals** within the agencies themselves. Whether a case originates in a court of law or in an administrative tribunal, a final judgment of that court or tribunal is usually subject to review by an appellate court. Appellate courts are designed primarily to correct errors committed by trial courts and administrative tribunals.

In reviewing cases, appellate courts interpret the federal and state constitutions and statutes and develop and harmonize the law, sometimes "filling in gaps" in the statutory and decisional law. Where a legislative body has left a gap with respect to an issue and there is no controlling judicial precedent, an appellate court must determine whether an administrative body has made a reasonable judgment in its interpretation and application of a statute. As the U.S. Supreme Court has noted: "The court need not conclude that the agency's construction was the only one it permissibly could have adopted to uphold the

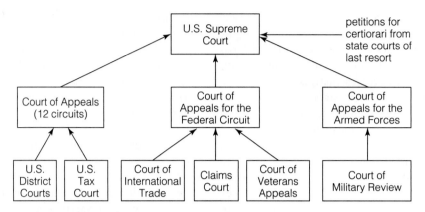

FIGURE 1.1 The Federal Court System

construction, or even the reading the court would have reached if the question initially had arisen in a judicial proceeding."[4]

Appellate courts are collegial courts, in that decisions are made by panels of judges who justify their interpretation of the law by producing written opinions. The process is designed to maximize rationality and minimize subjectivity while providing direction to lower courts and administrative agencies. In performing judicial review of administrative agency decisions, federal and state courts determine the meaning of legislation and can even invalidate statutes when the legislature has crossed constitutional boundaries, a particularly important aspect of administrative law.

Federal courts exercise judicial review over federal agencies, while state courts review actions of state and local administrative and regulatory agencies. In exercise of their jurisdiction they can issue **injunctions** and **restraining orders** to prevent an injury from taking place or continuing. Courts also have power to issue various orders, writs and decrees to effectuate their judgments.

The Federal Court System Article III of the United States Constitution provides that "[t]he judicial Power of the United States, shall be vested in one supreme Court, and in such inferior Courts as the Congress may from time to time ordain and establish." Beginning with the landmark Judiciary Act of 1789, Congress has used this authority to create, empower and regulate the federal court system (see Figure 1.1). Congress determines the structure of the federal judiciary, establishes the number of federal judges, determines the jurisdiction of the lower federal courts, and provides for the funding of the federal judiciary. Article III prescribes jurisdiction of the Supreme Court, although Congress may regulate to some extent the Supreme Court's authority to hear appeals.[5] Under this authority Congress has created a system of trial courts, known as District Courts, and intermediate courts, known as the United States Courts of Appeals, that handle appeals from district courts as well as from administrative agencies. In addition Congress, under authority of Article I of the Constitution, has created certain specialized courts. These include the Tax Court, which resolves disputes between taxpayers and the Internal Revenue Service, the Court of Veterans Appeals, which reviews administrative decisions involving veterans' claims for benefits, and the Claims Court, which adjudicates tort claims (civil suits for damages) against the United States.

The **United States District Courts** are the major trial courts in the federal system.[6] These courts conduct trials and hearings in civil and criminal cases arising under federal law and in certain civil cases arising under state law but where the parties reside in different states. Because the national government has exclusive

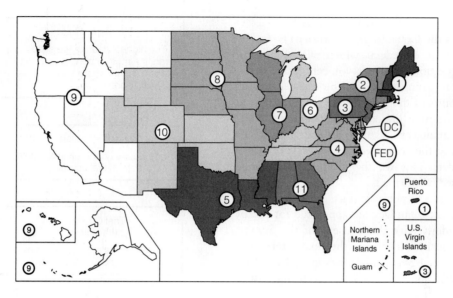

FIGURE 1.2 The Thirteen Federal Judicial Circuits

jurisdiction over bankruptcies, each of the federal district courts operates its own bankruptcy court.

There are currently ninety-four federal judicial districts, with each state being allocated at least one.[7] Some states have more districts, depending on population and geographical size. Normally only one judge presides at hearings and trials, although federal law permits certain exceptional cases to be decided by panels of three judges.[8]

The **United States Courts of Appeals** (also known as circuit courts) are the **intermediate appellate courts** in the federal system, although because of the limited jurisdiction of the Supreme Court these courts become final arbiters of most disputes in the federal system, an aspect of great importance in the field of administrative law. The nation is divided into twelve circuits, with each circuit comprising one or more federal judicial districts (see Figure 1.2.) There is also a "federal circuit" that is authorized to grant appeals from decisions of specialized federal courts. The circuit courts hear appeals from the federal districts within their circuits. The Court of Appeals for the District of Columbia Circuit, based in Washington, has the very important additional function of

hearing appeals from numerous administrative tribunals in the federal bureaucracy.

Generally, appeals in the circuit courts are decided by rotating panels of three judges that vote to affirm, reverse, or modify the lower court decisions under review. There is a procedure designed to resolve conflicts in decisions among the panels of judges who sit on the court by which the circuit courts provide **en banc hearings.** In an en banc hearing, all of the judges assigned to the court participate in a decision.[9]

The United States Supreme Court The highest appellate court in the federal judicial system is the **United States Supreme Court.** Because of the unique federal system in America, the Supreme Court sits at the apex of the nation's judicial system. The Supreme Court's **appellate jurisdiction** extends to all federal cases "with such Exceptions, and under such Regulations as the Congress shall make."[10] Today, the Court's appellate jurisdiction is exercised almost exclusively through the **writ of certiorari.** "Certiorari" is a Latin term meaning, "to be made certain." In American law, it refers an appellate court order to a lower court directing it to send up for review the record in a particular case. Federal law authorizes the Court to grant certiorari to review all cases, state or federal, which raise substantial federal questions. Petitions for certiorari usually come from losing parties in the thirteen federal circuit courts or the highest state courts. If at least four of the nine justices of the Supreme Court vote to "grant cert," as they say, the entire court will review the record of the lower court decision to determine whether that decision should be reversed or affirmed.

The nine Supreme Court justices, like district and circuit judges, are appointed for life by the president with the consent of the Senate. These nine individuals are the final interpreters of the United States Constitution and the final arbiter in respect to the law governing federal administrative agencies.

State Court Systems

Each of the fifty states has its own independent court system, responsible for cases arising under the state constitution, statutes enacted by the state legislature, orders issued by the governor, regulations promulgated by various state agencies, and local ordinances. State judicial systems are characterized by variations in structure, jurisdiction, and procedure but have certain commonalties. Every state has one or more levels of trial courts and at least one appellate court (see Figure 1.3). An increasingly significant area of state court jurisdiction involves review of decisions handed down by state and local administrative agencies.

Most states have **courts of general jurisdiction,** which conduct trials in major civil and criminal cases and **courts of limited jurisdiction,** which handle trials in cases involving less serious matters. In some states the courts of general jurisdiction review decisions by local administrative agencies that adjudicate licensing and zoning disputes.

Each state has a **court of last resort,** usually called the **state supreme court** (known as the Court of Appeals in New York and Maryland),

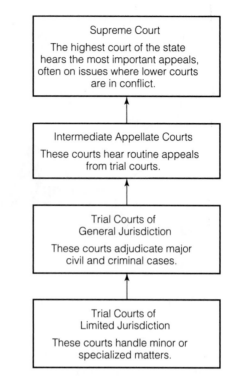

FIGURE 1.3 A Model State Court System

which speaks with finality on matters of state law.[11] The state supreme court has final jurisdiction on matters of state law in civil and criminal cases and generally supervises administration of the state court system.

Forty-four states now have some form of intermediate appellate courts that relieve the state supreme court from hearing routine appeals. This allows the state supreme court to focus on the most important cases and the resolution of conflicting decisions by these intermediate appellate courts. The jurisdictional characteristics of these intermediate appellate courts vary considerably.

Unlike the federal system, states select their judges in a variety of ways. Most state judges are elected. Some judges run for office on partisan ballots (as Republicans or Democrats) while others run in nonpartisan races. Many state judges are appointed by governors, either directly or through a nominating process known as merit selection. Even appointed judges typically must face the voters eventually in a contested election or a merit retention election in which voters are asked whether a judge should be given another term.

BUREAUCRACY, LAW, AND POLITICS

The legal framework for administrative law is defined by constitutional provisions, legislation, executive orders, and judicial decisions. But to really understand the theory, practical applications, and political role of administrative law, one must begin with the idea of **bureaucracy,** which is a fundamental concept in contemporary political science. The term "bureaucracy" was coined in the early nineteenth century. The word "bureau" is French, meaning literally a "writing desk." In English, the term "bureau" came to mean an "office for the transaction of business."[12] Literally, the term "bureaucracy" means "government by office." As the term is used in political science today, it refers to an organization established by government to perform administrative and/or regulatory functions.

Although the term "bureaucracy" is of relatively recent coinage, the concept of bureaucracy was not unknown to ancient civilizations. China and Egypt are good examples of ancient civilizations that were highly bureaucratized. Yet, along with democracy, bureaucracy is one of the leading characteristics of modern government. Governments around the world, both democratic and authoritarian, rely on bureaucracies to perform the everyday tasks of government: administration of programs, development and enforcement of regulations, and delivery of services. As will become evident in Chapter 2, the concept of bureaucracy in the United States took on new meaning in the era of the New Deal in the 1930s as a response to the Great Depression. Since that time much of the

lawmaking that affects the everyday life of Americans has become **administrative rulemaking,** a concept that requires an increased emphasis on accountability of government. Today, many of the rules affecting business and industry emanate not from Congress or state legislatures, but from agencies established by legislatures and invested with **quasi-legislative powers** to make and enforce rules governing particular activities. Likewise, many of the disputes that citizens and corporations become embroiled in as they cope with these rules are not decided by courts of law but by agencies invested with **quasi-judicial powers.** Bureaucracy in the United States, as in most advanced countries, has become pervasive and powerful. No citizen, business, profession, occupation, or industry is beyond its reach.

The Ideal-Type Bureaucracy

Max Weber, the eminent German sociologist, argued that bureaucracy is an essential part of modern life because it is the most rational way for society to achieve collective goals. Weber identified the characteristics of the "ideal type" bureaucracy as follows:

- Hierarchy—a chain of command from top to bottom.

- Division of labor—task specialization within the organization.

- Meritocracy—workers are recruited and retained on the basis of demonstrable competence, not family ties, personal favoritism, or political patronage.

- Rules-based decision making—decisions of the bureaucracy are based on the impersonal application of neutral rules. Personal, familial, social, economic, and political considerations are not supposed to influence decisions.

Figure 1.4 displays the organizational chart for the U.S. Department of Labor (DOL), which is one of fifteen major departments of the executive branch of the national government. The organiza-

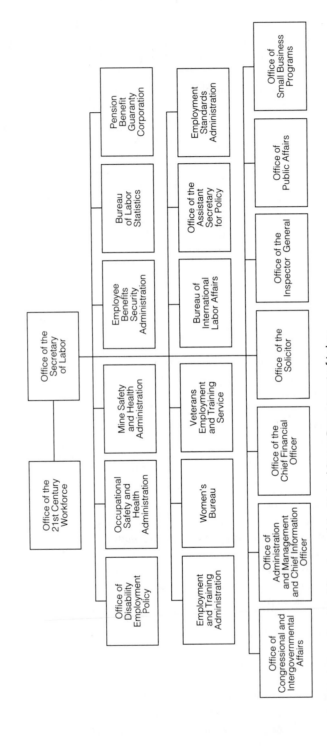

FIGURE 1.4 Organizational Structure of the United States Department of Labor

Source: U.S. Department of Labor, online at http://www.dol.gov/dol/aboutdol/orgchart.htm

tional chart nicely illustrates the bureaucratic characteristic of division of labor. Note that there are nineteen different offices, bureaus and administrations within DOL, each of which specializes in some aspect of DOL's broad mission of promoting "the welfare of the job seekers, wage earners, and retirees of the United States."[13]

Bureaucracy in the Real World

Anyone who has ever dealt with bureaucracies, and this includes almost everyone, knows that they do not always conform to the Weberian ideal. In American political culture, bureaucracy is often associated with delay, inefficiency, and mindless procedure. Americans routinely complain about "red tape"[14] and often suspect government agencies of waste, fraud, and abuse. In many cases, these complaints and suspicions are justified. Business people often complain about the burdens of complying with government regulations and record-keeping requirements. Anyone who has ever attempted to operate a small business in this country is well aware of the difficulties (not to mention costs) associated with compliance with myriad laws and regulations.

Perhaps one of the most dramatic displays of bureaucratic ineffectiveness occurred six months after the terrorist attacks of September 11, 2001. In March 2002, the Immigration and Naturalization Service (INS) issued student visas to two of the men who had crashed the planes into the World Trade Center. Voicing his anger when he heard the news report, President George W. Bush described the event as "a wake-up call for those who run the INS." A spokesman for the INS admitted that the agency's system for tracking foreign students was "antiquated, outdated, inaccurate and untimely."

Although citizens demand the many services furnished through the bureaucracy, the American public is impatient with the "red tape" that citizens often encounter in attempting to navigate through bureaucratic channels. Many regard governmental agencies as inefficient. They see bureaucratic agencies as being captivated by special interests and heavily influenced by lobbyists who wield too

Table 1.1 Public Attitudes toward the Federal Bureaucracy

"Overall, who do you think works harder—people in federal government jobs, or people in similar jobs outside the government?"

Government workers	9%
Nongovernment workers	80%
No difference	7%
Not sure	4%

"How about the number of people employed by the federal government: In general, do you think the federal government employs too many people or too few people to do the work that must be done?"

Too many	75%
About the right number	5%
Too few	11%
Too many in some areas, not enough in others	6%
Not sure	2%

"Do you believe that federal employees are paid more, less, or about the same as people in similar jobs outside the government?"

Paid more	58%
Paid less	17%
Paid about the same	19%
Not sure	5%

SOURCE: National telephone survey of 603 adults, conducted January 15–16, 1994, by the Social Science Research Institute at the University of Tennessee, Knoxville. The margin of error is +/− four percentage points at the 95 percent confidence level.

much control over the administrative processes of government.

Table 1.1 provides a glimpse of public opinion with respect to the federal bureaucracy. It shows that Americans tend to see federal workers as overpaid and underworked and federal agencies as being overstaffed. Such attitudes are not merely a function of recent events or circumstances; they are deeply rooted in American political culture. Given the depth and prevalence of such attitudes, it is not surprising that politicians often seek to exploit resentment of the federal bureaucracy. Voters often respond favorably to candidates who campaign on promises to rein in the bureaucracy.

Most people would agree that bureaucracy is inevitable in the administration of the American government. We the people simply expect more from government than can be performed by legislatures, courts, and small executive offices. As demands on government grow, government itself grows, not as an undifferentiated mass, but as a conglomeration of highly specialized agencies. From the time of the Great Depression (1930s) through the 1970s, the emphasis of leaders in both the legislative and executive arenas was on the creation of new government agencies and programs to meet the rising demands on government. Since that time, the focus has shifted to improving the effectiveness and efficiency of the administrative state while demanding agency accountability and protection of the rights of citizens, corporations, and public employees.

Political Perspectives on Bureaucracy

Bureaucracy has long been the subject of political conflict in America. In the early days of the Republic, the followers of Thomas Jefferson argued for limited government and opposed efforts of the Federalists to expand the powers, functions, and machinery of the national government. In the late nineteenth and early twentieth centuries, populists and progressives supported the creation of new government agencies to check the unbridled power of corporations, while more conservative forces argued for adherence to the ideal of laissez-faire capitalism. In the modern era, Democrats have by and large supported the growth of the administrative state to achieve important goals such as social welfare, consumer protection, civil rights, and environmental quality. Republicans have often (but not always) opposed such efforts, which they see as creating undesirable burdens on taxpayers and the business community.

The issue of the proper role of government is generally seen as a defining difference between classical and modern liberalism. The classical liberalism of the eighteenth and nineteenth centuries advocated limited government and individual self-reliance. Modern liberalism evolved as a reaction to the excesses of the Industrial Revolution. Thinkers such as John Dewey and Herbert Croly led the way in reformulating liberalism to conceive of the state in more positive terms—an antidote to the excesses of unregulated capitalism. Contemporary liberals tend to be sanguine about the role of government in improving society through regulation, provision of services, and redistribution of wealth. Contemporary conservatives are much more skeptical about the ability of government to improve society. They tend to agree with President Ronald Reagan that "government is not the solution to our problem; government is the problem."[15] However, it should be noted that conservatives tend to be supportive of big government when it is used to promote the national security and traditional moral values, and enforce public order. But they are much less likely to support government efforts to expand civil rights, provide social services, protect the environment, or engage in what they consider to be social engineering.

Libertarians (who are the contemporary manifestation of classical liberalism) tend to be the most consistent (and insistent) in calling for a diminution of the role of government, lowering taxes, easing regulations, and allowing individuals and corporations to function with a minimum of legal control. Like their classical liberal forebears, libertarians believe that social progress is best achieved by unleashing the potential of the individual and by allowing maximum freedom in social relations and in the marketplace. Libertarians may be few in number, but their message has deep resonance within American political culture.

These differing ideological orientations toward government are important in shaping administrative law. Liberal actors, whether they are legislators, judges, chief executives, media pundits, or interest group leaders, try to shape administrative law so as to empower government agencies to pursue liberal notions of social justice and progress. Conservative actors, on the other hand, see administrative law as a means of limiting the reach of bureaucracy. Many, though certainly not all, controversies in administrative law can be boiled down to competing liberal and conservative perspectives.

Academic Perspectives on the Administrative State

The scholarship in the administrative law field, both in the legal academy and in political science, often reflects the ideological divisions of the larger society. That does not mean that every scholar or academic perspective can be neatly classified as liberal or conservative. Scholarly commentary tends to be more sophisticated than political discourse and often the ideological orientation of the commentator may be subtle or muted. But there is clearly a liberal strain of administrative law scholarship that seeks to justify the modern administrative state and typically supports agency claims to legal authority. At the same time, liberal commentators often support public employees, students, environmental groups, welfare recipients, and others who might be regarded as underdogs in disputes with agencies. Conservative scholarship, on the other hand, tends to be very critical of the administrative state and generally argues in favor of stricter interpretation of legal controls on bureaucratic action. Conservative commentators will often take up the cause of parties who find themselves in disputes with agencies, especially when those parties are corporations, property owners, or taxpayers.

In examining the literature in the field of administrative law, one encounters several persistent themes. One theme is "bureaucracy and democracy." Given that public administrators are unelected, how can the administrative state be reconciled with democratic theory? Scholars who are motivated by this concern typically are interested in various mechanisms by which elected officials exercise control over the bureaucracy as well as mechanisms by which citizens can participate in bureaucratic decision making or at least have access to information about same.

Another basic theme is "bureaucracy and constitutionalism." Here the concern is over the extent to which the modern administrative state can be reconciled with constitutional principles such as separation of powers, checks and balances, federalism, and limited government. A related theme is that of constitutional adaptation—the extent to which these principles must change to adapt American constitutionalism to modern social and economic conditions. Does limited government mean the same thing today as it did in 1791? Does it make sense to view the fifty states as sovereign entities when they are components of a political system dominated by the national government? Is the principle of separation of powers a static one or does it evolve to allow branches of government to adopt procedures not contemplated by the founders? Are traditional constitutional powers and procedures sufficient to accommodate and control the administrative state or must there be an evolving system of checks and balances based on trial and error? Which is more compelling—the need to maintain formal constitutional procedures and traditional doctrines or the need to adapt constitutional forms and theories to contemporary realities?

A more contemporary theme in the literature is that of "bureaucracy and pluralism." The concern here is whether and how agencies respond to the constellation of stakeholder groups that surrounds every significant agency action. We can place under this same heading the difficult question of whether, in responding to the demands of particular interests, agencies are inhibited from promoting the larger public interest, assuming such a thing exists.

The preceding themes help to make sense of a rich and dynamic body of scholarship that helps to shape the evolution of American law. Courts in particular pay close attention to legal scholarship in addressing problems of administrative law they are called upon to solve.

ADMINISTRATIVE LAW: A ROADMAP

In succeeding chapters we discuss the constitutional and statutory underpinnings of administrative law, the processes of administrative decision making, and judicial review of administrative action. In addition we examine issues concerning political control of bureaucracy, the rights of public employees, and the liability of public agencies.

Constitutional Foundations

The United States Constitution and the original state constitutions were adopted at a time when relatively little was expected from government. People expected the national government to protect the nation from invasion and rebellion, provide a mechanism for the settlement of interstate disputes (the federal courts), enforce standards of weights and measures, provide a medium of exchange (money), enforce some simple rules of commerce, operate a system for the delivery of mail, and build a few highways and canals. The state and local governments were expected to maintain public peace and order, provide for the settlement of most legal disputes, and dispense justice to those guilty of crimes. Very little was expected of any level of government with respect to education or welfare. Most businesses operated with little or no regulation. The prevailing ethos was laissez-faire. The primary constitutional value was **limited government.**

Obviously, American government has changed dramatically over the last two centuries. Government is now involved in education, public welfare, research and development, agriculture, management of natural resources, environmental protection, regulation of business and industry, public utilities, transportation systems . . . the list goes on and on. People today expect government to solve problems, which government typically attempts to do by creating a new program or regulation along with the bureaucracy to administer

or enforce it. Yet the modern administrative state must operate according to the requirements and limitations of the federal and state constitutions. When it fails to do so, parties that are adversely affected may challenge agencies in court. If a court finds that an agency has acted unconstitutionally, it will declare that agency action null and void. In cases challenging agency actions, courts will often review the constitutionality of legislation from which agencies derive their powers.

In Chapter 3, we examine the constitutional foundations of, and limitations on, the modern administrative state.

Statutory Framework

Agencies must operate within the parameters of authority delineated by legislation. If an agency acts outside its statutory authority or in a manner contrary to a relevant statutory provision, a court may declare the agency action **ultra vires,** that is, "beyond its authority." For example, the federal Food and Drug Administration derives its authority from the Food, Drug and Cosmetics Act, enacted by Congress in 1938 and amended several times since then, as well as various other federal statutes. In 2000, the U.S. Supreme Court held that the FDA exceeded its statutory authority when it established regulations governing the sale of tobacco products.[16] In striking the regulations, the Court sought to ensure that a bureaucratic entity was operating within the boundaries established by the legislature.

In addition to enacting enabling legislation focusing on particular agencies, Congress and the state legislatures have enacted broad statutes that affect the administrative process generally. Most significant among these are the federal **Administrative Procedure Act (APA)** and its state counterparts. Adopted in 1946, the APA has been called the Magna Carta of the administrative state. It functions almost like a constitution in providing the broad outline of procedures that federal agencies must follow in establishing and enforcing regulation. The counterpart state-level

APAs perform the same function with respect to state agencies.

Another significant component of the statutory framework within which many agencies operate is the **Freedom of Information Act (FOIA),** which provides a right of public access to many types of records created by executive agencies. The purpose of the act is to prevent the bureaucracy from shrouding itself in a cloak of secrecy, which is something that agencies, left to their own devices, are prone to do. States have similar statutes, generally known as **open records laws.** In Chapter 4 we examine these and other important elements of the statutory framework in which administrative agencies operate.

Investigation and Enforcement

Agencies have the authority to conduct investigations within the purview of their regulatory authority. To facilitate investigations, agencies possess powers to compel the attendance of witnesses and production of documents. They also are empowered to conduct audits, inspections, searches, and seizures. Agencies are also authorized to impose sanctions on parties that violate agency regulations or statutes that agencies are empowered to enforce. Administrative enforcement mechanisms include revocation of licenses, issuance of cease and desist orders, civil litigation, referring cases for criminal prosecution, imposing liens, levies, and garnishments, and seizing assets. Of course, the powers of investigation and enforcement possessed by any particular agency must be exercised within both statutory and constitutional constraints. We examine the investigatory and enforcement powers of agencies in Chapter 5.

Rulemaking and Adjudication

Rulemaking occurs when agencies promulgate regulations affecting matters within their jurisdiction. **Adjudication** takes place when agencies settle disputes or determine the rights of parties that have dealings with agencies. When agencies engage in rulemaking, they are acting in a quasi-legislative fashion. Adjudication is a quasi-judicial process in which **administrative law judges (ALJs),** legally trained agency officials whose function is solely the adjudication of cases, play a prominent role. Absent specific constitutional language governing these agency functions, legislatures have provided statutory guidance. The APA and its state-level counterparts outline basic requirements for agency rulemaking and adjudication. (Excerpts from the federal APA are reprinted in the Appendix B.) We examine agency rulemaking in Chapter 6; adjudication is addressed in Chapter 7.

Political Control of the Bureaucracy

In a democracy, where power is presumed to flow from the people to their government, and not vice versa, bureaucracy must be subject to control by elected officials. While maintaining effective control over a massive bureaucracy is a constant challenge to presidents, governors, and legislators, these officials have at their disposal a number of mechanisms by which they can curtail the bureaucracy. Legislatures can always enact new legislation or amend existing laws affecting agency powers and procedures. Legislatures oversee the day-to-day activities of the bureaucracy through a variety of informal means. When necessary, legislative committees conduct formal investigations in which agency officials are required to appear and answer questions or produce documents. And legislatures possess the power of the purse. Agencies depend for their funding on the budgets enacted by Congress and the state assemblies. Therefore officials must be ever mindful of how their agencies' activities are perceived by the politicians who inhabit the legislative branches of government.

Presidents and governors also play an important role in the budgetary process, in that they develop the budget proposals to which legislatures respond. This allows the executive to maintain considerable control over the bureaucracy. Moreover, presidents and governors possess the power to appoint agency officials and, to a lesser degree, to remove them from office. Finally, chief executives can, pursuant to their statutory or constitutional powers, issue **executive orders** that impose responsibilities or limitations on executive agencies.

We examine political controls on the bureaucracy in Chapter 8.

Judicial Review of Agency Actions

Judicial review is the process whereby courts exercise control over agencies. Of course, courts do not initiate judicial review of agency actions. Rather, they resolve cases in which litigants challenge agency powers, rules, orders, etc. To get access to judicial review, litigants must overcome a number of barriers. Among other things, they must possess standing to sue, they must have exhausted their nonjudicial remedies, and they must file their cases in courts of appropriate jurisdiction. In addressing litigation involving agencies, courts will review particular agency actions in light of agency rules and procedures as well as the relevant statutory and constitutional provisions. Judicial review of agency actions is the subject of Chapter 9.

The Rights of Public Employees

Historically, public employees at all levels of government served at the pleasure of chief executives. Under the so-called **spoils system,** mayors, governors, and presidents had virtually total discretion in hiring and firing government employees. A new era in the federal bureaucracy began in 1883 when Congress enacted **civil service** laws and regulations, which established a merit system of employment, promotion, and discharge of public employees. In the twentieth century state and local governments followed suit. Today, most rank and file agency personnel at all levels of government are considered civil service employees, which is to say that they obtain their positions and advance within their agencies based on merit and are protected from

interference by politicians. Civil service laws also limit the political activities of employees, which sometimes raises First Amendment concerns. In the federal government and most states, once a civil service employee has completed a short probationary period, he or she may be terminated only for adequate cause. Civil service employees are entitled to procedural due process protections when subjected to termination or disciplinary actions. These protections, as well as other rights retained by public employees, are the subject of Chapter 10.

Liability of Public Agencies

Agencies and their personnel often commit acts that subject them to civil liability. The historic doctrine of **sovereign immunity** inherited from the English common law protects government agencies from civil liability, although Congress and many state legislatures have enacted laws waiving sovereign immunity with respect to particular types of claims. For example, the **Federal Tort Claims Act** exposes the United States government to limited liability for certain tort claims in the same manner as a private individual. Even where sovereign immunity has not been waived, agency personnel can be found personally liable for torts and other unlawful acts. Frequently suits are filed under provisions of federal or state civil rights statutes. Some of the most common types of civil suits involving government agencies or personnel allege wrongful termination of public employees, unfair hiring practices, or other types of discrimination, use of excessive force by police officers, and the failure to warn or protect parties from harm where agencies have a duty to do so. Chapter 11 examines civil suits against public agencies.

The Goals of Administrative Law

Officials responsible for public administration, including presidents, governors, mayors, and the people they appoint to run agencies, are constantly thinking about ways to make public agencies more efficient and effective. However, it must be understood at the outset that **administrative efficiency** and effectiveness are not the highest goals of administrative law. Rather, administrative law seeks to render bureaucracy compatible with democratic and constitutional values. Administrative law, while not at war with efficiency and effectiveness, is more concerned about the legal authority of agencies and the rights of those affected by agency actions. Administrative law seeks to make bureaucracy conform to the classical liberal ideal of the rule of law, which embodies notions of procedural regularity, limited government, and **individual rights.** It also fosters the democratic values of **accountability, openness,** and **participation.** Administrative law seeks to make bureaucracy responsive to the range of interest groups that are affected by bureaucratic action. Finally, administrative law seeks to enhance the quality of administrative decision making by promoting **rationality** and reliance on evidence. At the same time, administrative law assumes that agencies must be vested with a certain degree of discretion. Together these values—procedural regularity, limited government, individual rights, accountability, openness, participation, responsiveness, and rationality—form the outline of administrative law. Of course, the rich content within that outline is formed daily by the myriad actions of legislatures, courts, executive officials, agencies, interest groups, corporations, and private citizens. In Chapter 12, the final chapter of the book, we assess the extent to which administrative law succeeds in meeting these goals. We also mention some proposed reforms and speculate as to the challenges that administrative law will face in the future.

THE IMPACT ON HUMAN LIVES

Most textbooks on administrative law (and this one is no exception) focus primarily on issues and problems arising in the context of regulatory policies promulgated by federal agencies like the Occupational Safety and Health Administration, the Environmental Protection Agency, or the Securities and Exchange Commission. It is important to understand, however, that administrative law is not confined to federal regulatory issues. Administrative law comes into play, at least potentially, in every encounter between a citizen or company and an agency or official of government. Administrative law applies to the licensure of businesses we patronize, the zoning decisions that affect our neighborhoods, and the provision of social services that many of us depend on. The following are a few hypothetical examples of how administrative law can affect the lives of everyday people, sometimes in profound fashion.

- **Challenging a Parking Ticket.** Jenny Driver, a new resident of Metropolis, has received a parking ticket even though she was legally parked in a meter space and put the proper amount of money in the parking meter. Believing that the meter was defective and showed "violation" before her allotted time had expired, Jenny has chosen to challenge the parking ticket. Jenny has learned that she has the right to a hearing before an administrative officer with the Metropolis Parking Authority. She has to request the hearing in writing. The request must be postmarked no later than ten days after the date the ticket was issued. Failure to meet this deadline will result in the imposition of a penalty, even if the ticket is overturned. At her hearing, Jenny has the right to be represented by an attorney or other representative. She has the right to present evidence, including her own testimony, the testimony of witnesses, and any relevant physical evidence. If the hearing officer refuses to dismiss the ticket, Jenny has the right to file a timely appeal with the Metropolis Board of Administrative Appeals.

- **Dismissal from a University for Academic Dishonesty.** Steve Scholastic, a senior at Summit State University, has been accused of academic dishonesty by a professor who claims that he caught Steve cheating on his midterm examination. The professor has entered a failing grade for the course, which will prevent Steve from graduating this semester. The professor has also reported the violation to the university's Office of Student Conduct. Unless the charge is removed, Steve will be dismissed from the university and his permanent record will reflect that he was dismissed for academic dishonesty. Because his aspirations of attending medical school are now in jeopardy, Steve has chosen to retain an attorney and defend himself against the charge. After reviewing the university's student handbook and making inquiries of the university administration, the attorney advises Steve that a hearing will be conducted before a board of review consisting of two faculty members, two students, and one administrator. Steve will appear before the board, along with the professor who has made the allegation, as well as two fellow students Steve has requested to appear as witnesses. If the board finds that there is insufficient evidence to sustain the charge, the charge will be dismissed and Steve will be given the option of being reinstated in the class or receiving a grade of "withdraw passing." If the board sustains the charge of dishonesty, Steve may appeal the decision to the vice-chancellor for academic affairs. Within the university, his ultimate recourse lies with the board of trustees who oversee the institution. Convinced that he is being treated unjustly, Steve is determined to see the process through to the end, even if it means filing a lawsuit.

- **Violation of a Building Code.** Dave and Lisa Homebody decided to add on to their home. Without investigating local building regulations, Dave and Lisa hired a contractor who constructed a new bedroom wing without first obtaining a building permit. A local building inspector, prompted by a tip from a neighbor, has come to Dave and Lisa's house and informed them that the new addition is not "up to code" and must be removed. Hav-

ing spent $10,000 they obtained through a second mortgage on their home, Dave and Lisa are extremely upset and have decided to retain counsel to advise them as to what administrative and legal recourse may be available to them. Dave has also joined the Libertarian Party and begun a personal crusade against "unnecessary and unjust regulation of private property."

- **Fighting Neighborhood Blight.** Amanda Activo has just purchased an old, rundown house located in a blighted neighborhood in Brownfield. Amanda, a twenty-five-year-old single mother who works in a nearby paper mill, was able to purchase the home for a very low price and she is working hard to fix up the place and develop some "sweat equity." But she is understandably concerned about the neighborhood in which her property is located. There are many abandoned houses, some of which are frequented by homeless persons looking for shelter. Some are reputed to be "crack houses." Others are quite obviously firetraps and pose hazards to other nearby structures. Having learned about the new ordinance that permits the city of Brownfield to more easily condemn and demolish abandoned structures, Amanda has filed complaints with the Brownfield Urban Renewal Authority seeking to have the city demolish the many abandoned houses on her street. However, owners of several homes slated for demolition have gone to court challenging the constitutionality of the city ordinance. Amanda is now anxiously awaiting the outcome of this litigation.

- **Saving the Beaches.** Save Our Beaches (SOB), an interest group composed largely of outdoor enthusiasts and environmental activists, has successfully lobbied the city of Idyllia to enact an ordinance establishing strict controls over commercial and residential development along the city's famous beaches. Pursuant to the ordinance, the city has established the Beachfront Protection Commission and delegated to that body the authority to deny any building permit "that would substantially impair the public's access to or enjoyment of the public beaches of Idyllia." The agency has interpreted its mandate broadly and has denied almost all applications for building permits for properties along the beaches. Now a group of beachfront property owners, backed by the local chamber of commerce, has brought suit to challenge the legality of the commission's actions and is also lobbying the city council to repeal the ordinance and abolish the commission. SOB has assembled its own team of lawyers to support the city's position in the litigation and has hired a political consulting firm to assist in lobbying the city to retain the ordinance.

■ **Access to Health Care.** Jeremy is fifty-five years old and works for a small business. He has just learned that he has a rare, life-threatening medical condition for which there are no widely accepted medical treatments, only experimental treatments of questionable efficacy. In an effort to cut costs and improve profitability, Jeremy's company has dropped its group health insurance plan. Jeremy is above the federal poverty level, so he does not meet the federal eligibility requirements for the Medicaid program. However, Jeremy's state has just created a new program extending Medicaid benefits to uninsured persons who make less than $35,000 per year. Jeremy would seem to qualify for the coverage, but his attempt to obtain state coverage to pay for his experimental medical treatments has failed. The agency that administers the program has determined that its own criteria, and the statu-

tory language on which they are based, do not authorize the agency to cover experimental medical procedures. Jeremy is without legal representation, is becoming increasingly ill, and may soon have to quit his job. He is desperately seeking information and assistance that will help him convince the state agency to pay for treatments that he sees as his only chance. Jeremy is essentially fighting for his life.

CONCLUSION

As government in contemporary society has become more pervasive, every citizen has had or will have contact with an administrative agency. In modern America bureaucratic agencies have become the dominant force in carrying out administrative and regulatory functions at federal, state, and local levels of government. In their wide-ranging activities, nonelected administrators often exercise executive, quasi-legislative, and quasi-judicial powers. This suggests the importance of administrative law as that branch of public law that preserves the constitutional rights of citizens as it facilitates oversight of the procedures agencies employ in carrying out the responsibilities delegated by Congress, the president, and state and local executive authorities and legislative bodies. By becoming aware of the legal framework of administrative law and contrasting the ideal versus the reality of the bureaucracy in American life, the reader is poised to embark on an examination of the functions of administrative tribunals and the courts and their role in law and the administrative process.

KEY TERMS

accountability

adjudication

administrative agencies

administrative efficiency

administrative law

administrative law judges (ALJs)

Administrative Procedure Act (APA)

administrative rulemaking

administrative tribunals

appellate courts

appellate jurisdiction

bureaucracy	intermediate appellate courts	rules-based decision making
civil service	judicial review	separation of powers
constitutional law	limited government	session laws
cooperative federalism	meritocracy	sovereign immunity
court of last resort	modern administrative state	spoils system
courts of general jurisdiction	open records laws	state supreme court
courts of limited jurisdiction	openness	statutes
discretion	oversight	trial courts
division of labor	participation	*ultra vires*
en banc hearings	procedural regularity	*United States Code*
executive orders	public law	*United States Code Annotated* (U.S.C.A.)
Federal Tort Claims Act	quasi-judicial powers	United States Courts of Appeals
federalism	quasi-legislative powers	United States District Courts
Freedom of Information Act (FOIA)	rationality	*United States Statutes at Large*
hierarchy	regulatory agencies	United States Supreme Court
individual rights	restraining orders	writ of certiorari
injunctions	rule of law	
	rulemaking	

QUESTIONS FOR THOUGHT AND DISCUSSION

1. Why has bureaucracy become an essential feature of modern societies?

2. How do we reconcile the seeming incompatibility between bureaucracy and representative democracy?

3. What is the difference between an "administrative agency" and a "regulatory" agency?

4. How does bureaucracy in the real world compare to the ideal notions of bureaucracy?

5. In general, how do American citizens regard bureaucracy?

6. What is meant by the term "cooperative federalism"?

7. What is meant by an annotated version of a code of statutes?

8. What are the goals of administrative law?

9. What are the most common situations in which private citizens have dealings with administrative agencies and what types of legal issues can arise in such situations?

10. The law consists of rules, but administration of government often requires officials to exercise discretion. Is the reality of administrative discretion compatible with the American ideal of the rule of law?

ENDNOTES

1. The term "administrative state" was coined by Dwight Waldo in his 1948 book, *The Administrative State: A Study of the Political Theory of American Public Administration* (New York: Ronald Press).

2. Another important distinction is that between "independent agencies" and those that are located within the major departments of the executive branch. For example, at the federal level, the Food and Drug Administration is located within the Department of Health and Human Services, whereas the Consumer Products Safety Commission is an independent agency. Similarly, the Occupational Safety and Health Administration is located within the Department of Labor. The Environmental Protection Agency, by contrast, is an independent regulatory agency.

3. Go to http://www4.law.cornell.edu/uscode/.

4. *Chevron, U.S.A., Inc. v. Natural Resources Defenses Council, Inc.,* 467 U.S. 837, n.11 (1984).

5. There are two basic categories of federal jurisdiction. First is federal question jurisdiction. The essential requirement here is that a case must present a federal question, that is, a question arising under the United States Constitution, a federal statute, regulation, executive order, or treaty. The federal government has produced a myriad of statutes, regulations, and executive orders. Consequently, most important questions of public policy can be framed as issues of federal law, thus permitting the federal courts to play a tremendous role in the policy-making process. The second broad category, diversity of citizenship jurisdiction, applies only to civil suits and is unrelated to the presence of a question of federal law. To qualify under federal diversity jurisdiction, a case must involve parties from different states and an amount in controversy that exceeds $75,000. Federal courts also have sole jurisdiction over bankruptcies.

6. See 28 U.S.C.A. §§ 81-132.

7. There are also federal district courts in the District of Columbia, Guam, Puerto Rico, North Marianna Islands, and the Virgin Islands.

8. Federal magistrate judges (formerly called "federal magistrates") are appointed by the judges of the federal district courts for a period of eight years. Magistrate judges preside over pretrial proceedings in civil and criminal cases. They try misdemeanors and can preside over civil trials with the consent of both parties.

9. In the Ninth Circuit, which has jurisdiction over federal district courts in California, Oregon, Washington, Arizona, Montana, Idaho, Nevada, Alaska, Hawaii, Guam, and the Northern Mariana Islands, en banc rehearings are before randomly selected panels of eleven judges.

10. U.S. Const. Art. III, § 2.

11. Texas is unique in that it has two courts of last resort. The Court of Criminal Appeals is the last resort in criminal cases; the Texas Supreme Court is the last resort in civil matters.

12. *Black's Law Dictionary*, 5th edition (St. Paul: West Publishing Co., 1978), p. 278.

13. Quoted from the Mission Statement of the U.S. Department of Labor, online at http://www.dol.gov/opa/aboutdol/mission.htm.

14. The term "red tape" refers to unnecessarily complex and time-consuming procedures followed by bureaucracies. The term is thought to have originated from the practice of English lawyers and administrators tying bundles of papers with red tape to keep them organized.

15. Ronald Wilson Reagan, First Presidential Inaugural Address, January 20, 1981.

16. *Food & Drug Administration v. Brown & Williamson Tobacco Co.*, 529 U.S 120 (2000).

2

The Evolution of the Administrative State

The rise of administrative bodies probably has been the most significant legal
trend of the last century. . . . They have become a veritable fourth branch of
the Government, which has deranged our three-branch legal theories. . . .

JUSTICE ROBERT H. JACKSON
DISSENTING IN *FTC V. RUBEROID CO.*, 343 U.S. 470, 487 (1952).

INTRODUCTION

Government in the United States today is highly bureaucratized. Many critics believe that our government is excessively bureaucratic—to the detriment of democratic and constitutional values. On the other hand, most Americans have come to see bureaucracy as the inevitable offspring of modern government. Thus there is a general begrudging acceptance of the **modern administrative state.**

In the early days of the Republic it was not this way. In fact, well into the nineteenth century the prevailing ethos was "that government is best that governs least."[1] As the nation developed, individuals were viewed as responsible for their own welfare. Those looked upon as deserving assistance were aided by family, neighbors, and often by religious organizations. Some local communities established funds to provide "relief" to the destitute, but the citizenry did not look upon government to provide "welfare" or social services. Rather, the task of government was to keep the peace, preserve order, settle disputes, and provide for the common defense.

Until the Industrial Revolution, which occurred in the mid-nineteenth century, American society remained basically agrarian, with relatively little commercial activity. The prevailing philosophy of the day was *laissez-faire,* not so much because people were opposed to government intervention, but because the people did not perceive a need for government to intervene in economic affairs beyond the coining of money, the regulation of standards of weights and measures, and the settling of economic disputes.

In the decade that followed the Declaration of Independence, the national government of the United States was a very weak entity established by the Articles of Confederation (adopted in 1777; ratified in 1781). During this critical period of our nation's history, the real power of government existed in the separate states, each of which had its own governmental machinery owing to the fact that each was originally established as a separate British colony. During this time the national government consisted only of the Congress and a few administrative personnel. There was no national court system and no separate executive branch. The Congress lacked the power to tax, which made the national government solely dependent on the states. By the mid-1780s a national consensus emerged, at least among the elites, that a new constitution would be needed to remedy the deficiencies of the Articles of Confederation.

CREATION OF THE FEDERAL BUREAUCRACY

The framers of the United States Constitution wanted to create a strong national government—one that would not be hampered by the deficiencies of the national government under the Articles of Confederation—but they very much believed in the idea of limited government. In their view, government existed to do what individuals and communities could not do for themselves. The new national government would be designed to do that which the state governments could not do for themselves, including national defense, foreign relations, the regulation of interstate commerce, and the settlement of interstate disputes. Article I, Section 8 of the Constitution enumerates the powers of Congress. These include the power to declare war, raise and support armies, collect taxes, spend money for the common defense and general welfare, regulate interstate and foreign commerce, coin money, regulate standards of weights and measures, establish post offices and post roads, and, significantly, to "make all Laws which shall be necessary and proper for carrying into Execution the foregoing Powers."

Two centuries later, these **enumerated powers** look somewhat paltry, but in 1787 the prevailing sentiment in the United States was that most of the activities of government would take place at the state and local levels. As James Madison observed in *The Federalist* No. 45: "The powers delegated by the proposed Constitution to the federal government are few and defined. Those which are to remain in the State governments are numerous and indefinite."[2]

Aside from the mention of post offices in Article I, Section 8 the Constitution contains no direct authority for Congress to create **executive agencies.** However, this authority is implied by the **Necessary and Proper Clause** of Article I, Section 8 and by the following language from Article II, Section 2, which addresses the president's appointment powers:

> He shall have Power, by and with the Advice and Consent of the Senate, to make Treaties, provided two thirds of the Senators present concur; and he shall nominate, and by and with the Advice and Consent of the Senate, shall appoint Ambassadors, other public Ministers and Consuls, Judges of the Supreme Court, and all other Officers of the United States, whose Appointments are not herein otherwise provided for, and which shall be established by Law: but the Congress may by Law vest the Appointment of such inferior Officers, as they think proper, in the President alone, in the Courts of Law, or in the Heads of Departments.

There is little doubt that the framers did not intend for the president to have the power to create "departments." From the beginning it was understood that this power resided in the Congress. The First Congress created three major **executive departments**—State, Treasury, and War—as well as a number of lesser offices, including an attorney general and a postmaster general. By the end of 1789, there were roughly 800 civilian employees of the federal government, one for every 5,000 Americans.

The State Department and the Conduct of Foreign Affairs

Article II of the Constitution authorized the president to make treaties (with the advice and consent of the Senate), appoint ambassadors and consuls, and receive ambassadors from other countries. It soon became clear that an executive department would be necessary to assist President George Washington in the conduct of foreign affairs and administration of the diplomatic corps. In May of 1789, Congress created the Department of Foreign Affairs to be headed by a secretary of foreign affairs. Two months later Congress changed the name to the Department of State and expanded the department's administrative responsibilities. In addition to housing the nation's diplomatic corps, the Department of State was required to publish the laws of the United States, prepare and deliver commissions to presidential appointees, and take custody of official documents, including the Constitution and the Declaration of Independence.[3] In September of 1789, President Washington appointed Thomas Jefferson to be the first secretary of state. In March of 1790 Jefferson returned from France to assume his new post as secretary of state. He found that one of the duties assigned to him was the preservation of the Declaration of Independence, a document he had authored fourteen years earlier.

From the founding of the Republic to the end of the nineteenth century, the predominant view of the American people and its leaders was isolationism. Americans were preoccupied with building a nation on a huge, largely unexplored continent and were averse to having their government involve itself with foreign powers. By and large, Americans agreed with George Washington, who in his farewell address observed, "The great rule of conduct for us in regard to foreign nations is . . . to have with them as little political connection as possible."

Protection of Patents and Copyrights

The Constitution authorized Congress to "promote the Progress of Science and useful Arts, by securing for limited Times to Authors and Inventors the exclusive Right to their respective Writings and Discoveries . . ." Congress acted on this grant of authority in 1790 by establishing a system for the issuance of patents and adopting the first federal copyright law. This was the beginning of a system for the protection of intellectual property that has become widely emulated throughout the world. Originally, clerks of the federal district courts recorded copyrights. In 1870 the copyright function was transferred to the Library of Congress, where it remains today. Patents were issued originally by a Patent Board consisting of the secretary of state, the secretary of war, and the attorney general.[4] In 1793, the function was transferred to a superintendent of patents appointed by the secretary of state.[5] Today, the Patent and Trademark Office is located within the Department of Commerce, where it is headed by the undersecretary of commerce for intellectual property.

The Treasury Department

Although the Congress had first appointed a Treasurer in 1777, the Treasury Department was created by statute in September 1789. President Washington immediately appointed Alexander Hamilton to serve as the first Secretary of the Treasury. One scholar has written, "If anyone deserves a title as the founder of American administrative state . . . it is Alexander Hamilton."[6] Hamilton advocated a strong national government and within it an energetic executive branch. In 1788 Hamilton observed:

> A feeble Executive implies a feeble execution of the government. A feeble execution is but another phrase for a bad execution; and a government ill executed, whatever it may be in theory, must be, in practice, a bad government.[7]

In addition to serving as the repository of funds, the Treasury Department under Hamilton took on the role of advising the president on matters of economic policy. The First Bank of the United States, the forerunner of the contemporary Federal Reserve System, was Hamilton's brainchild. Although the Constitution did not specifically authorize the Congress to establish a national bank, Hamilton argued that Congress

could do so under **implied powers** conferred by the Necessary and Proper Clause of Article I, Section 8 of the Constitution. Hamilton's view prevailed, first in Congress and later in the Supreme Court. Congress established the First Bank of the United States in 1791, granting the institution a twenty-year charter. In 1816, on the recommendation of President James Monroe, Congress chartered a second Bank of the United States, which established branches throughout the country. In the landmark case of *McCulloch v. Maryland* (1819),[8] the Supreme Court upheld Congress's power to establish a national bank and, implicitly, the power to create a host of administrative and regulatory agencies. (An excerpt from Chief Justice John Marshall's opinion for the Supreme Court in *McCulloch v. Maryland* is reproduced in Box 2.1.)

The Customs Service

The U.S. Customs Service, which was actually the first executive agency created by the First Congress, was relocated to the Treasury Department in September of 1789. Its function was (and is) the enforcement of import/export laws at ports of entry, the control of smuggling, and the assessment and collection of duties on imported goods. Customs was the first federal administrative agency responsible for the **adjudication** of disputes, which is one of the principal functions of administrative and regulatory agencies today. Until the establishment of a permanent federal income tax in 1913, import duties collected by the Customs Service would be the principal source of revenue for the federal government. By 1835, these revenues had erased the national debt that had originated from the American Revolution.

The War Department

In the years following American Independence, popular suspicion of a permanent military establishment was powerful and pervasive. After the Revolution, Congress reduced the Continental Army to a standing force of eighty soldiers, just

---

BOX 2.1 Supreme Court Perspective McCulloch v. Maryland

McCulloch v. Maryland
17 U.S. (4 Wheat.) 316 (1819)

[In this landmark decision, the U.S. Supreme Court considers whether Congress has constitutional authority to establish a national bank.]

Chief Justice Marshall delivered the opinion of the Court.

. . . *This government is acknowledged by all to be one of enumerated powers. . . . But the question respecting the extent of the powers actually granted, is perpetually arising, and will probably continue to arise, as long as our system shall exist. . . .*

. . . *Among the enumerated powers, we do not find that of establishing a bank or creating a corporation. But there is no phrase in the instrument which, like the Articles of Confederation, excludes incidental or implied powers; and which requires that everything granted shall be expressly and minutely described. . . . A constitution, to contain an accurate detail of all the subdivisions of which its great powers will admit, and of all the means by which they may be carried into execution, would partake of a prolixity of a legal code, and could scarcely be embraced by the human mind. It would probably never be understood by the public. Its nature, therefore, requires, that only its great outlines should be marked, its important objects designated, and the minor ingredients which compose those objects be deduced from the nature of the*

objects themselves. . . . In considering this question, then, we must never forget that it is a constitution we are expounding.

To [the] enumeration of powers [in Art. I, Sec. 8] is added that of making "all laws which shall be necessary and proper, for carrying into execution the foregoing powers, and all other powers vested by this Constitution, in the government of the United States, or in any department thereof." . . . The result of the most careful and attentive consideration bestowed upon this clause is, that if it does not enlarge, it cannot be construed to restrain the powers of Congress, or to impair the right of the legislature to exercise its best judgment in the selection of measures to carry into execution the constitutional powers of the government. . . .

We admit, as all must admit, that the powers of the government are limited, and that its limits are not to be transcended. But we think the sound construction of the Constitution must allow to the national legislature that discretion, with respect to the means by which the powers it confers are to be carried into execution, which will enable the body to perform the high duties assigned to it, in the manner most beneficial to the people. Let the end be legitimate, let it be within the scope of the Constitution, and all means which are appropriate, which are plainly adapted to that end, which are not prohibited, but consist with the letter and spirit of the Constitution, are constitutional. . . .

---

barely enough to man the post at West Point. To defend the frontier, Congress relied on the states to furnish troops from their militias. The framers of the Constitution recognized the need for a more permanent military establishment. Thus, Article I, Section 8 of the Constitution allowed for a national regular army and navy with the president as commander in chief. In August 1789, Congress created the War Department to oversee the army and the navy, thus firmly cementing the policy of subordinating the military to civilian control. In 1798, the Quasi-War with France led Congress to establish a separate Navy Department. Ultimately, in 1949, administration of the nation's armed forces would be

brought under a massive new administrative structure called the Department of Defense.

The Office of Attorney General

Congress established the Office of the Attorney General in 1789 and authorized this official "to prosecute and conduct all suits in the Supreme Court in which the United States shall be concerned, and to give his advice and opinion upon questions of law when required by the president of the United States, or when requested by the heads of any of the departments."[9] Originally, the position was not designated as **cabinet** rank, but President Washington routinely involved his attorneys general in cabinet meetings and the position soon came to be recognized as a de facto member of the Cabinet. Originally a part-time position, by the end of the Civil War the Office of Attorney General had become so inundated with legal work on behalf of the federal government that private counsel had to be retained. This led Congress to establish the Department of Justice in 1870.[10] This act made the attorney general head of the Department of Justice and created the Office of the Solicitor General to represent the government in the Supreme Court. The 1870 legislation also gave the Justice Department control over federal law enforcement. Today, Department of Justice is the world's largest law office representing the interests of the world's most powerful government.

The Post Office

In 1790 Congress created the position of postmaster general and placed it within the Treasury Department. Much of the growth of the federal bureaucracy during the early nineteenth century is attributable to the expansion of the Post Office Department, which grew as the nation expanded westward. The post office became so large and so important that in 1829 Congress removed it from the Treasury and made it a separate department. The postmaster general was made a member of the cabinet. In 1970 the Post Office Department was converted into the U.S. Postal Service, an **independent agency** governed by an eleven-member board, and the postmaster general was removed from the cabinet.

The Department of the Interior

The First Congress in 1789 and 1790 had created the administrative structure needed to carry out the federal government's limited responsibilities. That structure would survive with only minor changes for more than half a century. In 1849, Congress established the Department of the Interior to take charge of the nation's internal affairs and improvements. The depart-

ment was given a wide range of responsibilities, including Indian affairs, management of public lands, exploration of the western frontier, and regulation of U.S. territories. The Patent Office was also moved from the State Department to the new Department of the Interior. Eventually the department would assume the responsibilities of managing the system of national parks, preserving historic sites, and protecting threatened populations of fish and wildlife.

STATE AND LOCAL GOVERNMENT IN THE EARLY YEARS OF THE REPUBLIC

From the American Revolution to the Civil War, states were the most important units of government. If citizens had contact with or even awareness of government, it was likely to be at the state or local level. The national government seemed remote and concerned itself with matters beyond the ken of the ordinary American.

After the Revolution states adopted their own constitutions reflecting the prevalent Republican political philosophy but also drawing on English legal tradition and colonial experience. These constitutions outlined the structure of government, but they were chiefly concerned with elaborating the rights of citizens. Little was said in these early charters about public administration.

The new Americans were familiar with the principles of the English common law, and either by constitutional provision or statute, the new states (except Louisiana) adopted the English common law, as it existed at the time of the Declaration of Independence, as their own state law. Early legislation was directed to organizational structures of the government, defining boundaries of local government units, establishing election laws, and providing for inheritance rights. Basic public health and safety measures and provision for construction of roads and bridges would come later.

State and local officials by and large subscribed to the philosophy of minimal government. The citizen's economic well-being was not seen as the concern of the government. People were to be helped by protection of the law, courts to settle their disputes, and eventually schools to teach the children. In the early nineteenth century, social services by the states focused largely on development of public schools and control of contagious diseases while churches began to address the most basic means of assisting the sick and impoverished.

The county sheriff kept order, tax collectors gathered minimal funds to support the sheriff and the jails, and volunteers often served as firefighters. As cities began to be chartered they directed attention to inspecting slaughterhouses, controlling nuisances, and quarantining those with contagious diseases. Local ordinances began to address the use of animals, prohibiting conduct of business on Sundays, and regulating the sale of alcoholic beverages. In some instances cities afforded their residents some limited police protection. Thus, in the formative days of the Republic, state and local governments created modest bureaucratic structures to perform the minimal tasks that people expected of government in those days.

EMERGENCE OF THE ADMINISTRATIVE STATE

The Civil War era witnessed a dramatic expansion of the size and responsibilities of the federal government. In 1862, at the behest of President Lincoln, Congress created the Department of Agriculture. The ostensible purpose was to assist American farmers by providing them better seed and better farming techniques. Lincoln called it the "people's department," reflecting the fact that 90 percent of Americans were engaged in agriculture. The real motivation, though, was to ensure that the Union Army had a steady supply of food.

The Civil War sparked the Industrial Revolution in the United States. Factories and mills sprouted everywhere, mines were dug to extract coal and iron, and railroads were built to carry troops, supplies, and munitions to the front. After the war ended, industrialization continued to accelerate. Waves of immigrants looking for better lives in America crowded into cities and took industrial jobs. Wages were low, and working conditions were often miserable. Children worked side by side with their parents. Those who subscribed to the principle of laissez-faire argued that government should not intervene on behalf of workers or consumers. Unrestricted capitalism would over the long run, they argued, produce the greatest good for the greatest number of people. On the other side of the issue were reformers backed by throngs of workers, many of whom were beginning to exercise their right to vote. Pressure was growing for the national government to become actively involved in the regulation of the economy.

Creation of the Civil Service

Historically, those who assisted the candidate who won the presidency were rewarded with jobs in the new administration. Government jobs were handed out based largely on partisan political considerations. The old adage "To the victor belong the spoils" was a truism until the late 1880s. President Andrew Jackson sought to justify this practice, which had been in place since the Washington Administration, by declaring that the administration of the federal government is improved by the principle of "rotation in office." By the administration of President Ulysses S. Grant, however, a consensus was emerging that the **spoils system** was responsible for inefficiency and corruption in government. The assassination of President James Garfield by a disgruntled job seeker in 1881 was the immediate catalyst for reform, which led Congress to adopt the Civil Service Reform Act of 1883. Better known as the Pendleton Act, it caused the demise of the spoils system and the emergence of a **civil service** designed to establish professionalism in government employment. The Pendleton Act provided that members of federal civil service would be selected based on merit, as determined by open, competitive examinations. Civil servants were to be protected from political coercion; they were also prohibited from engaging in political solicitation while on the job. The act created the Civil Service Commission, which was empowered to issue and enforce regulations governing the civil service.[11] The New York state legislature passed a similar reform bill in 1883 and Massachusetts followed suit in 1884. Eventually, all fifty states would adopt merit systems for their own bureaucracies.

The creation of the Civil Service was a very significant step in the bureaucratization of America. Recall that in Chapter 1 we discussed Max Weber's ideal type bureaucracy, one element of which is meritocracy. A civil service system is designed to make public employment a profession, as opposed to a payoff. Entry to the profession is based on demonstrable merit and not political or familial connections. Closely related to the principles of meritocracy and professionalism is the politics/administration dichotomy first propounded in 1887 by then-professor Woodrow Wilson. In a widely influential article in *Political Science Quarterly,* Wilson argued that

> Administration lies outside of the proper sphere of politics. Administrative questions are not political questions. Although politics sets the tasks for administration, it should not be suffered to manipulate its offices.[12]

Wilson's idea of a merit-based, politically neutral corps of public servants would figure prominently in subsequent arguments in favor of creating public agencies to engage in economic regulation. And the politics/administration dichotomy would become a fundamental tenet of the new "science" of public administration, as it would be taught in colleges and universities throughout America over the next century.

The Advent of Regulation

By the 1870s the Industrial Revolution was in full flower. Factories had sprung up everywhere. Railroads crisscrossed the country. The economy was booming. Exports were at an all-time high. Yet there was a wave of discontent sweeping across the hinterland. America's farms, at that time largely small enterprises owned and operated by single families, were not experiencing the same profitability as America's industrial corporations. Farmers blamed railroads for what they regarded as extortionate shipping rates and banks for what they saw as usurious rates of interest. Some went so far as to accuse the national government and big business of a massive conspiracy to exploit the nation's farmers, a theme that socialists would later echo in appealing to downtrodden industrial workers in the nation's cities.

From this agrarian discontent emerged the Populist Movement, which demanded government intervention to regulate the railroads and the free coinage of silver to increase the nation's money supply, thereby reducing interest rates. Over the next two decades the Democratic Party would respond to this wave of discontent by adopting most of the Populist agenda. This cemented the position of the Republican Party as the party of "big business," Wall Street, and the "Eastern Establishment." Whereas slavery and secession had once divided the major parties, the new dividing line was the doctrine of laissez faire.

Social Darwinists like William Graham Sumner[13] defended laissez-faire on evolutionary grounds, arguing that an economy based on the survival of the fittest would in the long run produce the greatest benefits to society. But the prevailing intellectual currents, as well as public opinion, were running in the opposite direction. A new understanding was emerging, one that called for government intervention to temper the excesses of an unregulated industrial economy.

During the 1870s farmers began to organize and in some of the Midwestern states were able to achieve considerable influence over state legislatures. This led to the adoption of the Granger Laws, state laws regulating railroads and grain storage facilities. In 1877, the U.S. Supreme Court upheld Illinois' Granger Law against a constitutional challenge brought by private industry. In its landmark decision in *Munn v. Illinois,*[14] the Court said that "business affected with a public interest" could be constitutionally subjected to government regulation. However, a decade later a more conservative Court reversed course, holding that states did not have the power to regulate railroad rates because this power was vested exclusively in Congress.[15] Naturally, this decision led reformers to call for Congress to act.

In 1887 Congress created the Interstate Commerce Commission (ICC), the first **independent regulatory commission** of the national government. The ICC was "independent" in the sense that commissioners held their positions for fixed terms, rather than simply serving at the pleasure of the president. The legislation creating the commission required "just and reasonable" rates for the interstate shipment of goods by rail. However, it was not until after World War I that the ICC was empowered to actually set rates. Nevertheless, the creation of the commission represented a major departure from the doctrine of laissez-faire on the part of the national government and a significant milestone in the evolution of the administrative state. Over time, the ICC's jurisdiction expanded to include the trucking industry, bus lines, and even oil and gas pipelines.

The Sherman Antitrust Act In the late nineteenth century, much of the public debate over laissez-faire versus government interventionism was centered on the problem of industrial **monopolies.** Apostles of laissez-faire argued that monopolies were temporary aberrations that would eventually give way to free market competition. To the farmer dependent on the one railroad company that provided service to his remote community, that argument was not very persuasive. By the close of the 1880s, there was substantial public support for federal legislation to curb monopolies. This led Congress to enact the first in a series of **antitrust laws.** The Sherman Act of 1890 prohibited "every contract, combination in the form of trust or otherwise, or conspiracy, in restraint of trade or commerce among the several States, or with foreign nations" and provided for criminal and civil sanctions to enforce these prohibitions.

The Sherman Act was based on Congress's power to regulate interstate commerce enumerated in Article I, Section 8 of the Constitution. Yet some believed that Congress had gone too far. In 1895, a conservative Supreme Court limited the application of the statute to matters of interstate trade and transportation, allowing manufacturing and refining monopolies to flourish.[16] This decision signaled the beginning of an era of conservative activism on the Supreme Court, in which the justices invoked various constitutional doctrines to block federal and state economic regulation. Eventually, this conservative activism would give way to a new understanding, but not until the country had experienced the Great Depression and the Court had been challenged by the most powerful and popular president in American history, Franklin D. Roosevelt.

THE ERA OF PROGRESSIVE REFORM

The first two decades of the twentieth century are known as the Era of Progressive Reform. This was the age of the "muckrakers," crusading journalists like Lincoln Steffens who exposed corruption in business and government. It was a time that communism and various permutations thereof were beginning to attract converts in the United States and other industrialized nations. The face of America was changing rapidly with the massive influx of immigrants and the emergence of giant cities. Intellectuals like Herbert Croly[17] and John Dewey[18] believed that the political and economic systems had to be reformed dramatically in order to stave off the challenge from radical left-wing ideologies. The progressive reformers advocated various measures to reduce government corruption, make politics more democratic, solve social problems, and curb the excesses of laissez-faire capitalism. Many of these measures involved the creation of new bureaucracies staffed by "experts" and "professionals" who would transcend partisan politics and serve the greater public interest.

Progressivism achieved its greatest influence during the presidential administrations of Theodore Roosevelt (1901–1909) and Woodrow Wilson (1913–1921). During this era the administrative state grew steadily, as most reforms involved the creation of new bureaucracies. Although the most significant developments took place at the federal level, reformers persuaded a number of state legislatures to enact progressive measures. The most notable state-level reforms took place in Wisconsin during the first decade of the twentieth century under the leadership of Governor Robert LaFollete. Many of the progressive reforms adopted by the Wisconsin legislature such as workers' compensation, the minimum wage, and regulation of banks would serve as models for programs adopted by other states and eventually the federal government in the decades to come.

The Pure Food and Drug Act

At the federal level, one of the first major victories of the progressive reformers was the adoption of the Pure Food and Drug Act, which was signed into law in 1906 by President Theodore Roosevelt. The law represented a major expansion of the responsibilities of the federal government. Theretofore, state and local governments were assumed to have sole responsibility for measures affecting the public health and welfare. Of course, most states had done little to regulate food and drugs, as the prevailing ethos inherited from the English common law was caveat emptor ("let the buyer beware"), under which consumers

were solely responsible for evaluating products in the marketplace. The Pure Food and Drug Act prohibited the interstate transport of "unlawful" food and drugs. Unlawful foods were defined as those that contained filthy or decomposed substances or otherwise posed a health hazard. Unlawful drugs were those that deviated from the standards of strength, quality, and purity published in the *United States Pharmacopoeia* and the *National Formulary*. The new law required that variations from these standards be plainly stated on product labels. Originally administered by the Bureau of Chemistry in the Department of Agriculture, the law came to be enforced by the Food and Drug Administration (FDA), which is now an agency within the Department of Health and Human Services. The law was significantly strengthened by the adoption of the Food, Drug and Cosmetic Act of 1938, which gave the FDA responsibility for the premarket testing of pharmaceutical products.

Regulating Commerce and Labor

In 1903 Congress created the Department of Commerce and Labor. This new department included the Bureau of Immigration, which had been created in 1891 as the Immigration Service in the Department of Treasury. In 1913, the department was bifurcated into separate departments, Labor and Commerce. In the words of the act establishing the Department of Labor, its main purpose was "to foster, promote and develop the welfare of working people, to improve their working conditions, and to enhance their opportunities for profitable employment."

The Federal Reserve System

Progressives and Populists had long argued for a centralized banking system under government control. Conservatives, Republicans, and most banking interests opposed this idea, preferring a completely private banking system with minimal government control. The panic of 1907 shifted the debate to favor reform. In 1913, Congress created the Federal Reserve System, a compromise of sorts in that it represented a "decentralized central bank." The system consisted of twelve regional banks operated by the government and governed by the Federal Reserve Board of Governors. By the 1920s, the Federal Reserve had begun the practice of "open market operations," which consists of buying and selling government securities through an auction. The Federal Reserve developed this practice as a means of setting **monetary policy** for the nation. By controlling the nation's money supply and interest rates, today the Federal Reserve System exerts a tremendous influence on the American economy.

The Federal Income Tax

In 1913, the Sixteenth Amendment was ratified, giving Congress power to enact a **federal income tax,** which Congress promptly did. Responsibility for collection fell to the Bureau of Internal Revenue, the predecessor of the Internal Revenue Service. Expanding revenues facilitated the growth of the federal government. Without the steady stream of income tax dollars flowing to Washington, there is simply no way that the federal government would have attained its current size and scope.

The Federal Trade Commission

Prior to 1914, enforcement of the nation's antitrust laws was the sole responsibility of the Department of Justice, which was authorized to file suits in federal court to prevent or remedy restraints of trade. While there were notable accomplishments, such as the dismantling of the Standard Oil Company in 1911,[19] critics charged that the Justice Department was too passive in exercising its enforcement powers and that the federal courts were too protective of large corporate interests. In 1914 Congress established the Federal Trade Commission (FTC) as an independent agency like the ICC. The FTC's creation was supported not only by consumers, but also by small businesses threatened by unfair competition from large-scale monopolies. The FTC was charged with maintaining free and fair competition, specifically by enforcing antitrust laws and preventing deceptive advertising. Eventually the FTC was empowered to issue cease-and-desist orders where its own investigations found evidence of unfair practices. The FTC was also given its own authority to file suit in federal court against companies deemed to be acting unlawfully.

THE GREAT DEPRESSION AND THE NEW DEAL

No single event in American history had more impact on the growth of the federal bureaucracy than did the election of Franklin D. Roosevelt (FDR) to the presidency in 1932. Roosevelt won the election by promising the American people a "New Deal" to cope with the economic dislocations brought on by the Great Depression that began with the stock market crash of 1929. The Great Depression provided a political opportunity for liberal and progressive thinkers to test their idea that government management of all sectors of the economy would prove more successful than the traditional laissez-faire approach. The American public, reeling from massive unemployment and shocked by the stock market crash and the widespread failures of banks, farms, and other enterprises, was ready for a new approach. Under the New Deal, FDR and the Democratic Congress established public works programs such as the Civilian Conservation Corps (CCC) and the Works Progress Administration (WPA), as well as a variety of regulatory programs affecting agriculture, banking, mining, manufacturing, telecommunications, utilities, and the stock market. Perhaps the most important achievement from the standpoint of average Americans was the establishment of the Social Security system.

All of these programs required new bureaucracies, and the size of the federal government grew dramatically as a consequence. President Roosevelt requested and received from Congress authority to reorganize the executive branch via executive order. (Previously, such reorganization required Congress to enact a statute.) Through numerous enactments, Congress delegated unprecedented policy-making authority to the President. And FDR asserted constitutional authority inherent in the term "executive power" in justifying various executive orders designed to cope with the Great Depression and, later, World War II.

Conservatives were alarmed by the scope of the New Deal, in particular its interference with business, as well as the centralization of power in the executive branch. Some conservatives argued that the New Deal represented a significant step toward the implementation of socialism. Defenders of the New Deal argued that to rely on the traditional laissez-faire approach in the face of a calamity of the magnitude of the Great Depression would simply pave the way for a more radical and authoritarian system on the model of Hitler's Germany or the Soviet Union. The New Deal was thus defended as a pragmatic alternative to communism or fascism.

Conservatives were not convinced. During the first Roosevelt Administration (1933–1936), they found a powerful ally in the United States Supreme Court. After adverse decisions striking down key elements of the New Deal, Roosevelt began to refer to the Supreme Court as the "nine old men" and characterized them as out of touch with modern economic problems. FDR even proposed a plan by which he would be able to "pack" the Court with justices who would support his ideas. Although FDR's court packing plan was never adopted, it did get the Court's attention.

President Roosevelt finally won the battle when the Supreme Court, perhaps fearing retaliation by Congress and the president, abruptly changed direction in what has been referred to as the "constitutional revolution of 1937."

Roosevelt's four-term presidency saw almost complete turnover in the membership of the Supreme Court. The Roosevelt Court, as it came to be known, firmly established the legitimacy of the modern regulatory state as well as the primacy of the presidency in the scheme of national governance.

The NRA: Centerpiece of the New Deal

The guiding principle of the New Deal was centralized planning and regulation, an idea very much at odds with laissez-faire capitalism and traditional notions of federalism. The National Industrial Recovery Act of 1933 epitomized the philosophy of the New Deal. The act permitted the president to impose "codes of fair competition" on particular industries. To this end, President Roosevelt issued an executive order creating the National Recovery Administration (NRA) and authorizing it to promulgate such codes. The leadership of the NRA worked with leaders of industry to produce codes regulating wages, prices, working hours, and trade practices. Small business owners, who by and large identified with the Republican Party and opposed the New Deal, objected that the NRA's codes of fair competition placed them at a competitive disadvantage. In a unanimous judgment, the U.S. Supreme Court in 1935 declared the statute unconstitutional on two grounds: first, that Congress had impermissibly delegated its legislative power to the executive branch and; second, that Congress had exceeded its constitutional power to regulate interstate commerce.[20] The decision dealt a body blow to the New Deal and President Roosevelt was extremely unhappy with the decision. Although the NRA was short-lived, many of the policies it pursued were later enacted into law and survived constitutional challenge before a reconstituted Supreme Court. For example, provisions governing minimum wages and maximum working hours were adopted in the Fair Labor Standards Act of 1938, which was upheld by the Supreme Court in 1941.[21]

Regulation of Agriculture

American agriculture was devastated by the Great Depression. Commodity prices collapsed, forcing many farmers out of business. The New Dealers in Washington called for extensive federal regulation of farm production and commodity prices. The Agricultural Adjustment Act of 1933 authorized the Department of Agriculture to do just that. Again, the Supreme Court held the statute unconstitutional.[22] After the constitutional revolution of 1937, Congress reenacted the statute and this time it survived judicial review.[23] Thus the federal government acquired extensive control over farm production in the United States, even to the extent of imposing production quotas on commodities produced for personal use. In the realm of agriculture, the old laissez faire system was no more.

Regulating and Insuring the Banking Industry

One of the more frightening aspects of the Great Depression was the loss of public confidence in the nation's banking system. As depositors rushed to withdraw their funds, nearly ten thousand banks failed during the period 1930–1933. To stem the crisis caused by the great surge in bank failures, FDR declared a bank holiday the day after he was inaugurated in March 1933. Then, at FDR's urging, Congress passed the Banking Act of 1933, which provided for an interim plan to insure deposits and which was superseded in 1935 by a plan operated by the new agency, the Federal Deposit Insurance Corporation (FDIC). Designed to protect the small depositor, the FDIC insured the first $10,000 in each deposit account (now raised to $100,000) against loss. Additionally, the FDIC examines and supervises the member banks whose accounts are insured. This includes all national banks and those state-chartered banks that participate. Although state banking authorities retained the right to grant charters for state banks, today many insist that such banks affiliate with the FDIC.

The Tennessee Valley Authority

One of the main goals of the New Deal was to foster social and economic development in regions of the country that lagged behind. One such area was the Tennessee Valley, which includes Tennessee, Northern Alabama and Western Kentucky. In 1933, Congress established the Tennessee Valley Authority (TVA) to develop this impoverished region. Using the federal government's power of **eminent domain,** TVA acquired lands along the Tennessee River in order to construct a series of dams and reservoirs. The dams provided electrical power to a region where many people were still without electricity. The reservoirs provided water supplies for growing cities and industrial uses. Without question, TVA was extremely successful in transforming the Tennessee Valley. Today, TVA persists, even though its basic mission was accomplished decades ago.

Regulation of Broadcasting

Under the Post Roads Act of 1866,[24] the Postmaster General was authorized to fix rates on government telegrams. In passing the Mann-Elkins Act of 1910,[25] Congress vested the Interstate Commerce Commission with general regulatory authority over telephone and telegraph carriers. The Radio Act of 1927[26] gave the new Federal Radio Commission authority over the licensing and regulation of radio facilities. The purpose of the Communications Act of 1934[27] was to centralize regulatory authority over electronic communications in one agency, the Federal Communications Commission (FCC). In an early decision upholding the authority of the FCC, the Supreme Court observed that "Congress endowed the Communications Commission with comprehensive powers to promote and realize the vast potentialities of radio."[28] In another early case the Court observed that "[u]nless Congress had exercised its power over interstate commerce to bring about allocation of available frequencies and to regulate the employment of transmission equipment the result would have been an impairment of the effective use of these facilities by anyone."[29]

Regulating the Stock Market

The stock market crash of 1929 devastated thousands of investors and shook public confidence in the stock markets. To restore this confidence and to prevent future calamities, Congress adopted the Securities Act of 1933.[30] Sometimes referred to as the "truth in securities law," the statute had two main goals: first, to ensure that investors would receive adequate information before investing in stocks and bonds; and second, to reduce fraud and misrepresentation in the sale of public securities. Congress reinforced this legislation by enacting the Securities Exchange Act of 1934,[31] which created the Securities and Exchange Commission (SEC) to enforce federal securities laws and regulate the stock markets and brokerage firms. During the New Deal, Congress would pass several other statutes strengthening federal regulation of securities markets.

Regulation of Utilities

Prior to the New Deal, electric and gas utilities were regulated by states and, in some instances, local governments. The Federal Power Act of 1935 established the Federal Power Commission (FPC) and authorized it to regulate natural gas and oil pipelines, natural gas prices, and issue hydroelectric dam licenses. One of the more obscure New Deal agencies, the FPC would be reorganized in 1977, when Congress established the Federal Energy Regulatory Commission (FERC). The Commission now approves rates for wholesale electric sales of electricity and transmission in interstate commerce for private utilities.

Regulation of Labor-Management Relations

One of the philosophical commitments of the New Deal was to recognize the right of industrial workers to unionize and bargain collectively with management over the terms of employ-

ment. This had been a major source of conflict since the beginning of the 20th century. In some quarters, labor unions were regarded as "un-American" or "socialist." On numerous occasions force had been used to put down strikes. In 1935, the New Deal Congress adopted the National Labor Relations Act, better known as the Wagner Act. The Act recognized "the right of employees to self-organization and to bargain collectively through representatives of their own choosing." It prohibited "unfair labor practices" and created the National Labor Relations Board to investigate allegations thereof and issue orders to remedy violations. The Wagner Act was upheld against a constitutional challenge in 1937 in a pivotal decision that reoriented the Supreme Court with respect to the New Deal.[32]

New Deal Measures to Stimulate Home Ownership and Provide Public Housing

At the time of the Great Depression it was common for home mortgage loans to require repayment in a short number of years. By 1932, when the Federal Home Loan Bank Act was enacted to provide mortgage loans, thousands of home mortgages were already being foreclosed. The New Deal sought to stabilize home ownership by enactment of several measures. Starting in 1933, the Home Owners Loan Corporation assisted by refinancing home mortgages. The Home Owners Loan Act authorized federal savings and loan associations to stimulate home building by providing local communities with home-financing organizations. In 1934 the National Housing Act created the Federal Savings and Loan Insurance Corporation to provide protection to those who invested in these savings and loan associations and provide for refinancing and extending the maturity of home mortgage obligations. It also created the Federal Housing Administration (FHA) that provided federal insurance for long-term home mortgages.

In addition to the plight of thousands of homeowners who were struggling to pay mortgage debts, the Great Depression revealed the unavailability of affordable housing for the masses of urban poor. For some time, several larger cities had attempted to deal with public housing issues on a local basis; however, prior to the New Deal there was no federal program. The National Housing Act of 1937, better known as the Wagner-Steagall Act, created the U.S. Housing Authority (USHA) to administer grants and low-interest loans to communities for the purpose of replacing slum housing with new housing for low-income residents. In response to the federal Act, communities created public housing authorities to oversee slum clearance and develop new housing projects. By 1941, the USHA had assisted in the construction of more than 120,000 units of low-income public housing.

As a result of the legislation enacted as part of the New Deal, the federal government became firmly entrenched in the nation's home building, financing, and slum clearance. This has led to a plethora of federal, state, and local governmental agencies to administer such programs.

Social Security

Although the Constitution authorized Congress to spend money to promote the general welfare, the federal government had traditionally left social welfare problems to the state and local governments. But the Great Depression of the 1930s overwhelmed the ability of state and local governments to provide relief and created widespread demands for the national government to get involved. These demands led to the passage of the Social Security Act of 1935, the federal government's first major foray into the realm of promoting social welfare. The Social Security Act established retirement insurance for older Americans, provided **unemployment compensation** for laid-off workers, and provided federal supplements to state and local welfare programs. The enactment of the Social Security Act signaled the emergence of another face of modern government: the **welfare state**. Initially, the program was very limited and was administered by a small independent agency called the Social Security Board.

The Rise of Administrative Adjudication

The proliferation of government agencies in the New Deal period brought about a fundamental change in the American legal system. Before the advent of the administrative state, enforcement of legal prohibitions and requirements was almost exclusively the responsibility of prosecutors (in criminal cases) and private parties (in civil cases). And the adjudication of those cases was the sole responsibility of the courts. The proliferation of the bureaucracy resulted in a massive shift in these responsibilities away from the judiciary. As the administrative state evolved, agencies became more involved in the adjudication of disputes.

Proponents of administrative adjudication claimed that it would be a more efficient and more accessible alternative to traditional adjudication by courts. Filing requirements, evidentiary rules, and adjudicatory procedures would be simplified. Not everyone was convinced. Some critics charged that the bureaucracy was usurping the constitutional role of the courts. Others noted that agencies operated according to their own internal rules and procedures with little guidance from Congress and little concern for due process of law. But even the critics knew that administrative adjudication was going to be a permanent feature of American government. The challenge would be to make administrative agencies across the board adopt more or less uniform standards of procedure.

WORLD WAR II AND THE COLD WAR ERA

By 1941, the New Deal had been put in place and its legitimacy had been firmly established by a reconstituted Supreme Court. During World War II (1941–1945), the federal government was preoccupied with mobilization of military forces, conversion to a wartime economy, and prosecution of the war itself. However, in 1942, when the outcome of the war was far from certain, the Roosevelt administration obtained from Congress authority to regulate the American economy to an extent theretofore unseen. The Emergency Price Control Act of 1942 established the Office of Price Administration and empowered this agency to impose price and rent controls throughout the country. Designed as a temporary measure "in the interest of the national defense and security and necessary to the effective prosecution of the present war," the act was sustained by the Supreme Court in 1944.[33]

In 1941 and 1942 Congress enacted legislation giving the president sweeping powers to delegate executive power to numerous agencies. By executive order FDR established the Office of Emergency Management (OEM) in 1940. OEM, in turn, spawned numerous administrative agencies to mobilize production of war material.

World War II reinforced an idea that gained widespread acceptance during the Great Depression: in times of national emergency, the federal government must be permitted to take action that might be deemed unconstitutional in ordinary times. Although FDR seized several industrial plants during the war when strikes threatened to paralyze war production, no statutory authority for such action existed until the War Labor Disputes Act was passed in 1943.

Providing for Veterans

The federal government had made some provisions for war veterans as far back as the American Revolution. In 1862 Congress provided for pensions for Civil War veterans who became disabled as the result of war injuries as well as death benefits to "war widows." In 1930, President Hoover signed an executive order creating the Veterans Administration to provide benefits to the nearly five million living veterans of the armed forces. When World War II ended, demands on the federal government changed: now the federal government assumed the responsibility for housing, educating, and providing medical care to many thousands of returning war veterans. The Servicemen's Readjustment

Act of 1944, popularly known as the "G.I. Bill of Rights," may have had a greater impact on American society than any law that preceded it. The new law provided veterans who attended college with tuition, a monthly allowance, and other educational expenses. This led to a boom in American higher education and helped to fuel the tremendous economic growth of the postwar period. It also led to greatly increased tax revenues from a new class of educated citizens. The GI Bill also provided mortgage subsidies, which led to a boom in housing and gave rise to the "American dream" of universal single-family home ownership. The Veterans Administration, which had been created in 1930, was assigned responsibility of administering the benefits of the GI Bill.

Adoption of the Administrative Procedure Act

By 1945 the modern administrative state was essentially in place—a panoply of agencies administering a variety of programs and regulating numerous aspects of economic life. FDR even referred to the federal bureaucracy as a "fourth branch of government." Unfortunately, there was little consistency across agencies in terms of the procedures by which they made rules and adjudicated disputes with regulated interests. The administrative state was governed by a patchwork of statutes and characterized by an extremely high level of discretion. Many charged that the concept of the rule of law required some overarching legislation to standardize rulemaking and adjudicatory procedures. Others argued that the principles of democracy demanded greater public participation in agency decision making. Congress responded to these concerns by adopting the **Administrative Procedure Act (APA)** of 1946, which has been described as the Magna Carta of administrative law.[34]

The APA provided for uniform standards of procedure that would be common to all agencies. The act established the "notice and comment" requirements for informal rule making (see Chapter 6) and trial-type procedures for formal agency adjudication (see Chapter 7). It also guaranteed the right of judicial review to any person "suffering legal wrong because of any agency action." Without question, the APA is the single most important piece of legislation in the development of the administrative process, and much attention will be devoted to this statute throughout this textbook. In Box 2.2, we present an excerpt from a Supreme Court opinion discussing the importance of the APA. (Note: The APA, as amended, excerpted in Appendix B.)

Creation of the Nuclear Energy Industry

The nuclear energy industry began with the federal government's development of the atomic bomb during World War II. Soon after the war ended, Congress passed the Atomic Energy Act of 1946, which established the Atomic Energy Commission (AEC) and gave it exclusive control over nuclear materials, technology or information. Scientists and policymakers knew the tremendous potential of atomic energy in meeting the Nation's energy needs. In his 1950 State of the Union Address, President Harry Truman stated that "in the peaceful development of atomic energy we stand on the threshold of new wonders." Yet profound concerns for public safety and national security dictated a cautious approach to the development and diffusion of this new technology. Hence the Atomic Energy Act prohibited private parties from owning nuclear materials and patenting inventions in the field of nuclear energy.

In the early 1950s national laboratories at Oak Ridge, Tennessee, and the University of Chicago carried on intensive research and development into nuclear energy production. In his "Atoms for Peace" address to the United Nations in 1953, President Dwight D. Eisenhower announced,

> The United States knows that peaceful power from atomic energy is no dream of the future. That capability, already proved, is here now—today. . . . [we must] hasten the day when fear of the atom will begin to disappear from the minds of the people and the governments of the East and West. . . . This greatest of destructive forces can be developed into a great boon for the benefit of all mankind.[35]

The following year, Congress enacted the Atomic Energy Act of 1954, which charged the AEC with encouraging the use of nuclear power and regulating its safety. Private companies would be permitted to own and operate nuclear plants under licenses and regulations issued by the AEC. The nuclear power industry was thus conceived and incubated by the federal government, but ultimately transferred to the private sector, albeit under close governmental supervision. In 1974 Congress passed the Energy Reorganization Act abolishing the Atomic Energy Commission. The AEC's research and development functions were transferred to the Energy Research and Development Administration, which would later become the Department of Energy. AEC's regulatory responsibilities passed to a new agency, the Nuclear Regulatory Commission (NRC).

The National Security State

In the wake of World War II the United States and its allies found themselves in a new and different kind of war. The Cold War with the Soviet Union and its communist allies around the world would last half a century and would profoundly affect the operations of government in this country. In the face of espionage and subversion, both real and imagined, national security and government secrecy became paramount values.

The Pentagon, the world's largest office building, was constructed during World War II to consolidate seventeen different structures that housed the Department of War. In 1947 the War Department was renamed the Department of the Army. In 1949, it was consolidated with the Department of the Navy and the Department of the Air Force to create the Department of Defense.

In passing the National Security Act of 1947, Congress established two crucial components of the **national security state:** the Central Intelligence Agency (CIA) and the National Security Council (NSC). An outgrowth of the Office of Strategic Services (OSS) that had been created in 1942, the CIA assumed primary responsibility for gathering information ("intelligence") to protect the national security. The CIA was also given responsibility for coordinating the activities of the intelligence community, which includes the Defense Intelligence Agency (DIA) and the National Security Agency (NSA), two agencies located within the Department of Defense. The NSC, located within the Executive Office of the President, was created to advise the president in matters of foreign policy and national security. Its members were to include the vice president, the secretaries of state and defense, the director of the CIA and the chairman of the Joint Chiefs of Staff. The NSC would become a major component of the process by which foreign policy is made.

Expansion of Social Security

By the 1950s, the Social Security program was in full flower. The number of beneficiaries had jumped from under a quarter million in 1940 to three and a half million in 1950. By amending the Social Security Act in 1954 and 1956, Congress created a program to provide benefits for disabled workers. By 1960, nearly fifteen million Americans were receiving Social Security benefits. Under President Dwight D. Eisenhower's 1953 Reorganization Plan, administration of Social Security, as well as the various federal programs dealing with public health and education, was transferred to the newly created Department of Health, Education and Welfare (HEW). Placing these programs in a cabinet-level department signaled their increasing importance in the domestic policy making process.

Regulating Aviation

The increasing popularity of air travel in the post–World War II period led to demands for an increased federal role in fostering and regulating the commercial aviation industry. The Federal Aviation Act of 1958[36] replaced earlier legislation with a comprehensive approach to the federal role in aviation. The statute created two independent agencies—the Federal Aviation Agency (FAA) and the Civil Aeronautics Board (CAB). The FAA took on responsibility for regulating airline safety and administering the air traffic control system. The CAB was made responsible for economic regulation of the airline industry as well as investigation of airplane accidents.

THE NEW FRONTIER, THE GREAT SOCIETY, AND THE WELFARE STATE

From his campaign and election in 1960 to his assassination in November 1963, President John F. Kennedy inspired his countrymen with his vision of the New Frontier. President Kennedy faced down the Soviet Union in the Cuban Missile Crisis of 1962 and put this country on track to land a man on the moon. In domestic policy, Kennedy championed civil rights, but his untimely death in 1963 prevented him from seeing the adoption of the landmark civil rights measures he supported. Kennedy's successor, Lyndon B. Johnson, was able to push through the Congress two statutes of fundamental importance to the Civil Rights Movement.

Landmark Civil Rights Legislation

The Civil Rights Act of 1964 prohibited racial discrimination in places of public accommodation and prohibited employers from discriminating against employees on the basis of race. The act also established the Equal Employment Opportunity Commission (EEOC), which, along with the Department of Justice, enforces the following **civil rights laws:**

- Title VII of the Civil Rights Act of 1964, as amended, prohibiting employment discrimination on the basis of race, color, religion, sex, or national origin;

- the Age Discrimination in Employment Act (ADEA) of 1967, as amended, prohibiting employment discrimination against individuals forty years of age and older;

- the Equal Pay Act (EPA) of 1963 prohibiting discrimination on the basis of gender in compensation for substantially similar work under similar conditions;

- Title I and Title V of the Americans with Disabilities Act (ADA) of 1990, prohibiting employment discrimination on the basis of disability in the private sector and state and local government;

- Section 501 and 505 of the Rehabilitation Act of 1973, as amended, prohibiting employment discrimination against federal employees with disabilities; and,

- the Civil Rights Act of 1991 providing monetary damages in cases of intentional discrimination and clarifying provisions regarding disparate impact actions.[37]

The Voting Rights Act

Aside from the Civil Rights Act of 1964, the most significant modern legislation in the field of civil rights is the Voting Rights Act of 1965. This far-reaching statute authorized the attorney general to suspend voting tests and assign federal voting registrars and poll watchers to any state or

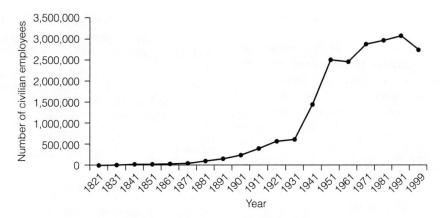

FIGURE 2.1 Growth in Federal Civilian Employment by Decade, 1821–1999

Source: U.S. Office of Personnel Management

political subdivision in which less than 50 percent of the voting age population was registered as of a specified date. In a civil action originating in the U.S. Supreme Court, South Carolina challenged the constitutionality of the Voting Rights Act. The Court, in an opinion by Chief Justice Warren, rejected this challenge, concluding that Congress had established an ample factual basis for the legislation and that the provisions in question "are a valid means for carrying out the commands of the Fifteenth Amendment."[38] The implementation of the Voting Rights Act brought additional administrative and regulatory responsibilities to the Department of Justice.

Expansion of the Welfare State

In 1965 President Johnson, a lifelong Democrat and admirer of Franklin Roosevelt, launched a broad range of initiatives to achieve what he called the "Great Society." Unlike the New Deal, which was conceived during a time of national crisis, the Great Society program was introduced during a period of economic vitality. The president's theme was that America could afford to do a better job of taking care of its people. Johnson, who in 1964 had been reelected in a landslide over conservative Republican Barry Goldwater, felt that he had a mandate from the American people to enact this

program, and Congress evidently agreed. In short order, Johnson proposed and Congress adopted the Medicare program, which provides health insurance for Americans over age sixty-five, and Medicaid, which provides health care for the poor. At Johnson's request, Congress greatly increased funding for Aid to Families with Dependent Children (AFDC), which had been established by the Social Security Act in 1935 as a means of helping children whose fathers were deceased. From 1965 to 1969, the federal government doubled the money it spent on AFDC, and the number of AFDC recipients increased by almost 60 percent. The administration of Social Security, Medicare, Medicaid, and AFDC required a large-scale bureaucracy, which was provided by the Department of Health, Education and Welfare, which had been established during the Eisenhower administration.

In 1965 Congress established the Department of Housing and Urban Development (HUD) to administer programs that provide federal aid for housing and community development. Acting under the mantle of **cooperative federalism,** HUD subsidized state and federal low-income housing projects. Two years later Congress created the Department of Transportation (DOT) to implement national transportation policy. Not since the New Deal had the federal government grown at this rate (see Figure 2.1).

The Freedom of Information Act (1966)

As we noted above, the Cold War era brought with it heightened concern for secrecy in government. By the mid-1960s, critics of various stripes were expressing concern about the inability of the public to gain access to information about activities of government agencies. To some extent, the concern was based on democratic theory: in a democracy the people should have access to information about *their* government. But some of the concern stemmed from the phenomenon of **regulatory capture** in which agencies become captives of the interest groups they are supposed to regulate. Obviously, this phenomenon is more likely to occur when information about agency activities is not publicly available.

Responding to these concerns, Congress enacted the **Freedom of Information Act (FOIA) in 1966**. Under FOIA, citizens can gain access to agency information that affects the public. While classified documents, medical records, proprietary matters, and various other types of information are not subject to FOIA, the act does provide a significant window through which citizens can monitor their government. FOIA has become an extremely important statutory component of administrative law, second in importance only to the Administrative Procedure Act. (FOIA is discussed at length in Chapter 4).

THE GOLDEN AGE OF REGULATION

In 1968, Republican Richard Nixon won the presidency on a promise to restore law and order to a turbulent society. While "law and order" is associated with conservatism, the Nixon Presidency is associated with some of the most significant advancements in the realm of government regulation. Herbert Stein, who served on the Council of Economic Advisers during the Nixon years, observed, "Probably more new regulation was imposed on the economy during the Nixon administration than in any other presidency since the New Deal."[39] The trend established during the Nixon presidency continued throughout the 1970s. The decade has been described as the "Golden Age of Regulation." During this period the term "regulatory state" was added to the political lexicon, joining "administrative state," "national security state," and "welfare state" as a popular characterization of the federal government.

Environmental Protection

Without question, the most significant development in the evolution of the contemporary regulatory state was the coming of far-ranging environmental regulation. The process began in earnest in 1969 with the enactment of the National Environmental Policy Act (NEPA).[40] This statute required all federal agencies to conduct environmental impact studies prior to undertaking or approving any major action affecting the environment, such as the construction of airports, office buildings, power plants, and highways. In 1973, Congress enacted the Endangered Species Act (ESA),[41] which prohibited government or private action that results in a "taking" of an endangered species of plant or animal designated by the Office of the Interior. ESA and NEPA are powerful tools used by the environmental community in opposing projects that in its judgment adversely affect the natural environment.

In 1970, President Nixon issued an **executive order** creating the Environmental Protection Agency (EPA) by consolidating a number of federal offices and programs. EPA soon became the most important and controversial federal regulatory agency as Congress vested it with broad regulatory authority and enforcement power in the environmental area. EPA was given rulemaking and/or enforcement authority under the following major environmental statutes:

- Clean Air Act (CLA)
- Clean Water Act (CWA)
- Resource Conservation and Recovery Act (RCRA)

- Toxic Substances Control Act (TSCA)
- Comprehensive Environmental Response, Compensation and Liability Act (CERCLA)

With its broad responsibilities for environmental protection, EPA quickly became a focal point for political controversy, as environmentalists, business interests, and state and local officials sought to advance or protect their interests. From the outset critics in business and industry charged that the EPA was imposing unreasonable policies that would threaten the economic health of the nation. On the other hand, environmentalists often accused EPA of dragging its feet in the face of political resistance to environmental progress.

Occupational Safety and Health

The Occupational Safety and Health Administration (OSHA), an agency within the Department of Labor, was established in 1970 to develop and enforce regulations for the safety and health of workers in major industries. Congress has given OSHA the power to make rules that are "reasonably necessary or appropriate to provide safe and healthful employment and places of employment." One of OSHA's principal concerns today is the exposure of workers to hazardous chemicals. OSHA routinely inspects workplaces and issues citations to companies that fail to comply with its regulations. Labor unions and environmentalists strongly support OSHA in these activities, but business interests often resent OSHA's "meddling."

The Consumer Product Safety Commission

In passing the Consumer Product Safety Act of 1972, Congress created the Consumer Product Safety Commission (CPSC) and directed it to protect the public "against unreasonable risks of injuries associated with consumer products." CPSC was given jurisdiction over a broad array of consumer products, virtually all products that were not subject to regulation by another federal agency.

Regulating Campaign Finance

In 1975, Congress created the Federal Election Commission (FEC) to administer and enforce the Federal Election Campaign Act (FECA)—the statute that governs the financing of federal elections. The duties of the FEC, which is an independent regulatory agency, are to disclose campaign finance information, to enforce the provisions of the law such as the limits and prohibitions on contributions, and to oversee the public funding of presidential elections. In 2002, Congress enacted new campaign finance legislation designed, among other things, to limit the influence of previously unregulated "soft money," that is, funds given to political parties and other organizations that are expended on behalf of candidates. On June 22, 2002, the FEC issued a new rule entitled "Prohibited and Excessive Contributions: Non-Federal Funds or Soft Money.[42] The new rule was published in the *Federal Register* on July 29, 2002.[43] Seventy-eight pages of the Federal Register are devoted to the publication and explanation of the new rule. A perusal of the new rule provides an immediate sense of the complexity of federal regulation.

Energy Policy

In response to the energy crisis of the 1970s, President Carter persuaded Congress in 1977 to enact legislation creating the Department of Energy. The Department brought together various federal programs and offices, including the nuclear weapons program previously housed in the Department of Defense. By assuming cabinet-level status, the new agency dramatized the importance of the energy issue at a time when future energy supplies were in doubt. In the 1980s, the nuclear weapons program became the department's top priority. In the 1990s, with the end of the Cold War, emphasis shifted to the cleanup of the toxic and radioactive wastes that had been produced by decades of nuclear weapons research and production.

Welfare and Education

When the Department of Health, Education and Welfare (HEW) was created in 1953, it had roughly 35,000 employees and a budget of $5.4 billion. By 1979, due to the growth of the welfare state, the Department employed nearly 160,000 workers and administered a budget of approximately $173 billion. At the same time, education, which had always been a state and local matter, was becoming a national policy concern. At the behest of President Carter, Congress in 1979 adopted the Department of Education Organization Act, providing for a separate Department of Education. Thus HEW became the Department of Health and Human Services (HHS).

Traditionally, public education in the United States had been primarily, if not exclusively, the domain of the state and local governments. Most public school districts were locally funded and administered with some degree of state-level control. The Supreme Court's decision in *Brown v. Board of Education* (1954), striking down state laws mandating racial segregation in the public schools, paved the way for the federal government to assume a greater role in public education. The Elementary and Secondary Education Act and the Higher Education Act, both passed in 1965, instituted a set of programs to provide federal financial assistance to public schools. Title VI of the Civil Rights Act of 1964 prohibited racial discrimination by all educational institutions that received federal funds. Title IX of the Education Amendments of 1972 prohibited gender-based discrimination and Section 504 of the Rehabilitation Act of 1973 prohibited discrimination based on disability. The administration of these programs and enforcement of these prohibitions was assigned to the Department of Health, Education and Welfare and passed to the newly created Department of Education in 1979. Within the Department of Education, enforcement of civil rights policies was assigned to the Office of Civil Rights.

THE REAGAN REVOLUTION

The election of Ronald Reagan to the presidency in 1980 was a watershed event in American political history. Reagan rode a wave of discontent in American society. To a great extent, the public was frustrated with the performance of the economy, which, shocked by spikes in oil prices, had experienced high levels of inflation combined with recession. Reagan also capitalized on widespread dissatisfaction with the federal government. Reagan's strongest support came from the business community, which demanded relief from government regulation it regarded as excessive and oppressive. The Reagan administration came to Washington with a clear agenda of reducing the size and scope of the federal government, at least in domestic affairs. The administration sought to curtail regulatory activity and even deregulate industries altogether. It sought to reduce the size of federal welfare programs. President Reagan went so far as to call for the abolition of the recently created Departments of Education and Energy. In his 1981 inaugural address, Reagan observed, "Government is not the solution to our problem; government is the problem."

"Reaganomics"

President Reagan's economic policy was predicated on the theory that federal income tax rates were too high and were depressing economic activity. Lowering tax rates would stimulate the economy and ultimately increase revenue flows to the federal government. In the short-run, however, government spending would have to be cut. At President Reagan's urging, Congress enacted the Economic Recovery Tax Act of 1981, which cut income tax rates by 25 percent over a three-year period. Eventually, these tax cuts did contribute to a revival of the economy. But the short-term effect was the creation of massive budget deficits. Some in the Reagan Administration wanted to balance the budget by drastically cutting social spending, but the Administration pursued a more moderate course. Substantial cuts were made in many social programs, but Social Security and Medicare were protected. At the same time, the military received a level of fiscal support not seen since World War II.

Deregulation

Essential to Ronald Reagan's conservative philosophy was the proposition that the federal government had imposed excessive regulation on American business, thereby depressing economic activity and stifling innovation. Actually, significant **deregulation** of industry had begun during the Carter Administration, as the airline industry was deregulated in 1978 and the trucking industry in 1980. Under Reagan, this process continued, as Congress enacted numerous deregulation statutes. For example, in 1982 Congress enacted a law allowing savings and loan institutions to make investments that had been previously prohibited. President Reagan appointed probusiness conservatives to head the Department of the Interior and the Environmental Protection Agency, which resulted in a relaxation of environmental restrictions and allowed for greater economic exploitation of public lands. On several occasions, the Reagan administration proposed the abolition of the Interstate Commerce Commission, which had been stripped of many of its regulatory functions, but Congress refused to accede to this demand.

Cabinet Status for the Veterans Administration

The United States has always provided assistance for veterans of the nation's wars. When the United States entered World War I in 1917, Congress included programs for disability compensation and rehabilitation programs and life insurance. Various government agencies handled different programs until 1930 when Congress authorized the president to "consolidate and coordinate Government activities affecting war veterans." This led to the establishment of the Veterans Administration (VA).

After World War II the VA assumed a greater role administering educational benefits for veterans. Further educational assistance acts were passed for the benefit of veterans of the Korean Conflict, the Vietnam Era, the Persian Gulf War, and the All-Volunteer Force.

In 1989, President Reagan's successor, President George H. W. Bush, signed legislation elevating the VA to a Cabinet-level department and renaming it the Department of Veterans Affairs. Its stated purpose is to administer laws providing benefits and services to veterans, their dependents, and their beneficiaries. In administering veterans' affairs today, the VA handles a panoply of veterans' benefits including educational assistance programs, life insurance, and disability compensation. It also operates a health-care system consisting of medical centers, outpatient clinics, and nursing home units.

REINVENTING GOVERNMENT? THE CLINTON YEARS

In 1992 presidential candidate Bill Clinton campaigned as a "New Democrat," meaning that he was willing to reevaluate his Party's long-standing positions on certain domestic policy issues. Yet in his first year in office President Clinton appointed First Lady Hillary Rodham Clinton to head the Task Force on National Health Care Reform, which resulted in a proposal to create a complex maze of regulation and bureaucracy to manage the Nation's health-care system. Popular disenchantment with this proposal was one factor that produced a landmark shift in the partisan balance of power in the 1994 midterm elections. The Republican Party gained control of both houses of Congress for the first time in a half century. Clearly, the public had sent a message that it wanted the scope and power of the federal government reduced. In his 1995 State of the Union Address, President Clinton proclaimed, "The era of big government is over."

Between 1995 and the Clinton impeachment saga of late 1998–early 1999, President Clinton and the Republican Congress were able to reach agreement on a number of important issues, including free trade, deregulation of agriculture, and welfare reform. Still, a number of policy and regulatory issues remained divisive, especially those pertaining to environmental protection.

NAFTA and the WTO

Much to the chagrin of its supporters in organized labor and the environmental community, the Clinton administration committed itself to a policy of free trade and worked to negotiate new agreements to eliminate or reduce trade barriers. The North American Free Trade Agreement, better known as NAFTA, sought to create a common market among the United States, Canada, and Mexico. Negotiated by the Bush Administration in 1991 and 1992 and pushed through Congress by the Clinton administration in 1993, NAFTA eliminated trade barriers, eased restrictions on foreign investment, and established common rules to protect intellectual property rights. One of the most controversial aspects of the Agreement, known as "investor-to-state" dispute resolution, allowed investors to seek monetary damages from signatory countries for the imposition of regulations that violate their "free trade rights." Claims were to be adjudicated by secret international tribunals. Critics of this process expressed concern that government regulations to protect public health and safety as well as the natural environment could be threatened.

In 1994, President Clinton secured congressional approval of a new international agreement that brought the United States into the World Trade Organization (WTO), a supranational agency devoted to issues of international commerce. The WTO acts as a quasi-judicial body with power to enforce sanctions against nations that violate international trade agreements. NAFTA and the WTO provided a glimpse of the powerful implications that the globalization of the world economy might hold for government regulation and, ultimately, the very concept of national sovereignty.

Deregulation and Reregulation of Agriculture

The Federal Agriculture Improvement and Reform Act of 1996[44] eliminated much of the agricultural regulation that had been in place since the New Deal. During an era of rising global demand for American farm products, price supports, quotas, and set asides were phased out as American farmers returned to free market agriculture. Farmers were once again free to make their own decisions as to what to plant and how much to plant. Of course, with this freedom came increased risk. In 1998, responding to low commodity prices and declining farm incomes, Congress enacted a $7 billion agricultural relief bill. The increasing globalization of the world economy created downward pressures on commodity prices and by 2000 many farming interests were calling for reregulation of agriculture. In 2002, Congress accommodated these demands by enacting the Farm Security and Rural Investment Act,[45] which boosted crop and dairy subsidies some 67 percent over a six-year period. Of course, the expanded farm subsidies continue to be administered by the U.S. Department of Agriculture.

Abolition of the Interstate Commerce Commission

When the Department of Transportation was created in 1966, it assumed the safety functions theretofore performed by the Interstate Commerce Commission (ICC). When the process of deregulation began during the Carter administration, the ICC's authority to regulate railroad and trucking routes and rates was eliminated. As noted above, the Reagan Administration sought unsuccessfully to abolish the Commission. President Clinton was able to do what President

Reagan could not. In December 1995, Clinton signed the Interstate Commerce Commission Termination Act,[46] which eliminated the ICC and transferred its remaining functions to the Surface Transportation Board, a smaller new agency located within the Department of Transportation.

Welfare Reform

One of the most dramatic consequences of the Republican takeover of Congress in 1994 was the enactment of **welfare reform.** Critics of the welfare state charged that welfare programs had created a class of people who were dependent solely on government and had contributed to the decline of the nuclear family among the poor. In 1996, Congress enacted the Personal Responsibility and Work Opportunity Reconciliation Act of 1996,[47] better known as the "welfare reform bill." The new law imposed a five-year lifetime limit on assistance to welfare recipients. Aid to Families with Dependent Children, the mainstay of federal welfare policy, was replaced by Temporary Aid to Needy Families (TANF). The new approach was that welfare assistance was to be temporary and not result in a dependency status.

In March 2002, Tommy Thompson, Secretary of Health and Human Services, testified before the Senate Finance Committee updating the Committee on the progress that has been achieved under the 1996 legislation. According to Secretary Thompson, the new law "dramatically shifted national welfare policy by promoting work, encouraging personal responsibility, discouraging out-of-wedlock pregnancies and supporting marriage."[48] He reported that as a result of the reforms nearly seven million fewer people are on welfare than in 1996; that 2.8 million fewer children are in poverty, there has been a dramatic rise in child support collection, and in employment of single mothers. Thompson outlined the president's proposals that include engaging all TANF families headed by an adult in activities leading to self-sufficiency.

The National Performance Review

Shortly after taking office in January 1993, President Bill Clinton appointed Vice President Albert Gore to head a task force called the National Performance Review. Operating under the banner of "reinventing government," Gore and his staff spent six months scouring the federal bureaucracy for waste, inefficiency, and needless or silly regulations. The National Performance Review generated considerable publicity for the Clinton administration. The degree to which government was in fact "reinvented" was certainly in doubt by the time Clinton and Gore left office in 2001. The level of regulatory activity by federal agencies remained very high, although the regulatory process was constrained somewhat. During the 2000 presidential campaign Al Gore made numerous references to the success of the Clinton administration in reducing the number of federal government employees. But to a great extent the reductions in the federal workforce targeted civilian employment within the Department of Defense.

Environmental Regulation
during the Clinton Administration

The policy area in which the Clinton Administration was most committed to regulation was environmental protection. The government's approach to managing public lands shifted decisively from exploitation of natural resources to protection of wilderness areas and endangered species. Perhaps the most significant regulatory development was EPA's toughening of the National Ambient Air Quality Standards (NAAQS). Many of the administration's most controversial rules were announced in the final year of the Clinton presidency, including tougher standards for drinking water, motor fuels, and energy efficiency of appliances. Ten days before President Clinton left the White House, the U.S. Forest Service announced a final rule restricting the building of new roads on public lands. Designed to protect animal habitat and preserve the integrity of wilderness areas, critics argued that the rule would have a significant adverse impact on economic development.

GEORGE W. BUSH
AND THE WAR ON TERRORISM

After a disputed election that placed a harsh spotlight on the system by which this country administers elections, President George W. Bush came into office in January 2001 promising, like Ronald Reagan twenty years before, to cut taxes, reduce bureaucracy, and rebuild the military. The terrorist attacks of September 11, 2001, would have a profound impact on the Bush agenda. Bush declared war on international terrorism and ordered American forces into action in Afghanistan and other hot spots around the globe. Suddenly, domestic security became an issue of paramount importance. This dramatic shift in national priorities was reflected by the fact that federal spending on domestic security doubled from roughly $20 billion in fiscal year (FY) 2002 to $40 billion in FY 2003. The war against Iraq in the spring of 2003 led to increased levels of concern about terrorism directed at American interests at home and abroad. Americans steeled themselves for a long period in which domestic security and counterterrorism would eclipse other governmental concerns.

Homeland Security

Responsibility for domestic security has long been spread across a host of federal agencies, including the Federal Aviation Administration, the Federal Bureau of Investigation, the Customs Service, the Coast Guard, the Immigration and Naturalization Service, and the Post Office, just to name a few of the more prominent ones. Believing that there needed to be one federal agency to oversee these efforts, President Bush issued Executive Order 13228, creating a new Office of Homeland Security within the Executive Office of the President. The office was charged with developing and coordinating a national strategy to protect the United States from terrorism and with disseminating information regarding the risk of terrorist attacks to federal, state, and local authorities and the American public. This would require extensive coordination with state, local, and other federal agencies. Critics charged that the new agency lacked sufficient power, i.e., statutory authority, to accomplish its mission.

During the summer of 2002, President Bush proposed a new cabinet-level Department of Homeland Security, which the White House called "the most significant transformation of the U.S. government in over a half-century."[49] A number of existing federal agencies would be brought into the new department, including the Coast Guard, the Immigration and Naturalization Service, and the Federal Emergency Management Agency. Of course, creation of this new department required an Act of Congress, which was introduced as the Homeland Security Act of 2002.[50] In November 2002, Congress enacted the measure creating the Department of Homeland Security as the fifteenth cabinet-level department within the executive branch.

The mission of the Department of Homeland Security (DHS) includes preparing for natural disasters and terrorist attacks through preventative planning, technology, and coordinated efforts. The Act establishes the post of Secretary, to be appointed by the President, and confirmed by the U.S. Senate and five under secretaries, who, subject to Senate confirmation oversee (1) Border and Transportation; (2) Emergency Preparedness (3) Science and Technology; (4) Information Analysis and Infrastructure; and (5) Management.

THE FEDERAL
BUREAUCRACY TODAY

The contemporary executive branch is comprised of the president, the vice president, their staffs, the president's cabinet, the **Executive Office of the President,** fifteen major departments and a host of independent agencies. All told, the executive branch employs about 2.9 million workers (not counting uniformed personnel in the military services).

The Executive Office of the President

One of the most striking developments in the growth of the administrative state is the bureaucratization of the presidency. Whereas George Washington sought advice from his cabinet, and Andrew Jackson employed a group of informal advisors known as the "Kitchen Cabinet," presidents today are surrounded by a massive staff and numerous offices. Collectively, these offices are known as the Executive Office of the President, which consists of the following entities:

- Council of Economic Advisers
- Council on Environmental Quality
- Domestic Policy Council
- National Economic Council
- National Security Council
- Office of Administration
- Office of Faith-Based and Community Initiatives
- Office of Management and Budget (OMB)
- Office of National AIDS Policy
- Office of National Drug Control Policy
- Office of Science and Technology Policy
- President's Foreign Intelligence Advisory Board
- United States Trade Representative (USTR)
- White House Staff

Of particular significance for administrative law is the Office of Management and Budget. By preparing the annual budget that the president submits to Congress, OMB serves as a device by which presidents maintain control over the massive executive branch. OMB evaluates agency policies, programs, and procedures in an ongoing effort to make agency activities comport with the philosophy of the president. (For further discussion of OMB, see Chapter 8.)

The Cabinet-Level Departments

As we noted earlier in the chapter, during the First Congress there were three major executive departments: Treasury, State, and War, as well as the offices of attorney general and postmaster general. Today, there are fifteen **cabinet-level departments:**

The Department of Agriculture. Despite the deregulation of American agriculture in the 1990s, the Department of Agriculture (USDA) continues to perform a number of important functions in the areas of research and development, food safety, foreign trade, conservation, rural economic development, and social welfare. USDA administers several important welfare programs, including Food Stamps, the Women and Infant Care (WIC) program, and the School Lunch program. USDA's Food Safety and Inspection Service inspects and grades meat, poultry, and eggs. USDA also houses the U.S. Forest Service, which is responsible for administering America's National Forests. USDA's legal authority is located in Title 7 of the United States Code.

The Department of Commerce. The Department of Commerce (DOC) is home to a number of bureaus that perform extremely important functions in the American economy. One of the most important of these bureaus is the Patent and Trademark Office (PTO). Its function is to "to promote the progress of science and the useful arts by securing for limited times to inventors the exclusive right to their respective discoveries."[51] The Bureau of Economic Analysis is one of the world's foremost statistical agencies, providing a constant stream of data on the performance of the American economy. These data are extremely important to policy makers and planners within government, but also to investors and to the business community. The Census Bureau, another agency within the DOC, conducts the constitutionally mandated decennial census, which is the basis of apportionment of representation in the U.S. House of Representatives and in the state legislatures and which provides crucial data for both government and business in this country. Many Americans depend heavily on weather data and forecasts provided by the National Oceanic and Atmospheric Administration, another agency within the DOC.

The Department of Defense. Since 1949 the Department of Defense (DOD) has retained the same basic structure. The National Command Authority (the president and the secretary of defense) direct military operations, with the president as the constitutional commander in chief of the armed forces. The DOD includes the three military departments, Army, Navy and Air Force, and fifteen defense agencies. All told, the Department of Defense consists of 1.37 million men and women in the active duty forces, another 1.28 million members in the reserve forces, and 669,000 civilian employees. It administers an annual budget in excess of $300 billion.

The Department of Education. The Department of Education administers more than $13 billion in federal grants to state and local school authorities to support elementary and secondary education. It also administers Pell Grants and student loans to students in higher education. The Office of Civil Rights (OCR) enforces a number of federal statutes prohibiting various forms of discrimination by educational institutions that receive federal financial assistance. To that end, OCR fields complaints, conducts investigations and hearings, and refers cases to the Department of Justice for further legal action.

The Department of Energy. The Department of Energy (DOE) is responsible for administering the nation's nuclear weapons research and development program. It also procures nuclear power plants for the Navy's nuclear powered ships and submarines. DOE also is responsible for research and development of technologies to increase domestic energy production. One of DOE's most controversial and difficult assignments is to develop a strategy for the long-term storage of radioactive waste. In February 2002, Energy Secretary Spencer Abraham, citing "sound science" and a "compelling national interest," formally recommended to President Bush that Yucca Mountain in Nevada be designated as "the nation's first geologic repository for high-level radioactive waste."

The Department of Health and Human Services. The Department of Health and Human Services (HHS) administers more than three hundred programs affecting public health and welfare. HHS runs Medicare, the nation's largest medical insurance program handling nearly a billion claims a year. HHS supervises Temporary Aid to Needy Families (TANF), the federal-state cooperative program that assists more than seven million persons. It also supervises Medicaid, the joint federal-state program providing medical care to the indigent. HHS incorporates the National Institutes of Health and the Centers for Disease Control and Prevention, the preeminent public health agencies in the country. It also includes the Food and Drug Administration (FDA), an important regulatory agency charged with assuring the safety of foods, cosmetics, pharmaceuticals, and medical products. During the Clinton administration, the FDA created controversy when it attempted to regulate tobacco products. Ultimately, the Supreme Court held that Congress did not intend for FDA to exercise such authority.[52]

The Department of Housing and Urban Development. The basic mission of the Department of Housing and Urban Development (HUD) is to provide housing to those who otherwise might not be able to secure it. To this end, HUD operates programs that seek to create, rehabilitate, and maintain affordable housing. It enforces laws prohibiting discrimination in housing. It funds public housing programs operated by local governments. HUD makes grants to local governments to promote urban renewal and economic development of inner cities and also offers mortgage subsidies to individuals to foster home ownership. HUD's Urban Revitalization Program, better known as HOPE VI, funds the demolition of Depression-era public housing projects and their replacement with affordable single-family homes.

The Department of the Interior. The Department of the Interior is responsible for managing the nation's parks and public lands and promoting conservation of the natural environment. Key agencies within DOI include:

- The National Park Service, which administers national parks, monuments, and historic areas.

- The U.S. Fish and Wildlife Service, which is responsible for promoting conservation of the nation's plants and animals and their habitats and has enforcement authority under the Endangered Species Act.

- The Bureau of Land Management, which is responsible for administering more than 62 million acres of public lands, most of which are located in the Western states.

- The Bureau of Indian Affairs, which provides assistance to Indian tribes and collects money from companies that drill for oil and gas on Indian reservations. The money goes into a trust fund to provide assistance to Native Americans.

The Department of Justice. The Department of Justice (DOJ) is the law firm for the executive branch of the federal government. The attorney general advises the president on legal policy issues. The solicitor general represents the United States before the Supreme Court. United States Attorneys are the prosecutors in the federal criminal justice system. DOJ has divisions devoted to the most important areas of federal law enforcement: civil rights, antitrust, criminal, environmental, and tax. DOJ also includes two of the most significant law enforcement agencies: the Federal Bureau of Investigation (FBI) and the Drug Enforcement Administration (DEA). Other important agencies within DOJ include the U.S. Marshals Service, the Bureau of Justice Statistics, and the Federal Bureau of Prisons.

The Department of Labor. The mission of the Department of Labor (DOL) is to promote the welfare of the American workforce. DOL enforces federal labor laws pertaining to discrimination, the minimum wage, unionization and collective bargaining, and workplace safety. It administers a workers' compensation program for federal government employees. Through the Bureau of Labor Statistics, DOL also collects data on the changing American workforce and the performance of the economy. It tracks unemployment, wages, and layoffs, as well as consumer and producer prices for goods and services. DOL is also home to OSHA, the Occupational Safety and Health Administration, the mission of which is the prevention of injuries and health problems stemming from conditions of employment. Established to implement the Occupational Safety and Health Act of 1970,[53] OSHA sets health and safety standards for virtually all workplaces in the United States.

The Department of State. The State Department plays a crucial role in the formulation and implementation of America's foreign policy. The secretary of state is a member of the National Security Council and a key advisor to the president on matters of foreign affairs. The State Department houses the nation's diplomatic corps—all of the ambassadors and members of the Foreign Service who represent the United States through embassies and consulates around the world. The State Department provides assistance to Americans abroad and issues passports to those who wish to travel abroad. The State Department houses the United States mission to the United Nations. It is also home to the Agency for International Development (USAID), which plays the leading role in the distribution of foreign aid.

The Department of Transportation. The Department of Transportation (DOT) was created in 1967 to coordinate policies and administer the transportation programs of the national government, especially urban mass transit systems. As a cabinet officer, the secretary of transportation is the principal adviser to the president in matters relating to federal transportation problems. Through the Federal Highway Administration, DOT administers federal grants to the states to construct and maintain federal highways. The DOT is also home to the Federal Aviation Administration, which regulates airport security and airline safety and administers the air traffic control system.

The Treasury Department. The Department of the Treasury collects taxes, issues money, and manages the finances of the federal government. Key agencies performing these functions are the Internal Revenue Service, the U.S. Mint, the Bureau of Engraving & Printing, the Comptroller of the Currency and the Bureau of the Public Debt. The Treasury also includes an important law enforcement agency, the Bureau of Alcohol, Tobacco & Firearms. Also located within Treasury, the Office of Thrift Supervision is the principal regulator of federally chartered savings and loan institutions.

The Department of Veterans Affairs. Better known as the VA, the Department of Veterans Affairs administers benefits and delivers services to American veterans and their families. Approximately seventy million people, nearly one-fourth of the nation's population, are potentially eligible for VA benefits. More than half of the VA's spending consists of direct payment to individuals through pensions and educational benefits. Another 40 percent of the budget is devoted to providing medical care.

The Department of Homeland Security. When the newest of the cabinet-level departments was established in November 2002, it represented the largest reorganization of the executive branch in fifty years (see Table 2.1). The new department merged more than twenty existing agencies, including the Immigration and Naturalization Service, the Coast Guard, the Secret Service, and the Customs Service into a massive new organization employing more than 175,000 workers and operating on an annual budget in the $40 billion range. The creation of the new department signals the high priority

that the national government assigns to domestic security as the nation prosecutes the "war on terrorism."

The Independent Agencies

Beginning with the creation of the Interstate Commerce Commission in 1887, Congress has created numerous agencies in the executive branch but located outside the cabinet-level departments. These "independent agencies," so called because agency heads are protected from presidential removal, include both regulatory and administrative agencies. Included among the more prominent of these agencies are the following:

- **Consumer Product Safety Commission (CPSC):** Protects the public against unreasonable risks of injuries associated with over 15,000 consumer products.[54]

- **Environmental Protection Agency (EPA):** Administers federal laws and regulations (Clean Air Act, Clean Water Act, etc.) to protect health and safeguard the natural environment.[55]

- **Federal Communications Commission (FCC):** Regulates interstate and international communications by radio, television, wire, satellite, and cable.[56]

- **Federal Deposit Insurance Corporation (FDIC):** Maintains stability of and public confidence in nation's financial system. Insures bank deposits; promotes sound banking practices.[57]

- **Federal Election Commission (FEC):** Administers and enforces laws governing financing of federal elections; oversees public funding of presidential elections.[58]

- **Federal Energy Regulatory Commission (FERC):** Regulates transmission and sale of natural gas, oil by pipeline, and sales of electricity in interstate commerce.[59]

- **Federal Reserve System (FRS):** Administers nation's credit and monetary policies;

Table 2.1 Constituent Agencies of the Department of Homeland Security

Directorate	Agency	Prior Location within Executive Branch
Border and Transportation Security	The U.S. Customs Service	Department of Treasury
	Immigration and Naturalization Service	Department of Justice
	Federal Protective Service	General Services Administration
	Transportation Security Administration	Department of Transportation
	Federal Law Enforcement Training Center	Department of Treasury
	Animal and Plant Health Inspection Service	Agriculture
	Office for Domestic Preparedness	Department of Justice
Emergency Preparedness and Response	The Federal Emergency Management Agency	Independent agency
	Strategic National Stockpile and National Disaster Medical System	Department of Health & Human Services
	Nuclear Incident Response Team	Department of Energy
	Domestic Emergency Support Teams	Department of Justice
	National Domestic Preparedness Office	Federal Bureau of Investigation
Science and Technology	CBRN Countermeasures Programs	Department of Energy
	Environmental Measurements Laboratory	Department of Energy
	National BW Defense Analysis Center	Department of Defense
	Plum Island Animal Disease Center	Department of Agriculture
Information Analysis and Infrastructure Protection	Critical Infrastructure Assurance Office	Department of Commerce
	Federal Computer Incident Response Center	General Services Administration
	National Communications System	Department of Defense
	National Infrastructure Protection Center	Federal Bureau of Investigation
	Energy Security and Assurance Program	Department of Energy

NOTE: The Secret Service and the Coast Guard are also located in the Department of Homeland Security, although not within one of the four "directorates."

SOURCE: U.S. Department of Homeland Security, online at http://www.dhs.gov

supervises and maintains stability of banking system; sets ceilings on interest rates.[60]

- **Federal Trade Commission (FTC):** Protects competitive economic system from monopolies and restraints on trade, and unfair and deceptive trade practices.[61]

- **Nuclear Regulatory Commission (NRC):** Licenses and regulates civilian use of nuclear energy; oversees reactor safety; investigates nuclear accidents.[62]

- **Securities and Exchange Commission (SEC):** Administers federal securities laws; protects investors from fraud and deception in sale of securities.[63]

CONTEMPORARY STATE AND LOCAL ADMINISTRATION

State governments and many local governments are highly bureaucratized. State governments administer major programs in public health, education, welfare, corrections, highway construction, and maintenance. They also regulate utilities, banking, insurance, and numerous professions. Local governments provide police and fire protection, waste collection and disposal, and operate public schools.

The Role of State Governments

The foundation of state government is the state constitution. The governor is the chief executive of the state with powers that vary somewhat in the individual states. Every state has a number of constitutional officers, that is, positions created by the state constitution. These usually include a lieutenant governor, secretary of state, treasurer, and attorney general. Like the governor, in most instances these officials are elected. Other state offices and agencies are created by legislation. Because taxation is an essential element of government, every state has an agency responsible for collection of revenues.

The voters elect members to serve specified terms in a bicameral (two-house) legislature in all states except Nebraska, which has a unicameral (one-house) legislative body. Likewise, each state has its own trial and appellate courts. In some states judges are elected while in others the governor appoints judges, often on recommendation of a merit selection committee.

States retain all powers inherent in sovereignty other than those that the thirteen original states delegated to the national government upon ratifying the federal constitution. Newer states agreed to this upon admission to the Union. This means the state has the power of eminent domain and the power to levy taxes and to enact laws in respect to crimes, property rights, education, and domestic relations. The state is also the repository of the police power, i.e., the power to enact laws to promote the health, safety, and welfare of the people. States, of course, are restricted from impinging on powers delegated to the federal government. Therefore, state laws must not contravene federal laws and the rights guaranteed under the federal constitution. Since the New Deal era the role of the states in exercising its police power has been somewhat diminished by the expanded role of the federal government.

State Administrative Agencies

Like the federal government, states exercise many of their executive and legislative powers through administrative agencies. States often have hundreds of agencies that administer and regulate in many and varied fields. The increased delegation of executive and legislative authorities in the twentieth century resulted in the creation of a plethora of state agencies. This caused a growing concern over the administrative procedures followed by state agencies. In the 1930s and 1940s state legislatures began enacting laws requiring publication of agency rules and regulations. A Model State Administrative Procedures Act (or similar legislation) has now been adopted by most states. These laws more or less parallel the Federal Administrative Procedure Act discussed earlier in this chapter and provide for publication of agency rules, procedures for handling disputes, and the right of judicial review of agency rulings. (The full text of the Model State Administrative Procedure Act can be easily found on various web sites.)

Some of the most common areas where states exercise administrative and regulatory authority include:

■ **Taxation and revenue.** States have a department of revenue responsible for administering the various taxes (income, intangible, excise, sales, etc.) that the state imposes.

■ **Environmental protection.** Every state has its own counterpart to the EPA. In fact, state environmental protection agencies have major responsibilities for enforcement of federal environmental statutes. However, some states go beyond federal standards in imposing various environmental regulations. States also have extensive regulations regarding hunting and fishing and have agencies to enforce these regulations.

■ **Social welfare programs.** All states have agencies dedicated to the delivery of social services to the indigent. For example, every state has an agency responsible for administering Temporary Aid to Needy Families (TANF), the principal federal welfare program for the poor. An example of cooperative federalism, TANF is funded principally by the federal government but administered by state agencies, which operate under federal guidelines. The degree of federal control of the program is less today, since Congress reformed welfare entitlements in 1996. Before then the chief welfare program was known as Aid to Families with Dependent Children. As with TANF, every state has an agency responsible for administering Medicaid, the federally funded program providing medical care to the poor. Like TANF, Medicaid is administered by state agencies under supervision of the federal government. States are free to establish their own rules of eligibility of Medicaid as long they meet the minimum standards enforced by the Health Care Finance Administration (HCFA). Medicaid is administered differently by agencies in each state. For example, in Alaska the Medicaid programs are administered by the Department of Health and Social Service. In Tennessee, Medicaid is called "TennCare" and is administered by the Department of Finance and Administration.

■ **Other social services.** States have long accepted a responsibility to care for those who cannot care for themselves, including orphans, abused or neglected children, the mentally ill, and the mentally retarded. In law this responsibility is termed *parens patriae,* literally "the parent of the country." Every state has agencies that operate programs for persons who are unable to care for themselves and have no one else to care for them. Every state operates hospitals for persons with mental illnesses and serious mental disabilities and has an agency to provide services to families. Serious administrative law issues can arise when the state, as *parens patriae,* takes custody of children who suffer from neglect or abuse and places them in foster care or in other supervised programs.

■ **Highway construction.** States are the primary units of government when it comes to construction and maintenance of roads and bridges. Another good example of cooperative federalism, state highway programs receive grants from the federal government to build and maintain federal highways such as the interstate highway system.

■ **Education.** State governments are responsible for operating systems of higher education, including universities, colleges, community colleges, and vocational-technical institutions. All states have executive agencies devoted to the administration of higher education. They also have agencies, typically large-scale departments, for the purpose of certifying elementary and secondary school teachers and assisting local school districts.

■ **Law enforcement and public safety.** Most states have a state-level counterpart to the FBI. Most have an agency responsible for maintaining safety on the state's highways, often known as the highway patrol or the state troopers. State agencies issue drivers' licenses and, in many states, operate motor vehicle inspection programs.

■ **Prisons.** Every state has a prison system and this agency is generally known as the Department of Corrections. In California, the Department of Corrections employs about fifty thousand people, has an annual budget of almost $5 billion, and maintains nearly a hundred separate facilities housing more than three hundred thousand convicted felons. Yet, as large as it is, the California Department of Corrections consumes only about 6 percent of the state budget.[64]

■ **Regulation of businesses and professions.** Every state has agencies that license and regulate certain professions, including law, medicine, psychology, architecture, contracting, real estate, and cosmetology. States have agencies that charter and regulate state banks and savings and loan institutions. Many have state agencies or commissions responsible for regulating the insurance industry.

■ **Workers compensation and unemployment insurance.** At the state level a department of labor often administers these programs.

■ **Public utilities.** In most states a public service commission regulates rates and service conditions of telephone companies, electric and gas utilities, and in some instances water and sewer utilities.

■ **Personnel and pensions.** Most states have agencies that administer health insurance programs for state officers and employees as well as pension plans for constitutional and statutory officials and employees who are under state civil service programs.

County Government

When the colonists arrived in America they organized local government along the lines of the counties that existed in England, where the principal local officers were the sheriff and justice of the peace. The county became and remains the basic unit of local government; however, in Louisiana this basic unit is known as the "parish" and in Alaska, the "borough." As a political subdivision of the state, the county plays an important role in local government throughout the United States, except in the New England states where, in most instances, the town is the primary instrument of local government. There is a considerable variation in the number of counties in each state. Texas comprises 254; Delaware has only three. Boundaries of the counties are usually set by the state constitution or the state legislature.

County offices are often delineated in state constitutions or by statutes enacted by the state legislature, although some county agencies are created by ordinances adopted by the governing body of the county. A board, often called the Board of County Commissioners, consisting of anywhere from three to ten elected members with one designated as chair, generally administers the county government. In addition to the elected commissioners, counties usually have an elected sheriff, clerk of the courts and recorder of public records, a prosecuting attorney, a tax assessor and collector, an elections supervisor, a coroner, and fiscal and auditing personnel. The fact that many of these officers fill specific posts leads to a decentralized administration. However, in recent years some counties have been granted "home rule" charters by the state legislatures. Home rule charters grant counties powers to enact ordinances and render municipal-type services in unincorporated areas. In many instances, counties operating under home rule charters grant franchises to private entities to furnish utility services to unincorporated areas. Where this has occurred there has been a trend for the elected body of commissioners to appoint a professionally trained county administrator. An elected or appointed county attorney usually serves as chief legal adviser to the governing body, although because of the decentralized character of country offices, some elected officials have their own legal counsel.

The functions served by counties vary considerably among the states and even among the counties in a particular state. For example, public schools fall under the jurisdiction of some county governments. More frequently, an elected school board with an elected or appointed superintendent of public instruction is responsible for the schools.

Among the most basic county functions are collection of taxes, conduct of elections, operation of jails, and provisions for maintenance of county roads. Counties frequently maintain parks and recreational facilities and libraries; some provide water and sewer and even electric services. Over the years operation of hospitals and airports has been undertaken by some counties, but the trend in recent years has been for these institutions to be operated by specially created districts.

City Government

Towns in colonial America existed by charter of the Crown. Once America became an independent nation of sovereign states, the state legislatures generally chartered cities or provided for incorporation of cites under general enabling statutes. Cities today are created by the grant of a special charter or by general law whereby the state legislature authorizes the residents of a specified contiguous area to create a municipality upon compliance with laws. In contrast to most counties, cities are usually granted corporate powers, including the power of eminent domain, to allow them to effectively govern an urban population. Increasingly, state constitutions have been amended to allow cities to adopt their own charters. The extent of "home rule" allowed cities varies in the states, but cities are not allowed to exercise powers that conflict with general laws of the state or federal laws.

Municipal charters usually define city offices, although many city agencies are created by ordinances adopted by city councils or commissions. Cities are responsible for public safety (i.e., police and fire protection), for maintenance of roads, sidewalks, and parks, and they usually operate municipal water and sewer systems. Many cities today provide expanded cultural and recreational amenities and share responsibility with federal and state governments for local transportation and for public housing.

Although there are various forms of municipal government, most fall under two principal forms: "mayor-council" and the "commission-manager." Under the mayor-council form of local government the mayor is elected, usually for a term of from one to four years, and is granted executive powers to enforce municipal ordinances, prepare a budget, and appoint and remove administrative heads. Council members are elected, often from specified districts, and enact ordinances and often exercise approval power of mayoral appointments and removals of administrative officials. The largest cities in the United States generally are governed under the mayor-council plan, often with a strong mayor.

The commission-manager form of municipal government is newer, having been first instituted in Staunton, Virginia, in 1908, and has since become the most popular form of municipal government in medium-sized cities. Under this plan the elected commissioners retain a professionally qualified city manager who serves as the chief executive officer of the city, submits a budget to the commission, sets the salaries of administrative personnel, and (often subject to civil service regulations for certain personnel) hires and fires employees. In some instances the mayor is elected; in others commissioners select one of their number to serve as mayor. The mayor chairs commission meetings and serves as the ceremonial head of the city. The commission adopts the budget and sets policy for the city through adoption of ordinances and resolutions,

but commissioners do not interfere with the day-to-day operations. Often the city commission appoints various municipal boards to advise the commission on planning, **zoning,** and environmental matters. In some instances the commission's approval is required in the appointment of major department heads, for example, the chief of police or fire chief.

Consolidation of County and City Governments—the Metro Concept

During the latter half of the twentieth century, a number of cities and counties opted for some form of consolidation of government. There are a number of variations in the form that such consolidations take. We cite two instances.

In 1956 the voters in Florida amended the state constitution to allow the city of Miami and Dade County to have a Home Rule Charter. The following year the charter was adopted by referendum, and Miami-Dade, as it is now known, is comprised of a large unincorporated area and thirty incorporated municipalities. In this form of "metro government" an executive mayor and the Miami-Dade Board of County Commissioners govern the county, enact ordinances, collect taxes, and provide for area wide administration. The individual municipalities retain their identities and continue to provide certain municipal services.

After the Tennessee Constitutional Convention of 1953, an attempt in 1958 to consolidate the city of Nashville and Davidson County failed. A subsequent attempt in 1962 won the approval of a consolidation charter and in ensuing years Nashville has become one of leading cities in the South. A proposal to consolidate the Knoxville-Knox County area in 1998 failed.

Functions Common to Local Governments

As noted, the structure of local government takes many forms. Nevertheless, all local governments must provide certain basic services. While police and fire protection and emergency services are among the oldest services provided, today most local governments deal with *ad valorem* tax disputes, local civil service (usually for police and fire personnel), and pensions, as well as the planning and zoning boards. Most have administrative departments or agencies to deal with the following matters:

■ **Waste collection and disposal.** In many unincorporated areas, residents obtain water from wells and dispose of wastes through septic systems. In more populated areas waste collection is now often **privatized,** which means that these services are delivered by private companies under contracts with local governments. City and county governments often operate sanitary landfills, although these facilities are also sometimes operated by private concerns. Regardless of whether landfills are operated by local governments or private companies, their operations are regulated by the U.S. Environmental Protection Agency.

■ **Public schools.** Although states maintain agencies that supervise public education, the actual administration of the public schools tends to occur at the local level, either by county agencies, city agencies, or independent school districts. Generally, an elected school board makes school policy and an elected or appointed superintendent supervises school administration. Public schools are often funded through a combination of state funds and proceeds from local property taxes.

■ **Land use planning and zoning.** Zoning is the means by which local government regulates the use of land. Parcels of land are classified as falling within residential, professional, commercial, industrial or agricultural uses. The first zoning ordinance was adopted by New York City in 1916. For much of the twentieth century, zoning was a very controversial idea in many parts of the country, inasmuch as it entails restrictions on private ownership.[65] Today, zoning is widely, but not universally accepted.[66] In New York City today, zoning laws are administered by the New York City Department of Planning. To obtain a change in zoning designation, a property owner must apply through this agency, although final approval rests with the City Council. Many local governments have planning boards to assist in comprehensive land use policies. In addition, they must maintain boards of zoning appeals, which act in a quasi-judicial capacity, to consider requests for variances or exceptions to zoning requirements.

■ **Building and trade codes.** In addition to zoning, local governments administer building codes for construction and remodeling of business buildings and residences, and codes regulating plumbing, electrical work, heating, and air conditioning.

■ **Regulatory ordinances.** Local governments also regulate many aspects of business and community life and usually impose occupation license fees. In addition to the major areas discussed above, cities typically enact local ordinances that regulate animals, billboards, noise, peddlers, pawnbrokers, restaurants, streets, sidewalks and parks, taxicabs, traffic, street vendors, and sales of alcoholic beverages.

■ **Administrative boards.** To carry out governmental functions local governments establish boards to deal with *ad valorem* tax disputes, local civil service regulations (usually for police and fire personnel), pension programs, as well as the planning and zoning boards mentioned above.

CONCLUSION

As America moved from a small agrarian nation through the industrial revolution, the role of government changed dramatically. The problems that accompanied "big business" and "big labor" led to "big government" being looked upon to provide solutions for economic and social problems. The administrative state emerged with its growth accelerated by the New Deal in response to problems of the Great Depression. That growth continues as the technological and information revolutions and the increasing longevity of a larger and more diverse population demand solutions to economic and social problems. However, the nature of the administrative state is changing. Over the last decade, the number of public employees has been declining, especially at the federal level, yet the scope of government activity has continued to increase. Many of the routine functions of government, from the basic services provided by cities to the social programs established by the federal government, have been turned over to private contractors. Mental health counseling and other social services are now often provided by not-for-profit organizations that receive government grants to deliver these services. Even some state prisons and local jails have been privatized. Privatization of government services has allowed the scope of government responsibility to grow without increasing the size of public sector employment.

The American people may dislike bureaucracy, but most of them understand that, given what they expect from government, bureaucracy is inevitable. Yet most also believe, rightly or wrongly, that the federal bureaucracy is beset by "waste, fraud, and abuse." It is a staple of presidential campaigns that candidates promise to go after the wasteful, inefficient or corrupt bureaucracy. Presidents, governors, and mayors can have a significant impact on the development and direction of bureaucracies, as can legislative bodies. But everyone realizes that, for better or worse, bureaucracy is here to stay at all levels of government. The goal of administrative law is to harmonize the operations of bureaucracy with the rule of law while effectively providing workable solutions for the problems now assigned to government.

KEY TERMS

adjudication

Administrative Procedure Act (APA)

antitrust laws

cabinet

cabinet-level departments

civil rights laws

civil service

cooperative federalism

deregulation

eminent domain

enumerated powers

executive agencies

executive departments

Executive Office of the President

executive order

federal income tax

Freedom of Information Act

implied powers

independent agency

independent regulatory commission

laissez-faire

modern administrative state

monetary policy

monopolies

national security state

Necessary and Proper Clause

parens patriae

privatized

regulatory capture

spoils system

unemployment compensation

welfare reform

welfare state

zoning

QUESTIONS FOR THOUGHT AND DISCUSSION

1. Contrast the powers now exercised by Congress with a strict constructionist interpretation of the powers enumerated in Article I, Section 8 of the United States Constitution.

2. Under what constitutional authority has Congress created administrative and regulatory agencies? What social and economic problems caused Congress to create these agencies?

3. Name some of the notable state reforms that served as models for programs later adopted by the federal government.

4. How did the National Recovery Act of 1933 epitomize the philosophy of the New Deal?

5. Which of the reforms adopted in the New Deal have the greatest effect on the present day economy of the United States? Support your answer with reasons.

6. What is the objective of the Administrative Procedure Act (APA) of 1946?

7. How did President Lyndon Johnson's administration expand the "welfare state"?

8. What principal administrative and regulatory developments occurred during the administration of President Richard Nixon?

9. Why do the authors describe the election of Ronald Reagan to the presidency in 1980 as a "watershed event" in American political history?

10. How can bureaucracy be harmonized with constitutional and democratic values?

ENDNOTES

1. This quotation is often attributed to Thomas Jefferson, but does not appear in his published writings. In his essay *Civil Disobedience* (1849), Henry David Thoreau wrote: "I heartily accept the motto, 'That government is best which governs least'; and I should like to see it acted up to more rapidly and systematically."

2. *The Federalist* No. 45, pp. 292–293 (C. Rossiter, ed. 1961).

3. In 1935 the function of preserving official documents was assigned to the National Archives and Records Administration, an independent agency.

4. See Patent Act of 1790, 1 Stat. 109.

5. See Patent Act of 1793, 1 Stat. 318.

6. Paul Van Riper, "The American Administrative State: Wilson and the Founders—An Unorthodox View." *Public Administration Review* 43 (Nov./Dec. 1983), p. 480.

7. Alexander Hamilton, *The Federalist* No. 70, p. 423 (C. Rossiter, ed. 1961).

8. See *McCulloch v. Maryland,* 4 Wheat. (17 U.S.) 316 (1819).

9. The Judiciary Act of 1789, ch. 20, sec. 35, 1 Stat. 73, 92–93 (1789).

10. Act to Establish the Department of Justice, ch. 150, 16 Stat. 162 (1870).

11. The Civil Service Commission was abolished in 1978 and its functions transferred to the new Office of Personnel Management.

12. Woodrow Wilson, The Study of Administration, *Political Science Quarterly* (June 1887), pp. 198–222.

13. William Graham Sumner (1840–1910) taught political science and sociology at Yale University. His ideas about politics, society, and the economy were much influenced by Charles Darwin's theory of evolution, hence the term Social Darwinist is often applied to Sumner.

14. 94 U.S. 113 (1877).

15. *Wabash, St. Louis & Pacific Railroad Company v. Illinois,* 118 U.S. 557 (1886).

16. *United States v. E. C. Knight Co.,* 156 U.S. 1 (1895).

17. Herbert Croly (1869–1930) was the first editor of the influential journal *The New Republic* and remained in that position until his death. Croly's early writings, in which he advocated a planned economy, social welfare programs, and universal public education, exerted strong influence on the Progressive Movement and the subsequent New Deal.

18. John Dewey (1859–1952) was a philosopher and social critic who contributed frequently to *The New Republic* and other progressive publications on topics such as democracy, women's suffrage, education, and organized labor.

19. *Standard Oil Co. v. United States,* 221 U.S. 1 (1911).

20. *A.L.A. Schechter Poultry Corp. v. United States,* 295 U.S. 495 (1935).

21. *United States v. Darby,* 312 U.S. 100 (1941).

22. *United States v. Butler,* 297 U.S. 1 (1936).

23. *Wickard v. Filburn,* 317 U.S. 111 (1942).

24. 14 Stat. 221, 47 U.S.C.A. § 1 *et seq.*

25. 36 Stat. 539, 49 U.S.C.A. § 1 *et seq.*

26. 44 Stat. 1162, 47 U.S.C.A. § 81 *et seq.*

27. 48 Stat. 1064, 47 U.S.C.A. § 151 *et seq.*

28. *National Broadcasting Co. v. United States,* 319 U.S. 190, 217 (1943).

29. *Federal Communications Commission v. Sanders Bros. Radio Station,* 309 U.S. 470 (1940).

30. 48 Stat. 74, 15 U.S.C.A. § 77a *et seq.*

31. 48 Stat. 896, 15 U.S.C.A. § 78a *et seq.*

32. *National Labor Relations Board v. Jones-Laughlin Steel Corporation,* 301 U.S. 1 (1937).

33. *Yakus v. United States,* 321 U.S. 414 (1944).

34. The APA is codified at 5 U.S.C.A. § 551 *et seq.*

35. President Dwight D. Eisenhower, Speech before the General Assembly of the United Nations, December 8, 1953.

36. Pub. L. 85-726.

37. Taken from the EEOC's web site, online at http://www.eeoc.gov/statauth.html.

38. *South Carolina v. Katzenbach,* 383 U.S. 301, 337 (1966).

39. Herbert Stein, *Presidential Economics: The Making of Economic Policy from Roosevelt to Clinton* (Washington, D.C.: AEI Press, 1994), p. 190.

40. Pub. L. 91-190, 42 U.S.C.A. §§ 4321-4347, January 1, 1970, as amended by Pub. L. 94-52, July 3, 1975, Pub. L. 94-83, August 9, 1975, and Pub. L. 97-258, § 4(b), Sept. 13, 1982.

41. Codified at 7 U.S.C.A. § 136; 16 U.S.C.A. § 460 *et seq.* (1973).

42. 11 CFR, Parts 100 *et al.*

43. *Federal Register,* Vol. 67, No. 145 (July 29, 2002), pp. 49064–49132.

44. Pub. L. 104–127, 110 Stat. 974.

45. Pub. L. No. 107-171, 116 Stat. 134.

46. Pub. L. No. 104-88, 109 Stat. 803 (1995).

47. Pub. L. No. 104-193, 110 Stat. 2105.

48. Testimony of Tommy G. Thompson before the Senate Finance Committee, March 12, 2002.

49. Taken from the White House web site, online at http://www.whitehouse.gov/deptofhomeland.

50. Pub. L. No. 107-296, 116 Stat. 2135.

51. U.S. Const., Art. I, § 8.

52. *Food and Drug Administration v. Brown and Williamson,* 529 U.S. 120 (2000).

53. Pub. L. No. 91-596, 84 Stat. 1590 (codified as amended at 29 U.S.C.A. §§ 651–678). (The act does not provide specific standards that employers must follow; rather, it authorizes the secretary of labor to promulgate occupational safety and health standards.)

54. Established by the Consumer Safety Act of 1972, codified at 15 U.S.C.A. § 2051 *et seq.*

55. Established by Reorganization Plan #3 (1970).

56. Established by the Communications Act of 1934, codified at 47 U.S.C.A. § 151 *et seq.*

57. Established by the Banking Act of 1933, codified at 12 U.S.C.A. § 227 *et seq.*

58. Established by the Federal Election Campaign Act of 1975, codified at 2 U.S.C.A. § 437c.

59. Established by the Department of Energy Organization Act of 1977, codified at 42 U.S.C.A. § 7131.

60. Established by the Federal Reserve Act of 1913, codified at 12 U.S.C.A. § 221.

61. Established by the Federal Trade Commission Act of 1914, codified at 15 U.S.C.A. § 41 *et seq.*

62. Established by the Energy Reorganization Act of 1974, codified at 42 U.S.C.A. § 5801 *et seq.*

63. Established by the Securities and Exchange Act of 1934, codified at 15 U.S.C.A. § 78a-78jj.

3

Constitutional Sources of Bureaucratic Power and Restraint

"The proliferation of Government, State and Federal, would amaze the Framers [of the Constitution], and the administrative state with its reams of regulations would leave them rubbing their eyes."

JUSTICE DAVID SOUTER
DISSENTING IN *ALDEN V. MAINE,* 527 U.S. 706, 807 (1999).

INTRODUCTION

The essential idea of **constitutionalism** is that government should be based on and limited by fundamental legal principles. In the American context these fundamental legal principles are found in the United States Constitution and the fifty state constitutions. American constitutionalism is distinguished not only by its emphasis on written constitutions, but on the theory of **separation of powers** under which the legislative, executive, and judicial functions are located within separate and to a great extent independent branches of government. American constitutionalism is also characterized by **federalism,** the division of sovereignty between the national government and the states. The national government is created and limited by the United States Constitution, adopted in 1787 and ratified the following year. The fifty state governments are based on their own constitutions, adopted when these states became part of the Union. In examining administrative law, one must be cognizant of these basic principles of American constitutionalism, for they have significant implications for the administrative process.

In this chapter we examine the constitutional aspects of the administrative state. Our examination begins with the constitutional parameters within which the federal bureaucracy emerged and developed and those under which it operates today. We then explore the constitutional dimensions of public administration at the state and local levels. Finally, we explain how rights guaranteed by the federal and state constitutions come into play in the bureaucratic realm.

CONSTITUTIONAL FOUNDATIONS OF THE FEDERAL BUREAUCRACY

As noted in Chapter 2, the United States Constitution says precious little about the executive branch of the national government. Yet there was little doubt that Congress is given authority to create agencies within the executive branch to carry out the essential operations of government. The Supreme Court's seminal decision in *McCulloch v. Maryland* (1819)[1] (see Chapter 2) implicitly recognized broad authority for the creation of new administrative agencies, as long as Congress was acting in furtherance of its enumerated or implied powers under the Constitution. As we pointed out in the preceding chapter, Congress has used this authority frequently, especially in the modern era, to create the massive executive bureaucracy we refer to as the administrative state.

Since its inception, the administrative state has aroused opposition, both political and constitutional. Some see "big government" as a threat to liberty. Others are concerned about the diminution of privacy. Many oppose government interference with private enterprise and believe that regulation hampers economic growth, while others object to "social engineering" and view government social programs as threats to traditional values and institutions. Still others perceive the administrative state to be a threat to democratic values of participation and accountability. The bureaucracy has numerous critics across the ideological spectrum, although contemporary opposition is most pronounced among political conservatives. In this chapter, our concern is with *constitutional*, as distinct from *ideological*, attacks on the administrative state.

We may divide constitutional objections to the administrative state into two broad categories. The first concerns the structural aspects of the administrative state; the second involves claims that particular exercises of bureaucratic power violate the constitutionally protected rights of private parties. We begin by examining the structural issues at the federal, state, and local level. We then examine issues involving assertions of constitutional rights.

In dealing with the structural constitutional issues, we focus on the basic challenges to Congress's authority to constitute administrative and regulatory agencies. (Constitutional issues relative to executive and legislative control of the bureaucracy are dealt with in Chapter 8.) Structural challenges to the administrative state can be placed in three broad categories:

- Congress has exceeded its legislative powers by impermissibly delegating its lawmaking power to the bureaucracy.

- In vesting executive agencies with legislative and judicial power, Congress has violated the principle of separation of powers.

- Congress has encroached on powers reserved to the states.

The Ideal of Limited Government

In keeping with the **classical liberalism** of the Enlightenment, the framers of the American Constitution sought to create a national government of limited powers. Moreover, they wanted to ensure that the newly created national government would not encroach on the powers of the sovereign states. They knew that if the proposed national government were vested with too much power, the people of the states would refuse to ratify the Constitution. Thus, in characterizing the power of the federal government vis-à-vis that of the states, James Madison observed: "The powers delegated by the proposed Constitution to the federal government are few and defined. Those which are to remain in the State governments are numerous and indefinite."[2]

The Enumerated Powers of Congress In writing of the "few and defined" powers of the federal government, Madison was referring to the **enumerated powers** of Congress set forth in Article I, Section 8 of the Constitution. These include the power to declare war, coin money, collect taxes, borrow money, raise and support armies, establish post offices, establish rules for naturalization, and so on. Basically, the enumerated powers of Congress were designed to allow the national government to do for the nation what the states could not do on their own. There is no question that the framers of the Constitution believed that they were creating a national government of limited powers. However, there were profound

disagreements among the founders as to how limited these powers should be. On the one hand, Federalists like Alexander Hamilton argued for a broad interpretation of Congress's powers, while Republicans like Thomas Jefferson advocated a stricter reading of Congressional authority. As Chief Justice John Marshall (who served 1801–1835), stated in *McCulloch v Maryland* (1819):

> The [federal] government is acknowledged by all to be one of enumerated powers. The principle, that it can exercise only the powers granted to it is now universally admitted. But the question respecting the extent of the powers actually granted, is perpetually arising, and will probably continue to arise, as long as our system shall exist.[3]

The Doctrine of Implied Powers Under Chief Justice Marshall the Supreme Court endorsed Hamilton's view, rejecting strict construction of the Constitution and recognizing broad congressional authority under both enumerated and **implied powers.** In the landmark *McCulloch* decision, Marshall opined:

> Let the end be legitimate, let it be within the scope of the constitution, and all means which are appropriate, which are plainly adapted to that end, which are not prohibited, but consist with the letter and spirit of the constitution, are constitutional.[4]

Under the doctrine of implied powers, scarcely any area exists in which Congress is absolutely barred from acting, since most problems have a conceivable relationship to the broad powers and objectives contained in the Constitution. Thomas Jefferson, an ardent opponent of the doctrine of implied powers, argued, "To take a single step beyond the boundaries thus specially drawn around the powers of Congress is to take possession of a boundless field of power, no longer susceptible of any definition."[5] Today, the powers of Congress, while not exactly "boundless," are certainly far greater than most of the founders could have imagined.

The Commerce Clause: The Power that Became the Tool for National Regulation

One of the "few and defined" powers explicitly granted by the Constitution to Congress is the power "[t]o regulate Commerce with foreign Nations, and among the several States, and with the Indian Tribes."[6] In the early days of the Republic, Congress seldom exerted legislative power under the **Commerce Clause.** However, the Commerce Clause was used by the courts to strike down protectionist state laws, the abolition of which was the principal motivation behind the adoption of the Clause. In *Gibbons v. Ogden* (1824), the Supreme Court struck down a monopoly on the steamboat trade established by the state of New York.[7] In his opinion for the Court, John Marshall defined interstate commerce as commercial intercourse, that is, transportation of goods and persons across state lines. Chief Justice Marshall observed:

Commerce among the states cannot stop at the external boundary line of each state, but may be introduced into the interior. It is not intended to say that these words comprehend that commerce which is completely internal, which is carried on between man and man in a state, or between different parts of the same state, and which does not extend to or affect other states. Such a power would be inconvenient and is certainly unnecessary. Comprehensive as the word *among* is, it may very properly be restricted to that commerce which concerns more states than one. The phrase is not one which would probably have been selected to indicate the completely interior traffic of a state, because it is not an apt phrase for that purpose; and the enumeration of the particular classes of commerce to which the power was to be extended would not have been made had the intention been to extend the power to every description. The enumeration presupposes something not enumerated; and that something, if we regard the language or the subject of the sentence, must be the exclusively internal commerce of a state.[8]

Marshall's formulation of interstate commerce was broader than that proposed by some of his contemporaries, but it nevertheless suggested that Congress's power to regulate interstate commerce was limited to movement of persons and goods across state lines. Certainly Marshall was not suggesting that the Commerce Clause would provide Congress a warrant to regulate all aspects of the national economy.

In 1887, Congress enacted the Interstate Commerce Act,[9] and in 1890 Congress passed the Sherman Antitrust Act.[10] These enactments represented the beginning of a new era of national regulation of business and a greatly expanded notion of congressional power under the Commerce Clause. For almost fifty years a conservative Supreme Court resisted this trend, culminating in the showdown with President Franklin D. Roosevelt (FDR) over the constitutionality of the New Deal.

In 1935, the Court struck down the National Industrial Recovery Act (NIRA) of 1933, in part because Congress had exceeded its powers under the Commerce Clause.[11] Under the NIRA, Congress had established an agency within the executive branch and vested it with power to regulate economic activities, even those that were wholly intrastate in nature. Writing for the Court, Chief Justice Hughes observed that unless Congress's power under the Commerce Clause were limited to matters of *inter*state, as distinct from *intra*state commerce, "there would be virtually no limit to the federal power, and for all practical purposes we should have a completely centralized government."[12]

The Constitutional Revolution of 1937 The centralized government managing the economy and the society, presumably in the "public interest," that the more radical New Dealers had in mind was a far cry from the limited government envisaged by the framers. In a 1968 essay aptly titled "Rewriting the Constitution," Rexford Tugwell, one of the architects of the New Deal, made a startling admission: "To the extent that these New Deal policies developed, they were tortured interpretations of a document intended to prevent them." Tugwell's admission suggests that the New Dealers were not at war merely with the "nine old men" of the Supreme Court, as FDR referred to them. Rather, they were on a mission to remake the American Constitution itself.

Of course, as we pointed out in Chapter 2, in 1937 the Court made a sudden about-face, owing to a shift in the position by the Court's two moderates, Justice Owen Roberts and Chief Justice Charles Evans Hughes. In *National Labor Relations Board v. Jones & Laughlin Steel Corporation*,[13] the Court upheld the National Labor Relations Act of 1935, which guaranteed the right of industrial workers to unionize and bargain collectively with management. In contrast to earlier Commerce Clause decisions where the Court drew a sharp distinction between manufacturing and commerce, Chief Justice Hughes' opinion in *NLRB* took note of the "intimate relation which a manufacturing industry may have to interstate commerce. . . ."[14]

By 1941 President Roosevelt had appointed seven of the nine justices then serving on the Supreme Court, not by any extraordinary means, but simply through natural attrition and replacement. Seven of the eight new justices were Democrats (one, Justice Frankfurter, was an Independent) and all eight were committed to a philosophy of judicial restraint with regard to legal challenges to government involvement in the economy. With this new attitude toward economic interventionism came a new view of the Commerce Clause. In upholding the Fair Labor Standards Act, another key piece of New Deal legislation, the reconstituted Court articulated the modern view of the Commerce Clause:

> The power of Congress over interstate commerce is not confined to the regulation of commerce among the states. It extends to those activities intrastate which so affect interstate commerce or the exercise of the power of Congress over it as to make regulation of them appropriate means to the attainment of a legitimate end, the exercise of the granted power of Congress to regulate interstate commerce.[15]

Since the **Constitutional Revolution of 1937**, the Commerce Clause has served as the constitutional basis for the enactment of far reaching social, economic, and environmental legislation and the creation of numerous federal agencies to promulgate and enforce social, economic and environmental regulations. In 1942, in *Wickard v. Filburn*,[16] under the reinterpreted Commerce Clause, the Court sustained a regulatory regime established by the Department of Agriculture under which farmers were penalized for producing commodities in excess of their quotas, even if the surplus was for personal consumption. In recent years the Commerce Clause has served as the basis for legislation prohibiting discrimination by "places of public accommodation"[17] and by private employers.[18]

During the 1970s, Congress relied heavily on the Commerce Clause in adopting an elaborate regime of environmental legislation enforced by the Environmental Protection Agency. These enactments include the Endangered Species Act,[19] the Clean Air Act,[20] the Hazardous Substances Act,[21] the Clean Water Act,[22] the Hazardous Materials Transportation Act,[23] and the Comprehensive Environmental Response, Compensation, and Liability Act (better known as the "Superfund" law).[24]

Congress invoked the Commerce Clause in enacting the Occupational Safety and Health Act of 1970.[25] This statute created the Occupational Safety and Health Administration, an agency within the Department of Labor, which is empowered to issue and enforce safety and health "standards" in the workplace. As the following excerpt demonstrates, the OSHA statute is quite explicit in its reliance on the Commerce Clause, stating:

> The Congress declares it to be its purpose and policy, through the exercise of its powers to regulate commerce among the several States and with foreign nations and to provide for the general welfare, to assure so far as possible every working man and woman in the Nation safe and healthful working conditions and to preserve our human resources . . . .

Congress has even used the Commerce Clause to enact a wide variety of criminal laws, including prohibitions against interstate transportation of kidnapped persons,[26] interstate transportation of stolen automobiles,[27] manufacture, sale, distribution, and possession of controlled substances,[28] racketeering and organized crime,[29] computer crimes,[30] loan sharking,[31] and even carjacking.[32]

Given the great variety of legislation enacted under the Commerce Clause, it appeared to many observers that Congress has utilized the clause as the basis for a federal **police power,** that is, a general legislative power to advance the public welfare. While there is substantial political support for defining congressional power under the Commerce Clause so broadly, this approach runs counter to the prevailing understanding of the framers of the Constitution. It has now run into some opposition from a conservative Supreme Court.

Has Judicial Deference to Congressional Authority under the Commerce Clause Ended?

After decades of deference to congressional assertions of power, the Supreme Court has recently shown an inclination to mark the outer limits of Congress's authority under the Commerce Clause. In *United States v. Lopez* (1995),[33] the Court, in a 5-4 decision, struck down a federal law prohibiting possession of a firearm in close proximity to a school. The Court rejected the government's argument that the law was rationally related to the protection of the educational process and thereby an enhancement of national commerce. Writing for the Court, Chief Justice Rehnquist observed that "if we were to accept the Government's arguments, we are hard-pressed to posit any activity by an individual that Congress is without power to regulate."[34] Rehnquist opined:

Admittedly, some of our prior cases have taken long steps down that road, giving great deference to congressional action. . . . The broad language in these opinions has suggested the possibility of additional expansion,

but we decline here to proceed any further. To do so would require us to conclude that the Constitution's enumeration of powers does not presuppose something not enumerated . . . and that there never will be a distinction between what is truly national and what is truly local. . . . This we are unwilling to do.[35]

Despite *Lopez* and other recent court decisions restricting its power, Congress retains ample legislative authority to address national problems, not only under the Commerce Clause, but also under its various enumerated and implied powers.

Federalism

The Tenth Amendment provides: "The powers not delegated to the United States by the Constitution, nor prohibited by it to the States, are reserved to the States respectively, or to the people." This amendment was adopted to allay fears that the national government might attempt to exercise powers not granted by the Constitution and, by so doing, encroach on the powers of the several states. Even after the Civil War, Chief Justice Salmon P. Chase would comment that

the preservation of the States, and the maintenance of their governments, are as much within the design and care of the Constitution as the preservation of the Union and the maintenance of the National government. The Constitution . . . looks to an indestructible Union, composed of indestructible States.[36]

Dual Federalism Under the doctrine of **dual federalism**, there was thought to be a bright line between the domain of the national government and that of the states. In *Hammer v. Dagenhart* (1918),[37] the Supreme Court invoked the doctrine of dual federalism in striking down a federal law restricting the use of child labor in factories. Writing for the Court, Justice William R. Day characterized the statute as an invasion by the federal government of an area reserved to the states by the Tenth Amendment: "The power of the states to regulate their purely internal affairs by such laws as seem wise to the local authority is inherent and has never been surrendered to the general government."[38]

As noted by Edward S. Corwin, the New Deal and its "enlarged theories of the function of government" led to the abandonment of dual federalism.[39] After the Constitutional Revolution of 1937, the Supreme Court repudiated the doctrine of dual federalism altogether. Speaking for the Court in *United States v. Darby* (1941), Justice Harlan F. Stone minimized the significance of the Tenth Amendment stating:

> The amendment states but a truism that all is retained which has not been surrendered. There is nothing in the history of its adoption to suggest that it was more than declaratory of the relationship between the national and state governments as it had been established by the Constitution before the amendment or that its purpose was other than to allay fears that the new national government might seek to exercise powers not granted, and that the states might not be able to exercise fully their reserved powers.[40]

Cooperative Federalism The *Darby* decision ushered in the age of **cooperative federalism,** under which the national government and the states are seen as interconnected, rather than as independent entities. This concept has served as the basis for federal programs in the areas of welfare, housing, education, environmental protection, and transportation. In these programs the national government establishes and largely funds programs, which are administered by state agencies under federal supervision.

Whereas regulations of the New Deal era targeted private actors, in the 1960s and 70s Congress made state and local governments the targets of regulation. During these decades, Congress established more than five hundred new regulatory programs affecting state and local governments. Many of these programs involved efforts to protect the environment or promote civil rights. Although the Supreme Court offered some resistance to these developments by invoking the Tenth Amendment, by the mid-1980s the Court reversed itself and acquiesced to federal mandates on state and local governments.[41] Early on, the federal government largely paid for the costs incurred by state and local governments in complying with federal regulations. During the 1980s federal fiscal aid to the states and cities declined markedly, but the imposition of federal regulations continued. This led state and local leaders to complain about **unfunded mandates.** Congress responded to this concern in 1995 with the adoption of the Unfunded Mandates Reform Act,[42] a largely symbolic gesture but with some impact on federal agency rulemaking (see Chapter 4).

Preemption of State Law and State Regulations Under the Supremacy Clause of Article VI of the U.S. Constitution, state and local laws that contravene valid federal laws are unconstitutional. Under modern constitutional doctrine, federal statutes, and federal regulations promulgated pursuant to those statutes, can (but do not always) preempt state laws and regulations. That is to say that by occupying a certain field of policy, the federal government can prevent states from moving into that field. Express preemption of state law occurs when Congress has through statutory language provided a clear indication of its intent to supplant state law.[43] But Congress may also preempt state law implicitly by enacting a comprehensive regulatory scheme that does not leave room for competing state regulation.[44] A recent example of federal preemption of state law can be seen in *Lorillard v. Reilly* (2001),[45] where the Supreme Court held that the Federal Cigarette Labeling and Advertising Act preempted state regulations governing outdoor and point-of-sale cigarette advertising.

The Supreme Court's *Lorillard Tobacco Company vs. Reilly* decision is excerpted at the end of the chapter.

BOX 3.1 Supreme Court Perspective

New York v. United States
505 U.S. 144 (1992)

[In this case the Supreme Court struck down a provision of the Low-Level Radioactive Waste Policy Amendments Act of 1985 that imposed upon the states the obligation to provide for the disposal of radioactive waste generated within their borders.]

Justice O'Connor delivered the opinion of the Court. *. . . The Federal Government undertakes activities today that would have been unimaginable to the Framers in two senses: first, because the Framers would not have conceived that any government would conduct such activities; and second, because the Framers would not have believed that the Federal Government, rather than the States, would assume such responsibilities. Yet the powers conferred upon the Federal Government by the Constitution were phrased in language broad enough to allow for the expansion of the Federal Government's role.*

. . . Some truths are so basic that, like the air around us, they are easily overlooked. Much of the Constitution is concerned with setting forth the form of our government, and the courts have traditionally invalidated measures deviating from that form. The result may appear "formalistic" in a given case to partisans of the measure at issue, because such measures are typically the product of the era's perceived necessity. But the Constitution protects us from our own best intentions: it divides

power among sovereigns and among branches of government precisely so that we may resist the temptation to concentrate power in one location as an expedient solution to the crisis of the day. . . .

States are not mere political subdivisions of the United States. State governments are neither regional offices nor administrative agencies of the Federal Government. The positions occupied by state officials appear nowhere on the Federal Government's most detailed organizational chart. The Constitution instead "leaves to the several States a residuary and inviolable sovereignty," . . . reserved explicitly to the States by the Tenth Amendment.

Whatever the outer limits of that sovereignty may be, one thing is clear: the Federal Government may not compel the States to enact or administer a federal regulatory program. The Constitution permits both the Federal Government and the States to enact legislation regarding the disposal of low level radioactive waste. The Constitution enables the Federal Government to pre-empt state regulation contrary to federal interests, and it permits the Federal Government to hold out incentives to the States as a means of encouraging them to adopt suggested regulatory schemes. It does not, however, authorize Congress simply to direct the States to provide for the disposal of the radioactive waste generated within their borders. While there may be many constitutional methods of achieving regional self-sufficiency in radioactive waste disposal, the method Congress has chosen is not one of them. . . .

Assessment of Contemporary Federalism
Despite the dramatic changes in the federal system, the concept of federalism and the Tenth Amendment in particular remain important values in the constitutional system. After decades of decisions promoting the dominance of the national government, the Supreme Court under Chief Justice Rehnquist has attempted to restore some balance to the federal system by recognizing limitations on national power and affirming the sovereignty of the states.[46] For a glimpse into the contemporary Court's approach to federalism, examine the excerpt from *New York v. United States* located in Box 3.1.

The national government is clearly the dominant actor in the federal system, yet the states are protected to some degree from overt national coercion. Although the federal government can make states the object of regulation, Congress cannot compel state governments to adopt or enforce federal programs.[47] Nor may Congress "circumvent that prohibition by conscripting the State's officers directly."[48] Of course, Congress can, and often does, encourage the states to participate in federal programs by offering fiscal incentives. The Supreme Court has held that Congress may impose reasonable requirements on the states as conditions of receiving federal grants.[49]

Without question, the national government, through congressional, bureaucratic, and judicial decision making, dominates the policymaking process throughout the United States. Yet the states remain viable actors in the political and legal systems.

Delegation of Legislative Power

In a democracy, the authority to make law resides in the legislature, the people's elected representatives. Yet in the modern era, Congress has delegated substantial lawmaking power to agencies within the federal bureaucracy. Indeed, the **delegation of legislative power** is the hallmark of the modern regulatory state. The Food and Drug Administration (FDA), the Nuclear Regulatory Commission (NRC), the Federal Aviation Administration (FAA), the Occupational Safety and Health Administration (OSHA), the Environmental Protection Agency (EPA), and the Securities and Exchange Commission (SEC) are just a few of the myriad agencies to which the Congress has delegated broad authority to make public policy.

A good recent example of this type of delegation is the Americans with Disabilities Act (ADA) of 1990.[50] The ADA, which builds upon the existing body of federal civil rights law, mandates the elimination of discrimination against individuals with disabilities. A number of federal agencies, including the Department of Justice (DOJ), the Department of Transportation (DOT), the Equal Employment Opportunity Commission (EEOC), and the Federal Communications Commission (FCC), are given regulatory and enforcement powers under the act.

Title II of the ADA provides that "no qualified individual with a disability shall, by reason of such disability, be excluded from participation in or be denied the benefits of the services, programs, or activities of a public entity, or be subjected to discrimination by any such entity." The Department of Justice has implemented this provision by issuing various rules. For example, DOJ's "integration rule" requires that a "public entity administer . . . programs . . . in the most

integrated setting appropriate to the needs of qualified individuals with disabilities."[51] In enforcing this rule, DOJ has required state institutions that house persons with mental disabilities to move their patients to community-based programs when mental health professionals determine that community placement is appropriate, irrespective of the substantial costs the state must bear in meeting this requirement.[52]

Another DOJ rule, known as the "reasonable-modifications regulation," requires public agencies to "make reasonable modifications" to avoid "discrimination on the basis of disability."[53] To further implement this rule, DOJ has issued "Accessibility Guidelines for Buildings and Facilities" that go so far as to specify the height of the arc of the stream of water the flows from drinking fountains. Critics have charged that these rules allow DOJ to "micromanage" hospitals, prisons, and other public institutions that house sick or disabled persons. They argue that Congress, by not clearly specifying the meaning of the term "discrimination," has allowed the DOJ to function as policy maker rather than faithful executor of the legislative will. Defenders argue that there is no way that Congress could be expected to specify in legislation all of the detailed requirements that are necessary to achieve the goals of the Americans with Disabilities Act and that any time Congress is unhappy with the DOJ's interpretation of the law, Congress can amend the ADA to constrain DOJ's rulemaking.

Is Delegation of Legislative Power Constitutional? Article I, Section 1 of the United States Constitution states: "All legislative Powers herein granted shall be vested in a Congress of the United States. . . ." Similarly, all fifty state constitutions vest lawmaking power in the state legislatures. In a typical formulation, Article II, Section 1 of the North Carolina Constitution states: "The legislative power of the State shall be vested in the General Assembly . . ." Under the separation of powers theory that undergirded the federal and state constitutions, the legislature would make the laws; the executive would "take

Care that the Laws be faithfully executed."[54] Moreover, under the prevailing constitutional theory, the legislature could not delegate its law-making power to the executive. John Locke, the English political thinker whose ideas were most influential among the founders, argued:

> The *Legislative cannot transfer the Power of Making Laws* to any other hands. For it being but a delegated Power from the People, they who have it, cannot pass it over to others."[55]

Locke borrowed the maxim *delegata potestas non potest delegari* ("a delegated power cannot itself be delegated") from the common law principle that an agent cannot redelegate the authority delegated by a principal without the permission of that principal and apply it to government. In the classical liberal view, the Constitution is a contract between the people (the principal) and the government (their agent). Under this contract the people, in whom sovereignty is ultimately vested, delegate to the legislature the authority to make laws that bind the people, as long as those laws are consistent with relevant constitutional provisions. For the legislature to be able to redelegate its power to another party, whether inside or outside the government, requires the specific consent of the people. Because there is no language in the Constitution that can be fairly interpreted to express or imply such consent, the legislature is barred from redelegating its power to make laws, unless and until the Constitution is amended to specifically authorize such redelegation.

In the nineteenth century, the "rule of nondelegation," as Sotirios Barber has called it, became firmly established in American constitutional law.[56] In his 1883 treatise on constitutional limitations, Thomas M. Cooley wrote:

> One of the settled maxims in constitutional law is, that the power conferred upon the legislature to make laws cannot be delegated by that department to any other body or authority. Where the sovereign power of the State has located the authority, there it must remain until the Constitution itself is changed.[57]

Early Supreme Court Rulings on Delegation of Legislative Power The Supreme Court first encountered the delegation issue in *Brig Aurora v. United States* (1813),[58] a case having to do with American efforts to remain neutral during the Napoleonic Wars. To ensure American neutrality, Congress enacted a law authorizing the president to impose an embargo against either Great Britain or France, depending on the president's determination of specific facts. If the president found that either nation ceased "to violate neutral commerce" involving American ships, he was free to impose an embargo on the remaining offender. President James Madison determined that France was the first to comply and thus initiated an embargo against Great Britain. The Supreme Court sustained the act against a constitutional challenge, holding that the president's role was merely one of fact finding, rather than lawmaking. Thus, in the Court's view, no unconstitutional delegation of power had taken place.

In 1892 in *Field v. Clark*,[59] the Supreme Court upheld the Tariff Act of 1890, which imposed tariffs on certain imports if, in the president's judgment, the exporting country placed "reciprocally unequal and unreasonable" tariffs on American products. Here again the Court viewed the president's role as one of fact finder, rather than lawmaker, and thus upheld the challenged act. Speaking for the majority, Justice John M. Harlan (the elder) noted that: "The Act does not in any real sense invest the President with the power of legislation. Legislative power was exercised when Congress declared that [enforcement of the tariffs] should take effect upon a named contingency."[60]

The Court's Approach in the Early Twentieth Century The Court confronted a more difficult case in *United States v. Grimaud* (1911).[61] The defendant was indicted for grazing his sheep in a national forest reserve without obtaining permission from the Department of Agriculture. Citing the nondelegation rule, the defendant challenged the Forest Reserve Act of 1897,[62] which authorized the department to make rules governing the national forests—rules to be enforced through criminal prosecution. The Supreme Court rejected the challenge, observing:

> From the beginning of the government, various acts have been passed conferring upon executive officers power to make rules and regulations—not for the government of their departments, but for administering the laws which did govern. None of these statutes could confer legislative power. But when Congress had legislated and indicated its will, it could give to those who were to act under such general provisions "power to fill up the details" by the establishment of administrative rules and regulations. . . .[63]

By the 1920s regulatory agencies were doing far more than "filling in the details" of policies enacted by Congress—they were becoming important policymakers. In 1928 the Supreme Court articulated a more permissive approach to the delegation problem. In *J. W. Hampton & Co. v. United States*, the Court held that as long as "Congress shall lay down by legislative act an intelligible principle to which [the agency] is directed to conform, such legislative action is not a forbidden delegation of legislative power."[64] As long as the thrust of the policy originated in Congress, the ancillary policymaking of the agency was permissible.

The New Deal and the Constitutional Revolution of 1937 As we saw in Chapter 2, the New Deal represented a quantum leap in the evolution of the administrative state. To an unprecedented extent, the federal government relied on bureaucracy to make policy. The centerpiece of the New Deal was the National Industrial Recovery Act (NIRA), which we discussed earlier in the context of congressional power under the Commerce Clause. The NIRA created a federal agency, the National Recovery Administration (NRA), and authorized that agency to promulgate "codes of fair competition" for a broad range of industries. These codes, developed in some cases in cooperation with targeted industries, were enforceable by criminal and civil penalties. The

Schechter Poultry Corporation was convicted on several counts of violating the NRA's Live Poultry Code. One of these counts involved the delivery of an "unfit chicken," hence the case is popularly known as the Sick Chicken Case.[65]

In 1935, the Supreme Court unanimously declared the NIRA unconstitutional, partly (as noted in the previous paragraph) because Congress had exceeded its powers under the Commerce Clause, but also because the statute impermissibly delegated legislative power to the executive branch. Writing for the Court, Chief Justice Charles Evans Hughes asserted that the NIRA granted "virtually unfettered" discretion to the president to enact "laws for the government of trade and industry throughout the country."[66] Justice Benjamin N. Cardozo concurred, characterizing the power granted by Congress as "delegation running riot."[67]

As we noted above, President Roosevelt remade the Supreme Court by appointing seven new justices between 1937 and 1941. Beginning in the 1940's, the Court manifested much more tolerance of delegation of legislative power. For example, in *Yakus v. United States* (1944), the Court upheld the Emergency Price Control Act of 1942, which established the Office of Price Administration and vested it with wide latitude to control prices and rents. The Court's decision in *Yakus* might be viewed as turning on the temporary nature of the act and the fact that the nation was at war. Subsequent decisions have made it clear, however, that *Yakus* was no fluke but rather represented a trend of judicial tolerance toward congressional delegations of power. In effect, the Roosevelt Court acknowledged the legitimacy of the modern administrative state. As Cass Sunstein has noted, President Roosevelt's remaking the Court "altered the constitutional system in ways so fundamental as to suggest that a constitutional amendment had taken place."[68]

The Permissiveness of the Modern Court The modern Supreme Court has shown little if any inclination to revive the nondelegation rule. In *Arizona v. California* (1963),[69] the

Court sustained an extremely vague delegation of power to the Secretary of the Interior. The Boulder Canyon Act of 1928[70] granted the Secretary almost unlimited discretion to allocate the water of the Colorado River (which had been dammed to create reservoirs) among seven states. In making such allocations, the secretary was to follow legislative priorities indicated in the act: "first, for river regulation, improvement of navigation and flood control; second, for irrigation and domestic uses and satisfaction of present perfected rights . . . ; and third, for [electrical] power." On the basis of these guidelines, it was difficult to determine whether the secretary was in fact acting within the "principles" established by Congress. The Court, however, gave Congress the benefit of the doubt, although not without a sharp dissent from Justice John M. Harlan (the younger). "Under the Court's construction of the Act," wrote Harlan, "Congress has made a gift to the Secretary of almost one million, five hundred thousand acre feet of water a year, to allocate virtually as he pleases. . . ." No doubt aware of the inherent vagueness of the delegation it had sustained, the Court suggested that if the secretary of the interior acted in a fashion not consistent with congressional intent, Congress could reduce his power through subsequent legislation.

In the 1970s, some members of the Supreme Court seemed ready to put the nondelegation doctrine to rest once and for all. For example, in *National Cable Association v. United States* (1974),[71] Justice Thurgood Marshall's concurring opinion characterized the antidelegation rule as a remnant of a bygone era, the period before the "Constitutional Revolution of 1937." According to Justice Marshall, the antidelegation rule "is surely as moribund as the substantive due process approach of the same era."[72] Marshall's comments notwithstanding, a number of scholars called for the revival of the nondelegation doctrine.[73]

The Court's reluctance to invoke the nondelegation doctrine was reaffirmed in its 1989 ruling upholding Congress's creation of the U.S. Sentencing Commission and recognizing the constitutionality of detailed sentencing guidelines

promulgated by the Commission in 1987.[74] Eight members of the Court rejected the argument that Congress had impermissibly delegated its power to prescribe ranges of criminal sentences that federal judges were required to impose on persons convicted of crimes. Writing for the Court in *Mistretta v. United States*, Justice Blackmun observed: "Our jurisprudence has been driven by a practical understanding that in our increasingly complex society, replete with ever changing and more technical problems, Congress simply cannot do its job absent an ability to delegate power under broad general directives."[75] In a lone dissent, Justice Antonin Scalia asserted that the separation of powers principle had been violated, concluding that the new sentencing commission amounted to a "junior varsity Congress with extensive lawmaking power."[76]

The contemporary Court's unwillingness to revive the nondelegation doctrine is illustrated by a 2001 decision upholding the broad regulatory authority of the Environmental Protection Agency. The EPA is perhaps the most powerful of the independent regulatory agencies of the federal government. Congress has delegated enormous responsibility to the EPA to deal with matters of air pollution, water pollution, environmental reclamation, and the transportation and disposal of hazardous chemicals and waste products. Accordingly, the EPA has long been a target for those who believe that the courts should more strictly apply the nondelegation doctrine. In *Whitman v. American Trucking Associations* (2001),[77] the Supreme Court was afforded such an opportunity. The American Trucking Associations and other business interests challenged new EPA limits on ozone and soot, arguing, among other things, that the Clean Air Act under which EPA promulgated the regulations constituted an impermissible delegation of legislative power.

To the surprise of many observers, the Court was unanimous in rejecting the challenge to the EPA's authority. Writing for the Court, Justice Scalia observed that "[t]he scope of discretion [the challenged provision] allowed is in fact well within the outer limits of our nondelegation precedents."[78] Some Court watchers were surprised by Scalia's position, given his dissent in *Mistretta*. Quoting his *Mistretta* dissent, Scalia noted that "a certain degree of discretion, and thus of lawmaking, inheres in most executive or judicial action."[79] The *Whitman* decision suggests strongly that the nondelegation doctrine, while officially viable, is not likely to be invoked to upset the institutional arrangements that have come to characterize the modern administrative state.

The Supreme Court's *Whitman* decision is excerpted at the end of the chapter.

Evaluation of the Delegation Issue Those who argue in favor of delegation present three arguments: First, in an increasingly complex society characterized by technological sophistication and economic interdependence, the sheer magnitude of problems demanding congressional attention and the practical difficulties of regulation limit the ability of Congress to legislate comprehensively, much less effectively. Second, the deliberate, tortoise-like pace of the legislative process makes it all but impossible for Congress to respond promptly to changing objective conditions, making meaningful legislative regulation almost inconceivable. Finally, many of the subjects of regulation are both complex and esoteric, requiring policymaking expertise not possessed within the Congress. Given these factors, proponents conclude that it is both desirable and inevitable that Congress rely more and more on "experts" for the development as well as the implementation of regulations.

In recent years, however, many critics have come to question the "expertise" of the bureaucracy. Some would argue that delegation of power to the bureaucracy merely changes the venue where politics, dominated by interest groups, takes place. Delegation can also be faulted for contributing to the growth of government. Jacob Weisberg has noted in the *New Republic*, "As a labor-saving device, delegation did for legislators what the washing machine did for the 1950s housewife. Government could now

penetrate every nook and cranny of American life in a way that was simply impossible before."[80] Those who champion limited government have every reason to be suspicious of the delegation of legislative power. Yet, as we have seen, even a conservative Supreme Court is unwilling to resurrect the nondelegation rule, for to do so would shake the very foundations of the administrative state. As Gary Lawson has noted, "When faced with a choice between the Constitution and the structure of modern governance, the Court has had no difficulty making the choice."[81] See Box 3.2 for further discussion of antidelegation.

Separation of Powers

As required by the federal and state constitutions, government in the United States is structured on the principle of separation of powers. That is, the legislative, executive, and judicial powers of government are assigned to separate and largely independent branches of government. As the Supreme Court has recognized, the founders "viewed the principle of separation of powers as a vital check against tyranny."[82] President James Madison observed that "accumulation of all powers, legislative, executive, and judiciary, in the same hands may justly be pronounced the very definition of tyranny."[83] At the same time, the Constitution "contemplates that practice will integrate the dispersed powers into a workable government."[84] In *J. W. Hampton & Co. v. United States,* discussed above in the context of the delegation issue, the Supreme Court said that the constitutional boundaries between the branches of government should be determined "according to common sense and the inherent necessities of the governmental co-ordination."[85] More recently, the Court has observed that "the accumulation of excessive authority in a single Branch . . . lies not in a hermetic division among the Branches, but in a carefully crafted system of checked and balanced power within each Branch."[86] In this view, the key to maintaining limited government and preventing one

---

BOX 3.2   Scholarly Perspectives on the Antidelegation Doctrine

"With the New Deal, and the attendant death of the nondelegation doctrine, the giveaway of what had been seen as legislative authority (or something close) became massive. . . . At least as important as the scope of modern delegation, however, is to whom the power has been delegated. If there has been any net beneficiary of Congress's abdication of authority, it has been the President. . . ." M. Elizabeth Magill, "Beyond Powers and Branches in Separation of Powers Law," 150 *U. Pa. L. Rev.* 603 (2001).

"The nondelegation doctrine could move the constitutional balance of power back toward the balance envisioned by the Framers by forcing legislators to make the law and by rendering it more difficult for the executive branch to enlarge its sphere of power." Marci A. Hamilton, "Representation and Nondelegation: Back to Basics," 20 *Cardozo L. Rev.* 807 (1999).

"The Supreme Court . . . has rejected so many delegation challenges to so many utterly vacuous statutes that modern delegation decisions now simply recite these past holdings and wearily move on. Anything short of the Goodness and Niceness Commission, it seems, is permissible." Gary Lawson, "The Rise and Rise of the Administrative State," 107 *Harv. L. Rev.* 1231 (1994).

"In our view, delegation is a self-regulating system, not in need of closer attention from the judiciary. Legislators will, over time, adjust the boundaries of the administrative state so that the executive branch considers those issue areas that Congress handles less effectively itself, keeping the system in a rough equilibrium. Forcing Congress to do more legislating would only push back into the halls of the legislature those issues on which the committee system, with its lack of expertise and tendency towards uncontrollable logrolls, produces policy most inefficiently. This would be hardly a step in the right direction." David Epstein and Sharyn O'Halloran, "The Nondelegation Doctrine and the Separation of Powers: A Political Science Approach," 20 *Cardozo L. Rev.* 947 (1999).

"In the end, . . . the nondelegation doctrine is a prescription for judicial supervision of both the substance and forms of legislation and hence of politics and public policy, without the existence or even the possibility of any coherent, principled, or manageable judicial standards." Peter H. Schuck, "Delegation and Democracy," 20 *Cardozo L. Rev.* 775 (1999).

". . . [F]or 60 years the nondelegation doctrine has existed only as part of the Constitution-in-exile, along with the doctrines of enumerated powers, unconstitutional conditions, and substantive due process, and their textual cousins, the Necessary and Proper, Contracts, Takings, and Commerce Clauses. The memory of these ancient exiles, banished for standing in opposition to unlimited government, is kept alive by a few scholars who labor on in the hope of a restoration, a second coming of the Constitution of liberty—even if perhaps not in their own lifetimes." Douglas Ginsburg, "Delegation Running Riot," 1 *Regulation* 83 (1995).

---

branch from becoming too powerful is to maintain a healthy system of **checks and balances.** (See the excerpt from the Supreme Court's opinion in *Mistretta v. United States* located in Box 3.3.)

The Progressive reformers and New Dealers who created the modern administrative state saw separation of powers as an outmoded concept, an invitation to "gridlock" and therefore an impediment to good government. Their solution was to create a host of subgovernments, agencies that would exercise legislative, executive, and judicial power. This phenomenon can be seen throughout the federal bureaucracy today. An agency promulgates rules using a **quasi-legislative** power delegated from the Congress. The agency enforces these rules, which is quite properly the function of an agency within the executive branch. In what is often termed an exercise of **quasi-judicial** power, the agency also adjudicates disputes with those parties against whom it has enforced rules. The agency is placed in the anomalous position of judging a case to which it is itself a party. Is this phenomenon "the very definition of tyranny" or merely reflective of the "inherent necessities of the governmental co-ordination"?

BOX 3.3 Supreme Court Perspective

Mistretta v. United States
488 U.S. 361 (1989).

[In this case the Court upheld an act of Congress creating the United States Sentencing Commission as an independent agency within the judicial branch and delegating to that agency the authority to establish sentencing guidelines for federal criminal cases. One of the grounds upon which the act was challenged was that it violated the separation of powers doctrine by permitting the Sentencing Commission to act as a legislative body. In rejecting this argument, Justice Blackmun summarized the Court's separation of powers jurisprudence.]

Justice Blackmun delivered the opinion of the Court.

. . . In applying the principle of separated powers in our jurisprudence, we have sought to give life to Madison's view of the appropriate relationship among the three coequal Branches. . . . Madison recognized that our constitutional system imposes upon the Branches a degree of overlapping responsibility, a duty of interdependence as well as independence . . . . In a passage now commonplace in our cases, Justice Jackson summarized the pragmatic, flexible view of differentiated governmental power to which we are heir: "While the Constitution diffuses power the better to secure liberty, it also contemplates that practice will integrate the dispersed powers into a workable government. It enjoins upon its branches separateness but interdependence, autonomy but reciprocity." . . .

In adopting this flexible understanding of separation of powers, we simply have recognized Madison's teaching that the greatest security against tyranny—the accumulation of excessive authority in a single Branch—lies not in a hermetic division among the Branches, but in a carefully crafted system of checked and balanced power within each Branch. . . . Accordingly, . . . the Framers "built into the tripartite Federal Government . . . a self-executing safeguard against the encroachment or aggrandizement of one branch at the expense of the other." . . .

It is this concern of encroachment and aggrandizement that has animated our separation-of-powers jurisprudence and aroused our vigilance against the "hydraulic pressure inherent within each of the separate Branches to exceed the outer limits of its power." . . . Accordingly, we have not hesitated to strike down provisions of law that either accrete to a single Branch powers more appropriately diffused among separate Branches or that undermine the authority and independence of one or another coordinate Branch. For example, just as the Framers recognized the particular danger of the Legislative Branch's accreting to itself judicial or executive power, so too have we invalidated attempts by Congress to exercise the responsibilities of other Branches or to reassign powers vested by the Constitution in either the Judicial Branch or the Executive Branch. . . . By the same token, we have upheld statutory provisions that to some degree commingle the functions of the Branches, but that pose no danger of either aggrandizement or encroachment. . . .

A 1991 Supreme Court decision indicates that the separation of powers doctrine is not completely defunct. In *Metropolitan Washington Airports Authority* (MWAA) *v. Citizens for the Abatement of Aircraft Noise* (CAAN),[87] the Court struck down an arrangement under which Congress sought to exercise control over an independent regulatory entity through nonlegislative means. The Court ruled that Congress violated separation of powers by authorizing the establishment of a board of review, consisting exclusively of members of Congress, with authority to veto decisions made by MWAA, an entity created by a compact between Virginia and Washington, D.C. The Court, in effect, saw the board of review as an agent of Congress and was not persuaded otherwise by the formal requirement that board members act "in their individual capacities as representatives of airport users nationwide."

Although the courts have invalidated a number of governmental polices and practices based on the separation of powers principle, they have been unwilling to apply a strict version of the doctrine to the federal bureaucracy. To do so would require a fundamental restructuring of the modern administrative state, a project that courts have been disinclined to address.

Defenders of the modern administrative state point to the controls that the three constitutional branches of government exercise over the bureaucracy (see Chapters 8 and 9). Congress, the White House, and the federal courts can (and sometimes do) nullify agency actions that go too far. But as long as effective legislative, executive, and judicial control remains in effect, the constitutional problems of the administrative state are overcome or at least attenuated.

THE STATE AND LOCAL CONTEXT

Unlike the national government, which theoretically derives its powers from the United States Constitution, states have the inherent power to govern. As the Washington Supreme Court has recognized,

> The state is inherently sovereign at all times and in every capacity. . . . By reason of this sovereignty, it possesses all powers, but only such powers as are within the limitations of the state Constitution and without the prohibitions of the federal Constitution. It can do no act except in the exercise of this sovereign power and within these constitutional limitations.[88]

The **sovereign states** thus possess all powers, except as limited by their own constitutions and the powers they delegated to the national government upon ratification of the United States Constitution or upon being admitted to the Union.

State Constitutions

Each of the states is governed under its own constitution. The **state constitution** is the basic law of the state and is supreme except insofar as it conflicts with the United States Constitution, federal laws, treaties, and regulations. Like the federal constitution, state constitutions are based on the doctrine of separation of the executive, legislative, and judicial powers. Some state constitutions emphasize the point by explicitly mandating that persons of one branch of state government shall not exercise powers belonging to another branch. And like the federal constitution, state constitutions provide for a system of checks and balances and include provisions similar to the Bill of Rights. State constitutions usually divide the state into counties (called parishes in Louisiana and boroughs in Alaska) for purposes of governmental administration.

As an attribute of sovereignty, states have police power, which is the authority to enact laws that promote the health, safety, morals, and welfare of the citizens. The police power evolves to meet the needs of a changing society. Some state constitutions detail such inherent sovereign powers as **eminent domain**, that is the power to take private property for public use, and provide limitations or restrictions on the exercise of this and other powers. Basic to state constitutions is the creation of the office of governor as the elected chief executive, an elected legislature, and a judicial system. The structure of these offices, terms of office holders, and qualifications to hold office are essential elements in state constitutions.

Unlike the federal constitution, state constitutions tend to be quite lengthy and to describe in great detail the structure and powers of the three branches of government. The process of amendment of a state constitution is much simpler than the requirements to effect an amendment to the federal constitution. Consequently, state constitutions have undergone frequent changes by amendments and many have become cluttered by numerous provisions concerning taxes, public education, utilities, and so forth that are not basic to state organization structure and powers.

Judicial Interpretation of State Constitutions

Like the federal Constitution, the state constitutions must be interpreted, and this function is performed by the state courts, most notably the state supreme courts. State supreme courts have the last word with respect to the interpretation of their respective state constitutions. Of course, if a state or federal court determines that a provision of a state constitution is in conflict with the United States Constitution, the court will declare the state constitutional provision to be null and void.[89]

Many provisions of the state constitutions have counterparts in the federal Constitution. For example, every state constitution has a due process clause or some equivalent provision. In interpreting provisions of their state constitutions that have federal counterparts, state courts may take three different approaches. Under the "independent approach" state courts interpret state constitutional provisions without relying on federal court interpretations of counterpart federal constitutional provisions. As Cooper and Marks note, this approach "is deferential to traditional notions of federalism because it promotes the development of state constitutions without effect from the intimidating shadow of federal decisional law."[90] The opposite approach, sometimes dubbed the "clone approach," calls for the state court to simply adopt the prevailing federal interpretation. "Under this approach, a state court only reaches a separate conclusion on a particular issue where it has not been addressed by the federal courts or when the federal answer is ambiguous or unclear."[91] Between these polar opposites lies a middle ground in which state courts are guided but not bound by the federal decisional law. Under this approach, "the state court is deferential to a federal interpretation of a federal provision when construing a similar state provision, but it is not bound by it, since local or special circumstances might suggest a differing result."[92] This approach is sensible and is probably the most commonly employed.

The State Bureaucracy

In addition to the governor, state constitutions usually create the offices of lieutenant-governor, secretary of state, treasurer (or comptroller), and attorney general. Some state constitutions create additional offices (for example, school superintendent, agricultural commissioner, secretary of labor, secretary of commerce, and so forth) as well as various state agencies. Additional offices and agencies are created by legislative enactments. As we mentioned in Chapter 2, state governments are highly bureaucratized in their collection of revenues, supervision of elections, and regulation of agriculture, conservation, business, and labor, and the administration of public health, education, and social welfare programs. Legislatively created boards and commissions administer state civil service and pension laws. They also include agencies that administer and regulate public utilities, transportation, state parks, public works, motor vehicles and highway safety, banking, insurance, professions and occupations, and other fields of government activity.

Critics argue that the structure of the usual state executive branch with its multiplicity of agencies leads to an overlapping of functions and results in an ineffective decentralization of government. The consequence, they point out, is an inefficient system that duplicates costs that burden the taxpayers. In response, there has been a trend to limit the number of elected officials at the state level in order to promote efficiency and allow the governor to exercise more control over functions of the government.

Separation of Powers at the State Level

The United States Constitution recognizes the doctrine of separation of powers by its separate treatment of powers of the legislative, executive, and judicial branches in Articles I, II, and III respectively. The objective is to prevent the concentration of power in one branch of government, prevent one branch from interfering with other branches, and provide for a system of checks and balances. State constitutions parallel this structure, often with explicit recognition of the doctrine. For example, Article II, Section 1 of the Nebraska Constitution provides:

> The powers of the government of this state are divided into three distinct departments,

the legislative, executive and judicial, and no person or collection of persons being one of these departments shall exercise any powers properly belonging to either of the others, except as hereinafter expressly directed or permitted appertaining to either of the other branches unless expressly provided herein.

It is uncommon for state courts to invalidate state laws or policies on this basis. By and large, the state courts take a pragmatic, rather than a formalistic, approach to separation of powers issues. It takes a fairly extreme case to prompt state courts to strike down policymaking arrangements as violations of the separation of powers principle. One such case occurred in New Mexico in 1998, when the governor vetoed a statute enacting a welfare reform policy and then undertook to develop an alternative policy through the administrative process. In *State ex rel. Taylor v. Johnson*,[93] the New Mexico Supreme Court held that the governor and other executive officials usurped the legislative function and violated the separation of powers clause of the state constitution. In a surprising decision, the court chastised the governor for ignoring an earlier court order and held him and other executive officials in contempt.

The New Mexico Supreme Court's decision in *State ex rel. Taylor v. Johnson* is excerpted at the end of the chapter.

State administrative agencies often combine legislative, executive, and judicial functions. Thus they appear to violate the doctrine of separation of powers. Yet, courts view the federal and state constitutions as workable documents of government and uniformly approve delegation of legislative, executive, and judicial powers to administrative agencies when such delegations are based on adequate standards. Delegation of executive functions usually involve no conflicts between the other branches of government and pose no constitutional problem as long as such functions are provided for within the constitution and laws of the state.

The Delegation of State Legislative Power to State and Local Agencies

As we noted above, federal courts rarely find the nondelegation doctrine to be a significant barrier to the exercise of legislation delegation. Some state courts, on the other hand, have taken a stricter approach in judicial review of legislative delegations. State courts vary somewhat in their approaches but they generally uphold delegations of power as long as the powers are exercised in accordance with legislative standards, do not invade the lawmaking function of the legislature or the core functions of the judiciary, and provide sufficient safeguards to those affected by agency actions. Actions beyond the scope of delegated authority are regarded as **ultra vires** and are subject to being invalidated by the courts.

Although the legislature cannot delegate its power to make laws, it can delegate to an administrative agency the power to make regulations and fill in the details necessary to implement a legislative enactment. Agency rules adopted pursuant to authority delegated by the legislature have the same legal force and effect as statutory provisions. For example, the state legislature cannot be expected to determine the speed limits for every stretch of highway throughout the state. Therefore, it delegates this power to a state agency, such as the Department of Transportation. The DOT determines the appropriate speed limit for a particular roadway and posts signs to that effect. As anyone who has ever received a citation for speeding knows, these posted speed limits are not mere suggestions for safe driving. They are laws, and those who violate them can be fined or have their driving privilege suspended or revoked.

Courts often characterize delegation of legislative powers as quasi-legislative or quasi-judicial. Quasi-legislative power involves rulemaking, a process whereby an administrative agency adopts policy statements to implement the intent of legislation. The legislature can validly delegate quasi-judicial power to an agency to enable it to settle disputes as long as the adjudicatory process does not invade the core functions of the judiciary. Quasi-judicial functions involve the application of laws and rules to the rights of persons in a dispute, and, where appropriate, the imposition of sanctions. One might liken the process of administrative adjudication to a nonjury proceeding in the court system. We discuss the rulemaking and adjudicatory functions of administrative agencies in detail in later chapters.

In some instances a state constitution will delegate authority to a specific board to regulate such basic functions as public utilities or regulation of banks and insurance companies. In other instances a legislative body will create an agency to handle specifically delegated responsibilities. Where the state legislature declares a policy, fixes a standard, and allows the agency to prescribe the rules and regulations to promote the purpose of the legislation, courts generally hold the delegation of quasi-legislative power to be constitutional. And while state courts generally uphold the constitutionality of a delegation of quasi-judicial functions, to allow an agency to award damages in a case involving a tort or a breach of contract violates the separation of powers doctrine.[94] Moreover, while an administrative agency may impose fines and forfeitures (see Chapter 5), it may not order persons to be incarcerated for violations of criminal law without a judicial finding of guilt.

Increasingly, state legislatures not only delegate legislative power to administrative agencies, they also provide for privatization of some historic governmental functions, for example, administration of state penal institutions by delegation of powers to private entities.[95]

The Historic Approach to Delegation of Legislative Powers In reviewing the constitutionality of delegation of legislative powers, some state courts require rather precise standards with limited or no discretion vested in agency personnel. Citing Article II, Section 1 of the Nebraska Constitution (quoted earlier), the Nebraska Supreme Court in *Bosselman, Inc. v. State*[96] found

that the legislature had unconstitutionally delegated its power when it enacted a statute empowering local governing bodies to adopt licensing regulations that must be met by an applicant before a license will issue, without providing the necessary standards to limit the contents of the regulations. The court noted that power [conferred] upon an administrative agency must not only be reasonably sufficient and definite for the guidance of the agency but must also be sufficient to enable those affected to know their rights and obligations.

Florida also has a separation of powers clause in its constitution similar to the Nebraska provision quoted earlier. In 1979, the Florida Supreme Court invalidated statutes that the court found to be "so lacking in guidelines that neither the agency nor the court [could] determine whether the agency [was] carrying out the intent of the legislature."[97]

The Modern View of Delegation of State Legislative Powers The trend is for courts to take a more liberal view of upholding a delegation statute that provides general standards and allows for exercise of discretion as long as sufficient procedural safeguards are in place. The Colorado Supreme Court's 1981 decision in *City and County of Denver v. Cottrell*,[98] exemplifies the more liberal approach. A delegation of state legislative power allowed the city, in determining water rates, to make provision for the municipal water system to serve the anticipated growth of metropolitan Denver. The state supreme court rejected the contention that, because the delegation of power lacked adequate standards, the statute was unconstitutional.

The court referred to the traditional nondelegation rule that requires the legislature to provide sufficient standards to guide the administrative agency's exercise of delegated powers, but declined to be bound by it. The court found the municipal board's charter required that the water rates be set at a public hearing at rates as low as possible and that the metro areas would reimburse the municipality for the additional costs of serving nonmunicipal areas. The court concluded that there were sufficient safeguards and procedural protections to allow it to uphold the delegation of legislative power. The court cited several recent decisions from various state courts and observed:

> The modern view is to recognize that the traditional standards test to determine the validity of delegation of legislative authority is inadequate, and the proper focus should be upon the totality of protection provided by standards and procedural safeguards at both the statutory and administrative levels. . . . We now make explicit that the test is not simply whether the delegation is guided by standards, but whether there are sufficient statutory standards and safeguards and administrative standards and safeguards, in combination, to protect against unnecessary and uncontrolled exercise of discretionary power.[99]

In 1976, the Supreme Judicial Court of Maine adhered to the modern view on delegation of legislative power in *State v. Boynton*.[100] Defendant Boynton challenged his conviction for violating a town ordinance regulating clam diggers. He argued that the town ordinance making it unlawful for any person to take shellfish from the coastal waters of the municipality without having a municipal license was an unlawful delegation of legislative power. In rejecting the defendant's contention, the court pointed out that the town was required to have a permit from and secure the approval of the Commissioner of Marine Resources before enacting the ordinance. The purpose of the nondelegation doctrine, the court explained, is to protect against arbitrary action and make certain that the powers delegated have meaningful standards. In view of the bifurcation of authority between the state and local levels of government, the court found that the enabling statute did not constitute an impermissible delegation of legislative authority to the town.

CONSTITUTIONAL RIGHTS AS LIMITATIONS ON BUREAUCRATIC POWER

Administrative agencies wield broad governmental powers. Yet, in exercising those powers, federal, state, and local agencies must cope with numerous constitutional limitations and restraints. Both federal and state constitutions mandate that agencies afford persons due process of law and not deny anyone the equal protection of the laws. In addition, administrative agencies at all levels must be conscious of specific constitutional guarantees in the Bill of Rights.

Although the Bill of Rights was designed to provide protection against the federal government, the United States Supreme Court has found that most provisions of the Bill of Rights are "incorporated" into the guarantees of the Fourteenth Amendment and thus effective against the states as well. As a result of this **doctrine of incorporation,** actions of state and local agencies that are alleged to violate Bill of Rights protections are subject to judicial review in federal courts. Of course, state and local agencies must also comply with the requirements of their respective state constitutions, and in some instances state courts interpret state constitutional provisions protecting rights more broadly than the federal courts interpret counterpart provisions of the United States Constitution. While state constitutional provisions are important in protecting rights threatened by state and local bureaucracies, our discussion here focuses on rights protected by the United States Constitution and, in particular, the interpretation of those rights by the United States Supreme Court.

First Amendment rights of free expression are of particular importance to officers and employees of administrative agencies as well as to those whose rights are affected by agency rulings. The strictures of the **Fourth Amendment** prohibition against unreasonable searches and seizures can come into play in administrative searches. The **Fifth Amendment** protections against self-incrimination can surface in administrative investigations and quasi-judicial hearings. And the requirement that an owner must be paid just compensation is an essential consideration in the taking of property for public use by condemnation or where such taking occurs by regulation. Although the Bill of Rights does not explicitly protect "privacy," the courts have ruled that there is a right of privacy that emanates from the Bill of Rights.[101] Thus, agencies whose policies intrude into the realm of individual privacy or family life are subject to challenge on the basis of this important constitutional right.

Due Process of Law

The exercise of police power—the power to legislate for the protection of the health, safety, morals, and general welfare—is very broad in its scope. Under this power the state legislature can regulate life, liberty, and property interests. Congress has acquired a similar power through the broad interpretation of the Commerce Clause. Laws that regulate life, liberty, and property interests are valid, even though they appear unwise, as long as they afford due process and equal protection of the laws, are not irrational, and do not violate specific constitutional protections.

Today the concept of due process is extremely important in administrative law because actions by administrative agencies affect the life, liberty, and property interests of millions of Americans. Due process of law is based on the requirement of the Fifth Amendment to the U.S. Constitution that provides that "[no person] shall be deprived of life, liberty, or property, without due process of law; nor shall private property be taken for public use, without just compensation." It is extended to cover actions by state and local governments by the Fourteenth Amendment, which provides that "nor shall any State deprive any person of life, liberty, or property, without due process of law; nor deny to any person within its jurisdiction the equal protection of the laws." Every state constitution contains some similar protection. In lan-

guage echoing Magna Carta, the medieval origin of the concept of due process, the Tennessee Constitution provides: "That no man shall be taken or imprisoned, or disseized of his freehold, liberties or privileges, or outlawed, or exiled, or in any manner destroyed or deprived of his life, liberty or property, but by the judgment of his peers or the law of the land."[102]

In its most general sense, due process refers to the exercise of governmental power under the rule of law with due regard for the rights and interests of individuals. The essence of due process is protection of the individual against arbitrary governmental action.[103] The courts have recognized that due process has two dimensions: substantive and procedural. **Substantive due process** is concerned with whether a law is substantively related to a valid legislative purpose and is neither arbitrary nor unfair. As the Supreme Court said in 1934, "the guaranty of due process . . . demands only that the law shall not be unreasonable, arbitrary, or capricious, and that the means selected shall have a real and substantial relation to the object sought to be attained."[104] **Procedural due process** is the requirement that government agencies follow proper legal procedures before acting to deprive persons of life, liberty, or property. The most fundamental requirement of procedural due process is that the individual be afforded a fair hearing before government takes action inimical to that individual's interests.[105] As Cooper and Marks have observed,

> While the doctrines of substantive and procedural due process play distinct roles in the judicial process, they frequently overlap. Hence, many cases do not expressly state the distinction between procedural and substantive due process.[106]

Substantive Due Process Historically, courts exercised considerable discretion in making determinations that laws or policies violated substantive due process. The classic case was decided by the United States Supreme Court in 1905. In

Lochner v. New York,[107] the Court struck down a state law setting maximum working hours in bakeries. Indeed, prior to the Constitutional Revolution of 1937, the Supreme Court invalidated laws designed to effect social and economic reforms. The Court based its rejection of such laws on the ground that they infringed "liberty of contract" without sufficient justification in terms of the public welfare (see discussion in Chapter 2). This became known as substantive due process analysis.

After 1937, the Supreme Court changed its approach dramatically in reviewing legislation involving economic regulation. When considering whether a law that limited economic liberty was constitutional the Court began to apply a **rational basis test** in which the key question is whether the challenged law has a rational relationship to a valid governmental objective. As a result, the legislative branch of the government was given broad discretion in enacting laws, and the modern administrative state began to flourish. Today, federal and state courts generally uphold legislative enactments or administrative regulations irrespective of the court's view as to the wisdom of the law or regulation as long as the court finds any rational relationship between a law and the public interest. But in reviewing the constitutionality of state laws, local ordinances, and administrative regulations, some state courts still apply a substantive due process approach similar to that taken in *Lochner v. New York*. Under this analysis administrative policies developed under the rulemaking process can be vulnerable to constitutional attack (see discussion on Fourteenth Amendment, which follows in the next section).

The Supreme Court takes an approach stricter than the rational basis test when it reviews the constitutionality of a law infringing **fundamental rights,** even those that are not explicitly identified in the Constitution. For example, the Court has held that **strict scrutiny** is warranted in reviewing laws that infringe the right to travel freely across state lines.[108] In the landmark decision in *Roe v. Wade* (1973),[109] the Court applied strict scrutiny in striking down a state law restrict-ing access to abortion. While the Court has since modified its approach somewhat in abortion cases,[110] some state courts continue to employ strict scrutiny in reviewing state abortion laws under their own state constitutions. For example, in *In re: T.W.*,[111] the Florida Supreme Court applied strict scrutiny in finding unconstitutional a statute requiring parental approval before a pregnant minor could obtain an abortion. The court concluded that the statute requiring parental consent intruded on the minor's right to privacy under the Florida Constitution. The court observed that the Florida Constitution embraced more privacy interests and extended more protection in this area than the federal constitution. (At the time of the court's decision Florida was one of the few states that had an independent privacy provision in its state constitution.)

Strict judicial scrutiny is also applied to forms of discrimination, such as that based on race, that have been held to be "inherently suspect."[112] When courts apply strict scrutiny, government carries the burden of proving that the challenged policy is narrowly tailored to the achievement of a **compelling governmental interest.** This is a difficult standard to meet. In most instances, invocation of strict scrutiny presages invalidation of a challenged policy.

Procedural Due Process Of far greater significance today than the doctrine of substantive due process is the doctrine of procedural due process. The Due Process Clauses of the Fifth and Fourteenth Amendments impose significant procedural constraints on the exercise of the police power. Procedural due process addresses the manner in which government undertakes to accomplish its objectives. It certainly relates to the activities of government agencies, most obviously to the adjudication of cases (see Chapter 7). Generally speaking, procedural due process is not a requirement in agency rulemaking because rulemaking relates to legislative functions.[113] Nevertheless, some state courts apply state procedural due process considerations to rulemaking directed at specific businesses or occupations.

Procedural due process is required when government seeks to deprive an individual of a liberty interest.[114] It is also clear that actions affecting a party's traditional property interests require the application of procedural due process. During the latter half of the twentieth century the United States Supreme Court expanded the scope of procedural due process to include interests beyond the traditional concept of property. Examples of this "new property" include government entitlements,[115] public employment[116] and licenses.[117]

To comply with the procedural due process requirements the government must provide a party with a **fair notice** and a **fair hearing** before an **impartial decision maker** with the authority to hear the evidence presented. A party must also be provided the **opportunity to present evidence** and arguments before an administrative agency deprives a person of life, liberty, or property. In *Goldberg v. Kelly* (1970),[118] the Supreme Court noted the importance of an impartial decision maker in an administrative hearing, affirmed a party's right to retain counsel at the party's own expense, and adopted a balancing approach to determine just what due process is due. In 1976, in *Mathews v. Eldridge*, the Court elaborated on this approach by stating:

> [O]ur prior decisions indicate that identification of the specific dictates of due process generally requires consideration of three distinct factors: First, the private interest that will be affected by the official action; second, the risk of an erroneous deprivation of such interest through the procedures used, and the probable value, if any, of additional or substitute procedural safeguards; and finally, the Government's interest, including the function involved and the fiscal and administrative burdens that the additional or substitute procedural requirement would entail.[119]

Procedural due process requires that notice to a party must fairly state the charges or claims that an agency is making against the party, define the procedural rights available, and afford adequate

time to prepare for a hearing. In some instances, statutes require agencies to engage in formal adjudication, a process that more or less resembles a civil trial. Formal adjudicatory procedures are outlined in the federal Administrative Procedure Act and its state counterparts (see Chapter 7). Although the specific procedural rights of parties in formal adjudications are defined by statute, they are based ultimately on the constitutional norm of procedural due process.

An agency's decision must be based on the law and evidence presented and the agency's order must contain essential **findings of fact** and **conclusions of law.** It is important that an adequate record be compiled so it can be available to be presented to a court should an interested party seek judicial review of the agency's actions. (Judicial review of agency action is discussed in depth in Chapter 9.)

In later chapters we will elaborate on the wide range of significant interests that administrative agencies deal with and describe instances where procedural due process is extremely important. But for now, just consider a few examples where the adjudicatory process comes into play:

- A state agency notifies a vendor that it proposes to revoke its license because the licensee has been found guilty of selling alcoholic beverages to a minor.

- A student is expelled from public school for violating a rule outlined in the students' handbook that prohibits wearing "inappropriate" clothing to class. The student plans to file an appeal with the local school board.

- A municipality grants a rezoning request contingent upon the developer dedicating a portion of the land being rezoned for a public park.

- A public hospital administrator denies a physician staff privileges because a court has found the physician liable for malpractice resulting in a patient's death. The physician files an appeal with the district hospital board.

- A state parole board informs a parolee that the board intends to revoke parole.

Equal Protection of the Laws

The **Fourteenth Amendment** to the U.S. Constitution guarantees that "[n]o State shall make or enforce any law which shall . . . deny to any person within its jurisdiction the equal protection of the laws." The amendment was adopted in 1868 to protect the rights of the newly freed slaves after the Civil War. Congress has also relied on the Amendment as a basis to enact civil rights laws. Section 5 of the Fourteenth Amendment provides that "The Congress shall have power to enforce, by appropriate legislation, the provisions of this article," meaning that Congress is authorize to enact legislation to implement the guarantee of equal protection of the laws.

Racial Discrimination The Fourteenth Amendment was adopted to protect persons of African descent from official discrimination. Since the Supreme Court's 1954 landmark decision in *Brown v. Board of Education*,[120] in which racial segregation in public schools was declared unconstitutional, the Equal Protection Clause of the Fourteenth Amendment has been used by state and federal courts to overturn laws that discriminate against persons based on their race. Courts employ strict scrutiny in cases of discrimination based on race, which means that the government is required to prove that such discrimination is necessary to achieve a compelling public purpose. This test is very difficult, if not impossible, to satisfy. In a 1995 decision with important implications for employment and contracting policies of administrative agencies, the Supreme Court has said that

> all governmental action based on race—a group classification long recognized as "in most circumstances irrelevant and therefore prohibited,". . . should be subjected to detailed judicial inquiry to ensure that the personal right to equal protection of the

laws has not been infringed. These ideas have long been central to this Court's understanding of equal protection, and holding "benign" state and federal racial classifications to different standards does not square with them. "[A] free people whose institutions are founded upon the doctrine of equality,". . . should tolerate no retreat from the principle that government may treat people differently because of their race only for the most compelling reasons. Accordingly, we hold today that all racial classifications, imposed by whatever federal, state, or local governmental actor, must be analyzed by a reviewing court under strict scrutiny. In other words, such classifications are constitutional only if they are narrowly tailored measures that further compelling governmental interests.[121]

Affirmative Action often defended as "benign" forms of discrimination in that they seek to compensate for historic "invidious" discrimination, **affirmative action programs** are also subject to strict judicial scrutiny under the Equal Protection Clause.[122] In 2003, the Supreme Court considered two cases involving the use of race in affirmative action programs for admission to institutions of higher learning. The Court struck down an affirmative action policy employed in undergraduate admissions to the University of Michigan. Applying strict scrutiny, the Court found the state had a compelling interest in increasing the diversity of student population. Nevertheless, the Court found that the preferential treatment, which allowed every "underrepresented minority" applicant a fixed number of points for admission because of race, was not narrowly tailored to achieve educational diversity.[123] In a related case, the Court upheld an affirmative action plan for admissions to the University of Michigan law school. There the Court found that the law school admission process was an individualized review that considered race as one of multiple factors for admission to the law school and was not unduly burdensome to nonminority applicants. Thus, the Court concluded the law school admissions process was narrowly tailored to achieve the educational benefits of a diverse student body.[124]

Gender-Based Discrimination Agencies must take care to avoid discriminating on the basis of gender among their employees, clients, or the parties they regulate. In gender discrimination cases, the courts employ "intermediate" or "heightened" scrutiny, which means that government must demonstrate an "exceedingly persuasive justification" before courts will approve such discrimination.[125] Although this level of judicial review theoretically is not as demanding as strict scrutiny, the Supreme Court's case law reveals "a strong presumption that gender classifications are invalid."[126] For example, in *United States v. Virginia* (1996),[127] the Court struck down the long-standing policy under which admission to Virginia Military Academy was limited to males. Writing for the Court, Justice Ruth Ginsburg observed that "generalizations about 'the way women are,' estimates of what is appropriate for most women, no longer justify denying opportunity to women whose talent and capacity place them outside the average description."[128]

Equal Protection and the Administration of Elections The Equal Protection Clause also extends to the exercise of the franchise. In *Reynolds v. Sims* (1964), the Supreme Court said:

> The right to vote freely for the candidate of one's choice is of the essence of a democratic society, and any restrictions on that right strike at the heart of representative government. And the right of suffrage can be denied by a debasement or dilution of the weight of a citizen's vote just as effectively as by wholly prohibiting the free exercise of the franchise.[129]

In the United States, state and local officials are responsible for conducting elections, even for federal office. State and local election officials must take care in administering elections that they do not run afoul of equal protection requirements. Readers will recall the heated conflict that arose in Florida concerning counting of ballots in the presidential contest between Al Gore and George W. Bush. The Florida Supreme Court interpreted the state election code to allow a manual recount of alleged undercounted ballots. After it did, the United States Supreme Court entered the picture on petition of the Bush Campaign. In *Bush v. Gore*,[130] the Court held that the manual recount of ballots in several Florida counties would violate the Equal Protection Clause because there were no uniform standards as to the recounting that could ensure uniform treatment in counting ballots in the various counties. The dissenters argued that the case involved construction of a state law and that the Court should accept the Florida Supreme Court's decision interpreting the Florida Statutes that define the standards required in a manual recount.[131]

More recently, a legal controversy erupted in California over the fact that counties used different types of voting mechanisms in the October 2003 referendum on the recall of Governor Gray Davis. Voters in counties that used punch-card machines filed suit in federal court in an effort to postpone the election. Citing *Bush v. Gore*, they argued that they would have a lesser chance of having their votes counted than voters in counties that use more reliable voting technologies. Ultimately, plaintiffs lost their case[132] and the election was held as scheduled. Governor Davis was recalled and the movie star Arnold Schwarzenegger was elected to replace him.

The First Amendment

The text of the First Amendment to the United States Constitution is brief, containing but forty-five words, yet it has become the basis for continuing legal issues. It states:

> Congress shall make no law respecting an establishment of religion, or prohibiting the free exercise thereof; or abridging the freedom of speech, or of the press; or the right of

the people peaceably to assemble, and to petition the Government for a redress of grievances.

The Supreme Court issued relatively few opinions construing the First Amendment until the 1930s. Since then it has been a prolific source of litigation concerning expression and religion. The First Amendment is perhaps the most basic of constitutional guarantees. It applies to various forms of expression and applies (to a lesser degree) to commercial speech. Consequently, it poses considerable restrictions on the activities of administrative agencies. Many of these restrictions concern public employment and public school policies. (The First Amendment rights of public employees are discussed in Chapter 10.)

First Amendment Issues in Public Schools Public school officials must be alert not to impose rules and regulations that transgress the First Amendment rights of expression and religion. Controversies often focus on whether rules violate the "establishment of religion" prong or the "free exercise of religion" prong of the First Amendment. It is clear that public schools may not indoctrinate students in religion. However, they may teach the historical background and context of various religions. Debate continues over the Supreme Court's decisions prohibiting prayer in schools.

In *Santa Fe Independent School District v. Doe*,[133] the Court in 2000 held that a school district's policy that permitted prayer initiated and led by a student over the school's public address system before football games violated the Establishment of Religion prong of the First Amendment. But the following year the Court ruled that a Christian club could meet after hours in a public school because the school had given similar access to other clubs.[134]

Like religion, freedom of expression under the First Amendment is an issue that continually confronts school officials. Students generally are permitted to engage in expressive activities as long as they do not substantially disrupt the educational

process.[135] However, the First Amendment rights of public school students "are not automatically coextensive with the rights of adults in other settings."[136] In applying all constitutional rights to the public school setting, courts consider the special characteristics of the school environment.[137]

Despite the First Amendment guarantee of freedom of the press, in 1988 in *Hazlewood School District v. Kuhlmeier*,[138] the Supreme Court in a 5-3 decision allowed a public school principal to excise controversial material concerning divorce and teenage pregnancy from the school newspaper. The Court observed that greater discretion was allowed over school-sponsored expression than over a student's individual exercise of First Amendment rights.

The United States Courts of Appeals in the various circuits have issued a number of rulings on the applicability to students of the First Amendment freedom of expression. Two decisions in 2001 illustrate the tenor of current judicial thinking in the lower federal courts:

- A high school could not suspend students for wearing T-shirts bearing a Confederate flag unless there was evidence of incidents of racial violence attributable to such display. (Case returned for a trial on the issue of whether display of Confederate symbols motivated violence.)[139]

- In another case, a female student was disappointed by not making the varsity basketball team and this apparently motivated her to write an inappropriate letter, which she distributed to members of the varsity team. In her letter she criticized the coach and used the crude term "bullshit." The court held the school did not abridge a student's free speech rights by disciplining her.[140]

Agency Restrictions on Commercial Speech There are numerous federal, state, and local regulations restricting various forms of commercial advertising and solicitation, from restrictions on "ambulance chasing" by attorneys to state and federal restrictions on telemarketing.

At one time, such regulations were not considered to raise any constitutional problem, because the courts did not regard commercial speech as protected by the First Amendment. That changed abruptly in 1976 when the Supreme Court struck down Virginia's ban on the advertisement of prescription drug prices.[141] In *Central Hudson Gas and Electric Corporation v. Public Service Commission of New York* (1980), Justice Lewis Powell articulated the general rationale for First Amendment protection in this area:

> Commercial expression not only serves the economic interest of the speaker, but also assists consumers and furthers the societal interest in the fullest possible dissemination of information. In applying the First Amendment to this area, we have rejected the "highly paternalistic" view that government has complete power to suppress or regulate commercial speech.[142]

In *Central Hudson*, Justice Powell outlined a four-part test seeking to balance the need for consumer protection on one hand with the value of a free marketplace of ideas on the other. To merit constitutional protection commercial speech must "concern lawful activity and not be misleading." If this prerequisite is met, then three additional questions must be considered: 1) Is the "asserted governmental interest" in regulation substantial? 2) Does the regulation directly advance the asserted governmental interest? 3) Finally, is the regulation more extensive than is necessary to serve that purpose?

Among the most controversial restrictions on commercial speech are regulations on the advertising of cigarettes. In 1969, Congress adopted the Public Health Cigarette Smoking Act,[143] which prohibits cigarette advertising on any medium of electronic communication under the jurisdiction of the Federal Communications Commission. And in 1984, Congress enacted the Comprehensive Smoking Education Act,[144] which, among other things, established a series of strong health warnings to appear in print and billboard adver-

tisements of cigarettes. While these measures have been criticized by libertarians and various interest groups, they have come to be widely accepted—by the courts, by the society, and even by the tobacco industry. In 2001, however, the Supreme Court held that the state of Massachusetts had gone too far in its attempt to regulate advertising of tobacco products. In *Lorillard Tobacco Co. v. Reilly*,[145] the Court held that Massachusetts' regulation of cigarette advertising was preempted by federal law. It further held that regulations with respect to other tobacco products (including cigars and smokeless tobacco) violated the First Amendment. Writing for a majority of five, Justice O'Connor observed that "so long as the sale and use of tobacco is lawful for adults, the tobacco industry has a protected interest in communicating information about its products and adult customers have an interest in receiving that information."[146]

The Supreme Court's decision in *Lorillard Tobacco Co. v. Reilly* is excerpted at the end of the chapter.

Regulation of Broadcasting Even though broadcasting involves expression, courts have taken the view that government may regulate the content of radio and television programs on the ground that the airwaves belong to the public. Indeed, one needs a license from the Federal Communications Commission to lawfully operate a radio or television station. In a regulation that would almost certainly be declared unconstitutional if applied to a magazine or newspaper, the Federal Communications Commission prohibits radio and television stations, whether public or private, from broadcasting "indecent" or "obscene" programs. The Supreme Court upheld this regulation in 1978.[147] During the 1970s and 1980s, the FCC reprimanded and threatened more severe disciplinary action against radio stations featuring so called "shock jocks" whose on-air comments were often vulgar and profane. In the 1990s the FCC became more tolerant, reflecting a more permissive social climate. But in 2004, after a widely publicized televised incident at the Super Bowl halftime show, the FCC moved to curb indecency on the airwaves by imposing substantial fines on violators.

The Fourth Amendment

The Fourth Amendment to the United States Constitution protects people from "unreasonable searches and seizures," not only by police, but by all government officials and their agents. The protection of the Fourth Amendment extends to houses, offices, stores, and places of business, with the exception of those business areas where the public is invited to enter. Generally speaking, authorities must have probable cause and, absent exigent circumstances, a warrant before conducting a search or making a seizure. But there are numerous exceptions to the probable cause and warrant requirements. Most fundamentally, searches and seizures must be "reasonable." In assessing the reasonableness of a particular search or seizure, courts consider a person's expectations of privacy, the intrusiveness of the search, the consequences that the person will face if the search proves fruitful, and the magnitude of the government's interest in conducting the search.

The Fourth Amendment applies to the states through the Due Process Clause of the Fourteenth Amendment.[148] States have counterparts in their constitutions that can afford more protection than the Fourth Amendment; they cannot afford less. Subject to certain exceptions, evidence seized in violation of the Fourth Amendment is excluded from proceedings in federal and state courts and administrative proceedings. This is known as the exclusionary rule.[149]

Standards Applicable to Administrative Searches The Fourth Amendment applies to government action, but not to private actors. Subject to a number of exceptions, it requires law enforcement officers to obtain a search warrant before conducting a search or seizure. Historically these requirements were not applied to **administrative searches;** however, in 1967, in *Camara v. Municipal Court of the City & County of San Francisco,*[150] the Supreme Court held that the Fourth Amendment does apply to administrative searches and seizures. Nevertheless, these searches and seizures are governed by a standard of "reasonableness," which is less rigorous than the "probable cause" requirement applicable to criminal investigations. Courts also apply the reasonableness standard to determine if there is cause to support issuance of an administrative search warrant as well as in determining whether a **warrantless search** is lawful. States, of course, can provide more protection for administrative searches and some state constitutions and statutes provide additional restrictions.

State statutes and municipal ordinances generally allow for routine and unannounced administrative inspections of **pervasively regulated businesses,** for example establishments that sell alcoholic beverages, as well as routine inspections for compliance with building and zoning laws. A few years after its decision in *Camara*, the Supreme Court announced that such administrative searches are not subject to Fourth Amendment protections.[151] Fourth Amendment protections also apply to searches of children in the public schools, but such searches are also judged by a reasonableness standard and are not subject to the requirement of probable cause, much less the warrant requirement.[152] (Fourth Amendment problems in the administrative context are dealt with much more extensively in Chapter 5.)

Drug Testing of Employees and Students
Many local, state and federal agencies, especially in the field of law enforcement, require their employees to submit to periodic or random drug testing as a condition of employment or promotion. In the "war on drugs" many government agencies have adopted **drug testing** requirements of employees and students. The Supreme Court has said that collection and testing of urine constitutes a "search" under the Fourth Amendment and has furnished some guidance in these areas.[153]

Courts have generally upheld drug testing of public safety officers where there is a reasonable suspicion of drug abuse. In 1989 the Court upheld drug testing of Customs Inspectors, who are directly involved in drug interdiction.[154] In 1997, however, the Court struck down a Georgia law requiring all candidates for state office to submit to drug tests.[155]

In 1995, in *Vernonia School District v. Acton*,[156] the Supreme Court recognized the decreased expectation of privacy of public school students and that public schools must exercise supervision of students. In a 6–3 decision, the Court held that a school district's random urinalysis drug testing of students who participated in its athletic programs did not violate their Fourth Amendment right to be free from unreasonable searches. Since then, the tendency of state and federal court decisions has been to uphold drug testing policies as they relate to both teachers and students in public schools.

Given the national concern over the use of illicit drugs, and the government's resolve to cope with the problem, there will likely be additional laws and regulations extending the use of random drug testing of public employees and public school students. As such policies often arouse intense opposition, we can also anticipate continuing litigation of the constitutional issues involved in these areas. (The drug testing issue, as it impacts public employees, is discussed more extensively in Chapter 10.)

The Right to Privacy

Although not mentioned in the U.S. Constitution, the Supreme Court has found that the **right to privacy** is implicit in the protections that the Constitution affords. The doctrine received its constitutional sanction in 1965 in *Griswold v. Connecticut*[157] where the Court overturned a Connecticut law that criminalized the sale and distribution of birth control devices. The *Griswold* decision was the precursor of the Court's 1973 decision in *Roe v. Wade*,[158] striking down the Texas law prohibiting abortions and causing a constitutional debate that still rages. The law concerning marital and reproductive privacy and the right to die appear to be well established. Nevertheless, the Court has upheld state laws that prohibit assisted suicide.[159]

Because our society relies so heavily on computerized databases capable of storing vast amounts of information about individuals, it was inevitable that the Supreme Court would be asked to determine the degree to which the right of privacy insulates a person from having to disclose personal information to government agencies. The question first arose in regard to a New York law that established a compulsory official record of prescriptions for drugs for which there is a substantial illegal market. In an effort to control the abuse and illegal sale of certain substances, the law required the recording of the names and addresses of individuals for whom prescriptions were written, as well as the pharmacies designated to fill such prescriptions. The law did, however, contain safeguards designed to preserve the confidentiality of these records so as to protect the reputations of those whose medical prescriptions contained substances popularly associated with "drug abuse." In *Whalen v. Roe* (1977),[160] the Supreme Court unanimously upheld the law, finding no invasion of protected privacy. Justice Stevens' opinion for the Court acknowledged the threat to privacy inherent in the collection of vast amounts of personal data but concluded that the New York law contained adequate safeguards. Justice Stevens concluded his opinion with the following observations:

> The collection of taxes, the distribution of welfare and social security benefits, the supervision of public health, the direction of our Armed Forces, and the enforcement of the criminal laws all require the orderly preservation of great quantities of information, much of which is personal in character and potentially embarrassing or harmful if disclosed. The right to collect and use such data for

public purposes is typically accompanied by a concomitant statutory or regulatory duty to avoid unwarranted disclosures. Recognizing that in some circumstances that duty arguably has its roots in the Constitution, nevertheless New York's statutory scheme, and its implementing administrative procedures, evidence a proper concern with, and protection of, the individual's interest in privacy. We therefore need not, and do not, decide any question which might be presented by the unwarranted disclosure of accumulated private data—whether intentional or unintentional—or by a system that did not contain comparable security provisions.[161]

The Fifth Amendment

Three provisions of the Fifth Amendment to the U.S. Constitution have special relevance to administrative law. The protection against self-incrimination stipulates that "No person . . . shall be compelled . . . to be a witness against himself." The Due Process Clause provides that no person shall "be deprived of life, liberty, or property, without due process of law." Finally, the Amendment includes the mandate that "nor shall private property be taken for public use, without just compensation." This latter proviso is commonly referred to as the **Takings Clause.**

The Privilege against Self-Incrimination Everyone is familiar with the witness who appears before a federal or state investigating committee and states words to the effect, "On advice of counsel, I respectfully decline to answer any questions based on my Fifth Amendment right against self-incrimination." The Fifth Amendment contains an express privilege against **self-incrimination** for individuals. A corporation does not have the privilege; therefore its records are subject to being subpoenaed by an administrative agency.[162] A person may exercise the right against self-incrimination in either criminal or civil proceedings wherever there is a reasonable basis to believe that the information

being sought can be used in a criminal prosecution. A witness before a court or an administrative agency can be required to give information, even though incriminating, if the witness is granted immunity from prosecution.

The Takings Clause of the Fifth Amendment The Takings Clause of the Fifth Amendment to the U.S. Constitution stipulates that "private property [shall not] be taken for public use without just compensation." In 1878 in *Boom Co. v. Patterson* the Supreme Court said:

> The right of eminent domain, that is, the right to take private property for public uses, appertains to every independent government. It requires no constitutional recognition; it is an attribute of sovereignty. The clause found in the Constitutions of the several States providing for just compensation for property taken is a mere limitation upon the exercise of the right. When the use is public, the necessity or expediency of appropriating any particular property is not a subject of judicial cognizance.[163]

The federal government and the government of each state have the power of eminent domain, that is the right to take private property for public use. State legislatures generally delegate this power to counties and cities, and in some instances to public utilities. The power to condemn property is used to acquire lands for government buildings, military bases, highways, parks, and recreation areas. The power of eminent domain can only be exercised for public purposes. In addition to establishing that property is being taken is for public purposes, a condemning authority must pay **just compensation** to the owners of the property taken. Thus, the cost of acquiring property for public purposes is borne by the taxpayers.

Regulatory Takings Courts have long recognized that the Takings Clause has applicability to governmental regulatory actions as well as to physical takings of property. In some instances government regulations have greatly affected the economic value of an owner's property. For example, in 1987 the U.S. Supreme Court ruled that land use regulation can effectively become a **regulatory taking** where the regulations do not substantially advance legitimate interests of the government or where such regulations deny the owners use of their land.[164]

The need to protect the environment has caused governmental agencies to take steps, for example, denying a permit to fill wetlands, that have greatly burdened an owner's use of private property. The Court has noted the Takings Clause is designed not to limit the governmental interference with property rights per se, but rather to secure compensation in the event of otherwise proper interference amounting to a taking.[165]

Frequently local governments require certain concessions from a property owner before approval of rezoning of land or issuance of a building permit. For example, a city might require an owner to grant an easement or dedicate land for public use. In such instances an issue of regulatory taking may come into play. In 1994, the Supreme Court held that requiring the owner to deed a portion of the property to the city for use as a public greenway along an adjoining portion of the property before allowing the owner to expand her store and add a paved parking lot went too far. The Court found such regulatory requirement to be inconsistent with the Takings Clause of the Fifth Amendment.[166]

It is not uncommon for local governments to grant a rezoning request subject to the applicant complying with specified conditions. In *Nollan v. California Coastal Commission*,[167] the California Coastal Commission granted the Nollans a permit to tear down a small house on their lot in Ventura Beach, California, and build a larger one. But the permit was granted only on the condition that the Nollans allow the public lateral access to pass across their land, which was situated between two public beaches. The required condition was "part of a comprehensive program to provide continuous public access along Faria Beach as the lots undergo development or redevelopment." The Nollans unsuccessfully

challenged this requirement in the California courts, arguing that their property was effectively being taken for public use without just compensation. But the United States Supreme Court agreed with the Nollans. Writing for the Court, Justice Antonin Scalia said, "California is free to advance its 'comprehensive program,' if it wishes, by using its power of eminent domain for this 'public purpose' . . . but if it wants an easement across the Nollans' property, it must pay for it." In dissent, Justice William Brennan castigated the Court's "narrow view" of the case, saying that its "reasoning is hardly suited to the complex reality of natural resource protection in the 20th century."[168]

The Supreme Court's decision in *Nollan v. California Coastal Commission* is excerpted at the end of the chapter.

Determination of Just Compensation When the **condemning authority** and the property owner cannot agree on what constitutes just compensation, the amount of compensation is determined by a court, usually in a jury trial. The condemning authority introduces evidence that the property being taken is required for public purposes. It then presents to the court real estate appraisers and other experts who offer opinions on the value of the property being condemned. The property owner, in turn, has the right to testify concerning the value and use of the property being taken and to present appraisers and other expert witnesses to testify as to the market value of the property. The testimony as to the amount of compensation to be awarded can become very technical when the condemning authority takes real estate that effectively abolishes or diminishes the value of the owner's ongoing business. In such instances accountants and economists often appear as expert witnesses on behalf of the owner.

Where a property owner contends that governmental action has caused a regulatory taking, the court must first resolve that issue. In effect, the property owner brings suit alleging that an **inverse condemnation** has occurred. If the court rules in favor of the property owner, then a proceeding along the lines outlined earlier in this chapter ensues to determine the just compensation due the owner.

CONCLUSION

Without question, the most significant change in the American republic over the last two centuries is the emergence of the administrative state. This development has brought about major changes in the prevailing understanding of the United States Constitution, especially as it relates to the scope of congressional authority, the delegation of legislative power, separation of powers, and federalism. Yet constitutional principles, especially those found in the Bill of Rights and the Fourteenth Amendment (and corresponding provisions of the fifty state constitutions) remain extremely important in the judicial oversight of the administrative state.

KEY TERMS

administrative searches

affirmative action programs

checks and balances

classical liberalism

Commerce Clause

compelling governmental interest

conclusions of law

condemning authority

Constitutional Revolution of 1937

constitutionalism

cooperative federalism

delegation of legislative power

doctrine of incorporation

drug testing

dual federalism

eminent domain

enumerated powers

fair hearing

fair notice

federalism

Fifth Amendment

findings of fact

First Amendment

Fourteenth Amendment

Fourth Amendment

fundamental rights

impartial decision maker

implied powers

inverse condemnation

just compensation

opportunity to present evidence

pervasively regulated businesses

police power

procedural due process

quasi-judicial

quasi-legislative

rational basis test

regulatory taking

right to privacy

self-incrimination

separation of powers

sovereign states

state constitution

strict scrutiny

substantive due process

Takings Clause

ultra vires

unfunded mandates

warrantless search

QUESTIONS FOR THOUGHT AND DISCUSSION

1. How and why are federalism and separation of powers bedrock principles of American constitutionalism?

2. What view did James Madison expound as to the nature of the powers delegated to the national government under the U.S. Constitution?

3. How did the Supreme Court explain the doctrine of implied powers in *McCulloch v. Maryland*? What has been the effect of that decision

on American constitutional law and the American economy?

4. Discuss the effect of the New Deal and the Constitutional Revolution of 1937 on the doctrine of nondelegation of legislative power.

5. Explain the evolution of the federal system from dual federalism to cooperative federalism.

6. Under what circumstances does the Fourth Amendment require municipal and state officials to obtain a warrant to search business premises for building code violations?

7. Contrast the historical and modern views that state courts take in regard to upholding state

statutes that delegate legislative powers to administrative agencies.

8. Describe the functions an agency performs in its exercise of quasi-legislative powers in contrast to the exercise of its quasi-judicial powers.

9. Explain the difference between "substantive due process" and "procedural due process."

10. Give an example of a regulatory measure that would be regarded by the courts as a "taking" that would subject a state or local government to the Fifth Amendment requirement of paying just compensation to the property owner.

EDITED CASE   Lorillard Tobacco Company v. Reilly
United States Supreme Court, 533 U.S. 525 (2001)

[In this case the Supreme Court reviews state regulations governing the advertising and sale of tobacco products. The Court considers whether these regulations are preempted by federal law and whether they violate the First Amendment's protection of free speech.]

Justice O'Connor delivered the opinion of the Court.
. . . In January 1999, pursuant to his authority to prevent unfair or deceptive practices in trade, . . . the Massachusetts Attorney General (Attorney General) promulgated regulations governing the sale and advertisement of cigarettes, smokeless tobacco, and cigars. The purpose of the cigarette and smokeless tobacco regulations is "to eliminate deception and unfairness in the way cigarettes and smokeless tobacco products are marketed, sold and distributed in Massachusetts in order to address the incidence of cigarette smoking and smokeless tobacco use by children under legal age . . . . [and] in order to prevent access to such products by underage consumers." . . . The similar purpose of the cigar regulations is "to eliminate deception and unfairness in the way cigars and little cigars are packaged, marketed, sold and distributed in Massachusetts [so that] . . . consumers may be adequately informed about the health risks associated with cigar smoking, its addictive properties, and the false perception that cigars are a safe alternative to cigarettes . . . [and so that] the incidence of cigar use by children under legal age is addressed . . . in order to prevent access to such products by under-

age consumers." . . . The regulations have a broader scope than the master settlement agreement, reaching advertising, sales practices, and members of the tobacco industry not covered by the agreement. The regulations place a variety of restrictions on outdoor advertising, point-of-sale advertising, retail sales transactions, transactions by mail, promotions, sampling of products, and labels for cigars. . . .

II
Before reaching the First Amendment issues, we must decide to what extent federal law pre-empts the Attorney General's regulations. The cigarette petitioners contend that the Federal Cigarette Labeling and Advertising Act (FCLAA), 15 U. S. C. § 1331 et seq., pre-empts the Attorney General's cigarette advertising regulations.

A
Article VI of the United States Constitution commands that the laws of the United States "shall be the supreme Law of the Land; . . . any Thing in the Constitution or Laws of any State to the Contrary notwithstanding." . . . This relatively clear and simple mandate has generated considerable discussion in cases where we have had to discern whether Congress has preempted state action in a particular area. State action may be foreclosed by express language in a congressional enactment, . . . by implication from the depth and breadth of

---

EDITED CASE   Lorillard Tobacco Company v. Reilly (Continued)

---

a congressional scheme that occupies the legislative field, . . . or by implication because of a conflict with a congressional enactment. . . .

In the FCLAA, Congress has crafted a comprehensive federal scheme governing the advertising and promotion of cigarettes. The FCLAA's preemption provision provides:

"(a) Additional statements

"No statement relating to smoking and health, other than the statement required by section 1333 of this title, shall be required on any cigarette package.

"(b) State regulations

"No requirement or prohibition based on smoking and health shall be imposed under State law with respect to the advertising or promotion of any cigarettes the packages of which are labeled in conformity with the provisions of this chapter." 15 U. S. C. § 1334.

The FCLAA's pre-emption provision does not cover smokeless tobacco or cigars.

In this case, our task is to identify the domain expressly pre-empted, . . . because "an express definition of the pre-emptive reach of a statute . . . supports a reasonable inference . . . that Congress did not intend to pre-empt other matters." . . . Congressional purpose is the "ultimate touchstone" of our inquiry. . . . Because "federal law is said to bar state action in [a] fiel[d] of traditional state regulation," namely, advertising, . . . we "wor[k] on the assumption that the historic police powers of the States [a]re not to be superseded by the Federal Act unless that [is] the clear and manifest purpose of Congress." . . .

Our analysis begins with the language of the statute. . . . In the pre-emption provision, Congress unequivocally precludes the requirement of any additional statements on cigarette packages beyond those provided in § 1333. . . . Congress further precludes States or localities from imposing any requirement or prohibition based on smoking and health with respect to the advertising and promotion of cigarettes. § 1334(b). Without question, the second clause is more expansive than the first; it employs far more sweeping language to describe the state action that is pre-empted. We must give meaning to each element of the pre-emption provision. We are aided in our interpretation by considering the predecessor pre-emption

provision and the circumstances in which the current language was adopted. . . .

In 1964, the groundbreaking Report of the Surgeon General's Advisory Committee on Smoking and Health concluded that "[c]igarette smoking is a health hazard of sufficient importance in the United States to warrant appropriate remedial action." . . . In 1965, Congress enacted the FCLAA as a proactive measure in the face of impending regulation by federal agencies and the States. . . . The purpose of the FCLAA was twofold: to inform the public adequately about the hazards of cigarette smoking, and to protect the national economy from interference due to diverse, nonuniform, and confusing cigarette labeling and advertising regulations with respect to the relationship between smoking and health. . . . The FCLAA prescribed a label for cigarette packages: "Caution: Cigarette Smoking May Be Hazardous to Your Health." . . . The FCLAA also required the Secretary of Health, Education, and Welfare (HEW) and the Federal Trade Commission (FTC) to report annually to Congress about the health consequences of smoking and the advertising and promotion of cigarettes. . . .

Section 5 of the FCLAA included a pre-emption provision in which "Congress spoke precisely and narrowly." . . . Subsection 5(a) prohibited any requirement of additional statements on cigarette packaging. Subsection 5(b) provided that "[n]o statement relating to smoking and health shall be required in the advertising of any cigarettes the packages of which are labeled in conformity with the provisions of this Act." Section 10 of the FCLAA set a termination date of July 1, 1969 for these provisions. As we have previously explained, "on their face, [the pre-emption] provisions merely prohibited state and federal rulemaking bodies from mandating particular cautionary statements on cigarette labels [subsection (a)] or in cigarette advertisements [subsection (b)]." . . .

The FCLAA was enacted with the expectation that Congress would reexamine it in 1969 in light of the developing information about cigarette smoking and health. . . . In the intervening years, Congress received reports and recommendations from the HEW Secretary and the FTC. . . .

(Continued)

EDITED CASE   Lorillard Tobacco Company v. Reilly (Continued)

. . . [T]he Public Health Cigarette Smoking Act of 1969 . . . made three significant changes to the FCLAA. . . . First, Congress drafted a new label that read: "Warning: The Surgeon General Has Determined That Cigarette Smoking Is Dangerous to Your Health." . . . Second, Congress declared it unlawful to advertise cigarettes on any medium of electronic communication subject to the jurisdiction of the FCC. . . . Finally, Congress enacted the current pre-emption provision, which proscribes any "requirement or prohibition based on smoking and health . . . imposed under State law with respect to the advertising or promotion" of cigarettes. . . . The new subsection . . . did not pre-empt regulation by federal agencies, freeing the FTC to impose warning requirements in cigarette advertising. . . . The new pre-emption provision, like its predecessor, only applied to cigarettes, and not other tobacco products.

In 1984, Congress again amended the FCLAA in the Comprehensive Smoking Education Act. . . . The purpose of the Act was to "provide a new strategy for making Americans more aware of any adverse health effects of smoking, to assure the timely and widespread dissemination of research findings and to enable individuals to make informed decisions about smoking." . . . The Act established a series of warnings to appear on a rotating basis on cigarette packages and in cigarette advertising, . . . and directed the Health and Human Services Secretary to create and implement an educational program about the health effects of cigarette smoking. . . .

The scope and meaning of the current pre-emption provision become clearer once we consider the original pre-emption language and the amendments to the FCLAA. Without question, "the plain language of the pre-emption provision in the 1969 Act is much broader." . . . Rather than preventing only "statements," the amended provision reaches all "requirement[s] or prohibition[s] . . . imposed under State law." And, although the former statute reached only statements "in the advertising," the current provision governs "with respect to the advertising or promotion" of cigarettes. . . . Congress expanded the pre-emption provision with respect to the States, and at the same time, it allowed the FTC to regulate cigarette advertising. Congress also prohibited cig-

arette advertising in electronic media altogether. Viewed in light of the context in which the current pre-emption provision was adopted, we must determine whether the FCLAA pre-empts Massachusetts' regulations governing outdoor and point-of-sale advertising of cigarettes. . . .

The context in which Congress crafted the current pre-emption provision leads us to conclude that Congress prohibited state cigarette advertising regulations motivated by concerns about smoking and health. Massachusetts has attempted to address the incidence of underage cigarette smoking by regulating advertising, . . . much like Congress' ban on cigarette advertising in electronic media. At bottom, the concern about youth exposure to cigarette advertising is intertwined with the concern about cigarette smoking and health. . . .

. . . [W]e fail to see how the FCLAA and its pre-emption provision permit a distinction between the specific concern about minors and cigarette advertising and the more general concern about smoking and health in cigarette advertising, especially in light of the fact that Congress crafted a legislative solution for those very concerns. We also conclude that a distinction between state regulation of the location as opposed to the content of cigarette advertising has no foundation in the text of the pre-emption provision. Congress pre-empted state cigarette advertising regulations like the Attorney General's because they would upset federal legislative choices to require specific warnings and to impose the ban on cigarette advertising in electronic media in order to address concerns about smoking and health. Accordingly, we hold that the Attorney General's outdoor and point-of-sale advertising regulations targeting cigarettes are pre-empted by the FCLAA. . . .

Although the FCLAA prevents States and localities from imposing special requirements or prohibitions "based on smoking and health" "with respect to the advertising or promotion" of cigarettes, that language still leaves significant power in the hands of States to impose generally applicable zoning regulations and to regulate conduct. . . .

The FCLAA also does not foreclose all state regulation of conduct as it relates to the sale or use of cigarettes. The FCLAA's pre-emption provision

---

EDITED CASE   Lorillard Tobacco Company v. Reilly (Continued)

---

explicitly governs state regulations of "advertising or promotion." Accordingly, the FCLAA does not pre-empt state laws prohibiting cigarette sales to minors. To the contrary, there is an established congressional policy that supports such laws; Congress has required States to prohibit tobacco sales to minors as a condition of receiving federal block grant funding for substance abuse treatment activities. . . .

In Massachusetts, it is illegal to sell or distribute tobacco products to persons under the age of 18. . . . Having prohibited the sale and distribution of tobacco products to minors, the State may prohibit common inchoate offenses that attach to criminal conduct, such as solicitation, conspiracy, and attempt. . . . States and localities also have at their disposal other means of regulating conduct to ensure that minors do not obtain cigarettes. . . .

III

By its terms, the FCLAA's pre-emption provision only applies to cigarettes. Accordingly, we must evaluate the smokeless tobacco and cigar petitioners' First Amendment challenges to the State's outdoor and point-of-sale advertising regulations. The cigarette petitioners did not raise a pre-emption challenge to the sales practices regulations. Thus, we must analyze the cigarette as well as the smokeless tobacco and cigar petitioners' claim that certain sales practices regulations for tobacco products violate the First Amendment.

. . . For over 25 years, the Court has recognized that commercial speech does not fall outside the purview of the First Amendment. . . . Instead, the Court has afforded commercial speech a measure of First Amendment protection commensurate with its position in relation to other constitutionally guaranteed expression. . . . In recognition of the distinction between speech proposing a commercial transaction, which occurs in an area traditionally subject to government regulation, and other varieties of speech, . . . we developed a framework for analyzing regulations of commercial speech that is substantially similar to the test for time, place, and manner restrictions. . . . The analysis contains four elements:

At the outset, we must determine whether the expression is protected by the First Amend-

ment. For commercial speech to come within that provision, it at least must concern lawful activity and not be misleading. Next, we ask whether the asserted governmental interest is substantial. If both inquiries yield positive answers, we must determine whether the regulation directly advances the governmental interest asserted, and whether it is not more extensive than is necessary to serve that interest. . . . [See *Central Hudson Gas & Electric v. Public Service Commission*, 447 U.S. 557 (1980).]

Petitioners urge us to reject the *Central Hudson* analysis and apply strict scrutiny. They are not the first litigants to do so. . . . Admittedly, several Members of the Court have expressed doubts about the *Central Hudson* analysis and whether it should apply in particular cases. . . . But . . . we see no need to break new ground. *Central Hudson*, as applied in our more recent commercial speech cases, provides an adequate basis for decision. . . .

The State's interest in preventing underage tobacco use is substantial, and even compelling, but it is no less true that the sale and use of tobacco products by adults is a legal activity. We must consider that tobacco retailers and manufacturers have an interest in conveying truthful information about their products to adults, and adults have a corresponding interest in receiving truthful information about tobacco products. . . .

In some instances, Massachusetts outdoor advertising regulations would impose particularly onerous burdens on speech. For example, we disagree with the Court of Appeals conclusion that because cigar manufacturers and retailers conduct a limited amount of advertising in comparison to other tobacco products, the relative lack of cigar advertising also means that the burden imposed on cigar advertisers is correspondingly small. . . . If some retailers have relatively small advertising budgets, and use few avenues of communication, then the Attorney General's outdoor advertising regulations potentially place a greater, not lesser, burden on those retailers speech. Furthermore, to the extent that cigar products and cigar advertising

(Continued)

EDITED CASE   Lorillard Tobacco Company v. Reilly (Continued)

differ from that of other tobacco products, that difference should inform the inquiry into what speech restrictions are necessary.

In addition, a retailer in Massachusetts may have no means of communicating to passersby on the street that it sells tobacco products because alternative forms of advertisement, like newspapers, do not allow that retailer to propose an instant transaction in the way that onsite advertising does. The ban on any indoor advertising that is visible from the outside also presents problems in establishments like convenience stores, which have unique security concerns that counsel in favor of full visibility of the store from the outside. It is these sorts of considerations that the Attorney General failed to incorporate into the regulatory scheme.

We conclude that the Attorney General has failed to show that the outdoor advertising regulations for smokeless tobacco and cigars are not more extensive than necessary to advance the State's substantial interest in preventing underage tobacco use. Justice Stevens urges that the Court remand the case for further development of the factual record. . . . We believe that a remand is inappropriate in this case because the State had ample opportunity to develop a record with respect to tailoring (as it had to justify its decision to regulate advertising), and additional evidence would not alter the nature of the scheme before the Court. . . .

A careful calculation of the costs of a speech regulation does not mean that a State must demonstrate that there is no incursion on legitimate speech interests, but a speech regulation cannot unduly impinge on the speaker's ability to propose a commercial transaction and the adult listeners opportunity to obtain information about products. After reviewing the outdoor advertising regulations, we find the calculation in this case insufficient for purposes of the First Amendment. . . .

Massachusetts has also restricted indoor, point-of-sale advertising for smokeless tobacco and cigars. Advertising cannot be placed lower than five feet from the floor of any retail establishment which is located within a one thousand foot radius of any school or playground. . . .

We conclude that the point-of-sale advertising regulations fail both the third and fourth steps of the Central Hudson analysis. A regulation cannot be sustained if it provides only ineffective or remote support for the governments purpose, . . . or if there is little chance that the restriction will advance the States goal. . . . As outlined above, the States goal is to prevent minors from using tobacco products and to curb demand for that activity by limiting youth exposure to advertising. The 5 foot rule does not seem to advance that goal. Not all children are less than 5 feet tall, and those who are certainly have the ability to look up and take in their surroundings. . . .

Massachusetts may wish to target tobacco advertisements and displays that entice children, much like floor-level candy displays in a convenience store, but the blanket height restriction does not constitute a reasonable fit with that goal. The Court of Appeals recognized that the efficacy of the regulation was questionable, but decided that [i]n any event, the burden on speech imposed by the provision is very limited. . . . There is no de minimis exception for a speech restriction that lacks sufficient tailoring or justification. We conclude that the restriction on the height of indoor advertising is invalid under Central Hudson's third and fourth prongs. . . .

We have observed that tobacco use, particularly among children and adolescents, poses perhaps the single most significant threat to public health in the United States. . . . From a policy perspective, it is understandable for the States to attempt to prevent minors from using tobacco products before they reach an age where they are capable of weighing for themselves the risks and potential benefits of tobacco use, and other adult activities. Federal law, however, places limits on policy choices available to the States.

In this case, Congress enacted a comprehensive scheme to address cigarette smoking and health in advertising and pre-empted state regulation of cigarette advertising that attempts to address that same concern, even with respect to youth. The First Amendment also constrains state efforts to limit advertising of tobacco products, because so long as the sale and use of tobacco is lawful for adults, the tobacco industry has a protected interest in communicating information about its products and adult customers have an interest in receiving that information.

EDITED CASE   Lorillard Tobacco Company v. Reilly (Continued)

To the extent that federal law and the First Amendment do not prohibit state action, States and localities remain free to combat the problem of underage tobacco use by appropriate means. The judgment of the United States Court of Appeals for the First Circuit is therefore affirmed in part and reversed in part, and the cases are remanded for further proceedings consistent with this opinion. . . .

Justice Kennedy, with whom *Justice Scalia* joins, concurring in part and concurring in the judgment.

Justice Thomas, concurring in part and concurring in the judgment. . . .

Justice Souter, concurring in part and dissenting in part. . . .

Justice Stevens, . . . concurring in part, concurring in the judgment in part, and dissenting in part.

This suit presents two separate sets of issues. The first—involving preemption—is straightforward. The second—involving the First Amendment—is more complex. Because I strongly disagree with the Court's conclusion that the Federal Cigarette Labeling and Advertising Act of 1965 . . . as amended, precludes States and localities from regulating the location of cigarette advertising, I dissent from [those portions of the] Court's opinion. On the First Amendment questions, I agree with the Court both that the outdoor advertising restrictions imposed by Massachusetts serve legitimate and important state interests and that the record does not indicate that the measures were properly tailored to serve those interests. Because the present record does not enable us to adjudicate the merits of those claims on summary judgment, I would vacate the decision upholding those restrictions and remand for trial on the constitutionality of the outdoor advertising regulations. Finally, because I do not believe that either the point-of-sale advertising restrictions or the sales practice restrictions implicate significant First Amendment concerns, I would uphold them in their entirety. . . .

EDITED CASE   Whitman v. American Trucking Associations
United States Supreme Court, 531 U.S. 457 (2001)

[In this case the Supreme Court considers whether a provision of the Clean Air Act (CAA) is an impermissible delegation of legislative power to the Environmental Protection Agency.]

Justice Scalia delivered the opinion of the Court.

. . . Section 109(a) of the CAA . . . requires the Administrator of the EPA to promulgate national ambient air quality standards [NAAQS] for each air pollutant for which "air quality criteria" have been issued. . . . Once a NAAQS has been promulgated, the Administrator must review the standard (and the criteria on which it is based) "at five-year intervals" and make "such revisions . . . as may be appropriate." . . .

These cases arose when, on July 18, 1997, the Administrator revised the NAAQS for particulate matter (PM) and ozone. . . . American Trucking Associations, Inc., and its co-respondents—which include, in addition to other private companies, the States of Michigan, Ohio, and West Virginia— challenged the new standards in the Court of Appeals for the District of Columbia Circuit. . . .

Section 109(b)(1) of the CAA instructs the EPA to set "ambient air quality standards the attainment and maintenance of which in the judgment of the Administrator, based on [the] criteria [documents of § 108] and allowing an adequate margin of safety, are requisite to protect the public health." . . . The Court of Appeals held that this section as interpreted by the Administrator did not provide an "intelligible principle" to guide the EPA's exercise of authority in setting NAAQS. "[The] EPA," it said, "lack[ed] any determinate criteria for drawing lines. It has failed to state intelligibly how much is too much." . . . The court hence found that the EPA's interpretation (but not the

(Continued)

EDITED CASE   Whitman v. American Trucking Associations (Continued)

---

statute itself) violated the nondelegation doctrine. . . . We disagree.

In a delegation challenge, the constitutional question is whether the statute has delegated legislative power to the agency. Article I, § 1, of the Constitution vests "[a]ll legislative Powers herein granted . . . in a Congress of the United States." This text permits no delegation of those powers, . . . and so we repeatedly have said that when Congress confers decision making authority upon agencies *Congress* must "lay down by legislative act an intelligible principle to which the person or body authorized to [act] is directed to conform." . . . We have never suggested that an agency can cure an unlawful delegation of legislative power by adopting in its discretion a limiting construction of the statute.

. . . The idea that an agency can cure an unconstitutionally standardless delegation of power by declining to exercise some of that power seems to us internally contradictory. The very choice of which portion of the power to exercise—that is to say, the prescription of the standard that Congress had omitted—would *itself* be an exercise of the forbidden legislative authority. Whether the statute delegates legislative power is a question for the courts, and an agency's voluntary self-denial has no bearing upon the answer.

We agree with the Solicitor General that the text of § 109(b)(1) of the CAA at a minimum requires that "[f]or a discrete set of pollutants and based on published air quality criteria that reflect the latest scientific knowledge, [the] EPA must establish uniform national standards at a level that is requisite to protect public health from the adverse effects of the pollutant in the ambient air." . . . Requisite, in turn, "mean[s] sufficient, but not more than necessary." . . .

These limits on the EPA's discretion are strikingly similar to the ones we approved in *Touby* v. *United States* (1991), which permitted the Attorney General to designate a drug as a controlled substance for purposes of criminal drug enforcement if doing so was " 'necessary to avoid an imminent hazard to the public safety.'" . . . They also resemble the Occupational Safety and Health Act provision requiring the agency to " 'set the standard which most adequately assures, to the extent feasible, on the basis of the best available evi-

dence, that no employee will suffer any impairment of health' "—which the Court upheld in *Industrial Union Dept., AFL-CIO* v. *American Petroleum Institute* (1980), and which even then-Justice Rehnquist, who alone in that case thought the statute violated the nondelegation doctrine, . . . would have upheld if, like the statute here, it did not permit economic costs to be considered. . . .

The scope of discretion § 109(b)(1) allows is in fact well within the outer limits of our nondelegation precedents. In the history of the Court we have found the requisite "intelligible principle" lacking in only two statutes, one of which provided literally no guidance for the exercise of discretion, and the other of which conferred authority to regulate the entire economy on the basis of no more precise a standard than stimulating the economy by assuring "fair competition." See *Panama Refining Co.* v. *Ryan* (1935); *A. L. A. Schechter Poultry Corp.* v. *United States,* (1935). We have, on the other hand, upheld the validity of § 11(b)(2) of the Public Utility Holding Company Act of 1935, 49 Stat. 821, which gave the Securities and Exchange Commission authority to modify the structure of holding company systems so as to ensure that they are not "unduly or unnecessarily complicate[d]" and do not "unfairly or inequitably distribute voting power among security holders." *American Power & Light Co.* v. *SEC* (1946). We have approved the wartime conferral of agency power to fix the prices of commodities at a level that "'will be generally fair and equitable and will effectuate the [in some respects conflicting] purposes of th[e] Act.'" *Yakus* v. *United States* (1944). And we have found an "intelligible principle" in various statutes authorizing regulation in the "public interest." . . . In short, we have "almost never felt qualified to second-guess Congress regarding the permissible degree of policy judgment that can be left to those executing or applying the law.". . .

It is true enough that the degree of agency discretion that is acceptable varies according to the scope of the power congressionally conferred. . . . While Congress need not provide any direction to the EPA regarding the manner in which it is to define "country elevators," which are to be exempt from new-stationary-source regulations governing grain elevators, . . . it must provide sub-

---

EDITED CASE Whitman v. American Trucking Associations (Continued)

---

stantial guidance on setting air standards that affect the entire national economy. But even in sweeping regulatory schemes we have never demanded, as the Court of Appeals did here, that statutes provide a "determinate criterion" for saying "how much [of the regulated harm] is too much." . . .

In *Touby*, for example, we did not require the statute to decree how "imminent" was too imminent, or how "necessary" was necessary enough, or even—most relevant here—how "hazardous" was too hazardous. . . . It is therefore not conclusive for delegation purposes that, as respondents argue, ozone and particulate matter are "non-threshold" pollutants that inflict a continuum of adverse health effects at any airborne concentration greater than zero, and hence require the EPA to make judgments of degree. "[A] certain degree of discretion, and thus of lawmaking, inheres in most executive or judicial action." . . . Section 109(b)(1) of the CAA, which to repeat we interpret as requiring the EPA to set air quality standards at the level that is "requisite"—that is, not lower or higher than is necessary—to protect the public health with an adequate margin of safety, fits comfortably within the scope of discretion permitted by our precedent.

We therefore reverse the judgment of the Court of Appeals remanding for reinterpretation that would avoid a supposed delegation of legislative power. . . .

Justice Thomas, concurring. . . .

Justice Stevens, with whom *Justice Souter* joins, concurring in part and concurring in the judgment.

Section 109(b)(1) delegates to the Administrator of the Environmental Protection Agency (EPA) the authority to promulgate national ambient air quality standards (NAAQS). . . . [T]he Court convincingly explains why the Court of Appeals erred when it concluded that § 109 effected "an unconstitutional delegation of legislative power." . . . I wholeheartedly endorse the Court's result and endorse its explanation of its reasons, albeit with the following caveat.

The Court has two choices. We could choose to articulate our ultimate disposition of this issue by frankly acknowledging that the power delegated to the EPA is "legislative" but nevertheless conclude that the delegation is constitutional because adequately limited by the terms of the authorizing statute. Alternatively, we could pretend, as the Court does, that the authority delegated to the EPA is somehow not "legislative power." Despite the fact that there is language in our opinions that supports the Court's articulation of our holding, I am persuaded that it would be both wiser and more faithful to what we have actually done in delegation cases to admit that agency rulemaking authority is "legislative power."

The proper characterization of governmental power should generally depend on the nature of the power, not on the identity of the person exercising it. . . . If the NAAQS that the EPA promulgated had been prescribed by Congress, everyone would agree that those rules would be the product of an exercise of "legislative power." The same characterization is appropriate when an agency exercises rulemaking authority pursuant to a permissible delegation from Congress.

My view is not only more faithful to normal English usage, but is also fully consistent with the text of the Constitution. In Article I, the Framers vested "All legislative Powers" in the Congress, Art. I, § 1, just as in Article II they vested the "executive Power" in the President, Art. II, § 1. Those provisions do not purport to limit the authority of either recipient of power to delegate authority to others. . . .

It seems clear that an executive agency's exercise of rulemaking authority pursuant to a valid delegation from Congress is "legislative." As long as the delegation provides a sufficiently intelligible principle, there is nothing inherently unconstitutional about it. Accordingly, . . . I would hold that when Congress enacted § 109, it effected a constitutional delegation of legislative power to the EPA.

Justice Breyer, concurring in part and concurring in the judgment. . . .

EDITED CASE   State ex rel. Taylor v. Johnson
Supreme Court of New Mexico, 961 P.2d 768 (N.M. 1998)

[In this case the New Mexico Supreme Court considers the constitutionality of a state welfare reform policy that is instituted via executive order rather than by legislation. The court concludes that the means by which the policy was made violates the separation of powers required by the New Mexico constitution.]

Justice Baca delivered the opinion of the court.

The Constitution of the State of New Mexico commands that "[t]he powers of the government of this state are divided into three distinct departments, the legislative, executive, and judicial, and no person or collection of persons charged with the exercise of powers properly belonging to one of these departments, shall exercise any powers properly belonging to either of the others. . . ." N.M. Const. art. III, § 1. The case before us does not concern the merits of public assistance reform or conflicts of political ideology. Rather, it concerns only the sanctity of the New Mexico Constitution and the judiciary's obligation to uphold the principles therein. . . .

This case began as a challenge of the power of the Executive to effect an extensive overhaul of the state's public assistance system without legislative participation. In the course of the proceedings before this Court, two issues presented themselves. First, the question arose whether Respondents had exceeded their constitutional powers in enacting and implementing certain welfare regulations. Subsequently, after this Court ruled Respondents had violated the constitutional provisions established by the separation of powers doctrine, the question arose whether Respondents had honored this Court's order. This question implicated an even more fundamental concept: respect for the rule of law. We address both questions in this opinion.

Petitioners filed a Verified Petition for a Writ of Mandamus directed at Governor Gary Johnson and the Secretary of the New Mexico Human Services Department (Respondents). Petitioners alleged that Respondents exceeded their constitutional authority by implementing significant public assistance policy changes without legislative approval. This Court, in a decision rendered from the bench on September 10, 1997, held that Respondents

violated the separation of powers provision in Article III, Section 1 of the New Mexico Constitution. Pursuant to this holding, we issued a Writ of Mandamus requiring Respondents: 1) to desist from the implementation of their public assistance changes; and 2) to administer the public assistance program in full compliance with existing law until it is constitutionally altered or amended by legislation signed into law by the Governor.

On October 24, 1997, Petitioners filed a motion to hold Respondents in contempt of court, alleging that Respondents were continuing to implement their public assistance changes. On December 10, 1997, the Court held a hearing requiring Respondents to show cause why this Court should not hold them in contempt for failing to comply with the Writ.

We first restate the holding and fully articulate the reasoning behind our September 10, 1997, decision holding that Respondents violated Article III, Section 1 of the state constitution. Second, we determine that Respondents have not complied with the Writ and, therefore, hold Respondents in indirect civil contempt.

I

Congress enacted the federal Aid to Families with Dependent Children program (AFDC) as part of the Social Security Act of 1935. . . . AFDC created a new federal-state public assistance partnership. The federal government established the primary framework for public assistance programs and offered funding for states that implemented their programs consistent with federal guidelines.

Soon after the federal government passed AFDC, New Mexico elected to join the federal program, passing implementing legislation now called the Public Assistance Act (NMPAA). . . . The NMPAA authorizes administration of the AFDC program and sets the basic formula for determining eligibility. . . . The Legislature also created the New Mexico Human Services Department (HSD) . . . to work with the federal government in administering public assistance programs. . . .

In the decades following passage of federal AFDC, Congress made major adjustments to the program. In such instances, the New Mexico Legis-

---

EDITED CASE   State ex rel. Taylor v. Johnson (Continued)

---

lature passed, and a governor signed into law, bills adopting the federal changes in New Mexico. . . .

The most recent change in federal AFDC occurred with the enactment of the Personal Responsibility and Work Opportunity Reconciliation Act of 1996 (PRA). . . . The PRA repealed federal statutory and regulatory constraints on state administration of public assistance, permitting the states to create their own programs. To increase states' flexibility, the PRA replaced the former AFDC funding structure with a block grant program called Temporary Assistance to Needy Families (TANF). States now are eligible to receive TANF funds and use them as they wish in their own programs, subject only to minimal federal PRA guidelines.

The PRA's passage spurred legislative and executive action in New Mexico. Anticipating federal public assistance reform legislation in 1995, Governor Johnson submitted a state public assistance reform bill to the New Mexico Legislature in the 1996 legislative session. However, the bill died after failing to reach the floor of the New Mexico House of Representatives. After Congress passed and the President signed the PRA in 1996, the New Mexico Legislature, this time on its own initiative, began considering public assistance reform during its 1997 session. The New Mexico House of Representatives and Senate both passed substantially identical bills both known as the Family Assistance and Individual Responsibility Act (FAIR). The Act would have created a new NMPAA section to accommodate the TANF block grant program requirements and would have authorized HSD to administer the program.

Soon thereafter, Governor Johnson vetoed the FAIR Act and line-item vetoed language in the General Appropriations Act that allotted money for the FAIR program. He stated in his veto messages that, as the Executive, he possessed authority to exercise the discretion left to the states under the PRA. . . . The Governor argued that the proposed state legislation encroached upon the executive's authority. . . .

Immediately following his veto, Governor Johnson announced the creation of his own public assistance reform plan, a program he labeled "PROGRESS." His proposed plan modified aspects of public assistance eligibility, support services, and

delivery in New Mexico. Governor Johnson also stated that he intended to implement the program's public assistance changes through administrative regulation. Subsequently, HSD held public hearings regarding the proposed regulatory changes, and Respondents' program was adopted, taking effect on July 1, 1997.

On July 21, 1997, Petitioners filed a Verified Petition for Writ of Mandamus. The Petitioners asserted that Governor Johnson and then-Secretary of HSD, Duke Rodriguez, unlawfully implemented Respondents' program without seeking legislative approval, in violation of both state statute and the New Mexico Constitution's separation of powers provision. This Court held oral argument on September 10, 1997. In a unanimous decision, the Court ruled from the bench that Respondents had violated the New Mexico Constitution, Article III, Section 1. The Court ordered Respondents to: a) desist from the implementation of their PROGRESS program, and b) to administer the Public Assistance Program in full compliance with New Mexico statutes until such time as existing law is altered or amended by the passage of a bill by the state legislature which is then signed into law by the governor in accordance with the provisions of the New Mexico Constitution. . . . When announcing the holding, the Chief Justice also asked the parties, "Are there any questions from counsel?" . . . There were none, and the Court issued the Writ.

II

. . . This Court has original jurisdiction in this proceeding pursuant to Article VI, Section 3 of the New Mexico Constitution.

. . . Petitioners are alleging that the Respondents engaged in unlawful or unconstitutional official acts, Petitioners may request mandamus as the necessary relief.

III

Next we address whether the Respondents' actions constituted a violation of the New Mexico Constitution's separation of powers provision. Respondents contend that implementation of Respondents' program does not unconstitutionally

(Continued)

EDITED CASE   State ex rel. Taylor v. Johnson (Continued)

infringe upon the Legislature's authority. Instead, they argue first that, as agents of the executive branch, they may implement the policy changes without seeking the direct participation of the Legislature. Respondents also contend that the Legislature conferred discretionary authority upon HSD to construct plans, make rules, and enact all regulations necessary to secure federal public assistance funds and to comply with federal law. As part of this position, Respondents assert not only that they were given discretionary authority to make such adjustments, but also that New Mexico and federal law compelled them to make the policy changes. We disagree.

A

Article III, Section 1 of the New Mexico Constitution prohibits any branch of government from usurping the power of the other branches: The powers of the government of this state are divided into three distinct departments, the legislative, executive and judicial, and no person or collection of persons charged with the exercise of powers properly belonging to one of these departments, shall exercise any powers properly belonging to either of the others. . . . This provision articulates one of the cornerstones of democratic government: that the accumulation of too much power within one branch poses a threat to liberty. . . .

Within our constitutional system, each branch of government maintains its independent and distinct function. . . . We have said that only the legislative branch is constitutionally established to create substantive law. . . . We also have recognized the unique position of the Legislature in creating and developing public policy. "[I]t is the particular domain of the legislature, as the voice of the people, to make public policy. Elected executive officials and executive agencies also make policy, [but] to a lesser extent, [and only] as authorized by the constitution or legislature." . . .

A governor's proper role is the execution of the laws. . . . Public assistance programs must be administered, and we recognize that such administration involves discretion by executive agencies. Yet, such discretion is not boundless. Generally, the Legislature, not the administrative agency, declares the policy and establishes primary standards to which the agency must conform. . . . The administrative agency's discretion may not justify altering,

modifying or extending the reach of a law created by the Legislature. . . .

While recognizing the specific roles of each branch of government, we also note that absolute separation of powers is "neither desirable nor realistic," . . . and that the constitutional doctrine of separation of powers permits some overlap of governmental functions. . . . Nonetheless, this Court must give effect to Article III, Section 1, and will not be reluctant to intervene where one branch of government unduly encroaches or interferes with the authority of another branch. . . . Such an infringement occurs when the action by one branch prevents another branch from accomplishing its constitutionally assigned functions. . . .

"The test is whether the Governor's action disrupts the proper balance between the executive and legislative branches." . . . If a governor's actions infringe upon "the essence of legislative authority—the making of laws—then the [g]overnor has exceeded his authority." . . . A violation occurs when the Executive, rather than the Legislature, determines "how, when, and for what purpose the public funds shall be applied in carrying on the government." . . . In addition, infringement upon legislative power may also occur where the executive does not "execute existing New Mexico statutory or case law [and rather attempts] to create new law." . . .

B

We have no doubt that Respondents' program implements the type of substantive policy changes reserved to the Legislature. Their changes substantially altered, modified, and extended existing law governing the structure and provision of public assistance in New Mexico. . . . Furthermore, by refusing to permit legislative participation in fashioning public assistance policy changes, Respondents "attempt to foreclose legislative action in [an] area[ ] where legislative authority is undisputed." . . . We hold that Respondents' program constitutes executive creation of substantive law, and as such, is an unconstitutional encroachment upon the Legislature's role of declaring public policy.

The substantial nature of the Respondents' adjustments to public assistance policy are best illustrated: 1) by comparing existing New Mexico public assistance standards with Respondents'

EDITED CASE   State ex rel. Taylor v. Johnson (Continued)

---

changes; and 2) by placing those changes in the context of the range of policy options available to the New Mexico Legislature.

First, federal AFDC statutes required that a child be "dependent" to qualify for assistance. Generally, this meant that a child had to be from a one-parent household to be eligible for benefits. . . . The PRA eliminated this federal requirement and gave the states the option to use TANF funds to support needy children in two-parent families as well. . . . Although New Mexico had the option under federal law to maintain its existing "dependent" requirement, Respondents eliminated the requirement in New Mexico through the new administrative regulations. Income Support Division Financial Assistance Program. . . . Respondents' actions effectively denied the Legislature any participation in this decision. Second, the old federal AFDC program contained ancillary job training and limited work requirements. . . . New Mexico's current law reflects this. . . . The PRA replaced these programs with mandatory work requirements. . . . Respondents' program imposed a mandatory work requirement through regulations and adopted work schedules that exceed those included in the PRA. . . . Again, the Legislature had no participation in deciding the extent of work requirements appropriate for New Mexico.

Third, under the old federal framework, eligible individuals were deemed "entitled" to benefits. This meant that states were not free to make waiting lists or establish limits on the duration of assistance. The new PRA permits states to limit or end this entitlement. . . . Respondents' program eliminated the entitlement in New Mexico. . . . The Legislature had no influence in deciding, as a matter of public assistance policy, whether an entitlement should have been maintained in New Mexico.

Finally, federal AFDC did not impose any durational limits on eligibility for benefits. However, according to the PRA, states cannot use TANF block grant money to provide assistance to persons for more than five years. . . . Hence, if a state chooses, it may provide assistance without durational limits, but public assistance payments exceeding five years must be funded entirely by state coffers. . . . Respondents' program set a durational limit of three years in New Mexico. . . . The Legislature, had it been given the option, might have chosen not to impose a durational limit. Or alternatively, it might have chosen to set a limit of shorter or longer duration. Promulgation of the new program's three year limitation denied the Legislature any participation in deciding what, if any, time limits would be appropriate for New Mexico.

Although this is not a complete list of the changes affected by Respondents' regulations, these examples represent a substantial change in New Mexico's public assistance eligibility or delivery standards without the participation of the Legislature. Indeed, little of New Mexico's public assistance program remains intact in the wake of Respondents' changes. Such results, by their very nature, set fundamental standards and make vital policy choices, a role reserved for the Legislature. . . .

We also believe that the past practices of the New Mexico Legislature and Executive are instructive on these issues. In the past, when states were given the option to adopt federal public assistance policy changes, such changes were examined and adopted through the full legislative process and eventually signed into law by a governor. . . . Thus, the Respondents' unilateral implementation of the public assistance changes represents a substantial break with past practice, ignoring the New Mexico Legislature's consistent role in creating state public assistance policy.

In sum, when the federal government enacted the PRA, New Mexico faced three questions: 1) whether to continue to use the state's existing public assistance framework; 2) whether to create a new program for the delivery of public assistance services, and if so, the identification of its essential structure and elements; and 3) whether to administer a program with federal funding which would be subject to new federal restrictions. These issues go to the core of public assistance policy. By implementing their plan through HSD regulations rather than through the required legislative process, Respondents made these core policy choices themselves, thereby preventing the constitutionally required input of the people's elected law-making representatives.

(Continued)

EDITED CASE   State ex rel. Taylor v. Johnson (Continued)

C

The NMPAA does not confer upon Respondents discretionary authority to implement the PROGRESS program changes. Respondents cite to eight primary sections of the NMPAA that they contend confer discretionary authority upon HSD. As a general matter, Respondents make much of the language calling for "consistency with federal law" included in some of these cited sections. Respondents argue that this language indicates that the New Mexico Legislature has delegated expansive authority to HSD to promulgate any necessary regulations which will maintain conformity between New Mexico and federal public assistance law. We disagree.

Taken as a whole, these references to consistency merely recognize that HSD acts with the federal government to cooperatively administer certain public assistance programs such as AFDC and Medicaid. Such "boilerplate" language recognizing the cooperative nature of the federal and state relationship cannot be used to justify the unfettered discretionary authority that Respondents urge. Nor can this language be used to ignore the substantive commands of the New Mexico Legislature.

The language invoked by Respondents is a limitation on HSD, not a carte blanche grant of discretionary authority. The language indicates that where joint federal/state programs are involved, New Mexico's regulation of the programs cannot violate federal guidelines. The phrases "must be consistent" or "as required by federal law" by their very nature suggest that, even though the programs are administered jointly, there are aspects of the programs that are regulated solely by federal law. The states are at liberty to determine some elements of the subject programs, but state power is limited in that the states cannot contradict federal controls over a program. Viewed in this context, we have no doubt that the "consistency" language is a limitation on HSD discretion and not a delegation of legislative power.

In addition, we reject any notion that the PRA confers authority upon the executive branch to ignore duly enacted state legislation or to make the legislative policy choices embodied in the new public assistance changes. The PRA confers upon the states the essential choices of public assistance

policy. . . . The PRA neither explicitly or implicitly gives that authority solely to the executive of the state. Furthermore, federal law cannot enlarge state executive power beyond that conferred by the state constitution. . . .

In a similar vein, Respondents also argue that the PRA imposes conditions on New Mexico and that the Legislature's acceptance of TANF funds, absent required changes in the NMPAA, leaves the implementation of those obligatory changes to the Executive. It is true that "under Congress' spending power, 'Congress may attach conditions on the receipt of federal funds.'" . . . However, as indicated above, we conclude that many provisions contained in Respondent's program were not required by the PRA.

Finally, we reject Respondents' contention that if the Legislature disagrees with Respondents' program, the appropriate remedy is for the Legislature to redirect HSD's discretionary authority with new statutes during the next legislative session. This argument has no merit. Only a simple majority is required to pass a bill through both legislative chambers. . . . A governor is constitutionally entitled to veto the legislation if he does not agree with it. . . . The Legislature then has the option of attempting to override the veto, by securing a two-thirds majority. . . . The counterbalance of a governor's veto power against the Legislature's ability to override the veto is the mechanism that forces the two branches to compromise and work together to create law.

The alleged remedy that Respondents' urge is impractical, and more importantly, it would subvert the system of checks and balances of the New Mexico Constitution. Through HSD regulation, Governor Johnson implemented new public assistance policies in exactly the form that he deemed appropriate for New Mexico. If the Legislature were now to pass statutory amendments by a simple majority in an attempt to "redirect" HSD's discretion, the Governor's signature would still be required for such changes to become law.

Respondents' position is impractical because the Governor would have no reason to accept, or even consider, such changes. He already has the public assistance policies in place that he favors via administrative regulation. Therefore, no incentive exists for him to consider any public assistance changes suggested by the Legislature. Conse-

---

EDITED CASE   State ex rel. Taylor v. Johnson (Continued)

---

quently, the Governor could, and almost certainly would, veto any bill submitted to him altering the program that he already put in place unilaterally.

With the administrative changes to public assistance already in place and a veto of any proposed amendments assured, the Legislature could convince the Governor to compromise only if, from the outset, the Legislature had the necessary votes for a veto-override. This scenario, in effect, would force the Legislature to garner a veto-override majority of two-thirds to bring about any consideration of amendments to the existing public assistance regulations.

Respondents' recommendation for further legislative action turns our constitutional system of checks and balances on its head. The New Mexico Constitution requires that the Legislature first have the opportunity to debate and vote on core policy changes; only then may the Governor exercise his veto powers and force the Legislature to consider a veto-override. In this case, the Governor already has usurped the legislative function, initiating public policy changes which should find their genesis only in the Legislature. Requiring legislative action to change the Governor's program now would place the Legislature in a position of responding to, rather than initiating, core public policy choices.

Because the substantive public assistance policy changes promulgated in Respondents' plan required legislative participation and because neither state statute nor federal law conferred discretionary authority upon Respondents to institute the policy changes, we conclude that Respondents violated Article III, Section 1 of the New Mexico Constitution. From this conclusion, a writ of mandamus was issued September 10, 1997.

IV

In the months that followed the Writ, Respondents made no attempt to comply with the Writ and openly defied this Court. During this time, Respondents were advised by several legal authorities that they should comply with this Court's Writ. The New Mexico Attorney General assured Respondents that no irreconcilable conflicts existed between state and federal law and stressed the importance of relinquishing the Respondents' public assistance program. HSD's general counsel also advised Respondents to return to New Mexico's existing program until the Legislature passed a bill and the

Governor signed it into law. Despite this overwhelming advice to comply with the Court's Order, Respondents continued implementation of their public assistance program.

After several failed attempts to seek Respondents' compliance, Petitioners filed a Motion for Supplemental and Further Relief. Respondents did not deny that they were disobeying the Court's Writ. Respondents admitted that the Writ compelled them to cease their public assistance program and reinstate New Mexico's existing program. However, HSD continued to encourage implementation of Respondents' new public assistance regulations, except with respect to a waiver of the work requirement penalty.

On October 24, 1997, Petitioners filed a motion to have this Court declare Respondents in contempt of court. The petition alleged that Respondents continued to carry out their public assistance program. Respondents replied that they could not comply with the Court's Writ because the existing state statutes were contrary to federal PRA guidelines. Specifically, Respondents asserted that state statutes: 1) provided benefits to unqualified aliens, felons, and parole violators, and 2) did not include mandatory work requirements.

Before considering contempt proceedings, the Chief Justice strongly encouraged the parties to engage in good-faith negotiations or mediation toward settlement. Despite the Chief Justice's encouragement, Respondents refused to consider any proposals, and they continued to implement their own public assistance program.

On December 8, 1997, the Petitioners filed a Supplemental Memorandum concerning possible sanctions and urged the Court to consider imposing contempt sanctions against both the Governor, and newly-appointed HSD Secretary Bill Johnson. In response, Respondents only repeated the argument that they could not comply with the Court's Writ because NMPAA conflicted with federal law. Pursuant to motion, the Court then initiated contempt proceedings, setting a hearing for Respondents to show cause why they should not be held in contempt.

At the contempt hearing, Respondents maintained that harmonizing the Court's Writ with the

(Continued)

EDITED CASE   State ex rel. Taylor v. Johnson (Continued)

---

federal funding requirements in the PRA was impossible. Respondents reasoned that because the federal government no longer funds the federal AFDC program, HSD was unable to return to the existing New Mexico law. Respondents also asserted that the state would lose federal public assistance funds as a result of complying with the Court's Writ.

Respondent's misrepresentation of the loss of federal funding was an attempt to mislead this Court. Respondents first asserted that reinstituting the prior AFDC program would result in the loss of the entire amount of federal welfare funding. Yet, the actual penalty for noncompliance with the PRA's requirements and penalties would be a loss of no more than 5% of the entire federal funding amount. Federal Register Vol. 62, No. 224, Nov. 20, 1997. Although this may be a substantial amount, it would not be the death knell for the state's welfare program that Respondents would have us believe. Second, Respondents suggested that New Mexico would suffer immediate funding consequences if they followed the Court's Writ. However, existing federal authority indicates that if any federal funds were going to be withheld from New Mexico, such a decision would not be made anytime in the near future. Id. Hence, the tone of urgency and desperation adopted by Respondents was at best unnecessary, and at worst, misleading. Third, contrary to Respondents' assertions, nothing in the record indicates that anyone from either HSD or the Governor's Office made any inquiries with federal agencies regarding the imposition of possible penalties or exceptions. We are not convinced that Respondents actually pursued this avenue as a possible solution to this case. Finally, Respondents' counsel misused legal authority in an attempt to mislead this Court. During oral argument, Respondents' counsel cited to a proposed rule, treating it as applicable federal law. We specifically object to this misrepresentation and to counsel's attempt to lead this Court astray.

FAIR, the Legislature's proposed public assistance program that the Governor vetoed, may not have been acceptable to the Governor, but it did comply with the PRA. The Governor has every right to veto legislation but he must be mindful of his veto's consequences. The Governor should have foreseen that vetoing the proposed public assistance program left the prior AFDC program as the only viable public assistance program. Implementing Respondents' own welfare program without legislative approval was not an option.

V

Next we address application of the appropriate contempt sanction. "Without question, the power of the judiciary to compel compliance with its orders, extends to the executive branch." . . . "The executive branch of government has no right to treat with impunity the valid orders of the judicial branch." . . . By statute, the New Mexico Supreme Court has the authority to hold an individual in contempt of court and to punish, by "reprimand, arrest, fine or imprisonment." . . . In determining the appropriate punishment for civil contempt, the Court exercises its discretion. The Court considers the character and degree of harm threatened by continued contemptuous acts and whether contemplated sanctions will cause compliance with the Court's order. . . . Courts consider the seriousness of the consequences of continued contemptuous behavior, the public's interest in ending defendants' defiance, and the importance of avoiding future defiance. . . . A court may directly order an individual to comply with its order to purge himself or herself of contempt and may stay further sanctions if the individual complies with the order by a specified date. . . . Other state courts have used direct orders or injunctions to compel executive branch members to comply with court orders. . . .

Some state courts have fined executive branch members in their individual capacities when their actions were willful and performed in bad faith. . . . Individual executive branch members have had to pay personal contempt fines when the individual has notice of the judgment and is able to comply with the court order and nonetheless refuses to comply with the judgment. . . . Some states also have restricted an individual member from using certain state funds to pay the fine. . . .

Courts may also impose imprisonment in a civil contempt action to coerce compliance. . . . It is clear this Court has authority to implement the full extent of contempt sanctions against executive branch members, including fines and imprisonment.

Petitioners urge this Court to consider appointing a special master to oversee the program and to

---

EDITED CASE State ex rel. Taylor v. Johnson (Continued)

---

ensure compliance. Under Petitioners' proposal, the special master would recommend to this Court the appropriate sanction. Petitioners suggest that if Respondents continue to refuse to comply with the Writ, then this Court could expand the special master's authority, assigning the special master to administer the entire public assistance program. However, we do not feel that such an appointment is appropriate.

We hold that the most appropriate contempt sanction is an order directing Respondents to cease and desist immediately from implementing the Respondents' public assistance program within seven days. The Court will consider imposing further sanctions if Respondents do not comply. Here, the Court's Writ requires Respondents to stop implementing an unconstitutional program.

Respondents do not have the discretion to continue an unconstitutional act. Moreover, Respondents had more than adequate notice and were advised to comply with the Writ.

We hold that Respondents acted in defiance of this Court's Order and have shown no justification for failing to comply with it. Accordingly, we find Respondents in indirect civil contempt, and after reviewing all sanctions within our contempt power, we hold that the most appropriate sanction is a direct order to comply within a specified time, with further sanctions if Respondents do not immediately comply. We maintain jurisdiction to impose additional contempt sanctions if we later determine that they are necessary and appropriate.

Justices FRANCHINI, MINZNER and McKINNON, concurring.

EDITED CASE Nollan v. California Coastal Commission
United States Supreme Court, 483 U.S. 825 (1987)

[James and Marilyn Nollan leased with an option to purchase a small bungalow situated on a beach-front lot in Ventura County, California. Their option to buy was conditioned on their promise to demolish the bungalow, which had fallen into disrepair, and replace it with a new structure. In order to do so, they had to obtain a development permit from the California Coastal Commission. The commission informed the Nollans that it would grant the permit only on the condition that they grant an easement allowing for public access to the beach across their property. The Nollans filed suit in the superior court, which invalidated the easement condition and ordered that it be stricken from the permit. The California Coastal Commission appealed to the California Court of Appeals, which reversed the superior court. The Nollans appealed to the U.S. Supreme Court.]

Justice Scalia delivered the Opinion of the Court.
. . . Had California simply required the Nollans to make an easement across their beachfront available to the public on a permanent basis in order to

increase public access to the beach, rather than conditioning their permit to rebuild their house on their agreeing to do so, we have no doubt there would have been a taking. To say that the appropriation of a public easement across a landowner's premises does not constitute a taking of a property interest but rather (as Justice Brennan contends) "a mere restriction on its use," . . . is to use words in a manner that deprives them of all their ordinary meaning. Indeed, one of the principal uses of the eminent domain power is to assure that government be able to require conveyance of such interests, so long as it pays for them. . . . Perhaps because the point is so obvious, we have never been confronted with a controversy that required us to rule upon it, but our cases' analysis of the effects of other governmental action lead us to the same conclusion. . . .

Given, then, that requiring uncompensated conveyance of the easement outright would violate the Fourteenth Amendment, the question becomes

(Continued)

EDITED CASE   Nollan v. California Coastal Commission (Continued)

---

whether requiring it to be conveyed as a condition for issuing a land-use permit alters the outcome. We have long recognized that land use regulation does not effect a taking if it "substantially advance[s] legitimate state interests" and does not "den[y] an owner economically viable use of his land." . . . Our cases have not elaborated on the standards for determining what constitutes a "legitimate state interest" or what type of connection between the regulation and the state interest satisfies the requirement that the former "substantially advance" the latter. They have made clear, however, that a broad range of governmental purposes and regulations satisfies these requirements. . . . The Commission argues that among these permissible purposes are protecting the public's ability to see the beach, assisting the public in overcoming the "psychological barrier" to using the beach created by a developed shorefront, and preventing congestion on the public beaches. We assume, without deciding, that this is so—in which case the Commission unquestionably would be able to deny the Nollans their permit outright if their new house (alone, or by reason of the cumulative impact produced in conjunction with other construction) would substantially impede these purposes, unless the denial would interfere so drastically with the Nollans use of their property as to constitute a taking. . . .

The Commission argues that a permit condition that serves the same legitimate police-power purpose as a refusal to issue the permit should not be found to be a taking if the refusal to issue the permit would not constitute a taking. We agree. . . . Although such a requirement, constituting a permanent grant of continuous access to the property, would have to be considered a taking if it were not attached to a development permit, the Commission's assumed power to forbid construction of the house in order to protect the public's view of the beach must surely include the power to condition construction upon some concession by the owner, even a concession of property rights, that serves the same end. If a prohibition designed to accomplish that purpose would be a legitimate exercise of the police power rather than a taking, it would be strange to conclude that providing the owner an alternative to that prohibition which accomplishes the same purpose is not.

The evident constitutional propriety disappears, however, if the condition substituted for the prohibition utterly fails to further the end advanced as the justification for the prohibition. When that essential nexus is eliminated, the situation becomes the same as if California law forbade shouting fire in a crowded theater, but granted dispensations to those willing to contribute $100 to the state treasury. While a ban on shouting fire can be a core exercise of the State's police power to protect the public safety, and can thus meet even our stringent standards for regulation of speech, adding the unrelated condition alters the purpose to one which, while it may be legitimate, is inadequate to sustain the ban. Therefore, even though, in a sense, requiring a $100 tax contribution in order to shout fire is a lesser restriction on speech than an outright ban, it would not pass constitutional muster. Similarly here, the lack of nexus between the condition and the original purpose of the building restriction converts that purpose to something other than what it was. The purpose then becomes, quite simply, the obtaining of an easement to serve some valid governmental purpose, but without payment of compensation. Whatever may be the outer limits of "legitimate state interests" in the takings and land use context, this is not one of them. In short, unless the permit condition serves the same governmental purpose as the development ban, the building restriction is not a valid regulation of land use but "an out-and-out plan of extortion." . . .

. . . It is quite impossible to understand how a requirement that people already on the public beaches be able to walk across the Nollans' property reduces any obstacles to viewing the beach created by the new house. It is also impossible to understand how it lowers any "psychological barrier" to using the public beaches, or how it helps to remedy any additional congestion on them caused by construction of the Nollans' new house. We therefore find that the Commission's imposition of the permit condition cannot be treated as an exercise of its land use power for any of these purposes. Our conclusion on this point is consistent with the approach of every other court that has considered the question, with the exception of the California state courts. . . .

EDITED CASE   Nollan v. California Coastal Commission (Continued)

Justice Brennan argues that imposition of the access requirement is not irrational. In his version of the Commission's argument, the reason for the requirement is that in its absence, a person looking toward the beach from the road will see a street of residential structures including the Nollans' new home and conclude that there is no public beach nearby. If, however, that person sees people passing and repassing along the dry sand behind the Nollans' home, he will realize that there is a public beach somewhere in the vicinity. The Commission's action, however, was based on the opposite factual finding that the wall of houses completely blocked the view of the beach and that a person looking from the road would not be able to see it at all. . . .

We are left, then, with the Commission's justification for the access requirement unrelated to land use regulation:

"Finally, the Commission notes that there are several existing provisions of pass and repass lateral access benefits already given by past Faria Beach Tract applicants as a result of prior coastal permit decisions. The access required as a condition of this permit is part of a comprehensive program to provide continuous public access along Faria Beach as the lots undergo development or redevelopment." . . .

That is simply an expression of the Commission's belief that the public interest will be served by a continuous strip of publicly accessible beach along the coast. The Commission may well be right that it is a good idea, but that does not establish that the Nollans (and other coastal residents) alone can be compelled to contribute to its realization. Rather, California is free to advance its "comprehensive program," if it wishes, by using its power of eminent domain for the "public purpose," but if it wants an easement across the Nollans' property, it must pay for it. . . .

Justice Brennan, with whom **Justice Marshall** joins, dissenting.

. . . The Court's conclusion that the permit rendition imposed on appellants is unreasonable cannot withstand analysis. First, the Court demands a degree of exactitude that is inconsistent with our standard for reviewing the rationality of a state's exercise of its police power for the welfare of its citizens. Second, even if the nature

of the public access condition imposed must be identical to the precise burden on access created by appellants, this requirement is plainly satisfied. . . .

Imposition of the permit condition in this case represents the State's reasonable exercise of its police power. The Coastal Commission has drawn on its expertise to preserve the balance between private development and public access, by requiring that any project that intensifies development on the increasingly crowded California coast must be offset by gains in public access. Under the normal standard for review of the police power, this provision is eminently reasonable. . . .

. . . State agencies . . . require considerable flexibility in responding to private desires for development in a way that guarantees public access to the coast. They should be encouraged to regulate development in the context of the overall balance of competing uses of the shoreline. The Court today does precisely the opposite, overruling an eminently reasonable exercise of an expert state agency's judgment, substituting its own narrow view of how this balance should be struck. Its reasoning is hardly suited to the complex reality of natural resource protection in the 20th century. I can only hope that today's decision is an aberration, and that a broader vision ultimately prevails. . . .

Justice Blackmun, dissenting.

. . . I disagree with the Court's rigid interpretation of the necessary correlation between a burden created by development and a condition imposed pursuant to the State's police power to mitigate that burden. The land-use problems this country faces require creative solutions. These are not advanced by an "eye for an eye" mentality. The close nexus between benefits and burdens that the Court now imposes on permit conditions creates an anomaly in the ordinary requirement that a State's exercise of its police power need be no more than rationally based. In my view, the easement exacted from appellants and the problems their development created are adequately related to the governmental interest in providing public access to the beach. Coastal development by its very nature

(Continued)

EDITED CASE   Nollan v. California Coastal Commission (Continued)

---

makes public access to the shore generally more difficult. Appellants' structure is part of that general development and, in particular, it diminishes the public's visual access to the ocean and decreases the public's sense that it may have physical access to the beach. These losses in access can be counteracted, at least in part, by the condition on appellants' construction permitting public passage that ensures access along the beach.

Traditional takings analysis compels the conclusion that there is no taking here. The govern-

mental action is a valid exercise of the police power, and, so far as the record reveals, has a nonexistent economic effect on the value of appellants' property. No investment-backed expectations were diminished. It is significant that the Nollans had notice of the easement before they purchased the property and that public use of the beach had been permitted for decades. . . .

Justice Stevens, with whom *Justice Blackmun* joins, dissenting. . . .

ENDNOTES

1. *McCulloch v. Maryland,* 4 Wheat. (17 U.S.) 316 (1819).

2. James Madison, *The Federalist* No. 45.

3. *McCulloch v. Maryland, supra, Id.* at 405.

4. *McCulloch v. Maryland, supra,* at 421.

5. Thomas Jefferson, Secretary of State, Memorandum to President George Washington opposing the establishment of the First Bank of the United States, 1790.

6. U.S. Const., Art. I, 8, cl. 3.

7. 22 U.S. 1 (1824).

8. *Id.,* at 194-195.

9. 24 Stat. 379.

10. 26 Stat. 209, as amended, 15 U.S.C.A. 1 *et seq.*

11. *A .L. A. Schechter Poultry Corp. v. United States,* 295 U.S. 495 (1935).

12. *Id.* at 548.

13. 301 U.S. 1 (1937).

14. *Id.* at 38.

15. *United States v. Darby,* 312 U. S. 100, 118 (1941).

16. 317 U.S. 111 (1942).

17. Title II of the Civil Rights Act of 1964, 204 (a), 78 Stat. 244, 42 U.S.C.A. 2000a-3 (a). Upheld by the Supreme Court in *Heart of Atlanta Motel v. United States,* 379 U.S. 241 (1964); and *Katzenbach v. McClung,* 379 U.S. 294 (1964).

18. Title VII of the Civil Rights Act of 1964, 42 U.S.C.A. § 2000e *et seq.* See *Griggs v. Duke Power Co.,* 401 U.S. 424 (1971) .

19. 7 U.S.C.A. 136;16 U.S.C.A. § 460 *et seq.*

20. 42 U.S.C.A. §§ 7401 *et seq.*

21. 15 U.S.C.A. § 1263.

22. 33 U.S.C.A. § 1251 *et seq.*

23. 49 U.S.C.A. § 5102(1).

24. 42 U.S.C.A. §§ 9601 *et seq.*

25. 29 U.S.C.A. § 651 *et seq.*

26. 18 U.S.C.A. § 1201.

27. 18 U.S.C.A. § 2312.

28. 21 U.S.C.A. § 801 *et seq.*

29. 18 U.S.C.A. §§ 1961–1963.

30. 18 U.S.C.A. § 1030.

31. 18 U.S.C.A. 891 *et seq.*

32. 18 U.S.C.A. § 2119.

33. 514 U.S. 549 (1995).

34. *Id.* at 567.

35. *Id.* at 567.

36. *Texas v. White,* 7 Wall. 700, 725 (1869).

37. 247 U.S. 251 (1918).

38. *Id.* at 275.

39. Edward S. Corwin, *The Passing of Dual Federalism,* 36 Va. L. Rev. 1 (1950).

40. *United States v. Darby,* 312 U.S. 100, 124 (1941).

41. See *National League of Cities v. Usery,* 426 U.S. 833 (1976), overruled in *Garcia v. San Antonio Metropolitan Transit Authority,* 469 U.S. 528 (1985).

42. 2 U.S.C.A. § 1501 *et seq.*

43. *Cipollone v. Liggett Group, Inc.,* 505 U.S. 504, 517 (1992).

44. *Pennsylvania v. Nelson,* 350 U.S. 497 (1956).

45. 533 U.S. 525 (2001).

46. This can be seen in decisions like *United States v. Lopez, supra, New York v. United States,* 505 U.S. 144 (1992), *Seminole Tribe of Florida v. Florida,* 517 U.S. 44 (1996), *Printz v. United States,* 521 U.S. 898 (1997), *Alden v. Maine,* 527 U.S. 706 (1999), and *United States v. Morrison,* 529 U.S. 598 (2000).

47. *Hodel v. Virginia Surface Mining & Reclamation Assn., Inc.,* 452 U.S. 264, 288 (1981); *New York v. United States, supra.*

48. *Printz v. United States, supra,* at 935.

49. *See, e.g., South Dakota v. Dole,* 483 U.S. 203 (1987).

50. Pub. L. 101-336, 104 Stat. 1337, 42 U.S.C.A. § 12101 *et seq.*

51. 28 C.F.R. § 35.130(d).

52. See *Olmstead v. L.C.,* 527 U.S. 581 (1999).

53. 28 C.F.R. § 35.130(b)(7).

54. U.S. Const., art I., § 3.

55. John Locke, *Second Treatise of Civil Government* (1690) § 141.

56. Sotirios A. Barber, *The Constitution and the Delegation of Congressional Power* (1975).

57. T. M. Cooley, *Constitutional Limitations* (5th ed. 1883).

58. 11 U.S. (7 Cranch) 382 (1813).

59. 143 U.S. 649 (1892).

60. *Id.* at 692.

61. 220 U.S. 506 (1911).

62. 30 Stat. at L. 35, chap. 2, U.S. Comp. Stat. 1901, p. 1540.

63. *United States v. Grimaud, supra,* at 517.

64. *J. W. Hampton & Company v. United States,* 276 U.S. 394, 409 (1928).

65. *A. L. A. Schechter Poultry Corporation v. United States, supra.*

66. *Id.* at 542.

67. *Id.* at 553.

68. Cass Sunstein, *Constitutionalism after the New Deal,* 101 Harv. L. Rev. 421, 447–448 (1987).

69. 373 U.S. 546 (1963).

70. 45 Stat. 1057.

71. 415 U.S. 352 (1974).

72. *Id.* at 353.

73. *See, e.g.,* Theodore J. Lowi, *The End of Liberalism* (1979).

74. *Mistretta v. United States,* 488 U.S. 361 (1989).

75. 488 U.S. at 372.

76. 488 U.S. at 427.

77. 531 U.S. 457 (2001).

78. *Id.* at 474.

79. *Id.* at 475.

80. Quoted in Cato Handbook for Congress: Policy Recommendations for the 107th Congress, Chapter 8, p. 101.

81. Gary Lawson, *The Rise and Rise of the Administrative State,* 107 Harv. L. Rev. 1231-1254 (1994).

82. *Buckley v. Valeo,* 424 U.S. 1, 121 (1976).

83. James Madison, *The Federalist,* No. 47.

84. *Buckley v. Valeo, supra,* at 121.

85. *J. W. Hampton & Co. v. United States, supra,* at 406.

86. *Mistretta v. United States, supra,* at 381.

87. 501 U.S. 252 (1991).

88. *Riddoch v. State,* 123 P. 450, 452–53 (1912).

89. See, for example, *Romer v. Evans,* 517 U.S. 620 (1996).

90. John Cooper and Thomas Marks, *Florida Constitutional Law* 617 (3d ed. 2001).

91. *Id.* at 617.

92. *Id.* at 618.

93. 961 P.2d 768 (N.M. 1998).

94. *Metro Dade County Fair Housing and Employment Appeals Board v. Sunrise Village Mobile Home Park, Inc.,* 511 So. 2d 962 (Fla. 1987).

95. See, for example, *Tulsa County Deputy Sheriffs v. Board of County Commissioners of Tulsa County,* 995 P.2d 1123 (Okla. 2000) (jail privatization statutes not an unconstitutional delegation of legislative authority with respect to jails or duties of sheriffs).

96. 432 N.W. 2d 225 (Neb. 1988).

97. *Askew v. Cross Key Waterways*, 372 So 2d 913, 918–919 (Fla. 1979). In *Askew* the court found certain environmental statutes designating the criteria for determining an area of critical state concern to be constitutionally defective because they reposed in the Administration Commission the fundamental legislative task of determining which geographic areas and resources were to be designated as needing the greatest protection.

98. 636 P. 2d 703 (Colo. 1981).

99. *Cottrell Id.* at 709.

100. 379 A. 2d 994 (Me. 1977).

101. *Griswold v. Connecticut*, 381 U.S. 479 (1965).

102. Tenn. Const., Art. I, Sec. 8 (1870).

103. *Dent v. West Virginia*, 129 U.S. 114, 123 (1889).

104. *Nebbia v. New York*, 291 U.S. 502, 524 (1934).

105. *Parratt v. Taylor*, 451 U.S. 527 (1981).

106. Cooper & Marks, *Florida Constitutional Law,* at 644.

107. 198 U.S. 45 (1905).

108. *Shapiro v. Thompson*, 394 U.S. 618 (1969).

109. 410 U.S. 113 (1973).

110. *Planned Parenthood v. Casey*, 505 U.S. 833 (1992).

111. 551 So. 2d 1186 (Fla. 1989).

112. *Korematsu v. United States*, 323 U.S. 214 (1944).

113. See, e.g., *Yankee Nuclear Power Corp. v. Natural Resources Defense Council, Inc.,* 435 U.S. 519 (1978).

114. *Board of Regents of State Colleges v. Roth*, 408 U.S. 564 (1972).

115. See, e.g., *Golberg v. Kelly*, 397 U.S. 254 (1970).

116. See, e.g., *Cleveland Board of Education v. Loudermill,* 470 U.S. 532 (1985).

117. See, e.g., *Withrow v. Larkin*, 421 U.S. 35 (1975).

118. 397 U.S. 254 (1970).

119. 424 U.S. 319, 334–335 (1976).

120. 347 U.S. 483 (1954).

121. *Adarand Constructors, Inc. v. Pena*, 515 U.S. 200, 225 (1995).

122. *Id.*

123. *Gratz v. Bollinger*, 539 U.S. 244 (2003).

124. *Grutter v. Bollinger*, 539 U.S. 306 (2003).

125. *Mississippi Univ. for Women v. Hogan*, 458 U.S. 718, 724 (1982).

126. *J. E. B. v. Alabama ex rel. T. B.*, 511 U.S. 127 (1994), Kennedy, J., concurring.

127. 518 U.S. 515 (1996).

128. *Id.* at 550.

129. 377 U.S. 533, 555 (1964).

130. 531 U.S. 98 (2000).

131. *Id.* at 139–140.

132. *Southwest Voter Registration Education Project v. Shelley*, 344 F.3d 914 (9th Cir. 2003).

133. 530 U.S. 290 (2000).

134. *Good News Club v. Milford Central School*, 533 U.S. 98 (2001).

135. *Tinker v. Des Moines*, 393 U.S. 403 (1968).

136. *Bethel School District No. 403 v. Fraser*, 478 U.S. 675, 682 (1986).

137. *New Jersey v. T. L. O.*, 469 U.S. 325, 341–343 (1985).

138. 484 U.S. 260 (1988).

139. *Castorina v. Madison County School Board*, 246 F.3d 536 (6th Cir. 2001).

140. *Wildman v. Marshalltown School District*, 249 F.3d 768 (8th Cir. 2001).

141. *Virginia State Board of Pharmacy v. Virginia Citizens Consumer Council*, 425 U.S. 748 (1976).

142. *Central Hudson Gas and Electric Corp. v. New York Public Service Commission*, 447 U.S. 557, 591 (1980).

143. Pub. L. 91-222, 84 Stat. 87, as amended, 15 U.S.C.A. §§ 1331–1340.

144. Pub. L. No. 98-474, 98 Stat. 2200, 15 U.S.C.A. § 1331 *et seq.*

145. 533 U.S. 525 (2001).

146. *Id.* at 571.

147. *FCC v. Pacifica Foundation*, 438 U.S. 726 (1978).

148. *Wolf v. Colorado*, 338 U.S. 25 (1949).

149. *Mapp v. Ohio*, 367 U.S. 643 (1961).

150. 387 U.S. 523 (1967).

151. *Colonnade Catering Corp. v. United States*, 397 U.S. 72 (1970).

152. *New Jersey v. T. L .O., supra.*

153. *Skinner v. Railway Labor Executives' Assn.*, 489 U.S. 602, 617 (1989).

154. *National Treasury Employees Union v. Von Raab*, 489 U.S. 656 (1989).

155. *Chandler v. Miller*, 520 U.S. 305 (1997).

156. 515 U.S. 646 (1995).

157. 381 U.S. 479 (1965).

158. 410 U.S. 113 (1973).

159. *Washington v. Glucksberg*, 521 U.S. 702 (1997).

160. 429 U.S. 589 (1977).

161. *Id.* at 605.

162. *Bellis v. United States,* 417 U.S. 85 (1974).

163. 98 U.S. 403, 406 (1878).

164. See *Bituminous Coal Association v. DeBenedictis,* 480 U.S. 470 (1987).

165. *First English Evangelical Church of Glendale v. County of Los Angeles,* 482 U.S. 304 (1987).

166. *Dolan v. City of Tigard,* 512 U.S. 374 (1994).

167. 483 U.S. 825 (1987).

168. *Id.* at 842.

4

The Statutory Framework
of the Administrative Process

"[A]n administrative agency's power to regulate in the public interest must
always be grounded in a valid grant of authority from Congress."

JUSTICE SANDRA DAY O'CONNOR
WRITING FOR THE MAJORITY IN *FOOD & DRUG ADMINISTRATION V. BROWN & WILLIAMSON
TOBACCO CO.*, 529 U.S. 120 (2000).

INTRODUCTION

Because American political culture stresses the rule of law, government agencies derive their authority from statutes enacted by legislatures. In this country we do not create agencies and endow them with roving commissions to solve problems or combat injustice. In adopting rules, conducting investigations, issuing licenses, or taking other actions, agencies must rely on specific statutory grants of authority. Actions beyond the scope of delegated authority are regarded as *ultra vires* ("beyond power") and are subject to invalidation by the courts.

At the same time, it is important to recognize that statutes often vest agencies with tremendous **discretion.** The fact that the legislature has authorized an agency to promulgate regulations in a certain area does not necessarily mean that the agency must do so. Moreover, as we saw in the previous chapter, statutes delegating **quasi-legislative power** to agencies often provide only the most general policy direction, allowing agencies to make policy within broad parameters. Sometimes legislatures simply require that regulations "serve the public interest," which allows agencies maximum policymaking discretion. In many instances statutes defining agency powers are ambiguous, which also allows agencies to exercise considerable discretion in interpreting their own statutory authority. In such situations, especially when the political or economic stakes are high, parties that are adversely affected by agency action will often ask the courts to render their own interpretations of the law.

THE STATUTORY AUTHORITY OF AGENCIES

In some instances, agencies derive their authority principally from a single statute. For example, the Food and Drug Administration is responsible for enforcing the Pure Food, Drugs and Cosmetics Act. More frequently, agencies are empowered by multiple statutes. The Environmental Protection Agency is an extreme example, in that it has rulemaking and/or enforcement authority under numerous statutes, including:

- National Environmental Policy Act (NEPA)
- Chemical Safety Information, Site Security, and Fuels Regulatory Relief Act
- Clean Air Act (CAA)
- Clean Water Act (CWA)
- Comprehensive Environmental Response, Compensation, & Liability Act (CERCLA)
- Emergency Planning & Community Right-To-Know Act (EPCRA)
- Endangered Species Act (ESA)
- Federal Insecticide, Fungicide, and Rodenticide Act (FIFRA)
- Federal Food, Drug, and Cosmetic Act (FFDCA)
- Food Quality Protection Act (FQPA)
- Occupational Safety and Health Act (OSHA)
- Oil Pollution Act (OPA)
- Pollution Prevention Act (PPA)
- Resource Conservation and Recovery Act (RCRA)
- Safe Drinking Water Act (SDWA)
- Superfund Amendments and Reauthorization Act (SARA)
- Toxic Substances Control Act (TSCA)

Frequently one statute confers responsibility and/or authority on multiple agencies. For example, consider the Americans with Disabilities Act (ADA) of 1990.[1] Title I of the ADA, which prohibits employment discrimination against persons with disabilities, is enforced primarily by the Equal Employment Opportunity Commission (EEOC), which is empowered to promulgate regulations under the statute.[2] Titles II and III of the ADA, which require reasonable accommodation of disabled persons by state and local agencies and places of public accommodation, respectively, are enforced by the Department of

Justice, which is likewise vested with regulatory authority.[3] Title II also requires reasonable accommodation by public transportation systems. To this end, regulatory power is vested in the Department of Transportation.[4] Title IV relates to access to electronic media.[5] The Federal Communications Commission has been given regulatory authority in this area.[6]

Other federal agencies having regulatory, administrative or enforcement responsibilities under the ADA include the Access Board, the Department of Agriculture, the Department of Education, the Department of the Interior, the Department of Labor, the Department of Housing and Urban Development, and the Department of Health and Human Services. Virtually all of the programs and facilities operated by the federal government are affected to some degree by the ADA.

Like many federal statutes, the ADA requires federal agencies to promulgate rules to effectuate the policy goals of the statute. Ultimately, these rules are incorporated into the **Code of Federal Regulations (CFR).** For example, one can find the rules that the Department of Transportation has adopted under the ADA in 49 CFR, Parts 37 and 38. The Department of Justice's rules implementing the ADA with respect to public accommodations and commercial facilities are found in 28 CFR Part 36. The EEOC's rules implementing ADA in the area of employment practices are found in 29 CFR Part 1630. And the FCC's rules effectuating the ADA with respect to telecommunications are located in 47 CFR Part 64.

INTERPRETATION
OF AGENCY POWERS

It is axiomatic that to be valid, an agency action must be authorized (explicitly or implicitly) by law. One of the principal problems of administrative law is that of determining when an agency is operating within its **jurisdiction** as defined by

statute. This is not always an easy task, as legislation is often ambiguous and sometimes internally contradictory (or in conflict with other laws).

Statutory ambiguity is sometimes the result of poorly drafted legislation. More frequently, though, it is the result of the politics of the legislative process. One needs to remember that the legislative process is highly political. Legislators, even within the same political party, will often disagree as to what policy objectives should be sought through legislation and what means should be employed to reach those objectives. Moreover, legislators are influenced by the myriad interest groups (and their lobbyists) that have a stake in a particular policy issue. Any bill that can muster a majority in both houses of the legislature will usually undergo significant changes along the way. Even if the original language of a bill was crystal clear, the need to build majority support for the bill within the legislature, or the need to engender the support of the president or governor (or at least avoid a veto) will often require the substitution of more ambiguous language. As Justice Rehnquist observed in 1981, "It is not unusual for the various factions supporting or opposing a proposal to accept some departure from the language they would prefer and to adopt substitute language agreeable to all."[7] That way, everyone who supports the bill can claim that the bill means what they prefer it to mean, even if that meaning was not intended by the sponsors of the bill or other legislators who voted for it. The need for political compromise usually trumps the desire for **statutory clarity.**

Agency Interpretation
of Their Own Powers

The agency to which power is delegated is the primary interpreter of its statutory authority. Decision makers within an agency are the first to decide what Congress or the state legislature meant when it enacted that statute. Because agencies have a vested interest in the programs they administer, every agency has its own legislative staff that includes policy specialists and staff attorneys. These actors often play key roles in developing proposed legislation. Once a bill is introduced into the legislature and is referred to committee, agency staff will often work closely with legislators and their staffs. Invariably, agencies are well acquainted with bills that affect them long before such bills become law and are typically in a strong position to defend their interpretations of the law.

An agency's interpretation of its statutory authority is often as much a political enterprise as it is a technical process of legal research and reasoning. Agency heads will usually have their own political agendas, which may or may not coincide with the policy preferences of the legislature or the chief executive. A broad delegation of power or a high level of statutory ambiguity will allow agencies more freedom of movement in interpreting the law in a way that comports with the agency's own political inclinations and policy objectives. Of course, when agencies act on the basis of broad or ambiguous grants of power, parties who are adversely affected by such actions will often resort to the courts in an attempt to have the agency's interpretation of its statutory powers judicially nullified. In some instances, parties will go to court to challenge an agency's refusal to promulgate regulations or take enforcement actions.[8] Federal law provides that "[a] person suffering legal wrong because of agency action, or adversely affected or aggrieved by agency action within the meaning of a relevant statute, is entitled to judicial review thereof."[9] Every state has a similar provision.

Two Case Studies in Statutory Interpretation

In Chapter 9, "Judicial Review of Agency Action," we examine in some depth judicial approaches to the interpretation of statutes empowering agencies. At this point it will suffice to briefly discuss two Supreme Court decisions that illustrate how statutes can be interpreted to expand or contract an agency's authority.

Bob Jones University v. United States Prior to 1975, Bob Jones University (BJU), a fundamentalist Christian college in South Carolina, refused to admit African-Americans as students. After 1975, African-Americans were admitted, but interracial dating and marriage among students were strictly prohibited. Like most other private colleges, BJU enjoyed tax-exempt status under 26 U.S.C.A. § 501(c)(3). The statute provided tax-exempt status for not-for-profit corporations "organized and operated exclusively for religious, charitable, scientific, testing for public safety, literary, or educational purposes, or to foster national or international amateur sports competition, . . . or for the prevention of cruelty to children or animals. . . ."[10]

In 1970 the Internal Revenue Service (IRS) determined, based on considerations of national policy, that private schools with racially discriminatory policies toward their students were not "charitable" institutions and therefore would no longer be eligible for tax-exempt status. Accordingly, in 1976 the IRS revoked BJU's federal tax exemption. Not surprisingly, BJU decided to challenge the IRS in federal court. Without question, the IRS's action was consistent with the thrust of national policy on racial discrimination, but was it consistent with the language of the relevant statute? A strict reading of § 501(c)(3) would suggest otherwise. Even granting the validity of the IRS's definition of the term "charitable," the statute granted tax exemption to "religious, charitable . . . *or* educational" organizations (emphasis added). Under a strict reading of the statute, an organization had to be "religious," "charitable," or "educational," but not necessarily all three. Lawyers for BJU pressed that argument in federal district court and prevailed—the court ruled that revocation of BJU's tax exemption exceeded the delegated powers of the IRS. The Fourth Circuit Court of Appeals in Richmond reversed, and BJU asked the Supreme Court to grant certiorari.

In *Bob Jones University v. United States*[11] the Supreme Court upheld the IRS's action. In his opinion for the Court, Chief Justice Warren E. Burger glossed over the question of **statutory interpretation,** stressing instead the "broad authority" that Congress has invested in the IRS. Burger noted that Congress, had it disagreed with the IRS's interpretation, could have rewritten the statute to make its intentions perfectly clear. During the thirteen years from the time that the IRS changed its policy to the time the Supreme Court decided the case, Congress did not act, suggesting that it acquiesced in the IRS's action. In his lone dissent, Justice William Rehnquist argued that this sort of policy change should emanate from Congress, not from the bureaucracy. In his view, the IRS had simply taken it upon itself to rewrite the law.

The Supreme Court's decision in *Bob Jones University v. United States* is excerpted at the end of the chapter.

Food and Drug Administration v. Brown and Williamson Tobacco Corporation As a dramatic example of judicial negation of agency authority, the Supreme Court's decision in *Food and Drug Administration v. Brown and Williamson Tobacco Corporation* (2000)[12] is the polar opposite of the *Bob Jones* decision. In *Brown and Williamson* the Court held that the Food and Drug Administration (FDA) had exceeded its statutory powers in attempting to regulate tobacco products. Relying on the Food, Drug, and Cosmetics Act (FDCA),[13] the FDA in 1996 promulgated regulations designed to limit young people's access to tobacco products. These regulations were immediately challenged by the tobacco industry.

Affirming a court of appeals decision, the Supreme Court held that the FDA did not have statutory authority to adopt the regulations at issue. Writing for the Court, Justice Sandra Day O'Connor acknowledged the serious public health problems posed by tobacco products, but concluded that Congress did not intend for the FDA to exercise authority over them. In dissent, Justices Breyer, Stevens, Souter, and Ginsburg argued that tobacco is a drug and that statutes enacted subsequent to the FDCA did not deprive the FDA of authority to regulate tobacco products.

Because the Court's decision was based solely on statutory interpretation, Congress may adopt legislation clearly authorizing the FDA to regulate tobacco products. Despite demands from antismoking and public health groups, Congress has yet to provide FDA with such authority. Others argue that Congress should face the essential policy question itself and not simply delegate new authority to the bureaucracy. As one observer has pointed out, "there's nothing scientifically complex about the question of whether to prohibit nicotine in cigarettes. Ultimately, it's a question for the people, through their elected representatives, to decide."[14]

The Supreme Court's decision in *FDA v. Brown and Williamson Tobacco Corp.* is excerpted at the end of the chapter.

THE ADMINISTRATIVE PROCEDURE ACT AND ITS STATE COUNTERPARTS

Aside from the legislation establishing agencies and enabling them to operate, the most important statute affecting administrative agencies is the **Administrative Procedure Act (APA).**[15] As we saw in Chapter 2, the New Deal created myriad federal agencies, but prior to the 1940s neither Congress nor the courts said much about agency procedures. Consequently, agency rulemaking and adjudicatory procedures varied widely. Enacted in 1946, the APA was designed to achieve a measure of uniformity in federal agencies' rulemaking and adjudicatory procedures. The act prescribes the basic requirements that agencies must follow in promulgating rules and adjudicating disputes. Of course, particular

Table 4.1 State Administrative Procedure Acts

Alabama: Ala. Code §§ 41-22-1 to 41-2-27	Nevada: Nev. Rev. Stat. 233B.010 to 233B.150
Alaska: Alaska Stat. §§ 24.20.400 to 24.20.460 and §§ 44.62.010 to 44.62.650	New Hampshire: N.H. Rev. Stat. Ann. §§ 541:1 to 541:22, 541-A:1 to 541-A:22
Arizona: Ariz. Rev. Stat. Ann. §§ 41-1001 to 41-1066	New Jersey: N.J. Stat. Ann. 52:14B-1 tp 52:14B-15
Arkansas: Ark. Code Ann. §§ 25-15-201 to 25-15-214	New Mexico: N.M. Stat. Ann. §§ 12-8-1 to 12-8-25
California: Cal. Govt. Code §§ 11340 to 11370.5 and §§ 11500 to 11528	New York: N.Y. A.P.A. §§ 101 to 501
Colorado: Colo. Rev. Stat. 224-4101 to 24-4-108	North Carolina: N.C. Gen. Stat. §§ 150B-1 to 150B-64
Connecticut: Conn. Gen. Stat. Ann. §§ 4-166 to 4-189	North Dakota: N.D. Cent. Code §§ 28-32-1 to 28-32-22
Delaware: Del. Code Ann. tit. 29, §§ 10101 to 10161	Ohio: Ohio Rev. Code §§ 119.01 to 119.13
District of Columbia: D.C. Code Ann. §§ 1-1501 to 1-1542	Oklahoma: Okl. St. Ann. tit. 75, §§ 250 to 323
Florida: Fla. Stat. §§ 120.50 to 120.81	Oregon: Or. Rev. Stat. §§ 183.025 to 183.725
Georgia: Ga. Code Ann. §§ 50-13-1 to 50-13-44	Pennsylvania: Pa. Stat. tit. 2 appendix §§ 101 to 754; tit. 45, §§ 1102 to 1208
Hawaii: Hawaii Rev. Stat. §§ 91-1 to 91-18	Rhode Island: R.I. Gen. Laws §§ 42-35-1 to 42-35-18
Idaho: Idaho Code §§ 67-5201 to 67-5292	South Carolina: S.C. Code §§ 1-23-10 to 1-23-400, 1-33-500 to 1-33-660
Illinois: S.H.A. 5 I.L.C.S. 100/1-1 to 100/15-10	South Dakota: S.D. Codified Laws §§ 1-26-1 to 1-26-41, 1-26A-1 to 1-26A-10, 1-26-B-1 to 1-26B-12, 1-26C-1 to 1-26C-25
Indiana: Ind. Code. Ann. §§ 4-22	
Iowa: Iowa Code Ann. §§ 17A.1 to 17A.33	Tennessee: Tenn. Code Ann. §§ 4-5-101 to 4-5-324
Kansas: Kan. Stat. Ann. §§ 77-501 to 77-550	Texas: Tex. Government Code Ann. §§ 2001.001 to 2001.902
Kentucky: Ky. Rev. Stat. §§ 13A.010 to 13A350	Utah: Utah Code Ann. 63-46a-1 to 63-46a-16, 63-46b-0.5 to 63-46b-22.
Louisiana: La. Rev. Stat. Ann. §§ 49:950 to 49:970	
Maine: Me. Rev. Stat. Ann. tit. 5, §§ 8001 to 11116	Vermont: Vt. Stat. Ann. tit. 3, §§ 801 to 849 [Title 3]
Maryland: Md. State Govt. Code §§ 10-101 to 10-905	Virginia: Va. Code §§ 9-6.14:1 to 9-6.14:25, 9-6.15 to 9-6.22
Massachusetts: Mass. Gen. Laws Ann. c. 30A, §§ 1 to 17	Washington: West's Rev. Code Wash. Ann. §§ 34.05.001 to 34.05.902
Michigan: Mich. Comp. Laws Ann. §§ 24.201 to 24.328	West Virginia: W. Va. Code §§ 29A-1-1 to 29A-7-4
Minnesota: Minn. Stat. Ann. §§ 14.01 to 14.69	Wisconsin: Wis. Stat. Ann. §§ 227.01 to 227.26
Mississippi: Miss. Code Ann. §§ 25-43-1 to 25-43-19	Wyoming: Wyo. Stat. §§ 16-3-101 to 16-3-115
Missouri: Mo. Ann. Stat. §§ 536.010 to 536.215	
Montana: Mont. Code Ann. §§ 2-4-101 to 2-4-711	
Nebraska: Neb. Rev. St. §§ 84-901 to 84-919	

agencies are required to follow additional or specialized procedures as provided by Congress.

Every state and the District of Columbia has its own counterpart to the APA. Many of these statutes are based, in varying degrees, on the Model State Administrative Procedure Act published in 1981 by the National Conference of Commissioners on Uniform State Laws. Table 4.1 lists the state administrative procedure acts and their statutory citations.

Rulemaking Distinguished from Adjudication

We discuss the APA in some depth as it relates to rulemaking in Chapter 6 and as it relates to adjudication in Chapter 7. But given the fundamental importance of rulemaking and adjudication in the administrative process, and the relevance of the APA to both of these core functions, we think it is useful at this juncture to

AGENCY FUNCTION ↓	STYLE OF PROCEDURE ↓	
	Informal	*Formal*
Rulemaking	Informal Rulemaking: Notice and Comment Procedure	Formal Rulemaking: Trial-Type Procedures
Adjudication	Informal Adjudication: No Set Procedure	Formal Adjudication: Trial-Type Procedures

FIGURE 4.1 A typology of agency decision-making procedures

provide an overview of these topics. At the outset we need to distinguish between rulemaking and adjudication.

The APA defines **rulemaking** as the agency process for formulating, amending, or repealing a rule."[16] The Model State Administrative Procedure Act, revised in 1981, defines rulemaking as "the process for formulation and adoption of a rule."[17] A "rule" is an agency statement issued to augment or interpret a law or to prescribe a policy or agency practice.

Rulemaking is an exercise of quasi-legislative power that formulates rules for the future. Rulemaking affects a category of parties, not an individual or single entity. **Adjudication**, on the other hand, is an exercise of **quasi-judicial power** and focuses on resolution of fact-specific disputes between an agency and one or more parties.[18] In other words, when an agency promulgates a rule, it is acting very much like a legislature. When it adjudicates a case, it is acting very much like a court of law.

Formality versus Informality in Administrative Decisions

Both adjudication and rulemaking can be formal or informal (see Figure 4.1). "Formal" procedures are more legalistic, that is, more elaborate and more standardized. The most formal administrative proceedings resemble a trial in court and are often referred to as **trial-type procedures.** Such proceedings afford interested parties an opportunity to testify, present witnesses and documentary evidence, cross-examine opposing witnesses, and present arguments.

Informal decisions are those that are least constrained by law. In other words, they are those in which officials have the most discretion. The overwhelming majority (probably 90 percent or more) of decisions made by agencies, whether adjudicatory or rulemaking, are of the informal variety. *The key to administrative law is to understand when the law requires formal procedures and what specific procedures are required.* The APA governs formal rulemaking and formal adjudication, as well as informal rulemaking. It does not impose procedural constraints on informal adjudication.

Informal Rulemaking

The federal Administrative Procedure Act and its state counterparts provide a template for informal rulemaking by agencies. The two essential requirements are 1) public notice of proposed rules and 2) the opportunity for interested parties to comment on proposed rules before they are adopted. 5 U.S.C.A. § 553(b). This informal approach, called **notice and comment rulemaking,** seeks to harmonize bureaucratic decision making with democratic values. One can argue that democracy is eroded to the extent that policy-making authority is vested in bureaucracies. Requiring bureaucracies to publicly announce their proposed rules and obtain public input prior to adopting such rules allows the public to know what its government is doing and provides at least minimal opportunities for public participation in policy making. Obviously, the mass public will not be much interested in most rules proposed by regulatory agencies. But particular segments of the public, i.e., interest groups, will often be highly interested. Notice and comment rulemaking is thus consistent with the theory of democratic pluralism under which all interest groups are entitled to compete on a level playing field. The late Kenneth Culp Davis, a great scholar of administrative law, claimed that informal notice-and-comment rulemaking is "one of the greatest inventions of modern government."[19]

The federal APA exempts an agency from following the notice and comment requirements in any rulemaking for which the agency finds "for good cause . . . that notice and public procedure thereon are impracticable, unnecessary, or contrary to the public interest." An agency invoking this exemption must incorporate both "the finding and a brief statement of reasons" for the finding in the rule.[20]

In recent years the trend has been for agencies to basically craft a rule before employing the notice and comment procedures, thus resulting in the public participation becoming more of a record-making device to document the rule should the courts review it.

Formal Rulemaking

Most federal administrative agencies develop their rules through the informal process described in the preceding topic. **Formal rulemaking** involves many of the procedural safeguards associated with a nonjury civil trial; however, federal agencies are required to proceed by formal rulemaking only when a Congressional statute requires that rulemaking proceed by an agency hearing that follows a trial-type format. This is referred to as "on the record" rulemaking. Formal rulemaking "on the record" is mandatory only when a statute so explicitly provides, a subject we discuss in Chapter 6.

Formal Adjudication

Formal adjudication (sometimes referred to as an evidentiary hearing) is designed to resolve factual disputes between individual and corporate parties and an administrative agency. A federal administrative agency is required to proceed with formal adjudication only when a Congressional statute so directs. Formal adjudications bear the trappings of a nonjury trial in a civil court and provide for adequate notice to interested parties, introduction of evidence, cross-examination of witnesses, and oral and written presentations. An agency head can conduct these adjudications, but typically they are conducted before an **administrative law judge** (ALJ), an impartial hearing officer with special training in administrative law.

Alternative Dispute Resolution In recent years there has been a movement away from formal adjudication and toward **alternative dispute resolution** (ADR). ADR includes a number of informal methods of settling disputes between agencies and outside parties, including negotiated settlements, mediation, and arbitration. ADR provides substantial benefits to agencies and outside parties in that it allows for disputes to be settled in a way that is usually less costly and less time-consuming. As federal agencies moved to embrace ADR in the 1980s, some observers raised questions about the legality of such procedures in light of the fact that the Administrative Procedure Act did not explicitly authorize them. In 1996 Congress amended the APA to allow federal agencies to utilize ADR in lieu of formal adjudication.[21] Many state legislatures have followed suit. For further discussion of ADR, see Chapter 7.

Informal Adjudication

Adjudication is an agency's determination of a person's legal rights in regard to a specific subject within an agency's jurisdiction. Everyday examples include an agency's decision to issue or revoke an occupational or professional license, to issue or decline to issue a building permit. Less frequent examples would be an agency's determination to issue or revoke a license for a radio or television station, approve a land development of regional impact, or to grant a pharmaceutical company approval to market a new drug.

The APA is specific as to the requirements for formal (trial-type) adjudication. This is also true of most state administrative procedure acts. Determinations in many of the less frequent examples cited above will be made in formal adjudication. But the vast majority of administrative adjudications, including those everyday examples listed above, at the federal and state levels are adjudicated on an informal basis. The APA provides no procedural framework for informal adjudication. In some instances a statute will specify requirements for adjudication of a particular class of disputes within a given agency's jurisdiction. Such statutes must comport with federal and state due process standards and must be observed by the agency. Absent such statutory requirements an adjudication that affects one's life, liberty, or property is subject to the requirements of the Due Process Clause of the U.S. Constitution and the extent of procedural requirements must be gleaned from judicial decisions. Much of the material in the later chapters addresses the procedural safeguards that the courts have mandated in various adjudicatory situations. As we noted above, the federal Administrative Procedure Act and its state counterparts provide no procedural framework for informal adjudication.

STATUTORY REQUIREMENTS PROMOTING OPENNESS IN PUBLIC ADMINISTRATION

Critics of the administrative state have long argued that bureaucratic secrecy threatens democratic values. Political scientists who study interest groups have long been aware of the tendency for particular interests to "capture" the agencies that are set up to regulate them. Moreover, the ever-increasing span of bureaucratic control has led to demands by the public that government actions be conducted openly and that records of such activities be made available to the citizenry on demand. These demands have been supported, indeed often initiated by the news media. Such concerns have led Congress and the state legislatures to enact laws designed to open up the administrative process—to "let the sun shine in." In the realm of governmental decision making, sunshine is thought to be the best disinfectant. Of course, there must be exceptions to this principle in order to protect personal privacy, ensure national security, and foster effective law enforcement.

The Freedom of Information Act

Adopted by Congress in 1966, the **Freedom of Information Act (FOIA)**[22] provides a right of access to federal agency records. Commenting on the scope of the statute in 1973, the Supreme Court observed:

> Without question, the Act is broadly conceived. It seeks to permit access to official information long shielded unnecessarily from public view and attempts to create a judicially enforceable public right to secure

---

BOX 4.1 E-FOIA and Electronic Reading Rooms

On October 2, 1996, President Clinton signed into law the Electronic Freedom of Information Act Amendments of 1996. E-FOIA, as it is often called, is codified at 5 U.S.C.A. § 552. A significant step in the emergence of electronic government, E-FOIA requires federal agencies to use the Internet to create "electronic reading rooms." Agencies are now required to make available through the Internet any records disclosed in response to an

FOIA request that "the agency determines have become or are likely to become the subject of subsequent requests for substantially the same records."

A good example of an electronic reading room can be easily located on the web site maintained by the U.S. Department of State, online at http://foia.state.gov/default.asp.

---

such information from possibly unwilling official hands.[23]

FOIA requires all federal agencies within the executive branch to disclose records upon receiving a written request, except for those records that are protected by nine "exemptions" and three "exclusions" provided in the statute. The Supreme Court has observed that "these limited exemptions do not obscure the basic policy that disclosure, not secrecy, is the dominant objective of the Act."[24] Frequently courts will be asked to determine the scope and applicability of FOIA exemptions and exclusions, as parties seeking agency records may go to court to challenge agency refusals to comply with FOIA requests.

FOIA establishes a presumption that records in the possession of agencies and executive departments of the U.S. Government are accessible to the people. The statute sets standards for determining which records must be disclosed and which records can be withheld. The law provides administrative and judicial remedies for those denied access to records. Above all, the statute requires federal agencies to provide the fullest possible **disclosure of information** to the public. Together with the **Privacy Act** (discussed below), FOIA restricts the **improper disclosure of personal information** and provides for civil remedies where an individual's rights have been violated.

The Freedom of Information Act applies to documents held by agencies in the executive branch of the Federal Government, including the cabinet-level departments, military departments, government corporations, independent regulatory agencies, law enforcement agencies, and other establishments in the executive branch. FOIA does not apply to elected officials of the federal government, including the president, vice president, and members of Congress. It does not apply to the federal courts. Nor does it apply to private companies or persons who receive federal contracts or grants. FOIA does not apply to state or local governments, but all states and some localities have passed **open records laws,** which like the FOIA and Privacy Act, permit individuals access to records.

FOIA provides that a party making a request must ask for existing records rather than information. The law requires that each request must reasonably describe the records being sought. A request must be specific enough to permit the agency to locate the record in a reasonable period of time. Once an FOIA request is filed, an agency is required to determine within ten days (excluding Saturdays, Sundays, and legal holidays) whether to comply. The actual disclosure of documents is required to follow promptly thereafter. FOIA permits an agency to extend the time limits up to ten days in unusual circumstances. If a request is denied, the agency must

---

BOX 4.2   Making an FOIA Request from the Social Security Administration

The Social Security Administration provides a very complete web page dealing with FOIA issues (http://www.ssa.gov/foia/foia_guide.htm). Among other things, the page provides the following information on how to file an FOIA request with the agency:

Making an FOIA Request
If you want to request a record which we don't publish or which we don't make available in one of our offices, give us a detailed description of the record(s) you want. You should give us as many details, such as names, dates, subject matter and location, if you know them. If you don't give us a good description, we may not be able to find the records you want, or it may take us longer. We will ask you to revise your request if we need more information to find the record(s).

It is easy to make a written FOIA request by mail. No form is needed. We process FOIA requests in two locations, depending on the type of request. Mark both the envelope and its contents: "FREEDOM OF INFORMATION REQUEST" or "INFORMATION REQUEST." Be sure to include your name and address on your request. It is a good idea to include a daytime phone number or e-mail address in case we need to contact you about your request. Do not include a return envelope.

Send FOIA requests to:
Social Security Administration
Office of Public Disclosure
3-A-6 Operations Building
6401 Security Boulevard
Baltimore, Maryland, 21235

---

provide reasons for the denial. FOIA contains a number of exemptions designed to protect against the disclosure of information that would jeopardize national security, privacy of individuals, proprietary interests of business, and the functioning of the government. For example, classified documents are exempt, as are records relating to internal personnel matters, internal government communications, and confidential business information. In denying a request, the agency must also indicate whether there is a mechanism internal to the agency to appeal a denial. Of course, the ultimate review lies with the federal courts. Often it is a federal court that must decide whether an agency has properly invoked one of the exemptions in denying an FOIA request. (See Box 4.2 for a description of how to make an FOIA request from the Social Security Administration.)

In 2001 some public interest groups sued Department of Justice (DOJ) under the FOIA, seeking information regarding persons the Government detained in wake of the terrorist attacks of 9/11. A federal district court ordered the release of certain information concerning those persons who were detained. The Government appealed and the U.S. Court of Appeals for the D.C. Circuit reversed the district court's decision and held that the Government could withhold such information pursuant to FOIA Exemption 7(A), which exempts "records or information compiled for law enforcement purposes . . . to the extent that the production" of them "could reasonably be expected to interfere with enforcement proceedings."[25]

FOIA also contains three "exclusions," which allow an agency to treat certain exempt records as if the records were not subject to the FOIA. An agency is not required even to confirm the existence of these types of records. The first exclusion applies to information that is exempt because disclosure might reasonably be expected to interfere with an ongoing law enforcement investigation. The second pertains to informant records maintained by a law enforcement agency under the informant's name or personal identifier. The third exclusion applies only to records maintained by the Federal Bureau of Investigation that deal with foreign intelligence, counter-intelligence, or terrorism. If such records are requested, the agency may respond that there are no disclosable records responsive to the request. However, these exclusions do not broaden the authority of any agency to withhold documents from the public. The exclusions are applicable only to information that is otherwise exempt from disclosure.

FOIA requires that federal administrative agencies publish in the *Federal Register* information concerning agency organization, functions, procedures, and policies.[26] Publication is not required as to matters that relate to internal rules, adjudicative opinions or to rules that are merely instructive. Matters not published may not bind or adversely affect a party unless that party has actual notice.[27] Courts, however, have held that FOIA and the *Federal Register* Act are "intended to protect persons who have no actual notice from being adversely affected."[28]

State Open Records Acts

Every state has its own version of the Freedom of Information Act. Collectively, these statutes are referred to as open records laws. State open records laws vary somewhat in their scope, and often require judicial interpretation. Because the California Public Records Act is modeled after the Freedom of Information Act, California courts look to the federal courts for interpretive guidance.[29] To determine the applicability of a state open records law a court must carefully scrutinize the wording of the particular state statute. Two statutory elements usually come into play: first, whether the entity from which records are sought is a "public agency," and second, whether the records being sought are "public records."

After the National Collegiate Athletic Association (NCAA) and the Southwest Athletic Conference (SWC) refused requests of several media organizations for information regarding possible violations of NCAA regulations, some media organizations brought suit under the Texas Open Records Act contending that NCAA and SWC were "governmental bodies" under the act and that the information requested was "public information." At the time, the Texas act defined a governmental body as one "which is supported in whole or in part by public funds, or which expends public funds."[30] The law defined "public information" as "all information collected, assembled or maintained by governmental bodies pursuant to law or ordinance or in connection with the transaction of official business. . . ."[31] In 1988, in *Kneeland v. NCAA*,[32] the U.S. Court of Appeals for the Fifth Circuit concluded that although the associations received some public funds, the receipt of those revenues did not constitute "support" as required by the act to qualify NCAA and SWC as governmental bodies. Thus, the court held the associations were not subject to the disclosure requirements of the Texas Open Records Act.

The Kentucky Open Records Act defines "public agency" as "[a]ny body which derives at least twenty-five percent (25%) of its funds expended by it in the Commonwealth of Kentucky from state or local authority funds."[33] The act provides that "[a]ll public records shall be opened for inspection by any person, except as otherwise provided . . . and suitable facilities shall be made available by each public agency for the exercise of this right." The term "public record" includes books, papers, maps, photographs, cards, tapes, discs, diskettes, recordings, software, or other documents prepared, owned, used, in the possession of or otherwise retained by a public agency.[34] However, not all records held by public agencies qualify as "public records." For example, where a hospital admitted it was a public agency under Kentucky law, a Kentucky appellate court denied public access to patient records retained by a public hospital, noting that "the medical records of those patients in a public hospital are not related to the functioning of the hospital, the activities carried on by the hospital, its programs, or its operations."[35]

Eco, Incorporated v. City of Elkhorn, **a Wisconsin appellate court decision involving the Wisconsin open records law, is excerpted at the end of the chapter.**

Open Meetings Laws

Congress and all fifty state legislatures have enacted laws requiring agencies to hold certain meetings in public. These **sunshine laws,** as they are generally known, do not necessarily allow members of the public or media to speak at such meetings, but they do allow attendance. The federal open meetings law applies only to multimember commissions and advisory committees. State laws vary, applying to a variety of state and local commissions, boards, and councils. Open meetings laws require affected agencies to provide advance public notice of meetings and in most instances to publish the agendas for such meetings. Moreover, these laws require that minutes be kept and that those minutes become accessible public records. There are numerous exceptions to the open meetings laws. Most laws exempt meetings on personnel matters, collective bargaining negotiations, meetings with counsel to discuss litigation, and discussions of the sale or acquisition of property. Like FOIA, open meetings laws are enforceable judicially.

The federal Government in the Sunshine Act[36] (informally called the Sunshine Act) requires federal agencies headed by a collegial body composed of two or more members to hold their meetings in public. There are numerous exceptions to this requirement, however. The Sunshine Act does not require agencies, for example, to hold public meetings that would reveal matters that must be kept secret for reasons of national security or those that relate solely to the internal agency personnel rules and practices. The act also exempts the disclosure of ongoing law enforcement investigations, personal information that would be an unwarranted invasion of personal privacy, as well as disclosures that would lead to speculation in currencies, securities, or commodities. The federal Sunshine Act is in fact fairly narrow in its requirements of open meetings.[37] For example, in *FCC v. ITT World Commuications* (1984),[38] the Supreme Court held that the Sunshine Act does not apply to informal, consultative meetings of members of the Federal Communications Commission, but only to those meetings where a quorum of commissioners is present.

State sunshine laws are often much broader. Florida has one of the strictest sunshine laws and violations are punishable by fine.[39] Florida appellate courts have said the law must be broadly construed to effectuate its remedial and protective purpose. That purpose, one court opined, is to prevent crystallization of secret governmental decisions at nonpublic meeting to the point just short of ceremonial acceptance.[40] The Florida Sunshine Law stipulates that all meetings of any board or commission of any state, county, political subdivision, or municipality at which official acts are to be taken, are to be public meetings open to the public at all times, except as otherwise provided in the state constitution. Minutes of all such meetings must be recorded and made available for public inspection. The law does permit agencies to meet in private to discuss pending litigation, but a record must be made of such discussions and it must be made available after the litigation has been concluded. The law has been held to apply only to a meeting of two or more public officials at which decision making, as opposed to fact finding or information gathering, will occur. At the point where decisions are being made, such discussions must be conducted in public meetings after notice to the public. In an early opinion construing the law, a Florida appellate court held that a junior college president was neither a "board" or "commission" nor an alter ego of the college board of trustees. Accordingly, the court held he was outside the ambit of the Sunshine Law and was not required to open his meetings with representatives of career employees of the college.[41]

Federal Advisory Committee Act

In an attempt to make federal advisory committees accountable to the public, Congress enacted the Federal Advisory Committee Act (FACA)[42] in 1972. The act applies to any committee not wholly composed of federal employees established by statute, or established or utilized by the executive branch, for the purpose of providing advice to the president or to one or more agencies or officers of the federal government.

An advisory committee is subject to the FACA only where it renders advice to the president, the Congress, or an executive branch agency, including any independent regulatory agency. An advisory committee subject to FACA must give notice of committee meetings (at least fifteen days in advance) by publication of its agenda in the *Federal Register*. Advisory committee meetings must be open to the public, unless the president or the head of the agency to which the advisory committee reports determines that the meeting may be closed in accordance with the exemptions listed in the Sunshine Act. Records, reports, transcripts, minutes, agendas, working papers, drafts, or other documents made available to or prepared by an advisory committee shall be made available to the public, except to the extent that the material is protected from disclosure under one or more applicable FOIA exemptions. Although the FACA does not specify remedies for violations, courts have granted injunctive and declaratory relief in instances of violations.

Critics argue that the burdensome requirements of the act have proved to be an incentive to avoid establishing advisory committees. In practice the FACA has not resulted in the laudable objectives that led it its passage. Many committees offering advice to the Congress or the executive branch of the federal government have not been found to be within the scope of the FACA. In *Public Citizen v. U.S. Dept. of Justice* (1989),[43] the U.S. Supreme Court held the act did not apply to the Justice Department's solicitation of views of the American Bar Association's Standing Committee on the Federal Judiciary, which renders advice on prospective judicial nominees. The Court found the committee was not an "advisory committee" within meaning of act, as it was not "utilized" within meaning of statute by president or the Department of Justice in connection with those evaluations of judicial nominees.

In 1993, in *Association of American Physicians and Surgeons, Inc. v. Clinton*,[44] the U.S. Court of Appeals for the D.C. Circuit treated the president's wife, Hillary Rodham Clinton, as a de facto officer or employee. As head of the President's Task Force on National Health Care Reform, the court held she was a "full-time officer or employee of the Federal Government" within meaning of provision of FACA provision exempting any committee which is composed wholly of full-time officers or employees of federal government.

STATUTORY PROTECTIONS FOR INDIVIDUAL PRIVACY

Critics of bureaucracy have for many years expressed concern about the tremendous volume of information that agencies collect about individuals. They believe that personal privacy is threatened by the collection and disclosure of information about individuals' educational achievements, financial status, and physical and mental health. Such concerns have prompted Congress and the state legislatures to enact statutes to protect the confidentiality of personal information obtained by government.

The Federal Privacy Act of 1974

The federal Privacy Act of 1974[45] requires that personal information files held by federal agencies are limited to those that are clearly necessary. It prohibits secret record-keeping systems. The law says that individuals must be afforded the opportunity to see what information about them is kept and to challenge its accuracy. It further provides that personal information collected for one purpose will not be used for another purpose without the consent of the affected person. Moreover, the law requires that if agencies make disclosures of personal information, they will inform the affected person as to whom the disclosure was made, for what purpose and on what date. The Privacy Act was amended in 1976 to require that social security numbers be kept confidential by the government agencies that collect them.[46]

State Laws Protecting Privacy

A number of states have adopted amendments to their constitutions to afford privacy protections to individuals. Other states have adopted statutes providing specific rights of privacy, often paralleling the federal protections by limiting government record-keeping about individuals. A good example of this is the Minnesota Data Privacy Act,[47] which classifies state government data on individuals into three categories: confidential, private, and public. Confidential data is that which is inaccessible to the public and to the individual who is the subject of the data. Private data is that which is inaccessible to the public but is accessible to the individual subject. Public data is that which is accessible to everyone and indeed must be provided to a requesting party under the applicable state open records law.

Minnesota Medical Association v. Minnesota Department of Public Welfare, **a Minnesota Supreme Court decision interpreting the Minnesota Data Privacy Act, is excerpted at the end of the chapter.**

The Family Educational Privacy Act
(Buckley Amendment)

The **Family Educational Rights Privacy Act** (FERPA),[48] better known as the **Buckley Amendment,** protects the privacy of students' educational records. The law applies to all state and local educational institutions that receive federal funds and provides that federal funds are to be withheld from school districts that have a policy or practice of permitting the release of education records without the students' written consent, or parental consent of minor students. FERPA defines educational records as "records, files, documents, and other materials" containing information directly related to a student, which "are maintained by an educational agency or institution or by a person acting for such agency or institution."[49] Lower federal courts disagreed on whether a violation of FERPA provides a private person a cause of action enforceable under 42 U.S.C.A. § 1983. (See the discussion in Chapter 11 of Section 1983, which creates a cause of action for intentional torts committed under cover of authority of law that deprives a person of rights protected by federal laws.) However, in *Gonzaga Univ. v. Doe,* (2002),[50] the Supreme Court held that FERPA does not provide private parties with a cause of action enforceable under § 1983.

Despite the broad statutory definition, questions have arisen as to whether specified records are "education records" within the statutory definition. For example, in 1997 a state appellate court in Ohio held that records sought by a student newspaper of proceedings before the university's disciplinary board did not contain "educationally related information such as grades or other academic data." Accordingly, the university was required to release the records under the Ohio Open Records Law by disclosing the general location of the incident, the age and sex of the student (which does not identify the student), the nature of the offense, and the type of disciplinary penalty imposed.[51] In 2002, where researchers sought disclosure of state university records pertaining to students and applicants, the Wisconsin Supreme Court held that the researchers were not requesting personally identifiable information that FERPA prohibited from disclosure and that the university must redact any information not subject to disclosure before releasing the records.[52]

The Arkansas Supreme Court held that records maintained by the Arkansas Intercollegiate Athletic Conference concerning sums paid by state universities to student athletes each year were not "educational records" required to be closed to the public under Family Educational Rights Privacy Act of 1974. Therefore, the conference was required to release those records because the sums paid were at least partially supported by public funds. The court observed that under the state's Freedom of Information Act "the public's fundamental right of access to public records is the general rule and secrecy is the exception."[53]

In *Owasso Independent School District v. Falvo* (2002), the U.S. Supreme Court ruled that peer-graded classroom work and assignments are not covered as educational records under FERPA (see the Supreme Court Perspective located in Box 4.3).

Right to Financial Privacy Act

In today's "information society" government agencies maintain enormous quantities of information about each of us. Much of this information is derived from our financial records, and increasingly Americans have indicated a strong interest in maintaining their privacy in such records. In 1976 the U.S. Supreme Court ruled that bank customers had no legal right to privacy in financial information held by financial institutions because these are the business records of the banks.[54] In order to ameliorate the effect of that decision, Congress enacted the Right to Financial Privacy Act (RFPA).[55] The act defines "financial institution" broadly and states that no government authority may have access to or obtain copies of, or the information contained in the financial records of any customer from a financial institution unless the financial records are reasonably described and the customer authorizes access or there is an appropriate administrative subpoena or summons; a search warrant, or subpoena or other appropriate written request from an authorized government authority.

RFPA provides exemptions that allow disclosure to a federal agency of information not specifically related to an individual or in regard to a financial institution's interest concerning its loans and loan guarantees, and where federal agencies are conducting supervisory investigations of institutions. In addition the IRS, which has its own statutory privacy protections, may obtain information from a bank about a customer without a summons or notice. Disclosures may be made pursuant to other federal statutes and, of course, in civil litigation information may be disclosed pursuant to Federal Rules of Civil Procedure. Finally, the federal government can obtain information if the institution's customer is suspected of terrorist action. The act requires the federal government to give an institution's customer notice when it is seeking disclosure in order to afford a person an opportunity to challenge such request. Further details of the RFPA are available on the Internet at http://www.epic.org/privacy/rfpa/.

Privacy of Medical Records

Along with financial records, medical records are an essential element of a person's individual privacy, but historically the law has not recognized a person's right to privacy in such records. In *Whalen v. Roe* (1977)[56] the U.S. Supreme Court recognized that disclosures of private medical information to doctors, hospital personnel, insurance companies, and to public health agencies are often an essential part of modern medical practice even when the disclosure may reflect unfavorably on the character of the patient. In recent years Congress has recognized this strong desire for privacy in medical records and when it enacted the Health Insurance Portability and Accountability Act of 1996 (HIPAA),[57] it mandated that the Department of Health and Human Services (HHS) develop privacy standards to protect patients' medical records and other health information furnished to physicians, hospitals, and other health-care providers. HHS subsequently promulgated a

---

BOX 4.3 Supreme Court Perspective

Owasso Independent School District v. Falvo
534 U.S. 426 (2002)

[Kristja J. Falvo's children were enrolled in a public school in a suburb of Tulsa, Oklahoma. She claimed that having students to score each other's tests and assignments embarrassed her children and violated the Family Educational Rights and Privacy Act (FERPA). When the school declined her request to ban peer grading she brought a class action against the school district and school officials. A federal district court ruled in her favor; the U.S. Court of Appeals for the Tenth Circuit reversed, reasoning that if Congress forbids teachers to disclose students' grades once written in a grade book, it makes no sense to permit the disclosure immediately beforehand. The Supreme Court granted certiorari to determine whether peer grading violates FERPA.]

Justice Kennedy delivered the opinion of the Court, stating in part:

The Court of Appeals' logic does not withstand scrutiny. Its interpretation, furthermore, would effect a drastic alteration of the existing allocation of responsibilities between States and the National Government in the operation of the Nation's schools. We would hesitate before interpreting the statute to effect such a substantial change in the balance of federalism unless that is the manifest purpose of the legislation. This principle guides our decision.

Two statutory indicators tell us that the Court of Appeals erred in concluding that an assignment satisfies the definition of education records as soon as it is graded by another student. First, the student papers are not, at that stage, "maintained" within the meaning of § 1232g(a)(4)(A). The ordinary meaning of the word "maintain" is "to keep in existence or continuance; preserve; retain." . . . Even assuming the teacher's grade book is an education record—a point the parties contest and one we do not decide here—the score on a student-graded assignment is not "contained therein," . . .

until the teacher records it. The teacher does not maintain the grade while students correct their peers' assignments or call out their own marks. Nor do the student graders maintain the grades within the meaning of § 1232g(a)(4)(A). The word "maintain" suggests FERPA records will be kept in a filing cabinet in a records room at the school or on a permanent secure database, perhaps even after the student is no longer enrolled. The student graders only handle assignments for a few moments as the teacher calls out the answers. It is fanciful to say they maintain the papers in the same way the registrar maintains a student's folder in a permanent file.

The Court of Appeals was further mistaken in concluding that each student grader is "a person acting for" an educational institution for purposes of § 1232g(a)(4)(A). . . . The phrase "acting for" connotes agents of the school, such as teachers, administrators, and other school employees. Just as it does not accord with our usual understanding to say students are "acting for" an educational institution when they follow their teacher's direction to take a quiz, it is equally awkward to say students are "acting for" an educational institution when they follow their teacher's direction to score it. . . . We do not think FERPA prohibits these educational techniques. We also must not lose sight of the fact that the phrase "by a person acting for [an educational] institution" modifies "maintain." Even if one were to agree students are acting for the teacher when they correct the assignment, that is different from saying they are acting for the educational institution in maintaining it.

We doubt Congress meant to intervene in this drastic fashion with traditional state functions. Under the Court of Appeals' interpretation of FERPA, the federal power would exercise minute control over specific teaching methods and instructional dynamics in classrooms throughout the country. The Congress is not likely to have mandated this result, and we do not interpret the statute to require it.

Privacy Protection Rule that represents the first comprehensive federal protection for the privacy of patients' medical records and other individually identifiable information. The new rule covers such medical information, whether communicated electronically, on paper, or orally, that is used or disclosed by entities subject to the rule. It grants patients access to their records and requires that they consent before release or disclosure of protected information. For example, patients have to grant authorization before an entity subject to the rule can release a patient's medical records to a bank or life insurance company. Affected entities were required to comply with the new rule by April 14, 2003. Those who violate the rule are subject to civil and criminal penalties.[58] HHS has announced that the new federal privacy standards simply set a national "floor" to protect persons and that any state law providing additional protections would continue to apply.[59]

The National Do-Not-Call Registry

In 2003 concern over intrusion into privacy by unwanted telemarketing phone calls prompted response by two federal agencies. The Federal Communications Commission (FCC), under authority of the Telephone Consumer Protection Act (TCPA), and the Federal Trade Commission (FTC) under authority of the Telemarketing and Consumer Fraud and Abuse Prevention of 1994, promulgated rules that together created the national do-not-call registry. The registry permits consumers to register their phone numbers on a list that prohibits telemarketers from making unwanted telephone calls.[60] The rules, which became effective October 1, 2003, are nationwide in scope and prohibit telemarketers from calling persons who have registered their phone numbers indicating they do not wish to have unsolicited telephone calls. Tax-exempt nonprofit organizations, political fund raising, and calls from those with which a person has an established business relationship are exempt from the prohibitions. Violation is subject to civil penalties of up to $11,000 per violation. In addition, violators may be subject to nationwide injunctions that prohibit certain conduct, and may be required to pay redress to injured consumers. The FTC, the states, and private citizens may bring civil actions in federal district courts to enforce the rule.

Some initial lower court decisions held that the regulations were beyond the statutory authority of the agencies and that the prohibition on telemarketers violated First Amendment rights on commercial free speech. But on February 17, 2004, the U.S. Court of Appeals for the Tenth Circuit upheld the do-not-call registry, noting that it is designed to reduce intrusions into personal privacy and to reduce the risk of telemarketing fraud and abuse that can accompany unwanted telephone solicitation. The court also ruled that the statutory interpretations under which the agencies acted were entitled to deference under the test the Supreme Court outlined in *Chevron, U.S.A., Inc. v. Natural Resources Defense Council* (1984).[61] The court concluded that the statutory authority to promulgate do-not-call regulations is at least a permissible construction of the federal statutes.[62] (The *Chevron* decision recognizes that agencies must be allowed to interpret complex statutes regulating their particular area of expertise without judicial second-guessing. We discuss this doctrine of deference to agency rulings more extensively in Chapter 9).

OTHER KEY STATUTES AFFECTING THE ADMINISTRATIVE PROCESS

Since the beginnings of the administrative state, critics have complained about the burdens of regulation. Early on, the principal opponents of regulation were the corporations and those who represented their interests. Later, as big business adjusted to the regulatory state and, in many instances, learned to benefit from it, corporate America became less vocal in its opposition to regulation. Since the 1970s, some of the most strident criticism of the regulatory state has come from small business, which is often less able to cope with the burdens of regulation. In particular, small business has struggled with environmental regulations and with rules governing labor practices and health and safety in the workplace. Small business owners have been especially vocal in complaining about the time and energy that must be devoted to filling out forms and reports that must be filed with various local, state, and federal agencies. In the 1990s, cities joined the chorus of criticism of the bureaucracy in opposing **unfunded mandates**—regulations that often cost municipalities millions of dollars to comply with. Congress has responded to these concerns by enacting laws that attempt to mitigate the impact of regulation. These include the **Paperwork Reduction Act,** the **Regulatory Flexibility Act,** and the **Unfunded Mandates Reform Act.**

The Paperwork Reduction Act

Throughout the modern era, citizens and companies have expressed concern about bureaucratic "red tape." In the 1970s, a rising tide of criticism led Congress to establish a commission to investigate the problem of excessive paperwork. The commission's report prompted Congress to enact legislation. First enacted in 1980, strengthened in 1995, and amended in 2000 and 2002, the Paperwork Reduction Act (PRA)[63] has as its goal the reduction of information collection burdens imposed on the public.

The PRA of 1980 created the **Office of Information and Regulatory Affairs (OIRA)** within the **Office of Management and Budget (OMB).** As we noted in Chap-ter 2, OMB is a critically important agency within the Executive Office of the President, the primary mission of which is to develop the budget proposal that the president submits to Congress each fiscal year. OIRA is charged with meeting annual paperwork reduction goals, reviewing every federal agency's information management activities, and improving federal information management generally. Before any agency conducts a survey, requires a client to complete a questionnaire, or imposes a record-keeping requirement on a regulated entity, it must obtain OMB approval. Under the statute, OMB must determine "whether the collection of information by an agency is necessary for the proper performance of the functions of the agency."[64] Before making a determination OMB may give the agency and other interested persons an opportunity to be heard or to submit statements in writing. To the extent, if any, that OMB determines that the collection of information by an agency is unnecessary for any reason, the agency may not engage in the collection of information.[65] OMB relies on OIRA in making this determination.

Although the ostensible purpose of OIRA review under the PRA is nonpolitical, critics have sometimes accused OIRA of using the PRA to frustrate certain federal agencies' efforts to achieve their statutory mandates. During the 1980s and early 1990s, critics charged that the Reagan and Bush Administrations were using OIRA to curtail regulatory initiatives. Under the Clinton administration the interactions between OIRA and other federal agencies were less confrontational. Throughout the 1980s and 1990s, regardless of the philosophy of the administration in power, the paperwork burden on the American economy continued to increase as Congress enacted new legislation calling for additional information collection by federal agencies. In FY 2001, citizens and companies spent more than 7.5 billion hours in complying with federal paperwork requirements. Not surprisingly, the agency most responsible for generating this paperwork is the Internal Revenue Service.[66]

The Regulatory Flexibility Act

During the 1970s small businesses complained vociferously about the economic impact of regulation. This led Congress to enact the Regulatory Flexibility Act of 1980.[67] The RFA applies to any rule required to be issued after notice and comment under the Administrative Procedure Act, § 553(b). On August 13, 2002, President Bush issued Executive Order 13272, which requires that agencies establish procedures and policies to promote compliance with the RFA. Under the statute, agencies proposing rules that would have a significant economic impact on small business are required to conduct a **regulatory flexibility analysis** (RFA) and submit the results of this analysis to the Small Business Administration (SBA). The purpose of the requirement is to ensure that agencies consider ways to minimize the burden that new regulations impose on small business. SBA does not have the authority to reject the analysis or the proposed rule that accompanies it; its only role is one of monitoring compliance with the requirement to conduct the analysis. For a deeper discussion of how the statute affects the agency rulemaking process, see Chapter 6.

The Unfunded Mandates Reform Act

During the 1980s and 1990s, state and local officials complained about the proliferation of federal regulations that mandated expenditures by state and local governments without providing federal funding. These unfunded mandates take the form of the federal government requiring state and local governments to pay for federally mandated benefits and regulatory activities. Former Congressman and Delaware Governor Pete duPont, remarked that "Unfunded mandates undermine political accountability, by placing the selection of policies in Washington and the execution of them in state capitals."[68] Fulfilling part of the "Contract with America," the Republican-controlled Congress in 1995 enacted the Unfunded Mandates Reform Act (UMRA).[69] The act prohibits Congress from considering legislation containing new unfunded mandates without a cost statement produced by the Congressional Budget Office. It also requires federal agencies to conduct a cost-benefit analysis before adopting new rules that mandate expenditures by state and local governments.

CONCLUSION

Subject to constitutional limitations, federal and state statutes empower administrative agencies to perform their functions. Although an agency's authority and mission are spelled out in one or more enabling statutes, agencies often must interpret ambiguities in these statutes. Of course, agency interpretations of statutory authority are subject to judicial interpretations. Several other statutes govern the bureaucracy generally. This statutory framework includes the federal Administrative Procedure Act and its state counterparts, which are of overarching importance in respect to procedural regularity in rulemaking and formal adjudication. In informal adjudication where agencies adjudications affect a person's life, liberty, or property, agencies must abide by appropriate constitutional requirements of due process of law. The statutory framework in which agencies operate also includes federal and state laws concerning access to government information, open meetings, privacy rights, paperwork reduction, and various acts requiring analyses of agency regulations and procedures. This statutory framework and the decisions of the Supreme Court and the lower federal and state courts are the threads that weave the tapestry of the administrative process in the United States.

KEY TERMS

adjudication

administrative law judge

Administrative Procedure
Act (APA)

alternative dispute resolution

Buckley Amendment

Code of Federal
Regulations (CFR)

disclosure of information

discretion

Family Educational Rights
Privacy Act

formal adjudication

formal rulemaking

Freedom of Information Act
(FOIA)

improper disclosure of personal
information

jurisdiction

notice and comment rulemaking

Office of Information and
Regulatory Affairs (OIRA)

Office of Management and
Budget (OMB)

open records laws

Paperwork Reduction Act

Privacy Act

quasi-judicial power

quasi-legislative power

Regulatory Flexibility Act

regulatory flexibility analysis

rulemaking

statutory ambiguity

statutory clarity

statutory interpretation

sunshine laws

trial-type procedures

ultra vires

unfunded mandates

Unfunded Mandates Reform Act

QUESTIONS FOR THOUGHT
AND DISCUSSION

1. Why did it become important for Congress and the state legislatures to adopt administrative procedural acts?

2. Explain the procedural difference involved in informal (notice and comment) rulemaking and formal rulemaking.

3. Describe the scope of: a) the Freedom of Information Act (FOIA); b) federal and state open meetings laws.

4. How do the objectives of the Freedom of Information and Sunshine Laws contrast with Privacy Acts?

5. To what extent is the privacy of students' educational records at state and local schools and universities protected by federal statute? How is the law enforced?

6. How did the implementation of the Paperwork Reduction Act affect presidential control of the executive bureaucracy?

7. Explain the purpose and operation of the Regulatory Flexibility Act (RFA).

8. What political consequences do unfunded mandates pose to the doctrine of federalism? How does the Unfunded Mandates Reform Act (UMRA) attempt to control federal rules that mandate expenses by state and local governments?

9. Give some examples of public records that are commonly exempted from disclosure under state "Open Records" laws. What is the rationale for these exemptions?

10. Give some examples of informal adjudication and formal (trial type) adjudication. To what extent must agencies follow due process of law requirements in each type of adjudication?

EDITED CASE   Bob Jones University v. United States
United States Supreme Court, 461 U.S. 574 (1983)

[In this case the Supreme Court considers whether the Internal Revenue Service acted properly in revoking tax-exempt status from a private religious college that practiced racial discrimination.]

Chief Justice Burger delivered the opinion of the Court.

. . . Bob Jones University is a nonprofit corporation located in Greenville, S.C. . . . "giving special emphasis to the Christian religion and the ethics revealed in the Holy Scriptures." . . . It is both a religious and educational institution. Its teachers are required to be devout Christians, and all courses at the University are taught according to the Bible. Entering students are screened as to their religious beliefs, and their public and private conduct is strictly regulated by standards promulgated by University authorities.

The sponsors of the University genuinely believe that the Bible forbids interracial dating and marriage. To effectuate these views, Negroes were completely excluded until 1971. From 1971 to May 1975, the University accepted no applications from unmarried Negroes, but did accept applications from Negroes married within their race.

Following the decision of the United States Court of Appeals for the Fourth Circuit in *McCrary v. Runyon* (1976), prohibiting racial exclusion from private schools, the University revised its policy. Since May 29, 1975, the University has permitted unmarried Negroes to enroll; but a disciplinary rule prohibits interracial dating and marriage. That rule reads:

> "There is to be no interracial dating.
> "1. Students who are partners in an interracial marriage will be expelled.
> "2. Students who are members of or affiliated with any group or organization which holds as one of its goals or advocates interracial marriage will be expelled.
> "3. Students who date outside of their own race will be expelled.
> "4. Students who espouse, promote, or encourage others to violate the University's dating rules and regulations will be expelled." . . .

The University continues to deny admission to applicants engaged in an interracial marriage or known to advocate interracial marriage or dating. . . .

Until 1970, the IRS extended tax-exempt status to Bob Jones University under [U.S. Code, Title 26,] § 501(c)(3). By the letter of November 30, 1970 . . . the IRS formally notified the University of the change in IRS policy, and announced its intention to challenge the tax-exempt status of private schools practicing racial discrimination in their admissions policies.

After failing to obtain an assurance of tax exemption through administrative means, the University instituted an action in 1971 seeking to enjoin the IRS from revoking the school's tax-exempt status. . . .

The United States District Court for the District of South Carolina held that revocation of the University's tax-exempt status exceeded the delegated powers of the IRS, was improper under the IRS rulings and procedures, and violated the University's rights under the Religion Clauses of the First Amendment. . . .

The Court of Appeals for the Fourth Circuit, in a divided opinion, reversed. . . .

In Revenue Ruling 71-447, the IRS formalized the policy, first announced in 1970, that § 170 and § 501(c)(3) embrace the common-law "charity" concept. Under that view, to qualify for a tax exemption pursuant to 501(c)(3), an institution must show, first, that it falls within one of the eight categories expressly set forth in that section, and second, that its activity is not contrary to settled public policy.

Section § 501(c)(3) provides that "[c]orporations . . . organized and operated exclusively for religious, charitable . . . or educational purposes" are entitled to tax exemption. Petitioners argue that the plain language of the statute guarantees them tax-exempt status. . . . The Court of Appeals rejected that contention and concluded that petitioners' interpretation of the statute "tears section § 501(c)(3) from its roots." . . .

(Continued)

EDITED CASE   Bob Jones University v. United States (Continued)

Section § 501(c)(3) . . . reveals unmistakable evidence that, underlying all relevant parts of the Code, is the intent that entitlement to tax exemption depends on meeting certain common-law standards of charity—namely, that an institution seeking tax-exempt status must serve a public purpose and not be contrary to established public policy. . . .

The form of § 170 simply makes plain what common sense and history tell us: in enacting both § 170 and § 501(c)(3), Congress sought to provide tax benefits to charitable organizations, to encourage the development of private institutions that serve a useful public purpose or supplement or take the place of public institutions of the same kind. . . .

. . . Charitable exemptions are justified on the basis that the exempt entity confers a public benefit—a benefit which the society or the community may not itself choose or be able to provide, or which supplements and advances the work of public institutions already supported by tax revenues. . . . The institution's purpose must not be so at odds with the common community conscience as to undermine any public benefit that might otherwise be conferred.

. . . Whatever may be the rationale for such private schools' policies, and however sincere the rationale may be, racial discrimination in education is contrary to public policy. Racially discriminatory educational institutions cannot be viewed as conferring a public benefit within the "charitable" concept discussed earlier, or within the congressional intent underlying § 170 and 501(c)(3).

Petitioners contend that, regardless of whether the IRS properly concluded that racially discriminatory private schools violate public policy, only Congress can alter the scope of § 170 and 501(c)(3). Petitioners accordingly argue that the IRS overstepped its lawful bounds in issuing its 1970 and 1971 rulings. . . .

In § 170 and 501(c)(3), Congress has identified categories of traditionally exempt institutions and has specified certain additional requirements for tax exemption. Yet the need for continuing interpretation of those statutes is unavoidable. For more than 60 years, the IRS and its predecessors have constantly been called upon to interpret these and comparable provisions, and in doing so

have referred consistently to principles of charitable trust law. . . .

Guided, of course, by the Code, the IRS has the responsibility, in the first instance, to determine whether a particular entity is "charitable" for purposes of § 170 and 501(c)(3). . . . We emphasize, however, that these sensitive determinations should be made only where there is no doubt that the organization's activities violate fundamental public policy.

On the record before us, there can be no doubt as to the national policy. In 1970, when the IRS first issued the ruling challenged here, the position of all three branches of the Federal Government was unmistakably clear. The correctness of the Commissioner's conclusion that a racially discriminatory private school "is not 'charitable' within the common law concepts reflected in . . . the Code" . . . is wholly consistent with what Congress, the Executive, and the courts had repeatedly declared before 1970." . . . We therefore hold that the IRS did not exceed its authority when it announced its interpretation of § 170 and § 501(c)(3) in 1970 and 1971.

The evidence of congressional approval of the policy embodied in Revenue Ruling 71-447 goes well beyond the failure of Congress to act on legislative proposals. Congress affirmatively manifested its acquiescence in the IRS policy when it enacted the present § 501(i) of the Code. . . . That provision denies tax-exempt status to social clubs whose charters or policy statements provide for "discrimination against any person on the basis of race, color, or religion." . . .

Petitioners contend that, even if the Commissioner's policy is valid as to nonreligious private schools, that policy cannot constitutionally be applied to schools that engage in racial discrimination on the basis of sincerely held religious beliefs. As to such schools, it is argued that the IRS construction of § 170 and § 501(c)(3) violates their free exercise rights under the Religion Clauses of the First Amendment. This contention presents claims not heretofore considered by this Court in precisely this context.

This Court has long held the Free Exercise Clause of the First Amendment to be an absolute prohibition against governmental regulation of religious beliefs. . . . As interpreted by this Court,

---

EDITED CASE   Bob Jones University v. United States (Continued)

---

moreover, the Free Exercise Clause provides substantial protection for lawful conduct grounded in religious belief. . . . However, "[n]ot all burdens on religion are unconstitutional. . . . The state may justify a limitation on religious liberty by showing that it is essential to accomplish an overriding governmental interest." . . .

The governmental interest at stake here is compelling. . . . [T]he Government has a fundamental, overriding interest in eradicating racial discrimination in education—discrimination that prevailed, with official approval, for the first 165 years of this Nation's constitutional history. That governmental interest substantially outweighs whatever burden denial of tax benefits places on petitioners' exercise of their religious beliefs. . . .

Petitioner Bob Jones University . . . contends that it is not racially discriminatory. It emphasizes that it now allows all races to enroll, subject only to its restrictions on the conduct of all students, including its prohibitions of association between men and women of different races, and of interracial marriage. Although a ban on intermarriage or interracial dating applies to all races, decisions of this Court firmly establish that discrimination on the basis of racial affiliation and association is a form of racial discrimination. . . . We therefore find that the IRS properly applied Revenue Ruling 71-447 to Bob Jones University. . . .

Justice Powell, concurring in part and concurring in the judgment. . . .

Justice Rehnquist, dissenting.

The Court points out that there is a strong national policy in this country against racial discrimination. To the extent that the Court states that Congress in furtherance of this policy could deny tax-exempt status to educational institutions that promote racial discrimination, I readily agree. But, unlike the Court, I am convinced that Congress simply has failed to take this action and, as this Court has said over and over again, regardless of our view on the propriety of Congress' failure to legislate we are not constitutionally empowered to act for it.

In approaching this statutory construction question the Court quite adeptly avoids the statute it is construing. This I am sure is no accident, for there is nothing in the language of § 501(c)(3) that supports the result obtained by the Court. . . .

With undeniable clarity, Congress has explicitly defined the requirements for § 501(c)(3) status. An entity must be (1) a corporation, or community chest, fund, or foundation, (2) organized for one of the eight enumerated purposes, (3) operated on a nonprofit basis, and (4) free from involvement in lobbying activities and political campaigns. Nowhere is there to be found some additional, undefined public policy requirement.

The Court first seeks refuge from the obvious reading of § 501(c)(3) by turning to § 170 of the Internal Revenue Code, which provides a tax deduction for contributions made to § 501(c)(3) organizations. In setting forth the general rule, § 170 states:

"There shall be allowed as a deduction any charitable contribution (as defined in subsection (c)) payment of which is made within the taxable year. A charitable contribution shall be allowable as a deduction only if verified under regulations prescribed by the Secretary." 26 U.S.C. § 170(a)(1).

The Court seizes the words "charitable contribution" and with little discussion concludes that "[o]n its face, therefore, § 170 reveals that Congress' intention was to provide tax benefits to organizations serving charitable purposes," intimating that this implies some unspecified common-law charitable trust requirement. . . .

The Court would have been well advised to look to subsection (c) where, as § 170(a)(1) indicates, Congress has defined a "charitable contribution": "For purposes of this section, the term 'charitable contribution' means a contribution or gift to or for the use of . . . [a] corporation, trust, or community chest, fund, or foundation . . . organized and operated exclusively for religious, charitable, scientific, literary, or educational purposes, or to foster national or international amateur sports competition (but only if no part of its activities involve the provision of athletic facilities or equipment), or for the prevention of cruelty to children or animals; . . . no part of the net earnings of which inures to the benefit of any private shareholder or individual; and . . . which is not disqualified for tax exemption under section 501(c)(3) by reason of attempting to influence legislation, and which does not participate in, or intervene in

(Continued)

EDITED CASE   Bob Jones University v. United States (Continued)

(including the publishing or distributing of statements), any political campaign on behalf of any candidate for public office." 26 U.S.C. § 170(c).

Plainly, § 170(c) simply tracks the requirements set forth in 501(c)(3). Since § 170 is no more than a mirror of § 501(c)(3) and, as the Court points out, § 170 followed § 501(c)(3) by more than two decades . . . , it is at best of little usefulness in finding the meaning of 501(c)(3). . . .

In 1970 the IRS was sued by parents of black public school children seeking to enjoin the IRS from according tax-exempt status under § 501(c)(3) to private schools in Mississippi that discriminated against blacks. The IRS answered, consistent with its longstanding position, by maintaining a lack of authority to deny the tax exemption if the schools met the specified requirements of 501(c)(3). Then "[i]n the midst of this litigation," . . . and in the face of a preliminary injunction, the IRS changed its position and adopted the view of the plaintiffs.

Following the close of the litigation, the IRS published its new position in Revenue Ruling 71-447, stating that "a school asserting a right to the benefits provided for in section § 501(c)(3) of the Code as being organized and operated exclusively for educational purposes must be a common law charity in

order to be exempt under that section." . . . The IRS then concluded that a school that promotes racial discrimination violates public policy and therefore cannot qualify as a common-law charity. . . .

I have no disagreement with the Court's finding that there is a strong national policy in this country opposed to racial discrimination. I agree with the Court that Congress has the power to further this policy by denying § 501(c)(3) status to organizations that practice racial discrimination. But as of yet Congress has failed to do so. Whatever the reasons for the failure, this Court should not legislate for Congress.

Petitioners are each organized for the "instruction or training of the individual for the purpose of improving or developing his capabilities," . . . and thus are organized for "educational purposes" within the meaning of 501(c)(3). Petitioners' nonprofit status is uncontested. There is no indication that either petitioner has been involved in lobbying activities or political campaigns. Therefore, it is my view that unless and until Congress affirmatively amends § 501(c)(3) to require more, the IRS is without authority to deny petitioners § 501(c)(3) status. For this reason, I would reverse the Court of Appeals.

EDITED CASE   Food and Drug Administration v. Brown & Williamson Tobacco Co.
United States Supreme Court, 529 U.S. 120 (2000)

[The Food, Drug, and Cosmetic Act (FDCA) grants the Food and Drug Administration (FDA) authority to regulate drugs and defines drug to include "articles (other than food) intended to affect the structure or any function of the body." In 1996 FDA issued a final rule determining that nicotine is a drug and that cigarettes and smokeless tobacco are "drug delivery devices." FDA adopted regulations that prohibited sale of tobacco products through vending machines and required retailers to require photo identification of persons under age twenty-seven who seek to buy tobacco products. Brown and Williamson, a manufacturer of tobacco products, filed suit challenging the FDA's authority in this area. The federal district court

upheld the FDA's authority, but the Court of Appeals reversed, holding that Congress had not granted the FDA jurisdiction over tobacco products. The Supreme Court granted review and struck down FDA's rule.]

Justice O'Connor delivered the opinion of the Court.

. . . The FDA's assertion of jurisdiction to regulate tobacco products is founded on its conclusions that nicotine is a "drug" and that cigarettes and smokeless tobacco are "drug delivery devices." Again, the FDA found that tobacco products are "intended" to deliver the pharmacological effects of satisfying addiction, stimulation and

EDITED CASE Food and Drug Administration v. Brown & Williamson Tobacco Co. (Continued)

tranquilization, and weight control because those effects are foreseeable to any reasonable manufacturer, consumers use tobacco products to obtain those effects, and tobacco manufacturers have designed their products to produce those effects. . . .

A threshold issue is the appropriate framework for analyzing the FDA's assertion of authority to regulate tobacco products. Because this case involves an administrative agency's construction of a statute that it administers, our analysis is governed by *Chevron U.S.A. Inc. v. Natural Resources Defense Council, Inc.* . . . (1984). Under *Chevron*, a reviewing court must first ask "whether Congress has directly spoken to the precise question at issue." . . . If Congress has done so, the inquiry is at an end; the court "must give effect to the unambiguously expressed intent of Congress." . . . But if Congress has not specifically addressed the question, a reviewing court must respect the agency's construction of the statute so long as it is permissible. Such deference is justified because "[t]he responsibilities for assessing the wisdom of such policy choices and resolving the struggle between competing views of the public interest are not judicial ones," . . . and because of the agency's greater familiarity with the ever-changing facts and circumstances surrounding the subjects regulated. . . .

In determining whether Congress has specifically addressed the question at issue, a reviewing court should not confine itself to examining a particular statutory provision in isolation. The meaning—or ambiguity—of certain words or phrases may only become evident when placed in context. . . . It is a "fundamental canon of statutory construction that the words of a statute must be read in their context and with a view to their place in the overall statutory scheme." . . . A court must therefore interpret the statute "as a symmetrical and coherent regulatory scheme," . . . and "fit, if possible, all parts into an harmonious whole." . . . Similarly, the meaning of one statute may be affected by other Acts, particularly where Congress has spoken subsequently and more specifically to the topic at hand. . . . In addition, we must be guided to a degree by common sense as to the manner in which Congress is likely to delegate a policy decision of such economic and political magnitude to an administrative agency. . . . With these principles in mind, we find that Congress has directly spoken to the issue here and precluded the FDA's jurisdiction to regulate tobacco products.

Considering the FDCA as a whole, it is clear that Congress intended to exclude tobacco products from the FDA's jurisdiction. A fundamental precept of the FDCA is that any product regulated by the FDA—but not banned—must be safe for its intended use. Various provisions of the Act make clear that this refers to the safety of using the product to obtain its intended effects, not the public health ramifications of alternative administrative actions by the FDA. That is, the FDA must determine that there is a reasonable assurance that the product's therapeutic benefits outweigh the risk of harm to the consumer. According to this standard, the FDA has concluded that, although tobacco products might be effective in delivering certain pharmacological effects, they are "unsafe" and "dangerous" when used for these purposes. Consequently, if tobacco products were within the FDA's jurisdiction, the Act would require the FDA to remove them from the market entirely. But a ban would contradict Congress' clear intent as expressed in its more recent, tobacco-specific legislation. The inescapable conclusion is that there is no room for tobacco products within the FDCA's regulatory scheme. If they cannot be used safely for any therapeutic purpose, and yet they cannot be banned, they simply do not fit. . . .

In determining whether Congress has spoken directly to the FDA's authority to regulate tobacco, we must also consider in greater detail the tobacco-specific legislation that Congress has enacted over the past 35 years. At the time a statute is enacted, it may have a range of plausible meanings. Over time, however, subsequent acts can shape or focus those meanings. The "classic judicial task of reconciling many laws enacted over time, and getting them to make sense' in combination, necessarily assumes that the implications of a statute may be altered by the implications of a later statute." . . . This is particularly so where the scope of the earlier statute is broad but the subsequent statutes more specifically address the topic at hand. . . .

(Continued)

EDITED CASE   Food and Drug Administration v. Brown &
Williamson Tobacco Co. (Continued)

Congress has enacted six separate pieces of legislation since 1965 addressing the problem of tobacco use and human health. . . . Those statutes, among other things, require that health warnings appear on all packaging and in all print and outdoor advertisements; . . . prohibit the advertisement of tobacco products through "any medium of electronic communication" subject to regulation by the Federal Communications Commission (FCC); . . . require the Secretary of Health and Human Services (HHS) to report every three years to Congress on research findings concerning "the addictive property of tobacco"; . . . and make States' receipt of certain federal block grants contingent on their making it unlawful "for any manufacturer, retailer, or distributor of tobacco products to sell or distribute any such product to any individual under the age of 18." . . .

In adopting each statute, Congress has acted against the backdrop of the FDA's consistent and repeated statements that it lacked authority under the FDCA to regulate tobacco absent claims of therapeutic benefit by the manufacturer. In fact, on several occasions over this period, and after the health consequences of tobacco use and nicotine's pharmacological effects had become well known, Congress considered and rejected bills that would have granted the FDA such jurisdiction. Under these circumstances, it is evident that Congress' tobacco-specific statutes have effectively ratified the FDA's long-held position that it lacks jurisdiction under the FDCA to regulate tobacco products. Congress has created a distinct regulatory scheme to address the problem of tobacco and health, and that scheme, as presently constructed, precludes any role for the FDA.

. . . By no means do we question the seriousness of the problem that the FDA has sought to address. The agency has amply demonstrated that tobacco use, particularly among children and adolescents, poses perhaps the single most significant threat to public health in the United States. Nonetheless, no matter how "important, conspicuous, and controversial" the issue, and regardless of how likely the public is to hold the Executive Branch politically accountable, . . . an administrative agency's power to regulate in the public interest must always be grounded in a valid grant of authority from Congress. And "'[i]n our anxiety to

effectuate the congressional purpose of protecting the public, we must take care not to extend the scope of the statute beyond the point where Congress indicated it would stop.'" . . . Reading the FDCA as a whole, as well as in conjunction with Congress' subsequent tobacco-specific legislation, it is plain that Congress has not given the FDA the authority that it seeks to exercise here. For these reasons, the judgment of the Court of Appeals for the Fourth Circuit is affirmed.

Justice Breyer, joined by *Justices Stevens, Souter,* and *Ginsburg,* dissenting.

The Food and Drug Administration (FDA) has the authority to regulate "articles (other than food) intended to affect the structure or any function of the body. . . ." . . . Unlike the majority, I believe that tobacco products fit within this statutory language.

In its own interpretation, the majority nowhere denies the following two salient points. First, tobacco products (including cigarettes) fall within the scope of this statutory definition, read literally. Cigarettes achieve their mood-stabilizing effects through the interaction of the chemical nicotine and the cells of the central nervous system. Both cigarette manufacturers and smokers alike know of, and desire, that chemically induced result. Hence, cigarettes are "intended to affect" the body's "structure" and "function," in the literal sense of these words.

Second, the statute's basic purpose—the protection of public health—supports the inclusion of cigarettes within its scope. . . . Unregulated tobacco use causes "[m]ore than 400,000 people [to] die each year from tobacco-related illnesses, such as cancer, respiratory illnesses, and heart disease." . . . Indeed, tobacco products kill more people in this country every year "than . . . AIDS, car accidents, alcohol, homicides, illegal drugs, suicides, and fires, *combined*." . . .

Despite the FDCA's literal language and general purpose (both of which support the FDA's finding that cigarettes come within its statutory authority), the majority nonetheless reads the statute as *excluding* tobacco products for two basic reasons:

(1) the FDCA does not "fit" the case of tobacco because the statute requires the

---

EDITED CASE   Food and Drug Administration v. Brown & Williamson Tobacco Co. (Continued)

FDA to prohibit dangerous drugs or devices (like cigarettes) outright, and the agency concedes that simply banning the sale of cigarettes is not a proper remedy; and

(2) Congress has enacted other statutes, which, when viewed in light of the FDA's long history of denying tobacco-related jurisdiction and considered together with Congress' failure explicitly to grant the agency tobacco-specific authority, demonstrate that Congress did not intend for the FDA to exercise jurisdiction over tobacco. . . .

In my view, neither of these propositions is valid. Rather, the FDCA does not significantly limit the FDA's remedial alternatives. . . . And the later statutes do not tell the FDA it cannot exercise jurisdiction, but simply leave FDA jurisdictional law where Congress found it. . . .

. . . In short, I believe that the most important indicia of statutory meaning—language and purpose—along with the FDCA's legislative history . . . are sufficient to establish that the FDA has authority to regulate tobacco. The statute-specific arguments against jurisdiction that the tobacco companies and the majority rely upon . . . are based on erroneous assumptions and, thus, do not defeat the jurisdiction-supporting thrust of the FDCA's language and purpose. The inferences that the majority draws from later legislative history are not persuasive, since . . . one can just as easily infer from the later laws that Congress did not intend to affect the FDA's tobacco-related authority at all. And the fact that the FDA changed its mind about the scope of its own jurisdiction is legally insignificant because . . . the agency's reasons for changing course are fully justified. Finally, . . . the degree of accountability that likely will attach to the FDA's action in this case should alleviate any concern that Congress, rather than an administrative agency, ought to make this important regulatory decision. . . .

According to the FDA, only 2.5% of smokers successfully stop smoking each year, even though 70% say they want to quit and 34% actually make an attempt to do so. . . . The fact that only a handful of those who try to quit smoking actually succeed illustrates a certain reality—the reality that the nicotine in cigarettes creates a powerful physiological addiction flowing from chemically induced changes in the brain. The FDA has found that the makers of cigarettes "intend" these physical effects. Hence, nicotine is a "drug"; the cigarette that delivers nicotine to the body is a "device"; and the FDCA's language, read in light of its basic purpose, permits the FDA to assert the disease-preventing jurisdiction that the agency now claims.

The majority finds that cigarettes are so dangerous that the FDCA would require them to be banned (a result the majority believes Congress would not have desired); thus, it concludes that the FDA has no tobacco-related authority. I disagree that the statute would require a cigarette ban. But even if I am wrong about the ban, the statute would restrict only the agency's choice of remedies, not its jurisdiction.

The majority also believes that subsequently enacted statutes deprive the FDA of jurisdiction. But the later laws say next to nothing about the FDA's tobacco-related authority. Previous FDA disclaimers of jurisdiction may have helped to form the legislative atmosphere out of which Congress' own tobacco-specific statutes emerged. But a legislative atmosphere is not a law, unless it is embodied in a statutory word or phrase. And the relevant words and phrases here reveal nothing more than an intent not to change the jurisdictional status quo.

The upshot is that the Court today holds that a regulatory statute aimed at unsafe drugs and devices does not authorize regulation of a drug (nicotine) and a device (a cigarette) that the Court itself finds unsafe. Far more than most, this particular drug and device risks the life-threatening harms that administrative regulation seeks to rectify. The majority's conclusion is counter-intuitive. And, for the reasons set forth, I believe that the law does not require it. . . .

EDITED CASE Department of Justice v. Reporters' Committee
United States Supreme Court, 489 U.S. 749 (1989)

[In this case the Supreme Court considers whether members of the media can get access to FBI "rap sheets" the Freedom of Information Act.]

Justice Stevens delivered the opinion of the Court.

. . . In 1924 Congress appropriated funds to enable the Department of Justice (Department) to establish a program to collect and preserve fingerprints and other criminal identification records. . . . That statute authorized the Department to exchange such information with "officials of States, cities and other institutions." . . . Six years later Congress created the FBI's identification division, and gave it responsibility for "acquiring, collecting, classifying, and preserving criminal identification and other crime records and the exchanging of said criminal identification records with the duly authorized officials of governmental agencies, of States, cities, and penal institutions." . . . Rap sheets compiled pursuant to such authority contain certain descriptive information, such as date of birth and physical characteristics, as well as a history of arrests, charges, convictions, and incarcerations of the subject. Normally a rap sheet is preserved until its subject attains age 80. Because of the volume of rap sheets, they are sometimes incorrect or incomplete and sometimes contain information about other persons with similar names.

The local, state, and federal law enforcement agencies throughout the Nation that exchange rap-sheet data with the FBI do so on a voluntary basis. The principal use of the information is to assist in the detection and prosecution of offenders; it is also used by courts and corrections officials in connection with sentencing and parole decisions. As a matter of executive policy, the Department has generally treated rap sheets as confidential and, with certain exceptions, has restricted their use to governmental purposes. Consistent with the Department's basic policy of treating these records as confidential, Congress in 1957 amended the basic statute to provide that the FBI's exchange of rap-sheet information with any other agency is subject to cancellation "if dissemination is made outside the receiving departments or related agencies." . . .

As a matter of Department policy, the FBI has made two exceptions to its general practice of prohibiting unofficial access to rap sheets. First, it allows the subject of a rap sheet to obtain a copy; and second, it occasionally allows rap sheets to be used in the preparation of press releases and publicity designed to assist in the apprehension of wanted persons or fugitives. . . .

In addition, on three separate occasions Congress has expressly authorized the release of rap sheets for other limited purposes. In 1972 it provided for such release to officials of federally chartered or insured banking institutions and "if authorized by State statute and approved by the Attorney General, to officials of State and local governments for purposes of employment and licensing. . . ." . . . In 1975, in an amendment to the Securities Exchange Act of 1934, Congress permitted the Attorney General to release rap sheets to self-regulatory organizations in the securities industry. . . . And finally, in 1986 Congress authorized release of criminal-history information to licensees or applicants before the Nuclear Regulatory Commission. . . . These three targeted enactments—all adopted after the FOIA was passed in 1966—are consistent with the view that Congress understood and did not disapprove the FBI's general policy of treating rap sheets as nonpublic documents.

Although much rap-sheet information is a matter of public record, the availability and dissemination of the actual rap sheet to the public is limited. Arrests, indictments, convictions, and sentences are public events that are usually documented in court records. In addition, if a person's entire criminal history transpired in a single jurisdiction, all of the contents of his or her rap sheet may be available upon request in that jurisdiction. That possibility, however, is present in only three States. All of the other 47 States place substantial restrictions on the availability of criminal-history summaries even though individual events in those summaries are matters of public record. Moreover, even in Florida, Wisconsin, and Oklahoma, the publicly available summaries may not include information about out-of-state arrests or convictions.

EDITED CASE Department of Justice v. Reporters' Committee (Continued)

II

The statute known as the FOIA is actually a part of the Administrative Procedure Act (APA). Section 3 of the APA as enacted in 1946 gave agencies broad discretion concerning the publication of governmental records. In 1966 Congress amended that section to implement "'a general philosophy of full agency disclosure.'" The amendment required agencies to publish their rules of procedure in the *Federal Register*, 5 U.S.C. 552(a)(1)(C), and to make available for public inspection and copying their opinions, statements of policy, interpretations, and staff manuals and instructions that are not published in the *Federal Register*, 552(a)(2). In addition, 552(a)(3) requires every agency "upon any request for records which . . . reasonably describes such records" to make such records "promptly available to any person." If an agency improperly withholds any documents, the district court has jurisdiction to order their production. Unlike the review of other agency action that must be upheld if supported by substantial evidence and not arbitrary or capricious, the FOIA expressly places the burden "on the agency to sustain its action" and directs the district courts to "determine the matter de novo."

Congress exempted nine categories of documents from the FOIA's broad disclosure requirements. Three of those exemptions are arguably relevant to this case. Exemption 3 applies to documents that are specifically exempted from disclosure by another statute. . . . Exemption 6 protects "personnel and medical files and similar files the disclosure of which would constitute a clearly unwarranted invasion of personal privacy." . . . Exemption 7(C) excludes records or information compiled for law enforcement purposes, "but only to the extent that the production of such [materials] . . . could reasonably be expected to constitute an unwarranted invasion of personal privacy." . . .

Exemption 7(C)'s privacy language is broader than the comparable language in Exemption 6 in two respects. First, whereas Exemption 6 requires that the invasion of privacy be "clearly unwarranted," the adverb "clearly" is omitted from Exemption 7(C). This omission is the product of a 1974 amendment adopted in response to concerns expressed by the President. Second, whereas Exemption 6 refers to disclosures that "would constitute" an invasion of privacy, Exemption 7(C) encompasses any disclosure that "could reasonably be expected to constitute" such an invasion. This difference is also the product of a specific amendment. Thus, the standard for evaluating a threatened invasion of privacy interests resulting from the disclosure of records compiled for law enforcement purposes is somewhat broader than the standard applicable to personnel, medical, and similar files.

III

This case arises out of requests made by a CBS news correspondent and the Reporters Committee for Freedom of the Press (respondents) for information concerning the criminal records of four members of the Medico family. The Pennsylvania Crime Commission had identified the family's company, Medico Industries, as a legitimate business dominated by organized crime figures. Moreover, the company allegedly had obtained a number of defense contracts as a result of an improper arrangement with a corrupt Congressman.

The FOIA requests sought disclosure of any arrests, indictments, acquittals, convictions, and sentences of any of the four Medicos. Although the FBI originally denied the requests, it provided the requested data concerning three of the Medicos after their deaths. In their complaint in the District Court, respondents sought the rap sheet for the fourth, Charles Medico (Medico), insofar as it contained "matters of public record." . . .

The parties filed cross-motions for summary judgment. Respondents urged that any information regarding "a record of bribery, embezzlement or other financial crime" would potentially be a matter of special public interest. . . . In answer to that argument, the Department advised respondents and the District Court that it had no record of any financial crimes concerning Medico, but the Department continued to refuse to confirm or deny whether it had any information concerning nonfinancial crimes. Thus, the issue was narrowed to Medico's nonfinancial-crime history insofar as it is a matter of public record.

(Continued)

EDITED CASE   Department of Justice v. Reporters' Committee (Continued)

The District Court granted the Department's motion for summary judgment, relying on three separate grounds. First, it concluded that 28 U.S.C. 534, the statute that authorizes the exchange of rap-sheet information with other official agencies, also prohibits the release of such information to members of the public, and therefore that Exemption 3 was applicable. Second, it decided that files containing rap sheets were included within the category of "personnel and medical files and similar files the disclosure of which would constitute an unwarranted invasion of privacy," and therefore that Exemption 6 was applicable. The term "similar files" applied because rap-sheet information "is personal to the individual named therein." . . . After balancing Medico's privacy interest against the public interest in disclosure, the District Court concluded that the invasion of privacy was "clearly unwarranted." Finally, the court held that the rap sheet was also protected by Exemption 7(C), but it ordered the Department to file a statement containing the requested data in camera to give it an opportunity to reconsider the issue if, after reviewing that statement, such action seemed appropriate. After the Department made that filing, the District Court advised the parties that it would not reconsider the matter, but it did seal the in camera submission and make it part of the record on appeal.

The Court of Appeals reversed. . . . It held that an individual's privacy interest in criminal-history information that is a matter of public record was minimal at best. Noting the absence of any statutory standards by which to judge the public interest in disclosure, the Court of Appeals concluded that it should be bound by the state and local determinations that such information should be made available to the general public. Accordingly, it held that Exemptions 6 and 7(C) were inapplicable. It also agreed with respondents that Exemption 3 did not apply because 28 U.S.C. 534 did not qualify as a statute "specifically" exempting rap sheets from disclosure.

In response to rehearing petitions advising the court that, contrary to its original understanding, most States had adopted policies of refusing to provide members of the public with criminal-history summaries, the Court of Appeals modified its holding. . . . With regard to the public interest side of the balance, the court now recognized that

it could not rely upon state policies of disclosure. However, it adhered to its view that federal judges are not in a position to make "idiosyncratic" evaluations of the public interest in particular disclosures, . . . instead, it directed district courts to consider "the general disclosure policies of the statute." . . . With regard to the privacy interest in nondisclosure of rap sheets, the court told the District Court "only to make a factual determination in these kinds of cases: Has a legitimate privacy interest of the subject in his rap sheets faded because they appear on the public record?" . . . In accordance with its initial opinion, it remanded the case to the District Court to determine whether the withheld information is publicly available at its source, and if so, whether the Department might satisfy its statutory obligation by referring respondents to the enforcement agency or agencies that had provided the original information. . . .

The Court of Appeals denied rehearing en banc, with four judges dissenting. . . . Because of the potential effect of the Court of Appeals' opinion on values of personal privacy, we granted certiorari. . . . We now reverse.

IV

Exemption 7(C) requires us to balance the privacy interest in maintaining, as the Government puts it, the "practical obscurity" of the rap sheets against the public interest in their release.

The preliminary question is whether Medico's interest in the nondisclosure of any rap sheet the FBI might have on him is the sort of "personal privacy" interest that Congress intended Exemption 7(C) to protect. As we have pointed out before, "[t]he cases sometimes characterized as protecting 'privacy' have in fact involved at least two different kinds of interests. One is the individual interest in avoiding disclosure of personal matters, and another is the interest in independence in making certain kinds of important decisions." . . . Here, the former interest, "in avoiding disclosure of personal matters," is implicated. Because events summarized in a rap sheet have been previously disclosed to the public, respondents contend that Medico's privacy interest in avoiding disclosure of a federal compilation of these events approaches zero. We reject respondents' cramped notion of personal privacy. . . .

EDITED CASE   Department of Justice v. Reporters' Committee (Continued)

. . . Specifically, the FOIA provides that "[t]o the extent required to prevent a clearly unwarranted invasion of personal privacy, an agency may delete identifying details when it makes available or publishes an opinion, statement of policy, interpretation, or staff manual or instruction." 5 U.S.C. 552(a)(2). Additionally, the FOIA assures that "[a]ny reasonably segregable portion of a record shall be provided to any person requesting such record after deletion of the portions which are exempt under [(b)]." . . . These provisions, for deletion of identifying references and disclosure of segregable portions of records with exempt information deleted, reflect a congressional understanding that disclosure of records containing personal details about private citizens can infringe significant privacy interests.

Also supporting our conclusion that a strong privacy interest inheres in the nondisclosure of compiled computerized information is the Privacy Act of 1974. . . . The Privacy Act was passed largely out of concern over "the impact of computer data banks on individual privacy." . . . The Privacy Act provides generally that "[n]o agency shall disclose any record which is contained in a system of records . . . except pursuant to a written request by, or with the prior written consent of, the individual to whom the record pertains." . . . Although the Privacy Act contains a variety of exceptions to this rule, including an exemption for information required to be disclosed under the FOIA, . . . Congress' basic policy concern regarding the implications of computerized data banks for personal privacy is certainly relevant in our consideration of the privacy interest affected by dissemination of rap sheets from the FBI computer.

Given this level of federal concern over centralized databases, the fact that most States deny the general public access to their criminal-history summaries should not be surprising. As we have pointed out, . . . States nonconviction data from criminal-history summaries are not available at all, and even conviction data are "generally unavailable to the public." . . . State policies, of course, do not determine the meaning of a federal statute, but they provide evidence that the law enforcement profession generally assumes—as has the Department of Justice—that individual subjects have a significant privacy interest in their criminal histories. It is reasonable to presume that Congress legislated with an understanding of this professional point of view. . . .

We have also recognized the privacy interest in keeping personal facts away from the public eye. In *Whalen v. Roe*, 429 U.S. 589 (1977), we held that "the State of New York may record, in a centralized computer file, the names and addresses of all persons who have obtained, pursuant to a doctor's prescription, certain drugs for which there is both a lawful and an unlawful market." . . . In holding only that the Federal Constitution does not prohibit such a compilation, we recognized that such a centralized computer file posed a "threat to privacy":

"We are not unaware of the threat to privacy implicit in the accumulation of vast amounts of personal information in computerized data banks or other massive government files. The collection of taxes, the distribution of welfare and social security benefits, the supervision of public health, the direction of our Armed Forces, and the enforcement of the criminal laws all require the orderly preservation of great quantities of information, much of which is personal in character and potentially embarrassing or harmful if disclosed. The right to collect and use such data for public purposes is typically accompanied by a concomitant statutory or regulatory duty to avoid unwarranted disclosures. Recognizing that in some circumstances that duty arguably has its roots in the Constitution, nevertheless New York's statutory scheme, and its implementing administrative procedures, evidence a proper concern with, and protection of, the individual's interest in privacy." . . .

In sum, the fact that "an event is not wholly 'private' does not mean that an individual has no interests in limiting disclosure or dissemination of the information." . . . The privacy interest in a rap sheet is substantial. The substantial character of that interest is affected by the fact that in today's society the computer can accumulate and store information that would otherwise have surely been forgotten long before a person attains age 80, when the FBI's rap sheets are discarded.

V

Exemption 7(C), by its terms, permits an agency to withhold a document only when revelation "could reasonably be expected to constitute an unwarranted invasion of personal privacy." We must next address what factors might warrant an invasion of the interest described in Part IV, *supra*.

(Continued)

EDITED CASE Department of Justice v. Reporters' Committee (Continued)

. . . As we have repeatedly stated, Congress "clearly intended" the FOIA "to give any member of the public as much right to disclosure as one with a special interest [in a particular document]." . . .

Thus whether disclosure of a private document under Exemption 7(C) is warranted must turn on the nature of the requested document and its relationship to "the basic purpose of the Freedom of Information Act 'to open agency action to the light of public scrutiny.'" . . . In our leading case on the FOIA, we declared that the Act was designed to create a broad right of access to "official information." *EPA v. Mink*, 410 U.S. 73, 80 (1973). . . .

This basic policy of "full agency disclosure unless information is exempted under clearly delineated statutory language," . . . indeed focuses on the citizens' right to be informed about "what their government is up to." Official information that sheds light on an agency's performance of its statutory duties falls squarely within that statutory purpose. That purpose, however, is not fostered by disclosure of information about private citizens that is accumulated in various governmental files but that reveals little or nothing about an agency's own conduct. In this case—and presumably in the typical case in which one private citizen is seeking information about another—the requester does not intend to discover anything about the conduct of the agency that has possession of the requested records. Indeed, response to this request would not shed any light on the conduct of any Government agency or official. . . .

Respondents argue that there is a twofold public interest in learning about Medico's past arrests or convictions: He allegedly had improper dealings with a corrupt Congressman, and he is an officer of a corporation with defense contracts. But if Medico has, in fact, been arrested or convicted of certain crimes, that information would neither aggravate nor mitigate his allegedly improper relationship with the Congressman; more specifically, it would tell us nothing directly about the character of the Congressman's behavior. Nor would it tell us anything about the conduct of the Department of Defense (DOD) in awarding one or more contracts to the Medico Company. Arguably a FOIA requests to the DOD for records relating to those contracts, or for documents describing the agency's

procedures, if any, for determining whether officers of a prospective contractor have criminal records, would constitute an appropriate request for "official information." Conceivably Medico's rap sheet would provide details to include in a news story, but, in itself, this is not the kind of public interest for which Congress enacted the FOIA. In other words, although there is undoubtedly some public interest in anyone's criminal history, especially if the history is in some way related to the subject's dealing with a public official or agency, the FOIA's central purpose is to ensure that the Government's activities be opened to the sharp eye of public scrutiny, not that information about private citizens that happens to be in the warehouse of the Government be so disclosed. Thus, it should come as no surprise that in none of our cases construing the FOIA have we found it appropriate to order a Government agency to honor a FOIA request for information about a particular private citizen.

What we have said should make clear that the public interest in the release of any rap sheet on Medico that may exist is not the type of interest protected by the FOIA. Medico may or may not be one of the 24 million persons for whom the FBI has a rap sheet. If respondents are entitled to have the FBI tell them what it knows about Medico's criminal history, any other member of the public is entitled to the same disclosure—whether for writing a news story, for deciding whether to employ Medico, to rent a house to him, to extend credit to him, or simply to confirm or deny a suspicion. There is, unquestionably, some public interest in providing interested citizens with answers to their questions about Medico. But that interest falls outside the ambit of the public interest that the FOIA was enacted to serve. . . .

VI

Both the general requirement that a court "shall determine the matter de novo" and the specific reference to an "unwarranted" invasion of privacy in Exemption 7(C) indicate that a court must balance the public interest in disclosure against the interest Congress intended the Exemption to protect. . . .

. . . The privacy interest in maintaining the practical obscurity of rap-sheet information will always be high. When the subject of such a rap

---

EDITED CASE   Department of Justice v. Reporters' Committee (Continued)

---

sheet is a private citizen and when the information is in the Government's control as a compilation, rather than as a record of "what the Government is up to," the privacy interest protected by Exemption 7(C) is in fact at its apex while the FOIA-based public interest in disclosure is at its nadir. . . . Such a disparity on the scales of justice holds for a class of cases without regard to individual circumstances; the standard virtues of bright-line rules are thus present, and the difficulties attendant to ad hoc adjudication may be avoided. Accordingly, we hold as a categorical matter that a third party's request for law enforcement records or information about a private citizen can reasonably be expected to invade that citizen's privacy, and that when the request seeks no "official information" about a Government agency, but merely records that the Government happens to be storing, the invasion of privacy is "unwarranted." The judgment of the Court of Appeals is reversed. . . .

Justice Blackmun, with whom *Justice Brennan* joins, concurring in the judgment.

I concur in the result the Court reaches in this case, but I cannot follow the route the Court takes to reach that result. In other words, the Court's use of "categorical balancing" under Exemption 7(C), I think, is not basically sound. Such a bright-line rule obviously has its appeal, but I wonder whether it would not run aground on occasion, such as in a situation where a rap sheet discloses a congressional candidate's conviction of tax fraud five years before. Surely, the FBI's disclosure of that information could not "reasonably be expected" to constitute an invasion of personal privacy, much less an unwarranted invasion, inasmuch as the candidate relinquished any interest in preventing the dissemination of this information when he chose to run for Congress. In short, I do not believe that Exemption 7(C)'s language and its legislative history, or the case law, support interpreting that provision as exempting all rap-sheet information from the FOIA's disclosure requirements. . . .

It might be possible to mount a substantial argument in favor of interpreting Exemption 3 and 28 U.S.C. 534 as exempting all rap-sheet information from the FOIA, especially in the light of the presence of the three post-FOIA, enactments the Court mentions. . . . But the federal parties before this Court have abandoned the Exemption 3 issue they presented to the Court of Appeals and lost, and it perhaps would be inappropriate for us to pursue an inquiry along this line in the present case.

For these reasons, I would not adopt the Court's bright-line approach but would leave the door open for the disclosure of rap-sheet information in some circumstances. Nonetheless, even a more flexible balancing approach would still require reversing the Court of Appeals in this case. I, therefore, concur in the judgment, but do not join the Court's opinion.

EDITED CASE   FCC v. ITT World Communications, Inc.
United States Supreme Court, 466 U.S. 463 (1984)

[In this case the Supreme Court considers whether the Government in the Sunshine Act applies to informal international conferences attended by members of the Federal Communications Commission.]

Justice Powell delivered the opinion of the Court.

. . . Members of petitioner Federal Communications Commission (FCC) participate with their European and Canadian counterparts in what is referred to as the Consultative Process. This is a series of conferences intended to facilitate joint planning of telecommunications facilities through an exchange of information on regulatory policies. At the time of the conferences at issue in the present case, only three American corporations— respondents ITT World Communications, Inc. (ITT), and RCA Global Communications, Inc., and Western Union International—provided overseas record telecommunications services. Although the FCC had approved entry into the market by other competitors, European regulators had been reluctant to do so. The FCC therefore added the topic of

(Continued)

EDITED CASE   FCC v. ITT World Communications, Inc. (Continued)

---

new carriers and services to the agenda of the Consultative Process, in the hope that exchange of information might persuade the European nations to cooperate with the FCC's policy of encouraging competition in the provision of telecommunications services.

Respondents, opposing the entry of new competitors, initiated this litigation. First, respondents filed a rulemaking petition with the FCC concerning the Consultative Process meetings. The petition requested that the FCC disclaim any intent to negotiate with foreign governments or to bind it to agreements at the meetings, arguing that such negotiations were *ultra vires* the agency's authority. Further, the petition contended that the Sunshine Act required the Consultative Process sessions, as "meetings" of the FCC, to be held in public. . . . The FCC denied the rulemaking petition, and respondents filed an appeal in the Court of Appeals for the District of Columbia Circuit.

Respondent ITT then filed suit in the District Court for the District of Columbia. The complaint, like respondents' rulemaking petition, contended (i) that the agency's negotiations with foreign officials at the Consultative Process were *ultra vires* the agency's authority and (ii) that future meetings of the Consultative Process must conform to the requirements of the Sunshine Act. The District Court dismissed the *ultra vires* count on jurisdictional grounds, but ordered the FCC to comply with the Sunshine Act. Respondent ITT appealed, and the Commission cross-appealed.

The Court of Appeals for the District of Columbia Circuit considered on consolidated appeal the District Court's judgment and the FCC's denial of the rulemaking petition. The District Court judgment was affirmed in part and reversed in part. . . . The Court of Appeals affirmed the District Court's ruling that the Sunshine Act applied to meetings of the Consultative Process. It reversed the District Court's dismissal of the *ultra vires* count, however. Noting that exclusive jurisdiction for review of final agency action lay in the Court of Appeals, that court held that the District Court nonetheless could entertain under 5 U.S.C. 703 a suit that alleged that FCC participation in the Consultative Process should be enjoined as *ultra vires* the agency's authority. The case was

remanded for consideration of the merits of respondents' *ultra vires* claim.

The Court of Appeals also concluded that the FCC erroneously had denied respondents' rulemaking petition. Consistent with its affirmance of the District Court, the Court of Appeals held that the FCC had erred in concluding that the Sunshine Act did not apply to the Consultative Process sessions. Further, the court found the record "patently inadequate" to support the FCC's conclusion that attendance at sessions of the Consultative Process was within the scope of its authority. . . . Although remanding to the FCC, the court suggested that the agency stay consideration of the rulemaking petition, as the District Court's action upon respondents' complaint might moot the question of rulemaking.

We granted certiorari, to decide whether the District Court could exercise jurisdiction over the *ultra vires* claim and whether the Sunshine Act applies to sessions of the Consultative Process. . . . We reverse.

II

We consider initially the jurisdiction of the District Court to enjoin FCC action as *ultra vires*. Exclusive jurisdiction for review of final FCC orders, such as the FCC's denial of respondents' rulemaking petition, lies in the Court of Appeals. . . . Litigants may not evade these provisions by requesting the District Court to enjoin action that is the outcome of the agency's order. . . . Yet that is what respondents have sought to do in this case. In substance, the complaint filed in the District Court raised the same issues and sought to enforce the same restrictions upon agency conduct as did the petition for rulemaking that was denied by the FCC. . . . The appropriate procedure for obtaining judicial review of the agency's disposition of these issues was appeal to the Court of Appeals as provided by statute.

The Administrative Procedure Act authorizes an action for review of final agency action in the District Court to the extent that other statutory procedures for review are inadequate. . . . Respondents contend that these provisions confer jurisdiction in the present suit because the record developed upon consideration of the rulemaking petition by the agency does not enable the Court of Appeals fairly to evaluate their *ultra vires* claim. If, how-

EDITED CASE   FCC v. ITT World Communications, Inc. (Continued)

ever, the Court of Appeals finds that the administrative record is inadequate, it may remand to the agency, . . . or in some circumstances refer the case to a special master. . . . Indeed, in the present case, the Court of Appeals has remanded the case to the agency for further proceedings. We conclude that the District Court lacked jurisdiction over respondents' *ultra vires* claim.

III

The Sunshine Act, 5 U.S.C. 552b(b), requires that "meetings of an agency" be open to the public. Section 552b(a)(2) defines "meetings" as "the deliberations of at least the number of individual agency members required to take action on behalf of the agency where such deliberations determine or result in the joint conduct or disposition of official agency business." Under these provisions, the Sunshine Act does not require that Consultative Process sessions be held in public, as the participation by FCC members in these sessions constitutes neither a "meeting" as defined by 552b(a)(2) nor a meeting "of the agency" as provided by 552b(b).

A

Congress in drafting the Act's definition of "meeting" recognized that the administrative process cannot be conducted entirely in the public eye. "[I]nformal background discussions [that] clarify issues and expose varying views" are a necessary part of an agency's work. . . . The Act's procedural requirements effectively would prevent such discussions and thereby impair normal agency operations without achieving significant public benefit. Section 552b(a)(2) therefore limits the Act's application to meetings "where at least a quorum of the agency's members . . . conduct or dispose of official agency business." . . .

Three Commissioners, the number who attended the Consultative Process sessions, did not constitute a quorum of the seven-member Commission. The three members were, however, a quorum of the Telecommunications Committee. That Committee is a "subdivision . . . authorized to act on behalf of the agency." The Commission had delegated to the Committee, pursuant to 5(d)(1) of the Communications Act of 1934, 48 Stat. 1068, as amended, 47 U.S.C. 155(d)(1), the power to approve applications for common carrier

certification. . . . The Sunshine Act applies to such a subdivision as well as to an entire agency. . . .

It does not appear, however, that the Telecommunications Committee engaged at these sessions in "deliberations [that] determine or result in the joint conduct or disposition of official agency business." This statutory language contemplates discussions that "effectively predetermine official actions." . . . Such discussions must be "sufficiently focused on discrete proposals or issues as to cause or be likely to cause the individual participating members to form reasonably firm positions regarding matters pending or likely to arise before the agency." . . . On the cross-motions for summary judgment, however, respondent ITT alleged neither that the Committee formally acted upon applications for certification at the Consultative Process sessions nor that those sessions resulted in firm positions on particular matters pending or likely to arise before the Committee. Rather, the sessions provided general background information to the Commissioners and permitted them to engage with their foreign counterparts in an exchange of views by which decisions already reached by the Commission could be implemented. As we have noted, Congress did not intend the Sunshine Act to encompass such discussions.

The Court of Appeals did not reach a contrary result by finding that the Commissioners were deliberating upon matters within their formally delegated authority. Rather, that court inferred from the members' attendance at the sessions an undisclosed authority, not formally delegated, to engage in discussions on behalf of the Commission. The court then concluded that these discussions were deliberations that resulted in the conduct of official agency business, as the discussions "play[ed] an integral role in the Commission's policymaking processes." . . .

We view the Act differently. It applies only where a subdivision of the agency deliberates upon matters that are within that subdivision's formally delegated authority to take official action for the agency. Under the reasoning of the Court of Appeals, any group of members who exchange views or gathered information on agency business

(Continued)

EDITED CASE   FCC v. ITT World Communications, Inc. (Continued)

---

apparently could be viewed as a "subdivision . . . authorized to act on behalf of the agency." The term "subdivision" itself indicates agency members who have been authorized to exercise formally delegated authority. . . . Moreover, the more expansive view of the term "subdivision" adopted by the Court of Appeals would require public attendance at a host of informal conversations of the type Congress understood to be necessary for the effective conduct of agency business. In any event, it is clear that the Sunshine Act does not extend to deliberations of a quorum of the subdivision upon matters not within the subdivision's formally delegated authority. Such deliberations lawfully could not "determine or result in the joint conduct or disposition of official agency business" within the meaning of the Act. As the Telecommunications Committee at the Consultative Process sessions did not consider or act upon applications for common carrier certification—its only formally delegated authority—we conclude that the sessions were not "meetings" within the meaning of the Sunshine Act.

B

The Consultative Process was not convened by the FCC, and its procedures were not subject to the FCC's unilateral control. The sessions of the Consultative Process therefore are not meetings "of an agency" within the meaning of 552b(b). The Act prescribes procedures for the agency to follow when it holds meetings and particularly when it chooses to close a meeting. . . . These provisions presuppose that the Act applies only to meetings that the agency has the power to conduct according to these procedures. And application of the Act to meetings not under agency control would restrict the types of meetings that agency members could attend. It is apparent that Congress, in enacting requirements for the agency's conduct of its own meetings, did not contemplate as well such a broad substantive restraint upon agency processes. . . .

IV

For these reasons, we reverse the judgment of the Court of Appeals and remand the case for further proceedings consistent with this opinion. . . .

EDITED CASE   Eco, Incorporated v. City of Elkhorn
Court of Appeals of Wisconsin, 655 N.W.2d 510 (Wis. App. 2002)

[In this case a Wisconsin Appellate Court reviews a city's refusal to provide information covered by the state open records law that was requested by a private company. The city argued that because the request was incorrectly filed under the federal Freedom of Information Act rather than the state open records law, the city had no duty to comply with the request.]

Justice Snyder delivered the opinion of the court.

ECO, Incorporated appeals from a judgment and orders of the circuit court ruling that ECO's two requests for records to the City of Elkhorn, filed pursuant to the Freedom of Information Act (FOIA), were not open records requests pursuant to Wis. Stat. §§ 19.31 through 19.37 (1999–2000) and thus not actionable via a writ of mandamus. ECO

argues that the two requests qualified as requests under Wisconsin open records law despite the mistaken reference to FOIA. We agree that the two requests required, at the very least, a response from the City. We therefore reverse the judgment and orders of the circuit court and remand for proceedings consistent with this opinion.

ECO is a Wisconsin corporation with its principal office in Elkhorn, Wisconsin. On or about April 24, 1996, ECO's president and CEO, E. Christian Olsen, submitted a written request to the City for access to various public records; the request was denominated a request pursuant to the Freedom of Information Act and read:

> Please provide us with the following information as allowed under F.O.I.A.: All engineering

---

EDITED CASE   Eco, Incorporated v. City of Elkhorn (Continued)

---

plans, prints, as built drawings, engineering and inspection reports as related to: 1. Deere Road sanitary sewer from a point 100' west of STH 67 to a point 800' west of STH 67. 2. Deere Road water main from and to points as defined in (1) above. 3. Deere Road storm sewer as defined in (1) above. 4. Deere Road as defined in (1) above. 5. Sanitary sewer main as is crossing property commonly referred to as lot # 's 2 and 3 of the Deere Road Industrial Park. 6. Storm sewer within a 100' range of the northerly boundary of lot 1 of the Deere Road Industrial Park. 7. Any and all underground utilities owned, operated, or controlled by the City of Elkhorn within a 200' range of the boundaries of lot 2 and 3 of the Deere Road Industrial Park.

ECO was looking for these records because of severe water problems occurring on its property; ECO suspected the problems were caused by a disruption of either a man-made or natural underground flowage as a result of utility construction.

ECO eventually received a copy of a letter to the City from the City's engineers, Crispell-Snyder, Inc., and an "as-built" map. . . . However, ECO did not receive any formal response from the City either granting or denying its request. Olsen contacted the city clerk and asked if there were additional records but was told there were not any more. . . .

On or about September 22, 2000, ECO submitted a second written request to the City virtually identical to the April 24, 1996 request; in addition, ECO requested the following:

> Please provide us with the following information as allowed under FOIA: 1. Any and all documents in your possession, your agents [sic] possession including but not limited to contracted insurance carriers and underwriters, their agents, engineering firms, or other contracted professional service offices, and in the possession of related City of Elkhorn affiliates or operating affiliates, past or present city officials and/or employees, including but not limited to the Elkhorn Light and Water Commission, relating to properties in the Deere Road Industrial Park North of the centerline of Deere Road [detailed description omitted]

> 2. Your written explanation of the inability to provide any of the aforementioned items.

On October 16, 2000, the City, via legal counsel, responded to ECO's request:

> Please be advised that we have received your request for information under the Freedom of Information Act. Your request has fallen upon my desk for a response. I have researched the Freedom of Information Act and your request. Please be advised that neither the State of Wisconsin nor the City of Elkhorn is subject to the Freedom of Information Act. The Act applies only to federal agencies and does not create a right of access to records held by any state or local government agency. As such, we will not be responding to your request. Wisconsin and the City of Elkhorn maintain open records pursuant to state law. Please feel free to make a request under a legitimate avenue.

On or about October 19, 2000, ECO resubmitted its requests for records to the City; the requests were identical to the September 22, 2000 requests except this time ECO specifically referenced Wisconsin public records law instead of FOIA. On December 1, 2000, ECO received a response from Elkhorn City Clerk Nancy B. Jacobson that read in relevant part as follows:

> I am writing in regards to your request for records. I apologize for the delay; however, other pressing business, which included the election and preparation of the tax roll, diverted my time to these and other matters. I am in the process of assembling your request and hope to complete it in a timely fashion. In order to fulfill your request of engineering plans, prints, as built drawings, engineering and inspection reports, I am requesting copies from the engineers. As soon as the engineers respond to my request, I will send you the cost of copies. Once I receive a check from you covering those costs, I will instruct the engineers to make the copies. There will also be a charge for time and copies made by City staff. Copies are 25 cents plus tax and staff time is $13.40 per hour.

(Continued)

EDITED CASE   Eco, Incorporated v. City of Elkhorn (Continued)

ECO never received any further response. ECO contacted the Walworth county district attorney's office for assistance in getting a response from the City; on at least two occasions, a Walworth county assistant district attorney contacted the City and urged them to comply with ECO's October 19, 2000 request.

On March 8, 2001, ECO filed a petition for writ of mandamus seeking disclosure of the requested documents and related damages, fees and costs; the circuit court signed the alternative writ of mandamus that same day, compelling the City to provide ECO with the requested information or show cause why not.

On March 23, 2001, ECO received a letter from Jacobson indicating that documents responsive to ECO's records requests were available for inspection and requesting a prepayment of $1137.70 for the City's related labor and copying costs.

On March 26, 2001, the circuit court held a "show cause" hearing. The City conceded a lack of defense to the open records request and agreed to produce the requested documents upon payment by ECO for its labor and copying costs. Based upon this representation, the circuit court declined to make the writ of mandamus absolute. That same day, Olsen paid the City's $1137.70 bill and was provided access to a large box of documents. Despite these disclosures, Olsen remained suspicious that additional records existed. Olsen went to the city engineer's office to inquire about the existence of additional engineering records regarding ECO's property. While at the office, Olsen spoke with a city employee, who showed him an entire drawer filled with files relating to the utilities on Deere Road near ECO's property. The city employee informed Olsen that the files contained all of the City's engineering records for ECO's property which would include as-built drawings, surveys, assessment notes, field notes and engineering drawings. The city employee informed Olsen that this file had been removed from the city engineer's office and sent to the city clerk's office to be copied in 1997, around the time ECO initiated its civil lawsuit against the City.

ECO's attorney then attempted to contact, via voice mail and a letter, the city attorney to inquire about the documents found in the city engineer's office. On March 29, 2001, the city attorney acknowledged receipt of these inquiries and declared that he

was investigating the allegations but would not respond "until [he] ha[d] all of the facts before [him]." That same day, ECO sent a letter to the city attorney reiterating its demand for the records. Neither the City nor its attorney ever responded to this letter. Nor did the City produce any of the documents stored in the city engineer's office.

ECO therefore moved the circuit court to make the writ of mandamus absolute. ECO also requested that it be awarded actual, consequential and punitive damages and costs and attorney's fees associated with its attempts to secure a response from the City to the various open records requests. . . .

The circuit court held that the April 24, 1996 request and September 22, 2000 requests were not "requests" pursuant to open records law because they were titled FOIA requests. Thus, according to the circuit court, the City was not required to adhere to the requirements of Wisconsin's open records law.

However, the circuit court found that the City violated Wis. Stat. § 19.35(4) in failing to timely respond to ECO's October 19, 2000 request. The circuit court also found that ECO's mandamus action was a "substantial factor" in the City's production of documents after the October 19, 2000 request and therefore ECO was entitled to $100 in damages and reasonable attorney's fees, but not punitive damages because neither the City nor Jacobson "acted arbitrarily or capriciously." The circuit court further held that ECO did not substantially prevail regarding the April 24, 1996 request or the September 22, 2000 request.

ECO submitted billing statements in support of its request for $14,351.42 in attorney's fees and actual costs of $861. The circuit court ultimately awarded ECO $11,951.42 in damages, attorney's fees and costs associated with the October 19, 2000 request. ECO appeals the circuit court's denial of its request for a writ of mandamus and associated damages, fees and costs relating to the April 24, 1996 and September 22, 2000 written requests. . . .

. . . Wisconsin Stat. § 19.31 sets forth this policy declaration regarding open records: In recognition of the fact that a representative government is dependent upon an informed electorate, it is declared to be the public policy of this state that all persons are entitled to the greatest possible information regarding the affairs of government

---

EDITED CASE   Eco, Incorporated v. City of Elkhorn (Continued)

---

and the official acts of those officers and employees who represent them. Further, providing persons with such information is declared to be an essential function of a representative government and an integral part of the routine duties of officers and employees whose responsibility it is to provide such information. To that end, §§ 19.32 to 19.37 shall be construed in every instance with a presumption of complete public access, consistent with the conduct of governmental business. The denial of public access generally is contrary to the public interest, and only in an exceptional case may access be denied. The open records law serves one of the basic tenets of our democratic system by providing an opportunity for public oversight of the workings of government. . . . This state recognizes a presumption of accessibility to public records, reflected in both the statutes and in our case law. . . .

. . . [T]he general presumption of our law is that public records shall be open to the public unless there is a clear statutory exception, unless there exists a limitation under the common law or unless there is an overriding public interest in keeping the public record confidential. . . .

Wisconsin Stat. § 19.31 must be broadly construed to favor disclosure. . . . Exceptions must be recognized for what they are, instances in derogation of the general legislative intent, and must therefore be narrowly construed. It would be contrary to general well-established principles of open records statutes to hold that, by implication only, any type of record can be held from public inspection. . . .

The City concedes that the April 24, 1996 request met the requirements of an open records request and that the body of the letter adequately describes open records. However, the City argues that because the request was filed pursuant to FOIA and the City is not subject to said Act, it did not have a duty to respond. Such assertions are contrary to the strong public policies behind open records law and the language of open records statutes. We conclude that because the letter clearly describes open records and the letter had all the earmarkings of an open records request, the April 24, 1996 letter was in fact an open records request and triggered, at a minimum, a duty to respond to the request. . . .

None of these statutes requires a request to contain any "magic words" nor do they prohibit the use of any words. While "request" is not

defined anywhere in open records law, a request is deemed sufficient if "it reasonably describes the requested record or the information requested." Wis. Stat. § 19.35(1)(h). Here, the City concedes as much. We conclude that the use of FOIA does not render it a nonrequest. Because a request must only reasonably describe the requested record or information requested, because nothing in open records law prohibits the use of any certain words, because the City concedes that the letter meets the requirements of an ope155n records request and because the legislature's well-established public policy presumes accessibility to public records and mandates that open records law be liberally construed to favor disclosure, we conclude that the April 24, 1996 letter was, in fact, an adequate open records request.

. . . Thus, under § 19.35(4)(a), receipt of an open records request triggers either a duty to respond to the request or a duty to produce the requested records. Here, the City neither responded to the April 24, 1996 request nor produced the requested documents. It is incumbent upon the custodian of the public record who refused the demand of inspection to "state specifically the reasons for this refusal." . . . A custodian's denial of access to a public record must be accompanied by a statement of the specific public policy reasons for the refusal. . . . The City did not provide any response whatsoever and therefore did not comply with open records law.

Because the City failed to respond to ECO's request and thus failed to comply with the requirements of Wis. Stat. § 19.35(4)(a), ECO is entitled to costs, fees and damages pursuant to Wis. Stat. § 19.37(2). The circuit court took the issue of damages under advisement pending a decision on whether the April 24, 1996 and September 22, 2000 letters constituted open records requests. Once the circuit court determined that the two letters were not open records requests, the issue of damages became moot and was not addressed. Because we conclude that both the April 24, 1996 letter and September 22, 2000 letter were, in fact, open records requests which were wrongfully denied, damages must be addressed. We therefore remand this matter to the circuit court to address the issue of damages.

Judgment and orders reversed and cause remanded with directions.

EDITED CASE   Minnesota Medical Association v.
Minnesota Department of Public Welfare
Supreme Court of Minnesota 274 N.W.2d 84 (Minn. 1978)

[In this case the Minnesota Supreme Court interprets the Minnesota Data Privacy Act in the context of an attempt by a Roman Catholic publication to obtain information about abortions provided to patients receiving state medical assistance.]

Chief Justice Sheran delivered the opinion of the court.

This is an appeal from an order of the Ramsey County District Court denying plaintiffs' motion for a temporary injunction restraining defendant Minnesota Department of Public Welfare from furnishing to the Catholic Bulletin Publishing Co. any Catholic Bulletin Publishing Company in 1976 and 1977. We affirm.

In June 1977, a Catholic Bulletin reporter requested the Department of Public Welfare to provide him a list of all physicians, clinics, and hospitals that had performed abortions for medical assistance patients in 1976 and 1977 and to disclose the amounts the state had paid each service provider for these procedures. The department agreed to provide the information, which is stored with other data furnished by the providers on computer tapes. The department informed the Bulletin that it would cost $2,500 to $4,000 to program and run the computer to retrieve the data, but later agreed to furnish it at no cost if the Bulletin would prepare the program.

At that time the Minnesota Medical Association and its president, Dr. Chester Anderson, brought an action for a temporary and permanent injunction to prohibit the department from disseminating information stored in state computers until administrative regulations governing access to computer-stored information were adopted and complied with, which regulations should require payment of retrieval costs, public hearings prior to dissemination, and protection of patients' and physicians' rights to receive and render medical treatment. On November 23, 1977, a temporary restraining order and order to show cause was issued. On December 14, 1977, a hearing was held on plaintiffs' motion for a temporary injunction "restraining and enjoining Defendants, their officers, agents and employees and all persons acting in concert or participation with them from publish-

ing, providing, disseminating or otherwise disclosing data in response to the request of the Catholic Bulletin that it be provided without cost and by use of its own computer program, any data relating to names of service providers and/or medical procedures and amount paid to service providers relating to 'abortions' during 1976 and 1977, including any portions or part thereof, and whether alone or in combination, until the final adjudication of Plaintiffs' claims for relief."

On December 20, 1977, the court issued its order denying the motion. It concluded that, with the exception of Dr. Chester Anderson's claim that providing the information to the Catholic Bulletin without cost would constitute an unlawful expenditure of public funds, the plaintiffs had "no constitutional or statutory right to the relief sought." It held that the information sought was "public" enjoying no classification of "private" or "confidential" under Minn.St. 15.1642, and that the fact that the information was stored on computer tapes does not remove it from the category of "public records" under Minn.St. 15.17. It further held that prohibiting disclosure would impose an unconstitutional prior restraint on publication by the Catholic Bulletin. With respect to Anderson's claim as a taxpayer, the court held that the Catholic Bulletin must pay the cost of providing the data. It ruled, however, that a claim that the department would not charge the full cost was not a ground for injunctive relief since the taxpayer could challenge the reasonableness of the department's charges in a taxpayer suit to recover the sum allegedly due.

Plaintiffs appeal, contending that they have standing to challenge alleged invasions of their right to administer medical treatment; that the use of the state's computers to compile, collate, and correlate the requested data will impair or defeat privacy rights, physicians' rights to administer medical treatment according to their professional judgment, and medical assistance patients' right to a free choice of physicians; that state agencies must adopt rules governing access to computer files before releasing any information stored therein; and that taxpayers may obtain injunctions prohibiting agencies from furnishing services or property until full payment is received.

EDITED CASE   Minnesota Medical Association v. Minnesota Department
of Public Welfare (Continued)

I. Statutory Bases for Injunctive Relief

A. Statutory Classification of the Requested Data
The purpose of Minn.St. 15.162 to 15.169, known
as the Minnesota Data Privacy Act, is to control the
state's collection, security, and dissemination
of information in order "to protect the privacy of
individuals while meeting the legitimate needs of
government and society for information." Minn.St.
15.169, subd. 3(3). To accomplish this purpose the
law provides for the classification of data on
individuals into three categories: "confidential,"
"private," and "public." "Confidential data on
individuals" is defined as data which is "(a) made
not public by statute or federal law applicable
to the data and is inaccessible to the individual
subject of that data." Minn.St. 15.162, subd. 2a.
"Private data on individuals" is data "which is
made by statute or federal law applicable to the
data: (a) not public; and (b) accessible to the individual subject of that data." Minn.St. 15.162, subd.
5a. "Public data on individuals" means "data
which is accessible to the public in accordance with
the provisions of section 15.17." Minn.St. 15.162,
subd. 5b. These definitions require that classifications as "confidential" or "private" be made by
"statute or federal law applicable to the data."

Appellant cites no statute or federal law which
makes the names of those receiving payments for
abortion services provided to medical assistance
patients or the amount of the payments received
"not public." Therefore, this information is neither
"confidential" nor "private." Appellants nevertheless contend that the information is not "public
data on individuals" because it does not fall
within the definition of "public records" under
Minn.St. 15.17.

A similar inference can be drawn from Minn.St.
145.413, which requires physicians to report to the
state board of health all abortions they perform.
The statute expressly provides that no part of such
reports may be disclosed and classifies as "confidential" all information reported.

Minn.St. 15.17, subd. 1, requires all state agencies to "make and keep all records necessary to
a full and accurate knowledge of their official
activities." The statute then provides that "(a)ll
such public records" shall be made on durable
paper, but that they may be photographed, photo-

stated, microphotographed, or microfilmed and
that the reproductions may be substituted for the
originals. Minn.St. 15.17, subd. 4, requires public
record custodians to keep the records "easily accessible for convenient use," and provides in part:
"Except as otherwise expressly provided by law, he
shall permit all public records in his custody to be
inspected, examined, abstracted, or copied at reasonable times and under his supervision and regulation by any person; and he shall, upon the
demand of any person, furnish certified copies
thereof on payment in advance of fees not to
exceed the fees prescribed by law."

Appellants contend that, because the information sought here was stored on computer tapes, it
is not a "public record" accessible to the public
under § 15.17. Rather, they argue, only the micro-
film copies of the practitioner invoices from which
the computer tapes are made constitute public
records. This argument is without merit.

The requirement of Minn.St. 15.17, subd. 1,
that public records be made on durable quality
paper does not constitute a definition of public
records. Rather, that requirement is imposed on
"(a)ll such public records." "Such" refers to the
sentence immediately preceding, which requires
officials to keep "all records necessary to a full and
accurate knowledge of their official activities."
Thus, whether records are "public records"
depends not on the form in which they are kept
but on whether they are "necessary to a full and
accurate knowledge" of official activities. The
form requirements merely ensure that the records
are made permanent. The department has complied with this provision by microfilming the practitioner invoices. Minn.St. 15.17, subd. 4, which
grants public access to all public records, "except
as otherwise expressly provided by law," places no
restrictions on the form in which the records shall
be made available other than that they shall be
"easily accessible for convenient use." While it
provides that "(p)hotographic, photostatic,
microphotographic, or microfilmed records shall
be considered as accessible for convenient use
regardless of the size of such records," it does not
proscribe furnishing the records in some other

(Continued)

EDITED CASE   Minnesota Medical Association v. Minnesota Department
of Public Welfare (Continued)

form acceptable to the requester. Therefore, Minn.St. 15.17 does not in any way prohibit the department from releasing data contained in its public records in the form of a computer printout. Minn.St. 256B.041 provides for the establishment of a system for the centralized disbursement of medical assistance payments to vendors by the commissioner of public welfare. Minn.St. 256B.064 provides for the termination of such payments to vendors of medical care who have been determined to be ineligible for payment. These provisions establish that the records of payments to individual providers of medical care are "necessary to a full and accurate knowledge" of the department's official activities. Without such records it could not be determined whether the department was making payments only to eligible providers or whether the payments made were reasonable for the services provided. Therefore, such records are public records accessible to the public under Minn.St. 15.17, and the information contained in such records is "public data on individuals" under Minn.St. 15.162, subd. 5b.

B. Patients' Right to Free Choice of Physician
Appellants argue that even if the disclosure of the information sought is not proscribed by statute, such disclosure would impair or defeat the statutory right of medical assistance patients to a free choice of physicians. They contend that, if the information is disclosed, fewer doctors will be willing to participate in the medical assistance program and the patients' right to free choice will thereby be impaired. Even if this is true, however, it does not serve as a ground for injunctive relief. The legislature has provided mechanisms by which the public may be denied access to information controlled by state agencies. It has further determined that public records are to be available to the public "except as otherwise expressly provided by law." Minn.St. 15.17, subd. 4. These provisions evidence a legislative intent to retain full control of public access to information. The power to restrict access is given to administrative agencies only in emergency situations, and even that power is subject to legislative action. No power to restrict access is granted to the courts.

   With such a clear statement of legislative intent, appellants' contention that the court should balance

the public's statutory right of access against medical assistance patients' statutory right to a free choice of physicians and the effectiveness of the medical assistance program is unacceptable. The legislature has expressly reserved the power to engage in such balancing to itself, and its failure to deny public access to the information sought here constitutes a legislative determination that the public's right to know outweighs the competing interests of the medical assistance program and its patients.

C. Necessity for Rules and Regulations Governing Access to Computer-Stored Data
Minn.St. 15.1641(e) provides: "The responsible authority shall establish procedures and safeguards to ensure that all public, private or confidential data on individuals is accurate, complete and current. Emphasis shall be placed on the data security requirements of computerized files containing private or confidential data on individuals which are accessible directly via telecommunications technology, including security during transmission." Minn.St. 15.1671 provides in part: "The commissioner (of administration) shall with the advice of the intergovernmental information services advisory council promulgate rules, in accordance with the rulemaking procedures in the administrative procedures act which shall apply to state agencies, statewide systems and political subdivisions to implement the enforcement and administration of sections 15.162 to 15.169." Appellants argue that since no rules have been adopted as required by § 15.1671, no information stored in the department's computer may be compiled or disseminated to the public. Appellants base their argument on the broad legal principle that important questions of social and political policy should not be decided by administrative agencies on an ad hoc basis. Yet, they fail to relate this principle to the facts of this case. Minn.St. 15.1641(e), quoted above, does not expressly require agencies to implement computer security procedures through rulemaking. The definition of "rule" in Minn.St. 15.0411, subd. 3, of the Administrative Procedures Act specifically excludes "rules concerning only the internal management of the agency or other agencies, and which do not directly affect the rights of or procedure available to the public." The "procedures

---

EDITED CASE   Minnesota Medical Association v. Minnesota Department
of Public Welfare (Continued)

---

and safeguards" to ensure the accuracy, completeness, and currency of agency data on individuals concern only the internal management of the agency since they provide guidance to the agency in its collection and storage of information. Therefore, such procedures and safeguards need not be adopted in the manner specified by the Administrative Procedures Act.

Minn.St. 15.1671 requires the commissioner of administration to adopt, in accordance with the Administrative Procedures Act, rules "to implement the enforcement and administration of sections 15.162 to 15.169." The commissioner has not done so. Nevertheless, this failure cannot affect public access to "public" information. Nothing in sections 15.162 to 15.169 purports to govern dissemination of public data.

Dissemination is governed by Minn.St. 15.17 to 15.174. Minn.St. 15.171 expressly authorizes the use of "alternative methods for the compilation, maintenance and storage of information contained in (official) records" and provides that such methods must provide for access to the information "by those authorized by law to have access." Since the information sought here is public information, the Catholic Bulletin is authorized to have access to it. Its access is thus determined under the Official Records Act, and the commissioner's failure to promulgate rules under the Data Privacy Act is immaterial. . . . Because the information sought by the Catholic Bulletin is "public data on individuals" accessible under the Official Records Act, because the statutory right of medical assistance patients has been legislatively subjected to the public's right to information contained in official records, and because the failure of the commissioner of administration to adopt rules under the Data Privacy Act does not affect the public's right to information, appellants have no statutory right to prevent the department from disclosing the requested information.

II. Constitutional Grounds for Injunctive Relief
Appellants assert that "collection and disclosure of data relating to abortions is constitutionally suspect, and may be sustained only upon a showing that it will be held in confidence and that it will not restrict the physicians' right to exercise of medical judgment or otherwise interfere with a pregnant woman's right to obtain an abortion

prior to viability of the embryo." This statement is overly broad and does not correctly state the holding of the court's decision in *Planned Parenthood of Central Missouri v. Danforth*, 428 U.S. 52, 96 S.Ct. 2831, 49 L.Ed.2d 788 (1976). The amicus brief of the Minnesota Civil Liberties Union provides a better statement of the constitutional issues. The M.C.L.U. contends that disclosure of the names of physicians who performed abortions on medical assistance patients would infringe the privacy rights of both the patients and the physicians.

A. Patients' Right to Privacy
. . . In *Planned Parenthood of Central Missouri v. Danforth*, 428 U.S. 52, 96 S.Ct. 2831, 49 L.Ed.2d 788 (1976), the court upheld a provision of a Missouri statute that required doctors to make and keep records on all abortions for the use of local, state, and national public health officers. The records were to be confidential and used only for statistical purposes to enhance medical knowledge for the preservation of maternal health. The recordkeeping requirement was challenged on the ground that it constituted an unconstitutional restriction on the patients' abortion decision during the first trimester. The court, however, found that the records served the state's interest in protecting the health of its female citizens and that, because the records were confidential, there was "no legally significant impact or consequence on the abortion decision or on the physician-patient relationship." . . .

Amicus M.C.L.U. contends that the proposed disclosure of the names of physicians who performed abortions will have the legally significant impact not found in *Danforth*. First, there is the danger that patients' names will be accidentally disclosed. Second, any disclosure will have a chilling effect in that women may be prevented from obtaining an abortion by the fear that their names might be accidentally disclosed. Third, a woman may be deterred from seeking an abortion from the doctor named because people might correctly infer the reason she saw that doctor. Fourth, disclosure may cause some doctors to discontinue performing abortions, thus making it more difficult for women to find a willing doctor and infringing their freedom of choice in the selection of a physician. M.C.L.U. also notes that the

(Continued)

EDITED CASE   Minnesota Medical Association v. Minnesota Department
of Public Welfare (Continued)

---

confidentiality of the physician- patient relationship
is protected under state law.

Nevertheless, the M.C.L.U.'s speculations on the
possible effects of the disclosure of the doctors'
names on women seeking abortions are not
sufficient grounds for injunctive relief. Whenever
the state acquires confidential information, the
possibility of accidental disclosure exists. That possibility is not sufficient to preclude the state from
acquiring the information, . . . and should also
not be sufficient to deprive the public of access to
other, nonconfidential information. Beyond simply
presenting the possibility of accidental disclosure
of patients' names, amicus offers nothing to show
that the procedures followed by the department in
this case are insufficient to protect patient
anonymity. Similarly there is no evidence to support the speculation that the mere possibility of
disclosure of patient identities, however slight, will
be a significant factor in a medical assistance
patient's decision not to seek an abortion. The
guilt-by-association argument is also without evidentiary support and appears even less reasonable.
The validity of that argument must rest on the
assumption that once a doctor is known to have
performed abortions, it may be inferred that all, or
at least the majority, of his female patients employ
him to perform abortions. Only if the doctor provides almost no services except abortions, does
such an assumption have merit. In such a case, it is
likely that the nature of the doctor's practice
would be known even without disclosure of the
department's information. Thus, it is improbable
that disclosure will have any significant effect on
the inferences that can be drawn from the fact
that a woman visits a particular physician.

A "radical restriction in the number of Minnesota
physicians willing to perform abortions" resulting
from disclosure would present a more difficult problem than the more direct effect on women themselves. Amicus contends that such a reduction would
infringe on a woman's right to make an independent abortion decision by making abortions less
available. Here again, however, there is no evidence
that such a reduction will occur. Robert G. Randle,
director of the Medical assistance division of the
state Medicaid program, states in his deposition that
disclosure of physicians' names "could have some
kind of an impact on participation" of medical

providers in the medical assistance program. He goes
on to state, however, that his "primary concern was
the relationship between the providers and the program." Nowhere does he forecast a "radical restriction" in the number of participating providers.

The affidavit of plaintiff Dr. Chester Anderson
states that disclosure of the names of physicians
and the nature of the treatments they provided
"would also discourage physicians and other medical providers from providing treatment covered by
the Medical Assistance program to patients eligible
for Medical Assistance and discourage physicians
and other medical providers from performing necessary medical procedures which are controversial
from a nonmedical point of view." He does not
allege any significant reduction in the number of
doctors willing to participate in the medical assistance program. Neither Randle nor Anderson
offers any support for his speculations. Moreover,
it seems unlikely that mere disclosure of the fact
that a doctor has performed abortions will cause
him to stop providing that service. Once that fact is
known, the doctor has little reason to stop. In fact,
disclosure could aid women seeking abortions to
find a doctor willing to provide the service. Of
course, disclosure may also permit those who
oppose abortions to focus pressure on the named
doctors to convince them that it would be in their
best interests to cease providing the service. The
propriety of such action, however, is not before
this court, which is concerned on this appeal only
with the effect of the disclosure itself.

The United States Supreme Court has indicated
that any state action that interferes with a
woman's right to make an independent abortion
decision or with her physician's exercise of medical
judgment constitutes an invasion of her right
to privacy, at least during the first trimester of
pregnancy. . . . The disclosure sought to be
prevented in this case would not constitute such an
"otherwise unconstitutional restriction." Disclosure
places no burden on the doctor, does not destroy
the confidentiality of his relationship with patients,
and does not restrict his freedom to exercise his
medical judgment. Disclosure itself does not have
any effect on the moral or ethical considerations
that affect his decision whether or not to perform
abortions. If antiabortion factions of the public
convince him to stop performing abortions, his

EDITED CASE Minnesota Medical Association v. Minnesota Department of Public Welfare (Continued)

---

decision will be the result of private, not state, actions. Therefore, even if the ultimate consequence of disclosure is a reduction in the number of physicians willing to perform abortions, that reduction will not constitute an unconstitutional infringement of women's rights of privacy. Plaintiffs thus have failed to establish that failure to grant the requested injunction will result in a deprivation of female medical assistance patients' rights to privacy in making an independent decision to seek termination of pregnancy.

B. Physicians' Right to Privacy
Amicus M.C.L.U. asserts that disclosure will deprive physicians of their rights to both privacy and property. The property right claimed is "to practice medicine according to his or her best judgment and without undue interference by the state." Whether physicians have the property right claimed, independent of their patients' rights to receive the services involved, has not been decided. . . . Even if such a right exists, as is noted in the preceding section, disclosure itself does not constitute "interference" by the state. Thus, the physician's right to privacy is the only right not derived from the patients that can serve as a ground for injunctive relief. In *Roe v. Wade*, . . . the court stated: "The Constitution does not explicitly mention any right of privacy. In a line of decisions, however, . . . the Court has recognized that a right of personal privacy, or a guarantee of certain areas or zones of privacy, does exist under the Constitution. These decisions make it clear that only personal rights that can be deemed 'fundamental' or 'implicit in the concept of ordered liberty,' . . . are included in this guarantee of personal privacy." Thus, the question presented by the assertion of the physicians' right of privacy is whether the personal right claimed that is, the right of medical assistance providers to keep the details of their dealings with the department of public welfare from becoming public knowledge is "fundamental" or "implicit in the concept of ordered liberty." The right claimed is not, as amicus argues, "the right not to have all their professional and business dealings made public." The department does not propose to disclose "all their professional and business dealings." Only services that are paid for with public funds are involved. The providers contracted with the department to provide medical care to medical assistance patients and were paid by

the department for services rendered pursuant to the agreement. The intervenors seek disclosure of information concerning only those services and payments. Viewed in this manner, the contention that disclosure would infringe the physicians' personal rights of privacy loses much of its force.

The public has a right to know about the workings of government. . . . Great responsibility is accordingly placed upon the news media to report fully and accurately the proceedings of government, and official records and documents open to the public are the basic data of governmental operations. Without the information provided by the press most of us and many of our representatives would be unable to vote intelligently or to register opinions on the administration of government generally." In opposition to the public's need for information in this case is the doctors' asserted right to prevent public disclosure of their names. In *Paul v. Davis*, 424 U.S. 693, 713, 96 S.Ct. 1155, 1166, 47 L.Ed.2d 405, 421 (1976), the court held that no personal right of privacy was infringed when a police department distributed a flyer identifying the plaintiff as an "Active Shoplifter" to local businesses. . . .

The instant case, like *Paul v. Davis*, involves the disclosure of records of official acts. As previously noted, that disclosure does not restrict the doctors' freedom of action in a private sphere. Moreover, the information to be disclosed cannot be characterized as purely "personal" since it concerns the expenditure of public funds. . . .

In *Nixon v. Administrator of General Services*, 433 U.S. 425, 459, 97 S.Ct. 2777, 2798, 53 L.Ed.2d 867, 901 (1977), the court distinguished between the former president's personal matters . . . and matters relating to acts done in his public capacity. The same distinction can be made between a doctor's private records and the records of the department of public welfare's payments to him. The latter records are not "extremely private communications." It must, therefore, be concluded that disclosure of the information sought here will not infringe physicians' constitutional rights of privacy. Appellants have failed to establish that they have any statutory or constitutional right to prevent disclosure of the requested information. Since disclosure will not violate appellants' rights, the district

(Continued)

EDITED CASE   Minnesota Medical Association v. Minnesota Department of Public Welfare (Continued)

---

court did not abuse its discretion in denying their plea for injunctive relief and its decision is affirmed. Affirmed.

Justice Otis, dissenting.

There are two areas of disagreement with the majority opinion which prompt me to dissent. They are, however, fundamental to the ultimate disposition of these proceedings. First, I have no trouble reconciling the Data Privacy Act with the Official Records Act insofar as they deal with the protection of a needy patient's privacy. In my opinion, they compel compliance with the statutory man-

date that the commissioner of administration adopt appropriate regulations to implement the Data Privacy Act. Such regulations can distinguish private detail from otherwise public Medicaid payment records. Second, the disclosure here sought, I submit, constitutes state action which results in a constitutional burden on the right of needy patients to obtain abortions. . . .

Justice Todd, dissenting. I join in the dissent of Mr. Justice Otis.

Justice Wahl, dissenting. I respectfully join in the dissent of Mr. Justice Otis.

ENDNOTES

1. Pub. L. 101–336, 42 U.S.C.A. § 12101 *et seq.*

2. 42 U.S.C.A. § 12116.

3. 42 U.S.C.A. §§ 12186(a)(1), (b).

4. 42 U.S.C.A. §§ 12143(b), 12149, 12164.

5. Amended Title II of the Communications Act of 1934, 47 U.S.C.A. § 201 *et seq.*

6. 47 U.S.C.A. § 610.

7. *American Textile Manufacturers Institute v. Donovan,* 452 U.S. 490, 547 (1981), Rehnquist, J., dissenting.

8. See, e.g., *NAACP v. Federal Power Commission,* 452 U.S. 662 (1976).

9. 5 U.S.C.A. § 702.

10. 26 U.S.C.A. § 501(c)(3).

11. 461 U.S. 574 (1983).

12. 529 U.S. 120 (2000).

13. 21 U.S.C.A. § 301 *et seq.*

14. Jerry Taylor, *Democracy's at Stake in the Fight over Tobacco Regulation,* Cato Institute, April 19, 2000. Retrieved from http://www.cato.org/dailys/ 04-19-00.html.

15. 5 U.S.C.A. §§ 551–559, §§ 701–706.

16. 5 U.S.C.A. § 551(5).

17. 1981 MSAPA § 1.102 (11).

18. *Bi-Metallic Investment Co. v. State Board of Equalization of Colorado,* 239 U.S. 44 (1915).

19. Kenneth Culp Davis, *Administrative Law Text* 142 (3d ed. 1972).

20. 5 U.S.C.A. § 553(b).

21. Pub. L. 104–320, 110 Stat. 3870, now codified at 5 U.S.C.A. § 571 *et seq.*

22. 5 U.S.C.A. § 552.

23. *EPA v. Mink,* 410 U.S. 73, 80 (1973).

24. *Department of Air Force v. Rose,* 425 U.S. 352, 361 (1976).

25. 5 U.S.C.A. § 552(B)(7)(A); *Center for National Security Studies v. U.S. Dept. of Justice,* 331 F.3d 918 (D.C. Cir. 2003).

26. 5 U.S.C.A. § 552(a)(1).

27. See *Morton v. Ruiz,* 415 U.S. 199 (1974).

28. See, e.g., *United States v. Floyd,* 477 F.2d 217 (10th Cir. 1973) (posted sign and the security guards gave demonstrators actual notice that they could not enter military base without permission of the base commander).

29. *American Civil Liberties Union Foundation v. Deukmejian,* 51 P.2d 822 (Cal. 1982).

30. Tex. Rev. Civ. Stat. Ann. art. 6252-17a, § 2(1)(F) (Vernon Supp.1986).

31. Tex. Rev. Civ. Stat. Ann. art. 6252-17a § 3(a) (Vernon Supp.1986).

32. 850 F.2d 224 (5th Cir. 1988).

33. KRS 61.870(1)(h).

34. KRS 61.870(2).

35. *Hardin County v. Valentine,* 894 S.W.2d 151, 152 (Ky. App. 1995).

36. 5 U.S.C.A. § 552b(b).

37. See, generally, R. Berg & S. Klitzman, *An Interpretive Guide to the Government in the Sunshine Act* (1978).

38. *FCC v. ITT World Commuications,* 466 U.S. 463 (1984).

39. Fla. Stat. Ch. 286.

40. *News-Press Publishing Co. v. Carlson,* 410 So.2d 546 (Fla. App. 1982).

41. *Bennett v. Warden,* 333 So.2d 97 (Fla. App. 1976).

42. 5 U.S.C.A. §§ 1 *et seq.*

43. 491 U.S. 440.

44. 997 F.2d 898 (D.C. Cir. 1993).

45. 5 U.S.C.A. § 552a.

46. 42 U.S.C.A. § 405(c)(2)(C).

47. Minn. Statutes §§ 15.162 to 15.169.

48. 20 U.S.C.A. 1232g.

49. 20 U.S.C.A. § 1232a(4)(A).

50. 534 U.S. 273.

51. *State ex rel. The Miami Student v. Miami University,* 680 N.E.2d 956 (Ohio App. 1997).

52. *Osborn v. Board of Regents,* 647 N.W.2d 158 (2002).

53. *Arkansas Gazette Co. v. Southern State College,* 620 S.W.2d 258, 259 (Ark. 1981).

54. *United States v. Miller,* 425 U.S. 435 (1976).

55. Pub. L. 95-630, Nov. 10, 1978, 92 Stat. 3697, codified at 12 U.S.C.A. §§ 3401-342.

56. 429 U.S. 589.

57. Pub.L. 104-191, 110 Stat. 1936.

58. 65 Fed. Reg. 82,462 (Dec. 28, 2000).

59. Further information about the new rule is available on the Department of Health and Human Services web site, online at http://www.hhs.gov/news.

60. See 16 C.F.R. 310.4(b)(1)(iii)(B) (FTC rule); 47 C.F.R. 64.1200(c)(2) (FCC rule).

61. *Chevron, U.S.A., Inc. v. Natural Resources Defense Council,* 467 U.S. 837 (1984).

62. *Mainstream Marketing Services, Inc. v. Federal Trade Commission,* (Nos. 03-1429, 03-6258, 03-9571, 03-9594. No 03-1429, 3rd Cir. Feb. 17, 2004).

63. 44 U.S.C.A. §§ 3501-3520.

64. 44 U.S.C.A. § 3504 (c)(2).

65. 44 U.S.C.A. § 3508.

66. Office of Management and Budget, Office of Information and Regulatory Affairs, *Managing Information Collection and Dissemination,* FY 2002.

67. Regulatory Flexibility Act of 1980; see 5 U.S.C.A. § 601.

68. Pete Du Pont, *Pleading the Tenth: With the Demise of Liberalism, Can Federalism Be Brought Back to Life?* National Review, Nov. 27, 1995, at 50.

69. See 2 U.S.C.A. § 1501 *et seq.*

5

Investigation
and Enforcement

"Regulatory or enforcement authority generally carries with it all the
modes of inquiry and investigation traditionally employed or useful to
execute the authority granted."

CHIEF JUSTICE WARREN E. BURGER
WRITING FOR THE SUPREME COURT
IN *DOW CHEMICAL COMPANY V. UNITED STATES,* 476 U.S. 227, 233 (1986).

INTRODUCTION

Administrative agencies require accurate information to carry out their functions. They receive the information from public sources and from persons for whom an agency administers government programs. Other data must be obtained from the businesses and industries that an agency regulates. When Congress or a state legislature delegates to an administrative agency investigative responsibilities, the agency must inform itself of violations of the laws and regulations that it is charged with enforcing. Those regulated by agencies are required to maintain certain records available for inspection and to make reports concerning their operations. The extent of these requirements varies according to the agency's statutory mandates. An agency charged with investigative duties is granted authority to make inspections, audits and examinations, and administrative inspections and searches, and where necessary, to obtain administrative search warrants, and issue subpoenas to compel individuals to testify and to produce records. When an agency must compel the production of information, the right of privacy often conflicts with the public's need for information and brings into play the Fourth Amendment prohibition against unreasonable searches and seizures and the Fifth Amendment privilege against self-incrimination.

To enforce the laws it administers and ensure compliance with its regulations and orders, an agency usually has available a panoply of enforcement mechanisms. These sanctions depend on the agency's statutory authority and may include issuance of cease and desist orders, suspension and revocation of licenses and permits, and imposition of administrative fines as well as liens, garnishments, and forfeitures. These sanctions must always be exercised within the bounds of constitutional constraints, especially the Fourth and Fifth Amendments. Courts tend to relax Fourth and Fifth Amendment protections considerably when the only sanctions to be imposed are administrative in nature. Where an administrative sanc-

tion is unavailing an agency can resort to civil litigation or refer a case for criminal prosecution. In that context courts tend to be much more solicitous of Fourth and Fifth Amendment rights.

COMPULSORY PROCESS

As pointed out, agencies obtain most of the information they require through voluntary compliance by those subject to the agency's regulations. But when an agency seeks information or the production of documents from an individual or entity subject to its authority it has available a tool called a **subpoena.** A subpoena is a court order requiring a person to appear before a court or other tribunal. A **subpoena** *duces tecum* requires the person to bring along specified documents. In conducting investigations, agencies have powers to subpoena records and compel individuals to testify, as long as compelled testimony is not used as evidence in a criminal prosecution.[1] Without these powers, the ability of agencies to fulfill their statutory missions would be seriously degraded. Unlike courts, which possess the inherent power to issue subpoenas, administrative agencies must acquire that authority by law, usually by the legislative act creating an agency. In some instances, statutes delegate administrative subpoena power directly to the chief executive (the president or governor) who, in turn, delegates this power to a particular agency head by way of an executive order.[2]

Both the federal Administrative Procedure Act (APA) and the Model State Administrative Procedure Act (MSAPA) recognize that it is essential that the power to issue subpoenas be conferred by law. Section 555(c) of the APA stipulates that compulsory process is to issue only in conformity with the law, and Section 555(d) of the APA provides:

> Agency subpoenas authorized by law shall
> be issued to a party on request and, when
> required by rules of procedures, on a statement

or showing of general relevance and reasonable scope of the evidence sought. On contest, the court shall sustain the subpoena or similar process or demand to the extent that it is found to be in accordance with law. In a proceeding for enforcement, the court shall issue an order requiring the appearance of the witness or the production of the evidence or data within a reasonable time under penalty of punishment for contempt in case of contumacious failure to comply.

When it becomes necessary to enforce compliance with an administrative subpoena, an agency must generally petition for enforcement through the appropriate federal or state court.[3] Often an agency requires that one who wishes to challenge a subpoena must first exhaust any administrative procedures.[4] Courts grant agencies considerable leeway in conducting investigations; however, one who has exhausted administrative remedies can raise a challenge to a subpoena in the appropriate federal or state court on grounds that the agency's action is beyond its powers or that the information being sought is not relevant to the agency's functions or the investigation it is pursuing. It is difficult, however, to prevail on such grounds, as historically the Supreme Court has looked upon administrative subpoenas as it does grand jury subpoenas[5] and has ruled that an administrative subpoena should be enforced where the evidence the agency is seeking is not "plainly incompetent or irrelevant to any lawful purpose" of the agency.[6] A party can challenge a subpoena *duces tecum* on the ground that the subpoena is not specific as to the information being sought, is unduly burdensome, or that it seeks **disclosure of trade secrets.** When a challenge is leveled at information claimed to be trade secrets a court will likely enter a protective order to assure protection for confidential documents.[7] See Box 5.1 for an excerpt from a landmark Supreme Court decision upholding the power of a federal agency to require production of certain documents by a regulated entity.

The Use of a "John Doe" Summons

A "John Doe" summons is a summons directed to a fictitious person whose identity is unknown at the time of issuing the summons. In 1975, the U.S. Supreme Court held that the Internal Revenue Service has the authority under 26 U.S.C.A. § 7601 and § 7602 to issue a John Doe summons to a bank or other depository to discover the identity of a person who has made bank transactions that suggest the possibility of income tax evasion.[8] The Court indicated the validity of such a summons assumes "that a legitimate investigation was being conducted and that the summons [is] no broader than necessary to achieve its purpose."[9] The Court admonished the government not to use this power to conduct "fishing expeditions" into the private affairs of bank depositors.

Constraints on Administrative Subpoenas

A person subpoenaed can invoke a common-law testimonial privilege. This includes the **attorney-client privilege** and the **spousal privilege.** A testimonial privilege protects confidential communications made during a privileged relationship and, subject to narrow exceptions, allows a person protected by the privilege to refuse to disclose such confidential communications. Some states have enacted statutes conferring additional privileges, for example, a physician-patient privilege. And even when a court enforces a subpoena an individual (but not a corporation) can raise the Fifth Amendment **privilege against self-incrimination.**[10] Although the Fifth Amendment was designed to prevent self-incrimination "in any criminal case," Supreme Court decisions have interpreted "criminal case" to include any proceeding in which a witness's testimony might render that witness liable in a subsequent criminal prosecution. Thus, the privilege against self-incrimination is available in civil or criminal, administrative or judicial, investigatory proceedings.

BOX 5.1 Supreme Court Perspective

United States v. Morton Salt Co.
338 U.S. 632 (1950)

[The Federal Trade Commission ordered Morton Salt and other companies to cease and desist from certain trade practices. The Court of Appeals affirmed the order and commanded compliance. FTC ordered Morton Salt to file reports to demonstrate compliance. The opinion of the Supreme Court states that "reports of compliance were subsequently filed and accepted, and there the matter appears to have rested for a little upwards of four years." The FTC subsequently ordered Morton Salt to produce "additional and highly particularized reports to show continuing compliance with the decree." The company refused to comply with the agency's demand, which led the government to file this lawsuit to seek compliance. In a unanimous decision, the Supreme Court upheld the government's position and ordered Morton Salt to comply with the FTC's order. In his opinion for the Court, Justice Robert Jackson expounds on the investigative powers of administrative agencies.]

Justice Jackson delivered the Opinion of the Court.
 . . . *This case illustrates the difference between the judicial function and the function the Commission is attempting to perform. The respondents argue that since the Commission made no charge of violation either of the decree or the statute, it is engaged in a mere "fishing expedition" to see if it can turn up evidence of guilt. We will assume for the argument that this is so. Courts have often disapproved the employment of the judicial process in such an enterprise. Federal judicial power itself extends only to adjudication of cases and controversies and it is natural that its investigative powers should be jealously confined to these ends. The judicial subpoena power not only is subject to specific constitutional limitations, which also apply to admin-istrative orders, such as those against self-incrimination, unreasonable search and seizure, and due process of law, but also is subject to those limitations inherent in the body that issues them because of the provisions of the Judiciary Article of the Constitution.*
 We must not disguise the fact that sometimes, especially early in the history of the federal administrative tribunal, the courts were persuaded to engraft judicial limitations upon the administrative process. The courts could not go fishing, and so it followed neither could anyone else. Administrative investigations fell before the colorful and nostalgic slogan "no fishing expeditions." It must not be forgotten that the administrative process and its agencies are relative newcomers in the field of law and that it has taken and will continue to take experience and trial and error to fit this process into our system of judicature. More recent views have been more tolerant of it than those which underlay many older decisions.
 The only power that is involved here is the power to get information from those who best can give it and who are most interested in not doing so. Because judicial power is reluctant if not unable to summon evidence until it is shown to be relevant to issues in litigation, it does not follow that an administrative agency charged with seeing that the laws are enforced may not have and exercise powers of original inquiry. It has a power of inquisition, if one chooses to call it that, which is not derived from the judicial function. It is more analogous to the Grand Jury, which does not depend on a case or controversy for power to get evidence but can investigate merely on suspicion that the law is being violated, or even just because it wants assurance that it is not. When investigative and accusatory duties are delegated by statute to an administrative body, it, too, may take steps to inform itself as to whether there is probable violation of the law. . . .

Where enforcement of a subpoena is contested a court must determine if the investigation is for a lawfully authorized purpose, whether the evidence sought is reasonably relevant to such purpose and the demand is sufficiently definite and not oppressive or unreasonably burdensome, and that the information sought is not privileged information.[11]

Sometimes an agency subpoenas a massive amount of information from a regulated industry. In such cases the subpoenaed party may succeed in contending that the demands made are unreasonably burdensome. An example is where an employer filed an action in federal court seeking to quash a subpoena *duces tecum* issued by Equal

Employment Opportunity Commission. The Commission's charges alleged racial discrimination in hiring, promotion, and discharge. The court held that the subpoena that sought production of documents related not only to racial discrimination but also to other forms of discrimination was unduly broad.[12] And in a case in which a Federal Trade Commission subpoena required a massive amount of work to produce records, a federal appellate court approved a reduced scope of demands.[13]

INSPECTIONS, SEARCHES, AND SEIZURES

One of the most important investigative tools agencies possess is that of search and seizure. Despite the Fourth Amendment's prohibition of unreasonable searches and seizures, agencies routinely conduct **administrative inspections** of the industries they regulate. In general, the courts are more permissive toward **administrative searches** directed at business and industry than toward searches directed at private individuals or their residences.

An Exception for Administrative Searches?

In 1959, the Supreme Court found no violation of the Fourth Amendment when administrative searches were conducted without notice and without search warrants. In *Frank v. Maryland*[14] the Court upheld the conviction of a Baltimore man who refused to allow a city health inspector to enter and inspect his home without a warrant. The inspector was looking for evidence of rat infestation. The Baltimore City Code provided: "Whenever the Commissioner of Health shall have cause to suspect that a nuisance exists in any house, cellar or enclosure, he may demand entry therein in the day time, and if the owner or occupier shall refuse or delay to open the same and admit a free examination, he shall forfeit and pay for every such refusal the sum of Twenty Dollars."

In his opinion for the Court sustaining the constitutionality of this ordinance, Justice Felix Frankfurter observed:

> Time and experience have forcefully taught that the power to inspect dwelling places . . . is of indispensable importance to the maintenance of community health; a power that would be greatly hobbled by the blanket requirement of the safeguards necessary for a search of evidence of criminal acts. The need for preventive action is great, and city after city has seen this need and granted the power of inspection to its health officials; and these inspections are apparently welcomed by all but an insignificant few.[15]

The *Frank* decision suggested that administrative searches were outside the prohibitions of the Fourth Amendment. In dissent, Justice Douglas averred, "The Court misreads history when it relates the Fourth Amendment primarily to searches for evidence to be used in criminal prosecutions."[16] In Douglas' view, the decision of the Court "greatly dilutes the right of privacy which every homeowner had the right to believe was part of our American heritage."[17]

The *Camara* and *See* Decisions

Frank v. Maryland was predicated on a bifurcation between administrative-type inspections and searches for evidence of crime. In the real world, though, the two are often intertwined. Indeed, warrantless administrative inspections can lead to criminal charges or serve as a pretext for the gathering of information to assist criminal investigations. In *Camara v. Municipal Court* (1967),[18] the Supreme Court recognized this and overruled *Frank v. Maryland*. Writing for the Court in *Camara*, Justice Byron White recognized that administrative searches "are significant intrusions upon the interests protected by the Fourth Amendment" and that "the reasons put forth in *Frank v. Maryland* and in other cases for upholding these warrantless searches are insufficient to justify so substantial a weakening of the Fourth

Amendment's protections."[19] In *Camara,* the Court held that, as a general rule, warrants must be obtained to permit administrative searches of private residences.

The Supreme Court's decision in *Camara v. Municipal Court* is excerpted at the end of the chapter.

The same day it decided *Camara,* the Court decided *See v. City of Seattle,*[20] in which it extended the *Camara* ruling to commercial establishments. In *See,* a Seattle businessman was convicted of a misdemeanor for refusing to allow a fire inspector to enter his locked warehouse without a warrant. Entry to the warehouse was requested as part of a routine citywide program to achieve compliance with fire regulations. Again, Justice White spoke for the Court:

> The businessman, like the occupant of a residence, has a constitutional right to go about his business free from unreasonable official entries upon his private commercial property. The businessman, too, has that right placed in jeopardy if the decision to enter and inspect for violation of regulatory laws can be made and enforced by the inspector in the field without official authority evidenced by a warrant."[21]

Closely Regulated Industries

Some commentators interpreted the *Camara* and *See* decisions as requiring that administrative searches should be subject to the same Fourth Amendment requirements that apply to criminal searches. In 1970, the Supreme Court invalidated that interpretation when it decided *Colonnade Corporation v. United States.*[22] At issue in the case was whether agents of the federal Bureau of Alcohol, Tobacco, and Firearms (ATF) needed a warrant before inspecting an establishment they had probable cause to believe was serving liquor from refilled bottles in violation of 26 U.S.C.A. § 5301(c). The Court held that "Congress has broad authority to fashion standards of reasonableness for searches and seizures" with respect to

an industry "long subject to close supervision and inspection."[23]

The Supreme Court's *Colonnade* decision is excerpted at the end of the chapter.

The Court reaffirmed and amplified its *Colonnade* decision in *Biswell v. United States* (1972).[24] In that case an ATF agent conducted a surprise warrantless inspection of a pawnshop that was federally licensed to sell guns for sporting use. The agent located and seized two sawed-off rifles that the proprietor was not licensed to possess. In reversing a lower court decision invalidating the seizure, the Court observed that

> regulation of the interstate traffic in firearms is not as deeply rooted in history as is governmental control of the liquor industry, but close scrutiny of this traffic is undeniably of central importance to federal efforts to prevent violent crime and to assist the States in regulating the firearms traffic within their borders. . . . Large interests are at stake, and inspection is a crucial part of the regulatory scheme, since it assures that weapons are distributed through regular channels and in a traceable manner and makes possible the prevention of sales to undesirable customers and the detection of the origin of particular firearms. . . . It is also apparent that if the law is to be properly enforced and inspection made effective, inspections without warrant must be deemed reasonable official conduct under the Fourth Amendment.[25]

The *Colonnade* and *Biswell* decisions stand for the proposition that the Fourth Amendment imposes only a basic standard of reasonableness with respect to searches and inspections of closely regulated industries. The underlying premise is that businesses that choose to operate in such fields knowingly subject themselves to pervasive regulation and therefore have minimal expectations of privacy. The obvious question raised by these decisions is: What constitutes a "closely regulated industry"?

In *Marshall v. Barlow's, Inc.* (1978),[26] the Supreme Court said that the mere fact that a business is involved in interstate commerce and is therefore subject to a variety of federal regulations does not make it a "closely regulated industry." Were it otherwise, virtually every business in America would be classified as such, because the courts have so liberally construed the terms "interstate commerce" and "affecting interstate commerce."[27] In *Marshall v. Barlow's* the Court struck down a provision of the Occupational Health and Safety Act of 1970 that allowed OSHA to conduct warrantless searches of the workplace. However, the Court was careful to point out that to obtain **administrative search warrants,** OSHA inspectors did not have to meet the same strict standards of probable cause that govern the issuance of warrants in criminal investigations.

The Supreme Court's decision in *Marshall v. Barlow's* is excerpted at the end of the chapter.

In the 1980s, a more conservative Supreme Court appeared to back away from the strict scrutiny of regulatory searches suggested by the *Barlow's* decision. In 1981 the Court refused to invalidate a provision of the Federal Mine Safety and Health Act of 1977 that allowed the Department of Labor to conduct **warrantless inspections** of mines on a regular basis.[28] Emphasizing the "certainty and regularity" of the inspection regime, the Court held that the Fourth Amendment warrant requirement was inapplicable.

> Under these circumstances, it is difficult to see what additional protection a warrant requirement would provide. The Act itself clearly notifies the operator that inspections will be performed on a regular basis. Moreover, the Act and the regulations issued pursuant to it inform the operator of what health and safety standards must be met in order to be in compliance with the statute. The discretion of Government officials to determine what facilities to search and what violations to search for is thus directly curtailed by the regulatory scheme. In addition, the statute itself embodies a means by which any special Fourth Amendment interests can

be accommodated. Accordingly, we conclude that the general program of warrantless inspections authorized by . . . the Act does not violate the Fourth Amendment.[29]

A Framework for Evaluating Warrantless Administrative Searches

By the early 1980s, it appeared to some observers that the Court's decisions with respect to **warrantless administrative searches** were somewhat ad hoc, lacking a clear framework to guide lower courts in their evaluation of such searches. In *New York v. Burger* (1987),[30] in upholding a warrantless inspection of a junkyard, the Court laid out such a framework. The Court said that such inspections should be upheld as long three conditions are met:

1. there is a substantial government interest that informs the regulatory scheme pursuant to which the inspection is made;

2. the warrantless inspection is necessary to further the regulatory scheme; and

3. the inspection program must provide a constitutionally adequate substitute for a warrant.

This approach gives government agencies considerable latitude in conducting warrantless inspections of regulated industries and, accordingly, has been criticized by commentators with libertarian sensibilities.

State Court Rulings on Administrative Searches

In interpreting their respective state constitutions, state courts have generally applied the criteria announced by the U.S. Supreme Court in *Burger,* but appellate courts have made differing judgments as to when a sufficient governmental interest in the regulated activity justifies dispensing with normal warrant requirements. This often involves determinations of whether a state statute authorizing warrantless searches is constitutional and a determination of what constitutes a pervasively regulated industry or business. Liquor establishments are the classic example of pervasively regulated businesses. Many state courts have held that pharmacies also fall in this category. But the classification extends to many other endeavors. A Washington appellate court held that commercial fishermen are subject to warrantless entry upon their boats by fisheries inspectors who have reason to believe that food fish or shellfish are on board in violation of agency regulations.[31] The Florida Supreme Court held that a statute allowing warrantless administrative searches of junkyards, scrap metal processing plants, motor vehicle salvage yards, licensed motor vehicle dealers' lots, and other establishments dealing with salvaged motor vehicle parts is constitutional, as it is limited to business establishments that easily could be involved in theft and unlawful disposition of vehicles, and is restricted to normal business hours.[32] But a New York court held that neither a used car business nor a repair shop business are in pervasively regulated industries such as would permit warrantless searches or seizures at places of business.[33] And a Texas court held that a warrantless administrative search of an oil lease and business office exceeded the state's authority under a regulatory statute.[34]

Courts universally hold that a warrantless administrative search cannot be used as a device to avoid the standard of probable cause required to obtain a judicial search warrant. For example, in 1988, the Ohio Supreme Court held that despite the fact that state statutes and administrative code provisions grant regulatory authority to Department of Liquor Control over the sale of intoxicating liquors, the statutes are unconstitutional insofar as they fail to establish time, place, and scope of limitations on warrantless administrative searches of liquor establishments. Thus, the court ruled that evidence obtained as result of warrantless administrative search of a liquor establishment may not be used in a prosecution under a statute of general criminality not related to liquor control or liquor permit statutes.[35]

This was further illustrated in 1991 when a Kansas court found a substantial government interest in regulating the operation of puppy mills (dog breeders that supply pet shops) allowed warrantless searches of the breeders' premises. Nevertheless, the court found that neither the law allowing such searches nor the administrative order obtained for the inspection of the puppy mill premises placed any limits on the discretion of the inspectors as to time, place, and scope of the inspection. Therefore, the court ruled that the evidence discovered during the inspection was not admissible in a criminal prosecution.[36]

What Constitutes a Search?

A warrant is not required for inspecting that which is visible from a public area. This has commonly been understood to allow agency inspectors to obtain any information that could be viewed from a road or park or other public place. Perhaps the most extreme example occurred when the Environmental Protection Agency (EPA) employed aerial photographers to conduct aerial surveillance and take pictures of the Dow Chemical Company's plant, the perimeter of which was walled in to protect its premises from observation. Dow Chemical contested the EPA's activity on the ground that it was an unreasonable search that violated its reasonable expectation of privacy. However, in 1986 the Supreme Court in a 5–4 decision upheld the flyover photography by EPA on the ground that it was not a "search" within the meaning of the Fourth Amendment.[37] The case discussed in Box 5.2 highlights some of the issues of warrantless inspection as they relate to a contractor's business.

An edited version of the Supreme Court's decision in *Dow Chemical v. United States* is included at the end of the chapter.

AUDITS AND EXAMINATIONS

When one thinks of an audit by a governmental agency the first thing that usually comes to mind is a tax audit by the Internal Revenue Service (IRS). In order to ascertain the correctness of any

---

BOX 5.2   Case in Point

Are a Contractor's Business Records Subject to Warrantless Inspection?
Pinney v. Phillips, as Registrar
California Court of Appeals
230 Cal. App. 1570 (1991)

David R. Phillips, as Registrar of the Contractors State License Board (Registrar), revoked Jay Scott Pinney's license as an electrical contractor for Pinney's failure to produce his business records after the Registrar had made a written demand for such records under section 7111 of the California Business and Professions Code. That section requires a contractor to retain records for not less than five years after completion of a project and provides that refusal to comply with the Registrar's request to inspect such records is ground for disciplinary action. Pinney refused the Registrar's request to produce his records, contending that their inspection was subject to the warrant requirements of the Fourth Amendment to the U.S. Constitution. Thus, he contended that their production could be compelled only by subpoena, which would afford certain protections under state law. A lower court agreed with Pinney and the Registrar appealed.

The appellate court recognized that a warrantless search of records is permitted in instances of closely regulated businesses, for example where it is necessary to regulate a licensed business engaged in activities with a high risk of illegal conduct or of serious danger to the public. But, the court said, "[C]ontractors in general and electrical contractors in particular are not engaged in any such activities. Nor can they fairly be classified as 'closely regulated.'" Thus the court ruled that section 7111 could not constitutionally be applied to permit a warrantless inspection or production of Pinney's records without a subpoena.

---

federal tax return or determine the liability of any person for any internal revenue tax, Congress has granted the IRS the authority to examine any books, papers, records, or other data relevant to such an inquiry and to summon persons liable for such taxes or those who have custody of their books or records to appear and produce such records.[38] Administrative agencies routinely provide for **audits and examinations.** For example, the Medicare program reimburses costs to provider hospitals through a "fiscal intermediary," usually an insurance company that acts under contract on behalf of the Secretary of Health and Human Services to determine a hospital's claimed Medicare reimbursement. The intermediary analyzes the claims submitted by providers, performs an audit, and determines the amount of reimbursement to which a hospital is entitled.

Although a tax or reimbursement audit may be the most common, Congress has granted many administrative agencies the authority to conduct audits and examinations. Congress created the Federal Deposit Insurance Corporation (FDIC) in 1933 to make savings accounts in banks secure. Today nearly everyone is familiar with the fact that the FDIC insures deposits up to $100,000 in all national and most state banks. To assure that institutions insured by the FDIC function properly, Congress has provided that the Comptroller General "shall have access to, and the right to examine and copy, all records and other recorded information in any form, and to examine any property, within the possession or control of any agency or person which is subject to audit."[39] The Comptroller's access to information is enforceable under 31 U.S.C.A. § 716.

Just how broad can an agency's request be when it examines an industry it regulates? In 1950 in *Morton Salt Co. v. United States*,[40] the Supreme Court observed, "[I]t is sufficient if the inquiry is within the authority of the agency, the demand is not too indefinite and the information sought is reasonably relevant. 'The gist of the protection is in the requirement, expressed in terms, that the disclosure sought shall not be unreasonable.' "[41]

In 1978 the U.S. Court of Appeals for the D.C. Circuit upheld a regulation promulgated by the Federal Savings and Loan Insurance Corporation (FSLIC) that authorized the FSLIC at any time to make, or cause to be made, an audit of an insured institution. The regulation that stipulated an audit could "be conducted by auditors and in a manner satisfactory to (FSLIC) in accordance with general policies from time to time established by the Board" was authorized by 12 U.S.C.A. § 1726(b).[42]

State legislatures customarily grant similar authority to agencies charged with enforcing state taxes and administering benefit programs. West's Annotated California Labor Code § 129 provides that to make certain that injured workers, and their dependents in the event of their death, receive promptly and accurately the full measure of compensation to which they are entitled, the administrative director shall audit insurers, self-insured employers, and third-party administrators to determine if they have met their obligations under this code.

Public utilities and corporations that hold permits for legalized gambling are always subject to administrative audit. Arkansas law requires franchisees to keep books and records of their activities and stipulates that "Within thirty (30) days after the conclusion of every race meeting, the franchise holder shall submit to the Arkansas Racing Commission a complete audit of receipts and admissions."[43]

Recordkeeping and Reporting Requirements

To facilitate agency oversight of regulated industries, Congress and the state legislatures have enacted laws requiring the keeping of certain records and, in some instances, regular reporting to agencies. For example, candidates for national elective office are required to make periodic reports of contributions and expenditures.[44] All fifty states have laws of this type, although they vary greatly as to the rigor of their reporting requirements.[45] In an effort to monitor abuse of prescription drugs, a number of states require pharmacies to maintain records of drug deliveries and prescriptions and, in some instances, to report names and addresses of persons to whom prescription drugs are provided.[46] In 1977 the U.S. Supreme Court upheld one such requirement against a constitutional challenge based on the right of privacy.[47]

Since the enactment of the Bank Secrecy Act of 1970,[48] the federal government has required banks to maintain records and make report of matters that "have a high degree of usefulness in criminal, tax, or regulatory investigations or proceedings" as well as in "the conduct of intelligence or counterintelligence activities, including analysis, to protect against domestic and international terrorism."[49] In particular, banks are required to report cash transactions exceeding $10,000.[50] It is illegal to break up a single transaction into two or more separate transactions "for the purpose of evading the reporting requirement."[51] In *California Bankers Assn. v. Shultz* (1974)[52] the Supreme Court upheld these requirements against constitutional challenges based on the First, Fourth, and Fifth Amendments. The Court stressed the federal government's long-standing regulation of the banking industry and minimized the threat these requirements might pose to individual rights. In dissent, Justice William O. Douglas posed an interesting rhetorical question:

> Suppose Congress passed a law requiring telephone companies to record and retain all telephone calls and make them available to any federal agency on request. Would we hesitate even a moment before striking it down? I think not, for we [have] condemned "the broad and unsuspected governmental incursions into conversational privacy which electronic surveillance entails." . . . A checking account . . . may well record a citizen's activities, opinions, and beliefs as fully as transcripts of his telephone conversations.[53]

Given the extensive electronic surveillance now being conducted by the government as part of the ongoing "war on terrorism," Justice Douglas's question takes on new significance.

BOX 5.3 Case in Point

Scope of IRS Discretion in Enforcing the Tax Laws
United States v. Fior D'italia, Inc.
United States Supreme Court
536 U.S. 238 (2002)

Federal law imposes a tax on employees and their employers to support the Social Security program. The tax is based on "remuneration" paid to employees by their employers. The law regards "tips" received by employees "as remuneration" deemed to have been paid by the employer for purposes of the Social Security tax and requires employees who receive tips to report the amount of those tips to their employers, who must in turn report those sums to the IRS.

Under 26 U.S.C. § 6201(a) the Internal Revenue Service (IRS) "is authorized and required to make the inquiries, determinations, and assessments of all taxes . . . which have not been duly paid. . . ." The IRS interprets this provision as allowing the agency to assess a restaurant for Social Security taxes based upon tips that its employees may have received but did not report. In making such assessments, IRS estimates the aggregate value of all the tips that the restaurant's customers paid its employees. It does this by examining charge card records, which show tips customers added to their bills, computing an average tip, then generalizing to cash transactions on the assumption that cash paying customers tip at the same rate.

In this case, Fior D'Italia, a long-standing and well-known eatery in San Francisco, objected to an IRS assessment against it and challenged the legality of the aggregate estimation procedure. In Fior D'Italia's view, the law requires IRS to estimate each employee's tip income separately, then sum these individual estimates to create a total. Clearly, this would be a much more difficult procedure.

In a 6–3 decision, the Supreme Court ruled in favor of the IRS. Justice Breyer's majority opinion examined the relevant statutory provisions and found no language that either required the IRS to adopt the individualized estimate procedure or prohibited it from using the aggregate estimate method. The Court noted the IRS's discretionary authority in the enforcement of the tax laws and refused to disallow a particular enforcement mechanism on the ground that it might possibly be subject to abuse. The majority opinion turned on the fact that 26 U.S.C.A. § 6201(a) grants the IRS assessment authority and hence it follows that IRS has the power to decide how to make that assessment as long as they adopt a reasonable method. Here the Court found IRS's aggregate method procedure was reasonable and would not allow a taxpayer to thwart IRS by insisting on another method.

Justices Souter, Thomas and Scalia dissented from the holding of the Court, observing that the Court's decision "saddles employers with a burden unintended by Congress."

See Box 5.3 for a summary of a recent decision in which the U.S. Supreme Court upheld the broad discretion of the Internal Revenue Service in enforcing the federal income tax laws.

DEPORTATION AND ADMINISTRATIVE DETENTION

The Bureau for Citizenship and Immigration Services (BCIS), located in the Department of Homeland Security (formerly the Immigration and Naturalization Service [INS], located within the Department of Justice), has primary responsibility for carrying out the nation's immigration laws.[54] Historically, federal immigration authorities have possessed broad discretion in enforcement of immigration law and adjudication of immigration cases.

Today a new agency known as Immigration and Customs Enforcement (ICE) (also located within Homeland Security) conducts immigration inspections of travelers entering the United States, regulates permanent and temporary immigration (including legal permanent residence status, non-immigrant status), and maintains control of the nation's borders. ICE identifies and removes people who do not have lawful immigration status, a process known as **deportation.** Under the Illegal Immigration and Immigrant Responsibility Act of 1996, immigration authorities can detain illegal aliens indefinitely without bond, regardless of whether they are likely to appear for deportation proceedings and pose no danger to the community.[55] **Administrative detention** in such cases is not subject to judicial review.[56] This approach is justified on the basis that illegal aliens are not entitled to the protections of the United States Constitution, a theory that not everyone accepts.[57]

The Supreme Court has said that the power to exclude or expel aliens, being a power affecting international relations, is vested in the political departments of the government.[58]

In 2002, two federal appellate courts issued conflicting decisions on whether there is a First Amendment right to attend "special interest" deportation hearings. These are hearings the Attorney General has determined may have a connection with or reveal knowledge of the September 11 terrorist attacks on the United States. In *Detroit Free Press v. Ashcroft,*[59] the media challenged the closure of "special interest" deportation proceedings claiming they violated the First Amendment. In affirming a district court judgment granting the requested relief, the Sixth Circuit held that there is a First Amendment right of access to deportation proceedings and the Attorney General's directive closing such proceedings impermissibly infringed on those rights. The court recognized: "The Government's ongoing anti-terrorism investigation implicates a compelling interest. However, the [attorney general's] directive is neither narrowly tailored, nor does it require particularized findings. Therefore, it impermissibly infringes on . . . First Amendment right of access."[60]

In *North Jersey Media Group, Inc. v. Ashcroft,*[61] a media group challenged the attorney general's directive that denied the media a right of access to "special interest" deportation hearings. The district court granted an injunction, but on appeal the Third Circuit reversed, observing:

[W]e are unable to conclude that openness plays a positive role in special interest deportation hearings at a time when our nation is faced with threats of such profound and unknown dimension. . . . We do not decide that there is no right to attend administrative proceedings, or even that there is no right to attend any immigration proceeding. Our judgment is confined to the extremely narrow class of deportation cases that are determined by the Attorney General to present significant national security concerns. In recognition of his experience (and our lack of experience) in this field, we will defer to his judgment. We note that although there may be no judicial remedy for these closures, there is, as always, the powerful check of political accountability on Executive discretion."[62]

SUSPENSION AND REVOCATION OF LICENSES

Administrative agencies that are empowered to issue licenses and permits have the power to suspend and revoke them; however, where a statute specifies the grounds for suspension or revocation the agency must follow those criteria. Agencies that issue licenses, such as the Federal Communications Commission and the Nuclear Regulatory Commission, have the authority to revoke such licenses where licensees engage in repeated violations of regulations.

At the state level regulatory agencies are responsible for the licensing of numerous occupations and professions and granting permits to perform various activities. Statutes generally provide standards and guidelines for **suspension and revocation of licenses and permits**; however, agencies are generally allowed to suspend or revoke a permit on an emergency basis where the agency determines it to be necessary in the interest of the public health, safety, or welfare.

Section 558 of the APA provides:

Except in cases of willfulness or those in which public health, interest, or safety requires otherwise, the withdrawal, suspension, revocation, or annulment of a license is lawful only if, before the institution of agency proceedings therefore, the licensee has been given—

1. notice by the agency in writing of the facts or conduct which may warrant the action; and
2. opportunity to demonstrate or achieve compliance with all lawful requirements.

Building and Environmental Permits

State and local governmental bodies issue environmental permits, which may be revoked administratively for failure of the holder to comply with statutory provisions authorizing the issuance of a permit.[63] As stated by a California appellate court,

> In determining that a permit, validly issued, should be revoked, the governing body of a municipality acts in a quasi-judicial capacity. In revoking a permit lawfully granted, due process requires that it act only upon notice to the permitee, upon a hearing, and upon evidence substantially supporting a finding of revocation."[64]

But the question often arises whether a building permit was lawfully granted, and if not, whether circumstances may give rise to the permit holder having vested rights in such a permit. Courts overwhelmingly hold that issuance of a building permit results in a vested right only when permit is legal and valid. Legal issues can arise when the permit holder incurs substantial expenditures in reliance on a permit that was issued without authority.

In Lamoni, Iowa, a property owner was erroneously issued a building permit for construction of a sawmill when the zoning ordinance did not

allow that use in that district. The permitee continued to build after receiving notice of revocation of permit, and the court held that the permitee did not have a vested right in permit that would prevent its being revoked by city.[65] Likewise, the Georgia Supreme Court has held that an illegal building permit issued to landowners after their subsequent expenditures on property did not give them vested right to develop property.[66]

On the other hand, whether a permit holder has in good faith incurred expenditures in reliance on a permit later determined to be invalid has caused some courts to hold that reliance upon informal city approvals (based upon city officials' mistaken impression of the zoning status of the subject property) can give rise to a vested rights where the property owner has made substantial expenditures pursuant to the permit.[67]

Drivers' Licenses

State statutes commonly provide for suspension or revocation of drivers' licenses upon conviction of offenses involving driving while intoxicated. Some states go further, for example South Carolina provides for suspension of a driver's license of a person convicted of controlled substances violations.[68] Many states have now adopted a "point system" assigning points for various motor vehicle violations. Georgia law, for example, authorizes its safety department to suspend the license of a driver without a preliminary hearing upon a showing by the records of the department or other sufficient evidence that the licensee is a habitually dangerous or negligent driver of a motor vehicle. This fact is established by the accumulation of points due to various infractions.[69]

Occupational and Professional Licenses

At the state level a department of professional regulation frequently handles suspension or revocations of occupational and professional licenses. It is common for a statute to provide: "The Board shall suspend or revoke the license of any licensee that

---

BOX 5.4 Case in Point

Is Sexual Misconduct Grounds to Revoke Teacher's Credentials?
Petit v. State Board of Education
California Supreme Court
513 P.2d 889 (Cal. 1973)

The California State Board of Education revoked the credential of a female elementary school teacher who had been teaching since 1957. In November 1967 she and her husband joined "The Swingers," a private club in Los Angeles that promoted diverse sexual activities between members at club parties. Los Angeles Police Department Sergeant Berk, working undercover, was accepted for membership, and at a party at a private residence in December 1967, he observed the teacher commit three separate acts of oral copulation with three different men at the party while others looked on. She pleaded guilty to the misdemeanor offense of outraging public decency, was fined and placed on probation. Upon payment of her fine her probation was terminated and the criminal proceedings dismissed.

After an administrative hearing where Sgt. Berk testified to the above facts and three ele-

mentary school superintendents opined that the teacher's conduct disclosed her unfitness to teach, the Board revoked her teaching credentials on the ground that her conduct demonstrated her unfitness to teach.

After her unsuccessful suit in the trial court, the California Supreme Court rejected the teacher's contention that the Board's actions invaded her right to privacy. The court cited several cases that hold that a teacher's inability to act in accordance with traditional moral principles may constitute sufficient ground for revocation or dismissal. Concluding that the teacher would be unable to act as an exemplar for her pupils and offer them suitable moral guidance, the court upheld the Board's revocation and the trial court's rejection of her appeal. Two dissenting justices pointed out that during the 13 years that the teacher had taught mentally retarded elementary school children there was no evidence that she ever failed to perform her professional responsibilities. Further, the ruling not only forced her discharge, but also barred any school district in California from hiring her.

---

has committed one or more of the enumerated violations." The enumerated violations include that the licensee is unfit to act in the field licensed or is guilty of a crime involving moral turpitude. Where an administrative proceeding establishes a licensee's incompetence or the licensee is convicted of a crime involving moral turpitude, courts usually uphold the suspension or revocation. For example, an Ohio appellate court found that the State Board of Embalmers and Funeral Directors properly revoked the funeral and embalming license of a licensee who embezzled funds from his employer.[70]

Persons who hold professional licenses, for example, a physician or lawyer, are expected to adhere to certain professional standards, and suspension of a license, for example, can pose problems concerning proof of violation of competency and ethical and moral standards. Box 5.4 describes

a situation where, despite a teacher's commendable record of teaching, the California Supreme Court in 1973 upheld revocation of her teaching certificate based on her sexual misconduct. Given the changes in societal standards, would a court reach the same result today?[71]

In *Gilpin v. Montana Board of Nursing* (1992), **the Montana Supreme Court upheld the revocation of a nursing license held by a man who had been convicted of sexually assaulting two minors. The decision is reprinted at the end of the chapter.**

Enforcement of Licensing Actions

Agency suspensions and revocations of licenses are self-executing. Thus, once an agency suspends or revokes a license or permit, its action becomes final unless the licensee seeks judicial review. Where a licensee contests a suspension or revocation of a professional or occupational license before a court the licensee bears the burden to prove that the agency acted illegally or arbitrarily. In such cases it is common for a court to grant a stay of the suspension or revocation pending the court's review unless the licensing agency can show good cause that the public health, safety, or welfare requires that an agency's action must take effect immediately.

Judicial review of an agency's decision is l imited to whether the agency's factual findings are against the manifest weight of the evidence, and whether these findings support the imposed sanctions.

Courts generally do not review the level of sanctions imposed as long as they are within the agency's statutory authority. In *State v. Hochhausler*,[72] the Ohio Supreme Court reviewed an appeal from an administrative suspension of a driver's license by a motorist who had been charged with a second offense of driving while intoxicated (DWI). In rejecting the driver's challenge to the statute for not providing a presuspension hearing, the court addressed due process considerations in applying an Ohio statute, which allows administrative suspension of a driver's license where a driver is charged with DWI without a prior opportunity for the driver to be heard on the issue of suspension.

The Ohio Supreme Court relied on the U.S. Supreme Court's decision in *Mackey v. Montrym*.[73] There the court applied the three-pronged test in *Mathews v. Eldridge*[74] in addressing the issue of due process required to protect an individual against the possibility of an erroneous deprivation of a property interest in a driver's license. In applying the *Mathews* factors the court in *Mackey v. Montrym* considered 1) the private interest affected by official action and probable value, if any, of additional or substitute procedural safeguards, 2) the risk of an erroneous deprivation of such interest through the procedures used; and 3) the government's interest, including the function involved and the fiscal and administrative burdens that the additional or substitute procedural requirement would entail.

In reviewing the Ohio statute that provided for a summary suspension of the defendant's license the Ohio Supreme Court likewise applied the *Mathews* factors. The court recognized the driver's obvious private interest in having a driver's license. But considering the duration of suspensions and because of the underlying circumstances—an arrest, reasonable grounds for the arrest, and either a refusal to take the chemical test, or taking the chemical test and failing—court found the risk of erroneous deprivation to be minimal. In view of the death and injury caused by persons driving on public roads and highways while intoxicated, the court had no problem in finding the state's interest served by the reasonable use of an administrative license suspension. Thus, the court rejected the driver's contention that due process of law required that he be given prior notice and an opportunity to be heard before his license was suspended. Although upholding the statutory provisions that allowed administrative suspension without a prior opportunity for a hearing, the Ohio court held that the section of the DWI statute that prevents a court from granting a stay of administrative license suspension was unconstitutional because it violated the separation of powers doctrine embedded in the state constitution.

The New Hampshire Supreme Court has stated that a driver's license is a state constitutionally protected interest, which may not be suspended without due process. But the court also held that there was no due process violation where a driver's license was suspended for failure to submit to chemical test for driving while intoxicated (DWI), as the driver was entitled to apply for an administrative hearing within thirty days after notice of the suspension.[75]

IMPOSITION OF ADMINISTRATIVE FINES

Federal and state statutes generally delegate to agencies the power to devise remedies and to impose **administrative fines** in order to effectuate the purposes of the law the agency is charged with administering. Administrative agencies have considerable latitude to shape their remedies within the scope of their statutory authority.[76] Courts hold that an administrative agency is entitled to substantial deference in assessing a civil penalty appropriate for violation of its regulations. Courts will not generally overturn an agency's "choice of a sanction unless the sanction 'is unwarranted in law' or 'without justification in fact.' "[77]

In 1970 Congress enacted the Occupational Safety and Health Act of 1970 (OSHA).[78] Under the statute, OSHA inspectors are authorized to conduct reasonable safety and health inspections. If a violation is discovered, the inspector, on behalf of the Secretary of Labor, issues a citation to the employer, fixing a reasonable time for its abatement and can propose a **civil penalty** of not more than $1,000 for serious violations, to a maximum of $10,000 for willful or repeated violations. An employer can contest the penalty or the abatement order by notifying the Secretary of Labor within fifteen days, in which case the abatement order is automatically stayed and an evidentiary hearing is held before an administrative law judge of the Occupational Safety and Health Review Commission.

In 1977 in *Atlas Roofing Co. v. Occupational Safety and Health Rev. Commission,*[79] the Supreme Court addressed the issue whether, consistent with the Seventh Amendment, Congress may create a new cause of action in the government for civil penalties enforceable in an administrative agency where there is no provision made for a jury trial. The Court rejected an attack on OSHA's enabling statute and ruled that

> when Congress creates new statutory "public rights," it may assign their adjudication to an administrative agency with which a jury trial would be incompatible, without violating the Seventh Amendment's injunction that jury trial is to be "preserved" in "suits at common law." Congress is not required by the Seventh Amendment to choke the already crowded

federal courts with new types of litigation or prevented from committing some new types of litigation to administrative agencies with special competence in the relevant field.[80]

CEASE AND DESIST ORDERS

A **cease and desist order** is an order issued by a regulatory agency prohibiting a named party from continuing a specific course of conduct. Many federal agencies have the authority to issue such orders. Three of the most prominent are National Labor Relations Board (NLRB), the Federal Trade Commission (FTC), and the Securities and Exchange Commission (SEC). The NLRB was established to prevent unfair labor practices by employers and labor unions. In context of an NLRB order on unfair labor practices, the Supreme Court observed that "The breadth of the order, like the injunction of a court, must depend upon the circumstances of each case, the purpose being to prevent violations, the threat of which in the future is indicated because of their similarity or relation to those unlawful acts which the Board has found to have been committed by the employer in the past."[81]

The Federal Trade Commission (FTC) seeks to prevent unfair methods of competition and unfair or deceptive acts or practices in interstate commerce. Following a suitable hearing and determination the FTC is empowered and directed to order those found guilty of such practices to cease and desist therefrom.

The Securities Act of 1933 and the Securities Exchange Act of 1934 empower the Securities and Exchange Commission (SEC) to investigate violations of securities laws such as insider trading, misrepresentation or omission of important information about securities; manipulating the market prices of securities; and sale of unregistered securities. These acts provide that the SEC may impose a cease and desist order upon any person who "is violating, has violated, or is about to violate any provision" of the federal securities laws.

BOX 5.5   Case in Point

**Order Barring Employer from Discriminating
against Pregnant Employees**
Franklin Publishing. Co., Inc. v.
Massachusetts Commission Against Discrimination
Appeals Court of Massachusetts
519 N.E.2d 798 (Mass.App.Ct. 1988).

After Franklin Publishing Co. (Franklin) discharged
its receptionist, Merle Gowen-Esdale, because of
her pregnancy, she filed a sex-discrimination complaint with the Massachusetts Commission Against
Discrimination. The Commission ordered Franklin
to cease and desist from further acts of discrimination against women on the basis of pregnancy,

and to compensate her for lost wages and medical
insurance premiums and for the emotional distress
she suffered. The local court affirmed the decision
regarding back pay and insurance premiums, but it
disallowed her recovery for emotional distress and
made no mention of the cease and desist provision. On appeal by the Commission, the Appeals
Court of Massachusetts reinstated the Commission's original order and award, which included
the damages for emotional injury. The court also
held that the Commission was authorized under
M.G.L.A. ch. 151B, § 5 to enter cease and desist
order against the employer where sex discrimination against a pregnant employee was established.

At the state level legislatures commonly grant
agencies that regulate banking, insurance, and environmental matters the power to issue cease and desist
orders. When contested these orders are subject
to judicial review. For example, the Texas Department of Insurance issued a cease and desist order
prohibiting an out-of-state insurance company
from engaging in unauthorized business of insurance, unfair methods of competition, and deceptive
acts or practices in business of insurance. On appeal
the Texas Court of Appeals found that the insurer
engaged in unlicensed business of insurance in state;
and that its failure to disclose unauthorized status
could mislead policyholders. Therefore, it upheld
the cease and desist order that prevented the insurer
from engaging in business until properly licensed.[82]
Box 5.5 describes a case in which cease and desist
was issued against an employer who was found to
be discriminating against a pregnant employee.

In addition to issuing cease and desist orders
in banking and insurance matters, states increasingly use the device to prevent violations of environmental laws. Typically, Arizona has enacted
statutes for enforcement of its Ground Water
Code that provide:

> if the director [of water resources] has reason
> to believe that a person is violating or has
> violated a provision of this chapter or a per-
> mit, rule or order issued or adopted pursuant

to this chapter, the director may give the person written notice that the person may appear
and show cause at an administrative hearing
why the person should not be ordered to
cease and desist from the violation.[83]

Local ordinances frequently provide for
issuance of cease and desist orders to enforce environmental regulations (see, for example, Box 5.6
displaying a section of the Santa Monica, California Municipal Code). Cease and desist orders play
an important role at the local level where zoning
authorities often issue such orders to prevent continuing violations of land use zoning regulations.[84]

CIVIL SUITS TO ENFORCE REGULATIONS AND ORDERS

A number of federal agencies have the authority
to file civil suits against violators. For example,
the Civil Rights Act of 1964 authorizes the
Department of Justice to file suit to vindicate citizens' civil rights:

> Whenever the Attorney General has reasonable
> cause to believe that any person or group of
> persons is engaged in a pattern or practice of
> resistance to the full enjoyment of any of the
> rights secured by this subchapter, and that the

BOX 5.6 Santa Monica Municipal Code

Chapter 5.20: Industrial Wastewater Control
Section 5.20.540 Cease and desist orders.

(a) When the Director finds that a user has violated, or continues to violate, any provision of this Chapter, a wastewater discharge permit or order issued hereunder, or any other pretreatment standard or requirement, or finds that the user's past violations are likely to recur, the Director may issue an order to the user directing it to cease and desist all such violations and directing the user to:

(1) Immediately comply with all requirements; and

(2) Take such appropriate remedial or preventative action as may be needed to properly address a continuing or threatened violation, including halting operations and/or terminating the discharge.

(b) Issuance of a cease and desist order shall not be a bar against, or prerequisite for, taking any other action against the user.

---

pattern or practice is of such a nature and is intended to deny the full exercise of the rights herein described, the Attorney General may bring a civil action in the appropriate district court of the United States by filing with it a complaint . . . setting forth facts pertaining to such pattern or practice, and . . . requesting such preventive relief, including an application for a permanent or temporary injunction, restraining order or other order against the person or persons responsible for such pattern or practice, as he deems necessary to insure the full enjoyment of the rights herein described.[85]

It was under this provision that the Justice Department filed a highly publicized suit in 1993 against Flagstar Corporation, the operator of Denny's Restaurants. The suit alleged racial discrimination against black patrons. In a settlement, Flagstar paid $45 million in damages and established a program to prevent future discrimination at its restaurants.[86]

Often the civil rights suits filed by the Justice Department are referred to it by other federal agencies. For example, the Office of Civil Rights (OCR) in the U.S. Department of Education is responsible for enforcing a number of civil rights laws that apply to public education, including Title VI of the Civil Rights Act of 1964, Title IX of the Education Amendments of 1972, Section 504 of the Rehabilitation Act of 1973, and Title II of the Americans with Disabilities Act of 1990. The

OCR investigates complaints filed by parties who believe they are the victims of unlawful discrimination, but it has no power to bring lawsuits on its own. The OCR prefers to settle discrimination complaints through negotiation with school officials, but in some instances it refers cases to the Justice Department, which then decides whether to file suit against the school district.

One agency that can bring civil suits directly against violators is the Securities and Exchange Commission. The SEC routinely files suit in federal district court against parties who are accused of securities fraud under federal law and the Commission's own regulations.[87] The SEC is empowered to seek injunctions, the "disgorgement" of ill-gotten gains, as well as civil penalties. For example, in *SEC v. Fabri-Centers of America, Inc.*, an SEC enforcement action resulted in an order requiring the defendant to pay a $50,000 civil penalty, more than $45,000 in disgorgement and more than $40,000 in prejudgment interest.[88]

In some instances citizens can go to court directly rather than wait for a government agency to act on a violation of public policy. For example, Section 505(a) of the Clean Water Act authorizes private citizens to commence a civil action for injunctive relief and/or the imposition of civil penalties in federal district court against any person "alleged to be in violation" of the conditions of a National Pollutant Discharge Elimination System (NPDES) permit. However, Section 505(a) does not allow citizen suits for "wholly past violations."[89]

Qui Tam Suits

An increasingly popular form of citizen-initiated litigation is the **qui tam action.** *Qui tam* is short for the Latin phrase *qui tam pro domino rege quam pro sic ipso in hoc parte sequitur,* which means "who sues for the king sues for himself as well." According to *Black's Law Dictionary,* a *qui tam* suit is "an action brought by an informer, under a statute which establishes a penalty for the commission or omission of a certain act, and provides that the same shall be recoverable in a civil action, part of the penalty to go to any person who will bring such action and the remainder to the state or some other institution." The Federal False Claims Act allows private citizens to file suit on behalf of the U.S. Government charging fraud by government contractors and others who receive federal funds.[90] If the plaintiff prevails, the government can recover triple its damages in addition to civil penalties ranging from $5,000 to $10,000 per violation. The citizen (referred to as the "relator") shares in the monetary damages collected up to a maximum of 30 percent. The False Claims Act was enacted by Congress during the Civil War in order to ferret out fraud in military procurement. Today, the law provides an incentive to **whistleblowers** to reveal evidence of fraud in programs like Medicare and Medicaid. In recent years there have been a number of hundred million-dollar settlements. Currently, about 500 *qui tam* actions are filed in federal courts each year and the number is growing rapidly. In *Vermont Agency of Natural Resources v. United States ex rel. Stevens* (2000),[91] the Supreme Court held that States are not "persons" subject to False Claims Act *qui tam* actions; however in 2003 in *Cook County, Illinois v. United States ex rel. Chandler,*[92] the Court held that municipalities are "persons" amenable to such *qui tam* actions.

CRIMINAL PROSECUTIONS

Administrative investigations sometime reveal evidence of criminal violations of federal or state law. Federal agencies (and generally state agencies) do not have the authority to initiate criminal prosecutions; however, when an agency investigation discloses evidence of criminal wrongdoing, it can refer the matter to the Department of Justice or a state prosecutor. If, at the federal level, the attorney general believes the matter warrants prosecution, the case is presented to a federal grand jury for indictment. A state prosecutor, when the situation warrants it, can seek an indictment from a grand jury or file an information (a charging document filed with a court), depending on the law of the particular state.[93]

Historically, administrative agencies referred relatively few violations to prosecuting authorities. Indeed, many violations of laws administered by government agencies resulted in administrative fines often viewed by violators as a "cost of doing business." In the 1970s Congress enacted major federal environmental legislation (the Clean Air Act, Clean Water Act, Toxic Substances Act, Endangered Species Act, etc.) providing for criminal sanctions. Agencies originally relied almost exclusively on civil penalties as an enforcement tool, but in the 1980s agencies began to refer cases for criminal sanctions.

In an effort to prosecute **white-collar crime** in recent years Congress and state legislatures have created new crimes. Investigative agencies such as the FBI and the IRS and their state counterparts have become more vigilant in investigating white-collar crime. Recent years have witnessed aggressive actions by state attorneys general in the prosecution the investigation of alleged irregularities in stock exchange, brokerage houses, and mutual fund practices. Increasingly, prosecutors at the state and local level have created special divisions within their offices for investigation and enforcement of regulatory offenses that focus on environmental violations, consumer fraud, and unlicensed occupational and professional practitioners.

There is a growing trend for criminal investigators to seek criminal penalties independently from agency referrals. Much of the effort is directed against those who commit fraud in government contracting and those who violate federal and state laws regulating securities, Medicare and Medicaid regulations, as well as environmental statutes. In addition, a whistleblower is likely to report evidence of wrongdoing directly to law enforcement or prosecutorial authorities.

The trend toward increased prosecution of regulatory violations is not without critics. Some critics argue that prosecutorial agencies are usurping the role of agencies in areas such as securities violations, health care policies, and environmental regulations. Many environmental statutes are enforceable by states where there are disparate standards and enforcement policies, and prosecuting authorities often act independently from administrative authorities. Consequently their actions result in regulatory policymaking outside the traditional processes of agency dispute resolution and without the benefit of the expertise of agencies.

LIENS, LEVIES, AND GARNISHMENTS

Without question, the federal agency most feared by average Americans is the Internal Revenue Service. It is also among the most vital, in that it collects 95 percent of the federal government's revenues through personal and corporate income taxes, excise, gift, and estate taxes, as well as Social Security employment taxes. The IRS is empowered to conduct audits of taxpayers' returns, impose **liens** and levies on assets in order to recover unpaid taxes, and even garnish wages. However, in 1988, 1996, and 1998 Congress enacted legislation to protect taxpayers from the abuse of IRS powers. A taxpayer's principal residence is now protected from **levy** to satisfy tax liabilities of less than $5,000. The taxpayer must be provided with a levy statement at least thirty days before property is seized, during which time the taxpayer may request a hearing to challenge the levy. With respect to garnishments, the law now requires a twenty-one-day hold on bank accounts garnished by the IRS, which provides more time to challenge an improper **garnishment.** Finally, taxpayers who are the victims of reckless or intentional disregard of proper tax collection procedures may sue the IRS in federal district court for damages up to $1 million.[94]

FORFEITURES

Federal law provides for the **forfeiture** of real estate and other property used in illegal drug trafficking and other criminal activities.[95] Cars, boats, and airplanes are commonly seized under the forfeiture laws. In 1984, federal law enforcement agencies began a program called "Equitable Sharing" under which federal agencies recruit state and local police to assist them in seizing property under federal statutes. Local or state police seize property and turn it over to the federal government. If the forfeiture is upheld, the state or local police agency that made the seizure shares equally in the proceeds when the forfeited assets are sold at auction.

In 1993 the Supreme Court held that a property forfeiture stemming from a drug crime is subject to limitation under the Eighth Amendment. Writing for the Court in *Austin v. United States*,[96] Justice Blackmun concluded that "forfeiture . . . constitutes 'payment to a sovereign as punishment for some offense,' and, as such, is subject to the limitations of the Eighth Amendment's Excessive Fines Clause."[97]

The Supreme Court's decision in *Austin v. United States* is excerpted at the end of the chapter.

Until recently, real estate, including a residence or business, could be seized on the basis of an ex parte seizure warrant, and the property owner ousted from the property pending trial—without notice or an opportunity to be heard. The Supreme Court has held that such practices are unconstitutional when they apply to seizures of real estate.[98] Due process requires notice and the opportunity to be heard before real estate can be seized, the Court held, and in most situations that should mean that the property owner not be disturbed in the right of possession of the property pending trial. But the Supreme Court expressly limited the holding to real property—residential or commercial. It did not affect pretrial detention of cars, bank accounts, cash, and other personal property.

The **USA PATRIOT Act** signed into law by President Bush on October 26, 2001, vests the federal government with new authorities to declare

---

BOX 5.7   An Overview of Federal Asset Forfeiture

Compiled by Steven M. Sucsy, Assistant United States Attorney

Administrative forfeiture is the process by which property may be forfeited to the United States by the investigative agency that seized it. It is an *in rem* (against the property) action that permits the federal seizing agency to forfeit the property without judicial involvement. The authority for a seizing agency to start an administrative forfeiture action is found in the Tariff Act of 1930, 19 U.S.C. §§ 1602-1621.

Property that can be administratively forfeited is: merchandise the importation of which is prohibited; a conveyance used to import, transport, or store a controlled substance; a monetary instrument; or other property that does not exceed $500,000 in value. Real property cannot be the subject of administrative forfeiture, regardless of its value.

Once the decision has been made by an agency to proceed with an administrative forfeiture, the seizing agency must pursue the matter promptly. Written notice must generally be provided not later than 60 days from the date of the seizure.

Publication and personal notice are also required. Notice of the seizure of the property and the intent to forfeit it must be published once each week for three successive weeks in a newspaper of general circulation in the judicial district in which the property was seized. Personal notice of the pending forfeiture and applicable procedures must also be given to all persons, including lienholders, whose identities and addresses are reasonably ascertainable and whose rights and interests in the subject property will or could be affected by the forfeiture. These persons include all possessors, owners, and lienholders.

In order to contest a proposed administrative forfeiture, a person asserting an interest in the subject property must file a verified claim with the seizing agency within 30 days of the date of the final publication of notice.

While the courts have allowed due process challenges under some circumstances, courts have been unwilling to consider challenges to the merits of administrative forfeitures.

SOURCE: Texas Association of Legal Professionals web site, online at http://www.texasals.org/federalasset.htm.

---

forfeitures of property.[99] The act allows confiscation of property located in the United States for a range of crimes committed in violation of foreign law. It also permits the United States to enforce foreign forfeiture orders, provides for seizure of correspondent accounts held in U.S. financial institutions for foreign banks holding forfeitable assets in other countries, and denies corporate entities the right to contest a confiscation if their principal shareholder is a fugitive. See Box 5.7 for an overview of federal asset forfeiture.

CONCLUSION

To effectively carry out the functions and responsibilities delegated to it by Congress or the state legislature an administrative agency must be continually informed of activities of those regulated or for whose benefits it administers programs. It must become aware of violations of the laws and regulations that it is charged with administering and enforcing. Regulated parties are required to maintain records and make reports of their operations. When an agency cannot obtain needed information voluntarily, it must pursue an investigation through inspections, audits, and examinations, and must conduct searches in order to compel the production of information. At such point the right of privacy often conflicts with the public's need for information. Thus in pursuing an investigation an agency must adhere to the constraints imposed by the constitutional protections. Statutory laws generally provide an agency with a variety of possible sanctions to enforce regulations and orders. But, as in its investigations, an agency must employ sanctions within its statutory authority and within the bounds of constitutional constraints. When an agency adheres to these requirements courts generally uphold its selection of remedies. Where an administrative sanction is unavailing, an agency can resort to civil litigation or refer a case for criminal prosecution.

KEY TERMS

administrative detention

administrative fines

administrative inspections

administrative search warrants

administrative searches

attorney-client privilege

audits and examinations

cease and desist order

civil penalty

deportation

disclosure of trade secrets

forfeiture

garnishment

levy

liens

privilege against self-incrimination

qui tam action

spousal privilege

subpoena

subpoena *duces tecum*

suspension and revocation of licenses and permits

USA PATRIOT Act

warrantless administrative searches

warrantless inspections

whistleblowers

white-collar crime

QUESTIONS FOR THOUGHT AND DISCUSSION

1. When is an administrative agency authorized to issue a subpoena? What is the distinction between a subpoena and a subpoena *duces tecum*?

2. On what grounds can a person subpoenaed challenge an agency's issuance of a subpoena?

3. In what instances can an agency conduct a warrantless search or seizure?

4. Give an example of when a regulatory agency might issue a "cease and desist" order. How are such orders enforced?

5. Under what circumstances can an agency revoke an occupational or professional license?

6. What is a *qui tam* suit? What incentive is provided by federal statute to encourage a person to file a *qui tam* suit?

7. What is the rationale for allowing the Bureau for Citizenship and Immigration Services to detain illegal aliens indefinitely without bond or legal recourse?

8. What restrictions does the U.S. Constitution impose on administrative forfeitures?

9. Explain the difference between a garnishment and a levy.

10. What factors account for the increased prosecutorial initiatives in enforcement of administrative laws?

EDITED CASE Camara v. Municipal Court
United States Supreme Court, 387 U.S. 523 (1967)

[In this case the Supreme Court reconsiders its 1957 decision in Frank v. Maryland, which essentially exempted administrative searches from Fourth Amendment challenge.]

Justice White delivered the opinion of the Court.
   In *Frank v. Maryland*, 359 U.S. 360, this Court upheld, by a five-to-four vote, a state court convic-

tion of a home-owner who refused to permit a municipal health inspector to enter and inspect his premises without a search warrant. In *Eaton v. Price*, 364 U.S. 263, a similar conviction was affirmed by an equally divided Court. Since those closely divided decisions, more intensive efforts at

(Continued)

EDITED CASE   Camara v. Municipal Court (Continued)

all levels of government to contain and eliminate urban blight have led to increasing use of such inspection techniques, while numerous decisions of this Court have more fully defined the Fourth Amendment's effect on state and municipal action. . . . In view of the growing nationwide importance of the problem, we noted probable jurisdiction in this case . . . to re-examine whether administrative inspection programs, as presently authorized and conducted, violate Fourth Amendment rights as those rights are enforced against the States through the Fourteenth Amendment. . . .

Appellant brought this action in a California Superior Court alleging that he was awaiting trial on a criminal charge of violating the San Francisco Housing Code by refusing to permit a warrantless inspection of his residence, and that a writ of prohibition should issue to the criminal court because the ordinance authorizing such inspections is unconstitutional on its face. The Superior Court denied the writ, the District Court of Appeal affirmed, and the Supreme Court of California denied a petition for hearing. Appellant properly raised and had considered by the California courts the federal constitutional questions he now presents to this Court.

Though there were no judicial findings of fact in this prohibition proceeding, we shall set forth the parties' factual allegations. On November 6, 1963, an inspector of the Division of Housing Inspection of the San Francisco Department of Public Health entered an apartment building to make a routine annual inspection for possible violations of the city's Housing Code. The building's manager informed the inspector that appellant, lessee of the ground floor, was using the rear of his leasehold as a personal residence. Claiming that the building's occupancy permit did not allow residential use of the ground floor, the inspector confronted appellant and demanded that he permit an inspection of the premises. Appellant refused to allow the inspection because the inspector lacked a search warrant.

The inspector returned on November 8, again without a warrant, and appellant again refused to allow an inspection. A citation was then mailed ordering appellant to appear at the district attorney's office. When appellant failed to appear, two inspectors returned to his apartment on November 22. They informed appellant that he was required by law to permit an inspection under § 503 of the Housing Code:

> Sec. 503 RIGHT TO ENTER BUILDING. Authorized employees of the City departments or City agencies, so far as may be necessary for the performance of their duties, shall, upon presentation of proper credentials, have the right to enter, at reasonable times, any building, structure, or premises in the City to perform any duty imposed upon them by the Municipal Code.

Appellant nevertheless refused the inspectors access to his apartment without a search warrant. Thereafter, a complaint was filed charging him with refusing to permit a lawful inspection in violation of § 507 of the Code. Appellant was arrested on December 2 and released on bail. When his demurrer to the criminal complaint was denied, appellant filed this petition for a writ of prohibition.

Appellant has argued throughout this litigation that § 503 is contrary to the Fourth and Fourteenth Amendments in that it authorizes municipal officials to enter a private dwelling without a search warrant and without probable cause to believe that a violation of the Housing Code exists therein. Consequently, appellant contends, he may not be prosecuted under § 507 for refusing to permit an inspection unconstitutionally authorized by § 503. Relying on *Frank v. Maryland*, *Eaton v. Price*, and decisions in other States, the District Court of Appeal held that § 503 does not violate Fourth Amendment rights because it "is part of a regulatory scheme which is essentially civil rather than criminal in nature, inasmuch as that section creates a right of inspection which is limited in scope and may not be exercised under unreasonable conditions." Having concluded that *Frank v. Maryland*, to the extent that it sanctioned such warrantless inspections, must be overruled, we reverse.

I

The Fourth Amendment provides that, "The right of the people to be secure in their persons, houses, papers, and effects, against unreasonable searches and seizures, shall not be violated, and no Warrants shall issue, but upon probable cause, supported by Oath or affirmation, and particularly describing the place to be searched, and the per-

EDITED CASE Camara v. Municipal Court (Continued)

sons or things to be seized." The basic purpose of this Amendment, as recognized in countless decisions of this Court, is to safeguard the privacy and security of individuals against arbitrary invasions by governmental officials. The Fourth Amendment thus gives concrete expression to a right of the people which "is basic to a free society.". . . As such, the Fourth Amendment is enforceable against the States through the Fourteenth Amendment. . . .

Though there has been general agreement as to the fundamental purpose of the Fourth Amendment, translation of the abstract prohibition against "unreasonable searches and seizures" into workable guidelines for the decision of particular cases is a difficult task which has for many years divided the members of this Court. Nevertheless, one governing principle, justified by history and by current experience, has consistently been followed: except in certain carefully defined classes of cases, a search of private property without proper consent is "unreasonable" unless it has been authorized by a valid search warrant. . . .

"The right of officers to thrust themselves into a home is also a grave concern, not only to the individual but to a society which chooses to dwell in reasonable security and freedom from surveillance. When the right of privacy must reasonably yield to the right of search is, as a rule, to be decided by a judicial officer, not by a policeman or government enforcement agent."

In *Frank v. Maryland*, this Court upheld the conviction of one who refused to permit a warrantless inspection of private premises for the purposes of locating and abating a suspected public nuisance. Although *Frank* can arguably be distinguished from this case on its facts, the *Frank* opinion has generally been interpreted as carving out an additional exception to the rule that warrantless searches are unreasonable under the Fourth Amendment. . . . The District Court of Appeal so interpreted *Frank* in this case, and that ruling is the core of appellant's challenge here. We proceed to a re-examination of the factors which persuaded the *Frank* majority to adopt this construction of the Fourth Amendment's prohibition against unreasonable searches.

To the *Frank* majority, municipal fire, health, and housing inspection programs "touch at most

upon the periphery of the important interests safeguarded by the Fourteenth Amendment's protection against official intrusion," . . . because the inspections are merely to determine whether physical conditions exist which do not comply with minimum standards prescribed in local regulatory ordinances. Since the inspector does not ask that the property owner open his doors to a search for "evidence of criminal action" which may be used to secure the owner's criminal conviction, historic interests of "self-protection" jointly protected by the Fourth and Fifth Amendments are said not to be involved, but only the less intense "right to be secure from intrusion into personal privacy." . . .

We may agree that a routine inspection of the physical condition of private property is a less hostile intrusion than the typical policeman's search for the fruits and instrumentalities of crime. For this reason alone, *Frank* differed from the great bulk of Fourth Amendment cases which have been considered by this Court. But we cannot agree that the Fourth Amendment interests at stake in these inspection cases are merely "peripheral." It is surely anomalous to say that the individual and his private property are fully protected by the Fourth Amendment only when the individual is suspected of criminal behavior. For instance, even the most law-abiding citizen has a very tangible interest in limiting the circumstances under which the sanctity of his home may be broken by official authority, for the possibility of criminal entry under the guise of official sanction is a serious threat to personal and family security. And even accepting *Frank's* rather remarkable premise, inspections of the kind we are here considering do in fact jeopardize "self-protection" interests of the property owner. Like most regulatory laws, fire, health, and housing codes are enforced by criminal processes. In some cities, discovery of a violation by the inspector leads to a criminal complaint. Even in cities where discovery of a violation produces only an administrative compliance order, refusal to comply is a criminal offense, and the fact of compliance is verified by a second inspection, again without a warrant. Finally, as this case demonstrates, refusal to permit an inspection is itself a crime, punishable by fine or even by jail sentence.

(Continued)

EDITED CASE　Camara v. Municipal Court (Continued)

The *Frank* majority suggested, and appellee reasserts, two other justifications for permitting administrative health and safety inspections without a warrant. First, it is argued that these inspections are "designed to make the least possible demand on the individual occupant." . . . The ordinances authorizing inspections are hedged with safeguards, and at any rate the inspector's particular decision to enter must comply with the constitutional standard of reasonableness even if he may enter without a warrant. In addition, the argument proceeds, the warrant process could not function effectively in this field. The decision to inspect an entire municipal area is based upon legislative or administrative assessment of broad factors such as the area's age and condition. Unless the magistrate is to review such policy matters, he must issue a "rubber stamp" warrant which provides no protection at all to the property owner.

In our opinion, these arguments unduly discount the purposes behind the warrant machinery contemplated by the Fourth Amendment. Under the present system, when the inspector demands entry, the occupant has no way of knowing whether enforcement of the municipal code involved requires inspection of his premises, no way of knowing the lawful limits of the inspector's power to search, and no way of knowing whether the inspector himself is acting under proper authorization. These are questions which may be reviewed by a neutral magistrate without any reassessment of the basic agency decision to canvass an area. Yet, only by refusing entry and risking a criminal conviction can the occupant at present challenge the inspector's decision to search. And even if the occupant possesses sufficient fortitude to take this risk, as appellant did here, he may never learn any more about the reason for the inspection than that the law generally allows housing inspectors to gain entry. The practical effect of this system is to leave the occupant subject to the discretion of the official in the field. This is precisely the discretion to invade private property which we have consistently circumscribed by a requirement that a disinterested party warrant the need to search. . . . We simply cannot say that the protections provided by the warrant procedure are not needed in this context; broad statutory safeguards are no substitute for individualized review,

particularly when those safeguards may only be invoked at the risk of a criminal penalty.

The final justification suggested for warrantless administrative searches is that the public interest demands such a rule: it is vigorously argued that the health and safety of entire urban populations is dependent upon enforcement of minimum fire, housing, and sanitation standards, and that the only effective means of enforcing such codes is by routine systematized inspection of all physical structures. Of course, in applying any reasonableness standard, including one of constitutional dimension, an argument that the public interest demands a particular rule must receive careful consideration. But we think this argument misses the mark. The question is not, at this stage at least, whether these inspections may be made, but whether they may be made without a warrant. For example, to say that gambling raids may not be made at the discretion of the police without a warrant is not necessarily to say that gambling raids may never be made. In assessing whether the public interest demands creation of a general exception to the Fourth Amendment's warrant requirement, the question is not whether the public interest justifies the type of search in question, but whether the authority to search should be evidenced by a warrant, which in turn depends in part upon whether the burden of obtaining a warrant is likely to frustrate the governmental purpose behind the search. . . . It has nowhere been urged that fire, health, and housing code inspection programs could not achieve their goals within the confines of a reasonable search warrant requirement. Thus, we do not find the public need argument dispositive. . . .

In summary, we hold that administrative searches of the kind at issue here are significant intrusions upon the interests protected by the Fourth Amendment, that such searches when authorized and conducted without a warrant procedure lack the traditional safeguards which the Fourth Amendment guarantees to the individual, and that the reasons put forth in *Frank v. Maryland* and in other cases for upholding these warrantless searches are insufficient to justify so substantial a weakening of the Fourth Amendment's protections. Because of the nature of the municipal programs under consideration, however, these conclusions must be the beginning, not the end, of

EDITED CASE   Camara v. Municipal Court (Continued)

our inquiry. The *Frank* majority gave recognition to the unique character of these inspection programs by refusing to require search warrants; to reject that disposition does not justify ignoring the question whether some other accommodation between public need and individual rights is essential.

II

The Fourth Amendment provides that, "no Warrants shall issue, but upon probable cause." Borrowing from more typical Fourth Amendment cases, appellant argues not only that code enforcement inspection programs must be circumscribed by a warrant procedure, but also that warrants should issue only when the inspector possesses probable cause to believe that a particular dwelling contains violations of the minimum standards prescribed by the code being enforced. We disagree.

In cases in which the Fourth Amendment requires that a warrant to search be obtained, "probable cause" is the standard by which a particular decision to search is tested against the constitutional mandate of reasonableness. To apply this standard, it is obviously necessary first to focus upon the governmental interest which allegedly justifies official intrusion upon the constitutionally protected interests of the private citizen. For example, in a criminal investigation, the police may undertake to recover specific stolen or contraband goods. But that public interest would hardly justify a sweeping search of an entire city conducted in the hope that these goods might be found. Consequently, a search for these goods, even with a warrant, is "reasonable" only when there is "probable cause" to believe that they will be uncovered in a particular dwelling.

Unlike the search pursuant to a criminal investigation, the inspection programs at issue here are aimed at securing city-wide compliance with minimum physical standards for private property. The primary governmental interest at stake is to prevent even the unintentional development of conditions which are hazardous to public health and safety. Because fires and epidemics may ravage large urban areas, because unsightly conditions adversely affect the economic values of neighboring structures, numerous courts have upheld the police power of municipalities to impose and enforce such minimum standards even upon existing structures. In determining whether a particular inspection is reasonable—and thus in determining whether there is probable cause to issue a warrant for that inspection—the need for the inspection must be weighed in terms of these reasonable goals of code enforcement.

There is unanimous agreement among those most familiar with this field that the only effective way to seek universal compliance with the minimum standards required by municipal codes is through routine periodic inspections of all structures. It is here that the probable cause debate is focused, for the agency's decision to conduct an area inspection is unavoidably based on its appraisal of conditions in the area as a whole, not on its knowledge of conditions in each particular building. Appellee contends that, if the probable cause standard urged by appellant is adopted, the area inspection will be eliminated as a means of seeking compliance with code standards and the reasonable goals of code enforcement will be dealt a crushing blow.

In meeting this contention, appellant argues first, that his probable cause standard would not jeopardize area inspection programs because only a minute portion of the population will refuse to consent to such inspections, and second, that individual privacy in any event should be given preference to the public interest in conducting such inspections. The first argument, even if true, is irrelevant to the question whether the area inspection is reasonable within the meaning of the Fourth Amendment. The second argument is in effect an assertion that the area inspection is an unreasonable search. Unfortunately, there can be no ready test for determining reasonableness other than by balancing the need to search against the invasion which the search entails. But we think that a number of persuasive factors combine to support the reasonableness of area code-enforcement inspections. First, such programs have a long history of judicial and public acceptance. . . . Second, the public interest demands that all dangerous conditions be prevented or abated, yet it is doubtful that any other canvassing technique would achieve acceptable results. Many such conditions—faulty wiring is an obvious example—are not observable from outside the building and

(Continued)

EDITED CASE   Camara v. Municipal Court (Continued)

indeed may not be apparent to the inexpert occupant himself. Finally, because the inspections are neither personal in nature nor aimed at the discovery of evidence of crime, they involve a relatively limited invasion of the urban citizen's privacy. Both the majority and the dissent in *Frank* emphatically supported this conclusion:

"Time and experience have forcefully taught that the power to inspect dwelling places, either as a matter of systematic area-by-area search or, as here. to treat a specific problem, is of indispensable importance to the maintenance of community health; a power that would be greatly hobbled by the blanket requirement of the safeguards necessary for a search of evidence of criminal acts. The need for preventive action is great, and city after city has seen this need and granted the power of inspection to its health officials; and these inspections are apparently welcomed by all but an insignificant few. Certainly, the nature of our society has not vitiated the need for inspections first thought necessary 158 years ago, nor has experience revealed any abuse or inroad on freedom in meeting this need by means that history and dominant public opinion have sanctioned." . . .

". . . This is not to suggest that a health official need show the same kind of proof to a magistrate to obtain a warrant as one must who would search for the fruits or instrumentalities of crime. Where considerations of health and safety are involved, the facts that would justify an inference of 'probable cause' to make an inspection are clearly different from those that would justify such an inference where a criminal investigation has been undertaken. Experience may show the need for periodic inspections of certain facilities without a further showing of cause to believe that substandard conditions dangerous to the public are being maintained. The passage of a certain period without inspection might of itself be sufficient in a given situation to justify the issuance of a warrant. The test of 'probable cause' required by the Fourth Amendment can take into account the nature of the search that is being sought." . . .

Having concluded that the area inspection is a "reasonable" search of private property within the meaning of the Fourth Amendment, it is obvious that "probable cause" to issue a warrant to inspect must exist if reasonable legislative or administrative standards for conducting an area inspection

are satisfied with respect to a particular dwelling. Such standards, which will vary with the municipal program being enforced, may be based upon the passage of time, the nature of the building (e.g., a multi-family apartment house), or the condition of the entire area, but they will not necessarily depend upon specific knowledge of the condition of the particular dwelling. It has been suggested that so to vary the probable cause test from the standard applied in criminal cases would be to authorize a "synthetic search warrant" and thereby to lessen the overall protections of the Fourth Amendment. . . . But we do not agree. The warrant procedure is designed to guarantee that a decision to search private property is justified by a reasonable governmental interest. But reasonableness is still the ultimate standard. If a valid public interest justifies the intrusion contemplated, then there is probable cause to issue a suitably restricted search warrant. . . . Such an approach neither endangers time-honored doctrines applicable to criminal investigations nor makes a nullity of the probable cause requirement in this area. It merely gives full recognition to the competing public and private interests here at stake and, in so doing, best fulfills the historic purpose behind the constitutional right to be free from unreasonable government invasions of privacy. . . .

III

Since our holding emphasizes the controlling standard of reasonableness, nothing we say today is intended to foreclose prompt inspections, even without a warrant, that the law has traditionally upheld in emergency situations. . . . On the other hand, in the case of most routine area inspections, there is no compelling urgency to inspect at a particular time or on a particular day. Moreover, most citizens allow inspections of their property without a warrant. Thus, as a practical matter and in light of the Fourth Amendment's requirement that a warrant specify the property to be searched, it seems likely that warrants should normally be sought only after entry is refused unless there has been a citizen complaint or there is other satisfactory reason for securing immediate entry. Similarly, the requirement of a warrant procedure does not suggest any change in what seems to be the prevailing local policy, in most situations, of authorizing entry, but not entry by force, to inspect.

EDITED CASE   Camara v. Municipal Court (Continued)

IV

In this case, appellant has been charged with a crime for his refusal to permit housing inspectors to enter his leasehold without a warrant. There was no emergency demanding immediate access; in fact, the inspectors made three trips to the building in an attempt to obtain appellant's consent to search. Yet no warrant was obtained and thus appellant was unable to verify either the need for or the appropriate limits of the inspection. No doubt, the inspectors entered the public portion of the building with the consent of the landlord, through the building's manager, but appellee does not contend that such consent was sufficient to authorize inspection of appellant's

premises. . . . Assuming the facts to be as the parties have alleged, we therefore conclude that appellant had a constitutional right to insist that the inspectors obtain a warrant to search and that appellant may not constitutionally be convicted for refusing to consent to the inspection. It appears from the opinion of the District Court of Appeal that under these circumstances a writ of prohibition will issue to the criminal court under California law.

The judgment is vacated and the case is remanded for further proceedings not inconsistent with this opinion.

Justice Clark, dissenting. . . .

EDITED CASE   Colonnade Corporation. v. United States
United States Supreme Court, 397 U.S. 72 (1970)

[Here the Supreme Court recognizes an exception to the Fourth Amendment warrant requirement for administrative searches of closely regulated industries.]

Justice Douglas delivered the opinion of the Court.

Petitioner, a licensee in New York authorized to serve alcoholic beverages and also the holder of a federal retail liquor dealer's occupational tax stamp, 26 U.S.C. § 5121 (a), brought this suit to obtain the return of seized liquor and to suppress it as evidence. The District Court granted the relief. The Court of Appeals reversed. . . .

Petitioner runs a catering establishment. A federal agent, a member of the Alcohol and Tobacco Tax Division of the Internal Revenue Service, was a guest at a party on petitioner's premises and noted a possible violation of the federal excise tax law. When federal agents later visited the place, another party was in progress. They noticed that liquor was being served. Without the manager's consent, they inspected the cellar. Then they asked the manager to open the locked liquor storeroom. He said that the only person authorized to open that room was one Rozzo, petitioner's president,

who was not on the premises. Later Rozzo arrived and refused to open the storeroom. He asked if the agents had a search warrant and they answered that they did not need one. When Rozzo continued to refuse to unlock the room, an agent broke the lock and entered. Then they removed the bottles of liquor now in controversy which they apparently suspected of being refilled contrary to the command of 26 U.S.C. § 5301 (c).

It is provided in 26 U.S.C. § 5146 (b) and in 26 U.S.C. § 7606 that the Secretary of the Treasury or his delegate has broad authority to enter and inspect the premises of retail dealers in liquors. And in case of the refusal of a dealer to permit the inspection, it is provided in 26 U.S.C. § 7342:

"Any owner of any building or place, or person having the agency or superintendence of the same, who refuses to admit any officer or employee of the Treasury Department acting under the authority of section 7606 (relating to entry of premises for examination of taxable articles) or refuses to permit him to examine such article or articles, shall, for every such refusal, forfeit $500."

(Continued)

EDITED CASE   Colonnade Corporation. v. United States (Continued)

The question is whether the imposition of a fine for refusal to permit entry—with the attendant consequences that violation of inspection laws may have in this closely regulated industry—is under this statutory scheme the exclusive sanction, absent a warrant to break and enter.

In *Frank v. Maryland*, . . . a case involving an inspection under a municipal code, we said: "[The] inspector has no power to force entry and did not attempt it. A fine is imposed for resistance, but officials are not authorized to break past the unwilling occupant."

Frank v. Maryland was overruled . . . insofar as it permitted warrantless searches or inspections under municipal fire, health, and housing codes. The dictum that the provision for a fine on refusal to allow inspection made the use of force improper when there was no warrant was not disturbed; and the question is whether that dictum contains the controlling principle for this case.

The Government, emphasizing that the Fourth Amendment bans only "unreasonable searches and seizures," relies heavily on the long history of the regulation of the liquor industry during pre-Fourth Amendment days, first in England and later in the American Colonies. It is pointed out, for example, that in 1660 the precursor of modern-day liquor legislation was enacted in England which allowed commissioners to enter, on demand, brewing houses at all times for inspection. Massachusetts had a similar law in 1692. And in 1791, the year in which the Fourth Amendment was ratified, Congress imposed an excise tax on imported distilled spirits and on liquor distilled here, under which law federal officers had broad powers to inspect distilling premises and the premises of the importer without a warrant. From these and later laws and regulations governing the liquor industry, it is argued that Congress has been most solicitous in protecting the revenue against various types of fraud and to that end has repeatedly granted federal agents power to make warrantless searches and seizures of articles under the liquor laws.

The Court recognized the special treatment of inspection laws of this kind in *Boyd v. United States*: "[I]n the case of excisable or dutiable articles, the government has an interest in them for the payment of the duties thereon, and until such duties are paid has a right to keep them under observation, or to pursue and drag them from concealment."

And it added:

"The seizure of stolen goods is authorized by the common law; and the seizure of goods forfeited for a breach of the revenue laws, or concealed to avoid the duties payable on them, has been authorized by English statutes for at least two centuries past; and the like seizures have been authorized by our own revenue acts from the commencement of the government. The first statute passed by Congress to regulate the collection of duties, the act of July 31, 1789, . . . contains provisions to this effect. As this act was passed by the same Congress which proposed for adoption the original amendments to the Constitution, it is clear that the members of that body did not regard searches and seizures of this kind as 'unreasonable,' and they are not embraced within the prohibition of the amendment." . . .

We agree that Congress has broad power to design such powers of inspection under the liquor laws as it deems necessary to meet the evils at hand. The general rule . . . "that administrative entry, without consent, upon the portions of commercial premises which are not open to the public may only be compelled through prosecution or physical force within the framework of a warrant procedure"—is therefore not applicable here. . . .

Where Congress has authorized inspection but made no rules governing the procedure that inspectors must follow, the Fourth Amendment and its various restrictive rules apply. . . .

What was said in *See* reflects this Nation's traditions that are strongly opposed to using force without definite authority to break down doors. We deal here with the liquor industry long subject to close supervision and inspection. As respects that industry, and its various branches including retailers, Congress has broad authority to fashion standards of reasonableness for searches and seizures. Under the existing statutes, Congress selected a standard that does not include forcible entries without a warrant. It resolved the issue, not by authorizing forcible, warrantless entries, but by making it an offense for a licensee to refuse admission to the inspector.

Reversed.

EDITED CASE Marshall v. Barlow's, Inc.
United States Supreme Court, 436 U.S. 307 (1978)

[In this case the Court reviews a provision of the Occupational Safety and Health Act of 1970 authorizing agents of the Occupational Safety and Health Administration (OSHA) to conduct unannounced, warrantless inspections of employment facilities within the OSHA's jurisdiction.]

Justice White delivered the opinion of the Court.

. . . On the morning of September 11, 1975, an OSHA inspector entered the customer service area of Barlow's, Inc., an electrical and plumbing installation business located in Pocatello, Idaho. The president and general manager, Ferrol G. "Bill" Barlow, was on hand; and the OSHA inspector, after showing his credentials, informed Mr. Barlow that he wished to conduct a search of the working areas of the business. Mr. Barlow inquired whether any complaint had been received about his company. The inspector answered no, but that Barlow's, Inc., had simply turned up on the agency's selection process. The inspector again asked to enter the nonpublic area of the business; Mr. Barlow's response was to inquire whether the inspector had a search warrant. The inspector had none. Thereupon, Mr. Barlow refused the inspector admission to the employee area of his business. He said he was relying on his rights as guaranteed by the Fourth Amendment of the United States Constitution. . . .

The Secretary [of Labor] urges that warrantless inspections to enforce [the Occupational Safety and Health Act] are reasonable within the meaning of the Fourth Amendment. Among other things, he relies on § 8(a) of the Act, . . . which authorizes inspection of business premises without a warrant and which the Secretary urges represents a congressional construction of the Fourth Amendment that the courts should not reject. Regrettably, we are unable to agree.

The Warrant Clause of the Fourth Amendment protects commercial buildings as well as private homes. To hold otherwise would belie the origin of that Amendment, and the American colonial experience. An important forerunner of the first ten Amendments to the United States Constitution, the Virginia Bill of Rights, specifically opposed "general warrants, whereby an officer or messenger may be commanded to search suspected places without evidence of a fact committed." The general warrant was a recurring point of contention in the Colonies immediately preceding the Revolution. The particular offensiveness it engendered was acutely felt by the merchants and businessmen whose premises and products were inspected for compliance with the several parliamentary revenue measures that most irritated the colonists. "[T]he Fourth Amendment's commands grew in large measure out of the colonists' experience with the writs of assistance . . . [that] granted sweeping power to customs officials and other agents of the king to search at large for smuggled goods." . . . Against this background, it is untenable that the ban on warrantless searches was not intended to shield places of business as well as of residence.

This Court has already held that warrantless searches are generally unreasonable, and that this rule applied to commercial premises as well as homes. In *Camara v. Municipal Court* . . . [1967], we held [that] "[E]xcept in certain carefully defined classes of cases, a search of private property without proper consent is 'unreasonable unless it has been authorized by a valid search warrant.'" On the same day, we also ruled:

> [A] search of private houses is presumptively unreasonable if conducted without a warrant. The businessman, like the occupant of a residence, has a constitutional right to go about his business free from unreasonable official entries upon his private commercial property. The businessman, too, has that right placed in jeopardy if the decision to enter and inspect for violation of regulatory laws can be made and enforced by the inspector in the field without official authority evidenced by a warrant. *See v. Seattle* . . . (1967).

These same cases also held that the Fourth Amendment prohibition against unreasonable searches protects against warrantless intrusions during civil as well as criminal investigations. The

(Continued)

EDITED CASE   Marshall v. Barlow's, Inc. (Continued)

reason is found in the "basic purpose of this Amendment . . . [which] is to safeguard the privacy and security of individuals against arbitrary invasions by governmental officials." . . . If the government intrudes on a person's property, the privacy interest suffers whether the government's motivation is to investigate violations of criminal law or breaches of other statutory or regulatory standards. It therefore appears that unless some recognized exception to the warrant requirement applies. *See v. Seattle* would require a warrant to conduct the inspection sought in this case.

The Secretary urges that an exception from the search warrant requirement has been recognized for "pervasively regulated" industries "long subject to close supervision and inspection." *Colonnade Catering Corp. v. United States* . . . (1970); *Biswell v. United States* . . . (1972). These cases are indeed exceptions, but they represent responses to relatively unique circumstances. Certain industries have such a history of government oversight that no reasonable expectation of privacy, could exist for a proprietor over the stock of such an enterprise. Liquor (*Colonnade*) and firearms (*Biswell*) are industries of this type; when an entrepreneur embarks upon such a business, he has voluntarily chosen to subject himself to a full arsenal of governmental regulations. . . .

The clear import of our cases is that the closely regulated industry of the type involved in *Colonnade* and *Biswell* is the exception. The Secretary would make it the rule. Invoking the Walsh-Healey Act of 1936, . . . the Secretary attempts to support a conclusion that all businesses involved in interstate commerce have long been subjected to close supervision of employee safety and health conditions. But the degree of federal involvement in employee working circumstances has never been of the order of specificity and pervasiveness that OSHA mandates. It is quite unconvincing to argue that the imposition of minimum wages and maximum hours on employers who contracted with the Government under the Walsh-Healey Act prepared the entirety of American interstate commerce for regulation of working conditions to the minutest detail. Nor can any but the most fictional sense of voluntary consent to later searches be found in the single fact that one conducts a business affecting interstate commerce; under current practice and law, few businesses can be conducted without having some effect on interstate commerce. . . .

The critical fact in this case is that entry over Mr. Barlow's objection is being sought by a government agent. Employees are not being prohibited from reporting OSHA violations. What they observe in their daily functions is undoubtedly beyond the employer's reasonable expectation of privacy. The Government inspector, however, is not an employee. Without a warrant he stands in no better position than a member of the public. What is observable by the public is observable, without a warrant, by the Government inspection as well. The owner of a business has not, by the necessary utilization of employees in his operation, thrown open the areas where employees alone are permitted to the warrantless scrutiny of Government agents. That an employee is free to report, and the government is free to use, any evidence of noncompliance with OSHA that the employee observes furnishes no justification for federal agents to enter a place of business from which the public is restricted and to conduct their own warrantless search.

The Secretary nevertheless stoutly argues that the enforcement scheme of the Act requires warrantless searches, and that the restrictions on search discretion contained in the Act and its regulations already protect as much privacy as a warrant would. The Secretary thereby asserts the actual reasonableness of OSHA searches, whatever the general rule against warrantless searches might be. Because "reasonableness is still the ultimate standard," . . . the Secretary suggests that the Court decide whether a warrant is needed by arriving at a sensible balance between the administrative necessities of OSHA inspections and the incremental protection of privacy of business owners a warrant would afford. He suggests that only a decision exempting OSHA inspections from the Warrant Clause would give "full recognition to the competing public and private interests here at stake." . . .

The Secretary submits that warrantless inspections are essential to the proper enforcement of OSHA because they afford the opportunity to inspect without prior notice and hence to preserve the advantages of surprise. While the dangerous conditions outlawed by the Act include structural defects that cannot be quickly hidden or remedied, the Act also regulates a myriad of safety

---

EDITED CASE   Marshall v. Barlow's, Inc. (Continued)

---

details that may be amenable to speedy alteration or disguise. The risk is that during the interval between an inspector's initial request to search a plant and his procuring a warrant following the owner's refusal of permission, violations of this latter type could be corrected and thus escape the inspector's notice. To the suggestion that warrants may be issued *ex parte* and executed without delay and without prior notice, thereby preserving the element of surprise, the Secretary expresses concern for the administrative strain that would be experienced by the inspection system, and by the courts, should ex parte warrants issued in advance become standard practice.

We are unconvinced, however, that requiring warrants to inspect will impose serious burdens on the inspection system or the courts, will prevent inspections necessary to enforce the statute, or will make them less effective. In the first place, the great majority of businessmen can be expected in normal course to consent to inspection without warrant; the Secretary has not brought to this Court's attention any widespread pattern of refusal. . . . Nor is it immediately apparent why the advantages of surprise would be lost if, after being refused entry, procedures were available for the Secretary to seek an ex parte warrant and to reappear at the premises without further notice to the establishment being inspected.

Whether the Secretary proceeds to secure a warrant or other process, with or without prior notice, his entitlement to inspect will not depend on his demonstrating probable cause to believe that conditions in violation of OSHA exist on the premises. Probable cause in the criminal law sense is not required. For purposes of an administrative search such as this, probable cause justifying the issuance of a warrant may be based not only on specific evidence of an existing violation but also on a showing that "reasonable legislative or administrative standards for conducting an . . . inspection are satisfied with respect to a particular [establishment]." . . . A warrant showing that a specific business has been chosen for an OSHA search on the basis of a general administrative plan for the enforcement of the Act derived from neutral sources such as, for example, dispersion of employees in various types of industries across a given area, and the desired frequency of searches

in any of the lesser divisions of the area, would protect an employer's Fourth Amendment divisions of the area, would protect an employer's Fourth Amendment rights. . . .

Finally, the Secretary urges that requiring a warrant for OSHA inspectors will mean that, as a practical matter, warrantless-search provisions in other regulatory statutes are also constitutionally infirm. The reasonableness of a warrantless search, however, will depend upon the specific enforcement needs and privacy guarantees of each statute. Some of the statutes cited apply only to a single industry, where regulations might already be so pervasive that a *Colonnade-Biswell* exception to the warrant requirement could apply. Some statutes already envision resort to federal-court enforcement when entry is refused, employing specific language in some cases and general language in others. In short, we base today's opinion on the facts and law concerned with OSHA and do not retreat from a holding appropriate to that statute because of its real or imagined effect on other, different administrative schemes.

Nor do we agree that the incremental protections afforded the employer's privacy by a warrant are so marginal that they fail to justify the administrative burdens that may be entailed. The authority to make warrantless searches devolves almost unbridled discretion upon executive and administrative officers, particularly those in the field, as to when to search and whom to search. A warrant, by contrast, would provide assurances from a neutral officer that the inspection is reasonable under the Constitution, is authorized by statute, and is pursuant to an administrative plan containing specific neutral criteria. Also, a warrant would then and there advise the owner of the scope and objects of the search, beyond which limits the inspector is not expected to proceed. These are important functions for a warrant to perform, functions which underlie the Court's prior decisions that the Warrant Clause applied to inspections for compliance with regulatory statutes. . . . We conclude that the concerns expressed by the Secretary do not suffice to justify warrantless inspections under OSHA or vitiate the general constitutional requirement that for a search to be reasonable a warrant must be obtained. . . .

(Continued)

EDITED CASE   Marshall v. Barlow's, Inc. (Continued)

Justice Brennan took no part in the consideration or decision of this case.

Justice Stevens, with whom *Justices Blackmun* and *Rehnquist* join, dissenting.

Congress enacted the Occupational Safety and Health Act to safeguard employees against hazards in the work areas of business subject to the act. To ensure compliance, Congress authorized the Secretary of Labor to conduct routine, nonconsensual inspections. Today the Court holds that the Fourth Amendment prohibits such inspections without a warrant. The Court also holds that the constitutionally required warrant may be issued without any showing of probable cause. I disagree with both of these holdings.

The Fourth Amendment contains two separate Clauses, each flatly prohibiting a category of governmental conduct. The first Clause states that the right to be free from unreasonable searches "shall not be violated"; the second unequivocally prohibits the issuance of warrants except "upon probable cause." In this case the ultimate question is whether the category of warrantless searches authorized by the statute is "unreasonable" within the meaning of the first Clause.

In cases involving the investigation of criminal activity, the Court has held that the reasonableness of a search generally depends upon whether it was conducted pursuant to a valid warrant. . . . There is, however, also a category of searches which are reasonable within the meaning of the first Clause even though the probable-cause requirement of the Warrant Clause cannot be satisfied. . . . The regulatory inspection program challenged in this case, in judgment, falls within this category.

The warrant requirement is linked "textually . . . to the probable-cause concept" in the Warrant Clause. . . . The routine OSHA inspections are, by definition, not based on cause to believe there is a violation on the premises to be inspected. Hence, if the inspections were measured against the requirements of the Warrant Clause, they would be automatically and unequivocally unreasonable.

Because of the acknowledged importance and reasonableness of routine inspections in the enforcement of federal regulatory statutes such as OSHA, the Court recognizes that requiring full compliance with the Warrant Clause would invalidate all such inspection programs. Yet, rather than simply analyzing such programs under the "Reasonableness" Clause of the Fourth Amendment, the Court holds the OSHA program invalid under the Warrant Clause and then avoids a blanket prohibition on all routine, regulatory inspections by relying on the notion that the "probable cause" requirement in the Warrant Clause may be relaxed whenever the Court believes that the governmental need to conduct a category of "search" outweighs the intrusion on interests protected by the Fourth Amendment.

The Court's approach disregards the plain language of the Warrant Clause and is unfaithful to the balance struck by the Framers of the Fourth Amendment—"the one procedural safeguard in the Constitution that grew directly out of the events which immediately preceded the revolutionary struggle with England."

Since the general warrant, not the warrantless search, was the immediate evil at which the Fourth Amendment was directed, it is not surprising that the Framers placed precise limits on its issuance. The requirement that a warrant only issue on a showing of particularized probable cause was the means adopted to circumscribe the warrant power. While the subsequent course of Fourth Amendment jurisprudence in this Court emphasizes the dangers posed by warrantless searches conducted without probable cause, it is the general reasonableness standard in the first Clause, not the Warrant Clause, that the Framers adopted to limit this category of searches. It is, of course, true that the existence of a valid warrant normally satisfied the reasonableness requirement under the Fourth Amendment. But we should not dilute the requirements of the Warrant Clause in an effort to force every kind of governmental intrusion which satisfied the Fourth Amendment definition of a "search" into a judicially developed, warrant-preference scheme.

Fidelity to the original understanding of the Fourth Amendment, therefore, leads to the conclusion that the Warrant Clause has no application to routine, regulatory inspections of commercial premises. If such inspections are valid, it is because they comport with the ultimate reasonableness standard of the Fourth Amendment. If the Court were correct in its view that such inspections, if undertaken without a warrant, are unreasonable in the constitutional sense, the issuance of a "new-

---

EDITED CASE   Marshall v. Barlow's, Inc. (Continued)

---

fangled warrant"—to use Mr. Justice Clark's characteristically expressive term—without any true showing of particularized probable cause would not be sufficient to validate them. . . .

The case before us involves an attempt to conduct a warrantless search of the working area of an electrical and plumbing contractor. The statute authorizes such an inspection during reasonable hours. The inspection is limited to those areas over which Congress has exercised its proper legislative authority. The area is also one to which employees have regular access without any suggestion that the work performed or the equipment used has any special claim to confidentiality. Congress had determined that industrial safety is an urgent federal interest requiring regulation and supervision, and further, that warrantless inspections are necessary to accomplish the safety goals of the legislation. While one may question the wisdom of pervasive governmental oversight of industrial life, I decline to question Congress' judgment that the inspection power is a necessary enforcement device in achieving the goals of a valid exercise of regulatory power.

I respectfully dissent.

EDITED CASE   Dow Chemical Company v. United States
United States Supreme Court, 476 U.S. 227 (1986)

[In this case, the Supreme Court reviews a court of appeals decision upholding the Environmental Protection Agency's aerial observation of a chemical plant complex. The key question is whether the EPA action constituted a search within the meaning of the Fourth Amendment.]

Chief Justice Burger delivered the opinion of the Court.

. . . Petitioner Dow Chemical Co. operates a 2,000-acre facility manufacturing chemicals at Midland, Michigan. The facility consists of numerous covered buildings, with manufacturing equipment and piping conduits located between the various buildings exposed to visual observation from the air. At all times, Dow has maintained elaborate security around the perimeter of the complex barring ground-level public views of these areas. It also investigates any low-level flights by aircraft over the facility. Dow has not undertaken, however, to conceal all manufacturing equipment within the complex from aerial views. Dow maintains that the cost of covering its exposed equipment would be prohibitive.

In early 1978, enforcement officials of EPA, with Dow's consent, made an on-site inspection of two power plants in this complex. A subsequent EPA request for a second inspection, however, was denied, and EPA did not thereafter seek an administrative search warrant. Instead, EPA employed a commercial aerial photographer, using a standard floor-mounted, precision aerial mapping camera, to take photographs of the facility from altitudes of 12,000, 3,000, and 1,200 feet. At all times the aircraft was lawfully within navigable airspace. . . .

EPA did not inform Dow of this aerial photography, but when Dow became aware of it, Dow brought suit in the District Court alleging that EPA's action violated the Fourth Amendment and was beyond EPA's statutory investigative authority. The District Court granted Dow's motion for summary judgment on the grounds that EPA had no authority to take aerial photographs and that doing so was a search violating the Fourth Amendment. EPA was permanently enjoined from taking aerial photographs of Dow's premises and from disseminating, releasing, or copying the photographs already taken. . . .

The District Court accepted the parties' concession that EPA's "quest for evidence" was a "search," . . . and limited its analysis to whether the search was unreasonable under *Katz v. United States* . . . (1967). Proceeding on the assumption that a search in Fourth Amendment terms had

(Continued)

EDITED CASE   Dow Chemical Company v. United States (Continued)

---

been conducted, the court found that Dow manifested an expectation of privacy in its exposed plant areas because it intentionally surrounded them with buildings and other enclosures. . . .

The District Court held that this expectation of privacy was reasonable, as reflected in part by trade secret protections restricting Dow's commercial competitors from aerial photography of these exposed areas. . . . The court emphasized that use of "the finest precision aerial camera available" permitted EPA to capture on film "a great deal more than the human eye could ever see." . . .

The Court of Appeals reversed. . . . It recognized that Dow indeed had a subjective expectation of privacy in certain areas from ground-level intrusions, but the court was not persuaded that Dow had a subjective expectation of being free from aerial surveillance since Dow had taken no precautions against such observation, in contrast to its elaborate ground-level precautions. . . . The court rejected the argument that it was not feasible to shield any of the critical parts of the exposed plant areas from aerial surveys. The Court of Appeals, however, did not explicitly reject the District Court's factual finding as to Dow's subjective expectations.

. . . Viewing Dow's facility to be more like the "open field" in *Oliver v. United States* . . . (1984), than a home or an office, [the court of appeals] held that the common-law curtilage doctrine did not apply to a large industrial complex of closed buildings connected by pipes, conduits, and other exposed manufacturing equipment. The Court of Appeals looked to "the peculiarly strong concepts of intimacy, personal autonomy and privacy associated with the home" as the basis for the curtilage protection. The court did not view the use of sophisticated photographic equipment by EPA as controlling.

The Court of Appeals then held that EPA clearly acted within its statutory powers even absent express authorization for aerial surveillance, concluding that the delegation of general investigative authority to EPA, similar to that of other law enforcement agencies, was sufficient to support the use of aerial photography. . . .

The photographs at issue in this case are essentially like those commonly used in mapmaking. Any person with an airplane and an aerial camera could readily duplicate them. In common with much else, the technology of photography has changed in this century. These developments have enhanced industrial processes, and indeed all areas of life; they have also enhanced law enforcement techniques. Whether they may be employed by competitors to penetrate trade secrets is not a question presented in this case. Governments do not generally seek to appropriate trade secrets of the private sector, and the right to be free of appropriation of trade secrets is protected by law.

Dow nevertheless relies heavily on its claim that trade secret laws protect it from any aerial photography of this industrial complex by its competitors, and that this protection is relevant to our analysis of such photography under the Fourth Amendment. That such photography might be barred by state law with regard to competitors, however, is irrelevant to the questions presented here. State tort law governing unfair competition does not define the limits of the Fourth Amendment. . . . The Government is seeking these photographs in order to regulate, not to compete with, Dow. If the Government were to use the photographs to compete with Dow, Dow might have a Fifth Amendment "taking" claim. Indeed, Dow alleged such a claim in its complaint, but the District Court dismissed it without prejudice. But even trade secret laws would not bar all forms of photography of this industrial complex; rather, only photography with an intent to use any trade secrets revealed by the photographs may be proscribed. Hence, there is no prohibition of photographs taken by a casual passenger on an airliner, or those taken by a company producing maps for its mapmaking purposes.

Dow claims first that EPA has no authority to use aerial photography to implement its statutory authority for "site inspection" under 114 (a) of the Clean Air Act . . . ; second, Dow claims EPA's use of aerial photography was a "search" of an area that, notwithstanding the large size of the plant, was within an "industrial curtilage" rather than an "open field," and that it had a reasonable expectation of privacy from such photography protected by the Fourth Amendment. . . .

Congress has vested in EPA certain investigatory and enforcement authority, without spelling out precisely how this authority was to be exer-

---

EDITED CASE Dow Chemical Company v. United States (Continued)

---

cised in all the myriad circumstances that might arise in monitoring matters relating to clean air and water standards. When Congress invests an agency with enforcement and investigatory authority, it is not necessary to identify explicitly each and every technique that may be used in the course of executing the statutory mission. Aerial observation authority, for example, is not usually expressly extended to police for traffic control, but it could hardly be thought necessary for a legislative body to tell police that aerial observation could be employed for traffic control of a metropolitan area, or to expressly authorize police to send messages to ground highway patrols that a particular over-the-road truck was traveling in excess of 55 miles per hour. Common sense and ordinary human experience teach that traffic violators are apprehended by observation.

Regulatory or enforcement authority generally carries with it all the modes of inquiry and investigation traditionally employed or useful to execute the authority granted. Environmental standards such as clean air and clean water cannot be enforced only in libraries and laboratories, helpful as those institutions may be.

Under 114(a)(2), the Clean Air Act provides that "upon presentation of . . . credentials," EPA has a "right of entry to, upon, or through any premises." . . . Dow argues this limited grant of authority to enter does not authorize any aerial observation. In particular, Dow argues that unannounced aerial observation deprives Dow of its right to be informed that an inspection will be made or has occurred, and its right to claim confidentiality of the information contained in the places to be photographed. . . . It is not claimed that EPA has disclosed any of the photographs outside the agency.

Section 114(a), however, appears to expand, not restrict, EPA's general powers to investigate. Nor is there any suggestion in the statute that the powers conferred by this section are intended to be exclusive. There is no claim that EPA is prohibited from taking photographs from a ground-level location accessible to the general public. EPA, as a regulatory and enforcement agency, needs no explicit statutory provision to employ methods of observation commonly available to the public at large: we hold that the use of aerial observation and photography is within EPA's statutory authority. . . .

We turn now to Dow's contention that taking aerial photographs constituted a search without a warrant, thereby violating Dow's rights. Under this contention, however, Dow concedes that a simple flyover with naked-eye observation, or the taking of a photograph from a nearby hillside overlooking such a facility, would give rise to no Fourth Amendment problem. . . .

Dow plainly has a reasonable, legitimate, and objective expectation of privacy within the interior of its covered buildings, and it is equally clear that expectation is one society is prepared to observe. . . . Moreover, it could hardly be expected that Dow would erect a huge cover over a 2,000-acre tract. In contending that its entire enclosed plant complex is an "industrial curtilage," Dow argues that its exposed manufacturing facilities are analogous to the curtilage surrounding a home because it has taken every possible step to bar access from ground level.

The Court of Appeals held that whatever the limits of an "industrial curtilage" barring ground-level intrusions into Dow's private areas, the open areas exposed here were more analogous to "open fields" than to a curtilage for purposes of aerial observation. In *Oliver*, the Court described the curtilage of a dwelling as "the area to which extends the intimate activity associated with the 'sanctity of a man's home and the privacies of life.' " The intimate activities associated with family privacy and the home and its curtilage simply do not reach the outdoor areas or spaces between structures and buildings of a manufacturing plant.

Admittedly, Dow's enclosed plant complex, like the area in *Oliver*, does not fall precisely with the "open fields" doctrine. The area at issue here can perhaps be seen as falling somewhere between "open fields" and curtilage, but lacking some of the critical characteristics of both. Dow's inner manufacturing areas are elaborately secured to ensure they are not open or exposed to the public from the ground. Any actual physical entry by EPA into any enclosed area would raise significantly different questions, because "the businessman, like the occupant of a residence, has a constitutional right to go about his business free from

(*Continued*)

EDITED CASE   Dow Chemical Company v. United States (Continued)

unreasonable official entries upon his private commercial property." The narrow issue raised by Dow's claim of search and seizure, however, concerns aerial observation of a 2,000-acre outdoor manufacturing facility without physical entry.

We pointed out in *Donovan v. Dewey* . . . (1981), that the Government has "greater latitude to conduct warrantless inspections of commercial property" because "the expectation of privacy that the owner of commercial property enjoys in such property differs significantly from the sanctity accorded an individual's home." We emphasized that unlike a homeowner's interest in his dwelling, the interest of the owner of commercial property is not one in being free from any inspections." And with regard to regulatory inspections, we have held that "[w]hat is observable by the public is observable without a warrant, by the Government inspector as well."

. . . Here, EPA was not employing some unique sensory device that, for example, could penetrate the walls of buildings and record conversations in Dow's plants, offices, or laboratories, but rather a conventional, albeit precise, commercial camera commonly used in mapmaking. The Government asserts it has not yet enlarged the photographs to any significant degree, but Dow points out that simple magnification permits identification of objects such as wires as small as 1/2-inch diameter.

It may well be, as the Government concedes, that surveillance of private property by using highly sophisticated surveillance equipment not generally available to the public, such as satellite technology, might be constitutionally proscribed absent a warrant. But the photographs here are not so revealing of intimate details as to raise constitutional concerns. Although they undoubtedly give EPA more detailed information than naked-eye views, they remain limited to an outline of the facility's buildings and equipment. The mere fact that human vision is enhanced somewhat, at least to the degree here, does not give rise to constitutional problems.

An electronic device to penetrate walls or windows so as to hear and record confidential discussions of chemical formulae or other trade secrets would raise very different and far more serious questions; other protections such as trade secret laws are available to protect commercial activities from private surveillance by competitors.

We conclude that the open areas of an industrial plant complex with numerous plant structures spread over an area of 2,000 acres are not analogous to the curtilage of a dwelling, [because they are] open to the view and observation of persons in aircraft lawfully in the public airspace immediately above or sufficiently near the area for the reach of cameras.

We hold that the taking of aerial photographs of an industrial plant complex from navigable airspace is not a search prohibited by the Fourth Amendment. . . .

Justice Powell, with whom *Justices Brennan, Marshall,* and *Blackmun* join, . . . dissenting in part.

The Fourth Amendment protects private citizens from arbitrary surveillance by their Government. For nearly 20 years, this Court has adhered to a standard that ensured that Fourth Amendment rights would retain their vitality as technology expanded the Government's capacity to commit unsuspected intrusions into private areas and activities. Today, in the context of administrative aerial photography of commercial premises, the Court retreats from that standard. It holds that the photography was not a Fourth Amendment "search" because it was not accompanied by a physical trespass and because the equipment used was not the most highly sophisticated form of technology available to the Government. Under this holding, the existence of an asserted privacy interest apparently will be decided solely by reference to the manner of surveillance used to intrude on that interest. Such an inquiry will not protect Fourth Amendment rights, but rather will permit their gradual decay as technology advances. . . .

I would reverse the decision of the Court of Appeals. EPA's aerial photography penetrated into a private commercial enclave, an area in which society has recognized that privacy interests legitimately may be claimed. The photographs captured highly confidential information that Dow had taken reasonable and objective steps to preserve as private. Since the Clean Air Act does not establish a defined and regular program of warrantless inspections, see *Marshall v. Barlow's, Inc.* . . . (1978), EPA should have sought a warrant from a neutral judicial officer. The Court's holding that the warrantless photography does not constitute

---

EDITED CASE Dow Chemical Company v. United States (Continued)

---

an unreasonable search within the meaning of the Fourth Amendment is based on the absence of any physical trespass—a theory disapproved in a line of cases beginning with the decision in *Katz v. United States* . . . (1967). These cases have provided a

sensitive and reasonable means of preserving interests in privacy cherished by our society. The Court's decision today cannot be reconciled with our precedents or with the purpose of the Fourth Amendment.

EDITED CASE Gilpin v. Montana Board of Nursing
Supreme Court of Montana 837 P.2d 1342 (Mont. 1992)

[The Montana Board of Nursing revoked Joel Gilpin's nursing license after he was convicted of two counts of sexual assault upon two minors.]

Chief Justice Turnage delivered the opinion of the court.

This is an appeal of an administrative action of the Montana Board of Nursing, which permanently revoked the license of Joel R. Gilpin to practice in Montana as a registered professional nurse. The District Court for the First Judicial District, Lewis and Clark County, affirmed, but it deleted a provision that the revocation is permanent. Gilpin appeals to this Court.

We affirm.

The issues are: 1. Does the Board have jurisdiction to revoke a Montana nursing license which expired before revocation? 2. Did the Board revoke Gilpin's Montana nursing license without affording him a proper hearing? 3. Did the Board properly consider criteria for licensure of criminal offenders in revoking Gilpin's nursing license?

Gilpin was licensed as a registered nurse in Montana from 1980 through 1990. The Board did not send him a license renewal application for 1991, and his license lapsed at the end of 1990. In 1987, Gilpin was convicted of two counts of sexual assault upon eleven- and twelve-year-old girls. He was sentenced to four years' imprisonment on each count, to be served consecutively. In June 1988, as a result of his criminal conviction, the Board initiated a license disciplinary proceeding against him. At Gilpin's request, the disciplinary proceeding was delayed while he appealed his criminal conviction to this Court and pursued a habeas corpus action in federal court.

This Court's opinion affirming Gilpin's criminal conviction sets forth the facts underlying the conviction. . . . That opinion is a public record and as such was available to the Board. In November 1990, the proceeding before the Board was reactivated. The parties submitted the matter on an agreed statement of facts. A hearing examiner heard the case and submitted findings, conclusions, and a recommended order to the Board. After hearing Gilpin's objections orally and receiving them in writing, the Board adopted the hearing examiner's findings, conclusions, and recommendations. Gilpin appealed to the District Court. The court heard the parties' arguments and then issued its written memorandum and order affirming the decision to revoke Gilpin's license. However, the court deleted the provision that the revocation is permanent.

I

Does the Board have jurisdiction to revoke a Montana nursing license which expired before revocation?

Gilpin argues that the Board lost jurisdiction over him after his nursing license lapsed in 1990. He claims that the Board is statutorily empowered to take action only on an application for a nursing license or on an issued license, not on an expired license.

Section 37-8-431(3), MCA, provides that a lapsed nursing license may be reinstated by the Board upon satisfactory explanation for the failure to renew the license and upon payment of current

(Continued)

EDITED CASE Gilpin v. Montana Board of Nursing (Continued)

---

fees. Section 37-1-141, MCA, provides that a lapsed occupational or professional license which is not renewed within three years of the most recent renewal date automatically terminates and a new original license must be obtained.

Because the above statutes give the Board the power to reinstate a nursing license for three years after it lapses, we conclude that the Board retains jurisdiction over a lapsed nursing license for three years following a failure to renew. This action took place within three years after Gilpin's license lapsed. We hold that the Board had jurisdiction to revoke Gilpin's license.

II

Did the Board revoke Gilpin's Montana nursing license without affording him a proper hearing?

Despite his consent to submit to the hearing examiner an agreed set of facts, Gilpin contends that he was entitled to a hearing before the Board on the merits of his case. He points out that, in the brief submitted to the Board in support of revoking his license, various harmful consequences were alleged as possible results of halting disciplinary proceedings. Gilpin maintains that a hearing should have been held to afford him an opportunity to rebut those "allegations of fact."

The material facts of this case were stipulated—that Gilpin stands convicted of sexually molesting two pre-teen girls. The results which were forecast if disciplinary proceedings were halted did not create material issues of fact. Gilpin was afforded a hearing before the Board at which he presented his arguments in opposition to the hearing examiner's findings and conclusions. We hold that Gilpin's criminal conviction and the facts to which he stipulated were a sufficient basis for summary judgment and that Gilpin was not entitled to any hearings in addition to those which he was given.

III

Did the Board properly consider criteria for licensure of criminal offenders in revoking Gilpin's nursing license?

Gilpin states that there is no indication, in either the record in this case or in this Court's decision in his appeal from his criminal conviction, of any connection between the conduct on which his criminal conviction was based and his nursing practice. He points out that the conduct occurred while he was off duty and away from his workplace. He quotes the following statutes dealing with the licensure of criminal offenders:

37-1-201. Purpose. It is the public policy of the legislature of the state of Montana to encourage and contribute to the rehabilitation of criminal offenders and to assist them in the assumption of the responsibilities of citizenship. The legislature finds that the public is best protected when such offenders are given the opportunity to secure employment or to engage in a meaningful occupation, while licensure must be conferred with prudence to protect the interests of the public.

37-1-202. Intent and policy. It is the intent of the legislature and the declared policy of the state that occupational licensure be granted or revoked as a police power of the state in its protection of the public health, safety, and welfare.

37-1-203. Conviction not a sole basis for denial. Criminal convictions shall not operate as an automatic bar to being licensed to enter any occupation in the state of Montana. No licensing authority shall refuse to license a person solely on the basis of a previous criminal conviction; provided, however, where a license applicant has been convicted of a criminal offense and such criminal offense relates to the public health, welfare, and safety as it applies to the occupation for which the license is sought, the licensing agency may, after investigation, find that the applicant so convicted has not been sufficiently rehabilitated as to warrant the public trust and deny the issuance of a license.

37-1-204. Statement of reasons for denial. When a licensing agency prohibits an applicant from being licensed wholly or partially on the basis of a criminal conviction, the agency shall state explicitly in writing the reasons for the decision.

37-1-205. Licensure on completion of supervision. Completion of probation or parole supervision without any subsequent criminal conviction shall be evidence of rehabilitation; provided, however, that the facts surrounding the situation that led to the probation or parole supervision may be considered as they relate to the occupation for which a license is sought and provided that nothing herein shall be construed to prohibit licensure of a person while he is under state supervision if the licensing agency finds insufficient evidence to preclude such licensure.

EDITED CASE   Gilpin v. Montana Board of Nursing (Continued)

Under the statutes set forth above, the policy of this State is to protect the public health, safety, and welfare. Gilpin cites this Court's holding in Mills v. Commissioner of Insurance (1987), 226 Mont. 387, 736 P.2d 102, that a finding that Mills had been convicted of a felony involving moral turpitude (felony theft) was an insufficient basis upon which to hold that the conviction was related to the public health, welfare, or safety through the licensed occupation of insurance sales. . . .

In the present case, the hearing examiner concluded that "[a] crime of sexual assault, especially on two young girls, is, in my mind, ipso facto, sufficient grounds for revocation of his license." The Board adopted the hearing examiner's further conclusions that, by reason of his criminal conviction of sexually assaulting two young girls, Gilpin was guilty of unprofessional conduct as a nurse within the meaning of § 37-8-441(5), MCA, and was unfit to practice nursing by reason of negligence, habits, or other causes, within the meaning of § 37-8-441(2), MCA.

The District Court noted that even though the sexual assaults did not occur while Gilpin was acting as a nurse, the conviction for those offenses causes great concern for public health, welfare, and safety. The court reasoned that the practice of nursing, by its very nature, involves the care of patients and brings the nurse into close physical contact with patients, including possible contact with intimate body areas of patients who are young, old, male, and female. . . .

Section 37-1-203, MCA, provides that when a person has been convicted of a criminal offense which relates to the public health, welfare, and safety, that person shall be granted a professional or occupational license only if he or she has been sufficiently rehabilitated to warrant the public trust. There is nothing in the record to show that Gilpin has been rehabilitated. In fact, he was still serving his sentence of imprisonment at the time of the hearing before the hearing examiner. In that respect, this case may be further distinguished from Mills. All but thirty days of Mills' prison sentence was suspended and she was not incarcerated at the time her case was heard before the licensing agency.

We hold that, in revoking Gilpin's license, the Board properly considered the criteria for licensing criminal defendants. We affirm the order of the District Court revoking Gilpin's license to practice in Montana as a registered professional nurse.

Justices Harrison, Gray, McDonald, and Trieweiler concur.

EDITED CASE   Austin v. United States
United States Supreme Court, 509 U.S. 602 (1992)

[Under the U.S. Code, § 881 (a)(4), a "conveyance" is subject to forfeiture if it is used to transport "controlled substances." Under § 881(a)(7), real estate may be forfeited if it is used to commit a drug-related felony. In this case the Supreme Court considers whether such forfeitures are limited by the Excessive Fines Clause of the Eighth Amendment.]

Justice Blackmun delivered the opinion of the Court.

. . . On August 2, 1990, petitioner Richard Lyle Austin was indicted on four counts of violating South Dakota's drug laws. Austin ultimately pleaded guilty to one count of possessing cocaine with intent to distribute and was sentenced by the state court to seven years' imprisonment. On September 7, the United States filed an *in rem* action in the United States District Court for the District of South Dakota seeking forfeiture of Austin's mobile home and auto body shop under 21 U.S.C. §§ 881 (a)(4) and (a)(7). Austin filed a claim and an answer to the complaint.

On February 4, 1991, the United States made a motion, supported by an affidavit from Sioux Falls Police Officer Donald Satterlee, for summary judgment. According to Satterlee's affidavit, Austin met Keith Engebretson at Austin's body shop on

(Continued)

EDITED CASE   Austin v. United States (Continued)

June 13, 1990, and agreed to sell cocaine to Engebretson. Austin left the shop, went to his mobile
home, and returned to the shop with two grams
of cocaine which he sold to Engebretson. State
authorities executed a search warrant on the body
shop and mobile home the following day. They
discovered small amounts of marijuana and
cocaine, a .22 caliber revolver, drug paraphernalia, and approximately $4,700 in cash. In opposing
summary judgment, Austin argued that forfeiture
of the properties would violate the Eighth
Amendment. The District Court rejected this argument and entered summary judgment for the
United States. . . .

The United States Court of Appeals for the
Eighth Circuit "reluctantly agree[d] with the government" and affirmed. . . . Although it thought
that "the principle of proportionality should be
applied in civil actions that result in harsh penalties," . . . and that the Government was "exacting
too high a penalty in relation to the offense committed," . . . the court felt constrained from holding the forfeiture unconstitutional. It cited this
Court's decision in *Calero-Toledo v. Pearson Yacht
Leasing Co.* . . . (1974) for the proposition that,
when the Government is proceeding against property *in rem*, the guilt or innocence of the property's owner "is constitutionally irrelevant." . . .

We granted certiorari . . . to resolve an apparent conflict . . . over the applicability of the
Eighth Amendment to *in rem* civil forfeitures. . . .

II
Austin contends that the Eighth Amendment's
Excessive Fines Clause applies to *in rem* civil forfeiture proceedings. . . . We have had occasion to
consider this Clause only once before. In *Browning-Ferris Industries v. Kelco Disposal, Inc.* . . .
(1989), we held that the Excessive Fines Clause
does not limit the award of punitive damages to a
private party in a civil suit when the government
neither has prosecuted the action nor has any
right to receive a share of the damages. . . . The
Court's opinion and Justice O'Connor's opinion,
concurring in part and dissenting in part, reviewed
in some detail the history of the Excessive Fines
Clause. . . . The Court concluded that both the
Eighth Amendment and § 10 of the English Bill of
Rights of 1689, from which it derives, were
intended to prevent the government from abusing

its power to punish, . . . and therefore "that the
Excessive Fines Clause was intended to limit only
those fines directly imposed by, and payable to,
the government." . . .

We found it unnecessary to decide in
Browning-Ferris whether the Excessive Fines
Clause applies only to criminal cases. . . .
The United States now argues that "any claim
that the government's conduct in a civil
proceeding is limited by the Eighth Amendment
generally, or by the Excessive Fines Clause in
particular, must fail unless the challenged governmental action, despite its label, would have
been recognized as a criminal punishment at the
time the Eighth Amendment was adopted." . . .
It further suggests that the Eighth Amendment
cannot apply to a civil proceeding unless that
proceeding is so punitive that it must be considered criminal. . . .

Some provisions of the Bill of Rights are
expressly limited to criminal cases. The Fifth
Amendment's Self-Incrimination Clause, for example, provides: "No person . . . shall be compelled
in any criminal case to be a witness against himself." The protections provided by the Sixth
Amendment are explicitly confined to "criminal
prosecutions." . . . The text of the Eighth Amendment includes no similar limitations. . . .

Nor does the history of the Eighth Amendment
require such a limitation. Justice O'Connor noted
in *Browning-Ferris*: "Consideration of the Eighth
Amendment immediately followed consideration
of the Fifth Amendment. After deciding to confine
the benefits of the Self-Incrimination Clause of the
Fifth Amendment to criminal proceedings, the
Framers turned their attention to the Eighth
Amendment. There were no proposals to limit that
Amendment to criminal proceedings. . . ." Section
10 of the English Bill of Rights of 1689 is not
expressly limited to criminal cases either. The original draft of § 10 as introduced in the House of
Commons did contain such a restriction, but only
with respect to the bail clause: "The requiring
excessive Bail of Persons committed in criminal
Cases, and imposing excessive Fines, and illegal
Punishments, to be prevented." . . . The absence
of any similar restriction in the other two clauses
suggests that they were not limited to criminal
cases. In the final version, even the reference to
criminal cases in the bail clause was omitted. . . .

EDITED CASE Austin v. United States (Continued)

The purpose of the Eighth Amendment, putting the Bail Clause to one side, was to limit the government's power to punish. . . . The Cruel and Unusual Punishments Clause is self-evidently concerned with punishment. The Excessive Fines Clause limits the Government's power to extract payments, whether in cash or in kind, "as punishment for some offense." . . . "The notion of punishment, as we commonly understand it, cuts across the division between the civil and the criminal law." . . . Thus, the question is not, as the United States would have it, whether forfeiture under §§ 881 (a)(4) and (a)(7) is civil or criminal, but rather whether it is punishment. . . .

In considering this question, we are mindful of the fact that sanctions frequently serve more than one purpose. We need not exclude the possibility that a forfeiture serves remedial purposes to conclude that it is subject to the limitations of the Excessive Fines Clause. We, however, must determine that it can only be explained as serving in part to punish. . . . We turn, then, to consider whether, at the time the Eighth Amendment was ratified, forfeiture was understood at least in part as punishment and whether forfeiture under §§ 881(a)(4) and (a)(7) should be so understood today.

III

A

Three kinds of forfeiture were established in England at the time the Eighth Amendment was ratified in the United States: deodand [forfeiture of an inanimate object causing the accidental death of a King's subject], forfeiture upon conviction for a felony or treason, and statutory forfeiture. . . . Each was understood, at least in part, as imposing punishment.

B

Of England's three kinds of forfeiture, only the third took hold in the United States. "Deodands did not become part of the common-law tradition of this country." . . . The Constitution forbids forfeiture of estate as a punishment for treason "except during the Life of the Person attainted," . . . , and the First Congress also abol-

ished forfeiture of estate as a punishment for felons. . . . But [l]ong before the adoption of the Constitution the common law courts in the Colonies—and later in the states during the period of Confederation—were exercising jurisdiction *in rem* in the enforcement of [English and local] forfeiture statutes." . . .

The First Congress passed laws subjecting ships and cargoes involved in customs offenses to forfeiture. It does not follow from that fact, however, that the First Congress thought such forfeitures to be beyond the purview of the Eighth Amendment. Indeed, examination of those laws suggests that the First Congress viewed forfeiture as punishment. . . . It is also of some interest that "forfeit" is the word Congress used for fine. . . . Other early forfeiture statutes follow the same pattern. . . .

Our cases also have recognized that statutory *in rem* forfeiture imposes punishment. In *Peisch v. Ware* . . . (1808), for example, the Court held that goods removed from the custody of a revenue officer without the payment of duties, should not be forfeitable for that reason unless they were removed with the consent of the owner or his agent. . . .

The same understanding of forfeiture as punishment runs through our cases rejecting the "innocence" of the owner as a common-law defense to forfeiture. . . . In these cases, forfeiture has been justified on two theories—that the property itself is "guilty" of the offense, and that the owner may be held accountable for the wrongs of others to whom he entrusts his property. Both theories rest, at bottom, on the notion that the owner has been negligent in allowing his property to be misused and that he is properly punished for that negligence. . . .

In sum, even though this Court has rejected the "innocence" of the owner as a common-law defense to forfeiture, it consistently has recognized that forfeiture serves, at least in part, to punish the owner. . . . We conclude, therefore, that forfeiture generally and statutory *in rem* forfeiture in particular historically have been understood, at least in part, as punishment.

(Continued)

EDITED CASE   Austin v. United States (Continued)

IV

We turn next to consider whether forfeitures under 21 U.S.C. §§ 881(a)(4) and (a)(7) are properly considered punishment today. We find nothing in these provisions or their legislative history to contradict the historical understanding of forfeiture as punishment. Unlike traditional forfeiture statutes, as 881(a)(4) and (a)(7) expressly provide an "innocent owner" defense. These exemptions serve to focus the provisions on the culpability of the owner in a way that makes them look more like punishment, not less. The inclusion of innocent-owner defenses in §§ 881(a)(4) and (a)(7) reveals a similar congressional intent to punish only those involved in drug trafficking.

Furthermore, Congress has chosen to tie forfeiture directly to the commission of drug offenses. Thus, under § 881 (a)(4), a conveyance is forfeitable if it is used or intended for use to facilitate the transportation of controlled substances, their raw materials, or the equipment used to manufacture or distribute them. Under § 881(a)(7), real property is forfeitable if it is used or intended for use to facilitate the commission of a drug-related crime punishable by more than one year's imprisonment. . . .

The Government argues that §§ 881(a)(4) and (a)(7) are not punitive but, rather, should be considered remedial in two respects. First, they remove the "instruments" of the drug trade "thereby protecting the community from the threat of continued drug dealing." . . . Second, the forfeited assets serve to compensate the Government for the expense of law enforcement activity and for its expenditure on societal problems such as urban blight, drug addiction, and other health concerns resulting from the drug trade. . . .

In our view, neither argument withstands scrutiny. Concededly, we have recognized that the forfeiture of contraband itself may be characterized as remedial because it removes dangerous or illegal items from society. . . . The Court, however, previously has rejected government's attempt to extend that reasoning to conveyances used to transport illegal liquor. . . . In that case it noted: "There is nothing even remotely criminal in possessing an automobile." . . . The same, without question, is true of the properties involved here, and the Government's attempt to characterize these properties as "instruments" of the drug trade must meet the same fate as Pennsylvania's effort to characterize the 1958 Plymouth Sedan as "contraband."

The Government's second argument about the remedial nature of this forfeiture is no more persuasive. We previously have upheld the forfeiture of goods involved in customs violations as "a reasonable form of liquidated damages." . . . But the dramatic variations in the value of conveyances and real property forfeitable under §§ 881(a)(4) and (a)(7) undercut any similar argument with respect to those provisions. The Court made this very point in Ward: the "forfeiture of property . . . [is] a penalty that ha[s] absolutely no correlation to any damages sustained by society or to the cost of enforcing the law." . . .

Fundamentally, even assuming that §§ 881(a)(4) and (a)(7) serve some remedial purpose, the Government's argument must fail. "[A] civil sanction that cannot fairly be said solely to serve a remedial purpose, but rather can only be explained as also serving either retributive or deterrent purposes, is punishment, as we have come to understand the term." . . . In light of the historical understanding of forfeiture as punishment, the clear forces of §§ 881(a)(4) and (a)(7) on the culpability of the owner, and the evidence that Congress understood those provisions as serving to deter and to punish, we cannot conclude that forfeiture under §§ 881(a)(4) and (a)(7) serves solely a remedial purpose. We therefore conclude that forfeiture under these provisions constitutes "payment to a sovereign as punishment for some offense," . . . and, as such, is subject to the limitations of the Eighth Amendment's Excessive Fines Clause.

V

Austin asks that we establish a multifactor test for determining whether a forfeiture is constitutionally "excessive." . . . We decline that invitation. Although the Court of Appeals opined "that the government is exacting too high a penalty in relation to the offense committed," . . . it had no occasion to consider what factors should inform such a decision because it thought it was foreclosed from engaging in the inquiry. Prudence dictates that we allow the lower courts to consider that question in the first instance.

EDITED CASE   Austin v. United States (Continued)

The judgment of the Court of Appeals is reversed and the case is remedied to that court for further proceedings consistent with this opinion. . . .

Justice Scalia, concurring in part and concurring in the judgment.

We recently stated that, at the time the Eighth Amendment was drafted, the term "fine" was "understood to mean a payment to a sovereign as punishment for some offense." . . . It seems to me that the Court's opinion obscures this clear statement, and needlessly attempts to derive from our sparse caselaw on the subject of in rem forfeiture the questionable proposition that the owner of property taken pursuant to such forfeiture is always blameworthy. I write separately to explain why I consider this forfeiture a fine, and to point out that the excessiveness inquiry for statutory in rem forfeitures is different from the usual excessiveness inquiry. . . .

. . . The relevant inquiry for an excessive forfeiture under § 881 is the relationship of the property to the offense: Was it close enough to render the property, under traditional standards, "guilty" and hence forfeitable?

I join the Court's opinion in part, and concur in the judgment.

Justice Kennedy, with whom the **Chief Justice** and **Justice Thomas** join, concurring in part and concurring in the judgment. . . .

ENDNOTES

1. *Murphy v. Waterfront Commission,* 378 U.S. 52 (1964).

2. For example, Section 104(e) of the Comprehensive Environmental Response, Compensation and Liability Act, 42 U.S.C.A. § 9604(e), delegates subpoena power to the executive branch generally. Exec. Order No. 12,580, Section 2(j), 52 *Fed. Reg.* 2923 (Jan. 29, 1987), delegates this power to various executive departments and agencies responsible for enforcing the statute.

3. *Interstate Commerce Commission v. Brimson,* 154 U.S. 447 (1894).

4. *McClendon v. Jackson Television,* 603 F.2d 1174 (5th Cir. 1979).

5. *Oklahoma Press Publishing Co. v. Walling,* 327 U.S. 186, 226 (1946).

6. *Endicott Johnson Corp. v. Perkins,* 317 U.S. 501 (1943).

7. *See Federal Trade Commission v. Texaco, Inc.,* 555 F.2d 862 (D.C. Cir. 1977).

8. *United States v. Bisceglia,* 420 U.S. 141 (1975).

9. *Id.* at 150.

10. *United States v. White,* 322 U.S. 694, 698 (1944).

11. *United States v. Powell,* 379 U.S. 48 (1964).

12. *New Orleans Public Service v. Brown,* 369 F. Supp. 702 (E.D. La. 1974).

13. *Hunt Foods & Industries, Inc. v. Federal Trade Commission,* 286 F.2d 803 (9th Cir. 1960).

14. *Frank v. Maryland,* 359 U.S. 360 (1959).

15. *Id.* at 372.

16. *Id.* at 376.

17. *Id.* at 374.

18. 387 U.S. 523 (1967).

19. *Id.* at 534.

20. 387 U.S. 541 (1967).

21. *Id.* at 543.

22. 397 U.S. 72 (1970).

23. *Id.* at 77.

24. 406 U.S. 311 (1972).

25. *Id.* at 316.

26. 436 U.S. 307 (1978).

27. See, e.g., *Katzenbach v. McClung,* 379 U.S. 294 (1964).

28. *Donovan v. Dewey,* 452 U.S. 594 (1981).

29. *Id.* at 605.

30. 482 U.S. 691 (1987).

31. *State v. Mach,* 594 P.2d 1361 (Wash. App. 1979).

32. *Moore v. State,* 442 So.2d 215 (Fla. 1983).

33. *People v. Robles,* 477 N.Y.S.2d 567 (N.Y. Sup. 1984).

34. *Weatherford v. State,* 822 S.W.2d 217 (Tex. App. 1991).

35. *State v. VFW Post 3562*, 525 N.E.2d 773 (Ohio 1988).

36. *State v. Marsh*, 823 P.2d 823 (Kan. App. 1991).

37. *Dow Chemical v. United States*, 476 U.S. 227 (1986).

38. 26 U.S.C.A. § 7602.

39. 12 U.S.C.A. § 1833c.

40. 338 U.S. 632 (1950).

41. *Id.* at 652–653, quoting *Oklahoma Press Publishing Co. v. Walling*, 327 U.S. 186, 226 (1946).

42. *Guardian Federal Savings and Loan Assn. v. Federal Savings and Loan Insurance Corp.*, 589 F.2d 658 (D.C. Cir. 1978).

43. A.C.A. § 23-110-412.

44. 2 U.S.C.A. § 434.

45. Campaign Disclosure Project, UCLA School of Law, online at www.campaigndisclosure.org.

46. See, e.g., Mo. Rev. Stat. § 195.400.

47. *Whalen v. Roe*, 423 U.S. 1313 (1975).

48. Pub. L. 91-508, 84 Stat. 1114.

49. 12 U.S.C.A. § 1829b(a)(1)(A).

50. 31 U.S.C.A. § 5313(a).

51. 31 U.S.C.A. § 5324(3).

52. 416 U.S. 21 (1974).

53. *Id.* at 89–90.

54. See 8 U.S.C.A. §§ 1181 *et seq.*

55. 8 U.S.C.A. § 1226a.

56. 8 U.S.C.A. § 1226e.

57. The counterargument is that illegal aliens, as persons within the jurisdiction of the United States, should be provided due process of law much in the same way that non-citizens accused of crimes are provided due process.

58. *Fong Yue Ting v. United States*, 149 U.S. 698, 711, 713 (1893).

59. 303 F.3d 681 (6th Cir. 2002).

60. *Id.* at 705.

61. 308 F.3d 198 (3d Cir. 198 (2002).

62. *Id.* at 220.

63. See, e.g., Fla. Stat. § 403.722(5) providing for revocation of permits for hazardous waste disposal, storage, and treatment facilities for failure to comply with statutory requirements and departmental standards, failure to allow inspections, or for submission of inaccurate information.

64. *City of San Marino v. Roman Catholic Archbishop*, 180 Cal. App. 2d 657, 668 (1960).

65. *City of Lamoni v. Livingston*, 392 N.W.2d 506 (Iowa 1986).

66. *McClure v. Davidson*, 373 S.E.2d 617 (Ga. 1988).

67. See, for example, *Abberville Arms v. City of Abberville*, 257 S.E.2d 716 (S.C. 1979).

68. S.C. Code 56-1-745.

69. Ga. Code § 40-5-57.

70. *Slowe v. Ohio Board of Embalmer and Funeral Directors*, 704 N.E.2d 633 (Ohio App. 1997).

71. *Peitit v. State Board of Education*, 513 P.2d 889 (Cal. 1973).

72. 668 N.E.2d 457 (Ohio 1996).

73. 403 U.S. 1 (1979).

74. 424 U.S. 319 (1976).

75. *Bragg v. Director, New Hampshire Div. of Motor Vehicles*, 690 A.2d 571 (N.H. 1997).

76. The relation of remedy to policy is peculiarly a matter for administrative competence. *Fibreboard Paper Products Corp. v. NLRB*, 379 U.S. 203, 216 (1964).

77. *Butz v. Glover Livestock Comm'n Co.*, 411 U.S. 182 (1973).

78. 29 U.S.C.A. § 657(a) *et seq.*

79. 430 U.S. 442 (1977).

80. *Id.* at 455.

81. *National Labor Relations Board v. Express Pub. Co.*, 312 U.S. 426, 436 (1941).

82. *Southwest Professional Indemnity Corp. v. Texas Dept. of Insurance*, 914 S.W.2d 256 (Tex. App. 1996).

83. A.R.S. § 45-634.

84. See, e.g., *Zeigler v. Town of Thomaston*, 654 A.2d 392 (Conn. Super 1994) (upholding the town's zoning enforcement officer's cease and desist order directing property owner to rectify eight specific violations on his premises).

85. 42 U.S.C.A. § 2000a-5.

86. *United States v. Flagstar Corporation*, Civ. No. 93-20208-JW (Amended Consent Decree).

87. See Section 17(a) of the Securities Act of 1933, Section 10(b) of the Securities Exchange Act of 1934, and SEC Rule 10b-5.

88. Case No. 5:97CV1216 (N.D. Ohio).

89. *Gwaltney v. Chesapeake Bay Foundation*, 484 U.S. 49 (1987).

90. 31 U.S.C.A. §§ 3729-33.

91. 529 U.S. 765 (2000).

92. 123 S.Ct. 1239 (2003).

93. See, e.g., Ga. Code, § 16-9-31 which states: "Whenever an investigation has been conducted by the Governor's Office of Consumer Affairs . . . and such investigation reveals conduct which constitutes a criminal offense, the administrator shall forward the results of such investigation to the Attorney General or other prosecuting attorney of this state who shall commence any criminal prosecution that he or she deems appropriative."

94. See Internal Revenue Code, 26 U.S.C.A. §§ 1-1563.

95. See, e.g., 21 U.S.C.A. § 881.

96. 509 U.S. 602 (1993).

97. *Id.* at 622.

98. *United States v. James Daniel Good Real Property*, 510 U.S. 43 (1992).

99. Uniting and Strengthening America Act by Providing Appropriate Tools Required to Intercept and Obstruct Terrorism (USA PATRIOT) Act of 2001, P.L. 107-56, 115 Stat. 272.

6

Rulemaking

"[T]he decision maker has the authority to rely on rulemaking to resolve certain issues of general applicability unless Congress clearly expresses an intent to withhold that authority."

JUSTICE RUTH BADER GINSBURG
WRITING FOR THE SUPREME COURT IN *LOPEZ V. DAVIS*, 531 U.S. 230, 243-244 (2001).

INTRODUCTION

In a republican form of government, legislatures comprised of elected representatives are empowered to make laws. Yet today there are more **rules** than laws. The distinction between laws and rules, however, is somewhat academic. Statutes and ordinances, of course, can only be enacted by legislative bodies and rules can only be properly promulgated by government agencies based on a delegation of legislative authority. However, properly promulgated, rules have the force of law.[1] Violations of agency rules can lead to the imposition of serious sanctions (see Chapter 5).

From the beginnings of the federal and state governments, agencies have promulgated rules to implement legislation; however, the process of administrative **rulemaking** was greatly accelerated during the 1930s and succeeding decades. Rules are the primary means used by administrative agencies to implement legislation and formulate policy. At the federal level they are generally promulgated under the rulemaking provisions of the **Administrative Procedure Act (APA)** (see Appendix B). Most states have adopted their own counterparts to the APA, which more or less follow the **Model State Administrative Procedure Act.** In all fifty states administrative rulemaking is authorized and limited by statutory frameworks enacted by the state legislatures.

Rules promulgated at the federal level deal with a wide variety of subjects. Some of these areas include antitrust regulations, rules concerning banking, securities, and financial services, communications, energy policies, environmental regulations, foods, drugs, and other consumer products, housing and urban developments, international trade, immigration, labor, Social Security and Medicare, transportation on land, air, and sea, revenue and tax issues, veterans affairs, and welfare benefits.

At the state and local levels many administrative rules cover education, elections, health and welfare, insurance, occupational and professional licensing, land development, public utilities, revenues and taxes, and zoning, as well as state and local aspects of some of the areas of federal regulation such as environmental protection and energy policy.

Federal and state agencies issue thousands of rules each year. Indeed, administrative rules are pervasive in governing everyday life in America. Consider the familiar case of the friendly neighborhood pizza delivery service. Numerous federal agencies (not to mention state and local ones), including the Department of Agriculture, the Food and Drug Administration, the Department of Labor, and the Occupational Safety and Health Administration regulate various aspects of this seemingly simple enterprise. The pizza example is by no means unique. Virtually all economic activities (at least the lawful ones) are regulated by various government agencies.

The discussion of rules and rulemaking in this chapter focuses primarily on activities of federal government agencies where the Administrative Procedure Act (APA) plays an important role. Enacted by Congress in 1946, and since amended, the APA basically governs rulemaking at the federal level. Most states have either adopted the Model State Administrative Procedure Act of 1961, its 1981 update, or have enacted other legislation to regulate rulemaking.

Section 553 of the APA describes the basic rulemaking processes and exempts several categories of rules from those processes. Rules are generally promulgated through the process of rulemaking; however, agencies can make rules through a process of **adjudication,** a subject we discuss in Chapter 7. As administrative agencies began to respond to increasing health, safety, and environmental concerns, the flexibility of rulemaking became preferable in most instances. Finally, it became the most common method of developing policies because it offers agencies the opportunity of addressing numerous issues in an efficient manner whereas adjudication usually focuses narrowly on a fact-specific controversy.

The rules the federal agencies produce are chronicled in the *Federal Register* and codified in the *Code of Federal Regulations,* publications

Table 6.1 Major and Minor Rules Promulgated by Federal Agencies, FY 1996–FY 2001

	Major Rules	Minor Rules	Total
FY 1996	35	2,024	2,059
FY 1997	59	3,873	3,932
FY 1998	70	4,672	4,742
FY 1999	58	4,495	4,553
FY 2000	65	4,528	4,593
FY 2001	48	1,718	1,766
Total	335	21,310	21,645

SOURCE: U.S. General Accounting Office

that we discuss later. Attempts are being made to provide convenient nontechnical access to the public concerning government. One of the latest attempts is the recently created web site, www.firstgov.gov, which, according to President George W. Bush, "is the official U.S. gateway to all government information" and "is the catalyst for a growing electronic government." Using this web site, citizens can gain access to information about all branches of the national government, including the myriad agencies of the executive branch. Users can access electronic versions of the *Federal Register* and the *Code of Federal Regulations,* and can even review regulations pending approval.

Note/Noticia: FirstGov en Espanol es el portal oficial del gobierno de los Estados Unidos. The site www.espanol.gov is a Spanish-language gateway to web sites for fifty-five federal agencies.

The magnitude of rulemaking by federal agencies is suggested by the following data: between FY 1996 and FY 2001, inclusive, federal agencies promulgated nearly 22,000 new rules (see Table 6.1). These rules were generated by, in descending order, the Department of Health and Human Services, the Federal Communications Commission, the Department of Agriculture, the Environmental Protection Agency, the U.S. Fish and Wildlife Service, the Securities and Exchange Commission, and various other agencies.

THE BASICS OF RULES AND RULEMAKING

Once Congress enacts a law, federal administrative agencies develop rules that describe how an agency will implement the legislative will of Congress. This is the essence of rulemaking. The same basic process occurs once a state legislature enacts a statute that requires implementation to carry out the legislature's intent.

At the federal level, Section 551 of the APA essentially defines a "rule" as: "[T]he whole or part of an agency statement of general or particular applicability and future effect designed to implement, interpret, or prescribe law or policy or describing the organization, procedure, or practice requirements of an agency. . . ."[2] The Model State Administrative Procedure Act (1981) states that "rule" means "the whole or the part of an agency statement of general applicability that implements, interprets, or prescribes (i) law or policy, or (ii) the organization, procedure or practice requirements of an agency. The term includes the amendment, repeal, or suspension of an existing rule."[3]

Thus, an administrative rule is a general statement having a future effect and addressed to a category of parties. This contrasts with an administrative decision or an order. The latter apply to a present factual situation and are usually addressed to specific parties.

Administrative agencies develop different categories of rules. **Legislative rules** are either substantive or procedural and have the force of law. **Substantive rules** affect the rights of persons. **Procedural rules** regulate agency decision-making and enforcement processes, but are exempt from the rulemaking requirements of the APA. **General statements of policy** and **interpretive rules** are also exempt from the APA rulemaking requirements and while they do not have the force of law, they must be published. Statements of policy simply state an agency's view of how it will likely act in the future. Interpretive rules interpret or clarify an agency's position as to its duties or responsibilities based on a controlling statute or a previously promulgated legislative rules. Even though they do not have the force of law, statements of policy and interpretive rules play an important role in the administrative process. As with laws, administrative rules are subject to judicial review.

Legal Parameters of Rulemaking

In reviewing agency rules and rulemaking procedures, courts are concerned primarily with statutory requirements. As we illustrated in Chapter 4, if an agency rule is outside the scope of power delegated to the agency by the legislature, the court may invalidate the rule as *ultra vires*. If an agency promulgates a rule without following procedures required by the Administrative Procedure Act or applicable statutes, that is also a basis upon which a court may invalidate the rule. As we explained in Chapter 3, courts will also entertain constitutional challenges to agency rules, especially where such rules infringe the constitutional rights of private parties.

Generally speaking, the constitutional concept of **procedural due process** does not apply to agency rulemaking. In 1915, in *Bi-Metallic Investment Co v. State Board of Equalization of Colorado*[4] (see the Supreme Court Perspective contained in Box 6.1), Justice Oliver Wendell Holmes, Jr. explained that because rulemaking is more akin to legislation, it is to be controlled by the political process and not by judicial oversight. Adjudication, on the other hand, because it deals with the rights of individual parties, must conform to the requirements of due process (see Chapter 7).

Rulemaking versus Adjudication

The distinction between rulemaking and adjudication is important because, as we will see later in this chapter, the modern innovation of **informal (notice-and-comment) rulemaking** allows agencies to make policy with considerable flexibility. Generally speaking, agencies have discretion in choosing whether to make policy via rulemaking or adjudication. As the Supreme Court stated in *Securities and Exchange Commission v. Chenery Corporation* (1947), "the choice between proceeding by general rule or by individual, ad hoc litigation is one that lies primarily in the informed discretion of the administrative agency."[5] Speaking for the Court in *Chenery*, Justice Frank Murphy observed that

> Not every principle essential to the effective administration of a statute can or should be cast immediately into the mold of a general rule. Some principles must await their own development, while others must be adjusted to meet particular, unforeseeable situations. In performing its important functions in these respects, therefore, an administrative agency must be equipped to act either by general rule or by individual order. To insist upon one form of action to the exclusion of the other is to exalt form over necessity.[6]

Justice Murphy also recognized that

> [P]roblems may arise in a case which the administrative agency could not reasonably foresee, problems which must be solved despite the absence of a relevant general rule. Or the agency may not have had sufficient experience with a particular problem to warrant rigidifying its tentative judgment into a hard and fast rule. Or the problem may be so

---

BOX 6.1   Supreme Court Perspective

Bi-Metallic Investment Co. v. State Board of Equalization of Colorado

239 U.S. 441 (1915)

[Prior to the adoption of the Administrative Procedure Act, courts grappled with the distinction between rulemaking and adjudication and the procedures that agencies were constitutionally obligated to employ in both instances. In the Bi-Metallic decision of 1915, the Supreme Court issued a landmark opinion in this area. The case involved a challenge to a state administrative decision to increase the valuation of all taxable property in Denver by 40%. The plaintiff objected to the fact that affected property owners were not provided an opportunity to be heard, claiming that this amounted to a denial of due process of law.]

Justice Holmes delivered the Opinion of the Court, saying in part:

Where a rule of conduct applies to more than a few people, it is impracticable that everyone should have a direct voice in its adoption. The Constitution does not require all public acts to be done in town meeting or an assembly of the whole. General statutes within the state power are passed that affect the person or property of individuals, sometimes to the point of ruin, without giving them a chance to be heard. Their rights are protected in the only way that they can be in a complex society,

by their power, immediate or remote, over those who make the rule. If the result in this case had been reached, as it might have been by the state's doubling the rate of taxation, no one would suggest that the 14th Amendment was violated unless every person affected had been allowed an opportunity to raise his voice against it before the body entrusted by the state Constitution with the power. In considering this case in this court we must assume that the proper state machinery has been used, and the question is whether, if the state Constitution had declared that Denver had been undervalued as compared with the rest of the state, and had decreed that for the current year the valuation should be 40 per cent higher, the objection now urged could prevail. It appears to us that to put the question is to answer it. There must be a limit to individual argument in such matters if government is to go on. In Londoner v. Denver . . . *[1908], a local board had to determine 'whether, in what amount, and upon whom' a tax for paving a street should be levied for special benefits. A relatively small number of persons was concerned, who were exceptionally affected, in each case upon individual grounds, and it was held that they had a right to a hearing. But that decision is far from reaching a general determination dealing only with the principle upon which all the assessments in a county had been laid.*

---

specialized and varying in nature as to be impossible of capture within the boundaries of a general rule. In those situations, the agency must retain power to deal with the problems on a case-to-case basis if the administrative process is to be effective. There is thus a very definite place for the case-by-case evolution of statutory standards.[7]

Initiation of Rulemaking

An agency can initiate a rule on its own, on petition of governmental officials, or at the request of interested persons. In some instances a statute will set a time to complete rulemaking. Absent such a mandate, agencies are to complete rules within a reasonable time. The process often takes a year or more. An agency must exercise its rulemaking authority in accordance with the standards mandated by the statute creating that particular agency. These standards vary from agency to agency. In most instances, federal agencies must also follow the procedures outlined in the APA; however, statutes prescribe certain procedures for rulemaking by specific agencies.

Types of Rulemaking

Rulemaking by agencies falls into three different categories: *exempt, informal,* and *formal.* In addition to these categories outlined in the APA, a hybrid type of rulemaking has developed.

Most rulemaking at the federal level follows the path of informal rulemaking. Far less rulemaking occurs on a formal basis. We now turn to an examination of each of these types of rulemaking.

EXEMPT RULEMAKING

Before discussing informal and formal rulemaking it is helpful to recognize a number of **exemptions from rulemaking procedures.** Initially it should be noted that rules relating to military and foreign affairs are exempt from rulemaking procedures, as are agency personnel rules, and matters relating to public property, loans, grants, benefits, or contracts.[8] These exemptions are understandable; however some commentators have criticized exempting rules concerning grants and benefits from rulemaking procedures. More complex are the exemptions for general statements of policy, interpretive rules, procedural rules, and rules that an agency develops where there is "good cause" not to follow rulemaking procedures. Section 553 of the APA exempts all these categories of rules from the usual rulemaking procedures.[9] But because exempting rules deprives the public of participation in the rulemaking process, courts narrowly construe these exemptions. It should be noted that agencies have discretion to use rulemaking procedures to adopt these types of rules, and many would argue that doing so is likely to enhance their legitimacy.

General Statements of Policy

The APA does not define a "general statement of policy." However, in *Pacific Gas and Electric Co. v. FPC* (1974),[10] the United States Court of Appeals for the D.C. Circuit observed that "[a] policy statement announces the agency's tentative intentions for the future."[11] In effect, a general statement of policy keeps the public informed as to an agency's intentions for positions it will likely take in the future, but it does not establish any legally binding rule.

Writing in the *Duke Law Journal*, Michael Asimow discusses the decision making aspect of general statements of policy, observing:

> General policy statements are well calculated to control staff action and, because they must be published in the *Federal Register*, to inform the public. They provide authoritative guidance on what the staff is likely to do, yet unlike legislative rules they remain tentative, not rigid. Consequently, they leave decision makers room for flexible application; they do not foreclose further experimentation and learning from experience.[12]

In *Chamber of Commerce of the United States v. United States Department of Labor*,[13] the D.C. Circuit in 1999 reviewed a directive issued by Occupational Safety and Health Administration (OSHA), pursuant to which each employer in selected industries would be inspected unless it adopted comprehensive safety and health program designed to meet certain standards. In some respects these standards exceeded those required by law. The directive further provided that the OSHA would remove a workplace from the primary inspection list, and reduce by 70 to 90 percent the probability that it will be inspected, if the employer participates in the agency's "Cooperative Compliance Program (CCP)." The Chamber of Commerce, as an organization of employers, challenged the directive contending it was an invalid legislative rule because OSHA had not adopted it through a notice-and-comment rulemaking proceeding. OSHA countered by arguing that its directive imposed no formal legal obligation upon an employer that chooses not to participate in the CCP. The D.C. Circuit Court of Appeals pointed out that it had previously held that whether a rule is a policy statement is to be determined by whether it (1) has only a prospective effect, and (2) leaves agency decision makers free to exercise their informed discretion in individual cases. "Both criteria," the court explained, "lead us here to the conclusion that the [OSHA] Directive is a substantive rule rather than a policy statement."[14] (The Case in Point

---

BOX 6.2   Case in Point

The Difference Between Policy Statements and Legislative Rules
General Electric Co. v. EPA
United States Court of Appeals for the District of Columbia Circuit 290 F.3d 377 (D.C. Cir. 2002)

The Toxic Substance Control Act (TSCA) prohibits the manufacture, processing, distribution, and use (other than in a "totally enclosed manner") of polychlorinated biphenyls (PCBs) unless the EPA determines that the activity will not result in an "unreasonable risk of injury to health or the environment." EPA regulations, adopted after notice-and-comment proceedings, specify methods for handling cleanup and disposal of PCB remediation waste and PCB bulk product waste. The regulations allow an applicant to establish a method of disposal that does not pose an unreasonable risk of injury to health or to the environment.

The Environmental Protection Administration (EPA) issued a "PCB Risk Assessment Review Guidance Document" explaining two acceptable methods of calculating cancer risks that an applicant for a PCB cleanup plan could follow in order to demonstrate no unreasonable risk. EPA promulgated this Guidance Document without notice or comment concerning permissible risk assessment techniques for parties who might wish to use some alternative method for disposal of PCBs.

General Electric contested the Guidance Document, arguing that it was, in effect, a legislative rule that was not properly promulgated as required by the APA. The court agreed and held that because an applicant for a disposal permit had to use one of the two approaches to risk assessment and no other, the Guidance Document was a legislative rule. Because EPA intended the rule to have binding effect, it could not rely upon the statutory exemption for policy statement; rather it was required to observe the rulemaking procedures set out in the APA.

---

located in Box 6.2 may help to illustrate the difference between a policy statement and a legislative rule.)

Interpretive Rules

An interpretive rule merely states an agency's understanding of existing laws and rules. Interpretive rules often take the form of policy statements, opinion letters, guidelines, and even agency manuals. Although they meet the definition of a "rule" under Section 551(4) of the APA, they are not promulgated under the rulemaking procedures specified in Section 553. Thus, while obviously intended to have an effect on persons, they do not have the force of law. As stated by the United States Court of Appeals for the D.C. Circuit in 1980 "a rule is interpretive, rather than legislative, if it is not issued under statutory authority to make rules having the force of law or if the agency intends the rule to be no more than an expression of its construction of a statute."[15] Interpretive rules do not create rights nor do they affect the rights of anyone; they do not have the force of law. Although not binding on a court, more than a half century ago the United States Supreme Court observed in *Skidmore v. Swift Co.* that interpretive rules "constitute a body of experience and informed judgment to which courts and litigants may properly resort for guidance."[16] Given the fact that agency rules are usually crafted by persons with expertise in the particular area being regulated, the Court's ruling is understandable. In *Chevron U.S.A. v. Natural Resources Defense Council* (1984),[17] the Supreme Court in a landmark opinion stated that where the intent of Congress is not clear that courts should give deference to an agency's construction of a statute. Over the years there has been a conflict in the Courts of Appeals as to whether this *Chevron* deference applies to interpretive rules. (The *Chevron* decision is excerpted and discussed extensively in Chapter 9.)

It becomes important to distinguish a legislative (substantive) rule from an interpretive rule for two reasons. First, if the rule is an interpretive one it is exempt from the notice and public participation requirements that we discuss later. Second, courts tend to give great weight to administrative interpretations, as long as they are reasonable and do not conflict with statutory or judicial interpretations. But determining whether a rule is interpretive is not always an easy task. Both classes of rules must be published in the *Federal Register*, but, as noted, an interpretive rule is exempt from being developed in a formal or informal rulemaking process.

In 2000 the Supreme Court addressed the conflict in the lower federal courts concerning application of the Fair Labor Standards Act (FLSA), which requires employers to pay overtime or grant "comp time" that allows employees to be off from work with full pay. Harris County, Texas established a plan that set a maximum number of "comp time hours" that an employee could accumulate. When an employee accumulated a certain number of comp time hours a supervisor could order the employee to use the accumulated comp time at specified times. The Department of Labor issued an opinion letter stating that employers could use compelled compensatory time as a means of complying with certain requirements of FLSA, but only if there was a prior agreement between the employer and the employee specifically providing for this practice. This conflicted with the county's approach. Several deputy sheriffs brought suit claiming that the FLSA does not permit an employer to compel an employee to use compensatory time in the absence of an agreement permitting the employer to do so. Their argument was consistent with the Department of Labor's opinion letter. The District Court ruled that the county's policy violated the FLSA, but the United States Court of Appeals for the Fifth Circuit reversed, holding that the FLSA did not speak to the issue and thus did not prohibit the county from implementing its policy. The Supreme Court granted review.

In *Christensen v. Harris County* (2000)[18] the Court found that nothing in the FLSA or its implementing regulations prohibits a public employer from compelling the use of compensatory time. But in an opinion by Justice Thomas, writing for a five-justice majority, the Court made a significant administrative law ruling. The Court held that interpretive rules such as the Department of Labor's opinion letter are "entitled to respect" pursuant to the Court's 1944 opinion in *Skidmore v. Swift Co.* referred to above, but they are not entitled to the "*Chevron* deference" announced by the Court in 1984. It follows that when a party challenges a rule promulgated by a federal agency it should be easier to prevail under the *Skidmore* doctrine applied in *Christensen* than to overturn an agency rule if the court were to apply the *Chevron* deference doctrine.

Following its approach in *Christensen*, the Supreme Court in *United States v. Mead Corporation* (2001) ruled that "a tariff classification has no claim to judicial deference under *Chevron*, there being no indication that Congress intended such a ruling to carry the force of law, but we hold that . . . the ruling is eligible to claim respect according to its persuasiveness . . . ."[19]

Even in an instance where an administrative agency labels a rule as "interpretive," courts look to the substance (and not merely the label) of the rule. In doing so courts apply different criteria to make a legal distinction between interpretive and legislative rules. Formerly, if a court found that a rule in controversy had a "substantial impact" on the rights and interests of private parties it would likely reject the agency's classification of a rule as interpretive. But since 1978 the substantial impact test is no longer considered an independent basis to invalidate an interpretive rule otherwise exempt under the APA. Yet, it remains a significant criterion for review of interpretive rules.[20]

In 1974, the Supreme Court ruled that a Department of the Interior regulation adopted as an interpretive rule purporting to make certain government benefits available only to Native Americans living on reservations was a legislative rule. Consequently, because the agency failed to comply with the APA notice-and-comment rulemaking procedures, the Court held the rule ineffective to extinguish benefits to Native Americans living off of reservations.[21]

Court decisions from the United States Courts of Appeals, most frequently from the District of Columbia Circuit, furnish numerous examples of judicial determinations whether a rule is legislative or interpretive. For example in 1983 in *General Motors Corporation v. Ruckelshaus*,[22] the D.C. Circuit reviewed a rule promulgated by the Environmental Protection Agency (EPA) construing the Clean Air Act. The rule allowed the EPA to require manufacturers to recall and repair a class of vehicles regardless of the age or mileage of a vehicle presented for repair. The court found the rule to be interpretative, not legislative, as the record did not indicate the EPA intended the rule to carry any weight beyond the agency's interpretation of the Clean Air Act.

On the other hand, several recent decisions from the U.S. Courts of Appeal have concluded that rules that an agency had characterized as interpretive were invalid. A recent decision from the U.S. Court of Appeals for the D.C. Circuit is illustrative. After originally complying with notice and comment requirements the Federal Communications Commission (FCC) issued a rule governing compensation to telecommunications companies for non-coin calls from pay phones. Later the FCC issued a First Reconsideration Order clarifying the original rule. More than four years after promulgating its initial rule the FCC issued a Second Reconsideration Order, which it characterized as an interpretive rule. But the effect was to change the original rule by altering existing payment arrangements to pay-phone service providers. In declaring the Second Reconsideration Order invalid, the court observed that while a clarification may be embodied in an interpretive rule that is exempt from notice and comment requirements, nevertheless a rule that works a substantive change in a prior regulation is subject to the APA's procedures. The court recognized that the FCC's First Reconsideration Order merely clarified the meaning of the original rule. But it found that

the Second Reconsideration Order could not stand because it changed not only the meaning, but also the very text of the original rule.[23]

Procedural Rules

Procedural rules are internal rules adopted by administrative agencies to assist in carrying out the agency's duties and responsibilities. Section 553(b)(a) of the APA permits agencies to adopt procedural rules without prior notice; nevertheless a procedural rule is legislative in character and therefore has a legally binding effect. For example, in *Inova Alexandria Hospital v. Shalala*,[24] an agency rule permitted a Provider Reimbursement Review Board to dismiss an appeal when a Medicare provider failed to submit a final position paper to the board by the due date. The hospital claimed that even if the Medicare Act allows for a dismissal, a rule dealing with the failure to file papers on appeal, the board was required to promulgate the rule under the APA's notice-and-comment procedure. The court rejected the hospital's contention, saying, "[R]ules of agency organization, procedure, or practice" are exempt from the notice-and-comment provisions of the APA. . . . A rule fits within this exemption if it does not "alter the rights or interests of parties."[25]

In *National Whistleblower Center v. Nuclear Regulatory Commission*,[26] the federal district court for the District of Columbia held that the Nuclear Regulatory Commission had authority to change a rule and apply an "unavoidable and extreme circumstances" test, in lieu of a "good cause" test, to assess requests for extensions of time in which to file contentions in nuclear power plant license renewal proceeding. The court pointed out that unless an agency's rules foreclose an effective opportunity for a party to make a case on the merits, rules need not be promulgated through notice-and-comment rulemaking.

Agencies are not required to adopt procedural rules, but if they do they are required to publish such rules in the *Federal Register*,[27] and once an agency adopts a procedural rule it is bound to adhere to that rule. As with interpretive rules, courts look to the substance of rules, not the label that an agency places on them. Therefore, if a court finds that a rule that an agency has labeled as procedural has a substantial effect on the parties it regulates, the court will likely reject such rule as having been improperly adopted. For example, in *Brown Express, Inc., v. United States,*[28] a federal appellate court in 1979 held that even though it was adopted as a procedural rule, the Interstate Commerce Commission's rule eliminating its forty-year-old practice of notifying competing carriers of pending emergency temporary authority applications had a substantial impact on the motor carrier industry. Thus, rather than being exempt, the rule was controlled by informal rulemaking (notice-and-comment) requirements of the Administrative Procedure Act. The issue, the court explained, was not just whether a rule is *substantive* or *procedural*, but rather whether the rule will have a substantial impact on those regulated.

Two recent federal appellate decisions illustrate limits the courts impose in respect to procedural rules. In 1999, the United States Court of Appeals for the Fifth Circuit held that an agency could not enforce a handbook provision that went beyond requirements established by the agency's procedural rules.[29] The same year the D.C. Circuit found that an agency action vacating a "directive" was not exempt either as procedural rule or as policy statement.[30]

In July 1998 the United States Department of Agriculture (USDA) Food Safety Inspection Service (FSIS) adopted a rule discontinuing face-to-face meetings with commercial food producers regarding proposed food labeling. The food producers brought suit challenging the rule. They conceded that USDA's rule appeared on its face to be procedural, but they contended it represented a significant value judgment and therefore was substantive and subject to rulemaking requirements. The Court of Appeals recognized that "agency housekeeping rules often embody a judgment about what mechanics and processes are most efficient" and held the USDA's rule was procedural, and thus not subject to notice-and-comment rulemaking under the APA.[31]

The Good Cause Exemption

The APA also exempts rulemaking when an agency finds "good cause" that notice and public procedure is impracticable, unnecessary, or contrary to the public interest. Good cause will excuse both notice of proposed rulemaking,[32] and notice of the rule by publication or service 30 days before its effective date.[33] For example, in *Northwest Airlines, Inc. v. Goldschmidt,*[34] the U.S. Court of Appeals for the Eighth Circuit court examined the validity of rules issued after an insufficient period for submission of comments. The court held that good cause was shown for limitation of the period for comment and for making the rule effective upon its being promulgated.

In 1973 the nation experienced gasoline shortages as a result of an embargo imposed by the Organization of Petroleum Exporting Countries (OPEC). The Federal Energy Office (FEO) found that the gasoline shortage was a temporary, but highly disruptive, national emergency, which had brought about long lines at gasoline stations and had prompted violence in some situations. It concluded that preferential treatment for regular customers was a serious alteration in established business practices—one that could result in some customers being served while others were wholly excluded. FEO adopted a rule prohibiting retail gasoline dealers from giving preference to regular customers and made its ruling effective immediately. In *Reeves v. Simon,*[35] a federal appeals court held that the agency had established good cause that the problem required immediate attention.

In *Pent-R-Books, Inc. v United States Postal Service,*[36] a federal district court agreed that the postal service had good cause to implement a law prohibiting the mailing of sexually oriented advertisements to persons who had notified the postal service that they did not wish to receive such material. Thus, the regulation became effective upon publication in the *Federal Register*.

When an agency invokes the **good cause exemption** it must incorporate its finding of good cause and a brief statement of reasons for the exception in the rules as issued.[37] An agency that adopts a rule under this exception effectively deprives the public from participation in the rulemaking process. Therefore, courts narrowly construe an agency's right to adopt rules under the good cause exemption to the APA.

Where an administrative rule has a bearing on proscribing criminal conduct, courts are likely to take a close look at the rule. In *United States v. Gavrilovic*,[38] the defendants were convicted of manufacturing a controlled substance. They argued on appeal that the drug mecloqualone was not a controlled substance at the time of their arrest. They contended the regulations placing the drug on a controlled list were invalid because they became effective less than 30 days after publication of the rules. The Eighth Circuit Court of Appeals said that the Administrator of the Drug Enforcement Administration had failed to show "good cause" within the meaning of Section 553(d)(3) of the APA to justify regulations which made mecloqualone a "controlled substance" just two days after publication of the agency's decision in the *Federal Register*.

INFORMAL AND FORMAL RULEMAKING

Rulemaking subject to the APA begins with notice. Section 553(b) of the APA stipulates that a **notice of proposed rule making (NPRM)** shall be published in the *Federal Register*, unless persons subject thereto are named and either personally served or otherwise have actual notice thereof in accordance with law. The notice must include:

1. a statement of the time, place, and nature of public rule making proceedings;

2. reference to the legal authority under which the rule is proposed; and

3. either the terms or substance of the proposed rule or a description of the subjects and issues involved.[39]

Congress obviously intended that these requirements would give interested citizens an opportunity to participate in rulemaking and cause administrative agencies to be accountable to the public. In *Utility Solid Waste Activities Group v. EPA*,[40] the EPA argued that the petitioners received "actual notice" when it published a notice of the change of a rule on its Internet site and held a meeting attended by counsel for Utility Solid Waste Activities Group. The court in 2001 rejected the argument saying, "This court has never found that Internet notice is an acceptable substitute for publication in the *Federal Register*, and we refuse to do so now."[41]

Agencies frequently include a proposed rule in the notice although federal courts have held that the notice is sufficient as long as it fairly apprises interested parties of the issues involved and affords interested persons a reasonable and meaningful opportunity to participate in the rulemaking process. It need not specify every precise proposal that the agency may consider.[42] Occasionally a proposed rule is relatively brief. More often the proposed rule is quite lengthy.

Informal "Notice-and-Comment" Rulemaking

Unless the statute creating the agency mandates to the contrary, Section 553 of the APA permits an agency to follow an informal (notice-and-comment) process of rulemaking. Informal rulemaking is designed to assist an agency in obtaining information and views from the public to enable it to promptly make a proper decision.

In an informal rulemaking procedure the agency is required to furnish interested persons an opportunity to participate through submission of written data, views, or arguments with or without opportunity for oral presentation, but the agency has considerable discretion as to whether to allow interested parties to present evidence and arguments to the agency.[43] After consideration of the relevant matter presented and review of other materials the agency considers relevant, the agency issues final rules and must incorporate a concise general statement of their basis and purpose.[44]

The APA requirements for informal rulemaking are relatively simple. Because formal rulemaking procedures are extremely time consuming, for the past several decades agencies have exhibited a definite preference to use informal rulemaking to administer federal laws. Probably over 90 percent of federal rulemaking is conducted on an informal basis. Congress, however, has required certain agencies to comply with additional procedures. For example, the Food and Drug Administration must follow extensive statutory procedures before granting approval of new drugs and medical devices.[45] Likewise the Environmental Protection Agency must follow elaborate procedures in regulating hazardous materials.[46]

In some instances agencies label rules as exempt, characterizing them as interpretive or procedural or stating that they come within the "good cause" exemption that we discussed earlier. Courts narrowly construe exemptions and not infrequently invalidate such rules. For example, in 1999 the EPA issued certain technical amendments.[47] The EPA claimed the amendments were minor and should fall within the good cause exemption. The D.C. Circuit Court of Appeals rejected the agency's claims.[48] Thus, the EPA was required to proceed under the informal rulemaking procedures.

The late Kenneth Culp Davis, the author of a leading treatise on administrative law and a strong supporter of administrative government, once observed that informal rulemaking is "one of the greatest inventions of modern government."[49] Without question, informal rulemaking facilitates regulation. Moreover, by allowing interested persons a channel to exercise a degree of political power, the notice-and-comment procedure tends to alleviate the undemocratic character of agency rulemaking. Those who are suspicious of the regulatory state tend to favor more demanding procedures that make it more difficult for agencies to impose rules.

Direct Final Rulemaking

A variation of informal (notice-and-comment) rulemaking is direct final rulemaking. The purpose is to expedite the rulemaking process when a rule is noncontroversial. It is a relatively new approach used by federal agencies. The agency publishes a final rule in the *Federal Register* with a statement that, unless a significant adverse comment is received within a specified period of time, the rule will become effective. At the same time an identical proposed rule is often published. If no significant comments are received the rule goes into effect. On the other hand, if such comments are received, the agency withdraws the direct final rule and proceeds to consider the comments as directed to a proposed rule. The Environmental Protection Agency, the Department of Agriculture, and the Department of Transportation are among the federal agencies that have extensively used direct final rulemaking.[50] Direct final rulemaking is distinguishable from "interim final rulemaking" discussed in Box 6.3.

Interim Rules

Although not specifically provided for in the APA, federal agencies often make an announcement that by a set date a particular rule is to be promulgated but may be changed after input to the agency as the notice-and-comment process ensues. The agency adopts a rule without prior public input and then invites postpromulgation comments directed toward the issue of whether the rule should be changed sometime in the future. The **interim rule** process is often used when there is urgency in reliance on the APA "good cause" provision that exempts prior notice and comment. It has the advantage of affording those who are to be affected an advance notice to "gear up" to comply with the proposed rule. After becoming effective,

---

BOX 6.3 Invitation for Public Comment on Proposed Change
in EPA

Permit Requirements for Municipal Wastewater Treatment Discharges

Summary: Today, EPA is inviting comment on a proposed policy regarding NPDES permit requirements for treatment plants in publicly owned treatment works (POTWs) under peak wet weather flow conditions. Regulatory agencies, municipal operators of POTWs, and representatives of environmental advocacy groups have expressed uncertainty about the appropriate regulatory interpretation for such situations. Today's document describes both a proposed interpretation of regulations, as well as draft guidance to implement such an interpretation. EPA's intention is to ensure that NPDES requirements be applied in a nationally-consistent manner

that improves the capacity, management, operation and maintenance of POTW treatment plants and collection systems and protects human health and the environment.

Dates: Written comments on this proposed policy must be received by EPA or postmarked by January 9, 2004.

Addresses: Comments may be submitted electronically, by mail, or through hand delivery/courier. . . .

For Further Information, Contact: For questions about the substance of this proposed policy, contact . . . Office of Wastewater Management.

SOURCE: *Federal Register*, Volume 68, Number 216 (November 7, 2003)

---

interim rules are not usually withdrawn absent a significant comment. Critics argue that the interim rule process evades the APA requirements designed to allow public participation and as a result the process tends to greatly limit the probability that public input will be effective in molding a rule.

Formal Rulemaking

In contrast to the informal rulemaking process, the APA states that "[w]hen rules are required by statute to be made on the record after opportunity for an agency hearing," rulemaking must follow the provisions for formal adjudication.[51] When **formal rulemaking** is mandated by a statute, an agency must conduct a **trial-type hearing** and afford interested parties an opportunity to testify, present witnesses and documentary evidence, cross-examine opposing witnesses, and present arguments.

As in informal rulemaking, the process of formal rulemaking starts with public notice of the proposed rule, but it then takes on a new dimension. The public comment that characterizes the notice-and-comment procedure of informal rulemaking is replaced by a trial-type hearing, cus-

tomarily presided over by an **administrative law judge (ALJ).**[52] The hearing has the trappings of an adversary court hearing with each party entitled to present a case or defense by oral or documentary evidence, to submit rebuttal evidence, and to conduct such cross-examination as may be required for a full and true disclosure of the facts.[53] The ALJ makes findings of fact and conclusions of law and issues a preliminary opinion and forwards it to the members of the administrative commission, who issue a final decision. Although the hearing resembles a nonjury trial, the procedures are not as technical and the rules of evidence are relaxed. Agencies receive evidence that is material and relevant without regard to such restrictions as the "hearsay rule" applicable in civil and criminal trials. Finally, it should be noted that in formal rulemaking there is a ban on **ex parte contacts** by agency personnel and interested parties relevant to the merits of a proceeding.[54]

When Formal Rulemaking Is Required An agency may opt to conduct formal rulemaking, but most do not. Before an agency is required to conduct a formal rulemaking proceeding there must be a statutory mandate to have rules made "on the record after an opportunity for an agency hearing."[55]

Questions as to just when a statute requires a formal (trial-type) hearing were resolved in 1973 by the Supreme Court in its landmark decision, *United States v. Florida East Coast Railroad.*[56] Historically the Interstate Commerce Commission (ICC) had conducted trial-type hearings when it established rules and regulations with regard to freight car service by railroads. But because of a shortage of freight cars on the nation's railroads, in 1966 Congress had enacted an amendment to the Interstate Commerce Act enlarging the ICC's authority to prescribe per diem charges for use by one railroad of freight cars owned by another. The statute stipulated that the ICC *"may, after hearing,"* issue rules to establish incentive per diem charges for use of freight cars. Florida East Coast Railroad sought to set aside the ICC rule that imposed a per diem charge on any railroad that retained a boxcar of another railroad. Florida East Coast argued that the rates established by the ICC were invalid because the ICC refused its request for a formal hearing. The Supreme Court rejected the argument and held that the informal (notice-and-comment) type hearing was sufficient. Writing for the Court, Justice Rehnquist opined:

> We think the treatment of the term "hearing" in the Administrative Procedure Act affords a sufficient basis for concluding that the requirement of a "hearing" contained in § 1(14)(a) [referring to the ICC Act]; in a situation where the Commission was acting under the 1966 statutory rulemaking authority that Congress had conferred upon it, did not by its own force require the Commission either to hear oral testimony, to permit cross-examination of Commission witnesses, or to hear oral argument. . . . The parties had fair notice of exactly what the Commission proposed to do, and were given an opportunity to comment, to object, or to make some other form of written submission. The final

order of the Commission indicates that it gave consideration to the statements of the two appellees here. . . .[57]

The Court's ruling meant that the statutory language *"after hearing"* was not equivalent to the APA requirement that a rule be made *"on the record after opportunity for an agency hearing."* After the Supreme Court's decision it was clear that unless the agency statute specifically provided for a hearing "on the record" or a reasonable equivalent thereof, an informal rulemaking procedure would suffice. Relatively few federal statutes require "on the record" hearings, so the Court's decision had the effect of greatly increasing the use of informal rulemaking by federal administrative agencies.

HYBRID RULEMAKING

By the late 1960s the efficiency of informal rulemaking and the complexity of formal rulemaking caused informal rulemaking to become increasingly important. Yet critics complained that informal rulemaking did not satisfy traditional due process of law concerns because agencies were resolving contested factual issues without an opportunity for challengers to cross-examine the proponents of such facts. There was no legal difficulty if an agency chose to adopt additional procedural safeguards beyond the notice-and-comment type of rulemaking. Yet, in reviewing informal rulemaking, federal appellate courts began compelling agencies to provide procedures that were neither required by the APA nor mandated by Congress in the agency's enabling statute. Such enhanced procedures came to be known as **hybrid rulemaking.** Hybrid rulemaking is procedurally more elaborate than informal notice-and-comment rulemaking, but less elaborate than formal, adjudicatory rulemaking.

In a series of decisions during the 1970s the United States Court of Appeals for the D.C. Circuit reversed a number of informal rulemaking decisions because the agencies failed to provide due process procedures that were neither required by the Constitution, the agencies' enabling statutes, nor the APA. One of the most notable of the cases involved a proceeding by the Federal Power Commission (FPC) to set rates to be charged by pipelines that transported hydrocarbon products. In 1973, in *Mobil Oil Corporation v. Federal Power Commission*,[58] the issue involved an agency ratemaking rule promulgated through informal proceedings. The Court of Appeals for the D.C. Circuit held that the informal "notice-and-comment" rulemaking process of setting rates did not create a record that satisfied the standard of review to enable the court to determine if there was substantial evidence to support an agency's decision. The court observed:

> Even if adverse parties submit controverting information in the form of comments, the procedure employed cannot be relied upon as adequate. A "whole record" . . . includes the process of testing and illumination ordinarily associated with adversary, adjudicative procedures. . . . Thus, it is adversary procedural devices, which permit testing and elucidation that raise information from the level of mere inconsistent data to evidence "substantial" enough to support rates.[59]

The court stopped short of requiring a formal rulemaking, adding:

> The defect we find in the Commission's procedures here, and the resulting inadequacy of the evidence could be remedied by according the procedure described under sections 556 and 557 of the APA, but such complete adjudicatory procedures are not required. . . . What are required are procedures, which will . . . create a record that will allow a reviewing court to examine the agency's actions.[60]

Even after the Supreme Court's 1973 ruling in *United States v. Florida East Coast Railroad,* federal appellate courts continued to impose procedural requirements for informal rulemaking. For example, the D.C. Circuit required agencies to disclose data to interested parties in advance of rulemaking to enable interested parties to respond.[61] These decisions caused the congressionally mandated informal proceedings to more closely mirror the requirements of formal rulemaking. As procedures for adoption of rules became very protracted some agencies even substituted adjudication as a policymaking alternative. Critics of these judicially imposed requirements often termed the result an ossification of the rulemaking process.

In 1973 the Court of Appeals for the D.C. Circuit reviewed a decision of the Atomic Energy Commission (AEC). AEC had initiated an informal rulemaking proceeding to determine the manner in which potential environmental damage resulting from disposal of spent nuclear fuel should be reflected in deciding whether to license nuclear power plants. The agency refused to grant the Natural Resources Defense Council's request to cross-examine witnesses. The Court of Appeals reversed the agency's ruling because the agency had failed to adopt procedures that would assure a "thorough ventilation of the issues."[62]

The *Vermont Yankee* Case

The stage was now being set for a resolution of the problem of the judicially imposed requirements on informal rulemaking by federal agencies. The United States Supreme Court entered the picture to clarify an agency's procedural responsibilities. In 1978 the Court issued its landmark opinion in *Vermont Yankee Nuclear Power Corp. v. Natural Resources Defense Council.*[63] The Supreme Court noted that the AEC had complied with the required APA procedures for informal rulemaking, and reversed the D.C. Circuit's decision. The Court recognized that agencies are free to grant additional procedural rights in the exercise of their discretion. Nevertheless, the Court ruled that reviewing courts are generally not free to impose such procedural rights if the agencies have not chosen to grant them. Writing for the Supreme Court, Justice Rehnquist cautioned reviewing courts against engrafting their own notions of proper procedures upon agencies entrusted with substantive functions by Congress, observing:

> . . . [I]f courts continually review agency proceedings to determine whether the agency employed procedures which were, in the court's opinion, perfectly tailored to reach what the court perceives to be the "best" or "correct" result, judicial review would be totally unpredictable. And the agencies, operating under this vague injunction to employ the "best" procedures and facing the threat of reversal if they did not, would undoubtedly adopt full adjudicatory procedures in every instance. Not only would this totally disrupt the statutory scheme, through which Congress enacted "a formula upon which opposing social and political forces have come to rest," . . . but all the inherent advantages of informal rulemaking would be totally lost.[64]

Thus, after the Court's decision the issue of whether procedural due process requires rulemaking procedures beyond those required by the APA became an agency question, not a judicial issue.

The Supreme Court's opinion in *Vermont Yankee Nuclear Power Corp. v. Natural Resources Defense Council* **is excerpted at the end of this chapter.**

NEGOTIATED RULEMAKING

Congress enacted the Negotiated Rulemaking Act of 1990 (NRMA)[65] to encourage innovation in rulemaking consistent with the informal (notice-and-comment) rulemaking process. Congress now encourages the use of **negotiated rulemaking** (often referred to as "regneg") by certain agencies in the development of specific regulations. Likewise, the executive branch has now become an advocate for negotiated rulemaking.

To initiate negotiated rulemaking an agency must publish a notice in the *Federal Register* announcing the establishment of a negotiated rulemaking committee and inviting persons to apply for, or nominate persons for, membership. If after considering comments and applications, the agency decides not to establish a negotiated rulemaking committee, it must publish notice of such a decision and the reasons for it in the *Federal Register*. To go forward, the committee meets publicly with a mediator and seeks to formulate a proposed rule. The negotiating process takes place before an agency issues a proposed regulation. If successful, the agency may, but is not required to, adopt the text arrived at by consensus as a proposed rule. At that point the agency follows the notice-and-comment requirements of informal rulemaking. Proponents of negotiated rulemaking claim that it speeds up the process of rulemaking and limits court challenges to final rules. Commentators have been favorably impressed with the idea of negotiated rulemaking; however, to date the process has been used in a relatively small number of rulemaking procedures.

ELECTRONIC RULEMAKING

Electronic rulemaking refers to the use of the Internet, email, and other electronic information technologies as means of enhancing public knowledge of and participation in agency rulemaking. This new phenomenon was given substantial impetus when Congress enacted E-Government Act of 2002.[66] The act is aimed at requiring federal agencies to expand their use of the Internet as a vehicle to deliver information to the public. This new statute creates a Federal Chief Information Officer within the **Office of Management and Budget (OMB)** and mandates the use of Internet-based technologies to enhance the management and promotion of electronic government services and public access to government information and services by establishing a broad framework of measures using Internet-based information technology.

Section 205 of the new act requires each federal court to maintain a website that contains pertinent information about the court, its functions, local rules, and so forth. Section 206(a) states that Congress intends the new law to "improve performance in the development and issuance of agency regulations by using information technology to increase access, accountability, and transparency; and enhance public participation in Government by electronic means." Subsection (b) states that agencies shall ensure that a publicly accessible Federal Government website includes all information about that agency required to be published in the *Federal Register* under paragraphs (1) and (2) of 5 U.S.C.A. § 552(a) of the Freedom of Information Act (FOIA) including:

1. descriptions of its central and field organizations, contact information, and methods to request information or make submittals;

2. statements that explain its functions and formal and informal procedures;

3. rules of procedures, places where forms may be obtained, and instructions as to the scope and content of reporting requirements;

4. substantive rules, statements of general policy, and generally applicable interpretations; and

5. any amendments, revisions, or repeals.

The goal of electronic rulemaking is to present information to the public and to foster use of the Internet for receiving and displaying public comments during the rulemaking process thereby increasing public participation. To achieve this goal, Section 206(d) directs each agency to build publicly accessible web sites that contain all the comments submitted to a rulemaking docket under § 553(c) of the APA along with other materials by agency rule or practice that are included in a rulemaking docket. Providing docket information does not pose a problem, but making available effective means of dialogue is a greater challenge. Greater public participation should be valuable, but as Jeffrey S. Lubbers has pointed out, the goal of increasing participation by the citizenry raises some important issues. Those issues he mentions include whether rule-making "chat rooms" should be governed by rules and whether they should be moderated or not, how to cope with incivility or high-volume posting, and how to deal with mail attachments of huge files.[67] Electronic rulemaking is in its infancy, but holds great potential to increase public participation in an area of government where federal agencies produce some four thousand regulations each year. We should see considerable progress in this area in 2005 and later years.[68]

PUBLICATION AND CODIFICATION OF RULES

As noted earlier in the chapter, agencies begin the rulemaking process by publishing a notice of proposed rule making (NPRM) in The *Federal Register*. Likewise, the APA requires that a **final rule** must be published in the same publication thirty days before it becomes effective; however, the time requirement does not apply to interpretive rules and statements of policy or rules covered by the good cause exemption but the requirement for publication of the rule still applies.[69] After new rules are published they are codified and incorporated into the *Code of Federal Regulations* (CFR), which prints the text of each regulation. The CFR is updated annually. In addition to subject indexes, the CFR includes information to enable the reader to locate regulations by reference to federal statutes indexed in the United States Code Annotated (USCA).

The *Code of Federal Regulations*

The *Code of Federal Regulations* (CFR) is a codification of general and permanent rules published in the *Federal Register* by Executive departments and agencies of the United States Government. The CFR embraces fifty titles, each divided into chapters usually bearing the name of the issuing agency. Table 6.2 lists the various titles. Each

chapter is further subdivided into parts covering specific regulatory areas. Each volume is revised at least once a year. A subject matter index is contained in a separate volume that is revised annually. This volume contains the parallel Table of Statutory Authorities and Agency Rules, a list of CFR titles, chapters, and parts, and an alphabetical list of agencies.

The *Code of Federal Regulations* as a Research Tool College and local libraries usually include the *Code of Federal Regulations* in their collections. An hour spent in browsing the CFR will acquaint the reader with the availability of valuable resources of government rules and regulations. Moreover, research into the CFR can be very enlightening on a wide variety of subjects governed by rules adopted by the numerous federal agencies. For example, pick up a can of your favorite fruit or vegetables in the supermarket and check out the valuable nutrition information on the label. What is required? How specific must the information be? How is it to be presented to the consumer? The rules adopted by the Food and Drug Administration are revelatory. As an example, we researched the CFR to check out regulations on the labeling of canned and packaged food. The Subject Matter Index led us to Title 21, which contains eight volumes of rules of the Food and Drug Administration, Department of Health and Human Services. The Title is divided into Chapters with each subdivided into separate Parts. The Index revealed that food labeling is included in Part 101 and consists of Sections 101.01–101.108. Within these sections we found a storehouse of information on labeling requirements, nutrition information, and health claims in regard to food sold for human consumption.

THE RULEMAKING RECORD

In formal rulemaking a complete record of agency proceedings must include the transcript of testimony and exhibits, together with all papers and requests filed in the proceeding.[70]

Table 6.2 Overview of Code of Federal Regulations

Title 1	General Provisions	Title 26	Internal Revenue
Title 2	[Reserved]	Title 27	Alcohol, Tobacco Products, and Firearms
Title 3	The President	Title 28	Judicial Administration
Title 4	Accounts	Title 29	Labor
Title 5	Administrative Personnel	Title 30	Mineral Resources
Title 6	[Reserved]	Title 31	Money and Finance: Treasury
Title 7	Agriculture	Title 32	National Defense
Title 8	Aliens and Nationality	Title 33	Navigation and Navigable Waters
Title 9	Animals and Animal Products	Title 34	Education
Title 10	Energy	Title 35	Panama Canal
Title 11	Federal Elections	Title 36	Parks, Forests, and Public Property
Title 12	Banks and Banking	Title 37	Patents, Trademarks, and Copyrights
Title 13	Business Credit and Assistance	Title 38	Pensions, Bonuses, and Veterans' Relief
Title 14	Aeronautics and Space	Title 39	Postal Service
Title 15	Commerce and Foreign Trade	Title 40	Protection of Environment
Title 16	Commercial Practices	Title 41	Public Contracts and Property Management
Title 17	Commodity and Securities Exchanges	Title 42	Public Health
Title 18	Conservation of Power and Water	Title 43	Public Lands: Interior
Title 19	Customs Duties	Title 44	Emergency Management and Assistance
Title 20	Employees' Benefits	Title 45	Public Welfare
Title 21	Food and Drugs	Title 46	Shipping
Title 22	Foreign Relations	Title 47	Telecommunication
Title 23	Highways	Title 48	Federal Acquisition Regulations System
Title 24	Housing and Urban Development	Title 49	Transportation
Title 25	Indians	Title 50	Wildlife and Fisheries

Historically, in informal rulemaking the record has been rather informally prepared, usually consisting of a compilation of the various materials considered by the agency. This was generally deemed to be adequate, as courts presumed a factual basis for the informal creation of rules. In 1935, in *Pacific States Box & Basket Co. v. White*, the Supreme Court observed that "where the regulation is within the scope of authority legally delegated, the presumption of the existence of facts justifying its specific exercise attaches alike to statutes, to municipal ordinances, and to orders of administrative bodies.[71] The Supreme Court's 1978 opinion in *Vermont Yankee* seemed to support this view. But in *Motor Vehicle Manufacturers Ass'n. v. State Farm Mutual Automobile Ins. Co.*,[72] the Supreme Court intimated that in some instances reviewing courts might look more

closely at the factual basis for choices made by an agency in informal rulemaking. Therefore in order to produce a rule that will survive judicial review it now seems prudent for agencies to build a **rulemaking record,** even in an informal rulemaking procedure, that demonstrates a factual connection between the evidence before the agency and the agency's decision.

REGULATORY FLEXIBILITY ANALYSIS

In 1953 Congress passed the Small Business Act[73] to advance the goal of a freely competitive economy by promoting economic viability of small business.[74] The act describes a small business as an independently owned and operated enterprise that is not dominant in its field and gives the Small Business Administration (SBA) the power to define such enterprises, considering such factors as the number of employees, dollar volume of business, net worth, net income, or a combination of factors. The SBA has outlined in detail those factors it considers. These include economic characteristics comprising the structure of an industry, including degree of competition, average firm size, start-up costs and entry barriers, distribution of firms by size, as well as technological changes in the industry, which may distinguish small firms from other firms.[75]

In 1980 Congress enacted the Regulatory Flexibility Act[76] to minimize the effects of administrative regulations on small businesses and not-for-profit organizations. The act requires federal agencies to file initial and final regulatory flexibility analyses (RFAs) to accompany notices of proposed rules and final rules where regulations have a significant impact on small businesses. A **regulatory flexibility analysis** seeks to not only minimize the economic effects of regulations on small businesses, but also to consider any flexible measures that could be incorporated to assist small businesses in compliance and reporting requirements. The act encourages comments during the notice-and-comment period directed at how proposed regulations can be adapted to small business requirements, and requires that small businesses be given an opportunity to participate in the rulemaking for any rule that has an appreciable impact on small businesses. These RFAs are monitored by the Small Business Administration. The act does not apply when the head of an agency certifies that a rule or regulation will not affect a substantial number of small business entities.[77] But if an agency certifies that a rule will not, if promulgated, have a significant economic impact on a substantial number of small entities, and that a regulatory flexibility analysis is, therefore, not required, that certification is subject to judicial review.[78] The act also provides that two agencies, the Environmental Protection Agency (EPA) and

the Occupational Safety and Health Administration of the Department of Labor (OSHA) are required to participate in a process that involves small entities in the rulemaking for development of the rule through various methods.[79]

WAIVERS AND VARIANCES

The United States Constitution is the supreme law of the land and statutory law has become increasingly important. Yet, the American legal system is essentially based on the English common law and the concept of equity, which allows exceptions based on specific circumstances. This thread of flexibility also exists in the rulemaking process at the federal and state levels. Thus, where the strict application of a rule can lead to unreasonable or unintended results in a specific situation, one who is covered by the rule may apply for relief in the form of a waiver or variance from the agency's interpretation or enforcement of a given rule.

As administrative law developed in the twentieth century, the Supreme Court recognized that reasons might be advanced to justify a **waiver** of or **variance** from agency rules.[80] For many years the Environmental Protection Agency has provided for variances from its regulations. Today the practice of agencies granting waivers or variances from the strict application of rules is widely accepted. The grant or denial of a request is a matter for agency discretion that should be accompanied by a meaningful explanation by the agency.[81] Courts have not indicated that an agency must be statutorily authorized to grant waivers and variances.

In 1985 in *Chemical Mfrs. Ass'n. v. Natural Resources Defense Council, Inc.*,[82] the Supreme Court reviewed a federal appellate court decision that barred the EPA from issuing variances from toxic pollutant effluent limitations under the Clean Water Act. Under the act, the EPA was required to promulgate regulations establishing categories of pollution sources and setting effluent limitations for those categories. EPA developed a "fundamentally different factor" (FDF) variance to ensure that its necessarily rough-hewn categories of sources did not unfairly burden atypical dischargers of waste. Interested parties could seek an FDF variance to make effluent limitations either more or less stringent. If the standards applied to a given source because of factors fundamentally different from those considered by EPA in setting the limitation were either too lenient or too strict, EPA could grant a variance. The lower court based its ruling barring the EPA from issuing variances on the fact that the Clean Water Act provided that EPA could not "modify" any effluent-limitation requirement insofar as toxic materials are concerned.

The Supreme Court reversed, holding that the word "modify" was the proper subject of construction by EPA and the courts. The Court said that EPA's regulation as to such variances was an acknowledgment that not all relevant factors were sufficiently taken into account in framing that requirement originally. The Court went on to explain that those relevant factors, properly considered, would have justified—indeed, required—the creation of a subcategory for the discharger in question. The Court concluded that the availability of FDF variances makes bearable the enormous burden faced by EPA in promulgating categories of sources and setting effluent limitations.

Although there is no requirement that an agency's enabling legislation grant specific authority for the grant or denial of waivers and variances, there has been a trend for Congress to make such provision in certain enactments. For example, Congress included a stipulation that "any person to whom a rule . . . applies may petition the Commission for an exemption from such rule" in the Magnuson-Moss Warranty Act that provides for rulemaking by the Federal Trade Commission.[83] The Occupation Safety and Health Act (OSHA) provisions dealing with variances are now statutorily provided and its variance policies are codified.[84]

Today courts generally recognize that in promulgating rules, agencies should make some provision for exemption. Waivers and variances are the recognized administrative devices to accomplish such individualized justice. In 1993 the D.C. Circuit held that waiver processes are a permissible device for fine-tuning regulations and an appropriate method of curtailing the inevitable excesses of the agency's general rule.[85] Because an agency has considerable discretion in determining whether to grant a waiver or variance, a party who challenges an agency's denial of its request for a waiver faces the difficult task of showing that the agency's reasons are "so insubstantial as to render that denial an abuse of discretion."[86]

EXECUTIVE OVERSIGHT OF RULEMAKING

The United States Constitution vests the executive power of the federal government in the president and directs the president to see that the laws are faithfully executed."[87] The framers of the Constitution could not have foreseen the development of administrative functions that were to become part of the federal government in the twentieth century. Yet, the presidency of Franklin Delano Roosevelt (1933–1945) and the years that followed witnessed a multitude of federal agencies that promulgated a massive number of rules and regulations. By the 1970s there was a heightened concern over the economic impact of government regulations. Since then several **executive orders** have been issued by presidents as a means of providing **executive oversight** over the federal administrative process.

Key Executive Orders Affecting Rulemaking

In 1974 President Ford issued Executive Order 11,821, which authorized the Office of Management and Budget (OMB) to require inflation impact assessments by agencies before they promulgate new rules. To ensure that economic costs were taken into account President Carter issued Executive Order 12,044 in 1978 requiring federal agencies to conduct a "regulatory analysis" before adopting new rules.

Shortly after his election, President Reagan issued Executive Order 12,291 in 1981 mandating that agencies conduct cost-benefit analyses and adopt only those rules that maximized net benefits to society. In 1985 President Reagan issued Executive Order 12,498 that required executive agencies to submit their anticipated regulatory programs to OMB annually. The Reagan orders only applied to executive, not independent, agencies.

In 1993 President Bill Clinton issued Executive Order 12,866 to replace the two Executive Orders issued by President Reagan. The Clinton order modified some of the regulatory features of the Reagan orders, extended the regulatory aspects to independent federal agencies, and delegated responsibility for regulatory review to the vice president. It provided that the Office of Information and Regulatory Affairs (OIRA) "shall provide meaningful guidance and oversight so that each agency's regulatory actions are consistent with applicable law, the President's priorities, and the principles set forth in this Executive order and do not conflict with the policies or actions of another agency." In 1999 President Clinton issued Executive Order 13,132 entitled "Federalism," designed to guide agencies in formulating policies that have implications between the federal government and the states. The order prohibits an agency, to the extent practicable, from promulgating a regulation that imposes substantial direct compliance costs on state and local governments. If an agency foresees a conflict between federal interests and state law, the agency is to consult with state and local officials.

In May 2001, President George W. Bush issued Executive Order 13,211. The order was based on the premise that the federal government can significantly affect the supply, distribution, and use of energy. It requires that before taking any "significant agency actions" federal agencies must prepare a Statement of Energy Effect (SEE) and present the Office of Information and Regulatory Affairs (OIRA), Office of the Management of the Budget (OMB) with a detailed statement regarding any adverse effects the action would have on energy supply or use.

Preclearance of Proposed Rules

As a result of executive orders issued by recent presidents, most notably E.O. 12,866, **preclearance of proposed rules** has come to be institutionalized as a part of the rulemaking process. As noted, preclearance is effectuated by the Office of Information and Regulatory Affairs (OIRA) within the Office of Management and Budget (OMB), which is located within the Executive Office of the President. Agencies that fail to obtain preclearance of proposed rules are prevented from publishing NPRMs in the *Federal Register*. Preclearance insures that new agency rules are consistent with the Presidents policy agenda. It also facilitates interagency regulatory coordination—preventing agencies from issuing rules that are inconsistent or redundant.

LEGISLATIVE CONTROL OF RULEMAKING

Congress oversees executive agencies through its elaborate committee system. Committees in both the House and Senate are assigned responsibility for overseeing particular agencies or government functions. For example, the U.S. Department of Agriculture is overseen by the Agriculture Committee in the House and the Agriculture, Nutrition, and Forestry Committee in the Senate. Congressional committees receive **oversight briefings** from agency officials and, if necessary, conduct **oversight hearings** in which agency personnel are invited (or subpoenaed) to appear and give testimony. In conducting oversight, congressional committees rely heavily on information provided by the **General Accounting**

Office (GAO), an investigatory agency located within the legislative branch. GAO monitors and evaluates agency rulemaking as part of its broader function of auditing the expenditures of the federal government. GAO reports to congressional committees often contain specific recommendations with respect to agency rules, powers, and procedures. If Congress is dissatisfied with the performance of a particular agency, it can punish the agency through the budgetary process or it can amend existing legislation affecting the agency's powers or procedures. Because agencies owe their very existence to legislation, Congress has ultimate control over agency performance.

The Legislative Veto

A **legislative veto** is a provision typically written into the original act delegating legislative power to an executive agency. Congress and state legislative bodies, employing different types of vetoes, used the device to control administrative rulemaking. Congress enacted statutes giving the entire Congress, one house thereof, or committees in both chambers the prerogative to override an agency decision. In *Immigration and Naturalization Service v. Chadha*,[88] the Supreme Court in 1983 held that the legislative veto is unconstitutional. The Court ruled that legislative vetoes are invalid because the President is not given the opportunity to veto the legislative veto of the agency's action. (The *Chadha* decision is excerpted and discussed more extensively in Chapter 8.)

In 1996 Congress amended the APA to allow it to retain control over agency decisions in a manner functionally similar to the legislative veto. Under a section titled "Congressional Review of Agency Decisionmaking," before the rule can take effect Congress now requires agencies to submit to the U.S. House and Senate and the Comptroller General a report that includes a copy of the rule, a statement of its basis and purpose, and its effective date.[89] The report must include any cost-benefit analysis for the rule, a copy of any proposed or final regulatory flexibil-

ity analyses required by the Regulatory Flexibility Act,[90] and information relevant to compliance with the Unfunded Mandates Reform Act of 1995.[91] Under the 1996 amendments federal agencies must assess the effects of their regulatory actions on state, local, and tribal governments and the private sector. Agencies must also show compliance with the Paperwork Reduction Act of 1995,[92] and where relevant, with the National Environmental Policy Act (NEPA),[93] as well as compliance with any relevant Executive Orders.

The requirements are quite broad. As used in the subtitle, "rule" has the meaning given such term under the Administrative Procedure Act, and thus includes both legislative and interpretive rules. Congress is thus given an opportunity to adopt a resolution of approval or disapproval of a proposed rule. The act distinguishes between major rules and all other rules, a major rule being one that the OIRA finds likely to have a major effect on the economy. Rules, other than major rules, take effect in their normal course; however, if Congress disapproves of a rule that has taken effect, the rule is treated as having never taken effect. For major rules the General Accounting Office submits a report to Congress and Congress has sixty days after it receives the report to disapprove the rule. A presidential veto and possible override of such veto can affect time requirements, and the act contains some exceptions.

EX PARTE CONTACTS BY DECISION MAKERS

To ensure the independent judgment of administrative judges and agency decision makers Section 557 of the APA, which outlines the procedures for formal rulemaking and adjudication, forbids "[an] interested person outside the agency" from communicating off-the-record with any agency official "who is or may reasonably be expected to be involved in the decisional process of the proceeding."[94] In contrast, Section 553 of the APA, which addresses informal rulemaking, is silent concerning ex parte contacts between decision makers and interested parties.[95]

Historically courts looked upon rulemaking much as they do adjudication and held that agency personnel involved in decision-making processes should insulate themselves from ex parte contacts with interested parties. In 1977 in *Home Box Office, Inc. v. FCC*,[96] the Court of Appeals for the D.C. Circuit reviewed a rulemaking proceeding involving subscription broadcast television rules. The court found evidence of undue industry influence over Commission proceedings and observed: "We are particularly concerned that the final shaping of the rules we are reviewing here may have been by compromise among the contending industry forces, rather than by exercise of the independent discretion in the public interest the Communications Act vests in individual commissioners."[97] In order to determine the effect of those ex parte communications, the court required the FCC to hold an evidentiary hearing to ascertain the nature of all ex parte pleas and other approaches that were made to the Commission or its employees after the issuance of the first notice of proposed rulemaking.

Four years later in *Sierra Club v. Costle*[98] the same court ruled that the EPA did not exceed its statutory authority under the Clean Air Act in promulgating new source performance standards governing emission control by coal-burning power plants. The court again addressed ex parte contacts between agency officials and interested parties and distinguished the administrators and lobbyists from the role judges play, noting that informal contacts may enable an agency to gain support for its programs. In contrast to its decision in *Home Box Office*, this time the court observed:

> Under our system of government, the very legitimacy of general policymaking performed by unelected administrators depends in no small part upon the openness, accessibility, and amenability of these officials to the needs and ideas of the public from whom their ultimate authority derives, and upon whom their commands must fall. As judges we are insulated

from these pressures because of the nature of the judicial process in which we participate; but we must refrain from the easy temptation to look askance at all face-to-face lobbying efforts, regardless of the forum in which they occur, merely because we see them as inappropriate in the judicial context.[99]

Both *Home Box Office* and *Sierra Club* involved informal rulemaking. Recall that in 1978 the Supreme Court in *Vermont Yankee* cautioned lower courts not to impose requirements in informal rulemaking beyond those required by statute. Moreover, since the *Sierra Club* decision federal courts tend to view the informal rulemaking process more as a political function, and one not to be likened to formal rulemaking and adjudicative processes that prohibit "off the record" contacts. Many federal administrative agencies now have their own standards and maintain some form of a public ex parte file for "off-the-record" comments from interested parties including those from the legislative and executive branch members.

RULEMAKING AT THE STATE LEVEL

Rulemaking by state administrative agencies covers a broad spectrum of human activities. Revenue and tax rules, health and welfare regulations, public schools and higher educational institutions, elections, energy policies, licensure of occupations and professions, control of alcoholic beverages, corrections systems, environmental standards, building codes, transportation, and maintenance of parks and recreation are among the more prominent areas where state agencies develop rules.

Earlier in the chapter we discussed definitions of rules and rulemaking under the Model State Administrative Procedure Act (MSAPA), as revised in 1981. Rulemaking in most states generally follows the principles outlined in the MSAPA as over half the states have an Administrative Procedure

Act (State APA) based, at least in part, on the 1981 revision or its predecessors. Procedures, however, vary somewhat among the states.

In *Detroit Base Coalition for the Human Rights of the Handicapped v. Dept. of Social Services*, **the Michigan Supreme Court determines that procedures established by a state social services agency are inconsistent with agency rules and rule-making provisions of the state administrative procedures act. This case is excerpted at the end of the chapter.**

Model State Administrative Procedure Act

The MSAPA allows an agency or any interested citizen to petition for adoption or repeal of a rule and provides for notice and hearings on proposed rules. Like the federal APA, the MSAPA allows a "good cause" exception from its rulemaking requirements, but it places the burden on the agency to establish good cause. It allows agencies to issue statements that define the meaning of a statute or other provision of law or precedent (interpretive rules) but they must be so labeled.[100]

Generally the MSAPA follows the federal APA requirements for rulemaking, yet it departs from the federal procedures in specific instances. MSAPA requires the notice of rulemaking to set out the text of a proposed rule as well as including the authority for its adoption and a brief explanation of the proposed rule. An agency is prohibited from adopting a rule that is not substantially as proposed.[101] The agency must promptly furnish copies of the proposed rule to any person who has so requested.[102] The MSAPA provides that certain special classes of rules are exempt from the informal (notice-and-comment) form of rulemaking.[103] These include rules concerning agency budgets and internal management, those relating to use of facilities or property owned, operated, or maintained by the state, and rules concerning inmates of correctional facilities.

Not later than 180 days after publication of a proposed rule, or close of the proceedings, MSAPA requires that an agency either adopt the proposed rule or terminate the proceedings.[104] The MSAPA requires filing and publication of rules as adopted and makes provision for agencies to issues declaratory statements as to rules and for courts to issue declaratory judgments as to the validity of rules.

Some Specific Provisions in State Administrative Procedure Acts

State statutes delegate rulemaking authority to agencies. A legion of state court decisions admonish administrative agencies that their rulemaking authority is limited to powers granted by statutes and that they are not to attempt to exercise their powers in such a way as to enlarge or modify an enabling statute. Some state legislatures emphasize this principle by requiring a very specific delegation of authority before an agency engages in rulemaking. Florida law, for example, stipulates:

> A grant of rulemaking authority is necessary but not sufficient to allow an agency to adopt a rule; a specific law to be implemented is also required. An agency may adopt only rules that implement or interpret the specific powers and duties granted by the enabling statute.[105]

State legislatures place great importance on administrative agencies providing fair notice of rulemaking describing the subject of a proposed rule. All states require publication of notices of intention to adopt proposed rules and publication of rules as adopted. Some even require that an agency allow oral argument on proposed rules. North Carolina, for instance, allows an agency to either publish the text of a proposed rule or the subject matter of the proposal, but if the agency chooses not to publish the text of a proposed rule, any party may insist on an oral hearing before the rule becomes effective.[106] Texas requires an agency to mail notice of a proposed rule to each person who has made a timely written request of the agency for advance notice of its rulemaking proceedings. Subject to certain exceptions, the notice becomes effective when published in the *Texas Register*.[107] The *Texas Register* serves a function similar to the *Federal Register.*

After publication of a notice of a proposed rule, persons affected are usually afforded an opportunity to present evidence and arguments, sometimes at a public hearing. If a person has a substantial interest that will be affected by rulemaking proceedings, such person may be able to "draw out" of the proceedings and begin a separate proceeding.[108]

In some states the law requires an agency to submit copies of proposed rules with an explanatory justification to a legislative review committee for review and recommendation. Committees of this type have varying authorities. In several instances state legislatures have enacted legislative veto provisions similar to those we discussed in respect to federal agency rules, but laws allowing legislative vetoes over administrative agency rules have not fared well in the courts. In *Barker v. Manchin,*[109] the West Virginia Supreme Court held that a statute allowing the legislature to veto administrative rules violated the separation of powers principle. In *State ex rel. Stephan v. Kansas House of Reps.,*[110] the Kansas Supreme Court held unconstitutional a statute empowering the legislature to revoke administrative rules by concurrent resolution.

State agencies must deal with many problems that require emergency attention, for instance, childcare, disease prevention, nursing home regulations and so forth. States generally grant some form of exemption from notice requirements when an agency has to issue a rule on an emergency basis. Typically, the Arkansas Administrative Procedures Act specifies:

> If an agency finds that imminent peril to the public health, safety, or welfare requires adoption of a rule upon less than thirty (30) days' notice and states in writing its reasons for that finding, it may proceed without prior notice or hearing, or upon any abbreviated notice and hearing that it may choose, to adopt an emer-

gency rule. The rule may be effective for no longer than one hundred twenty (120) days.[111]

The Arkansas APA further provides that an emergency rule may become effective immediately upon filing if the agency finds it is necessary because of imminent peril to the public health, safety, or welfare.[112]

State laws frequently make provision for an agency to issue a declaratory ruling as to the validity of a rule or as to the applicability to a given state of facts of a statute administered by the agency. Michigan law stipulates:

> On request of an interested person, an agency may issue a declaratory ruling as to the applicability to an actual state of facts of a statute administered by the agency or of a rule or order of the agency. . . . A declaratory ruling is binding on the agency and the person requesting it unless it is altered or set aside by any court. An agency may not retroactively change a declaratory ruling, but nothing in this subsection prevents an agency from prospectively changing a declaratory ruling. A declaratory ruling is subject to judicial review in the same manner as an agency final decision or order in a contested case.[113]

Just as Congress has assisted small businesses in coping with governmental regulation, states often attempt to alleviate the effect of governmental regulations that have a potential economic impact on businesses. Among other forms of relief, states seek to accomplish this by simplifying reporting requirements and establishing less stringent deadlines for compliance by small businesses. The California legislature has been in the forefront in the effort to assist businesses. State law provides that early in the process of proposals to adopt, amend, or repeal an administrative rule, an agency must address several economic considerations. Among other factors, the agency must assess whether its action will create or eliminate jobs and how it will affect businesses in competing with businesses in other states.[114]

State laws often include provisions for granting waivers and variances where the strict application of an administrative regulation would likely cause undue hardship. In most states these provisions are found in statutes governing particular agencies. For example, Minnesota law specifies the criteria for granting hospitals variances or waivers.[115] Indiana provides procedures for granting variances or waivers of rules governing child-care institutions, foster family homes, and group homes.[116]

The Rulemaking Record

States require agencies to prepare rulemaking records with copies of notices, petitions, requests, responses, submissions, and comments concerning rules along with analyses of regulatory costs and so forth prepared for the proceedings on which a regulation is based. If an agency conducts an evidentiary hearing, the record must include a transcript of those proceedings.

Section 3-112 of the 1981 MSAPA is specific in calling for an agency to maintain an official rulemaking record for each rule it proposes or adopts. It recommends a comprehensive rulemaking record that should include copies of the rule and petitions for exceptions, any objections filed by an administrative rules review committee and any executive order filed with respect to the rule. It also requires that the record include copies of all publications with respect to a rule, all docket entries, petitions, requests, submissions, comments, and written materials, transcripts of oral presentations, regulatory analyses, and explanatory statements that have been filed with the secretary of state or other official office where rules are filed.

State Administrative Publications

Most states have an administrative publication similar in scope to the *Federal Register* where notices of proposed rules and the text of final rules are published. In Florida this publication is known as *Florida Administrative Weekly*. Box 6.5 displays an excerpt from the *Florida Administrative Weekly* of April 26, 2002, illustrating the format of a proposed rule.

In addition to publications that include proposed and final rules, most states now periodically codify all rules of a general and permanent nature. For example, there is the *New Jersey Administrative Code*, the *Missouri Administrative Code* and so forth. These codes usually have a table of contents organized by departments of state government and then by chapters covering the functions of those departments. Most also have a subject index and reference to relevant state statutes as well. This type of publication is a valuable tool for researching rules covering a wide range of activities.

In Florida this publication is supervised by the Secretary of State and is known as the *Florida Administrative Code*. A glance through the general subject index of the *Florida Administrative Code* reveals rules concerning such matters as abortion clinics, banks, cemeteries, drivers licenses, environmental programs, fishing, gas services, hospital licensing, juvenile boot camps, lotteries, motor vehicles, nursing homes, optometry, parole regulations, revenue rules, sexual harassment, telephones, unemployment compensation, veterans affairs, weights and measures, youthful offenders, and zoning. We mention these few of the hundreds of subjects regulated by state rules to give the reader an idea of the value of a state code of regulations to one who is researching administrative law.

In *State v. Peters,* a Missouri appellate court invalidates a state health department rule prescribing a method of determining blood alcohol from a blood sample because the department failed to comply with statutory requirements of publication and filing of the rule. This case is excerpted at the end of the chapter.

Box 6.6 gives an example of a state agency requesting exemption from rulemaking in order to reduce its vulnerability to terrorism.

BOX 6.5 Florida Department of Corrections
Rule No. 33-108.101

33-108.101. Inmate Substance Abuse Testing.
The Office of the Inspector General shall be responsible for the development and implementation of the department's substance abuse testing program.

(1) Definitions.
(a) Random Selection—A computerized random selection model utilized to obtain a sample of inmates to be tested for drugs or alcohol.

(b) Tester—a correctional officer who has been trained and certified as competent by the manufacturer of the onsite testing device or certified training personnel, affiliated with the department, on the proper procedures for collecting urine specimens, including the completion and maintenance of the Chain of Custody Form, the handling and disposing of urine specimens, and the administration and interpretation of the on-site testing device. All testing personnel must be approved by the Office of the Inspector General. The Chain of Custody Form is incorporated by reference in paragraph (3)(g) of this rule.

(c) Random List—the randomly selected sample of inmates to be tested for drugs or alcohol.

(d) Chain of Custody Form—the form used to document the identity and integrity of an inmate's specimen from time of collection until the specimen is prepared for shipment to a designated outside laboratory for confirmation testing. This form will be provided by the laboratory conducting confirmation tests on specimens that had a positive result on the on-site testing device.

(e) Test refusal—failure on the part of an inmate to fully comply with the department's substance abuse testing procedures, which includes failing to provide a valid urine specimen, attempting to alter his or her urine specimen with adulterants, as established by an on-site specimen validity testing device, and using substitute urine in makeshift devices or objects. Any inmate who refuses to comply with the testing process or fails to provide a valid specimen, within the specified time frames as stipulated in Section (3)(b)8. and (3)(b)10., shall be given a disciplinary report in accordance with Rules 33-601.301—.314, F.A.C.

(f) Dry cell—refers to a secure cell without a water supply or one in which the water supply has been interrupted.

(2) The Department of Corrections conducts the following types of inmate substance abuse testing:
(a) For-Cause or Reasonable Suspicion Testing.
1. Inmates suspected of involvement with drugs or alcohol shall be subject to for-cause testing upon order of the warden or duty warden of the institution, or the correctional officer chief of the facility, or their designees, or the Office of the Inspector General. An inmate should only be tested for a maximum of four drugs on a for-cause basis, unless extenuating circumstances exist. For-cause tests will only be conducted on inmates who meet the criteria outlined in 2.a. through c. below.
2. For-cause drug testing (also referred to as reasonable suspicion drug testing) means drug testing based on a belief that an inmate is using or has used drugs or alcohol based on specific facts and reasonable inferences drawn from those facts in light of experience. Such facts and inferences shall be based upon:
    a. Observable phenomena such as direct observation of drug or alcohol use or of the physical symptoms or manifestations of being under the influence of drugs or alcohol (such as slurred or incoherent speech, erratic or violent behavior, uneven gait, or other behaviors or physical symptoms unusual for the inmate based on the staff member's knowledge of the inmate).
    b. Evidence that the inmate has tampered with or attempted to tamper with a urine specimen.
    c. Evidence or intelligence reports indicating that an inmate has used, possessed, sold, solicited or transferred drugs or alcohol.
3. When for-cause testing is ordered, an incident report shall be prepared including:
    a. Dates and times of reported drug-related events;
    b. Rationale leading to the request for testing.

(Continued)

BOX 6.5   Florida Department of Corrections (Continued)

4. The senior correctional officer on duty shall be notified that the staff member has identified a suspicious inmate who meets the for-cause drug testing criteria. The highest ranking correctional officer shall ensure that an incident report is prepared. The incident report shall contain all pertinent information concerning the inmate which prompted the request for testing, to include any supporting evidence.

5. Upon approval of the warden, duty warden, correctional officer chief, or their designees, or the Office of the Inspector General, collection and testing procedures shall be conducted immediately pursuant to this rule.

6. A copy of the Incident Report, Form DC6-210, shall be attached to the facility's copy of the Chain of Custody Form for positive specimens sent to the laboratory for confirmation testing. Form DC6-210 is incorporated in Rule 33-602.210, F.A.C. The Chain of Custody Form is incorporated by reference in paragraph (3)(g) of this rule.

(b) Random Substance Abuse Testing. All correctional facilities shall receive on a weekly basis a list of the names and DC numbers of inmates generated through random selection for substance abuse testing. The list will be electronically transmitted from the Offender Base Information System to the secure printer of the warden of each major institution or the correctional officer chief of the correctional facility. Any facility that does not have a secure printer will have their respective list printed to a secure printer at another facility as designated by the warden of the institution or correctional officer chief of the facility. The list is considered confidential and shall not be disseminated to inmates or non-essential staff members prior to testing. Each time an inmate's name appears on the random list, he or she shall be tested regardless of whether or not he or she has been previously tested.

(c) Substance Abuse Program Testing. Inmates participating in substance abuse programs will be subject to substance abuse testing as a condition of the program.

(3) Procedures.

(a) Chain of Custody.

1. At a minimum, the Chain of Custody Form must include inmate and tester identification, initialed by both the inmate and the tester, date and time of collection, type of test (i.e., random, for-cause or substance abuse program participation), and identification of all individuals who had custody of the specimen from the time of collection until the specimen was prepared for shipment to the laboratory. Once the outside laboratory receives the specimen, it will become the laboratory's responsibility to maintain a chain of custody throughout the testing process.

2. The Chain of Custody Form allows for any comments by the tester regarding any unusual observations. Any failure by the inmate to cooperate with the collection process, and the unusual nature (e.g., discolored urine or urine containing foreign objects) of any specimen provided shall be noted.

3. The tester shall ensure that all collected urine specimens, being sent to a designated outside laboratory for confirmation testing, are properly labeled and sealed with a security label as provided on the Chain of Custody Form. The tester shall also ensure that the Chain of Custody Form for all collected urine specimens is completed in accordance with procedures.

4. If an inmate is unable or unwilling to enter his or her initials on the Chain of Custody Form, the tester will make a notation in the comment section of the Chain of Custody Form and leave the space blank. The tester will not under any circumstances sign the Chain of Custody Form for an inmate.

(b) Specimen Collection Procedures.

1. The tester shall ensure that all urine specimens are collected in accordance with procedures. All collections shall be performed under direct observation, where the tester directly observes the voiding of urine into the specimen cup. Direct observation may also be accomplished through use of mirrors strategically mounted in the collection rest room.

BOX 6.5 Florida Department of Corrections (Continued)

2. Under no circumstances is direct observation by a tester of the opposite sex from the inmate allowed.

3. The tester shall ensure that there is positive inmate identification prior to collecting the inmate's urine specimen. Sight, name, DC number, and examination of picture identification card shall provide positive identification of the inmate selected for drug testing.

4. The tester shall search the inmate to ensure that the inmate is not concealing any substances or materials that could be used to alter or substitute his or her urine specimen. If any such substances or materials are found, the inmate will be charged with refusing to submit to a substance abuse test.

5. If an inmate attempts to alter his or her urine specimen during the collection process through the use of adulterants or substitute urine, the inmate will be charged with refusing to submit to substance abuse testing.

6. The tester shall give each inmate a closed specimen cup with an identification label containing the inmate's name and DC number prior to collecting the inmate's urine specimen. The tester shall ensure that the inmate acknowledges his or her correct identity information on the label of the specimen cup.

7. The inmate is expected to provide a minimum of 30 ml of urine. If the inmate provides less than this amount, the tester shall again attempt to collect an adequate specimen. If the inmate cannot immediately submit another urine specimen, then the procedure outlined in 8. below for a claimed inability to provide a urine specimen shall apply.

8. An inmate who has not provided an adulterated urine specimen and who indicates a claimed inability to provide an adequate urine specimen shall be detained in the presence of the tester or other designated person for a period not to exceed 1 hour to provide an adequate specimen. During that time, the inmate shall be allowed to consume one cup (8 oz.) of water or other beverage every 1/2 hour, not to exceed a total of 2 cups during this time period and an Acknowledgement of Beverage Form,

DC1-823, shall be completed. Form DC1-823, Acknowledgement of Beverage Form, is incorporated by reference in paragraph (3)(g) of this rule. If after the 1-hour period an inmate still fails to submit a valid adequate urine specimen, the inmate shall be considered to have refused to provide a urine specimen and a disciplinary report shall be prepared in accordance with Rules 33-601.301—.314, F.A.C. If an inmate claims an inability to urinate due to a medical condition, procedures set forth in (3)(c) shall apply.

9. After the inmate has voided a urine specimen into the cup, the tester will visually inspect the urine specimen to make sure that the specimen appears to be valid and unadulterated. If the tester suspects that the specimen has been adulterated based upon observation, experience, or prior training, the tester will utilize the on-site specimen validity-testing device in front of the inmate following the manufacturer's testing protocols. If a positive result is received on the on-site specimen validity testing device indicating that the urine specimen was adulterated, the adulterated specimen will not be accepted as a valid specimen and will be discarded. The inmate will be required to submit a valid and unadulterated specimen. If the inmate cannot submit a valid and unadulterated specimen, then the procedure outlined below in subparagraph (3)(b)10 shall apply.

10. Inmates who have adulterated their urine specimen by ingesting substances, as established by the on-site testing device, shall be detained in the presence of the tester or placed in a "dry cell" for a period not to exceed two (2) hours. During that time, the inmate shall not be allowed to consume any water or other beverage. If, after the two-hour period, an inmate still fails to submit an unadulterated valid urine specimen, the inmate shall be considered to have refused to provide a urine specimen and a disciplinary report shall be prepared in accordance with Rules 33-601.301—.314, F.A.C.

(Continued)

BOX 6.5   Florida Department of Corrections (Continued)

11. Once the tester has determined that the urine specimen is valid and unadulterated, the tester shall direct the inmate where to place the urine specimen so that the on-site test can be conducted. The specimen must be in view of the inmate throughout the entire testing process.

12. If a urine specimen contains blood or appears to contain blood, the inmate who produced the specimen shall be referred immediately to the medical department for evaluation. If no valid reason exists for having blood in the specimen, the inmate will be required to provide another urine specimen. If the inmate cannot submit a urine specimen, then the procedure outlined above for a claimed inability to provide a urine specimen shall apply.

(c) Upon notification from an inmate that he is unable to urinate due to a medical condition, the officer shall verify with medical staff that the inmate possesses a specific medical condition or is taking medication which inhibits the inmate from urinating within the designated time frame. Upon receiving such verification, the inmate shall be given the opportunity to provide a urine specimen under the following conditions:

1. The inmate shall be informed that he or she will be placed in a dry cell until he or she can provide a valid urine specimen. The inmate shall be issued a hospital or other type privacy gown during the time that he or she is housed in the dry cell.

2. The inmate shall remove the contents of his or her pockets, and his or her shirt, shoes, pants and hat. The inmate shall be thoroughly searched prior to entering the dry cell to prevent him or her from using any adulterants such as bleach or cleanser to alter his or her urine specimen.

3. The tester shall give the inmate a closed specimen cup with an identification label containing the inmate's name and DC number. The testing officer shall ensure that the inmate acknowledges his or her correct identity information on the label of the specimen cup.

4. The inmate shall be allowed to consume one cup (8 oz.) of water or other beverage every 1/2 hour, not to exceed a total of two cups during the time spent in the dry cell and an Acknowledgement of Beverage Form, DC1-823, shall be completed.

5. A physical check shall be made on the inmate once every 30 minutes to see if he or she has provided a valid urine specimen.

6. Upon receipt of the urine specimen the tester shall visually inspect the urine specimen to ensure it appears valid and unadulterated and the procedures outlined in (3)(d)1. for the testing of urine specimens shall be followed.

(d) Testing of urine specimens.

1. Only certified testing personnel are authorized to utilize the on-site testing equipment. For every on-site test conducted, regardless of purpose, the Inmate Scannable Drug Testing Control Card shall be filled out. The Inmate Scannable Drug Testing Control Card, DC1-826 is incorporated in paragraph (3)(g) of this rule.

2. Certified testers shall follow collection procedures in paragraph (3)(b).

3. All on-site testing procedures shall be conducted in the presence of the inmate in accordance with the manufacturer's protocols.

4. After the tester has taken a sample of urine from the specimen cup for the on-site testing device, the tester shall close the cup tightly.

5. Negative test results. The tester shall inform the inmate of the negative test results of the on-site testing device. The tester shall record all negative test results on the Inmate Scannable Drug Testing Control Card and the OBIS printout. The tester will then dispose of the remaining specimen, specimen cup and testing device. All forms shall be retained in accordance with state law and rules governing the retention of records.

6. Positive test results. The tester shall inform the inmate of the positive results of the on-site testing device. The inmate will then be given the opportunity to sign an Affidavit for Admission of Drug Use, DC1-824. Form DC1- 824, Affidavit for Admission of Drug Use, is incorporated by reference in paragraph (3)(g) of this rule.

BOX 6.5 Florida Department of Corrections (Continued)

a. If the inmate chooses to sign the Affidavit for Admission of Drug Use, DC1-824, the testing officer shall complete the affidavit form and have the inmate swear to its content, with the officer witnessing the inmate's signature. The inmate will be placed into administrative confinement and a disciplinary report written. The signed Affidavit for Admission of Drug Use, DC1-824, will be attached to the disciplinary report to be used as evidence in the disciplinary report hearing.

b. The testing officer will complete the Inmate Scannable Drug Testing Control Card indicating the positive results of the on-site testing device.

c. If the inmate does not sign the Affidavit for Admission of Drug Use, DC1-824, the following steps shall be taken:

   i. Once the urine specimen has been securely closed by the tester, the tester shall attach a security seal from the Chain of Custody Form across the lid of the sample cup under the inmate's observation.

   ii. The tester shall instruct the inmate to place his or her initials on the Chain of Custody Form verifying that the urine specimen was collected and sealed under the inmate's observation and that the specimen cup identification is correct.

   iii. The tester shall then prepare the urine specimen for shipment, by a commercial carrier, to the designated outside laboratory for confirmation testing.

   iv. Inmates with positive test results on the on-site testing device shall immediately be placed in administrative confinement pending investigation until results of the confirmation test are received.

7. Once received from the outside laboratory, the confirmation testing results will be entered onto the respective Inmate Scannable Drug Testing Control Card. If the confirmation testing results are positive, a copy of the results will be attached to the disciplinary report for use as evidence during the disciplinary hearing.

(e) Other on-site testing device procedures.

   1. Due to product limitations, it may become necessary to utilize other noninvasive on-site testing devices for alcohol testing. In such instances, the certified tester will utilize the on-site testing device in the presence of the inmate following the manufacturer's testing protocols. If the initial result of the on-site testing device is positive, and the inmate declines to sign the Affidavit for Admission of Drug Use Form, DC1-824, then a urine specimen will be obtained from the inmate and sent to a designated outside laboratory for confirmation testing, in accordance with the procedures outlined in paragraph (3)(b), specimen collection procedures, and paragraph (3)(d), testing of urine specimens.

   2. All correctional facilities shall maintain a record of all reasonable suspicion substance abuse tests conducted. This record shall be maintained by the correctional officer chief or his designee. Form DC1-827, Reasonable Suspicion Testing Tracking Form, shall be utilized for this purpose. Form DC1-827, Reasonable Suspicion Testing Tracking Form, is incorporated by reference in paragraph (3)(g) of this rule.

(f) Record keeping. Each facility shall keep all records pertaining to the testing program. This includes the drug testing list and results, Chain of Custody forms, laboratory confirmation reports, and inventory control logs. All records shall be kept in accordance with state law and rules regarding retention of records.

(g) Forms. The following forms referenced in this rule are hereby incorporated by reference. Copies of these forms, unless otherwise indicated, may be obtained from the Forms Control Administrator, Office of the General Counsel, 2601 Blair Stone Road, Tallahassee, Florida 32399-2500.

   1. Form DC1-823, Acknowledgement of Beverage, effective date February 5, 2001.

   2. Form DC1-824, Affidavit for Admission of Drug Use, effective date February 5, 2001.

(Continued)

BOX 6.5 Florida Department of Corrections (Continued)

3. Chain of Custody, effective date February 5, 2001, is a vendor form that may be obtained directly from the vendor or through the Office of the Inspector General, 2601 Blair Stone Road, Tallahassee, Florida 32399-2500.
4. Form DC1-826, Inmate Scannable Drug Testing Control Card, effective date February 5,

2001, may be obtained directly from the vendor or through the Office of the Inspector General, 2601 Blair Stone Road, Tallahassee, Florida 32399-2500.
5. Form DC1-827, Reasonable Suspicion Testing Tracking Form, effective date February 5. 2001.

SOURCE: 28 Florida Administrative Weekly, No. 17, April 26, 2002

BOX 6.6 Case in Point

The Threat of Terrorism as a Basis for Exempting an Agency from Rulemaking
Jewish Community Action v. Commissioner of Public Safety
Minnesota Court of Appeals
657 N.W.2d 604 (Minn. App. 2003)

In the wake of the terrorist attacks of September 11, 2001, the Minnesota Department of Public Safety (DPS) adopted new rules governing proof of identity for the issuance of drivers' licenses. The new rules provided that an applicant who could not prove identity through a previously issued Minnesota license must present certain primary and secondary documents to prove identification. The DPS characterized licenses as "gateway documents," which enable holders to establish ostensibly accurate and legitimate identities. Given the urgency of dealing with the threat of terrorism, the DPS determined that public rulemaking would have been contrary to the public interest. The Chief Administrative Law Judge determined use of the good cause exemption was proper.

In reviewing the matter, the Court of Appeals recognized the DPS had demonstrated a serious and immediate threat from domestic terrorism. But the court held the DPS had not established that the normal rulemaking process was unnecessary, impracticable or contrary to the public interest as required by the rulemaking statute to justify exempt rulemaking. The court explained that the good cause exception is an exceptional procedure reserved for emergencies where the agency finds the usual requirements "unnecessary, impracticable, or contrary to public interest" and the rule addresses "a serious and immediate threat to the public health, safety, or welfare."

The court found that the record before it was more conclusory than factual on the 'contrary-to-public-interest standard.' Here the DPS simply asserted that delays in implementing the rules would be inimical to the public safety; but failed to quantify the delay that would occur if formal rulemaking was undertaken or how the exempt rulemaking procedure would better serve the public interest. Because the DPS failed to carry such burden, the court declared the rules to be invalid as having been improperly adopted.

CONCLUSION

Rulemaking is one of the most essential functions of administrative agencies. Agencies make rules in the administration of the programs they manage. They also make rules to regulate areas of economic and social life over which legislatures have given them jurisdiction. Rulemaking procedures range from the informal, notice-and-comment approach to the highly formal, adjudicatory approach. The style of rulemaking procedures used by an agency depends on the statutory framework under which the agency must operate. Section 553 of the Administrative Procedure Act simply provides a minimal standard for informal rulemaking by federal agencies. Informal rule-making is defined by two principal factors: 1) the public is notified that an agency is considering a new rule; and 2) members of the public are given a meaningful opportunity to provide input into the agency's decision. Other statutes require specific agencies or specific types of agency decisions to follow the formal, adjudicatory approach. When formal rulemaking is required, an agency must conduct a trial-type hearing in which parties are afforded the opportunity to testify, present witnesses and documentary evidence, cross-examine opposing witnesses, and present arguments. The situation is much the same at the state level, where state counterparts to the Administrative Procedure Act are in effect. Generally, state agencies follow the informal approach to rule-making except where they are mandated by law to follow more elaborate procedures.

Courts are hesitant to require agencies to adopt rulemaking procedures beyond those required by statutes. In general, courts have taken the view that, because agency rulemaking is quasi-legislative in character, the constitutional concept of procedural due process does not apply. Courts do review the substance of agency rules, however, typically using the rational basis test. Therefore, it is incumbent upon agencies to create a record of rulemaking process to allow for judicial review.

In addition to judicial review, agency rule-making is subject to oversight and control by chief executives and by legislatures. Both chief executives and legislatures can use the budgetary process to reward or punish agencies. Legislative committees receive briefings and hold hearings as means of maintaining oversight of agencies. If necessary, legislatures can amend legislation affecting the structure, procedures, and powers of agencies. Thus, while agency rulemaking is a significant exercise of governmental authority, it is subject to most of the checks and balances that characterize the constitutional system generally.

KEY TERMS

adjudication

administrative law judge (ALJ)

Administrative Procedure Act (APA)

Code of Federal Regulations

direct final rulemaking

electronic rulemaking

ex parte contacts

executive orders

executive oversight

exemptions from rulemaking procedures

Federal Register

final rule

formal rulemaking

General Accounting Office (GAO)

general statements of policy

good cause exemption

hybrid rulemaking

informal (notice-and-comment) rulemaking

interim rule

interpretive rules

legislative rules

legislative veto

Model State Administrative Procedure Act

negotiated rulemaking

notice of proposed rule making (NPRM)

Office of Management and Budget (OMB)

oversight briefings

oversight hearings

preclearance of proposed rules

procedural due process

procedural rules

regulatory flexibility analysis

rulemaking

rulemaking record

rules

substantive rules

trial-type hearing

ultra vires

variance

waiver

QUESTIONS FOR THOUGHT
AND DISCUSSION

1. What essential characteristics distinguish rule-making from adjudication under the APA?

2. Describe the difference between the procedural requirements in formal and informal rulemaking under the APA.

3. What does it mean to say that agency rulemaking is "quasi-legislative" in character? What implications does this characterization have for judicial review?

4. What advantages do you see in negotiated rulemaking a) from the agency's standpoint, and b) from the standpoint of an industry being subjected to a new rule?

5. What constitutional and political values are advanced by the APA requirements for informal rulemaking?

6. What is the purpose of "regulatory flexibility analysis" with respect to agency rulemaking?

7. How has Congress required federal agencies to protect the interests of small businesses in rulemaking?

8. Explain the role of waivers and variances in rulemaking by federal agencies.

9. In what ways does Congress retain control over rulemaking by federal agencies?

10. On what basis did the United States Supreme Court invalidate the legislative veto developed by Congress to control agency decision making?

11. What is the significance of the Office of Management and Budget with respect to federal agency rulemaking?

12. What is the rationale for the Administrative Procedure Act's prohibition against ex parte between agency members and interested parties in formal rulemaking while not mandating such a prohibition in informal (notice-and-comment) rulemaking?

13. What is the effect of a declaratory ruling by an agency under a state APA?

14. What materials generally comprise the record in state administrative rulemaking?

15. On what basis is a state court most likely to invalidate a new rule issued by an independent agency of that state?

EDITED CASE   Vermont Yankee Nuclear Power Corp. v.
Natural Resources Defense Council
United States Supreme Court, 435 U.S. 519 (1978)

[In a proceeding growing out of the licensing of two nuclear power plants, the Atomic Energy Commission (AEC) (predecessor to the Nuclear Regulatory Commission), promulgated a "spent fuel cycle rule." Although AEC was authorized to follow informal rulemaking procedures, it received oral comments at a hearing. But AEC did not allow discovery proceedings or cross-examination of the witnesses who appeared at the hearing. On review, the U.S. Court of Appeals for the D.C. Circuit overturned the rule, holding that the procedures followed by AEC were insufficient because they did not allow discovery of evidence or cross-examination of key witnesses. The U.S. Supreme Court granted review.]

Justice Rehnquist delivered the Opinion of the Court.

In 1946, Congress enacted the Administrative Procedure Act, which . . . was not only "a new and comprehensive regulation of procedures in many agencies," . . . but was also a legislative enactment

---

EDITED CASE Vermont Yankee Nuclear Power Corp. v. Natural Resources Defense Council (Continued)

---

which settled "long continued and hard-fought contentions, and enacts a formula upon which opposing social and political forces have come to rest." . . . Section 553 of the Act, dealing with rulemaking, requires that ". . . notice of proposed rulemaking shall be published in the *Federal Register*" . . . describes the contents of that notice, and goes on to require in subsection (c) that after the notice the agency "shall give interested persons an opportunity to participate in the rulemaking through submission of written data, views, or arguments with or without opportunity for oral presentation." After consideration of the relevant matter presented the agency shall incorporate in the rules adopted a general statement of their basis and purpose." 5 U.S.C.A. § 553. . . .

Interpreting this provision of the Act . . . we [have] held that generally speaking this section of the Act established the maximum procedural requirements which Congress was willing to have the courts impose upon agencies in conducting rulemaking procedures. Agencies are free to grant additional procedural rights in the exercise of their discretion, but reviewing courts are generally not free to impose them if the agencies have not chosen to grant them. This is not to say necessarily that there are no circumstances which would ever justify a court in overturning agency action because of a failure to employ procedures beyond those required by the statute. But such circumstances, if they exist, are extremely rare. . . .

It is in the light of this background of statutory and decisional law that we granted certiorari to review two judgments of the Court of Appeals for the District of Columbia Circuit because of our concern that they had seriously misread or misapplied this statutory and decisional law cautioning reviewing courts against engrafting their own notions of proper procedures upon agencies entrusted with substantive functions of Congress. . . .

. . . [B]efore determining whether the Court of Appeals reached a permissible result, we must determine exactly what result it did reach, and in this case that is no mean feat. Vermont Yankee argues that the court invalidated the rule because of the inadequacy of the procedures employed in the proceedings. Respondent NRDC, on the other hand, labeling

petitioner's view of the decision a "straw man," argues to this Court that the court merely held that the record was inadequate to enable the reviewing court to determine whether the agency had fulfilled its statutory obligation. . . .

After a thorough examination of the opinion itself, we conclude that while the matter is not entirely free from doubt, the majority of the Court of Appeals struck down the rule because of the perceived inadequacies of the procedures employed in the rulemaking proceedings. The court first determined the intervenors' primary argument to be "that the decision to preclude 'discovery or cross-examination' denied them a meaningful opportunity to participate in the proceedings as guaranteed by due process." . . . The court also refrained from actually ordering the agency to follow any specific procedures, but there is little doubt in our minds that the ineluctable mandate of the court's decision is that the procedures afforded during the hearings were inadequate. This conclusion is particularly buttressed by the fact that after the court examined the record, . . . and declared it insufficient, the court proceeded to discuss at some length the necessity for further procedural devices or a more "sensitive" application of those devices employed during the proceedings. . . .

In prior opinions we have intimated that even in a rulemaking proceeding when an agency is making a "quasi-judicial" determination by which a very small number of persons are "exceptionally affected". . . , in some circumstances additional procedures may be required in order to afford the aggrieved individuals due process. . . . It might also be true, although we do not think the issue is presented in this case and accordingly do not decide it, that a totally unjustified departure from well settled agency procedures of long standing might require judicial correction.

But this much is absolutely clear. Absent constitutional constraints or extremely compelling circumstances, "the administrative agencies should be free to fashion their own rules of procedure and to pursue methods of inquiry capable of permitting them to discharge their multitudinous duties." . . .

(Continued)

EDITED CASE   Vermont Yankee Nuclear Power Corp. v.
Natural Resources Defense Council (Continued)

. . . NRDC argues that Sec. 553 of the Administrative Procedure Act merely establishes lower procedural bounds and that a court may routinely require more than the minimum when an agency's proposed rule addresses complex or technical factual issues or "issues of great public import." . . . We have, however, previously shown that our decisions reject this view.

We also think the legislative history, even the part which it cites, does not bear out its contention. . . . Congress intended that the discretion of the agencies and not that of the courts be exercised in determining when extra procedural devices should be employed.

There are compelling reasons for construing Sec. 553 in this manner. In the first place, if courts continually review agency proceedings to determine whether the agency employed procedures which were, in the court's opinion, perfectly tailored to reach what the court perceives to be the "best" or "correct" result, judicial review would be totally unpredictable. And the agencies, operating under this vague injunction to employ the "best" procedures and facing the threat of reversal if they did not, would undoubtedly adopt full adjudicatory procedures in every instance. Not only would this totally disrupt the statutory scheme, through which Congress enacted "a formula upon which opposing social and political forces have come to rest," . . . but all the inherent advantages of informal rulemaking would be totally lost.

Secondly, it is obvious that the court in this case reviewed the agency's choice of procedures on the basis of the record actually produced at the hearing, and not on the basis of the information available to the agency when it made the decision to structure the proceedings in a certain way. This sort of Monday morning quarterbacking not only encourages but almost compels the agency to conduct all rulemaking proceedings with the full panoply of procedural devices normally associated only with adjudicatory hearings.

Finally, and perhaps more importantly, this sort of review fundamentally misconceives the nature of the standard for judicial review of an agency rule. The court below uncritically assumed that additional procedures will automatically result in a more adequate record because it will give interested parties more of an opportunity to participate and contribute to the proceedings. But informal rulemaking need not be based solely on the transcript of a hearing held before an agency. Indeed, the agency need not even hold a formal hearing. . . . Thus, the adequacy of the "record" in this type of proceeding is not correlated directly to the type of procedural devices employed, but rather turns on whether the agency has followed the statutory mandate of the Administrative Procedure Act or other relevant statutes. If the agency is compelled to support the rule which it ultimately adopts with the type of record produced only after a full adjudicatory hearing, it simply will have no choice but to conduct a full adjudicatory hearing prior to promulgating every rule. In sum, this sort of unwarranted judicial examination of perceived procedural shortcomings of a rulemaking proceeding can do nothing but seriously interfere with that process prescribed by Congress. . . .

Justices Blackmun and *Powell* took no part in . . . [this decision].

EDITED CASE   Detroit Base Coalition for the Human Rights
of the Handicapped v. Department of Social Services
Supreme Court of Michigan, 431 Mich. 172, 428 N.W.2d 335 (Mich. 1988)

[In this case the Michigan Supreme Court determines that procedures established by a state social services agency are inconsistent with agency rules and rule-making provisions of the state administrative procedures act.]

Justice Boyle delivered the opinion of the court.
. . . The DSS [Department of Social Services] is required to conduct administrative hearings for individuals who contest the denial or reduction of public assistance. . . . Michigan law also requires

---

EDITED CASE   Detroit Base Coalition for the Human Rights
of the Handicapped v. Department of Social Services (Continued)

---

the DSS to promulgate rules which must provide adequate procedures by which to conduct the hearings. M.C.L. S 400.9(1); M.S.A. S 16.409(1):

> "[T]he director shall promulgate rules for the conduct of hearings within the state department. The rules shall provide adequate procedure for a fair hearing of appeals and complaints, when requested in writing by an applicant for or recipient of assistance or service, financed in whole or in part by federal funds." . . .

Since the adoption of a rule by an agency has the force and effect of law and may have serious consequences of law for many people, the Legislature has proscribed an elaborate procedure for rule promulgation. As set forth in the APA, . . . that process requires public hearings, public participation, notice, approval by the joint committee on administrative rules, and preparation of statements, with intervals between each process.

This action was taken because, in recent years, legislative bodies have delegated to administrative agencies increasing authority to make public policy and, consequently, have recognized a need to "ensure that none of the essential functions of the legislative process are lost in the course of the performance by agencies of many law-making functions once performed by our legislatures." . . . Thus, the question whether the policy may be adopted without compliance with the APA is more than a question of notice and hearing requirements. It is a question of the allocation of decision-making authority.

. . . Two rules are applicable here. 1979 AC, R 400.907 provides that hearings be held at "a reasonable time, date, and place which normally shall be in the county where a claimant resides." Second, 1979 AC, R 400.912 provides that a party to a DSS hearing is guaranteed six specific rights for prehearing and hearing procedures.

Prior to 1980, administrative hearings for clients whose benefits had been denied, reduced, or terminated were conducted before a hearing officer at the DSS office of a client's county of residence. Between 1980 and 1984, an applicant for or recipient of benefits had the option of appearing in-person at a hearing at a local DSS office or permitting a hearing referee to hear the case by telephone. In an in-person hearing, the hearing

referee traveled to the local office and had an opportunity to view all the witnesses and evidence. In a telephone hearing, the claimant, any witnesses, and the local DSS worker were in the local office, and the hearing referee was in either the department's Lansing or Detroit office. The hearing was conducted by speakerphones in each office.

In 1984, the DSS issued the policy bulletin which presents the issue in this case, Program Policy Bulletin No. 84-16, to provide for a telephone hearing using the same procedure in effect since 1980 or for a modified face- to-face hearing on written request. . . . Under the "modified in-person hearing" a claimant could travel to one of four hearing sites (Detroit, Escanaba, Grayling, or Lansing) and be present in the same room with the hearing referee, and the department representative would remain in the local office and participate by speakerphone. The case file would remain in the local office. The policy provides that, upon request, the department could schedule an in-person hearing in the county where the client lives if the client has an impairment which is in issue or which makes travel to one of the four sites impossible or impractical. . . .

The plaintiffs maintain that Program Policy Bulletin No. 84-16 is inconsistent with and alters the existing rules. Specifically, plaintiffs contend that the policy conflicts with Rule 400.907 which states that hearings shall be conducted at "a reasonable time, date, and place which normally shall be in the county where a claimant resides." (Emphasis added.) The plaintiffs submit that Rule 400.907 provides public assistance claimants who request a hearing with the right to have their appeal heard and conducted in the county where the claimant resides, and that the policy bulletin provides only for telephone hearings conducted outside the referee's presence or for regional hearings in the presence of the hearing referee, but without the presence of the department representative. . . .

The defendants reply that when the hearing is conducted by telephone, it actually takes place at both the place where the claimant is present and the place where the hearing referee is present. The defendants thus contend that the hearing contemplated by the policy bulletin is consistent with Rule 400.907 because it is conducted in the county where the plaintiff resides. . . .

(Continued)

EDITED CASE   Detroit Base Coalition for the Human Rights
of the Handicapped v. Department of Social Services (Continued)

For purposes of Rule 400.907, we reject defendants' argument that the location of the telephone hearing is in two places simultaneously and hold that the hearing is considered and conducted at the place where the hearing referee is present. Therefore, telephone hearings or the modified face-to-face hearings which are the options available to claimants under the 1984 policy revision do not take place "in the county" in which the claimant resides.

A policy mandating telephone hearing procedures would mean that as a rule the hearings will not take place in the county in which a claimant resides, and therefore does not meet the statutory requirement of 1979 AC, R 400.907 that the hearing be held at "a reasonable time, date, and place which normally shall be in the county where a claimant resides." Contrary to defendants' characterization, the policy mandating telephone hearings or modified in-person hearings represents a modification of the manner in which fair hearings are conducted and thus is inconsistent with the existing rules. . . .

It is undisputed that the policy bulletin at issue here was not issued pursuant to the requirements for promulgation of an agency rule. A rule that does not comply with the procedural requirements of the APA is invalid under Michigan law. . . .

The Legislature has defined "rule" broadly so as to defeat the inclination of "agencies to label as 'bulletins,' 'announcements,' 'guides,' 'interpretive bulletins,' . . . which, in legal operation and effect, really amount to rules. . . ."

"'Rule' means an agency regulation, statement, standard, policy, ruling or instruction of general applicability, which implements or applies law enforced or administered by the agency, or which prescribes the organization, procedure or practice of the agency, including the amendment, suspension or rescission thereof. . . ."

The second portion of the definition of "rule" is a series of specific exclusions from the broader concept. The classes of rules which are exempt from the rule-making requirements represent an effort to strike a fair balance between the need for adequate procedures to govern the proposal, adoption, and effectiveness of rules on the one hand, and the conflicting need for workable, efficient, economical, and effective government on the other. . . .

We are unable to accept the Court of Appeals conclusion that the telephone hearing procedure is excepted from the APA. . . .

"'Rule' means . . . but does not include the following:

. . .

"(h) A form with instructions, an interpretive statement, a guideline, an informational pamphlet or other material which in itself does not have the force and effect of law but is merely explanatory."

This exception has been narrowly construed and requires that the interpretive statement at issue be merely explanatory. . . .

This construction follows from the principle that the preferred method of policymaking is by promulgation of rules. When action taken by an agency alters the status quo, those who will be affected by its future application should have the opportunity to be heard and to participate in the decisionmaking. . . .

In construing administrative rules, courts apply principles of statutory construction. . . . In addition, § 32(1) of the APA provides that any statutory definitions of words, phrases, or rules of construction made applicable to all statutes also apply to rules unless it is clear that such definition or construction was not intended. . . .

The general rule when interpreting the language of a statute is to construe it according to its plain meaning. A fair interpretation of Rule 400.907 would be that at the time the rule was promulgated a fair hearing was a hearing which must generally take place in the county in which the claimant resides. It is clear that the rule as stated did not envision telephone hearings. Rather, it clearly contemplated a hearing in which all parties and the hearing referee were in attendance at one site, generally the place where the claimant resided. . . .

The telephone hearing procedures are binding and affect the rights of the public to administrative hearings and the conduct of those hearings. The new procedures are not merely mechanical details for the conduct of hearings, but, rather, represent substantial changes in the detailed requirements for the conduct of fair hearings to determine claimants' rights under the Social Welfare Act and applicable federal law. The rules are extensive and

EDITED CASE Detroit Base Coalition for the Human Rights
of the Handicapped v. Department of Social Services (Continued)

were adopted, without notice and comment from the general public and interested parties and consideration by a joint committee, as rules which would provide "adequate procedure for a fair hearing." . . . An agency is under a duty to follow its own rules. . . . This policy bulletin represents an alteration of the present rules and therefore must be promulgated as a rule under the proper procedures set out by the APA.

In sum, the telephone hearing policy is inconsistent with the existing rules and therefore cannot be implemented without benefit of rulemaking. The telephone hearing procedure has the full force and effect of law and represents an alteration or change from the rule. The department's effort to change substantially the manner in which it conducts its hearings solely through an internal policy bulletin and manual revision undermines the fundamental purpose of the APA:

"[B]ecause the adoption of a rule by an agency has the force and effect of law and may have serious consequences for many people, the legislature prescribed an elaborate procedure for rule promulgation in Chapter 3 of the Michigan Administrative Procedures Act. . . . These provisions are calculated to invite public participation in the rule-making process, prevent precipitous action by the agency, prevent the adoption of rules that are illegal or that may be beyond the legislative intent, notify affected and interested persons of the existence of the rules, and make the rules readily accessible after adoption." . . .

In the absence of rulemaking then, appellants have been deprived of rights under the APA 1) to receive notice of the telephone hearing policy as a proposed rule, 2) to comment on the rule at public hearings, and 3) to review the rule through the joint committee on administrative rules of the Michigan Legislature.

The telephone hearing policy adopted by the Department of Social Services was not promulgated as a rule within the meaning of the APA and therefore, absent full compliance with the rule-making provisions of the APA, the policy cannot be implemented because it is without legal authority or effect under Michigan law.

The decision of the Court of Appeals which affirmed the trial court's dismissal of plaintiff's complaint is reversed. Program Policy Bulletin No. 84-16 is inconsistent with the existing rules governing administrative hearings and, unless promulgated pursuant to the rule-making procedures of the APA, the DSS cannot implement a mandatory telephone hearing policy.

Justices Levin, Archer, Riley, Griffin, Cavanagh, and *Brickley,* concurring.

EDITED CASE State v. Peters
Missouri Court of Appeals, Southern District, Division One
729 S.W.2d 243 (Mo.App. S.D. 1987)

[Here a Missouri appellate court invalidates a state health department rule prescribing a method of determining blood alcohol from a blood sample because the department failed to comply with statutory requirements of publication and filing of the rule.]

Judge Holstein delivered the opinion of the court.

This is an appeal by the State of the trial court's order suppressing evidence of a blood test in a case in which the defendant is charged with the misdemeanors of driving while intoxicated and driving on the wrong side of the road. The action of the trial court in suppressing the evidence of the blood test is affirmed.

The motion to suppress pointed out that inasmuch as §§ 577.020 and 577.026 RSMo 1986 require that chemical analysis of a person's blood be performed according to satisfactory techniques, devices, equipment, or methods

(Continued)

EDITED CASE State v. Peters (Continued)

approved by the department of health and the department of health has failed to issue any regulations approving techniques, devices, equipment or methods for determining blood alcohol content from blood samples, such analysis is inadmissible in evidence.

The "Department of Health" includes what was formerly referred to as the "Division of Health." In the regulations hereafter cited the same agency is referred to as "the division." We use the terms interchangeably herein.

For the purposes of the hearing on the motion to suppress, the parties stipulated that a trained technician, doctor or nurse had drawn blood from the defendant in compliance with § 577.029 RSMo 1986 and the blood sample was subjected to alcohol content analysis using the gas chromatography method by chemist Bill Marbaker of the Missouri State Highway Patrol Laboratory, who holds a Type I permit. The court took judicial notice of the pertinent portions of the Code of State Regulations, 13 CSR 50-140.

The only testimony at the hearing was by Richard Gnaedinger PhD, chief of chemistry for the Missouri Department of Health. Dr. Gnaedinger testified that it was his duty to approve methods for determining blood alcohol from a blood sample. He is also involved in approving applicants for Type I permits. Each such applicant when approved, is approved only to use the method of blood alcohol analysis upon which he successfully was tested. Three scientifically accepted methods have been approved by Dr. Gnaedinger. These are (1) the gas chromatography method mentioned above, (2) the enzymatic method, and (3) the distillation and titration method. None of the three methods are listed as an "approved" method in the Code of State Regulations. The rationale offered by Dr. Gnaedinger for not specifically approving methods was the "endless list of variations" in the principal methods, all of which would produce an accurate result. He identified State's Exhibit 3 as a list of eleven variations of the three methods which he, on behalf of his agency, had approved for use in various laboratories in the state.

After the trial court sustained the motion to suppress, the State perfected its appeal. . . .

The State does not argue nor does the record indicate that the blood sample might be admissible as evidence seized pursuant to a lawful arrest, independent of the "implied consent" law. The sole basis urged for admissibility of the blood sample is §§ 577.020 et seq. We decide this case only on the issue presented.

This court has previously decided that under the former "implied consent" law, . . . (now repealed), for a chemical analysis of a person's breath to be valid it must be performed according to methods approved by the department of health. . . . The current "implied consent" law uses almost identical language but expands the scope of the implied consent, authorizing the taking of blood, urine or saliva samples, in addition to breath samples. The principles enunciated in cases construing the former statute are applicable here.

Section 577.020 provides:

(1) Any person who operates a motor vehicle upon the public highways of this state shall be deemed to have given consent to, subject to the provisions of sections 577.020 to 577.041, a chemical test or tests of his breath, blood, saliva or urine for the purpose of determining the alcohol or drug content of his blood if arrested for any offense arising out of acts which the arresting officer had reasonable grounds to believe were committed while the person was driving a motor vehicle while in an intoxicated or drugged condition . . .

(3) Chemical analysis of the person's breath, blood, saliva, or urine to be considered valid under the provision of sections 577.020 to 577.041 shall be performed according to methods approved by the state division of health by licensed medical personnel or by a person possessing a valid permit issued by the state division of health for this purpose . . .

(4) The state division of health shall approve satisfactory techniques, devices, equipment, or methods to be considered valid under the provisions of sections 577.020 to 577.041 and shall establish standards to ascertain the qualifications and competence of individuals to conduct analyses and to issue permits which shall be subject to termination or revocation by the state division of health.

EDITED CASE State v. Peters (Continued)

Section 577.026 provides:

(1) Chemical tests of the person's breath, blood, saliva, or urine to be considered valid under the provisions of sections 577.020 to 577.041, shall be performed according to methods and devices approved by the state division of health by licensed medical personnel or by a person possessing a valid permit issued by the state division of health for this purpose.

(2) The state division of health shall approve satisfactory techniques, devices, equipment, or methods to conduct tests required by sections 577.020 to 577.041, and shall establish standards as to the qualifications and competence of individuals to conduct analyses and to issue permits which shall be subject to termination or revocation by the state division of health.

The above legislative enactments are a substitute for the common law foundation for the introduction of evidence of analyses for blood alcohol, and are mandatory. . . . If the State has failed to comply with these statutes the blood analysis is inadmissible and prejudicial.

The department of health has adopted administrative rules relating to the determination of blood alcohol by blood, breath, saliva, and urine analysis. 13 CSR 50-140.020(1) describes the five types of permits issued by the department including the Type I permit, the holder of which is permitted ". . . to determine the alcoholic content of blood from a sample of expired (alveolar) air, blood, saliva or urine utilizing standard quantitative chemical analytical methods as approved by the division . . ." The same section of the regulation makes provision for testing of applicants for a Type I permit. 13 CSR 50-140.020(5). The regulations also make provision for the qualifications of a person seeking to become the holder of a Type I permit. . . . Finally, the regulations provide for the duties and responsibilities of a Type I permittee. Those duties and responsibilities are set forth as follows:

(1) Permittee, Type I, is for the determination of the alcoholic content of the blood from a sample of expired (alveolar) air, blood, saliva, or urine utilizing standard quantitative chemical analytical methods.

(A) The permittee shall accept for test only specimens properly identified and submitted in a manner so that reliable results are possible.

(B) He shall conduct all analyses in a fair, impartial and competent manner.

(C) He shall keep adequate records of receipts and analysis of all specimens.

(D) Permittee shall examine and report results on check specimens for alcohol provided by the division, at intervals deemed to be appropriate by the division.

No other reference is made in the regulations describing the "techniques, devices, equipment or methods" approved for analysis of a blood sample.

The statutory word "method" refers to the method of testing whether it be a breathalyzer, gas chromatography or other method which might find approval by the department of health. . . . The State's position is that the department's regulations authorize the Type I permit and prior to the issuance of the permit the applicant is required to ". . . supply his analytical method, prove his accuracy and possess or have access to satisfactory techniques. . . ." Thus, the State argues, the regulations approve methods, devices, equipment or techniques for conducting blood alcohol tests. This tortured argument would result in a situation in which the department of health has delegated its responsibility to the Type I permittee. This conclusion is contrary to the clear and redundant statutory language which requires a specific approval of methods by the department of health.

The State's evidence suggested that the list of methods contained in State's Exhibit 3 are "approved in the State of Missouri for determining alcohol in blood." Unfortunately, the exhibit has never been adopted as an administrative rule.

Section 536.010(4) sets out the definition of the term "rule" as follows: "Rule" means each agency statement of general applicability that implements, interprets, or prescribes law or policy, or that describes the organization, procedure, or practice requirements of any agency. The term includes the amendment or repeal of an existing rule, but does not include . . . (exceptions are thereafter listed not applicable here).

(Continued)

EDITED CASE   State v. Peters (Continued)

Inasmuch as the approval of the methods of blood analysis contained in Exhibit 3 is an attempt by the department of health to implement the law, as well as prescribe a policy of the department, the agency was required to comply with the statutory publication and filing procedure for adopting rules. . . .

In an analogous case, another state agency, the division of family services, had published a manual setting forth methods for computing the amount of Medicaid to be paid on behalf of a recipient of benefits to a nursing home. The court found such policy was a "rule" which affected substantial legal rights of the recipient and to be effective must satisfy the statutory publication and filing requirements. . . . In the absence of compliance with the statute the "rule" is void. . . .

Finally, the State urges the court to avoid requiring the department of health to publish the specific analytical methods to be used because of the "endless list of variations" involved. We point out to the State that it is the statute, not this court, that requires publication of such methods. While it may be true that numerous inconsequential variations may exist in performing chemical analyses, we find it difficult to believe that the department of health cannot adequately describe the techniques, devices, equipment or methods in broad enough terms to allow for such variations and yet assure accurate results. In view of the gaping deficiencies in the regulations and the dangers posed by drunk drivers on the public highways, we urge the department of health to take appropriate steps to promulgate rules prescribing the methods or techniques approved for the analysis of blood samples for alcohol content.

The order suppressing the evidence of the blood alcohol test is affirmed.

Justices Crow and **Greene,** concurring.

ENDNOTES

1. *Chrysler Corp. v. Brown*, 441 U.S. 281 (1979).

2. 5 U.S.C.A. § 551(4).

3. 1981 MSAPA § 1.102 (10).

4. 239 U.S. 44 (1915).

5. 332 U.S. 194, 203 (1947).

6. *Id.* at 202.

7. *Id.*, at 202-203

8. 5 U.S.C.A. § 553(a).

9. 5 U.S.C.A. § 553(a)&(b).

10. 506 F.2d 33 (D.C.Cir. 1974).

11. *Id.* at 38.

12. Michael Asimow, *Nonlegislative Rulemaking and Regulatory Reform*, 1985 Duke L.J. 381, 388.

13. 174 F.3d 206 (D.C. Cir. 1999).

14. *Id.* at 213.

15. *Chamber of Commerce v. Occupational Safety and Health Agency*, 636 F.2d 464, 488 (D.C. Cir. 1983).

16. *Skidmore v. Swift & Co.*, 323 U.S. 134, 140 (1944).

17. 467 U.S. 837 (1984).

18. 529 U.S. 576 (2000).

19. 533 U.S. 218, 221 (2001).

20. See *Vermont Yankee Nuclear Power Corp. v. Natural Resources Defense Council, Inc.*, 435 U.S. 519 (1978).

21. *Morton v. Ruiz*, 415 U.S. 199 (1974).

22. 724 F.2d 979 (D.C. Cir. 1983).

23. *Sprint Corp. v. Federal Communications Commission*, 315 F.3d 369 (D.C. Cir. 2003).

24. 244 F.3d 342 (4th Cir. 2001).

25. *Id.* at 349.

26. 208 F.3d 256, 262 (D.C. Cir. 2000).

27. 5 U.S.C.A. § 552(a)(1)(c).

28. 607 F.2d 695 (5th Cir. 1979).

29. *Davidson v. Glickman*, 169 F.3d 996, 999 (5th Cir. 1999).

30. *Chamber of Commerce of the United States v. U.S. Dept. of Labor*, 174 F.3d 206, 211-13 (D.C. Cir. 1999).

31. *James V. Hurson Associates, Inc. v. Glickman*, 229 F.3d 277, 281 (D.C. Cir. 2000).

32. 5 U.S.C.A. § 553(b)(B).

33. 5 U.S.C.A. S 553(d)(3).

34. 645 F.2d 1309, 1321 (8th Cir. 1981).

35. 507 F.2d 455 (Em. Ct App. 1974).

36. 328 F. Supp 297, (E.D. N.Y. 1977).

37. 5 U.S.C.A § 553(b).

38. 551 F.2d 1099 (8th Cir.1977).

39. 5 U.S.C.A. § 553(b).

40. 236 F.3d 749 (D.C. Cir. 2001).

41. *Id.* at 754.

42. See, e.g., *Action for Children's Television v. FCC*, 564 F.2d 458, 470 (D.C. Cir. 1977).

43. 5 U.S.C.A. § 553(b).

44. 5 U.S.C.A. § 553(c).

45. 21 U.S.C.A. § 355.

46. 15 U.S.C.A. § 2601.

47. 64 Fed. Reg. 33,756 (1999).

48. *Utility Solid Waste Activities Group v. Environmental Protection Agency*, 236 F.3d 749 (2001).

49. Kenneth Culp Davis, *Administrative Law Treatise* (1970 Supplement) (§ 6.15); reaffirmed in 1 Administrative Law Treatise (2nd ed. 1978) (§ 6.1).

50. Ronald M. Levin, *Direct Final Rulemaking*, 64 Geo. Wash. L. Rev. 1 (Nov. 1995).

51. 5 U.S.C.A. §§ 556, 557.

52. 5 U.S.C.A. § 556(b).

53. 5 U.S.C.A. § 556(d).

54. 5 U.S.C.A. § 557(d)(1).

55. 5 U.S.C.A. § 553(c).

56. 410 U.S. 224 (1973).

57. *Id.* at 241.

58. 483 F.2d 1238 (D.C. Cir. 1973).

59. *Id.* at 1260.

60. *Id.* at 1262.

61. See, e.g., *Portland Cement Ass'n v. Ruckelshaus*, 486 F.2d 375 (D.C. Cir. 1973).

62. *Vermont Yankee Nuclear Power Corp. v. Natural Resources Defense Council*, 483 F.2d 1238 (D.C. Cir. 1973).

63. 435 U.S. 519 (1978).

64. *Id.* at 546-547.

65. 5 U.S.C.A. § 561 *et seq.*

66. P.L. 107-347, 116 Stat. 2915.

67. J. Lubbers, The Future of Electronic Rulemaking, Admin. & Reg. Law News, p. 6 (Summer 2002).

68. For a more complete discussion of the future of electronic rulemaking, see "Electronic Rulemaking at HHS," online at http://globe.lmi.org/erm/docs/erm525.htm.

69. 5 U.S.C.A. § 553(d).

70. 5 U.S.C.A. § 556.

71. 296 U.S. 176, 186 (1935).

72. 463 U.S. 29 (1983).

73. 15 U.S.C.A. § 631 *et seq.*

74. See *SGA Financial Corp. v. U.S. Small Business Administration*, 509 F. Supp. 392 (D.C.N.J. 1981), *affirmed* 673 F.2d 1301.

75. See 13 C. F. R. § 121.102.

76. 5 U.S.C.A. §§ 601-612.

77. 5 U.S.C.A. § 605(b).

78. 5 U.S.C.A. § 611.

79. 5 U.S.C. A. § 609.

80. See, e.g., *United States v. Storer Broadcasting Co.*, 351 U.S. 192 (1956).

81. See, e.g., 5 U.S.C.A. § 555(3) (reasons for denial of any petition requires an agency to set forth its reasons).

82. 470 U.S. 116 (1985).

83. 15 U.S.C.A. S 57a(g).

84. 29 U.S.C.A. §§ 655(b)(6), 655(d); See also 29 C.F.R. pt. 1905.

85. *National Rural Telecom Ass'n v. FCC*, 988 F.2d 174, 181 (D.C. Cir. 1993).

86. *MacLeod v. ICC*, 54 F.3d 888, 891 (D.C. Cir. 1995).

87. U.S. Const. art. II, sec. 1.

88. 462 U.S. 919 (1983).

89. 5 U.S.C.A. § 801(a)(1)(A).

90. 5 U.S.C.A. §§ 602-603.

91. 2 U.S.C.A. § 1531 *et seq.*

92. 44 U.S.C.A. § 3501 *et seq.*

93. 42 U.S.C.A. § 4321 *et seq.*

94. 5 U.S.C.A. § 557(d)(1).

95. See 5 U.S.C.A. § 553.

96. 567 F.2d 9 (D.C. Cir. 1977).

97. *Id.* at 53.

98. 657 F.2d 298 (D.C. Cir.1981).
99. *Id*. at 400–401.
100. 1981 MSAPA § 3-109(a).
101. 1981 MSAPA 3-103(a).
102. 1981 MSAPA § 3-103(b).
103. 1981 MSAPA § 3-116(1)&(4).
104. 1981 MSAPA § 3-106(b).
105. Fla. Stat. Ann. § 120.536(1).
106. N.C. Gen. Stat. §§ 150B-21.2(a)(1).
107. Tex. Govt. Code Ann. § 2001.026.

108. See, e.g., Fla. Stat. Ann. § 120.54(3)c(2).
109. 279 S.E.2d 622 (W.Va. 1981).
110. 687 P.2d 622 (Kan. 1984).
111. Ark. Code Ann. § 25-15-204 (b).
112. Ark. Code Ann. § 25-15-204 (e)(2)(A).
113. Mich. Comp. Laws Ann. § 24.263.
114. See West's Ann. Cal. Gov. Code § 11346.3.
115. Minn. Stat. Ann. § 144.6535.
116. Ind. Stat. Ann. § 12-17.4-2-8.

7

Adjudication

"[T]he laws under which these agencies operate prescribe the foundations of fair play. They require that interested parties be granted an opportunity for hearing and that judgment must express a reasoned conclusion."

JUSTICE FELIX FRANKFURTER
WRITING FOR THE U.S. SUPREME COURT IN *FEDERAL COMMUNICATIONS COMMISSION V. POTTSVILLE BROADCASTING CO.*, 309 U.S. 134, 143 (1940).

INTRODUCTION

Courts issue orders to adjudicate disputes based on constitutional and statutory proscriptions, procedural rules, and common-law traditions. Within the sphere of administrative law agencies carry out their adjudicative functions by issuing orders of particular applicability to settle the rights and obligations of parties in accordance with statutory requirements and agency regulations.

Historically, American courts have given great effect to precedent. Attempts to solve the economic problems of the 1930s resulted in the creation of numerous administrative agencies largely unguided by precedent. As these agencies carried out their functions designed to accomplish a fair and efficient resolution of disputes, a massive number of agency rules developed. Perhaps it was this proliferation of rules that in 1932 led Thurman Arnold, a former Yale law professor, to characterize the difference in court and administrative adjudication by saying, "Courts are bound by precedent and bureaus are bound by red tape."[1] Although court adjudications do follow a formal trial process and adhere to precedent, this may or may not be true of administrative adjudication.

In some instances federal statutes require agencies to conduct **formal adjudication** in a trial-type manner; however, the great majority of administrative actions at the federal level are decided through **informal adjudication.** States also make provision for formal administrative adjudications, but again most administrative actions at the state level are decided through informal adjudication. Informal agency processes at both the federal and state levels run the gamut from relatively simple processes to procedures akin to formal adjudications.

Adjudication is designed to settle disputes between parties; yet, historically, federal agencies also utilized formal adjudications to establish administrative policy. When disputing parties litigate in court there is an expectation the court will resolve any factual disputes and interpret and apply the law to resolve their controversy. Under the common-law approach, court decisions become precedents to guide others as to the likely outcome of similar disputes. Similarly, when agencies adjudicate disputes, especially in such fields as licensing and ratemaking, their determinations often establish the agency's policy in a particular area. As pointed out in the preceding chapter, where the subject matter lends itself to a policy of general applicability, most commentators recommend that an agency formulate its policies by rulemaking, where interests broader than those in a specific controversy can be addressed.

Participation in adjudicatory proceedings is limited to those with **standing,** that is, those who have a direct stake in the outcome of the controversy (see Chapter 9). In contrast, when administrative policy is established by rulemaking, affected parties can participate in the policymaking process or at least be notified that the process is underway and have the opportunity to comment. For this and other reasons outlined in Chapter 6, the trend has been for both federal and state agencies to make policy through rulemaking rather than through formal adjudication. Unlike rulemaking, which is a **quasi-legislative** function, adjudicatory processes are **quasi-judicial** and are therefore subject to the protections of the due process clauses of the Fifth and Fourteenth Amendments to the United States Constitution and the interpretations of these clauses by federal and state courts (see Chapter 3). Due process comes into play in an administrative adjudication when a party's property or liberty interests are at stake. Among the considerations that gauge the extent of due process that must be afforded are the interest to be affected by the government action, relevant constitutional and statutory requirements, rules of the specific agency, and the administrative costs entailed.

Formal, i.e., trial type, agency hearings generally follow a prescribed format designed to emulate the judicial process and fulfill the constitutional requirements of due process. In this chapter we discuss the various elements of a formal agency hearing, including the right to counsel, the prehearing, hearing, decisional, and post-hearing processes and the roles played by administrative law judges and the other actors. We also discuss informal adjudications, but the diversity of informal adjudicatory procedures makes it impossible to generalize as to their format. Nevertheless, they must comport with the due process provisions of federal, and where applicable, state constitutions, as well as agencies' enabling statutes and agency regulations.

Before reviewing formal and informal adjudication procedures, consider a few examples of administrative adjudication at the federal and state and local levels. The federal Clean Water Act provides for formal adjudicatory hearing in accordance with the provisions of the **Administrative Procedure Act (APA)** where the Environmental Protection Agency sets effluent limitations pursuant to application by operators of offshore oil platforms. Likewise, the Federal Communications Act requires a formal hearing before revocation of a broadcasting or television license. On the other hand, while the Social Security Agency must afford claimants certain procedural rights before terminating their disability payments, a formal **predetermination hearing** is not required. And the federal government contracts with private insurance companies to resolve disputed claims for services of healthcare providers with a process for contesting non-payment of claims that consist largely of a "paper review."

State agencies administer a wide variety of administrative matters. For example, when a discharged employee files a claim for unemployment compensation, the employer may contend the employee was guilty of misconduct and therefore not entitled to compensation. A hearing officer conducts a formal evidentiary hearing, makes **findings of fact**, **conclusions of law,** and recommendations to an agency, which enters an order adjudicating the rights of the parties. On the other hand, a public school can suspend a student for a short period with only minimal due process procedures that generally do not include a predetermination hearing.

Cities and counties establish boards to consider whether to grant special exceptions and variances from comprehensive zoning ordinances based on specified criteria. Local ordinances usually afford interested parties an opportunity for a formal hearing. Yet a local agency may deny a homeowner a permit for removal of a tree without resort to any predetermination hearing.

These examples illustrate different administrative approaches to adjudication. As will become evident, the degree of formality of a hearing, or, indeed, whether a hearing is even required, varies considerably across situations.

APPLICABILITY OF ADMINISTRATIVE PROCEDURE ACTS

The federal Administrative Procedure Act (APA) sets out requirements for both formal and informal rulemaking by federal agencies (see Chapter 6). Yet in respect to adjudication, the APA focuses on procedures for formal adjudication. The APA is procedural, not substantive, that is, it does not create the right to a hearing in administrative adjudication; rather, it defines the procedural rights where another statute requires a formal hearing. Section 551(6) defines an **order** as "the whole or part of a final disposition, whether affirmative, negative, injunctive, or declaratory in form, of an agency in a matter other than rule making but including licensing." Subsection (7) defines **adjudication** as "agency process for the formulation of an order." Section 554(a) provides the procedures to be followed when an administrative adjudication is "required by statute to be determined on-the-record after opportunity for an agency hearing."

The APA does not set out requirements for informal adjudications; however, Section 555(e) does require prompt notice of the denial of a written application, petition, or other request by an interested person in connection with any agency proceeding, and except when an agency affirms a prior denial or when the denial is self-explanatory, the notice is to be accompanied by a brief statement of the grounds for denial.

The APA does not apply to matters subject to a subsequent trial of the law and the facts on a **de novo** basis in a court of law. Moreover, it exempts proceedings in which decisions rest solely on inspections, tests, or elections, the selection or tenure of employees (other than administrative law judges), and matters involving the conduct of military or foreign affairs. Otherwise, where a statute requires an adjudication to be determined on the record after opportunity for an agency hearing, the agency must follow formal (trial-type) proceedings, unless Congress directs a different form of procedure.[2]

In *Marcello v. Bonds* (1955),[3] the Supreme Court recognized that Congress can require different procedures for adjudication of disputes as long as the procedures do not fall below the constitutional requirements of due process of law. In many instances the applicable agency statute is either silent or requires only minimal procedures to assure interested persons due process of law. Where there is no statutory requirement for a hearing an agency may determine its own procedures for informal adjudication. Thus, a multiplicity of statutes and agency rules makes it difficult to generalize as to procedural requirements when a statute directs less than formal adjudications. Nevertheless, wherever a person's **liberty** or **property rights** as defined by the Supreme Court are involved, administrative proceedings must comport with constitutional requirements of due process of law under the **Fifth Amendment** to the U.S. Constitution. The **Fourteenth Amendment** binds the states to afford due process of law. Although a state constitution may afford more protection than afforded by the federal constitution, it cannot afford less. Over the years the Supreme Court has interpreted the due process requirements in a series of opinions that we discuss later.

State Administrative Procedure Acts

Many state administrative procedure statutes were adapted from the **1961 Model State Administrative Procedure Act (MSAPA)**, which sets out basic procedures for adjudication. Section 1(2) requires a hearing in a **contested case** defined as "a proceeding, including but not restricted to ratemaking, and licensing, in which the legal rights, duties, or privileges of a party are *required by law* to be determined by an agency after an opportunity for hearing." Thus, in many states before being eligible for a hearing, a party must be involved in a contested case or there must be a constitutional provision, statute, or agency rule apart from the MSAPA that requires an adjudicatory hearing.

The **1981 Model State Administrative Procedure Act (MSAPA)** takes a much more progressive approach. Whereas the federal APA and the 1961 Model Act provide the rules for formal hearings when another statute so requires, Section 4-102(b)(3) of the 1981 Model Act provides that an agency shall conduct an adjudicative proceeding upon application before issuing an order unless "a statute vests the agency with discretion to conduct or not conduct an adjudicative hearing before issuing an order to resolve the matter, and, in the exercise of that discretion, the agency has determined not to conduct an adjudicative proceeding." Section 4-102(b)(4) requires an adjudicative proceeding unless "resolution of the matter does not require the agency to issue an order that determines the applicant's legal rights, duties, privileges, immunities, or other legal interests."

State Administrative Procedure Acts are generally applicable to the executive, but not to legislative or judicial branches of state government. One must examine the state statutes to determine applicability. In Florida, for example, all state agencies, boards, commissions, educational units, and regional planning districts (e.g., transportation authorities and water management districts) are subject to the State APA. The legislature, however, has not elected to place counties and municipalities under the Act.[4]

Recent state statutes tend to follow the 1981 MSAPA approach and create different adjudicatory procedures for different classes of agency matters. For example, Delaware law provides:

> When required by law or when the parties do not consent to informal proceedings, or when the matters at issue involve price fixing, rate making or similar matters of general public interest, as determined by the agency, the agency shall conduct a formal, public evidentiary hearing to which the following provisions shall apply:
>
> 1. The notice required by § 10122 of this title shall be published in at least 2 Delaware newspapers of general circulation; and
>
> 2. Applicants for licenses, renewals and other rights or benefits shall not be entitled to prior notice of application requirements but shall receive notice of any proposed contest of such applications.[5]

The Florida APA requires formal adjudicatory proceedings when a party's substantial interests are involved and there is a disputed issue of material fact, unless the interested parties waive a formal hearing. In absence of a disputed material fact adjudicatory proceedings are informal unless the interested parties agree to a formal proceeding.[6]

Local Administrative Procedure Ordinances

Some of the larger cities have their own administrative procedure acts. For example, the New York City Charter, Chapter 45 contains the City Administrative Procedure Act. Section 1046 embraces adjudication. In absence of a state statute to the contrary, most cities and counties either prescribe adjudication procedures by ordinance or develop their procedures on a case-by-case basis.

FORMAL AND INFORMAL ADJUDICATIONS

As noted, the federal APA provides procedures for formal adjudicatory hearings when federal statutes direct on-the-record hearings. States vary in their requirements as to when a formal hearing is required. Many state administrative procedure acts follow the tenor of the federal APA and direct a formal hearing only in a "contested case." Although this chapter discusses formal adjudication in detail, it must be remembered that most administrative adjudication is classified as informal.

Some administrative actions are very informal. Government agencies routinely issue drivers' licenses based on vision and hearing tests, determine whether motor vehicles pass safety inspections or whether certain products meet quality standards, and administer tests to determine licenses to pilot ships and aircraft. As previously pointed out, the APA (and state statutes generally) exempt proceedings in which decisions rest solely on inspections, tests, or elections, the selection or tenure of employees (other than administrative law judges), and matters involving the conduct of military or foreign affairs. But even in these instances due process of law mandates that there must be some recourse to review an administrator's decision.

Procedures for informal adjudication are governed by constitutional provisions, statutes, agency regulations, and in some instances, by courts. Unlike in formal adjudication, procedures in informal adjudication vary from the most simple (for example, a conference with an administrative official) to complex procedures approaching those required in formal adjudication. Some federal and state statutes describe the specific adjudicatory procedures that must be followed. More commonly, however, the detailed procedures for informal adjudication are found in agency rules.

An agency rule providing for informal adjudication is illustrated by the Connecticut Department of Motor Vehicles Agency Regulations, which make two informal methods available to licensees affected by the department's orders or license requirements. The department may schedule an informal conference on its own initiative or on request of a licensee in an attempt to resolve a dispute. Notice may be by telephone or mail and conference proceedings need not be recorded. Alternatively, the agency may notify a licensee by certified mail affording the licensee an opportunity to show compliance with requirements for retention of a license. In either instance the agency's rules provide that an alleged violator must be given a concise written factual statement of any violation alleged with reference to the statute or regulation allegedly violated, and notifying the alleged violator that he or she may be represented by counsel. Formal rules of evidence are not to be observed in either instance; however, in a compliance conference a hearing officer presides, the proceedings are recorded, and the hearing officer makes a written report and recommendations to the commissioner.[7]

At least one commentator has lamented the fact that the federal APA has had such a great effect on state laws. Arthur Earl Bonfield has urged that instead of following the APA that states should give serious consideration to emulating the 1981 MSAPA by "creating several different classes of agency adjudication, each subject to procedural requirements specially tailored to its needs and circumstances."[8]

In some states agencies develop their own procedures for informal adjudication. Other states have enacted statutes governing informal adjudication. For example, Delaware law provides:

> Where a formal hearing is not required by law and where the parties agree in advance to proceed in such manner, the agency shall acquire the information upon which it bases its decision by means of informal conference or consultation among the parties as follows:
>
> 1. The agency shall conduct the conference itself or may designate a subordinate to do so;
>
> 2. The parties may appear in person and by counsel; and

> 3. The parties may submit any relevant factual data, documents, testimony, and argument. Only such evidence and argument presented at such conference or presented to the agency and opposing parties before the conference may be taken into consideration by the agency in making its findings and rendering its decision.[9]

Other states have enacted statutes that classify administrative proceedings as requiring different degrees of administrative formality. Because of the disparities in procedures in agency adjudication where the law does not require a formal proceeding, informal adjudications are often challenged on the basis of the agency's failure to afford due process of law to interested parties. In the following section we offer an extended discussion of due process of law with emphasis on when due process must be accorded and the extent of that due process.

AGENCY ADJUDICATION AND DUE PROCESS OF LAW

The Fifth Amendment to the U.S. Constitution provides that "no person shall be deprived of life, liberty, or property, without due process of law." The Fourteenth Amendment includes a similar provision that binds state and local agencies. These core proscriptions are not detailed; rather they assume that law and custom have expressed or will declare the fundamental values they address. Indeed, the judicial interpretations of these constitutional proscriptions have been the dominant factors in the development of the procedural aspects of the administrative process.

Interests Triggering Procedural Due Process

When administrative agencies act to the detriment of any person's life, liberty, or property, they are subject to constitutional **procedural due process** requirements as determined by the courts. Of course, administrative agencies must also adhere to procedural requirements stipulated by statutes, agency rules, and by applicable judicial interpretations of same. Administrative agencies never threaten to take a person's life, as capital punishment can be imposed only by a court of law in a criminal prosecution. Thus litigation and commentary have focused on the terms "liberty" and "property" found in the due process clauses of the Fifth and Fourteenth Amendments.

As we have noted in previous chapters, the complexity of modern life has led to the creation of many administrative agencies at all levels of government. In turn, this has brought about considerable litigation over the extent to which due process of law must be observed in administrative matters. Just as administrative proceedings have evolved over time, so have the decisions of the U.S. Supreme Court interpreting when and to what extent due process protections must be afforded to persons whose liberty and property interests are affected by agency actions. These decisions must be read in light of the time when rendered and in the context of the particular circumstance surrounding administrative action.

Liberty One could take a narrow perspective of the term "liberty" as it appears in the Fifth and Fourteenth Amendments and argue that deprivation of liberty refers only to the physical restraint of the individual. This would have the effect of limiting due process protections to those situations where agencies actually take persons into custody. Although some administrative agencies (such as the Bureau for Citizenship and Immigration Services and the Federal Bureau of Prisons) have authority to do this under some circumstances, most administrative actions that adversely affect individuals do not involve any sort of physical restraint. In any event, the Supreme Court long ago rejected this narrow conception of liberty. For example, in 1923, the Court said that liberty

> denotes not merely freedom from bodily restraint but also the right of the individual

to contract, to engage in any of the common occupations of life, to acquire useful knowledge, to marry, establish a house and bring up children, to worship God according to the dictates of his own conscience, and generally to enjoy those privileges long recognized . . . as essential to the orderly pursuit of happiness by free men.[10]

More recently, the Court has noted, "In a Constitution for a free people, there can be no doubt that the meaning of 'liberty' must be broad indeed."[11] Thus administrative actions that impair individual freedom, including but not limited to the freedoms enumerated in the Bill of Rights, are subject to due process requirements.

Property Historically the Supreme Court defined "property rights" subject to due process of law in the restrictive common-law context of real estate, chattels, and money. When the government sought to deprive an owner of these types of property rights, there was no question that due process had to be observed. On the other hand, government jobs, benefits, licenses, grants, etc. were seen as **privileges** that could be revoked without notice or hearing.[12] In the modern era, commentators pointed out that much of the country's wealth was linked to government benefits.[13] Essentially adopting this idea of "the new property," the modern Supreme Court has taken a much broader perspective, rejecting traditional distinctions between rights and privileges and going so far as to recognize welfare benefits as a form of property.[14]

What Process Is Due?

In the line of cases interpreting due process protections in the context of administrative actions, questions of whether due process protections are applicable are often intermingled with questions regarding the nature and degree of the procedural protections that must be afforded. Even if due process applies to a given administrative action, the question remains: What process is due?

Notice and hearing are traditionally considered to be the core elements of procedural due process, but they have not always been viewed by the courts as essential to due process in the administrative context. Early in the twentieth century the U.S. Supreme Court sustained a state law requiring compulsory vaccination,[15] and upheld the seizure of putrid food[16] without requiring these administrative norms be followed.

In *Londoner v. Denver* (1908) the Supreme Court ruled that individual property owners in Denver, Colorado were denied due process when the city refused to grant them a hearing to allow each property owner to challenge a special assessment for street paving.[17] The decision had broad implications in respect to governmental action and needed clarification. In 1915, in *Bi-Metallic Investment Co. v. State Board of Equalization*,[18] the Court provided the necessary clarification when it rejected the contention of property owners that Denver's across-the-board revaluation of real estate without a prior hearing violated their rights to due process of law. On the surface the Court's decision in *Bi-Metallic* appeared to conflict with *Londoner*. But in writing for the Court, Justice Oliver Wendell Holmes distinguished *Bi-Metallic* from *Londoner* by pointing out that whereas in *Londoner* only a small number of property owners were affected, *Bi-Metallic* involved numerous people broadly affected by action closely akin to general legislative enactments that do not require notice and hearing.

The late Kenneth Culp Davis, an eminent scholar in the administrative law field, argued that the real distinction between the two cases is that in *Londoner* the facts were adjudicative—that is, facts in dispute needed to be found through trial-type procedures—while in *Bi-Metallic* the facts were legislative because they affected all real property in Denver.[19] In 1973 in *United States v. Florida East Coast Ry. Co.*,[20] the Supreme Court continued to recognize the *Londoner/Bi-Metallic* distinction between rulemaking and the adjudication of disputed facts.

An excerpt from the Supreme Court's decision in *United States v. Florida East Coast Ry. Co.* is reprinted at the end of the chapter.

Broadening the Scope of Procedural Due Process In 1933 the Supreme Court voided a Virginia statute that authorized the state highway commissioner to order a railroad company to eliminate a grade crossing and require an overhead crossing where necessary for public safety and convenience. The Court held that "before its [the railroad's] property can be taken under the edict of an administrative officer the appellant [railroad] is entitled to a fair hearing upon the fundamental facts."[21]

With the proliferation of the administrative state, the *Londoner/Bi-Metallic* tests did not provide a workable solution to afford due process protections where government action affected the property interests of large numbers of people. After its 1955 decision in *Marcello v. Bonds*,[22] the Supreme Court began to look upon the procedures required in administrative adjudication by relating the procedural safeguards to agency functions.

If administrative action infringes a person's significant liberty or property interests the question arises as to what procedures will satisfy constitutional due process requirements. Historically courts accorded due process to "rights" but not to "privileges." Government benefits (including employment, licenses, and the right to contract with government) were looked upon as a gratuity or privilege and not as a right. But by the 1960s the nation had become an administrative state and it was evident that this old dichotomy was no longer useful. The 1960s witnessed an increased emphasis on the individual's "liberties." At the same time, society began to demand an expansion of the historic common-law concept that limited procedural due process protection to traditional forms of ownership of real and personal property.

During the 1960s the New York City Department of Social Services followed the procedure

BOX 7.1 Supreme Court Perspective

MORRISSEY V. BREWER
408 U.S. 471 (1972)

Chief Justice Burger, writing for the Court:
. . . "[T]his Court now has rejected the concept that constitutional rights turn upon whether a governmental benefit is characterized as a 'right' or as a 'privilege.'" . . . Whether any procedural protections are due depends on the extent to which an individual will be "condemned to suffer grievous loss." . . . The question is not merely the "weight" of the individual's interest, but whether the nature of the interest is one within the contemplation of the "liberty or property" language of the Fourteenth Amendment. . . . Once it is determined that due process applies, the question remains what

process is due. It has been said so often by this Court and others as not to require citation of authority that due process is flexible and calls for such procedural protections as the particular situation demands. "[C]onsideration of what procedures due process may require under any given set of circumstances must begin with a determination of the precise nature of the government function involved as well as of the private interest that has been affected by governmental action." . . . To say that the concept of due process is flexible does not mean that judges are at large to apply it to any and all relationships. Its flexibility is in its scope once it has been determined that some process is due; it is a recognition that not all situations calling for procedural safeguards call for the same kind of procedure.

of furnishing a welfare recipient a seven-day notice before it terminated federally assisted welfare benefits. A welfare recipient who objected was permitted to file a written statement in protest; however, no provision was made for a predetermination evidentiary hearing. A welfare recipient filed suit contending that lack of a predetermination hearing before termination of his welfare benefits denied him due process of law. In the landmark case of *Goldberg v. Kelly* (1970),[23] the Supreme Court phrased the issue as: "[W]hether a State that terminates public assistance payments to a particular recipient without affording him the opportunity for an evidentiary hearing prior to termination denies the recipient procedural due process in violation of the Due Process Clause of the Fourteenth Amendment." The Court held that although New York was not required to conduct a full judicial or quasi-judicial hearing, a welfare recipient must be given an opportunity to confront and cross-examine witnesses before the agency could terminate public assistance benefits.

An extract of the Supreme Court's decision in *Goldberg v. Kelly* appears at the end of the chapter.

The Supreme Court used *Goldberg* as a vehicle to inject the concept that government benefits were an **entitlement** that required protection afforded by the constitutional mandate to due process of law. By the 1970s the Court extended this protection to various regulatory entitlements such as rights of civil servants and licensees. The Court also became very sensitive to "liberty interests." In 1972, in *Morrissey v. Brewer*,[24] it held that the Due Process Clause of the Fourteenth Amendment required a State to afford a parolee a notice and hearing with basic trial-type rights before it could revoke parole (see the Supreme Court Perspective feature contained in Box 7.1).

The same day the Court decided *Morrissey v. Brewer* it handed down its decision in *Board of Regents v. Roth*.[25] The Wisconsin State University-Oshkosh had hired David Roth as an assistant professor of political science for a one-year term. When he completed his term the University informed him he would not be rehired for the next academic year. Professor Roth contended that the University's failure to provide him an opportunity for a hearing violated his right to procedural due process of law. Because Roth was not a tenured professor the Court found that he had no legitimate property interest in continuing his employment and therefore was not entitled to a hearing when the university dismissed him. More significant than the result was Justice Potter Stewart's summary of the Court's recently developed views on the right to due process when either property or liberty interests are at stake:

> [T]he Court has fully and finally rejected the wooden distinction between 'rights' and 'privileges' that once seemed to govern the applicability of procedural due process rights. The Court has also made clear that the property interests protected by procedural due process extend well beyond actual ownership of real estate, chattels, or money. By the same token, the Court has required due process protection for deprivation of liberty beyond the sort of formal constraints imposed by the criminal process.[26]

In *Perry v. Sinderman*, also decided on the same day as *Roth* and *Morrissey*, the Court expounded a broad view of "property" for purposes of due process analysis, saying that one's "interest in a benefit is a 'property' interest for due process purposes if there are such rules or mutually explicit understandings that support his claim of entitlement to the benefit and that he may invoke at a hearing."[27]

The Supreme Court's decision in *Perry v. Sinderman* is excerpted at the end of the chapter.

In *Goss v. Lopez* (1975),[28] the Supreme Court split 5-4 in ruling that a ten-day suspension from public school deprived students of a property interest because state law created an entitlement for them to receive a public education and their suspension deprived them of liberty by interfering with that right. Thus, it held that the Due Process Clause required the school to provide students facing suspension basic procedural safeguards. The Court said, "At the very minimum, therefore, students facing suspension and the consequent interference with a protected property interest must be given "some kind of notice and some kind of hearing."[29] By this time a majority of the Court

appeared committed to an expanded construction of the Due Process Clause.

A New Pragmatic Approach to Procedural Due Process

The *Goldberg* requirement for a predetermination hearing was not a workable solution for administrative adjudication in a modern administrative state. The Supreme Court came to grips with the problem after George Eldridge brought suit contending that the Court's decision in *Goldberg* entitled him to a trial-type hearing before the Social Security Administration (SSA) could terminate his disability benefits. In its seminal decision in *Mathews v. Eldridge*,[30] the Court allowed the SSA, based on medical reports and examinations and without a predetermination hearing, to adjudge that Eldridge was no longer entitled to receive his disability benefits. Although the SSA did provide for a post-termination evidentiary hearing, payments could be terminated without a hearing. In a landmark ruling upholding the SSA's procedures Justice Lewis Powell announced a **three-part balancing test** to determine whether due process of law necessitates that trial-type procedures be employed in agency proceedings before an agency makes an adjudication. The new test would consider:

1. the private interest that will be affected by the official action;

2. the risk of an erroneous deprivation of such interest through the procedures used, and the probable value, if any, of additional or substitute safeguards; and

3. the administrative burdens that the additional or substitute procedural requirements would entail.[31]

An excerpt from the Supreme Court's decision in *Mathews v. Eldridge* (1976) is included at the end of the chapter.

The Supreme Court's decision in *Mathews v. Eldridge* soon became the basis for courts to employ a balancing test that enabled courts to uphold a variety of administrative actions without first holding an evidentiary hearing as long as provision is made for a **post–agency action hearing.** By the late 1970s and in the 1980s the Supreme Court seemed to have reached an accommodation between the rights of individuals to due process of law and the necessity for government to function effectively in the modern administrative environment. Thus, without a prior hearing it became possible for administrative authorities to revoke a driver's license where the driver had repeated convictions[32] and to uphold a suspension of a driver's license when a driver arrested for driving under the influence of alcoholic beverages refused to take a blood-alcohol or urinalysis test.[33] In each case a post-revocation or suspension hearing was provided.

The Court's new restrained approach was further evident when it reviewed a case involving two junior high school students in Dade County, Florida, who instituted suit against a certain public school official, alleging that the school's infliction of corporal punishment violated their constitutional rights. When the Court eventually reviewed the case in 1977 a key issue in *Ingraham v. Wright*,[34] was whether the Due Process Clause of the Fourteenth Amendment requires prior notice and an opportunity to be heard before the school could paddle the students for misconduct. The Court concluded that in light of the three-factor test delineated in *Mathews v. Eldridge*, the common-law remedies available under Florida law for excessive corporal punishment afforded the students sufficient due process of law. Again, writing for the majority of the Court, Justice Powell opined:

> If the punishment inflicted is later found to have been excessive . . . the school authorities inflicting it may be held liable in damages to the child and, if malice is shown, they may be subject to criminal penalties . . . the fact that any student injured could bring an action under Florida law for a teacher's use of excessive force adequately provided the necessary due process of law.[35]

In 1978 the Supreme Court found a city's notice threatening to cut off utility service was inadequate because it did not spell out a procedure that could be availed of by the homeowner. Yet the Court went on to say that an opportunity for an informal meeting with a responsible employee empowered to resolve the dispute in advance of the scheduled date of termination of utility service would be sufficient to satisfy due process consideration in such an instance.[36] The same year the Court held that a medical school did not have to hold a formal hearing before dismissing a student based on her inadequate performance in clinical functions.[37]

In 1979 the Court ruled that due process did not require a predetermination hearing before a horse trainer's license could be suspended when the trainer was suspected of drugging horses.[38] But the Court stated that due process required a prompt **postsuspension hearing.**

During the 1980s the Supreme Court appeared reluctant to insist on formal proceedings when informal procedures could reasonably protect an individual's right to due process. A prime case in point is *Cleveland Board of Education v. Loudermill*.[39] In 1979 the Cleveland, Ohio Board of Education employed James Loudermill as a security guard. He stated on his application that he had never been convicted of a felony. Some eleven months later the board discovered that he had been convicted of grand larceny several years before his application with the board. It then informed him he was being dismissed because of the false statement he made in filling out his employment application. Although classified as a civil service employee, Loudermill was not afforded an opportunity to respond to the charge or to challenge his dismissal. Loudermill challenged his dismissal, contending that he was unconstitutionally denied of a property right in his continued employment. In reviewing his challenge, the Supreme Court observed that property interests are not created by the Constitution. Rather, "they are created and their dimensions are defined by existing rule or understandings that stem from an independent source such as state law. . . ."[40] Because Loudermill was a civil service employee under Ohio law he could not be dismissed "except . . . for . . . misfeasance."[41] Reiterating that an essential principle of due process is that a deprivation of life, liberty, or property be preceded by notice and opportunity for hearing appropriate to the nature of the case, the Court held that this principle requires "some kind of a hearing" prior to the discharge of an employee such as Loudermill because he has a constitutionally protected property interest in his employment. The Court recognized that Loudermill was entitled to a full post-termination hearing, but concluded that prior to being terminated he was constitutionally entitled only to notice and some opportunity to respond.

> [A] tenured public employee is entitled to oral or written notice of the charges against him, an explanation of the employer's evidence, and an opportunity to present his side of the story. . . . To require more than this prior to termination would intrude to an unwarranted extent on the government's interest in quickly removing an unsatisfactory employee."[42]

The Supreme Court's decision in *Cleveland Board of Education v. Loudermill* (1985) is excerpted at the end of the chapter.

By the late 1980s the Supreme Court's decisions trended toward an expanded interpretation of "liberty" and "property" but with a pragmatic retraction of the extent that an administrative agency must go to satisfy the requirements of due process of law in specific situations. In November 1988, in a cogent analysis, Shapiro and Glicksman observed, "[T]his retraction of due process rights was motivated by concerns that elaborate procedures were inefficient and did little to make agencies' decisions more accurate."[43]

Due Process in the 1990s and 2000s

Having expanded the definitions of liberty and property, in the 1990s and 2000s the courts addressed the extent of due process that must be

accorded in a number of areas that affect the liberty and property interests of individuals. Among these have been immigration, licensure, pensions, and school and college issues.

Immigration Issues Efforts by immigration authorities to deport aliens to other countries continue to involve serious questions of procedural due process. For example, in *Kuhai v. INS*, (1999)[44] the Seventh Circuit Court of Appeals rejected an Immigration and Naturalization Service (INS) order deporting an alien to the Ukraine because she had not been given notice and the opportunity to brief the issue of whether she was deportable. Although born in the Ukraine, Ms. Kuhai was residing in Uzbekistan when that former Soviet republic became an independent nation. The Board of Immigration Appeals modified an administrative order changing the country of Kuhai's deportation from Uzbekistan to Ukraine. The court found the agency violated due process by not affording Ms. Kuhai an opportunity to brief the issue of changing the designation of countries for deportation from Uzbekistan to Ukraine, noting that "a deportation order without a fair hearing concerning that deportation violates due process."[45] The following year, in *Perez-Lastor v. INS* (2000),[46] the U.S. Court of Appeals for the Ninth Circuit found the translation at a hearing on Perez-Lastor's deportation hearing was incompetent. The court held that an incompetent translation at a deportation hearing deprives aliens of their due process rights to a fair and full hearing and remanded the case to the Board of Immigration Appeals with instructions to afford Perez-Lastor a new hearing.

Licensure Licensure involves the issuance, suspension and revocation of licenses. Cases involve property rights as well as procedural due process. Consider the case of Marc La Cloche, who served a prison term for conviction of robbery. During his time in prison he completed a vocational course in barbering. In anticipation of parole, he applied to the New York Secretary of State's division of licensing for a license as a barber appren-

---

BOX 7.2 Case in Point

Was a Former Municipal Employee Deprived of Due Process of Law by Being Denied a Jury Trial Before He Forfeited His Pension Rights?
Doherty v. Retirement Board of Medford
Massachusetts Supreme Judicial Court
680 N.E.2d 45 (Mass. 1997)

The Medford, Massachusetts, Retirement Board found that Thomas E. Doherty, a former city police officer, had misappropriated city funds when he provided his son with an advance copy of a police entrance examination to enable him to obtain city employment. After a lower court affirmed the board's ruling that Doherty had forfeited his retirement benefits, he obtained review in the Supreme Judicial Court, where he argued that the statute authorizing forfeiture violated his right to a jury

trial and that the board had denied him due process of law.

The court concluded that by permitting forfeiture of an employee's pension, the statute provided an equitable remedy of restitution. Thus, there was no violation of the state's guarantees to the right to trial by jury in controversies involving property. Moreover, the Seventh Amendment to the U.S. Constitution does not apply "where jury trials would be incompatible with the whole concept of administrative adjudication." Doherty was permitted to present evidence, cross-examine witnesses, and seek judicial review, and there was substantial evidence to uphold the board's findings and judgment. Thus, the board did not deny him due process of law. The court affirmed the board's judgment.

---

tice. The agency denied his request on the ground that his criminal history indicated a lack of good moral character required for licensure. On appeal, the New York court pointed out that having taught him a trade so he could earn a living, the state could not deny him a license solely because he had been convicted of a crime. The court remanded for a hearing before an administrative law judge (ALJ) on whether La Cloche is of sufficient moral character to receive a license.[47]

An interesting scenario arose in a case in Illinois involving the due process rights of the holders of liquor licenses. The case bears some resemblance to the *Londoner/Bi-Metallic* distinction discussed earlier. The Seventh Circuit had previously upheld an Illinois law that allowed the local electorate to prohibit the sale of liquor anywhere in a given precinct. An amendment to the state law allowed voters in a given precinct to elect to revoke a particular liquor license without the necessity of voting the entire precinct dry. In *Club Misty, Inc. v. Laski* (2000),[48] the court said the election under the original law was legislative in character in that it affected liquor licenses generally. But when it came to the electorate voting about a specific licensee without

affording proper notice and a hearing, it violated the due process rights of liquor licensees.

Pension Rights Because a vested right to a pension involves property interests, procedural due process increasingly comes into play in such instances as forfeiture of benefits of public officers and employees. The Case-in-Point found in Box 7.2 is illustrative.

Dismissal of Students from Public Educational Institutions for Academic Reasons
Public educational institutions are required to provide a level of due process rights to their students because they act as an arm of the state. In contrast to being suspended for disciplinary reasons, dismissal from a public school or college for academic reasons generally requires only minimal procedural protections. Yet, in *Nickerson v. University of Alaska, Anchorage*,[49] the Supreme Court of Alaska heard an appeal from Wayne Nickerson, who was dismissed from a teaching practicum in a special education course because of his inability to interact effectively with students and colleagues. Despite the fact Nickerson's dismissal was premised largely upon conduct, the court

accepted the university's characterization of his dismissal being for academic reasons. The court held that Nickerson was entitled to adequate notice of his pending dismissal to afford him a reasonable time to correct deficiencies, and, because the record was unclear, the court remanded the case to the lower court for further findings as to whether Nickerson had been given adequate notice of his dismissal.

Although academic institutions are generally held to a lower standard of procedural due process in academic suspensions, courts hold they must carefully observe the rules they prescribe for an administrative appeal from a decision adversely affecting a student's rights. This is exemplified in *Van Morfit v. University of South Florida*,[50] a Florida appellate court decision in 2001. The University of South Florida sent Van Morfit, a graduate student in anthropology, a letter alleging misconduct during a research project and informing him of his immediate suspension. After Van Morfit's administrative appeal resulted in the suspension being upheld, he sought relief from the state appellate court. The court found that the university violated the student's rights to the due process by its failure to follow its own disciplinary procedures, which included the student's right to have the witnesses testify in front of a hearing officer and the right to question witnesses. Thus, the case was one in which the university violated its own procedures, so the court remanded for a new administrative hearing to be conducted according to the university's rules.

An excerpt from *Van Morfit v. University of South Florida* is reprinted at the end of the chapter.

ALTERNATIVE FORMS
OF DISPUTE RESOLUTION

Recent years have witnessed a growing interest in **alternative dispute resolution (ADR)** both in civil and administrative disputes. Commonly referred to as "ADR," these methods of resolving

disputes take several forms, with negotiation, mini-trials, arbitration, and mediation being the most common. Much civil litigation is settled informally by negotiation between lawyers for contesting parties and by utilizing ADR methods.

In a mini-trial each side presents their proposed evidence and arguments before an impartial decision maker in an attempt to arrive at a settlement after considering the strength and weaknesses of a case. In arbitration parties select an impartial arbitrator and either privately, or under court supervision, agree to accept the results of an informal out-of-court adjudication. Mediation is the fastest growing form of ADR. In mediation a neutral third party, often one who has special qualifications in a particular field, acts as a facilitator in an informal nonadversarial process and assists disputants in reaching an acceptable settlement. Some mediation is conducted on a private basis; in other instances it is court-supervised. One key factor in mediation is that it is confidential and the statements made by parties cannot later be introduced in evidence if the mediation is unsuccessful.

By the 1980s ADR had become a popular form of resolving disputes in civil court proceedings, yet it was only in the last decade of the twentieth century that it came on the administrative law scene. Although there was considerable interest in ADR, it was legally questionable whether a federal administrative agency was authorized to agree to resolve disputes through ADR. Congress determined that the delay and costs involved in administrative proceedings had become too great. It settled the issue of ADR being authorized for administrative proceedings when it enacted the Administrative Dispute Resolution Act in 1990. The act was amended in 1996 and has become part of the APA in Sections 571 et seq. It defines alternative dispute resolution as "any procedure that is used, in lieu of an adjudication as defined in 5 U.S.C.A. § 551(7), to resolve issues in controversy, including, but not limited to, settlement negotiations, conciliation, facilitation, mediation, factfinding, minitrials, and arbitration, or any combination thereof."[51] The procedures are voluntary and parties involved must consent to such a proceeding.[52] The act provides for selection of mediators and arbitrators and for confidentiality of the settlement procedures.[53]

The act provides that an agency shall consider not using a dispute resolution proceeding if

1. a definitive or authoritative resolution of the matter is required for precedential value, and such a proceeding is not likely to be accepted generally as an authoritative precedent;

2. the matter involves or may bear upon significant questions of government policy that require additional procedures before a final resolution may be made;

3. maintaining established policies is of special importance, so that variations among individual decisions are not increased and such a proceeding would not likely reach consistent results among individual decisions; if maintaining established policies is of special importance, so that variations among individual decisions are not increased;

4. the matter significantly affects persons or organizations who are not parties to the proceeding;

5. a full public record of the proceeding is important, and a dispute resolution proceeding cannot provide such a record; and

6. the agency must maintain continuing jurisdiction over the matter with authority to alter the disposition of the matter in the light of changed circumstances, and a dispute resolution proceeding would interfere with the agency's fulfilling that requirement.[54]

States have become active supporters of settling administrative disputes through informal procedures. The North Carolina legislature has declared that it is the policy of that state that any dispute between an agency and another person that involves the person's rights, duties, or privileges, including licensing or the levy of a monetary penalty, should be settled through informal procedures.[55] In many states specific agencies, for example, motor vehicle departments and environmental commissions, have procedures that involve the forms of dispute resolution just mentioned.

THE RIGHT TO COUNSEL

There is no express **right to counsel** in administrative proceedings under the U.S. Constitution. The Sixth Amendment provides for the assistance of counsel to an accused in criminal proceedings, but this is not applicable to administrative proceedings. Nevertheless, the right to counsel in administrative proceedings in some instances can be read into the Due Process Clause of the federal and state constitutions. In addition, some federal and state statutes and some administrative regulations expressly confer the right to counsel in administrative proceedings.

Section 555(b) of the APA provides that "[a] person compelled to appear in person before an agency or representative thereof is entitled to be accompanied, represented, and advised by counsel." Note, however, this only applies to adjudications subject to the APA. And, of course, it has no applicability to state and local administrative agencies. Section 4-203(b) of the 1981 MSAPA provides: "Whether or not participating in person, any party may be advised and represented at the party's own expense by counsel or, if permitted by law, other representative."

The fact is that federal and state agencies routinely allow parties in administrative hearings to be represented by counsel. Therefore, the Supreme Court is not likely to be confronted with the issue, although in 1970 in *Goldberg v. Kelly*, the Court upheld the right of a welfare recipient in an agency hearing to be represented by counsel at his or her own expense.

The right to counsel is not applicable to investigatory as opposed to adjudicatory proceedings; however, the D.C. Circuit has held that the right to counsel was violated by a rule adopted by the National Regulatory Commission (NRC) governing investigations and inspections of licensed facilities. The NRC rule authorized exclusion of witnesses' counsel if there was a "reasonable basis for believing that counsel's presence would impair the investigation." The D.C. Circuit held the portion of the rule excluding attorneys violated the APA provision concerning the right to counsel.[56]

The right to counsel in adjudicatory proceedings does not mean that the government must provide counsel. As in civil court proceedings, the usual rule is that the party who retains counsel is responsible to pay that counsel's fees. Section 504 of the APA (incorporated as part of the Equal Access to Justice Act of 1980) does provide that if a party prevails in a formal adjudication or in court, that party may seek to have the government pay counsel fees and expenses unless the agency's position was "substantially justified" or unless it would be unjust to require the government to pay. To be liable for payment of fees and expenses the agency must have been a party involved. Some states have statutes that award attorney's fees to a prevailing party when the ALJ determines that a nonprevailing adverse party participated in a proceeding for an improper purpose.[57]

There is abundant authority that counsel's ineffectiveness can lead to a new trial for a defendant in a criminal case.[58] This has no applicability to administrative proceedings. Indeed, in some administrative proceedings, for example, claimants in Social Security hearings, a party may be represented by someone who is not a member of the legal profession. In university disciplinary hearings involving issues of student misconduct, students are often represented by faculty members, other students or other persons who are not members of the bar.

PREHEARING PROCESSES IN FORMAL ADJUDICATION

The federal APA provides procedural requirements for formal adjudication, often referred to as "on-the-record" or "trial-type" hearings, but Section 554(a) stipulates that these requirements apply only when a statute mandates that an agency adjudication be determined on-the-record after an opportunity for an agency hearing. Proceedings must be presided over by the agency head, a member of the agency, or by an **administrative law judge (ALJ)**.[59]

The Administrative Law Judge

In practice, an ALJ, formerly referred to as a "hearing examiner," conducts almost all adjudications at the federal level. At the federal level ALJs are selected on a merit basis and often have expertise peculiar to the agency. The Office of Personnel Management (OPM) oversees the selection of ALJs using methods designed to exclude politics from the appointment process.

State counterparts, often known as **hearing officers,** usually conduct state proceedings. The 1981 MSAPA recommends an office of administrative hearings headed by a director appointed by the governor and confirmed by the state senate. The office would employ persons admitted to practice law in the particular state and makes them available to agencies.[60] Some states follow this method; in other states agencies select their hearing officers, often opting to employ qualified lawyers who have specialized knowledge in the field of the particular agency's activities.

Personal or Financial Interest, Bias, Conflict, and Prejudgment ALJs function as impartial arbiters of disputes and federal law provides they may not be assigned to duties beyond their judicial functions. At the federal level they may be removed or disciplined only for good cause.[61] An ALJ who has any basis to be partial may recuse himself or herself. It is a basic principle of procedural due process that an ALJ who has a financial stake in a controversy or who exhibits a bias or hostility in favor or against a party or a party's counsel is disqualified from hearing a particular dispute. Section 556(b) of the APA provides that should a party in good faith timely file an affidavit alleging grounds for disqualification, the agency must make a determination on the record as to whether the ALJ is legally qualified to sit on a case. State procedures vary, but always there are similar requirements for recusal or disqualification of an administrative judge or hearing officer.

An ALJ regulates the course of a formal federal agency hearing. In the process ALJs administer oaths and affirmations, issue subpoenas, rule on offers of proof and receive relevant evidence, make findings of fact, and issue either an initial or recommended decision.[62] At the state level an administrative law judge or hearing officer usually performs the same functions and conducts the proceedings in contested adjudicatory cases in much the same manner.

To an onlooker a formal adjudicatory hearing resembles a nonjury civil trial in federal or state courts. But when one looks beyond the appearance there are some rather significant differences between a trial in a court of law and an administrative adjudication. In a judicial proceeding the decision maker (judge or jury) generally reviews a case without prior knowledge of the evidence whereas in an agency adjudication, it is considered beneficial that the agency head responsible for the final decision have an awareness of the facts involved in the general area of a dispute.

The Notice Requirement

Basic to any formal adjudication is the **notice requirement** that requires that affected parties be given notice of the time, place, and nature of the hearing to be held. Writing for the Supreme Court in 1950, Justice Robert Jackson admonished, "An elementary and fundamental requirement of due process in any proceeding which is to be accorded finality is notice reasonably calculated, under all the circumstances, to apprise interested parties of the pendency of the action and afford them an opportunity to present their objections."[63]

Section 554(b) of the APA requires that persons entitled to notice of an agency hearing shall be timely informed of: the time, place, and nature of the hearing; the legal authority and jurisdiction under which the hearing is to be held; and the matters of fact and law asserted.

The 1981 Model State Administrative Procedure Act provides that the presiding officer shall set the time and place of the hearing and give reasonable written notice to all parties and to all persons who have filed written petitions to intervene in the matter.[64] State laws impose similar requirements.

Motion Practice

Prior to an adjudicatory hearing counsel may seek various forms of relief by filing written **motions** with the agency. Among the more common objectives of motion practice are to seek a continuance, to intervene, to add parties, to dismiss a proceeding for lack of evidence, to disqualify a presiding officer, to consolidate one case with another, and to direct discovery or grant protection from discovery. Agency rules often set forth the administrative requirements for presentation and disposition of motions.

Intervention The results of an adjudicatory proceeding may affect others than the named parties. Those whose business interests are allied with or competitive to the named parties and public interest groups, for example, environmental organizations, may seek to become involved in the process of adjudication so they can have input into the resolution of the issues. The APA makes no provision for **intervention** by nonparties in formal adjudication; however, as in judicial proceedings, parties with a definite interest in the outcome of a case and who can show "good cause" may be permitted to intervene in accordance with statutory and agency regulations.

Many administrative agencies make provision for intervention. For example, Rule 3.14 of the Federal Trade Commission's (FTC's) Rules of Practice for Adjudication stipulates that "any individual, partnership, unincorporated association, or corporation desiring to intervene in an adjudicative proceeding shall make written application in the form of a motion setting forth the basis therefor. Such application shall have attached to it a certificate showing service thereof upon each party to the proceeding. . . ." The rule further provides that the ALJ or the Commission may by order permit the intervention to such extent and upon such terms as are provided by law or as otherwise may be deemed proper.

The 1981 MSAPA includes express provisions concerning intervention and allows the presiding officer to "grant a petition for intervention at any time, upon determining that the intervention sought is in the interests of justice and will not impair the orderly and prompt conduct of the proceedings."[65]

A California statute permits an applicant seeking to intervene to file a motion demonstrating that the applicant's legal rights, duties, privileges, or immunities will be substantially affected by the proceeding or that the applicant qualifies as an intervenor under a statute or regulation. The motion must be filed before the prehearing conference, and if granted, the presiding officer of the agency may limit the intervenor's participation to issues in which the intervenor has a particular interest. The California statute is nonexclusive, applying only when an agency opts to be governed by its provisions.[66]

Often the statutory and agency criteria for allowing intervention are somewhat vague. Consequently courts are sometimes called upon to determine whether individuals and organizations have a sufficient interest in a controversy to be allowed to intervene in an adjudication proceeding. The leading case in this field is *United Church of Christ v. Federal Communications Commission* (1966),[67] otherwise known as "the WLBT case," in which activists within the Civil Rights movement successfully challenged the broadcast license of a Mississippi radio station. After WLBT in Jackson, Mississippi filed for renewal of its broadcast license with the Federal Communications Commission (FCC), the United Church of Christ (UCC) asserted that it was a "party in interest" within the meaning of the Communications Act of 1934 and filed a petition to deny the station

renewal of its license. UCC alleged that "WLBT failed to serve the general public because it provided a disproportionate amount of commercials and entertainment and did not give a fair and balanced presentation of controversial issues, especially those concerning Negroes, who comprise almost forty-five per cent of the total population within its prime service area." Because of its policy to only allow competitors of existing stations to intervene, the FCC refused to allow UCC to be a party. On appeal, the D.C. Circuit disagreed. The court saw no reasons to exclude those with such an obvious and acute concern as the listening audience. The court observed:

> We can see no reason to exclude those with such an obvious and acute concern as the listening audience. This much seems essential to insure that the holders of broadcasting licenses be responsive to the needs of the audience, without which the broadcaster could not exist.[68]

In this and later cases federal courts equated the right to intervene with a petitioner's standing to seek judicial review, reasoning that intervention is essential for the right of judicial review to be effective.

Consolidation of Hearings In some instances an agency, on motion of interested parties, or on its own motion may consolidate two or more proceedings. Agency rules usually provide the ALJ with discretion to consolidate cases. There are some cases where **consolidation** may be required, for instance where more than one applicant is seeking a license or permit and only one can be issued. Such was the situation the Supreme Court addressed in 1945 in *Ashbacker Radio Corp. v. Federal Communications Commission.*[69] Two companies applied to the FCC for a broadcast license in adjoining communities. If the FCC were to grant both applications the stations would interfere with reception in the area. The Federal Communications Act provided that the FCC could grant a license without a formal hearing but it could not deny an application without one. After the FCC granted the first applicant a license without a formal hearing it scheduled the other applicant's request for a formal hearing. The Supreme Court held the FCC was required to consolidate the applications in order to determine which applicant was better qualified to serve the public interest. This requirement became known as the *Ashbacker* doctrine and mandates consolidation when two or more parties compete for a single license or permit.

Discovery Proceedings Discovery The process of obtaining information relevant to issues in judicial or administrative litigation is known as **discovery.** Federal and state rules of civil procedure authorize pretrial discovery that can lead to discovery of evidence that would be admissible at trial in civil litigation.[70] Discovery in a civil case may take the form of:

- interrogatories, that is written questions submitted by one party to another to be answered under oath;

- oral depositions, where, in advance of trial, a party or witness must answer under oath, usually before a court reporter, questions that may lead to relevant evidence (a subpoena is usually issued to compel a nonparty witness to give a deposition); and

- requests for production of relevant documents in advance of trial, or requests for a party to admit certain facts

Many lawyers contend these broad discovery rules often lead to out-of-court settlements and prevent litigants from being taken by surprise when a case must be tried. Courts have considerable discretion to control discovery and issue **protective orders** to protect privileged information (for example, spousal and clergy-penitent communications, trade secrets and so forth) and to curb abuse of the discovery process.

Administrative agencies often require information about the entities the agency regulates. Private parties also have the need to obtain information to assist in preparation of their posi-

tions in agency adjudication. Sometimes the processes of discovery yield this information. In other instances an agency may have to subpoena witnesses or records or issue subpoenas to assist private parties.

The federal APA contains no provision concerning discovery. When permitted by statute or agency rule, discovery in administrative adjudication is usually a matter of agency discretion controlled by the ALJ or presiding officer, who has the power to issue protective orders to avoid any abuses in discovery practices.

Some federal agencies have comprehensive discovery rules. Rule 3.31 of the Federal Trade Commission's Rules of Practice for Adjudication is an example. In addition to permitting discovery along the lines that courts permit, Rule 3.31(b)(2) requires counsel for parties to disclose to each other "a copy of, or a description by category and location of, all documents, data, compilations, and tangible things in the possession, custody, or control of the Commission or respondent(s) that are relevant to the allegations of the Commission's complaint, to the proposed relief, or to the defenses of the respondent. . . ." Rule 3.31(c)(2) provides the ALJ "may enter a protective order denying or limiting discovery to preserve the privilege of a witness, person, or governmental agency as governed by the Constitution, any applicable act of Congress, or the principles of the common law. . . ."

Several U.S. Courts of Appeals have ruled that there is no constitutional right to prehearing discovery in administrative proceedings; however, in 1973 the Court of Appeals for the D.C. Circuit stated that "discovery must be granted if in the particular situation a refusal to do so would so prejudice a party as to deny him due process."[71]

Apart from any permitted discovery processes three valuable resources at the federal level substitute to some degree for the broad discovery allowed in courts of law. First, the **Freedom of Information Act (FOIA),** which has become codified in Section 552 of the APA, allows any person to obtain copies of documents in agency files, subject to certain exemptions (see Chapter 4).

Second, parties have the right to subpoena persons and documents. Finally, under the **Jencks Act,**[72] a litigant in federal court is entitled, on demand, to a copy of a statement made by a prosecution witness after that witness has testified in court. The rule is generally invoked in criminal cases; however, at least one federal appellate court has ruled that when the government relies upon a witness's testimony in support of the government's claim it cannot deny access to that witness's prior statements, which might impeach the witness's testimony.[73]

The 1981 MSAPA allows the presiding officer to "issue subpoenas, discovery orders and protective orders, in accordance with the rules of civil procedure."[74] The reference to the rules of civil procedure would incorporate rules in each particular state, which rules tend to allow liberal rules of discovery through interrogatories, depositions, and requests for admissions.

Prehearing Conferences

Section 556(c)(6) of the APA requires the ALJ (or other presiding officer) to hold conferences for settlement or simplification of the issues in formal adjudications. A **prehearing conference** is similar to the pretrial conference in civil court, but may take place weeks or months in advance of the hearing. The conference affords counsel and the ALJ an opportunity to determine (and possibly simplify) the issues to be tried and to ascertain what facts the parties are willing to stipulate to as being undisputed. Section 554(b) of the APA requires agencies to entertain "offers of settlement, or proposals of adjustment when time, the nature of the proceedings, and the public interest permit." The prehearing conference affords the opportunity for arriving at a settlement between the agency and parties involved.

State administrative codes, or in some instances agency regulations, usually provide for prehearing conferences in trial-type adjudications. The Texas Administrative Code provides that the examiner conducting the conference may enter appropriate orders concerning prehearing discovery, stipulations of uncontested matters, and presentation of evidence, and should consider the following matters:

1. simplifying issues;

2. amending the pleadings;

3. making admissions of fact or stipulations to avoid the unnecessary introduction of proof;

4. designating parties;

5. setting the order of procedure at a hearing;

6. identifying and limiting the number of witnesses; and

7. resolving other matters which may expedite or simplify the disposition of the controversy, including settling issues in dispute.[75]

Today prehearing conferences are sometimes conducted by telephone, television, or other electronic means. The 1981 MSAPA expressly includes a provision to this effect.[76] Video conferencing and the Internet provide new opportunities to expand participation.

FORMAL ADJUDICATORY HEARINGS

Where a federal statute requires an adjudicatory hearing to be determined "on the record after an opportunity for an agency hearing" the conduct of a formal adjudicatory hearing bears a close resemblance to a nonjury trial in a civil court. As in a judicial proceeding, a formal adjudicatory hearing follows a definite format with an ALJ or other agency official presiding. A complete record is compiled of all pleadings, exhibits, testimony, and arguments. Table 7.1, which displays the index to the Federal Trade Commission Rules of Practice for Adjudicative Proceedings, provides a good illustration of the breadth of procedural rules in adjudication before federal agencies.

Table 7.1 Chapter I—Federal Trade Commission
Part 3—Rules of Practice for Adjudicative Proceedings

- 3.1   Scope of the rules in this part.
- 3.2   Nature of adjudicative proceedings.
- 3.11   Commencement of proceedings.
- 3.11A   Fast-track proceedings.
- 3.12   Answer.
- 3.13   Adjudicative hearing on issues arising in rulemaking proceedings under Fair Packaging and Labeling Act.
- 3.14   Intervention.
- 3.15   Amendments and supplemental pleadings.
- 3.21   Prehearing procedures.
- 3.22   Motions.
- 3.23   Interlocutory appeals.
- 3.24   Summary decisions.
- 3.25   Consent agreement settlements.
- 3.26   Motions following denial of preliminary injunctive relief.
- 3.31   General provisions.
- 3.32   Admissions.
- 3.33   Depositions.
- 3.34   Subpoenas.
- 3.35   Interrogatories to parties.
- 3.36   Applications for subpoenas for records, or appearances by officials or employees, of governmental agencies other than the Commission, and subpoenas to be served in a foreign country.
- 3.37   Production of documents and things; access for inspection and other purposes.
- 3.38   Motion for order compelling disclosure or discovery; sanctions.
- 3.38A   Withholding requested material.
- 3.39   Orders requiring witnesses to testify or provide other information and granting immunity.
- 3.40   Admissibility of evidence in advertising substantiation cases.
- 3.41   General rules.
- 3.42   Presiding officials.
- 3.43   Evidence.
- 3.44   Record.
- 3.45   In camera orders.
- 3.46   Proposed findings, conclusions, and order.
- 3.51   Initial decision.
- 3.52   Appeal from initial decision.
- 3.53   Review of initial decision in absence of appeal.
- 3.54   Decision on appeal or review.
- 3.55   Reconsideration.
- 3.56   Effective date of orders; application for stay.
- 3.71   Authority.
- 3.72   Reopening.
- 3.81   General provisions.
- 3.82   Information required from applicants.
- 3.83   Procedures for considering applicants.

Opening Statements

At the opening of an adjudicatory hearing the ALJ makes preliminary remarks and then administers oaths or affirmations to those who will testify. Counsel for the agency and the parties are each permitted to make a brief **opening statement.** The opening statement is not evidence, but it affords each counsel an opportunity to outline the issues and state what he or she intends to establish during the hearing.

Official Notice

In a court trial the judge may take judicial notice of the law and of certain well-known facts. For example, it is not necessary to prove who is president of the United States or matters that are commonly established by the calendar. Likewise, in administrative adjudications an ALJ may take **official notice** of applicable laws and commonly acknowledged facts.[77] This is similar to "judicial notice," but an ALJ has broader authority in this respect. While judges are limited to taking notice of facts that are commonly understood and beyond dispute, ALJs are permitted to take official notice of matters in agency files and of well-established facts peculiar to the area of the agency's expertise. The APA assumes that administrative agencies are authorized to take official notice of commonly acknowledged facts, but alludes to the doctrine only in Section 556(e), which states: "When an agency decision rests on official notice of a fact not appearing in the evidence in the record, a party is entitled, on timely request, to an opportunity to show to the contrary."[78]

Section 4-212(f) of the 1981 MSAPA includes a comprehensive provision that allows a presiding officer to take official notice. It states:

> Official notice may be taken of (i) any fact that could be judicially noticed in the court of this State, (ii) the record of other proceedings before the agency, (iii) technical or scientific matters within the agency's specialized knowledge, and (iv) codes or standards that have been adopted by an agency of the United States, of this State or of another state, or by a nationally recognized organization or association. Parties must be notified before or during the hearing, or before the issuance of any initial or final order that is based in whole or in part on facts or material noticed, of the specific facts or material noticed and the source thereof, including any staff memoranda and data, and be afforded an opportunity to contest and rebut the facts or material so noticed.

The Evidentiary Phase

After completing opening statements, counsel for the parties in an adjudicatory hearing present their **documentary exhibits** and their witnesses. After a direct examination by the counsel presenting a witness, that witness is subject to **cross-examination** by counsel for other parties "as may be required for a full and true disclosure of the facts."[79] Cross-examination can be very challenging in agency proceedings because many witnesses are highly qualified experts in technical fields. (See Box 7.3 for further discussion of expert testimony.) ALJs exercise considerable discretion in the extent of cross-examination permitted, but they tend to be liberal in order to insulate the proceedings from reversal should the case be reviewed by a court.

Although largely based on the common law, the rules of evidence in civil and criminal cases are codified at the federal and usually at the state level. Numerous rules restrict the introduction of most hearsay evidence, require the best available evidence of writings, and limit opinion evidence from lay witnesses. Courts strictly enforce the rules of evidence in jury trials but sometimes relax those rules in nonjury (bench) trials. In contrast, liberal standards on the admissibility of evidence apply in administrative adjudications. Section 556(d) of the APA states:

> Except as otherwise provided by statute, the proponent of a rule or order has the burden of proof. Any oral or documentary evidence may be received, but the agency as a matter

BOX 7.3   Case in Point

When Is Expert Testimony Necessary to Revoke a Doctor's License?
Medical Licensing Board of Indiana v. Ward
Indiana Court of Appeals
449 N.E.2d 1129 (Ind. App. 1983)

The Indiana Medical Licensing Board revoked Dr. Joseph M. Ward's chiropractor's license on the ground that he was guilty of willful or wanton conduct for having massaged the genitalia of several female patients. The Superior Court of Marion County found the Board's findings legally insufficient because its findings were not supported by expert medical testimony.

In reversing, the Court of Appeals found that the Board properly reached its decision without expert testimony. The court pointed out that where a question of medical diagnosis or treatment is crucial to the Board's decision, expert testimony is vital. Here, however, there was no justification for Dr. Ward's "treatments." Rejecting Dr. Ward's contention that expert testimony was required, the court observed that the charges against Dr. Ward related to his misconduct, not to an issue of alleviation of his patients' ills. The court reinstated the revocation of Dr. Ward's license to practice chiropractic medicine.

---

of policy shall provide for the exclusion of irrelevant, immaterial, or unduly repetitious evidence.

The rationale for allowing agencies flexibility in receiving evidence goes to the core function of the administrative process. Congress and state legislatures have determined that many disputes can be more expeditiously and satisfactorily resolved by allowing agencies to avoid many of the technical aspects of litigation in the civil courts. As a result much of the evidence in adjudicatory hearings is received in written form prepared by experts in the area of the dispute being adjudicated. Even if inadmissible evidence is admitted in an adjudicatory proceeding, such an error is not necessarily grounds to vacate the agency's decision. In reviewing administrative proceedings courts follow the **harmless error** rule set out in Section 706 of the APA and unless the error had a definite impact on the agency's decision the error is generally considered harmless.[80]

ALJs apply the **preponderance of evidence** standard in adjudicatory hearings. This is the standard applied to most civil cases in federal and state courts and is usually defined as "the greater weight of the evidence." In some civil

cases courts require a "clear and convincing" standard of proof, for example before a court severs parental rights. Statutes may provide for a higher standard of evidence.

Federal administrative agencies are not to deviate from the preponderance of evidence standard, absent statutory directive. This was highlighted in *Steadman v. United States*,[81] where the petitioner sought review of an order issued by the Securities and Exchange Commission (SEC). The petitioner leveled a major challenge against the SEC's use of the preponderance of the evidence standard in determining whether he had violated antifraud provisions of the federal securities laws. Because of the severity of sanctions involved, the petitioner argued that the SEC was required to apply the stricter "clear and convincing" standard in weighing the evidence. The Court rejected the contention, observing that Congress had the power to prescribe the evidentiary standards in administrative adjudications and it had directed the SEC to follow the preponderance of the evidence standard.

Where formal adjudication is conducted at the state level, the ALJ or hearing officer follows procedures in the evidentiary phase that closely track those under the federal APA. In some instances state courts impose a standard higher than the preponderance of evidence standard in certain types of adjudication. For example, the Florida Supreme Court holds that because of the gravity of revocation of a professional license (lawyer, real estate broker, teacher and so forth), the evidence must be clear and convincing.[82]

Closing Arguments

At the conclusion of an adjudicatory hearing, the ALJ or hearing officer customarily permits counsel a reasonable time for a **closing argument.** In some instances the arguments are oral; in others they are submitted in writing. Agency rules may provide for filing briefs by counsel for the parties involved. Absent such rules, an ALJ may exercise discretion to permit or require briefs to be filed.

DECISIONAL PROCESSES IN FORMAL ADJUDICATION

As noted above, an agency head may conduct an adjudicatory hearing, but in practice most hearings are conducted by an ALJ. Section 557(c) of the APA provides that in formal adjudication the parties are entitled to submit proposed findings and conclusions to the ALJ and the record must show the ALJ's ruling on each finding and conclusion before the ALJ issues either an **initial decision** or a **recommended decision.**[83] Likewise, Section 4-215(c) of the 1981 MSAPA states, "If a party has submitted proposed findings of fact, the order must include a ruling on the proposed findings."

The Requirement for a Reasoned Decision

It is basic to administrative adjudication that the decision maker states findings of fact and provides reasons for a decision. The Supreme Court emphasized this requirement in its 1970 decision in *Goldberg v. Kelly, supra.* Section 557 of the

federal APA includes this requirement, as does Section 4-215(c) of the 1981 MSAPA.

In *Matlovich v. Secretary of the Air Force,*[84] the D.C. Circuit in 1978 explained that the requirement that the ALJ make findings and provide reasons for a decision serves the following purposes:

> . . . Enabling the court to give proper review to the administrative determination; helping to keep the administrative agency within proper authority and discretion, as well as helping to avoid and prevent arbitrary, discriminatory, and irrational action by the agency, and informing the aggrieved person of the grounds of the administrative action so that he can plan his course of action (including the seeking of judicial review).

Initial and Recommended Decisions

An agency head who presides at a hearing can issue a final decision at the conclusion of proceedings. But in most instances an ALJ presides and issues an **initial decision,** which becomes the agency's decision unless review is sought from an appeal to the board or agency head. If, however, the adjudicatory hearing presents an issue where the decision will establish a new or revised policy, the agency may require the ALJ to issue only a **recommended decision.** A recommended decision must be considered by and acted upon by the agency before it can become effective.[85] The 1981 MSAPA is similar. It provides that if the presiding officer is the agency head, the presiding officer shall render a final order. Otherwise the presiding officer (usually the ALJ) renders an initial order, which becomes final unless revised by the agency head.[86]

Postdecisional Review

Review of decisions by the agency is either heard by the agency head or a subordinate official or review board. The APA stipulates that upon appeal from or review of a decision "the agency has all the powers which it would have in making the initial decision, except as it may limit the issues on notice or by rule."[87]

Rule 3.55 of the FTC's Rules of Practice for Adjudication illustrates one federal agency's approach to reconsideration. It provides:

Within fourteen (14) days after completion of service of a Commission decision, any party may file with the Commission a petition for reconsideration of such decision, setting forth the relief desired and the grounds in support thereof. Any petition filed under this subsection must be confined to new questions raised by the decision or final order and upon which the petitioner had no opportunity to argue before the Commission. Any party desiring to oppose such petition shall file an answer thereto within ten (10) days after service upon him of the petition. The filing of a petition for reconsideration shall not operate to stay the effective date of the decision or order or to toll [stop] the running of any statutory time period affecting such decision or order unless specifically so ordered by the Commission.

Section 4-216 of the 1981 MSAPA is to the same effect but covers the subject in more detail than the federal APA by including:

(e) The presiding officer shall afford each party an opportunity to present briefs and may afford each party an opportunity to present oral argument.

(f) Before rendering a final order, the presiding officer may cause a transcript to be prepared, at the agency's expense, of such portions of the proceeding under review, as the presiding officer considers necessary.

Unlike appellate courts, which defer to factual findings of the trial courts, an agency can disregard or revise an ALJ's findings and conclusions. The rationale for this rule is to preserve the policymaking authority of an agency.

EX PARTE CONTACTS

The term "ex parte" means "by one party." An **ex parte contact** is an **off the record communication** between an interested party and a person who has the responsibility for decision making out of the presence of other parties to the proceeding. Originally the APA did not include any provisions concerning ex parte contacts. Rather, in administrative proceedings courts considered whether such contacts had a bearing on whether parties involved were afforded due process of law.

The Codification of Restrictions on Ex Parte Contacts

In 1955, while hearings involving a Federal Trade Commission (FTC) complaint against the Pillsbury Company concerning acquisition of competing flour millers were ongoing before the ALJ, the U.S. Senate Judiciary Committee under the chairmanship of Senator Estes Kefauver summoned the chair and several members of the FTC to testify. Several senators voiced criticisms of the FTC's earlier decision involving the Pillsbury Company. Five years later the FTC ordered Pillsbury to divest itself of several companies it had acquired. Pillsbury attacked the order on several grounds, one of which alleged that Pillsbury had been denied due process because of Congressional interference with the decisional process while the case was under consideration.

In 1966, in *Pillsbury Company v. Federal Trade Commission*,[88] the Fifth Circuit Court of Appeals reviewed the FTC order that required the Pillsbury Company to divest itself of some baking companies. The court focused on the Congressional interference and remanded the case to the FTC for a new decision. In writing the court's opinion, Chief Judge Tuttle observed that. "[T]o subject an administrator to a searching examination as to how and why he reached his decision in a case still pending before him, and to criticize him for reaching the "wrong decision" . . . sacrifices the appearance of impartiality. . . ."[89]

Recognizing that formal adjudication should be conducted on basis of law and the evidence, Congress codified the *Pillsbury* doctrine by amending Section 557(d)(1) of the APA to prohibit any "interested person outside the agency" from making, or knowingly causing to be made to any decision-making official, "an ex parte communication relevant to the merits of the proceeding." Likewise it prohibits "any member of the agency, administrative law judge, or other employee involved in the decision-making process" from making or knowingly causing to be made to any interested person outside the agency "an ex parte communication relevant to the merits of the proceedings."

Long before Congress amended the APA to proscribe ex parte contacts, the 1961 MSAPA prohibited agency personnel responsible for decision making from communicating with persons in connection with contested cases except on notice and opportunity for all parties to participate. The 1981 MSAPA enlarged the prohibitions against ex parte contacts.[90]

Rules regarding ex parte contacts in informal adjudication are less certain. In recognition of the fact that some ex parte contacts between citizens and governmental administrators are useful many federal, state, and local agencies publish certain ethical standards in respect to contacts between citizens and agency officials.

Remedies Where an Improper Ex Parte Contact Occurs

If an improper ex parte contact occurs, APA Section 557(d)(1)(c) requires that a memorandum summarizing the contact must be filed in the record of the proceedings. It also includes administrative remedies for improper ex parte communications.

In *Professional Air Traffic Controllers Organization (PATCO) v. Federal Labor Relations Authority*

(FLRA) (1982)[91] the D.C. Circuit discussed the remedies for improper ex parte contacts.

> Section 557(d) contains two possible administrative remedies for improper ex parte communications. The first is disclosure of the communication and its content. . . . The second requires the violating party to "show cause why his claim or interest in the proceeding should not be dismissed, denied, disregarded, or otherwise adversely affected on account of (the) violation." . . . Congress did not intend, however, that an agency would require a party to "show cause" after every violation or that an agency would dismiss a party's interest more than rarely. . . . Indeed, the statutory language clearly states that a party's interest in the proceeding may be adversely affected only "to the extent consistent with the interests of justice and the policy of the underlying statutes." . . .[92]

Although the court found some improper contact it concluded there was insufficient reason to vacate the FLRA's decision or to remand the case for further proceedings.

CONCLUSION

Adjudication is a quasi-judicial agency process for formulating an order—the administrative counterpart of a nonjury trial in a civil court proceeding. If a federal agency's enabling statute requires a formal adjudicatory hearing, the Administrative Procedure Act, and at the state level a similar statute, usually requires a formal (trial-type) adjudicatory hearing in which ex parte contacts with the administrative law judge are prohibited. These hearings are conducted with many of the judicial trappings associated with a nonjury civil trial in a court of law and are designed to provide a full panoply of constitutional protections. But formal administrative hearings are infrequent. Rather, most adjudications are informal and the diversity of statutory requirements and agency rules makes it difficult to generalize as to when an adjudicatory hearing is required and, if required, the type of hearing that suffices. It is even more difficult to determine the extent to which ex parte contacts with an adjudicating agency are impermissible in such informal adjudications.

Irrespective of statutory requirements the Fifth and Fourteenth Amendments to the U.S. Constitution guarantee due process of law, which comes into play only when an agency adjudication affects liberty or property. In interpreting this broadly written guarantee, the U.S. Supreme Court has expanded traditional definitions of "property" and has afforded due process protections to persons who have "a legitimate entitlement" to government benefits. Consequently, when administrative action threatens a person's substantial liberty or property interests, the Supreme Court often insists that there be "some kind of hearing" even when statutory law provides for none. But with the rise of the administrative state, and the expansion of the concepts of "liberty" and "property," the Court has taken a pragmatic approach that does not always require a predetermination hearing even when one's liberty or property rights are affected. Rather, the trend is to look upon due process as a flexible concept and to allow informal actions to suffice as long as a **postdetermination hearing** is available.

KEY TERMS

1961 Model State Administrative Procedure Act (MSAPA)

1981 Model State Administrative Procedure Act (MSAPA)

adjudication

administrative law judge (ALJ)

Administrative Procedure Act (APA)

alternative dispute resolution (ADR)

closing argument

conclusions of law

consolidation

contested case

cross-examination

de novo

discovery

documentary exhibits

entitlement

ex parte contact

Fifth Amendment

findings of fact

formal adjudication

Fourteenth Amendment

Freedom of Information Act (FOIA)

harmless error

hearing officers

informal adjudication

initial decision

intervention

Jencks Act

liberty

motions

notice and hearing

notice requirement

"off the record" communication

official notice

opening statement

order

post-agency action hearing

postdetermination hearing

postsuspension hearing

predetermination hearing

prehearing conference

preponderance of evidence

privileges

procedural due process

property rights

protective orders

quasi-judicial

quasi-legislative

recommended decision

right to counsel

standing

three-part balancing test

QUESTIONS FOR THOUGHT
AND DISCUSSION

1. When does the federal Administrative Procedure Act require that an adjudicatory proceeding be conducted on a formal, i.e., "trial-type" basis?

2. What are the two basic requirements of due process of law when a person's property or liberty is significantly affected by administrative process?

3. What forms of alternative dispute resolution are authorized in federal administrative adjudications?

4. What effect did the Supreme Court's 1976 decision in *Matthews v. Eldridge* have on administrative adjudicatory proceedings?

5. To what extent have federal appellate courts continued to rely on the distinctions in the Supreme Court's *Londoner* and *BiMetallic* opinions?

6. What objectives are usually sought by filing motions in an adjudicatory proceeding?

7. Under what circumstances would an ALJ likely allow a conservancy association to intervene in a proceeding where the Environmental Protection Agency is adjudicating a case involving an oil company's alleged violation of the Clean Water Act?

8. What is meant by "discovery" in administrative proceedings? Name three types of discovery proceedings.

9. What is a prehearing conference before an ALJ designed to accomplish?

10. Identify the principal elements of a formal adjudicatory hearing.

11. Compare the functions performed by an administrative law judge to those performed by a judge in a nonjury trial in a civil court.

12. What is "official notice?" Give an example. How does this vary from the standard of "judicial notice" in civil court trials?

13. Compare the standards for admissibility of evidence in administrative proceedings to the standards applicable in civil proceedings in a court of law.

14. What is the difference in the effect of an "initial decision" and a "recommended decision" by an ALJ in a federal adjudicatory proceeding?

15. What is meant by an "ex parte contact?" To what extent are ex parte contacts regulated in formal administrative adjudications?

EDITED CASE   United States v. Florida East Coast Ry. Co.
United States Supreme Court, 410 U.S. 224 (1973)

[In this case the Supreme Court holds that a statutory requirement directing the Interstate Commerce Commission to conduct a "hearing" before establishing certain charges was governed by Section 553 of the APA and required neither a formal rulemaking procedure or a trial-type hearing.]

Justice Rehnquist delivered the opinion of the Court.

Appellees, two railroad companies, brought this action in the District Court for the Middle District of Florida to set aside the incentive per diem rates established by appellant Interstate Commerce Commission in a rulemaking proceeding. . . . The District Court held that the language of . . . the Interstate Commerce Act, 24 Stat. 379, as amended, 49 U.S.C. §1 (14) (a), required the Commission in a proceeding such as this to act in accordance with the Administrative Procedure Act, 5 U.S.C. §556 (d), and that the Commission's determination to receive submissions from the appellees only in written form was a violation of that section

---

EDITED CASE   United States v. Florida East Coast Ry. Co. (Continued)

---

because the appellees were "prejudiced" by that determination within the meaning of that section.

Following our decision last Term in *United States v. Allegheny-Ludlum Steel Corp.*, 406 U.S. 742 (1972), we . . . requested the parties to brief the question of whether the Commission's proceeding was governed by 5 U.S.C. §553, or by §556 and §557, of the Administrative Procedure Act. We here decide that the Commission's proceeding was governed only by §553 of that Act, and that appellees received the "hearing" required by §1 (14) (a) of the Interstate Commerce Act. We, therefore, reverse the judgment of the District Court and remand the case to that court for further consideration of appellees' other contentions that were raised there, but which we do not decide. . . .

This case arises from the factual background of a chronic freight-car shortage on the Nation's railroads. . . . Congressional concern for the problem was manifested in the enactment in 1966 of an amendment to §1 (14) (a) of the Interstate Commerce Act, enlarging the Commission's authority to prescribe per diem charges for the use by one railroad of freight cars owned by another. . . .

In December 1967, the Commission initiated the rulemaking procedure giving rise to the order that appellees here challenge. It directed Class I and Class II line-haul railroads to compile and report detailed information with respect to freight-car demand and supply at numerous sample stations for selected days of the week during 12 four-week periods, beginning January 29, 1968. . . .

The Commission . . . issued in December 1969 an interim report announcing its tentative decision to adopt incentive per diem charges on standard boxcars based on the information compiled by the railroads. The substantive decision reached by the Commission was that so-called "incentive" per diem charges should be paid by any railroad using on its lines a standard boxcar owned by another railroad. Before the enactment of the 1966 amendment to the Interstate Commerce Act, it was generally thought that the Commission's authority to fix per diem payments for freight car use was limited to setting an amount that reflected fair return on investment for the owning railroad, without any regard being had for the desirability of prompt return to the owning line or for the encouragement of additional purchases of freight cars by the

railroads as a method of investing capital. The Commission concluded . . . that in view of the 1966 amendment it could impose additional "incentive" per diem charges to spur prompt return of existing cars and to make acquisition of new cars financially attractive to the railroads. . . .

Both appellee railroads filed statements objecting to the Commission's proposal and requesting an oral hearing. . . . In April 1970, the Commission, without having held further "hearings," issued a supplemental report making some modifications in the tentative conclusions earlier reached, but overruling in toto the requests of appellees. The District Court held that in so doing the Commission violated 556 (d) of the Administrative Procedure Act, and it was on this basis that it set aside the order of the Commission. . . .

In *United States v. Allegheny-Ludlum Steel Corp.*, supra, we held that the language of §1 (14) (a) of the Interstate Commerce Act authorizing the Commission to act "after hearing" was not the equivalent of a requirement that a rule be made "on the record after opportunity for an agency hearing" as the latter term is used in §553 (c) of the Administrative Procedure Act. Since the 1966 amendment to §1 (14) (a), under which the Commission was here proceeding, does not by its terms add to the hearing requirement contained in the earlier language, the same result should obtain here unless that amendment contains language that is tantamount to such a requirement. Appellees contend that such language is found in the provisions of that Act requiring that: "[T]he Commission shall give consideration to the national level of ownership of such type of freight car and to other factors affecting the adequacy of the national freight car supply, and shall, on the basis of such consideration, determine whether compensation should be computed. . . ."

While this language is undoubtedly a mandate to the Commission to consider the factors there set forth in reaching any conclusion as to imposition of per diem incentive charges, it adds to the hearing requirements of the section neither expressly nor by implication. We know of no reason to think that an administrative agency in reaching a decision cannot accord consideration to factors such as those set forth in the 1966 amendment by means

(*Continued*)

EDITED CASE   United States v. Florida East Coast Ry. Co. (Continued)

other than a trial-type hearing or the presentation of oral argument by the affected parties. Congress by that amendment specified necessary components of the ultimate decision, but it did not specify the method by which the Commission should acquire information about those components. . . .

Inextricably intertwined with the hearing requirement of the Administrative Procedure Act in this case is the meaning to be given to the language "after hearing" in §1 (14) (a) of the Interstate Commerce Act. Appellees, both here and in the court below, contend that the Commission procedure here fell short of that mandated by the "hearing" requirement of §1 (14) (a), even though it may have satisfied §553 of the Administrative Procedure Act. The Administrative Procedure Act states that none of its provisions "limit or repeal additional requirements imposed by statute or otherwise recognized by law." 5 U.S.C. §559. Thus, even though the Commission was not required to comply with §556 and §557 of that Act, it was required to accord the "hearing" specified in §1 (14) (a) of the Interstate Commerce Act. Though the District Court did not pass on this contention, it is so closely related to the claim based on the Administrative Procedure Act that we proceed to decide it now. . . .

The term "hearing" in its legal context undoubtedly has a host of meanings. Its meaning undoubtedly will vary, depending on whether it is used in the context of a rulemaking-type proceeding or in the context of a proceeding devoted to the adjudication of particular disputed facts. . . .

Section 553 excepts from its requirements rulemaking devoted to "interpretative rules, general statements of policy, or rules of agency organization, procedure, or practice," and rulemaking "when the agency for good cause finds . . . that notice and public procedure thereon are impracticable, unnecessary, or contrary to the public interest." This exception does not apply, however, "when notice or hearing is required by statute"; in those cases, even though interpretative rulemaking be involved, the requirements of §553 apply. But since these requirements themselves do not mandate any oral presentation, . . . it cannot be doubted that a statute that requires a "hearing" prior to rulemaking may in some circumstances be satisfied by procedures that meet only the standards of §553. . . .

Similarly, even where the statute requires that the rulemaking procedure take place "on the record after opportunity for an agency hearing," thus triggering the applicability of §556, subsection (d) provides that the agency may proceed by the submission of all or part of the evidence in written form if a party will not be "prejudiced thereby." Again, the Act makes it plain that a specific statutory mandate that the proceedings take place on the record after hearing may be satisfied in some circumstances by evidentiary submission in written form only.

We think this treatment of the term "hearing" in the Administrative Procedure Act affords a sufficient basis for concluding that the requirement of a "hearing" . . . in a situation where the Commission was acting under the 1966 statutory rulemaking authority that Congress had conferred upon it, did not by its own force require the Commission either to hear oral testimony, to permit cross-examination of Commission witnesses, or to hear oral argument. Here, the Commission promulgated a tentative draft of an order, and accorded all interested parties 60 days in which to file statements of position, submissions of evidence, and other relevant observations. The parties had fair notice of exactly what the Commission proposed to do, and were given an opportunity to comment, to object, or to make some other form of written submission. The final order of the Commission indicates that it gave consideration to the statements of the two appellees here. Given the "open-ended" nature of the proceedings, and the Commission's announced willingness to consider proposals for modification after operating experience had been acquired, we think the hearing requirement of §1 (14) (a) of the Act was met. . . .

The basic distinction between rulemaking and adjudication is illustrated by this Court's treatment of two related cases under the Due Process Clause of the Fourteenth Amendment. In *Londoner v. Denver*, cited in oral argument by appellees, 210 U.S. 373 (1908), the Court held that due process had not been accorded a landowner who objected to the amount assessed against his land as its share of the benefit resulting from the paving of a street. Local procedure had accorded him the right to file a written complaint and objection, but not

---

EDITED CASE   United States v. Florida East Coast Ry. Co. (Continued)

---

to be heard orally. This Court held that due process of law required that he "have the right to support his allegations by argument however brief, and, if need be, by proof, however informal." . . . But in the later case of *Bi-Metallic Investment Co. v. State Board of Equalization*, 239 U.S. 441 (1915), the Court held that no hearing at all was constitutionally required prior to a decision by state tax officers in Colorado to increase the valuation of all taxable property in Denver by a substantial percentage. The Court distinguished *Londoner* by stating that there a small number of persons "were exceptionally affected, in each case upon individual grounds." . . .

Later decisions have continued to observe the distinction adverted to in *Bi-Metallic Investment Co.*, supra. . . . While the line dividing [rulemaking and adjudication] may not always be a bright one, these decisions represent a recognized distinction in administrative law between proceedings for the purpose of promulgating policy-type rules or standards, on the one hand, and proceedings designed to adjudicate disputed facts in particular cases on the other.

Here, the incentive payments proposed by the Commission in its tentative order, and later adopted in its final order, were applicable across the board to all of the common carriers by railroad subject to the Interstate Commerce Act. No effort was made to single out any particular railroad for special consideration based on its own peculiar circumstances. Indeed, one of the objections of appellee Florida East Coast was that it and other terminating carriers should have been treated differently from the generality of the railroads. But the fact that the order may in its effects have been thought more disadvantageous by some railroads than by others does not change its generalized nature. Though the Commission obviously relied on factual inferences as a basis for its order, the source of these factual inferences was apparent to anyone who read the order of December 1969. The factual inferences were used in the formulation of a basically legislative-type judgment, for prospective application only, rather than in adjudicating a particular set of disputed facts.

The Commission's procedure satisfied both the provisions of §1 (14) (a) of the Interstate Commerce Act and of the Administrative Procedure Act, and were not inconsistent with prior decisions of this Court. We, therefore, reverse the judgment of the District Court, and remand the case so that it may consider those contentions of the parties that are not disposed of by this opinion. . . .

Justice Powell took no part in the consideration or decision of this case.

Justice Douglas, with whom *Justice Stewart* concurs, dissenting.

The present decision makes a sharp break with traditional concepts of procedural due process. The Commission order under attack is tantamount to a rate order. . . .

The question is whether the Interstate Commerce Commission procedures used in this rate case "for the submission of . . . evidence in written form" avoided prejudice to the appellees so as to comport with the requirements of the Administrative Procedure Act. . . .

The more exacting hearing provisions of the Administrative Procedure Act . . . are only applicable, of course, if the "rules are required by statute to be made on the record after opportunity for an agency hearing." . . .

Section 1 (14) (a) of the Interstate Commerce Act bestows upon the Commission broad discretionary power to determine incentive rates. These rates may have devastating effects on a particular line. . . . [T]he amount of incentive compensation paid by debtor lines amounts to millions of dollars each six-month period. Nevertheless, the courts must defer to the Commission as long as its findings are supported by substantial evidence and it has not abused its discretion. "All the more insistent is the need, when power has been bestowed so freely, that the 'inexorable safeguard' . . . of a fair and open hearing be maintained in its integrity." . . .

Accordingly, I would hold that appellees were not afforded the hearing guaranteed by §1 (14) (a) of the Interstate Commerce Act and 5 U.S.C. §553, §556, and §557, and would affirm the decision of the District Court.

EDITED CASE   Goldberg v. Kelly
United States Supreme Court, 397 U.S. 254 (1970)

[A group of welfare recipients from New York City brought suit challenging an action by a state social services agency terminating their benefits without a prior evidentiary hearing. They claimed that the agency's action violated the Due Process Clause of the Fourteenth Amendment.]

Justice Brennan delivered the opinion of the Court.

The constitutional issue to be decided . . . is the narrow one whether the Due Process Clause requires that the recipient be afforded an evidentiary hearing before the termination of benefits. . . .

The constitutional challenge cannot be answered by an argument that public assistance benefits are "a 'privilege' and not a 'right.'" . . . Relevant constitutional restraints apply as much to the withdrawal of public assistance benefits as to disqualification for unemployment compensation, . . . or to denial of a tax exemption, . . . or to discharge from public employment. . . . The extent to which procedural due process must be afforded the recipient is influenced by the extent to which he may be "condemned to suffer grievous loss," . . . depends upon whether the recipient's interest in avoiding that loss outweighs the governmental interest in summary adjudication. Accordingly, . . . "consideration of what procedures due process may require under any given set of circumstances must begin with a determination of the precise nature of the government function involved as well as of the private interest that has been affected by governmental action." . . .

It is true, of course, that some governmental benefits may be administratively terminated without affording the recipient a pre-termination evidentiary hearing. But we agree . . . that when welfare is discontinued, only a pre-termination evidentiary hearing provides the recipient with procedural due process. For qualified recipients, welfare provides the means to obtain essential food, clothing, housing, and medical care. . . . Thus the crucial factor in this context—a factor not present in the case of the blacklisted government contractor, the discharged government employee, the taxpayer denied a tax exemption, or virtually anyone else whose governmental entitlements are ended—is that termination of aid pending resolution of a controversy over eligibility may deprive an eligible recipient of the very means by which to live while he waits. Since he lacks independent resources, his situation becomes immediately desperate. His need to concentrate upon finding the means for daily subsistence, in turn, adversely affects his ability to seek redress from the welfare bureaucracy.

Moreover, important governmental interests are promoted by affording recipients a pre-termination evidentiary hearing. From its founding the Nation's basic commitment has been to foster the dignity and well-being of all persons within its borders. We have come to recognize that forces not within the control of the poor contribute to their poverty. This perception, against the background of our traditions, has significantly influenced the development of the contemporary public assistance system. Welfare, by meeting the basic demands of subsistence, can help bring within the reach of the poor the same opportunities that are available to others to participate meaningfully in the life of the community. At the same time, welfare guards against the societal malaise that may flow from a widespread sense of unjustified frustration and insecurity. Public assistance, then, is not mere charity, but a means to "promote the general Welfare, and secure the Blessings of Liberty to ourselves and our Posterity." The same governmental interests that counsel the provision of welfare, counsel as well its uninterrupted provision to those eligible to receive it; pre-termination evidentiary hearings are indispensable to that end.

Appellant does not challenge the force of these considerations but argues that they are outweighed by countervailing governmental interests in conserving fiscal and administrative resources. These interests, the argument goes, justify the delay of any evidentiary hearing until after discontinuance of the grants. Summary adjudication protects the public fisc by stopping payments promptly upon discovery of reason to believe that a recipient is no longer eligible. Since most terminations are accepted without challenge, summary adjudication also conserves both the fisc and administrative

EDITED CASE　Goldberg v. Kelly (Continued)

time and energy by reducing the number of evidentiary hearings actually held.

We agree . . . however, that these governmental interests are not overriding in the welfare context. The requirement of a prior hearing doubtless involves some greater expense, and the benefits paid to ineligible recipients pending decision at the hearing probably cannot be recouped, since these recipients are likely to be judgment-proof. But the State is not without weapons to minimize these increased costs. Much of the drain on fiscal and administrative resources can be reduced by developing procedures for prompt pre-termination hearings and by skillful use of personnel and facilities. Indeed, the very provision for a post-termination evidentiary hearing in New York's Home Relief program is itself cogent evidence that the State recognizes the primacy of the public interest in correct eligibility determinations and therefore in the provision of procedural safeguards. Thus, the interest of the eligible recipient in uninterrupted receipt of public assistance, coupled with the State's interest that his payments not be erroneously terminated, clearly outweighs the State's competing concern to prevent any increase in its fiscal and administrative burdens. . . .

The city's procedures presently do not permit recipients to appear personally with or without counsel before the official who finally determines continued eligibility. Thus a recipient is not permitted to present evidence to that official orally, or to confront or cross-examine adverse witnesses. These omissions are fatal to the constitutional adequacy of the procedures.

The opportunity to be heard must be tailored to the capacities and circumstances of those who are to be heard. It is not enough that a welfare recipient may present his position to the decision maker in writing or secondhand through his caseworker. Written submissions are an unrealistic option for most recipients, who lack the educational attainment necessary to write effectively and who cannot obtain professional assistance. Moreover, written submissions do not afford the flexibility of oral presentations; they do not permit the recipient to mold his argument to the issues the decision maker appears to regard as important. Particularly where credibility and veracity are at

issue, as they must be in many termination proceedings, written submissions are a wholly unsatisfactory basis for decision. The secondhand presentation to the decision maker by the caseworker has its own deficiencies; since the caseworker usually gathers the facts upon which the charge of ineligibility rests, the presentation of the recipient's side of the controversy cannot safely be left to him. Therefore a recipient must be allowed to state his position orally. Informal procedures will suffice; in this context due process does not require a particular order of proof or mode of offering evidence.

In almost every setting where important decisions turn on questions of fact, due process requires an opportunity to confront and cross-examine adverse witnesses. . . .

Welfare recipients must therefore be given an opportunity to confront and cross-examine the witnesses relied on by the department. . . .

Finally, the decisionmaker's conclusion as to a recipient's eligibility must rest solely on the legal rules and evidence adduced at the hearing. . . . To demonstrate compliance with this elementary requirement, the decision maker should state the reasons for his determination and indicate the evidence he relied on, . . . though his statement need not amount to a full opinion or even formal findings of fact and conclusions of law. And, of course, an impartial decision maker is essential. . . . We agree with the District Court that prior involvement in some aspects of a case will not necessarily bar a welfare official from acting as a decision maker. He should not, however, have participated in making the determination under review. . . .

Chief Justice Burger*,** and ***Justices Stewart and ***Black,*** dissenting. . . .

In the last half century the United States, along with many, perhaps most, other nations of the world, has moved far toward becoming a welfare state, that is, a nation that for one reason or another taxes its most affluent people to help support, feed, clothe, and shelter its less fortunate citizens. The result is that today more than nine million men, women, and children in the United States receive some kind of state or federally

(Continued)

EDITED CASE   Goldberg v. Kelly (Continued)

---

financed public assistance in the form of allowances or gratuities, generally paid them periodically, usually by the week, month, or quarter. Since these gratuities are paid on the basis of need, the list of recipients is not static, and some people go off the lists and others are added from time to time. These ever-changing lists put a constant administrative burden on government and it certainly could not have reasonably anticipated that this burden would include the additional procedural expense imposed by the Court today. . . .

The procedure required today as a matter of constitutional law finds no precedent in our legal system. Reduced to its simplest terms, the problem in this case is similar to that frequently encountered when two parties have an ongoing legal relationship that requires one party to make periodic payments to the other. Often the situation arises where the party "owing" the money stops paying it and justifies his conduct by arguing that the recipient is not legally entitled to payment. The recipient can, of course, disagree and go to court to compel payment. But I know of no situation in our legal system in which the person alleged to owe money to another is required by law to continue making payments to a judgment-proof claimant without the benefit of any security or bond to insure that these payments can be recovered if he wins his legal argument. Yet today's decision in no way obligates the welfare recipient to pay back any benefits wrongfully received during the pre-termination evidentiary hearings or post any bond, and in all "fairness" it could not do so. These recipients are by definition too poor to post a bond or to repay the benefits that, as the majority assumes, must be spent as received to insure survival.

The Court apparently feels that this decision will benefit the poor and needy. In my judgment the eventual result will be just the opposite. While today's decision requires only an administrative, evidentiary hearing, the inevitable logic of the approach taken will lead to constitutionally imposed, time-consuming delays of a full adversary process of administrative and judicial review. In the next case the welfare recipients are bound to argue that cutting off benefits before judicial review of the agency's decision is also a denial of due process. Since, by hypothesis, termination of aid at that point may still "deprive an eligible recipient of the very means by which to live while he waits," . . . I would be surprised if the weighing process did not compel the conclusion that termination without full judicial review would be unconscionable. After all, at each step, as the majority seems to feel, the issue is only one of weighing the government's pocketbook against the actual survival of the recipient, and surely that balance must always tip in favor of the individual. Similarly today's decision requires only the opportunity to have the benefit of counsel at the administrative hearing, but it is difficult to believe that the same reasoning process would not require the appointment of counsel, for otherwise the right to counsel is a meaningless one since these people are too poor to hire their own advocates. . . . Thus the end result of today's decision may well be that the government, once it decides to give welfare benefits, cannot reverse that decision until the recipient has had the benefits of full administrative and judicial review, including, of course, the opportunity to present his case to this Court. Since this process will usually entail a delay of several years, the inevitable result of such a constitutionally imposed burden will be that the government will not put a claimant on the rolls initially until it has made an exhaustive investigation to determine his eligibility. While this Court will perhaps have insured that no needy person will be taken off the rolls without a full "due process" proceeding, it will also have insured that many will never get on the rolls, or at least that they will remain destitute during the lengthy proceedings followed to determine initial eligibility.

. . . The operation of a welfare state is a new experiment for our Nation. For this reason, among others, I feel that new experiments in carrying out a welfare program should not be frozen into our constitutional structure. They should be left, as are other legislative determinations, to the Congress and the legislatures that the people elect to make our laws.

EDITED CASE   Perry v. Sinderman
United States Supreme Court, 408 U.S. 593 (1972)

[Robert Sinderman, a professor at Odessa Junior College in Texas, became embroiled in a political controversy with the administration of the College and, as a result, his one-year contract was not renewed. Sinderman brought suit in federal court alleging that the College's decision not to renew his contract was in retaliation for his political statements and therefore violated his constitutional rights under the First Amendment. He also claimed that the College's failure to provide him an opportunity for a hearing violated the Due Process Clause of the Fourteenth Amendment. Readers should pay particular attention to Justice Stewart's discussion of Sinderman's due process claim.]

Justice Stewart delivered the opinion of the Court.

From 1959 to 1969 the respondent, Robert Sindermann, was a teacher in the state college system of the State of Texas. After teaching for two years at the University of Texas and for four years at San Antonio Junior College, he became a professor of Government and Social Science at Odessa Junior College in 1965. He was employed at the college for four successive years, under a series of one-year contracts. He was successful enough to be appointed, for a time, the cochairman of his department.

During the 1968-1969 academic year, however, controversy arose between the respondent and the college administration. The respondent was elected president of the Texas Junior College Teachers Association. In this capacity, he left his teaching duties on several occasions to testify before committees of the Texas Legislature, and he became involved in public disagreements with the policies of the college's Board of Regents. In particular, he aligned himself with a group advocating the elevation of the college to four-year status—a change opposed by the Regents. And, on one occasion, a newspaper advertisement appeared over his name that was highly critical of the Regents.

Finally, in May 1969, the respondent's one-year employment contract terminated and the Board of Regents voted not to offer him a new contract for the next academic year. The Regents issued a press release setting forth allegations of the respondent's insubordination. But they provided him no official statement of the reasons for the nonrenewal of his contract. And they allowed him no opportunity for a hearing to challenge the basis of the nonrenewal. . . .

I

The first question presented is whether the respondent's lack of a contractual or tenure right to re-employment, taken alone, defeats his claim that the nonrenewal of his contract violated the First and Fourteenth Amendments. We hold that it does not.

For at least a quarter-century, this Court has made clear that even though a person has no "right" to a valuable governmental benefit and even though the government may deny him the benefit for any number of reasons, there are some reasons upon which the government may not rely. It may not deny a benefit to a person on a basis that infringes his constitutionally protected interests—especially, his interest in freedom of speech. For if the government could deny a benefit to a person because of his constitutionally protected speech or associations, his exercise of those freedoms would in effect be penalized and inhibited. This would allow the government to "produce a result which [it] could not command directly." . . . Such interference with constitutional rights is impermissible.

We have applied this general principle to denials of tax exemptions, . . . unemployment benefits, . . . and welfare payments. . . . But, most often, we have applied the principle to denials of public employment. . . . We have applied the principle regardless of the public employee's contractual or other claim to a job. . . .

Thus, the respondent's lack of a contractual or tenure "right" to re-employment for the 1969-1970 academic year is immaterial to his free speech claim. Indeed, twice before, this Court has specifically held that the nonrenewal of a nontenured public school teacher's one-year contract may not be predicated on his exercise of First and Fourteenth Amendment rights. . . . We reaffirm those holdings here.

In this case, of course, the respondent has yet to show that the decision not to renew his contract was, in fact, made in retaliation for his exercise of the constitutional right of free speech. The District

(Continued)

EDITED CASE   Perry v. Sinderman (Continued)

Court foreclosed any opportunity to make this showing when it granted summary judgment [for the Board of Regents]. Hence, we cannot now hold that the Board of Regents' action was invalid.

But we agree with the Court of Appeals that there is a genuine dispute as to "whether the college refused to renew the teaching contract on an impermissible basis—as a reprisal for the exercise of constitutionally protected rights." . . . The respondent has alleged that his nonretention was based on his testimony before legislative committees and his other public statements critical of the Regents' policies. And he has alleged that this public criticism was within the First and Fourteenth Amendments' protection of freedom of speech. Plainly, these allegations present a bona fide constitutional claim. For this Court has held that a teacher's public criticism of his superiors on matters of public concern may be constitutionally protected and may, therefore, be an impermissible basis for termination of his employment. . . .

For this reason we hold that the grant of summary judgment against the respondent, without full exploration of this issue, was improper. . . .

II

The respondent's lack of formal contractual or tenure security in continued employment at Odessa Junior College, though irrelevant to his free speech claim, is highly relevant to his procedural due process claim. But it may not be entirely dispositive.

We have held . . . that the Constitution does not require opportunity for a hearing before the nonrenewal of a nontenured teacher's contract, unless he can show that the decision not to rehire him somehow deprived him of an interest in "liberty" or that he had a "property" interest in continued employment, despite the lack of tenure or a formal contract. . . .

. . . [T]he respondent here has yet to show that he has been deprived of an interest that could invoke procedural due process protection. . . .

But the respondent's allegations—which we must construe most favorably to the respondent at this stage of the litigation—do raise a genuine issue as to his interest in continued employment at Odessa Junior College. He alleged that this interest, though not secured by a formal contractual tenure provision, was secured by a no less binding understanding fostered by the college administration. In particular, the respondent alleged that the college had a de facto tenure program, and that he had tenure under that program. He claimed that he and others legitimately relied upon an unusual provision that had been in the college's official Faculty Guide for many years:

> "Teacher Tenure: Odessa College has no tenure system. The Administration of the College wishes the faculty member to feel that he has permanent tenure as long as his teaching services are satisfactory and as long as he displays a cooperative attitude toward his co-workers and his superiors, and as long as he is happy in his work."

Moreover, the respondent claimed legitimate reliance upon guidelines promulgated by the Coordinating Board of the Texas College and University System that provided that a person, like himself, who had been employed as a teacher in the state college and university system for seven years or more has some form of job tenure. Thus, the respondent offered to prove that a teacher with his long period of service at this particular State College had no less a "property" interest in continued employment than a formally tenured teacher at other colleges, and had no less a procedural due process right to a statement of reasons and a hearing before college officials upon their decision not to retain him.

We have made clear . . . that "property" interests subject to procedural due process protection are not limited by a few rigid, technical forms. Rather, "property" denotes a broad range of interests that are secured by "existing rules or understandings." . . . A person's interest in a benefit is a "property" interest for due process purposes if there are such rules or mutually explicit understandings that support his claim of entitlement to the benefit and that he may invoke at a hearing. . . .

A written contract with an explicit tenure provision clearly is evidence of a formal understanding that supports a teacher's claim of entitlement to continued employment unless sufficient "cause" is shown. Yet absence of such an explicit contractual provision may not always foreclose the possibility that a teacher has a "property" interest in re-employment. For example, the law of contracts in most, if not all, jurisdictions long has employed a process by which agreements, though not formal-

EDITED CASE Perry v. Sinderman (Continued)

ized in writing, may be "implied." . . . Explicit contractual provisions may be supplemented by other agreements implied from "the promisor's words and conduct in the light of the surrounding circumstances." . . . And, "[t]he meaning of [the promisor's] words and acts is found by relating them to the usage of the past." . . .

A teacher, like the respondent, who has held his position for a number of years, might be able to show from the circumstances of this service—and from other relevant facts—that he has a legitimate claim of entitlement to job tenure. Just as this Court has found there to be a "common law of a particular industry or of a particular plant" that may supplement a collective-bargaining agreement, . . . so there may be an unwritten "common law" in a particular university that certain employees shall have the equivalent of tenure. This is particularly likely in a college or university, like Odessa Junior College, that has no explicit tenure system even for senior members of its faculty, but that nonetheless may have created such a system in practice. . . .

In this case, the respondent has alleged the existence of rules and understandings, promulgated and fostered by state officials, that may justify his legitimate claim of entitlement to continued employment absent "sufficient cause." We disagree with the Court of Appeals insofar as it held that a mere subjective "expectancy" is protected by procedural due process, but we agree that the respondent must be given an opportunity to prove the legitimacy of his claim of such entitlement in light of "the policies and practices of the institution." . . . Proof of such a property interest would not, of course, entitle him to rein-

statement. But such proof would obligate college officials to grant a hearing at his request, where he could be informed of the grounds for his nonretention and challenge their sufficiency. . . .

Justice Powell took no part in the decision of this case.

Chief Justice Burger, concurring. . . .

Justices Brennan and **Douglas**, dissenting . . .

Justice Marshall, dissenting in part.

Respondent was a teacher in the state college system of the State of Texas for a decade before the Board of Regents of Odessa Junior College decided not to renew his contract. He brought this suit in Federal District Court claiming that the decision not to rehire him was in retaliation for his public criticism of the policies of the college administration in violation of the First Amendment, and that because the decision was made without giving him a statement of reasons and a hearing, it denied him the due process of law guaranteed by the Fourteenth Amendment. The District Court granted summary judgment for petitioners, but the Court of Appeals reversed and remanded the case for further proceedings. This Court affirms the judgment of the Court of Appeals.

I agree with Part I of the Court's opinion holding that respondent has presented a bona fide First Amendment claim that should be considered fully by the District Court. But . . . I would modify the judgment of the Court of Appeals to direct the District Court to enter summary judgment for respondent entitling him to a statement of reasons why his contract was not renewed and a hearing on disputed issues of fact.

EDITED CASE Mathews v. Eldridge
United States Supreme Court, 424 U.S. 319 (1976)

[In this case the Supreme Court considers the scope of constitutional due process protections in the context of termination of Social Security disability benefits. George Eldridge, who had been disabled due to "chronic anxiety and back strain," was informed by an official letter that, according to

medical reports, his disability no longer existed and that benefit payments would be terminated. Although agency procedures required ample notification and an evidentiary hearing prior to

(Continued)

EDITED CASE   Mathews v. Eldridge (Continued)

final termination, the payments could be stopped initially without a hearing. Provision was also made for retroactive payments to any recipient whose disability was later determined not to have ended. Eldridge brought suit in federal district court, arguing that the Due Process Clause as interpreted in Goldberg v. Kelly *required an evidentiary hearing before any termination of benefits.]*

Justice Powell delivered the opinion of the Court.

The issue in this case is whether the Due Process Clause of the Fifth Amendment requires that prior to the termination of Social Security disability benefit payments the recipient be afforded an opportunity for an evidentiary hearing.

Cash benefits are provided to workers during periods in which they are completely disabled under the disability insurance program created by the 1956 amendments to . . . the Social Security Act. . . . Eldridge was first awarded benefits in June 1968. In March 1972, he received a questionnaire from the state agency charged with monitoring his medical condition. Eldridge completed the questionnaire, indicating that his condition had not improved and identifying the medical sources, including physicians, from whom he had received treatment recently. The state agency then obtained reports from his physician and a psychiatric consultant. After considering these reports and other information in his file the agency informed Eldridge by letter that it has made a tentative determination that his disability had ceased in May 1972. The letter included a statement of reasons for the proposed termination of benefits, and advised Eldridge that he might request reasonable time in which to obtain and submit additional information pertaining to his condition.

In his written response, Eldridge disputed one characterization of his medical condition and indicated that the agency already had enough evidence to establish his disability. The state agency then made its final determination that he had ceased to be disabled in May 1972. This determination was accepted by the Social Security Administration (SSA), which notified Eldridge in July that his benefits would terminate after that month. The notification also advised him of his right to seek reconsideration by the state agency of this initial determination within six months.

Instead of requesting reconsideration Eldridge commenced this action challenging the constitutional validity of the administrative procedures established by the Secretary of Health, Education, and Welfare for assessing whether there exists a continuing disability. He sought an immediate reinstatement of benefits pending a hearing on the issue of his disability. . . . The secretary moved to dismiss on the grounds that Eldridge's benefits had been terminated in accordance with valid administrative regulations and procedures and that he had failed to exhaust available remedies. . . .

. . . [The] District Court held that prior to termination of benefits Eldridge had to be afforded an evidentiary hearing of the type required for welfare beneficiaries under . . . the Social Security Act. . . . [T]he Court of Appeals for the Fourth Circuit affirmed. . . . We reverse. . . .

Procedural due process imposes constraints on governmental decisions which deprive individuals of "liberty" or "property" interests within the meaning of the Due Process Clause of the Fifth or Fourteenth Amendment. The Secretary does not contend that procedural due process is inapplicable to terminations of Social Security disability benefits. He recognizes, as has been implicit in our prior decisions, . . . that the interest of an individual in continued receipt of these benefits is a statutorily created "property" interest protected by the Fifth Amendment. . . . Rather, the Secretary contends that the existing administration procedures . . . provide all the process that is constitutionally due before a recipient can be deprived of that interest.

This Court consistently has held that some form of hearing is required before an individual is finally deprived of a property interest. . . . The "right to be heard before being condemned to suffer grievous loss of any kind, even though it may not involve the stigma and hardships of a criminal conviction, is a principle basic to our society." . . . The fundamental requirement of due process is the opportunity to be heard "at a meaningful time and in a meaningful manner." . . . Eldridge agrees that the review procedures available to a claimant before the initial determination of ineligibility becomes final would be adequate if disability benefits were not terminated until after the evidentiary hearing stage of the administrative process. The dispute centers upon what process is due prior to the initial termination of benefits, pending review.

EDITED CASE Mathews v. Eldridge (Continued)

In recent years this Court increasingly has had occasion to consider the extent to which due process requires an evidentiary hearing prior to the deprivation of some type of property interest even if such a hearing is provided thereafter. In only one case, *Goldberg v. Kelly,* . . . has the Court held that a hearing closely approximating a judicial trial is necessary. In other cases requiring some type of pretermination hearing as a matter of constitutional right the Court has spoken sparingly about the requisite procedures. . . .

These decisions underscore the truism that " '[d]ue process,' unlike some legal rules, is not a technical conception with a fixed content unrelated to time, place, and circumstances." . . . "[D]ue process is flexible and calls for such procedural protections as the particular situation demands." . . . Accordingly, resolution of the issue whether the administrative procedures provided here are constitutionally sufficient requires analysis of the governmental and private interests that are affected. . . . More precisely, our prior decisions indicate that identification of the specific dictates of due process generally requires consideration of three distinct factors: first, the private interest that will be affected by the official action; second, the risk of an erroneous deprivation of such interest through the procedures used, and the probable value, if any, of additional or substitute procedural safeguards; and finally, the Government's interest, including the function involved and the fiscal and administrative burdens that the additional or substitute procedural requirement would entail. . . .

Despite the elaborate character of the administrative procedures provided by the Secretary, the courts below held them to be constitutionally inadequate, concluding that due process requires an evidentiary hearing prior to termination. In light of the private and governmental interests at stake here and the nature of the existing procedures, we think this was error.

Since a recipient whose benefits are terminated is awarded full retroactive relief if he ultimately prevails, his sole interest is in the uninterrupted receipt of this course of income pending final administrative decision on his claim. . . .

Only in *Goldberg* has the Court held that due process requires an evidentiary hearing prior to a temporary deprivation. It was emphasized there

that welfare assistance is given to persons on the very margin of subsistence. . . . Eligibility for disability benefits, in contrast, is not based upon financial need. Indeed, it is wholly unrelated to the worker's income or support from many other sources, such as earnings of other family members, workmen's compensation awards, tort claims awards, savings, private insurance, public or private pensions, veterans' benefits, food stamps, public assistance, or the "many other important programs, both public and private, which contain provisions for disability payments affecting a substantial portion of the work force." . . .

As *Goldberg* illustrates, the degree of potential deprivation that may be created by a particular decision is a factor to be considered in assessing the validity of any administrative decisionmaking process. . . . The potential deprivation here is generally likely to be less than in *Goldberg,* although the degree of difference can be overstated. . . . [T]o remain eligible for benefits a recipient must be "unable to engage in substantial gainful activity." . . .

As we recognized last Term, . . . "the possible length of wrongful deprivation of . . . benefits [also] is an important factor in assessing the impact of official action on the private interests." The Secretary concedes that the delay between a request for a hearing before an administrative law judge and a decision on the claim is currently between 10 and 11 months. Since a terminated recipient must first obtain a reconsideration decision as a prerequisite to invoking his right to an evidentiary hearing, the delay between the actual cut off of benefits and final decision after a hearing exceeds one year.

In view of the torpidity of this administrative review process, . . . and the typically modest resources of the family unit of the physically disabled worker, the hardship imposed upon the erroneously terminated disability recipient may be significant. Still, the disabled worker's need is likely to be less than that of a welfare recipient. In addition to the possibility of access to private resources, other forms of government assistance will become available where the termination of disability benefits places a worker or his family below the subsistence level. . . . In view of these potential

(Continued)

EDITED CASE   Mathews v. Eldridge (Continued)

---

sources of temporary income, there is less reason here than in *Goldberg* to depart from the ordinary principle, established by our decisions, that something less than an evidentiary hearing is sufficient prior to adverse administrative action.

An additional factor to be considered here is the fairness and reliability of the existing pretermination procedures, and the probable value, if any, of additional procedural safeguards. Central to the evaluation of any administrative process is the nature of the relevant inquiry. . . . In order to remain eligible for benefits the disabled worker must demonstrate by means of "medically acceptable clinical and laboratory diagnostic techniques" . . . that he is unable "to engage in any substantial gainful activity by reason of any medically determinable physical or mental impairment." . . . (emphasis supplied). In short, a medical assessment of the worker's physical or mental condition is required. This is a more sharply focused and easily documented decision than the typical determination of welfare entitlement. In the latter case, a wide variety of information may be deemed relevant, and issues of witness credibility and veracity often are critical to the decisionmaking process. . . .

By contrast, the decision whether to discontinue disability benefits will turn, in most cases, upon "routine, standard, and unbiased medical reports by physician specialists," . . . concerning a subject whom they have personally examined. . . . To be sure, credibility and veracity may be a factor in the ultimate disability assessment in some cases. But procedural due process rules are shaped by the risk of error inherent in the truthfinding process as applied to the generality of cases, not the rare exceptions. The potential value of an evidentiary hearing, or even oral presentation to the decisionmaker, is substantially less in this context than in *Goldberg.* . . .

A further safeguard against mistake is the policy of allowing the disability recipient's representative full access to all information relied upon by the state agency. In addition, prior to the cutoff of benefits the agency informs the recipient of its tentative assessment, the reasons therefore, and provides a summary of the evidence that it considers most relevant. Opportunity is then afforded the recipient to submit additional evidence or arguments, enabling him to challenge directly the accuracy of information in his field as well as the correctness of the agency's tentative conclusions. These procedures . . . enable the recipient to "mold" his argument to respond to the precise issues which the decisionmaker regards as crucial. . . .

In striking the appropriate due process balance the final factor to be assessed is the public interest. This includes the administrative burden and other societal costs that would be associated with requiring, as a matter of constitutional right, an evidentiary hearing upon demand in all cases prior to the termination of disability benefits. The most visible burden would be the incremental cost resulting from the increased number of hearings and the expense of providing benefits to ineligible recipients pending decision. No one can predict the extent of the increase, but the fact that full benefits would continue until after such hearings would assure the exhaustion in most cases of this attractive option. Nor would the theoretical right of the Secretary to recover undeserved benefits result, as a practical matter, in any substantial offset of the added outlay of public funds. . . . [E]xperience with the constitutionalizing of government procedures suggests that the ultimate additional cost in terms of money and administrative burden would not be insubstantial.

Financial cost alone is not a controlling weight in determining whether due process requires a particular procedural safeguard prior to some administrative decision. But the Government's interest, and hence that of the public, in conserving scarce fiscal and administrative recourses, is a factor that must be weighed. At some point the benefit of an additional safeguard to the individual affected by the administrative action and to society, in terms of increased assurance that the action is just, may be outweighed by the cost. Significantly, the cost of protecting those whom the preliminary administrative process had identified as likely to be found undeserving may in the end come out of the pockets of the deserving since resources available for any particular program of social welfare are not unlimited. . . .

But more is implicated in cases of this type than ad hoc weighing of fiscal and administrative burdens against the interests of a particular category of claimants. The ultimate balance involves a determination as to when, under our constitutional

---

EDITED CASE Mathews v. Eldridge (Continued)

system, judicial-type procedures must be imposed upon administrative action to assure fairness. We reiterate the wise admonishment of Mr. Justice Frankfurter that differences in the origin and function of administrative agencies "preclude wholesale transplantation of the rules of procedure, trial, and review which have evolved from the history and experience of courts." . . . The judicial model of an evidentiary hearing is neither a required, nor even the most effective, method of decisionmaking in all circumstances. The essence of due process is the requirement that "a person in jeopardy of serious loss [be given] notice of the case against him and opportunity to meet it." . . . All that is necessary is that the procedures be tailored, in light of the decision to be made, to "the capacity and circumstances of those who are to be heard," . . . to insure that they are given a meaningful opportunity to present their case. In assessing what process is due in this case, substantial weight must be given to the good-faith judgments of the individuals charged by Congress with the administration of social welfare programs that the procedures they have provided assure fair consideration of the entitlement claims of individuals. . . . This is especially so where, as here, the prescribed procedures not only provide the claimant with an effective process for asserting his claim prior to any administrative action, but also assure a right to an evidentiary hearing, as well as to subsequent judicial review, before the denial of his claim becomes final. . . .

We conclude that an evidentiary hearing is not required prior to the termination of disability benefits and that the present administrative procedures fully comport with due process. . . .

Justices Brennan and ***Marshall***, dissenting.
. . . I agree with the District Court and the Court of Appeals that, prior to termination of benefits, Eldridge must be afforded an evidentiary hearing of the type required for welfare beneficiaries. . . . I would add that the Court's consideration that a discontinuance of disability benefits may cause the recipient to suffer only a limited deprivation is no argument. It is speculative. Moreover, the very legislative determination to provide disability benefits, without any prerequisite determination of need in fact, presumes a need by the recipient which is not this Court's function to denigrate. Indeed, in the present case, it is indicated that because disability benefits were terminated there was a foreclosure upon the Eldridge home and the family's furniture was repossessed, forcing Eldridge, his wife and children to sleep in one bed. . . . Finally, it is also no argument that a worker, who has been placed in the untenable position of having been denied disability benefits, may still seek other forms of public assistance.

Justice Stevens took no part in the consideration or decision of this case.

EDITED CASE Cleveland Board of Education v. Loudermill
United States Supreme Court, 470 U.S. 532 (1985)

[James Loudermill was hired to work as a school security guard in Cleveland, Ohio. On his job application, Loudermill stated that he had never been convicted of a felony. Eleven months later, upon discovering that he had in fact been convicted of grand theft, the Board of Education dismissed Loudermill for dishonesty in filling out his application. He was not given an opportunity to respond to the dishonesty charge nor to challenge the dismissal in a hearing before the Board. Under Ohio law, Loudermill was a "classified civil servant" and as such

could be terminated only for cause. The law also provided that, if dismissed from their jobs, classified civil servants discharged were entitled to administrative review. Accordingly, Loudermill filed an appeal with the Cleveland Civil Service Commission, which upheld the Board of Education's action. Loudermill then filed suit in federal district court, claiming an abridgment of his due process rights under the Fourteenth

(Continued)

EDITED CASE   Cleveland Board of Education v. Loudermill (Continued)

Amendment. In this case, the Supreme Court considers whether Loudermill had a "property right" in his employment that would trigger due process protection and, if so, what process was due. Specifically, was Loudermill entitled to a hearing before the Board of Education before that body voted to terminate his employment?]

Justice White delivered the opinion of the Court.

Property interests are not created by the Constitution, "they are created and their dimensions are defined by existing rules or understandings that stem from an independent source such as state law. . . ." . . . The Ohio statute plainly creates such an interest. Respondents were "classified civil service employees," . . . entitled to retain their positions "during good behavior and efficient service," who could not be dismissed "except . . . for . . . misfeasance, malfeasance, or nonfeasance in office." . . . The statute plainly supports the conclusion, reached by both lower courts, that respondents possessed property rights in continued employment. Indeed, this question does not seem to have been disputed below.

The . . . Board argues, however, that the property right is defined by, and conditioned on, the legislature's choice of procedures for its deprivation. . . . The Board stresses that in addition to specifying the grounds for termination, the statute sets out procedures by which termination may take place. The procedures were adhered to in these cases. According to petitioner, "[t]o require additional procedures would in effect expand the scope of the property interest itself." . . .

This argument . . . has its genesis in the plurality opinion in *Arnett v. Kennedy,* 416 U.S. 134 (1974). Arnett involved a challenge by a former federal employee to the procedures by which he was dismissed. The plurality reasoned that where the legislation conferring the substantive right also sets out the procedural mechanism for enforcing that right, the two cannot be separated: "The employee's statutorily defined right is not a guarantee against removal without case in the abstract, but such a guarantee as enforced by the procedures which Congress has designated for the determination of cause." . . . "[W]here the grant of a substantive right is inextricably intertwined with the limitations on the procedures which are to be employed in determining that right, a litigant . . . must take the bitter with the sweet." . . .

This view garnered three votes in Arnett, but was specifically rejected by the other six Justices. . . . More recently, however, the Court has clearly rejected it. . . .

. . . [T]he "bitter with the sweet" approach misconceives the constitutional guarantee. If a clearer holding is needed, we provide it today. The point is straightforward: the Due Process Clause provides that certain substantive rights—life, liberty, and property—cannot be deprived except pursuant to constitutionally adequate procedures. The categories of substance and procedure are distinct. Were the rule otherwise, the Clause would be reduced to a mere tautology. "Property" cannot be defined by the procedures provided for its deprivation any more than can life or liberty. The right to due process "is conferred, not by legislative grace, but by constitutional guarantee. While the legislature may elect not to confer a property interest in [public] employment, it may not constitutionally authorize the deprivation of such an interest, once conferred, without appropriate procedural safeguards." . . .

In short, once it is determined that the Due Process Clause applies, "the question remains what process is due." . . . The answer to that question is not to be found in the Ohio statute. . . .

An essential principle of due process is that a deprivation of life, liberty, or property "be preceded by notice and opportunity for hearing appropriate to the nature of the case." . . . We have described "the root requirement" of the Due Process Clause as being "that an individual be given an opportunity for a hearing before he is deprived of any significant property interest." . . . This principle requires "some kind of a hearing" prior to the discharge of an employee who has a constitutionally protected property interest in his employment. . . .

The need for some form of pretermination hearing . . . is evident from a balancing of the competing interests at stake. These are the private interest in retaining employment, the governmental interest in the expeditious removal of unsatisfactory employees and the avoidance of administrative burdens, and the risk of an erroneous termination. . . .

First, the significance of the private interest in retaining employment cannot be gainsaid. We have frequently recognized the severity of depriving a person of the means of livelihood. . . . While

EDITED CASE   Cleveland Board of Education v. Loudermill (Continued)

a fired worker may find employment elsewhere, doing so will take some time and is likely to be burdened by the questionable circumstances under which he left his previous job. . . .

Second, some opportunity for the employee to present his side of the case is recurringly of obvious value in reaching an accurate decision. Dismissals for cause will often involve factual disputes. . . . Even where the facts are clear, the appropriateness or necessity of the discharge may not be; in such cases, the only meaningful opportunity to invoke the discretion of the decisionmaker is likely to be before the termination takes effect. . . .

. . . As for Loudermill, given the Commission's ruling we cannot say that the discharge was mistaken. . . . [N]either can we say that a fully informed decisionmaker might not have exercised its discretion and decided not to dismiss him, notwithstanding its authority to do so. In any event, the termination involved arguable issues, and the right to a hearing does not depend on a demonstration of certain success. . . .

The governmental interest in immediate termination does not outweigh these interests. As we shall explain, affording the employee an opportunity to respond prior to termination would impose neither a significant administrative burden nor intolerable delays. Furthermore, the employer shares the employee's interest in avoiding disruption and erroneous decisions; and until the matter is settled, the employer would continue to receive the benefit of the employee's labors. It is preferable to keep a qualified employee on than to train a new one. A governmental employer also has an interest in keeping citizens usefully employed rather than taking the possibly erroneous and counterproductive step of forcing its employees onto the welfare rolls. Finally, in those situations where the employer perceives a significant hazard in keeping the employee on the job, it can avoid the problem by suspending with pay. . . .

The foregoing considerations indicate that the pretermination "hearing," though necessary, need not be elaborate. We have pointed out that "[t]he formality and procedural requisites for the hearing can vary, depending upon the importance of the interests involved and the nature of the subsequent proceedings." . . . In general, "something less" than a full evidentiary hearing is sufficient prior to adverse administrative action. . . .

The essential requirements of due process . . . are notice and an opportunity to respond. The opportunity to present reasons, either in person or in writing, why proposed action should not be taken is a fundamental due process requirement. . . . The tenured public employee is entitled to oral or written notice of the charges against him, an explanation of the employer's evidence, and an opportunity to present his side of the story. . . . To require more than this prior to termination would intrude to an unwarranted extent on the government's interest in quickly removing an unsatisfactory employee. . . .

We conclude that all the process that is due is provided by a pretermination opportunity to respond, coupled with posttermination administrative procedures as provided by the Ohio statute. . . .

Justice Marshall, concurring in part and concurring in the judgment.

I agree wholeheartedly with the Court's express rejection of the theory of due process, urged upon us by the petitioner Boards of Education, that a public employee who may be discharged only for cause may be discharged by whatever procedures the legislature chooses. I therefore join Part II of the opinion for the Court. I also agree that, before discharge, the respondent employees were entitled to the opportunity to respond to the charges against them (which is all they requested), and that the failure to accord them that opportunity was a violation of their constitutional rights. Because the Court holds that the respondents were due all the process they requested, I concur in the judgment of the Court.

I write separately, however, to reaffirm my belief that public employees who may be discharged only for cause are entitled, under the Due Process Clause of the Fourteenth Amendment, to more than respondents sought in this case. I continue to believe that before the decision is made to terminate an employee's wages, the employee is entitled to an opportunity to test the strength of the evidence "by confronting and cross-examining adverse witnesses and by presenting witnesses on his own behalf, whenever there are substantial disputes in testimonial evidence." . . . Because the Court suggests that even in this situation due process requires no more than notice and an opportunity to be heard before wages are cut off, I

(Continued)

EDITED CASE   Cleveland Board of Education v. Loudermill (Continued)

---

am not able to join the Court's opinion in its entirety. . . .

Justice Brennan, concurring in part and dissenting in part. . . .

Justice Rehnquist, dissenting.

In *Arnett v. Kennedy*, 416 U.S. 134 (1974), six Members of this Court agreed that a public employee could be dismissed for misconduct with-out a full hearing prior to termination. A plurality of Justices agreed that the employee was entitled to exactly what Congress gave him, and no more. . . .

Because I believe that the Fourteenth Amendment of the United States Constitution does not support the conclusion that Ohio's effort to confer a limited form of tenure upon respondents resulted in the creation of a "property right" in their employment, I dissent.

EDITED CASE   Van Morfit v. University of South Florida
District Court of Appeal of Florida, Second District. 794 So.2d 655
(Fla. App. 2001)

[In this case, a Florida intermediate appellate court reviews a University decision to suspend a graduate student who allegedly engaged in academic misconduct. The issue is whether in suspending the student the University observed due process of law as well as its own procedural rules.]

Justice Davis delivered the opinion of the court.

Van Morfit, a graduate student at the University of South Florida, appeals the school's decision to suspend him from classes at the school. He argues that the school did not follow its own rules and failed to afford him due process. We agree and reverse.

Morfit was a graduate student in the anthropology program. He also was working as a research assistant for the USF College of Public Health in a project at the Veterans Administration Hospital. When subjects in the research project made allegations regarding Morfit's misconduct during his work on the project, Anthony J. Joiner, the university's associate dean of student judicial services, sent a letter to Morfit detailing the allegations and imposing an immediate suspension from the school. Morfit was advised that he could request an emergency administrative hearing and that he could appeal the decision of the hearing officer to the vice president for student life and wellness. Finally, Morfit was advised that he was "trespassed" from the campus during the suspension. Morfit hired an attorney and requested a hearing.

At the January 25, 2000, hearing, Dean Joiner served as the hearing officer. The basis of the charge against Morfit was a report filed by a security officer who had interviewed one alleged victim. No witnesses were called. Morfit moved to dismiss the charge for lack of evidence and on other procedural grounds. Dean Joiner denied the motion. Although Morfit denied any wrongdoing, Dean Joiner found that Morfit had violated the Student Code of Conduct based on the charges brought against him. He suspended Morfit through the end of the 2000 spring semester.

Morfit timely appealed Dean Joiner's decision to Dr. Wilma Henry, associate vice president for student life and wellness. Dr. Henry wrote Morfit on March 8, 2000, to advise him that she had reviewed the proceedings and concluded that Morfit had been afforded due process. She upheld Dean Joiner's decision. Morfit then filed this appeal.

Section 120.68, Florida Statutes (2000), provides that a party who is adversely affected by final agency action is entitled to judicial review. The finality of an agency action depends on whether it has brought the administrative adjudicative process to a close. . . . There is no question here that the letter from Dean Henry was final agency action under that standard.

Pursuant to section 120.81(1)(g), Florida Statutes (2000), educational units follow a different procedure than other agencies. In any proceeding in which the substantial interests of a student

---

EDITED CASE Van Morfit v. University of South Florida (Continued)

---

are determined by the state university system or a community college district, sections 120.569 and 120.57 (the general due process provisions of the Administrative Procedure Act) do not apply. Rather, the Board of Regents is directed to establish a committee that will establish rules and guidelines ensuring fairness and due process in judicial proceedings involving students in the state university system. To that end, section 6C4-6.0021 of the Florida Administrative Code, the Student Code of Conduct, was adopted.

Subsection 6 of the code describes the student judicial process and proceedings, and subsection 7(b) delineates the student's due process rights. Specifically, section 7(b)5 gives the student the right to question witnesses: "The student may hear and question adverse witnesses, except in cases of violent misconduct where the student may submit questions to the hearing officer for use in questioning adverse witnesses." Although Morfit claims several other violations of his due process rights, the violation of this right is sufficient to require reversal of the dean's decision.

The complaining witnesses were never called. In fact, the only statements from the alleged victims were contained in the investigation report written by an officer who talked with them. Morfit was entitled to have the witnesses make their statements directly to the hearing officer, and he was entitled to question them. This is a fundamental ingredient of due process in any judicial or quasi-judicial proceeding. It is recognized that in school suspension cases, a relaxed due process standard is followed. . . . However, the school's own code guaranteed Morfit this right. We must conclude that the school denied Morfit his right to due process, and, therefore, this decision must be reversed. Not only did the initial hearing deny him his due process rights, but the appeals determination, finding as it did that he had been afforded due process, was also in error. Accordingly, we reverse Morfit's suspension with directions that the school afford Morfit a new hearing in compliance with the Student Code of Conduct.

Justices Parker and **Casanueva**, concurring.

ENDNOTES

1. T. Arnold, *The Role of Substantive Law and Procedure in the Legal Practice.* 45 Harv. L. Rev. 617, 624 (1932).

2. 5 U.S.C.A. § 554.

3. 349 U.S. 302 (1955).

4. Fla. Stat. Ann. Ch. 120.

5. 29 Del.Code Ann. § 10124.

6. Fla. Stat. Ann. §§ 120.569; 120.57.

7. Regs. Conn. State Agencies, § 14-137-37.

8. A. Bonfield, *The Federal and State Administrative Law*, 72 Va. L. Rev. 297, 324 (1986).

9. 29 Del.Code Ann. § 10123.

10. *Meyer v. Nebraska*, 262 U.S. 390, 394 (1923).

11. *Board of Regents v. Roth*, 408 U.S. 564, 572 (1972).

12. See, e.g., *Bailey v. Richardson*, 341 U.S. 918 (1951).

13. See, generally, Reich, *The New Property*, 73 Yale L.J. 733 (1964).

14. See, e.g., *Goldberg v. Kelly*, 397 U.S. 254 (1970).

15. *Jacobson v. Massachusetts*, 197 U.S. 11 (1905).

16. *North American Cold Storage Co. v. Chicago*, 211 U.S. 206 (1908).

17. *Londoner v. Denver*, 210 U.S. 373 (1908).

18. 239 U.S. 441 (1915).

19. K. Davis, Administrative Law Treatise § 7.19 (2d ed. 1979).

20. 410 U.S. 224 (1973).

21. *Southern Railway Co. v. Virginia*, 290 U.S. 190, 199 (1933).

22. 349 U.S. 302 (1955).

23. 397 U.S. 254 (1970).

24. 408 U.S. 471 (1972).

25. 408 U.S. 564 (1972).

26. *Id.* at 571-572.

27. 408 U.S. 593, 600 (1972).

28. 419 U.S. 565 (1975).

29. *Id.* at 579.

30. 424 U.S. 319 (1976).

31. *Id.* at 334.

32. *Dixon v. Love*, 431 U.S. 105 (1977).

33. *Mackey v. Monty*, 443 U.S. 1 (1979).

34. 430 U.S. 651 (1977).

35. *Id.* at 677.

36. *Memphis Light, Gas & Water Div. v. Graft*, 436 U.S. 1, 18 (1978).

37. *Board of Curators v. Horowitz*, 435 U.S. 78 (1978).

38. *Barry v. Barchi*, 443 U.S. 55 (1979).

39. 470 U.S. 532 (1985).

40. *Id.* at 538.

41. *Id.* at 539.

42. *Id.* at 546.

43. S. Shapiro & R. Glicksman, *Congress, the Supreme Court and the Quiet Revolution in Administrative Law.* 1988 Duke LJ 819, 850.

44. 199 F.3d 909 (7th Cir. 1999).

45. *Id.* at 911.

46. 208 F.3d 773 (9th Cir. 2000).

47. *Matter of Marc La Cloche*, 755 N.Y. Supp. 827 (2003).

48. 208 F.3d 615 (7th Cir. 2000).

49. 975 P.2d 46 (Alaska 1999).

50. 794 So.2d 655 (Fla. App. 2001).

51. 5 U.S.C.A. § 571(3).

52. 5 U.S.C.A. § 572(a).

53. 5 U.S.C.A. §§ 573; 574.

54. 5 U.S.C.A. § 572(b).

55. N.C.G.S.A. § 150B-22.

56. *Professional Reactor Operator Society v. National Regulatory Commission*, 939 F.2d 1047, 1051-1052 (D.C. Cir. 1991).

57. See, e.g., Fla. Stat. Ann. § 120.595.

58. The leading case in this area is *Strickland v. Washington*, 466 U.S. 668 (1984).

59. 5 U.S.C.A. § 556(b) .

60. MSAPA 1981 § 4-301.

61. 5 U.S.C.A. §§ 3105, 5372, 7521.

62. 5 U.S.C.A. § 556.

63. *Mullane v. Central Hanover Bank & Trust Co.*, 339 U.S. 306, 314.

64. MSAPA 1981 § 4-206.

65. MSAPA 1981 § 4-109(b).

66. West's Ann. Cal. Gov. Code § 11440.50.

67. 359 F.2d 994 (D.C. Cir. 1966).

68. *Id.* at 1002.

69. 326 U.S. 327 (1945).

70. *See, e.g.*, Fed. R. Civ. P. 21.

71. *McClelland v. Andrews*, 606 F.2d 1278, 1286 (D.C. Cir. 1973).

72. 18 U.S.C.A. § 3500.

73. *Harvey Aluminum, Inc. v. N.L.R.B.*, 335 F.2d 749 (9th Cir. 1964).

74. MSAPA 1981 § 4-210.

75. 13 TAC § 27.111.

76. MSAPA 1981 § 4-205.

77. *Kaczmarczyk v. INS*, 933 F.2d 588, 593, 596 (7th Cir. 1991).

78. 5 U.S.C.A. § 556(d).

79. 5 U.S.C.A. § 556(d).

80. See, for example, *Kerner v. Celebrezze*, 340 F.2d 736 (2nd Cir. 1965).

81. 450 U.S. 91 (1981).

82. *Ferris v. Turlington*, 510 So.2d 292 (Fla. 1987).

83. 5 U.S.C.A. § 557(c).

84. 591 F.2d 852, 857 (D.C. Cir. 1978).

85. 5 U.S.C.A. § 557(b).

86. MSAPA 1981 § 4-215.

87. 5 U.S.C.A. § 557(b).

88. 354 F.2d 952 (5th Cir. 1966).

89. *Id.* at 964.

90. MSAPA 1981 § 4-213.

91. 685 F.2d 547 (D.C. Cir. 1982).

92. *Id.* at 564.

8

Political Control of Agencies

"The accumulation of all powers, legislative, executive, and judiciary, in the same hands . . . may justly be pronounced the very definition of tyranny."

JAMES MADISON
THE FEDERALIST NO. 47

INTRODUCTION

During the Progressive Era (the first two decades of the twentieth century), the prevailing intellectual currents supported the creation of bureaucratic entities to handle highly specialized policy problems with a minimum of political control or accountability. The prevailing idea was that many problems could be better addressed by experts unhampered by meddling politicians. "Politics" was seen as a corrupting force from which agencies should be insulated. The most radical architects of the administrative state envisioned a new **technocracy** that would replace both the eighteenth century republican constitutionalism with its emphasis on limited government, as well as nineteenth century democratic ideas, which emphasized popular sovereignty, majoritarianism, and political parties.

Today, due to the proliferation of bureaucracy at all levels of government, there are far more administrative regulations in effect than there are federal or state statutes or local ordinances. In promulgating and enforcing these myriad regulations, federal, state, and local agencies affect nearly every facet of our lives. In a democratic society, it is vital that the people's elected representatives monitor and control the activities of a powerful, unelected bureaucracy. This is especially the case when a bureaucratic organization acts as a quasi-legislative body in making rules, an executive agency in enforcing those rules, and a quasi-judicial entity in adjudicating disputes over the application of such rules. In a constitutional republic based on the principle of **separation of powers,** this concentration of power in the hands of unelected bureaucrats, if left unsupervised and unchecked, "may justly be pronounced the very definition of tyranny."[1] Thus it is necessary that officials conduct the business of government with adherence to the **checks and balances** inherent in the concept of separation of powers delineated in the federal and state constitutions.

The responsibility for monitoring and controlling the federal bureaucracy is shared by Congress and the president, although both receive important assistance from staff and key support agencies. At the state level, legislators, governors, and other elected officials exercise political control of the bureaucracy. At the local level, political responsibility for public administration varies considerably across cities and counties. Mayors, county executives, city and county commissioners, school board members, sheriffs, and various other elected officials keep watch over local agencies and government personnel.

The process by which elected officials keep tabs on the bureaucracy is known as **oversight.** Oversight can be formal or informal. **Formal oversight** occurs when elected officials invoke mechanisms of control that are explicitly provided for in law. **Informal oversight** is much more common; indeed it is an ongoing process. Informal oversight refers to the day-to-day process in which elected officials monitor and communicate with agencies.

In a constitutional order committed to the **rule of law,** one can argue that courts should play a significant role in overseeing the bureaucracy, and indeed they do. However, the nature of **judicial oversight** differs dramatically from that performed by legislatures and chief executives. Judicial oversight of bureaucracy takes place in the context of lawsuits filed by agencies or parties seeking to challenge agency actions. More commonly, it occurs in the appellate review of cases originally adjudicated by quasi-judicial bodies within the executive branch. Judicial review of administrative action is so important in the development of administrative law that it warrants its own chapter (see Chapter 9).

In this chapter we discuss executive and legislative oversight functions and explore the formal and informal means of political control over administrative agencies asserted by Congress and presidents. We also provide some insights as to political control of state agencies by governors and state legislatures. However, because local governments vary so widely in structure and function, and because the concept of separation of powers often does not apply at the local level, we do not attempt to describe and explain political control of local bureaucracies.

LEGISLATIVE OVERSIGHT

Federal administrative agencies are created by and are accountable to the elected representatives in Congress. At the state level these agencies are created by the state constitution or by legislative enactments. Here also the agencies are accountable to the legislative branch of state government. In our republican form of government citizens rightfully look to their elected representatives to assist them in dealing with the bureaucracy. Administrative agencies are directly dependent on the elected members of Congress or the state legislature to provide funding for their programs and activities. Thus, their accountability to the legislative branch is more direct and often more important than the prospect of judicial review, a subject we discuss in Chapter 9. **Legislative oversight** of the bureaucracy occurs in both formal and informal ways.

At the federal level the U.S. Senate exercises an area of political control over executive agencies because of the constitutional "advice and consent" stipulation in respect to appointment of federal judges and "officers of the United States."[2] Congress at the federal level (and state legislatures at the state level) exercise formal oversight over the objectives and policies of independent agencies by **statutory directives.** In their enactment of appropriations bills Congress can control the operating funds of agencies, thereby rewarding or punishing an agency based on performance. Congressional committees can summon representatives of the independent agencies to testify as to agency activities.

Public dissatisfaction can also invoke **formal legislative action.** For example, in 1977 the Food and Drug Administration (FDA) proposed a ban on saccharin, but Congress intervened and enacted legislation that allowed it to remain on the market with a warning label. And in response to constituents' complaints concerning activities of the Internal Revenue Service (IRS), Congress passed the Internal Revenue Service Restructure and Reform Act in 1998 (found in various sections of 26 U.S.C.A.). The new act revised the structure of IRS and provided numerous areas of relief for taxpayers.

At the federal level, legislative control of the bureaucracy originates with the **Ways and Means Committee** of the U.S. House of Representatives and the **Finance Committee** in the U.S. Senate. These committees hold **hearings** in every session of Congress on significant legislative proposals that affect federal agencies. Through these hearings the committees receive input both from agencies and from **lobbyists** representing **interest groups** that may be affected by agency action. After hearings are completed, a proposed bill is considered in a **mark-up session** where the committee votes to accept or reject changes proposed by members. From the mass of bills submitted, eventually the committees shape legislation for Congress to consider.

The Interplay of Congress, Agencies, and Interest Groups

Although Congress exercises substantial control of the bureaucracy through the legislative process, it is important to recognize the role that interest groups and the agencies themselves play in influencing Congress. Every agency has a legislative staff that includes specialists and staff attorneys who assist in developing proposed legislation, which is introduced by senators and representatives, often at the request of the White House. Interest groups also play an important role in shaping legislation, both by lobbying members of Congress (and, arguably, supporting their campaigns) and by developing relationships with agency officials.

In 1949, when radio was the principal electronic medium, the Federal Communications Commission (FCC) determined that broadcast licensees had an obligation to afford reasonable opportunity for discussion of contrasting points of view on controversial issues of public importance. This became known as the fairness doctrine and was designed to assure that coverage of all public issues on the airwaves was full and fair.

When a station sought renewal of its broadcast license, an assessment was made of its fulfillment of obligations of fair coverage of public issues. By the 1980s there were abundant competing radio and television stations to offer competing points of view. Journalists were raising their voices about the "chilling effect" on free speech presented by the Fairness Doctrine. By 1985, the FCC issued its *Fairness Report,* asserting that the doctrine was no longer having its intended effect and, in fact, might have a "chilling effect" and be in violation of the freedom of expression guaranteed by the First Amendment. The FCC discontinued the fairness doctrine in 1987; however, shortly before the FCC's action, Congress voted to enact into law the fairness doctrine, which the FCC would then have to enforce. This interplay culminated in a veto by President Reagan, who was actively pursuing an agenda of deregulation. Efforts to override the veto were unsuccessful.

Another example of the interplay of Congress, agencies, and interest groups can be seen in the area of health-care policy. The Social Security Act (SSA), originally adopted in 1935, is the largest, most comprehensive, and complex social legislation ever enacted by the Congress. It has been amended many times, most importantly in 1965 when Congress included Medicare to assist persons over age 65 in covering medical expenses, and Medicaid to assist states in financing medical services for low-income persons. Each time amendments to the Medicare and Medicaid programs are considered, congressional committees receive input from officials at the Department of Health and Human Services (HHS) as well as from lobbyists from state governments and organizations including the American Medical Association (AMA), the American Hospital Association (AHA), nursing associations, and the pharmaceutical industry. These organizations represent the health-care providers and are vitally interested in the reimbursement aspects of medical programs. In addition, the American Association for Retired People (AARP) and labor organizations, for example, the AFL-CIO, represent the recipients of benefits and seek to persuade the HHS and Congress to shape legislation to benefit their constituents. After years of intense lobbying efforts, Congress passed and on December 8, 2003, President George W. Bush signed the Medicare Prescription Drug Improvement and Modernization Act of 2003. The act provides drug benefits for Medicare beneficiaries beginning in 2006 with interim benefits, especially for low-income Medicare beneficiaries.

The influence of interest groups is hard to reconcile with classical republican or traditional democratic theories of government. Political scientists in the twentieth century developed the theory of **pluralism** to take into account the proliferation and influence of interest groups in American politics. According to this theory, political participation consists primarily of joining organizations that represent the interests of their members and seek to advance those interests by influencing the political process. In pluralist theory, the role of democratic government is to adopt policies that balance the competing demands of interest groups. The role of the law is to create a level playing field for the competition among organized interests. And the role of the courts is to referee the competition to make sure that the game is played fairly. Pluralism is held to be "democratic" in the sense that everyone has an equal right to "petition government for a redress of their grievances" by joining, supporting, or actively working in one or more interest groups. Moreover, pluralist theorists will argue, policies that emerge from the free competition among interest groups are most likely to meet the utilitarian criterion of promoting the "greatest good for the greatest number."

Not everyone accepts pluralism as an explanation or justification of the political process. Those of a classical republican orientation advocate a style of governance in which both legislators and executive officials look beyond the conflicting demands of organized interests and seek a transcendent public interest. Those of a more populist orientation believe that legislators should be driven by the will of the people and should make sure that majoritarian preferences are imposed on bureaucratic entities. Both classical republicans and populists tend to see pluralism as a corruption of American democracy. Classical republicans bemoan the fact that pluralism does not even acknowledge the existence of the public interest. Populists object to the fact that the policies that emerge from the interest group struggle are not necessarily those favored by the majority of voters.

Critics of the role that interest groups play in the political system will often point out the very cozy relationships that can develop among lobbyists, agency officials, and members of Congress. When these three-way relationships become cemented, they are known as **iron triangles.** Iron triangles are generally seen as antithetical to notions of good government and the public interest. Iron triangles depend on control of information and a minimal degree of media or public scrutiny. To a great extent, the Freedom of Information Act and the Open Meetings Law were intended to prevent the formation of iron triangles. While iron triangles still exist in narrow areas of policy that are not on the "radar screen" of the mass media or the mass public, they have largely been replaced by **issue networks.** An issue network is a loose collection of actors inside and outside government who regularly interact in a particular area of policy. An issue network includes not only agency officials, members of Congress, and lobbyists, but also congressional staff members, members of the media, academics, and researchers from think tanks. In general, expertise and information tend to be the keys to influence within an issue network. The shift from iron triangles to issue networks has rendered the policymaking process more visible to the public but also more conflictual and less predictable.[3]

Legislative Investigations

One of the most formal and visible mechanisms of oversight of the bureaucracy is the legislative investigation. Over the years Congress and state legislatures have conducted hundreds of investigations and called thousands of witnesses to testify before committee hearings. Sometimes these investigations have been great public events, such as the hearings that followed the collapse of

Enron Corporation in late 2001. More often, they have involved relatively mundane questions of regulatory policy or governmental administration, and quite frequently agency officials have been called to testify. Committee hearings are thus important means of legislative oversight of the bureaucracy. In a classic work in American political science, Woodrow Wilson discussed the importance of **legislative investigations** of government operations:

> It is the proper duty of a representative body to look diligently into every affair of government and to talk much about what it sees. It is meant to be the eyes and the voice, and to embody the wisdom and will of its constituents. Unless Congress have and use every means of acquainting itself with the acts and the disposition of the administrative agents of the government, the country must be helpless to learn how it is being served; and unless Congress both scrutinize these things and sift them by every form of discussion, the country must remain in embarrassing, crippling ignorance of the very affairs which it is most important that it should understand and direct. The informing function of Congress should be preferred even to its legislative function.[4]

In most cases agency officials are invited to testify and do so voluntarily. Failure to do so might well jeopardize agency budgets or authority. In the event that bureaucrats are unwilling to appear before legislative committees, Congress and all fifty state legislatures have the power to compel testimony by the issuance of subpoenas, which are backed up by the threat of criminal prosecution. One who disobeys a legislative **subpoena** is subject to prosecution for **legislative contempt.** In *McGrain v. Daugherty* (1927),[5] a case stemming from a Senate investigation into the lease of oil reserves without competitive bidding (the Teapot Dome scandal) during the administration of President Warren G. Harding, the Supreme Court upheld Congress's power to enforce a subpoena. Speaking for the Court, Justice Willis Van Devanter concluded that "the power of inquiry—with the process to enforce it—is an essential and appropriate auxiliary to the legislative function."[6]

During the 1950s congressional and state legislative committees conducted far-reaching investigations of alleged communist infiltration of government, education, and organized labor. In many instances private citizens were subpoenaed and subjected to relentless questioning about their political beliefs, activities, and associations. It was in that context that the Supreme Court observed in 1957:

> The power of the Congress to conduct investigations is inherent in the legislative process. That power is broad. It encompasses inquiries concerning the administration of existing laws as well as proposed or possibly needed statutes. It includes surveys of defects in our social, economic or political system for the purpose of enabling the Congress to remedy them. It comprehends probes into departments of the Federal Government to expose corruption, inefficiency or waste. But, broad as is this power of inquiry, it is not unlimited. There is no general authority to expose the private affairs of individuals without justification in terms of the functions of the Congress.[7]

Executive Privilege When agency officials are called to testify before Congress, they can be caught in the middle of a political dispute between Congress and the White House. Presidents sometimes withhold certain information from Congress using what is termed **executive privilege.** In some instances they invoke executive privilege to prevent subordinate officials from testifying or producing requested documents.

The Supreme Court has recognized that executive privilege "is fundamental to the operation of Government and inextricably rooted in the separation of powers under the Constitution."[8] It is generally accepted that executive privilege extends to communications within the White House staff and between the president and members of the cabinet. But there is considerable controversy as to how far down the chain of command the privilege extends. Both Presidents Bill

Clinton and George W. Bush invoked executive privilege to prevent congressional committees from obtaining documents from various government agencies. Courts are often reluctant to intervene in disputes between the "political" branches of government and there is precious little case law on the scope of executive privilege.

The General Accounting Office

Created by the Budget and Accounting Act of 1921,[9] the **General Accounting Office (GAO)** is a congressional support agency that performs a key role in legislative oversight of the bureaucracy. Whereas congressional committee investigations tend to focus on particular problems or issues, the GAO monitors activities in the executive branch on a routine basis. Many of the scandals on excessive government spending, such as the notorious $500 toilet seats and $100 screwdrivers being purchased by the Pentagon, have been uncovered by GAO studies. Figure 8.1 provides the organizational structure of the GAO. Headed by the Comptroller General, the GAO is the largest congressional support agency, with more than 5,000 employees.

In 2002, the General Accounting Office (GAO) filed suit to obtain records of meetings between Vice President Dick Cheney and various energy industry executives who helped the Bush administration develop a national energy policy during 2001. Apparently, some of the meetings included executives from Enron Corporation, the now bankrupt energy-trading firm that was the target of congressional investigations and federal prosecution. Critics charged that Enron, a contributor to the Bush presidential campaign in 2000, had undue influence over public policy. In its lawsuit, the GAO argued that the information it was seeking would "enable GAO to report fully to Congress on the process through which the proposed national energy policy was developed, and [would] thereby assist Congress in the discharge of its legislating and oversight functions." Responding to the unprecedented lawsuit, Justice Department lawyers asserted that the GAO lacked standing to bring the case against

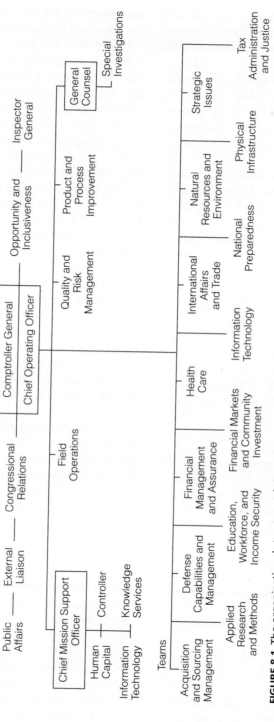

FIGURE 8.1 The organizational structure of the general accounting office.

SOURCE: U.S. General Accounting Office, online at http://www.gao.gov/.

the vice president and that, in any event, the vice president "is entitled to executive privilege based on the significance of his role in national security and public safety in general." On December 9, 2002, the United States District Court for the District of Columbia dismissed the case, holding that the GAO lacked standing to bring the suit. The court recognized the significant constitutional issues in the case, but held that the lawsuit was not appropriately before the court.[10] After consulting with congressional leaders, the Comptroller General, who heads the General Accounting Office, decided not to appeal the decision. But he did not rule out going to court in the future to obtain information that the executive branch refused to disclose.

Although the Comptroller General did not file an appeal to obtain records of meetings between Vice President Dick Cheney and various energy industry executives who helped the Bush Administration develop a national energy policy during 2001, the controversy has continued. In other litigation, Judicial Watch, a non-profit organization involved in issues of public concern, and Sierra Club, a nonprofit group involved in promotion of preservation of environmental resources, sued the National Energy Policy Development Group (NEPDG), Vice President Cheney, and other federal officials alleging that NEPDG failed to comply with the procedural requirements of the Federal Advisory Committee Act (FACA). The federal district court ordered the vice president and others to comply with certain discovery requests to determine whether the FACA applies to the meetings involving energy policy. The Vice President unsuccessfully appealed to the D.C. Circuit.[11] In April 2004, the case was argued before the U.S. Supreme Court. (Unfortunately, the Court's decision came down after this book went to press.)

The Legislative Veto

One of the boldest means of Congress (and several state legislatures) of exercising control of administrative decisions was writing a **legislative veto** into numerous congressional and state enactments. This device allowed one house of Congress to invalidate agency rules by action other than a legislative enactment. The authority was first provided Congress in the Reorganization Act of 1932 and effectively allowed Congress to exercise control over rulemaking actions of federal agencies. But it was not until the 1970s, when Congress became increasingly concerned over the flood of administrative regulations, that it began to rely on the legislative veto device.

Proponents of the legislative veto claim that it provides for agency accountability, particularly in instances where statutory enactments may be susceptible of varying interpretations. Opponents argue that the device encourages agencies to develop law through adjudication rather than using rulemaking, which is made subject to the veto.

In 1983, Congress's use of the legislative veto came to a halt. In that year in *Immigration and Naturalization Service v. Chadha*,[12] the U.S. Supreme Court reviewed a House of Representatives resolution reversing a decision by the Immigration and Naturalization Service. In a 7-2 landmark decision the Court held that a "one-house veto" that Congress inserted into the Immigration and Nationality Act violated Article I, Section 7 of the U.S. Constitution that requires legislation to pass both houses of Congress. The Court's decision in *Chadha* rendered presumptively invalid veto provisions that Congress had inserted in over two hundred other Acts.[13] The Court obviously assumed that a legislative veto is a legislative act that must conform to the requirements of Article I of the U.S. Constitution. In explaining that legislative action must conform to the constitutional provision that requires bicameral passage of laws and presentment of such laws to the president for approval or veto, Chief Justice Burger observed:

> The bicameral requirement, the Presentment Clauses, the President's veto, and Congress' power to override a veto were intended to erect enduring checks on each Branch and to protect the people from the improvident

exercise of power by mandating certain pre-scribed steps. To preserve those checks, and maintain the separation of powers, the care-fully defined limits on the power of each Branch must not be eroded.[14]

Two justices dissented. In a powerful dissent Justice White wrote:

> If Congress may delegate lawmaking power to independent and executive agencies, it is most difficult to understand Article I as forbidding Congress from also reserving a check on legislative power for itself. Absent the veto, the agencies receiving delegations of legislative or quasi-legislative power may issue regulations having the force of law without bicameral approval and without the President's signature.[15]

The Supreme Court's decision in *Chadha* focused on a one-house veto, but it was followed by *Process Gas Consumers Group v. Consumers Energy Council of America,*[16] in which the Court made clear that a two-house veto provision was equally unconstitutional. The Court also made it clear that although *Chadha* involved adjudication, it applied with equal force to rulemaking.

Many scholars have found the majority's reasoning in *Chadha* unpersuasive. In particular, critics have faulted the Court for being excessively formalistic in insisting that legislative vetoes are subject to the bicameralism and presentment requirements of Article I. Some have noted that the *Chadha* decision places the Court in an anomalous situation with respect to the modern administrative state. On one hand, the Court permits broad and sometimes vague delegations of power from Congress to the executive branch. On the other hand, it refuses to allow Congress to create a device by which it may check the exercise of the very power it delegated. How can the Court be so permissive in its interpretation of the Constitution on the delegation issue and so strict on the issue of the legislative veto? It would appear that the Court is not operating from a coherent theoretical perspective in this area of constitutional law.

An excerpt of the Court's opinion in *Immigration and Naturalization Service v. Chadha* is reprinted at the end of this chapter.

The legislative veto was a congressional response to the increased discretionary authority exercised by regulatory agencies. As agencies broadened their exercise of administrative discretion, congressional use of the legislative veto proliferated. Arguably the demise of the legislative veto resulted in Congress losing a powerful form of control over regulatory policymaking. Yet, the practical effect of *Chadha* is more limited. Congress can still enact legislation to overrule a regulatory decision, and, of course, it can still alter regulatory policy through the appropriations process when it reviews an agency's budget.

It is interesting that, notwithstanding the *Chadha* decision, Congress has not eliminated many of the legislative veto provisions in existing law and has even included legislative veto provisions in a number of statutes passed since *Chadha* was decided. Some of these provisions require executive agencies to obtain approval of certain actions by congressional committees. Others authorize Congress to approve or disapprove agency decisions made pursuant to delegated authority. Thus, although presumptively invalid, the legislative veto survives, at least in the statute books. In 1993, Louis Fisher concluded: "In one form or another, legislative vetoes will remain an important mechanism for reconciling legislative and executive interests. The executive branch wants to retain access to discretionary authority; Congress wants to control some of those discretionary decisions without having to pass another public law."[17]

The Congressional Review of Agency Decisionmaking Act Congress has found other means to exercise control over agency rulemaking. The Contract with America Act of 1996 included a section entitled the **Congressional Review of Agency Decisionmaking Act**[18] that requires federal agencies to submit all newly issued rules to Congress before they can take effect.

The law makes a distinction between "major rules" and all other rules. A major rule is defined as one that has resulted in or is likely to have "an annual effect on the economy of $100 million or more, resulted in "a major increase in costs or prices," or resulted in "significant adverse effects" on domestic economic indicators.[19] Federal agencies must submit all final and interim rules to the General Accounting Office (GAO) which, in turn, must submit a report to Congress. A major rule ordinarily takes effect sixty days after the date on which Congress receives a report from the GAO, or the rule is published in the *Federal Register,* which occurs later. If, within such time, a resolution disapproving the rule is passed by both houses of Congress and signed by the president (or if the joint resolution is vetoed by the president and subsequently passed over the president's veto) the rule "shall be treated as though such rule had never taken effect." An agency may not reissue a rule that is disapproved in a substantially similar form unless authorized by subsequent legislation.[20]

The new law places congressional review of agency rules on a "fast track." Although it remains to be seen how it will work out in practice, this approach has the virtue of allowing the people's elected representatives to exercise substantial direct control over rulemaking without producing undue delay in the implementation of new agency rules.

Legislative Oversight at the State Level

The **1981 Model State Administrative Procedure Act (1981 MSAPA)** does not include a provision for legislative veto. Nevertheless, to exercise control over state administrative agencies many state legislatures have included legislative veto provisions in statutory enactments. Since the Supreme Court's decision in *Chadha,* several state courts have found these provisions to offend their own constitutions. In *Blank v. Department of Corrections,*[21] the Michigan Supreme Court recently held such legislation unconstitutional as being in violation of the requirements of the Michigan Constitution con-

cerning separation of powers and its requirement of presentment of legislation to the governor. The Michigan court pointed out that the highest courts in eight other states have also declared this form of legislative oversight of rulemaking to be unconstitutional.

Not all state courts agree. The highest state courts in two states have upheld legislative vetoes. In 1990 the Idaho Supreme Court agreed with the dissent in *Chadha* and held that Idaho's executive branch agencies were not executing the law by promulgating rules but were acting according to a legislative delegation of power.[22] Therefore, the court found that it was constitutional for the legislature to override agency rulemaking activities without adhering to the formality of the enactment and presentment requirements of the Idaho Constitution. Two years later the Wisconsin Supreme Court upheld a statute that authorized a joint committee to suspend the implementation of administrative rules pending bicameral legislative review and presentment to the governor.[23] There, the legislature can permanently block the promulgation of agency rules only through a legislative act that complies with constitutional requirements of the state constitution.

At the state level, devices beyond the legislative veto allow state legislatures to exercise control of agency rulemaking. The 1981 Model State Administrative Procedure Act[24] provides for establishing a bipartisan Administrative Rules Review Committee composed of legislators to review state agency rules. If the committee objects to all or a portion of a rule because it considers it to be beyond the procedural or substantive authority delegated to the adopting agency, the committee may file objections. The agency may then respond to the committee's objections. But, if the objection remains, the burden is on the agency in any proceeding for judicial review or for enforcement of the rule to establish that the rule (or the part objected to) is within the procedural and substantive authority delegated to the agency.

The Florida legislature has established an Administrative Procedures Committee somewhat different from the MSAPA model, yet it provides the state legislature a measure of political control. The Florida committee consists of three members of the state Senate and three members of the House of Representatives. The committee is directed to maintain a continuous review of administrative rules and the rulemaking processes and request an agency to repeal any rule that reiterates or paraphrases any statute or for which statutory authority has been repealed. The committee also reports annually to the state legislature on needed legislation.[25]

Prohibition from Exercising a Power Delegated to Another Branch of Government

The U.S. Supreme Court has made it clear that in its legislative oversight Congress cannot exercise a power that the Constitution properly delegates to another branch of government. In 1926 in *Myers v. United States,*[26] at issue was a statute that provided certain postmasters could be removed only "by and with the advice and consent of the Senate." At the time, the post office was a department of the president's cabinet so the focus of the Court's inquiry was on an executive official. Chief Justice Taft, a former president, writing for the Supreme Court, found the statute unconstitutional because it allowed Congress to "draw to itself, or to either branch of it, the power to remove or the right to participate in the exercise of that power . . . would be . . . to infringe on the constitutional principle of the separation of governmental powers." The Court took note of the fact the president must ensure that the laws "be faithfully executed" and stated:

> . . . [A]rticle 2 grants to the President the executive power of the government—i.e., the general administrative control of those executing the laws, including the power of appointment and removal of executive officers—a conclusion confirmed by his obligation to take care that the laws be faithfully executed; . . . Article 2 excludes the

exercise of legislative power by Congress to provide for appointments and removals, except only as granted therein to Congress in the matter of inferior offices. . . .[27]

Sixty years later in *Bowsher v. Synar,*[28] the Supreme Court referred to its decision in *Myers v. United States* and struck down a key provision of the Gramm-Rudman-Hollings Act, which set maximum deficits for federal spending for the years 1986-1991. Congress had provided that if it did not agree on the necessary budgetary cuts to meet the requirements of the act, the comptroller general would specify annual cuts in the federal budget. The Court held that specifying budget cuts was an executive function and observed that because Congress could remove the comptroller general, to grant executive powers to that office violated the Constitutional doctrine of separation of powers.

The Supreme Court's decision in *Bowsher v. Synar* is excerpted at the end of the chapter.

According to Bernard Schwartz, Chief Justice Burger's first draft opinion in *Bowsher v. Synar* included language to the effect that "the sole power of removal of an officer charged with the execution of the laws . . . resides in the President." Schwartz points out that "[s]ince the independent agencies are 'charged with the execution of the laws,' the implication is that their members must be subject to removal at will by the President—which would, of course, completely destroy their independence."[29]

In 1984 Congress enacted the Sentencing Reform Act in response to the widespread dissatisfaction with disparities in the sentencing processes then in place. The act created the U.S. Sentencing Commission. The commission consisted of six members appointed by the president and was authorized to establish ranges of sentences to be imposed by judges on those convicted of federal crimes.

John Mistretta, a federal prisoner, challenged his sentence that was imposed under guidelines established by the act. He contended that the act was unconstitutional because it violated the doctrine of separation of powers and because Congress had delegated excessive authority to the Sentencing Commission. In 1989, in *Mistretta v. United States,*[30] Justice Blackmun, writing for an 8-1 majority of the Supreme Court, held that Congress's delegation of authority was sufficiently specific to meet Constitutional requirements. He opined that while the principle of separation of powers is essential, that principle does not require the three branches of government to be entirely distinct from one another. Justice Blackmun also noted that although the Commission was established within the judicial branch its powers were not united with the judiciary. Justice Scalia, the lone dissenter, argued that the act violated the doctrine of separation of powers. He described the new Sentencing Commission as "a sort of junior-varsity Congress" which "exercises no governmental powers except the making of rules that have the effect of laws."[31]

The Budgetary Process

Article 1, Section 9 of the U.S. Constitution vests the power in Congress to budget and spend money. The **budgetary process** represents a significant phase of formal legislative oversight where political agendas, partisan differences, and the effects of special interests are all melded into the mix that becomes the national budget.

The Congressional Budget Office In 1974 Congress created the **Congressional Budget Office (CBO)**. Its mission is to provide Congress with objective, timely, nonpartisan analyses needed for making budgetary decisions. It keeps track of spending and revenue legislation, supports the work of House and Senate Budget Committees, and helps Congress stay within its budget. To better assess the impact of laws on state and local governments and the private sector, Congress enacted the **Unfunded Mandates Reform Act of 1995,**[32] requiring the CBO to furnish the budget committees information as to costs and funding requirements where bills contain federal mandates. (We discuss unfunded mandates in more detail in Chapter 4).

During its review of the president's budget, the Senate and House Committees receive reports, hear requests, debate the merits of the proposed budget, propose revisions, and finally submit the budget to Congress. The budgetary process consists of enactment first of Authorizing Bills followed by an Appropriations Act, which is enacted by Congress following House and Senate Budget Committee action, Congressional Budget Office (CBO) analysis, and floor debate.

The Line Item Veto Historically the president has been required to accept or veto a bill in its entirety. Many states allow the governor to veto individual items in appropriation bills. Several recent presidents have sought such power either through constitutional amendment or statute. Proponents of the **line item veto** argue that while members of Congress were forced to fight for local spending projects to insure their reelection, the president, by virtue of a national mandate, could "trim the fat" that could not otherwise be eliminated from the national budget. Finally, in 1996 Congress enacted the Line Item Veto Act (LIVA),[33] which gave the president the authority to veto certain items in appropriations bills, thus allowing the president an effective means to control federal spending by being able to veto individual line items.

President Clinton used the line item veto device in 1997; however, in 1998 in *Clinton v. City of New York,*[34] the Supreme Court ruled the statute unconstitutional. (See Supreme Court Perspective located in Box 8.1.)

Many state constitutions allow the governor to exercise the line item veto power in respect to appropriations. In California, as in many states, the governor may reduce or eliminate one or more items from the appropriations bill.[35]

Informal Legislative Oversight

More than two hundred congressional committees and subcommittees of Congress attempt to exercise broad discretionary power over administrative agencies. Some committees exercise oversight over a particular agency or group of

---

BOX 8.1 Supreme Court Perspective

Clinton v. City of New York
524 U.S. 417 (1998)

[In 1996 Congress enacted the Line Item Veto Act, which gave the president power to cancel discretionary budget items, items of new direct spending, or any limited tax benefit. When President Clinton used the device in 1997 to cancel some spending items, the matter ended up in the Supreme Court. Relying on its decision in INS v. Chadha, 462 U.S. 919 (1983), the Court found that the act allowing the president to exercise the line item veto was unconstitutional.]

Justice Stevens, writing for a 7-2 majority, explained:

. . . [O]ur decision rests on the narrow ground that the procedures authorized by the Line Item Veto Act are not authorized by the Constitution. The Balanced Budget Act of 1997 is a 500-page document that became "Public Law 105-33" after three procedural steps were taken: (1) a bill containing the exact text was approved by a majority of the Members of the House of Representatives,

(2) the Senate approves precisely the same text, and (3) that text was signed into law by the President. The Constitution explicitly requires that each of those three steps be taken before a bill may "become a law." Art 1, § 7. If one paragraph of that text had been omitted at any one of those three stages, Public Law 105-33 would not have been validly enacted. If the Line Item Veto Act were valid, it would authorize the President to create a different law—one whose text was not voted on by either House of Congress or presented to the President for signature. Something that might be known as "Public Law 105-33 as modified by the President" may or may not be desirable, but it is surely not a document that may "become a law" pursuant to the procedures designed by the Framers of Article I, § 7, of the Constitution. If there is to be a new procedure in which the President will play a different role in determining the final text of what may "become a law," such change must come not by legislation but through the amendment procedure set forth in Article V of the Constitution. . . .

---

agencies; others exercise control over appropriations and budgetary matters.

In addition to Congress, legislative staff members through their requests to agencies, exercise an informal oversight. As legislation has increased to cope with the technological developments in society, the legislative staff members have assumed a role of greater importance in the political oversight of agency action.

Congress can investigate agencies and require reports; however, courts have ruled that congressional committees cannot inject themselves into adjudications pending before agencies. In *Pillsbury Co. v. FTC*,[36] in questioning Federal Trade Commission (FTC) commissioners, several subcommittee members of the Senate Judiciary Committee expressed strong views on a key issue pending before the FTC. The FTC subsequently ruled on the issue as the senators had suggested. In holding that the senate committee's actions deprived the Pillsbury Co. of a fair adjudication of disputed issues, the court observed:

To subject an administrator to a searching examination as to how and why he reached his decision in a case still pending before him, and to criticize him for reaching the 'wrong' decision, as the Senate subcommittee did in this case, sacrifices the appearance of impartiality—the *sine qua non* of American judicial justice—in favor of some short-run notions regarding the Congressional intent underlying an amendment to a statute, unfettered administration of which was committed by Congress to the Federal Trade Commission.[37]

Improper Political Interference with Matters Committed to Agency Discretion
Because administrative agencies are creatures of Congress, citizens and special interest groups often look to their congressional representatives to assist them in navigating through the bureaucracy. Legislators often assist their constituents by checking up on agency action or inaction. In

Sierra Club v. Costle,[38] a federal appeals court observed:

> We believe it entirely proper for Congressional representatives vigorously to represent the interest of their constituents before administrative agencies engaged in informal, general policy rulemaking, so long as individual Congressmen do not frustrate the intent of Congress as a whole as expressed in statute nor undermine applicable rules or procedures.[39]

Within bounds members of Congress can strongly assert their views. However, when a member of Congress exerts influence to shape an agency's determination of the merits, or causes an agency to depart from relevant statutory requirements, the courts will step in. The classic case in point is *D.C. Federation of Civic Associations v. Volpe*,[40] where the U.S. Court of Appeals for the District of Columbia Circuit invalidated the secretary of transportation's decision to build a controversial bridge across the Potomac River. The court concluded that the secretary's decision was possibly influenced by the threat of a House subcommittee chairman to scuttle funding for the D.C. subway system if the bridge project was abandoned. The court directed the secretary to "make new determinations based strictly on the merits and completely without regard to any considerations not made relevant by Congress in the applicable statutes."[41] Writing for the court, Judge David Bazelon observed:

> So long as the Secretary applies his expertise to considerations Congress intended to make relevant, he acts within his discretion and our role as a reviewing court is constrained. We do not hold, in other words, that the bridge can never be built. Nor do we know or mean to suggest that the information now available to the Secretary is necessarily insufficient to justify construction of the bridge. We hold only that the Secretary must reach his decision strictly on the merits and in the manner prescribed by statute, without reference to irrelevant or extraneous considerations.[42]

See Box 8.2 for more detail regarding the scope of Congress's influence on the validity of administrative decisions.

EXECUTIVE CONTROL OF THE BUREAUCRACY

Because the president is the chief executive, he exercises substantial control over executive agencies. The independent agencies are less subject to direct presidential control. All presidents, regardless of political party, struggle to maintain oversight and control over the bureaucracy. The federal government is so massive, so involved in so many different programs and activities at home and abroad, that it is impossible for any president to know exactly what is going on in every agency at any point in time. That is why presidents rely so heavily on staff and on key support agencies within the Executive Office. State and local governments are not so large, not so complex and not so far-flung. Still, governors, county executives, and mayors rely on key advisors and agencies to help them manage their respective bureaucracies.

In addition to their power of persuasion, which may be the ultimate presidential power,[43] presidents can use executive orders, their role in the budget process, their **powers of appointment and removal,** and their control over agency litigation as means of controlling the bureaucracy. At the state level, these powers are available to most governors, although the measure of any governor's control is largely based on the state constitution and statutes, and there is considerable variance from state to state.

Constitutional Powers Provide for Direct Oversight

The U.S. Constitution and the constitutions of many states provide express means of oversight by the president of the United States or the governor of a state. At the federal level Article II, Section 3 of the U.S. Constitution requires the president to "take care that the laws be faithfully

---

BOX 8.2   Case in Point

When Does Congressional Influence Render an Administrative Decision Invalid?
ATX, INC. v. United States Department of Transportation
United States Court of Appeals for the District of Columbia Circuit
41 F.3d 1522 (D.C. Cir. 1994)

ATX filed an application with the Department of Transportation (DOT) for operation of a new airline. The record established that members of Congress repeatedly contacted Secretary of Transportation Pena to voice their opposition to the ATX application for certification. Secretary Pena received at least 60 letters commenting negatively on Frank Lorenzo, founder of ATX Airline, almost all concluding that he was not fit to return to the airline industry and urging the Secretary to deny ATX's petition outright. DOT denied the application, and ATX sought review before the D.C. Circuit of the United States Court of Appeals. ATX contended that Congressional interference rendered the DOT's denial invalid. In rejecting ATX's petition the Court of Appeals pointed out that while Congressional interference in the administrative process is of heightened concern in a quasi-judicial proceeding, that concern is guided by two principles. First, "the appearance of bias or pressure may

be no less objectionable than the reality . . . Second, judicial evaluation of the pressure must focus on the nexus between the pressure and the actual decision maker." The court found evidence to suggest that the congressional letters influenced Secretary Pena's decision to set the ATX application for hearing, but noted that such "influence" is not the improper influence that concerns the court. "We are concerned," the court noted "when congressional influence shapes the agency's determination of the merits." The court further observed, "Here, we have no reason to doubt that the decision to hold a hearing was made to ensure the fairness and impartiality of the process, as evidenced by Assistant Secretary Murphy's statement that a hearing would provide 'maximum possible due process to interested parties.' " . . . "Murphy issued a lengthy opinion based on the administrative record, the basis of his decision was clear and open to scrutiny and his decision was fully supported by the record. Finally, the record manifests that both the Secretary and his acting Assistant Secretary were non-committal in their reactions to the congressional contacts. Secretary Pena's response to the correspondence stressed that it was inappropriate for him to discuss the merits of the case with the congressmen . . ."

---

executed," a provision construed by the Supreme Court in *Myers v. United States,* which we discussed earlier. Article II, Section 2, cl.1 provides that the president may "require the opinion, in writing, of the principal officer in each of the executive departments, upon any subject relating to the duties of their respective offices." Whether this provides authority for the president to require reports from independent agencies is an undecided issue. The president and heads of agencies have access to the Office of Legal Counsel, which serves as legal adviser to the executive branch of the federal government. At the state level the attorney general issues advisory opinions on the law to the governor and other state officials. State statutes usually stipulate which state officials are eligible to receive opinions. Although opinions of attorneys general are

not binding on the courts, nevertheless judges tend to give considerable weight to such opinions, particularly if an official or agency has acted pursuant to an attorney general's opinion for a considerable time.

Under Article II, Section 2, cl. 2 of the U.S. Constitution the president has primary responsibility for the appointment of high executive officials. The appointment power is an important mechanism for controlling the bureaucracy and has over the years been a source of disagreement between Congress and the president. We discuss the appointment power in greater detail in the following section. State constitutions grant varying powers to governors to make administrative appointments. In some states the governor appoints the heads of executive offices and independent agencies, sometimes with the consent of

Table 8.1 Executive Orders Issued, Presidents Hoover through Clinton

President	Years in office	First E.O. #	Last E.O. #	Number issued
Herbert Hoover	1929–1933	5075	6070	995
Franklin D. Roosevelt	1933–1945	6071	9537	3466
Harry S. Truman	1945–1953	9538	10431	893
Dwight D. Eisenhower	1953–1961	10432	10913	481
John F. Kennedy	1961–1963	10914	11127	213
Lyndon B. Johnson	1963–1969	11128	11451	323
Richard Nixon	1969–1974	11452	11797	345
Gerald R. Ford	1974–1977	11798	11966	168
Jimmy Carter	1977–1981	11967	12286	319
Ronald Reagan	1981–1989	12287	12667	380
George H. W. Bush	1989–1993	12668	12833	165
William J. Clinton	1993–2001	12834	13197	363

SOURCE: *Federal Register.*

one or both houses of the state legislature. In some instances executive officers are elected, as are heads of some independent agencies. The 1981 Model State Administrative Procedure Act provides for the governor to appoint a "rules counsel" and allows the governor by executive order "to suspend all or a severable portion of an agency rule."[44]

Executive Orders

An **executive order** is a presidential directive to officials and agencies. Executive orders are not mentioned in the U.S. Constitution; however, they have a long history of being used for a variety of purposes. Historically, two of the most significant executive orders were President Lincoln's Emancipation Proclamation in 1863, an important step in the abolition of slavery, and President Truman's 1948 order ending racial segregation in the armed forces, an important step in the desegregation of American society.

Throughout this text we have noted numerous instances of modern presidents issuing executive orders. President Franklin D. Roosevelt was the most prolific in the use of executive orders, issuing nearly 3,500 of them in the twelve and a half years he occupied the White House (see

Table 8.1). Recognizing the increasing use of executive orders, Congress enacted legislation in 1935 requiring that every executive order be filed with the Office of the Federal Register, and that, beginning in 1936, all such orders of general applicability be published in the *Federal Register*.

Although there is no specific language in the Constitution authorizing presidents to issue executive orders, the Supreme Court has recognized the constitutionality of executive orders as an inherent power of the president.[45] Unless they are invalidated by congressional or judicial action, executive orders have the force of law. Indeed, John E. Noyes has characterized executive orders as "the most important type of 'Presidential legislation.'"[46] Executive orders to administrative agencies are generally looked upon as a means of carrying out the president's directions to executive agencies.

Although no general statute provides for their issuance, in many instances executive orders are issued pursuant to specific statutory authority. In one instance the Supreme Court recognized the statutory basis of an executive order, noting that

the Executive Order finds express statutory authorization in 5 U.S.C. § 7301, which provides that "(t)he President may prescribe regulations for the conduct of employees in the executive branch." In view of the substantial federal interests in effective management of the business of the National Government and exclusive control over the conduct of federal employees, and this congressional authorization, we have no difficulty concluding that the Executive Order is valid and may create rights protected against inconsistent state laws through the Supremacy Clause.[47]

In 1981 President Reagan issued Executive Order 12291 instructing federal agencies, "to the extent permitted by Law" to take regulatory action only if "the potential benefits to society for the regulation outweigh the potential costs to society." In 1993 President Clinton replaced the Reagan approach with Executive Order 12,866. Although it retained the basic framework of regulatory review established in 1981, the new order effected several changes in response to criticisms that had been voiced against the Reagan/Bush programs. One of the changes directed the **Office of Management and Budget (OMB)** to focus its review on the most important rules. President Clinton charged Vice President Albert Gore with heading the National Performance Review (NPR), which sought to "reinvent government" by making agencies act more like businesses in dealing with customers. Clinton accepted strong bipartisan measures to reform the nation's welfare system. In his last State of the Union message to Congress, Clinton recognized that the mood of the country was to simplify government when he declared, "The era of big government is over."

Controversial Orders Issued by President George W. Bush Shortly after taking office in 2001, President George W. Bush issued two controversial executive orders designed to increase involvement of religious organizations in furnishing services under various programs administered by the federal government. Executive Order 13198 concerns agency responsibilities with respect to faith-based and community initiatives. Executive Order 13199 established within the Executive Office of the President, the Office of Faith-Based and Community Initiatives. These orders were based on the president's general executive power, not on specific statutory authority. Following the issuance of these orders, federal agencies moved to eliminate regulations that barred religiously oriented charities from receiving federal grants and contracts for the delivery of social services. Critics charged that the new policy toward faith-based organizations breached the wall of separation between church and state.

Three days after the infamous terrorist attacks of September 11, 2001, President Bush issued Executive Order 13223 ordering the Ready Reserve of the Armed Forces to active duty and delegating certain authorities to the Secretary of Defense and the Secretary of Transportation. This was followed by Order 13224, issued on September 23, prohibiting transactions with persons who commit, threaten to commit, or support terrorism, and was designed to give the U.S. government tools to impede terrorist funding. Both of these orders were issued pursuant to specific statutory authority.

On November 13, 2001, President Bush issued a military order entitled "Detention, Treatment, and Trial of Certain Non-Citizens in the War Against Terrorism." Based primarily on the president's constitutional powers as commander in chief, the controversial order allows the use of military commissions to try foreign nationals accused of terrorism. Under the order, the secretary of defense is directed to establish these tribunals and promulgate rules governing their operation. On March 21, 2002, Secretary of Defense Donald Rumsfeld issued an order specifying the procedures to be followed by the military tribunals. Critics claimed that the new military tribunals deprived persons under the jurisdiction of the United States due process of law and that the president's order exceeded his constitutional authority. In testimony before the Senate Judiciary Committee on November 28, 2001, Professor Philip B. Heymann of the Harvard Law School referred to President Bush's order as "one of the clearest mistakes and one of

---

BOX 8.3   Case in Point

Was the Administrative Law Judge an "Inferior Officer"?
Landry v. Federal Deposit Insurance Corporation
United States Court of Appeals for the District
of Columbia Circuit
204 F.3d 1125 (D.C. Cir. 1998)

The Federal Deposit Insurance Corporation (FDIC)
notified Michael D. Landry, a bank officer in a
bank in Hammond, Louisiana, that it intended to
seek an order to remove him from his position and
to prohibit him from further operations of a federally insured depository institution. As required by
statute, the FDIC assigned the matter for a formal
on-the-record hearing to one of the administrative
law judges (ALJs) appointed by the FDIC. After a
lengthy hearing, the ALJ issued a recommended
decision that the FDIC issue its proposed order. The
Board of Directors of the FDIC agreed with the ALJ
and issued an order of removal and prohibition.

In a petition to the U.S. Court of Appeals for
the District of Columbia Circuit, Landry sought to
challenge the FDIC's decision that mandated his
removal from office and barred him from any
further participation in the operation of a federally insured institution. He contended the ALJ that
conducted the hearing was an "inferior officer"
who had not been properly appointed since he had
not been appointed by the President, the head of
a department, or the courts of law as required by
the Appointment Clause of the U.S. Constitution.
Art. II, § 2, cl. 2.

The court denied Landry's petition. In doing so it
distinguished the case from the U.S. Supreme Court's
decision in *Freytag v. Commissioner of Internal Revenue Service*, 501 U.S. 868 (1991). In *Freytag*, the
Court held that special trial court judges of the U.S.
Tax Courts were inferior officers whose appointments must conform to the Appointments Clause of
the U.S. Constitution. The Court of Appeals pointed
out that unlike the judges in *Freytag*, who possessed
the power to render final decisions in certain tax
cases, the FDIC's ALJ's could not render final decisions and the FDIC Board of Directors owed no deference to the ALJ's factual findings.

---

the most dangerous claims of executive power in
the almost fifty years that I have been in and out
of government."

The Power to Appoint Officers

The **Appointments Clause** found in Article III,
Section 2 of the Constitution provides that the
president "by and with the Advice and Consent of
the Senate, shall appoint Ambassadors, other public Ministers and Consuls, Judges of the Supreme
Court, and all other Officers of the United States,
whose Appointments are not herein otherwise
provided for . . ." But it also provides that "Congress may by Law vest the Appointment of such
inferior Officers, as they think proper, in the President alone, in the Courts of Law, or in the Heads
of Departments." This power to appoint officers
affords the president the opportunity to shape the
administrative policy of the federal government.
The line between **Officers of the United**
States and **inferior officers** is not a clear one
and remains to be defined by the Supreme Court
on a case-by-case basis. See Box 8.3 for an example in which the controversy over whether an
administrative law judge was an "inferior officer"
was critical to the outcome of a case.

In *Buckley v. Valeo*,[48] the Supreme Court recognized that "[P]rincipal officers are selected by
the President with the advice and consent of the
Senate. Inferior officers Congress may allow to
be appointed by the President alone, by the
heads of departments, or by the Judiciary." But
the Court invalidated federal legislation creating
the Federal Election Commission (FEC) that
provided that four of the six voting members of
the FEC would be appointed by the Speaker of
the House and the president pro tem of the Senate. The Court held that the Appointments
Clause applies to all officers who exercise significant authority pursuant to the laws of the
United States such as rulemaking, adjudication,

or enforcement functions, but noted it would have reached a different conclusion if the FEC had merely been assigned investigative and informative powers.

Congress can set qualifications for offices, such as limiting the number of members of an agency that can be appointed from one political party. Congress can defer from approving presidential nominees as it did in 1995 when President Clinton sought to appoint Jocelyn Elders to be surgeon general. During the 2001–2003 period President George W. Bush experienced difficulties in securing Senate approval of several of his nominations of federal judges. In 2001 and 2002, the problem stemmed primarily from the fact that a Senate Judiciary Committee controlled by Democrats scrutinized a Republican president's judicial nominees. The situation changed considerably when the president's party regained control of the Senate through the November 2002 midterm congressional elections. However, during 2003, the Democrats used the tactic of the "filibuster" (i.e., protracted debate) to prevent the Senate from voting on several of President Bush's key judicial nominees.

In *Morrison v. Olson,* the Supreme Court upheld the constitutionality of the Ethics in Government Act in which Congress authorized appointment of a special prosecutor (independent counsel) by a federal court of appeals to investigate allegations of criminal wrongdoing by high officials of the executive branch. Referring to the Appointments Clause, the Court observed, "[T]he inclusion of 'as they think proper' seems clearly to give Congress significant discretion to determine whether it is 'proper' to vest the appointment of, for example, executive officials in the courts of Law."[49]

In *Freytag v. Commissioner of Internal Revenue Service* (1991),[50] a federal statute authorized the chief judge of the U.S. Tax Court to appoint special trial judges. The Commissioner argued that the Tax Court was a "Department," since it had been an agency in the executive branch before Congress designated it as a "court" and the change in name did not remove it to a different branch. It was also argued that the delegation by the chief judge violated the Appointments Clause of the Constitution, because a special trial judge is an "Officer" of the United States who must be appointed in compliance with the clause. But the Supreme Court held that the court was one of the "Courts of Law" mentioned in the Appointments Clause of the Constitution and upheld the authority of the chief judge of the Tax Court to make the appointments.

The Power to Remove Officers

Except for impeachment the Constitution does not address circumstances under which agency personnel may be removed from office. Heads of "executive agencies" (e.g., cabinet departments) serve at the pleasure of the president. Presidents not only appoint their cabinet officers and heads of executive agencies, they frequently reorganize executive agencies and fill key positions with officials sympathetic to the approach of their administration.

On the other hand, commissioners of independent federal agencies (e.g., SEC, FCC, NLRB) are appointed for fixed terms and statutory law protects them from arbitrary removal during their terms of office. As we noted, these independent agencies of the federal government are often described as the "fourth branch of government" because of the power they wield in American government.

In *Humphrey's Executor v. United States* (1935),[51] the issue before the Supreme Court was whether a statute restricting the president's power to remove commissioners of the Federal Trade Commission (FTC) was constitutional. President Roosevelt had removed William E. Humphrey as chair of the FTC. The relevant statute permitted the president to remove a commissioner only for inefficiency, neglect of duty, or malfeasance in office. Humphrey died and his executor contested his removal in the U.S. Court of Claims. Eventually the case wound up in the Supreme Court, which held that the statutory removal-for-cause limit on the president's removal power prevented

President Roosevelt from removing Humphrey as the chair of the FTC. The Court ruled that the president's right to remove an executive officer did not apply to officers of the FTC because it "occupies no place in the executive department" and "acts in part quasi-legislatively and part quasi-judicially."

Removal of Officers of Independent Agencies In 1958 in *Wiener v. United States*,[52] President Eisenhower sought to remove a commissioner from the War Claims Commission in order to replace him with his own appointee. Wiener was one of three commissioners appointed by President Truman pursuant to the War Claims Act of 1948 to adjudicate claims for compensating internees, prisoners of war, and religious organizations that suffered personal injury or property damage at the hands of the enemy in World War II. Noting the adjudicatory character of the commission, Justice Frankfurter stated for the Court that "it must be inferred that Congress did not wish to have hang over the Commission the Damocles' sword of removal by the President for no other reason than that he preferred to have on the Commission men of his own choosing."[53] The Court thus rejected Eisenhower's attempt to remove Wiener without cause.

The Supreme Court's opinion in *Wiener v. United States* is excerpted at the end of the chapter.

The Supreme Court's decisions in this area suggest that the legality of presidential removal of an official in the executive branch depends on the nature of the duties performed by the official in question. Officials performing purely executive functions may be removed by the president at will; those performing quasi-legislative or quasi-judicial functions can be removed by the president only for cause, assuming that is what Congress has provided by statute. Although Congress may determine the basis for removal of officials in independent agencies, the ultimate power to remove officials in the executive branch belongs to the president. In practice the president exercises considerable authority over

independent agencies because the president's request for an administrator's resignation is generally honored. Otherwise it could trigger a **removal-for-cause** controversy.

The Executive Role in the Budgetary Process

As we noted above, the budgetary process is essentially a legislative function. Nevertheless the president has a vital role in budgeting. The Budget and Accounting Act of 1921[54] requires the president to submit a budget to the Congress by February 1 each year. The president's budget proposal is essentially a statement of the administration's priorities and is an important means of controlling the bureaucracy. Agencies whose activities are consistent with presidential philosophy are typically rewarded with budget increases, while those that displease the president often find their budgets reduced. Of course, Congress may disagree with the president's priorities, as well as with his assessment of the performance of particular agencies. The final budget is always a compromise between the two branches of government. The failure of the two branches to reach agreement by the beginning of a new fiscal year can result in a partial shutdown of the federal government such as that which occurred in 1995. To prevent this drastic consequence, Congress can adopt a continuing resolution to keep the government running according to the previous budget.

The Office of Management and Budget To assist the president in performing the budgetary function, Congress created the Bureau of the Budget (BOB) in 1921. Prior to that time, executive branch agencies made their budget requests directly to Congress. Centralizing this process under an agency under presidential control improved the efficiency of the budget process but resulted in a significant shift of power to the executive branch. First housed within the Treasury Department, the BOB was moved to the Executive Office of the President in 1939. In

1970 Congress created the Office of Management and Budget (OMB) from the BOB.[55]

The OMB develops the president's annual budget for submission to Congress. Agencies submit their budgets to the OMB, which attempts to shape their proposals to reflect the president's priorities. In assisting the president in formulating a budget proposal, OMB evaluates the effectiveness of agency programs, policies, and procedures. It also ensures that agency reports, rules, testimony, and proposed legislation are consistent with the president's budgetary priorities and with the president's policies. OMB is widely regarded as one of the most powerful agencies within the executive branch and obviously exerts significant influence over public policy.

As citizens became disenchanted with the growing size and power of the federal bureaucracy during the last quarter of the twentieth century, calling for bureaucratic reform became a political mantra for presidential candidates. In 1976 Jimmy Carter ran for president claiming to have successfully reorganized state government while he was governor of Georgia. After assuming office in 1977, President Carter told Congress that it was essential that it review the laws that established the regulatory process of the federal government. He proceeded to establish the Regulatory Analysis Review Group (RARG) to review proposed new administrative rules. He championed enactment of the Civil Service Reform Act of 1978. To reduce the burden of paperwork associated with regulatory agencies, he vigorously supported the **Paperwork Reduction Act (PRA).**[56] Enacted by Congress in 1980, the new act created the **Office of Information and Regulatory Affairs (OIRA),** which continues to play an important role in review of agency regulations. Before an agency makes any new demand for information, it must satisfy the Office of Information and Regulatory Affairs within OMB that the information is required by the agency to perform its functions.

During the Reagan and elder Bush administrations, OIRA served as a significant brake on regulation. While this aroused considerable criticism from interests that favored regulation, at least one commentator has defended the overtly political role that OIRA can play in the regulatory process:

> OIRA is more politically accountable than a reviewing court. As numerous commentators and jurists have demonstrated, rulemaking is, and should be, a political process. The informal rulemaking process has features that simultaneously approximate the process of communication and debate used to resolve policy disputes through the legislative process and that allow effective participation by the diverse elected officials who participate in the legislative process . . . Moreover, the president will be held politically accountable for the results of the OIRA review process.[57]

Executive Control of Agency Litigation

Because judicial decisions can effect changes in administrative policies and in some instances can nullify administrative rulings, litigation and threats of litigation can shape governmental policy. Therefore, the **power to control litigation** involving federal agencies is an important tool in the hands of the president. Where the United States is a party, litigation is generally under control of the Department of Justice (DOJ), established in 1870, and headed by the **attorney general.** It is the **solicitor general,** based on authority delegated by the attorney general, who represents the United States before the Supreme Court. The president appoints these officials to implement the president's constitutional mandate to "take Care that the Laws be faithfully executed,"[58] so one may assume their views will be compatible with the president's administration.

Federal law provides: "Except as otherwise authorized by law, the conduct of litigation in which the United States, an agency, or officer thereof is a party, or is interested, and securing evidence therefor, is reserved to officers of the Department of Justice, under the direction of the Attorney General."[59] Thus, the attorney general generally controls litigation involving federal agencies.

Representation of the executive agencies is routinely handled by the DOJ, but in many instances Congress has exercised its political will by vesting varying measures of litigating authority in independent agencies. The Internal Revenue Service (IRS) is authorized to litigate in the Tax Court.[60] Some agencies, for example, the Federal Trade Commission has much broader authority to litigate.[61] Neal Devins observes that "[T]he patchwork nature of governmental representation is often an outgrowth of political conflict" yet most independent agencies "are able to conduct the bulk of their own litigation using agency attorneys."[62]

Even when Congress allows certain independent agencies to litigate outside the control of the DOJ, it seldom grants these agencies the right to handle cases before the U.S. Supreme Court. This reserves the political control over Supreme Court litigation to the solicitor general, who is influential in deciding whether to ask the Court to grant certiorari review in cases involving the United States and federal agencies. Moreover, in reviewing an agency's statutory authority, the Court has been inclined to reserve the right to petition for certiorari to the solicitor general. For example, Congress provided the Federal Election Commission (FEC) with broad litigating authority on all matters, including the right to appeal and petition for certiorari in actions to enforce the presidential election fund laws.[63] Yet, in 1994 the Supreme Court ruled that the FEC did not have authority to petition the Supreme Court for certiorari in an action involving enforcement of campaign laws against a political action committee because a different section of the same enabling statute[64] did not contain an express grant of the power to petition the Supreme Court for a writ of certiorari.[65]

The relationship between the president and the solicitor general assures the president of maintaining a large measure of policy control over the most significant legal proceedings affecting the federal government, and assures the federal government that it will speak before the Court with one voice. Traditionally the office of solicitor general has exercised a high degree of objectivity in deciding whether to seek Supreme Court review in administrative agency matters. Nevertheless, given that several independent agencies have litigating authority before the lower courts, some argue that these agencies should have the right to independently determine whether to seek Supreme Court review. They contend that allowing the solicitor general to become the "gatekeeper to the Supreme Court" not only limits the autonomy of independent agencies, but in some cases places the solicitor general in a position of divided loyalty between the agency's position and the solicitor general's loyalty to the president.

There have been some highly visible examples of conflicts between a president's administration and the position of an independent governmental agency. For example, in 1985 the Reagan administration directed the solicitor general to file an amicus curiae brief in *Thornburg v. American College of Obstetricians*[66] asking the Supreme Court to overturn its 1973 decision in *Roe v. Wade* establishing the constitutional right to obtain an abortion.

In 1992, in the latter days of the elder President Bush's administration, the DOJ directed the Postal Service's Board of Governors to withdraw from a case before the U.S. Court of Appeals for the D.C. Circuit. The court rejected the president's position and later approved the Postal Service's right to litigate.[67]

In *Bob Jones University v. United States* (1983),[68] a case we discussed in Chapter 4, the IRS denied federal tax-exempt status to a university that practiced racial discrimination. After the Treasury Department had taken conflicting positions, the Supreme Court appointed counsel to represent the treasury's earlier position that the IRS should not grant the exemption, while an assistant attorney general represented the government's final position that there was no statutory authority for the IRS to deny the exemption.[69]

Thus, although the president maintains a large measure of political control over litigation involving federal agencies, Congress exercises a degree of political control by authorizing independent agencies to conduct litigation on their own behalf. Nevertheless, the president through the attorney general and the solicitor general generally control whether to seek Supreme Court review of lower court decisions. In the final analysis, it is the Supreme Court that resolves controversies that have the most significant bearing on public administration.

At the state level the attorney general usually maintains control over litigation involving the state; however, in some instances legislatures have authorized independent agencies to handle litigation. In most states the attorney general is an elected officer; in a few the governor appoints the attorney general.[70] In sum, unless the attorney general is a gubernatorial appointee, the governor's political control over litigation is generally limited, especially when the governor and attorney general are members of different political parties.

DIRECT CONTROL OF THE BUREAUCRACY BY THE ELECTORATE

Because the framers of the United States Constitution believed in a "republican" rather than a "democratic" form of government, voters have no direct control over policies adopted by the federal government. Rather, they must rely on elected officials who in turn must act through the mechanisms described previously in this chapter if they are to bend bureaucratic actions to the popular will. On the other hand, voters in many states exercise a significant degree of direct political control over policy via the processes of the **initiative and referendum.** In some instances, voters adopt measures designed to directly control bureaucratic policymaking. For example, in 1996 California voters were successful in amending the state constitution by adopting Proposition 209, which provides that state

and local government agencies may not discriminate against or grant preferential treatment to any individual or group on the basis of race, sex, color, ethnicity, or national origin. Similarly, Colorado voters in 1992 amended the state constitution to prevent state and local legislative bodies and administrative agencies from adopting policies granting protected status or preferential treatment to persons based on their sexual orientation. However, the Supreme Court declared this amendment unconstitutional on the basis of the Equal Protection Clause of the Fourteenth Amendment, saying, "It is not within our constitutional tradition to enact laws of this sort."[71] Voters in states with the initiative and referendum procedure may exert significant control over the bureaucracy, but such initiatives are still subject to attack under applicable provisions of state and federal constitutions.

CONCLUSION

The modern administrative state, with its multiplicity of agencies, promulgates a massive number of regulations that affect our everyday lives. This poses serious problems to our traditional democratic values and to our understanding of the constitutional doctrine of separation of powers. Individual citizens can hardly be expected to monitor the activities of regulatory agencies; nevertheless, the "democracy problem" is attenuated to a considerable extent by the fact that elected officials, who are expected to voice the criticisms and expectations of their constituents, maintain a significant degree of political control over bureaucratic action. The "constitutional problem" is addressed, at least in a functional sense, as each branch of government attempts to influence the regulatory process, thereby ensuring that agencies operate within an effective system of checks and balances and by the availability of judicial review. Political control over agencies can be a valuable check, yet there are instances in which political controls can undermine the effectiveness of agency action. For example, executive branch staff members, often with minimal technical expertise, are sometimes called on to exercise oversight over agencies with a scientific mission. The challenge in the American system is to find the appropriate balance between political control and agency independence, while maintaining a viable republican form of government and preserving basic democratic values.

KEY TERMS

1981 Model State Administrative Procedure Act (1981 MSAPA)

Appointments Clause

attorney general

budgetary process

checks and balances

Congressional Budget Office (CBO)

Congressional Review of Agency Decisionmaking Act

executive order

executive privilege

Finance Committee

formal legislative action

formal oversight

General Accounting Office (GAO)

hearings

inferior officers

informal oversight

initiative and referendum

interest groups

iron triangles

issue networks

judicial oversight

legislative contempt

legislative investigations

legislative oversight

legislative veto

line item veto

lobbyists

mark-up session

Office of Information and Regulatory Affairs (OIRA)

Office of Management and Budget (OMB)

Officers of the United States

oversight

Paperwork Reduction Act (PRA)

pluralism

power to control litigation

powers of appointment and removal

removal-for-cause

rule of law

separation of powers

solicitor general

statutory directives

subpoena

technocracy

Unfunded Mandates Reform Act of 1995

Ways and Means Committee

QUESTIONS FOR THOUGHT AND DISCUSSION

1. What are the two principal ways in which Congress and state legislatures exercise oversight of administrative agencies?

2. What was the Supreme Court's rationale for declaring the "legislative veto" unconstitutional? How have state courts reacted to challenges of legislative vetoes?

3. After the legislative veto was declared unconstitutional, what means did Congress resort to in order to have an effective formal oversight over agency regulations?

4. What is a "line item veto" and why did the Supreme Court declare it unconstitutional in *Clinton v. City of New York?*

5. In what ways does the budgeting process lend itself to political control of administrative policymaking by the executive and legislative branches of the government?

6. How does the Office of Management and Budget (OMB) play a role in carrying out the president's agenda?

7. How does the role of the Congressional Budget Office (CBO) differ from that of the Office of Management and Budget (OMB)?

8. Under what circumstances can the president remove an officer from (a) a federal executive agency; (b) an independent federal agency?

9. Why has the Supreme Court rejected the power of the president to remove without cause officers of quasi-judicial agencies?

10. In what ways does the Office of Solicitor General afford the president a measure of policy control over independent federal agencies?

EDITED CASE Immigration and Naturalization Service v. Chadha
United States Supreme Court, 462 U.S. 919 (1983)

[Jagdish Rai Chadha was lawfully admitted to the United States in 1966 on a non-immigrant student visa. After his visa expired the Immigration and Naturalization Service (INS) ordered Chadha to show cause why he should not be deported. An immigration judge found that Chadha met the requirements of section 244(a) of the Immigration and Nationality Act, which allowed for a suspension of deportation of a person found to be of good moral character, who had resided continuously in the United States for over seven years and who would suffer extreme hardship if deported. The judge's findings were transmitted to Congress and would take effect unless, under the power provided in section 244(c)(2) of the act, the Senate or the House of Representatives adopted a resolution vetoing such findings. The House adopted such a resolution and ordered that Chadha be deported. Chadha then sought to have the immigration judge rule that section 244(c)(2) was unconstitutional, but the Board of Immigration Appeals dismissed the proceedings, holding that it had no power to declare an act of Congress unconstitutional. Chadha next petitioned for review in the U.S. Court of Appeals for the Ninth Circuit, which held that the House was without constitutional authority to order Chadha's deportation. The Supreme Court granted certiorari and in this case considers whether the veto action of one House of Congress under section 244(c)(2) of the act is constitutional.]

Chief Justice Burger delivered the opinion of the Court.

. . . We turn now to the question whether action of one House of Congress under § 244(c)(2)

violates strictures of the Constitution. We begin, of course, with the presumption that the challenged statute is valid. Its wisdom is not the concern of the courts; if a challenged action does not violate the Constitution, it must be sustained. . . .

By the same token, the fact that a given law or procedure is efficient, convenient, and useful in facilitating functions of government, standing alone, will not save it if it is contrary to the Constitution. Convenience and efficiency are not the primary objectives—or the hallmarks—of democratic government and our inquiry is sharpened rather than blunted by the fact that Congressional veto provisions are appearing with increasing frequency in statutes which delegate authority to executive and independent agencies:

Since 1932, when the first veto provision was enacted into law, 295 congressional veto-type procedures have been inserted in 196 different statutes as follows: from 1932 to 1939, five statutes were affected; from 1940–49, nineteen statutes; between 1950–59, thirty-four statutes; and from 1960–69, forty-nine. From the years 1970 through 1975, at least one hundred sixty-three such provisions were included in eighty-nine laws. . . .

Justice White undertakes to make a case for the proposition that the one-House veto is a useful "political invention," and we need not challenge that assertion. We can even concede this utilitarian argument although the long-range political wisdom of this "invention" is arguable. It has been vigorously debated and it is instructive to compare the views of the protagonists. But policy arguments

(Continued)

EDITED CASE   Immigration and Naturalization Service v. Chadha (Continued)

---

supporting even useful "political inventions" are subject to the demands of the Constitution which defines powers and, with respect to this subject, sets out just how those powers are to be exercised.

Explicit and unambiguous provisions of the Constitution prescribe and define the respective functions of the Congress and of the Executive in the legislative process. Since the precise terms of those familiar provisions are critical to the resolution of this case, we set them out verbatim. Art. I provides:

All legislative Powers herein granted shall be vested in a Congress of the United States, which shall consist of a Senate and a House of Representatives. [Art. I, Sec. 1. Emphasis added.] Every Bill which shall have passed the House of Representatives and the Senate, shall, before it becomes a Law, be presented to the President of the United States; . . .

Every Order, Resolution, or Vote to which the Concurrence of the Senate and House of Representatives may be necessary (except on a question of Adjournment) shall be presented to the President of the United States; and before the Same shall take Effect, shall be approved by him, or being disapproved by him, shall be repassed by two thirds of the Senate and House of Representatives, according to the Rules and Limitations prescribed in the Case of a Bill.

These provisions of Art. I are integral parts of the constitutional design for the separation of powers. We have recently noted that "[t]he principle of separation of powers was not simply an abstract generalization in the minds of the Framers: it was woven into the documents that they drafted in Philadelphia in the summer of 1787." . . . Just as we relied on the textual provision of Art. II, Sec. 2, cl. 2, to vindicate the principle of separation of powers . . . , we find that the purposes underlying the Presentment Clauses, Art. I, Sec. 7, cls. 2, 3, and the bicameral requirement of Art. I, Sec. 1 and 7, cl. 2, guide our resolution of the important question presented in this case. The very structure of the articles delegating and separating powers under Arts. I, II, and III exemplify the concept of separation of powers and we now turn to Art. I.

The records of the Constitutional Convention reveal that the requirement that all legislation be presented to the President before becoming law was uniformly accepted by the Framers. Presentment to the President and the Presidential veto were considered so imperative that the draftsmen took special pains to assure that these requirements could not be circumvented. During the final debate on Art. I, Sec. 7, cl. 2, James Madison expressed concern that it might easily be evaded by the simple expedient of calling a proposed law a "resolution" or "vote" rather than a "bill." As a consequence, Art. I, Sec. 7, cl. 3, was added.

The decision to provide the President with a limited and qualified power to nullify proposed legislation by veto was based on the profound conviction of the Framers that the powers conferred on Congress were the powers to be most carefully circumscribed. It is beyond doubt that lawmaking was a power to be shared by both Houses and the President. . . .

The President's role in the law-making process also reflects the Framers' careful efforts to check whatever propensity a particular Congress might have to enact oppressive, improvident, or ill-considered measures.

The bicameral requirement of Art. I, Sec. 1, 7 was of scarcely less concern to the Framers than was the Presidential veto and indeed the two concepts are interdependent. By providing that no law could take effect without the concurrence of the prescribed majority of the Members of both Houses, the Framers reemphasized their belief, already remarked upon in connection with the Presentment Clauses, that legislation should not be enacted unless it has been carefully and fully considered by the Nation's elected officials. . . .

However familiar, it is useful to recall that apart from their fear that special interests could be favored at the expense of public needs, the Framers were also concerned, although not of one mind, over the apprehensions of the smaller states. Those states feared a commonality of interest among the larger states would work to their disadvantage; representatives of the larger states, on the other hand, were skeptical of a legislature that could pass laws favoring a minority of the people. It need hardly be repeated here that the Great Compromise, under which one House was viewed as representing the people and the other the states, allayed the fears of both the large and small states.

We see therefore that the Framers were acutely conscious that the bicameral requirement and the Presentment Clauses would serve essential consti-

---

EDITED CASE Immigration and Naturalization Service v. Chadha (Continued)

---

tutional functions. The President's participation in the legislative process was to protect the Executive Branch from Congress and to protect the whole people from improvident laws. The division of the Congress into two distinctive bodies assures that the legislative power would be exercised only after opportunity for full study and debate in separate settings. The President's unilateral veto power, in turn, was limited by the power of two thirds of both Houses of Congress to overrule a veto thereby precluding final arbitrary action of one person. . . . [This] represents the Framers' decision that the legislative power of the Federal government be exercised in accord with a single, finely wrought and exhaustively considered, procedure.

. . . The Constitution sought to divide the delegated powers of the new federal government into three defined categories, legislative, executive and judicial, to assure, as nearly as possible, that each Branch of government would confine itself to its assigned responsibility. The hydraulic pressure inherent within each of the separate Branches to exceed the outer limits of its power, even to accomplish desirable objectives, must be resisted.

Although not "hermetically" sealed from one another, the powers delegated to the three Branches are functionally identifiable. When any Branch acts, it is presumptively exercising the power the Constitution has delegated to it. When the Executive acts, it presumptively acts in an executive or administrative capacity as defined in Art. II. And when, as here, one House of Congress purports to act, it is presumptively acting within its assigned sphere.

Beginning with this presumption, we must nevertheless establish that the challenged action under § 244(c)(2) is of the kind to which the procedural requirements of Art. I, Sec. 7 apply. Not every action taken by either House is subject to the bicameralism and presentment requirements of Art. I. Whether actions taken by either House are, in law and fact, an exercise of legislative power depends not on their form but upon "whether they contain matter which is properly to be regarded as legislative in its character and effect." . . .

Examination of the action taken here by one House pursuant to § 244(c)(2) reveals that it was essentially legislative in purpose and effect. In purporting to exercise power defined in Art. I, Sec. 8, cl. 4 to "establish an uniform Rule of Naturaliza-

tion," the House took action that had the purpose and effect of altering the legal rights, duties and relations of persons, including the Attorney General, Executive Branch officials and Chadha, all outside the legislative branch. Section 244(c)(2) purports to authorize one House of Congress to require the Attorney General to deport an individual alien whose deportation otherwise would be cancelled under 244. The one-House veto operated in this case to overrule the Attorney General and mandate Chadha's deportation; absent the House action, Chadha would remain in the United States. Congress has acted and its action has altered Chadha's status.

The legislative character of the one-House veto in this case is confirmed by the character of the Congressional action it supplants. Neither the House of Representatives nor the Senate contends that, absent the veto provision in § 244(c)(2), either of them, or both of them acting together, could effectively require the Attorney General to deport an alien once the Attorney General, in the exercise of legislatively delegated authority, had determined the alien should remain in the United States. Without the challenged provision in 244(c)(2), this could have been achieved, if at all, only by legislation requiring deportation. Similarly, a veto by one House of Congress under § 244(c)(2) cannot be justified as an attempt at amending the standards set out in 244(a)(1), or as a repeal of 244 as applied to Chadha. Amendment and repeal of statutes, no less than enactment, must conform with Art. I.

The nature of the decision implemented by the one-House veto in this case further manifests its legislative character. After long experience with the clumsy, time-consuming private bill procedure, Congress made a deliberate choice to delegate to the Executive Branch, and specifically to the Attorney General, the authority to allow deportable aliens to remain in this country in certain specified circumstances. It is not disputed that this choice to delegate authority is precisely the kind of decision that can be implemented only in accordance with the procedures set out in Art. I. Disagreement with the Attorney General's decision on Chadha's deportation—that is, Congress' decision to deport Chadha—no less than Congress' original choice to delegate to the Attorney General the authority to

(Continued)

EDITED CASE Immigration and Naturalization Service v. Chadha (Continued)

make that decision, involves determinations of policy that Congress can implement in only one way; bicameral passage followed by presentment to the President. Congress must abide by its delegation of authority until that delegation is legislatively altered or revoked.

Finally, we see that when the Framers intended to authorize either House of Congress to act alone and outside of its prescribed bicameral legislative role, they narrowly and precisely defined the procedure for such action. There are but four provisions in the Constitution, explicit and unambiguous, by which one House may act alone with the unreviewable force of law, not subject to the President's veto:

(a) The House of Representatives alone was given the power to initiate impeachments. Art. I, Sec. 2, cl. 6;

(b) The Senate alone was given the power to conduct trials following impeachment on charges initiated by the House and to convict following trial. Art. I, Sec. 3, cl. 5;

(c) The Senate alone was given final unreviewable power to approve or to disapprove presidential appointments. Art. II, Sec. 2, cl. 2;

(d) The Senate alone was given unreviewable power to ratify treaties negotiated by the President. Art. II, Sec. 2, cl. 2.

Clearly, when the Draftsmen sought to confer special powers on one House, independent of the other House, or of the President, they did so in explicit, unambiguous terms. Those carefully defined exceptions from presentment and bicameralism underscore the difference between the legislative functions of Congress and other unilateral but important and binding one-House acts provided for in the Constitution. These exceptions are narrow, explicit, and separately justified; none of them authorize the action challenged here. On the contrary, they provide further support for the conclusion that Congressional authority is not to be implied and for the conclusion that the veto provided for in § 244(c)(2) is not authorized by the constitutional design of the powers of the Legislative Branch.

Since it is clear that the action by the House under § 244(c)(2) was not within any of the express constitutional exceptions authorizing one House to act alone, and equally clear that it was an exercise of legislative power, that action was subject to the standards prescribed in Article I. The bicameral requirement, the Presentment Clauses, the President's veto, and Congress' power to override a veto were intended to erect enduring checks on each Branch and to protect the people from the improvident exercise of power by mandating certain prescribed steps. To preserve those checks, and maintain the separation of powers, the carefully defined limits on the power of each Branch must not be eroded. To accomplish what has been attempted by one House of Congress in this case requires action in conformity with the express procedures of the Constitution's prescription for legislative action: passage by a majority of both Houses and presentment to the President.

The veto authorized by § 244(c)(2) doubtless has been in many respects a convenient shortcut; the "sharing" with the Executive by Congress of its authority over aliens in this manner is, on its face, an appealing compromise. In purely practical terms, it is obviously easier for action to be taken by one House without submission to the President; but it is crystal clear from the records of the Convention, contemporaneous writings and debates, that the Framers ranked other values higher than efficiency. The records of the Convention and debates in the States preceding ratification underscore the common desire to define and limit the exercise of the newly created federal powers affecting the states and the people. There is unmistakable expression of a determination that legislation by the national Congress be a step-by-step, deliberate and deliberative process.

The choices we discern as having been made in the Constitutional Convention impose burdens on governmental processes that often seem clumsy, inefficient, even unworkable, but those hard choices were consciously made by men who had lived under a form of government that permitted arbitrary governmental acts to go unchecked. There is no support in the Constitution or decisions of this Court for the proposition that the cumbersomeness and delays often encountered in complying with explicit Constitutional standards may be avoided, either by the Congress or by the President. With all the obvious flaws of delay, untidiness, and potential for abuse, we have not yet found a better way to preserve freedom than by making the exercise of

---

EDITED CASE   Immigration and Naturalization Service v. Chadha (Continued)

power subject to the carefully crafted restraints, spelled out in the Constitution.

. . . We hold that the Congressional veto provision in § 244(c)(2) is severable from the Act and that it is unconstitutional. Accordingly, the judgment of the Court of Appeals is affirmed.

Justice Powell, concurring in the judgment.

The Court's decision, based on the Presentment Clauses, Art. I, Sec. 7, cl. 2 and 3, apparently will invalidate every use of the legislative veto. The breadth of this holding gives one pause. Congress has included the veto in literally hundreds of statutes, dating back to the 1930s. Congress clearly views this procedure as essential to controlling the delegation of power to administration agencies. One reasonably may disagree with Congress' assessment of the veto's utility, but the respect due its judgment as a coordinate branch of Government cautions that our holding should be no more extensive than necessary to decide this case. In my view, the case may be decided on a narrower ground. When Congress finds that a particular person does not satisfy the statutory criteria for permanent residence in this country it has assumed a judicial function in violation of the principle of separation of powers. Accordingly, I concur only in the judgment. . . .

Justice White, dissenting.

Today the Court not only invalidates § 244(c)(2) of the Immigration and Nationality Act, but also sounds the death knell for nearly 200 other statutory provisions in which Congress has reserved a "legislative veto." For this reason, the Court's decision is of surpassing importance. And it is for this reason that the Court would have been well-advised to decide the case, if possible, on the narrower grounds of separation of powers, leaving for full consideration the constitutionality of other congressional review statutes operating on such varied matters as war powers and agency rulemaking, some of which concern the independent regulatory agencies.

The prominence of the legislative veto mechanism in our contemporary political system and its importance to Congress can hardly be overstated. It has become a central means by which Congress secures the accountability of executive and independent agencies. Without the legislative veto, Congress is faced with a Hobson's choice: either to refrain from delegating the necessary authority, leaving itself with a hopeless task of writing laws with the requisite specificity to cover endless special circumstances across the entire policy landscape, or in the alternative, to abdicate its lawmaking function to the executive branch and independent agencies. To choose the former leaves major national problems unresolved; to opt for the latter risks unaccountable policymaking by those not elected to fill that role. Accordingly, over the past five decades, the legislative veto has been placed in nearly 200 statutes. The device is known in every field of governmental concern: reorganization, budgets, foreign affairs, war powers, and regulation of trade, safety, energy, the environment and the economy.

The legislative veto developed initially in response to the problems of reorganizing the sprawling government structure created in response to the Depression.

. . . [T]he legislative veto is more than "efficient, convenient, and useful." . . . It is an important if not indispensable political invention that allows the President and Congress to resolve major constitutional and policy differences, assures the accountability of independent regulatory agencies, and preserves Congress' control over lawmaking. Perhaps there are other means of accommodation and accountability, but the increasing reliance of Congress upon the legislative veto suggests that the alternatives to which Congress must now turn are not entirely satisfactory.

The history of the legislative veto also makes clear that it has not been a sword with which Congress has struck out to aggrandize itself at the expense of the other branches—the concerns of Madison and Hamilton. Rather, the veto has been a means of defense, a reservation of ultimate authority necessary if Congress is to fulfill its designated role under Article I as the nation's lawmaker. While the President has often objected to particular legislative vetoes, generally those left in the hands of congressional committees, the Executive has more often agreed to legislative review as the price for a broad delegation of authority. To be sure, the President may have preferred unrestricted power, but that could be precisely why Congress thought it essential to retain a check on the exercise of delegated authority.

(Continued)

EDITED CASE Immigration and Naturalization Service v. Chadha (Continued)

For all the reasons, the apparent sweep of the Court's decision today is regrettable. The Court's Article I analysis appears to invalidate all legislative vetoes irrespective of form or subject. Because the legislative veto is commonly found as a check upon rulemaking by administrative agencies and upon broad-based policy decisions of the Executive Branch, it is particularly unfortunate that the Court reaches its decision in a case involving the exercise of a veto over deportation decisions regarding particular individuals. Courts should always be wary of striking statutes as unconstitutional; to strike an entire class of statutes based on consideration of a somewhat atypical and more-readily indictable exemplar of the class is irresponsible.

If the legislative veto were as plainly unconstitutional as the Court strives to suggest, its broad ruling today would be more comprehensible. But, the constitutionality of the legislative veto is anything but clear-cut. The issue divides scholars, courts, attorneys general, and the two other branches of the National Government. If the veto devices so flagrantly disregarded the requirements of Article I as the Court today suggests, I find it incomprehensible that Congress, whose members are bound by oath to uphold the Constitution, would have placed these mechanisms in nearly 200 separate laws over a period of 50 years.

I do not suggest that all legislative vetoes are necessarily consistent with separation of powers principles. A legislative check on an inherently executive function, for example that of initiating prosecutions, poses an entirely different question. But the legislative veto device here—and in many other settings—is far from an instance of legislative tyranny over the Executive. It is a necessary check on the unavoidably expanding power of the agencies, both executive and independent, as they engage in exercising authority delegated by Congress.

I regret that I am in disagreement with my colleagues on the fundamental questions that this case presents. But even more I regret the destructive scope of the Court's holding. It reflects a profoundly different conception of the Constitution than that held by the courts which sanctioned the modern administrative state. Today's decision strikes down in one fell swoop provisions in more laws enacted by Congress than the Court has cumulatively invalidated in its history. I fear it will now be more difficult "to insure that the fundamental policy decisions in our society will be made not by an appointed official but by the body immediately responsible to the people." . . . I must dissent.

Justice Rehnquist, dissenting . . .

EDITED CASE Wiener v. United States
United States Supreme Court, 357 U.S. 349 (1958)

[This case examines the president's power to remove without adequate cause appointed officials in the independent agencies.]

Justice Frankfurter delivered the opinion of the Court.

This is a suit for back pay, based on [Wiener's] alleged illegal removal as a member of the War Claims Commission. The facts are not in dispute. By the War Claims Act of 1948, . . . Congress established that Commission with "jurisdiction to

receive and adjudicate according to law" . . . claims for compensating internees, prisoners of war, and religious organizations . . . who suffered personal injury or property damage at the hands of the enemy in connection with World War II. The Commission was to be composed of three persons, at least two of whom were to be members of the bar, to be appointed by the President, by and with the advice and consent of the Senate. The Commission was to wind up its affairs not later than three years after the expiration of the

EDITED CASE Wiener v. United States (Continued)

time for filing claims, originally limited to two years but extended by successive legislation. . . . This limit on the Commission's life was the mode by which the tenure of the Commissioners was defined, and Congress made no provision for removal of a Commissioner.

Having been duly nominated by President Truman, [Wiener] was confirmed on June 2, 1950, and took office on June 8. . . . On his refusal to heed a request for his resignation, he was, on December 10, 1953, removed by President Eisenhower in the following terms: "I regard it as in the national interest to complete the administration of the War Claims Act of 1948, as amended, with personnel of my own selection." The following day, the President made recess appointments to the Commission, including petitioner's post. After Congress assembled, the President, on February 15, 1954, sent the names of the new appointees to the Senate. The Senate had not confirmed these nominations when the Commission was abolished, July 1, 1954. . . . Thereupon, [Wiener] brought this proceeding in the Court of Claims for recovery of his salary as a War Claims Commissioner from December 10, 1953, the day of his removal by the President, to June 30, 1954, the last day of the Commission's existence. . . . We brought the case here. . . . Controversy pertaining to the scope and limits of the President's power of removal fills a thick chapter of our political and judicial history. The long stretches of its history, beginning with the very first Congress, with early echoes in the Reports of this Court, were laboriously traversed in *Myers v. United States* . . . and need not be retraced. President Roosevelt's reliance upon the pronouncements of the Court in that case in removing a member of the Federal Trade Commission on the ground that "the aims and purposes of the Administration with respect to the work of the Commission can be carried out most effectively with personnel of my own selection" reflected contemporaneous professional opinion regarding the significance of the *Myers* decision. Speaking through a Chief Justice who himself had been President, the Court did not restrict itself to the immediate issue before it, the President's inherent power to remove a postmaster, obviously an executive official. As of set purpose and not by way of

parenthetic casualness, the Court announced that the President had inherent constitutional power of removal also of officials who have "duties of a quasi-judicial character . . . whose decisions after hearing affect interests of individuals, the discharge of which the President can not in a particular case properly influence or control." . . . This view of presidential power was deemed to flow from his "constitutional duty of seeing that the laws be faithfully executed." . . .

The assumption was short-lived that the *Myers* case recognized the President's inherent constitutional power to remove officials, no matter what the relation of the executive to the discharge of their duties and no matter what restrictions Congress may have imposed regarding the nature of their tenure. . . . Within less than ten years a unanimous Court, in *Humphrey's Executor v. United States* . . . narrowly confined the scope of the *Myers* decision to include only "all purely executive officers," . . . The Court explicitly "disapproved" the expressions in *Myers* supporting the President's inherent constitutional power to remove members of quasi-judicial bodies. . . . Congress had given members of the Federal Trade Commission a seven-year term and also provided for the removal of a Commissioner by the President for inefficiency, neglect of duty or malfeasance in office. . . .

Humphrey's case . . . drew a sharp line of cleavage between officials who were part of the Executive establishment and were thus removable by virtue of the President's constitutional powers and . . . those whose tasks require absolute freedom from Executive interference. "For it is quite evident," again to quote *Humphrey's Executor*, "that one who holds his office only during the pleasure of another, cannot be depended upon to maintain an attitude of independence against the latter's will." . . .

Thus, the most reliable factor for drawing an inference regarding the President's power of removal in our case is the nature of the function that Congress vested in the War Claims Commission. What were the duties that Congress confided

(Continued)

EDITED CASE   Wiener v. United States (Continued)

---

to this Commission? And can the inference fairly be drawn from the failure of Congress to provide for removal that these Commissioners were to remain in office at the will of the President? For such is the assertion of power on which [Wiener's] removal must rest. The ground of President Eisenhower's removal . . . was precisely the same as President Roosevelt's removal of Humphrey. Both Presidents desired to have Commissioners to be their men. The terms of removal in the two cases are identical and express the assumption that the agencies of which the two Commissioners were members were subject in the discharge of their duties to the control of the Executive. An analysis of the Federal Trade Commission Act left this Court in no doubt that such was not the conception of Congress in creating the Federal Trade Commission. The terms of the War Claims Act of 1948 leave no doubt that such was not the conception of Congress regarding the War Claims Commission.

The history of this legislation emphatically underlines this fact. The short of it is that the origin of the Act was a bill . . . passed by the House that placed the administration of a very limited class of claims in the hands of the Federal Security Administrator . . . The Federal Security Administrator was indubitably an arm of the President. When the House bill reached the Senate, it struck out all but the enacting clause, rewrote the bill, and established a Commission with "jurisdiction to receive and adjudicate according to law." . . . The Commission was established as an adjudicating body with all the paraphernalia by which legal claims are put to the test of proof, with finality of determination "not subject to review by any other official of the United States or by any court, by mandamus or otherwise." . . . Awards were to be paid out of a War Claims fund in the hands of the Secretary of the Treasury, whereby such claims were given even more assured collectability than adheres to judgments rendered in the Court of Claims. . . . With minor amendment . . . this Senate bill became a law.

. . . For Congress itself to have made appropriations for the claims with which it dealt under the War Claims Act was not practical in view of the large number of claimants and the diversity in the specific circumstances giving rise to the claims. The House bill in effect put the distribution of the narrow class of claims that it acknowledged into Executive hands, by vesting the procedure in the Federal Security Administrator. The final form of the legislation, as we have seen, left the widened range of claims to be determined by adjudication. Congress could, of course, have given jurisdiction over these claims to the District Courts or to the Court of Claims. The fact that it chose to establish a Commission to "adjudicate according to law" the classes of claims defined in the statute did not alter the intrinsic judicial character of the task with which the Commission was charged. The claims were to be "adjudicated according to law," that is, on the merits of each claim, supported by evidence and governing legal considerations, by a body that was "entirely free from the control or coercive influence, direct or indirect," . . . of either the Executive or the Congress. If, as one must take for granted, the War Claims Act precluded the President from influencing the Commission in passing on a particular claim, a fortiori must it be inferred that Congress did not wish to have hang over the Commission the Damocles' sword of removal by the President for no reason other than that he preferred to have on that Commission men of his own choosing.

For such is this case. We have not a removal for cause involving the rectitude of a member of an adjudicatory body, nor even a suspensory removal until the Senate could act upon it by confirming the appointment of a new Commissioner or otherwise dealing with the matter. Judging the matter in all the nakedness in which it is presented, . . . we are compelled to conclude that no such power is given to the President directly by the Constitution, and none is impliedly conferred upon him by statute simply because Congress said nothing about it. The philosophy of *Humphrey's Executor,* in its explicit language as well as its implications, precludes such a claim. . . .

EDITED CASE   Bowsher v. Synar
United States Supreme Court, 478 U.S. 714 (1986)

[In this case the Supreme Court considers whether provisions of the Gramm-Rudman-Hollings Act of 1985 violated the constitutional requirement of separation of powers.]

Chief Justice Burger delivered the opinion of the Court.

. . . On December 12, 1985, the President signed into law the Balanced Budget and Emergency Deficit Control Act of 1985, . . . popularly known as the "Gramm-Rudman-Hollings Act." The purpose of the Act is to eliminate the federal budget deficit. To that end, the Act sets a "maximum deficit amount" for federal spending for each of fiscal years 1986 through 1991. The size of that maximum deficit amount progressively reduces to zero in fiscal year 1991. If in any fiscal year the federal budget deficit exceeds the maximum deficit amount by more than a specified sum, the Act requires across-the-board cuts in federal spending to reach the targeted deficit level, with half of the cuts made to defense programs and the other half made to non-defense programs. The Act exempts certain priority programs from these cuts. . . .

These "automatic" reductions are accomplished through a rather complicated procedure, spelled out in Sec. 251, the so-called "reporting provisions" of the Act. Each year, the Director of the Office of Management and Budget (OMB) and the Congressional Budget Office (CBO) independently estimate the amount of the federal budget deficit for the upcoming fiscal year. If that deficit exceeds the maximum target deficit amount for that fiscal year by more than a specified amount, the Directors of OBM and CBO independently calculate, on a program-by-program basis, the budget reductions necessary to ensure that the deficit does not exceed the maximum deficit amount. The Act then requires the Directors to report jointly their deficit estimates and budget reduction calculations to the Comptroller General.

The Comptroller General, after reviewing the Directors' reports, then reports his conclusions to the President. . . . The President in turn must issue a "sequestration" order mandating the spending reductions specified by the Comptroller General. . . . There follows a period during which Congress may by legislation reduce spending to obviate, in whole or in part, the need for the sequestration order. If such reductions are not enacted, the sequestration order becomes effective and the spending reductions included in that order are made. . . .

Within hours of the President's signing of the Act, Congressman Synar, who had voted against the Act, filed a complaint seeking declaratory relief that the Act was unconstitutional. Eleven other Members later joined Congressman Synar's suit. A virtually identical lawsuit was also filed by the National Treasury Employees Union. The Union alleged that its members had been injured as a result of the Act's automatic spending reduction provisions, which have suspended certain cost-of-living benefit increases to the Union's members. . . .

The District Court rejected appellees' challenge that the Act violated the delegation doctrine. The court expressed no doubt that the Act delegated broad authority, but delegation of similarly broad authority has been upheld in past cases. The District Court observed that in *Yakus v. United States* . . . (1944), this Court upheld a statute that delegated to an unelected "Price Administrator" the power "to promulgate regulations fixing prices of commodities." Moreover, in the District Court's view, the Act adequately confined the exercise of administrative discretion. The District Court concluded that "the totality of the Act's standards, definitions, context, and reference to past administrative practice provides an adequate 'intelligible principle' to guide and confine administrative decision-making." . . .

Although the District Court concluded that the Act survived a delegation doctrine challenge, it held that the role of the Comptroller General in the deficit reduction process violated the constitutionally imposed separation of powers. The court first explained that the Comptroller General exercises executive functions under the Act. However, the Comptroller General, while appointed by the President with the advice and consent of the Senate, is removable not by the President but only by a joint resolution of Congress or by impeachment. The District Court reasoned that this arrangement could not be sustained under this Court's decisions in *Myers v. United States* . . . (1926) and

(Continued)

EDITED CASE Bowsher v. Synar (Continued)

Humphrey's Executor v. United States . . . (1935). Under the separation of powers established by the Framers of the Constitution, the court concluded, Congress may not retain the power of removal over an officer performing executive functions. The congressional removal power created a "here-and-now subservience" of the Comptroller General to Congress. . . . The District Court therefore held that "since the powers conferred upon the Comptroller General as part of the automatic deficit reduction process are executive powers, which cannot constitutionally be exercised by an officer removable by Congress, those powers cannot be exercised and therefore the automatic deficit reduction process to which they are central cannot be implemented." . . .

Appeals were taken directly to this Court. . . . We noted probable jurisdiction and expedited consideration of the appeals. . . . We affirm.

We noted recently that "[t]he Constitution sought to divide the delegated powers of the new Federal Government into three defined categories, Legislative, Executive, and Judicial. . . . The declared purpose of separating and dividing the powers of government, of course, was to "diffus[e] power the better to secure liberty." . . .

That this system of division and separation of powers produces conflicts, confusion, and discordance at times is inherent, but it was deliberately so structured to assure full, vigorous and open debate on the great issues affecting the people and to provide avenues for the operation of checks on the exercise of governmental power.

The Constitution does not contemplate an active role for Congress in the supervision of officers charged with the execution of the laws it enacts. The President appoints "Officers of the United States" with the advice and Consent of the Senate. . . . Once the appointment has been made and confirmed, however, the Constitution explicitly provides for removal of Officers of the United States by Congress only upon impeachment by the House of Representatives and conviction by the Senate. An impeachment by the House and trial by the Senate can rest only on "Treason, Bribery or other high Crimes and Misdemeanors." Article II, Sec. 4. A direct congressional role in the removal of officers charged with the execution of the laws beyond this limited one is inconsistent with separation of powers. . . .

This Court first directly addressed this issue in *Myers v. United States* . . . (1925). At issue in Myers was a statute providing that certain postmasters could be removed only "by and with the advice and consent of the Senate." The President removed one such postmaster without Senate approval, and a lawsuit ensued. Chief Justice Taft, writing for the Court, declared the statute unconstitutional on the ground that for Congress to "draw to itself, or to either branch of it, the power to remove or the right to participate in the exercise of that power . . . would be . . . to infringe the constitutional principle of the separation of governmental powers." . . .

A decade later, in *Humphrey's Executor v. United States* . . . (1935), relied upon heavily by appellants, a Federal Trade Commissioner who had been removed by the President sought back pay. Humphrey's Executor involved an issue not presented either in the Myers case or in this case—i.e., the power of Congress to limit the President's powers of removal of a Federal Trade Commissioner. . . . The relevant statute permitted removal "by the President," but only "for inefficiency, neglect of duty, or malfeasance in office." Justice Sutherland, speaking for the Court, upheld the statute, holding that "illimitable power of removal is not possessed by the President [with respect to Federal Trade Commissioners]." . . . The Court distinguished *Myers*, reaffirming its holding that congressional participation in the removal of executive officers is unconstitutional. . . .

In light of these precedents, we conclude that Congress cannot reserve for itself the power of removal of an officer charged with the execution of the laws except by impeachment. To permit the execution of the laws to be vested in an officer answerable only to Congress would, in practical terms, reserve in Congress control over the execution of the laws. As the District Court observed, "Once an officer is appointed, it is only the authority that can remove him, and not the authority that appointed him, that he must fear and, in the performance of his functions, obey." The structure of the Constitution does not permit Congress to execute the laws; it follows that Congress cannot grant to an officer under its control what it does not possess.

To permit an officer controlled by Congress to execute the laws would be, in essence, to permit a

---

EDITED CASE   Bowsher v. Synar (Continued)

---

congressional veto. Congress could simply remove, or threaten to remove, an officer for executing the laws in any fashion found to be unsatisfactory to Congress. This kind of congressional control over the execution of the laws, Chadha makes clear, is constitutionally impermissible.

The dangers of congressional usurpation of Executive Branch functions have long been recognized. "[T]he debates of the Constitutional Convention, and the Federalist Papers, are replete with expressions of fear that the Legislative Branch of the National Government will aggrandize itself at the expense of the other two branches." . . . Indeed, we also have observed only recently that "[t]he hydraulic pressure inherent within each of the separate Branches to exceed the outer limits of its power, even to accomplish desirable objectives, must be resisted." . . . With these principles in mind, we turn to consideration of whether the Comptroller General is controlled by Congress.

Appellants urge that the Comptroller General performs his duties independently and is not subservient to Congress. We agree with the District Court that this contention does not bear close scrutiny.

The critical factor lies in the provisions of the statute defining the Comptroller General's Office relating to removability. Although the Comptroller General is nominated by the President from a list of three individuals recommended by the Speaker of the House of Representatives and the President pro tempore of the Senate, . . . and confirmed by the Senate, he is removable only at the initiative of Congress. He may be removed not only by impeachment but also by Joint Resolution of Congress. . . .

Although the President could veto such a joint resolution, the veto could be overridden by a two-thirds vote of both Houses of Congress. Thus, the Comptroller General could be removed in the face of Presidential opposition. Like the District Court, we therefore read the removal provision as authorizing removal by Congress alone. . . .

It is clear that Congress has consistently viewed the Comptroller General as an officer of the Legislative Branch. The Reorganization Acts of 1945 and 1949, for example, both stated that the Comptroller General and the GAO are "a part of the legislative branch of the Government." . . . Similarly, in the Accounting and Auditing Act of 1950, Con-

gress required the Comptroller General to conduct audits "as an agent of the Congress." . . .

Over the years, the Comptrollers General have also viewed themselves as part of the Legislative Branch. . . .

Against this background, we see no escape from the conclusion that, because Congress had retained removal authority over the Comptroller General, he may not be entrusted with executive powers. The remaining question is whether the Comptroller General has been assigned such powers in the Balanced Budget and Emergency Deficit Control Act of 1985. The primary responsibility of the Comptroller General under the instant Act is the preparation of a "report." This report must contain detailed estimates of projected federal revenues and expenditures. The report must also specify the reductions, if any, necessary to reduce the deficit to the target for the appropriate fiscal year. The reductions must be set forth on a program-by-program basis.

In preparing the report, the Comptroller General is to have "due regard" for the estimates and reductions set forth in a joint report submitted to him by the Director of CBO and the Director of OMB, the President's fiscal and budgetary advisor. However, the Act plainly contemplates that the Comptroller General will exercise his independent judgment and evaluation with respect to those estimates. The Act also provides that the Comptroller General's report "shall explain fully any differences between the contents of such report and the report of the Directors." . . .

. . . [T]he Act . . . gives the Comptroller General the ultimate authority to determine the budget cuts to be made. Indeed, the Comptroller General commands the President himself to carry out, without the slightest variation (with exceptions not relevant to the constitutional issues presented), the director of the Comptroller General as to the budget reductions:

The [Presidential] order must provide for reductions in the manner specified, . . . must incorporate the provisions of the [Comptroller General's] report, and must be consistent with such report in all respects. The President may not modify or recalculate any of the estimates, determinations, specifications, bases, amounts, or percentages set forth

(Continued)

EDITED CASE   Bowsher v. Synar (Continued)

---

in the report submitted under Sec. 251 (b) in determining the reductions to be specified in the order with respect to programs, projects, and activities, or with respect to budget activities, within an account. . . .

Congress of course initially determined the content of the Balanced Budget and Emergency Deficit Control Act; and undoubtedly the content of the Act determines the nature of the executive duty. However, as Chadha makes clear, once Congress makes its choice in enacting legislation, its participation ends. Congress can thereafter control the execution of its enactment only indirectly—by passing new legislation. By placing the responsibility for execution of the Balanced Budget and Emergency Deficit Control Act in the hands of an officer who is subject to removal only by itself, Congress in effect has retained control over the execution of the Act and has intruded into the executive function. The Constitution does not permit such intrusion. . . .

Because we conclude that the Comptroller General, as an officer removable by Congress, may not exercise the powers conferred upon him by the Act, we have no occasion for considering appellees' other challenges to the Act, including their argument that the assignment of powers to the Comptroller General . . . violates the delegation doctrine. . . .

No one can doubt that Congress and the President are confronted with fiscal and economic problems of unprecedented magnitude, but "the fact that a given law or procedure is efficient, convenient, and useful in facilitating functions of government, standing alone, will not save it if it is contrary to the Constitution. Convenience and efficiency are not the primary objectives—or the hallmarks—of democratic government. . . ."

We conclude the District Court correctly held that the powers vested in the Comptroller General under Sec. 251 violate the command of the Constitution that the Congress play no direct role in the execution of the laws. Accordingly, the judgment and order of the District Court are affirmed. . . .

Justice Stevens, with whom *Justice Marshall* joins, concurring in the judgment.

When this Court is asked to invalidate a statutory provision that has been approved by both Houses of the Congress and signed by the President, particularly an act of Congress that confronts a deeply vexing national problem, it should only do so for the most compelling constitutional reasons. I agree with the Court that the "Gramm-Rudman-Hollings" Act contains a constitutional infirmity so severe that the flawed provision may not stand. I disagree with Court, however, on the reasons why the Constitution prohibits the Comptroller General from exercising the powers assigned to him by . . . the Act. It is not the dormant, carefully circumscribed congressional removal power that represents the primary constitutional evil. Nor do I agree with the conclusion of both the majority and the dissent that the analysis depends on a labeling of the functions assigned to the Comptroller General as "executive powers." . . . Rather, I am convinced that the Comptroller General must be characterized as an agent of Congress because of his longstanding statutory responsibilities; that the powers assigned to him under the Gramm-Rudman-Hollings Act require him to make policy that will bind the Nation; and that, when Congress, or a component or an agent of Congress, seeks to make policy that will bind the Nation, it must follow the procedures mandated by Article I of the Constitution—through passage by both Houses and presentment to the President. In short, Congress may not exercise its fundamental power to formulate national policy by delegating that power to one of its two Houses, to a legislative committee, or to an individual agent of the Congress such as the Speaker of the House of Representatives, the Sergeant at Arms of the Senate, or the Director of the Congressional Budget Office. . . . That principle, I believe, is applicable to the Comptroller General. . . .

Justice White, dissenting.

The Court, acting in the name of separation of powers, takes upon itself to strike down the Gramm-Rudman-Hollings Act, one of the most novel and far-reaching legislative responses to a national crisis since the New Deal. The basis of the Court's action is a solitary provision of another statute that was passed over sixty years ago and has lain dormant since that time. I cannot concur in the Court's action. Like the Court, I will not purport to speak to the wisdom of the policies incorporated in the legislation the Court invalidates; that is a matter for the Congress and the Executive, both of

---

EDITED CASE   Bowsher v. Synar (Continued)

which expressed their assent to the statute barely half a year ago. I will, however, address the wisdom of the Court's willingness to interpose its distressingly formalistic view of separation of powers, . . . [which rests] on untenable constitutional propositions . . . [and leads] to regrettable results. . . . Today's result is even more misguided. As I will explain, the Court's decision rests on a feature of the legislative scheme that is of minimal practical significance and that presents no substantial threat to the basic scheme of separation of powers. . . .

The majority's . . . conclusion rests on the rigid dogma that, outside of the impeachment process, any "direct congressional role in the removal of officers charged with the execution of the laws . . . is inconsistent with separation of powers." . . . Reliance on such an unyielding principle to strike down a statute posing no real danger of aggrandizement of congressional power is extremely misguided and insensitive to our constitutional role. The wisdom of vesting "executive" powers in an officer removable by joint resolution may indeed debatable—as may be the wisdom of the entire scheme of permitting an unelected official to revise the budget enacted by Congress—but such matters are for the most part to be worked out between the Congress and the President through the legislative process, which affords each branch ample opportunity to defend its interests. The Act vesting budget-cutting authority in the Comptroller General represents Congress' judgment that the delegation of such authority to counteract ever-mounting deficits is "necessary and proper" to the exercise of the powers granted the Federal Government by the Constitution; and the President's approval of the statute signifies his unwillingness to reject the choice made by Congress. . . . Under such circumstances, the role of this Court should be limited to determining whether the Act so alters the balance of authority among the branches of government as to pose a genuine threat to the basic division between the lawmaking power and the power to execute the law. Because I see no such threat, I cannot join the Court in striking down the Act. . . .

Justice Blackmun, dissenting.

The Court may be correct when it says that Congress cannot constitutionally exercise removal authority over an official vested with the budget-reduction powers that Sec. 251 of the Balanced Budget and Emergency Deficit Control Act of 1985 gives to the Comptroller General. This, however, is not because "[t]he removal powers over the Comptroller General's office dictate that he will be subservient to Congress." . . . I agree with Justice White that any such claim is unrealistic. Furthermore, I think it is clear under *Humphrey's Executor v. United States* . . . (1935), that "executive" powers of the kind delegated to the Comptroller General under the Deficit Control Act need not be exercised by an officer who serves at the President's pleasure; Congress certainly could prescribe the standards and procedures for removing the Comptroller General. But it seems to me that an attempt by Congress to participate directly in the removal of an executive officer—other than through the constitutionally prescribed procedure of impeachment—might well violate the principle of separation of powers by assuming for Congress part of the President's constitutional responsibility to carry out the laws.

In my view, however, that important and difficult question need not be decided in this case, because no matter how it is resolved the plaintiffs, now appellees, are not entitled to the relief they have requested. Appellees have not sought invalidation of the 1921 provision that authorizes Congress to remove the Comptroller General by joint resolution; indeed, it is far from clear they would have standing to request such a judgment. The only relief sought in this case is nullification of the automatic budget-reduction provisions of the Deficit Control Act, and that relief should not be awarded even if the Court is correct that those provisions are constitutionally incompatible with Congress' authority to remove the Comptroller General by joint resolution. Any incompatibility, I feel, should be cured by refusing to allow congressional removal—if it ever is attempted—and not by striking down the central provisions of the Deficit Control Act. However wise or foolish it may be that statute unquestionably ranks among the most important federal enactments of the past several decades. I cannot see the sense of invalidating legislation of this magnitude in order to preserve a cumbersome, 65-year-old removal power that has never been exercised and appears to have been all but forgotten until this litigation. . . .

ENDNOTES

1. James Madison, *The Federalist* No. 47 (C. Rossiter ed. 1961).

2. U.S. Const. Art. II, § 2.

3. David M. Ricci, *The Transformation of American Politics* (1993); Jeffrey M. Berry, *The Interest Group Society,* 3rd ed. (1977).

4. W. Wilson, *Congressional Government* (1885), 303.

5. 273 U.S. 135 (1927).

6. *Id.* at 177.

7. *Watkins v. United States,* 354 U.S. 178 (1957).

8. *United States v. Nixon,* 418 U.S. 683, 708 (1974).

9. 42 Stat. 20, 31 U.S.C.A. § 702.

10. *Walker v. Cheney,* 230 F. Supp. 51 (D.D.C. 2002).

11. *In re: Richard B. Cheney, et al.,* 334 F.3d 1096 (2003). On September 30, 2003, the U.S. Supreme Court granted certiorari. 114 S.Ct. 958 (Mem.).

12. 462 U.S. 919 (1983).

13. The Court noted that since 1932, when the first veto provision was enacted into law, 295 congressional veto-type procedures have been inserted in 196 different statutes as follows: from 1932 to 1939, five statutes were affected; from 1940-49, nineteen statutes; between 1950 and 1959, thirty-four statutes; and from 1960 to 1969, forty-nine. From the years 1970 through 1975, at least 163 such provisions were included in eighty-nine laws. *Id.* at 944.

14. *Id.* at 957-58.

15. *Id.* at 986-87.

16. 463 U.S. 1216 (1983).

17. L. Fisher, *The Legislative Veto: Invalidated, It Survives,* Law and Contemporary Problems, 1993, 273, 291.

18. 5 U.S.C.A. § 801 *et seq.*

19. 5 U.S.C.A. § 804(2).

20. 5 U.S.C.A. § 801(b)(2).

21. 611 N.W. 2d 530 (Mich. 2000).

22. *Mead v. Arnell,* 791 P.2d 410 (Idaho 1990).

23. *Martinez v. Dep't of Industry, Labor & Human Relations,* 478 N.W.2d 582 (Wis. 1992).

24. § 3-203, § 3-204 1981 MSAPA.

25. Fla. Stat. Ann. § 11.60.

26. 272 U.S. 52 (1926).

27. 272 U.S. *Id.* at 163-64.

28. 478 U.S. 714 (1986).

29. B. Schwartz, *An Administrative Law Might Have Been-Chief Justice Burger's* Bowsher v. Synar *Draft,* 42 Admin. L. Rev. 221, 232 (Spring 1990).

30. 488 U.S. 361 (1989).

31. 488 U.S. at 427.

32. 2 U.S.C.A. § 1501.

33. 2 U.S.C.A. Ch. 17B, Subch. III, Refs. & Annos.

34. 524 U.S. 417 (1998).

35. Cal. Const., Art. IV, §10(b).

36. 345 F.2d 952 (5th Cir. 1966).

37. 345 F.2d *Id.* at 964.

38. 657 F.2d 298 (D.C. Cir. 1981).

39. *Id.* at 409.

40. 459 F.2d 1231 (D.C. Cir. 1971).

41. *Id.* at 1246.

42. *Id.* at 1248.

43. Richard E. Neustadt, *Presidential Power* (1960).

44. MSAPA, 1981, § 3-202.

45. See *In re Neagle,* 135 U.S. 1 (1890); *Korematsu v. United States,* 323 U.S. 214 (1944).

46. John E. Noyes, *Executive Orders, Presidential Intent, and Private Rights of Action,* 59 Tex. L. Rev. 837, 839 (1981).

47. *Letter Carriers v. Austin,* 418 U.S. 264, 273 (1974).

48. 424 U.S. 1 (1976).

49. 487 U.S. 654, 673 (1988).

50. 501 U.S. 868 (1991).

51. 295 U.S. 602 (1935).

52. 357 U.S. 349 (1958).

53. *Id.* at 356.

54. Budget and Accounting Act, 1921 (June 10, 1921, ch. 18, 42 Stat. 20).

55. Title 5, U.S.C.A., Appendix, Reorganization Plan No. 2 of 1970 (Part I).

56. 44 U.S.C.A. §§ 3501-20.

57. Richard J. Pierce, Jr., *Seven Ways To Deossify Agency Rulemaking,* Administrative Law Review 59, 70 (Winter 1995).

58. Art. II, § 3, U.S. Const.

59. 28 U.S.C.A. § 516.

60. 26 U.S.C.A. § 7452.

61. Pub. L. No. 93-637, § 204, 88 Stat. 2183, 2199 (1975) (codified as amended at 15 U.S.C.A. § 56 (1994)) (granting FTC authority to represent itself before the Supreme Court); Act of Nov. 16, 1973, Pub. L. No. 93-153, § 408, 87 Stat. 576, 591-92 (1973) (authorizing FTC to represent itself on lower federal courts).

62. Neal Devins, *Unfairness and Independence: Solicitor General Control Over Independent Agency Litigation,* 82 Cal. L. Rev. 255, 269 (March 1994).

63. 26 U.S.C.A. § 9010(a).

64. 26 U.S.C.A. § 437d(a)(6).

65. *Federal Election Commission v. NRA Political Victory Fund,* 513 U.S. 88 (1994).

66. 476 U.S. 574 (1983).

67. *Mail Order Ass'n of America v. United States Postal Service,* 986 F.2d 509 (D.C. Cir. 1993).

68. 461 U.S. 574 (1983).

69. Thomas McCoy and Neal E. Devins, *Standing and Adverseness in Challenges of Tax Exemptions for Discriminatory Private Schools,* 52 Fordham L. Rev. 441, 464 (1984).

70. In one state, Tennessee, the state Supreme Court appoints the attorney general.

71. *Romer v. Evans,* 517 U.S. 620, 633 (1996).

9

Judicial Review
of Agency Actions

"If the action rests upon . . . an exercise of judgment in an area which
Congress has entrusted to the agency . . . it must not be set aside because the
reviewing court might have made a different determination. . . . But if the
action is based upon a determination of law . . . an order may not stand if the
agency has misconceived the law."

JUSTICE FELIX FRANKFURTER

WRITING FOR THE UNITED STATES SUPREME COURT IN *SECURITIES AND EXCHANGE
COMMISSION V. CHENERY CORPORATION,* 318 U.S. 80, 94 (1943).

INTRODUCTION

Judicial review is the process whereby courts exercise control over the findings of fact and interpretations of law by governmental agencies. Although judicial review is not explicitly provided for in the United States Constitution, the doctrine has firm constitutional underpinnings emanating from Chief Justice Marshall's historic opinion in *Marbury v. Madison.*[1] In Marshall's oft-quoted words, "It is emphatically the province and duty of the judicial department to say what the law is." In matters of law, both constitutional and statutory, the judiciary is the preeminent branch of government. Courts determine the meaning of legislation and can even invalidate statutes when the legislature has crossed constitutional boundaries. Courts also review the legality and constitutionality of executive action, from the police officer on the street, to the president of the United States. Judicial review certainly plays an enormous role in the realm of public administration. In fact, administrative law consists chiefly, but not entirely, of the opinions of the courts in cases where administrative action has been subjected to judicial review.

Judicial review permits affected parties to challenge administrative rulemaking and adjudications. It has become essential to maintaining the legitimacy of the administrative process by requiring agencies to make a record of proceedings, by establishing the boundaries of administrative authority, and by assuring the public that exercise of discretion by an administrative agency will be kept within proper bounds. Finally, it reduces the opportunity for political interference in agency decision making, thereby buttressing public confidence in public administration.

REVIEWABILITY OF ADMINISTRATIVE ACTIONS

Judicial review of agency actions is generally authorized by the statute creating an administrative agency and, as we point out later, may take the form of appellate review, agency enforcement, or an independent lawsuit. If there is no prescribed method of review, final agency action is still subject to judicial review, unless review is statutorily precluded, a topic we discuss later. But even when judicial review is precluded by statute, courts may still entertain challenges based on allegations of constitutional violations. Statutes, court rules, and judicial precedents all govern access to judicial review.

Relevance of the Administrative Procedure Act

The federal **Administrative Procedure Act (APA)** provides for judicial review of actions of agencies created by the federal government. Section 702 states: "A person suffering legal wrong because of agency action, or adversely affected or aggrieved by agency action within the meaning of a relevant statute, is entitled to judicial review thereof." Courts have sometimes referred to the APA as the basis for "reasoned decision making." In some instances legislation creating an agency, particularly at the federal level, will specify the scope of judicial review available, or state that no judicial review is available to challenge an agency's discretionary actions. Courts usually require that a litigant must have raised an issue or objected to an action before an administrative agency before raising such issue on review. This is derived from the **preservation of error rule** that applies in civil litigation; however, courts often are more lenient in enforcing such a rule in appeals from administrative agency proceedings. A contention that the agency lacked **subject matter jurisdiction** may be made at judicial review, irrespective of whether it was challenged before the agency.

Many states have statutes similar to the federal APA. A few provide for judicial review as outlined in the **1981 Model State Administrative Procedure Act (1981 MSAPA).** In other states the statutes governing review vary. Some include all administrative agencies; others exclude certain agencies, most commonly local governmental units such as counties, cities, and school boards. For example, the Kansas Act for Judicial Review and Civil Enforcement of Agency Action[2] establishes the exclusive means of review of agency action. On the other hand, the Florida Administrative Procedure Act[3] provides for judicial review of state agency action but excludes counties and municipalities, unless the legislature chooses to bring them under the act. Because the legislature has not chosen to do so, review of local agency actions in Florida is conducted in circuit court, the trial court of general jurisdiction.

Judicial review is generally limited to final agency action. An agency order, including a rule adopted by the agency, is generally considered final when it is reduced to writing and filed as provided by law. We discuss **finality** later; however, note that Section 704 of the APA stipulates that a preliminary, procedural, or intermediate agency action or ruling not directly reviewable may be reviewed from final agency action. Likewise, at the state and local level, preliminary agency action is generally reviewable only if the action taken by an agency imposes immediate adverse consequences for which final review would be inadequate.[4]

SELECTING THE PROPER JUDICIAL FORUM

To select the proper forum for judicial review one must refer to the statute creating the particular agency to determine which court has jurisdiction. **Jurisdiction** is the power of a court to hear and determine a case or controversy. Although the APA prescribes the standard of review, it does not provide the basis of jurisdiction for judicial review.[5] Without jurisdiction over the parties and the subject matter, a court has no authority to proceed. A court acquires jurisdiction over the parties once the notice of appeal from agency action has been filed within the time specified in applicable statutes. The time requirement varies, but often statutes allow at least twenty or thirty days for filing the required notice. In independent actions the court acquires jurisdiction when a complaint is filed in a court of competent jurisdiction and process is properly served.

At the federal level, judicial review of agency orders is generally before the United States Court of Appeals for the appropriate circuit, unless a statute indicates that such review is to be performed by a United States District Court. The time for filing is generally specified by statute. Rule 15 of the Federal Rules of Appellate Procedure stipulates that the timely filing of a petition for review with the clerk of a court of appeals (or in some instances a district court) is necessary for the reviewing court to have jurisdiction. If a petition for review is filed in the wrong court, the court where the petition is filed is authorized to transfer it to the correct court.[6]

At the federal level, where statutory review procedures are prescribed, they are exclusive, and **collateral review,** i.e., by an independent lawsuit is generally not permitted.[7] So long as effective means for judicial review are ultimately available where a constitutional claim can be raised, an plaintiff may not dispense with the requirement of prior administrative review; otherwise judicial review would be an abstract process.

Judicial review of administrative action generally takes the form of an appeal that involves the parties to the proceedings and in some instances the agency concerned. But when judicial review in the traditional sense is unavailable or legally inadequate, a petitioner may generally pursue any applicable independent legal action, including a suit for **declaratory judgments** or **mandatory injunction** or by seeking to have a court of competent jurisdiction issue a common-law **writ of prohibition, mandamus,** or **habeas corpus.** If no special statutory review proceeding is applicable, the action for judicial review of federal agency action may be brought against the United States, the agency by its official title, or the appropriate officer. Except to the extent that prior, adequate, and exclusive opportunity for judicial review is provided by law, agency action is subject to judicial review in civil or criminal proceedings for judicial enforcement.[8]

All states have enacted statutes concerning administrative agency procedures. Often the state constitution or a state administrative procedure act dictates the court that has jurisdiction to review agency orders. This can vary depending on whether the agency is a state agency, for example, a state department of environmental protection, or local administrative body, for example, a county, city, or municipal public housing agency. At the state level a notice of appeal or petition for review must be filed as prescribed by statute or rule of court. Often a petitioner is allowed twenty or thirty days after rendition of an order before review must be sought.

Relief from federal decisions or from the decisions of the highest state courts is discretionary with the U.S. Supreme Court and is limited to cases the Court finds to be of extreme public importance. Such relief occurs through issuance of a **writ of certiorari,** a judicial order directing review of lower court proceedings. Before the Court grants certiorari (commonly referred to as **"granting cert"**) at least four of the nine justices must vote to hear the case.

In the discussion of judicial review that follows, the reader will observe a number of citations to Supreme Court decisions. Nevertheless, one must realize that the Court grants only a very small number of petitions seeking certiorari review. Most decisional law that governs federal agencies results from the decisions of the United States Courts of Appeals for the D.C. Circuit, the eleven numbered circuits, and the federal circuit. In most instances the highest court of a state (usually called the state supreme court) is the final arbiter of interpretation of state administrative law. However, intermediate appellate courts frequently review appeals from administrative agencies.

STATUTORY PRECLUSION OF JUDICIAL REVIEW

Although the provision of the APA providing for judicial review is broad in scope, Section 701(a) states that it is not applicable to statutes that (1) preclude judicial review or (2) to agency action committed by law to agency discretion. Further, Section 701(b)(1) stipulates that "agency"

within the context of the APA, does not include Congress, courts of the United States, governments of territories or possessions of the United States, the government of the District of Columbia, courts-marital, military commissions, and some other entities. These exceptions result in **statutory preclusion of judicial review.** Nevertheless, even a statute that precludes judicial review of agency action does not preclude a petitioner from asserting constitutional claims.[9]

Matters "Committed to Agency Discretion"

Courts have frequently said that absent clear legislative intent, judicial review is not precluded. In *Traynor v. Turnage* (1988)[10] the U.S. Supreme Court recognized that there is a strong presumption that Congress intends to allow judicial review of administrative action, and that this presumption may be overcome only by clear and convincing evidence of a contrary legislative intent. But, as noted, the court must have jurisdiction, and jurisdiction of the lower federal courts is wholly dependent on Acts of Congress, which can preclude judicial review altogether or under certain circumstances. Review is generally statutorily precluded from agencies concerned with national defense and security matters. For example, in 1988, the Supreme Court held that the National Security Act of 1947 precludes judicial review of the CIA director's decisions to terminate employees regardless of cause.[11] In another instance, a federal appeals court pointed out that the Base Closure and Realignment Act stipulates that the Defense Department's decision to close military bases is a **matter committed to agency discretion,** and therefore a claim under the APA would be dismissed.[12]

The *Overton Park* Case Traditionally courts did not become involved in administrative decisions such as those involving the building of highways. The rise of environmentalism and citizen activism in the 1960s and 1970s changed that. The Supreme Court's decision in *Citizens to Preserve Overton Park v. Volpe* (1971)[13] is a classic example of how interest groups can invoke judicial review in an effort to defeat a bureaucratic decision. The controversy began when state and federal highway authorities decided to extend Interstate 40 through Memphis, Tennessee by using a right of way through a public park. An ad hoc citizens' group filed suit in federal court against Secretary of Transportation John Volpe in an effort to defeat this decision. Secretary Volpe claimed that his decision was an "agency action committed to agency discretion by law" and therefore not subject to judicial review.[14] In reviewing the case, the Supreme Court cited two statutes governing the use of public parkland as evidence that Secretary Volpe did not have unfettered discretion over the location of the interstate highway:

> Both the Department of Transportation Act and the Federal-Aid Highway Act provide that the Secretary "shall not approve any program or project" that requires the use of any public parkland "unless (1) there is no feasible and prudent alternative to the use of such land, and (2) such program includes all possible planning to minimize harm to such park. . . ." . . . This language is a plain and explicit bar to the use of federal funds for construction of highways through parks—only the most unusual situations are exempted.[15]

The Court found that there was "law to apply" and that the exemption for action "committed to agency discretion" was inapplicable. Ultimately, the citizens group won the litigation, Overton Park was preserved, and I-40 was built along another route.

The Supreme Court's decision in *Citizens to Preserve Overton Park v. Volpe* is excerpted at the end of the chapter.

The Hard Look Doctrine The Supreme Court's decision in *Overton Park* gave rise to a higher level of activism with respect to judicial review of decisions alleged to be committed to agency discretion. In the 1970s federal courts developed the **hard look doctrine**, under which courts closely examine the record of an agency's decision to determine whether the agency made a "clear error of judgment." A good example of this approach can be seen in *Motor Vehicle Manufacturers Association v. State Farm* (1983),[16] where the Supreme Court invalidated a decision by the National Highway Traffic Safety Administration (NHTSA) to rescind a requirement that motor vehicles produced after 1982 be equipped with airbags. The Court found that the NHTSA's decision to rescind the requirement was "arbitrary and capricious" inasmuch as the agency failed to present an adequate basis for rescinding the airbag requirement.

Judicial Review of Agency Refusals to Take Action

Another aspect of statutory preclusion of review is in the area of enforcement actions. The Supreme Court has said that an agency's decision not to take enforcement action is presumed to be immune from judicial review. *Heckler v. Chaney* (1985)[17] presented the question of whether an administrative agency's decision not to exercise its "discretion" to undertake enforcement actions is subject to judicial review under the APA.[18] Several prison inmates convicted of capital offenses and sentenced to die by lethal injection brought the suit, contending that the use of drugs to inflict capital punishment violated the Federal Food, Drug, and Cosmetic Act. The Supreme Court held that the Food and Drug Administration was not required to take the enforcement action requested by prison inmates. The Court observed that the "general exception to reviewability provided by Section 701(a)(2) of the APA for action 'committed to agency discretion' remains a narrow one . . . but within that exception are included agency refusals to institute investigative or enforcement proceedings, unless Congress has indicated otherwise."[19]

The Court identified three policy grounds for concluding that in enacting the APA Congress intended to exempt determinations not to enforce regulations from judicial inquiry. First, the Court said: "A decision not to enforce often involves a complicated balancing of a number of factors which are peculiarly within its expertise." Second, the Court pointed out that when an agency refuses to act "it generally does not exercise its coercive power over an individual's liberty or property rights." Finally, the Court observed that "an agency's refusal to institute proceedings shares to some extent the characteristics of the decision of a prosecutor in the Executive Branch not to indict—a decision which has long been regarded as the special province of the Executive Branch, inasmuch as it is the Executive who is charged by the Constitution to 'take Care that the Laws be faithfully executed.' "[20]

An excerpt from the Supreme Court's decision in *Heckler v. Chaney* is reprinted at the end of the chapter.

JUSTICIABILITY

Justiciability refers to a case being eligible for judicial consideration. As noted, before being entitled to seek judicial review a petitioner must select a forum that has jurisdiction, the indispensable prerequisite to a review of an administrative agency order. Beyond that, in federal courts there must be a **case or controversy,** because Article III of the U.S. Constitution limits the ability of courts to determine issues that do not meet this threshold. With the rise of the administrative state (see Chapter 2) the U.S. Supreme Court has developed a number of additional criteria that a petitioner must meet before a federal court will consider the merits of a case. These criteria have become doctrinal and control access to judicial review. They are sometimes referred to as **gatekeeping devices** and provide courts with a large measure of discretion. These devices evolved into judicial doctrines known as **standing, ripeness, exhaustion of administrative remedies** and **mootness** that bind the lower federal courts.

In states where the state constitution does not expressly restrict judicial review to a "case or controversy," state legislatures and courts have more leeway in prescribing requirements for judicial review. Nevertheless, irrespective of constitutional requirements, state courts have largely followed the tenor of the federal decisions by adopting similar gatekeeping devices that limit access to judicial review. By limiting access, courts refrain from interference with administrative adjudication, maintain manageable caseloads and maintain **comity** (harmonious relations) with the executive branch of government.

The Doctrine of Standing

The petitioner seeking judicial review of administrative action must have "standing to sue." Standing is a legal doctrine derived from the case or controversy requirement of the federal constitution. The historic "legal interest" test has yielded to a test that now limits access to review by judicial tribunals to those who have or will suffer an **injury in fact** as a result of an agency's decision.

To demonstrate an injury in fact is generally not a problem for a party whose rights have been adjudicated by an administrative tribunal. Courts have said the injury can be (and usually is) economic. But standing is not confined to those who can show economic harm. Indeed, with the enlarged scope of administrative agency authority there has been a trend to liberalize the requirement for standing, and the Supreme Court has said that "aesthetic, conservational, or recreational interests" may qualify.[21] Noneconomic grounds for standing are more difficult to establish. Notwithstanding the trend to liberalize standing, in recent years courts have opined that nonconstitutional prudential considerations require that an aggrieved litigant demonstrate that a complaint falls within a **"zone of interests** to be protected or regulated by the statute or constitutional guarantee in question."[22]

The 1960s witnessed the rise of interest groups that often were dissatisfied with the decisions of regulatory agencies, particularly in the field of environmental regulation. Where these interest groups are not direct parties to agency

---

BOX 9.1   Supreme Court Perspective

Sierra Club v. Morton
405 U.S. 727 (1972)

[The Sierra Club brought suit to restrain federal officials from approving a ski resort in the Sequoia National Forest. The Supreme Court ruled that the group lacked standing, holding that a group has standing to seek judicial review under the Administrative Procedure Act only if it can show that it has itself suffered or will suffer injury. In the following extract, the Court discusses the rationale for this holding.]

Justice Stewart delivered the opinion of the Court, saying in part:
   . . . The trend of cases arising under the APA and other statutes authorizing judicial review of federal agency action has been toward recognizing that injuries other than economic harm are sufficient to bring a person within the meaning of the statutory language, and toward discarding the notion that an injury that is widely shared is ipso facto not an injury sufficient to provide the basis for judicial review. . . . But broadening the categories of injury that may be alleged in support of standing is a different matter from abandoning the requirement that the party seeking review must himself have suffered an injury.
   Some courts have indicated a willingness to take this latter step by conferring standing upon organizations that have demonstrated "an organizational interest in the problem" of environmental or consumer protection. . . . But a mere "interest in a problem," no matter how longstanding the interest and no matter how qualified the organization is in evaluating the problem, is not sufficient by itself to render the organization "adversely affected" or "aggrieved" within the meaning of the APA. . . .
   The requirement that a party seeking review must allege facts showing that he is himself adversely affected does not insulate executive action from judicial review, nor does it prevent any public interests from being protected through the judicial process. It does serve as at least a rough attempt to put the decision as to whether review will be sought in the hands of those who have a direct stake in the outcome. That goal would be undermined were we to construe the APA to authorize judicial review at the behest of organizations or individuals who seek to do no more than vindicate their own value preferences through the judicial process.

---

proceedings they experience difficulty in establishing standing to challenge agency actions. An interest group or its members must show **individualized harm,** to meet the standing criteria. Obviously, under this standard the mere fact that an interest group or its members oppose what the agency has done does not meet the standard.[23] (For an excerpt from a key Supreme Court decision on this point, see Supreme Court Perspective in Box 9.1.) On the other hand, if a group can show that agency action adversely affects the quality of life of its members, it may be successful in overcoming this threshold issue.[24]

   Supreme Court decisions on standing often provide an insight as to the activism or conservatism of the Court in instances where the Court reviews standing of interest groups and organizations. The Court's decision and the

views of the dissenting justices in *Lujan v. National Wildlife Federation* (1990)[25] are illustrative. The National Wildlife Federation (NWF) filed suit against the Secretary of the Interior (Lujan) challenging the Bureau of Land Management's (BLM's) handling of certain public lands. NWF asserted the BLM's policies would lead to increased mining on public land and that this would damage the environment and diminish NWF's members' recreational opportunities. In a 5-4 decision, the Supreme Court denied NWF standing, holding that it had failed to show that its members would be "adversely affected or aggrieved by agency action." Justice Blackmun, writing for the four dissenters, asserted that the evidence supported NWF's contention that mining activities can be expected to cause severe environmental damage to the affected lands.[26]

BOX 9.2   Contrasting Judicial Perspectives on Standing

The doctrine of standing to sue is much more than a technical aspect of the judicial process. The doctrine determines who may challenge government policies and, to some extent, what types of policies may be challenged. Arguments over standing reflect different conceptions of the role of the federal courts in the political system.

Dissenting in *Warth v. Seldin* (1975), Justice William O. Douglas observed that "standing has become a barrier to access to the federal courts." Douglas insisted that "the American dream teaches that if one reaches high enough and persists there is

a forum where justice is dispensed." He concluded that the "technical barriers" should be lowered so that the courts could "serve that ancient need."

A sharply contrasting position is offered by Justice Lewis Powell. Concurring in *United States v. Richardson* (1975), Powell observed, "Relaxation of standing requirements is directly related to the expansion of judicial power." In Powell's view, "allowing unrestricted . . . standing would significantly alter the allocation of power at the national level, with a shift away from a democratic form of government."

The Supreme Court's decision in *Lujan v. National Wildlife Federation* is excerpted at the end of the chapter.

For additional information on contrasting judicial perspectives about standing, see Box 9.2.

May a Taxpayer Challenge Governmental Actions? Simply because a citizen is a taxpayer does not confer standing to challenge actions of the federal government. In *Frothingham v. Mellon* (1923),[27] the U.S. Supreme Court rejected an individual taxpayer's suit against the Secretary of Treasury of the United States seeking to invalidate a federal statute whereby the federal government would contribute funds to the states for certain maternal health programs. The Court held that the petitioner's interest as a taxpayer in federal appropriations was so remote that she had no standing to bring suit against the Secretary of the Treasury. The Court's decision remained the law until 1968 when it decided *Flast v. Cohen*.[28] There a more activist court under Chief Justice Earl Warren rejected the *Frothingham* absolute bar to taxpayers' suits and modified the Court's earlier view to allow suit by a taxpayer who could show a violation of the First Amendment establishment of religion clause to challenge federal expenditures.

Lawyers viewed the *Flast* decision as liberally allowing taxpayer suits to redress constitutional

grievances; however, in *Valley Forge Christian College v. Americans United for Separation of Church and State* (1982),[29] a more conservative Supreme Court with Warren Burger as chief justice rejected the underpinnings of *Flast*. Americans United for Separation of Church and State claimed that the federal government's delegation of authority to the Secretary of Health, Education, and Welfare allowing transfer of surplus property to a religious organization without payment violated the Establishment of Religion Clause of the First Amendment. The Court disagreed and in a 5-4 decision stated that a taxpayer's suit must show that a challenged enactment is prohibited by a specific limitation on Congress's taxing and spending powers under Article I, Section 8 of the United States Constitution. The Court held that because the source of the complaint was not congressional action, rather the decision by the Department of Health, Education, and Welfare and in view of fact that property transfer was not an exercise of authority conferred by the Taxing and Spending Clause of the Constitution, Americans United for Separation of Church and State lacked standing as taxpayers to complain. Four justices dissented. Writing for three of the dissenting justices, Justice Brennan placed great importance on the fact that the case involved a First Amendment issue concerning the establishment of religion.

***Qui Tam* Actions in Federal Courts** Congress has enacted legislation conferring standing on taxpayers for the purpose of deterring and punishing false claims against the federal government. As we saw in Chapter 5, the False Claims Act allows private citizens to file ***qui tam* actions** on behalf of the U.S. government charging fraud by government contractors, Medicare, and Medicaid providers, and others who receive federal funds. This creates a strong incentive for persons who become aware of fraud to "blow the whistle." The citizen who initiates the suit shares in the monetary damages by receiving up to a maximum of 30 percent of the amount recovered. This provides an incentive to whistleblowers to reveal evidence of fraud in government programs.

The Standing Doctrine in the State Courts State courts also apply the doctrine of standing to control access to the courts and to respect the autonomy of administrative agencies. Courts impose the doctrine in land use zoning cases to preclude someone who does not suffer an injury differing in kind rather than degree from that of the community from attacking zoning regulations. The courts usually find that the fact that a plaintiff would suffer from competition or increased traffic congestion because of zoning would not constitute a sufficient difference in kind from the general public.

In *Boucher v. Novotny,*[30] a leading Florida Supreme Court decision on standing, the court held that the plaintiff, who owned property across the street from a motel, did not have standing to seek redress against the alleged violation of a zoning ordinance because the plaintiff's damages did not differ in kind from those suffered by the community as a whole.

In *Pontiac Osteopathic Hospital v. Dept. of Public Health,*[31] a Michigan appellate court held that unsuccessful applicants for certificates of need to construct an acute care hospital facility lacked standing to challenge the Department of Public Health's issuance of a certificate of need to a competing applicant seeking to establish two surgical ambulatory suites.

On the issue of taxpayer suits, many states have enacted statutes that allow taxpayers to challenge state and local expenditures. Some state laws require that a certain number of taxpayers must first petition a governing body before bringing an action challenging an alleged illegal expenditure of public funds. Other statutes permit taxpayers to file suit upon failure of a local governing body. For example, resident city taxpayers in Oklahoma may bring a statutory *qui tam* action to recover city money that was paid out illegally or without authority; but the taxpayers must first demand in writing that city officers institute proceedings to recover the money. The right to bring suit accrues when the city officers either neglect or fail to act upon the demand.[32]

The Ripeness Requirement

In addition to the requirement that a petitioner seeking judicial review must have standing, the administrative decision to be reviewed must be "ripe" for review. In *Abbott Laboratories v. Gardner* (1967)[33] the Supreme Court explained:

> A controversy must be "ripe" for judicial resolution in order "to prevent the courts, through avoidance of premature adjudication, from entangling themselves in abstract disagreements over administrative policies, and also to protect the agencies from judicial interference until an administrative decision has been formalized and its effects felt in a concrete way by the challenging parties."[34]

The ripeness doctrine represents a prudential attempt to balance the interest of the court and the agency in delaying review against the petitioner's interest in obtaining prompt consideration of an agency action that the petitioner deems to be unlawful.[35]

To be ripe means the decision must have reached the point of finality where it is real and not speculative or hypothetical. In *Bennett v. Spear* (1997),[36] the Supreme Court observed

> As a general matter, two conditions must be satisfied for agency action to be "final." First,

the action must mark the "consummation" of the agency's decision making process—it must not be of a merely tentative or interlocutory nature. And second, the action must be one by which "rights or obligations have been determined," or from which "legal consequences will flow."[37]

In *Ash Creek Mining Co. v. Lujan* (1991),[38] the owner of surface rights in a tract of land challenged the Department of the Interior's decision to withhold the tract from the Department's coal leasing program pending a final decision on a proposed change of tract for other private lands. The U.S. Court of Appeals for the Tenth Circuit concluded that the case was not ripe for review. The court observed that the doctrine of ripeness prevents federal courts from interfering with actions of administrative agencies except when a specific final agency action has an actual or immediately threatened effect.

State courts, as well as federal courts, apply the doctrine of ripeness. In *Maine AFL-CIO v. Superintendent of Insurance,*[39] the AFL-CIO sought review of a lower court ruling dismissing for lack of ripeness its challenge to a rule promulgated by the Bureau of Insurance governing "pilot projects" for workers' compensation insurance. In upholding the lower court decision, the Supreme Judicial Court of Maine held that the rule assailed by the AFL-CIO was not ripe for review because no programs had yet been approved, and thus no specific legal issue was presented.

Exhaustion of Administrative Remedies

When a statute provides for administrative review within an agency, one who seeks such review must ordinarily first pursue any available administrative remedies. The rationale is that administrative agencies should be given every opportunity to correct their own errors before courts become involved. This exhaustion of remedies doctrine prevents judicial review that is premature or unnecessary, protects agency autonomy, and promotes efficiency and economy.

In *McCarthy v. Madigan* (1992),[40] the Supreme Court acknowledged the general rule that parties must exhaust prescribed administrative remedies before seeking relief from the federal courts. However, the following year in *Darby v. Cisneros,*[41] the Court ruled on a consolidated appeal from decisions by the Department of Housing and Urban Development (HUD) to initiate administrative sanctions against petitioners. There an **administrative law judge (ALJ)** concluded that petitioners should be debarred from participating in federal programs for eighteen months. Under HUD regulations, an ALJ's determination "shall be final unless . . . the Secretary . . . within 30 days of receipt of a request decides as a matter of discretion to review the [ALJ's] finding. . . ." Neither party sought further administrative review, but petitioners filed suit in the U.S. District Court, seeking an injunction and declaration that the sanctions were not in accordance with law within the meaning of the APA. Respondents moved to dismiss the complaint on the ground that petitioners, by foregoing the option to seek review by the secretary, had failed to exhaust their administrative remedies. The district court denied the motion and granted the petitioners summary judgment on the merits. The Court of Appeals reversed, holding that the district court erred in denying the motion to dismiss. The Supreme Court granted certiorari and reversed the decision by the Court of Appeals. The Court held that lower federal courts do not have the authority to require a plaintiff to exhaust available administrative remedies before seeking judicial review under the APA, where neither the relevant statute nor agency rules specifically mandate exhaustion as a prerequisite to judicial review. By the end of the 1990s many federal agencies had included explicit exhaustion requirements to satisfy Section 704.

State courts generally require that a party seeking judicial review exhaust all administrative remedies where there is a possibility of obtaining relief through administrative channels. Thus in *Lindsay v. Sterling*[42] the Texas Supreme Court pointed out that under Section 16 of the Administrative Procedure and Texas Register Act the requirement of having a motion for rehearing overruled, thus exhausting administrative remedies, is a jurisdictional prerequisite to judicial review by the district court and cannot be waived by action of the parties. But some state courts have made exceptions. For example, in New York if "an agency's action is challenged as either unconstitutional or wholly beyond its grant of power . . . or when resort to an administrative remedy would be futile . . . or when its pursuit would cause irreparable injury," then exhaustion of administrative remedies may be excused.[43]

Primary Jurisdiction Somewhat related to the doctrine of exhaustion of administrative remedies is the doctrine of **primary jurisdiction.** In instances where an independent lawsuit is filed and the matters involved fall clearly within the jurisdiction of an administrative agency, the court will often defer ruling on the substance of the plaintiff's complaint pending resolution of the issue by the appropriate administrative agency. In reality, the doctrine of primary jurisdiction is one of comity, not jurisdiction, and is invoked as a matter of judicial discretion to afford the court the benefit of an agency's expertise and to promote consistency in public policy.

In explaining the difference between exhaustion of remedies and the primary jurisdiction doctrines, the Supreme Court has said:

The doctrine of primary jurisdiction, like the rule requiring exhaustion of administrative remedies, is concerned with promoting proper relationships between the courts and administrative agencies charged with particular regulatory duties. "Exhaustion" applies where a claim is cognizable in the first instance by an administrative agency alone; judicial interference is withheld until the administrative process has run its course. "Primary jurisdiction," on the other hand, applies where a claim is originally cognizable in the courts, and comes into play whenever enforcement of the claim requires the resolution of issues which, under a regulatory scheme, have been placed within the special

competence of an administrative body; in such a case the judicial process is suspended pending referral of such issues to the administrative body for its views.[44]

State courts recognize the expertise of agencies and generally apply the doctrine of primary jurisdiction. In their opinions state appellate courts often point out that a court should not act in respect to a matter that is peculiarly within an administrative agency's specialized field without first giving the agency an opportunity to apply its expertise. This is illustrated by the Connecticut Supreme Court's decision in *Sharkey v. City of Stamford*[45] where the court reviewed a case involving several Stamford police officers who sought to enjoin the city from changing the testing procedures for promotions of officers. In ruling that the doctrine of primary jurisdiction required the validity of procedures to be challenged initially through municipal agency procedures, rather than through court action, the court explained how the application of the doctrine of primary jurisdiction is distinguishable from the exhaustion of remedies doctrine.

The doctrine of exhaustion of administrative remedies contemplates a situation where some administrative action has begun, but has not yet been completed; where there is no administrative proceeding under way, the exhaustion doctrine has no application. In contrast, primary jurisdiction situations arise in cases where a plaintiff, in the absence of pending administrative proceedings, invokes the original jurisdiction of a court to decide the merits of a controversy. We describe the circumstances herein as a primary jurisdiction case, because the plaintiffs, prior to filing their complaint, had sought no administrative action.[46]

The Mootness Doctrine

Because the United States Constitution limits the judicial power to "cases or controversies," a federal court will not consider a case that has become moot. A case is said to be moot if the parties have voluntarily complied with an agency decision or reached an amicable settlement of the issues involved. Other examples of mootness would be the payment of taxes that are the subject of litigation, and passage of legislation that resolves the problem being litigated. If a case becomes moot during the litigation a federal court will note its lack of jurisdiction and dismiss the case.[47]

In the 1998 case of *Knaust v. City of Kingston, New York*,[48] the plaintiffs claimed the city was in violation of certain environmental laws in connection with a federal grant of funds for development of a park. The federal district court denied their petition for a temporary injunction to halt the development. By the time the appellate court reviewed the denial of preliminary injunction the park was completed and all federal funds allocated to the project were disbursed. The Second Circuit Court of Appeals dismissed the appeal on the ground that it was moot.

Not all state constitutions have a "case or controversy requirement" similar to the federal constitution. The lack of such a provision gives a court some leeway in deciding a case even if it becomes moot. But even when not constitutionally bound to adhere to the case or controversy requirement, state courts generally will not hear and determine a case that has become moot. An exception is where an issue, although moot, is "capable of repetition, yet evading review." For example, a state court might review an administrative determination if a government agency denies access to public records, but provides such records while litigation to compel production is pending.

Florida's Public Records Act provides (with certain exceptions) that state and local government agencies must release public records on demand of citizens. In *Times Publishing Company, Inc. v. Butterworth*,[49] a Florida appeals court in 1990 reviewed an action where a city denied the media access to lease records concerning negotiations between the city and a major league baseball team. Pending an appeal, the city made the requested documents available. Although recognizing that "the issue regarding whether the lease documents are public records is now moot," the court held that because "the instant situation is capable of repetition while evading review, we find it appropriate to address the issues before us concerning applicability of the Public Records Act for future reference."[50]

REVIEW ON THE MERITS

At the threshold of seeking judicial review the petitioner (or plaintiff) must select the proper forum, then demonstrate standing to litigate and the ripeness of the controversy and administrative finality. In many cases the petitioner must have first exhausted any available administrative remedies, and, subject to narrow exceptions, must be able to show the controversy is not moot. These procedural mechanisms, often referred to as "gatekeeping devices," were discussed earlier. But the objective of seeking judicial review is to obtain a review on the merits of an administrative agency's decision. In this section we discuss the scope of review and the standards courts apply in reviewing the merits of administrative decisions.

Recall that Section 702 of the Administrative Procedure Act states: "A person suffering legal wrong because of agency action, or adversely affected or aggrieved by agency action within the meaning of a relevant statute, is entitled to judicial review thereof." In detailing the scope of review, Section 706 provides:

> To the extent necessary to decision and when presented, the reviewing court shall decide all relevant questions of law, interpret constitutional and statutory provisions, and determine the meaning or applicability of the terms of an agency action. The reviewing court shall
>
> (1) compel agency action unlawfully withheld or unreasonably delayed; and
>
> (2) hold unlawful and set aside agency action, findings, and conclusions found to be
>
> (A) arbitrary, capricious, an abuse of discretion, or otherwise not in accordance with law;

(B) contrary to constitutional right, power, privilege, or immunity;

(C) in excess of statutory jurisdiction, authority, or limitations, or short of statutory right;

(D) without observance of procedure required by law;

(E) unsupported by substantial evidence in a case subject to Sections 556 and 557 [refers to evidentiary hearings] of this title or otherwise reviewed on the record of an agency hearing provided by statute; or

(F) unwarranted by the facts to the extent that the facts are subject to trial de novo by the reviewing court.

In making the foregoing determinations, the court shall review the whole record or those parts of it cited by a party, and due account shall be taken of the rule of prejudicial error.

Thus, in reviewing an administrative agency decision a court serves several functions. It reviews the record to determine if the agency action conformed to constitutional requisites, was statutorily authorized, and afforded the parties administrative due process of law. Where the agency order is based on an evidentiary hearing, the reviewing court determines whether the agency's factual findings are supported by substantial evidence, and whether its conclusion is rational and neither arbitrary nor capricious.

In referring to the APA requirements, the U.S. Court of Appeals for the Federal Circuit recently explained:

> For judicial review to be meaningfully achieved within these strictures, the agency tribunal must present a full and reasoned explanation of its decision. The agency tribunal must set forth its findings and the grounds thereof, as supported by the agency record, and explain its application of the law to the found facts. . . . Not only must an agency's decreed result be within the scope of its lawful authority, but the process by

which it reaches that result must be logical and rational.[51]

The Mechanics of Judicial Review

The reviewing court conducts its review based on the record of agency proceedings. In some instances a court will hear testimony, for example, where irregularities of the agency proceedings are made apparent. Federal and state courts require the petitioner to assure that an accurate record of agency proceedings is presented to the reviewing court. The petitioner directs the clerk of the agency or the lower court to transmit the record to the reviewing court. The contents of the record will vary according to the issues raised, but generally it contains the pleadings (documents with allegations and responses by the parties) and a transcript of testimony before the agency or lower court along with pertinent exhibits. A respondent has the option of adding selected documents, where necessary. The petitioner and the respondent file briefs on the law, and in many instances courts hear oral argument by counsel for the parties much as prevails in appeals from judgments in civil actions. These procedural requirements are included in the Federal Rules of Appellate Procedure, the Supreme Court Rules, and comparable state court rules of procedure.

The above procedure may vary when an independent action rather than a petition for review is filed. In either event, federal and state courts act based on the issues the parties raise. In doing so a court can determine whether the agency action offends the federal constitution (and where applicable, the state constitution) and whether the agency acted without or beyond its statutory jurisdiction, violated basic rules of procedure (including the agency's own rules), whether the agency misinterpreted the law or acted in an arbitrary or capricious manner or denied interested parties administrative due process of law.

The reviewing court may affirm the agency's decision, reverse that decision, or remand the case to the agency with directions to conduct further proceedings. In conducting a review, courts apply three basic standards: First, a **de novo standard,** i.e., a review without deference to an agency ruling, when reviewing questions of law; for example, an agency's conclusion as to the legal effect of its findings and the application of the law to those findings. Second, when an agency's factual findings are challenged, the reviewing court determines if the agency's decision is supported by **substantial evidence.** Finally, courts apply an **abuse of discretion standard** when reviewing discretionary actions by an agency. (As previously pointed out, in instances where actions are statutorily "committed to the agency's discretion," that discretion is unreviewable.) Not infrequently a reviewing court will find it necessary to apply different standards to various issues raised.

Section 557 of the APA requires that a final agency order must include findings of fact and conclusions of law stated separately. This enables the reviewing court to perform meaningful review within the strictures of the APA and to determine "whether the decision was based on the relevant factors and whether there has been a clear error of judgment."[52]

Availability of Relief Pending Review

When an agency finds that justice so requires, it may postpone, i.e., **"stay"** the effective date of action taken by it, pending judicial review. Under the APA simply seeking judicial review does not stay an agency order, unless so provided by statute; however, a petitioner may apply to the agency for a stay pending review. A stay, of course, does not grant affirmative relief. Review of the denial of a stay generally takes place by an aggrieved party filing a motion in the court having jurisdiction to review the agency proceedings. At the federal level, Section 705 of the APA stipulates that a reviewing court may issue "all necessary and appropriate legal process to postpone the effective date of an agency action or to preserve status or rights pending conclusion of the review proceedings."

State courts are largely governed by statutory law and procedural rules. Indiana law appears typical. There, if a petition for judicial review concerns a matter other than an assessment of or determination of taxes, and the law does not preclude a stay, the reviewing court may stay the agency order pending a final judicial determination, provided the petitions for review and for a stay order show a reasonable probability that the order or determination appealed from is invalid or illegal. Indiana law requires that a bond be posted to guarantee that the petitioner will pay court costs and abide by the court's ruling if the administrative agency's order is not set aside.[53]

DEFERENCE TO AGENCY DETERMINATIONS

Judicial review is characterized by deference to the findings of fact and interpretations of law and rules by administrative agencies. Courts accord a **presumption of correctness** to actions taken by administrative agencies. It follows that one who challenges agency action that is constitutionally permissible and statutorily authorized must carry the burden of demonstrating to a judicial tribunal that such action is incorrect. In judicial review the extent of deference granted to administrative action depends on whether the issue involves factual findings, interpretation of statutes and agency rules, or rulemaking.

Deference to Findings of Fact

Section 706(2)(e) of the APA provides that a reviewing court shall set aside agency action, findings, and conclusions found to be unsupported by substantial evidence. In general, a reviewing court will defer to an administrative agency when the agency is performing its function as a fact finder. The APA sets three standards for judicial review of administrative findings of fact. On review courts may hold unlawful and set aside agency findings and conclusions found to be:

(1) arbitrary, capricious, an abuse of discretion, or otherwise not in accordance with law;

(2) unsupported by substantial evidence (in certain types of cases); or

(3) unwarranted by the facts to the extent that the facts are subject to trial de novo by the reviewing court.

Federal courts defer to administrative agency **findings of fact** when such findings are based on substantial evidence. State courts phrase their standards of review in various ways, but essentially they hold that a finding of facts of a state or local agency will not be set aside if based on competent substantial evidence. "Substantial evidence is relevant evidence which a reasonable mind might accept in support of the conclusions of the agency."[54]

But what does a reviewing court do when there is substantial evidence before an administrative tribunal that supports not only the agency's findings but also alternative findings? The U.S. Supreme Court answered that question in 1996, observing: "[T]he possibility of drawing two inconsistent conclusions from the evidence does not prevent an administrative agency's finding from being supported by substantial evidence."[55] More recently, the Court criticized lower courts that have reviewed administrative agency findings and then proceeded to make their own findings. In 1992 the Supreme Court cautioned, "A court reviewing an agency's adjudicative action should accept the agency's factual findings if those findings are supported by substantial evidence on the record as a whole. . . . The court should not supplant the agency's findings merely by identifying alternative findings that could be supported by substantial evidence."[56]

Statutory Interpretation

Statutes that delegate authority to administrative agencies frequently require interpretation. Although courts apply different rules in interpreting statutes, the cardinal principle is for the court to look to the **plain meaning of statutory language.** In some instances courts attempt to divine the **legislative intent** or purpose of the statute. Courts generally apply a de novo standard of review to an agency's conclusion of law; however, they grant reasonable deference to an **agency's construction of a statute** it is charged with administering if a statutory term is undefined, has no settled meaning or is ambiguous.[57]

One of the canons of statutory construction is that courts must consider the disputed provision in the context of other provisions of the statute as well as the general policy objective the legislature evidently sought to achieve. In 1857, the Supreme Court said that "in interpreting a statute, the court will not look merely to a particular clause in which general words may be used, but will take in connection with it the whole statute . . . and the objects and policy of the law."[58] More recently, the Supreme Court has observed that it is a "fundamental canon of statutory construction that the words of a statute must be read in their context and with a view to their place in the overall statutory scheme."[59] In other words, a court should interpret the provision at issue as part of a "symmetrical and coherent regulatory scheme."[60] An agency action that fits nicely into a symmetrical and coherent regulatory scheme is not likely to be invalidated by the courts. Courts are likely to closely scrutinize regulations that deviate from or upset such a scheme.

The *Chevron* Decision: Deference to Agency Interpretations of Law

In *Chevron U.S.A. v. Natural Defense Council* (1984)[61] the U.S. Supreme Court issued a landmark opinion written by Justice Stevens on the issue of judicial deference to an agency's interpretation of a statute that it administers. The Court's opinion has been cited in over 10,000 decisions by state and federal courts. Justice Stevens held that if a reviewing court

> determines Congress has not directly addressed the precise question at issue, the court does not simply impose its own construction on the statute, as would be necessary in the absence of an administrative

interpretation. Rather, if the statute is silent or ambiguous with respect to the specific issue, the question for the court is whether the agency's answer is based on a permissible construction of the statute.[62]

The *Chevron* decision recognizes that agencies must be allowed to interpret complex statutes regulating their particular area of expertise without judicial second-guessing. Thus, *Chevron* shifts the power away from unelected federal judges making policy through disparate decisions to agencies where decisions are to be made, at least in theory, by those who are politically accountable.

The Supreme Court's landmark decision in *Chevron U.S.A. v. Natural Resources Defense Council* is excerpted at the end of the chapter.

Reaffirmation and Refinement of the *Chevron* Standard The Supreme Court in *Chevron* held that a court, in reviewing an agency's interpretation of a statute it administers, must perform a two-step analysis. First, it must give effect to the congressional intent if it is clear on the precise question at issue. Second, if the statute is silent or ambiguous on that point, the court must sustain the agency's interpretation if it is based on a permissible construction of the statute. In 1998, the Supreme Court reaffirmed the principle that deference should be given to an agency's construction of a statute. Writing for the Court, Justice Ginsburg stated: "If the agency's reading fills a gap or defines a term in a reasonable way in light of the legislature's design, we give that reading controlling weight, even if it is not the answer 'the court would have reached if the question initially had arisen in a judicial proceeding.' "[63]

It is important to recognize that *Chevron* does not control every administrative interpretation by agencies. In 2001, in *United States v. Mead Corp.*,[64] the Supreme Court held that tariff classification rulings by the U.S. Customs Service are not entitled to judicial deference under the *Chevron* doctrine because such rulings do not

have the "force of law."[65] Writing for the Court, Justice Souter stated:

> [A]dministrative implementation of a particular statutory provision qualifies for *Chevron* deference when it appears that Congress delegated authority to the agency generally to make rules carrying the force of law, and that the agency interpretation claiming deference was promulgated in the exercise of that authority. Delegation of such authority may be shown in a variety of ways, as by an agency's power to engage in adjudication or notice-and-comment rulemaking, or by some other indication of a comparable congressional intent.[66]

Notwithstanding its conclusion that Custom Service's tariff rulings are not entitled to *Chevron* deference, the Court in *Mead* remanded the case to the lower court to consider whether the agency's rulings were entitled to deference under the Court's 1944 decision in *Skidmore v. Swift & Co.*[67] In *Skidmore* the Court examined an administrator's interpretations under the Fair Labor Standards Act where the administrator's ruling did not have the force of law. The Court stated that "[R]ulings, interpretations and opinions of the Administrator . . . while not controlling upon the courts by reason of their authority do constitute a body of experience and informed judgment to which courts and litigants may properly resort for guidance."[68] In *Mead* the Court mentioned, "Customs can bring the benefit of specialized experience to bear on this case's questions."[69]

Thus, it would seem that courts must apply the *Chevron* standard to legislative rules made by an agency where Congress has delegated such lawmaking authority to the agency. As to agency rulings made outside the ambit of lawmaking authority, courts should give weight to the "factors which give it power to persuade."[70]

A Contemporary Illustration of *Chevron* Deference The *Chevron* doctrine came into play again in 2002 in a case involving Social Security benefits. Cleveland Walton lost his position as a teacher as a result of mental illness. In 1996 he applied to the Social Security Administration for disability benefits under the Social Security Act, which defines "disability" as an "inability to engage in any substantial gainful activity by reason of any medically determinable physical or mental impairment which can be expected to result in death or which has lasted or can be expected to last for a continuous period of not less than 12 months."[71]

Although the statutory definition explicitly applies the 12-month requirement only to the physical or mental impairment, the agency's regulation construed it to require that a person be unable to engage in substantial gainful activity for not less than 12 months. Since Walton's illness kept him from working for only 11 months, he was denied disability benefits. Walton challenged the agency's determination that he was not entitled to benefits, arguing that even though he returned to work after 11 months, his impairment and his *inability* to work were nonetheless expected to last for at least 12 months before he returned to work. The U.S. Court of Appeals for the Fourth Circuit held the statute was clear and unambiguous and therefore precluded the agency's interpretation.

In *Barnhart v. Walton* (2002),[72] the Supreme Court reversed. In an opinion by Justice Stephen Breyer, the Court addressed whether the agency's interpretation of the durational requirement of the statutory provision was unlawful where the provision made no explicit statements about the duration of the claimant's "inability" to return to work. The Court agreed the provision made no explicit statement about the duration of the claimant's "inability" but further found that the statute did not unambiguously forbid the regulation. Noting that the agency's interpretation was consistent with the statute's basic objectives, Justice Breyer observed: "The Agency's interpretation supplies a duration requirement, which the statute demands, while doing so in a way that consistently reconciles the statutory 'impairment' and 'inability' language."[73] Finally, the Court noted that the agency's regulation was consistent

with its long-standing interpretation, and although Congress has frequently amended the statute it has made no attempt to alter the provision defining disability. Citing the *Chevron* decision, the Court deferred to the agency's interpretation of the statutory provisions of the Social Security Act and concluded the statutory language was ambiguous and the agency's regulation and its interpretation were reasonable. Interestingly, Justice Scalia, who concurred in the judgment, took exception to one point in the Court's opinion. He noted that *Chevron* did not rely on the long-standing nature of an agency's interpretation. For another noteworthy example of judicial deference to an administrative agency's interpretation of its statutory authority, see Box 9.3.

The Limits of Judicial Deference

Judicial deference to agency interpretations of statutory authority is not unlimited; however, and there are certainly a number of instances where courts have declared agency actions *ultra vires*. For example, as we discussed in Chapter 4, in 2000 the Supreme Court rejected the Food and Drug Administration's decision to regulate tobacco products as "drug delivery devices."[74] Generally speaking, courts will defer to an agency's own interpretation of its statutory mandate, especially when the agency action in question is consistent with the broad contours of public policy. However, in cases where an agency asserts unprecedented powers to make policy on salient political or economic issues, courts are more likely to strictly scrutinize the agency's interpretation of its statutory authority.[75]

A good example of this can be seen in *Industrial Union Department v. American Petroleum Institute* (1980).[76] In this case an interest group representing the oil refining industry challenged the authority of the Occupational Safety and Health Administration to dramatically lower the level at which benzene, a known carcinogen, would be permitted in the workplace. OSHA based its action on Section 6(b)(5) of the Occupational

---

BOX 9.3 Case in Point

Deference to Administrative Agencies: The Elian Gonzales Case

Gonzales v. Reno

United States Court of Appeals, 11th Circuit

212 F.3d 1338 (11th Cir. 2000)

[In late 1999 and early 2000, the Immigration and Naturalization Service (INS) became the focus of national and international attention for its handling of the unusual case of Elian Gonzales, a six-year-old Cuban boy who was rescued at sea after his mother and nine other people drowned when their boat capsized. The INS gave temporary custody of the boy to relatives in Miami. When the boy's natural father came from Cuba to claim Elian, the Miami relatives refused to relinquish custody. After negotiations between the INS and the Miami relatives broke down, the INS used force to remove the boy from the home of the Miami relatives and reunite him with his father. While they had custody of Elian, the Miami relatives initiated a federal lawsuit to force the INS to grant Elian a political asylum hearing. The INS took the position that legally, only Elian's father could speak for him in this regard. The federal district court in Miami dismissed the case. The Miami relatives appealed to the U.S. Court of Appeals for the Eleventh Circuit in Atlanta. On June 1, 2000, the 11th Circuit ruled that the INS had acted within its legal authority in refusing to hold a political asylum hearing. The Miami relatives sought review in the Supreme Court but their petition for certiorari was denied. The following is an excerpt from the 11th Circuit's opinion.]

Circuit Judge Edmondson delivers the opinion of the court:

. . . As policymakers, it is the duty of the Congress and of the executive branch to exercise political will. Although courts should not be unquestioning, we should respect the other branches' policymaking powers. The judicial power is a limited power. It is the duty of the judicial branch not to exercise political will, but only to render judicial judgment under the law.

When the INS was confronted with Plaintiff's purported asylum applications, the immigration law of the United States provided the INS with no clear answer. The INS accordingly developed a policy to deal with the extraordinary circumstances of asylum applications filed on behalf of a six-year-old child, by the child himself and a non-parental relative, against the express wishes of the child's parents (or sole parent). The INS then applied this new policy to Plaintiff's purported asylum applications and rejected them as nullities.

Because the preexisting law compelled no particular policy, the INS was entitled to make a policy decision. The policy decision that the INS made was within the outside border of reasonable choices. And the INS did not abuse its discretion or act arbitrarily in applying the policy and rejecting Plaintiff's purported asylum applications. The Court neither approves nor disapproves the INS's decision to reject the asylum applications filed on Plaintiff's behalf, but the INS decision did not contradict [the law].

Safety and Health Act of 1970, which permits regulators to "set the standard which most adequately assures, to the extent feasible, on the basis of the best available evidence, that no employee will suffer material impairment of health or functional capacity." In lowering the permitted level of benzene by a factor of ten, from 10 parts per million to 1 ppm, OSHA claimed that it was merely reducing "to the extent feasible" workers' exposure to a known carcinogen. In challenging the new regulation, the industry claimed that compliance would entail tremendous economic costs and that OSHA had failed to produce evidence that reducing the level of benzene in the workplace would actually result in a reduced incidence of cancer among exposed workers. In a 5-4 decision, the Supreme Court invalidated the regulation. Writing for a plurality of the Court, Justice Stevens observed:

In the absence of a clear mandate in the Act, it is unreasonable to assume that Congress intended to give [OSHA] the unprecedented power over American industry that would result from the Government's view [of the provision in question]. . . . In light of the fact that there are literally thousands of substances used in the workplace that have been identified as carcinogens or suspect carcinogens, the Government's theory would give OSHA the power to impose enormous costs that might produce little, if any, benefit.[77]

Another example of judicial negation of the Environmental Protection Agency's interpretation of its statutory mandate occurred in 2001 when the U.S. Supreme Court invalidated an EPA interpretation of the Clean Air Act. Writing for the Court in *Whitman v. American Trucking Associations* (2001),[78] Justice Scalia found that the EPA's policy violated the clear intent of Congress by considering implementation costs in setting air quality standards for ozone.

Section 109(b)(1) [of the Clean Air Act] instructs the EPA to set primary ambient air quality standards "the attainment and maintenance of which . . . are requisite to protect the public health" with "an adequate margin of safety." . . .Were it not for the hundreds of pages of briefing respondents have submitted on the issue, one would have thought it fairly clear that this text does not permit the EPA to consider costs in setting the standards. The language, as one scholar has noted, "is absolute." . . .The EPA, "based on" the information about health effects contained in the technical "criteria" documents compiled under § 108(a)(2), 42 U. S. C. § 7408(a)(2), is to identify the maximum airborne concentration of a pollutant that the public health can tolerate, decrease the concentration to provide an "adequate" margin of safety, and set the standard at that level. Nowhere are the costs of achieving such a standard made part of that initial calculation.[79]

Cases involving assertions of regulatory power by the EPA and OSHA often pit business and industry against environmentalists. In comparing *Industrial Union Department v. American Petroleum*

Institute to the more recent *Whitman* decision, the reader should note that in the former case, the proindustry position prevailed, while in the latter decision, the proenvironmental position prevailed. Given that the contemporary Supreme Court is usually characterized as "conservative," some commentators were surprised that the Court would read the Clean Air Act to prohibit EPA from considering implementation costs in setting air quality standards. Apparently, the Court was obviously more concerned about maintaining bureaucratic fidelity to law than with the public policy merits of EPA's position.

Judicial Deference in Cases Raising Constitutional Concerns

In general, courts are less likely to defer to agency interpretations of statutes where such interpretations allow agencies to act in ways that generate serious constitutional concerns.[80] Thus, in 1988 the Supreme Court held that "where an otherwise acceptable construction of a statute would raise serious constitutional problems, the Court will construe the statute to avoid such problems unless such construction is plainly contrary to the intent of Congress."[81] Yet there are numerous instances where courts have upheld dubious agency interpretations of statutes notwithstanding the existence of serious constitutional concerns. A good example of this can be seen in *Rust v. Sullivan*,[82] in which the Supreme Court upheld a controversial Department of Health and Human Services (HHS) regulation that limited the ability of recipients of federal funds to engage in abortion-related counseling. The regulation was adopted pursuant to an act of Congress that provided federal funding for family planning services but also provided that such grants were to be made in accordance with regulations promulgated by HHS. Not only was the regulation at issue arguably inconsistent with the will of Congress, it raised serious constitutional questions involving freedom of speech and abortion rights. The Court ultimately rejected the constitutional challenges to the HHS rule, but it could have avoided the constitutional questions altogether had it held that the agency adopted a rule contrary to congressional intent. In dissent, Justice O'Connor argued that the Court

> need only tell the Secretary that his regulations are not a reasonable interpretation of the statute; we need not tell Congress that it cannot pass such legislation. If we rule solely on statutory grounds, Congress retains the power to force the constitutional question by legislating more explicitly. It may instead choose to do nothing. That decision should be left to Congress; we should not tell Congress what it cannot do before it has chosen to do it.[83]

State Court Deference to Agency Construction of Statutes

In general, state courts follow the same approach in reviewing agency actions that are challenged as transcending state legislation. Following the *Chevron* doctrine, the Hawaii Supreme Court has said that "[j]udicial deference to agency expertise is a guiding precept where the interpretation and application of broad or ambiguous statutory language by an administrative tribunal are the subject of review."[84] The Washington Supreme Court observed:

> At times, administrative interpretation of a statute may approach "lawmaking," but we have heretofore recognized that it is an appropriate function for administrative agencies to "fill in the gaps" where necessary to the effectuation of a general statutory scheme. . . . It is likewise valid for an administrative agency to "fill in the gaps" via statutory construction— as long as the agency does not purport to "amend" the statute.[85]

The New Jersey Supreme Court has gone so far as to hold that "[t]he absence of an express statutory authorization in the enabling legislation will not preclude administrative agency action where, by reasonable implication, that action can be said to promote or advance the policies and findings that served as the driving force for the enactment of the legislation."[86]

Judicial Deference to Rules and Rulemaking Procedures

In addition to reviewing statutory interpretations, courts are also called on to review an agency's interpretation of the rules and regulations it has promulgated. Courts afford considerable deference to an agency's construction of its own rules and regulations. One reason often advanced by the courts is that the agency's expertise in its field makes it uniquely qualified to interpret its own rules. It follows that although an agency's interpretation is merely one of several reasonable interpretations, the agency interpretation generally stands, even though it may not appear to the reviewing court to be as reasonable as other alternative interpretations.[87]

As we pointed out in Chapter 6, agencies may conduct rulemaking pursuant to either informal or formal procedures. In *Association of National Advertisers, Inc. v. Federal Trade Commission* (1979), the U.S. Court of Appeals for the District of Columbia Circuit cited section 706(a) of the APA in pointing out that "reviewing courts are required to uphold informal rulemaking decisions unless those decisions are 'arbitrary, capricious, an abuse of discretion, or otherwise not in accordance with law.' "[88] The court observed, however, that formal rulemaking is governed by the substantial evidence rule.[89] Although there is a judicial deference to formulation of agency rules, the Supreme Court noted in *Christensen v. Harris County* (2000)[90] that the deference accorded to agency interpretations of statutes in the Court's 1984 decision in *Chevron U.S.A. v. Natural Defense Council* does not normally apply to informal rulemaking.

In 2001 the Court extended its holding in *Christensen*. In *United States v. Mead Corporation*[91] the Court ruled that a tariff classification in a ruling letter issued by the U.S. Customs Service was "beyond the *Chevron* pale" yet entitled to respect "proportional to its power to persuade."[92]

The Court explained that the Custom Service's ruling letters bind only the parties to ruling and not third parties; thus, they do not constitute the kind of rulemaking that has the force of law entitled to the deference accorded under the *Chevron doctrine.* Consequently, the Court afforded the Custom Service's ruling letter only the deference allowed agency positions under *Skidmore v. Swift & Co.*[93]

The U.S. Court of Appeals for the Seventh Circuit applied the *Mead* approach in 2002 in *U.S. Freightways Corp. v. Comm'r. of Internal Revenue.*[94] In *U.S. Freightways* the court explained that it was following *Mead* rather than *Chevron* in reviewing an interpretation that emerged inferentially as a result of IRS applying a rule that developed as a result of positions IRS had taken in a series of litigated cases.

When a rule is assailed on the basis of constitutionality, courts tend to uphold the rule if it bears a reasonable relationship to a legitimate governmental end and the record reveals that the rule effectuates the governmental policy objective the agency has sought to attain, and is not arbitrary. They apply a *de novo* standard when they review an agency's application of the law in rulemaking and insist on adherence to statutory procedures when agencies formulate rules. Reviewing courts often apply the "substantial evidence" standard on a less stringent basis because the record in rulemaking proceedings often includes technical literature, expert advice, and empirical data.

Little v. Traynor,[95] a 1997 decision of the North Dakota Supreme Court typifies the approach of state courts to judicial review of rulemaking. There the court explained that in an appeal from an administrative agency's rulemaking action, the court must affirm the agency's rulemaking action unless: the provisions of North Dakota law[96] have not been substantially complied with in the proceedings, the rule is unconstitutional on the face of the language adopted, the rule is beyond the scope of the agency's authority to adopt, or the rule is on the face of the language adopted an arbitrary or capricious application of authority granted by statute. Box 9.4 describes a case in which an appellate court remands a lower court decision with instructions to consider whether a zoning board's decision was supported by competent, substantial evidence.

Legal Rules Affecting Administrative Review

Judicial opinions on administrative law are likely to employ unfamiliar legal terms. These include *res judicata,* **collateral estoppel, laches,** and **harmless error.**

Under the common law the doctrine of *res judicata* (a matter adjudicated) prevents a party from relitigating a matter that has once been judicially determined. The doctrine comes into play less frequently in administrative law; nevertheless, if there has been a prior judicial or administrative proceeding with the same parties involving the same claim, the prior final order or judgment becomes *res judicata* and bars relitigation of the claim. A related term is collateral estoppel, which "estops" (i.e., prevents) a party from relitigating an issue that has been determined as between them in a prior administrative or judicial proceeding. In administrative law, collateral estoppel is often referred to as the doctrine of **issue preclusion.** The third term, laches, is a common-law doctrine that holds that one who unreasonably delays asserting a right and thereby prejudices another party, is barred from asserting a claim.

Courts sometimes refer to a **waiver,** which is a voluntary relinquishment of a known right. Finally, courts will sometimes decide that an error is so grave that the reviewing court will recognize it even though no one brought the matter to the attention of the administrative agency or lower court. This is referred to as **fundamental error.** Courts more frequently cite to errors committed in the lower court or administrative agency, but denominate them as harmless errors. A "harmless" error is one that does not affect the substantive rights of a party or affect the outcome of a court proceeding.

Freeman Hall, d/b/a Freeman's College City Lounge v. Alabama Alcoholic Beverage Control

---

BOX 9.4 Case in Point

Judicial Review of Legislative and Quasi-Judicial Actions in Land Use Zoning
Hirt v. Board of County Commissioners of Polk County
Florida Court of Appeal, Second District
578 So. 2d 415 (Fla. App. 1991)

After a zoning hearing before the Board of County Commissioners where an opportunity for cross-examination was afforded, and a verbatim transcript of the proceedings was made, the Board approved Jack M. Watkins' petition to allow a planned unit development of 258 home sites on a 58.6 acre tract of land. Thomas J. Hirt, an adjacent landowner, petitioned the local circuit court for review, alleging a lack of substantial evidence to support the Board's decision. The court dismissed Hirt's petition and the Court of Appeals granted review.

The appellate court pointed out that land use zoning decisions are usually classified as legislative, for example, enactment of an ordinance, or quasi-judicial, for example, where compliance with an ordinance must be measured according to stated criteria. In challenging a legislative enactment petitioners generally seek an injunction or declaratory judgment and, if the ordinance was properly enacted and constitutional, courts generally uphold a zoning ordinance as long as it is "fairly debatable."

Hirt was not contesting validity of the underlying ordinance; rather he was challenging the Board's decision as to whether Watkins's proposed planned unit development met the required zoning criteria. The Board was acting in a quasi-judicial capacity, and the standard for judicial review is whether there was competent, substantial evidence before the Board that the proposed development met the required criteria of the zoning ordinance. Accordingly the appellate court remanded Hirt's petition to the lower court with directions that it review the Board's decision to determine if it was supported by competent, substantial evidence.

Board, **a decision of the Alabama Court of Civil Appeals, is reprinted at the end of the chapter. This decision nicely illustrates, in a state context, the following concepts discussed in this chapter: 1) Failure to preserve error in lower proceeding; 2) Adequacy of notice; 3) Presumption of correctness based on the agency's presumed expertise; 4) Standard of review: substantial evidence to support agency findings, whether the agency's decision is reasonable and not arbitrary; and 5) Whether the agency acted within its constitutional and statutory powers.**

CONCLUSION

Judicial review of administrative agency action and lower court decisions ruling on agency actions is firmly established in the federal and state judicial systems. Although essential to the conduct of an orderly review, the rules that govern judicial review are not merely mechanical, they have a sound rationale. Litigants who seek review must meet threshold requirements of justiciability by demonstrating a protected interest. This avoids unnecessary litigation and under the doctrine of primary jurisdiction respects the authority of administrative agencies to apply their expertise to resolve the economic and social problems committed to their jurisdiction. Courts further protect the autonomy of agencies by limiting review to constitutional issues, compliance with statutory mandates, and by deferring to an agency's interpretation of a statute it administers, rather than substituting their own judgment. Reviewing courts protect the legitimate interests of litigants by assuring that factual findings by agencies are based on substantial evidence and that agency rulings correctly apply the law and are not arbitrary or capricious.

KEY TERMS

1981 Model State Administrative Procedure Act (1981 MSAPA)

abuse of discretion standard

administrative law judge (ALJ)

Administrative Procedure Act (APA)

agency's construction of a statute

case or controversy

collateral estoppel

collateral review

comity

de novo standard

declaratory judgments

exhaustion of administrative remedies

finality

findings of fact

fundamental error

gatekeeping devices

granting cert

habeas corpus

hard look doctrine

harmless error

individualized harm

injury in fact

issue preclusion

judicial review

jurisdiction

justiciability

laches

legislative intent

mandamus

mandatory injunction

matter committed to agency discretion

mootness

plain meaning of statutory language

preservation of error rule

presumption of correctness

primary jurisdiction

qui tam actions

res judicata

ripeness

standing

statutory preclusion of judicial review

stay

subject matter jurisdiction

substantial evidence

waiver

writ of certiorari

writ of prohibition

zone of interests

QUESTIONS FOR THOUGHT AND DISCUSSION

1. What functions do judicial reviews serve for (a) litigants in administrative proceedings? (b) the general public?

2. Where judicial review is precluded by federal statute, what methods can be employed to attack the constitutionality of an order rendered by a federal administrative agency?

3. Under what circumstances do federal courts not require a litigant to exhaust administrative remedies before seeking judicial review?

4. What criteria do courts impose before a public interest group has standing to seek judicial review of administrative action?

5. Give an example of a scenario when a state court would likely review an issue even if that issue had become moot.

6. Explain how federal courts apply the "case or controversy" clause of Article III of the U.S. Constitution to impose the doctrines of "finality" and "ripeness."

7. What standard of review do courts apply in reviewing agency (a) interpretations of law? (b) findings of fact? (c) discretionary action?

8. Under what circumstances would a petitioner seek a "stay" pending review of an agency decision?

9. What rationale supports the judicial view of upholding an agency's interpretation of its own rules even when the court may conclude that an alternative interpretation may better define an agency rule?

10. Explain the difference between *res judicata* and collateral estoppel.

EDITED CASE Citizens to Preserve Overton Park v. Volpe
United States Supreme Court, 401 U.S. 402 (1971)

Justice Marshall wrote the opinion of the Court, as delivered by Justice Stewart.

The growing public concern about the quality of our natural environment has prompted Congress in recent years to enact legislation designed to curb the accelerating destruction of our country's natural beauty. We are concerned in this case with § 4 (f) of the Department of Transportation Act of 1966, as amended, and § 18 (a) of the Federal-Aid Highway Act of 1968, 82 Stat. 823, 23 U.S.C. § 138 (1964 ed., Supp. V) (hereafter § 138). These statutes prohibit the Secretary of Transportation from authorizing the use of federal funds to finance the construction of highways through public parks if a "feasible and prudent" alternative route exists. If no such route is available, the statutes allow him to approve construction through parks only if there has been "all possible planning to minimize harm" to the park.

Petitioners, private citizens as well as local and national conservation organizations, contend that the Secretary has violated these statutes by authorizing the expenditure of federal funds for the construction of a six-lane interstate highway through a public park in Memphis, Tennessee. Their claim was rejected by the District Court, which granted the Secretary's motion for summary judgment, and the Court of Appeals for the Sixth Circuit affirmed. After oral argument, this Court granted a stay that halted construction and, treating the application for the stay as a petition for certiorari, granted review. . . . We now reverse the judgment below and remand for further proceedings in the District Court.

Overton Park is a 342-acre city park located near the center of Memphis. The park contains a zoo, a nine-hole municipal golf course, an outdoor theater, nature trails, a bridle path, an art academy, picnic areas, and 170 acres of forest. The proposed highway, which is to be a six-lane, high-speed, expressway, will sever the zoo from the rest of the park. Although the roadway will be depressed below ground level except where it crosses a small creek, 26 acres of the park will be destroyed. The highway is to be a segment of Interstate Highway I-40, part of the National System of Interstate and Defense Highways. I-40 will provide Memphis with a major east-west expressway which will allow easier access to downtown Memphis from the residential areas on the eastern edge of the city.

Although the route through the park was approved by the Bureau of Public Roads in 1956 and by the Federal Highway Administrator in 1966, the enactment of § 4 (f) of the Department of Transportation Act prevented distribution of federal funds for the section of the highway designated to go through Overton Park until the Secretary of Transportation determined whether the requirements of § 4 (f) had been met. Federal funding for the rest of the project was, however, available; and the state acquired a right-of-way on both sides of the park. In April 1968, the Secretary announced that he concurred in the judgment of local officials that I-40 should be built through the park. And in September 1969 the State acquired the right-of-way inside Overton Park from the city. Final approval for the project—the route as well as the design—was not announced until November 1969, after Congress had reiterated in § 138 of the Federal-Aid Highway Act that highway construction through public parks was to be restricted. Neither announcement approving the route and design of I-40 was accompanied by a statement of the Secretary's factual findings. He did not indicate why he believed there were no feasible and prudent alternative routes or why design changes could not be made to reduce the harm to the park.

Petitioners contend that the Secretary's action is invalid without such formal findings and that the Secretary did not make an independent determination but merely relied on the judgment of the Memphis City Council. They also contend that it would be "feasible and prudent" to route I-40 around Overton Park either to the north or to the south. And they argue that if these alternative routes are not "feasible and prudent," the present plan does not include "all possible" methods for reducing harm to the park. Petitioners claim that I-40 could be built under the park by using either of two possible tunneling methods, and they claim that, at a minimum, by using advanced drainage techniques the expressway could be depressed below ground level along the entire route through the park including the section that crosses the small creek.

(Continued)

EDITED CASE   Citizens to Preserve Overton Park v. Volpe (Continued)

Respondents argue that it was unnecessary for the Secretary to make formal findings, and that he did, in fact, exercise his own independent judgment which was supported by the facts. In the District Court, respondents introduced affidavits, prepared specifically for this litigation, which indicated that the Secretary had made the decision and that the decision was supportable. These affidavits were contradicted by affidavits introduced by petitioners, who also sought to take the deposition of a former Federal Highway Administrator who had participated in the decision to route I-40 through Overton Park.

The District Court and the Court of Appeals found that formal findings by the Secretary were not necessary and refused to order the deposition of the former Federal Highway Administrator because those courts believed that probing of the mental processes of an administrative decision-maker was prohibited. And, believing that the Secretary's authority was wide and reviewing courts' authority narrow in the approval of highway routes, the lower courts held that the affidavits contained no basis for a determination that the Secretary had exceeded his authority.

We agree that formal findings were not required. But we do not believe that in this case judicial review based solely on litigation affidavits was adequate.

A threshold question—whether petitioners are entitled to any judicial review—is easily answered. Section 701 of the Administrative Procedure Act . . . provides that the action of "each authority of the Government of the United States," which includes the Department of Transportation, is subject to judicial review except where there is a statutory prohibition on review or where "agency action is committed to agency discretion by law." In this case, there is no indication that Congress sought to prohibit judicial review and there is most certainly no "showing of 'clear and convincing evidence' of a . . . legislative intent" to restrict access to judicial review. . . .

Similarly, the Secretary's decision here does not fall within the exception for action "committed to agency discretion." This is a very narrow exception. . . . The legislative history of the Administrative Procedure Act indicates that it is applicable in those rare instances where "statutes are drawn in such broad terms that in a given case there is no law to apply." . . .

Section 4(f) of the Department of Transportation Act and § 138 of the Federal-Aid Highway Act are clear and specific directives. Both the Department of Transportation Act and the Federal-Aid Highway Act provide that the Secretary "shall not approve any program or project" that requires the use of any public parkland "unless (1) there is no feasible and prudent alternative to the use of such land, and (2) such program includes all possible planning to minimize harm to such park . . . ." . . . This language is a plain and explicit bar to the use of federal funds for construction of highways through parks—only the most unusual situations are exempted.

Despite the clarity of the statutory language, respondents argue that the Secretary has wide discretion. They recognize that the requirement that there be no "feasible" alternative route admits of little administrative discretion. For this exemption to apply the Secretary must find that as a matter of sound engineering it would not be feasible to build the highway along any other route. Respondents argue, however, that the requirement that there be no other "prudent" route requires the Secretary to engage in a wide-ranging balancing of competing interests. They contend that the Secretary should weigh the detriment resulting from the destruction of parkland against the cost of other routes, safety considerations, and other factors, and determine on the basis of the importance that he attaches to these other factors whether, on balance, alternative feasible routes would be "prudent."

But no such wide-ranging endeavor was intended. It is obvious that in most cases considerations of cost, directness of route, and community disruption will indicate that parkland should be used for highway construction whenever possible. Although it may be necessary to transfer funds from one jurisdiction to another, there will always be a smaller outlay required from the public purse when parkland is used since the public already owns the land and there will be no need to pay for right-of-way. And since people do not live or work in parks, if a highway is built on parkland no one will have to leave his home or give up his business. Such factors are common to substantially all highway construction. Thus, if Congress intended these factors to be on an equal footing with preservation of parkland there would have been no need for the statutes.

EDITED CASE   Citizens to Preserve Overton Park v. Volpe (Continued)

Congress clearly did not intend that cost and disruption of the community were to be ignored by the Secretary. But the very existence of the statutes indicates that protection of parkland was to be given paramount importance. The few green havens that are public parks were not to be lost unless there were truly unusual factors present in a particular case or the cost or community disruption resulting from alternative routes reached extraordinary magnitudes. If the statutes are to have any meaning, the Secretary cannot approve the destruction of parkland unless he finds that alternative routes present unique problems.

Plainly, there is "law to apply" and thus the exemption for action "committed to agency discretion" is inapplicable. But the existence of judicial review is only the start: the standard for review must also be determined. For that we must look to § 706 of the Administrative Procedure Act, . . . which provides that a "reviewing court shall . . . hold unlawful and set aside agency action, findings, and conclusions found" not to meet six separate standards. In all cases agency action must be set aside if the action was "arbitrary, capricious, an abuse of discretion, or otherwise not in accordance with law" or if the action failed to meet statutory, procedural, or constitutional requirements. . . . In certain narrow, specifically limited situations, the agency action is to be set aside if the action was not supported by "substantial evidence." And in other equally narrow circumstances the reviewing court is to engage in a de novo review of the action and set it aside if it was "unwarranted by the facts." . . .

Petitioners argue that the Secretary's approval of the construction of I-40 through Overton Park is subject to one or the other of these latter two standards of limited applicability. First, they contend that the "substantial evidence" standard of § 706 (2) (E) must be applied. In the alternative, they claim that § 706 (2) (F) applies and that there must be a de novo review to determine if the Secretary's action was "unwarranted by the facts." Neither of these standards is, however, applicable.

Review under the substantial-evidence test is authorized only when the agency action is taken pursuant to a rulemaking provision of the Administrative Procedure Act itself, . . . or when the agency action is based on a public adjudicatory hearing. . . . The Secretary's decision to allow the expenditure of federal funds to build I-40 through Overton Park was plainly not an exercise of a rule-making function. . . . And the only hearing that is required by either the Administrative Procedure Act or the statutes regulating the distribution of federal funds for highway construction is a public hearing conducted by local officials for the purpose of informing the community about the proposed project and eliciting community views on the design and route. . . . The hearing is nonadjudicatory, quasi-legislative in nature. It is not designed to produce a record that is to be the basis of agency action—the basic requirement for substantial-evidence review. . . .

Petitioners' alternative argument also fails. De novo review of whether the Secretary's decision was "unwarranted by the facts" is authorized by § 706 (2) (F) in only two circumstances. First, such de novo review is authorized when the action is adjudicatory in nature and the agency factfinding procedures are inadequate. And, there may be independent judicial fact-finding when issues that were not before the agency are raised in a proceeding to enforce nonadjudicatory agency action. . . . Neither situation exists here.

Even though there is no de novo review in this case and the Secretary's approval of the route of I-40 does not have ultimately to meet the substantial-evidence test, the generally applicable standards of 706 require that the reviewing court engage in a substantial inquiry. Certainly, the Secretary's decision is entitled to a presumption of regularity. . . . But that presumption is not to shield his action from a thorough, probing, in-depth review.

The court is first required to decide whether the Secretary acted within the scope of his authority. . . . This determination naturally begins with a delineation of the scope of the Secretary's authority and discretion. . . . As has been shown, Congress has specified only a small range of choices that the Secretary can make. Also involved in this initial inquiry is a determination of whether on the facts the Secretary's decision can reasonably be said to be within that range. The reviewing court must consider whether the Secretary properly construed his authority to approve the use of parkland as limited to situations where there are no

(Continued)

EDITED CASE   Citizens to Preserve Overton Park v. Volpe (Continued)

---

feasible alternative routes or where feasible alternative routes involve uniquely difficult problems. And the reviewing court must be able to find that the Secretary could have reasonably believed that in this case there are no feasible alternatives or that alternatives do involve unique problems.

Scrutiny of the facts does not end, however, with the determination that the Secretary has acted within the scope of his statutory authority. Section 706 (2) (A) requires a finding that the actual choice made was not "arbitrary, capricious, an abuse of discretion, or otherwise not in accordance with law." . . . To make this finding the court must consider whether the decision was based on a consideration of the relevant factors and whether there has been a clear error of judgment. . . . Although this inquiry into the facts is to be searching and careful, the ultimate standard of review is a narrow one. The court is not empowered to substitute its judgment for that of the agency.

The final inquiry is whether the Secretary's action followed the necessary procedural requirements. Here the only procedural error alleged is the failure of the Secretary to make formal findings and state his reason for allowing the highway to be built through the park.

Undoubtedly, review of the Secretary's action is hampered by his failure to make such findings, but the absence of formal findings does not necessarily require that the case be remanded to the Secretary. Neither the Department of Transportation Act nor the Federal-Aid Highway Act requires such formal findings. Moreover, the Administrative Procedure Act requirements that there be formal findings in certain rulemaking and adjudicatory proceedings do not apply to the Secretary's action here. . . . And, although formal findings may be required in some cases in the absence of statutory directives when the nature of the agency action is ambiguous, those situations are rare. . . . Plainly, there is no ambiguity here; the Secretary has approved the construction of I-40 through Overton Park and has approved a specific design for the project.

Petitioners contend that although there may not be a statutory requirement that the Secretary make formal findings and even though this may not be a case for the reviewing court to impose a requirement that findings be made, Department of Transportation regulations require them. This

argument is based on DOT Order 5610.1, which requires the Secretary to make formal findings when he approves the use of parkland for highway construction but which was issued after the route for I-40 was approved. Petitioners argue that even though the order was not in effect at the time approval was given to the Overton Park project and even though the order was not intended to have retrospective effect the order represents the law at the time of this Court's decision and under *Thorpe v. Housing Authority*, 393 U.S. 268, 281-282 (1969), should be applied to this case.

The *Thorpe* litigation resulted from an attempt to evict a tenant from a federally funded housing project under circumstances that suggested that the eviction was prompted by the tenant's objections to the management of the project. Despite repeated requests, the Housing Authority would not give an explanation for its action. The tenant claimed that the eviction interfered with her exercise of First Amendment rights and that the failure to state the reasons for the eviction and to afford her a hearing denied her due process. After denial of relief in the state courts, this Court granted certiorari "to consider whether [the tenant] was denied due process by the Housing Authority's refusal to state the reasons for her eviction and to afford her a hearing at which she could contest the sufficiency of those reasons." . . .

While the case was pending in this Court, the Department of Housing and Urban Development issued regulations requiring Housing Authority officials to inform tenants of the reasons for an eviction and to give a tenant the opportunity to reply. The case was then remanded to the state courts to determine if the HUD regulations were applicable to that case. The state court held them not to be applicable and this Court reversed on the ground that the general rule is "that an appellate court must apply the law in effect at the time it renders its decision." . . .

While we do not question that DOT Order 5610.1 constitutes the law in effect at the time of our decision, we do not believe that *Thorpe* compels us to remand for the Secretary to make formal findings. Here, unlike the situation in *Thorpe*, there has been a change in circumstances— additional right-of-way has been cleared and the 26-acre right-of-way inside Overton Park has been purchased by the State. Moreover, there is an

---

EDITED CASE   Citizens to Preserve Overton Park v. Volpe (Continued)

---

administrative record that allows the full, prompt review of the Secretary's action that is sought without additional delay which would result from having a remand to the Secretary.

That administrative record is not, however, before us. The lower courts based their review on the litigation affidavits that were presented. These affidavits were merely "post hoc" rationalizations, . . . which have traditionally been found to be an inadequate basis for review. . . . And they clearly do not constitute the "whole record" compiled by the agency: the basis for review required by § 706 of the Administrative Procedure Act. . . .

Thus it is necessary to remand this case to the District Court for plenary review of the Secretary's decision. That review is to be based on the full administrative record that was before the Secretary at the time he made his decision. But since the bare record may not disclose the factors that were considered or the Secretary's construction of the evidence it may be necessary for the District Court to require some explanation in order to determine if the Secretary acted within the scope of his authority and if the Secretary's action was justifiable under the applicable standard.

The court may require the administrative officials who participated in the decision to give testimony explaining their action. Of course, such inquiry into the mental processes of administrative decisionmakers is usually to be avoided. . . . And where there are administrative findings that were made at the same time as the decision, as was the case in Morgan, there must be a strong showing of bad faith or improper behavior before such inquiry may be made. But here there are no such formal findings and it may be that the only way there can be effective judicial review is by examining the decisionmakers themselves. . . .

The District Court is not, however, required to make such an inquiry. It may be that the Secretary can prepare formal findings including the information required by DOT Order 5610.1 that will provide an adequate explanation for his action. Such an explanation will, to some extent, be a "post hoc rationalization" and thus must be viewed critically. If the District Court decides that additional explanation is necessary, that court should consider which method will prove the most expeditious so that full review may be had as soon as possible.

Reversed and remanded.

Justice Douglas took no part in the consideration or decision of this case.

Separate opinion of *Justice Black*, with whom *Justice Brennan* joins.

I agree with the Court that the judgment of the Court of Appeals is wrong and that its action should be reversed. I do not agree that the whole matter should be remanded to the District Court. I think the case should be sent back to the Secretary of Transportation. It is apparent from the Court's opinion today that the Secretary of Transportation completely failed to comply with the duty imposed upon him by Congress not to permit a federally financed public highway to run through a public park "unless (1) there is no feasible and prudent alternative to the use of such land, and (2) such program includes all possible planning to minimize harm to such park . . . ." That congressional command should not be taken lightly by the Secretary or by this Court. It represents a solemn determination of the highest law-making body of this Nation that the beauty and health-giving facilities of our parks are not to be taken away for public roads without hearings, fact-findings, and policy determinations under the supervision of a Cabinet officer— the Secretary of Transportation. The Act of Congress in connection with other federal highway aid legislation, it seems to me, calls for hearings— hearings that a court can review, hearings that demonstrate more than mere arbitrary defiance by the Secretary. Whether the findings growing out of such hearings are labeled "formal" or "informal" appears to me to be no more than an exercise in semantics. Whatever the hearing requirements might be, the Department of Transportation failed to meet them in this case. I regret that I am compelled to conclude for myself that, except for some too-late formulations, apparently coming from the Solicitor General's office, this record contains not one word to indicate that the Secretary raised even a finger to comply with the command of Congress. It is our duty, I believe, to remand this whole matter back to the Secretary of Transportation for him to give this matter the hearing it deserves in full good-faith obedience to the Act of Congress. That Act was obviously passed to protect our public parks from forays by road builders except in the

(Continued)

EDITED CASE   Citizens to Preserve Overton Park v. Volpe (Continued)

---

most extraordinary and imperative circumstances. This record does not demonstrate the existence of such circumstances. I dissent from the Court's failure to send the case back to the Secretary, whose duty has not yet been performed.

Mr. Justice Blackmun, concurring.

I fully join the Court in its opinion and in its judgment. I merely wish to state the obvious: (1) The case comes to this Court as the end product of more than a decade of endeavor to solve the interstate highway problem at Memphis. (2) The administrative decisions under attack here are not those of a single Secretary; some were made by the present Secretary's predecessor and, before him, by the Department of Commerce's Bureau of Public Roads. (3) The 1966 Act and the 1968 Act have cut across former methods and here have imposed new standards and conditions upon a situation that already was largely developed.

This undoubtedly is why the record is sketchy and less than one would expect if the project were one which had been instituted after the passage of the 1966 Act.

EDITED CASE   Heckler v. Chaney
United States Supreme Court, 470 U.S. 821 (1985)

[In this case the Supreme Court considers whether an agency's decision not to pursue an enforcement action is subject to judicial review under the Administrative Procedure Act.]

Justice Rehnquist delivered the opinion of the Court.

. . . Respondents are several prison inmates convicted of capital offenses and sentenced to death by lethal injection of drugs. They petitioned the Food and Drug Administration, alleging that under the circumstances the use of these drugs for capital punishment violated the Federal Food, Drug, and Cosmetic Act . . . (FDCA), and requesting that the FDA take various enforcement actions to prevent these violations. The FDA refused their request. We review here a decision of the Court of Appeals for the District of Columbia Circuit, which held the FDA's refusal to take enforcement actions both reviewable and an abuse of discretion, and remanded the case with directions that the agency be required "to fulfill its statutory function." . . .

I

Respondents have been sentenced to death by lethal injection of drugs under the laws of the States of Oklahoma and Texas. Those States, and several others, have recently adopted this method for carrying out the capital sentence. Respondents first petitioned the FDA, claiming that the drugs used by the States for this purpose, although approved by the FDA for the medical purposes stated on their labels, were not approved for use in human executions. They alleged that the drugs had not been tested for the purpose for which they were to be used, and that, given that the drugs would likely be administered by untrained personnel, it was also likely that the drugs would not induce the quick and painless death intended. They urged that use of these drugs for human execution was the "unapproved use of an approved drug" and constituted a violation of the Act's prohibitions against "misbranding." They also suggested that the FDCA's requirements for approval of "new drugs" applied, since these drugs were now being used for a new purpose. Accordingly, respondents claimed that the FDA was required to approve the drugs as "safe and effective" for human execution before they could be distributed in interstate commerce. . . . They therefore requested the FDA to take various investigatory and enforcement actions to prevent these perceived violations; they requested the FDA to affix warnings to the labels of all the drugs stating that they were unapproved and unsafe for human execution, to send statements to the drug manu-

---

EDITED CASE   Heckler v. Chaney (Continued)

---

facturers and prison administrators stating that the drugs should not be so used, and to adopt procedures for seizing the drugs from state prisons and to recommend the prosecution of all those in the chain of distribution who knowingly distribute or purchase the drugs with intent to use them for human execution.

The FDA Commissioner responded, refusing to take the requested actions. The Commissioner first detailed his disagreement with respondents' understanding of the scope of FDA jurisdiction over the unapproved use of approved drugs for human execution, concluding that FDA jurisdiction in the area was generally unclear but in any event should not be exercised to interfere with this particular aspect of state criminal justice systems. He went on to state:

> "Were FDA clearly to have jurisdiction in the area, moreover, we believe we would be authorized to decline to exercise it under our inherent discretion to decline to pursue certain enforcement matters. The unapproved use of approved drugs is an area in which the case law is far from uniform. Generally, enforcement proceedings in this area are initiated only when there is a serious danger to the public health or a blatant scheme to defraud. We cannot conclude that those dangers are present under State lethal injection laws, which are duly authorized statutory enactments in furtherance of proper State functions. . . ."

Respondents then filed the instant suit in the United States District Court for the District of Columbia, claiming the same violations of the FDCA and asking that the FDA be required to take the same enforcement actions requested in the prior petition. Jurisdiction was grounded in the general federal-question jurisdiction statute, . . . and review of the agency action was sought under the judicial review provisions of the APA. . . . The District Court granted summary judgment for petitioner. It began with the proposition that "decisions of executive departments and agencies to refrain from instituting investigative and enforcement proceedings are essentially unreviewable by the courts." . . . The court then cited case law stating that nothing in the FDCA indicated an intent to circumscribe the FDA's enforcement discretion or to make it reviewable.

A divided panel of the Court of Appeals for the District of Columbia Circuit reversed. The majority began by discussing the FDA's jurisdiction over the unapproved use of approved drugs for human execution, and concluded that the FDA did have jurisdiction over such a use. The court then addressed the Government's assertion of unreviewable discretion to refuse enforcement action. It first discussed this Court's opinions which have held that there is a general presumption that all agency decisions are reviewable under the APA, at least to assess whether the actions were "arbitrary, capricious, or an abuse of discretion." . . . It noted that the APA . . . only precludes judicial review of final agency action—including refusals to act—when review is precluded by statute, or "committed to agency discretion by law."

. . . We granted certiorari to review the implausible result that the FDA is required to exercise its enforcement power to ensure that States only use drugs that are "safe and effective" for human execution. . . . We reverse.

II

The Court of Appeals' decision addressed three questions: (1) Whether the FDA had jurisdiction to undertake the enforcement actions requested, (2) whether if it did have jurisdiction its refusal to take those actions was subject to judicial review, and (3) whether if reviewable its refusal was arbitrary, capricious, or an abuse of discretion. In reaching our conclusion that the Court of Appeals was wrong, however, we need not and do not address the thorny question of the FDA's jurisdiction. For us, this case turns on the important question of the extent to which determinations by the FDA not to exercise its enforcement authority over the use of drugs in interstate commerce may be judicially reviewed. That decision in turn involves the construction of two separate but necessarily interrelated statutes, the APA and the FDCA.

The APA's comprehensive provisions for judicial review of "agency actions" are contained in 5 U.S.C. §§ 701-706. Any person "adversely affected or aggrieved" by agency action, see § 702, including a "failure to act," is entitled to "judicial review thereof," as long as the action is a "final agency action for which there is no other adequate

(Continued)

EDITED CASE   Heckler v. Chaney (Continued)

---

remedy in a court," see 704. The standards to be applied on review are governed by the provisions of § 706. But before any review at all may be had, a party must first clear the hurdle of § 701(a). That section provides that the chapter on judicial review "applies, according to the provisions thereof, except to the extent that—(1) statutes preclude judicial review; or (2) agency action is committed to agency discretion by law." Petitioner urges that the decision of the FDA to refuse enforcement is an action "committed to agency discretion by law" under § 701(a)(2).

This Court has not had occasion to interpret this second exception in § 701(a) in any great detail. On its face, the section does not obviously lend itself to any particular construction; indeed, one might wonder what difference exists between (a)(1) and (a)(2). The former section seems easy in application; it requires construction of the substantive statute involved to determine whether Congress intended to preclude judicial review of certain decisions. . . . But one could read the language "committed to agency discretion by law" in (a)(2) to require a similar inquiry. In addition, commentators have pointed out that construction of (a)(2) is further complicated by the tension between a literal reading of (a)(2), which exempts from judicial review those decisions committed to agency "discretion," and the primary scope of review prescribed by § 706(2)(A)—whether the agency's action was "arbitrary, capricious, or an abuse of discretion." How is it, they ask, that an action committed to agency discretion can be unreviewable and yet courts still can review agency actions for abuse of that discretion? . . . The APA's legislative history provides little help on this score. Mindful, however, of the common-sense principle of statutory construction that sections of a statute generally should be read "to give effect, if possible, to every clause," . . . we think there is a proper construction of (a)(2) which satisfies each of these concerns.

This Court first discussed (a)(2) in *Citizens to Preserve Overton Park v. Volpe*, 401 U.S. 402 (1971). That case dealt with the Secretary of Transportation's approval of the building of an interstate highway through a park in Memphis, Tennessee. The relevant federal statute provided that the Secretary "shall not approve" any program or project using public parkland unless the Secretary

first determined that no feasible alternatives were available. . . . Interested citizens challenged the Secretary's approval under the APA, arguing that he had not satisfied the substantive statute's requirements. This Court first addressed the "threshold question" of whether the agency's action was at all reviewable. After setting out the language of § 701(a), the Court stated:

> "In this case, there is no indication that Congress sought to prohibit judicial review and there is most certainly no 'showing of "clear and convincing evidence" of a . . . legislative intent' to restrict access to judicial review. . . . "Similarly, the Secretary's decision here does not fall within the exception for action 'committed to agency discretion.' This is a very narrow exception. . . . The legislative history of the Administrative Procedure Act indicates that it is applicable in those rare instances where 'statutes are drawn in such broad terms that in a given case there is no law to apply.' " . . .

The above quote answers several of the questions raised by the language of § 701(a), although it raises others. First, it clearly separates the exception provided by (a)(1) from the (a)(2) exception. The former applies when Congress has expressed an intent to preclude judicial review. The latter applies in different circumstances; even where Congress has not affirmatively precluded review, review is not to be had if the statute is drawn so that a court would have no meaningful standard against which to judge the agency's exercise of discretion. In such a case, the statute ("law") can be taken to have "committed" the decisionmaking to the agency's judgment absolutely. This construction avoids conflict with the "abuse of discretion" standard of review in 706—if no judicially manageable standards are available for judging how and when an agency should exercise its discretion, then it is impossible to evaluate agency action for "abuse of discretion." In addition, this construction satisfies the principle of statutory construction mentioned earlier, by identifying a separate class of cases to which § 701(a)(2) applies.

To this point our analysis does not differ significantly from that of the Court of Appeals. That court purported to apply the "no law to apply" standard of *Overton Park*. We disagree, however,

---

EDITED CASE   Heckler v. Chaney (Continued)

---

with that court's insistence that the "narrow construction" of (a)(2) required application of a presumption of reviewability even to an agency's decision not to undertake certain enforcement actions. Here we think the Court of Appeals broke with tradition, case law, and sound reasoning.

Overton Park did not involve an agency's refusal to take requested enforcement action. It involved an affirmative act of approval under a statute that set clear guidelines for determining when such approval should be given. Refusals to take enforcement steps generally involve precisely the opposite situation, and in that situation we think the presumption is that judicial review is not available. This Court has recognized on several occasions over many years that an agency's decision not to prosecute or enforce, whether through civil or criminal process, is a decision generally committed to an agency's absolute discretion. . . . This recognition of the existence of discretion is attributable in no small part to the general unsuitability for judicial review of agency decisions to refuse enforcement.

The reasons for this general unsuitability are many. First, an agency decision not to enforce often involves a complicated balancing of a number of factors which are peculiarly within its expertise. Thus, the agency must not only assess whether a violation has occurred, but whether agency resources are best spent on this violation or another, whether the agency is likely to succeed if it acts, whether the particular enforcement action requested best fits the agency's overall policies, and, indeed, whether the agency has enough resources to undertake the action at all. An agency generally cannot act against each technical violation of the statute it is charged with enforcing. The agency is far better equipped than the courts to deal with the many variables involved in the proper ordering of its priorities. Similar concerns animate the principles of administrative law that courts generally will defer to an agency's construction of the statute it is charged with implementing, and to the procedures it adopts for implementing that statute. . . .

In addition to these administrative concerns, we note that when an agency refuses to act it generally does not exercise its coercive power over an individual's liberty or property rights, and thus does not infringe upon areas that courts often are called upon to protect. Similarly, when an agency does act to enforce, that action itself provides a focus for judicial review, inasmuch as the agency must have exercised its power in some manner. The action at least can be reviewed to determine whether the agency exceeded its statutory powers. . . . Finally, we recognize that an agency's refusal to institute proceedings shares to some extent the characteristics of the decision of a prosecutor in the Executive Branch not to indict—a decision which has long been regarded as the special province of the Executive Branch, inasmuch as it is the Executive who is charged by the Constitution to "take Care that the Laws be faithfully executed." . . .

We of course only list the above concerns to facilitate understanding of our conclusion that an agency's decision not to take enforcement action should be presumed immune from judicial review under § 701(a)(2). For good reasons, such a decision has traditionally been "committed to agency discretion," and we believe that the Congress enacting the APA did not intend to alter that tradition. . . . In so stating, we emphasize that the decision is only presumptively unreviewable; the presumption may be rebutted where the substantive statute has provided guidelines for the agency to follow in exercising its enforcement powers. Thus, in establishing this presumption in the APA, Congress did not set agencies free to disregard legislative direction in the statutory scheme that the agency administers. Congress may limit an agency's exercise of enforcement power if it wishes, either by setting substantive priorities, or by otherwise circumscribing an agency's power to discriminate among issues or cases it will pursue. How to determine when Congress has done so is the question left open by *Overton Park*.

. . . The danger that agencies may not carry out their delegated powers with sufficient vigor does not necessarily lead to the conclusion that courts are the most appropriate body to police this aspect of their performance. That decision is in the first instance for Congress, and we therefore turn to the FDCA to determine whether in this case Congress has provided us with "law to apply." If it

(Continued)

EDITED CASE   Heckler v. Chaney (Continued)

---

has indicated an intent to circumscribe agency enforcement discretion, and has provided meaningful standards for defining the limits of that discretion, there is "law to apply" under § 701(a)(2), and courts may require that the agency follow that law; if it has not, then an agency refusal to institute proceedings is a decision "committed to agency discretion by law" within the meaning of that section.

III

To enforce the various substantive prohibitions contained in the FDCA, the Act provides for injunctions, 21 U.S.C. § 332, criminal sanctions, § 333 and § 335, and seizure of any offending food, drug, or cosmetic article, § 334. The Act's general provision for enforcement, § 372, provides only that "[t]he Secretary is authorized to conduct examinations and investigations . . ." (emphasis added). . . . § 332 gives no indication of when an injunction should be sought, and § 334, providing for seizures, is framed in the permissive—the offending food, drug, or cosmetic "shall be liable to be proceeded against." The section on criminal sanctions states baldly that any person who violates the Act's substantive prohibitions "shall be imprisoned . . . or fined." Respondents argue that this statement mandates criminal prosecution of every violator of the Act but they adduce no indication in case law or legislative history that such was Congress' intention in using this language, which is commonly found in the criminal provisions of Title 18 of the United States Code. . . . We are unwilling to attribute such a sweeping meaning to this language, particularly since the Act charges the Secretary only with recommending prosecution; any criminal prosecutions must be instituted by the Attorney General. The Act's enforcement provisions thus commit complete discretion to the Secretary to decide how and when they should be exercised.

Respondents nevertheless present three separate authorities that they claim provide the courts with sufficient indicia of an intent to circumscribe enforcement discretion. Two of these may be dealt with summarily. First, we reject respondents' argument that the Act's substantive prohibitions of "misbranding" and the introduction of "new drugs" absent agency approval . . . supply us with "law to apply." These provisions are simply irrele-

vant to the agency's discretion to refuse to initiate proceedings.

We also find singularly unhelpful the agency "policy statement" on which the Court of Appeals placed great reliance. We would have difficulty with this statement's vague language even if it were a properly adopted agency rule. Although the statement indicates that the agency considered itself "obligated" to take certain investigative actions, that language did not arise in the course of discussing the agency's discretion to exercise its enforcement power, but rather in the context of describing agency policy with respect to unapproved uses of approved drugs by physicians. In addition, if read to circumscribe agency enforcement discretion, the statement conflicts with the agency rule on judicial review, . . . which states that "[t]he Commissioner shall object to judicial review . . . if (i) [t]he matter is committed by law to the discretion of the Commissioner, e. g., a decision to recommend or not to recommend civil or criminal enforcement action. . . ." But in any event the policy statement was attached to a rule that was never adopted. Whatever force such a statement might have, and leaving to one side the problem of whether an agency's rules might under certain circumstances provide courts with adequate guidelines for informed judicial review of decisions not to enforce, we do not think the language of the agency's "policy statement" can plausibly be read to override the agency's express assertion of unreviewable discretion contained in the above rule.

Respondents' third argument, based upon § 306 of the FDCA, merits only slightly more consideration. That section provides: "Nothing in this chapter shall be construed as requiring the Secretary to report for prosecution, or for the institution of libel or injunction proceedings, minor violations of this chapter whenever he believes that the public interest will be adequately served by a suitable written notice or ruling." . . .

Respondents seek to draw from this section the negative implication that the Secretary is required to report for prosecution all "major" violations of the Act, however those might be defined, and that it therefore supplies the needed indication of an intent to limit agency enforcement discretion. We think that this section simply does not give rise to

---

EDITED CASE Heckler v. Chaney (Continued)

---

the negative implication which respondents seek to draw from it. The section is not addressed to agency proceedings designed to discover the existence of violations, but applies only to a situation where a violation has already been established to the satisfaction of the agency. We do not believe the section speaks to the criteria which shall be used by the agency for investigating possible violations of the Act.

IV

We therefore conclude that the presumption that agency decisions not to institute proceedings are unreviewable under 5 U.S.C. § 701(a)(2) is not overcome by the enforcement provisions of the FDCA. The FDA's decision not to take the enforcement actions requested by respondents is therefore not subject to judicial review under the APA. The general exception to reviewability provided by § 701(a)(2) for action "committed to agency discretion" remains a narrow one, . . . but within that exception are included agency refusals to institute investigative or enforcement proceedings, unless Congress has indicated otherwise. In so holding, we essentially leave to Congress, and not to the courts, the decision as to whether an agency's refusal to institute proceedings should be judicially reviewable. No colorable claim is made in this case that the agency's refusal to institute proceedings violated any constitutional rights of respondents, and we do not address the issue that would be raised in such a case. . . . The fact that the drugs involved in this case are ultimately to be used in imposing the death penalty must not lead this Court or other courts to import profound differences of opinion over the meaning of the Eighth Amendment to the United States Constitution into the domain of administrative law. . . .

Justice Brennan, concurring. . . .

Justice Marshall, concurring in the judgment.

Easy cases at times produce bad law, for in the rush to reach a clearly ordained result, courts may offer up principles, doctrines, and statements that calmer reflection, and a fuller understanding of their implications in concrete settings, would eschew. In my view, the "presumption of unreviewability" announced today is a product of

that lack of discipline that easy cases make all too easy. The majority, eager to reverse what it goes out of its way to label as an "implausible result," . . . not only does reverse, as I agree it should, but along the way creates out of whole cloth the notion that agency decisions not to take "enforcement action" are unreviewable unless Congress has rather specifically indicated otherwise. Because this "presumption of unreviewability" is fundamentally at odds with rule-of-law principles firmly embedded in our jurisprudence, because it seeks to truncate an emerging line of judicial authority subjecting enforcement discretion to rational and principled constraint, and because, in the end, the presumption may well be indecipherable, one can only hope that it will come to be understood as a relic of a particular factual setting in which the full implications of such a presumption were neither confronted nor understood.

I write separately to argue for a different basis of decision: that refusals to enforce, like other agency actions, are reviewable in the absence of a "clear and convincing" congressional intent to the contrary, but that such refusals warrant deference when, as in this case, there is nothing to suggest that an agency with enforcement discretion has abused that discretion. . . .

The problem of agency refusal to act is one of the pressing problems of the modern administrative state, given the enormous powers, for both good and ill, that agency inaction, like agency action, holds over citizens. . . . [T]he problems and dangers of agency inaction are too important, too prevalent, and too multifaceted to admit of a single facile solution under which "enforcement" decisions are "presumptively unreviewable." Over time, I believe the approach announced today will come to be understood, not as mandating that courts cover their eyes and their reasoning power when asked to review an agency's failure to act, but as recognizing that courts must approach the substantive task of reviewing such failures with appropriate deference to an agency's legitimate need to set policy through the allocation of scarce budgetary and enforcement resources. Because the Court's approach, if taken literally, would take the courts out of the role of reviewing agency inaction in far too many cases, I join only the judgment today.

EDITED CASE Lujan v. National Wildlife Federation
United States Supreme Court, 497 U.S. 871 (1990)

[In this case the Supreme Court considers whether the National Wildlife Federation (an environmental interest group) has standing to challenge decisions of the Department of the Interior relative to the management of public lands.]

Justice Scalia delivered the opinion of the Court.

. . . Respondent filed this action in 1985 in the United States District Court for the District of Columbia against petitioners the United States Department of the Interior, the Secretary of the Interior, and the Director of the Bureau of Land Management (BLM), an agency within the Department. In its amended complaint, respondent alleged that petitioners had violated the Federal Land Policy and Management Act of 1976 (FLPMA), . . . the National Environmental Policy Act of 1969 (NEPA), . . . and 10(e) of the Administrative Procedure Act (APA), . . . in the course of administering what the complaint called the "land withdrawal review program" of the BLM. . . .

In 1976, Congress passed the FLPMA, which repealed many of the miscellaneous laws governing disposal of public land, . . . and established a policy in favor of retaining public lands for multiple use management. It directed the Secretary to "prepare and maintain on a continuing basis an inventory of all public lands and their resource and other values," . . . required land use planning for public lands, and established criteria to be used for that purpose. . . . It provided that existing classifications of public lands were subject to review in the land use planning process, and that the Secretary could "modify or terminate any such classification consistent with such land use plans." . . . It also authorized the Secretary to "make, modify, extend or revoke" withdrawals. . . . Finally it directed the Secretary, within 15 years, to review withdrawals in existence in 1976 in 11 western States, . . . and to "determine whether, and for how long, the continuation of the existing withdrawal of the lands would be, in his judgment, consistent with the statutory objectives of the programs for which the lands were dedicated and of the other relevant programs." . . . The activities undertaken by the BLM to comply with these various provisions constitute what respondent's amended complaint styles the BLM's "land with-

drawal review program," which is the subject of the current litigation.

. . . Respondent alleged that petitioners, in the course of administering the Nation's public lands, had violated the FLPMA by failing to "develop, maintain, and, when appropriate, revise land use plans which provide by tracts or areas for the use of the public lands," . . . failing to submit recommendations as to withdrawals in the 11 western States to the President, . . . failing to consider multiple uses for the disputed lands, . . . focusing inordinately on such uses as mineral exploitation and development; and failing to provide public notice of decisions. . . . Respondent also claimed that petitioners had violated NEPA, which requires federal agencies to "include in every recommendation or report on . . . major Federal actions significantly affecting the quality of the human environment, a detailed statement by the responsible official on . . . the environmental impact of the proposed action." . . . Finally, respondent alleged that all of the above actions were "arbitrary, capricious, an abuse of discretion, or otherwise not in accordance with law," and should therefore be set aside. . . .

In December 1985, the District Court granted respondent's motion for a preliminary injunction prohibiting petitioners from "[m]odifying, terminating or altering any withdrawal, classification, or other designation governing the protection of lands in the public domain that was in effect on January 1, 1981," and from "[t]aking any action inconsistent" with any such withdrawal, classification, or designation. . . . In a subsequent order, the court denied petitioners' motion under Rule 12(b) of the Federal Rules of Civil Procedure to dismiss the complaint for failure to demonstrate standing to challenge petitioners' actions under the APA. . . . The Court of Appeals affirmed both orders. . . . As to the motion to dismiss, the Court of Appeals found sufficient to survive the motion the general allegation in the amended complaint that respondent's members used environmental resources that would be damaged by petitioners' actions. . . . It held that this allegation, fairly read along with the balance of the complaint, both identified particular land-status actions that respondent sought to challenge—since at least some of the actions complained of were

---

EDITED CASE Lujan v. National Wildlife Federation (Continued)

---

listed in the complaint's appendix of Federal Register references—and asserted harm to respondent's members attributable to those particular actions. . . . To support the latter point, the Court of Appeals pointed to the affidavits of two of respondent's members, Peggy Kay Peterson and Richard Erman, which claimed use of land "in the vicinity" of the land covered by two of the listed actions. Thus, the Court of Appeals concluded, there was "concrete indication that [respondent's] members use specific lands covered by the agency's Program and will be adversely affected by the agency's actions," and the complaint was "sufficiently specific for purposes of a motion to dismiss." . . . On petitions for rehearing, the Court of Appeals stood by its denial of the motion to dismiss, and directed the parties and the District Court "to proceed with this litigation with dispatch." . . .

Back before the District Court, petitioners again claimed, this time by means of a motion for summary judgment under Rule 56 of the Federal Rules of Civil Procedure (which motion had been outstanding during the proceedings before the Court of Appeals), that respondent had no standing to seek judicial review of petitioners' actions under the APA. After argument on this motion, and in purported response to the court's postargument request for additional briefing, respondent submitted four additional member affidavits pertaining to the issue of standing. The District Court rejected them as untimely, vacated the injunction, and granted the Rule 56 motion to dismiss. It noted that neither its earlier decision nor the Court of Appeals' affirmance controlled the question, since both pertained to a motion under Rule 12(b). It found the Peterson and Erman affidavits insufficient to withstand the Rule 56 motion, even as to judicial review of the particular classification decisions to which they pertained. And even if they had been adequate for that limited purpose, the court said, they could not support respondent's attempted APA challenge to "each of the 1250 or so individual classification terminations and withdrawal revocations" effected under the land withdrawal review program. . . .

This time the Court of Appeals reversed. . . . It both found the Peterson and Erman affidavits sufficient in themselves, and held that it was an abuse of discretion not to consider the four additional

affidavits as well. The Court of Appeals also concluded that standing to challenge individual classification and withdrawal decisions conferred standing to challenge all such decisions under the land withdrawal review program. We granted certiorari. . . .

We first address respondent's claim that the Peterson and Erman affidavits alone suffice to establish respondent's right to judicial review of petitioners' actions. Respondent does not contend that either the FLPMA or NEPA provides a private right of action for violations of its provisions. Rather, respondent claims a right to judicial review under 10(a) of the APA, which provides: "A person suffering legal wrong because of agency action, or adversely affected or aggrieved by agency action within the meaning of a relevant statute, is entitled to judicial review thereof." . . .

This provision contains two separate requirements. First, the person claiming a right to sue must identify some "agency action" that affects him in the specified fashion; it is judicial review "thereof" to which he is entitled. . . . When, as here, review is sought not pursuant to specific authorization in the substantive statute, but only under the general review provisions of the APA, the "agency action" in question must be "final agency action." . . .

Second, the party seeking review under § 702 must show that he has "suffer[ed] legal wrong" because of the challenged agency action, or is "adversely affected or aggrieved" by that action "within the meaning of a relevant statute." Respondent does not assert that it has suffered "legal wrong," so we need only discuss the meaning of "adversely affected or aggrieved . . . within the meaning of a relevant statute." As an original matter, it might be thought that one cannot be "adversely affected or aggrieved within the meaning" of a statute unless the statute in question uses those terms (or terms like them)—as some pre-APA statutes in fact did when conferring rights of judicial review. . . . We have long since rejected that interpretation, however, which would have made the judicial review provision of the APA no more than a restatement of preexisting law. Rather, we have said that, to be "adversely affected or

(Continued)

EDITED CASE Lujan v. National Wildlife Federation (Continued)

aggrieved . . . within the meaning" of a statute, the plaintiff must establish that the injury he complains of (his aggrievement, or the adverse effect upon him) falls within the "zone of interests" sought to be protected by the statutory provision whose violation forms the legal basis for his complaint. . . . Thus, for example, the failure of an agency to comply with a statutory provision requiring "on the record" hearings would assuredly have an adverse effect upon the company that has the contract to record and transcribe the agency's proceedings; but since the provision was obviously enacted to protect the interests of the parties to the proceedings, and not those of the reporters, that company would not be "adversely affected within the meaning" of the statute. . . .

We turn, then, to whether the specific facts alleged in the two affidavits considered by the District Court raised a genuine issue of fact as to whether an "agency action" taken by petitioners caused respondent to be "adversely affected or aggrieved . . . within the meaning of a relevant statute." We assume, since it has been uncontested, that the allegedly affected interests set forth in the affidavits—"recreational use and aesthetic enjoyment"—are sufficiently related to the purposes of respondent association that respondent meets the requirements of § 702 if any of its members do. . . .

As for the "agency action" requirement, we think that each of the affidavits can be read, as the Court of Appeals believed, to complain of a particular "agency action" as that term is defined in 551. The parties agree that the Peterson affidavit, judging from the geographic area it describes, must refer to . . . an order captioned W-6228 and dated April 30, 1984, terminating the withdrawal classification of some 4,500 acres of land in that area. . . . The parties also appear to agree, on the basis of similar deduction, that the Erman affidavit refers to . . . an order captioned Public Land Order 6156 and dated February 18, 1982.

We also think that whatever "adverse effect" or "aggrievement" is established by the affidavits was "within the meaning of the relevant statute"—i.e., met the "zone of interests" test. The relevant statute, of course, is the statute whose violation is the gravamen of the complaint—both the FLPMA and NEPA. We have no doubt that

"recreational use and aesthetic enjoyment" are among the sorts of interests those statutes were specifically designed to protect. The only issue, then, is whether the facts alleged in the affidavits showed that those interests of Peterson and Erman were actually affected.

The Peterson affidavit averred:

"My recreational use and aesthetic enjoyment of federal lands, particularly those in the vicinity of South Pass-Green Mountain, Wyoming, have been and continue to be adversely affected in fact by the unlawful actions of the Bureau and the Department. In particular, the South Pass-Green Mountain area of Wyoming has been opened to the staking of mining claims and oil and gas leasing, an action which threatens the aesthetic beauty and wildlife habitat potential of these lands." . . .

Erman's affidavit was substantially the same as Peterson's, with respect to all except the area involved; he claimed use of land "in the vicinity of Grand Canyon National Park, the Arizona Strip (Kanab Plateau), and the Kanab National Forest." . . .

It is impossible that the affidavits would suffice . . . to enable respondent to challenge the entirety of petitioners' so-called "land withdrawal review program." That is not an "agency action" within the meaning of § 702, much less a "final agency action" within the meaning of 704. The term "land withdrawal review program" (which as far as we know is not derived from any authoritative text) does not refer to a single BLM order or regulation, or even to a completed universe of particular BLM orders and regulations. It is simply the name by which petitioners have occasionally referred to the continuing (and thus constantly changing) operations of the BLM in reviewing withdrawal revocation applications and the classifications of public lands and developing land use plans as required by the FLPMA. It is no more an identifiable "agency action"—much less a "final agency action"—than a "weapons procurement program" of the Department of Defense or a "drug interdiction program" of the Drug Enforcement Administration. As the District Court explained, the "land withdrawal review program" extends to, currently at least, "1250 or so individual classification terminations and withdrawal revocations." . . .

EDITED CASE Lujan v. National Wildlife Federation (Continued)

Respondent alleges that violation of the law is rampant within this program—failure to revise land use plans in proper fashion, failure to submit certain recommendations to Congress, failure to consider multiple use, inordinate focus upon mineral exploitation, failure to provide required public notice, failure to provide adequate environmental impact statements. Perhaps so. But respondent cannot seek wholesale improvement of this program by court decree, rather than in the offices of the Department or the halls of Congress, where programmatic improvements are normally made. Under the terms of the APA, respondent must direct its attack against some particular "agency action" that causes it harm. Some statutes permit broad regulations to serve as the "agency action," and thus to be the object of judicial review directly, even before the concrete effects normally required for APA review are felt. Absent such a provision, however, a regulation is not ordinarily considered the type of agency action "ripe" for judicial review under the APA until the scope of the controversy has been reduced to more manageable proportions, and its factual components fleshed out, by some concrete action applying the regulation to the claimant's situation in a fashion that harms or threatens to harm him. (The major exception, of course, is a substantive rule which, as a practical matter, requires the plaintiff to adjust his conduct immediately. Such agency action is "ripe" for review at once, whether or not explicit statutory review apart from the APA is provided. . . .

In the present case, the individual actions of the BLM identified in the six affidavits can be regarded as rules of general applicability . . . announcing, with respect to vast expanses of territory that they cover, the agency's intent to grant requisite permission for certain activities, to decline to interfere with other activities, and to take other particular action if requested. It may well be, then, that even those individual actions will not be ripe for challenge until some further agency action or inaction more immediately harming the plaintiff occurs. But it is at least entirely certain that the flaws in the entire "program"—consisting principally of the many individual actions referenced in the complaint, and presumably actions yet to be taken as well—cannot be laid before the courts for wholesale correction under the APA, simply because one of them that is ripe for review adversely affects one of respondent's members.

The case-by-case approach that this requires is understandably frustrating to an organization such as respondent, which has as its objective across-the-board protection of our Nation's wildlife and the streams and forests that support it. But this is the traditional, and remains the normal, mode of operation of the courts. Except where Congress explicitly provides for our correction of the administrative process at a higher level of generality, we intervene in the administration of the laws only when, and to the extent that, a specific "final agency action" has an actual or immediately threatened effect. . . . Such an intervention may ultimately have the effect of requiring a regulation, a series of regulations, or even a whole "program" to be revised by the agency in order to avoid the unlawful result that the court discerns. But it is assuredly not as swift or as immediately far-reaching a corrective process as those interested in systemic improvement would desire. Until confided to us, however, more sweeping actions are for the other branches. . . .

Respondent's final argument is that we should remand this case for the Court of Appeals to decide whether respondent may seek § 702 review of petitioners' actions in its own right, rather than derivatively through its members. Specifically, it points to allegations in the amended complaint that petitioners unlawfully failed to publish regulations, to invite public participation, and to prepare an environmental impact statement with respect to the "land withdrawal review program" as a whole. In order to show that it is a "person . . . adversely affected or aggrieved" by these failures, it submitted to the District Court a brief affidavit (two pages in the record) by one of its vice-presidents, Lynn A. Greenwalt, who stated that respondent's mission is to "inform its members and the general public about conservation issues" and to advocate improvements in laws and administrative practices "pertaining to the protection and enhancement of federal lands," . . . and that its ability to perform this mission has been impaired by

(Continued)

EDITED CASE   Lujan v. National Wildlife Federation (Continued)

---

petitioners' failure "to provide adequate information and opportunities for public participation with respect to the Land Withdrawal Review Program." . . . The District Court found this affidavit insufficient to establish respondent's right to seek judicial review, since it was "conclusory and completely devoid of specific facts." . . . The Court of Appeals, having reversed the District Court on the grounds discussed above, did not address the issue.

We agree with the District Court's disposition. Even assuming that the affidavit set forth "specific facts," . . . adequate to show injury to respondent through the deprivation of information; and even assuming that providing information to organizations such as respondent was one of the objectives of the statutes allegedly violated, so that respondent is "aggrieved within the meaning" of those statutes; nonetheless, the Greenwalt affidavit fails to identify any particular "agency action" that was the source of these injuries. The only sentences addressed to that point are as follows:

"NWF's ability to meet these obligations to its members has been significantly impaired by the failure of the Bureau of Land Management and the Department of the Interior to provide adequate information and opportunities for public participation with respect to the Land Withdrawal Review Program. These interests of NWF have been injured by the actions of the Bureau and the Department, and would be irreparably harmed by the continued failure to provide meaningful opportunities for public input and access to information regarding the Land Withdrawal Review Program." . . .

As is evident, this is even more deficient than the Peterson and Erman affidavits, which contained geographical descriptions whereby at least an action as general as a particular classification decision could be identified as the source of the grievance. As we discussed earlier, the "land withdrawal review program" is not an identifiable action or event. With regard to alleged deficiencies in providing information and permitting public participation, as with regard to the other illegalities alleged in the complaint, respondent cannot demand a general judicial review of the BLM's day-to-day operations. The Greenwalt affidavit, like the others, does not set forth the specific facts necessary to survive a Rule 56 motion. . . .

For the foregoing reasons, the judgment of the Court of Appeals is reversed.

Justice Blackmun, with whom *Justices Brennan*, *Marshall*, and *Stevens* join, dissenting.

In my view, the affidavits of Peggy Kay Peterson and Richard Loren Erman, in conjunction with other record evidence before the District Court on the motions for summary judgment, were sufficient to establish the standing of the National Wildlife Federation (Federation or NWF) to bring this suit. I also conclude that the District Court abused its discretion by refusing to consider supplemental affidavits filed after the hearing on the parties' cross-motions for summary judgment. I therefore would affirm the judgment of the Court of Appeals. . . .

The Federation's asserted injury in this case rested upon its claim that the Government actions challenged here would lead to increased mining on public lands; that the mining would result in damage to the environment; and that the recreational opportunities of NWF's members would consequently be diminished. Abundant record evidence supported the Federation's assertion that, on lands newly opened for mining, mining in fact would occur. Similarly, the record furnishes ample support for NWF's contention that mining activities can be expected to cause severe environmental damage to the affected lands. The District Court held, however, that the Federation had not adequately identified particular members who were harmed by the consequences of the Government's actions. Although two of NWF's members expressly averred that their recreational activities had been impaired, the District Court concluded that these affiants had not identified with sufficient precision the particular sites on which their injuries occurred. The majority, like the District Court, holds that the averments of Peterson and Erman were insufficiently specific to withstand a motion for summary judgment. Although these affidavits were not models of precision, I believe that they were adequate at least to create a genuine issue of fact as to the organization's injury. . . .

The requirement that evidence be submitted is satisfied here: the Federation has offered the sworn statements of two of its members. . . . The question, it should be emphasized, is not whether the NWF has proved that it has standing to bring this action, but simply whether the materials before the District Court established "that there is a genuine issue for trial," . . . concerning the Federation's standing. . . .

EDITED CASE Lujan v. National Wildlife Federation (Continued)

. . . The Administrative Procedure Act permits suit to be brought by any person "adversely affected or aggrieved by agency action." . . . In some cases the "agency action" will consist of a rule of broad applicability; and if the plaintiff prevails, the result is that the rule is invalidated, not simply that the court forbids its application to a particular individual. Under these circumstances, a single plaintiff, so long as he is injured by the rule, may obtain "programmatic" relief that affects the rights of parties not before the court. On the other hand, if a generally lawful policy is applied in an illegal manner on a particular occasion, one who is injured is not thereby entitled to challenge other applications of the rule. . . .

The majority, quoting the District Court, characterizes the Bureau's land management program as

"'1250 or so individual classification terminations and withdrawal revocations.'" . . . The majority offers no argument in support of this conclusory assertion, and I am far from certain that the characterization is an accurate one. Since this issue bears on the scope of the relief ultimately to be awarded should the plaintiff prevail, rather than on the jurisdiction of the District Court to entertain the suit, I would allow the District Court to address the question on remand. . . .

Since I conclude that the Peterson and Erman affidavits provided sufficient evidence of NWF's standing to withstand a motion for summary judgment, and that the District Court abused its discretion by refusing to consider the Federation's supplemental affidavits, I would affirm the judgment of the Court of Appeals. I respectfully dissent.

EDITED CASE Chevron U.S.A. v. Natural Resources Defense Council
United States Supreme Court, 467 U.S. 837 (1984)

[In this landmark decision involving an EPA interpretation of the Clean Air Act Amendments of 1977, the Supreme Court establishes a policy under which federal courts defer to agency constructions of statutes where congressional intent is ambiguous.]

Justice Stevens delivered the opinion of the Court.

In the Clean Air Act Amendments of 1977, Pub. L. 95-95, 91 Stat. 685, Congress enacted certain requirements applicable to States that had not achieved the national air quality standards established by the Environmental Protection Agency (EPA) pursuant to earlier legislation. The amended Clean Air Act required these "nonattainment" States to establish a permit program regulating "new or modified major stationary sources" of air pollution. Generally, a permit may not be issued for a new or modified major stationary source unless several stringent conditions are met. The EPA regulation promulgated to implement this permit requirement allows a State to adopt a plantwide definition of the term "stationary source." Under this definition, an existing plant that contains several pollution-emitting devices may install or modify one piece of equipment with-

out meeting the permit conditions if the alteration will not increase the total emissions from the plant. The question presented by these cases is whether EPA's decision to allow States to treat all of the pollution-emitting devices within the same industrial grouping as though they were encased within a single "bubble" is based on a reasonable construction of the statutory term "stationary source." . . .

The EPA regulations containing the plantwide definition of the term stationary source were promulgated on October 14, 1981. . . . Respondents filed a timely petition for review in the United States Court of Appeals for the District of Columbia Circuit pursuant to 42 U.S.C. 7607(b) (1). The Court of Appeals set aside the regulations. . . .

The court observed that the relevant part of the amended Clean Air Act "does not explicitly define what Congress envisioned as a 'stationary source,' to which the permit program . . . should apply," and further stated that the precise issue was not "squarely addressed in the legislative history." . . .

(Continued)

EDITED CASE   Chevron U.S.A. v. Natural Resources Defense Council (Continued)

In light of its conclusion that the legislative history bearing on the question was "at best contradictory," it reasoned that "the purposes of the nonattainment program should guide our decision here." . . . Based on two of its precedents concerning the applicability of the bubble concept to certain Clean Air Act programs, the court stated that the bubble concept was "mandatory" in programs designed merely to maintain existing air quality, but held that it was "inappropriate" in programs enacted to improve air quality. . . . Since the purpose of the permit program—its "raison d'etre," in the court's view—was to improve air quality, the court held that the bubble concept was inapplicable in these cases under its prior precedents. . . . It therefore set aside the regulations embodying the bubble concept as contrary to law. We granted certiorari to review that judgment . . . and we now reverse.

The basic legal error of the Court of Appeals was to adopt a static judicial definition of the term "stationary source" when it had decided that Congress itself had not commanded that definition. Respondents do not defend the legal reasoning of the Court of Appeals. Nevertheless, since this Court reviews judgments, not opinions, we must determine whether the Court of Appeals' legal error resulted in an erroneous judgment on the validity of the regulations. . . .

When a court reviews an agency's construction of the statute which it administers, it is confronted with two questions. First, always, is the question whether Congress has directly spoken to the precise question at issue. If the intent of Congress is clear, that is the end of the matter; for the court, as well as the agency, must give effect to the unambiguously expressed intent of Congress. If, however, the court determines Congress has not directly addressed the precise question at issue, the court does not simply impose its own construction on the statute, as would be necessary in the absence of an administrative interpretation. Rather, if the statute is silent or ambiguous with respect to the specific issue, the question for the court is whether the agency's answer is based on a permissible construction of the statute.

"The power of an administrative agency to administer a congressionally created . . . program necessarily requires the formulation of policy and the making of rules to fill any gap left, implicitly or explicitly, by Congress." . . . If Congress has explicitly left a gap for the agency to fill, there is an express delegation of authority to the agency to elucidate a specific provision of the statute by regulation. Such legislative regulations are given controlling weight unless they are arbitrary, capricious, or manifestly contrary to the statute. Sometimes the legislative delegation to an agency on a particular question is implicit rather than explicit. In such a case, a court may not substitute its own construction of a statutory provision for a reasonable interpretation made by the administrator of an agency. . . .

In light of these well-settled principles it is clear that the Court of Appeals misconceived the nature of its role in reviewing the regulations at issue. Once it determined, after its own examination of the legislation, that Congress did not actually have an intent regarding the applicability of the bubble concept to the permit program, the question before it was not whether in its view the concept is "inappropriate" in the general context of a program designed to improve air quality, but whether the Administrator's view that it is appropriate in the context of this particular program is a reasonable one. Based on the examination of the legislation and its history which follows, we agree with the Court of Appeals that Congress did not have a specific intention on the applicability of the bubble concept in these cases, and conclude that the EPA's use of that concept here is a reasonable policy choice for the agency to make. . . .

In August 1980, however, the EPA adopted a regulation that, in essence, applied the basic reasoning of the Court of Appeals in these cases. The EPA took particular note of the two then-recent Court of Appeals decisions, which had created the bright-line rule that the "bubble concept" should be employed in a program designed to maintain air quality but not in one designed to enhance air quality. Relying heavily on those cases, EPA adopted a dual definition of "source" for nonattainment areas that required a permit whenever a change in either the entire plant, or one of its components, would result in a significant increase in emissions even if the increase was completely offset by reductions elsewhere in the plant. The EPA expressed the opinion that this interpretation was "more consistent with congressional intent" than

---

EDITED CASE Chevron U.S.A. v. Natural Resources Defense Council (Continued)

---

the plantwide definition because it "would bring in more sources or modifications for review," . . . but its primary legal analysis was predicated on the two Court of Appeals decisions.

In 1981 a new administration took office and initiated a "Government-wide reexamination of regulatory burdens and complexities." . . . In the context of that review, the EPA reevaluated the various arguments that had been advanced in connection with the proper definition of the term "source" and concluded that the term should be given the same definition in both nonattainment areas and PSD areas.

In explaining its conclusion, the EPA first noted that the definitional issue was not squarely addressed in either the statute or its legislative history and therefore that the issue involved an agency "judgment as how to best carry out the Act." . . . It then set forth several reasons for concluding that the plantwide definition was more appropriate. . . .

In these cases the Administrator's interpretation represents a reasonable accommodation of manifestly competing interests and is entitled to deference: the regulatory scheme is technical and complex, the agency considered the matter in a detailed and reasoned fashion, and the decision involves reconciling conflicting policies. Congress intended to accommodate both interests, but did not do so itself on the level of specificity presented by these cases. Perhaps that body consciously desired the Administrator to strike the balance at this level, thinking that those with great expertise and charged with responsibility for administering the provision would be in a better position to do so; perhaps it simply did not consider the question at this level; and perhaps Congress was unable to forge a coalition on either side of the question, and those on each side decided to take their chances with the scheme devised by the agency. For judicial purposes, it matters not which of these things occurred.

Judges are not experts in the field, and are not part of either political branch of the Government.

Courts must, in some cases, reconcile competing political interests, but not on the basis of the judges' personal policy preferences. In contrast, an agency to which Congress has delegated policy-making responsibilities may, within the limits of that delegation, properly rely upon the incumbent administration's views of wise policy to inform its judgments. While agencies are not directly accountable to the people, the Chief Executive is, and it is entirely appropriate for this political branch of the Government to make such policy choices—resolving the competing interests which Congress itself either inadvertently did not resolve, or intentionally left to be resolved by the agency charged with the administration of the statute in light of everyday realities.

When a challenge to an agency construction of a statutory provision, fairly conceptualized, really centers on the wisdom of the agency's policy, rather than whether it is a reasonable choice within a gap left open by Congress, the challenge must fail. In such a case, federal judges—who have no constituency—have a duty to respect legitimate policy choices made by those who do. The responsibilities for assessing the wisdom of such policy choices and resolving the struggle between competing views of the public interest are not judicial ones: "Our Constitution vests such responsibilities in the political branches." . . .

We hold that the EPA's definition of the term "source" is a permissible construction of the statute which seeks to accommodate progress in reducing air pollution with economic growth. "The Regulations which the Administrator has adopted provide what the agency could allowably view as . . . [an] effective reconciliation of these twofold ends. . . ." . . .

The judgment of the Court of Appeals is reversed.

Justices Marshall and *Rehnquist* took no part in the consideration or decision of these cases.

Justice O'Connor took no part in the decision of these cases.

EDITED CASE Freeman Hall, D/B/A Freeman's College City
Lounge v. Alabama Alcoholic Beverage Control Board
Alabama Court of Civil Appeals, 631 So.2d 1047 (Ala. Civ. App. 1993)

*[In this case the holder of a retail liquor license
sought judicial review of the Alcoholic Beverage
Control Board's denial of renewal of his license
after a local court had affirmed the Control Board's
decision.]*

Per Curiam [decision delivered by the collective
members of the court].

This is an appeal from a judgment affirming the
decision of the Alabama Alcoholic Beverage Control Board (Board), which denied the renewal of a
retail liquor license. The Board held a hearing on
citizen protests of the renewal of Freeman Hall's,
d/b/a Freeman's College City Lounge, lounge retail
liquor license.

The Board denied Hall's application for renewal
of his alcoholic beverage license, and Hall filed a
petition for judicial review in the Perry County Circuit Court.

After reviewing the testimony presented at the
hearing before the Board and the briefs filed by
the parties, the trial court entered judgment,
affirming the decision of the Board. Hall appeals,
contending that the Board violated his right to
Due Process and Equal Protection under the United
States Constitution and that the Board misapplied
the law in reaching its decision.

Hall first argues that he was denied due process
and that his equal protection rights were violated.
His equal protection argument was not raised previously and will not be considered on appeal. . . .
Our review reveals that pursuant to § 41-22-12,
Ala.Code 1975, Hall was afforded ample notice
that protests had been filed against the renewal of
his license, he was apprised of his right to respond,
and he was forewarned to present all evidence
supporting his position at a hearing. Hall was represented by legal counsel throughout the proceedings. The record clearly discloses that even under
the relaxed standards of an administrative
proceeding, Hall was provided adequate notice
regarding the protests, he was afforded an

opportunity to respond and present evidence on
his behalf, and he received an impartial hearing.
There is nothing in the record to disclose that Hall
was denied due process of law.

Judicial review of administrative acts and decisions is limited in scope to whether the order is
supported by substantial evidence, whether the
agency's decision is reasonable and not arbitrary,
and whether the agency acted within its power
conferred upon it by law and the
Constitution. . . . A presumption of correctness
attaches to the decision of an administrative
agency due to its recognized expertise in a specific,
specialized area. . . .

The chief of police of the City of Marion, Henry
Wright, testified that the police department had
received numerous calls from citizens complaining
about the lounge since the lounge had been open.
He testified that the lounge's bouncer had been
arrested for selling controlled substances; however,
testimony conflicted concerning whether the
bouncer's arrest arose out of the sale of controlled
substances at the lounge. The chief further testified that the Marion police had observed the
lounge open past 2:00 A.M. on Sunday mornings, a
violation of state law.

A couple living next-door to the lounge testified about loud music coming from the lounge,
loud voices coming from the area of the lounge,
and finding beer bottles, whiskey bottles, and
other debris in their yard. A local pastor testified
that while visiting the couple one night, he heard
noise coming from the area of the lounge. He further testified that people leaving from the lounge
had "panhandled" him and that he had seen
drunks staggering in the streets in the area of the
lounge.

After a careful review of the record evidence,
we cannot hold that the Board's decision was so
unsupported by the evidence as to be unreasonable and arbitrary. The judgment of the trial court
is affirmed.

ENDNOTES

1. 5 U.S. 137 (1803).

2. K.S.A. 77-603.

3. Fla. Stat. Ann. § 120.68.

4. See, e.g., 5 Maine R.S.A. § 11,001.

5. *Califano v. Sanders,* 430 U.S. 99 (1977).

6. 28 U.S.C.A. §§ 610; 1631.

7. *Gaunce v. deVincentis,* 708 F.2d 1290 (7th Cir. 1983).

8. See, generally, § 703 A.P.A.

9. See *Rodrigues v. Donovan,* 769 F.2d 1344 (9th Cir. 1985).

10. 485 U.S. 535 (1988).

11. *Webster v. Doe,* 486 U.S. 592 (1988).

12. *National Federation of Federal Employees v. United States,* 905 F.2d 400 (D.C. Cir. 1990).

13. 401 U.S. 402 (1971).

14. Section 701 of the Administrative Procedure Act, 5 U.S.C.A. § 701.

15. 401 U.S. at 411.

16. 463 U.S. 29 (1983).

17. 470 U.S. 821 (1985).

18. 5 U.S.C.A. § 501 *et seq.*

19. *Heckler v. Chaney,* 470 U.S. at 838.

20. *Id.* at 831-832.

21. See *Association of Data Processing Service Organizations v. Camp,* 397 U.S. 150, 154 (1970).

22. *Id.* at 153.

23. *Sierra Club v. Morton,* 405 U.S. 727 (1972).

24. See, e.g., *United States v. Students Challenging Regulatory Agency Procedures,* 412 U.S. 669 (1973).

25. 497 U.S. 871 (1990).

26. *Id.* at 900-901.

27. *Frothingham v. Mellon,* cited as *Massachusetts v. Mellon,* 262 U.S. 447 (1923), the two cases having been consolidated.

28. 392 U.S. 83 (1968).

29. 454 U.S. 464 (1982).

30. 102 So.2d 132 (Fla. 1958).

31. 403 N.W.2d 82 (Mich. App. 1986).

32. *State ex rel. Trimble v. City of Moore,* 818 P.2d 889 (Okla. 1991).

33. 387 U.S. 136 (1967).

34. *Id.* at 148-49.

35. *Florida Power & Light Co. v. E.P.A.,* 345 F.3d 1414 (D.C. Cir. 1998).

36. 529 U.S. 154 (1997).

37. *Id.* at 176.

38. 934 F.2d 240 (10th Cir. 1991).

39. 732 A.2d 633 (Me. 1998).

40. 503 U.S. 140 (1992).

41. 509 U.S. 137 (1993).

42. 690 S.W.2d 560 (Tex. 1985).

43. *Watergate II Apts. v. Buffalo Sewer Auth.,* 385 N.E.2d 560, 563 (N.Y. 1978).

44. *United States v. Western Pacific Railroad Co.,* 352 U.S. 59, 63 (1956).

45. 492 A.2d 171 (Conn.1985).

46. *Id.* at 173.

47. See, e.g., *Honig v. Doe,* 484 U.S. 305 (1988).

48. 157 F.3d 86 (2nd Cir. 1998).

49. 558 So.2d 487 (Fla. App. 1990).

50. *Id.* at 491. Unlike the federal constitution, the Florida Constitution does not include a "case or controversy" requirement that would preclude Florida courts from deciding a case that has become moot.

51. *In re: Sang-Su Lee,* 277 F.3d 1338, 1342 (Fed. Cir. 2001).

52. *Citizens to Preserve Overton Park v. Volpe,* 401 U.S. 402, 416 (1971).

53. See West's Ann. Ind. Code, Ch. 5, Judicial Review, § 9(a).

54. *Mitchell v. State,* 968 P.2d 37 (Wyo. 1998).

55. *Consolo v. Federal Maritime Comm'n,* 383 U.S. 607 (1996).

56. *Arkansas v. Oklahoma et al. Environmental Protection Agency,* 503 U.S. 91, 113 (1992).

57. See, for example, *Mester Mfg. Co. v. INS,* 879 F.2d 561 (9th Cir.1989).

58. *Brown v. Duchesne,* 19 How. 183, 194 (1857).

59. *Davis v. Michigan Dept. of Treasury,* 489 U.S. 803, 809 (1989).

60. *Gustafson v. Alloyd Co.,* 513 U. S. 561, 569 (1995).

61. 467 U.S. 837 (1984).

62. *Id.* at 843.

63. *Regions Hospital v. Shalala,* 522 U.S. 448, 457 (1998).

64. 533 U.S. 218 (2001).

65. *Id.* at 221.

66. *Id.* at 226-27.

67. 323 U.S. 134 (1944).

68. *Id.* at 140.

69. *United States v. Mead Corp.,* 533 U.S. at 220.

70. *Id.* at 130.

71. 42 U.S.C.A. § 423(d)(1).

72. 535 U.S. 212 (2002).

73. *Id.* at 219.

74. In See *Food and Drug Administration et al. v. Brown & Williamson Tobacco Corporation,* 529 U.S 120 (2000).

75. See *MCI Telecommunications Corp. v. American Telephone & Telegraph Co.,* 512 U.S. 218, 231 (1994).

76. 448 U.S. 607 (1980).

77. *Id.* at 645.

78. 531 U.S. 457 (2001).

79. *Id.* at 465.

80. *Hooper v. California,* 155 U.S. 648, 657 (1895); *Crowell v. Benson,* 285 U.S. 22, 62 (1932); *Machinists v. Street,* 367 U.S. 740, 749 (1961); *United States v. Security Industrial Bank,* 459 U.S. 70, 78 (1982).

81. *Edward J. DeBartolo Corp. v. Florida Gulf Coast Building & Construction Trades Council,* 485 U.S. 568, 575 (1988).

82. 500 U.S. 173 (1991).

83. *Id.* at 224.

84. *Richard v. Metcalf,* 921 P.2d 169, 172 (Hawaii 1996).

85. *Hama Hama Company v. Shorelines Hearings Board,* 536 P.2d 157, 161-62 (Wash. 1975).

86. *A.A. Mastrangelo, Inc. v. Commissioner, Dep't of Environmental Protection,* 449 A.2d 516, 525 (N.J. 1982).

87. *Expedient Services, Inc., v. Weaver,* 614 F.2d 56 (5th Cir. 1980); *Pan Am World Airways, Inc. v. Florida Public Service Comm'n,* 427 So. 2d 716 (Fla. 1983).

88. 627 F.2d 1151, 1160 (D.C. Cir. 1979).

89. *Id.* at 1160–61 See § 706(e) of the APA.

90. 529 U.S. 576 (2000).

91. *United States v. Mead Corporation,* 533 U.S. 218 (2001).

92. *Id.* at 234, 235.

93. 323 U.S. 134 (1944).

94. 270 F.3d 1137 (7th Cir. 2002).

95. 565 N.W.2d 766 (N.D. 1997).

96. N.D.C.C. § 28-32-19-1.

10

The Rights of Public Employees

"A State may not condition public employment on an employee's exercise of
his or her First Amendment rights. . . . Absent some reasonably appropriate
requirement, government may not make public employment subject to the
express condition of political beliefs or prescribed expression."

JUSTICE ANTHONY KENNEDY
WRITING FOR THE SUPREME COURT IN *O'HARE TRUCK SERVICE V. CITY OF NORTHLAKE*,
518 U.S. 712, 717 (1996).

INTRODUCTION

Citizens who find themselves in an adversarial posture with respect to a public agency often believe that their rights have been ignored or violated by bureaucrats. Yet bureaucrats are citizens too and, accordingly, have rights that must be respected by the agencies in which they are employed. This chapter examines the rights of public employees. Primary attention is accorded to those rights protected by the federal and state constitutions, including the freedoms of expression, religion, and association, the freedom from unreasonable searches and seizures, and the all-important rights to due process and equal protection of the law. As the Supreme Court observed in 1968 "public employees are entitled, like all other persons, to the benefit of the Constitution. . ."[1] But public employees also derive protection from federal and state statutes. These laws address such matters as hiring, promotion and job security, unionization, collective bargaining and the right to strike, the "whistleblower" phenomenon, discrimination, and sexual harassment. This chapter looks at those statutory sources of protection as well.

All public officials, from presidents, governors, and mayors, to clerks, administrative assistants, and secretaries, hold positions created by federal or state constitutions, federal or state statutes, or local ordinances. To be eligible to be elected or appointed to a public office one must possess the qualifications prescribed by law. When a period of residency in a given state or locality is a prerequisite, such requirement is generally upheld by courts if it is of a reasonable duration. Likewise prohibitions against one who has been convicted of a felony involving moral turpitude from holding a public office are usually upheld. A public officer is required to take an oath to uphold the U.S. Constitution before assuming official duties as a member of Congress, state legislature, or as a federal or state executive or judicial officer. States require that the oath include the obligation to uphold the constitution of the state. Even cities often require their officers to take an oath to uphold the city's charter.

THE CIVIL SERVICE

Historically, public employees at all levels of government served at the pleasure of chief executives. Under the so-called **spoils system**, mayors, governors, and presidents had virtually total discretion in hiring and firing government employees. President Andrew Jackson is most closely associated with this system, which he referred to as "rotation in office." To Jackson, it was imperative that an incoming president should be able to reward his political supporters with federal employment and he believed that their complete dependence on his good graces was consistent with democratic principles. To Jackson, the idea of a professional bureaucracy was anathema. Of course, in those days the federal workforce hovered around twenty thousand employees, and most of the jobs federal workers performed were fairly rudimentary. In 1829, Jackson asserted that "the duties of all public officers are, or at least admit of being made, so plain and simple that men of intelligence may readily qualify themselves for their performance."[2] The demands of the Civil War and the increasing responsibilities being assumed by the federal government would eventually cast widespread doubt on President Jackson's thesis.

The Pendleton Act

In the years following the Civil War there was much discussion of the need for civil service reform, but very little concrete action beyond a short-lived experiment in which a merit-based civil service was put in place from 1871 to 1873. But a bizarre event would galvanize public opinion and lead to permanent change. On July 2, 1881, President James Garfield was mortally shot by Charles Guiteau, an angry office-seeker who believed that Garfield had played a key role in preventing him from getting an appointment to the diplomatic corps. As Garfield lingered on his deathbed, public support for civil service reform mounted. Five months after President Garfield's death in September 1882, Congress passed the seminal legislation that would lead to the

---

BOX 10.1 Excerpts from the Pendleton Act (1883)

An act to regulate and improve the civil service of the United States.

Be it enacted . . . That the President is authorized to appoint, by and with the advice and consent of the Senate, three persons, not more than two of whom shall be adherents of the same party, as Civil Service Commissioners, and said three commissioners shall constitute the United States Civil Service Commission. Said commissioners shall hold no other official place under the United States.

Sec. 2. That it shall be the duty of said commissioners:

First. To aid the President, as he may request, in preparing suitable rules for carrying this act into effect, and when said rules shall have been promulgated it shall be the duty of all officers of the United States in the departments and offices to which any such rules may relate to aid, in all proper ways, in carrying said rules, and any modifications thereof, into effect.

Second. And, among other things, said rules shall provide and declare, as nearly as the conditions of good administration will warrant, as follows:

First, for open, competitive examinations for testing the fitness of applicants for the public service now classified or to be classified hereunder. Such examinations shall be practical in their character, and so far as may be shall relate to those matters which will fairly test the relative capacity and fitness of the persons examined to discharge the duties of the service into which they seek to be appointed.

Second, that all the offices, places, and employments so arranged or to be arranged in classes shall be filled by selections according to grade from among those graded highest as the results of such competitive examinations.

Third, appointments to the public service aforesaid in the departments at Washington shall be apportioned among the several States and Territories and the District of Columbia upon the basis of population as ascertained at the last preceding census . . .

Fourth, that there shall be a period of probation before any absolute appointment or employment aforesaid.

Fifth, that no person in the public service is for that reason under any obligations to contribute to any political fund, or to render any political service, and that he will not be removed or otherwise prejudiced for refusing to do so.

Sixth, that no person in said service has any right to use his official authority or influence to coerce the political action of any person or body.

Seventh, there shall be non-competitive examinations in all proper cases before the commission, when competent persons do not compete, after notice has been given of the existence of the vacancy, under such rules as may be prescribed by the commissioners as to the manner of giving notice . . .

Third. Said commission shall, subject to the rules that may be made by the President, make regulations for, and have control of, such examinations . . .

SOURCE: U.S. Statutes at Large 22 (1883): 403.

---

dismantling of the spoils system and the establishment of a merit-based civil service within the federal government.

The **Pendleton Act**[3] created a "classified" civil service and required people seeking to enter the civil service to take a competitive examination. The act established the **U.S. Civil Service Commission** (CSC), an independent agency within the executive branch, to develop and administer civil service exams. The act also prohibited agencies from dismissing employees for refusing to support or contribute to a political campaign. (An abridged version of the Pendleton Act is reprinted in Box 10.1.) While these were significant measures, the 1883 legislation said nothing about problems such as promotions, disciplinary action, pensions, unionization, and collective bargaining. These issues would be addressed by subsequent legislation.

The Lloyd-LaFollette Act

In 1897, President William McKinley issued an order providing that "[n]o removal shall be made from any position subject to competitive examination except for just cause and upon written

---

BOX 10.2   The Hatch Act: Dos and Don'ts

Federal employees may not:

Use official authority or influence to interfere with an election

Solicit or discourage political activity of anyone with business before their agency

Solicit or receive political contributions

Be candidates for public office in partisan elections

Engage in political activity in a government office, wearing an official uniform, or using a government vehicle

Wear partisan political buttons on duty

Federal employees may:

Be candidates for public office in nonpartisan elections

Register and vote as they choose

Assist in voter registration drives

Express opinions about candidates and issues

Contribute money to political organizations

Attend political fundraising functions

Attend and be active at political rallies and meetings

Join and be an active member of a political party or club

Sign nominating petitions

Campaign for or against referendum questions, constitutional amendments, municipal ordinances

Campaign for or against candidates in partisan elections

Make campaign speeches for candidates in partisan elections

Distribute campaign literature in partisan elections

Hold office in political clubs or parties

SOURCE: Adapted from U.S. Department of Education web site, online at http://www.ed.gov/offices/OGC/ogcethics.html

---

charges filed with the head of the Department or other appointing officer, and of which the accused shall have full notice and an opportunity to make defense."[4] Yet the order failed to provide for any administrative appeals process in cases where agencies violated the new rule, and the federal courts refused to enforce the rule in the absence of legislation. Such legislation came in 1912 when Congress enacted the **Lloyd-LaFollette Act**. The act provided that

> no person in the classified civil service of the United States shall be removed therefrom except for such cause as will promote the efficiency of said service and for reasons given in writing, and the person whose removal is sought shall have notice of the same and of any charges preferred against him, and be furnished with a copy thereof, and also be allowed a reasonable time for personally answering the same in writing; and affidavits in support thereof; but no examination of witnesses nor any trial or hearing shall be required except in the discretion of the officer making the removal;

and copies of charges, notice of hearing, answer, reasons for removal, and of the order of removal shall be made a part of the records of the proper department or office, as shall also the reasons for reduction in rank or compensation; and copies of the same shall be furnished to the person affected upon request, and the Civil Service Commission also shall, upon request, be furnished copies of the same. . . .[5]

The Hatch Act

An important aspect of the professionalization of the civil service is the removal of partisan politics from public administration. Since 1908 the Pendleton Act had been interpreted by the Civil Service Commission to prohibit members of the classified civil service from actively participating in political campaigns.[6] Named after its sponsor, Senator Carl Hatch of New Mexico, The **Hatch Act** of 1939[7] codified this prohibition and significantly expanded the restrictions on the political activities of the federal civil service (see Box 10.2).

In 1940 Congress extended the Hatch Act to cover state and local employees "whose principal employment is in connection with any activity which is financed in whole or in part by loans or grants made by the United States."[8] The 1940 legislation also placed limits on political campaign contributions by federal civil servants. The Hatch Act was controversial from the outset due to the restrictions it placed on citizens simply because they work for the government. Some of its more general provisions are subject to constitutional challenge using the doctrines of vagueness and overbreadth. Nevertheless, the Supreme Court upheld the Hatch Act in *United Public Workers v. Mitchell* (1947)[9] and *Civil Service Commission v. National Association of Letter Carriers* (1973).[10] Writing for the Court in the latter decision, Justice White observed that "it is in the best interest of the country, indeed essential, that federal service should depend upon meritorious performance rather than political service, and that the political influence of federal employees on others and on the electoral process should be limited."[11]

The Civil Service Reform Act of 1978

One of the goals of the Carter Administration was to modernize the federal civil service, which had not been significantly altered since the New Deal era. One of the Administration's concerns was the Civil Service Commission, which had developed into an "omnibus personnel agency" for the Executive Branch. The **Civil Service Reform Act** (CSRA) of 1978[12] abolished the CSC and created a new independent agency, the **Office of Personnel Management** (OPM), to serve as the federal government's personnel recruitment agency. OPM administers the civil service laws, and conducts civil service exams.

CSRA also established the **Merit Systems Protection Board** (MSPB), an independent, quasi-judicial agency charged with hearing appeals from federal employees who are terminated or subjected to other major personnel actions. Federal law provides that "an employee, former employee, or applicant for employment

may, with respect to any personnel action taken, or proposed to be taken, against such employee, former employee, or applicant for employment, as a result of a prohibited personnel practice . . . , seek corrective action from the Merit Systems Protection Board."[13]

One of the hallmarks of the civil service is that employees may be discharged only for "cause." Generally speaking, cause includes: **malfeasance** (the commission of illegal acts under "color of office"); **misfeasance** (performing legal acts in an improper or illegal manner); and **nonfeasance** (neglect of duties). Federal civil service employees who believe that they were terminated without just cause and who have passed a one-year probationary period, or who are in the "excepted service" and have completed two years of service in the same or similar position, can appeal their terminations to the MSPB. The appeal must be filed within thirty days of the effective date of the termination. In most cases, MSPB cases are heard by an administrative law judge, whose decision is appealable to the full three-member board appointed by the president. Final decisions of the MSPB are appealable to the United States Court of Appeals for the Federal Circuit.

Protection of Whistleblowers

A **whistleblower** is an employee of a government agency or contractor who discloses improper or illegal activity within the organization. Bureaucracies are known for their tendency to "circle the wagons" when subjected to external scrutiny. They also frequently seek to punish members of the organization who reveal "damaging" information to "outsiders." (A good example of this phenomenon is described in Box 10.3.) From the analyst in the Department of Defense who reveals cost overruns or doctored test results on new weapons systems, to the scientist at the Department of Energy who publicly questions official conclusions about the safety of DOE plans for the storage of nuclear waste, whistleblowers can find themselves ostracized,

---

Box 10.3   Excerpts from Memorandum from Inspector General,
                       Department of Energy, January 28, 2003

Memorandum for the Secretary

From: Gregory H. Friedman, Inspector General

Subject: Special Inquiry Regarding Operations at
Los Alamos National Laboratory

On November 18, 2002, the Office of Inspector
General began a fact finding inquiry into allegations that senior management of the Los Alamos
National Laboratory engaged in a deliberate
cover-up of security breaches and illegal activities,
in particular, with respect to reported instances of
property loss and theft. The Acting Administrator
of the National Nuclear Security Administration
requested this inquiry based, in part, on media
reports that Los Alamos employees had misused
the Government purchase order system to buy millions of dollars worth of goods for personal use
and that Los Alamos management had attempted
to hide these events from the Department of
Energy and the public.

Shortly after our review began, Los Alamos terminated the employment of two security officials
who had been vocal in criticizing Los Alamos management's handling of property loss and theft
issues. We expanded our review to evaluate the circumstances surrounding those terminations. . . .

Our inquiry disclosed a series of actions by Laboratory officials that had the effect of obscuring
serious property and procurement management
problems and weakened or overrode relevant
internal controls. These actions created an
atmosphere in which Los Alamos employees were

discouraged from, or had reason to believe they
were discouraged from, raising concerns to appropriate authorities. In short, management's
actions—whether intended as a cover-up or not—
resulted in delayed identification and resolution of
the underlying property and procurement weaknesses, and related security concerns. . . .

Our inquiry corroborated a number of the
concerns expressed by the terminated security
officials related to weak internal controls and
other property management issues. The Laboratory's decision to terminate the two security officials during ongoing external reviews that were
addressing some of the very same issues raised by
these officials, and which were later corroborated,
was, in our judgment, incomprehensible. These
events raise doubt about Los Alamos' commitment
to solving noted problems, had the potential to
have a chilling effect on employees who may have
been willing to speak out on matters of
concern, and were inconsistent with Laboratory
and University of California obligations under its
contract with the Department of Energy. As you
know, the University recently announced that the
two security officials had been re-hired.

Our report of inquiry contains recommendations for corrective action. In particular, responsible
Department officials must ensure that the
University of California and the Laboratory's
management is held accountable for implementing
and executing corrective actions resulting from
the current situation at the Laboratory. . . .

---

reprimanded, passed over for promotion, or even
terminated.

The Civil Service Reform Act of 1978 prohibits reprisal against federal employees[14] or
applicants for federal jobs for "whistleblowing."
This prohibition was significantly strengthened
by the Whistleblower Protection Act of 1989 and
its 1994 amendments. Today, there are provisions
in at least thirty federal statutes protecting
whistleblowers in various contexts. Some critics
charge that the existing patchwork of laws is
confusing and contains too many gaps. Others

complain that existing laws have been inade-
quately enforced. Whistleblower cases are often
complicated by the fact that the agency or contractor accused of reprisal cites other reasons for
taking action against the employee. Whistleblowers are often accused of insubordination, nonfeasance, or violation of various agency policies.

The Office of Special Counsel The **Office
of Special Counsel** (OSC)[15] is an independent
agency within the executive branch established to
protect federal employees and job applicants from

BOX 10.4 Prohibited Personnel Practices Defined By 5 U.S.C.A. § 2302(B)

(1) discrimination against an employee or applicant based on race, color, religion, sex, national origin, age, handicapping condition, marital status, or political affiliation;

(2) soliciting or considering employment recommendations based on factors other than personal knowledge or records of job-related abilities or characteristics;

(3) coercing the political activity of any person;

(4) deceiving or willfully obstructing anyone from competing for employment;

(5) influencing anyone to withdraw from competition for any position so as to improve or injure the employment prospects of any other person;

(6) giving unauthorized preference or advantage to anyone so as to improve or injure the employment prospects of any particular employee or applicant;

(7) engaging in nepotism (hiring, promoting, or advocating the hiring or promotion of relatives);

(8) taking, failing to take, or threatening to take or fail to take a personnel action with respect to any employee or applicant because of any disclosure of information by the employee or applicant that he or she reasonably believes evidences a violation of a law, rule or regulation; gross mismanagement; gross waste of funds; an abuse of authority; or a substantial and specific danger to public health or safety;

(9) taking, failing to take, or threatening to take or fail to take a personnel action against an employee or applicant for exercising an appeal, complaint, or grievance right; testifying for or assisting another in exercising such a right; cooperating with or disclosing information to the Special Counsel or to an Inspector General; or refusing to obey an order that would require the individual to violate a law;

(10) discrimination based on personal conduct which is not adverse to the on-the-job performance of an employee, applicant, or others; or

(11) taking or failing to take, recommend, or approve a personnel action if taking or failing to take such an action would violate a veterans' preference requirement; and

(12) taking or failing to take a personnel action, if taking or failing to take action would violate any law, rule or regulation implementing or directly concerning merit system principles.

SOURCE: Adapted from Office of Special Counsel web site, online at http://www.osc.gov.

---

prohibited personnel practices, including retaliation for whistleblowing (see Box 10.4). OSC is designed to provide a "secure channel" through which agency employees can reveal information regarding agency improprieties that might lead to reprisals from supervisors. After receiving the allegation, OSC directs the head of the relevant agency to conduct an investigation. After doing so, the agency head must report the findings to the OSC, which in turn forwards these findings along with its own comments and recommendations to both Congress and the president. During this process, the OSC does not divulge the identity of the whistleblower without that party's consent. OSC conducts its own investigations of allegations of reprisals against whistleblowers. If its investigation substantiates a whistle-blower's complaint, OSC will request the agency involved to take remedial action with respect to the affected employee. If the agency refuses to comply or fails to implement the proposed remedy, OSC is empowered to file a petition with the Merit Systems Protection Board. MSPB is authorized to issue stays of pending personnel actions and to impose remedies that include reinstatement of terminated employees, reversal of suspensions and other adverse actions, reimbursement of attorney's fees, and issuance of back pay.

State Civil Service Laws

Every state has its own civil service system based on statutes enacted by its own legislature. Likewise, every state has some sort of executive or independent agency to administer the system and adjudicate cases involving termination or discipline of public employees.[16] Most states have their own versions of the Hatch Act[17] and their own statutory protections for whistleblowers.[18]

In *Kenner Police Dept. v. Kenner Municipal Fire & Police Civil Service Board*, **a Louisiana appellate court upheld the termination of five police officers who were fired for violating Louisiana's "Little Hatch Act." The decision is excerpted at the end of the chapter.**

DUE PROCESS PROTECTIONS FOR PUBLIC EMPLOYEES

The Due Process Clause of the Fifth Amendment states that the federal government may not deprive people of life, liberty, or property without due process of law. The Fourteenth Amendment applies this same requirement to state and local governments. Due process requires government to treat people fairly, but only where government action threatens life, liberty, or property. As the Supreme Court observed in 1972, "[t]he requirements of procedural due process apply only to the deprivation of interests encompassed by the . . . protection of liberty and property."[19]

Is There a Property Interest in Public Employment?

Traditionally, courts declined to view a job held by a public employee as a property interest entitled to **due process protection,** but that view no longer prevails. Public employment and other government benefits can be considered aspects of "the new property" that modern courts have come to recognize.[20] However, not all public employees automatically have the right to procedural due process; they must first demonstrate they have a property interest in their position. In *Board of Regents v. Roth* (1972),[21] the Supreme Court noted that "the range of interests protected by procedural due process is not infinite"[22] and that property interests are "defined by existing

rules or understandings that stem from an independent source such as state law—rules or understandings that secure certain benefits and that support claims of entitlement to those benefits."[23] Thus, in determining if a property interest exists, courts consider whether there is an employment contract, the past practices of the agency, as well as the laws and rules defining the position. For example, a tenured professor at the state university clearly has a property interest in maintaining his or her position, as the policies of the state university system permit the professor to be dismissed only for cause. Likewise, where the law states that a member of the civil service may be terminated only for cause, in effect a grant of tenure, such an employee has acquired a property interest in maintaining that position and may seek the protections of due process.

What Process Is Due?

Assuming a public employee can assert a property interest that triggers due process protections, the question becomes: What process is due before an agency can terminate the employee? In *Arnett v. Kennedy* (1974)[24] the Supreme Court addressed the requirement of affording due process of law where a tenured employee was discharged for cause. Wayne Kennedy, a Civil Service employee in the Office of Economic Opportunity (OEO) was discharged for allegedly having made recklessly false and defamatory statements about other OEO employees. Kennedy was given written notice of the reasons for his discharge and offered an opportunity to respond in person or in writing. The Court upheld the government's use of this informal, written decision-making procedure given the fact that under Civil Service regulations he had the right to a post-discharge trial-type hearing.

Following its decision in *Arnett v. Kennedy*, the Supreme Court in *Matthews v. Eldridge* (1976), delineated the factors to be considered in determining the extent of due process of law that must be afforded to a person whose liberty or property interests are to be adversely affected by government action. As we explained in Chapter 7, the

Court's 1976 decision in *Matthews v. Eldridge*[25] became the basis for lower courts to employ a balancing test that enabled them to uphold a variety of administrative actions without first holding an evidentiary hearing as long as provision is made for a post-agency action hearing.

In *Cleveland Board of Education v. Loudermill* (1985), another case discussed in Chapter 7, the Supreme Court held that a "tenured public employee is entitled to oral or written notice of the charges against him, an explanation of the employer's evidence, and an opportunity to present his side of the story."[26] The **pretermination hearing** need not be of the formal, adversary nature, because that "would intrude to an unwarranted extent on the government's interest in quickly removing an unsatisfactory employee."[27]

In 1997 the Supreme Court reviewed a case where Richard J. Homar, employed as a police officer at East Stroudsburg University (ESU), was immediately suspended without pay when the university learned he had been arrested on drug-related charges. Homar brought action against university officials alleging due process violations because he was not afforded a presuspension hearing. The U.S. Court of Appeals ruled in his favor, but the Supreme Court reversed and held that although Homar was a public employee with a protected interest, he was constitutionally entitled only to a "very limited hearing prior to his termination, to be followed by a more comprehensive post-termination hearing."[28] In discussing what process is constitutionally due a public employee who has a protected interest in continued employment the Court reiterated the need to balance the three it articulated in its 1976 decision in *Matthews v. Eldridge*: "First, the private interest that will be affected by the official action; second, the risk of an erroneous deprivation of such interest through the procedures used, and the probable value, if any, of additional or substitute procedural safeguards; and finally, the Government's interest."[29] The Court explained that the concept of due process of law is flexible and noted that the need for immediate action can permit an employer to dispense with a predeprivation hear-

ing. "The purpose on any pre-suspension hearing would be to assure that there are reasonable grounds to support the suspension without pay. . . . But here that has already been assured by the arrest and filing of charges."[30]

It is difficult to say with certainty just when a public agency can dispense with a predeprivation hearing when it discharges a tenured employee. Rather, it appears that the Court will continue to make an ad hoc review of such cases in determining the extent of pretermination due process that must be afforded. At some point, a public agency that dismisses a tenured employee must provide him or her with a **full-blown evidentiary hearing.** At this hearing the agency must produce witnesses or other evidence to show cause for the employee's dismissal. In most cases, the employee has the right to confront witnesses and challenge evidence submitted by the agency. The hearing must be presided over by an impartial decision maker.

Federal and state statutes enacted in the 1970s and 1980s have gone a long way toward expanding the procedural protections available to public employees who are terminated, suspended, or subjected to disciplinary actions. Consequently, there are fewer cases today where public employees invoke the due process protections of the Fifth or Fourteenth Amendments. But those vital clauses remain available in instances where statutory protections are inadequate to insure fundamental fairness.

EMPLOYEES' UNIONS, COLLECTIVE BARGAINING, AND THE RIGHT TO STRIKE

Federal workers began to join labor unions in 1889 with the formation of the National Association of Letter Carriers. There was considerable opposition to this development, which in some quarters was equated with "creeping socialism." In 1895, the postmaster general prohibited postal workers from visiting the nation's capital to influence legislation. And in 1902, President Teddy Roosevelt issued a so-called "gag order" prohibiting federal employees from soliciting members of Congress for wage increases or for other legislation. The Lloyd–LaFollette Act of 1912 rescinded the gag rule and guaranteed all federal workers the right to petition Congress. While the new law recognized federal employees' right to join labor organizations, it prohibited them from joining unions that would require them to strike, a prohibition that remains in effect today.[31]

Private sector employees gained the right to unionize via the National Labor Relations Act (NLRA) of 1935. The statute also prohibited employers from committing unfair labor practices that might impede organizing or prevent workers from negotiating a union contract. To this end, NLRA created the National Labor Relations Board (NLRB) to enforce these provisions. The law did not, however, apply to public sector personnel.

In 1962, President Kennedy issued an executive order providing that federal employees "shall have, and shall be protected in the exercise of, the right, freely and without feel of penalty or reprisal, to form, join and assist any employee organization or to refrain from any such activity."[32] In the wake of President Kennedy's order, union membership among federal civil service employees increased dramatically.

In 1978, Congress enacted the Federal Service Labor-Management Relations Statute.[33] The statute requires federal employers to meet with employees' collective-bargaining representative and to "negotiate in good faith for the purposes of arriving at a **collective bargaining agreement.**"[34] The statute also created the **Federal Labor Relations Authority (FLRA)** to oversee the relationship between federal agencies and labor unions and vested the FLRA with broad rulemaking and adjudicatory powers.[35]

Today, about 32 percent of the more than three million employees of the federal government are represented by labor unions.[36] The largest of these unions is the American Federation of Government Employees, which represents more than six hundred thousand federal employees.

In January 2002, President George W. Bush issued an executive order barring union representation at five offices of the U.S. Department of Justice.[37] The order affected more than five hundred employees in various agencies within the Justice Department, including the offices of U.S. Attorneys across the country. After the Republican Party regained control of Congress via the 2002 midterm congressional elections, President Bush was successful in getting Congress to pass legislation allowing the president to waive collective bargaining rights for employees in the new Department of Homeland Security. However, the law requires the president to notify Congress of his reasons for exercising such a waiver ten days before it takes effect.

Unionization of State and Local Employees

Because there is no federal statute providing state and local government employees the right to collective bargaining, such rights depend on applicable state statutes and, in some instances, local ordinances. Today, only about half the states allow state employees' unions to collectively bargain with state agencies regarding all terms of employment. Several other states permit collective bargaining only with regard to working conditions. In North Carolina, for instance, state law prohibits collective bargaining agreements between any government agency and any organization representing state employees.[38] The statute does not prohibit state employees from joining a union, which is an aspect of the freedom of association implicitly protected by the federal Constitution, but it does prevent any such union from engaging in collective bargaining. Advocates of organized labor argue that the right to unionize is hollow without the power of collective bargaining. Twenty-eight states allow local government employees' unions full collec-

---

BOX 10.5   Case in Point

Air Traffic Controllers Go on Strike
Professional Air Traffic Controllers v. Federal Labor
Relations Authority
United States Court of Appeals for the District
of Columbia Circuit
685 F.2d 547 (D.C. Cir. 1982)

The Professional Air Traffic Controllers Organization (PATCO) was the recognized exclusive bargaining representative for air traffic controllers
employed by the Federal Aviation Administration.
Following a breakdown in negotiations for a new
contract PATCO announced a strike deadline, and
on August 3, 1981, over 70 percent of the nation's
federally employed air traffic controllers walked
off the job, resulting in the cancellation of nearly

40 percent of flights nationwide. Two days after
the strike began, President Reagan fired the striking air traffic controllers. The FAA revoked
PATCO's status as bargaining representative and
obtained a restraining order against the strike. This
was followed by civil and criminal contempt citations when the restraining order was not heeded.
The Federal Labor Relations Authority (FLRA)
upheld the FAA's actions and eventually the case
came before the U.S. Court of Appeals for the D.C.
Circuit. In 1985 that court upheld the FLRA's
actions in revoking PATCO's status as union representative for the Air Controllers. In 1993, President
Bill Clinton issued an executive order permitting
former strikers to be rehired as air traffic
controllers.

---

tive bargaining rights. Nine other states allow
certain types of employees, such as teachers or
firefighters, to engage in collective bargaining.[39]
The largest union representing state and local
employees is the American Federation of State,
County and Municipal Employees (AFSCME),
which has over 1.3 million members in 3,500
local unions in forty-seven states.

Do Employees Have a Right to Strike against the Government?

Prior to the 1960s, nearly all states had laws prohibiting state and local employees from going
out on strike. Today, about one-fourth of the
states have enacted laws granting the **right to
strike** to public employees, although all of these
states still prohibit strikes by certain classes of
workers (e.g., police officers, prison guards, firefighters, hospital workers, court employees, etc.).
Federal law provides that a person "may not
accept or hold a position in the Government of
the United States or be a member of an organization of employees of the Government if he
participates in a strike, or asserts the right to
strike, against the Government of the United

States."[40] Participation in a strike against the federal government is also defined as a misdemeanor punishable by a fine and up to one year
in prison.[41] When members of the Professional
Air Traffic Controllers Union walked off the job
in 1981, they were summarily fired by President
Reagan (see the Case in Point in Box 10.5).

Rights of Union Members

Congress has provided that federal civil service
employees "shall have the right to form, join, or
assist any labor organization, or to refrain from
any such activity, freely and without fear of
penalty or reprisal, and each employee shall be
protected in the exercise of such right."[42] Federal
law also requires unions that represent federal
employees to follow democratic procedures, treat
members fairly, and maintain fiscal integrity.[43]
Congress has delegated authority to the secretary
of labor to adopt regulations to implement these
goals. These regulations are administered by the
Office of Labor Management Standards (OLMS),
located within the Employment Standards
Administration of the Department of Labor.[44]
The regulations require federal employees'

unions to conduct free and fair elections of union leaders, to utilize democratic procedures in raising union dues, and to provide full and fair hearings before imposing disciplinary measures on members. The regulations also guarantee union members freedom of speech and assembly with respect to union meetings, equal voting rights in union elections, and full access to collective bargaining agreements.

A federal employee who believes that one or more of these rights have been violated by union officials must first avail himself or herself of internal union procedures for filing and resolving complaints of this nature. Once these internal remedies are exhausted, the union member may file a complaint with a district office of the OLMS. If an initial screening by the district director indicates "reasonable grounds" for the complaint, the matter is referred to an administrative law judge for a hearing. At the hearing the union member carries the burden of proving that the union violated his or her rights. The ALJ's findings and recommendations are forwarded to the Assistant Secretary of Labor for Employment Standards who is empowered to dismiss the complaint or order the Union to take appropriate remedial action. There are no additional administrative appeals available; further recourse lies to the courts.[45]

Unions representing state and local employees are not covered by these federal statutes or regulations. Members of these unions must look to state laws and regulations for protection of their rights vis-à-vis union officials.

Right to Work Laws

Not all employees wish to join labor unions. Some are philosophically opposed to unions; many others prefer to be "free riders"—workers who benefit from collective bargaining agreements without paying union dues. Section 14(b) of the Taft-Hartley Act of 1947 affirmed the right of states to pass **right to work laws.** Under these laws, employees cannot be forced to pay union dues as a condition of employ-

ment. Right to work laws exist in about half the states. (Virginia's right to work law is featured in Box 10.6.) Obviously, such laws are anathema to labor unions, which argue that such laws "vastly decrease union membership, thus dramatically diminishing unions' bargaining power."[46] But many Americans see compulsory unionization as antithetical to traditional notions of individual freedom.

Negotiated Grievance Procedures

Most government agencies have internal grievance systems to resolve various disputes between an employee and the agency without the need for external intervention. One of the benefits of union representation is that collective bargaining agreements usually contain provisions under which agency employees may file grievances with their unions. Under what are termed **negotiated grievance procedures,** union officials work with agency officials to negotiate settlements of employee grievances. Often, collective bargaining agreements permit unions to refer grievances to an arbitrator jointly selected by the union and the agency.

CIVIL RIGHTS PROTECTIONS FOR PUBLIC EMPLOYEES

The Fourteenth Amendment to the U.S. Constitution prohibits states (and their political subdivisions) from denying to persons within their jurisdiction the **equal protection of the laws.** The Supreme Court has held that the Fifth Amendment imposes the same prohibition on the federal government.[47] Historically, these prohibitions were applied primarily to problems of racial discrimination. But in the modern era courts have recognized that a number of forms of discrimination are subject to equal protection challenges. For example, in 1973, the Supreme Court held that the Air Force violated the equal protection component of the Fifth Amendment

---

BOX 10.6 Virginia's Right to Work Law

Va. Code Ann. §§ 40.1-58 through 40.1-69

Article 3. *Denial or Abridgment of Right to Work*
§ 40.1-58. Policy of article.—*It is hereby declared to be the public policy of Virginia that the right of persons to work shall not be denied or abridged on account of membership or nonmembership in any labor union or labor organization.*

§ 40.1-58.1. Application of article to public employers and employees.—As used in this article, the words, *"person," "persons," "employer," "employees," "union," "labor union," "association," "organization"* and *"corporation"* shall include but not be limited to public employers, public employees and any representative of public employees in this State. The application of this article to public employers, public employees and their representatives shall not be construed as modifying in any way the application of § 40.1-55 to government employees.

§ 40.1-59. Agreements or combinations declared unlawful.—Any agreement or combination between any employer and any labor union or labor organization whereby persons not members of such union or organization shall be denied the

right to work for the employer, or whereby such membership is made a condition of employment or continuation of employment by such employer, or whereby any such union or organization acquires an employment monopoly in any enterprise, is hereby declared to be against public policy and an illegal combination or conspiracy.

§ 40.1-60. Employers not to require employees to become or remain members of union.—No person shall be required by an employer to become or remain a member of any labor union or labor organization as a condition of employment or continuation of employment by such employer.

§ 40.1-61. Employers not to require abstention from membership in union.—No person shall be required by an employer to abstain or refrain from membership in any labor union or labor organization as a condition of employment or continuation of employment.

§ 40.1-62. Employer not to require payment of union dues, etc.—No employer shall require any person, as a condition of employment or continuation of employment, to pay any dues, fees or other charges of any kind to any labor union or labor organization.

---

in requiring women, but not men, to demonstrate that their spouses were in fact dependents for the purpose of receiving medical and dental benefits.[48] Government employees and applicants for government jobs can invoke equal protection in challenging discriminatory policies and requirements, but in general they must show that the government intended to discriminate against them based on some impermissible criterion.[49]

The Fourteenth Amendment also authorizes Congress to enact laws to enforce the guarantee of equal protection. Congress has made extensive use of this authority and has also relied on its broad power to regulate interstate commerce in enacting laws that prohibit discrimination in the workplace. Generally speaking, these prohibitions apply to the governmental workplace as well as the private sector. Most cases alleging discrimination in the governmental workplace are brought on

the basis of federal statutes prohibiting **employment discrimination.** In many instances these statutes do not require plaintiffs to prove intentional discrimination—a showing of an unjustifiable discriminatory effect is often sufficient to prevail. Some states have enacted antidiscrimination laws that go beyond the prohibitions of the federal civil rights statutes.

Federal Laws Prohibiting Employment Discrimination

Title VII of the **Civil Rights Act of 1964**, as amended, prohibits employment discrimination on the basis of race, color, religion, sex, or national origin. These prohibitions now apply to federal, state, and local agencies as well as to the private sector.[50] Actionable issues include racial and gender discrimination in hiring and promotions, including the controversial question of affirmative action, as well as racial and sexual harassment.

Other federal civil rights laws provide significant protection to public employees. These include:

- The **Equal Pay Act** of 1963 (EPA). Protects men and women who perform substantially equal work in the same establishment from wage discrimination.

- The **Age Discrimination in Employment Act** of 1967 (ADEA). Protects people forty and over from age discrimination.

- **Title IX** of the Education Amendments of 1972. Prohibits discrimination based on sex in education programs or activities that receive federal funding. Title IX can be used to challenge sex discrimination in the compensation of teachers and other public school employees.

- Sections 501, 505 and 508 of the **Rehabilitation Act** of 1973. Prohibit discrimination against qualified individuals with disabilities who work in the federal government.

- Title I and Title V of the **Americans with Disabilities Act** of 1990 (ADA). Prohibit employment discrimination against qualified individuals with disabilities in the private sector and in state and local governments.

- The Civil Service Reform Act of 1978. Requires the federal government to provide fair and equitable treatment in all personnel matters without regard to political affiliation, race, color, religion, national origin, sex, marital status, age, or disabling condition.

Equal Employment Opportunity Commission

The **Equal Employment Opportunity Commission** (EEOC) is an independent agency created by Congress in 1964 to enforce Title VII of the Civil Rights Act of 1964. The EEOC enforces all of the federal laws pertaining to employment discrimination. The EEOC also provides oversight and coordination of all federal equal employment opportunity regulations, practices, and policies. Employees who believe they have been subjected to unlawful employment discrimination must first file a complaint with the EEOC. After investigating the complaint, the EEOC will make a determination as to whether there are grounds for a lawsuit. If so, the EEOC will provide the complainant with a **right-to-sue letter.**

Remedies available for employment discrimination include back pay, hiring, promotion, reinstatement, reasonable accommodation, and other remedies designed to restore the plaintiff to the condition he or she would have been in absent the unlawful discrimination. Under most of the civil rights statutes enforced by the EEOC, monetary damages also may be available where intentional discrimination is found. Damages may be awarded to compensate for actual or future monetary losses, for mental anguish, and for inconvenience. In most federal civil rights cases, **punitive damages** may be imposed if an employer acted with malice or reckless indifference.[51] However, punitive damages are not available against the federal, state, or local governments.

As a result of the Civil Service Reform Act of 1978, EEOC assumed responsibility for enforcing antidiscrimination laws applicable to the civilian federal workforce as well as coordinating all federal equal employment opportunity programs.

State and Local Laws Prohibiting Employment Discrimination

Most states and many cities have enacted civil rights laws pertaining to employment and the use of public accommodations. In many instances state laws mirror federal civil rights statutes, but some states have gone beyond the prohibitions and remedies of the federal law. In some instances state and local government employees may have additional protections against employment discrimination based on applicable provisions of state statutes and/or local ordinances. For example, there is no federal law prohibiting employment discrimination based on sexual orientation. But thirteen states and the District of Columbia have enacted laws prohibiting this type of discrimination in public and private employment. Another eight states have statutes prohibiting discrimination on the basis of sexual orientation in public employment only, and several other states have established this prohibition via executive order. It is important to remember that in a federal system, the rights of public employees are not defined solely by the United States Constitution, the statutes enacted by Congress, or the rules promulgated by federal agencies. State constitutions and statutes, local ordinances, and state and local administrative orders and rules can provide significant protections to public employees. Consequently, state and local employees who encounter discrimination may have remedies available to them in state courts and state and local administrative agencies.

Disparate Impact of Job Qualifications

In *Washington v. Davis* (1976),[52] the Supreme Court considered a challenge to the practice of requiring applicants to a police department to pass a verbal skills test that was used widely in the federal civil service. African-American applicants were approximately four times as likely to fail this test as white applicants. The Supreme Court rejected the argument that the testing requirement should be subjected to strict scrutiny under the Equal Protection Clause. Under *Washington v. Davis* and similar decisions, a policy that is racially neutral on its face but has a **disparate impact** on people of different races will be upheld unless plaintiffs can show that it was adopted to serve a racially discriminatory purpose.

As we noted above, plaintiffs proceeding under Title VII need not concern themselves with proving an employer's discriminatory intent. In *Griggs v. Duke Power Co.* (1971),[53] the Supreme Court held that Title VII

. . . proscribes not only overt discrimination but also practices that are fair in form, but discriminatory in operation. The touchstone is business necessity. . . . [G]ood intent or absence of discriminatory intent does not redeem employment procedures or testing mechanisms that operate as "built-in headwinds" for minority groups and are unrelated to measuring job capability.[54]

Employment practices that are subject to a disparate impact challenge include height and weight requirements, educational requirements, and written tests given to applicants. In challenging such practices, a plaintiff must prove that the challenged practice produces a disparate impact on a protected class (i.e., a group of persons defined by race, gender, religion, or national origin). If the plaintiff establishes this disparate impact by a preponderance of the evidence, the burden shifts to the agency, which has to prove, again by a preponderance of the evidence, that the challenged practice is "job-related for the position in question and consistent with business necessity."[55] Assuming the agency is able to do this, the plaintiff can still prevail in the lawsuit by showing that the agency refused to adopt a less discriminatory employment practice that would satisfy its legitimate interests.[56]

Affirmative Action

During the late 1960s and early 1970s federal agencies began to develop **affirmative action programs** with respect to hiring, contracting, and dispensing grants. These programs provided preferential treatment to members of racial and ethnic minorities, and often to women as well, in order to bring them into the economic and social mainstream. Historically, women and minorities were underrepresented in most public agencies, especially in leadership and managerial positions. State and local agencies followed suit, sometimes establishing affirmative action programs on their own initiative, but often goaded into adopting them by federal agencies using the highly effective inducement of federal grant money.

Proponents of affirmative action programs justified racial and gender preferences in hiring on the basis of the federal government's overarching commitment to the desegregation of public institutions and the need to enhance economic opportunities for members of traditionally disfavored groups.

From the outset, affirmative programs were extremely controversial. Opponents characterized affirmative action as "reverse discrimination," which they believed violated the principle of equal opportunity. Persons who believed that they were the victims of reverse discrimination sought relief in the courts under the Equal Protection Clause of the Fourteenth Amendment and the Civil Rights Act of 1964. Defenders of affirmative action admitted that it involved discrimination, but they characterized it as "benign discrimination," as distinct from the "invidious discrimination" to which women and minorities were traditionally subjected.

Early on the Supreme Court was favorably disposed toward affirmative action programs.[57] In a key decision in 1987, the Court upheld an affirmative action program for hiring and promoting minorities and women by a county transportation agency. Writing for the Court in *Johnson v. Transportation Agency*, Justice William Brennan concluded that the program involved "a moderate, flexible, case-by-case approach to effecting a gradual improvement in the representation of minorities and women in the Agency's work force."[58]

The Supreme Court's decision in *Johnson v. Transportation Agency* is excerpted at the end of the chapter.

As the Supreme Court became more conservative in the late 1980s and 1990s, it indicated in a number of decisions that it would not tolerate affirmative action programs unless they were tailored to remedy specific instances of discrimination. For example, in 1989, the Court struck down a Richmond, Virginia, policy that set aside a certain proportion of city public works contracts for "minority business enterprises."[59] In a key

decision in 1994, the Court said that it would subject all affirmative action programs established by government agencies to the highest level of judicial scrutiny.[60] The late 1990s witnessed a rollback of affirmative action programs across the country, either as the result of lawsuits or merely in response to the threat of litigation.

In 1998, civil rights organizations paid to fund an out-of-court settlement of an affirmative action case that was before the Supreme Court, thus preventing the Court from ruling on the issue (see the Case in Point in Box 10.7).

In 2003, the Court handed down two important rulings in the affirmative action area. In *Grutter v. Bollinger*,[61] the Court upheld the use of race in the admissions process of the law school at the University of Michigan. Writing for the Court, Justice Sandra Day O'Connor concluded that "in the context of its individualized inquiry into the possible diversity contributions of all applicants, the Law School's race-conscious admissions program does not unduly harm nonminority applicants."[62] But in *Gratz v. Bollinger*,[63] decided the same day, the Court invalidated the affirmative action program in use for undergraduate admissions at the same university. In both decisions, the Court held that the pursuit of "diversity" in the student population is a compelling interest that overrides the prohibition against racial discrimination. But in the undergraduate case, the Court ruled that the university's use of race in its admissions policy was not "narrowly tailored" to achieve this goal. Many commentators, hoping the Court would render greater clarity to a murky area of law, bemoaned what seemed to be a "split decision" on affirmative action.

Preferential Treatment of Veterans and Residents

Race, ethnicity, and gender are not the only bases upon which government agencies grant preferences in hiring. Since the Civil War, federal law has given preference to veterans who apply for federal jobs.[64] Nearly all the states also grant pref-

---

BOX 10.7   Case in Point

Affirmative Action
Taxman v. Board of Education
of the Piscataway Township
United States Court of Appeals for the Third Circuit
91 F.3d 1547 (3rd Cir. 1996)

This case involved a local school board's decision to lay off a teacher in the township's high school. The secretarial studies program had two teachers, one white and one African-American, who had been hired the same day, so they had equal seniority. The school board decided to keep the African-American teacher, and lay off Taxman, the white teacher, to further its "diversity objectives." Taxman filed a complaint with the Equal Employment Opportunity Commission. After a favorable finding by EEOC, Taxman brought suit under Title VII. The federal district court ruled for Taxman and ordered the board to pay her $144,000. The Court of Appeals for the Third Circuit affirmed, stating that Title VII did not allow race to be taken into

account in making any employment decision except those necessary to remedy proven past discrimination. Because there was no allegation of a pattern of past discrimination in the Piscataway school system, the Board of Education could not rely on this defense.

In 1998 the Supreme Court agreed to hear the case. Civil rights groups were concerned that the conservative majority of the Rehnquist Court might use the case to further weaken or even abolish affirmative action in the workplace. In order to prevent the case from going to the Court, civil rights groups donated substantial sums of money to fund a $435,000 out-of-court settlement. Supporters of affirmative action knew that another affirmative action case would eventually reach the Supreme Court, but they hoped that the Democratic candidate would win the presidency in 2000, and that a Democratic president might appoint justices to the Supreme Court who would be more sympathetic to affirmative action.

---

erences to veterans seeking state and government jobs. Not only do such preferences reward veterans for their service to their country, they facilitate the transition from military to civilian life. Of course, any official preference for one group of citizens over another is likely to raise an equal protection question. Because persons in military service historically have been disproportionately male, **veterans' preferences** has been criticized as a de facto form of sex discrimination.[65] In 1979, the Supreme Court rejected a sex discrimination challenge to a Massachusetts statute granting an employment preference to veterans.[66] The Court pointed out, as it has many times, that for there to be an equal protection violation, there must be discriminatory intent. The Court found no intent by the state of Massachusetts to discriminate against women. Of course, as the number of women in military service increases, the degree of de facto discrimination produced by veterans' preferences is attenuated.

States and cities often grant preferences to their own residents in the allocation of government jobs. For example, the Colorado Constitution requires that applicants for state jobs be residents of that state, although the State Personnel Board may waive this requirement with respect to specific positions.[67] Similarly, Montana law provides that a "state agency that operates within an Indian reservation shall give a preference in hiring for employment with the state agency to an Indian resident of the reservation who has substantially equal qualifications for the position."[68] Such preferences are subject to judicial challenge under the Privileges and Immunities Clause of Article IV, Section 2 of the U.S. Constitution, which provides: "The Citizens of each State shall be entitled to all Privileges and Immunities of Citizens in the several States." However, the courts have shown a willingness to invalidate only the most exclusionary **residential preferences.**[69]

Sexual Harassment

In *Meritor Savings Bank v. Vinson* (1986),[70] the Supreme Court held that **sexual harassment** in the workplace that is so "severe or pervasive" as to "alter the conditions of employment and create an abusive working environment" constitutes a violation of Title VII. Writing for the Court, Justice Rehnquist observed that sexual harassment "is every bit the arbitrary barrier to sexual equality at the workplace that racial harassment is to racial equality."[71] This decision produced a tidal wave of sexual harassment complaints. The Equal Employment Opportunity Commission now receives more than fifteen thousand such complaints each year and federal courts continue to grapple with difficult legal questions in this area. What exactly is sexual harassment? How is it to be differentiated from simple teasing? To what extent and under what circumstances are supervisors liable for harassment committed by subordinates? Because sexual harassment involves communication, to what extent does the First Amendment protect public employees from punitive action stemming from charges of harassment? While all of these questions have to be fully resolved, the Supreme Court has rendered several rulings in recent years that have helped to clarify the legal responsibilities of public administrators in dealing with sexual harassment in the government workplace. For example, in 1998 the Court ruled that a city may be found vicariously liable for sexual harassment of an employee by a supervisor, unless the city can show that it made reasonable efforts to prevent the harassment from taking place.[72] The same year, the Court held that Title IX of the Education Amendments of 1972 permits school districts to be held liable for sexual harassment by their teachers only if they know about the behavior and are "deliberately indifferent" to it.[73] Perhaps, as people become more accustomed to having persons of the opposite sex in the workplace and more aware of their legal rights and responsibilities in this area, sexual harassment will subside somewhat. Nevertheless, agencies must take all reasonable measures to insure that sexual harassment does not occur.

Age Discrimination

The Age Discrimination in Employment Act (ADEA)[74] protects workers who are forty and over from **age discrimination** in employment. The statutory protection applies not only to hiring and firing, but also to pay levels, promotions, layoffs, benefits, job assignments, training programs, and retirement policies. Originally, the ADEA was limited to private sector employers, but in 1974 Congress amended the statute to cover state governments and their political subdivisions.[75] In 1978, the statute was extended to cover federal agencies as well. The original ADEA permitted employers to impose **mandatory retirement** on their employees who had reached age sixty-five. In 1978 Congress raised the minimum mandatory retirement age to seventy. And in 1986 Congress prohibited mandatory retirement ages altogether for most workers. However, the prohibition of mandatory retirement ages does not apply to local, state, or federal public safety agencies. Police officers, firefighters, and air traffic controllers can still be subjected to mandatory retirement. For example, federal air traffic controllers are required to retire after twenty years service or age fifty-six, whichever comes later.[76]

Like Title VII, the ADEA is enforced primarily by the Equal Employment Opportunity Commission. EEOC's Age Discrimination Rules place the burden on employers to establish that policies that discriminate against older workers are based on "business necessity."[77] As in Title VII cases, EEOC issues right-to-sue letters to employees; it may also bring suit on the employee's behalf. In January 2003, the EEOC announced a record $250 million age-discrimination settlement in a suit claiming age discrimination by a state retirement program.[78] The suit alleged that the California Public Employees Retirement System shorted disability payments to 1,700 police, firefighters and other public safety personnel.

Employment Discrimination against Persons with Disabilities

As we noted above, Sections 501 and 505 of the Rehabilitation Act of 1973[79] prohibit discrimination against qualified individuals with disabilities who work in the federal government. Title I and Title V of the Americans with Disabilities Act (ADA) impose the same prohibition on state and local agencies. Thus all government agencies in the United States must take steps to ensure that they do not unnecessarily exclude or limit employees with disabilities. Qualifications and selection criteria that tend to screen out applicants with disabilities must be based on "business necessity." Agencies must provide **reasonable accommodation** to applicants and employees with disabilities unless doing so would cause undue hardship. Federal agencies are required by executive order to "establish effective written procedures for processing requests for reasonable accommodation by employees and applicants with disabilities."[80]

The Workforce Investment Act of 1998[81] requires that federal employees with disabilities have "comparable access" to and use of information and data stored by federal agencies. A new federal agency, the Center for Information Technology Accommodation (CITA), located within the General Services Administration, has responsibility for educating federal employees in this area and building the infrastructure needed to implement the accessibility requirements.

Declaring that "the federal government should be a model employer of individuals with disabilities" the EEOC has clarified the application of the ADA to federal workers by adopting a rule that became effective June 20, 2002. The new rule

- makes reassignment a reasonable accommodation that federal agencies can deny a worker only if it imposes an undue hardship;
- limits pre-employment inquiries into whether an applicant's medical condition will impair his or her performance of a job; and
- allows an employer to disqualify an individual from employment for health or safety reasons only if the individual poses "a significant risk of substantial harm" to oneself or others, even with a reasonable accommodation.[82]

Protection against Discrimination Based on Sexual Orientation

As we noted above, there is no federal statute that specifically prohibits government agencies from discriminating against employees on the basis of sexual orientation. However, the Civil Service Reform Act of 1978 (CSRA) provides that certain personnel actions can not be based on attributes or conduct that do not adversely affect employee performance.[83] In May 1998, President Clinton issued Executive Order 13087, which prohibits employment **discrimination based upon sexual orientation** within the executive branch of the federal government. Because this prohibition is not of a statutory nature, remedies lie not with the Equal Employment Opportunity Commission or the courts, but with the Merit Systems Protection Board, the Office of Special Counsel and with employees' own agencies. Federal employees who are covered by a collective bargaining agreement may file a grievance with their union.[84]

As we noted above, a number of states have enacted laws prohibiting sexual orientation discrimination in public employment.[85] In other states, governors have issued executive orders much like President Clinton did with respect to the federal executive agencies. For example, in March 2002, Alaska's governor signed an order prohibiting sexual orientation discrimination in state employment.[86] A number of cities have adopted ordinances prohibiting employment discrimination on the basis of sexual orientation. For example, even though the state of Texas has no such prohibition, Austin, Houston, and Dallas all have ordinances prohibiting employment discrimination based on sexual orientation. A number of cities around the country, from Anchorage to Ypsilanti, have enacted similar ordinances.

The Family Medical and Leave Act

Congress enacted the Family and Medical Leave Act (FMLA)[87] in 1993 to (1) balance the demands of the workplace with the needs of families, to promote the stability and economic security of families, and to promote national interests in preserving family integrity; and (2) entitle employees to take reasonable leave for medical reasons, for the birth or adoption of a child, and for the care of a child, spouse, or parent who has a serious health condition.

The act covers private employers with fifty or more employees, but federal, state, and local public agencies are covered regardless of the number of employees. A covered employer must grant an eligible employee up to a total of twelve workweeks of unpaid leave during any twelve-month period because of the:

- birth of a son or daughter of the employee and in order to care for such son or daughter;

- placement of a son or daughter with the employee for adoption or foster care;

- necessity to care for the spouse, or a son, daughter, or parent of the employee, if such spouse, son, daughter, or parent has a serious health condition; or

- a serious health condition that makes the employee unable to perform the functions of the position of such employee.

The FMLA makes it unlawful for any employer to interfere with, restrain, or deny the exercise of any right provided under the act or to discharge or discriminate against any person for opposing any practice made unlawful by the act or for involvement in any proceeding under or relating to the FMLA. The U.S. Department of Labor is authorized to investigate and resolve complaints of violations and is granted the power to subpoena necessary records in connection with investiga-

tions. An eligible employee may bring a civil action against an employer for violations. The FMLA does not affect any federal or state law prohibiting discrimination, or supersede any state or local law or collective bargaining agreement that provides greater family or medical leave rights.

FIRST AMENDMENT RIGHTS

The **First Amendment** protects citizens from governmental abridgments of their freedoms of speech, press, religion, and assembly. Implicitly, it protects their freedom of association as well.[88] Although the First Amendment was adopted to protect citizens from the federal government, the Supreme Court has held that First Amendment rights are enforceable against state and local governments inasmuch as they are incorporated within the liberty the **Fourteenth Amendment** protects against state action.[89] Thus public employees often invoke the First Amendment when the federal, state, or local agencies they work for threaten or limit their fundamental freedoms. Of course, these freedoms are not absolute, and courts must balance public employees' rights against the legitimate needs for order, security, and discipline in the governmental workplace.

Freedom of Speech

Just as students and teachers do not "shed their constitutional rights to **freedom of speech** or expression at the schoolhouse gate,"[90] "a public employee does not relinquish First Amendment rights to comment on matters of public interest by virtue of government employment."[91] The classic case in this area is *Pickering v. Board of Education* (1968),[92] in which a public school teacher was dismissed for sending a letter to a newspaper criticizing the local board of education. The teacher sued for reinstatement and eventually the Supreme Court held that the school board could not deprive Pickering, the teacher, of his right as a citizen to comment on matters of public concern. In 1983 the Supreme Court emphasized that in applying standards it articulated in *Pickering* courts must determine whether a public employee's speech touches on a matter of public concern and look to the content, form, and context of a given statement as revealed by the whole record. When the employee's expression does not satisfy this inquiry, the First Amendment does not offer protection.[93]

In 1987, the Court held that dismissal of a worker in a constable's office violated the First Amendment when the employee was fired after making an intemperate political remark. When Ardith McPherson heard that John Hinckley had tried unsuccessfully to assassinate former President Ronald Reagan, she remarked, "If they go for him again, I hope they get him." In *Rankin v. McPherson* (1987),[94] the Supreme Court held that McPherson's First Amendment rights had been violated. Her speech, while distasteful to many (including her superiors), addressed a matter of public concern. Moreover, her comment was made in a nonthreatening context.

The Supreme Court's decision in *Rankin v. McPherson* is excerpted at the end of the chapter.

In *United States v. National Treasury Employees Union* (1995),[95] the Court struck down a provision of the Ethics in Government Act that barred federal civil service employees from accepting honoraria for speeches and articles. Although the ban was content-neutral, it applied to all honoraria, even those received for speeches and writings having nothing to do with civil servants' jobs. Writing for the dissenters, Chief Justice Rehnquist complained that the majority's "application of the First Amendment understates the weight which should be accorded to the governmental justifications for the honoraria ban and overstates the amount of speech which actually will be deterred."[96]

An area of public employment which always provides fertile ground for First Amendment controversies is public education. Over the years there have been numerous disputes, many of which have led to litigation, over what teachers and professors may say in the classroom. Quite frequently these disputes have involved the expression of unpopular or controversial views on political issues. In other instances teachers have been disciplined for addressing sexual topics in a manner deemed inappropriate by school authorities (see, for example, the Case in Point in Box 10.8). While courts have taken the view that public school authorities may circumscribe classroom expression, courts insist that such restrictions are clear, reasonable, and applied evenhandedly.

Freedom of Religion

In addition to guaranteeing **free exercise of religion,** the U.S. Constitution stipulates that no religious test may be required to hold office.[97] In *Torcaso v. Watkins* (1961),[98] the Supreme Court struck down a provision of the Maryland Constitution that prohibited anyone who would not profess belief in God from holding public office. Seldom, especially today, do laws and policies affecting public employment intrude so blatantly into matters of religion. More often, public agencies are challenged because they are unable or unwilling to accommodate employees' religious practices and preferences.

As we noted above in the discussion of federal civil rights laws, Title VII prohibits **employment discrimination based on religion.** Today, most of the legal action dealing with religious freedom in the public workplace takes place under Title VII rather than the First Amendment. Not only does Title VII prohibit public agencies from hiring, firing, and promoting employees with regard to their religion, agencies must make "reasonable accommodation" for religious expression by their employees, unless doing so would create "undue hardship" for the agency in the performance of its duties.[99] Of course, terms like "reasonable accommodation" and "undue hardship" are terms about which reasonable people can disagree and about which there has been considerable litigation. The courts generally take the position that "reasonable accommodation" does not mean that agencies must provide the specific accommodation requested by the employee (see, for example, the

---

BOX 10.8 Case in Point

A College Professor Accused of Sexual Harassment
Cohen v. San Bernardino Valley College
United States Court of Appeals
for the Ninth Circuit
92 F.3d 968 (9th Cir. 1996)

Dean Cohen, a tenured English professor at a California community college, was disciplined for violating the college's policy against sexual harassment. Cohen's teaching emphasized controversial subjects, his teaching style was highly confrontational, and his language in the classroom was often vulgar and profane. During a classroom discussion on pornography, Cohen read Hustler and Playboy articles out loud in class. When Cohen assigned his students to write a paper defining pornography, a female student requested an alternative assignment. Cohen refused to give her one; the student stopped attending class and received a failing grade. After unsuccessfully complaining to Cohen's department chair, the student subsequently filed a formal grievance against Cohen, asserting that he had sexually harassed her. After conducting

a hearing on the matter, a college grievance committee found that Professor Cohen had violated the institution's sexual harassment policy by creating a hostile learning environment in his classroom. The board of trustees imposed a number of disciplinary measures against Professor Cohen, who responded by filing a federal lawsuit claiming deprivation of his First Amendment rights. The trial court dismissed the case against the college and granted summary judgment to the school officials named as defendants in the suit, ruling that the college did not violate Cohen's First Amendment rights. On appeal, the Ninth Circuit Court of Appeals reversed. The court held that the sexual harassment policy was "simply too vague as applied to Cohen in this case." The court observed that "Cohen's speech did not fall within the core region of sexual harassment as defined by the Policy." Rather, the court found that "officials of the College, on an entirely ad hoc basis, applied the Policy's nebulous outer reaches to punish teaching methods that Cohen had used for many years." The Supreme Court denied the College's petition for certiorari.

Case in Point in Box 10.9). The Supreme Court has said that

> . . . where the employer has already reasonably accommodated the employee's religious needs, the statutory inquiry is at an end. The employer need not further show that each of the employee's alternative accommodations would result in undue hardship. [The question of] undue hardship . . . is at issue only where the employer claims that it is unable to offer any reasonable accommodation without such hardship.[100]

In *Shelton v. University of Medicine & Dentistry of New Jersey* a federal appeals court considers whether a state hospital discriminated against an employee based on her religious beliefs and practices in violation of Title VII of the Civil Rights Act and infringed her First Amendment right to free exercise of religion. The decision is excerpted at the end of the chapter.

FOURTH AMENDMENT RIGHTS

The **Fourth Amendment** to the U.S. Constitution prohibits unreasonable searches and seizures conducted by police and other officials. The Fourth Amendment applies to the federal government; the Fourteenth Amendment extends the prohibition of unreasonable searches and seizures to state and local officials.[101] Of course, state constitutions contain similar provisions, and state courts are free to interpret those provisions so as to provide higher levels of protection than are afforded by the Fourth Amendment. In some instances public employees may find their state courts more solicitous of their privacy rights than are the federal courts. The Fourth Amendment protects citizens' **reasonable expectations of privacy**.[102] Unless there is a reasonable expectation of privacy in a particular setting or situation, the protections of the Fourth Amendment do not apply. This is often a serious obstacle for public employees seeking to invoke Fourth

---

BOX 10.9 Case in Point

Reasonable Accommodation of an Employee's Religious Beliefs
Rodriguez V. City of Chicago
United States Court of Appeals
for the Seventh Circuit
156 F.3d 771 (7th Cir. 1998)

Rodriguez, a police officer, refused for religious reasons to guard an abortion clinic and protect its employees from protesters. When he requested an exemption from this duty, his supervisor informed him he could not refuse an assignment. However, the department provided Rodriguez the opportu-

nity to transfer to another district (in which there was no abortion clinic) at the same pay and benefit levels. Rodriguez refused the offer, took the assignment under protest, and brought suit under Title VII of the 1964 Civil Rights Act. The federal district court granted the police department's motion for summary judgment. The Court of Appeals affirmed, ruling the police department had reasonably accommodated the officer's religious beliefs. The court held that the accommodation available to Rodriguez was not unreasonable simply because it would have prevented Rodriguez from staying in a district of his choosing.

Amendment protections, as courts generally do not regard privacy expectations in the workplace to be as great as those associated with one's home. Generally speaking, employees working in airports, schools, prisons, military installations, government laboratories, and other security-conscious environments will have lower expectations of privacy than employees working in more conventional office buildings.

A public employee has virtually no expectation of privacy in the common areas of the workplace. There may be some expectation of privacy in one's own office, especially if it is configured in such a way to allow for privacy. Expectations of privacy are much higher with respect to personal effects the employee brings to the office. Today, a problem that is vexing the courts is the degree of privacy that an employee should expect with regard to communications such as telephone calls, faxes, and emails. One could argue that because the employee is using the agency's equipment and facilities, that there is no reasonable expectation of privacy. Yet telephone conversations, and, increasingly, email messages are used by employees all the time for personal communications. Should these communications not be entitled to some degree of privacy?

Assuming a public employee does have a reasonable expectation of privacy in a particular

setting or situation, the reasonableness of a given search "depends upon all of the circumstances surrounding the search or seizure and the nature of the search or seizure itself."[103] The reasonableness of a search "is judged by balancing its intrusion on the individual's Fourth Amendment interests against its promotion of legitimate governmental interests."[104]

When a search is conducted by law enforcement officers seeking to discover evidence of crime, the Fourth Amendment generally requires a **search warrant.** Search warrants are issued by judges or magistrates upon a showing of **probable cause.** Warrantless searches are permissible under **exigent circumstances,** assuming police have probable cause to search. Courts are generally reluctant to apply these requirements to the government workplace. Most searches of the public workplace are not conducted by police and most are not criminal in nature. Some searches conducted by agency personnel are investigatory in nature; others are merely routine or precautionary. **Administrative searches** that involve only minor inconvenience to employees are not apt to cause serious Fourth Amendment problems. Searches that potentially subject employees to embarrassment, disciplinary action, termination or criminal prosecution are scrutinized more closely by the courts. (We discuss administrative searches in Chapter 5.)

BOX 10.10   Supreme Court Perspective

O'Connor v. Ortega
480 U.S. 709 (1987)

[Dr. Magno Ortega had primary responsibility for training physicians in the psychiatric residency program at Napa State Hospital in California for seventeen years. Hospital officials became concerned about possible improprieties in his management of the program. While he was on administrative leave pending investigation of the charges, hospital officials, allegedly in order to inventory and secure state property, searched his office and seized personal items from his desk and file cabinets that were used in administrative proceedings resulting in his discharge. No formal inventory of the property in the office was ever made, and all the other papers in the office were merely placed in boxes for storage. Ortega filed a federal lawsuit against hospital officials under 42 U.S.C. § 1983, alleging that the search of his office violated the Fourth Amendment. The federal district court granted hospital officials' motion for summary judgment, finding that there was no Fourth Amendment violation. After the Ninth Circuit Court of Appeals reversed, the hospital officials obtained review in the Supreme Court. In a plurality opinion, Justice O'Connor found that Dr. Ortega had a "reasonable expectation of privacy" in his hospital office and therefore the protections of the Fourth Amendment applied. However, O'Connor took the position that the special environment of the public hospital made the probable cause and warrant requirements inapplicable. The Supreme Court remanded the case to the Ninth Circuit for reconsideration. In the following excerpt from the plurality opinion, Justice O'Connor considers Fourth Amendment requirements in the context of the public workplace.]

Justice O'Connor delivered the opinion of the Court . . .

The legitimate privacy interests of public employees in the private objects they bring to the workplace may be substantial. Against these privacy interests, however, must be balanced the realities of the workplace, which strongly suggest that a warrant requirement would be unworkable. . . .

In our view, requiring an employer to obtain a warrant whenever the employer wished to enter an employee's office, desk, or file cabinets for a work-related purpose would seriously disrupt the routine conduct of business and would be unduly burdensome. Imposing unwieldy warrant procedures in such cases upon supervisors, who would otherwise have no reason to be familiar with such procedures, is simply unreasonable. . . .

Whether probable cause is an inappropriate standard for public employer searches of their employees' offices presents a more difficult issue. . . .

The governmental interest justifying work-related intrusions by public employers is the efficient and proper operation of the workplace. Government agencies provide myriad services to the public, and the work of these agencies would suffer if employers were required to have probable cause before they entered an employee's desk for the purpose of finding a file or piece of office correspondence. Indeed, it is difficult to give the concept of probable cause, rooted as it is in the criminal investigatory context, much meaning when the purpose of a search is to retrieve a file for work-related reasons. Similarly, the concept of probable cause has little meaning for a routine inventory conducted by public employers for the purpose of securing state property. . . . To ensure the efficient and proper operation of the agency, therefore, public employers must be given wide latitude to enter employee offices for work-related, noninvestigatory reasons. . . .

As Justice O'Connor observed in 1987, "requiring an employer to obtain a warrant whenever the employer wished to enter an employee's office, desk, or file cabinets for a work-related purpose would seriously disrupt the routine conduct of business and would be unduly burdensome. Imposing unwieldy warrant procedures in such cases upon supervisors, who would otherwise have no reason to be familiar with such procedures, is simply unreasonable."[105] While recognizing that probable cause is "a more difficult issue," O'Connor likewise concluded that imposing the probable cause requirement in such cases "would impose intolerable burdens on public employers."[106] (See the Supreme Court Perspective in Box 10.10.)

BOX 10.10 Supreme Court Perspective (Continued)

. . . In contrast to law enforcement officials, . . . public employers are not enforcers of the criminal law; instead, public employers have a direct and overriding interest in ensuring that the work of the agency is conducted in a proper and efficient manner. In our view, therefore, a probable cause requirement for searches of the type at issue here would impose intolerable burdens on public employers. The delay in correcting the employee misconduct caused by the need for probable cause rather than reasonable suspicion will be translated into tangible and often irreparable damage to the agency's work, and ultimately to the public interest. . . . Additionally, while law enforcement officials are expected to 'schoo[l] themselves in the niceties of probable cause,' . . . no such expectation is generally applicable to public employers, at least when the search is not used to gather evidence of a criminal offense. It is simply unrealistic to expect supervisors in most government agencies to learn the subtleties of the probable cause standard. . . .

Balanced against the substantial government interests in the efficient and proper operation of the workplace are the privacy interests of government employees in their place of work which, while not insubstantial, are far less than those found at home or in some other contexts. . . . [T]he employer intrusions at issue here 'involve a relatively limited invasion' of employee privacy. . . . Government offices are provided to employees for the sole purpose of facilitating the work of an agency. The employee may avoid exposing personal belongings at work by simply leaving them at home.

In sum, we conclude that the "special needs, beyond the normal need for law enforcement make the . . . probable-cause requirement impracticable," . . . for legitimate work-related, noninvestigatory intrusions as well as investigations of work-related misconduct. A standard of reasonableness will neither unduly burden the efforts of government employers to ensure the efficient and proper operation of the workplace, nor authorize arbitrary intrusions upon the privacy of public employees. . . .

Drug Testing

One of the more controversial constitutional questions involving public employees today is **drug testing.** Many local, state, and federal agencies, especially in the fields of law enforcement and education (see the Case in Point in Box 10.11), require their employees to submit to periodic or random drug testing as a condition of employment or promotion. In *National Treasury Employees Union v. Von Raab* (1989),[107] the Supreme Court recognized that drug testing by public agencies is a form of search and is therefore subject to challenge under the Fourth Amendment. At the same time the Court upheld drug testing of Customs Inspectors, who are directly involved in drug interdiction. In 1997, however, the Court struck down a Georgia law requiring all candidates for state office to submit to drug tests.[108] Between the two decisions lies a gray area that is now the subject of considerable litigation in state and federal courts.

The Supreme Court's decision in *National Treasury Employees Union v. Von Raab* is excerpted at the end of the chapter.

CONCLUSION

By the end of the nineteenth century employees of the federal government had evolved from being a part of the "spoils system" to positions of dignity under civil service protection. The twentieth century witnessed them being rewarded based on meritorious performance and not political activity, and later gaining the right to opt for unionization. In the 1960s laws were enacted to prohibit employment discrimination on the basis of race, color, religion, sex, or national origin, followed by decades that focused on interpreting such laws and providing a forum to enforce the rights of public employees. The mandates of the 1990s were to end

---

BOX 10.11   Case in Point

Drug Testing of Public School Teachers
Knox County Education Association v. Knox
County Board of Education
United States Court of Appeals for the Sixth Circuit
158 F. 3d 361 (6th Cir. 1998)

In 1994 the Knox County, Tennessee, Board of Education adopted a drug-testing program requiring all new teachers, principals and assistant principals, secretaries, and bus drivers to undergo drug testing via urinalysis. The local teachers' union sued, claiming the policy violated the Fourth Amendment prohibition of unreasonable searches and seizures. A federal district judge agreed and enjoined the school board from enforcing the policy. The U.S.

Court of Appeals for the Sixth Circuit reversed, saying that even without evidence of a drug problem among teachers, drug testing is justified by the "unique role" teachers play in school children's lives. The court observed that teachers "leave indelible impressions on the minds of their young students, because they are entrusted with the safe keeping and education of children during their most impressionable and formative years. Therefore, teachers must expect that with this extraordinary responsibility, they will be subject to scrutiny to which other civil servants or professionals might not be subjected, including drug testing." In 1999, the Supreme Court denied the Knox County Education Association's petition for certiorari.

---

employment discrimination against qualified individuals with disabilities and provide administrative and judicial protection to whistleblowers. Although many reforms in the civil service originated in the federal system, states have also made significant reforms in the field of public employment.

In the twenty-first century the ramifications of affirmative action and some aspects of discrimination in public employment remain to be clarified judicially. Litigation, however, has not proven to be the ideal method of resolving most contemporary claims of public employees.

Rather, today most issues of accommodation of religious practices, defining the extent of privacy of public employees, and arriving at workable definitions of sexual harassment in the workplace can be resolved administratively within the framework of the federal and state constitutions and statutes. The present challenge in administrative law is to strike an appropriate balance between the necessities of the government as employer and the legitimate rights of its employees. But always this must be accomplished with the recognition that the bureaucracy exists to serve the citizens of the nation.

KEY TERMS

administrative searches

affirmative action programs

age discrimination

Age Discrimination in
Employment Act

Americans with Disabilities Act

Civil Rights Act of 1964

Civil Service Reform Act

collective bargaining agreement

discrimination based upon
sexual orientation

disparate impact

drug testing

due process protection

employment discrimination

employment discrimination
based on religion

Equal Employment Opportunity
Commission

Equal Pay Act

equal protection of the laws

exigent circumstances

Federal Labor Relations Authority

First Amendment

Fourteenth Amendment

Fourth Amendment

free exercise of religion

freedom of speech

full-blown evidentiary hearing

Hatch Act

Lloyd-LaFollette Act

malfeasance

mandatory retirement

Merit Systems Protection Board

misfeasance

negotiated grievance procedures

nonfeasance

Office of Personnel Management

Office of Special Counsel

Pendleton Act

pretermination hearing

probable cause

prohibited personnel practices

punitive damages

reasonable accommodation

reasonable expectations of privacy

Rehabilitation Act

residential preferences

right to strike

right to work laws

right-to-sue letter

search warrant

sexual harassment

spoils system

Title VII

Title IX

U.S. Civil Service Commission

veterans' preferences

whistleblower

QUESTIONS FOR THOUGHT AND DISCUSSION

1. Do the restrictions the Hatch Act imposes on political activities of federal employees strike a fair balance between the rights of the government employees to participate in the nation's political system and the objective that public employment be governed by meritorious service rather than political influence?

2. What is a "whistleblower"? How does the Civil Service Reform Act of 1978 and the Whistleblower Protection Act of 1989, as amended in 1994, seek to afford protection to whistleblowers? What, if any, additional protections should be provided?

3. What is a "collective bargaining agreement"? What is the role of the Federal Labor Relations Authority (FLRA) in respect to unions and collective bargaining?

4. Under what circumstance can a public employee who has been discharged establish that he or she had a "property interest" in employment sufficient to be entitled to an evidentiary hearing on the reasons for being terminated?

5. The Taft-Hartley Act of 1947 affirmed the right of states to pass "right to work laws" providing that workers cannot be forced to pay union dues as a condition of employment. Those who support such laws see compulsory unionization as antithetical to individual freedom, while labor unions argue that such controversial laws, which exist in about half the states, diminish their power to negotiate collective bargaining agreements. Assume you are a staff member for a state senator and the legislature is considering the repeal of its right to work law. What arguments would you present for the legislator to consider in determining whether to vote to uphold or repeal the law?

6. Title VII of the Civil Rights Act of 1964, as amended, prohibits employment discrimination on the basis of race, color, religion, sex, or national origin in federal, state, and local agencies as well as in the private sector. What role does the Equal Employment Opportunity Commission (EEOC) play in enforcement of the act?

7. Assume you are a staff member of a state environmental agency. Agency regulations prohibit any unwelcome sexual advances, requests for sexual favors, physical or verbal conduct of a sexual nature, or visual exposure of sexual materials in the workplace. You are asked to review the present regulations and draft any proposals that would better define the agency's prohibition against sexual harassment. How would you respond?

8. What classes of employees are still subject to mandatory retirement despite the protections of the Age Discrimination in Employment Act (ADEA)? What is the rationale for exempting such employees from the protections of the ADEA?

9. Ima Academic, a public school teacher, has a desk with unlocked drawers in her classroom, where only she teaches. She keeps her purse in a drawer along with students' papers. One day she stashed a letter from her boyfriend in the drawer. In his letter the boyfriend sympathized with her concern that she might be found to have violated the school's policy that prohibits anyone from bringing any alcoholic beverages on the campus. That afternoon an assistant principal, while conducting a routine search of classroom equipment, read the letter and then handed it to the principal. The principal initiated disciplinary action against Ms. Academic whom she had already suspected of having brought alcoholic beverages on campus. At the disciplinary hearing Ms. Academic objected to the school board considering the letter on the ground that seizure of the letter violated her constitutional right of expectation of privacy. What ruling is the school board likely to make on this issue? Why?

10. On the basis of your study of this chapter, do you think a court would likely approve a requirement that employees of a public day-care center for preschool-age children be subjected to random drug testing? Why or why not?

EDITED CASE Kenner Police Dept. v. Kenner Municipal Fire & Police Civil Service Board

Louisiana Court of Appeals, 5th Circuit 783 So.2d 392 (La.App. 5 Cir. 2001)

[This appeal was brought by five former police officers that were fired for violating Louisiana's "Little Hatch Act" prohibiting political activity by civil service employees. A lower court determined that the officers were properly terminated in that they did violate the law.]

Judge McManus delivered the opinion of the court.

. . . These appeals arise from a ruling of the Kenner Municipal Fire and Police Civil Service Board. The five Appellants in this case, Wesley T. West, Sr., Dennis Lynch, Robert Polito, Henry Jaume and Bruce Verrette, were Kenner Police Department employees. They were terminated by the Appointing Authority of the City of Kenner Police Department, for alleged violations of La.R.S. 33:2504 [which] prohibits political activity by civil service employees.

The Appellants appealed their termination to the Kenner Municipal Fire and Police Civil Service Board, and also sought injunctive relief in federal court. The federal district court denied summary judgment on the Appellants' civil-rights claims concluding that the employees had violated provisions prohibiting political activity. The United States Court of Appeals for the Fifth Circuit affirmed the district court's decision.

On June 25, 1999, the Civil Service Board found violations of La.R.S. 33:2504, but concluded that termination was inappropriate and reinstated the five employees. Both the Appointing Authority and the five Appellants appealed the decision of the Civil Service Board. On appeal, the district court affirmed the decision by the Civil Service Board . . . , but reversed the decision that termination was inappropriate and that Appellants be reinstated. The five Appellants now appeal that judgment. . . .

Appellants, Wesley T. West, Sr., Dennis Lynch, Robert Polito, Henry Jaume, and Bruce Verrette, were former police officers for the city of Kenner. They were also members of an organization called the Police Association of the City of Kenner (PACK). In fact, the Appellants made up the entire executive board of PACK. On March 3, 1998, each appellant signed and mailed a letter to the members of PACK announcing the Executive Board's decision to endorse and support Joe Stagni in his campaign for political office. The Appellants did not obtain the approval of the entire organization before making

---

EDITED CASE Kenner Police Dept. v. Kenner Municipal Fire &
Police Civil Service Board (Continued)

---

this decision. In fact, thirteen members of PACK wrote a letter to the PACK Executive Board objecting to the manner in which the decision to endorse and support Mr. Stagni was made.

Despite this objection, on March 13, 1998, the PACK Executive Board conducted a meeting of just the Board and voted to make a campaign contribution to candidate Joe Stagni. The five Appellants voted 5-0 in favor of the financial contribution, and on March 30, 1998, the Appellants did in fact make a $300.00 financial contribution to the Joseph Stagni Campaign Fund.

Subsequently, the Appointing Authority conducted a formal investigation for possible violations of La.R.S. 33:2504. On June 15, 1998, the Appellants were terminated under La.R.S. 33:2504(3). The statute provides, in pertinent part: "No employee in the classified service shall, directly or indirectly, pay, or promise to pay, any assessment, subscription, or contribution for any political organization or purpose, or solicit or take part in soliciting any such assessment, subscription, or contribution."

The Civil Service Board concluded that the five officers both directly and indirectly caused a $300 contribution to the Stagni campaign in violation of La.R.S. 33:2504(3). The Civil Service Board also found that the PACK Executive Board did not notify the rest of the PACK membership of the decision to endorse and support Mr. Stagni until after the decision was already made, and financially contributed to the Stagni campaign fund without getting the approval of PACK as a whole.

The district court concluded that the Civil Service Board had legal cause for its findings. The court found that the Appellants controlled PACK and did in fact violate the provisions of La.R.S. 33:2504. The district court further found that the endorsement of Mr. Stagni and contribution to his campaign amounted to political activity prohibited by the statute. Finally, the district court also found that the appropriate penalty is termination. . . .

It is well settled that a court of appeal may not upset the factual findings of a trial court absent manifest error or unless they are clearly wrong. . . . Where there is conflict in the testimony, reasonable evaluations of credibility and reasonable inferences of fact should not be disturbed upon review, even though the appellant

court may feel that its own evaluations and inferences are as reasonable. When findings are based on determinations regarding the credibility of witnesses, the manifest error standard demands great deference to the trier of fact's findings. . . . Only the factfinder can be aware of the variations in demeanor and tone of voice that bear so heavily on the listener's understanding and belief in what is said. . . .

The first question is whether there was a violation of La.R.S. 33:2504. This requires us to determine who made the campaign contribution at issue, the five Appellants or PACK. It is true that the money came from PACK funds, and that the Appellants signed the contribution check as the PACK Executive Board. However, we conclude that the weight of the evidence points towards this contribution being a personal action taken by the five Appellants individually, and not an action of PACK as an organization.

The evidence reveals that the five Appellants, as members of the PACK Executive Board, decided to endorse and support candidate Joe Stagni. No formal vote or poll of the PACK membership was taken to approve or disapprove of this action. A letter was sent to the PACK membership welcoming any objection to the endorsement, but this letter came after the decision to endorse the candidate was already made. The Appellants then conducted a meeting of just the PACK Executive Board. In this meeting, the five Appellants voted 5-0 in favor of the campaign contribution.

As pointed out above, the Appellants did address a letter to the membership of PACK concerning the endorsement. We find the language of this letter quite instructive. It reads: "At this time we, the Executive Board of the Police Association City of Kenner (P.A.C.K.), have decided to endorse and support Mr. Stagni in his endeavor to seek political office."

We note that the letter clearly demonstrates that the Appellants made the decision to endorse and support Mr. Stagni. We also point out that several members of PACK did indeed object to the process by which the Executive Board decided to endorse Mr. Stagni. The PACK members expressed

(Continued)

EDITED CASE   Kenner Police Dept. v. Kenner Municipal Fire &
Police Civil Service Board (Continued)

---

disapproval that they were not included in the decision. Nevertheless, the Appellants then held a meeting of only the Executive Board, and individually voted to contribute to Mr. Stagni's campaign fund. No member of PACK testified that they were aware of the financial campaign contribution in advance of it being given to candidate Stagni. We also find it significant that prior to the Appellants in this case, PACK has never before been involved with the endorsement of a candidate for political office. We see no manifest error in the district court's finding that the Appellants individually endorsed and contributed to a political candidate in violation of La.R.S. 33:2504. . . .

The statute prohibits political activity by civil service employees and mandates that the appropriate disciplinary action for such activity is termination. There is no inherent conflict between La.R.S. 33:2504 and La.R.S. 33:2507, as suggested by the Appellants. La.R.S. 33:2507 states that anyone who "willfully" violates any provision in this section shall be fined and deemed ineligible for any position in the classified service, and "shall forfeit his office or position" if he is an officer or employee of the classified civil service. Applying La.R.S. 33:2507, the Civil Service Board concluded that the Appellants should not have been terminated because the violations were not done willfully. The district court reversed this decision to reinstate the Appellants relying instead on La.R.S. 33:2504(B). The language of La.R.S. 33:2504(B) is mandatory and clearly states that "the appointing authority shall discharge from

the service any employee whom he deems guilty of violating any or more of the provisions of this Section." We find that the district court correctly applied La.R.S. 33:2504(B). The language of La.R.S. 33:2507 provides for additional penalties beyond termination for civil service employees who willfully participate in political activity. However, neither statute allows for a penalty of less than termination for a violation of La.R.S. 33:2504.

Finally, we address the Appellants' argument that "causing" a contribution to be made is not the same as directly or indirectly making a contribution. The Appellants submit that the Civil Service Board and the district court are adding a prohibition not contained in the statute, that is "causing" a third party to make a contribution. In its decision, the Civil Service Board concluded: the five officers, both indirectly and directly, caused a $300 contribution to the Stagni campaign in violation of La.R.S. 33:2504(3).

The statute prohibits direct or indirect contributions to political candidates. We note that the Appellants were the sole members of the PACK Executive Board, and by virtue of this position they controlled the funds of the organization. At the very least, the evidence shows that the Appellants indirectly contributed funds to Mr. Stagni's campaign fund, and therefore violated the statute. . . .

This Court affirms the decision of the district court that there was a violation of La.R.S. 33:2504. We further find that the appropriate penalty under the statute is termination.

EDITED CASE   Johnson v. Transportation Agency
United States Supreme Court, 480 U.S. 616 (1987)

[In this case, the Supreme Court approves an affirmative action plan established by a county transportation agency. Pursuant to the plan, the agency passed over Paul Johnson, a male employee, and promoted a female employee applicant, Diane Joyce. After receiving a right-to-sue letter from the Equal Employ- *ment Opportunity Commission (EEOC), Johnson brought suit in the District Court for the Northern District of California, arguing that the plan violated Title VII of the Civil Rights Act of 1964. The Court of Appeals for the Ninth Circuit reversed and the Supreme Court affirmed the circuit court's decision.]*

EDITED CASE Johnson v. Transportation Agency (Continued)

Justice Brennan delivered the opinion of the Court.

I

In December 1978, the Santa Clara County Transit District Board of Supervisors adopted an Affirmative Action Plan (Plan) for the County Transportation Agency. The Plan implemented a County Affirmative Action Plan, which had been adopted, declared the County, because "mere prohibition of discriminatory practices is not enough to remedy the effects of past practices and to permit attainment of an equitable representation of minorities, women and handicapped persons." . . . Relevant to this case, the Agency Plan provides that, in making promotions to positions within a traditionally segregated job classification in which women have been significantly underrepresented, the Agency is authorized to consider as one factor the sex of a qualified applicant.

In reviewing the composition of its work force, the Agency noted in its Plan that women were represented in numbers far less than their proportion of the County labor force in both the Agency as a whole and in five of seven job categories. Specifically, while women constituted 36.4% of the area labor market, they composed only 22.4% of Agency employees. Furthermore, women working at the Agency were concentrated largely in EEOC job categories traditionally held by women: women made up 76% of Office and Clerical Workers, but only 7.1% of Agency Officials and Administrators, 8.6% of Professionals, 9.7% of Technicians, and 22% of Service and Maintenance Workers. As for the job classification relevant to this case, none of the 238 Skilled Craft Worker positions was held by a woman. . . . The Plan noted that this underrepresentation of women in part reflected the fact that women had not traditionally been employed in these positions, and that they had not been strongly motivated to seek training or employment in them "because of the limited opportunities that have existed in the past for them to work in such classifications." . . . The Plan also observed that, while the proportion of ethnic minorities in the Agency as a whole exceeded the proportion of such minorities in the County work force, a smaller percentage of minority employees held management, professional, and technical positions.

The Agency stated that its Plan was intended to achieve "a statistically measurable yearly improvement in hiring, training and promotion of minorities and women throughout the Agency in all major job classifications where they are underrepresented." . . . As a benchmark by which to evaluate progress, the Agency stated that its long-term goal was to attain a work force whose composition reflected the proportion of minorities and women in the area labor force. . . . Thus, for the Skilled Craft category in which the road dispatcher position at issue here was classified, the Agency's aspiration was that eventually about 36% of the jobs would be occupied by women.

The Plan acknowledged that a number of factors might make it unrealistic to rely on the Agency's long-term goals in evaluating the Agency's progress in expanding job opportunities for minorities and women. Among the factors identified were low turnover rates in some classifications, the fact that some jobs involved heavy labor, the small number of positions within some job categories, the limited number of entry positions leading to the Technical and Skilled Craft classifications, and the limited number of minorities and women qualified for positions requiring specialized training and experience. . . . As a result, the Plan counseled that short-range goals be established and annually adjusted to serve as the most realistic guide for actual employment decisions. Among the tasks identified as important in establishing such short-term goals was the acquisition of data "reflecting the ratio of minorities, women and handicapped persons who are working in the local area in major job classifications relating to those utilized by the County Administration," so as to determine the availability of members of such groups who "possess the desired qualifications or potential for placement." . . . These data on qualified group members, along with predictions of position vacancies, were to serve as the basis for "realistic yearly employment goals for women, minorities and handicapped persons in each EEOC job category and major job classification." . . .

The Agency's Plan thus set aside no specific number of positions for minorities or women, but

(Continued)

EDITED CASE   Johnson v. Transportation Agency (Continued)

---

authorized the consideration of ethnicity or sex as a factor when evaluating qualified candidates for jobs in which members of such groups were poorly represented. One such job was the road dispatcher position that is the subject of the dispute in this case.

On December 12, 1979, the Agency announced a vacancy for the promotional position of road dispatcher in the Agency's Roads Division. Dispatchers assign road crews, equipment, and materials, and maintain records pertaining to road maintenance jobs. Id., at 23-24. The position requires at minimum four years of dispatch or road maintenance work experience for Santa Clara County. The EEOC job classification scheme designates a road dispatcher as a Skilled Craft Worker.

Twelve County employees applied for the promotion, including Joyce and Johnson. Joyce had worked for the County since 1970, serving as an account clerk until 1975. She had applied for a road dispatcher position in 1974, but was deemed ineligible because she had not served as a road maintenance worker. In 1975, Joyce transferred from a senior account clerk position to a road maintenance worker position, becoming the first woman to fill such a job. Tr. 83-84. During her four years in that position, she occasionally worked out of class as a road dispatcher.

Petitioner Johnson began with the County in 1967 as a road yard clerk, after private employment that included working as a supervisor and dispatcher. He had also unsuccessfully applied for the road dispatcher opening in 1974. In 1977, his clerical position was downgraded, and he sought and received a transfer to the position of road maintenance worker. . . . He also occasionally worked out of class as a dispatcher while performing that job.

Nine of the applicants, including Joyce and Johnson, were deemed qualified for the job, and were interviewed by a two-person board. Seven of the applicants scored above 70 on this interview, which meant that they were certified as eligible for selection by the appointing authority. The scores awarded ranged from 70 to 80. Johnson was tied for second with a score of 75, while Joyce ranked next with a score of 73. A second interview was conducted by three Agency supervisors, who ultimately recommended that Johnson be promoted. Prior to the second interview, Joyce had

contacted the County's Affirmative Action Office because she feared that her application might not receive disinterested review. The Office in turn contacted the Agency's Affirmative Action Coordinator, whom the Agency's Plan makes responsible for, inter alia, keeping the Director informed of opportunities for the Agency to accomplish its objectives under the Plan. At the time, the Agency employed no women in any Skilled Craft position, and had never employed a woman as a road dispatcher. The Coordinator recommended to the Director of the Agency, James Graebner, that Joyce be promoted.

Graebner, authorized to choose any of the seven persons deemed eligible, thus had the benefit of suggestions by the second interview panel and by the Agency Coordinator in arriving at his decision. After deliberation, Graebner concluded that the promotion should be given to Joyce. As he testified: "I tried to look at the whole picture, the combination of her qualifications and Mr. Johnson's qualifications, their test scores, their expertise, their background, affirmative action matters, things like that. . . . I believe it was a combination of all those." . . .

The certification form naming Joyce as the person promoted to the dispatcher position stated that both she and Johnson were rated as well qualified for the job. The evaluation of Joyce read: "Well qualified by virtue of 18 years of past clerical experience including 3 1/2 years at West Yard plus almost 5 years as a [road maintenance worker]." . . . The evaluation of Johnson was as follows: "Well qualified applicant; two years of [road maintenance worker] experience plus 11 years of Road Yard Clerk. Has had previous outside Dispatch experience but was 13 years ago." Ibid. Graebner testified that he did not regard as significant the fact that Johnson scored 75 and Joyce 73 when interviewed by the two-person board. . . .

Petitioner Johnson filed a complaint with the EEOC alleging that he had been denied promotion on the basis of sex in violation of Title VII. He received a right-to-sue letter from the EEOC on March 10, 1981, and on March 20, 1981, filed suit in the United States District Court for the Northern District of California. The District Court found that Johnson was more qualified for the dispatcher position than Joyce, and that the sex of Joyce was the "determining factor in her selection." . . . The

---

EDITED CASE Johnson v. Transportation Agency (Continued)

court acknowledged that, since the Agency justified its decision on the basis of its Affirmative Action Plan, the criteria announced in *Steelworkers v. Weber*, 443 U.S. 193 (1979), should be applied in evaluating the validity of the Plan. . . . It then found the Agency's Plan invalid on the ground that the evidence did not satisfy *Weber*'s criterion that the Plan be temporary. . . . The Court of Appeals for the Ninth Circuit reversed, holding that the absence of an express termination date in the Plan was not dispositive, since the Plan repeatedly expressed its objective as the attainment, rather than the maintenance, of a work force mirroring the labor force in the County. . . . The Court of Appeals added that the fact that the Plan established no fixed percentage of positions for minorities or women made it less essential that the Plan contain a relatively explicit deadline. . . . The Court held further that the Agency's consideration of Joyce's sex in filling the road dispatcher position was lawful. The Agency Plan had been adopted, the court said, to address a conspicuous imbalance in the Agency's work force, and neither unnecessarily trammeled the rights of other employees, nor created an absolute bar to their advancement. . . .

II

. . . The assessment of the legality of the Agency Plan must be guided by our decision in *Weber*, supra. In that case, the Court addressed the question whether the employer violated Title VII by adopting a voluntary affirmative action plan designed to "eliminate manifest racial imbalances in traditionally segregated job categories." . . . The respondent employee in that case challenged the employer's denial of his application for a position in a newly established craft training program, contending that the employer's selection process impermissibly took into account the race of the applicants. The selection process was guided by an affirmative action plan, which provided that 50% of the new trainees were to be black until the percentage of black skilled craftworkers in the employer's plant approximated the percentage of blacks in the local labor force. Adoption of the plan had been prompted by the fact that only 5 of 273, or 1.83%, of skilled craftworkers at the plant were black, even though the work force in the area was approximately 39% black. Because of the historical exclusion of blacks from craft positions,

the employer regarded its former policy of hiring trained outsiders as inadequate to redress the imbalance in its work force.

We upheld the employer's decision to select less senior black applicants over the white respondent, for we found that taking race into account was consistent with Title VII's objective of "break[ing] down old patterns of racial segregation and hierarchy." . . .

. . . In reviewing the employment decision at issue in this case, we must first examine whether that decision was made pursuant to a plan prompted by concerns similar to those of the employer in *Weber*. Next, we must determine whether the effect of the Plan on males and non-minorities is comparable to the effect of the plan in that case.

The first issue is therefore whether consideration of the sex of applicants for Skilled Craft jobs was justified by the existence of a "manifest imbalance" that reflected underrepresentation of women in "traditionally segregated job categories." . . . In determining whether an imbalance exists that would justify taking sex or race into account, a comparison of the percentage of minorities or women in the employer's work force with the percentage in the area labor market or general population is appropriate in analyzing jobs that require no special expertise, . . . or training programs designed to provide expertise. . . . Where a job requires special training, however, the comparison should be with those in the labor force who possess the relevant qualifications. . . . The requirement that the "manifest imbalance" relate to a "traditionally segregated job category" provides assurance both that sex or race will be taken into account in a manner consistent with Title VII's purpose of eliminating the effects of employment discrimination, and that the interests of those employees not benefiting from the plan will not be unduly infringed. . . .

It is clear that the decision to hire Joyce was made pursuant to an Agency plan that directed that sex or race be taken into account for the purpose of remedying underrepresentation. The Agency Plan acknowledged the "limited opportunities that have existed in the past," . . . for women to find employment in certain job classifications "where

(Continued)

EDITED CASE   Johnson v. Transportation Agency (Continued)

women have not been traditionally employed in significant numbers." . . . As a result, observed the Plan, women were concentrated in traditionally female jobs in the Agency, and represented a lower percentage in other job classifications than would be expected if such traditional segregation had not occurred. . . . The Plan sought to remedy these imbalances through "hiring, training and promotion of . . . women throughout the Agency in all major job classifications where they are underrepresented." . . .

As an initial matter, the Agency adopted as a benchmark for measuring progress in eliminating underrepresentation the long-term goal of a work force that mirrored in its major job classifications the percentage of women in the area labor market. Even as it did so, however, the Agency acknowledged that such a figure could not by itself necessarily justify taking into account the sex of applicants for positions in all job categories. For positions requiring specialized training and experience, the Plan observed that the number of minorities and women "who possess the qualifications required for entry into such job classifications is limited." . . . The Plan therefore directed that annual short-term goals be formulated that would provide a more realistic indication of the degree to which sex should be taken into account in filling particular positions. . . . The Plan stressed that such goals "should not be construed as 'quotas' that must be met," but as reasonable aspirations in correcting the imbalance in the Agency's work force. . . . These goals were to take into account factors such as "turnover, lay-offs, lateral transfers, new job openings, retirements and availability of minorities, women and handicapped persons in the area work force who possess the desired qualifications or potential for placement." . . . The Plan specifically directed that, in establishing such goals, the Agency work with the County Planning Department and other sources in attempting to compile data on the percentage of minorities and women in the local labor force that were actually working in the job classifications constituting the Agency work force. . . . From the outset, therefore, the Plan sought annually to develop even more refined measures of the underrepresentation in each job category that required attention.

As the Agency Plan recognized, women were most egregiously underrepresented in the Skilled Craft job category, since none of the 238 positions was occupied by a woman. In mid-1980, when Joyce was selected for the road dispatcher position, the Agency was still in the process of refining its short-term goals for Skilled Craft Workers in accordance with the directive of the Plan. This process did not reach fruition until 1982, when the Agency established a short-term goal for that year of 3 women for the 55 expected openings in that job category—a modest goal of about 6% for that category.

We reject petitioner's argument that, since only the long-term goal was in place for Skilled Craft positions at the time of Joyce's promotion, it was inappropriate for the Director to take into account affirmative action considerations in filling the road dispatcher position. The Agency's Plan emphasized that the long-term goals were not to be taken as guides for actual hiring decisions, but that supervisors were to consider a host of practical factors in seeking to meet affirmative action objectives, including the fact that in some job categories women were not qualified in numbers comparable to their representation in the labor force.

By contrast, had the Plan simply calculated imbalances in all categories according to the proportion of women in the area labor pool, and then directed that hiring be governed solely by those figures, its validity fairly could be called into question. This is because analysis of a more specialized labor pool normally is necessary in determining underrepresentation in some positions. If a plan failed to take distinctions in qualifications into account in providing guidance for actual employment decisions, it would dictate mere blind hiring by the numbers, for it would hold supervisors to "achievement of a particular percentage of minority employment or membership . . . regardless of circumstances such as economic conditions or the number of available qualified minority applicants. . . ."

The Agency's Plan emphatically did not authorize such blind hiring. It expressly directed that numerous factors be taken into account in making hiring decisions, including specifically the qualifications of female applicants for particular jobs. Thus, despite the fact that no precise short-term goal

---

EDITED CASE   Johnson v. Transportation Agency (Continued)

---

was yet in place for the Skilled Craft category in mid-1980, the Agency's management nevertheless had been clearly instructed that they were not to hire solely by reference to statistics. The fact that only the long-term goal had been established for this category posed no danger that personnel decisions would be made by reflexive adherence to a numerical standard.

Furthermore, in considering the candidates for the road dispatcher position in 1980, the Agency hardly needed to rely on a refined short-term goal to realize that it had a significant problem of underrepresentation that required attention. Given the obvious imbalance in the Skilled Craft category, and given the Agency's commitment to eliminating such imbalances, it was plainly not unreasonable for the Agency to determine that it was appropriate to consider as one factor the sex of Ms. Joyce in making its decision. The promotion of Joyce thus satisfies the first requirement enunciated in *Weber,* since it was undertaken to further an affirmative action plan designed to eliminate Agency work force imbalances in traditionally segregated job categories.

We next consider whether the Agency Plan unnecessarily trammeled the rights of male employees or created an absolute bar to their advancement. In contrast to the plan in *Weber,* . . . the Plan sets aside no positions for women. The Plan expressly states that "[t]he 'goals' established for each Division should not be construed as 'quotas' that must be met." . . . Rather, the Plan merely authorizes that consideration be given to affirmative action concerns when evaluating qualified applicants. As the Agency Director testified, the sex of Joyce was but one of numerous factors he took into account in arriving at his decision. . . . [T]he Agency Plan requires women to compete with all other qualified applicants. No persons are automatically excluded from consideration; all are able to have their qualifications weighed against those of other applicants.

In addition, petitioner had no absolute entitlement to the road dispatcher position. Seven of the applicants were classified as qualified and eligible, and the Agency Director was authorized to promote any of the seven. Thus, denial of the promotion unsettled no legitimate, firmly rooted expectation on the part of petitioner.

Furthermore, while petitioner in this case was denied a promotion, he retained his employment with the Agency, at the same salary and with the same seniority, and remained eligible for other promotions.

Finally, the Agency's Plan was intended to attain a balanced work force, not to maintain one. The Plan contains 10 references to the Agency's desire to "attain" such a balance, but no reference whatsoever to a goal of maintaining it. The Director testified that, while the "broader goal" of affirmative action, defined as "the desire to hire, to promote, to give opportunity and training on an equitable, non-discriminatory basis," is something that is "a permanent part" of "the Agency's operating philosophy," that broader goal "is divorced, if you will, from specific numbers or percentages." . . .

The Agency acknowledged the difficulties that it would confront in remedying the imbalance in its work force, and it anticipated only gradual increases in the representation of minorities and women. It is thus unsurprising that the Plan contains no explicit end date, for the Agency's flexible, case-by-case approach was not expected to yield success in a brief period of time. Express assurance that a program is only temporary may be necessary if the program actually sets aside positions according to specific numbers. . . . This is necessary both to minimize the effect of the program on other employees, and to ensure that the plan's goals "[are] not being used simply to achieve and maintain . . . balance, but rather as a benchmark against which" the employer may measure its progress in eliminating the underrepresentation of minorities and women. . . . In this case, however, substantial evidence shows that the Agency has sought to take a moderate, gradual approach to eliminating the imbalance in its work force, one which establishes realistic guidance for employment decisions, and which visits minimal intrusion on the legitimate expectations of other employees. Given this fact, as well as the Agency's express commitment to "attain" a balanced work force, there is ample assurance that the Agency does not seek to use its Plan to maintain a permanent racial and sexual balance.

(Continued)

EDITED CASE   Johnson v. Transportation Agency (Continued)

III

In evaluating the compliance of an affirmative action plan with Title VII's prohibition on discrimination, we must be mindful of "this Court's and Congress' consistent emphasis on 'the value of voluntary efforts to further the objectives of the law.'" . . . The Agency in the case before us has undertaken such a voluntary effort, and has done so in full recognition of both the difficulties and the potential for intrusion on males and nonminorities. The Agency has identified a conspicuous imbalance in job categories traditionally segregated by race and sex. It has made clear from the outset, however, that employment decisions may not be justified solely by reference to this imbalance, but must rest on a multitude of practical, realistic factors. It has therefore committed itself to annual adjustment of goals so as to provide a reasonable guide for actual hiring and promotion decisions. The Agency earmarks no positions for anyone; sex is but one of several factors that may be taken into account in evaluating qualified applicants for a position. As both the Plan's language and its manner of operation attest, the Agency has no intention of establishing a work force whose permanent composition is dictated by rigid numerical standards.

We therefore hold that the Agency appropriately took into account as one factor the sex of Diane Joyce in determining that she should be promoted to the road dispatcher position. The decision to do so was made pursuant to an affirmative action plan that represents a moderate, flexible, case-by-case approach to effecting a gradual improvement in the representation of minorities and women in the Agency's work force. Such a plan is fully consistent with Title VII, for it embodies the contribution that voluntary employer action can make in eliminating the vestiges of discrimination in the workplace. Accordingly, the judgment of the Court of Appeals is . . . Affirmed.

Justice Stevens, concurring. . . .

Justice O'Connor, concurring in the judgment.

. . . I concur in the judgment of the Court in light of our precedents. I write separately, however, because the Court has chosen to follow an expansive and ill-defined approach to voluntary affirmative action by public employers despite the limitations imposed by the Constitution and by the provisions of Title VII, and because Justice Scalia's dissent rejects the Court's precedents and addresses the question of how Title VII should be interpreted as if the Court were writing on a clean slate. The former course of action gives insufficient guidance to courts and litigants; the latter course of action serves as a useful point of academic discussion, but fails to reckon with the reality of the course that the majority of the Court has determined to follow.

In my view, the proper initial inquiry in evaluating the legality of an affirmative action plan by a public employer under Title VII is no different from that required by the Equal Protection Clause. In either case, consistent with the congressional intent to provide some measure of protection to the interests of the employer's nonminority employees, the employer must have had a firm basis for believing that remedial action was required. An employer would have such a firm basis if it can point to a statistical disparity sufficient to support a prima facie claim under Title VII by the employee beneficiaries of the affirmative action plan of a pattern or practice claim of discrimination. . . .

In sum, I agree that respondents' affirmative action plan as implemented in this instance with respect to skilled craft positions satisfies the requirements of [the Court's precedents in this area.] Accordingly, I concur in the judgment of the Court.

Justice White, dissenting.

. . . My understanding of *Weber* was, and is, that the employer's plan did not violate Title VII because it was designed to remedy the intentional and systematic exclusion of blacks by the employer and the unions from certain job categories. That is how I understood the phrase "traditionally segregated jobs" that we used in that case. The Court now interprets it to mean nothing more than a manifest imbalance between one identifiable group and another in an employer's labor force. As so interpreted, that case, as well as today's decision . . . is a perversion of Title VII. I would overrule *Weber* and reverse the judgment below.

Justice Scalia, with whom *The Chief Justice* joins, and with whom *Justice White* joins [in part], dissenting.

. . . The most significant proposition of law established by today's decision is that racial or sexual discrimination is permitted under Title VII when it is intended to overcome the effect, not of the employer's own discrimination, but of societal attitudes that have limited the entry of certain races, or of a particular sex, into certain jobs.

EDITED CASE Johnson v. Transportation Agency (Continued)

. . . In fact, however, today's decision goes well beyond merely allowing racial or sexual discrimination in order to eliminate the effects of prior societal discrimination. The majority opinion often uses the phrase "traditionally segregated job category" to describe the evil against which the plan is legitimately (according to the majority) directed. As originally used in *Steelworkers v. Weber,* 443 U.S. 193 (1979), that phrase described skilled jobs from which employers and unions had systematically and intentionally excluded black workers—traditionally segregated jobs, that is, in the sense of conscious, exclusionary discrimination. . . . But that is assuredly not the sense in which the phrase is used here. It is absurd to think that the nationwide failure of road maintenance crews, for example, to achieve the Agency's ambition of 36.4% female representation is attributable primarily, if even substantially, to systematic exclusion of women eager to shoulder pick and shovel. It is a "traditionally segregated job category" not in the *Weber* sense, but in the sense that, because of longstanding social attitudes, it has not been regarded by women themselves as desirable work. Or as the majority opinion puts the point, quoting approvingly the Court of Appeals: "'A plethora of proof is hardly necessary to show that women are generally underrepresented in such positions and that strong social pressures weigh against their participation.'" . . . Given this meaning of the phrase, it is patently false to say that "[t]he requirement that the 'manifest imbalance' relate to a 'traditionally segregated job category' provides assurance . . . that sex or race will be taken into account in a manner consistent with Title VII's

purpose of eliminating the effects of employment discrimination." . . . There are, of course, those who believe that the social attitudes which cause women themselves to avoid certain jobs and to favor others are as nefarious as conscious, exclusionary discrimination. Whether or not that is so (and there is assuredly no consensus on the point equivalent to our national consensus against intentional discrimination), the two phenomena are certainly distinct. And it is the alteration of social attitudes, rather than the elimination of discrimination, which today's decision approves as justification for state-enforced discrimination. This is an enormous expansion, undertaken without the slightest justification or analysis. It is unlikely that today's result will be displeasing to politically elected officials, to whom it provides the means of quickly accommodating the demands of organized groups to achieve concrete, numerical improvement in the economic status of particular constituencies. Nor will it displease the world of corporate and governmental employers . . . for whom the cost of hiring less qualified workers is often substantially less—and infinitely more predictable—than the cost of litigating Title VII cases and of seeking to convince federal agencies by nonnumerical means that no discrimination exists. In fact, the only losers in the process are the Johnsons of the country, for whom Title VII has been not merely repealed but actually inverted. The irony is that these individuals—predominantly unknown, unaffluent, unorganized—suffer this injustice at the hands of a Court fond of thinking itself the champion of the politically impotent. I dissent.

EDITED CASE Rankin v. McPherson
United States Supreme Court, 483 U.S. 378 (1987)

[In this case a clerical employee in a county constable's office was discharged for remarking, after hearing of an attempt on the life the of the President, "If they go for him again, I hope they get him." The Supreme Court must decide whether the dismissal was a violation of the First Amendment.]

Justice Marshall delivered the opinion of the Court.

. . . On January 12, 1981, respondent Ardith McPherson was appointed a deputy in the office of the constable of Harris County, Texas. The constable

(Continued)

EDITED CASE   Rankin v. McPherson (Continued)

---

is an elected official who functions as a law enforcement officer. At the time of her appointment, McPherson, a black woman, was 19 years old and had attended college for a year, studying secretarial science. Her appointment was conditional for a 90-day probationary period.

Although McPherson's title was "deputy constable," this was the case only because all employees of the constable's office, regardless of job function, were deputy constables. She was not a commissioned peace officer, did not wear a uniform, and was not authorized to make arrests or permitted to carry a gun. McPherson's duties were purely clerical. . . .

On March 30, 1981, McPherson and some fellow employees heard on an office radio that there had been an attempt to assassinate the President of the United States. Upon hearing that report, McPherson engaged a co-worker, Lawrence Jackson, who was apparently her boyfriend, in a brief conversation . . . [According to McPherson's uncontroverted testimony, she remarked,] ". . . shoot, if they go for him again, I hope they get him."

McPherson's . . . remark was overheard by another deputy constable, who, unbeknownst to McPherson, was in the room at the time. The remark was reported to Constable Rankin, who summoned McPherson. McPherson readily admitted that she had made the statement, but testified that she told Rankin, upon being asked if she made the statement, "Yes, but I didn't mean anything by it." After their discussion, Rankin fired McPherson.

McPherson brought suit in the United States District Court for the Southern District of Texas under 42 U.S.C. sec 1983, alleging that petitioner Rankin, in discharging her, had violated her constitutional rights under color of state law. She sought reinstatement, back pay, costs and fees, and other equitable relief. . . .

[T]he District Court held . . . that the statements were not protected [under the First Amendment]. . . . [In reversing the District Court], the Court of Appeals concluded that the Government's interest did not outweigh the First Amendment interest in protecting McPherson's speech. Given the nature of McPherson's job and the fact that she was not a law enforcement officer, was not brought by virtue of her job into contact with the public, and did not have access to sensitive infor-

mation, the Court of Appeals deemed her "duties . . . so utterly ministerial and her potential for undermining the office's mission so trivial" as to forbid her dismissal for expression of her political opinions. "However ill-considered Ardith McPherson's opinion was," the Court of Appeals concluded, "it did not make her unfit" for the job she held in Constable Rankin's office. . . .

We . . . affirm [the judgment of the Court of Appeals]. . . .

The determination whether a public employer has properly discharged an employee for engaging in speech requires "a balance between the interests of the [employee], as a citizen, in commenting upon matters of public concern and the interest of the State, as an employer, in promoting the efficiency of the public services it performs through its employees." . . . This balancing is necessary in order to accommodate the dual role of the public employer as a provider of public services and as a government entity operating under the constraints of the First Amendment. On one hand, public employers are employers, concerned with the efficient function of their operations; review of every personnel decision made by a public employer could, in the long run, hamper the performance of public functions. In the other hand, "the threat of dismissal from public employment is . . . a potent means of inhibiting speech." . . . Vigilance is necessary to ensure that public employers do not use authority over employees to silence discourse, not because it hampers public functions but simply because superiors disagree with the content of employees' speech.

The threshold question in applying this balancing test is whether McPherson's speech may be "fairly characterized as constituting speech on a matter of public concern." . . . "Whether an employee's speech addresses a matter of public concern must be determined by the content, form, and context of a given statement, as revealed by the whole record." . . . The District Court apparently found that McPherson's speech did not address a matter of public concern. The Court of Appeals rejected this conclusion, finding that "the life and death of the President are obviously matters of public concern" . . .

Considering the statement in context discloses that it plainly dealt with a matter of public con-

---

EDITED CASE   Rankin v. McPherson (Continued)

---

cern. The statement was made in the course of a conversation addressing the policies of the President's administration. . . . While a statement that amounted to a threat to kill the President would not be protected by the First Amendment, the District Court concluded, and we agree, that McPherson's statement did not amount to a threat punishable under [the federal statute proscribing threats against public officials], or, indeed, that could properly be criminalized at all. The inappropriate or controversial character of a statement is irrelevant to the question whether it deals with a matter of public concern. . . .

Because McPherson's statement addressed a matter of public concern . . . we [must] balance McPherson's interest in making her statement against "the interest of the State, as an employer, in promoting the efficiency of the public services it performs through its employees." . . . The State bears a burden of justifying the discharge on legitimate grounds. . . .

[T]he very nature of the balancing test make[s] apparent that the state interest element of the test focuses on the effective functioning of the public employer's enterprise. Interference with work, personnel relationships, or the speaker's job performance can detract from the public employer's function; avoiding such interference can be a strong state interest. From this perspective, however, petitioner fails to demonstrate a state interest that outweighs McPherson's First Amendment rights. While McPherson's statement was made at the workplace, there is no evidence that it interfered with the efficient functioning of the office. . . .

While the facts underlying Rankin's discharge of McPherson are, despite extensive proceedings in the District Court, still somewhat unclear, it is undisputed that he fired McPherson based on the content of her speech. Evidently because McPherson had made the statement, and because the constable believed that she "meant it," he decided that she was not a suitable employee to have in a law enforcement agency. But in weighing the State's interest in discharging an employee based on any claim that the content of a statement made by the employee somehow undermines the mission of the public employer, some attention must be paid to the responsibilities of the employee within

the agency. The burden of caution employees bear with respect to the words they speak will vary with the extent of authority and public accountability the employee's role entails. Where, as here, an employee serves no confidential, policymaking, or public contact role, the danger to the agency's successful function from threat employee's private speech is minimal. We cannot believe that every employee in Constable Rankin's office, whether computer operator, electrician, or file clerk, is equally required, on pain of discharge, to avoid any statement susceptible of being interpreted by the Constable as an indication that the employee may be unworthy of employment in his law enforcement agency. At some point, such concerns are so removed from the effective function of the public employer that they cannot prevail over the free speech rights of the public employee.

This is such a case. McPherson's employment-related interaction with the Constable was apparently negligible. Her duties were purely clerical and were limited solely to the civil process function of the constable's office. There is no indication that she would ever be in a position to further—or indeed to have any involvement with—the minimal law enforcement activity engaged in by the constable's office. Given the function of the agency, McPherson's position in the office, and the nature of her statement, we are not persuaded that Rankin's interest in discharging her outweighed her rights under the First Amendment.

Justice Powell, concurring. . . .

Justice Scalia, with whom the **Chief Justice, Justice White**, and **Justice O'Connor** join, dissenting.

I agree with the proposition, felicitously put by Constable Rankin's counsel, that no law enforcement agency is required by the First Amendment to permit one of its employees to "ride with the cops and cheer for the robbers." . . . The issue in this case is whether Constable Rankin, a law enforcement official, is prohibited by the First Amendment from preventing his employees from saying of the attempted assassination of President Reagan—on the job within hearing of other employees—"If they go for him again, I hope they get him." The Court holds that McPherson's statement was protected by the First Amendment because (1) it "addressed a

(Continued)

EDITED CASE   Rankin v. McPherson (Continued)

---

matter of public concern," and (2) McPherson's interest in making the statement outweighs Rankin's interest in suppressing it. In so doing, the Court significantly and irrationally expands the definition of "public concern"; it also carves out a new and very large class of employees—i.e. those in "nonpolicy-making" positions—who, if today's decision is to be believed , can never be disciplined for statements that fall within the Court's expanded definition. Because I believe the Court's conclusions rest upon a distortion of both the record and the Court's prior decisions, I dissent. . . .

[S]peech on matters of public concern is that speech which lies "at the heart of the First Amendment's protection." . . . If, but only if, an employee's speech falls within this category, a public employer seeking to abridge or punish it must show that the employee's interest is outweighed by the government's interest, "as an employer, in promoting the efficiency of the public services it performs through its employees." . . .

McPherson fails this threshold requirement. The statement for which she was fired—and the only statement the Constable heard—was, "If they go for him again, I hope they get him." . . .

The District Judge rejected McPherson's argument that her statement was "mere political hyperbole," finding, to the contrary, that it was, "in context," "violent words." "This is not, he said, "the situation where one makes an idle threat to kill someone for not picking them [sic] up on time, or not picking up their [sic] clothes. It was more than that." . . . He ruled against McPherson at the conclusion of the second hearing because "I don's think it is a matter of public concern to approve even more to [sic] the second attempt at assassination." . . .

McPherson's statement . . . is only one step removed from statements that we have previously held entitled to no First Amendment protection

even in the nonemployment context—including assassination threats against the President . . . , "fighting words," epithets or personal abuse, and advocacy of force or violence. A statement lying so near the category of completely unprotected speech cannot fairly be viewed as lying within the "heart" of the First Amendment's protection; it lies within that category of speech that can neither be characterized as speech on matters of public concern nor properly subject to criminal penalties. Once McPherson stopped explicitly criticizing the President's policies and expressed a desire that he be assassinated, she crossed the line.

The Court reaches the opposite conclusion only by distorting the concept of "public concern." It does not explain how a statement expressing approval of a serious and violent crime—assassination of the President—can possibly fall within that category. It simply rehearses the "context" of McPherson's statement, and then concludes that because of that context, and because the statement "came on the heels of a news bulletin regarding what is certainly a matter of heightened public attention; an attempt on the life of the President," the statement "plainly dealt with a matter of public concern." . . . I cannot respond to this progression of reasoning except to say I do not understand it. . . .

Even if I agreed that McPherson's statement was speech on a matter of "public concern," I would still find it unprotected. It is important to be clear on what the issue is in this part of the case. . . . We are asked to determine whether, given the interests of this law enforcement office, McPherson had a right to say what she did—so that she could not only be fired for it, but could not be formally reprimanded for it, or even prevented from repeating it endlessly into the future. It boggles the mind to think that she has such a right.

EDITED CASE Shelton v. University of Medicine & Dentistry of New Jersey
United States Court of Appeals for the Third Circuit 223 F.3d 220 (2000)

[In this case a federal appeals court considers whether a state hospital discriminated against an employee based on her religious beliefs and practices in violation of Title VII of the Civil Rights Act and infringed her First Amendment right to free exercise of religion.]

Circuit Judge Scirica delivered the opinion of the court.

. . . Yvonne Shelton worked as a staff nurse in the Labor and Delivery section of the Hospital at the University of Medicine and Dentistry of New Jersey. The Hospital's Labor and Delivery section provides patients with routine vaginal and cesarean-section deliveries. The Labor and Delivery section does not perform elective abortions. On occasion, Labor and Delivery section patients require emergency procedures that terminate their pregnancies. Labor and Delivery section nurses are required to assist in emergency procedures as part of their job responsibilities.

Shelton is a member of the Pentecostal faith; her faith forbids her from participating "directly or indirectly in ending a life." The proscription includes abortions of live fetuses. Shelton claims she notified the Hospital in writing about her religious beliefs when she first joined the Hospital in 1989, and again in 1994. During this time, the Hospital accommodated Shelton's religious beliefs by allowing her to trade assignments with other nurses rather than participate in emergency procedures involving what Shelton considered to be abortions.

Two events precipitated Shelton's termination. In 1994, Shelton refused to treat a patient. According to the Hospital, the patient was pregnant and suffering from a ruptured membrane (which the Hospital describes as a life-threatening condition). Shelton learned the Hospital planned to induce labor by giving the patient oxytocin. Shelton refused to assist or participate.

After the incident, Shelton's supervisor asked her to provide a note from her pastor about her religious beliefs. Instead, Shelton submitted her own note: "Before the foundations of the earth, God called me to be Holy. For this cause I must be obedient to the word of God. From his own mouth he said 'Thou shalt not kill.' Therefore, regardless of the situation, I will not participate directly or indirectly in ending a life." . . .

In November 1995, Shelton refused to treat another emergency patient. This patient—who was "standing in a pool of blood"—was diagnosed with placenta previa. The attending Labor and Delivery section physician determined the situation was life-threatening and ordered an emergency cesarean-section delivery. When Shelton arrived for her shift, she was told to "scrub in" on the procedure. Because the procedure would terminate the pregnancy, Shelton refused to assist or participate. Eventually, another nurse took her place. The Hospital claims Shelton's refusal to assist delayed the emergency procedure for thirty minutes.

Two months later, the Hospital informed Shelton she could no longer work in the Labor and Delivery section because of her refusal to assist in "medical procedures necessary to save the life of the mother and/or child." The Hospital claimed that staffing cuts prevented it from allowing Shelton to continue to trade assignments when situations arose she considered would lead to an abortion. The Hospital believed Shelton's refusals to assist risked patients' safety.

But the Hospital did not terminate Shelton. Instead, it offered her a lateral transfer to a staff nurse position in the Newborn Intensive Care Unit ("Newborn ICU"). The Hospital also invited Shelton to contact its Human Resources Department, which would help her identify other available nursing positions.

Shelton undertook her own investigation of the Newborn ICU position. She claims she spoke with a nurse (whose name she does not remember) in that unit, who said that "extremely compromised" infants who were not expected to survive would be "set aside" and allowed to die. Shelton did not attempt to confirm this information with the Hospital. Nor did she contact the Human Resources Department to investigate other available positions. Shelton claims she believed no other positions would be available.

(Continued)

EDITED CASE Shelton v. University of Medicine & Dentistry
of New Jersey (Continued)

The Hospital gave Shelton thirty days to accept the position in Newborn ICU, or to apply for another nursing position. Shelton did neither. . . . On February 15, 1996, the Hospital terminated Shelton. . . .

Title VII of the 1964 Civil Rights Act requires employers to make reasonable accommodations for their employees' religious beliefs and practices, unless doing so would result in "undue hardship" to the employer. . . . To establish a prima facie case, the employee must show:

1. she holds a sincere religious belief that conflicts with a job requirement;
2. she informed her employer of the conflict; and
3. she was disciplined for failing to comply with the conflicting requirement.

. . . If the employee establishes a prima facie case, the burden shifts to the employer to show that it made good faith efforts to accommodate, or that the requested accommodation would work an undue hardship. . . .

The District Court held Shelton established a prima facie case. We agree. There is no dispute that Shelton's religious beliefs are sincere, and that the Hospital ultimately terminated Shelton. Although the parties dispute when Shelton first notified the Hospital she would not participate in abortions (Shelton claims she notified the Hospital when she commenced work), they do not dispute the Hospital was on notice by at least 1994. Although the Hospital claims Shelton failed to establish notice because she never provided the requested note from her pastor, we disagree. Under the facts presented, Shelton provided sufficient notice.

Because Shelton established her prima facie case, the burden shifts to the Hospital to show either that it offered Shelton a reasonable accommodation, or that it could not do so because of a resulting undue hardship. . . . The Hospital claims it satisfied the former.

Title VII does not define what is a "reasonable accommodation." But the Supreme Court [has] made clear what it need not be: a sufficient religious accommodation need not be the "most" reasonable one (in the employee's view), it need not be the one the employee suggests or prefers, and

it need not be the one that least burdens the employee. . . . In short, the employer satisfies its Title VII religious accommodation obligation when it offers any reasonable accommodation. . . .

Shelton argues there is a fact issue whether the Hospital reasonably accommodated her by offering a transfer to the Newborn ICU. The core of her argument is that the transfer would not have resolved the religious conflict; in the Newborn ICU she would again be asked to undertake religiously untenable nursing actions (or inactions). The Hospital countered Shelton's claim with testimony that infants in Newborn ICU are not denied medical treatment. Carolyn Franklin, the Hospital's Director of Patient Care Services, testified that she had no knowledge that any baby in Newborn ICU had been taken off of life support, or denied nourishment. Furthermore, there is no evidence that if Shelton worked in the unit, she would be asked to deny care to any infant. Indeed, Shelton admitted that her conclusion about what she might be asked to do in the Newborn ICU was self-drawn.

In sum, Shelton has not established she would face a religious conflict in the Newborn ICU. The Hospital's offer of a lateral transfer to that unit thus constituted a reasonable accommodation. . . .

In another attempt to accommodate Shelton's religious conflict, the Hospital invited Shelton to meet with its Human Resources Department to discuss other available nursing positions. Once the Hospital initiated discussions with that proposal, Shelton had a duty to cooperate in determining whether the proposal was a reasonable one. . . . By refusing to meet with Human Resources to investigate available positions, Shelton failed to satisfy her duty. . . . Shelton does not dispute that at the relevant time, staff nursing positions may have been available in other departments. But she claims her duty to cooperate in finding an accommodation never arose because a transfer to any other department was not a viable option. Not surprisingly, she does not base this claim on any religious conflict. Instead, she claims a transfer to any other department would have required her to "give up eight years of specialized training and education," and to undertake retraining.

EDITED CASE   Shelton v. University of Medicine & Dentistry
of New Jersey (Continued)

The District Court found unconvincing Shelton's claim that a transfer to another staff nurse position would require her to "give up" all of her years of training and education. We agree. Shelton has not come forward with any evidence that a lateral transfer would have affected her salary or benefits. Indeed, Shelton testified that she did not pursue a meeting with Human Resources to identify other lateral transfers because she believed positions were not available. She never expressed a concern that she would be forced to accept a lower salary or benefits. Instead, conceding that a lateral transfer "may have resulted in no immediate economic impact," Shelton offered only the generic speculation that lateral transfers may result in "long-term economic consequences as to the employee's career prospects." Such speculation is insufficient to raise a fact issue precluding summary judgment.

Although there is evidence that Shelton likely would have to undergo some retraining if she took a position outside of the Labor and Delivery section, there is no evidence that she would lose pay or benefits by accepting a new staff nurse position. On this point, the Hospital's Nursing Manager, Edyth Stroud, testified that although a staff nurse who transferred to another nursing unit would need some training, the relocation would not be burdensome. We agree with the District Court that there was no evidence in this case that a lateral transfer would be unreasonable or burdensome.

In sum, Shelton's refusal to cooperate in attempting to find an acceptable religious accommodation was unjustified. Her unwillingness to pursue an acceptable alternative nursing position undermines the cooperative approach to religious accommodation issues that Congress intended to foster. . . .

. . . [W]e believe public trust and confidence requires that a public hospital's health care practitioners—with professional ethical obliga-

tions to care for the sick and injured—will provide treatment in time of emergency. Shelton refused the Hospital's efforts to accommodate her religious beliefs and practices. Having done so, she cannot successfully challenge those efforts as legally inadequate. . . .

. . . Shelton also alleges the Hospital violated Shelton's First Amendment right to free exercise of religion by engaging in improper viewpoint discrimination. Specifically, she claims the Hospital fired her because its viewpoint on abortion conflicted with hers. In support of this argument Shelton cites *Rosenberger v. Rector and Visitors of Univ. of Virginia*, 515 U.S. 819 (1995). We fail to see how *Rosenberger*—or Shelton's viewpoint argument—applies here. *Rosenberger* dealt with whether a public university violated students' First Amendment free speech rights by providing funds to non-religious student publications, but denying funds to a religious publication. The alleged viewpoint discrimination comprised the university's different treatment of two student publications that espoused different views. Here, Shelton has not attempted to establish that the Hospital treated her differently from any other staff nurse who refused to participate in procedures. Nor does it appear that she could, for the evidence was to the contrary: one of the Hospital's representatives testified that when nurses developed sensitivities to latex gloves and could not perform work in their unit, the Hospital "was able to accommodate some of those situations." Thus, it appears that the Hospital has dealt consistently with nurses who could not or would not refuse to perform their nursing duties, regardless of reason.

In sum, Shelton has failed to establish that the Hospital was anything but neutral with respect to religion. Thus we see no error in the District Court's grant of summary judgment to the Hospital on Shelton's First Amendment claim. . . .

For the reasons stated, we will affirm the judgment of the District Court.

EDITED CASE   National Treasury Employees Union v. Von Raab
United States Supreme Court, 489 U.S. 656 (1989)

[Here the Supreme Court considers whether the Fourth Amendment permits the U.S. Customs Service to require that employees who seek transfer or promotion to certain positions undergo drug testing.]

Justice Kennedy delivered the opinion of the Court.

. . . The United States Customs Service, a bureau of the Department of the Treasury, is the federal agency responsible for processing persons, carriers, cargo, and mail into the United States, collecting revenue from imports, and enforcing customs and related laws. . . . An important responsibility of the Service is the interdiction and seizure of contraband, including illegal drugs. In 1987 alone, Customs agents seized drugs with a retail value of nearly $9 billion. . . .

In December 1985, respondent, the Commissioner of Customs, established a Drug Screening Task Force to explore the possibility of implementing a drug-screening program within the Service. . . . After extensive research and consultation with experts in the field, the task force concluded that "drug screening through urinalysis is technologically reliable, valid and accurate." Citing this conclusion, the Commissioner announced his intention to require drug tests of employees who applied for, or occupied, certain positions within the Service. . . .

In May 1986, the Commissioner announced implementation of the drug-testing program. Drug tests were made a condition of placement or employment for positions that meet one or more of three criteria. The first is direct involvement in drug interdiction or enforcement of related laws, an activity the Commissioner deemed fraught with obvious dangers to the mission of the agency and the lives of Customs agents. . . . The second criterion is a requirement that the incumbent carry firearms, as the Commissioner concluded that "[p]ublic safety demands that employees who carry deadly arms and are prepared to make instant life or death decisions be drug free." The third criterion is a requirement for the incumbent to handle "classified" material, which the Commissioner determined might fall into the hands of smugglers if accessible to employees who, by reason of their own illegal drug use, are susceptible to bribery or blackmail. . . .

After an employee qualifies for a position covered by the Customs testing program, the Service advises him by letter that his final selection is contingent upon successful completion of drug screening. An independent contractor contacts the employee to fix the time and place for collecting the sample. On reporting for the test, the employee must produce photographic identification and remove any outer garments, such as a coat or a jacket, and personal belongings. The employee may produce the sample behind a partition, or in the privacy of a bathroom stall if he so chooses. To ensure against adulteration of the specimen, or substitution of a sample from another person, a monitor of the same sex as the employee remains close at hand to listen for the normal sounds of urination. Dye is added to the toilet water to prevent the employee from using the water to adulterate the sample.

Upon receiving the specimen, the monitor inspects it to ensure its proper temperature and color, places a tamper-proof custody seal over the container, and affixes an identification label indicating the date and the individual's specimen number. The employee signs a chain-of-custody form, which is initialed by the monitor, and the urine sample is placed in a plastic bag, sealed, and submitted to a laboratory.

The laboratory tests the sample for the presence of marijuana, cocaine, opiates, amphetamines, and phencyclidine. Two tests are used. An initial screening test uses the enzyme-multiplied-immunoassay technique (EMIT). Any specimen that is identified as positive on this initial test must then be confirmed using gas chromatography/mass spectrometry (GC/MS). Confirmed positive results are reported to a "Medical Review Officer." . . . After verifying the positive result, the Medical Review Officer transmits it to the agency.

Customs employees who test positive for drugs and who can offer no satisfactory explanation are subject to dismissal from the Service. Test results may not, however, be turned over to any other agency, including criminal prosecutors, without the employee's written consent. . . .

EDITED CASE National Treasury Employees Union v. Von Raab (Continued)

Petitioners, a union of federal employees and a union official, commenced this suit in the United States District Court for the Eastern District of Louisiana on behalf of current Customs Service employees who seek covered positions. Petitioners alleged that the Custom Service drug-testing program violated . . . the Fourth Amendment. The District Court agreed. . . . The court acknowledged "the legitimate governmental interest in a drug-free work place and work force," but concluded that "the drug testing plan constitutes an overly intrusive policy of searches and seizures without probable cause or reasonable suspicion, in violation of legitimate expectations of privacy." . . . The court enjoined the drug-testing program, and ordered the Customs Service not to require drug tests of any applicants for covered positions.

A divided panel of the United States Court of Appeals for the Fifth Circuit vacated the injunction. . . .The court agreed with petitioners that the drug-screening program, by requiring an employee to produce a urine sample for chemical testing, effects a search within the meaning of the Fourth Amendment. The court held further that the searches required by the Commissioner's directive are reasonable under the Fourth Amendment. It first noted that "[t]he Service has attempted to minimize the intrusiveness of the search" by not requiring visual observation of the act of urination and by affording notice to the employee that he will be tested. . . . The court also considered it significant that the program limits discretion in determining which employees are to be tested, . . . and noted that the tests are an aspect of the employment relationship. . . .

. . . Illicit drug users, the court found, are susceptible to bribery and blackmail, may be tempted to divert for their own use portions of any drug shipments they interdict, and may, if required to carry firearms, "endanger the safety of their fellow agents, as well as their own, when their performance is impaired by drug use." "Considering the nature and responsibilities of the jobs for which applicants are being considered at Customs and the limited scope of the search," the court stated, "the exaction of consent as a condition of assignment to the new job is not unreasonable." . . .

The dissenting judge concluded that the Customs program is not an effective method for achieving the Service's goals. He argued principally that an employee "given a five day notification of a test date need only abstain from drug use to prevent being identified as a user." . . . He noted also that persons already employed in sensitive positions are not subject to the test. Because he did not believe that the Customs program can achieve its purposes, the dissenting judge found it unreasonable under the Fourth Amendment.

. . . We now affirm so much of the judgment of the Court of Appeals as upheld the testing of employees directly involved in drug interdiction or required to carry firearms. We vacate the judgment to the extent it upheld the testing of applicants for positions requiring the incumbent to handle classified materials, and remand for further proceedings.

II

In *Skinner v. Railway Labor Executives' Assn.*, . . . decided today, we held that federal regulations requiring employees of private railroads to produce urine samples for chemical testing implicate the Fourth Amendment, as those tests invade reasonable expectations of privacy. Our earlier cases have settled that the Fourth Amendment protects individuals from unreasonable searches conducted by the Government, even when the Government acts as an employer, . . . and, in view of our holding in *Railway Labor Executives* that urine tests are searches, it follows that the Customs Service's drug-testing program must meet the reasonableness requirement of the Fourth Amendment.

. . . [O]ur decision in *Railway Labor Executives* reaffirms the longstanding principle that neither a warrant nor probable cause, nor, indeed, any measure of individualized suspicion, is an indispensable component of reasonableness in every circumstance. . . . As we note in *Railway Labor Executives*, our cases establish that where a Fourth Amendment intrusion serves special governmental needs, beyond the normal need for law enforcement, it is necessary to balance the individual's privacy expectations against the Government's interests to determine whether it is impractical to require a warrant or some level of individualized suspicion in the particular context. . . .

(Continued)

EDITED CASE   National Treasury Employees Union v. Von Raab (Continued)

It is clear that the Customs Service's drug-testing program is not designed to serve the ordinary needs of law enforcement. Test results may not be used in a criminal prosecution of the employee without the employee's consent. The purposes of the program are to deter drug use among those eligible for promotion to sensitive positions within the Service and to prevent the promotion of drug users to those positions. These substantial interests, no less than the Government's concern for safe rail transportation at issue in Railway Labor Executives, present a special need that may justify departure from the ordinary warrant and probable-cause requirements.

A

. . . The Customs Service has been entrusted with pressing responsibilities, and its mission would be compromised if it were required to seek search warrants in connection with routine, yet sensitive, employment decisions.

Furthermore, a warrant would provide little or nothing in the way of additional protection of personal privacy. A warrant serves primarily to advise the citizen that an intrusion is authorized by law and limited in its permissible scope and to interpose a neutral magistrate between the citizen and the law enforcement officer "engaged in the often competitive enterprise of ferreting out crime." . . . But in the present context, "the circumstances justifying toxicological testing and the permissible limits of such intrusions are defined narrowly and specifically . . . , and doubtless are well known to covered employees." . . . Under the Customs program, every employee who seeks a transfer to a covered position knows that he must take a drug test, and is likewise aware of the procedures the Service must follow in administering the test. A covered employee is simply not subject "to the discretion of the official in the field." . . . The process becomes automatic when the employee elects to apply for, and thereafter pursue, a covered position. Because the Service does not make a discretionary determination to search based on a judgment that certain conditions are present, there are simply "no special facts for a neutral magistrate to evaluate." . . .

B

Even where it is reasonable to dispense with the warrant requirement in the particular circumstances, a search ordinarily must be based on probable cause. . . . Our cases teach, however, that the probable-cause standard "'is peculiarly related to criminal investigations.'" . . . In particular, the traditional probable-cause standard may be unhelpful in analyzing the reasonableness of routine administrative functions, . . . especially where the Government seeks to prevent the development of hazardous conditions or to detect violations that rarely generate articulable grounds for searching any particular place or person. . . . We think the Government's need to conduct the suspicionless searches required by the Customs program outweighs the privacy interests of employees engaged directly in drug interdiction, and of those who otherwise are required to carry firearms. . . .

It is readily apparent that the Government has a compelling interest in ensuring that front-line interdiction personnel are physically fit, and have unimpeachable integrity and judgment. Indeed, the Government's interest here is at least as important as its interest in searching travelers entering the country. We have long held that travelers seeking to enter the country may be stopped and required to submit to a routine search without probable cause, or even founded suspicion, "because of national self protection reasonably requiring one entering the country to identify himself as entitled to come in, and his belongings as effects which may be lawfully brought in." . . .

The public interest likewise demands effective measures to prevent the promotion of drug users to positions that require the incumbent to carry a firearm, even if the incumbent is not engaged directly in the interdiction of drugs. Customs employees who may use deadly force plainly "discharge duties fraught with such risks of injury to others that even a momentary lapse of attention can have disastrous consequences." Ante, at 628. We agree with the Government that the public should not bear the risk that employees who may suffer from impaired perception and judgment will be promoted to positions where they may need to employ deadly force. Indeed, ensuring against the creation of this dangerous risk will itself further Fourth Amendment values, as the use of deadly force may violate the Fourth Amendment in certain circumstances. . . .

Against these valid public interests we must weigh the interference with individual liberty that results from requiring these classes of employees

---

EDITED CASE   National Treasury Employees Union v. Von Raab (Continued)

---

to undergo a urine test. The interference with individual privacy that results from the collection of a urine sample for subsequent chemical analysis could be substantial in some circumstances. . . . We have recognized, however, that the "operational realities of the workplace" may render entirely reasonable certain work-related intrusions by supervisors and co-workers that might be viewed as unreasonable in other contexts. . . . While these operational realities will rarely affect an employee's expectations of privacy with respect to searches of his person, or of personal effects that the employee may bring to the workplace, . . . it is plain that certain forms of public employment may diminish privacy expectations even with respect to such personal searches. Employees of the United States Mint, for example, should expect to be subject to certain routine personal searches when they leave the workplace every day. Similarly, those who join our military or intelligence services may not only be required to give what in other contexts might be viewed as extraordinary assurances of trustworthiness and probity, but also may expect intrusive inquiries into their physical fitness for those special positions. . . .

We think Customs employees who are directly involved in the interdiction of illegal drugs or who are required to carry firearms in the line of duty likewise have a diminished expectation of privacy in respect to the intrusions occasioned by a urine test. Unlike most private citizens or government employees in general, employees involved in drug interdiction reasonably should expect effective inquiry into their fitness and probity. Much the same is true of employees who are required to carry firearms. Because successful performance of their duties depends uniquely on their judgment and dexterity, these employees cannot reasonably expect to keep from the Service personal information that bears directly on their fitness. . . . While reasonable tests designed to elicit this information doubtless infringe some privacy expectations, we do not believe these expectations outweigh the Government's compelling interests in safety and in the integrity of our borders.

. . . [P]etitioners . . . contend that the Service's drug-testing program is unreasonable in two particulars. First, petitioners argue that the program is unjustified because it is not based on a belief that testing will reveal any drug use by covered employees. In pressing this argument, petitioners point out that the Service's testing scheme was not implemented in response to any perceived drug problem among Customs employees, and that the program actually has not led to the discovery of a significant number of drug users . . . Counsel for petitioners informed us at oral argument that no more than 5 employees out of 3,600 have tested positive for drugs. . . . Second, petitioners contend that the Service's scheme is not a "sufficiently productive mechanism to justify [its] intrusion upon Fourth Amendment interests," . . . because illegal drug users can avoid detection with ease by temporary abstinence or by surreptitious adulteration of their urine specimens. . . . These contentions are unpersuasive.

Petitioners' first contention evinces an unduly narrow view of the context in which the Service's testing program was implemented. Petitioners do not dispute, nor can there be doubt, that drug abuse is one of the most serious problems confronting our society today. There is little reason to believe that American workplaces are immune from this pervasive social problem, as is amply illustrated by our decision in *Railway Labor Executives*. . . .

The mere circumstance that all but a few of the employees tested are entirely innocent of wrongdoing does not impugn the program's validity. The same is likely to be true of householders who are required to submit to suspicionless housing code inspections, . . . and of motorists who are stopped at the checkpoints we approved in *United States v. Martinez-Fuerte*, 428 U.S. 543 (1976). . . .

We think petitioner's second argument—that the Service's testing program is ineffective because employees may attempt to deceive the test by a brief abstention before the test date, or by adulterating their urine specimens—overstates the case. As the Court of Appeals noted, addicts may be unable to abstain even for a limited period of time, or may be unaware of the "fade-away effect" of certain drugs. . . . More importantly, the avoidance techniques suggested by petitioners are fraught with uncertainty and risks for those employees who venture to attempt them. A particular employee's pattern of elimination for a given

(Continued)

EDITED CASE   National Treasury Employees Union v. Von Raab (Continued)

drug cannot be predicted with perfect accuracy, and, in any event, this information is not likely to be known or available to the employee. Petitioners' own expert indicated below that the time it takes for particular drugs to become undetectable in urine can vary widely depending on the individual, and may extend for as long as 22 days. . . . Thus, contrary to petitioners' suggestion, no employee reasonably can expect to deceive the test by the simple expedient of abstaining after the test date is assigned. Nor can he expect attempts at adulteration to succeed, in view of the precautions taken by the sample collector to ensure the integrity of the sample. In all the circumstances, we are persuaded that the program bears a close and substantial relation to the Service's goal of deterring drug users from seeking promotion to sensitive positions.

In sum, we believe the Government has demonstrated that its compelling interests in safeguarding our borders and the public safety outweigh the privacy expectations of employees who seek to be promoted to positions that directly involve the interdiction of illegal drugs or that require the incumbent to carry a firearm. We hold that the testing of these employees is reasonable under the Fourth Amendment.

C

We are unable, on the present record, to assess the reasonableness of the Government's testing program insofar as it covers employees who are required "to handle classified material." . . . We readily agree that the Government has a compelling interest in protecting truly sensitive information from those who, "under compulsion of circumstances or for other reasons, . . . might compromise [such] information." . . . We also agree that employees who seek promotions to positions where they would handle sensitive information can be required to submit to a urine test under the Service's screening program, especially if the positions covered under this category require background investigations, medical examinations, or other intrusions that may be expected to diminish their expectations of privacy in respect of a urinalysis test. . . .

It is not clear, however, whether the category defined by the Service's testing directive encompasses only those Customs employees likely to gain access to sensitive information. . . . We assume these positions were selected for coverage under the Service's testing program by reason of the incumbent's access to "classified" information, as it is not clear that they would fall under either of the two categories we have already considered. Yet it is not evident that those occupying these positions are likely to gain access to sensitive information, and this apparent discrepancy raises in our minds the question whether the Service has defined this category of employees more broadly than is necessary to meet the purposes of the Commissioner's directive.

We cannot resolve this ambiguity on the basis of the record before us, and we think it is appropriate to remand the case to the Court of Appeals for such proceedings as may be necessary to clarify the scope of this category of employees subject to testing. Upon remand the Court of Appeals should examine the criteria used by the Service in determining what materials are classified and in deciding whom to test under this rubric. In assessing the reasonableness of requiring tests of these employees, the court should also consider pertinent information bearing upon the employees' privacy expectations, as well as the supervision to which these employees are already subject.

III

Where the Government requires its employees to produce urine samples to be analyzed for evidence of illegal drug use, the collection and subsequent chemical analysis of such samples are searches that must meet the reasonableness requirement of the Fourth Amendment. Because the testing program adopted by the Customs Service is not designed to serve the ordinary needs of law enforcement, we have balanced the public interest in the Service's testing program against the privacy concerns implicated by the tests, without reference to our usual presumption in favor of the procedures specified in the Warrant Clause, to assess whether the tests required by Customs are reasonable.

We hold that the suspicionless testing of employees who apply for promotion to positions directly involving the interdiction of illegal drugs, or to positions that require the incumbent to carry a firearm, is reasonable. The Government's compelling interests in preventing the promotion of drug users to positions where they might endanger

---

EDITED CASE   National Treasury Employees Union v. Von Raab (Continued)

---

the integrity of our Nation's borders or the life of the citizenry outweigh the privacy interests of those who seek promotion to these positions, who enjoy a diminished expectation of privacy by virtue of the special, and obvious, physical and ethical demands of those positions. We do not decide whether testing those who apply for promotion to positions where they would handle "classified" information is reasonable because we find the record inadequate for this purpose.

The judgment of the Court of Appeals for the Fifth Circuit is affirmed in part and vacated in part, and the case is remanded for further proceedings consistent with this opinion.

Justice Marshall, with whom *Justice Brennan* joins, dissenting. . . .

Justice Scalia, with whom *Justice Stevens* joins, dissenting.

The issue in this case is not whether Customs Service employees can constitutionally be denied promotion, or even dismissed, for a single instance of unlawful drug use, at home or at work. They assuredly can. The issue here is what steps can constitutionally be taken to detect such drug use. . . .

Until today this Court had upheld a bodily search separate from arrest and without individualized suspicion of wrongdoing only with respect to prison inmates, relying upon the uniquely dangerous nature of that environment. Today, in *Skinner*, we allow a less intrusive bodily search of railroad employees involved in train accidents. I joined the Court's opinion there because the demonstrated frequency of drug and alcohol use by the targeted class of employees, and the demonstrated connection between such use and grave harm, rendered the search a reasonable means of protecting society. I decline to join the Court's opinion in the present case because neither frequency of use nor connection to harm is demonstrated or even likely. In my view the Customs Service rules are a kind of immolation of privacy and human dignity in symbolic opposition to drug use. . . .

What is absent in the Government's justifications— notably absent, revealingly absent, and as far as I am concerned dispositively absent—is the recitation of even a single instance in which any of the speculated horribles actually occurred: an instance, that is, in which the cause of bribetaking, or of poor aim, or of unsympathetic law enforcement, or of compromise of classified infor-

mation, was drug use. Although the Court points out that several employees have in the past been removed from the Service for accepting bribes and other integrity violations, and that at least nine officers have died in the line of duty since 1974, . . . there is no indication whatever that these incidents were related to drug use by Service employees. Perhaps concrete evidence of the severity of a problem is unnecessary when it is so well known that courts can almost take judicial notice of it; but that is surely not the case here. The Commissioner of Customs himself has stated that he "believe[s] that Customs is largely drug-free," that "[t]he extent of illegal drug use by Customs employees was not the reason for establishing this program," and that he "hope[s] and expect[s] to receive reports of very few positive findings through drug screening." . . . The test results have fulfilled those hopes and expectations. According to the Service's counsel, out of 3,600 employees tested, no more than 5 tested positive for drugs. . . .

The Court's response to this lack of evidence is that "[t]here is little reason to believe that American workplaces are immune from [the] pervasive social problem" of drug abuse. . . . Perhaps such a generalization would suffice if the workplace at issue could produce such catastrophic social harm that no risk whatever is tolerable—the secured areas of a nuclear power plant, for example. . . . But if such a generalization suffices to justify demeaning bodily searches, without particularized suspicion, to guard against the bribing or blackmailing of a law enforcement agent, or the careless use of a firearm, then the Fourth Amendment has become frail protection indeed. . . .

Today's decision would be wrong, but at least of more limited effect, if its approval of drug testing were confined to that category of employees assigned specifically to drug interdiction duties. Relatively few public employees fit that description. But in extending approval of drug testing to that category consisting of employees who carry firearms, the Court exposes vast numbers of public employees to this needless indignity. Logically, of course, if those who carry guns can be treated in this fashion, so can all others whose work, if performed under the influence of drugs, may endanger others—automobile drivers, operators of

(Continued)

EDITED CASE National Treasury Employees Union v. Von Raab (Continued)

other potentially dangerous equipment, construction workers, school crossing guards. A similarly broad scope attaches to the Court's approval of drug testing for those with access to "sensitive information." Since this category is not limited to Service employees with drug interdiction duties, nor to "sensitive information" specifically relating to drug traffic, today's holding apparently approves drug testing for all federal employees with security clearances—or, indeed, for all federal employees with valuable confidential information to impart. Since drug use is not a particular problem in the Customs Service, employees throughout the Government are no less likely to violate the public trust by taking bribes to feed their drug habit, or by yielding to blackmail. Moreover, there is no reason

why this super-protection against harms arising from drug use must be limited to public employees; a law requiring similar testing of private citizens who use dangerous instruments such as guns or cars, or who have access to classified information, would also be constitutional. . . .

Those who lose because of the lack of understanding that begot the present exercise in symbolism are not just the Customs Service employees, whose dignity is thus offended, but all of us who suffer a coarsening of our national manners that ultimately give the Fourth Amendment its content, and who become subject to the administration of federal officials whose respect for our privacy can hardly be greater than the small respect they have been taught to have for their own.

ENDNOTES

1. *Sanitation Men v. Sanitation Commissioner,* 392 U.S. 280, 284 (1968).

2. President Andrew Jackson, First Annual Message to Congress, 1829.

3. Act of Jan. 16, 1883, c. 27, 22 Stat. 403.

4. Civil Service Rule II, Fifteenth Report of the Civil Service Commission 70 (1897–1898).

5. Act of Aug. 24, 1912, c. 389, 6, 37 Stat. 555. Codified at 5 U.S.C.A. § 7501.

6. Twenty-fourth Annual Report of the Civil Service Commission 104 (1908).

7. 53 Stat. 1147, codified at 18 U.S.C.A. § 61 *et seq.*

8. Act of July 19, 1940, 54 Stat. 767.

9. *United Public Workers v. Mitchell,* 330 U.S. 75 (1947).

10. 413 U.S. 548 (1973).

11. *Id.* at 557.

12. Public Law No. 95-454.

13. 5 U.S.C.A. § 1221(a).

14. The CSRA applies to most federal agency employees but does not include employees of a government corporation, the Federal Bureau of Investigation, the Central Intelligence Agency, the Defense Intelligence Agency, the National Security Agency, the General Accounting Office, or any agency involved in the foreign intelligence or counterintelligence activities.

15. http://www.osc.gov.

16. See, e.g., the New York State Department of Civil Service, online at http://www.cs.state.ny.us.

17. See, e.g., Tennessee's "Little Hatch Act," Tenn. Code Ann. §§ 2-19-201 to 2-19-208.

18. See, e.g., the California Whistleblower Protection Act, California Government Code Article 3 § 8547.

19. *Board of Regents v. Roth,* 408 U.S. 564, 569 (1972).

20. See Reich, *The New Property,* 73 Yale L. J. 733 (1964).

21. 408 U.S. 564 (1972).

22. *Id.* at 570.

23. *Id.* at 577.

24. *Arnett v. Kennedy,* 416 U.S. 134 (1974).

25. 424 U.S. 319 (1976).

26. 470 U.S. 532, 546 (1985).

27. *Id.* at 546.

28. *Gilbert v. Homar,* 520 U.S. 924, 929 (1997).

29. *Id.* at 932.

30. *Id.* at 933-34.

31. 5 U.S.C.A. § 7311.

32. Executive Order 10988, Section 1(a), January 17, 1962.

33. Codified at 5 U.S.C.A. § 7101 *et seq.*

34. 5 U.S.C.A. § 7114(a)(4).

35. See *National Federation of Federal Employees, Local 1309 v. Department of the Interior,* 526 U.S. 86 (1999).

36. U.S. Department of Labor Press Release, January 17, 2002.

37. Executive Order 13252, January 7, 2002.

38. N.C. Gen. Stat. § 95-98.

39. *Public Employees Bargain for Excellence:* A Compendium of State Public Sector Labor Relations Laws, Public Employees Department, AFL-CIO, 1997, pp. 1-2.

40. 5 U.S.C.A. § 7311.

41. 18 U.S.C.A. § 1918.

42. 5 U.S.C.A. § 7102.

43. 5 U.S.C.A. § 7120.

44. The regulations are codified at 29 CFR 458.2.

45. The procedures for filing and processing complaints are described in a Department of Labor publication entitled "Bill of Rights of Members of Federal Sector Unions—A Complainant's Guide," online at [URL]http://www.dol.gov/esa/regs/compliance/olms/bill_right.htm.

46. Ralph Nader, "The Taft-Hartley Act," July 18, 2002. Online at http://www.nader.org/interest/071802.html.

47. *Bolling v. Sharpe,* 347 U.S. 497 (1954).

48. *Frontiero v. Richardson,* 411 U.S. 677 (1973).

49. *Washington v. Davis,* 426 U.S. 229 (1976).

50. 42 U.S.C.A. § 2000e.

51. The Civil Rights Act of 1991, Pub. L. 102-166, expanded the remedies available in employment discrimination cases. In cases of intentional discrimination, plaintiffs are entitled to seek compensatory and punitive damages. Prior to the enactment of this statute, plaintiffs could seek reinstatement, back pay and other "equitable remedies."

52. 426 U.S. 229 (1976).

53. 401 U.S. 424 (1971).

54. *Id.* at 431-432.

55. 42 U.S.C.A. § 2000e-2(k)(1)(A)(i).

56. 42 U.S.C.A. § 2000e-2(k)(1)(A)(ii).

57. *United Steelworkers of America v. Weber,* 443 U.S. 193, (1979).

58. 480 U.S. 616, 641 (1987).

59. *City of Richmond v. J.A. Croson Co.,* 488 U.S. 469 (1989).

60. *Adarand Constructors, Inc. v. Pena,* 512 U.S. 1288 (1994).

61. 539 U.S. 306 (2003).

62. *Id.* at 341.

63. 539 U.S. 244 (2003).

64. 5 U.S.C.A. § 2108.

65. See, e.g., Blumberg, *De Facto and De Jure Sex Discrimination Under the Equal Protection Clause: A Reconsideration of the Veterans' Preference in Public Employment,* 26 Buffalo L. Rev. 3 (1977).

66. *Personnel Administrator of Mass. v. Feeney,* 442 U.S. 256 (1979).

67. Colo. Const. Article XII, Section 13.

68. Mont. Code Ann. § 2-18-111.

69. See, e.g., *Hicklin v. Orbeck,* 437 U.S. 518 (1978) (finding the privileges and immunities clause rendered unconstitutional an Alaska statute that required all employment connected with oil and gas leases to which the state was a party to be offered first to Alaska residents).

70. 477 U.S. 57 (1986).

71. *Id.* at 67.

72. *Faragher v. Boca Raton,* 525 U.S. 775 (1998).

73. *Gebser v. Lago Vista Independent School District,* 118 S. Ct. 1989 (1998).

74. 81 Stat. 602, as amended, 29 U.S.C.A. § 621 *et seq.*

75. However, in *Kimel v. Florida Board of Regents,* 528 U.S. 62 (2000), the Supreme Court held that the Eleventh Amendment limits the right of employees to sue state governments under the ADEA.

76. 5 U.S.C.A. § 8425(a).

77. 29 C.F.R. § 1620.

78. The case was styled *Arnett v. California Public Employees Retirement System.*

79. 29 U.S.C.A. § 701 *et seq.*

80. Executive Order 13164, July 26, 2000, Sec. 1(a).

81. Pub. L. 105-220, enacted on August 7, 1998, 112 Stat 936, codified as Section 504 of the Rehabilitation Act, 29 U.S.C.A. § 794d.

82. Federal Sector Equal Employment Opportunity, 67 Fed. Reg. 35,732 (May 21, 2002).

83. 5 U.S.C.A. § 2302(b)(10).

84. 5 U.S.C.A. § 7121.

85. See, e.g., 4 Colo. Code Regs. § 801, R-9-3 (2002).

86. Admin. Order No. 195 (2002).

87. 29 U.S.C.A. § 2601 *et seq.*

88. *NAACP v. Alabama ex rel. Patterson,* 357 U.S. 449 (1958).

89. *Gitlow v. New York,* 268 U.S. 652 (1925); *Cantwell v. Connecticut,* 310 U.S. 296 (1940); *DeJonge v. Oregon,* 299 U.S. 353 (1937).

90. *Tinker v. Des Moines School District,* 393 U.S. 503, 505 (1969).

91. *Connick v. Myers,* 461 U.S. 138, 140 (1983).

92. 391 U.S. 563 (1968).

93. *Connick v. Myers,* 461 U.S. 138 (1983).

94. 483 U.S. 378 (1987).

95. 513 U.S. 454 (1995).

96. *Id.* at 489.

97. U.S. Const. art. VI § 3.

98. 367 U.S. 488 (1961).

99. 42 U.S.C.A. § 2000e(j).

100. *Ansonia Board of Education v. Philbrook,* 479 U.S. 60, 68 (1986).

101. *Wolf v. Colorado,* 338 U.S. 25 (1949).

102. *Katz* v. *United States,* 389 U.S. 347 (1967), Harlan, J., concurring.

103. *New Jersey v. T.L.O.,* 469 U.S. 325, 337-342 (1985).

104. *Delaware v. Prouse,* 440 U.S. 648, 654 (1979).

105. *O'Connor v. Ortega,* 410 U.S. 709, 722 (1987).

106. *Id.* at 724.

107. 489 U.S. 656 (1989).

108. *Chandler v. Miller,* 520 U.S. 305 (1997).

11

Governmental Liability

It is an established principle of jurisprudence in all civilized nations that the
sovereign cannot be sued in its own courts, or in any other, without its consent
and permission; but it may, if it thinks proper, waive this privilege, and permit
itself to be made a defendant in a suit by individuals, or by another state.
And . . . it follows that it may prescribe the terms and conditions on
which it consents to be sued.

CHIEF JUSTICE ROGER B. TANEY
WRITING FOR THE SUPREME COURT IN *BEERS V. ARKANSAS,* 61 U.S. (20 HOW.) 527, 529 (1858).

INTRODUCTION

Given the size and scope of modern American government, there are myriad ways in which private citizens, corporations, and public employees can suffer violations of their rights at the hands of governmental actors. From traditional **torts** and **breaches of contract** to more contemporary wrongs such as sexual harassment, excessive use of force by police, and other types of civil rights violations, there are countless situations in which aggrieved parties look to the courts to remedy injuries visited upon them by public agencies or officials. The basic question addressed in this chapter is: Under what circumstances and to what extent can government be held liable for the wrongful acts of its officials and employees?

Liability of federal and state governments has evolved from government originally being immune from suit to the present status of general liability subject to certain exceptions based on statutory law and judicial decisions. In this chapter we briefly recount the historical foundations of **sovereign immunity**. We then discuss the statutory basis of liability enacted by Congress to allow citizens to sue the federal government, the applicable exceptions, and the basis of immunity of federal agents. Next we review the liability of public officials who violate a person's constitutional rights. Finally, we discuss sovereign immunity of state governments and statutes and judicial decisions waiving immunity of state and local governments.

SOVEREIGN IMMUNITY

The English common law concept of sovereign immunity was an outgrowth of the feudal system and was derived from the ancient notion that "the king can do no wrong." William Blackstone, the great commentator on the common law, observed "no suit or action can be brought against the king, even in civil matters, because no court can have jurisdiction over him. For all jurisdiction implies superiority of power."[1]

Although the United States Constitution makes no mention of the doctrine, it was generally well known if not universally accepted at the time of the American Revolution. Even as recently as 1999, the Supreme Court observed that

> The generation that designed and adopted our federal system considered immunity from private suits central to sovereign dignity. When the Constitution was ratified, it was well established in English law that the Crown could not be sued without consent in its own courts. . . . Although the American people had rejected other aspects of English political theory, the doctrine that a sovereign could not be sued without its consent was universal in the States when the Constitution was drafted and ratified.[2]

Historically, the Supreme Court treated sovereign immunity as a necessary incident to governmental sovereignty. In *United States v. Lee* (1882), the Supreme Court recognized that sovereign immunity has no basis in constitutional text; nevertheless the Court noted the principle has been repeatedly asserted yet "the principle has never been discussed or the reasons for it given, but it has always been treated as an established doctrine."[3] The notion that the sovereign, whether king or democratically elected government, "can do no wrong," does not comport with modern American political sensibilities. The doctrine has also been justified on the grounds that "the diversion of funds required for other governmental purposes could bankrupt the State and retard its growth, the State could perform its duties more efficiently and effectively if it were not faced with the threat of a floodgate of actions involving tort liability, and it [is] more expedient for an individual to suffer than for society to be inconvenienced."[4] These justifications, while not totally lacking in merit, are much less compelling today than they were when the country was in its infancy. Despite widespread criticism attacking sovereign immunity as undemocratic, unjust, outmoded, and contrary to the rule of law, the doctrine remains in effect today in the federal system and in many states. The effect of sovereign immunity is to immunize both federal and state governments from being sued without their consent.[5] However, in the modern era Congress and most state legislatures have enacted laws consenting to suits to redress a variety of injuries.

An Early Exception to Sovereign Immunity

As the growth of government in the early twentieth century fostered the development of administrative agencies, the Supreme Court recognized an important exception to the doctrine of sovereign immunity. In *Philadelphia Co. v. Stimson* (1912), the Court held that a federal government official who threatened to cause injury by an illegal action "cannot claim immunity from the injunctive process."[6] Courts have applied this principle when litigants have brought actions seeking **injunctions** against officials accused of exceeding their statutory powers or seeking to enforce unconstitutional enactments. In addition to actions seeking injunctions these suits have sometimes taken the form of requests for declaratory judgment and petitions for the **writ of mandamus.**[7] Despite the Court's decision in *Stimson,* the doctrine of sovereign immunity continued to insulate the federal government and all its agencies from suits to recover damages for torts committed by its agents and employees.

The Tucker Act

Historically the only recourse available to private claimants who sought monetary relief against the federal government was to petition Congress to grant relief through passage of a **private legislative act.** To relieve it from examining the merits of such private bills, in 1855 Congress created the Court of Claims Act. The act provided for that court to hear claims founded on any act of Congress, executive department regulation, or upon any contract with the government. When appropriate, the court would submit to Congress a draft of a private bill to compensate a claimant.

In 1863 Congress adopted President Lincoln's recommendation that the court be authorized to render final judgments. Finally, in 1887 Congress enacted a bill introduced by Representative John Randolph Tucker to replace most provisions of the 1855 and 1863 legislation by providing that claimants could bring suits against United States in specified matters.[8]

Today under the **Tucker Act,** the Court of Federal Claims has jurisdiction to render judgment on claims against the United States founded on the U.S. Constitution, acts of Congress, regulations of an executive department, or based on an express or implied contract with the United States. This includes actions against the United States for "takings" of property, for example, when government condemns someone's land.[9] The Supreme Court has held that the Tucker Act constitutes a **waiver of sovereign immunity** with respect to those claims against the government.[10] The Tucker Act is itself only a jurisdictional statute; it does not create any substantive right enforceable against the United States for money damages.[11] In addition to having jurisdiction for suits seeking the recovery of any internal revenue tax alleged to have been erroneously or illegally assessed or collected, federal district courts now have concurrent jurisdiction with the Court of Federal Claims where these cases do not involve more than $10,000 in controversy.[12]

Sovereign Immunity Does Not Bar Judicial Review of Agency Actions

It appeared that when Congress enacted the Administrative Procedure Act (APA) in 1946 it waived immunity of the federal government for proceedings involving agency actions. Yet court decisions were not in accord as to whether the APA waived sovereign immunity, and if so, to what extent. As amended in 1976, Section 702 provides "A person suffering legal wrong because of agency action, or adversely affected or aggrieved by agency action within the meaning of a relevant statute, is entitled to judicial review thereof." It then goes on to provide for relief "other than money damages." Thus, the 1976 amendments to Section 702 of the APA removed the defense of sovereign immunity as a bar review of federal administrative action otherwise subject to judicial review (see Chapter 9).

Although the APA continues to bar recovery of money damages, the Supreme Court has held that it does not bar specific relief such as reimbursement of specific sums as opposed to compensatory damages. Thus in 1988 the Court held that a federal district court had jurisdiction to order the Secretary for Health and Human Services to reimburse the state for expenditures under the Medicaid program.[13]

THE FEDERAL TORT CLAIMS ACT

As the functions performed by the federal government increased, the number of claims submitted to Congress increased dramatically. Despite enactment of the Tucker Act, those seeking redress for torts committed by government agencies were still without an effective remedy. To alleviate the injustices to citizens that occurred as a consequence of sovereign immunity, on August 2, 1946, Congress enacted the **Federal Tort Claims Act** (FTCA) effective as to all claims accruing on or after January 1, 1945.[14] The FTCA waives immunity for torts committed by agents of the federal government acting within the **scope of employment** and provides that "the United States is liable for money damages only for injury or loss of property or personal injury or death caused by the negligent or wrongful act or omission of any employee of the agency while acting within the scope of his office or employment, under circumstances where the United States, if a private person, would be liable to the claimant, in accordance with the law of the place where the act or omission occurred."[15]

The FTCA defines a "federal agency" to include "executive departments, military departments, independent establishments of the United States, and corporations primarily acting as instrumentalities or agencies of the United States but does not include any contractor with the United States."[16]

In addition to determining when personal injury or death or the loss of property is caused by the negligent or wrongful act or omission of a person acting within the scope of employment, it must be determined if the claim is barred by one of the foregoing exceptions. Torts are defined by state law, and federal courts hold that the law of the place where the alleged tort occurred controls as to what constitutes a tort and as to whether a person is "acting within the scope of employment." The fact that there is no counterpart in private law for certain governmental activity often poses a problem in applying the tort law of the state where a tort occurs. Courts uniformly hold that an independent contractor is not an "employee" of the United States within the meaning of the FTCA, but when is one who is an employee "acting within the scope of employment"?

In the Case in Point in Box 11.1 the court had to determine whether the legal doctrine of **respondeat superior** was controlling. *Respondeat superior* is a Latin term that means "let the superior answer." Courts apply the doctrine to hold a principal liable for the actions of an agent who acts in the "scope of employment." In military parlance the scope of employment is referred to as "line of duty."

The *Feres* Doctrine

The FTCA was designed to waive the immunity from tort actions for which a private party would be liable. In *Feres v. United States* (1950),[17] the Court held the government was not liable under the FTCA for death of active duty service members resulting from a barracks fire or from negligent medical treatment by military surgeons. The Court observed, "[P]laintiffs can point to no liability of a 'private individual' even remotely analogous to that which they are asserting against the United States. We know of no American law which ever has permitted a soldier to recover for

---

BOX 11.1 Case in Point

Is the Government Liable for the Wrongful Death of a Person When a Military Member Deviates from the Line of Duty?
Cannon v. United States
243 F.2d 71 (5th Cir. 1957)

On September 30, 1954, the U.S. Army dispatched two soldiers to take an army truck from Camp Rucker, Alabama, to Camp Stewart, Georgia, to pick up a roll of cable and transport it back to Camp Rucker. While proceeding along the highway the following day on their return to Camp Rucker, the soldiers were attracted to two young women sitting by the roadside in front of Club 84 near Bainbridge, Georgia. After they drove past the women, they turned the truck around and headed back to join them. Shortly thereafter one of the women got in the truck with one of the soldiers, who drove a short distance, tarried for awhile, and then headed back to Club 84. En route to Club 84 the army truck collided with a car driven by Mrs. Cannon, who was killed in the accident.

The plaintiff sued under Federal Tort Claims Act to recover damages for the wrongful death of Mrs. Cannon. The U.S. District Court rendered a judgment for the United States and the plaintiff appealed to the U.S. Court of Appeals. The appellate court pointed out that there was a distinct interruption of the soldier's duties for the government when the soldiers first turned the truck around and headed back to Club 84 to see the women. This interruption became more definite and final when one soldier drove the truck on a trip of his own with the return trip made necessary by his wrongful deviation from his duties. Thus, at the time of the collision the soldier had not resumed the service for which the government employed him. Thus the Court of Appeals found the case to be controlled by the Georgia doctrine of *respondeat superior* and held the government not liable because when the accident occurred the soldier driving the army truck was not within the scope of employment, that is his "in line of duty."

---

negligence, against either his superior officers or the Government he is serving."[18]

The *Feres* **doctrine** immunizes the government from liability for injuries or death of service-persons that arise out of or are in the course of activity incident to their military or naval service; however, retired military members or military dependents are allowed to sue for malpractice of military doctors.[19]

Common Exceptions to Governmental Liability under the Federal Tort Claims Act

As detailed in Box 11.2, the FTCA contains numerous exceptions that distinguish the government's liability from that of a private employer. For example, the government is not strictly liable in tort for extraordinary hazardous activities (as are private parties in some instances). Therefore, to recover damages under the FTCA a claimant must establish that the government's agent was negligent. Of the numerous exceptions under the

FTCA, three categories stand out as giving rise to considerable litigation in the federal courts.

- First, the exception for claims based on a government employee who is acting with due care while executing a government statute or regulation;

- Second, acts or omissions by a federal agency or employee who is carrying out a discretionary function; and

- Third, claims for injuries arising out of intentional torts, except in some instances when the tort is committed by an investigative or law enforcement officer.

The Exception for Executing Statutes and Regulations Litigation under the **exception for executing statutes and regulations** has been more limited than the other two exceptions named. Perhaps this is attributable to the fact that this exception more easily lends itself to clarity than the second and third exceptions

BOX 11.2

Exceptions to Federal Government Liability: Excerpts from the Federal Tort Claims Act

(a) Any claim based upon an act or omission of an employee of the Government, exercising due care, in the execution of a statute or regulation, whether or not such statute or regulation be valid, or based upon the exercise or performance or the failure to exercise or perform a discretionary function or duty on the part of a federal agency or an employee of the Government, whether or not the discretion involved be abused.

(b) Any claim arising out of the loss, miscarriage, or negligent transmission of letters or postal matter.

(c) Any claim arising in respect of the assessment or collection of any tax or customs duty, or the detention of any goods, merchandise, or other property by any officer of customs or excise or any other law enforcement officer, except that the provisions of this chapter and section 1346(b) of this title apply to any claim based on injury or loss of goods, merchandise, or other property, while in the possession of any officer of customs or excise or any other law enforcement officer, if—

    (1) the property was seized for the purpose of forfeiture under any provision of Federal law providing for the forfeiture of property other than as a sentence imposed upon conviction of a criminal offense;

    (2) the interest of the claimant was not forfeited;

    (3) the interest of the claimant was not remitted or mitigated (if the property was subject to forfeiture); and

    (4) the claimant was not convicted of a crime for which the interest of the claimant in the property was subject to forfeiture under a Federal criminal forfeiture law.

(d) Any claim for which a remedy is provided by sections 741-752, 781-790 of Title 46, relating to claims or suits in admiralty against the United States.

(e) Any claim arising out of an act or omission of any employee of the Government in administering the provisions of sections 1-31 of Title 50, Appendix.

(f) Any claim for damages caused by the imposition or establishment of a quarantine by the United States.

(g) Repealed. Sept. 26, 1950, c. 1049, § 13(5), 64 Stat. 1043.]

(h) Any claim arising out of assault, battery, false imprisonment, false arrest, malicious prosecution, abuse of process, libel, slander, misrepresentation, deceit, or interference with contract rights: Provided, That, with regard to acts or omissions of investigative or law enforcement officers of the United States Government, the provisions of this chapter and section 1346(b) of this title shall apply to any claim arising, on or after the date of the enactment of this proviso, out of assault, battery, false imprisonment, false arrest, abuse of process, or malicious prosecution. For the purpose of this subsection, "investigative or law enforcement officer" means any officer of the United States who is empowered by law to execute searches, to seize evidence, or to make arrests for violations of Federal law.

(i) Any claim for damages caused by the fiscal operations of the Treasury or by the regulation of the monetary system.

(j) Any claim arising out of the combatant activities of the military or naval forces, or the Coast Guard, during time of war.

(k) Any claim arising in a foreign country.

(l) Any claim arising from the activities of the Tennessee Valley Authority.

(m) Any claim arising from the activities of the Panama Canal Company.

(n) Any claim arising from the activities of a Federal land bank, a Federal intermediate credit bank, or a bank for cooperatives.

SOURCE: 28 U.S.C.A. § 2680.

named above. Several years after the FTCA was enacted, a maritime worker brought suit under the FTCA for the alleged negligence of the U.S. Coast Guard in refusing to certify him for employment on a merchant vessel. In *Dupree v. United States* the U.S. Court of Appeals ruled that because the plaintiff made no allegation of the lack of due care in application of regulations, the suit did not state a basis of a claim under the FTCA.[20] Numerous federal decisions have cited the *Dupree* case with approval.

In 1988 the United States Court of Appeals, District of Columbia Circuit, reviewed an appeal by a military veteran who filed suit under the FTCA challenging the Veterans Administration's (VA's) release of his medical records in response to a grand jury subpoena. He based his suit on the physician-patient privilege and provisions of the District of Columbia Mental Health Information Act, as well as the alleged intrusive invasion of his privacy by the VA. The court cited 28 U.S.C.A. § 2680(a), which excepts from the government's waiver of immunity, "[a]ny claim based upon an act or omission of an employee of the Government, exercising due care, in the execution of a statute or regulation, whether or not such statute or regulation [is] valid" and found the exception barred the plaintiff's claim for damages based on the VA's actions.[21]

The Discretionary Functions Exception

Perhaps the single most important exception to the waiver of immunity under the FTCA is the provision concerning the exercise of a "discretionary function" by federal employees. Specifically, 28 U.S.C.A. § 2680(a) provides that courts are without jurisdiction to consider:

> Any claim based upon an act or omission of an employee of the Government, exercising due care in the execution of a statute or regulation, whether or not such statute or regulation be valid, based upon the exercise or performance or the failure to exercise or perform a discretionary function or duty on the part of a Federal agency or an employee

of the Government; whether or not the discretion involved be abused.

The **discretionary function exception** has resulted in considerable litigation in part because what is "discretionary" is often unclear. In its initial interpretation of the provision, the Supreme Court held that the United States was not liable for the disastrous consequences resulting in 576 deaths from an explosion of a ship loaded with ammonium nitrate at the pier in Texas City, Texas, on April 16, 1947. Despite the risks involved, the government had made a policy decision to expedite shipments of fertilizer overseas at the end of World War II. A trial court found the government negligent in preparing the materials for shipment, but in a 4-3 decision the Supreme Court reversed, a majority of the justices stressing that the discretionary exception to the FTCA was designed to apply to those governmental functions that entail a policy judgment.[22] Later cases focused on the policy judgment aspect of the circumstances in determining whether the exception is applicable.

In 1984, in *United States v. Varig Airlines*,[23] the Supreme Court reviewed a lower court decision where the Federal Aviation Authority (FAA) and its predecessor the Civil Aeronautics Authority (CAA) certified as airworthy some of the airline's planes. Several passengers died as a result of some of the planes being damaged by fire. The owner of the planes and the families and representatives of the deceased passengers sued the United States under the FTCA claiming the government agencies had been negligent in inspecting the planes and issuing certificates showing compliance with safety requirements.

The claimants contended that the FAA was negligent in failing to inspect certain elements of aircraft design before certifying the aircraft involved. Specifically they contended FAA's "spot check" program was flawed. In ruling for government, Chief Justice Burger recognized that it was "impossible to define with precision every contour of the discretionary function exception" and opined that it is "the nature of the conduct, rather than the status of the actor, that governs whether the discretionary function exception applied in a given case."[24] In rejecting the claimants' contentions, Burger noted, "When an agency determines the extent to which it will supervise the safety procedures of private individuals, it is exercising discretionary regulatory authority of the most basic kind."[25] The Court went on to hold that the decision to "spot check" designs of aircraft rather than checking every detail of a design was a policy decision in accordance with agency directives and therefore was protected by the discretionary function exception under the FTCA.

Four years later the Court again considered the exception for discretionary acts in the FTCA and limited to some extent its holding in *Varig Airlines*. The Court held that the FTCA did not bar a claim of an infant who suffered from receiving an injection of polio vaccine manufactured by a civilian laboratory licensed to produce the vaccine by a bureau of the Food and Drug Administration (FDA). The infant became inflicted with polio and the parents sued under the FTCA seeking damages from the FDA's approval of the faulty vaccine. The plaintiff in *Berkovitz v. United States* (1988)[26] alleged that, under authority granted by regulations, the FDA had a policy of testing all lots of oral polio vaccine for compliance with safety standards and preventing public distribution of any lot that failed to comply. Notwithstanding the FDA's mandatory policy, the claimant contended that it was negligent in approving release of the unsafe lot of vaccine. The Court held that its decision in *Varig Airlines* did not bar the claim. Instead, it held that the discretionary exception, properly construed, protects only governmental actions and decisions based on considerations of public policy. The Court said that a requirement of judgment or choice is not satisfied if a "federal statute, regulation, or policy specifically prescribes a course of action for an employee to follow," because "the employee has no rightful option but to adhere to the directive."[27] The Court found that the Court of Appeals erred in holding that the discretionary function exception required

the dismissal of petitioners' claims and remanded the case to the lower court to further consider the plaintiff's claim.

In 1991 in *United States v. Gaubert*,[28] the Supreme Court reviewed a Court of Appeals decision and rejected the *Varig* planning/operational distinction concerning the FTCA "discretionary exception." In *Gaubert* the plaintiff, a former director and major stockholder of the Independent American Savings Association (IASA), filed a claim against the Federal Home Loan Bank Board (Board), the administrative agency that governs savings and loan (S&L) institutions. The plaintiff claimed when the Board took over IASA it had been negligent in its selection of new officials and in management of IASA and that such negligence caused the plaintiff large losses when the market price of IASA stock dramatically declined. A federal district court dismissed the suit on the ground that the discretionary exception to FTCA barred the plaintiff's recovery for any alleged acts of negligence. The Court of Appeals for the Fifth Circuit reversed, holding that while some of the Board's decisions were protected by the discretionary exception, others, for example, its negligent operational activities, were not. It found that the claims concerning the regulators' activities after they assumed a supervisory role in IASA's day-to-day affairs were not "policy decisions," which fall within the exception, but were "operational actions," which do not.

The Supreme Court reversed the Court of Appeals and reinstated the district court's dismissal of the suit. Writing for the Court, Justice White explained:

> Where Congress has delegated the authority to an independent agency or to the Executive Branch to implement the general provisions of a regulatory statute and to issue regulations to that end, there is no doubt that planning-level decisions establishing programs are protected by the discretionary function exception, as is the promulgation of regulations by which the agencies are to carry out the programs. In addition, the actions of Government agents involving the necessary

element of choice and grounded in the social, economic, or political goals of the statute and regulations are protected. . . .[29]

Day-to-day management of banking affairs, like the management of other businesses, regularly requires judgment as to which of a range of permissible courses is the wisest. Discretionary conduct is not confined to the policy or planning level. "[I]t is the nature of the conduct, rather than the status of the actor, that governs whether the discretionary function exception applies in a given case."[30]

It is often said that the exception for discretionary acts allows effective decision making by removing the threat of liability. Not everyone agrees. After a thorough examination of the FTCA and the discretionary function exception, Mark C. Niles notes that, after *Gaubert*, the plaintiff will have to demonstrate that policy considerations could not possibly have affected the decision. He concludes that "the Supreme Court's current interpretation of the exception expands the provision's limitations well beyond their intended scope, undermining the central purpose of the provision."[31]

The Supreme Court's decision in *United States v. Gaubert* is excerpted at the end of the chapter.

The Government Contractor Defense

A rather unique application of the discretionary functions exception in the FTCA surfaced in *Boyle v. United Technologies Corporation* (1988).[32] During a training exercise off the coast of Virginia, Boyle, a U.S. Marine co-pilot, survived the impact of the crash of a helicopter into the ocean. But he drowned when he was unable to escape from the helicopter because of his inability to open the escape hatch. Boyle's father sued the United Technologies Corporation, which built the helicopter for the Marine Corps, claiming an alleged design defect in the helicopter was the cause of his son's death and therefore United Technologies was liable under state tort law.

In a 5-4 decision, the Supreme Court held *United Technologies* was not liable. The Court found this to be one of the special instances where state tort claims are preempted by "federal common law," the injury having occurred as a result of federal governmental discretion in design. This is sometimes referred to as the **government contractor defense** and absolves the contractor from liability for design defects in military equipment being imposed pursuant to state law, when (1) the United States approved reasonably precise specifications; (2) the equipment conformed to those specifications; and (3) the supplier warned the United States about the dangers in the use of the equipment that were known to the supplier but not to the United States."[33]

The Intentional Torts Exception

FTCA did not waive governmental immunity for intentional torts, for example, assault, battery, libel, and slander; however as amended in 1974 it does waive immunity for intentional torts such as assault, battery, false imprisonment, false arrest, abuse of process, or malicious prosecution committed by "investigative or law enforcement officers." As amended, 28 U.S.C.A. § 2680(h) now excepts from the Government's waiver of liability:

(h) Any claim arising out of assault, battery, false imprisonment, false arrest, malicious prosecution, abuse of process, libel, slander, misrepresentation, deceit, or interference with contract rights: Provided, That, with regard to acts or omissions of investigative or law enforcement officers of the United States Government, the provisions of this chapter and section 1346(b) of this title shall apply to any claim arising, on or after the date of the enactment of this proviso, out of assault, battery, false imprisonment, false arrest, abuse of process, or malicious prosecution. For the purpose of this subsection, "investigative or law enforcement officer" means any officer of the United States who is empowered by law to execute searches, to seize evidence, or to make arrests for violations of Federal law.

Courts have struggled with the question of when the **intentional tort exception** in 28 U.S.C.A. § 2680(h) applies. In *Sheridan v. United States*,[34] the claimants brought suit under

---

BOX 11.3 Case in Point

**Was the Plaintiff's Injury Caused by Negligence
or by a Battery Committed by a Department
of Agriculture Meat Inspector?**
Lambertson v. United States
United States Court of Appeals for the Second Circuit
528 F.2d 441 (2nd Cir. 1976)

Richard Lambertson, an employee of Armour &
Company, was unloading a truck shipment of beef
at Armour's Syracuse plant, when suddenly and
without warning he was jumped by a Department
of Agriculture meat inspector. The inspector pulled
Lambertson's wool stocking hat over his eyes,
climbed on his back, and began to ride him piggy-
back. As a result, Lambertson fell forward and
struck his face on some meat hooks and suffered
severe injuries to his mouth and teeth. Lambertson
filed suit seeking to hold the government liable
under the FTCA predicated on the Department of
Agriculture's meat inspector's negligence.
The lower court rendered judgment for the
government and Lambertson appealed.

The U.S. Court of Appeals for the Second Circuit
explained that under the FTCA the law of the place
where the act occurs is controlling for a common-
law tort; that in New York, as in most other jurisdictions, the intent that is an essential element of
battery is the intent to make contact, not to do
injury to the victim. The court determined that the
meat inspector's conduct could not have been accidental. Therefore the "assault and battery" exception in 28 U.S.C.A. § 2680(h) barred Lambertson
from recovering damages.

In affirming the lower court's judgment in
favor of the government the court observed:
"We would find it much more pleasant to reach
a decision based on what we wish Congress had
said, rather than what it did say. However, to
permit plaintiff to recover by 'dressing up the
substance' of battery in the 'garments' of negligence would be to 'judicially admit at the back
door that which has been legislatively turned
away at the front door.'"

---

the FTCA alleging that an intoxicated member
of the naval service stood at the edge of the naval
base in Maryland and fired a rifle at cars on an
adjacent public road. As a result, Mrs. Sheridan
was injured and she and her husband sought to
hold the United States liable under the FTCA on
basis of the service member's alleged negligence.
The court, however, held the service member's
actions were an intentional tort and any injury
was not proximately caused by breach of government regulations.

Courts, however, have responded differently
where the government has assumed the duty to
care for persons under its supervision. Thus where
the evidence established that government was
negligent in hiring and continuing to employ a
teacher despite indications of predilections
towards sexual abuse, the assault and battery
[intentional tort] exception to FTCA liability did
not insulate the government from liability for the
teacher's sexual assault of students.[35] Nor did the
intentional tort exception preclude the United
States from being held liable for sexual abuse of

children while in the care of an Air Force base
day-care center. Such claims were not barred as
"arising out of assault." Instead, they arose out of a
breach of affirmative duty to the victim prior to
assault.[36] Likewise the Ninth Circuit Court of
Appeals held that the assault and battery exception did not bar a Forest Service employee's claim
alleging negligent supervision of a superior who
allegedly raped an employee.[37] The Case in Point
in Box 11.3 discusses an incident in which the
plaintiff blamed the U.S. Department of Agriculture for injuries that occurred at a private meat-
packing company.

Pursuing a Claim under the Federal Tort Claims Act

Congress amended the FTCA in 1966 to
authorize agency heads to settle all administrative
tort claims, regardless of amount, and required
that all claims be submitted as administrative
claims before commencement of suit. The claim
for a tort accruing on or after January 18, 1967,

BOX 11.4   Instances Where Courts Have Found the United States Liable
Under the Federal Tort Claims Act

Dishman v. United States, 93 F. Supp. 567 (D. Md. 1950): During the course of treating the plaintiff's ear, a physician at a Veterans Administration hospital mistakenly selected the wrong bottle from the medicine cabinet and poured carbolic acid in the plaintiff's ear, causing partial deafness. The court awarded the plaintiff $1,500.

Dean v. United States, 239 F. Supp. 167 (M.D. Ala. 1965): The court awarded the decedent's parents $14,641.40 and burial expenses to compensate them for the negligence of government employees who mistakenly administered a lethal dosage of medicine to their three-year-old son while he was a patient in an Air Force medical dispensary.

Swanner v. United States, 309 F. Supp. 1183 (M.D. Ala. 1970): Plaintiff Jesse E. Swanner was employed by the Alcohol and Tobacco Tax Division of the Internal Revenue Service to aid in the under-

cover investigation of illicit whisky operations in Tennessee. In his suit seeking damages, the court found the government was negligent in failing to exercise a special duty it had to use reasonable care for the protection of the plaintiff and his family who suffered injuries when a bomb exploded under their house. The court awarded claimants a total of $28,500.

Goudeau v. Christ, 325 F. Supp. 1154 (W.D. La. 1971): The court found that a U.S. Air Force airman who was driving a government vehicle was negligent in following other vehicles so closely that when other vehicles stopped at an intersection with yellow caution light, he had to slam on his brakes. When he did, it caused his vehicle to veer left into an approaching car. The court awarded the plaintiff, a motorist who was injured in a resulting vehicular accident, $10,000 for pain, suffering, etc. and $429.74 for medical expenses.

---

is barred unless presented to the federal agency within two years after the claim accrues or unless action is begun within six months after the date of mailing, by certified or registered mail, of notice of final denial of the claim by the agency to which it was presented.[38] A legion of federal court decisions holds that filing a claim is a prerequisite to an action under the FTCA and without it the court has no jurisdiction.

To recover against the government under the FTCA, a plaintiff must prove that there was (1) negligence; (2) by an agent of the United States; (3) acting within the scope of his or her employment (line of duty); (4) under circumstances where the United States would be liable if a private person would be liable to the claimant in the same manner and to the same extent in accordance with the law of the State where the negligent act or omission occurred.

In an action against the United States under the FTCA, a plaintiff cannot seek damages in excess of the claim presented to the federal agency unless there is newly discovered evidence that was not reasonably discoverable when the claim was

presented to the agency or where there have been intervening facts relating to the amount of the claim. In 1988, a federal appellate court ruled that when a claim had been pending for some ten years that courts could allow the claim to be pursued for a greater amount because the inflation over the years qualified as an intervening factor.[39]

Because claims are adjudicated on basis of the law of the place where the act or omission occurred, such defenses as contributory or comparative negligence, or assumption of risk, may be available to the government as the United States is entitled to raise all defenses available to a private defendant under state law.[40] The FTCA stipulates that suits against the United States are to be tried without a jury.[41] When the U.S. Constitution was adopted there was no common-law right to bring a suit against the sovereign. This is the constitutional justification for not allowing a jury trial as is provided for civil trials under the Seventh Amendment to the United States Constitution. Instances in which courts have found the United States liable under the Federal Tort Claims Act are discussed in Box 11.4.

The Westfall Act Amends the Federal Tort Claims Act

The FTCA waived the immunity of the federal government for acts of federal employees acting within the scope of their duties. Nevertheless, government employees could be sued individually, as the Supreme Court, in 1988, in *Westfall v. Erwin,*[42] held that federal employees acting within the scope of their office or employment were immune from tort liability only if their actions were of a discretionary nature. In response Congress enacted the **Westfall Act,** which amended the provisions of the Federal Tort Claims Act to provide that in court suits under the FTCA the federal government is to be substituted for employees acting within the scope of their employment. The act provides for the attorney general to certify that the government employee was acting within scope of his or her employment.[43]

In 1995, Justice Ginsburg, writing for the Court in *Martinez v. Lamagno,*[44] explained:

> When a federal employee is sued for a wrongful or negligent act, the Federal Employees Liability Reform and Tort Compensation Act of 1988 (commonly known as the Westfall Act) empowers the Attorney General to certify that the employee "was acting within the scope of his office or employment at the time of the incident out of which the claim arose. . . ." Upon certification, the employee is dismissed from the action and the United States is substituted as defendant. The case then falls under the governance of the Federal Tort Claims Act (FTCA). . . . Generally, such cases unfold much as cases do against other employers who concede *respondeat superior* liability. If, however, an exception to the FTCA shields the United States from suit, the plaintiff may be left without a tort action against any party.[45]

In 1990 the U.S. Court of Appeals for the First Circuit noted that 28 U.S.C.A. § 2679(d)(2) provides that the attorney general's certification conclusively establishes the scope of office or employment. Nevertheless, the court did not read that provision as manifesting a Congressional intent that the certification be beyond judicial review for all purposes.[46]

VIOLATION OF CONSTITUTIONAL RIGHTS

At a critical time in the history of the United States when social and political upheavals followed the end of the Civil War, Congress enacted a number of laws designed to protect civil rights of individuals. One of these laws, the **Civil Rights Act of 1871,** authorized individuals to bring civil suits in federal court against those who violate their constitutional rights under the **color of state law.** This statute was originally designed to enforce the Fourteenth Amendment. Section 1983 of the act is codified in Title 42 of the U.S. Code and now provides:

> Every person who, under color of any statute, ordinance, regulation, custom, or usage, of any State or Territory or the District of Columbia, subjects, or causes to be subjected, any citizen of the United States or other person within the jurisdiction thereof to the deprivation of any rights, privileges, or immunities secured by the Constitution and laws, shall be liable to the party injured in an action at law, suit in equity, or other proper proceeding for redress.

Scope of Section 1983

Actions brought under the authority of 42 U.S.C.A. § 1983 are commonly referred to as **Section 1983 actions.** Historically the Court gave a very limited construction to both the definition of conduct under color of state law and the definition of persons who could be subject to liability under section 1983, having held in 1904 in *Barney v. City of New York,*[47] that damages were not available when an individual had been injured by unauthorized conduct of state officials. But this changed in 1961 when in *Monroe v. Pape,* the Court held that § 1983 covered unauthorized as well as authorized actions by state officials who abused their positions of authority.[48] This decision and the nation's heightened sensitivity to civil rights in the 1960s resulted in a vast increase in civil litigation seeking recourse for violations of civil rights.

In 1941, the Supreme Court said that "color of any statute, ordinance, regulation, custom, or usage" refers to "misuse of power, possessed by virtue of state law and made possible only because the wrongdoer is clothed with the authority of state law."[49] "Deprivation of any rights, privileges, or immunities secured by the Constitution and laws" does not include violations of state constitutions and laws or torts committed by state official. Those state violations, of themselves, are not sufficient to show an invasion of a person's right as contemplated by Section 1983.[50] Finally, the phrase, "shall be liable . . . in an action at law, suit in equity, or other proper proceeding . . ." allows for actions seeking money damages, including punitive damages, as well as equitable relief by obtaining injunctions or declaratory judgments. In 1992 the Supreme Court observed that Section 1983 basically seeks "to deter state actors from using the badge of their authority to deprive individuals of their federally guaranteed rights" and to provide related relief to victims if such deterrence fails."[51]

Redress under Section 1983 is not available against a state as such; however, state officers can be sued individually. For purposes of Section 1983 the term "person" includes local and state officers acting under color of state law.[52] Corporations and partnerships are also "persons," but federal court decisions hold that colleges, universities, arms of state government, and state governmental agencies, are not. An earlier ruling indicated that a municipality could not be sued under Section 1983, but in 1978 in *Monell v. Department of Social Services,*[53] the Supreme Court ruled that municipal corporations, including cities and counties, are "persons" within the meaning of Section 1983. Therefore, although the Court said that local governments cannot be held liable under an employer-employee (*respondeat superior*) relationship, they are liable if their official policy has caused a constitutional deprivation. Writing for the majority of the Court in *Monell,* Justice Brennan explained that local governments may be sued directly under Section 1983 for monetary, declaratory, or injunctive relief where "the action that is alleged to be unconstitutional implements or executes a policy, statement, ordinance, regulation or decision officially adopted and promulgated by that body's officers."[54] Brennan observed that

> local governments like every other § 1983 "person," by the very terms of the statute, may be sued for constitutional deprivations . . . even though such a custom has not received formal approval through the body's official decision making channels. . . . On the other hand, Congress did not intend municipalities to be held liable unless action pursuant to official policy of some nature caused a constitutional tort. In particular . . . a municipality cannot be held liable under § 1983 on a *respondeat superior* theory.[55]

Justice Rehnquist, with whom Chief Justice Burger agreed, argued that the Court erred in abandoning the settled interpretation of the law based on *Monroe v. Pape.*

Punitive damages may be awarded to punish a tortfeasor's reckless and wanton conduct. In 1975 the city council in Newport, Rhode Island, canceled a license permitting a rock concert because of a dispute over the content of the music. Three years after *Monell,* in *Newport v. Fact Concerts, Inc.,*[56] the Court, in a 6-3 decision, with Justice Brennan dissenting, held that municipalities are immune from liability for punitive damages in a Section 1983 action. The Court found no evidence that Congress intended to disturb the settled common-law immunity, which precluded an award of punitive damages against a municipality.[57]

Constitutional Torts

The Civil Rights Act of 1871 permitted injured parties to bring federal civil suits to redress **constitutional torts;** that is, injuries resulting from the deprivation of constitutional rights. Section 1983 does not confer substantive rights. Therefore, a plaintiff seeking relief must bring an action in conjunction with some other statute or constitutional provision that provides substantive rights.

As Section 1983 was adopted shortly after ratification of the Fourteenth Amendment (1868), it was intended to allow for redress of violations of the Due Process and Equal Protection Clauses of the Fourteenth Amendment as well as the "appropriate legislation" Congress would enact to enforce these broad protections. However, because the modern Supreme Court has "incorporated" virtually all of the protections of the Bill of Rights into the Fourteenth Amendment (see Chapter 3), persons acting under color of state law who deprive persons of their freedoms of speech, assembly, religion, etc., are subject to civil liability under 42 U.S.C.A. § 1983.

The most highly publicized Section 1983 action in the last decade was Rodney King's suit, where King won a $3.8 million jury award against the City of Los Angeles based on the city's police officers having used excessive force in arresting him after stopping his car following a high-speed chase. The underlying constitutional violation in the Rodney King case was the deprivation of the Fourth Amendment right to be free from unreasonable searches and seizures, which the Supreme Court has interpreted to prohibit the excessive use of force by police officers attempting to make arrests.[58] The award in the federal civil case came after the officers were first acquitted of criminal charges in a state court, an event that sparked a riot that swept South-Central Los Angeles in late April and early May 1992, resulting in numerous deaths and vast property damage. (Later two police officers involved in the incident were convicted of civil rights violations under federal law).

In addition to suits involving law enforcement, Section 1983 actions have focused on a variety of situations involving education, employment, use of public facilities, rights of prisoners, and other areas (see Box 11.5.)

When Is a State's Failure to Protect Children a Constitutional Tort? The Constitution was adopted, among other things, to protect persons from government. But in the modern era, as government has assumed a more paternalistic role, some commentators have argued that government has a constitutional duty to provide security, protection, and subsistence to persons within its jurisdiction. In general, the courts have rejected this notion.[59] However, the Supreme Court has said that when a person is in the custody of the state, a constitutional duty arises to protect that person from harm. This duty obviously arises in the context of prisons, mental institutions, juvenile detention facilities, etc.[60]

Today, courts are beginning to consider the claim that states have a constitutional duty to protect children in foster care. The issue arises not only from the growing numbers of children who are removed from their homes and placed in foster care due to abuse or neglect, but a number of horrific instances where state agencies lost track of children under their jurisdiction. Some courts have held that state and local officials can be held liable in such cases only when they manifest "deliberate indifference" to the interests of children. Other courts impose a higher standard. For example, in *Kara B. v. Dane County,*[61] the Wisconsin Supreme Court reviewed a case in which young children were subjected to physical and sexual abuse in their foster homes. The court held that foster children have a clearly established constitutional right under the due process clause to safe and secure placement in a foster home and that public officials entrusted with the task of ensuring that children are placed in a safe and secure foster home owe a constitutional duty that is determined by a **professional judgment standard** rather than a **deliberate indifference standard.**

BOX 11.5

Instances Where Claimants Stated a Cause of Action Against a State Government Under 42 U.S.C.A. § 1983

Right to Read Defense Committee v. School Committee of Chelsea, 454 F. Supp. 703 (D. Mass. 1978): By removing an anthology of writings by students from the high school library because it felt that language and theme of a poem might have a damaging impact on high school students, the court held the School Committee infringed the First Amendment rights of students.

Ponton v. Newport News School Board, 632 F. Supp. 1056 (E.D. Va. 1986): The court held that an unmarried teacher's constitutional right of privacy was violated when she was forced to take a leave of absence for becoming pregnant.

Moody v. Ferguson, 732 F. Supp. 627 (D. S.C.1989): The court found that a state trooper had no reasonable basis for believing that a motorist had committed the crime of assault with intent to kill with which trooper charged him, and,

thus, the trooper was liable in a civil rights action for depriving motorist of the Fourth Amendment right to be free from an unlawful arrest. The trooper testified that he did not believe that the motorist intended to do any harm, much less kill him, and the facts did not reasonably support an intent to kill.

Cullen v. New York State Civil Service Commission, 435 F. Supp. 546 (E.D. N.Y. 1977): The court determined that conditioning promotions on making a financial contribution to a political party by persons in official positions constituted an invasion of constitutional rights actionable under § 1983.

Rose v. Village of Peninsula, 839 F. Supp. 517 (N.D. Ohio 1993): A motorist who was arrested for speeding alleged that he was seized pursuant to illicit law designed purposefully to create pretext for seizing citizens and trying to collect fines from them based on false appearance of wrongdoing created by illicit speed limit signs. These allegations in a lawsuit stated the basis for a claim under § 1983.

A related issue is whether officials in social services agencies can be held liable for failing to remove children from violent homes. In *DeShaney v. Winnebago County Department of Social Services,*[62] the Supreme Court, dividing 6 to 3, held that a local social services agency, regardless of its prior knowledge of the danger, did not violate the Fourteenth Amendment by failing to protect a child from domestic abuse. Four-year-old Joshua DeShaney was severely beaten by his father, resulting in extensive brain damage that required the boy to be institutionalized for the rest of his life. The boy's mother brought suit under Section 1983, alleging that county social workers had deprived Joshua of his "liberty interest in bodily integrity" in violation of the Fourteenth Amendment by failing to intervene to protect him from his father. Writing for the Court, Chief Justice Rehnquist recognized a state's constitutional obligation to protect the safety and well-being of those within its custody. However, in Rehnquist's view, this "affirmative duty to protect arises not from the

State's knowledge of the individual's predicament or from its expressions of intent to help him, but from the limitation which it has imposed on his freedom to act on his own behalf."[63] Because the state had no affirmative obligation to protect Joshua from his father, its failure to do so, although calamitous, did not constitute a violation of the Fourteenth Amendment. Dissenting in the case, Justice Harry Blackmun called for a more "sympathetic reading" of the Fourteenth Amendment that recognized that "compassion need not be exiled from the province of judging."

The Supreme Court's decision in *DeShaney v. Winnebago Social Services* is excerpted at the end of the chapter.

Pursuing a Claim under Section 1983

Federal district courts have jurisdiction to hear actions brought pursuant to § 1983. A plaintiff files a suit in the district where the defendant resides or where the events or omissions took place. Alternatively, a section 1983 action may be brought in state court,[64] and the attorney's fee provision that is part of the § 1983 remedy applies whether the action is brought in federal or state court.[65]

Unlike where a party seeks juridical review of an administrative action, it is not necessary for a litigant to exhaust state remedies before filing an action under Section 1983.[66] Actions brought pursuant to 42 U.S.C.A. § 1983 are governed by the state statutes of limitations for personal injury actions.[67] Although state law determines the length of the limitations period, federal law determines when a civil rights claim accrues and "[U]nder federal law, a claim accrues when the plaintiff knows or has reason to know of the injury which is the basis of the action."[68] Where the suit seeks money damages there is a right to jury trial, but traditional equity suits, such as seeking an injunction, are heard by the court without a jury. The court may award punitive damages where justified and a successful plaintiff may recover a reasonable attorney's fee.[69]

Liability of Federal Officials for Violations of Constitutional Rights

Section 1983 actions are designed to impose liability against persons who operate under the color of state law and to make liable those local governments whose policies cause deprivations of federal constitutional rights. Congress has not enacted a specific statute that parallels § 1983 to cause federal officials to be held personally liable for constitutional or statutory violations. However, this gap has been filled by judicial decision making.

In the 1960s the nation became very sensitive to the civil rights of its citizens. Indeed, in the following decade, the United States Supreme Court made statutory action by Congress unnecessary when in *Bivens v. Six Unknown Federal Narcotics Agents*[70] it ruled that a person who suffers injuries when federal officers violate the Fourth Amendment to the U.S. Constitution

may bring suit in federal court against these officers holding them personally liable for such constitutional torts.

The *Bivens* case began on the morning of November 26, 1965, when federal narcotics agents without a warrant raided Webster Bivens' apartment in search for contraband. Finding none, they nevertheless arrested and handcuffed him and brought him before a U.S. Commissioner who found no basis to detain him. Bivens then filed suit in federal court seeking damages from the FBI agents. Both the district court and the United States Court of Appeals for the Second Circuit dismissed his case as not stating a cause of action for relief.

The Supreme Court granted review. Writing in 1971 for a 7-2 majority, Justice Brennan simplified the issue before the Court saying, "The question is merely whether petitioner [Bivens] if he can demonstrate an injury consequent upon the violation by federal agents of his Fourth Amendment rights, is entitled to redress his injury through a particular remedial mechanism normally available in the federal courts."[71] The Court concluded that Bivens' complaint stated a cause of action for money damages for any injuries he suffered as a result of the narcotics agents' violation of his rights under the Fourth Amendment to the U.S. Constitution. Because the lower court had not considered whether the agents were immune from liability because of their official position, the Court remanded the case to the U.S. Court of Appeals for Second Circuit to determine if the agents should be afforded immunity.

The Court of Appeals held the officers were not to be accorded immunity from liability because they were not performing "discretionary" functions. Nevertheless the court stated, "[I]t is a defense to allege and prove good faith and reasonable belief in the validity of the arrest and search and in the necessity for carrying out the arrest and search in the way the arrest was made and the search was conducted. We think, as a matter of constitutional law and as a matter of common sense, a law enforcement officer is entitled to this protection."[72] Thus the court suggested that the agents might be entitled to a defense that has come to be known as qualified immunity. (We discuss the applicability of the doctrines of absolute immunity and qualified immunity in topics that follow.)

The Supreme Court soon extended the *Bivens* rationale to cover violations of the Due Process Clause of the Fifth Amendment[73] and to violations of the Cruel and Unusual Punishment Clause of the Eighth Amendment.[74] Lower federal courts have applied the *Bivens* rationale to various other protections under the U.S. Constitution. (See the examples in Box 11.5.)

The Supreme Court's decision in *Bivens v. Six Unknown Federal Narcotics Agents* is excerpted at the end of the chapter.

When Is Relief under the *Bivens* Doctrine Unavailable? There are situations where the *Bivens* doctrine does not permit a claimant a cause of action against the federal government. In 1980, in *Carlson v. Green*,[75] Justice Brennan explained:

> *Bivens* established that the victims of a constitutional violation by a federal agent have a right to recover damages against the official in federal court despite the absence of any statute conferring such a right. Such a cause of action may be defeated in a particular case, however, in two situations. The first is when defendants demonstrate "special factors counseling hesitation in the absence of affirmative action by Congress." . . . The second is when defendants show that Congress has provided an alternative remedy, which it explicitly declared to be a substitute for recovery directly under the Constitution, and viewed as equally effective.[76]

In 1983 in *Bush v. Lucas*,[77] Bush, an aerospace engineer, asked the Supreme Court to allow a new ***Bivens*-type remedy** for federal employees whose First Amendment rights are violated by their superiors. The Court declined, concluding that

because such claims arise out of an employment relationship governed by comprehensive procedural and substantive provisions of the Civil Service Reform Act (CSRA) that gives meaningful remedies against the United States, it would be inappropriate to supplement that regulatory scheme with a new judicial remedy.

In a 1988 *Harvard Law Review* note,[78] the author refers to the "Special Factor" and "Substitute for Recovery" that Justice Brennan mentioned in *Bivens*. In discussing *Bush v. Lucas*, the author points out that while nonprobationary employees receive a variety of procedural protections from arbitrary adverse personnel actions such as dismissal or demotion by their supervisors, such protections are not available under the CSRA for probationary employees. The author concludes:

> Congressional statutory schemes should serve as "special factors" precluding *Bivens* actions only when they provide effective remedies or, perhaps, when Congress has clearly stated its intent to preclude those actions. This conclusion follows from either of two premises: either the Constitution requires the provision of effective remedies for rights violations, or, even if it does not, prudential considerations dictate that courts should ensure that constitutional rights are not left without effective protection unless as a result of a considered decision by Congress. In the civil service context, the remedies for less-protected employees are not sufficiently effective because they rely entirely on the discretion of an administrative body; moreover, Congress has not clearly expressed an intent to preclude *Bivens* actions. Therefore, less-protected civil service employees should be allowed to bring *Bivens* actions to remedy violations of their constitutional rights; denial of such actions eviscerates the safeguards of the Constitution.[79]

The Supreme Court's 1983 decision in *Chappell v. Wallace*[80] illustrates a unique instance where "special factors" preclude relief under

42 U.S. § 1983. In 1983, writing for a unanimous Court, Chief Justice Burger stated: "[T]he unique disciplinary structure of the military establishment and Congress' activity in the field constitute 'special factors' which dictate that it would be inappropriate to provide enlisted military personnel a *Bivens*-type remedy against their superior officers."[81]

In a free and open society it is important that individuals have a means to impose limits on the ability of government to take actions that inflict injury on persons. Constitutional tort actions under Section 1983 and *Bivens v. Six Unknown Named Federal Narcotics Agents* have become the vehicle that enables a private citizen to challenge the government's infliction of injury. The Supreme Court's broad interpretation of "under color of law" has enabled individuals to play an important role in the shaping of constitutional rights.

IMMUNITY OF FEDERAL AND STATE OFFICIALS

Simply stated, **immunity** is the freedom from lawsuits and liability. In some instances such immunity is "absolute," while in others it is said to be "qualified." **Absolute immunity** insulates a selected class of officials including judges, prosecutors, and legislators from legal action for their official actions. On the other hand, **qualified immunity,** under current judicial interpretation, protects public officials in instances unless they violate "clearly established statutory or constitutional rights of which a reasonable person would have known." Officials who claim qualified immunity can be subjected to lawsuits as their entitlement may depend on a factual resolution.

Clearly no one has the discretion to violate another person's constitutional rights. Although 42 U.S.C.A. § 1983 made available a right of action for violations of constitutional rights by state officials, the Supreme Court has held that such officials are entitled to a certain degree of immunity in "constitutional tort" suits as they are in com-

mon-law tort suits.[82] As we have seen, *Bivens v. Six Unknown Named Federal Narcotics Agents* created a right of action for certain constitutional violations by federal officials. However, the issue of when a federal official may be entitled to immunity was not before the Court in *Bivens*.

To appreciate the concept of immunity and the distinction between absolute and qualified immunity some background is essential. In 1959, in *Barr v. Matteo,* the Supreme Court stated that a federal employee enjoys absolute immunity from tort liability for any act performed "within the outer perimeter of [his] line of duty."[83] *Barr* concerned an administrative agency official that allegedly libeled some agency employees. The Court held that Barr was absolutely immune because his allegedly libelous statement was an exercise of discretion that he possessed as a public official. This concept precluded most suits seeking damages against federal employees. In the 1970s the Supreme Court began to clarify when a government employee was entitled to absolute immunity in contrast to his or her entitlement to qualified immunity.

Absolute Immunity

The right of representatives of the people to enjoy a free and robust debate over public issues led the framers of the U.S. Constitution to include in Article I, Section 6 that Senators and Representative shall not be questioned "for any speech or debate in either House." This is known as the **Speech and Debate Clause.** Its purpose is to protect the integrity of the legislative process by insuring the independence of individual legislators so that the Congress can perform its legislative function independently.[84]

Judges have absolute immunity in their performance of judicial functions.[85] Likewise prosecutors have been held to have absolute immunity.[86] Legislators and witnesses also enjoy absolute immunity, as does the president. Likewise, because of the unique structure of the military and Congress's activity in that field, the Supreme Court has held that there is no *Bivens*

BOX 11.6 Case in Point

Judicial Immunity
Stump v. Sparkman
United States Supreme Court
435 U.S. 349 (1978)

On July 9, 1971, Linda Kay Spitler's mother presented to Judge Harold D. Stump of the Circuit Court of DeKalb County, Indiana, a petition to have a tubal ligation performed on her 15-year-old daughter. The petitioner stated under oath that her daughter was "somewhat retarded," had been associating with "older youth or young men" and that it would be in the daughter's best interest if she underwent a tubal ligation in order "to prevent unfortunate circumstances . . ." Judge Stump approved the petition on July 15 and the following day tubal ligation was performed. The young woman was released from the hospital apparently without knowledge of the nature of the surgical procedure.

Approximately two years after the operation, Linda Spitler married Leo Sparkman. Her inability to become pregnant led her to discover that she had been sterilized. As a result, the Sparkmans filed suit seeking damages in the U.S. District Court for the Northern District of Indiana against Judge Stump [and others] claiming Fourteenth Amendment Due Process and Equal Protection violations of her right to privacy and her right to procreate. The District Court dismissed the suit against the

judge; the Court of Appeals reversed, holding that the judge had forfeited his immunity "because of his failure to comply with elementary principles of procedural due process."

The U.S. Supreme Court granted certiorari. After citing precedents establishing the historic absolute immunity of judges, the Court, in an opinion by Justice White, explained that Judge Stump was protected by judicial immunity because he "performed the type of act normally performed only by judges and . . . he did so in his capacity as a Circuit Court Judge." Justice White observed that "The Indiana law vested in Judge Stump the power to entertain and act upon the petition for sterilization. He is, therefore, under the controlling cases, immune from damages liability even if his approval of the petition was in error."

Justice Stewart, with whom Justices Marshall and Powell joined dissenting, observed "[W]hat Judge Stump did on July 9, 1971, was in no way an act "normally performed by a judge. Indeed, there is no reason to believe that such an act has ever been performed by any other Indiana judge, either before or since.". . . "It is true that Judge Stump affixed his signature to the approval of the petition as 'Judge, DeKalb Circuit Court.' But the conduct of a judge surely does not become a judicial act merely on his own say-so. A judge is not free, like a loose cannon, to inflict indiscriminate damage whenever he announces that he is acting in his judicial capacity."

---

remedy available for injuries that arise out of or that occur in the course of activities incident to military service.[87]

(The Case in Point in Box 11.6 provides an example of judicial immunity being upheld even in extreme circumstances.)

Qualified Immunity

In 1975 in *Wood v. Strickland*,[88] the U.S. Supreme Court stated that an official would not be immune from liability if he knew or reasonably should have known that his actions violated plaintiff's clearly established constitutional rights

or if he acted with the malicious intention to cause injury. Thus, the availability of qualified immunity involved both objective and subjective elements.

In 1970 the U.S. Department of Agriculture charged Arthur N. Economou and Company, a dealer in commodity futures, with having willfully failed to maintain the capital requirements prescribed by the department under the Commodity Exchange Act. When the department sought to suspend or revoke Economou's registration, the company brought an action for damages against the department, the Commodity Exchange Authority, the Secretary of Agriculture, and other government officials alleging that they had deprived Economou of constitutional rights by wrongfully initiating administrative action. The district court dismissed actions against the government agencies on the ground of sovereign immunity; it dismissed the actions against the individual defendants because their alleged unconstitutional acts were discretionary. The Court of Appeals affirmed as to the government agencies but reversed as to the individual defendants. That court reasoned that the individuals were not entitled to absolute immunity but only to a qualified immunity of good faith and reasonable grounds similar to that accorded state officers who are sued for constitutional violations under the Civil Rights Act. The Supreme Court granted review.

In *Butz v. Economou* (1978)[89] the Supreme Court held that federal executive officials exercising discretion are entitled only to qualified immunity unless absolute immunity is essential for the conduct of public business. Qualified immunity is available only if the official had a good faith belief that his or her conduct was lawful. The Court said that good faith belief must be a reasonable one, noting that in suits brought directly under the Constitution against federal officers that they are entitled to assert the same immunity defenses as those that apply in "constitutional tort" actions against state officials under 42 U.S.C.A. § 1983.

The Supreme Court's decision in *Butz v. Economou* is excerpted at the end of the chapter.

In *Harlow v. Fitzgerald* (1982),[90] the issue focused on the scope of the immunity available to the senior aides and advisers of the president of the United States in a suit for damages based upon their official acts. The Supreme Court reduced the qualified immunity test to the question of whether the official violated "clearly established statutory or constitutional rights of which a reasonable person would have known." Justice Powell, writing for the Court observed:

Reliance on the objective reasonableness of an official's conduct, as measured by refer-

ence to clearly established law, should avoid excessive disruption of government and permit the resolution of many insubstantial claims on summary judgment. . . . If the law at that time was not clearly established, an official could not reasonably be expected to anticipate subsequent legal developments, nor could he fairly be said to "know" that the law forbade conduct not previously identified as unlawful.[91]

The doctrine of qualified immunity is designed to permit aggrieved individuals to seek redress for violations of their constitutional rights while at the same time protecting federal officials from the inhibiting effect such suits can create. A government official sued for a constitutional tort typically responds to the complaint by filing a motion to dismiss, contending that he or she has qualified immunity from such action. The standard articulated by the Court in *Harlow v. Fitzgerald* can enable a court to dispose of a suit against a public official in summary judgment proceedings, thereby avoiding the costs and delays of a trial (see the Case in Point in Box 11.7).

LIABILITY OF STATE AND LOCAL GOVERNMENTS

Thus far we have considered liability of state officials (and in some instances local governments) operating under color of state law for constitutional torts based on 42 U.S.C.A. § 1983. This federal statute targets individuals but is not a basis of the liability of a state or local government for wrongful acts of its employees. Instead, when a person seeks to hold a state or local government liable, different rules come into play.

Like the federal government, states by virtue of their sovereignty are immune from liability. But just as Congress by enactment of the Federal Tort Claims Act has waived sovereign immunity for damage or injury in certain instances where a private person would be liable, states have waived their sovereign immunity through constitutional provisions or legislative acts.

BOX 11.7 Case in Point

**Applicability of Summary Judgment Procedure
When the Court Finds the Actions of Defendants
to Be Objectively Reasonable
Glass v. Mayas**
United States Court of Appeals for the Second Circuit
984 F.2d 55 (2nd Cir. 1993)

In September 1990 Kendall Glass brought a Section
1983 action against several doctors and nurses for
allegedly violating his constitutional rights by
involuntarily hospitalizing him for psychiatric care.
The U. S. District Court for the Eastern District of
New York granted the defendants' motion for
summary judgment, and plaintiff appealed. The
Court of Appeals noted that Glass had an extensive
history of mental illness and was hospitalized following two reports that he was threatening an
individual with a gun and observations of strange
behavior. Those professionals who examined him
described him as hostile, guarded, angry, suspicious, uncooperative, and paranoid.

Quoting from *Harlow v. Fitzgerald*, the appellate court observed: "Qualified immunity shields
a government official from the liability in civil
actions if the official's conduct does not violate
clearly established statutory or constitutional
rights of which a reasonable person would have
known." The court continued: "The numerous
examinations of plaintiff reveal that plaintiff
exhibited dangerous tendencies in the past and
furthermore, there was an objectively reasonable
basis to believe, at the time in question, that
plaintiff posed a danger to himself or others.
A review of the notes made by defendants at
the time reveals sufficient evidence to support
defendants' decision to commit plaintiff. Accordingly, defendants are shielded by the doctrine of
qualified immunity and are entitled to summary
judgment." Thus the court affirmed the lower
court's finding granting a summary judgment in
favor of the defendants.

In some instances the abolition of state sovereign immunity has come about through judicial
decision. In the 1950s and 1960s, there was a
trend in which state supreme courts abolished
the doctrine in their states. To date, less than ten
states have followed this course. In abolishing
sovereign immunity in North Dakota, that state's
supreme court observed in 1994:

> Whatever justifications initially existed for
> sovereign immunity, they are no longer valid
> in today's society. . . . Sovereign immunity
> contradicts the essence of tort law that liabil-
> ity follows negligence and that individuals
> and corporations are responsible for the neg-
> ligence of their agents and employees acting
> in the course of their employment. We do
> not believe it requires laborious analysis to
> assert that the harshness and inequity of the
> doctrine of sovereign immunity are counter-
> intuitive to any ordinary person's sense of
> justice. It is sufficient to comment that, even
> under the earliest common law of England,
> sovereign immunity did not produce the
> harsh results it does today and only rarely

did it completely deny relief. We are aware
of no persuasive public policy reasons to
continue a constitutional interpretation that
condones an absolute bar to tort liability.[92]

Not to be confused with the sovereign
immunity of states, the **Eleventh Amendment**
to the United States Constitution prohibits federal courts from entertaining suits by individuals
against a state, but again there can be exceptions.
In the following sections we discuss waiver of
sovereign immunity when a state consents to be
sued, the effect of the Eleventh Amendment, and
the extent to which the U.S. Congress may by
explicit legislation authorize a suit against a state.

Sovereign Immunity of Local Governments

The historic immunity of state governments
from suits resulting from torts extended to political subdivisions of the state, for example, counties. Yet, the courts held that the immunity from
suits by local governmental bodies was limited
to cases where local government was acting in
a "governmental" as opposed to a "proprietary"

capacity. Immunity of local government when performing legislative, judicial, and other strictly governmental functions was reasonably clear, but increasingly local governments were performing many different functions. This led to courts creating a confusing patchwork of finding liability when local governments performed "proprietary" as opposed to "governmental" functions. It was relatively easy for a court to determine that protecting the community from fire and disease and maintaining jails was governmental while operating a transit system was proprietary. But courts struggled with the distinction when it involved such operations as a swimming pool, an off-street parking lot, a hospital, and an airport.

Statutory Waivers of Sovereign Immunity

The threat to state treasuries made state legislatures reluctant to waive sovereign immunity. But by the 1960s state courts began to point out that sovereign immunity was inconsistent with fairness and the realities of the modern social order. State legislatures began to enact statutes waiving immunity. Today most states have waived sovereign immunity at least to the extent of allowing injured parties to maintain a civil suit against public officials. Although there are some statutorily or judicially imposed limitations, in general these **statutory waivers of sovereign immunity** usually subject the state and its agencies and other units of government to the same liability as private entities. We illustrate contemporary approaches to waiver of sovereign immunity by three states: Ohio, Pennsylvania, and Florida.

The Ohio Approach Writing in the *Ohio State University Law Journal,* Robert Northness explains that "State statutes waiving immunity have generally taken three different forms: (1) absolute waivers; (2) limited waivers that allow only certain claims; and (3) general waivers subject to specific exceptions waivers of immunity." He describes the waiver under Ohio law as falling in the first category:

Ohio's statutory waiver in the Court Claims Act is absolute and contains few exceptions. . . . The definitional section of the Ohio Court of Claims Act specifically exempts political subdivisions of the state from the waiver of sovereign immunity contained in the Act. . . . The only other significant limitation to the waiver specifies that it shall be void if . . . "the act or omission was manifestly outside the scope of the officer's or employee's office or employment or that the officer or employee . . . acted with malicious purpose, in bad faith, or in a wanton or reckless manner."[93]

In 1984 in *Reynolds v. State,*[94] the Ohio Supreme Court held that a plaintiff who had been raped and assaulted could not bring an action against the state for its decision to furlough a prisoner but once the decision had been made an action can be maintained against the state for personal injuries resulting from the failure of the state to have confined the furloughed prisoner during nonworking hours as required by state law. The court observed:

The language in R.C. 2743.02 that "the state" shall "have its liability determined . . . in accordance with the same rules of law applicable to suits between private parties" . . . means that the state cannot be sued for its legislative or judicial functions or the exercise of an executive or planning function involving the making of a basic policy decision which is characterized by the exercise of a high degree of official judgment or discretion. However, once the decision has been made to engage in a certain activity or function, the state may be held liable, in the same manner as private parties, for the negligence of the actions of its employees and agents in the performance of such activities.[95]

Northness points out that the Ohio Court of Claims Act is the statutory provision that permitted the plaintiff in Reynolds to sue the state.[96]

The Pennsylvania Approach In 1978 the Pennsylvania Supreme Court stated, "Under the doctrine of sovereign immunity a plaintiff's opportunity for justice depends, irrationally, not upon the nature of his injury or of the act which caused it, but upon the identity or status of the wrongdoer . . . We today abrogate this doctrine of 'sovereign immunity.' "[97] The state legislature disagreed with the court's decision and promptly restored sovereign immunity except where it had previously been waived by statute. The Pennsylvania approach appears to fall in the second category that Northness mentions. Its limited waiver statute waives immunity in such instances as operation of state motor vehicles, defects in highways, sidewalks, and state real estate, sale of liquor at Pennsylvania liquor stores, and health personnel of medical facilities or institutions.[98] The Pennsylvania Supreme Court has since on several occasions noted that because of the clear intent to insulate government from exposure to tort liability, the exceptions to immunity are to be strictly construed.[99]

The Florida Approach Article X, Section 13 of the Florida Constitution authorizes the state legislature to abrogate sovereign immunity through enactment of a general law or by bringing suit against the state or its subdivisions. Pursuant to this authority, in 1973 the legislature adopted Section 768.28(1) that allows individuals to sue the state or any of its agencies as well as counties, and municipalities. The Florida statute falls within the third category, that Northness mentions, that is a general waiver; however it is subject to certain specific limitations as to the money damages a person may recover in a tort action for loss of property, personal injury, or death. The damage or injury must have been caused by the negligent or wrongful act or omission of a state or other entity while acting within the scope of employment under circumstances in which the state or other entity, if a private person, would have been liable to the claimant. (Note the parallels to the FTCA in several provisions.)

Under the Florida statute "State agencies or subdivisions" include the executive departments, the legislature, the judicial branch (including public defenders), and the independent establishments of the state; counties and municipalities; and corporations primarily acting as instrumentalities or agencies of the state, counties, or municipalities.

Historically the Florida Legislature has placed monetary limits on recovery under its waiver of sovereign liability. Effective January 7, 2003, Section 788.28 (5) provides:

> The state and its agencies and subdivisions shall be liable for tort claims in the same manner and to the same extent as a private individual under like circumstances, but liability shall not include punitive damages or interest for the period before judgment. Neither the state nor its agencies or subdivisions shall be liable to pay a claim or a judgment by any one person which exceeds the sum of $100,000 or any claim or judgment, or portions thereof, which, when totaled with all other claims or judgments paid by the state or its agencies or subdivisions arising out of the same incident or occurrence, exceeds the sum of $200,000. However, a judgment or judgments may be claimed and rendered in excess of these amounts and may be settled and paid pursuant to this act up to $100,000 or $200,000, as the case may be; and that portion of the judgment that exceeds these amounts may be reported to the Legislature, but may be paid in part or in whole only by further act of the Legislature. Notwithstanding the limited waiver of sovereign immunity provided herein, the state or an agency or subdivision thereof may agree, within the limits of insurance coverage provided, to settle a claim made or a judgment rendered against it without further action by the Legislature, but the state or agency or subdivision thereof shall not be deemed to have waived any defense

of sovereign immunity or to have increased the limits of its liability as a result of its obtaining insurance coverage for tortious acts in excess of the $100,000 or $200,000 waiver provided above. . . .

Unlike the Federal Tort Claims Act, the Florida act does not specifically exempt discretionary activities; however, the state Supreme court has ruled that actions against governmental entities engaged in "planning functions" involving discretionary or policy-making activities are still barred by the doctrine of sovereign immunity whereas "operational functions" that concern the implementation of those activities are subject to the waiver of immunity.

In 1979 in *Commercial Carrier Corp. v. Indian River County*,[100] the Florida Supreme Court acknowledged that Florida Statute § 768.28 does not contain an exception for discretionary acts, as does the Federal Tort Claims Act, nevertheless, the court concluded that "certain policy-making, planning or judgmental governmental functions cannot be the subject of traditional tort liability."[101]

Six years later in *Trianon Park Condominium Assn. v. City of Hialeah*,[102] the same court held that a municipality was not liable in tort to condominium owners who sustained damages from leaky roofs where the owners alleged the roofing defects arose out of allegedly negligent actions of city building inspectors in enforcing provisions of building code. The court pointed out that government's exercise of its discretionary power to enforce compliance with the laws is a matter of governance, for which there never has been a common-law duty of care. The court then observed:

> This discretionary power to enforce compliance with the law as well as the authority to protect the public safety is most notably reflected in the discretionary power given to judges, prosecutors, arresting officers, and other law enforcement officials, as well as the discretionary authority given fire protection agencies to suppress fires. This same

discretionary power to enforce compliance with the law is given to regulatory officials such as building inspectors, fire department inspectors, health department inspectors, elevator inspectors, hotel inspectors, environmental inspectors, and marine patrol officers."[103]

The court further observed that a discretionary function exception, within which these types of activities fall, was expressly recognized in the Federal Tort Claims Act . . . and has also been recognized as inherent in the act of governing by this Court and a majority of the other jurisdictions that have addressed this issue."[104]

As the Florida court held in *Commercial Carrier Corp. v. Indian River County, supra,* planning or judgmental functions do not generally subject a government to tort liability. But in some instances a claimant will contend that a state's failure to consider certain options or by implementing a revision from an original plan for construction of a public improvement the state loses its immunity from tort liability. For example, in 1992 in *Manna v. State,*[105] the Supreme Court of New Jersey reviewed a case where Joseph Manna was killed in a car accident when his car went out of control when he applied his brakes on a wet and slippery bridge that had been built in 1960. The administratrix of his estate sued the state, claiming it was not protected by immunity. The court summarized her arguments as follows:

> The State had to show that at the time it approved the plans for the bridge, it (1) "contemplated that the bridge surface would erode with time, and (2) [intended] to ignore it [as part of] a reasonably calculated plan which would maintain the bridge safe for its intended purposes." "Moreover, she implies that because studs were not considered in the original plan or design, the State's decision regarding whether to install studs now is not protected by the immunity. Alternatively, she characterizes the installation of studs as a

maintenance function that is not protected by the plan-or-design immunity."[106]

The court rejected her arguments and found the New Jersey Tort Claims Act provided the State with immunity for claims stemming from design of the bridge surface even though the condition of the surface of the bridge changed over time. The court observed, "The State is not required to explicitly consider and reject all conceivable design options before receiving immunity for the option chosen. Immunity attaches to the State's decision regarding how to design a particular feature, and does not turn on explicit consideration of specific options."[107] Two justices dissented, arguing that the condition that purportedly led to the accident—failure to maintain the bridge surface—was not contemplated by the original plans and should not apply to plaintiff's claims. They viewed the majority decision as obviating the State's duty to maintain and repair its roads and bridges. Finally, they contended the state legislature did not intend "to immunize the State from the negligent failure to maintain a . . . bridge that had been worn smooth from regular use over a period of twenty-six years."[108]

The New Jersey Supreme Court's decision in _Manna v. State_ is excerpted at the end of this chapter.

The Eleventh Amendment

In _Chisholm v. Georgia_ (1793),[109] the Supreme Court held that states could be sued in federal courts in actions at common law. The _Chisholm_ decision "fell upon the country with a profound shock."[110] The negative reaction to the Court's decision led to adoption of the Eleventh Amendment to United States Constitution in 1798. The Eleventh Amendment provides: "The Judicial power of the United States shall not be construed to extend to any suit in law or equity, commenced or prosecuted against one of the United States by Citizens of another State, or by

Citizens or Subjects of any Foreign State." Courts have interpreted the Eleventh Amendment to mean that a state is immune from suits brought in federal courts by citizens of any state.[111]

As previously noted, state officials can be sued directly in their individual capacities; however absent a waiver by a state, the Eleventh Amendment bars a damages action against a state in federal court, a bar that remains in effect when state officials are sued for damages in their official capacity.[112] In 1908 the Supreme Court recognized an important exception to this general rule: a suit challenging the constitutionality of a state official's action is not one against the State per se and therefore does not fall within the prohibition of the Eleventh Amendment.[113] Federal courts have since recognized that to avoid being barred by the Eleventh Amendment actions against a state official must be based on a theory that the officer acted beyond the scope of his or her statutory authority or, if within that authority, that such authority is unconstitutional.

Adjudication by Federal Administrative Tribunals The Eleventh Amendment limits the "Judicial power" of the United States with respect to suits "in law or equity." But as we have seen in previous chapters, many disputes today are adjudicated by administrative tribunals. Does the Eleventh Amendment preclude a federal agency from adjudicating a case in which a state is a party? In 2002, the Supreme Court answered this question in the affirmative.[114] Writing for the Court, Justice Thomas observed that by "guarding against encroachments by the Federal Government on fundamental aspects of state sovereignty, such as sovereign immunity, we strive to maintain the balance of power embodied in our Constitution."[115] In dissent, Justice Breyer insisted that "[f]ederal administrative agencies do not exercise the '[j]udicial power of the United States.'"[116] Excerpts from the majority opinion and Justice Breyer's dissent are presented in the Supreme Court Perspective in Box 11.8.

BOX 11.8   Supreme Court Perspective

**Federal Maritime Commission v.
South Carolina State Ports Authority**
535 U.S. 743 (2002)

*[In this case the Supreme Court must determine
whether state sovereign immunity precludes a federal administrative agency (the Federal Maritime
Commission) from adjudicating a private party's
complaint that a state-run port has violated
a federal shipping law.]*

Justice Thomas delivered the opinion of the Court.
. . . *"[L]ook[ing] first to evidence of the original understanding of the Constitution,"* . . . *as
well as early congressional practice, . . . we find
a relatively barren historical record, from which the
parties draw radically different conclusions. Petitioner FMC, for instance, argues that state sovereign immunity should not extend to administrative
adjudications because "[t]here is no evidence that
state immunity from the adjudication of complaints by executive officers was an established
principle at the time of the adoption of the Constitution." The SCSPA, on the other hand, asserts that
it is more relevant that "Congress did not attempt
to subject the States to private suits before federal
administrative tribunals" during the early days of
our Republic. . . .*

*In truth, the relevant history does not provide
direct guidance for our inquiry. The Framers, who
envisioned a limited Federal Government, could not
have anticipated the vast growth of the administrative state. . . . Because formalized administrative
adjudications were all but unheard of in the late
18th century and early 19th century, the dearth of
specific evidence indicating whether the Framers
believed that the States' sovereign immunity would
apply in such proceedings is unsurprising.*

*This Court, however, has applied a presumption
. . . that the Constitution was not intended to
"rais[e] up" any proceedings against the States
that were "anomalous and unheard of when the
Constitution was adopted." . . . We therefore
attribute great significance to the fact that States
were not subject to private suits in administrative
adjudications at the time of the founding or for
many years thereafter. . . .*

*To decide whether [this] presumption applies
here, however, we must examine FMC adjudications to determine whether they are the type of*
*proceedings from which the Framers would have
thought the States possessed immunity when they
agreed to enter the Union. . . .*

*. . .[N]either the Commission nor the United
States disputes the Court of Appeals' characterization below that such a proceeding "walks, talks,
and squawks very much like a lawsuit." . . .*

*In short, the similarities between FMC proceed-
ings and civil litigation are overwhelming. In fact,
to the extent that situations arise in the course of
FMC adjudications "which are not covered by a
specific Commission rule," the FMC's own Rules
of Practice and Procedure specifically provide that
"the Federal Rules of Civil Procedure will be
followed to the extent that they are consistent
with sound administrative practice." . . .*

*The preeminent purpose of state sovereign
immunity is to accord States the dignity that is consistent with their status as sovereign entities. . . .*

*Given both this interest in protecting States'
dignity and the strong similarities between FMC
proceedings and civil litigation, we hold that state
sovereign immunity bars the FMC from adjudicating complaints filed by a private party against a
nonconsenting State. Simply put, if the Framers
thought it an impermissible affront to a State's
dignity to be required to answer the complaints of
private parties in federal courts, we cannot imag-
ine that they would have found it acceptable to
compel a State to do exactly the same thing before
the administrative tribunal of an agency, such as
the FMC. . . . The affront to a State's dignity does
not lessen when an adjudication takes place in an
administrative tribunal as opposed to an Article III
court. In both instances, a State is required to
defend itself in an adversarial proceeding against a
private party before an impartial federal officer.
Moreover, it would be quite strange to prohibit
Congress from exercising its Article I powers to
abrogate state sovereign immunity in Article III
judicial proceedings, . . . but permit the use of
those same Article I powers to create court-like
administrative tribunals where sovereign immunity
does not apply. . . .*

Justice Breyer, *with whom* **Justice Stevens, Justice Souter,** *and* **Justice Ginsburg** *join, dissenting.*

*. . . The Court's decision threatens to deny
the Executive and Legislative Branches of Government the structural flexibility that the Constitu-*

> **BOX 11.8**   Supreme Court Perspective (Continued)
>
> *tion permits and which modern government demands. The Court derives from the abstract notion of state "dignity" a structural principle that limits the powers of both Congress and the President. Its reasoning rests almost exclusively upon the use of a formal analogy, which, as I have said, jumps ordinary separation-of-powers bounds. It places "great significance" upon the 18th century absence of 20th century administrative proceedings. . . . And its conclusion draws little support from considerations of constitutional purpose or related consequence. In its readiness to rest a structural limitation on so little evidence and in its willingness to interpret that limitation so broadly, the majority ignores a historical lesson, reflected in a constitutional understanding that the Court adopted long ago: An overly restrictive judicial interpretation of the Constitution's structural constraints (unlike its protections of certain basic liberties) will undermine the Constitution's own efforts to achieve its far more basic structural aim, the creation of a representative form of government capable of translating the people's will into effective public action.*
>
> *This understanding, underlying constitutional interpretation since the New Deal, reflects the Constitution's demands for structural flexibility sufficient to adapt substantive laws and institutions to rapidly changing social, economic, and technological conditions. It reflects the comparative inability of the Judiciary to understand either those conditions or the need for new laws and new administrative forms they may create. It reflects the Framers' own aspiration to write a document that would "constitute" a democratic, liberty-protecting form of government that would endure through centuries of change. This understanding led the New Deal Court to reject overly restrictive formalistic interpretations of the Constitution's structural provisions, thereby permitting Congress to enact social and economic legislation that circumstances had led the public to demand. And it led that Court to find in the Constitution authorization for new forms of administration, including independent administrative agencies, with the legal authority flexibly to implement, i.e., to "execute," through adjudication, through rulemaking, and in other ways, the legislation that Congress subsequently enacted.*

Congressional Abrogation of State Sovereign Immunity

The Fourteenth Amendment prohibits states from denying due process and equal protection of the laws to persons within their jurisdictions. Section 5 of that amendment authorizes Congress to implement these prohibitions by enacting "appropriate legislation." Notwithstanding the Eleventh Amendment, the Supreme Court has held that Section 5 allows Congress to enact laws that permit suits for damages against state governments. Thus the Fourteenth Amendment permits Congress to abrogate state sovereign immunity with respect to suits seeking to vindicate civil rights and liberties. However, Congress may do so "only by making its intention unmistakably clear in the language of the statute."[117]

In 1972 Congress amended Title VII of the Civil Rights Act of 1954 to authorize federal courts to award money damages to a private individual against a state government found to have subjected that person to employment discrimination on the basis of "race, color, religion, sex, or national origin." An issue arose as to whether, in view of the Eleventh Amendment prohibition on citizens bringing suit against a state in federal courts, Congress could enact a law allowing individuals to sue a state for money damages. In *Fitzpatrick v. Bitzer* (1976),[118] the Supreme Court upheld this law, with Justice Rehnquist stating that

> the Eleventh Amendment, and the principle of state sovereignty which it embodies, . . . are necessarily limited by the enforcement

provisions of section 5 of the Fourteenth Amendment. . . . When Congress acts pursuant to section 5, not only is it exercising legislative authority that is plenary within the terms of the constitutional grant, it is exercising that authority under one section of a constitutional Amendment whose other sections by their own terms embody limitations on state authority. We think that Congress may, in determining what is "appropriate legislation" for the purpose of enforcing the provisions of the Fourteenth Amendment, provide for private suits against States or state officials which are constitutionally impermissible in other contexts.[119]

In the past decade the Supreme Court under Chief Justice Rehnquist has placed considerable emphasis on the rights of the states. Accordingly, it has limited Congress' power to abrogate states' sovereign immunity. For example, in *Seminole Tribe of Florida v. Florida* (1996),[120] the Court struck down a provision of the Indian Gaming Regulatory Act that allowed Indian tribes to bring federal lawsuits against states to require them to engage in good faith negotiations to establish "Tribal–State Gaming Compacts." In abrogating state sovereign immunity in this context, Congress relied on its broad powers under the Commerce Clause of Article I, Section 8 (see Chapter 3). In striking down the law, the Court adopted the view that nothing in Article I gives Congress authority to abrogate state sovereign immunity and that such power stems only from the Fourteenth Amendment and must be confined to congressional efforts to enforce the guarantees of that amendment. In a protracted dissenting opinion, Justice Souter took strong issue with the majority's interpretation of the Eleventh Amendment. Souter expressed shock at the Court's holding "for the first time since the founding of the Republic that Congress has no authority to subject a State to the jurisdiction of a federal court at the behest of an individual asserting a federal right."[121]

The Rehnquist Court's philosophy of protecting states' rights by limiting **congressional power to abrogate state sovereign immunity** was dramatically illustrated in the Court's 5-4 decision in *Kimel v. Florida Board of Regents* (2000).[122] Writing for the Court in *Kimel,* Justice O'Connor acknowledged that the enforcement clause of the Fourteenth Amendment grants Congress the authority to abrogate the states' sovereign immunity but held that enactment by Congress of the Age Discrimination in Employment Act (ADEA) of 1967, as amended, did not abrogate the state's Eleventh Amendment immunity from suit by private individuals. Justice O'Connor emphasized the historic power of the states and quoted from a former decision of the Court that noted:

> Congress cannot decree the substance of the Fourteenth Amendment's restrictions on the States. . . . It has been given the power to enforce, not the power to determine what constitutes a constitutional violation. . . . The ultimate interpretation and determination of the Fourteenth Amendment's substantive meaning remains the province of the Judicial Branch.[123]

Justice Stevens' dissent was aimed not only at the Court's opinion in *Kimel,* but at the Rehnquist Court's Eleventh Amendment jurisprudence:

> Congress' power to regulate the American economy includes the power to regulate both the public and the private sectors of the labor market. Federal rules outlawing discrimination in the workplace, like the regulation of wages and hours or health and safety standards, may be enforced against public as well as private employers. In my opinion, Congress' power to authorize federal remedies against state agencies that violate federal statutory obligations is coextensive with its power to impose those obligations on the States in the first place. Neither the Eleventh Amendment nor the

doctrine of sovereign immunity places any limit on that power.[124]

It is important to recognize that the Court's decision does not preclude those who claim age bias from seeking a remedy in court under ADEA, but it does mean that plaintiffs cannot bring their actions in federal court.

Under the Court's recent Eleventh Amendment decisions, Congress does have power under the Fourteenth Amendment to abrogate state sovereign immunity, as long as it does so through clear statutory language and in a way that is consistent with the Fourteenth Amendment's substantive limitations on state power. Congress does not have power to abrogate state sovereign immunity under the Commerce Clause of Article I, Section 8. As the Court observed in *Seminole Tribe*, "Even when the Constitution vests in Congress complete law-making authority over a particular area, the Eleventh Amendment prevents congressional authorization of suits by private parties against unconsenting States."[125]

Liability of Local Governments in Section 1983 Actions

The Eleventh Amendment applies to damage actions against states but not to actions against local governments. Whether a particular defendant is an "arm of the State partaking of the State's Eleventh Amendment immunity" depends on "the nature of the entity created by state law."[126] As previously discussed, the Supreme Court now considers cities and counties to be "persons" that can be sued within the meaning of 42 U.S.C.A. § 1983, even though cities and counties are political subdivisions of their respective states. However, local governments cannot be held liable under an employer-employee (*respondeat superior*) relationship but can be held liable if their official policy has caused a constitutional deprivation. Local governments are not liable for the actions of their employees unless they are acting pursuant to policy. In the words

of Justice O'Connor, writing for the Court in *Board of County Commissioners v. Brown* (1997), "a plaintiff must show that the municipal action was taken with the requisite degree of culpability and must demonstrate a direct causal link between the municipal action and the deprivation of federal rights."[127] This makes it difficult, though certainly not impossible, for plaintiffs to prevail in civil suits alleging civil rights violations by cities and counties.

CONCLUSION

The ancient common-law doctrine of sovereign immunity runs counter to the American concept of providing redress for wrongs. Although the framers of the U.S. Constitution were not presented with an issue of governmental liability, the rise of the administrative state caused Congress to waive sovereign immunity to the extent of providing a system to compensate those who suffer injuries at the hands of the government officials while enabling those officials to carry out their responsibilities. This action, the increased accessibility to recourse based on historic civil rights laws, and the Supreme Court's modern decisions in the field of constitutional torts have afforded citizens a means to secure redress for violations of their rights by governmental officials.

The Eleventh Amendment prohibits federal courts from adjudicating suits against states. But the Supreme Court has construed the Fourteenth Amendment to permit Congress to abrogate state sovereign immunity with respect to suits to redress violations of civil rights and liberties. Moreover, the trend of legislative and judicial action in the states in recent decades has been to waive sovereign immunity to the extent of allowing private parties to secure redress for the injuries inflicted by governmental actors at the state and local levels. Availability of insurance allows governments to budget for compensating victims.

In implementing a fair system to compensate those who suffer injury, it is essential to protect the ability of government officials to carry out their responsibilities without the fear of being targeted by litigation. To accomplish the latter the law has accorded judges, prosecutors, and legislators with absolute immunity from legal action for their official actions while it has conferred qualified immunity against lawsuits unless their official acts violate clearly established rights.

The right to effective legal recourse against government officials whose actions or omissions cause injury is an important aspect of administrative law. Although redress can take many forms, the right to money damages is all-important because it not only compensates those who are injured; it deters government officials from acting illegally.

KEY TERMS

absolute immunity

Bivens-type remedy

breaches of contract

Civil Rights Act of 1871

color of state law

congressional power to abrogate state sovereign immunity

constitutional torts

deliberate indifference standard

discretionary function exception

Eleventh Amendment

exception for executing statutes and regulations

Federal Tort Claims Act

Feres doctrine

government contractor defense

immunity

injunctions

intentional tort exception

private legislative act

professional judgment standard

punitive damages

qualified immunity

respondeat superior

scope of employment

Section 1983 actions

sovereign immunity

Speech and Debate Clause

statutory waivers of sovereign immunity

torts

Tucker Act

waiver of sovereign immunity

Westfall Act

writ of mandamus

QUESTIONS FOR THOUGHT AND DISCUSSION

1. What is the historical basis of the doctrine of sovereign immunity?

2. What role has the Tucker Act played with respect to the federal government's waiver of sovereign immunity?

3. To what extent does the Federal Tort Claims Act waive the immunity of the United States for tort liability?

4. To what extent does the law of a state where a wrongful act or omission takes place affect the liability of the United States under the Federal Tort Claims Act?

5. How and why did Congress amend the Federal Tort Claims Act by enactment of the Westfall Act?

6. To what extent can state officials be held liable for violations of the federal constitution and laws under 42 U.S.C.A. § 1983?

7. To what extent have the Supreme Court's decisions since 1971 held federal officials liable for violation of an individual's constitutional rights?

8. Under what circumstances can a municipality be held liable under 42 U.S.C.A. § 1983?

EDITED CASE United States v. Gaubert
United States Supreme Court, 499 U.S. 315 (1991)

Justice White delivered the opinion of the Court.

. . . In this case, the FHLBB and the Federal Home Loan Bank-Dallas (FHLB-D) undertook to advise about and oversee certain aspects of the operation of a thrift institution. Their conduct in this respect was challenged by a suit against the United States under the Federal Tort Claims Act, 28 U.S.C. § 1346(b), § 2671 et seq. (FTCA), asserting that the FHLBB and FHLB-D had been negligent in carrying out their supervisory activities. The question before us is whether certain actions taken by the FHLB-Band FHLB-D are within the "discretionary function" exception to the liability of the United States under the FTCA. The Court of Appeals for the Fifth Circuit answered this question in the negative. We have the contrary view, and reverse.

I

This FTCA suit arises from the supervision by federal regulators of the activities of Independent American Savings Association (IASA), a Texas-chartered and federally insured savings and loan. Respondent Thomas A. Gaubert was IASA's chairman of the board and largest shareholder. In 1984, officials at the FHLBB sought to have IASA merge with Investex Savings, a failing Texas thrift. Because the FHLBB and FHLB-D were concerned about Gaubert's other financial dealings, they requested that he sign a "neutralization agreement" which effectively removed him from IASA's management. They also asked him to post a $25 million interest in real property as security for his personal guarantee that IASA's net worth would exceed regulatory minimums. Gaubert agreed to both conditions. Federal officials then provided regulatory and financial advice to enable IASA to consummate the merger with Investex. Throughout this period, the regulators instituted no formal action against IASA. Instead, they relied on the likelihood that IASA and Gaubert would follow their suggestions and advice.

In the spring of 1986, the regulators threatened to close IASA unless its management and board of directors were replaced; all of the directors agreed to resign. The new officers and directors, including the chief executive officer who was a former FHLB-D employee, were recommended by FHLB-D. After the new management took over, FHLB-D officials became more involved in IASA's day-to-day business. They recommended the hiring of a certain consultant to advise IASA on operational and financial matters; they advised IASA concerning whether, when, and how its subsidiaries should be placed into bankruptcy; they mediated salary disputes; they reviewed the draft of a complaint to be used in litigation; they urged IASA to convert from state to federal charter; and they actively intervened when the Texas Savings and Loan Department attempted to install a supervisory agent at IASA. In each instance, FHLB-D's advice was followed.

Although IASA was thought to be financially sound while Gaubert managed the thrift, the new directors soon announced that IASA had a substantial negative net worth. On May 20, 1987, Gaubert filed an administrative tort claim with the FHLBB, FHLB-D, and FSLIC, seeking $75 million in damages for the lost value of his shares and $25 million for the property he had forfeited under his personal guarantee. That same day, the FSLIC assumed the receivership of IASA. After Gaubert's administrative claim was denied six months later, he filed the instant FTCA suit in United States District Court for the Northern District of Texas, seeking $100 million in damages for the alleged negligence of federal officials in selecting the new officers and directors and in participating in the day-to-day management of IASA. The District Court granted the motion to dismiss filed by the United States, finding that all of the challenged actions of the regulators fell within the discretionary function exception to the FTCA, found in 28 U.S.C. 2680(a). . . .

The Court of Appeals for the Fifth Circuit affirmed in part and reversed in part. . . . Relying on this Court's decision in *Indian Towing Co. v.*

(Continued)

---

9. What is the difference between "absolute immunity" and "qualified immunity"? Who are eligible for each class of immunity?

10. Under what circumstances can a state and local unit of government be held liable for torts committed by its employees?

EDITED CASE United States v. Gaubert (Continued)

United States, 350 U.S. 61 (1955), the court distinguished between "policy decisions," which fall within the exception, and "operational actions," which do not. . . . After claiming further support for this distinction in this Court's decisions in *United States v. Varig Airlines*, 467 U.S. 797 (1984), and *Berkovitz v. United States*, 486 U.S. 531 (1988), the court explained:

> "The authority of the FHLBB and FHLB-Dallas to take the actions that were taken in this case, although not guided by regulations, is unchallenged. The FHLBB and FHLB-Dallas officials did not have regulations telling them, at every turn, how to accomplish their goals for IASA; this fact, however, does not automatically render their decisions discretionary and immune from FTCA suits. Only policy-oriented decisions enjoy such immunity. Thus, the FHLBB and FHLB-Dallas officials were only protected by the discretionary function exception until their actions became operational in nature, and thus crossed the line established in Indian Towing."
>
> . . .

In the court's view, that line was crossed when the regulators "began to advise IASA management and participate in management decisions." . . . Consequently, the Court of Appeals affirmed the District Court's dismissal of the claims which concerned the merger, neutralization agreement, personal guarantee, and replacement of IASA management, but reversed the dismissal of the claims which concerned the regulators' activities after they assumed a supervisory role in IASA's day-to-day affairs. We granted certiorari . . . and now reverse.

II

The liability of the United States under the FTCA is subject to the various exceptions contained in § 2680, including the "discretionary function" exception at issue here. That exception provides that the Government is not liable for "[a]ny claim based upon an act or omission of an employee of the Government, exercising due care, in the execution of a statute or regulation, whether or not such statute or regulation be valid, or based upon the exercise or performance or the failure to exercise or perform a discretionary function or duty on the part of a federal agency or an employee of the

Government, whether or not the discretion involved be abused." 28 U.S.C. § 2680(a).

The exception covers only acts that are discretionary in nature, acts that "involv[e] an element of judgment or choice," . . . and "it is the nature of the conduct, rather than the status of the actor," that governs whether the exception applies. . . . The requirement of judgment or choice is not satisfied if a "federal statute, regulation, or policy specifically prescribes a course of action for an employee to follow," because "the employee has no rightful option but to adhere to the directive." . . .

Furthermore, even "assuming the challenged conduct involves an element of judgment," it remains to be decided "whether that judgment is of the kind that the discretionary function exception was designed to shield." . . . Because the purpose of the exception is to "prevent judicial 'second-guessing' of legislative and administrative decisions grounded in social, economic, and political policy through the medium of an action in tort," . . . when properly construed, the exception "protects only governmental actions and decisions based on considerations of public policy." . . .

Where Congress has delegated the authority to an independent agency or to the executive branch to implement the general provisions of a regulatory statute and to issue regulations to that end, there is no doubt that planning-level decisions establishing programs are protected by the discretionary function exception, as is the promulgation of regulations by which the agencies are to carry out the programs. In addition, the actions of Government agents involving the necessary element of choice and grounded in the social, economic, or political goals of the statute and regulations are protected. . . .

Under the applicable precedents, therefore, if a regulation mandates particular conduct, and the employee obeys the direction, the Government will be protected, because the action will be deemed in furtherance of the policies which led to the promulgation of the regulation. . . . If the employee violates the mandatory regulation, there will be no shelter from liability, because there is no room for choice, and the action will be contrary to policy. On the other hand, if a regulation allows the employee discretion, the very existence of the regulation creates a strong presumption that a discre-

---

EDITED CASE   United States v. Gaubert (Continued)

---

tionary act authorized by the regulation involves consideration of the same policies which led to the promulgation of the regulations.

Not all agencies issue comprehensive regulations, however. Some establish policy on a case-by-case basis, whether through adjudicatory proceedings or through administration of agency programs. Others promulgate regulations on some topics, but not on others. In addition, an agency may rely on internal guidelines, rather than on published regulations. In any event, it will most often be true that the general aims and policies of the controlling statute will be evident from its text.

When established governmental policy, as expressed or implied by statute, regulation, or agency guidelines, allows a Government agent to exercise discretion, it must be presumed that the agent's acts are grounded in policy when exercising that discretion. For a complaint to survive a motion to dismiss, it must allege facts which would support a finding that the challenged actions are not the kind of conduct that can be said to be grounded in the policy of the regulatory regime. The focus of the inquiry is not on the agent's subjective intent in exercising the discretion conferred by statute or regulation, but on the nature of the actions taken and on whether they are susceptible to policy analysis.

III

In light of our cases and their interpretation of § 2680(a), it is clear that the Court of Appeals erred in holding that the exception does not reach decisions made at the operational or management level of the bank involved in this case. A discretionary act is one that involves choice or judgment; there is nothing in that description that refers exclusively to policymaking or planning functions. Day-to-day management of banking affairs, like the management of other businesses, regularly require judgment as to which of a range of permissible courses is the wisest. Discretionary conduct is not confined to the policy or planning level. "[I]t is the nature of the conduct, rather than the status of the actor, that governs whether the discretionary function exception applies in a given case." . . .

In *Varig Airlines,* the Federal Aviation Administration had devised a system of "spot-checking" airplanes. We held that not only was this act discretionary, but so too were the acts of agency

employees in executing the program, since they had a range of discretion to exercise in deciding how to carry out the spot-check activity. . . . Likewise, in *Berkovitz,* although holding that some acts on the operational level were not discretionary, and therefore were without the exception, we recognized that other acts, if held to be discretionary on remand, would be protected. . . .

IV

. . . These claims asserted that the regulators had achieved "a constant federal presence" at IASA. . . . In describing this presence, the Amended Complaint alleged that the regulators "consult[ed] as to day-to-day affairs and operations of IASA," . . . "participated in management decisions" at IASA board meetings, . . . "became involved in giving advice, making recommendations, urging, or directing action or procedures at IASA," . . . and "advised their hand-picked directors and officers on a variety of subjects." . . . Specifically, the complaint enumerated seven instances or kinds of objectionable official involvement. First, the regulators "arranged for the hiring for IASA of . . . consultants on operational and financial matters and asset management." . . . Second, the officials "urged or directed that IASA convert from a state-chartered savings and loan to a federally-chartered savings and loan, in part so that it could become the exclusive government entity with power to control IASA." . . . Third, the regulators "gave advice and made recommendations concerning whether, when, and how to place IASA subsidiaries into bankruptcy." . . . Fourth, the officials "mediated salary disputes between IASA and its senior officers." . . . Fifth, the regulators "reviewed a draft complaint in litigation" that IASA's board contemplated filing and were "so actively involved in giving advice, making recommendations, and directing matters related to IASA's litigation policy that they were able successfully to stall the Board of Directors' ultimate decision to file the complaint until the Bank Board in Washington had reviewed, advised on, and commented on the draft." . . . Sixth, the regulators "actively intervened with the Texas Savings and Loan Department (IASA's principal regulator) when the State attempted to install a supervisory agent at

(Continued)

EDITED CASE   United States v. Gaubert (Continued)

IASA." . . . Finally, the FHLB-D president wrote the IASA board of directors "affirming that his agency had placed that Board of Directors into office, and describing their mutual goal to protect the FSLIC insurance fund." . . . According to Gaubert, the losses he suffered were caused by the regulators' "assumption of the duty to participate in, and to make, the day-to-day decisions at IASA and [the] negligent discharge of that assumed duty." . . . Moreover, he alleged that "[t]he involvement of the FHLB-Dallas in the affairs of IASA went beyond its normal regulatory activity, and the agency actually substituted its decisions for those of the directors and officers of the association." . . .

We first inquire whether the challenged actions were discretionary, or whether they were instead controlled by mandatory statutes or regulations. . . . Although the FHLBB, which oversaw the other agencies at issue, had promulgated extensive regulations which were then in effect, . . . neither party has identified formal regulations governing the conduct in question. As already noted, 12 U.S.C. § 1464(a) authorizes the FHLBB to examine and regulate FSLA's, "giving primary consideration to the best practices of thrift institutions in the United States." Both the District Court and the Court of Appeals recognized that the agencies possessed broad statutory authority to supervise financial institutions. The relevant statutory provisions were not mandatory, but left to the judgment of the agency the decision of when to institute proceedings against a financial institution and which mechanism to use. For example, the FSLIC had authority to terminate an institution's insured status, issue cease-and-desist orders, and suspend or remove an institution's officers, if, "in the opinion of the Corporation," such action was warranted because the institution or its officers were engaging in an "unsafe or unsound practice" in connection with the business of the institution. . . . The FHLBB had parallel authority to issue cease-and-desist orders and suspend or remove an institution's officers. . . . Although the statute enumerated specific grounds warranting an appointment by the FHLBB of a conservator or receiver, the determination of whether any of these grounds existed depended upon "the opinion of the Board." . . . The agencies here were not bound to act in a particular way; the exercise of their authority involved a great "element of judgment or choice." . . .

We are unconvinced by Gaubert's assertion that, because the agencies did not institute formal proceedings against IASA, they had no discretion to take informal actions as they did. Although the statutes provided only for formal proceedings, there is nothing in the language or structure of the statutes that prevented the regulators from invoking less formal means of supervision of financial institutions. Not only was there no statutory or regulatory mandate which compelled the regulators to act in a particular way, but there was no prohibition against the use of supervisory mechanisms not specifically set forth in statute or regulation.

This is the view of the FHLBB; for, in a resolution passed in 1982, the FHLBB adopted "a formal statement of policy regarding the Bank Board's use of supervisory actions. . . ."

From this statement, it is clear that the regulators had the discretion to supervise IASA through informal means, rather than invoke statutory sanctions.

Gaubert also argues that the challenged actions fall outside the discretionary function exception because they involved the mere application of technical skills and business expertise. . . . But this is just another way of saying that the considerations involving the day-to-day management of a business concern such as IASA are so precisely formulated that decisions at the operational level never involve the exercise of discretion within the meaning of § 2680(a), a notion that we have already rejected in disapproving the rationale of the Court of Appeals' decision. It may be that certain decisions resting on mathematical calculations, for example, involve no choice or judgment in carrying out the calculations, but the regulatory acts alleged here are not of that genre. Rather, it is plain to us that each of the challenged actions involved the exercise of choice and judgment. . . .

We are also convinced that each of the regulatory actions in question involved the kind of policy judgment that the discretionary function exception was designed to shield. The FHLBB Resolution quoted above, coupled with the relevant statutory provisions, established governmental policy which is presumed to have been furthered when the regulators exercised their discretion to choose from various courses of action in supervising IASA. Although Gaubert contends that day-to-day decisions concerning IASA's affairs did not implicate social, economic, or political policies, even the

---

EDITED CASE United States v. Gaubert (Continued)

Court of Appeals recognized that these day-to-day "operational" decisions were undertaken for policy reasons of primary concern to the regulatory agencies:

"[T]he federal regulators here had two discrete purposes in mind as they commenced day-to-day operations at IASA. First, they sought to protect the solvency of the savings and loan industry at large, and maintain the public's confidence in that industry. Second, they sought to preserve the assets of IASA for the benefit of depositors and shareholders, of which Gaubert was one." . . .

Consequently, Gaubert's assertion that the day-to-day involvement of the regulators with IASA is actionable because it went beyond "normal regulatory activity" is insupportable.

We find nothing in Gaubert's Amended Complaint effectively alleging that the discretionary acts performed by the regulators were not entitled to the exemption. By Gaubert's own admission, the regulators replaced IASA's management in order to protect the FSLIC's insurance fund; thus, it cannot be disputed that this action was based on public policy considerations. The regulators' actions in urging IASA to convert to federal charter and in intervening with the state agency were directly related to public policy considerations regarding federal oversight of the thrift industry. So were advising the hiring of a financial consultant, advising when to place IASA subsidiaries into bankruptcy, intervening on IASA's behalf with Texas officials, advising on litigation policy, and mediating salary disputes. There are no allegations that the regulators gave anything other than the kind of advice that was within the purview of the policies behind the statutes.

There is no doubt that, in advising IASA, the regulators used the power of persuasion to accomplish their goals. Nevertheless, we long ago recognized that regulators have the authority to use such tactics in supervising financial institutions. . . . Moreover, the agencies' ability to terminate a bank's insured status and invoke other less drastic sanctions meant that "recommendations by the agencies concerning banking practices tend to be followed by bankers without the necessity of formal compli-ance proceedings." . . . These statements apply with equal force to supervision by federal agencies of the savings and loan industry. . . . Consequently, neither the pervasiveness of the regulators' presence at IASA nor the forcefulness of their recommendations is sufficient to alter the supervisory nature of the regulators' actions.

In the end, Gaubert's Amended Complaint alleges nothing more than negligence on the part of the regulators. Indeed, the two substantive counts seek relief for "negligent selection of directors and officers" and "negligent involvement in day-to-day operations." . . . Gaubert asserts that the discretionary function exception protects only those acts of negligence which occur in the course of establishing broad policies, rather than individual acts of negligence which occur in the course of day-to-day activities. . . . But we have already disposed of that submission. . . . If the routine or frequent nature of a decision were sufficient to remove an otherwise discretionary act from the scope of the exception, then countless policy-based decisions by regulators exercising day-to-day supervisory authority would be actionable. This is not the rule of our cases.

V

Because, from the face of the Amended Complaint, it is apparent that all of the challenged actions of the federal regulators involved the exercise of discretion in furtherance of public policy goals, the Court of Appeals erred in failing to find the claims barred by the discretionary function exception of the Federal Tort Claims Act. We therefore reverse the decision of the Court of Appeals for the Fifth Circuit and remand for proceedings consistent with this opinion. . . .

Justice Scalia, concurring in part and concurring in the judgment.

I concur in the judgment and in much of the opinion of the Court. I write separately because I do not think it necessary to analyze individually each of the particular actions challenged by Gaubert, nor do I think an individualized analysis necessarily leads to the results the Court obtains. . . .

EDITED CASE   Deshaney v. Winnebago County Department of Social Services
United States Supreme Court, 489 U.S. 1989 (1989)

[At issue before the Supreme Court in this case is whether the failure of a local social services agency to take action to prevent a boy from his abusive father constitutes "state action" for the purposes of the Fourteenth Amendment. Following his parents' divorce, one-year-old Joshua DeShaney was placed in the custody of his father, who soon established legal residence in Winnebago County, Wisconsin. Two years later, county social workers began to receive reports that the father was physically abusing the child. When Joshua was four years old, his father beat him so severely as to inflict permanent brain damage, leaving the child profoundly retarded and institutionalized for life. Joshua's mother brought suit on her son's behalf under 42 U.S.C.A. § 1983, alleging that the agency's failure to protect her son constituted an abridgment of his rights under the Due Process Clause of the Fourteenth Amendment.]

Chief Justice Rehnquist delivered the opinion of the Court.

. . . The Due Process Clause of the Fourteenth Amendment provides that "[n]o State shall . . . deprive any person of life, liberty, or property, without due process of law." Petitioners contend that the State deprived Joshua of his liberty interest in "free[dom] from . . . unjustified intrusions on personal security," . . . by failing to provide him with adequate protection against his father's violence. The claim is one invoking the substantive rather than procedural component of the Due Process Clause; petitioners do not claim that the State denied Joshua protection without according him appropriate procedural safeguards . . . but that it was categorically obligated to protect him in these circumstances.

But nothing in the language of the Due Process Clause itself requires the State to protect the life, liberty, and property of its citizens against invasion by private actors. The Clause is phrased as a limitation on the State's power to act, not as a guarantee of certain minimal levels of safety and security. It forbids the State itself to deprive individuals of life, liberty, or property without "due process of law," but its language cannot fairly be extended to impose an affirmative obligation on the State to ensure that those interests do not come to harm through other means. Nor does history support such an expansive reading of the constitutional text. Like its counterpart in the Fifth Amendment, the Due Process Clause of the Fourteenth Amendment was intended to prevent government "from abusing [its] power, or employing it as an instrument of oppression. . . ." Its purpose was to protect the people from the State, not to ensure that the State protected them from each other. The Framers were content to leave the extent of governmental obligation in the latter area to the democratic political processes.

Consistent with these principles, our cases have recognized that the Due Process Clauses generally confer no affirmative right to governmental aid, even where such aid may be necessary to secure life, liberty, or property interests of which the government itself may not deprive the individual. . . . If the Due Process Clause does not require the State to provide its citizens with particular protective services, it follows that the State cannot be held liable under the Clause for injuries that could have been averted had it chosen to provide them. As a general matter, then, we conclude that a State's failure to protect an individual against private violence simply does not constitute a violation of the Due Process Clause.

Petitioners contend, however, that even if the Due Process Clause imposes no affirmative obligation on the State to provide the general public with adequate protective services, such a duty may arise out of certain "special relationships" created or assumed by the State with respect to particular individuals. . . . Petitioners argue that such a "special relationship" existed here because the State knew that Joshua faced a special danger of abuse at his father's hands, and specifically proclaimed, by word and by deed, its intention to protect him against that danger. . . . Having actually undertaken to protect Joshua from this danger—which petitioners concede the State played no part in creating—the State acquired an affirmative "duty," enforceable through the Due Process Clause, to do so in a reasonably competent fashion. Its failure to discharge that duty, so the argument goes, was an abuse of governmental power that so "shocks the conscience," . . . as to constitute a substantive due process violation. . . .

> **EDITED CASE** Deshaney v. Winnebago County Department of Social Services (Continued)

We reject this argument. It is true that in certain limited circumstances the Constitution imposes upon the State affirmative duties of care and protection with respect to particular individuals. . . .

. . . While the State may have been aware of the dangers that Joshua faced in the free world, it played no part in their creation, nor did it do anything to render him any more vulnerable to them. That the State once took temporary custody of Joshua does not alter the analysis, for when it returned him to his father's custody, it placed him in no worse position than that in which he would have been had it not acted at all; the State does not become the permanent guarantor of an individual's safety by having once offered him shelter. Under these circumstances, the State had no constitutional duty to protect Joshua. . . .

Judges and lawyers, like other humans, are moved by natural sympathy in a case like this to find a way for Joshua and his mother to receive adequate compensation for the grievous harm inflicted upon them. But before yielding to that impulse, it is well to remember once again that the harm was inflicted not by the State of Wisconsin, but by Joshua's father. The most that can be said of the state functionaries in this case is that they stood by and did nothing when suspicious circumstances dictated a more active role for them. In defense of them it must also be said that had they moved too soon to take custody of the son away from the father, they would likely have been met with charges of improperly intruding into the parent-child relationship. . . .

The people of Wisconsin may well prefer a system of liability which would place upon the State and its officials the responsibility for failure to act in situations such as the present one. They may create such a system, if they do not have it already, by changing the tort law of the State in accordance with the regular law-making process. But they should not have it thrust upon them by this Court's expansion of the Due Process Clause of the Fourteenth Amendment. . . .

Justice Brennan, with whom *Justice Marshall* and *Justice Blackmun* join, dissenting. . . .

Justice Blackmun, dissenting.

Today, the Court purports to be the dispassionate oracle of the law, unmoved by "natural sympathy." But, in this pretense, the Court itself retreats into a sterile formalism which prevents it from recognizing either the facts of the case before it or the legal norms that should apply to those facts. As Justice Brennan demonstrates, the facts here involve not mere passivity, but active state intervention in the life of Joshua DeShaney—intervention that triggered a fundamental duty to aid the boy once the State learned of the severe danger to which he was exposed.

The Court fails to recognize this duty because it attempts to draw a sharp and rigid line between action and inaction. But such formalistic reasoning has no place in the interpretation of the broad and stirring clauses of the Fourteenth Amendment. . . .

Like the antebellum judges who denied relief to fugitive slaves, the Court today claims that its decision, however harsh, is compelled by existing legal doctrine. On the contrary, the question presented by this case is an open one and our Fourteenth Amendment precedents may be read more broadly or narrowly depending upon how one chooses to read them. Faced with the choice, I would adopt a "sympathetic" reading, one which comports with dictates of fundamental justice and recognizes that compassion need not be exiled from the province of judging. . . .

Poor Joshua! Victim of repeated attacks by an irresponsible, bullying, cowardly, and intemperate father, and abandoned by respondents who placed him in a dangerous predicament and who knew or learned what was going on, and yet did essentially nothing except, as the Court revealing observes, . . . "dutifully recorded these incidents in [their] files." It is a sad commentary upon American life, and constitutional principles—so full of late patriotic fervor and proud proclamations about "liberty and justice for all," that this child, Joshua DeShaney, now is assigned to live out the remainder of his life profoundly retarded. Joshua and his mother, as petitioners here, deserve—but now are denied by this Court—the opportunity to have the facts of their case considered in the light of the constitutional protection that 42 U.S.C. Sec. 1983 is meant to provide.

EDITED CASE   Bivens v. Six Unknown Federal Narcotics Agents
United States Supreme Court, 403 U.S. 388 (1971)

[Bivens filed suit in federal district court against "six unknown federal narcotics agents," alleging that they violated his Fourth Amendment rights by making an impermissible search of his apartment. The district court dismissed the case on the grounds that it failed to state a federal cause of action and that respondents were immune from suit by virtue of their official position. The Court of Appeals affirmed on the first ground.]

Mr. Justice Brennan delivered the opinion of the Court.

The Fourth Amendment provides that: "The right of the people to be secure in their persons, houses, papers, and effects, against unreasonable searches and seizures, shall not be violated. . . ." In *Bell v. Hood*, 327 U.S. 678 (1946), we reserved the question whether violation of that command by a federal agent acting under color of his authority gives rise to a cause of action for damages consequent upon his unconstitutional conduct. Today we hold that it does.

This case has its origin in an arrest and search carried out on the morning of November 26, 1965. Petitioner's complaint alleged that on that day respondents, agents of the Federal Bureau of Narcotics acting under claim of federal authority, entered his apartment and arrested him for alleged narcotics violations. The agents manacled petitioner in front of his wife and children, and threatened to arrest the entire family. They searched the apartment from stem to stern. Thereafter, petitioner was taken to the federal courthouse in Brooklyn, where he was interrogated, booked, and subjected to a visual strip search.

On July 7, 1967, petitioner brought suit in Federal District Court. In addition to the allegations above, his complaint asserted that the arrest and search were effected without a warrant, and that unreasonable force was employed in making the arrest; fairly read, it alleges as well that the arrest was made without probable cause. Petitioner claimed to have suffered great humiliation, embarrassment, and mental suffering as a result of the agents' unlawful conduct, and sought $15,000 damages from each of them. The District Court, on respondents' motion, dismissed the complaint on the ground, inter alia, that it failed to state a cause of action. . . . The Court of Appeals, one judge concurring specially, affirmed on that basis. . . . We granted certiorari. . . . We reverse.

I

Respondents do not argue that petitioner should be entirely without remedy for an unconstitutional invasion of his rights by federal agents. In respondents' view, however, the rights that petitioner asserts—primarily rights of privacy—are creations of state and not of federal law. Accordingly, they argue, petitioner may obtain money damages to redress invasion of these rights only by an action in tort, under state law, in the state courts. In this scheme the Fourth Amendment would serve merely to limit the extent to which the agents could defend the state law tort suit by asserting that their actions were a valid exercise of federal power: if the agents were shown to have violated the Fourth Amendment, such a defense would be lost to them and they would stand before the state law merely as private individuals. Candidly admitting that it is the policy of the Department of Justice to remove all such suits from the state to the federal courts for decision, respondents nevertheless urge that we uphold dismissal of petitioner's complaint in federal court, and remit him to filing an action in the state courts in order that the case may properly be removed to the federal court for decision on the basis of state law.

We think that respondents' thesis rests upon an unduly restrictive view of the Fourth Amendment's protection against unreasonable searches and seizures by federal agents, a view that has consistently been rejected by this Court. Respondents seek to treat the relationship between a citizen and a federal agent unconstitutionally exercising his authority as no different from the relationship between two private citizens. In so doing, they ignore the fact that power, once granted, does not disappear like a magic gift when it is wrongfully used. An agent acting—albeit unconstitutionally—in the name of the United States possesses a far greater capacity for harm than an individual trespasser exercising no authority other than his own. . . . Accordingly, as our cases make clear, the Fourth Amendment operates as a limitation upon the exercise of federal power regardless of

---

EDITED CASE   Bivens v. Six Unknown Federal Narcotics Agents (Continued)

whether the State in whose jurisdiction that power is exercised would prohibit or penalize the identical act if engaged in by a private citizen. It guarantees to citizens of the United States the absolute right to be free from unreasonable searches and seizures carried out by virtue of federal authority. And "where federally protected rights have been invaded, it has been the rule from the beginning that courts will be alert to adjust their remedies so as to grant the necessary relief." . . .

First. Our cases have long since rejected the notion that the Fourth Amendment proscribes only such conduct as would, if engaged in by private persons, be condemned by state law. Thus in *Gambino v. United States*, 275 U.S. 310 (1927), petitioners were convicted of conspiracy to violate the National Prohibition Act on the basis of evidence seized by state police officers incident to petitioners' arrest by those officers solely for the purpose of enforcing federal law. . . . Notwithstanding the lack of probable cause for the arrest, . . . it would have been permissible under state law if effected by private individuals. It appears, moreover, that the officers were under direction from the Governor to aid in the enforcement of federal law. . . . Accordingly, if the Fourth Amendment reached only to conduct impermissible under the law of the State, the Amendment would have had no application to the case. Yet this Court held the Fourth Amendment applicable and reversed petitioners' convictions as having been based upon evidence obtained through an unconstitutional search and seizure. Similarly, in *Byars v. United States*, 273 U.S. 28 (1927), the petitioner was convicted on the basis of evidence seized under a warrant issued, without probable cause under the Fourth Amendment, by a state court judge for a state law offense. At the invitation of state law enforcement officers, a federal prohibition agent participated in the search. This Court explicitly refused to inquire whether the warrant was "good under the state law . . . since in no event could it constitute the basis for a federal search and seizure." . . . And our recent decisions regarding electronic surveillance have made it clear beyond peradventure that the Fourth Amendment is not tied to the niceties of local trespass laws. . . . In light of these cases, respondents' argument that the Fourth Amendment serves only as a limitation on federal defenses to a state law claim, and not as an independent limitation upon the exercise of federal power, must be rejected.

Second. The interests protected by state laws regulating trespass and the invasion of privacy, and those protected by the Fourth Amendment's guarantee against unreasonable searches and seizures, may be inconsistent or even hostile. Thus, we may bar the door against an unwelcome private intruder, or call the police if he persists in seeking entrance. The availability of such alternative means for the protection of privacy may lead the State to restrict imposition of liability for any consequent trespass. A private citizen, asserting no authority other than his own, will not normally be liable in trespass if he demands, and is granted, admission to another's house. . . . But one who demands admission under a claim of federal authority stands in a far different position. . . . The mere invocation of federal power by a federal law enforcement official will normally render futile any attempt to resist an unlawful entry or arrest by resort to the local police; and a claim of authority to enter is likely to unlock the door as well. "In such cases there is no safety for the citizen, except in the protection of the judicial tribunals, for rights which have been invaded by the officers of the government, professing to act in its name. There remains to him but the alternative of resistance, which may amount to crime." . . . Nor is it adequate to answer that state law may take into account the different status of one clothed with the authority of the Federal Government. For just as state law may not authorize federal agents to violate the Fourth Amendment, . . . neither may state law undertake to limit the extent to which federal authority can be exercised. . . .The inevitable consequence of this dual limitation on state power is that the federal question becomes not merely a possible defense to the state law action, but an independent claim both necessary and sufficient to make out the plaintiff's cause of action. . . .

Third. That damages may be obtained for injuries consequent upon a violation of the Fourth Amendment by federal officials should hardly seem a surprising proposition. Historically, damages have

(Continued)

EDITED CASE   Bivens v. Six Unknown Federal Narcotics Agents (Continued)

---

been regarded as the ordinary remedy for an invasion of personal interests in liberty. . . . Of course, the Fourth Amendment does not in so many words provide for its enforcement by an award of money damages for the consequences of its violation. But "it is . . . well settled that where legal rights have been invaded, and a federal statute provides for a general right to sue for such invasion, federal courts may use any available remedy to make good the wrong done." . . . Nor are we asked in this case to impose liability upon a congressional employee for actions contrary to no constitutional prohibition, but merely said to be in excess of the authority delegated to him by the Congress. . . . Finally, we cannot accept respondents' formulation of the question as whether the availability of money damages is necessary to enforce the Fourth Amendment. For we have here no explicit congressional declaration that persons injured by a federal officer's violation of the Fourth Amendment may not recover money damages from the agents, but must instead be remitted to another remedy, equally effective in the view of Congress. The question is merely whether petitioner, if he can demonstrate an injury consequent upon the violation by federal agents of his Fourth Amendment rights, is entitled to redress his injury through a particular remedial mechanism normally available in the federal courts. . . . Having concluded that petitioner's complaint states a cause of action under the Fourth Amendment, . . . we hold that petitioner is entitled to recover money damages for any injuries he

has suffered as a result of the agents' violation of the Amendment.

II

In addition to holding that petitioner's complaint had failed to state facts making out a cause of action, the District Court ruled that in any event respondents were immune from liability by virtue of their official position. This question was not passed upon by the Court of Appeals, and accordingly we do not consider it here. The judgment of the Court of Appeals is reversed and the case is remanded for further proceedings consistent with this opinion.

  Mr. Justice Harlan, concurring in the judgment.

  My initial view of this case was that the Court of Appeals was correct in dismissing the complaint, but for reasons stated in this opinion I am now persuaded to the contrary. Accordingly, I join in the judgment of reversal. . . .

  Mr. Chief Justice Burger, dissenting.

  I dissent from today's holding which judicially creates a damage remedy not provided for by the Constitution and not enacted by Congress. We would more surely preserve the important values of the doctrine of separation of powers—and perhaps get a better result—by recommending a solution to the Congress as the branch of government in which the Constitution has vested the legislative power. Legislation is the business of the Congress, and it has the facilities and competence for that task—as we do not. . . .

EDITED CASE   Butz v. Economou
United States Supreme Court, 438 U.S. 478 (1978)

[In this case the Supreme Court considers the scope of immunity afforded to federal officials in the executive branch in cases where they are sued for violating citizens' constitutional rights. The reader should pay careful attention to the distinction the Court draws between officials performing executive functions and those performing quasi-prosecutorial and quasi-judicial functions.]

Justice White delivered the opinion of the Court.

  . . . Respondent controls Arthur N. Economou and Co., Inc., which was at one time registered with the Department of Agriculture as a commodity futures commission merchant. Most of respondent's factual allegations in this lawsuit focus on an earlier administrative proceeding in which the Department of Agriculture sought to revoke or suspend the com-

---

EDITED CASE Butz v. Economou (Continued)

---

pany's registration. On February 19, 1970, following an audit, the Department of Agriculture issued an administrative complaint alleging that respondent, while a registered merchant, had willfully failed to maintain the minimum financial requirements prescribed by the Department. After another audit, an amended complaint was issued on June 22, 1970. A hearing was held before the Chief Hearing Examiner of the Department, who filed a recommendation sustaining the administrative complaint. The Judicial Officer of the Department, to whom the Secretary had delegated his decisional authority in enforcement proceedings, affirmed the Chief Hearing Examiner's decision. On respondent's petition for review, the Court of Appeals for the Second Circuit vacated the order of the Judicial Officer. It reasoned that "the essential finding of willfulness . . . was made in a proceeding instituted without the customary warning letter, which the Judicial Officer conceded might well have resulted in prompt correction of the claimed insufficiencies." . . .

While the administrative complaint was pending before the Judicial Officer, respondent filed this lawsuit in Federal District Court. Respondent sought initially to enjoin the progress of the administrative proceeding, but he was unsuccessful in that regard. On March 31, 1975, respondent filed a second amended complaint seeking damages. Named as defendants were the individuals who had served as Secretary and Assistant Secretary of Agriculture during the relevant events; the Judicial Officer and Chief Hearing Examiner; several officials in the Commodity Exchange Authority; the Agriculture Department attorney who had prosecuted the enforcement proceeding; and several of the auditors who had investigated respondent or were witnesses against respondent.

The complaint stated that prior to the issuance of the administrative complaints respondent had been "sharply critical of the staff and operations of Defendants and carried on a vociferous campaign for the reform of Defendant Commodity Exchange Authority to obtain more effective regulation of commodity trading." . . . The complaint also stated that, some time prior to the issuance of the February 19 complaint, respondent and his company had ceased to engage in activities regulated by the defendants. The complaint charged that each of the administrative complaints had been issued without the notice or warning required by

law; that the defendants had furnished the complaints "to interested persons and others without furnishing respondent's answers as well"; and that following the issuance of the amended complaint, the defendants had issued a "deceptive" press release that "falsely indicated to the public that [respondent's] financial resources had deteriorated, when Defendants knew that their statement was untrue and so acknowledge[d] previously that said assertion was untrue." . . .

The complaint then presented 10 "causes of action," some of which purported to state claims for damages under the United States Constitution. For example, the first "cause of action" alleged that respondent had been denied due process of law because the defendants had instituted unauthorized proceedings against him without proper notice and with the knowledge that respondent was no longer subject to their regulatory jurisdiction. The third "cause of action" stated that by means of such actions "the Defendants discouraged and chilled the campaign of criticism [plaintiff] directed against them, and thereby deprived the [plaintiff] of [his] rights to free expression guaranteed by the First Amendment of the United States Constitution." The defendants moved to dismiss the complaint on the ground that "as to the individual defendants it is barred by the doctrine of official immunity. . . ." . . . The defendants relied on an affidavit submitted earlier in the litigation by the attorney who had prosecuted the original administrative complaint against respondent. He stated that the Secretary of Agriculture had had no involvement with the case and that each of the other named defendants had acted "within the course of his official duties." . . .

The District Court, apparently relying on the plurality opinion in *Barr v. Matteo*, 360 U.S. 564 (1959), held that the individual defendants would be entitled to immunity if they could show that "their alleged unconstitutional acts were within the outer perimeter of their authority and discretionary." . . . After examining the nature of the acts alleged in the complaint, the District Court concluded: "Since the individual defendants have shown that their alleged unconstitutional acts were both within the scope of their authority and

(Continued)

EDITED CASE   Butz v. Economou (Continued)

---

discretionary, we dismiss the second amended complaint as to them." . . .

The Court of Appeals for the Second Circuit reversed the District Court's judgment of dismissal with respect to the individual defendants. . . . The Court of Appeals reasoned that *Barr v. Matteo . . .* did not "represen[t] the last word in this evolving area," . . . because principles governing the immunity of officials of the Executive Branch had been elucidated in later decisions dealing with constitutional claims against state officials. . . . These opinions were understood to establish that officials of the Executive Branch exercising discretionary functions did not need the protection of an absolute immunity from suit, but only a qualified immunity based on good faith and reasonable grounds. The Court of Appeals rejected a proposed distinction between suits against state officials sued pursuant to 42 U.S.C. § 1983 and suits against federal officials under the Constitution, noting that "[o]ther circuits have also concluded that the Supreme Court's development of official immunity doctrine in § 1983 suits against state officials applies with equal force to federal officers sued on a cause of action derived directly from the Constitution, since both types of suits serve the same function of protecting citizens against violations of their constitutional rights by government officials." . . . The Court of Appeals recognized that under *Imbler v. Pachtman*, 424 U.S. 409 (1976), state prosecutors were entitled to absolute immunity from § 1983 damages liability but reasoned that Agriculture Department officials performing analogous functions did not require such an immunity because their cases turned more on documentary proof than on the veracity of witnesses and because their work did not generally involve the same constraints of time and information present in criminal cases. . . . The court concluded that all of the defendants were "adequately protected by permitting them to avail themselves of the defense of qualified 'good faith, reasonable grounds' immunity of the type approved by the Supreme Court. . . . After noting that summary judgment would be available to the defendants if there were no genuine factual issues for trial, the Court of Appeals remanded the case for further proceedings. . . .

The single submission by the United States on behalf of petitioners is that all of the federal officials sued in this case are absolutely immune from any liability for damages even if in the course of enforcing the relevant statutes they infringed respondent's constitutional rights and even if the violation was knowing and deliberate. Although the position is earnestly and ably presented by the United States, we are quite sure that it is unsound and consequently reject it. In *Bivens v. Six Unknown Fed. Narcotics Agents*, 403 U.S. 388 (1971), the victim of an arrest and search claimed to be violative of the Fourth Amendment brought suit for damages against the responsible federal agents. Repeating the declaration in *Marbury v. Madison*, 1 Cranch 137, 163 (1803), that "'[t]he very essence of civil liberty certainly consists in the right of every individual to claim the protection of the laws,'" . . . and stating that "[h]istorically, damages have been regarded as the ordinary remedy for an invasion of personal interests in liberty," . . . we rejected the claim that the plaintiff's remedy lay only in the state court under state law, with the Fourth Amendment operating merely to nullify a defense of federal authorization. We held that a violation of the Fourth Amendment by federal agents gives rise to a cause of action for damages consequent upon the unconstitutional conduct. . . .

Bivens established that compensable injury to a constitutionally protected interest could be vindicated by a suit for damages invoking the general federal-question jurisdiction of the federal courts, but we reserved the question whether the agents involved were "immune from liability by virtue of their official position," and remanded the case for that determination. On remand, the Court of Appeals for the Second Circuit, as has every other Court of Appeals that has faced the question, held that the agents were not absolutely immune and that the public interest would be sufficiently protected by according the agents and their superiors a qualified immunity.

In our view, the Courts of Appeals have reached sound results. We cannot agree with the United States that our prior cases are to the contrary and support the rule it now urges us to embrace. Indeed, as we see it, the Government's submission is contrary to the course of decision in this Court from the very early days of the Republic.

The Government places principal reliance on *Barr v. Matteo*, 360 U.S. 564 (1959). . . . *Barr* does not control this case. It did not . . . purport

---

EDITED CASE   Butz v. Economou (Continued)

---

to depart from the general rule, which long prevailed, that a federal official may not with impunity ignore the limitations which the controlling law has placed on his powers. The immunity of federal executive officials began as a means of protecting them in the execution of their federal statutory duties from criminal or civil actions based on state law. . . . A federal official who acted outside of his federal statutory authority would be held strictly liable for his trespassory acts. . . .

. . . [W]e are confident that *Barr* did not purport to protect an official who has not only committed a wrong under local law, but also violated those fundamental principles of fairness embodied in the Constitution. Whatever level of protection from state interference is appropriate for federal officials executing their duties under federal law, it cannot be doubted that these officials, even when acting pursuant to congressional authorization, are subject to the restraints imposed by the Federal Constitution.

. . . [I]n the absence of congressional direction to the contrary, there is no basis for according to federal officials a higher degree of immunity from liability when sued for a constitutional infringement as authorized by *Bivens* than is accorded state officials when sued for the identical violation under § 1983. The constitutional injuries made actionable by § 1983 are of no greater magnitude than those for which federal officials may be responsible. The pressures and uncertainties facing decisionmakers in state government are little if at all different from those affecting federal officials. We see no sense in holding a state governor liable but immunizing the head of a federal department; in holding the administrator of a federal hospital immune where the superintendent of a state hospital would be liable; in protecting the warden of a federal prison where the warden of a state prison would be vulnerable; or in distinguishing between state and federal police participating in the same investigation. Surely, federal officials should enjoy no greater zone of protection when they violate federal constitutional rules than do state officers. . . .

Accordingly, without congressional directions to the contrary, we deem it untenable to draw a distinction for purposes of immunity law between suits brought against state officials under § 1983 and suits brought directly under the Constitution against federal officials. The § 1983 action was provided to vindicate federal constitutional rights. That Congress decided, after the passage of the Fourteenth Amendment, to enact legislation specifically requiring state officials to respond in federal court for their failures to observe the constitutional limitations on their powers is hardly a reason for excusing their federal counterparts for the identical constitutional transgressions. To create a system in which the Bill of Rights monitors more closely the conduct of state officials than it does that of federal officials is to stand the constitutional design on its head. . . .

. . . *Bivens* established that a citizen suffering a compensable injury to a constitutionally protected interest could invoke the general federal-question jurisdiction of the district courts to obtain an award of monetary damages against the responsible federal official. . . .

Our opinion in *Bivens* put aside the immunity question; but we could not have contemplated that immunity would be absolute. If, as the Government argues, all officials exercising discretion were exempt from personal liability, a suit under the Constitution could provide no redress to the injured citizen, nor would it in any degree deter federal officials from committing constitutional wrongs. Moreover, no compensation would be available from the Government, for the Tort Claims Act prohibits recovery for injuries stemming from discretionary acts, even when that discretion has been abused.

The extension of absolute immunity from damages liability to all federal executive officials would seriously erode the protection provided by basic constitutional guarantees. The broad authority possessed by these officials enables them to direct their subordinates to undertake a wide range of projects—including some which may infringe such important personal interests as liberty, property, and free speech. It makes little sense to hold that a Government agent is liable for warrantless and forcible entry into a citizen's house in pursuit of evidence, but that an official of higher rank who actually orders such a burglary is immune simply because of his greater authority. Indeed, the greater power of such officials affords a greater potential for a regime of lawless conduct. Extensive Government operations offer opportunities for unconstitutional action on a massive scale. In situations of abuse,

(Continued)

EDITED CASE   Butz v. Economou (Continued)

---

an action for damages against the responsible official can be an important means of vindicating constitutional guarantees. Our system of jurisprudence rests on the assumption that all individuals, whatever their position in government, are subject to federal law. . . . In light of this principle, federal officials who seek absolute exemption from personal liability for unconstitutional conduct must bear the burden of showing that public policy requires an exemption of that scope.

This is not to say that considerations of public policy fail to support a limited immunity for federal executive officials. We consider here . . . the need to protect officials who are required to exercise their discretion and the related public interest in encouraging the vigorous exercise of official authority. Yet . . . it is not unfair to hold liable the official who knows or should know he is acting outside the law, and that insisting on an awareness of clearly established constitutional limits will not unduly interfere with the exercise of official judgment. We therefore hold that, in a suit for damages arising from unconstitutional action, federal executive officials exercising discretion are entitled only to . . . qualified immunity . . . subject to those exceptional situations where it is demonstrated that absolute immunity is essential for the conduct of the public business. . . .

. . . Federal officials will not be liable for mere mistakes in judgment, whether the mistake is one of fact or one of law. But we see no substantial basis for holding, as the United States would have us do, that executive officers generally may with impunity discharge their duties in a way that is known to them to violate the United States Constitution or in a manner that they should know transgresses a clearly established constitutional rule. The principle should prove as workable in suits against federal officials as it has in the context of suits against state officials. Insubstantial lawsuits can be quickly terminated by federal courts alert to the possibilities of artful pleading. Unless the complaint states a compensable claim for relief under the Federal Constitution, it should not survive a motion to dismiss. . . . In responding to such a motion, plaintiffs may not play dog in the manger; and firm application of the Federal Rules of Civil Procedure will ensure that federal officials are not harassed by frivolous lawsuits. . . .

Although a qualified immunity from damages liability should be the general rule for executive officials charged with constitutional violations, our decisions recognize that there are some officials whose special functions require a full exemption from liability. . . . In each case, we have undertaken "a considered inquiry into the immunity historically accorded the relevant official at common law and the interests behind it." . . .

We think that adjudication within a federal administrative agency shares enough of the characteristics of the judicial process that those who participate in such adjudication should also be immune from suits for damages. The conflicts which federal hearing examiners seek to resolve are every bit as fractious as those which come to court. . . . Moreover, federal administrative law requires that agency adjudication contain many of the same safeguards as are available in the judicial process. The proceedings are adversary in nature. . . . They are conducted before a trier of fact insulated from political influence. . . . A party is entitled to present his case by oral or documentary evidence, . . . and the transcript of testimony and exhibits together with the pleadings constitute the exclusive record for decision. . . . The parties are entitled to know the findings and conclusions on all of the issues of fact, law, or discretion presented on the record. . . .

There can be little doubt that the role of the modern federal hearing examiner or administrative law judge within this framework is "functionally comparable" to that of a judge. His powers are often, if not generally, comparable to those of a trial judge: He may issue subpoenas, rule on proffers of evidence, regulate the course of the hearing, and make or recommend decisions. . . . More importantly, the process of agency adjudication is currently structured so as to assure that the hearing examiner exercises his independent judgment on the evidence before him, free from pressures by the parties or other officials within the agency. Prior to the Administrative Procedure Act, there was considerable concern that persons hearing administrative cases at the trial level could not exercise independent judgment because they were required to perform prosecutorial and investigative functions as well as their judicial work, . . . and because they were often subordinate to executive officials within the agency. . . . Since the securing

---

EDITED CASE Butz v. Economou (Continued)

---

of fair and competent hearing personnel was viewed as "the heart of formal administrative adjudication," . . . the Administrative Procedure Act contains a number of provisions designed to guarantee the independence of hearing examiners. They may not perform duties inconsistent with their duties as hearing examiners. . . . When conducting a hearing under § 5 of the APA . . . a hearing examiner is not responsible to, or subject to the supervision or direction of, employees or agents engaged in the performance of investigative or prosecution functions for the agency. . . . Nor may a hearing examiner consult any person or party, including other agency officials, concerning a fact at issue in the hearing, unless on notice and opportunity for all parties to participate. . . . Hearing examiners must be assigned to cases in rotation so far as is practicable. . . . . They may be removed only for good cause established and determined by the Civil Service Commission after a hearing on the record. . . . Their pay is also controlled by the Civil Service Commission.

In light of these safeguards, we think that the risk of an unconstitutional act by one presiding at an agency hearing is clearly outweighed by the importance of preserving the independent judgment of these men and women. We therefore hold that persons subject to these restraints and performing adjudicatory functions within a federal agency are entitled to absolute immunity from damages liability for their judicial acts. Those who complain of error in such proceedings must seek agency or judicial review.

We also believe that agency officials performing certain functions analogous to those of a prosecutor should be able to claim absolute immunity with respect to such acts. The decision to initiate administrative proceedings against an individual or corporation is very much like the prosecutor's decision to initiate or move forward with a criminal prosecution. An agency official, like a prosecutor, may have broad discretion in deciding whether a proceeding should be brought and what sanctions should be sought. The Commodity Futures Trading Commission, for example, may initiate proceedings whenever it has "reason to believe" that any person "is violating or has violated any of the provisions of this chapter or of the rules, regulations, or orders of the Commission." . . . A range of sanctions is open to it. . . .

The discretion which executive officials exercise with respect to the initiation of administrative proceedings might be distorted if their immunity from damages arising from that decision was less than complete. . . . While there is not likely to be anyone willing and legally able to seek damages from the officials if they do not authorize the administrative proceeding, . . . there is a serious danger that the decision to authorize proceedings will provoke a retaliatory response. An individual targeted by an administrative proceeding will react angrily and may seek vengeance in the courts. A corporation will muster all of its financial and legal resources in an effort to prevent administrative sanctions. "When millions may turn on regulatory decisions, there is a strong incentive to counter-attack." . . .

The defendant in an enforcement proceeding has ample opportunity to challenge the legality of the proceeding. An administrator's decision to proceed with a case is subject to scrutiny in the proceeding itself. The respondent may present his evidence to an impartial trier of fact and obtain an independent judgment as to whether the prosecution is justified. His claims that the proceeding is unconstitutional may also be heard by the courts. Indeed, respondent in this case was able to quash the administrative order entered against him by means of judicial review. . . .

We believe that agency officials must make the decision to move forward with an administrative proceeding free from intimidation or harassment. Because the legal remedies already available to the defendant in such a proceeding provide sufficient checks on agency zeal, we hold that those officials who are responsible for the decision to initiate or continue a proceeding subject to agency adjudication are entitled to absolute immunity from damages liability for their parts in that decision.

We turn finally to the role of an agency attorney in conducting a trial and presenting evidence on the record to the trier of fact. We can see no substantial difference between the function of the agency attorney in presenting evidence in an agency hearing and the function of the prosecutor who brings evidence before a court. In either case, the evidence will be subject to attack through cross-examination, rebuttal, or reinterpretation by opposing counsel. Evidence which is false or unpersuasive should be

(Continued)

EDITED CASE   Butz v. Economou (Continued)

---

rejected upon analysis by an impartial trier of fact. If agency attorneys were held personally liable in damages as guarantors of the quality of their evidence, they might hesitate to bring forward some witnesses or documents. "This is particularly so because it is very difficult if not impossible for attorneys to be absolutely certain of the objective truth or falsity of the testimony which they present." . . . Apart from the possible unfairness to agency personnel, the agency would often be denied relevant evidence. . . . Administrative agencies can act in the public interest only if they can adjudicate on the basis of a complete record. We therefore hold that an agency attorney who arranges for the presentation of evidence on the record in the course of an adjudication is absolutely immune from suits based on the introduction of such evidence. . . .

    Justice Rehnquist, with whom *The Chief Justice*, *Justice Stewart*, and *Justice Stevens* join, concurring in part and dissenting in part.

    I concur in that part of the Court's judgment which affords absolute immunity to those persons performing adjudicatory functions within a federal agency, . . . those who are responsible for the decision to initiate or continue a proceeding subject to agency adjudication, . . . and those agency personnel who present evidence on the record in the course of an adjudication. . . . I cannot agree, however, with the Court's conclusion that in a suit for damages arising from allegedly unconstitutional action federal executive officials, regardless of their rank or the scope of their responsibilities, are entitled to only qualified immunity even when acting within the outer limits of their authority. The Court's protestations to the contrary notwithstanding, this decision seriously misconstrues our prior decisions, finds little support as a matter of logic or precedent, and perhaps most importantly, will, I fear, seriously "dampen the ardor of all but the most resolute, or the most irresponsible, in the unflinching discharge of their duties." . . .

    History will surely not condemn the Court for its effort to achieve a more finely ground product from the judicial mill, a product which would both retain the necessary ability of public officials to govern and yet assure redress to those who are the victims of official wrongs. But if such a system of redress for official wrongs was indeed

capable of being achieved in practice, it surely would not have been rejected by this Court speaking through the first Mr. Justice Harlan in 1896, by this Court speaking through the second Mr. Justice Harlan in 1959, and by Judge Learned Hand speaking for the Court of Appeals for the Second Circuit in 1948. These judges were not inexperienced neophytes who lacked the vision or the ability to define immunity doctrine to accomplish that result had they thought it possible. Nor were they obsequious toadies in their attitude toward high-ranking officials of coordinate branches of the Federal Government. But they did see with more prescience than the Court does today, that there are inevitable trade-offs in connection with any doctrine of official liability and immunity. They forthrightly accepted the possibility that an occasional failure to redress a claim of official wrongdoing would result from the doctrine of absolute immunity which they espoused, viewing it as a lesser evil than the impairment of the ability of responsible public officials to govern.

    But while I believe that history will look approvingly on the motives of the Court in reaching the result it does today, I do not believe that history will be charitable in its judgment of the all but inevitable result of the doctrine espoused by the Court in this case. That doctrine seeks to gain and hold a middle ground which, with all deference, I believe the teachings of those who were at least our equals suggest cannot long be held. That part of the Court's present opinion from which I dissent will, I fear, result in one of two evils, either one of which is markedly worse than the effect of according absolute immunity to the Secretary and the Assistant Secretary in this case. The first of these evils would be a significant impairment of the ability of responsible public officials to carry out the duties imposed upon them by law. If that evil is to be avoided after today, it can be avoided only by a necessarily unprincipled and erratic judicial "screening" of claims such as those made in this case, an adherence to the form of the law while departing from its substance. Either one of these evils is far worse than the occasional failure to award damages caused by official wrongdoing. . . .

EDITED CASE Manna v. State
Supreme Court of New Jersey, 609 A.2d 757 (1992)

[In this case the New Jersey Supreme Court considers whether the state of New Jersey is immune from liability in a civil suit stemming from a fatal traffic accident on a wet and slippery bridge. Joseph Manna died as a result of injuries he received when his car slid out of control on the bridge and crashed into an oncoming vehicle. Manna's wife filed suit against the state, claiming that it had been negligent in the construction and maintenance of the bridge and in its failure to provide adequate warnings of the bridge's dangerous condition.]

Justice Garibaldi delivered the opinion of the court. . . . We address the State's liability under the New Jersey Tort Claims Act, N.J.S.A. §§ 59:1-1 to 12-3 (the Act), the statute governing tort suits against public entities. The Act creates an underlying presumption of immunity, N.J.S.A. § 59:2-1, unless liability is specified. Even when that liability exists, however, it may be subject to specific statutory immunities. In this appeal we address the applicability of two such immunities: (1) the immunity for dangerous conditions caused solely by the weather, N.J.S.A. § 59:4-7; and (2) the immunity for dangerous conditions attributable to the plan or design of the public property, N.J.S.A. § 59:4-6.

In July 1986 Joseph Manna was driving northbound on Route 35 toward the Matawan Creek Bridge in Aberdeen. The bridge was wet from an earlier rain and very slippery. As Manna approached the bridge, the driver of the car in front of him applied his brakes. In response, Manna applied his brakes. When the car reached the open-steel-grid deck of the bridge, it slid out of control and into the oncoming lane of traffic, striking another car head-on. Ten days later Manna died from his injuries.

The bridge was originally built as a drawbridge in the 1920s. When the present bridge was constructed in 1960, the wood-block deck was replaced by an open-steel-grid deck. The steel grid was constructed with raised blocks to prevent skidding. According to plaintiff's expert, by the time of the accident the raised blocks had worn down and created a smooth surface that would "retain a water film and allow hydroplaning." Numerous accidents had been associated with the bridge in the past.

Gail Manna, the Administratrix for Joseph Manna's estate, filed a survival and wrongful death action against the State of New Jersey and the State Department of Transportation (State) under the New Jersey Tort Claims Act. She alleged that by failing to provide adequate warnings and failing to install metal studs to prevent skidding, the State was liable for the dangerous condition it had created. Because plaintiff has conceded that N.J.S.A. § 59:4-5 grants immunity for the failure to post warning signals, that issue is no longer in dispute.

The State moved for summary judgment. Reviewing the condition of the bridge, the trial court held that "the plaintiff would be able to establish a prima facie case that a dangerous condition existed." However, the court noted that the purpose of the Act was to grant immunity, and that "any immunity provisions provided in the Act, or by common law, will prevail over the liability provisions." Finding that "the sole cause of the accident was the wet condition of the . . . bridge deck," the court held that § 59:4-7, the weather-immunity provision, provided the State with immunity from Manna's suit. The court also held that the plan-or-design immunity, § 59:4-6, protected the State from liability for Manna's injuries. The court reasoned that the immunity was designed to be perpetual, and hence protected the State from liability when its original design choice proved hazardous. The court therefore granted the State's motion for summary judgment.

The Appellate Division affirmed. . . . We granted Manna's petition for certification. . . .

II

In 1972 the Legislature passed the New Jersey Tort Claims Act in response to the judiciary's weakening of the traditional doctrine of sovereign immunity. . . . Although the Legislature recognized that the strict application of the doctrine of sovereign immunity could lead to inequitable results, it chose to create an initial presumption of immunity to limit State liability. The Legislative Declaration states that the area within which government has the power to act for the public

(Continued)

EDITED CASE Manna v. State (Continued)

---

good is almost without limit and therefore government should not have the duty to do everything that might be done.

> Consequently, it is hereby declared to be the public policy of this State that public entities shall only be liable for their negligence within the limitations of this act and in accordance with the fair and uniform principles established herein. [N.J.S.A. § 59:1-2.]

Section 59:2-1(a) makes the presumption of immunity explicit, stating that "[e]xcept as otherwise provided by this act, a public entity is not liable for an injury . . ."

III

Dr. Richard A. Haber, a professional engineer. He stated that the original steel-grid pattern constructed in 1960 had "presented square ends and sharp edges to directional traffic and acted as a deterrent in the 1960 era of lesser speeds and different tread tires." The raised portions have now worn away, leaving a "smooth, skidprone surface." The expert concluded that the existing structure will retain a film of water and allow hydroplaning. He noted that the vehicle's tires had had good tread and so were probably not the cause of skidding, and noted the police report's observation that the bridge surface was "very slippery." Because forty-eight accidents had occurred on the road between January 1975 and July 1986, he indicated the State had to have been on notice of the dangerous condition of the bridge.

The trial court held that plaintiff had presented a prima facie case demonstrating that the bridge presented a dangerous condition. On appeal, the State did not contest that conclusion. However, plaintiff cannot proceed to demonstrate the State's liability for that dangerous condition under § 59:4-2 until the applicability of the Act's specific immunities to liability is determined.

IV

Both the trial court and the Appellate Division held that the State was immune from liability under the Act's provision establishing immunity for injuries caused solely by inclement weather. Section 59:4-7 states: Neither a public entity nor a public employee is liable for an injury caused solely by the effect on the use of streets and highways of weather conditions.

[Note: In the remaining parts of Part IV the court's opinion, the court concludes that the existing record does not resolve the material factual question of whether the bridge's dangerous condition contributed to the weather in causing Manna's accident. The court holds that the trial court's grant of summary judgment on that point was therefore improper.]

V

The State also asserts that it is immunized from suit by the Tort Claims Act's plan-or-design immunity. . . .

Application of plan-or-design immunity turns on whether the public entity has approved the feature in question so as to immunize it from challenge. . . .

The trial court found that plaintiff did not contest that "the actual bridge deck[ ] was constructed in conformity with the standards previously approved by the authorized entity or person." Moreover, the evidence supports the conclusion that the surface of the bridge was constructed according to approved plans. The State submitted an affidavit from a Regional Director of the New Jersey Department of Transportation, Nicholas J. Cifelli, which stated that "[t]he design of the bridge, including but not limited to the steel grid section was approved in advance of construction by the State Highway Commissioner and public employees exercising discretionary authority to give such approvals." He further stated that "[t]he bridge was constructed in accordance with the plans[,]" and that the bridge "was substantially the same as was shown in the various as-built plans." No improvements have been made to the bridge deck since its original installation.

In addition, plaintiff's expert presented evidence that the original plans not only encompassed the basic steel structure but specifically addressed the design necessary to create sufficient traction. The expert's report stated:

The configuration on the surface of the steel deck members is a series of metal parallagrams [sic] 1/4 inch to 3/8 inch above the surface of the member when new. They are placed in series as follows: 2 inch block 1/2 inch space, 1 inch block, 1/2 inch space, 1 inch block, 1/2 inch space, 2 inch block, etc. When new these blocks presented square ends and sharp edges to directional traffic and acted as a deterrent . . .

EDITED CASE   Manna v. State (Continued)

In a subsequent letter to clarify the meaning of "deterrent," plaintiff's expert stated that "the original design for the grid provided the required traction to permit safe passage across the bridge deck."

Because the evidence demonstrates that the bridge's steel grid was an approved feature of the original design, and in light of the additional evidence that the original plans specifically considered how to create traction on the bridge's surface, we conclude that the trial court correctly determined that the State has met its burden of proof in establishing the applicability of plan-or-design immunity.

Plaintiff disagrees and posits her claim on several grounds. She argues that for plan-or-design immunity to insulate the State from liability for the bridge's current condition, the State must show that, at the time it approved the plans for the bridge, it (1) "contemplated that the bridge surface would erode with time, and (2) [intended] to ignore it [as part of] a reasonably calculated plan which would maintain the bridge safe for its intended purposes." Moreover, she implies that because studs were not considered in the original plan or design, the State's decision regarding whether to install studs now is not protected by the immunity. Alternatively, she characterizes the installation of studs as a maintenance function that is not protected by the plan-or-design immunity.

Essentially, all of plaintiff's arguments fail because they improperly attempt to circumvent the perpetual nature of plan-or-design immunity. . . .

Thus, any claim that undermines the State's perpetual immunity unduly interferes with the protection accorded the State's decisions.

Plaintiff argues that the State must have specifically considered the bridge's future deterioration and decided not to maintain it in order to have the benefit of plan-or-design immunity for its present condition. That contention ignores the legislative comment's clear statement that "changed" or "unanticipated" circumstances do not defeat the plan-or-design immunity. As we have frequently observed, the immunity is not lost even if new knowledge demonstrates the dangerousness of the design, or the design presents a dangerous condition in light of a new context. . . .

Immunity applies regardless of whether the "changed condition" is external, like the advent of faster automobiles . . . or intrinsic to the design of the infrastructure in question, like the deteriora-

tion of the bridge's surface in the present dispute. Were we to agree with plaintiff and hold that the deterioration of the original structure abrogates the immunity because that deterioration was not an approved feature of the design, we would undermine the perpetual nature of the immunity. As the official Comment discloses, the Legislature specifically intended to create perpetual immunity and specifically rejected California's decision to forego it. Hindsight may frequently reveal the error of an earlier decision. The Legislature, however, has determined that the burden of that error is not to be borne by the public coffer.

Plaintiff also implies that because the original plans did not include the installation of metal studs to increase traction, the studding option was not explicitly considered and the decision on whether to install studs is therefore not immune. . . .

If we were to hold that immunity attaches to the consideration of the option rather than the feature, then the State's perpetual immunity might be undermined whenever the suggested option was a recent scientific advance. By definition, a recent advance could not have been considered in the original planning process. If the decision regarding its adoption were therefore not immune, then the immunity accorded the original decision would be jeopardized by every new scientific advance. . . .

Alternatively, plaintiff argues that she is not challenging the original design of the bridge. Rather, she asserts that the State had a duty to maintain it, and that that duty required the State to install metal studs. . . .

Notwithstanding plaintiff's phrasing, the facts of this case and the arguments presented simply do not present the issue of maintenance. Plaintiff argues that installing metal studs is a "maintenance" activity because it recreates the traction the bridge has lost over the years. We disagree. Installing studs cannot be termed maintenance. Simply put, studs were not part of the original design of the bridge, and adding them does much more than return the bridge to the status quo. Instead, it fundamentally changes the design of the bridge surface and constitutes a new and improved design to increase traction. No one argues that the State has a duty to undertake

(Continued)

EDITED CASE   Manna v. State (Continued)

---

design improvements. That fact cannot be avoided by labeling the desired improvement a "maintenance" activity. We thus believe the dissent takes too literally plaintiff's unsupported claim that the source of the danger stems from the State's failure to maintain the bridge. Had plaintiff alleged, for example, that the State's failure to paint the bridge caused rust that rendered the bridge a "dangerous condition" causing plaintiff's injuries, we would be confronted with the question of the State's liability for its failure to maintain. Because plaintiff raises only the State's failure to install studs, however, the issue of the State's failure to maintain is not properly before us.

In sum, the Act's perpetual plan-or-design immunity provides immunity for an approved feature of a system even if, over time, the condition of the feature, such as the bridge surface, changes. Moreover, immunity for an original design does not fail because alternative options regarding the feature of concern, such as studding, were not considered in the original plans. Finally, a plaintiff cannot cast a design improvement as a "maintenance" action to circumvent the immunity given the original design. The Legislature's grant of perpetual plan-or-design immunity evidences its intent to protect the State when its planning decisions have resulted in dangerous conditions. . . .

Justice Stein, concurring in part and dissenting in part.

Reduced to its simplest terms, the Court's opinion today holds that when the State builds a bridge with a steel-grid deck that eventually will be worn smooth, the State need not maintain the surface to make it safe again. Accordingly, the State may stand by while motorists are put at risk, and will enjoy immunity if injuries result. That cannot be the intended application of the Tort Claims Act. . . .

The "plan or design" immunity provision of the Tort Claims Act, N.J.S.A. 59:4-6(a), immunizes the State from liability stemming from injuries "caused by the plan or design of public property, either in its original construction or any improvement thereto, where such plan or design has been approved in advance of the construction or improvement" by the Legislature or authorized officials. We have held that for "plan or design" immunity to attach, the public entity must demonstrate that an approved feature of the plan

adequately addressed the dangerous condition that is causally related to the accident. . . .

According to the majority, the State established the applicability of the plan-or-design immunity because of evidence, presented by both the State's and plaintiff's experts, that "the bridge's steel grid was an approved feature of the original design," and that the original plans "specifically considered how to create traction on the bridge's surface.". . . That analysis, however, misconstrues the issue before the Court. Plaintiff does not contend that the bridge design was faulty or that it should not have required maintenance. Nor does plaintiff contend that the original design should have required installation of metal studs to increase traction. Rather, plaintiff asserts that the State is liable because the State failed adequately to maintain the bridge's surface, which it could have accomplished by replacing the steel-grid surface, by installing studs, or by some other method that retained the steel-grid design but provided adequate traction. . . .

. . . To establish plan-or-design immunity, the State would have had to prove that the original plan specifically contemplated that no maintenance or resurfacing would be performed when the original steel deck became worn. Here, no such proof was offered. Consequently, the condition that purportedly led to the accident—failure to maintain the bridge surface—was not contemplated by the original plans, and the plan-or-design immunity does not apply to plaintiff's claims. . . .

Extended to its logical limit, the majority's holding might immunize the State if, for example, an accident resulted from a bridge that had collapsed due to lack of maintenance, provided that the original plan and design had been properly approved. Further, the majority's result contradicts our prior acknowledgment that plan-or-design immunity "does not immunize a governmental body from responsibility for dangerous conditions created by its careless or negligent affirmative acts arising out of its maintenance." . . .

I cannot conceive that the Legislature intended the Act to immunize the State from the negligent failure to maintain a steel-deck bridge that had been worn smooth from regular use over twenty-six years. Accordingly, I would reverse the judgment of the Appellate Division. . . .

ENDNOTES

1. 1 W. Blackstone, Commentaries on the Laws of England 234–235 (1765).

2. *Alden v. Maine*, 527 U.S. 706, 715 (1999).

3. 106 U.S. 196, 207 (1882).

4. *Bulman v. Hulstrand Construction Co.*, 521 N.W.2d 632, 638 (N.D. 1994).

5. *United States v. Thompson*, 98 U.S. 486 (1878).

6. *Philadelphia Company v. Stimson*, 223 U.S. 605, 620 (1912).

7. According to the The 'Lectric Law Library's Lexicon, the writ of mandamus "is a command issuing in the name of the sovereign authority from a superior court having jurisdiction, and is directed to some person, corporation, or, inferior court, within the jurisdiction of such superior court, requiring them to do some particular thing therein specified, which appertains to their office and duty, and which the superior court has previously determined, or at least supposes to be consonant to right and justice." To this definition we would add that the writ of mandamus issues only to compel the performance of a nondiscretionary duty.

8. Act of March 3, 1887, ch. 359, 24 Stat. 505.

9. 28 U.S.C.A. § 1491.

10. *United States v. Mitchell*, 463 U.S. 206 (1983).

11. *United States v. Testan*, 424 U.S. 392 (1976).

12. 28 U.S.C.A. § 1346(a)(2).

13. *Bowen v. Massachusetts*, 487 U.S. 879 (1988).

14. 28 U.S.C.A. § 1346(b) and 28 U.S.C.A. §§ 2671–2680.

15. 28 U.S.C.A. § 1346(b).

16. 28 U.S.C.A. § 2671.

17. 340 U.S. 135 (1950).

18. *Id.* at 141.

19. *United States v. Brown*, 348 U.S. 110 (1954); *McNeill v. United States*, 519 F. Supp. 283 (D.S.C. 1981).

20. 247 F.2d 819 (3rd Cir. 1957).

21. *Doe v. Stephens*, 851 F.2d 1457, 1461 (D.C. Cir. 1988).

22. *Dalehite v. United States*, 346 U.S. 15, 36 (1953).

23. 467 U.S. 797 (1984).

24. *Id.* at 813.

25. *Id.* at 819.

26. 486 U.S. 531 (1988).

27. *Id.* at 536.

28. 499 U.S. 315 (1991).

29. *Id.* at 323.

30. *Id.* at 325.

31. M. Niles, *Nothing But Mischief: The Federal Tort Claims Act and The Scope of Discretionary Immunity*, 54 Admin. L. Rev. 1275, 1353 (Fall 2002).

32. 487 U.S. 500 (1988).

33. *Id.* at 512.

34. 969 F.2d 72 (4th Cir. 1992).

35. *Bennett v. United States*, 803 F.2d 1502 (9th Cir. 1986).

36. *Doe v. United States*, 838 F.2d 220 (7th Cir. 1988).

37. *Brock v. United States*, 64 F.3d 1421 (9th Cir. 1995).

38. 28 U.S.C.A. § 2401(b).

39. *McMichael v. United States*, 856 F.2d 1026 (8th Cir. 1988).

40. *Massey v. United States*, 733 F.2d 760 (11th Cir. 1984).

41. 28 U.S.C. A. § 2402.

42. 484 U.S. 292 (1988).

43. 28 U.S.C.A. § 2679.

44. 515 U.S. 417 (1995).

45. *Id.* at 419–420.

46. *Nasuti v. Scannell*, 906 F.2d 802 (1st Cir. 1990).

47. 193 U.S. 430 (1904).

48. 365 U.S. 167, 171 (1961) (holding that an unlawful search by police was "under color of law" even though not authorized).

49. *United States v. Classic*, 313 U.S. 299, 326 (1941).

50. See, e.g., *Kent v. Prasse*, 385 F.2d 406 (3rd Cir. 1967).

51. *Wyatt v. Cole*, 504 U.S. 158, 161 (1992).

52. *Carver v. Foerster*, 102 F.3d 96 (3rd Cir. 1996).

53. 436 U.S. 658 (1978).

54. *Id.* at 690.

55. *Id.* at 691.

56. 453 U.S. 247 (1981).

57. *Id.* at 266.

58. See *Tennessee v. Garner*, 471 U.S. 1 (1985).

59. See, e. g., *Harris v. McRae*, 448 U.S. 297, 317–318 (1980); *Lindsey v. Normet*, 405 U.S. 56, 74 (1972); *Youngberg v. Romeo*, 457 U.S. 307, 317 (1982).

60. In *Estelle v. Gamble*, 429 U.S. 97 (1976), the Supreme Court held that deliberate indifference by prison personnel to a prisoner's serious illness or injury constitutes cruel and unusual punishment under the Eighth Amendment, which applies to the states via the fourteenth Amendment.

61. 555 N.W.2d 630 (Wis. 1996).

62. 489 U.S. 189 (1989).

63. *Id.* at 198.

64. *Martinez v. California*, 444 U.S. 277, 283 n. 7, (1980).

65. *Maine v. Thiboutot*, 448 U.S. 1, 11 (1980).

66. *Patsy v. Board of Regents*, 457 U.S. 496 (1982).

67. See *Wilson v. Garcia*, 471 U.S. 261, 276 (1985).

68. *Morales v. City of Los Angeles*, 214 F.3d 1151, 1153-54 (9th Cir. 2000).

69. *Busche v. Burkee*, 649 F.2d 509 (7th Cir.1981).

70. 403 U.S. 388 (1971).

71. *Id.* at 397.

72. *Bivens v. Six Unknown Federal Narcotics Agents*, 456 F.2d 1339, 1348 (2nd Cir. 1972).

73. *Davis v. Passman*, 442 U.S. 228 (1979).

74. *Carlson v. Green*, 446 U.S. 14 (1980).

75. 446 U.S. 14 (1980).

76. *Id.* at 18-19.

77. 462 U.S.367 (1983).

78. Bivens *Doctrine in Flux: Statutory Preclusion of a Constitutional Cause of Action*, 101 Harv. L. Rev. 1251 (Apr. 1988).

79. *Id.* at 1268.

80. 462 U.S. 296 (1983).

81. *Id.* at 304.

82. *Imbler v. Pachtman*, 424 U.S. 409 (1976).

83. 360 U.S. 564 (1959).

84. *United States v. Brewster*, 408 U.S. 507 (1972).

85. *Pierson v. Ray*, 386 U.S. 547, 553-54 (1967); See also *Stump v. Sparkman*, 435 U.S. 349 (1978) (holding that a judge who ordered a woman to be sterilized enjoyed absolute immunity from suit).

86. *Imbler v. Pachtman*, 424 U.S. at 424.

87. *U.S. v. Stanley*, 483 U.S. 669 (1987).

88. 420 U.S. 308, 322 (1975).

89. 438 U.S. 478 (1978).

90. 457 U.S. 800 (1982).

91. *Id.* at 818.

92. *Bulman v. Hulstrand Construction Co.*, 521 N.W.2d at 638-639.

93. R. Northness, *Interpreting Tort Liability of the State of Ohio:* Reynolds v. State, 48 Ohio St. L.J. 577, 582-583 (1987).

94. 471 N.E. 2d 776 (1984).

95. *Id.* at 778.

96. R. Northness, *supra* at 583.

97. *Mayle v. Pennsylvania Dept. of Highways*, 388 A.2d 709, 710 (1978).

98. 42 Pa. C.S.A. § 8522(b).

99. See, e.g., *Dean v. Commonwealth of Pennsylvania Dept. of Transportation*, 751 A.2d 1130 (Pa. 2000).

100. 371 So. 2d 1010 (Fla. 1979).

101. *Id.* at 1020.

102. 468 So. 2d 912 (Fla. 1985).

103. *Id.* at 919.

104. *Id.* at 919-920.

105. 609 A.2d 757 (N. J. 1992).

106. *Id.* at 763.

107. *Id.* at 765.

108. *Id.* at 768.

109. 2 U.S. (2 Dall) 419 (1793).

110. 1 C. Warren, The Supreme Court in United States History 96 (rev. ed. 1926).

111. See *Employees v. Dept. of Public Health and Welfare*, 411 U.S. 279 (1973).

112. *Kentucky v. Graham*, 473 U.S. 159 (1985).

113. *Ex parte Young*, 209 U.S. 123 (1908).

114. *Federal Maritime Commission v. South Carolina State Ports Authority*, 535 U.S. 743 (2002).

115. *Id.* at 769.

116. *Id.* at 777.

117. *Atascadero State Hospital v. Scanlon*, 473 U.S. 234, 242 (1985).

118. 427 U.S. 445 (1976).

119. *Id.* at 456.

120. 517 U.S. 44 (1996).

121. *Id.* at 100.

122. 528 U.S. 62 (2000).

123. *Id.* at 81.

124. *Id.* at 92-93.

125. *Seminole Tribe of Florida v. Florida*, 517 U.S. at 72.

126. *Mt. Helathy City School District v. Doyle*, 429 U.S. 274 (1977).

127. 520 U.S. 397, 404 (1997).

12

The Future of
Administrative Law

CHAPTER OUTLINE

Introduction

**Deregulation, Devolution, and the
Neoadministrative State**

The Rise of E-Government

**The Expanding Fourth Branch of
Government: Initiative and Referendum**

**Globalization and the Rise
of International Institutions**

Conclusion

Key Terms

Questions for Thought and Discussion

Endnotes

INTRODUCTION

Although administrative law is a relatively new branch of the law, it has achieved a level of importance comparable to the criminal and civil law. This is because the bureaucratic state, which administrative law was developed to regulate, touches our lives in countless ways. In this text, we have focused on how administrative law has evolved along with modern bureaucratic government. We have also examined how administrative law relates (not always comfortably) to our constitutional structures and principles.

A brief review of history provides context. A few decades after its agrarian beginnings, the nation entered a new era of industrialization. As the Industrial Revolution progressed, the common law, with its emphasis on private initiation of dispute resolution in an adversarial setting, was not adequate to assure the rights of the masses of people whose lives were affected by the social and economic consequences of the Industrial Revolution. By the late nineteenth century, Congress and the state legislatures responded with new laws redefining the relationship between the government and the economy, which had since the founding of the country been defined by the concept of laissez-faire. These legislative responses, while adequate to establish overall policy, were inadequate to ensure the application of new laws to the problems wrought by the rapid industrialization of American society. Presidents and governors were likewise ill-equipped for this task. Government responded by developing the modern administrative state in which legislative bodies created myriad new administrative agencies and delegated to these new bureaucracies the authority to promulgate and enforce rules and adjudicate disputes arising under these new regulations.

Initially the judiciary resisted the creation and expansion of the administrative state. The new administrative agencies did not fit into the historic separation of powers and the dichotomy of federal and state authority contemplated by the framers of the U.S. Constitution. Beginning in the late 1930s, the judiciary reformulated these traditional constitutional doctrines to accommodate the administrative state. In ensuing years the courts expanded the concept of due process to assume a new role of monitoring the bureaucracy to prevent agencies from acting arbitrarily and capriciously or with callous disregard of citizens' constitutional rights.

It is fair to say that the modern administrative state, with its panoply of specialized agencies and experts, was very successful in addressing many of the problems created by the Industrial Revolution. Yet over time, as new agencies exercised vastly increased responsibilities, many became excessively hierarchical and their rulemaking processes became ossified. Many of the agencies established to promote the public interest through regulation were captured by the very industries they were designed to regulate. The private sector, especially small business, increasingly complained of stifling regulations. Economists began to speak of the stultifying effects of excessive regulation on the economy. By the 1980s, the administrative state came under increasing pressure. Antigovernment sentiments took hold in the electorate and politicians capitalized on this trend by "running against the bureaucracy." The Reagan Revolution of the 1980s produced cutbacks in government programs, downsizing of agencies, the **deregulation** of industry, and eventually the **devolution** of power and responsibility from the national government to the states.

Behind the political and economic pressures on the administrative state, more fundamental forces are at work. Over the last several decades the bureaucracy created during the industrialization of America has been transformed by what has been termed the "third wave" of history—the movement out of the Industrial Era and into the Information Age.[1] As the third wave rolls on, we are witnessing significant changes in government and, consequently, in administrative law. One of the most important of these changes is the movement away from centralized, hierarchical, and rigid structures of decision making to more decentralized, negotiative, and fluid models.[2] In keeping with this trend, agencies are now relying more on **negotiated rulemaking** and **alternative dispute resolution (ADR).**

Electronic government, which promises great benefits in terms of citizen participation and the use of information in policymaking, is fast becoming a reality. Still another important trend is the upsurge in **direct democracy,** manifested primarily through the process of **initiative and referendum,** which is having a significant impact on political institutions and administrative process in many American states. Finally, the increasingly rapid **globalization** of markets and governance is exerting new pressures on American legal institutions. In this final chapter, we briefly examine how each of these trends is likely to shape the evolution of administrative law in the United States.

DEREGULATION, DEVOLUTION, AND THE NEOADMINISTRATIVE STATE

As we pointed out in Chapter 2, the process of **deregulation** actually began during the Carter administration in the late 1970s but accelerated greatly during the Reagan years. Thus, years before President Clinton proclaimed that "the era of big government is over" the emphasis had shifted to downsizing bureaucracy, privatizing public services, and devolving power from the federal government to the states and local governments. The Supreme Court's recent decisions in the area of federalism have contributed to the process of **devolution.**[3] As a consequence, we have witnessed the emergence of what Robert Durant calls the **neoadministrative state,**[4] a paradigm shift in which authority is diffused "from the public sphere to the market and civic spheres of the nation."

Related to this is the rise of the **shadow government** consisting of networks of consultants, contractors, and grantees.[5] Today, most government services, from trash collection at the

municipal level to the federal government's Medicare program, are actually delivered by private firms under contract with government agencies. Because the members of the shadow government are not public officials, they operate largely outside the realm of administrative law. Increasingly, commentators are suggesting that laws designed to regulate the administrative state, such as the Freedom of Information Act, the Administrative Procedure Act, and the Hatch Act, be expanded to apply to the shadow government as well. This would appear to be one of great debates on the horizon, calling into question traditional notions about the distinction between the public and private sectors.

"Regneg" and ADR

One of the most significant changes in administrative law that is attributable to the emergence of the neoadministrative state is the decline of the adversarial legal model. As we explained in Chapter 6, negotiated rulemaking ("regneg") has become an important supplement to notice and comment rulemaking. In essence, an agency assembles a representative body of stakeholders and develops a proposed rule by consensus building. After the consensus emerges, the agency publishes a Notice of Proposed Rulemaking in the *Federal Register* (or counterpart state publication) and the normal rulemaking process ensues. Ideally, the process is less conflictual and more efficient, and the policy that results is more likely to be accepted by affected parties, which means that costly and time-consuming litigation is apt to be avoided. At the federal, state, and local levels agencies and interested parties are increasingly relying on alternative dispute resolution (ADR) in lieu of formal adjudication. As we discussed in Chapter 7, ADR includes arbitration, mediation, and negotiation. These mechanisms for resolving disputes have become increasingly popular because they are typically less conflictual and less costly than traditional adversarial adjudication and offer a degree of confidentiality in dispute resolution. As the neoadministrative state moves farther away from the Weberian model of bureaucracy (see Chapter 1), we would expect that agencies would rely increasingly on regneg and ADR.

Is the APA Still Relevant?

Congress adopted the Administrative Procedure Act (APA) in 1946 to require administrative agencies to make public their activities, provide procedural uniformity in their rulemaking and adjudicative functions, and prescribe methods to review their decisions. In the decades that followed, states adopted similar administrative acts. Today, there are those who believe that the Administrative Procedure Act is not relevant to the neoadministrative state. Indeed, some critics believe that the act was outmoded when it was enacted in 1946. Edward Rubin argues that the APA is flawed because it is based on a legalistic model and that it should be replaced with a statute that is built on a more political and administrative model.[6] But the general consensus is that the act has worked reasonably well and will continue to work well as long as Congress enacts amendments necessary to maintain the act's relevance to the changing realities of public administration. The reality is that the APA is the effective "constitution" of the modern administrative state, and despite the fact that there may now exist a postmodern neoadministrative state, the APA is not likely to be abolished.

THE RISE OF E-GOVERNMENT

We are now witnessing the rise of e-government. This entails more than the storage of records electronically. It means that communications within government agencies, and between agencies and their attentive public, is becoming increasingly electronic. The *Code of Federal Regulations* and *Federal Register* are now online and nearly every federal and state agency has its own web site. And, as Jeffrey S. Lubbers points out,

"the Electronic Freedom of Information Act Amendments of 1996 have geometrically increased the amount of information provided proactively by agencies."[7]

E-government is touted as a means of conserving tax dollars, simplifying the delivery of services, and expanding citizens' opportunities to learn about and participate in their government. Indeed, the Democracy in Cyberspace Initiative at the Yale Law School is dedicated to the promotion of information technologies as a means of enhancing citizen awareness and public participation.[8]

Electronic Rulemaking

As we discussed in Chapter 6, agencies are now engaged in **Electronic rulemaking.** Spurred on by the enactment of the E-Government Act of 2002, agencies are increasingly making use of the Internet, email, and other electronic information technologies as means of enhancing public knowledge of and participation in agency rulemaking. Electronic methodology is especially suitable for direct final rulemaking discussed in Chapter 6.

A recent survey revealed that one in three users of government web sites have used the Internet to send comments to government officials relating to public policy matters; that as of January 2002, some 68 million persons had visited at least one government site.[9] Without question, this trend will continue and will no doubt result in agencies receiving much more input during the comment phase of rulemaking.

On its face, electronic government would appear to be very democratic. Facilitating public participation is generally seen as a means of enhancing democracy. Of course, computer technology and literacy are not evenly distributed within the society. The term **digital divide** has been coined to refer to the fact that a substantial proportion of society is not equipped with the skills or does not have access to the technologies that allow for the meaningful exercise of electronic citizenship.

Although most citizens may have greater opportunities to participate in rulemaking via electronic communications, this does not mean that agencies will respond to or even seriously consider the content of those communications. In the past, some agencies have been accused of engaging in notice and comment rulemaking only as a legal formality. By itself, electronic rulemaking does nothing to alter this possibility.

Concern about Privacy

Advances in technology have facilitated the collection, storage, and sharing of information about citizens. The development of massive databases by government agencies is enormously useful in crime detection, intelligence gathering, research, and the dissemination of information. But it also threatens individual privacy. Congress has already enacted significant legislation in this area, including the Right to Financial Privacy Act,[10] the Fair Credit Reporting Act,[11] and the Health Insurance Portability and Accountability Act.[12] Regulations for the last of these statutes, which became effective in 2003, have caused all of us to receive numerous privacy notices from our doctors, insurers, etc. The emergence of new and unanticipated threats to privacy will require continued vigilance by Congress and the courts.

In addition to expressing concern about privacy of the individual because of the massive databases of federal information, in 2003 Congress began to address the privacy of consumers from electronic spam, which now accounts for over half of e-mail traffic. To protect consumers from the rise in unsolicited commercial e-mail and unmarked sexually oriented materials, it enacted, and on December 16, 2003, President Bush signed into law the Controlling the Assault of Non-Solicited Pornography and Marketing Act of 2003, commonly referred to as the "CAN SPAM Act." The new Act requires an e-mail sender's postal address and warning labels of adult contents of a message. It prohibits false or misleading e-mail transmissions, deceptive subject headings that mislead the recipient as to the nature of a message, and sending messages more than 10 days after a recipient has opted out of a mailing list. It also prohibits commercial e-mail that is sent to addresses collected from the Internet without permission or compiled by automated means. The Federal Trade Commission (FTC) is responsible for enforcement and can bring suit against violators, who are subject to fines. On March 11, 2004, the FTC published a notice in the Federal Register seeking public comment on whether it should adopt regulations to clarify certain provisions of the new Act. The FTC is due to report on the effectiveness of the Act by December 16, 2005.

THE EXPANDING FOURTH BRANCH OF GOVERNMENT: INITIATIVE AND REFERENDUM

Various commentators have used the term "fourth branch of government" to describe different aspects of the American political system, including the bureaucracy, the media, and even the "military-industrial complex." Today the term might be used to also describe the process of initiative and referendum. The United States Constitution makes no provision for initiative and referendum, but many state constitutions do. Today, about half the states have some form of initiative and referendum process.[13] Many municipal charters also provide this option. In general, the process begins with the filing with the appropriate state or local authorities of a preliminary proposal to amend the state constitution or municipal charter, or to propose a specific statutory measure. The next step is the circulation of a petition to get the proposal on the ballot. If the requisite number of signatures is obtained, a referendum is held in which voters of the state or city are asked to approve the proposed change to the state constitution or municipal charter or to enact a specific statutory measure. Increasingly, interest groups are making use of such provisions to achieve policy changes they cannot achieve through the legislative process.

Changing state and local policies via initiative and referendum poses new challenges for regulators. Constitutional changes achieved through initiative and referendum often require legislators to amend existing statutes. Agencies in turn must revise rules to make them conform with new constitutional and statutory language. For example, in 1996 California voters approved Proposition 209, which amended the state constitution to prohibit preferential treatment on the basis of race or sex in admissions to public schools and in government employment and contracts. After the extensive litigation failed to invalidate the measure, government agencies in California were forced to rewrite regulations regarding discrimination in employment and contracting as well as policies governing admission to institutions of higher learning. At the same time, these agencies had to remain in compliance with federal law, which had in some instances been interpreted to require affirmative action programs by educational institutions receiving federal assistance.

The recent movement to legalize marijuana for medical use provides another example of how changes in a state constitution achieved through initiative and referendum can result in conflicts between state and federal regulations. Since 1970, thirty-five states have enacted laws recognizing the legitimate medical use of marijuana. In eight states, voters have amended their state constitutions to exempt medical use of marijuana from criminal prosecution. Some states have attempted to establish registries to keep track of patients for whom marijuana is lawfully prescribed. Of course, possession and distribution of marijuana are violations of federal drug laws, and federal authorities have threatened criminal prosecution of doctors and patients who attempt to avail themselves of state medical marijuana initiatives. In 1996, after voters in California and Arizona approved medical marijuana initiatives, federal officials began to send letters to doctors in those states, warning them that prescribing marijuana could jeopardize their legal authority to issue any drug prescriptions to their patients.[14]

The process of initiative and referendum is an extremely significant one, both legally and politically. But dramatic changes in policy brought about through initiative and referendum can produce significant problems for regulators and can place states in a position of conflict with the federal government.

GLOBALIZATION AND THE RISE OF INTERNATIONAL INSTITUTIONS

By far the most significant change on the world scene is the increasing globalization of markets and governments. In the legal realm, the most important development is the increased prominence of **international law** and the emergence of **international tribunals** and agencies. These developments have come about through multilateral treaties, most of them negotiated under the auspices of the United Nations. Numerous treaties have emerged through this process, including agreements affecting human rights, the environment, terrorism, war crimes, and many other subjects.

Under the Constitution, the president has the power, "by and with the Advice and Consent of the Senate, to make Treaties, provided two thirds of the Senators present concur."[15] Most of the treaties that have come about through the United Nations have been signed by the president of the United States and ratified by the Senate. Some, like the Convention on the Elimination of All Forms of Discrimination Against Women (CEDAW), have been signed by the president but have not been ratified by the Senate. In other instances, such as the controversial Kyoto Protocol on global warming, one presidential administration (Bill Clinton's) has signed the treaty, but the succeeding administration (George W. Bush's) has repudiated it.

Once a treaty has been signed and ratified, it becomes the "supreme law of the land," and all federal, state, and local laws must be subordinated to it.[16] In some cases, the United States has resisted compliance with decisions rendered by international bodies established under treaties to which the United States is a party. For example, after World War II the United States ratified the Statute on the International Court of Justice,[17] but on several occasions the United States has ignored orders from the International Court of Justice to stay the execution of prisoners on death row. Many people in the United States no doubt regard such orders as unwarranted meddling in our domestic affairs, but a strong argument can be made that the United States is legally, as well as ethically, obligated to abide by such orders.

In some instances international treaties require domestic regulatory actions. For example, the Montreal Protocol on Substances that Deplete the Ozone Layer, which became effective in 1989, required the U.S. Environmental Protection Agency (EPA) and its counterparts in other countries to promulgate stricter regulations regarding the use of chlorofluorocarbons (CFCs) and other substances that harm the Earth's protective layer of ozone. As treaties continue to be adopted, the body of international law grows and gains legitimacy. The next stage of the process is the emergence of international regulatory institutions with powers of rulemaking and adjudication.

The World Trade Organization

One of the most powerful international institutions today is the **World Trade Organization (WTO),** which has considerable authority in matters of international trade. The WTO resulted from an agreement signed by representatives of 125 countries in 1994. Today, there are 134 signatories to the treaty that gave rise to the WTO. The mission of the WTO is to achieve worldwide free trade—in other words, the abolition of tariffs, import quotas, and other trade barriers. The methodology by which this goal is pursued is the ongoing negotiation of multilateral trade agreements that bind countries to lower trade barriers with respect to particular goods and services. In a sense, the WTO is a rulemaking body, not unlike a regulatory agency in the United States. But the

process by which the WTO makes rules governing international trade is one of secret negotiations by representatives of the countries involved. There is no provision for public notice or comment. Critics of the WTO, and they are numerous, argue that it is controlled by powerful economic interests and is insulated from those forces that advocate on behalf of human rights, social welfare, and environmental protection. Today, there are those who argue that a new international treaty modeled after the Administrative Procedure Act is needed to require WTO and other international bodies to allow greater public participation in policymaking.[18]

The WTO also has powers of adjudication. Its Dispute Settlement Body (DSB) hears complaints by member states that other states are in violation of trade rules. Findings of the DSB are subject to review by the Appellate Body of the WTO. As an illustration of how these bodies function, consider the case of *Venezuela v. United States*. In 1995, Venezuela lodged a complaint with the DSB accusing the United States of violating trade rules by imposing stricter rules on the chemical characteristics of imported gasoline than it imposed on domestically refined gasoline. In 1996, the DSB released its report sustaining Venezuela's complaint. The United States then sought review in the WTO Appellate Body, which upheld the findings of the DSB. Ultimately, the United States agreed to change its regulations on imported gasoline, which required the EPA to promulgate new regulations. Administrative law in the United States had been changed as the result of adjudication by an international tribunal. As the world becomes more of a "global village," one can expect similar episodes to occur with increasing frequency.

CONCLUSION

Administrative law is a dynamic branch of law that covers the broad spectrum of governmental operations. Its dynamism is characterized by the ongoing devolution and decentralization of governmental power and the deregulation of industry as the Information Age progresses. Dispute resolution is moving from the adjudicative to the negotiative model, as is rulemaking. With the Internet now widely accessible, electronic government is becoming a reality and potential threats to individual privacy are becoming an issue of major public concern. The mythical fourth branch of government is expanding to recognize the significance of citizen participation through the initiative and referendum, causing state agencies to revisit their regulatory measures. Finally, and perhaps most significantly, the increasing globalization of markets and governments is giving rise to international institutions possessing powers of regulation and adjudication. As the twenty-first century advances, the most exciting developments in administrative law will take place at the international level, but these developments will surely have enormous consequences for domestic administrative law in the United States.

Assessing Administrative Law

We noted in Chapter 1 that administrative law seeks to achieve several important goals. The highest goal is to assure that the bureaucracy functions in a manner that is consonant with the "rule of law." The concept of the rule of law has both substantive and procedural aspects. Substantive policies are to be expressed in laws, including the statutes enacted by legislatures and, increasingly, the regulations promulgated by agencies. Equally important is the process by which these laws and rules are developed, adopted, implemented and enforced. The rule of law requires that such procedures are regular, orderly, and fairly applied. For the most part, administrative law has succeeded in assuring procedural regularity in agency rulemaking, enforcement actions, and adjudication.

Administrative law also seeks to promote the democratic values of accountability, openness and participation. In the absence of legal compulsion, bureaucracies are unlikely to foster these values on their own volition. There is no question that over the last several decades public agencies have generally become more transparent, responsive, and accountable, although many commentators would argue that more progress is needed in these areas. Undoubtedly, legislators, chief executives and judges must continue to exercise substantial oversight over agency action.

Finally, we noted in chapter 1 that administrative law seeks to enhance the quality of administrative decision making by promoting rationality and reliance on evidence. Clearly there has been a significant increase at all levels of government in the extent to which agencies rely on science and technology in formulating, implementing and evaluating policies and programs. Yet the increasing reliance on technocracy does not negate the fundamentally political character of bureaucratic decision making. At the end of the day, administrative law is as much a part of political science as it is of the discipline of the law.

KEY TERMS

alternative dispute resolution (ADR)

deregulation

devolution

digital divide

direct democracy

electronic government

electronic rulemaking

globalization

initiative and referendum

international law

international tribunals

negotiated rulemaking

neoadministrative state

shadow government

World Trade Organization (WTO)

QUESTIONS FOR THOUGHT AND DISCUSSION

1. What trends in administrative law are developing in the Information Age?

2. Is electronic government likely to make government more democratic?

3. Evaluate Professor Rubin's comment to the effect that the Administrative Procedure Act is outmoded.

4. How can the initiative and referendum process be used to affect policymaking by state regulatory agencies?

5. Does the Administrative Procedure Act provide a template for rulemaking and adjudication by international agencies established pursuant to treaties? Why or why not?

6. Are state and local agencies in the United States bound by rulings of international tribunals that are based on treaties to which the United States is a signatory?

ENDNOTES

1. A. Toffler, *The Third Wave* (1980).

2. See, generally, Durant, *Agenda Setting, the Third Wave, and the Administrative State,* 30 Administration & Society 211 (1998).

3. See, e.g., *New York v. United States*, 505 U.S. 144 (1992); *United States v. Lopez*, 514 U.S. 549 (1995); *Seminole Tribe of Florida v. Florida*, 517 U.S. 44 (1996); *Printz v. United States*, 521 U. S. 898 (1997); *Alden v. Maine*, 527 U.S. 706 (1999);and *United States v. Morrison*, 529 U.S. 598 (2000).

4. Durant, *Agenda Setting, the Third Wave, and the Administrative State, supra.*

5. P. Light, *The True Size of Government* (1999).

6. See, e.g., Rubin, *It's Time to Make the Administrative Procedure Act Administrative,* 89 Cornell L. Rev. 95 (2003).

7. Lubbers, *The Future of Electronic Rulemaking; A Research Agenda,* 27 Administrative and Regulatory Law News 6, at 6.

8. http://islandia.law.yale.edu/isp/strongdem/overview.html.

9. Pew Internet & American Life Project, The Rise of the E-Citizen (2002).

10. Pub. L. 104-66, 109 Stat. 734.

11. Pub. L. 91-508, 84 Stat 1127.

12. Pub. L. 104-191, 110 Stat. 1936.

13. The Initiative and Referendum Institute is affiliated with the Center for Study of Law and Politics at the University of Southern California. Its website: http://www.iandrinstitute.org/ provides comprehensive information about the history of the initiative and referendum process, the forms it takes in the various states, and the outcome of questions submitted to the voters in recent years.

14. Peter Baker and William Claiborne, "Plan Targets Medical Use of Marijuana," *Washington Post*, December 29, 1996, p. A1

15. U.S. Const., Art. II, Sec. 2.

16. *Missouri v. Holland,* 252 U.S. 416 (1920).

17. ICJ Statute, June 26, 1945, Art. 58, 59 Stat. 1055, TS No. 993.

18. See, e.g., Aman, *Globalization, Democracy, and the Need for a New Administrative Law,* 10 Indiana J. Global Legal Studies 125 (2003).

Appendix A

The Constitution of the United States of America

We the People of the United States, in Order to form a more perfect Union, establish Justice, insure domestic Tranquility, provide for the common defense, promote the general Welfare, and secure the Blessings of Liberty to ourselves and our Posterity, do ordain and establish this Constitution for the United States of America.

ARTICLE I

Section 1. All legislative Powers herein granted shall be vested in a Congress of the United States, which shall consist of a Senate and House of Representatives.

Section 2. (1) The House of Representatives shall be composed of Members chosen every second Year by the People of the several States, and the Electors in each State shall have the Qualifications requisite for Electors of the most numerous Branch of the State Legislature.

(2) No Person shall be a Representative who shall not have attained to the age of twenty-five Years, and been seven Years a Citizen of the United States, and who shall not, when elected, be an Inhabitant of that State in which he shall be chosen.

(3) Representatives and direct Taxes shall be apportioned among the several States which may be included within this Union, according to their respective Numbers, which shall be determined by adding to the whole Number of free Persons, including those bound to Service for a Term of Years, and excluding Indians not taxed, three fifths of all other Persons. The actual Enumeration shall be made within three Years after the first Meeting of the Congress of the United States, and within every subsequent Term of ten Years, in such Manner as they shall by Law direct. The Number of Representatives shall not exceed one for every thirty Thousand, but each State shall have at Least one Representative; and until such enumeration shall be made, the State of New Hampshire shall be entitled to chuse three, Massachusetts eight, Rhode Island and Providence Plantations one, Connecticut five,

New York six, New Jersey four, Pennsylvania eight, Delaware one, Maryland six, Virginia ten, North Carolina five, South Carolina five, and Georgia three.

(4) When vacancies happen in the Representation from any State, the Executive Authority thereof shall issue Writs of Election to fill such Vacancies.

(5) The House of Representatives shall chuse their Speaker and other Officers; and shall have the sole Power of Impeachment.

Section 3. (1) The Senate of the United States shall be composed of two Senators from each State, chosen by the Legislature thereof, for six Years; and each Senator shall have one Vote.

(2) Immediately after they shall be assembled in Consequence of the first Election, they shall be divided as equally as may be into three Classes. The Seats of the Senators of the first Class shall be vacated at the Expiration of the second Year, of the second Class at the Expiration of the fourth Year, and of the third Class at the Expiration of the sixth Year, so that one third may be chosen every second Year; and if Vacancies happen by Resignation, or otherwise, during the Recess of the Legislature of any State, the Executive thereof may make temporary Appointments until the next Meeting of the Legislature, which shall then fill such Vacancies.

(3) No Person shall be a Senator who shall not have attained, to the Age of thirty Years, and been nine Years a Citizen of the United States, and who shall not, when elected, be an Inhabitant of that State for which he shall be chosen.

(4) The Vice President of the United States shall be President of the Senate, but shall have no Vote, unless they be equally divided.

(5) The Senate shall chuse their other Officers, and also a President pro tempore, in the Absence of the Vice President, or when he shall exercise the Office of the President of the United States.

(6) The Senate shall have the sole Power to try all Impeachments. When sitting for that Purpose, they shall be on Oath or Affirmation.

When the President of the United States is tried, the Chief Justice shall preside: And no Person shall be convicted without the Concurrence of two thirds of the Members present.

(7) Judgment in Cases of Impeachment shall not extend further than to removal from Office, and disqualification to hold and enjoy any Office of honor, Trust or Profit under the United States: but the Party convicted shall nevertheless be liable and subject to Indictment, Trial, Judgment and Punishment, according to Law.

Section 4. (1) The Times, Places and Manner of holding Elections for Senators and Representatives, shall be prescribed in each State by the Legislature thereof; but the Congress may at any time by Law make or alter such Regulations, except as to the Places of chusing Senators.

(2) The Congress shall assemble at least once in every Year, and such Meeting shall be on the first Monday in December, unless they shall by Law appoint a different Day.

Section 5. (1) Each House shall be the Judge of the Elections, Returns and Qualifications of its own Members, and a Majority of each shall constitute a Quorum to do Business; but a smaller Number may adjourn from day to day, and may be authorized to compel the Attendance of absent Members, in such Manner, and under such Penalties as each House may provide.

(2) Each House may determine the Rules of its Proceedings, punish its Members for disorderly Behavior, and, with the Concurrence of two thirds, expel a Member.

(3) Each House shall keep a Journal of its Proceedings, and from time to time publish the same, excepting such Parts as may in their Judgment require Secrecy; and the Yeas and Nays of the Members of either House on any question shall, at the Desire of one fifth of those Present, be entered on the Journal.

(4) Neither House, during the Session of Congress, shall, without the Consent of the other, adjourn for more than three days, nor to any other Place than that in which the two Houses shall be sitting.

Section 6. (1) The Senators and Representatives shall receive a Compensation for their Services, to be ascertained by Law, and paid out of the Treasury of the United States. They shall in all Cases, except Treason, Felony and Breach of the Peace, be privileged from Arrest during their Attendance at the Session of their respective Houses, and in going to and returning from the same; and for any Speech or Debate in either House, they shall not be questioned in any other Place.

(2) No Senator or Representative shall, during the Time for which he was elected, be appointed to any civil Office under the Authority of the United States, which shall have been created, or the Emoluments whereof shall have been increased during such time; and no Person holding any Office under the United States, shall be a Member of either House during his Continuance in Office.

Section 7. (1) All Bills for raising Revenue shall originate in the House of Representatives; but the Senate may propose or concur with Amendments as on other Bills.

(2) Every Bill which shall have passed the House of Representatives and the Senate, shall, before it become a Law, be presented to the President of the United States; If he approve he shall sign it, but if not he shall return it, with his Objections to that House in which it shall have originated, who shall enter the Objections at large on their Journal, and proceed to reconsider it. If after such Reconsideration two thirds of that House shall agree to pass the Bill, it shall be sent, together with the Objections, to the other House, by which it shall likewise be reconsidered, and if approved by two thirds of that House, it shall become a Law. But in all such Cases the Votes of both Houses shall be determined by Yeas and Nays, and the Names of the Persons voting for and against the Bill shall be entered on the Journal of each House respectively. If any Bill shall not be returned by the President within ten Days (Sunday excepted) after it shall have been presented to him, the Same shall be a Law, in like Manner as if he had signed it, unless the Congress by their Adjournment prevent its Return, in which Case it shall not be a Law.

(3) Every Order, Resolution, or Vote to which the Concurrence of the Senate and House of Representatives may be necessary (except on a question of Adjournment) shall be presented to the President of the United States; and before the Same shall take Effect, shall be approved by him, or being disapproved by him, shall be repassed by two thirds of the Senate and House of Representatives, according to the Rules and Limitations prescribed in the Case of a Bill.

Section 8. (1) The Congress shall have Power To lay and collect Taxes, Duties, Imposts and Excises, to pay the Debts and provide for the common Defense and general Welfare of the United States; but all Duties, Imposts and Excises shall be uniform throughout the United States;

(2) To borrow Money on the credit of the United States;

(3) To regulate Commerce with foreign Nations, and among the several States, and with the Indian Tribes;

(4) To establish an uniform Rule of Naturalization, and uniform Laws on the subject of Bankruptcies throughout the United States;

(5) To coin Money, regulate the Value thereof, and of foreign Coin, and to fix the Standard of Weights and Measures;

(6) To provide for the Punishment of counterfeiting the Securities and current Coin of the United States;

(7) To establish Post Offices and post Roads;

(8) To promote the Progress of Science and useful Arts, by securing for limited Times to Authors and Inventors the exclusive Right to their respective Writings and Discoveries;

(9) To constitute Tribunals inferior to the supreme Court;

(10) To define and punish Piracies and Felonies committed on the high Seas, and Offenses against the Law of Nations;

(11) To declare War, grant Letters of Marque and Reprisal, and make Rules concerning Captures on Land and Water;

(12) To raise and support Armies, but no Appropriation of Money to that Use shall be for a longer Term than two Years;

(13) To provide and maintain a Navy;

(14) To make Rules for the Government and Regulation of the land and naval Forces;

(15) To provide for calling forth the Militia to execute the Laws of the Union, suppress Insurrections and repel Invasions;

(16) To provide for organizing, arming, and disciplining, the Militia, and for governing such Part of them as may be employed in the Service of the United States, reserving to the States respectively, the Appointment of the Officers, and the Authority of training the Militia according to the discipline prescribed by Congress;

(17) To exercise exclusive Legislation in all Cases whatsoever, over such District (not exceeding ten Miles square) as may, by Cession of particular States, and the Acceptance of Congress, become the Seat of the Government of the United States, and to exercise like Authority over all Places purchased by the Consent of the Legislature of the State in which the Same shall be, for the Erection of Forts, Magazines, Arsenals, dock-Yards, and other needful Buildings;—And

(18) To make all Laws which shall be necessary and proper for carrying into Execution the foregoing Powers, and all other Powers vested by this Constitution in the Government of the United States, or in any Department or Officer thereof.

Section 9. (1) The Migration or Importation of such Persons as any of the States now existing shall think proper to admit, shall not be prohibited by the Congress prior to the Year one thousand eight hundred and eight, but a Tax or Duty may be imposed on such Importation, not exceeding ten dollars for each Person.

(2) The Privilege of the Writ of Habeas Corpus shall not be suspended unless when in Cases of Rebellion or Invasion the public Safety may require it.

(3) No Bill of Attainder or ex post facto Law shall be passed.

(4) No Capitation, or other direct, Tax shall be laid, unless in Proportion to the Census or Enumeration herein before directed to be taken.

(5) No Tax or Duty shall be laid on Articles exported from any State.

(6) No Preference shall be given by any Regulation of Commerce or Revenue to the Ports of one State over those of another; nor shall Vessels bound to, or from, one State, be obliged to enter, clear or pay Duties in another.

(7) No Money shall be drawn from the Treasury, but in Consequence of Appropriations made by Law; and a regular Statement and Account of the Receipts and Expenditures of all public Money shall be published from time to time.

(8) No Title of Nobility shall be granted by the United States: And no Person holding any Office of Profit or Trust under them, shall, without the Consent of the Congress, accept of any present, Emolument, Office, or Title, of any kind whatever, from any King, Prince or foreign State.

Section 10. (1) No State shall enter into any Treaty, Alliance, or Confederation; grant Letters of Marque and Reprisal; coin Money; emit Bills of Credit; make any Thing but gold and silver Coin a Tender in Payment of Debts; pass any Bill of Attainder, ex post facto Law, or Law impairing the Obligation of Contracts, or grant any Title of Nobility.

(2) No State shall, without the Consent of Congress, lay any Imposts or Duties on Imports or Exports, except what may be absolutely necessary for executing its inspection Laws: and the net Produce of all Duties and Imposts, laid by any State on Imports or Exports, shall be for the Use of the Treasury of the United States; and all such Laws shall be subject to the Revision and Control of the Congress.

(3) No State shall, without the Consent of Congress, lay any Duty of Tonnage, keep Troops, or Ships of War in time of Peace, enter into any

Agreement or Compact with another State, or with a foreign Power, or engage in War, unless actually invaded, or in such imminent Danger as will not admit of Delay.

ARTICLE II

Section 1. (1) The executive Power shall be vested in a President of the United States of America. He shall hold his Office during the Term of four Years, and, together with the Vice President, chosen for the same Term, be elected, as follows:

(2) Each State shall appoint, in such Manner as the Legislature thereof may direct, a Number of Electors, equal to the whole Number of Senators and Representatives to which the State may be entitled in the Congress: but no Senator or Representative, or Person holding an Office of Trust or Profit under the United States, shall be appointed an Elector.

The Electors shall meet in their respective States, and vote by Ballot for two Persons, of whom one at least shall not be an Inhabitant of the same State with themselves. And they shall make a List of all the Persons voted for, and of the Number of Votes for each; which List they shall sign and certify, and transmit sealed to the Seat of the Government of the United States, directed to the President of the Senate. The President of the Senate shall, in the presence of the Senate and House of Representatives, open all the Certificates, and the Votes shall then be counted. The Person having the greatest Number of Votes shall be the President, if such Number be a Majority of the whole Number of Electors appointed; and if there be more than one who have such Majority, and have an equal Number of Votes, then the House of Representatives shall immediately chuse by Ballot one of them for President; and if no Person have a Majority, then from the five highest on the List the said House shall in like Manner chuse the President. But in chusing the President, the Votes shall be taken by States, the Representation from each State having one Vote; a quorum for this Purpose shall consist of a Member or Members from two thirds of the States, and a Majority of all the States shall be necessary to a Choice. In every Case, after the Choice of the President, the Person having the greatest Number of Votes of the Electors shall be the Vice President. But if there should remain two or more who have equal Votes, the Senate shall chuse from them by Ballot the Vice President.

(3) The Congress may determine the Time of chusing the Electors, and the Day on which they shall give their Votes; which Day shall be the same throughout the United States.

(4) No Person except a natural born Citizen, or a Citizen of the United States, at the time of the Adoption of this Constitution, shall be eligible to the Office of President; neither shall any Person be eligible to that Office who shall not have attained to the Age of thirty five Years, and been fourteen Years a Resident within the United States.

(5) In Case of the Removal of the President from Office, or of his Death, Resignation, or Inability to discharge the Powers and Duties of the said Office, the Same shall devolve on the Vice President, and the Congress may by Law provide for the Case of Removal, Death, Resignation or Inability, both of the President and Vice President, declaring what Officer shall then act as President, and such Officer shall act accordingly, until the Disability be removed, or a President shall be elected.

(6) The President shall, at stated Times, receive for his Services, a Compensation, which shall neither be increased nor diminished during the Period for which he shall have been elected, and he shall not receive within that Period any other Emolument from the United States, or any of them.

(7) Before he enter on the Execution of his Office, he shall take the following Oath or Affirmation:—"I do solemnly swear (or affirm) that I will faithfully execute the Office of President of the United States, and will to the best of my Ability, preserve, protect and defend the Constitution of the United States."

Section 2. (1) The President shall be Commander in Chief of the Army and Navy of the United States, and of the Militia of the several States, when called into the actual Service of the United States; he may require the Opinion, in writing, of the principal Officer in each of the executive Departments, upon any Subject relating to the Duties of their respective Offices, and he shall have Power to grant Reprieves and Pardons for Offenses against the United States, except in Cases of Impeachment.

(2) He shall have Power, by and with the Advice and Consent of the Senate, to make Treaties, provided two thirds of the Senators present concur; and he shall nominate, and by and with the Advice and Consent of the Senate, shall appoint Ambassadors, other public Ministers and Consuls, Judges of the supreme Court, and all other Officers of the United States, whose Appointments are not herein otherwise provided for, and which shall be established by Law: but the Congress may by Law vest the Appointment of such inferior Officers, as they think proper, in the President alone, in the Courts of Law, or in the Heads of Departments.

(3) The President shall have Power to fill up all Vacancies that may happen during the Recess of the Senate, by granting Commissions which shall expire at the End of their next Session.

Section 3. He shall from time to time give to the Congress Information of the State of the Union, and recommend to their Consideration such Measures as he shall judge necessary and expedient; he may, on extraordinary Occasions, convene both Houses, or either of them, and in Case of Disagreement between them, with Respect to the Time of Adjournment, he may adjourn them to such Time as he shall think proper; he shall receive Ambassadors and other public Ministers; he shall take Care that the Laws be faithfully executed, and shall Commission all the Officers of the United States.

Section 4. The President, Vice President and all Civil Officers of the United States, shall be removed from Office on Impeachment for, and Conviction of, Treason, Bribery, or other high Crimes and Misdemeanors.

ARTICLE III

Section 1. The judicial Power of the United States, shall be vested in one supreme Court, and in such inferior Courts as the Congress may from time to time ordain and establish. The Judges, both of the supreme and inferior Courts, shall hold their Offices during good Behavior, and shall, at stated Times, receive for their Services, a Compensation, which shall not be diminished during their Continuance in Office.

Section 2. (1) The judicial Power shall extend to all Cases, in Law and Equity, arising under this Constitution, the Laws of the United States, and Treaties made, or which shall be made, under their Authority;—to all Cases affecting Ambassadors, other public Ministers and Consuls;—to all Cases of admiralty and maritime Jurisdiction;—to Controversies to which the United States shall be a party;—to Controversies between two or more States;—between a State and Citizens of another State;—between Citizens of different States;—between Citizens of the same State claiming Lands under Grants of different States, and between a State, or the Citizens thereof, and foreign States, Citizens or Subjects.

(2) In all Cases affecting Ambassadors, other public Ministers and Consuls, and those in which a State shall be Party, the supreme Court shall have original Jurisdiction. In all the other Cases before mentioned, the supreme Court shall have appellate Jurisdiction, both as to Law and Fact, with such Exceptions, and under such Regulations as the Congress shall make.

The Trial of all Crimes, except in Cases of Impeachment, shall be by Jury; and such Trial shall be held in the State where the said Crimes shall have been committed; but when not committed within any State, the Trial shall be at such Place or Places as the Congress may by Law have directed.

Section 3. (1) Treason against the United States, shall consist only in levying War against them, or in adhering to their Enemies, giving them Aid and Comfort. No Person shall be convicted of Treason unless on the Testimony of two Witnesses to the same overt Act, or on Confession in open Court.

(2) The Congress shall have Power to declare the Punishment of Treason, but no Attainder of Treason shall work Corruption of Blood, or Forfeiture except during the Life of the Person attained.

ARTICLE IV

Section 1. Full Faith and Credit shall be given in each State to the public Acts, Records, and judicial Proceedings of every other State. And the Congress may by general Laws prescribe the Manner in which such Acts, Records and Proceedings shall be proved, and the Effect thereof.

Section 2. (1) The Citizens of each State shall be entitled to all privileges and Immunities of Citizens in the several States.

(2) A Person charged in any State with Treason, Felony, or other Crime, who shall flee from Justice, and be found in another State, shall on Demand of the executive Authority of the State from which he fled, be delivered up, to be removed to the State having Jurisdiction of the Crime.

(3) No Person held to Service of Labor in one State, under the Laws thereof, escaping into another, shall, in Consequence of any Law or Regulation therein, be discharged from such Service or Labor, but shall be delivered up on Claim of the Party to whom such Service or Labor may be due.

Section 3. (1) New States may be admitted by the Congress into this Union; but no new State shall be formed or erected within the Jurisdiction of any other State; nor any State be formed by the Junction of two or more States, or Parts of States, without the Consent of the Legislatures of the States concerned as well as of the Congress.

(2) The Congress shall have power to dispose of and make all needful Rules and Regulations respecting the Territory or other Property

belonging to the United States; and nothing in this Constitution shall be so construed as to Prejudice any Claims of the United States, or of any particular State.

Section 4. The United States shall guarantee to every State in this Union a Republican Form of Government, and shall protect each of them against Invasion; and on Application of the Legislature, or of the Executive (when the Legislature cannot be convened) against domestic Violence.

ARTICLE V

The Congress, whenever two thirds of both Houses shall deem it necessary, shall propose Amendments to this Constitution, or, on the Application of the Legislatures of two thirds of the several States, shall call a Convention for proposing Amendments, which, in either Case, shall be valid to all Intents and Purposes, as Part of this Constitution, when ratified by the Legislatures of three fourths of the several States, or by Conventions in three fourths thereof, as the one or the other Mode of Ratification may be proposed by the Congress; Provided that no Amendment which may be made prior to the Year One thousand eight hundred and eight shall in any Manner affect the first and fourth Clauses in the Ninth Section of the first Article; and that no State, without its Consent, shall be deprived of its equal Suffrage in the Senate.

ARTICLE VI

(1) All Debts contracted and Engagements entered into, before the Adoption of this Constitution, shall be as valid against the United States under this Constitution, as under the Confederation.

(2) This Constitution, and the Laws of the United States which shall be made in Pursuance thereof; and all Treaties made, or which shall be made, under the Authority of

the United States, shall be the supreme Law of the Land; and the Judges in every State shall be bound thereby, any Thing in the Constitution or Laws of any State to the Contrary notwithstanding.

(3) The Senators and Representatives before mentioned, and the Members of the several State Legislatures, and all executive and judicial Officers, both of the United States and of the several States, shall be bound by Oath or Affirmation, to support this Constitution; but no religious Test shall ever be required as a Qualification to any Office or public Trust under the United States.

ARTICLE VII

The Ratification of the Conventions of nine States, shall be sufficient for the Establishment of this Constitution between the States so ratifying the Same.

Articles in addition to, and amendment of, the constitution of the United States of America, proposed by congress, and ratified by the several states, pursuant to the fifth article of the original constitution.

AMENDMENT I (1791)

Congress shall make no law respecting an establishment of religion, or prohibiting the free exercise thereof; or abridging the freedom of speech, or of the press; or the right of the people peaceably to assemble, and to petition the Government for a redress of grievances.

AMENDMENT II (1791)

A well regulated Militia, being necessary to the security of a free state, the right of the people to keep and bear Arms, shall not be infringed.

AMENDMENT III (1791)

No Soldier shall, in time of peace be quartered in any house, without the consent of the Owner, nor in time of war, but in a manner to be prescribed by law.

AMENDMENT IV (1791)

The right of the people to be secure in their persons, houses, papers, and effects, against unreasonable searches and seizures, shall not be violated, and no Warrants shall issue, but upon probable cause, supported by Oath or affirmation, and particularly describing the place to be searched, and the persons or things to be seized.

AMENDMENT V (1791)

No person shall be held to answer for a capital, or otherwise infamous crime, unless on a presentment or indictment of a Grand Jury, except in cases arising in the land or naval forces, or in the Militia, when in actual service in time of War or public danger; nor shall any person be subject for the same offense to be twice put in jeopardy of life or limb; nor shall be compelled in any criminal case to be a witness against himself, nor be deprived of life, liberty, or property, without due process of law; nor shall private property be taken for public use, without just compensation.

AMENDMENT VI (1791)

In all criminal prosecutions, the accused shall enjoy the right to a speedy and public trial, by an impartial jury of the State and district wherein the crime shall have been committed, which district shall have been previously ascertained by law, and to be informed of the nature and cause of the accusation; to be confronted with the witnesses against him; to have compulsory process for obtaining witnesses in his favor, and to have the Assistance of Counsel for his defense.

AMENDMENT VII (1791)

In Suits at common law, where the value in controversy shall exceed twenty dollars, the right of trial by jury shall be preserved, and no fact tried by a jury, shall be otherwise re-examined in any Court of the United States, than according to the rules of the common law.

AMENDMENT VIII (1791)

Excessive bail shall not be required, nor excessive fines imposed, nor cruel and unusual punishments inflicted.

AMENDMENT IX (1791)

The enumeration in the Constitution, of certain rights, shall not be construed to deny or disparage others retained by the people.

AMENDMENT X (1791)

The powers not delegated to the United States by the Constitution, nor prohibited by it to the States, are reserved to the States respectively, or to the people.

AMENDMENT XI (1798)

The Judicial power of the United States shall not be construed to extend to any suit in law or equity, commenced or prosecuted against one of the United States by Citizens of another State, or by Citizens or Subjects of any Foreign State.

AMENDMENT XII (1804)

The Electors shall meet in their respective states and vote by ballot for President and Vice-President, one of whom, at least, shall not be an inhabitant of the same state with themselves; they shall name in their ballots the person voted for as President, and in distinct ballots the person voted for as Vice-President, and they shall make distinct lists of all persons voted for as President, and of all persons voted for as Vice-President, and of the number of votes for each, which lists they shall sign and certify, and transmit sealed to the seat of the government of the United States, directed to the President of the Senate;—The President of the Senate shall, in the presence of the Senate and House of Representatives, open all the certificates and the votes shall then be counted;—The person having the greatest number of votes for President, shall be the President, if such number be a majority of the whole number of Electors appointed; and if no person have such majority, then from the persons having the highest numbers not exceeding three on the list of those voted for as President, the House of Representatives shall choose immediately, by ballot, the President. But in choosing the President, the votes shall be taken by states, the representation from each state having one vote; a quorum for this purpose shall consist of a member or members from two-thirds of the states, and a majority of all the states shall be necessary to a choice. And if the House of Representatives shall not choose a President whenever the right of choice shall devolve upon them, before the fourth day of March next following, then the Vice-President shall act as President, as in the case of the death or other constitutional disability of the President—The person having the greatest number of votes as Vice-President, shall be the Vice-President, if such number be a majority of the whole number of Electors appointed, and if no person have a majority, then from the two highest numbers on the list, the Senate shall choose the Vice-President; A quorum for the purpose shall consist of two-thirds of the whole number of Senators, and a majority of the whole number shall be necessary to a choice. But no person constitutionally ineligible to the office of President shall be eligible to that of Vice-President of the United States.

AMENDMENT XIII (1865)

Section 1. Neither slavery nor involuntary servitude, except as a punishment for crime whereof the party shall have been duly convicted, shall exist within the United States, or any place subject to their jurisdiction.

Section 2. Congress shall have power to enforce this article by appropriate legislation.

AMENDMENT XIV (1868)

Section 1. All persons born or naturalized in the United States and subject to the jurisdiction thereof, are citizens of the United States and of the State wherein they reside. No State shall make or enforce any law which shall abridge the privileges or immunities of citizens of the United States; nor shall any State deprive any person of life, liberty, or property, without due process of law; nor deny to any person within its jurisdiction the equal protection of the laws.

Section 2. Representatives shall be apportioned among the several States according to their respective numbers, counting the whole number of persons in each State, excluding Indians not taxed. But when the right to vote at any election for the choice of electors for President and Vice-President of the United States, Representatives in Congress, the Executive and Judicial officers of a State, or the members of the Legislature thereof, is denied to any of the male inhabitants of such State, being twenty-one years of age, and citizens of the United States, or in any way abridged, except for participation in rebel-

lion, or other crime, the basis of representation therein shall be reduced in the proportion which the number of such male citizens shall bear to the whole number of male citizens twenty-one years of age in such State.

Section 3. No person shall be a Senator or Representative in Congress, or elector of President and Vice-President, or hold any office, civil or military, under the United States, or under any State, who, having previously taken an oath, as a member of Congress, or as an officer of the United States, or as a member of any State legislature, or as an executive or judicial officer of any State, to support the Constitution of the United States, shall have engaged in insurrection or rebellion against the same, or given aid or comfort to the enemies thereof. But Congress may by a vote of two-thirds of each House, remove such disability.

Section 4. The validity of the public debt of the United States, authorized by law, including debts incurred for payment of pensions and bounties for services in suppressing insurrection or rebellion, shall not be questioned. But neither the United States nor any State shall assume or pay any debt or obligation incurred in aid of insurrection or rebellion against the United States, or any claim for the loss or emancipation of any slave; but all such debts, obligations and claims shall be held illegal and void.

Section 5. The Congress shall have power to enforce, by appropriate legislation, the provisions of this article.

AMENDMENT XV (1870)

Section 1. The right of citizens of the United States to vote shall not be denied or abridged by the United States or by any State on account of race, color, or previous condition of servitude.

Section 2. The Congress shall have power to enforce this article by appropriate legislation.

AMENDMENT XVI (1913)

The Congress shall have power to lay and collect taxes on incomes, from whatever source derived, without apportionment among the several States, and without regard to any census or enumeration.

AMENDMENT XVII (1913)

The Senate of the United States shall be composed of two Senators from each State, elected by the people thereof, for six years; and each Senator shall have one vote. The electors in each State shall have the qualifications requisite for electors of the most numerous branch of the State legislatures.

When vacancies happen in the representation of any State in the Senate, the executive authority of such State shall issue writs of election to fill such vacancies: Provided, That the legislature of any State may empower the executive thereof to make temporary appointments until the people fill the vacancies by election as the legislature may direct.

This amendment shall not be so construed as to affect the election or term of any Senator chosen before it becomes valid as part of the Constitution.

AMENDMENT XVIII (1919)

Section 1. After one year from the ratification of this article the manufacture, sale, or transportation of intoxicating liquors within, the importation thereof into, or the exportation thereof from the United States and all territory subject to the jurisdiction thereof for beverage purposes is hereby prohibited.

Section 2. The Congress and the several States shall have concurrent power to enforce this article by appropriate legislation.

Section 3. This article shall be inoperative unless it shall have been ratified as an amendment to the Constitution by the legislatures of the several States, as provided in the Constitution, within seven years from the date of the submission hereof to the States by the Congress.

AMENDMENT XIX (1920)

The right of citizens of the United States to vote shall not be denied or abridged by the United States or by any State on account of sex.

Congress shall have power to enforce this article by appropriate legislation.

AMENDMENT XX (1933)

Section 1. The terms of the President and Vice President shall end at noon on the 20th day of January, and the terms of Senators and Representatives at noon on the 3rd day of January, of the years in which such terms would have ended if this article had not been ratified; and the terms of their successors shall then begin.

Section 2. The Congress shall assemble at least once in every year, and such meeting shall begin at noon on the 3rd day of January, unless they shall by law appoint a different day.

Section 3. If, at the time fixed for the beginning of the term of the President, the President elect shall have died, the Vice President elect shall become President. If a President shall not have been chosen before the time fixed for the beginning of his term, or if the President elect shall have failed to qualify, then the Vice President elect shall act as President until a President shall have qualified; and the Congress may by law provide for the case wherein neither a President elect nor a Vice President elect shall have qualified, declaring who shall then act as President, or the manner in which one who is to act shall be selected, and such person shall act accordingly until a President or Vice President shall have qualified.

Section 4. The Congress may by law provide for the case of the death of any of the persons from whom the House of Representatives may choose a President whenever the right of choice shall have devolved upon them, and for the case of the death of any of the persons from whom the Senate may choose a Vice President whenever the right of choice shall have devolved upon them.

Section 5. Sections 1 and 2 shall take effect on the 15th day of October following the ratification of this article.

Section 6. This article shall be inoperative unless it shall have been ratified as an amendment to the Constitution by the legislatures of three-fourths of the several States within seven years from the date of its submission.

AMENDMENT XXI (1933)

Section 1. The eighteenth article of amendment to the Constitution of the United States is hereby repealed.

Section 2. The transportation or importation into any State, Territory or possession of the United States for delivery or use therein of intoxicating liquors, in violation of the laws thereof, is hereby prohibited.

Section 3. This article shall be inoperative unless it shall have been ratified as an amendment to the Constitution by conventions in the several States, as provided in the Constitution, within seven years from the date of the submission hereof to the States by the Congress.

AMENDMENT XXII (1951)

Section 1. No person shall be elected to the office of the President more than twice, and no person who has held the office of President, or acted as President, for more than two years of a term to which some other person was elected President shall be elected to the office of the President more than once. But this Article shall not apply to any person holding the office of President when this Article was proposed by the

Congress, and shall not prevent any person who may be holding the office of President, or acting as President, during the term within which this Article becomes operative from holding the office of President or acting as President during the remainder of such term.

Section 2. This Article shall be inoperative unless it shall have been ratified as an amendment to the Constitution by the legislatures of three-fourths of the several States within seven years from the date of its submission to the States by the Congress.

AMENDMENT XXIII (1961)

Section 1. The District constituting the seat of Government of the United States shall appoint in such manner as the Congress may direct:

A number of electors of President and Vice President equal to the whole number of Senators and Representatives in Congress to which the District would be entitled if it were a State, but in no event more than the least populous State; they shall be in addition to those appointed by the States, but they shall be considered, for the purposes of the election of President and Vice President, to be electors appointed by a State; and they shall meet in the District and perform such duties as provided by the twelfth article of amendment.

Section 2. The Congress shall have power to enforce this article by appropriate legislation.

AMENDMENT XXIV (1964)

Section 1. The right of citizens of the United States to vote in any primary or other election for President or Vice President, for electors for President or Vice President, or for Senator or Representative in Congress, shall not be denied or abridged by the United States or any State by reason of failure to pay any poll tax or other tax.

Section 2. The Congress shall have power to enforce this article by appropriate legislation.

AMENDMENT XXV (1967)

Section 1. In case of the removal of the President from office or of his death or resignation, the Vice President shall become President.

Section 2. Whenever there is a vacancy in the office of the Vice President, the President shall nominate a Vice President who shall take office upon confirmation by a majority vote of both Houses of Congress.

Section 3. Whenever the President transmits to the President pro tempore of the Senate and the Speaker of the House of Representatives his written declaration that he is unable to discharge the powers and duties of his office, and until he transmits to them a written declaration to the contrary, such powers and duties shall be discharged by the Vice President as Acting President.

Section 4. Whenever the Vice President and a majority of either the principal officers of the executive departments or of such other body as Congress may by law provide, transmit to the President pro tempore of the Senate and the Speaker of the House of Representatives their written declaration that the President is unable to discharge the powers and duties of his office, the Vice President shall immediately assume the powers and duties of the office as Acting President.

Thereafter, when the President transmits to the President pro tempore of the Senate and the Speaker of the House of Representatives his written declaration that no inability exists, he shall resume the powers and duties of his office unless the Vice President and a majority of either the principal officers of the executive department or of such other body as Congress may by law provide, transmit within four days to the President pro tempore of the Senate and the Speaker of the House of Representatives their written declaration that the President is unable to discharge the powers and duties of his office. Thereupon Congress shall decide the issue, assembling within forty-eight hours for that purpose if not in session. If the Congress, within twenty-one days after receipt of the latter written declaration, or, if Congress is not in session, within twenty-one days after Congress is required to assemble, determines by two-thirds vote of both Houses that the President is unable to discharge the powers and duties of his office, the Vice President shall continue to discharge the same as Acting President; otherwise, the President shall resume the powers and duties of his office.

AMENDMENT XXVI (1971)

Section 1. The right of citizens of the United States, who are eighteen years of age or older, to vote shall not be denied or abridged by the United States or by any State on account of age.

Section 2. The Congress shall have power to enforce this article by appropriate legislation.

AMENDMENT XXVII (1992)

No law, varying the compensation for the services of the Senators and Representatives, shall take effect, until an election of Representatives shall have intervened.

Appendix B

The Federal Administrative Procedure Act

Selected Provisions of Title 5, U.S. Code

§ 551. Definitions

For the purpose of this subchapter—

(1) 'agency' means each authority of the Government of the United States, whether or not it is within or subject to review by another agency, but does not include—(A) the Congress; (B) the courts of the United States; (C) the governments of the territories or possessions of the United States; (D) the government of the District of Columbia; or except as to the requirements of section 552 of this title—(E) agencies composed of representatives of the parties or of representatives of organizations of the parties to the disputes determined by them; (F) courts martial and military commissions; (G) military authority exercised in the field in time of war or in occupied territory; or (H) functions conferred by sections 1738, 1739, 1743, and 1744 of title 12; chapter 2 of title 41; or sections 1622, 1884, 1891–1902, and former section 1641(b)(2), of title 50, appendix;

(2) 'person' includes an individual, partnership, corporation, association, or public or private organization other than an agency;

(3) 'party' includes a person or agency named or admitted as a party, or properly seeking and entitled as of right to be admitted as a party, in an agency proceeding, and a person or agency admitted by an agency as a party for limited purposes;

(4) 'rule' means the whole or a part of an agency statement of general or particular applicability and future effect designed to implement, interpret, or prescribe law or policy or describing the organization, procedure, or practice requirements of an agency and includes the approval or prescription for the future of rates, wages, corporate or financial structures or reorganizations thereof, prices, facilities, appliances, services or allowances therefor or of valuations,

costs, or accounting, or practices bearing on any of the foregoing;

(5) 'rule making' means agency process for formulating, amending, or repealing a rule;

(6) 'order' means the whole or a part of a final disposition, whether affirmative, negative, injunctive, or declaratory in form, of an agency in a matter other than rule making but including licensing;

(7) 'adjudication' means agency process for the formulation of an order;

(8) 'license' includes the whole or a part of an agency permit, certificate, approval, registration, charter, membership, statutory exemption or other form of permission;

(9) 'licensing' includes agency process respecting the grant, renewal, denial, revocation, suspension, annulment, withdrawal, limitation, amendment, modification, or conditioning of a license;

(10) 'sanction' includes the whole or a part of an agency—(A) prohibition, requirement, limitation, or other condition affecting the freedom of a person; (B) withholding of relief; (C) imposition of penalty or fine; (D) destruction, taking, seizure, or withholding of property; (E) assessment of damages, reimbursement, restitution, compensation, costs, charges, or fees; (F) requirement, revocation, or suspension of a license; or (G) taking other compulsory or restrictive action;

(11) 'relief' includes the whole or a part of an agency—(A) grant of money, assistance, license, authority, exemption, exception, privilege, or remedy; (B) recognition of a claim, right, immunity, privilege, exemption, or exception; or (C) taking of other action on the application or petition of, and beneficial to, a person;

(12) 'agency proceeding' means an agency process as defined by paragraphs (5), (7), and (9) of this section;

(13) 'agency action' includes the whole or a part of an agency rule, order, license, sanction, relief, or the equivalent or denial thereof, or failure to act; and

(14) 'ex parte communication' means an oral or written communication not on the public record with respect to which reasonable prior notice to all parties is not given, but it shall not include requests for status reports on any matter or proceeding covered by this subchapter.

§ 553. Rule Making

(a) This section applies, according to the provisions thereof, except to the extent that there is involved—

(1) a military or foreign affairs function of the United States; or

(2) a matter relating to agency management or personnel or to public property, loans, grants, benefits, or contracts.

(b) General notice of proposed rule making shall be published in the Federal Register, unless persons subject thereto are named and either personally served or otherwise have actual notice thereof in accordance with law. The notice shall include—

(1) a statement of the time, place, and nature of public rule making proceedings;

(2) reference to the legal authority under which the rule is proposed; and

(3) either the terms or substance of the proposed rule or a description of the subjects and issues involved. Except when notice or hearing is required by statute, this subsection does not apply—(A) to interpretative rules, general statements of policy, or rules of agency organization, procedure, or practice; or (B) when the agency for good cause finds (and incorporates the finding and a brief statement of reasons therefor in the rules issued) that notice and public procedure thereon are impracticable, unnecessary, or contrary to the public interest.

(c) After notice required by this section, the agency shall give interested persons an opportunity to participate in the rule making through submission of written data, views, or arguments with or without opportunity for oral presentation. After consideration of the relevant matter presented, the agency shall incorporate in the rules adopted a concise general statement of their basis and purpose. When rules are required by statute to be made on the record after opportunity for an agency hearing, sections 556 and 557 of this title apply instead of this subsection.

(d) The required publication or service of a substantive rule shall be made not less than 30 days before its effective date, except—

(1) a substantive rule which grants or recognizes an exemption or relieves a restriction;

(2) interpretative rules and statements of policy; or

(3) as otherwise provided by the agency for good cause found and published with the rule.

(e) Each agency shall give an interested person the right to petition for the issuance, amendment, or repeal of a rule.

§ 554. Adjudications

(a) This section applies, according to the provisions thereof, in every case of adjudication required by statute to be determined on the record after opportunity for an agency hearing, except to the extent that there is involved—

(1) a matter subject to a subsequent trial of the law and the facts de novo in a court;

(2) the selection or tenure of an employee, except a administrative law judge appointed under section 3105 of this title;

(3) proceedings in which decisions rest solely on inspections, tests, or elections;

(4) the conduct of military or foreign affairs functions;

(5) cases in which an agency is acting as an agent for a court; or

(6) the certification of worker representatives.

(b) Persons entitled to notice of an agency hearing shall be timely informed of—

(1) the time, place, and nature of the hearing;

(2) the legal authority and jurisdiction under which the hearing is to be held; and

(3) the matters of fact and law asserted. When private persons are the moving parties, other parties to the proceeding shall give prompt notice of issues controverted in fact or law; and in other instances agencies may by rule require responsive pleading. In fixing the time and place for hearings, due regard shall be had for the convenience and necessity of the parties or their representatives.

(c) The agency shall give all interested parties opportunity for—

(1) the submission and consideration of facts, arguments, offers of settlement, or proposals of adjustment when time, the nature of the proceeding, and the public interest permit; and

(2) to the extent that the parties are unable so to determine a controversy by consent, hearing and decision on notice and in accordance with sections 556 and 557 of this title.

(d) The employee who presides at the reception of evidence pursuant to section 556 of this title shall make the recommended decision or initial decision required by section 557 of this title, unless he becomes unavailable to the agency. Except to the extent required for the disposition of ex parte matters as authorized by law, such an employee may not—

(1) consult a person or party on a fact in issue, unless on notice and opportunity for all parties to participate; or

(2) be responsible to or subject to the supervision or direction of an employee or agent engaged in the performance of investigative or prosecuting functions for an agency. An employee or agent engaged in the performance of investigative or prosecuting functions for an agency in a case may not, in that or a factually related case, participate or advise in the decision, recommended decision, or agency review pursuant to section 557 of this title, except as witness or counsel in public proceedings. This subsection does not apply—(A) in determining applications for initial licenses; (B) to proceedings involving the validity or application of rates, facilities, or practices of public utilities or carriers; or (C) to the agency or a member or members of the body comprising the agency.

(e) The agency, with like effect as in the case of other orders, and in its sound discretion, may issue a declaratory order to terminate a controversy or remove uncertainty.

§ 555. Ancillary Matters

(a) This section applies, according to the provisions thereof, except as otherwise provided by this subchapter.

(b) A person compelled to appear in person before an agency or representative thereof is entitled to be accompanied, represented, and advised by counsel or, if permitted by the agency, by other qualified representative. A party is entitled to appear in person or by or with counsel or other duly qualified representative in an agency proceeding. So far as the orderly conduct of public business permits, an interested person may appear before an agency or its responsible employees for the presentation, adjustment, or determination of an issue, request, or controversy in a proceeding, whether interlocutory, summary, or otherwise, or in connection with an agency function. With due regard for the convenience and necessity of the parties or their representatives and within a reasonable time, each agency shall proceed to conclude a matter presented to it. This subsection does not grant or deny a person who is not a lawyer the right to appear for or represent others before an agency or in an agency proceeding.

(c) Process, requirement of a report, inspection, or other investigative act or demand may not be issued, made, or enforced except as authorized by law. A person compelled to submit data or evidence is entitled to retain or, on payment of lawfully prescribed costs, procure a copy or transcript thereof, except that in a nonpublic investigatory proceeding the witness may for good cause be limited to inspection of the official transcript of his testimony.

(d) Agency subpoenas authorized by law shall be issued to a party on request and, when required by rules of procedure, on a statement or showing of general relevance and reasonable scope of the evidence sought. On contest, the court shall sustain the subpoena or similar process or demand to the extent that it is found to be in accordance with law. In a proceeding for enforcement, the court shall issue an order requiring the appearance of the witness or the production of the evidence or data within a reasonable time under penalty of punishment for contempt in case of contumacious failure to comply.

(e) Prompt notice shall be given of the denial in whole or in part of a written application, petition, or other request of an interested person made in connection with any agency proceeding. Except in affirming a prior denial or when the denial is self-explanatory, the notice shall be accompanied by a brief statement of the grounds for denial.

§ 556. Hearings; Presiding Employees; Powers and Duties; Burden of Proof; Evidence; Record as Basis of Decision

(a) This section applies, according to the provisions thereof, to hearings required by section 553 or 554 of this title to be conducted in accordance with this section.

(b) There shall preside at the taking of evidence—

(1) the agency;

(2) one or more members of the body which comprises the agency; or

(3) one or more administrative law judges appointed under section 3105 of this title. This subchapter does not supersede the conduct of specified classes of proceedings, in whole or in part, by or before boards or other employees specially provided for by or designated under statute. The functions of presiding employees and of employees participating in decisions in accordance with section 557 of this title shall be conducted in an impartial manner. A presiding or participating employee may at any time disqualify himself. On the filing in good faith of a timely and sufficient affidavit of personal bias or other disqualification of a presiding or participating employee, the agency shall determine the

matter as a part of the record and decision in the case.

(c) Subject to published rules of the agency and within its powers, employees presiding at hearings may—

(1) administer oaths and affirmations;

(2) issue subpoenas authorized by law;

(3) rule on offers of proof and receive relevant evidence;

(4) take depositions or have depositions taken when the ends of justice would be served;

(5) regulate the course of the hearing;

(6) hold conferences for the settlement or simplification of the issues by consent of the parties or by the use of alternative means of dispute resolution as provided in subchapter IV of this chapter;

(7) inform the parties as to the availability of one or more alternative means of dispute resolution, and encourage use of such methods;

(8) require the attendance at any conference held pursuant to paragraph (6) of at least one representative of each party who has authority to negotiate concerning resolution of issues in controversy;

(9) dispose of procedural requests or similar matters;

(10) make or recommend decisions in accordance with section 557 of this title; and

(11) take other action authorized by agency rule consistent with this subchapter.

(d) Except as otherwise provided by statute, the proponent of a rule or order has the burden of proof. Any oral or documentary evidence may be received, but the agency as a matter of policy shall provide for the exclusion of irrelevant, immaterial, or unduly repetitious evidence. A sanction may not be imposed or rule or order issued except on consideration of the whole record or those parts thereof cited by a party and supported by and in accordance with the reliable, probative, and substantial evidence. The agency may, to the extent consistent with the interests of justice and the policy of the underlying statutes administered by the agency, consider a violation of section 557(d) of this title suffi-

cient grounds for a decision adverse to a party who has knowingly committed such violation or knowingly caused such violation to occur. A party is entitled to present his case or defense by oral or documentary evidence, to submit rebuttal evidence, and to conduct such cross-examination as may be required for a full and true disclosure of the facts. In rule making or determining claims for money or benefits or applications for initial licenses an agency may, when a party will not be prejudiced thereby, adopt procedures for the submission of all or part of the evidence in written form.

(e) The transcript of testimony and exhibits, together with all papers and requests filed in the proceeding, constitutes the exclusive record for decision in accordance with section 557 of this title and, on payment of lawfully prescribed costs, shall be made available to the parties. When an agency decision rests on official notice of a material fact not appearing in the evidence in the record, a party is entitled, on timely request, to an opportunity to show the contrary.

§ 557. Initial Decisions; Conclusiveness; Review by Agency; Submissions by Parties; Contents of Decisions; Record

(a) This section applies, according to the provisions thereof, when a hearing is required to be conducted in accordance with section 556 of this title.

(b) When the agency did not preside at the reception of the evidence, the presiding employee or, in cases not subject to section 554 (d) of this title, an employee qualified to preside at hearings pursuant to section 556 of this title, shall initially decide the case unless the agency requires, either in specific cases or by general rule, the entire record to be certified to it for decision. When the presiding employee makes an initial decision, that decision then becomes the decision of the agency without further proceedings unless there is an appeal to, or review on motion of, the agency within time provided by rule. On appeal from or review of the initial decision, the agency has all the powers which it would have in making the initial decision except as it may limit the issues on notice or by rule. When the agency makes the decision without having presided at the reception of the evidence, the presiding employee or an employee qualified to preside at hearings pursuant to section 556 of this title shall first recommend a decision, except that in rule making or determining applications for initial licenses—

(1) instead thereof the agency may issue a tentative decision or one of its responsible employees may recommend a decision; or

(2) this procedure may be omitted in a case in which the agency finds on the record that due and timely execution of its functions imperatively and unavoidably so requires.

(c) Before a recommended, initial, or tentative decision, or a decision on agency review of the decision of subordinate employees, the parties are entitled to a reasonable opportunity to submit for the consideration of the employees participating in the decisions—

(1) proposed findings and conclusions; or

(2) exceptions to the decisions or recommended decisions of subordinate employees or to tentative agency decisions; and

(3) supporting reasons for the exceptions or proposed findings or conclusions. The record shall show the ruling on each finding, conclusion, or exception presented. All decisions, including initial, recommended, and tentative decisions, are a part of the record and shall include a statement of—(A) findings and conclusions, and the reasons or basis therefor, on all the material issues of fact, law, or discretion presented on the record; and (B) the appropriate rule, order, sanction, relief, or denial thereof.

(d) (1) In any agency proceeding which is subject to subsection (a) of this section, except to the extent required for the disposition of ex parte matters as authorized by law—(A) no interested person outside the agency shall make or knowingly cause to be made to any member of the body comprising the agency, administra-

tive law judge, or other employee who is or may reasonably be expected to be involved in the decisional process of the proceeding, an ex parte communication relevant to the merits of the proceeding; (B) no member of the body comprising the agency, administrative law judge, or other employee who is or may reasonably be expected to be involved in the decisional process of the proceeding, shall make or knowingly cause to be made to any interested person outside the agency an ex parte communication relevant to the merits of the proceeding; (C) a member of the body comprising the agency, administrative law judge, or other employee who is or may reasonably be expected to be involved in the decisional process of such proceeding who receives, or who makes or knowingly causes to be made, a communication prohibited by this subsection shall place on the public record of the proceeding: (i) all such written communications; (ii) memoranda stating the substance of all such oral communications; and (iii) all written responses, and memoranda stating the substance of all oral responses, to the materials described in clauses (i) and (ii) of this subparagraph; (D) upon receipt of a communication knowingly made or knowingly caused to be made by a party in violation of this subsection, the agency, administrative law judge, or other employee presiding at the hearing may, to the extent consistent with the interests of justice and the policy of the underlying statutes, require the party to show cause why his claim or interest in the proceeding should not be dismissed, denied, disregarded, or otherwise adversely affected on account of such violation; and (E) the prohibitions of this subsection shall apply beginning at such time as the agency may designate, but in no case shall they begin to apply later than the time at which a proceeding is noticed for hearing unless the person responsible for the communication has knowledge that it will be noticed, in which case the prohibitions shall apply beginning at the time of his acquisition of such knowledge.

(2) This subsection does not constitute authority to withhold information from Congress.

§ 558. Imposition of Sanctions; Determination of Applications for Licenses; Suspension, Revocation, and Expiration of Licenses

(a) This section applies, according to the provisions thereof, to the exercise of a power or authority.

(b) A sanction may not be imposed or a substantive rule or order issued except within jurisdiction delegated to the agency and as authorized by law.

(c) When application is made for a license required by law, the agency, with due regard for the rights and privileges of all the interested parties or adversely affected persons and within a reasonable time, shall set and complete proceedings required to be conducted in accordance with sections 556 and 557 of this title or other proceedings required by law and shall make its decision. Except in cases of willfulness or those in which public health, interest, or safety requires otherwise, the withdrawal, suspension, revocation, or annulment of a license is lawful only if, before the institution of agency proceedings therefor, the licensee has been given—

(1) notice by the agency in writing of the facts or conduct which may warrant the action; and

(2) opportunity to demonstrate or achieve compliance with all lawful requirements. When the licensee has made timely and sufficient application for a renewal or a new license in accordance with agency rules, a license with reference to an activity of a continuing nature does not expire until the application has been finally determined by the agency.

§ 559. Effect on Other Laws; Effect of Subsequent Statute

This subchapter, chapter 7, and sections 1305, 3105, 3344, 4301 (2)(E), 5372, and 7521 of this title, and the provisions of section 5335(a)(B) of this title that relate to administrative law judges, do not limit or repeal additional requirements imposed by statute or otherwise recognized by law. Except as otherwise required by law, requirements or privileges relating to evidence or procedure apply equally to agencies and persons. Each agency is granted the authority necessary to comply with the requirements of this subchapter through the issuance of rules or otherwise. Subsequent statute may not be held to supersede or modify this subchapter, chapter 7, sections 1305, 3105, 3344, 4301(2)(E), 5372, or 7521 of this title, or the provisions of section 5335(a)(B) of this title that relate to administrative law judges, except to the extent that it does so expressly.

§ 701. Application; Definitions

(a) This chapter applies, according to the provisions thereof, except to the extent that—

(1) statutes preclude judicial review; or

(2) agency action is committed to agency discretion by law.

(b) For the purpose of this chapter—

(1) "agency" means each authority of the Government of the United States, whether or not it is within or subject to review by another agency, but does not include—(A) the Congress; (B) the courts of the United States; (C) the governments of the territories or possessions of the United States; (D) the government of the District of Columbia; (E) agencies composed of representatives of the parties or of representatives of organizations of the parties to the disputes determined by them; (F) courts martial and military commissions; (G) military authority exercised in the field in time of war or in occupied territory; or (H) functions conferred by sections 1738, 1739, 1743, and 1744 of title 12; chapter 2 of title 41; or sections 1622, 1884, 1891–1902, and former section 1641(b)(2), of title 50, appendix; and

(2) "person", "rule", "order", "license", "sanction", "relief", and "agency action" have the meanings given them by section 551 of this title.

§ 702. Right of Review

A person suffering legal wrong because of agency action, or adversely affected or aggrieved by agency action within the meaning of a relevant statute, is entitled to judicial review thereof. An action in a court of the United States seeking relief other than money damages and stating a claim that an agency or an officer or employee thereof acted or failed to act in an official capacity or under color of legal authority shall not be dismissed nor relief therein be denied on the ground that it is against the United States or that the United States is an indispensable party. The United States may be named as a defendant in any such action, and a judgment or decree may be entered against the United States: Provided, That any mandatory or injunctive decree shall specify the Federal officer or officers (by name or by title), and their successors in office, personally responsible for compliance. Nothing herein

(1) affects other limitations on judicial review or the power or duty of the court to dismiss any action or deny relief on any other appropriate legal or equitable ground; or

(2) confers authority to grant relief if any other statute that grants consent to suit expressly or impliedly forbids the relief which is sought.

§ 703. Form and Venue of Proceeding

The form of proceeding for judicial review is the special statutory review proceeding relevant to the subject matter in a court specified by statute or, in the absence or inadequacy thereof, any applicable form of legal action, including actions for declaratory judgments or writs of prohibitory or mandatory injunction or habeas corpus, in a court of competent jurisdiction. If no special statutory review proceeding is applicable, the action for judicial review may be brought against the United States, the agency by its official title, or the appropriate officer. Except to the extent that prior, adequate, and exclusive opportunity for judicial review is provided by law, agency action is subject to judicial review in civil or criminal proceedings for judicial enforcement.

§ 704. Actions Reviewable

Agency action made reviewable by statute and final agency action for which there is no other adequate remedy in a court are subject to judicial review. A preliminary, procedural, or intermediate agency action or ruling not directly reviewable is subject to review on the review of the final agency action. Except as otherwise expressly required by statute, agency action otherwise final is final for the purposes of this section whether or not there has been presented or determined an application for a declaratory order, for any form of reconsideration, or, unless the agency otherwise requires by rule and provides that the action meanwhile is inoperative, for an appeal to superior agency authority.

§ 705. Relief Pending Review

When an agency finds that justice so requires, it may postpone the effective date of action taken by it, pending judicial review. On such conditions as may be required and to the extent necessary to prevent irreparable injury, the reviewing court, including the court to which a case may be taken on appeal from or on application for certiorari or other writ to a reviewing court, may issue all necessary and appropriate process to postpone the effective date of an agency action or to preserve status or rights pending conclusion of the review proceedings.

§ 706. Scope of Review

To the extent necessary to decision and when presented, the reviewing court shall decide all relevant questions of law, interpret constitutional and statutory provisions, and determine the meaning or applicability of the terms of agency action. The reviewing court shall–

(1) compel agency action unlawfully withheld or unreasonably delayed; and

(2) hold unlawful and set aside agency action, findings, and conclusions found to be—(A) arbitrary, capricious, an abuse of discretion, or otherwise not in accordance with law; (B) contrary to constitutional right, power, privilege, or immunity; (C) in excess of statutory jurisdiction, authority, or limitations, or short of statutory right; (D) without observance of procedure required by law; (E) unsupported by substantial evidence in a case subject to sections 556 and 557 of this title or otherwise reviewed on the record of an agency hearing provided by statute; or (F) unwarranted by the facts to the extent that the facts are subject to trial de novo by the reviewing court.

In making the foregoing determinations, the court shall review the whole record or those parts of it cited by a party, and due account shall be taken of the rule of prejudicial error.

Appendix C

Basic Legal Research

THE IMPORTANCE OF LEGAL RESEARCH IN ADMINISTRATIVE LAW

Legal research is a systematic method of finding the law applicable to a given factual scenario. The goal is to make a determination that will resolve a dispute or enable one to follow an advised course of action. After formulating the facts and attempting to develop the issue to be resolved, a legal researcher must seek to find the **constitutional and statutory sources of law,** the applicable regulations, and then ascertain relevant **judicial and administrative interpretations.** A grasp of basic legal research is a vital tool for a student or a professional working in the field of administrative law.

Once you become familiar with basic legal research you will discover that the books we discuss below are found in law school libraries. Many college (and even many local) libraries include many of these publications in their reference sections. Like so many other areas of research, legal research today is moving rapidly into the age of computers and the Internet. But before undertaking **on-line research** it is essential that the legal researcher understand the basic structure and functions of government and become knowledgeable about the books that are the traditional professional tools for legal research.

THE ROLES OF THE LEGISLATIVE, EXECUTIVE, AND JUDICIAL BRANCHES

In Chapter 1 we discussed the role of the executive branch of government and the enactment of statutory laws by Congress and state legislatures and how these bodies authorize regulatory agencies to promulgate and enforce rules. Familiarity with these concepts and the jurisdiction and functions of the federal and state courts, also discussed in Chapter 1, should provide a student with a head start in navigating the channels of legal authorities in administrative law.

Throughout the text we have referred to many precedent-setting decisions of the United States Supreme Court; however, most of the interpretations of law affecting the administrative process come from the lower federal and state appellate courts. Many of the significant interpretations at the federal level emanate from the U.S. Courts of Appeals, particularly the court that serves the District of Columbia Circuit. At the state level most administrative law interpretations come from the decisions of the intermediate appellate courts and the state's highest court, usually known as the state supreme court. Before undertaking legal research the student might find it helpful to review our discussion of the role of the executive, legislative, and judicial branches in Chapter 1.

GETTING STARTED
IN LEGAL RESEARCH

Once you become knowledgeable about the sources of the law and the process of its development of the law by courts and administrative agencies and you develop the skill of analyzing a problem, you can get started in legal research. Here is a suggestion that can help. If you attend a college at or near a law school, a law librarian might help you in the use of law books or electronic media. Or you might get assistance from a law student, as they usually take a course in legal research in their first year. In many instances legal research in administrative law may simply begin with use of a law dictionary. There are several fine law dictionaries. *Black's Law Dictionary* (7th ed.), available in both print and computer disk, is one of the best known and will be found in all law libraries and in many college and local libraries. If you are working from home do not overlook the fact that in many communities local governments, courthouses, and bar associations have established law libraries that are usually available to the public.

SOURCES OF THE LAW

Lawyers refer to constitutions, statutes, executive orders, agency regulations, ordinances, and court decisions as **primary legal authorities.** This is because they are official pronouncements of the law. Encyclopedias, textbooks, and scholarly articles are very helpful in understanding the law, but they are not official sources. They are, therefore, classified as **secondary legal authorities** and, while not official, they give the researcher considerable background in specialized areas and frequently are cited by courts and commentators as persuasive authorities in legal proceedings.

Primary Authorities of Administrative Law in the United States

The United States Constitution and the Federal Administrative Procedure Act are basic to administrative law. The Constitution is reprinted in Appendix A; excerpts from the APA are reprinted in Appendix B.

Federal statutes begin as "bills" introduced by a U.S. Senator or U.S. Congressperson in a session of Congress. Each bill is assigned a number. For example, a bill originating in the Senate may be numbered "S-10." One introduced in the House of Representatives will also carry a numerical designation, for example, "H.R. 90." During the legislative process bills introduced go through a process of committee action and floor debate. Some are rejected; some are combined with other bills. Once a bill is passed by both the Senate and the House and signed by the president, or if the bill is passed over the president's veto, it gets a new label as a Public Law and carries the year of the Congress and a numerical designation. For example, a bill that is enacted into law by the 102nd Congress might be labeled, "P.L. 102-300." Once a proposed bill becomes a federal law, it is published in the *United States Statutes at Large* and eventually becomes a part of the U.S. Code.

The United States Code Annotated (U.S.C.A.) A popular compilation of the federal law widely used by lawyers, judges, and other professionals is the *United States Code Annotated* (U.S.C.A.). Published by the West Group, the U.S.C.A. contains the entire current United States Code, with each section of statutory law followed by annotations consisting of court decisions interpreting the particular statute along with historical notes, cross-references, and other editorial features.

In various chapters of this text we have referred to a number of federal statutes by reference to the U.S.C.A. The researcher can locate a section of the U.S. Code identified numerically and can access such statutory reference in the code. A researcher who is proceeding on a "fact or subject basis" should note that the U.S.C.A. is divided by subject matter into 50 Titles. A list of the 50 Titles is published in the front section of each U.S.C.A. volume. For example, Title 20 relates to education; Title 21 concerns Food and Drugs. Each of these topics is of considerable interest in the administrative process. Having selected the appropriate topic, the researcher can then proceed to make a selection from the table of contents for that title. The U.S.C.A. also has a general index, printed annually, which will guide the researcher to a particular title and section number by subject.

Annually pocket parts are placed in the back of each volume of the U.S.C.A. to update federal statutory and decisional law in each volume. The use of pocket parts is common to legal reference books as it saves the expense of publishing revised volumes and has become a common method of keeping legal treatises current. Eventually volumes are completely revised and the process of supplementation begins again.

State Laws and Annotated State Codes State legislatures enact laws during each session of the legislature. These laws are called **session laws** and are initially compiled in sequence of their adoption. Later they are systematically arranged by subject in official compilations. In addition, many states have annotated statutes published either by the state or private publishers. Many follow a somewhat similar format to that discussed in the preceding section and research proceeds accordingly. For example, *West's Annotated California Codes* follows the same general format as the U.S.C.A.

The American Common Law Despite the growing importance of statutes and regulations, the decisions of federal and state courts (primarily appellate courts) in the United States basically follow the tradition of the common law developed in England after the Norman Conquest in 1066 and received in America as part of our legal heritage. Courts follow the principle of *stare decisis*, Latin for "let the decision stand." Even when reviewing statutes and regulations, judges look at prior decisions and court opinions and usually apply such decisions as "precedents." Nevertheless, courts sometimes veer from precedent, especially when societal values change. A classic example is the well-known decision of the U.S. Supreme Court in 1954 that outlawed racial segregation in the nation's public schools. Therefore, it is essential that a researcher have access to the up-to-date judicial decisions of the federal and state appellate courts. Fortunately, we have tools that enable us to locate those decisions in a rather expeditious manner.

The National Reporter System Decisions of the United States Supreme Court are officially published in the *United States Reports* (abbreviated U.S.) and in certain commercial publications, called **reporters**. For example, in the text we refer to *Chevron U.S.A. v. Natural Defense Council,* a landmark 1984 Supreme Court decision on judicial deference to an agency's interpretation of a statute. The decision is cited as 467 U.S. 837, which means it is found in volume 467 at page 837 of the *United States Reports.* Although in this text we cite to the official *U.S. Reports,* the same decision may be cited as 104 S.Ct. 2778, 81 L.Ed.2d 694 (1984). These latter **citations** refer to volumes published by two private organizations: The *Supreme Court Reporter* (abbreviated S.Ct.) is published by the West Group, and *Lawyers Edition,* now in its second series (abbreviated L.Ed.2d), is now published by the West Group. Reporters have somewhat different editorial features; but the opinions of the Supreme Court are reproduced identically in all three reporters.

Since 1889, the decisions of the United States Courts of Appeals have been published in *West's Federal Reporter,* now in its third series (abbreviated F.3d). Decisions of federal district (trial) courts are published in *West's Federal Supplement* (abbreviated F. Supp.). For example, a citation to a case in *Federal Reporter* may read, *Rodriguez v. Donovan,* 769 F.2d 1344 (9th Cir. 1985). This refers to a 1985 decision by the United States Court of Appeals for the 9th Circuit reported in volume 769, page 1344 of the *Federal Reporter,* second series. A citation to *Delgado v. Pung,* 704 F. Supp. 922 (D. Minn. 1977) refers to a 1977 federal district court decision from the Minnesota district reported in volume 704, page 922 of the *Federal Supplement.* Additional federal reporters publish the decisions from other federal courts (for example, bankruptcy and military appeals), but the federal reporters referred to above are those most frequently used in researching judicial decisions on administrative law.

The decisions of the highest state courts (usually but not always called supreme courts) and the decisions of other state appellate courts (usually referred to as intermediate appellate courts) are found in seven **regional reporters,** *West's California Reporter,* and the *New York Supplement.* Regional reporters, with their abbreviation in parentheses, include decisions from the following states:

- *Atlantic Reporter:* (A. and A.2d) Maine, Vermont, New Hampshire, Connecticut, Rhode Island, Pennsylvania, New Jersey, Maryland, Delaware, and the District of Columbia
- *North Eastern Reporter:* (N.E. and N.E.2d) Illinois, Indiana, Massachusetts, New York (court of last resort only), and Ohio

- *North Western Reporter:* (N.W. and N.W.2d) North Dakota, South Dakota, Nebraska, Minnesota, Iowa, Michigan, and Wisconsin
- *Pacific Reporter:* (P. and P.2d) Washington, Oregon, California, Montana, Idaho, Nevada, Utah, Arizona, Wyoming, Colorado, New Mexico, Kansas, Oklahoma, Alaska, and Hawaii
- *Southern Reporter:* (So. and So.2d) Florida, Alabama, Mississippi, and Louisiana
- *South Eastern Reporter:* (S.E. and S.E.2d) Georgia, North Carolina, South Carolina, Virginia, and West Virginia
- *South Western Reporter:* (S.W. and S.W.2d) Arkansas, Kentucky, Missouri, Tennessee, and Texas

For example: *Maine AFL-CIO v. Superintendent of Insurance,* a 1998 decision of the Supreme Judicial Court of Maine, is cited in the text with an endnote reference to 732 A.2d 633 (Me. 1998). This citation refers to the court's 1998 decision found in volume 732, page 633 of the *Atlantic Reporter,* Second Series.

These reporters are part of the National Reporter System published by the West Group. They include decisions from the United States Supreme Court, the lower federal courts, and the state appellate courts. The reporters contain not only the official text of each reported decision but also a brief summary of the decision, called the **syllabus,** and one or more topically indexed **headnotes.** The syllabus briefly identifies the court's decision and the headnotes concisely identify the main principles of law expounded by the court in its written opinion. The headnotes are indexed by a series of topics on legal subjects arranged alphabetically and by **key numbers.** West assigns these key numbers to specific points of decisional law of the topics it covers.

The West Group also publishes *Decennial Digests* that topically index all the appellate court decisions from the state and federal courts. Digests are tools that enable the researcher to locate cases in point through topics and key numbers. For instance, decisions dealing with the discretion that agencies exercise in rulemaking authority are found under Administrative Law and Procedure, Key number 385. Using this key number system, a researcher can locate headnotes of various appellate decisions on this aspect of administrative law. As of 2003, the most recent *Decennial Digest* embraces federal and state appellate court decisions from 1996–2001. The *Decennial Digests* are kept current by a set called the General Digests, so that the researcher can always find the latest cases.

As the decisional law develops, legal precedents are sometimes modified or even overruled. To assist the researcher in determining the current status of an appellate opinion, LEXIS/NEXIS publishes *Shepard's Citations,* a series of books that provide the judicial history of cases by reference to the volume and page number of the cases in the particular reporters. By using the symbols explained in this work, the researcher can determine whether a particular decision has been affirmed, followed, distinguished, modified, or reversed by subsequent court decisions. Most attorneys "Shepardize" the cases they cite in their law briefs to support various principles of law to make certain their research is current. There is a separate set of *Shepard's Citations* for the United States Supreme Court decisions, the federal appellate and district courts, for each regional reporter, and for each state that has an official reporter.

Federal Materials Three federal government publications that are of great value to the serious student of administrative law are available in many college libraries:

- The *United States Government Manual* provides basic information on all federal government agencies, including their histories, functions, programs, officials, etc. It is updated annually. This manual includes organization charts for each major agency, which can be a valuable assist to the researcher.

- The *Federal Register* contains all executive orders, presidential proclamations, notice of agency hearings, proposed and adopted rules, and amendments to proposed or adopted rules. It is published daily.

- The *Code of Federal Regulations* (CFR) is the codification of all final rules of all federal agencies. It is updated annually.

- Links to all three of these publications can be found on the Internet at http://thomas.loc.gov/home/legbranch/otherleg.html#govpub, or at http://www.access.gpo.gov/.

Some states publish codes of state administrative regulations. Most of these states will also have their regulations available on the Internet; you can usually find them at, or linked from, the official state web site.

The Secondary Legal Authorities

As we noted above, legal authorities other than constitutions, statutes, ordinances, agency regulations, and court decisions are called secondary authorities, yet they too are essential tools in legal research. In fact, a good way to seek general information on a legal topic is to research secondary authorities.

The Legal Encyclopedias; Textbooks; Law Reviews Beyond dictionaries, the most common secondary legal authorities are **legal encyclopedias.** These encyclopedias are arranged alphabetically by subject and are used much like any standard encyclopedia. There are two principal national encyclopedias of the law: *Corpus Juris Secundum* (C.J.S.), published by West, and *American Jurisprudence,* second edition (Am.Jur.2d), published by Lawyers Cooperative Publishing Company of Rochester, New York. The publishers of *American Jurisprudence* also publish encyclopedias of state law in the more populous states; for example, *Florida Jurisprudence.* The statements of the law in these encyclopedias are based on reported decisions of federal and state courts with footnotes directing the researcher to the cases that support the statements of law. As with U.S.C.A. and many other law books, these encyclopedias are supplemented annually with pocket parts identifying recent decisions and keyed to the appropriate sections of the text. A general index for each encyclopedia is issued annually, and researchers should use these first to find their specific subjects and section numbers.

Textbooks and other treatises on legal subjects often read much like encyclopedias; however, most address specific subjects in great depth. In addition, the leading law schools publish law reviews that contain articles, commentaries, and notes by academics, judges, lawyers, and law students who exhaustively research topics. These can be rather conveniently accessed through use of the *Index to Legal Periodicals.* This index is a valuable tool to find current information on administrative law subjects; it is published by the H.W. Wilson Company and is found in all law school libraries. Current articles on administrative law are listed under categories such as administrative agencies, administrative procedure, government contracts, rulemaking, judicial review of administrative action, and other topics in the field of administrative law.

Many law reviews publish articles and comments on administrative law topics. Prominent among these is the *Administrative Law Review,* published quarterly by the Washington College of Law of American University and the Section of Administrative Law and Regulatory Practice of the American Bar Association. It provides a forum for views on developments pertaining to administrative law. Recent issues have included articles on such timely topics as the Federal Tort Claims Act, standards of review of administrative judges' findings, and the movement toward on-line rulemaking.

Computerized Legal Research

Increasingly, **computerized legal research** is supplementing traditional use of books. Using computerized legal databases and retrieval system like Westlaw®, which operates from a central computer system where databases for state and federal statutes, appellate decisions, and other legal materials are stored, can be advantageous. Westlaw allows retrieval of statutes and cases when the correct citation is entered. It also allows users to enter "queries" into the system to receive relevant data and has a searching method that uses natural language that allows queries to be entered in plain English. Westlaw will retrieve a number of documents that have a likelihood of matching the search description. One can also retrieve proposed and adopted federal regulations. A prominent feature of Westlaw is its Key Cite service. This enables a researcher to check citations, prior and later case history, determine the number of times a given decision has been cited by the courts, and review a list of secondary authorities mentioning the decision. The researcher can also do a key number search on Westlaw, using the topic and key number system contained in the printed digests to quickly find the very latest cases.

LEXIS/NEXIS is an excellent competing system. As with Westlaw, researchers can use Lexis/Nexis to find cases, regulations, statutes, and other primary sources of law; they can search for items either by forming queries or using natural language; and they can find documents or cases by typing in the citations. Unlike Westlaw, which has KeyCite to check citation history, Lexis has an electronic version of *Shepard's* to check cites; it is a bit easier to use, and more up to date, than the printed *Shepard's* volumes.

The growth of the Internet makes it possible to search for legal information from federal government and most state governments on the World Wide Web (www). One way to start research on the Internet is by using a comprehensive site, such as www.findlaw.com or www.lawsource.com; these sites will tell you what is available on-line for a particular area of law or jurisdiction. More and more courts, at both federal and state levels, are putting up their own web sites and making their decisions available quickly and without charge. Also, many federal and state administrative agencies have their own web sites, which often include their regulations, pending rules, and even administrative decisions. (An example of this is the Social Security Administration's web site, at www.ssa.gov, which gives the user everything from forms and publications to information about obtaining a Social Security card.) The Internet has much to offer for legal research, and a resourceful student should be able to access considerable information on legal subjects from official government sites, free.

Also, CD-ROMs containing statutes, court decisions, and related materials are now commercially available. You might use these at a law school or court law library. The resourceful student should be able to access considerable information on legal subjects by exploring the Internet and other new technologies.

In addition to Findlaw, there is a web site to the Government Printing Office that lists publications and databases. Many federal and state administrative agencies have their own web pages that detail information concerning the agencies and their activities.

Glossary

1981 Model State Administrative Procedure Act (1981 MSAPA)   See *Model State Administrative Procedure Act.*

absolute immunity   Doctrine under which selected classes of officials, including judges, prosecutors, and legislators are completely insulated from lawsuits stemming from their official actions.

abuse of discretion   Failure to exercise reasonably sound judgment in decision making.

abuse of discretion standard   The standard of judicial review in which the decision of an agency or lower court is upheld unless it is unreasonable or "shocks the conscience" of the reviewing court.

accountability   The state of being answerable to another authority.

adjudication   The process by which courts or agencies decide cases involving the rights of parties.

adjudicatory procedures   Processes by which administrative or judicial bodies decide cases involving the rights of parties.

administrative agencies   Offices of federal, state, and local governments exercising authority over designated services or functions.

administrative detention   Incarceration of a person by an administrative agency, e.g., the detention of illegal aliens by immigration authorities.

administrative efficiency   The condition under which an agency achieves its goals with a minimum of resources.

administrative fines   Fines imposed by administrative agencies on violators of regulations.

administrative inspections   Examinations of the premises of regulated facilities by officials of administrative agencies.

administrative law   The branch of the public law dealing with the structure, authority, policies, and procedures of administrative and regulatory agencies.

administrative law judges (ALJs)   Officers appointed to hear and determine controversies before administrative agencies of governments.

Administrative Procedure Act (APA)   A 1946 Act of Congress specifying rulemaking and adjudicatory procedures for federal agencies.

administrative review   Review of an administrative proceeding within the agency itself.

administrative rulemaking   Rulemaking by administrative agencies pursuant to authority delegated by Congress or the state legislatures.

administrative search warrants   Court orders authorizing searches to determine if there are violations of regulatory laws and ordinances.

administrative searches   Searches of premises by a government official to determine compliance with applicable regulations.

administrative tribunals   Bodies established within administrative agencies for the purpose of conducting formal adjudication of cases involving disputing parties.

adversarial system   A system of justice involving conflicting parties where opposing parties advocate their legal positions before an independent judge or other neutral decision maker.

advice and consent   The constitutional power of the Senate to ratify treaties and confirm presidential appointments.

affirm   To uphold, ratify, or approve.

affirmative action programs   Controversial programs under which women and/or persons of particular minority groups are granted special consideration in public employment, government contracts, and admission to public institutions of higher education.

age discrimination   Especially applicable to employment situations, this involves the giving of unequal consideration to persons because of their age.

Age Discrimination in Employment Act (ADEA)   Enacted in 1967, the ADEA protects people aged forty and above from discrimination in the area of employment.

agency point of view   The attitude of bureaucrats that stresses the protection of their own agency's budget, powers, staff, and routines, often at the expense of what elected officials may desire.

agency records   Documents created by or in control of an official government agency.

agency's construction of a statute   An agency's official interpretation of its enabling legislation or some statute it is responsible for implementing or enforcing.

agenda setting   The stage of the policy-making process in which different political actors attempt to get an issue in the public view so that government officials will take action on it.

alternative dispute resolution (ADR)   Refers to methods of resolving disputes without judicial adjudication. Usual means employed are arbitration and mediation.

ambiguity   The condition in which the meanings of words in a statute, regulation, or contract are unclear or uncertain.

Americans with Disabilities Act (ADA)   Landmark federal statute enacted in 1990 forbidding discrimination on grounds of disability and guaranteeing access for the handicapped to public buildings, transportation facilities, communications technologies, and places of public accommodation.

antitrust law   The body of federal and state law defining antitrust violations, e.g., monopolies, price-fixing, etc., and providing remedies for such violations.

antitrust violations   Violations of laws designed to protect the public from price-fixing, price discrimination, and monopolistic practices in trade and commerce.

appeals of right   Appeals brought to higher courts as a matter of right under federal or state law.

appellant   A person that takes an appeal to a higher court.

appellate courts   Judicial tribunals that review decisions from lower tribunals.

appellate jurisdiction   The legal authority of a court of law to hear an appeal from or otherwise review a decision by a lower court.

appellate procedure   The rules of procedure followed by appellate courts in deciding appeals.

appellee   The party against whom a case is appealed to a higher court.

appointment power   The power of the president to appoint, with the consent of the Senate, judges, ambassadors, and high-level executive officials.

Appointments Clause   Located in Article II, Section 2 of the U.S. Constitution, this clause provides that the president "by and with the advice and consent of the senate, shall appoint ambassadors, other public ministers and consuls, judges of the supreme court, and all other officers of the United States, whose appointments are not herein otherwise provided for . . ."

appropriations   Money that is allocated by Congress or a state legislature for the purpose of funding government programs.

arbitration   Procedure whereby controversies are resolved by a referee or a panel of referees who make a decision on the merits of a controversy after presentations by the disputants.

attorney general   The highest legal officer of a state or of the United States.

attorney-client privilege   The right of a person (client) not to disclose and to prevent others from disclosing information about matters discussed in confidence with an attorney in the course of the attorney's representation.

audits and examinations   Formal reviews of financial records to determine compliance with law or regulations, e.g., a tax audit by Internal Revenue Service to determine a taxpayer's compliance with the law.

bankruptcy   Legal process by which honest debtors obtain relief under laws designed to protect them from their creditors.

bid rigging   An illegal manipulation in submitting bids to obtain a contract, usually from a public body.

Bill of Rights   The first ten amendments to the Constitution, enumerating rights that are protected from government infringement.

***Bivens*-type remedy**   A suit for damages against a federal official accused of violating the plaintiff's constitutional rights.

block grants   Federal moneys provided to state and local governments that are to be spent in specified general areas, such as housing or law enforcement, but do not carry the restrictions and requirements of categorical grants.

board of adjustment   A local board authorized to grant exceptions and variances from land use zoning ordinances and regulations.

board of equalization   A local board authorized to revise the assessed values of properties subject to *ad valorem* taxation.

breach of contract   The violation of a provision in a legally enforceable agreement that gives the damaged party the right to recourse in a court of law.

briefs   Written documents containing legal arguments in support of a party's position before a court or governmental agency.

Buckley Amendment   Popular name of the Family Educational Rights and Privacy Act of 1974, which protects the confidentiality of student educational records.

budgetary process   The administrative and legislative procedures by which governments formulate and enact budgets.

building codes   Governmental regulations specifying the requirements for the construction, remodeling, repair, and demolition of buildings.

Bureau of Alcohol, Tobacco and Firearms (ATF)   Federal agency located within the Department of the Treasury empowered to enforce federal statutes dealing with intoxicating beverages, tobacco products, guns, and explosives.

bureaucracy   Any large, complex, hierarchical organization staffed by appointed officials.

cabinet   The collective term for the heads of the executive departments of the federal or state government, which includes such offices as secretary of state, the attorney general, and the secretary of agriculture.

cabinet-level departments The fifteen major departments within the executive branch of the federal government headed by officials who are members of the president's cabinet.

career civil servants Members of the bureaucracy who occupy the middle-management, professional, technical, and clerical positions; career civil servants obtain their jobs on the basis of merit and are protected from being fired for political reasons.

case or controversy Article III of the U.S. Constitution extends the federal judicial power to actual cases or controversies, not to hypothetical or abstract questions of law. Many, but not all, state constitutions include such a clause as relates to the jurisdiction of state courts.

categorical grant Federal moneys provided to state and local governments for a narrowly defined purpose.

caveat emptor "Let the buyer beware." Common-law maxim requiring the consumer to judge the quality of a product before making a purchase, i.e., the buyer makes a purchase at his or her own risk.

cease and desist order An order issued by a court or an administrative agency requiring a person to stop certain designated activities.

certiorari Meaning "to be informed," this is an order from a higher court to a lower court to send up the record in a particular case so that it may be reviewed. The U.S. Supreme Court issues writs of certiorari (commonly referred to as "granting cert") to review decisions of lower federal courts and in some instances the highest state courts.

checks and balances Fundamental principle underlying the American constitutional system whereby institutions of government can check one another in order to prevent one branch from becoming too powerful or from exercising the powers of another branch.

chief of staff The head of the White House staff; the person responsible for controlling the president's calendar and advising the president on all aspects of domestic and foreign policy.

citation (1) A summons to appear in court, often used in traffic violations. (2) A reference to a statute or court decision, often designating a publication where the law or decision appears.

city manager A professionally trained public administrator hired by a city council to oversee the day-to-day operations of the city government.

civil case A judicial proceeding, outside the criminal law, by which a party seeks to enforce rights or to obtain redress for wrongs, often seeking monetary damages.

civil contempt Intentional disobedience of a court order.

civil law (1) The law relating to rights and obligations of private parties; (2) The body of law, based essentially on Roman Law, that prevails in most non-English speaking nations.

civil liberties The freedoms protected by the Constitution and statutes, for example, freedom of speech, religion, and assembly.

civil penalty A fine assessed for a noncriminal violation of a law or regulation.

civil procedure The rules of procedure followed by courts in adjudicating civil cases.

civil rights Rights guaranteed by the U.S. Constitution, federal statutes, state constitutional provisions, state statutes, and local ordinances that protect individuals from various forms of discrimination.

Civil Rights Act of 1871 This post–Civil-War statute made individuals acting under color of state law personally liable for acts violating the constitutional rights of others. Civil actions under this statute are commonly referred to as "Section 1983 actions" because the act is codified at 42 U.S.C.A. § 1983.

Civil Rights Act of 1964 Landmark civil rights statute aimed at ending racial discrimination in employment and by places of public accommodation.

civil rights laws Local, state, and federal laws protecting persons against various forms of discrimination.

civil rights legislation Statutes protecting persons against various forms of unlawful discrimination.

civil service The system under which government employees are selected and retained based on merit, rather than political patronage.

Civil Service Reform Act of 1883 Known as the Pendleton Act, this statute established the federal civil service whose members would be selected by competitive examinations. The act also created the Civil Service Commission, which was empowered to issue and enforce regulations governing the civil service.

Civil Service Reform Act of 1978 This statute abolished the U.S. Civil Service Commission and transferred its functions to three new agencies, the Merit Systems Protection Board, the Office of Personnel Management, and the Federal Labor Relations Authority.

civil suit Any legal action (other than a criminal prosecution) that is brought to enforce a legal right.

class action A civil suit brought by one or more parties on behalf of themselves and others similarly situated. Class actions are usually brought in civil court where the parties affected are so numerous as to make individual court actions impracticable.

classical liberalism The tradition of political philosophy beginning with John Locke advocating popular sovereignty, limited government, the rule of law, and the rights of individuals.

closing argument Statement presented by counsel at the conclusion of the presentation of evidence at a trial or administrative hearing.

Code of Federal Regulations (CFR) The codification of all federal agency regulations currently in effect.

collateral estoppel A rule barring a party from making of a claim in one judicial proceeding that has been adjudicated against that party in another, earlier proceeding.

collective bargaining Negotiations between representatives (usually union leaders) on behalf of employees and representatives on behalf of an employer. Bargaining usually focuses on wages, benefits, and working conditions.

color of law Acting under the appearance of law or of being cloaked with legal authority.

comity Courtesy, respect, civility. A matter of good will and tradition, rather than of right. Particularly important in a federal system where one jurisdiction is bound to respect the judgments of another.

commander in chief Refers to the president's authority to command the armed forces of the nation.

Commerce Clause Provision found in Article I, Section 8 of the United States Constitution authorizing Congress to "regulate Commerce with foreign Nations, and among the several States, and with the Indian Tribes."

common law The body of judge-made law inherited from England; also refers to the legal tradition that accepts judicial decisions as the source of law.

compelling government interest A government interest sufficiently strong that it overrides the fundamental rights of persons adversely affected by government action or policy. Courts employ the compelling interest test in exercising strict scrutiny in cases alleging racial discrimination by government or the abridgment of fundamental rights.

compensatory damages Amount of money awarded a plaintiff to compensate for injury or losses suffered.

competent Legally qualified. Often refers to a witness who is legally qualified to testify or to evidence that qualifies to be admitted in a judicial or administrative proceeding.

complaint An initial document filed in court to inform the defendant of the nature and extent of the plaintiff's claim against the defendant.

compulsory process The requirement that witnesses appear and testify in court or before a legislative committee. See also *subpoena*.

compulsory self-incrimination The requirement that an individual give testimony leading to his or her own criminal conviction. Forbidden by the U.S. Constitution, Amendment V.

conclusions of law A court's determination as to the principles of law applicable to a particular case.

concurrent jurisdiction Jurisdiction that is shared by different agencies or courts of law.

concurrent powers Powers exercised jointly by the state and federal governments.

concurring in the judgment A judicial opinion agreeing with the judgment of an appellate court without agreeing with the court's reasoning.

concurring opinion An opinion written by an appellate judge agreeing with the decision of the court, which may or may not agree with the rationale adopted in the majority opinion.

condemning authority Federal and state governments (and where authorized, local governments) that exercise the right of eminent domain, i.e., the right to take private property for public use upon payment of just compensation. A condemning authority that is unable to negotiate the taking of private property for public use, for example, for a road, park etc., can exercise such authority by initiation of a judicial proceeding.

Congressional Budget Office (CBO) Agency within the legislative branch of the federal government established in 1974 to provide Congress with analysis of budgetary matters.

congressional power to abrogate state sovereign immunity The power of Congress to authorize private lawsuits against states in federal courts, notwithstanding the states' sovereign immunity, in order to vindicate individual rights protected from state action by the Fourteenth Amendment to the U.S. Constitution.

Congressional Review of Agency Decisionmaking Act 1996 act of Congress that requires federal agencies to submit all newly issued rules to Congress before they can take effect.

consolidation (1) The act of combining city and county governments into one metropolitan government. (2) The decision of an appellate court to decide two or more cases at the same time where the cases present the same legal question.

constitution A nation or state's fundamental law defining the structure and powers of government and the rights of individuals vis-à-vis government.

constitutional law A body of law developed by the courts in cases interpreting the provisions of the federal and state constitutions.

Constitutional Revolution of 1937 Dramatic about-face by the Supreme Court in 1937 after which the Court accepted a broader role for the federal government in the management of the nation's economy.

constitutional torts Deprivations of constitutional rights for which the remedy is a civil suit for damages.

constitutionalism The legal and political tradition of subordinating government to principles enshrined in written constitutions.

contempt An action that embarrasses, hinders, obstructs, or is calculated to lessen the dignity of a judicial or legislative body.

contempt of court Any action that embarrasses, hinders, obstructs, or is calculated to lessen the dignity of a court of law.

contested case A case in which there are two or more parties contesting a factual or legal allegation.

contingent fee A fee to be paid to an attorney only in the event the attorney prevails in court on behalf of the client. Contingent fees are commonly applicable to actions by plaintiffs seeking money damages for suffering personal injuries. In such cases attorneys commonly agree to be compensated by receiving a certain percentage of the plaintiff's award, contingent on the plaintiff being successful.

continuing resolution A legislative act that continues the current level of funding for a program until a permanent budget can be passed.

cooperative federalism A modern approach to American federalism in which powers and functions are shared among national, state, and local authorities.

cost-benefit analysis Systematic assessment of the costs and benefits that will result from a given policy.

county manager   A professional administrator hired by a county commission to oversee the administration of the county government.

court of last resort   The highest court in a judicial system, the last resort for deciding appeals.

courts of general jurisdiction   Refers to courts that have jurisdiction to hear major civil and criminal cases.

courts of law   Judicial tribunals; governmental institutions established for the purpose of resolving legal disputes and interpreting the law.

courts of limited jurisdiction   Courts that handle pretrial matters and conduct trials in minor civil (small claims) and criminal (misdemeanor) cases.

cross-examination   The process of interrogating a witness who has testified on direct examination by asking the witness questions concerning testimony given. Cross-examination is designed to bring out any bias or inconsistencies in the witness's testimony.

cutback   In general, any reduction in spending for a particular government program. The term was often used in the 1980s to refer to the Reagan administration's efforts to reduce the fiscal role of the federal government in state and local affairs.

damages   Monetary compensation awarded by a court to a person who has suffered injuries or losses to person or property as a result of someone else's wrongful or negligent conduct.

de novo   Anew; for a second time. The term "trial *de novo*" refers to a new trial of a case with a complete new review of the facts and applicable law.

de novo standard   A standard of judicial review without granting any deference to the decision by the lower court or government agency.

debt ceiling   A restriction on how much money the Treasury Department can borrow without obtaining congressional approval again.

decisional law   The law as declared by appellate courts in their written decisions and opinions.

declaratory judgment   A judicial ruling conclusively declaring the rights, duties, or status of the parties but imposing no additional order, restriction, or requirement on them.

declaratory relief   A court decision establishing rights of parties but not ordering enforcement.

default   Failure to do some act required by contract or by law.

default judgment   A judgment entered by a court due to a defendant's failure to respond to legal process or to appear in court to contest the plaintiff's claim.

defendant   A person charged with a crime or against whom a civil action has been initiated.

deficit   The condition that occurs when spending exceeds revenues in a given fiscal year.

delagatee   One to whom a power, authority, or responsibility has been transferred.

delagator   One who transfers a power, authority, or responsibility to another party.

delegation   Act of transferring a power, authority, or responsibility to a person or agency.

delegation of legislative power   A legislative act authorizing an administrative agency to promulgate rules and regulations having the force of law.

deliberate indifference standard   Doctrine under which public officials can be held liable for their failure to act to protect persons under their jurisdiction only when they manifest deliberate indifference to their welfare.

Department of Justice   The department of the executive branch of the federal government that is headed by the Attorney General and staffed by United States Attorneys.

deportation   The legal process by which an alien is expelled from a host country.

deposition   The recorded sworn testimony of a party or a witness; not given in open court.

digital divide   Term referring to the unequal access of members of society to computer skills and technology.

equality before the law The status of being treated equally and fairly according to established norms of justice.

equality of opportunity The norm under which members of society are afforded an equal chance to succeed.

equality of result The condition in which wealth is distributed equally among the members of a society.

equity The body of law originating in the English Court of Chancery that makes determinations based on principles of what is fair and just rather than following the narrow provisions of the common law.

evidentiary hearing A judicial or administrative proceeding in which evidence is presented.

evidentiary presumption Establishment of one fact allows inference of another fact or circumstance.

ex parte Refers to a proceeding in which only one party is involved or represented.

ex parte contacts "Off the record" communications between an interested party and a person who has the responsibility for decision making out of the presence of other parties to the proceeding.

ex post facto law A legislative act that retroactively criminalizes some action that was not a crime when committed.

exception (1) An exemption from a rule; (2) A formal objection to a judicial or administrative ruling, as in "taking exception."

exception for executing statutes and regulations An exception to governmental liability under the Federal Tort Claims Act under which a federal employee acting with due care in the execution of statutes and/or administrative regulations may not be held liable in a lawsuit seeking damages for a negligent tort.

executive agencies Institutions located within the executive branch of government responsible for implementing and enforcing laws passed by the legislature.

executive agreements Agreements between the United States and one or more foreign countries, entered into by the president without the necessity of ratification by the Senate.

executive departments The fifteen major departments of the executive branch of the federal government or their counterparts at the state level.

Executive Office of the President The set of agencies under the direct control and supervision of the president, including the Office of Management and Budget, the National Security Council, the Council of Economic Advisers, and the White House Staff.

executive order An order by a president or governor directing some particular action to be taken.

executive oversight Refers to the role of presidents, governors, and local chief executives in overseeing the activities of subordinate executive agencies.

executive power The power to enforce the law and administer the government.

executive privilege The right of the president or governor to withhold certain information from the legislature or a court of law.

exemptions from rulemaking procedures Situations to which legal requirements governing agency rulemaking do not apply.

exhaustion of administrative remedies The requirement that a party seeking review by a court first exhaust all legal options for resolution of the issue by nonjudicial authorities or lower courts.

fair hearing A hearing in a court of law or administrative agency that conforms to standards of procedural justice.

fair notice The requirement stemming from due process that government provide adequate notice to a person before it deprives that person of life, liberty, or property.

Fairness Doctrine A requirement developed by the Federal Communications Commission that required broadcasters to allow equal opportunities for expression of differing views on controversial issues or policies.

Family Educational Privacy Act Also known as the Buckley Amendment, this 1974 federal statute protects the confidentiality of student educational records.

Federal Bureau of Investigation (FBI)   Located within the U.S. Department of Justice, the FBI is the primary federal agency charged with investigating violations of federal criminal laws.

federal bureaucracy   The collective term for the myriad departments, agencies, and bureaus of the federal government.

federal income tax   The federal government's program for taxing the incomes of Americans, the principal means of financing the activities of the federal government.

Federal Labor Relations Authority (FLRA)   An independent agency responsible for administering labor-management relations programs for employees of the federal government.

federal law   The body of law that consists of the U.S. Constitution, statutes enacted by Congress, regulations of federal government agencies, and U.S. treaties. (In some contexts this includes the decisional law of the U.S. courts, sometimes known as the federal common law.)

federal magistrate judges   Judges appointed to preside over pretrial proceedings, try misdemeanor cases, and with consent of parties, handle civil trials in federal courts.

federal question jurisdiction   The authority of federal courts to decide issues of national law.

Federal Register   An official publication of the U.S. government containing all the regulations proposed and promulgated by federal agencies.

federal system   A political system in which there is a division of authority and responsibility between a central government and a set of regional governments.

Federal Tort Claims Act   Enacted by Congress in 1946, this statute waives sovereign immunity for torts committed by agents of the federal government acting within the scope of employment.

federalism   The constitutional distribution of government power and responsibility between the national government and the states.

Feres **doctrine**   Derived from *Feres v. United States* (1950), this doctrine immunizes the government from liability for injuries or death of servicepersons that arise out of or are in the course of activity incident to their military or naval service; however, retired military members or military dependents are allowed to sue for malpractice of military doctors.

Fifth Amendment   Provisions of the Bill of Rights providing for due process of law and prohibiting compulsory self-incrimination.

final rule   An administrative agency's determination stating the text and purpose of the rule.

finality   A legal doctrine that holds that a court will not review an administrative agency's action until the agency has completed its rulemaking or adjudication.

Finance Committee   A Congressional committee assigned the task of reviewing proposed federal laws and policies relating to the management of money.

findings of fact   Determinations by a judge or administrator as to evidence presented at a trial or hearing. For example, administrative law judges are required to make findings of fact in adjudicating disputes.

fines   Sums of money exacted from criminal defendants as punishment for wrongdoing.

First Amendment   Provisions of the Bill of Rights protecting the freedoms of religion, expression and assembly.

fiscal federalism   Characterization of the American federal system that emphasizes the dominant role of intergovernmental transfers of public moneys among the three levels of government.

fiscal policy   A government's taxing and spending policies.

fiscal year   A twelve-consecutive-month period in which a budget is implemented. A fiscal year usually varies from the calendar year.

forfeiture   Sacrifice of ownership or some right (usually property) as a penalty.

formal adjudication Official determination usually by an administrative tribunal using trial-type procedures, for example, allowing cross-examination of witnesses.

formal legislative action The final enactment of a law or resolution by following all established rules of a legislative body.

formal oversight Legislative supervision of administrative agency through formal means such as committee hearings.

formal rulemaking The making of rules by an administrative agency which, by statute, are required to be made "on the record" by following trial-type procedures; for example, allowing cross-examination of witnesses.

Fourteenth Amendment Amendment to the U.S. Constitution, ratified in 1868, prohibiting states from depriving persons in their jurisdiction of life, liberty or property without due process of law or denying them equal protection of the laws.

Fourth Amendment Amendment within the Bill of Rights prohibiting unreasonable searches and seizures.

Freedom of Information Act (FOIA) Federal statute providing citizens a broad right of access to government information.

freedom of religion The First Amendment right to free exercise of one's religion.

freedom One of the core values of democracy—the idea that citizens should be free from unwarranted governmental control.

full-blown evidentiary hearing A hearing in which evidence is presented that is conducted using trial-type procedures and practices.

fundamental error An error in a judicial proceeding that adversely affects the substantial rights of the accused or the jurisdiction of the court to hear and determine a matter.

fundamental rights Those rights, whether or not explicitly stated in the Constitution, deemed to be basic and essential to a person's liberty and dignity.

gag order An order by a judge prohibiting certain parties from speaking publicly or privately about a specific matter before the court.

garnishment Court action requiring a party (garnishee) who is indebted to a person to withhold payment and pay a sum over to a creditor (garnishor) who instituted garnishment proceedings.

gatekeeping devices Legal doctrines that are prerequisites to seeking relief in a court of law. See *ripeness, standing, exhaustion of remedies*.

globalization The rapidly increasing interdependence of the world's societies, markets, and governments.

good cause exemption In administrative rulemaking, notice of proposed rulemaking is excused when an agency finds that notice and public procedure concerning rulemaking is impracticable, unnecessary, or contrary to the public interest.

government contractor defense A defense that absolves a contractor from tort liability for design defects in military equipment when (1) the United States approved reasonably precise specifications; (2) the equipment conformed to those specifications; and (3) the supplier warned the United States about the dangers in the use of the equipment that were known to the supplier but not to the United States.

grand jury A group of twelve to twenty-three citizens convened to investigate a public issue or to hear evidence in criminal cases to determine whether indictment is warranted.

grandfathered in Allowed to continue. Example: If a land use zoning ordinance changes the classification of zoning, an existing use that is permitted to continue is said to be "grandfathered in."

grantee One to whom a grant is made. Usually refers to a person or entity that acquires title to real estate.

granting cert The exercise of judicial discretion to accept for review a decision of a lower court. Commonly refers to the U.S. Supreme Court's agreement to hear a case.

grantor One who makes a grant. Usually refers to a person or entity that deeds property to another person or entity.

grants-in-aid   Federal moneys that are provided to state and/or local governments for particular projects, usually following an application and review process.

habeas corpus   "You have the body." See *habeas corpus, writ of.*

habeas corpus, writ of   A judicial order issued to an official holding someone in custody, requiring the official to bring the person being detained to court for the purpose of allowing the court to determine whether that person is being held legally.

harmless error   A procedural or substantive error that does not affect the outcome of a judicial proceeding.

Hatch Act   A federal law that prohibits federal employees from taking active part in political campaigns.

hazardous waste regulations Government regulations affecting the shipment, storage, and disposal of toxic and radioactive waste products.

hearing   A public proceeding in a court of law, legislature, or administrative body for the purpose of ascertaining facts and deciding matters of law or policy.

hearing officer   An official who presides at an administrative hearing. See *Administrative Law Judge.*

hearsay evidence   An out-of-court statement made by someone other than a witness that is offered in evidence at a trial or hearing to prove the truth of the matter asserted.

hierarchy   A group of officials organized by rank where each rank is subordinate to the one above it.

Home rule   Refers to a municipal charter or state constitutional provision that empowers a city to make governmental decisions without the concurrence of the state legislature.

hybrid rulemaking   A rulemaking procedure that is more elaborate than informal notice-and-comment rulemaking, but less elaborate than formal, adjudicatory-type rulemaking.

hyperpluralism   A condition in which the prevalence of group demands makes it impossible for government to plan, deal with long-term problems, and make policies that further the public interest.

immunity   Exemption from civil suit or prosecution.

impartial decision maker   An unbiased, neutral person charged with determining the facts and applying the law.

impeachment   (1) A legislative act bringing a charge against a public official that, if proven in a legislative trial, will cause his or her removal from public office; (2) impugning the credibility of a witness by introducing contradictory evidence or proving his or her bad character.

implementation   The stage of the policy-making process when an adopted policy is carried out.

implied powers   Governmental powers not stated in but implied by a constitution or statute as being necessary to carry out enumerated powers.

implied powers, doctrine of   A basic doctrine of American constitutional law derived from the Necessary and Proper Clause. Article I, Section 8 of the U.S. Constitution provides that Congress is not limited to exercising those powers specifically enumerated in Article I but rather may exercise powers reasonably related to the fulfillment of its broad constitutional powers and responsibilities.

impoundment   The refusal of the president to allow expenditure of funds appropriated by Congress.

improper disclosure of personal information   Revealing a person's private information without that person's consent and when not required by law.

impute   To attribute to; for example, to ascribe that a person receives a certain income based on his or her activities; to impute that a party has received notice because of the method notice was furnished.

in camera   "In a chamber." In private. Refers to a judicial proceeding or conference from which the public is excluded.

in camera inspection   A private review of evidence, usually a document, by a judge with the public excluded.

in re   "In the matter of."

in rem   "In the thing." Refers to legal actions brought against things rather than persons.

independent agencies Government agencies that are part of the bureaucratic structure but do not serve at the pleasure of the president. Examples include the Federal Labor Relations Authority and the Federal Reserve Board.

independent counsel A special prosecutor appointed to investigate and, if warranted, prosecute official misconduct.

independent regulatory commission A governmental body located outside one of the major executive departments, the function of which is to promulgate and enforce regulations in a particular field, and which is led by a group of commissioners appointed by the chief executive.

indictment A formal criminal charge handed down by a grand jury.

indirect evidence Inferences and presumptions (and not on personal knowledge) that tend to establish a fact or issue.

individual rights Legal rights of a person.

individualism The ideal of self-reliance and self-determination, especially as it applies to economic and social activities.

individualized harm An injury, loss, or impairment that directly affects a person.

inferior officers Officers that are subordinate to other officers. Article II, Section 2 of the U.S. Constitution provides Congress "may by Law vest the Appointment of such inferior Officers, as they think proper, in the President alone, in the Courts of Law, or in the Heads of Departments."

inflation A decline in the purchasing power of money.

informal adjudication A form of administrative adjudication that observes only minimal procedural requirements.

informal (notice-and-comment) rulemaking A rulemaking procedure where the agency is required to furnish interested persons an opportunity to participate through submission of written data, views, or arguments with or without opportunity for oral presentation.

informal oversight Refers to the day-to-day activities in which elected officials monitor and communicate with agencies.

inherent power The power existing in an agency, institution, or individual by definition of the office.

initial brief Appellant's brief filed in support of issues raised in appellate court.

initial decision A recommended decision in agency adjudication.

initial pleading Petition or complaint filed to initiate a proceeding in a judicial tribunal.

initiative and referendum A process by which a state constitution or local charter may be amended by direct popular action. "Initiative" refers to the act of petitioning the state or local government to put an issue before the voters in a "referendum."

injunction A court order prohibiting someone from doing some specified act or commanding someone to undo some wrong or injury.

injury in fact An actual invasion or abridgment of a person's legal rights.

insider information Information concerning financial matters and prospective actions of a corporation available only to persons within the corporation.

insider trading Transactions in securities by a person who operates "inside" a corporation and by using material nonpublic information trades to his or her advantage without first disclosing that information to the public.

institution An established pattern of behavior that transcends and outlives the individuals who occupy it.

institutional agenda The set of issues that are being actively considered by some governmental authority.

intelligence Information about activities in other countries that is used in making foreign policy decisions.

intentional acts Acts committed purposely.

intentional tort exception A limitation under the Federal Tort Claims Act that prevents a claimant from recovering damages for acts intentionally caused by federal employees.

inter alia "Among other things."

interest groups Private organizations formed to advance the shared interest of their members.

interim rule A rule adopted by an administrative agency without prior public input but which allows postpromulgation comments directed toward the issue of whether the rule should be be withdrawn or revised.

intermediate appellate courts Judicial tribunals consisting of three or more judges that review decisions of trial courts but which are subordinate to the final appellate tribunals.

international law A set of legal principles, derived primarily from treaties, governing legal relationships among nations.

international tribunals Courts established under International Law.

interpretive rules Administrative rules that interpret or clarify an agency's position as to its duties or responsibilities based on a controlling statute or a previously promulgated legislative rule.

intervention Process whereby a third party participates in administrative or judicial proceedings.

inverse condemnation Action by government that results in a taking of private property for public use without the exercise of the power of eminent domain. A private property owner may seek compensation for such governmental action by filing a suit alleging inverse condemnation. In some instances an extreme regulatory action by government will constitute inverse condemnation.

iron triangle A three-way symbiotic relationship involving a legislative committee, an executive agency, and an interest group.

issue network A small group of political actors involved in a particular policy area.

issue preclusion See *collateral estoppel*.

item veto The power of the chief executive to veto one or more parts of a bill without rejecting the bill in its entirety.

Jencks **Act** The common name for a federal statute that permits a defendant to review a witness' prior written or recorded statement after the witness has testified on direct examination.

judicial oversight A court's authority to oversee the exercise of specific governmental activities.

judicial review Generally, the review of any issue by a court of law. In American constitutional law, judicial review refers to the authority of a court to invalidate acts of government on constitutional grounds.

jurisdiction "To speak the law." The geographical area within which, the subject matter with respect to which, and the persons over whom a court or agency can properly exercise its power.

just compensation The constitutional requirement that a party whose property is taken by government under the power of eminent domain be justly compensated for the loss.

justiciability The quality of appropriateness for judicial decision. A justiciable dispute is one that can be effectively decided by a court of law.

laches An unreasonable delay in asserting one's legal rights.

laissez-faire The theory holding that a capitalist economy functions best when government refrains from interfering with the marketplace.

land use planning Developing criteria for present and future uses of lands. Land use zoning is a principal tool in land use planning.

land use zoning See *zoning*.

legislative contempt Actions or conduct evincing disrespect before a legislative committee that is conducting authorized proceedings.

legislative intent An indication perceived of the plan or purpose of a legislative body, often considering the problem legislature addressed or gleaned from debates preceding enactment of the statute.

legislative investigation A systematic inquiry by a legislative committee into a matter of concern to the legislature.

legislative oversight The monitoring of an administrative agency by the legislature through formal and informal means.

legislative rules (1) Standards adopted by legislative bodies for transaction of business relating to introduction of bills, debate, voting, and other practices prescribed by the body; (2) Substantive or procedural rules adopted by administrative agencies and having the force of law.

legislative supremacy A characteristic of parliamentary systems of government in which other agencies of government are subordinate to the legislature.

legislative veto A statutory provision under which a legislative body is permitted to overrule a decision of an executive agency.

legislators Members of a legislature.

legislature An elected lawmaking body such as the Congress of the United States or a state assembly.

liberty The absence of restraint.

licensee A party who holds a license.

licenses Permits to act for specified purposes.

lien A claim of a right or interest in or charge against another's property.

limited government A government that is limited to certain powers and responsibilities and is prohibited from transgressing the rights of citizens.

line-item veto See *item veto*.

Lloyd-La Follette Act A federal statute that provides federal civil service employees are to be removed only for cause stated in writing and allowing employees an opportunity to answer the grounds stated for removal.

lobbying Any effort by an individual or group to contact public officials for the purpose of influencing their policy decisions.

lobbyists Professionals whose job it is to contact public officials for the purpose of influencing their policy decisions.

Magna Carta The "Great Charter" of 1215 in which King John guaranteed the rights of English subjects.

malfeasance Misconduct that adversely affects the performance of official duties.

managed care Medical services generally furnished through a health maintenance organization (HMO).

mandamus, writ of A court order commanding a public official or an organization to perform a specified nondiscretionary duty.

mandatory injunction A court order requiring the doing of a specified act.

mandatory retirement Required termination of employment when an employee attains a certain age or completes a certain number of years of service.

mark-up session A legislative committee meeting when a vote is taken to accept or reject changes proposed by committee members to a bill.

material Important, relevant, necessary.

matter committed to agency discretion Administrative action that by law is committed to agency discretion is not subject to judicial review.

mediation An informal, nonadversarial process whereby a neutral third person facilitates resolution of a dispute between parties by exploring issues and settlement alternatives.

Medicaid A joint program between the states and the federal government whereby the national government provides matching funding, but the states decide which indigent persons are eligible for medical care.

Medicare A federal program approved in 1965 that provided for a payroll tax to be split between employers and employees to fund medical care for the elderly and disabled.

Merit Systems Protection Board Established by the Civil Service Reform Act of 1978, this independent agency is responsible for ensuring that federal agencies follow merit principles in recruiting, hiring, promoting, and dismissing employees.

meritocracy A hiring system in which officials are recruited, selected, and retained on the basis of demonstrable merit.

misfeasance The improper performance of a lawful act.

Model State Administrative Procedure Act Published in 1981 by the National Conference of Commissioners on Uniform State Laws, this model statute has served as a template for states in enacting their own counterparts to the federal Administrative Procedure Act.

modern administrative state Refers to the highly bureaucratized federal government that emerged in the twentieth century.

monetary policy Government policy aimed at controlling the supply of money and controlling interest rates.

money laundering The offense of disguising illegal income to make it appear legitimate.

monopolies Commercial entities that exercise exclusive control over the pricing and distribution of goods; certain monopolies are illegal under federal or state antitrust laws.

mootness Refers to a question that does not involve rights currently at issue in, or pertinent to, the outcome of a case.

motion An application to a court to obtain a particular ruling or order.

motion for continuance A formal request to a court to postpone a hearing or trial.

motion for rehearing A formal request made to a court of law to convene another hearing in a case in which the court has already ruled.

motion to dismiss (1) A formal request to a court to dismiss a plaintiff's complaint, often on the ground the complaint fails to state a legal basis for relief sought by the plaintiff; (2) A formal request to a trial court to dismiss the criminal charges against the defendant.

motions Formal applications to courts to obtain an order or grant some relief to the movant.

motive A person's conscious reason for acting.

municipal charter An act of a state legislature authorizing the creation of a city government.

national security state Term coined during the Cold War to characterize the national government's emphasis on defense and security issues.

Necessary and Proper Clause The final paragraph of Article I, Section 8 of the Constitution that allows Congress to make laws that are necessary and proper to further its enumerated powers.

negotiated grievance procedures Internal systems to resolve disputes between an employee and a government agency without the need for external intervention.

negotiated rulemaking Known as "regneg," an informal process designed to facilitate agreement to a proposed agency regulation. An agency may, but is not required to, adopt the text arrived at by consensus as a proposed rule.

negotiation (1) As respects commercial paper: a transfer in a manner that the transferee becomes a holder in due course; (2) Method of settling a dispute between parties without a formal trial.

neoadministrative state Term coined by political scientist Robert Durant to refer to a paradigm shift in which authority is diffused "from the public sphere to the market and civic spheres of the nation."

New Deal Policy initiatives of President Franklin D. Roosevelt consisting of unprecedented efforts by the federal government to regulate and manage the economy.

nonfeasance Failure to perform a duty.

notice-and-comment rulemaking An informal rulemaking procedure where an administrative agency furnishes interested persons an opportunity to submit written data, views, or arguments with or without opportunity for oral presentation.

notice and hearing Legal notification given to persons whose interests may be affected by an agency or court session.

notice of appeal Document filed notifying an appellate court of an appeal from a judgment of a lower court. The notice of appeal invokes the court's jurisdiction to hear a case.

notice of proposed rulemaking (NPRM) Formal public announcement of an agency's intention to promulgate a rule.

notice requirement Legal notification essential to be given to interested parties before administrative or judicial action takes place.

nuisance An unlawful or unreasonable use of a person's property that results in an injury to another or to the public.

off the record Refers to communication between an interested party and a person who has the responsibility for decision making out of the presence of other parties to the proceeding.

offer   Statement or conduct by a person constituting a proposal to enter a contract.

offeree   One to whom an offer has been made.

offeror   One who makes an offer.

Office of Information and Regulatory Affairs (OIRA)   An agency within the Executive Office of the President responsible to meet annual paperwork reduction goals, review every federal agency's information management activities, and improve federal information management.

Office of Management and Budget (OMB)   An agency within the Executive Office of the President whose primary mission is to develop the budget proposal the president submits to Congress each fiscal year.

Office of Personnel Management (OPM)   An independent federal agency that administers civil service laws and conducts civil service exams.

Office of Special Counsel   An independent agency within the executive branch established to protect federal employees and job applicants from prohibited personnel practices, including retaliation for whistleblowing.

Officers of the United States   Article II, Section 2 of the Constitution (Appointments Clause) provides that the president "by and with the Advice and Consent of the Senate, shall appoint Ambassadors, other public Ministers and Consuls, Judges of the supreme Court, and all other Officers of the United States, whose Appointments are not herein otherwise provided for . . ."

official notice   Legal notification by an agency or court in compliance with law or regulation.

ombudsman   An official who investigates and tries to resolve problems that people have with public agencies.

open meetings   Meetings of government agencies that are by law required to be open to the general public.

open records laws   Federal and state statutes that permit individuals access to public records of government agencies.

opening statement   A lawyer's initial statement to the judge or jury in a trial or hearing.

openness   State of being accessible to the public.

opinion   A written statement accompanying a judicial decision, authored by one or more judges, supporting or dissenting from that decision.

opinion of the court   The opinion expressing the views of the majority of judges participating in a judicial decision.

opportunity to present evidence   A right of due process that enables one to appear and present evidence to a court or administrative agency.

oral argument   Verbal presentation made to an appellate court in an attempt to persuade the court to affirm, reverse, or modify a lower court decision.

order   A direction or command, usually in writing, from a court or government agency.

ordinance   A law enacted by a local governing body such as a city council or county commission.

original jurisdiction   The authority of a court of law to hear a case for the first time, usually for the purpose of conducting a trial or holding a hearing.

original writs   Orders issued by a court in an original, as opposed to an appellate, proceeding. Original writs include mandamus, prohibition, *quo warranto,* and habeas corpus.

out-of-court settlements   Compromises arrived at between parties that result in dismissal of cases before formal trials occur.

oversight   Refers to the responsibility of a legislative body to monitor the activities of government agencies it created.

oversight briefings   Meeting in which agency officials provide pertinent information to legislators or other officials that have supervising authority.

oversight hearings   Formal hearings conducted for the purpose of monitoring actions by government agencies.

Paperwork Reduction Act (PRA)   An Act enacted by Congress in 1980 and since amended that is designed to reduce the information collection burdens the bureaucracy has imposed on the public.

participation   The act of being involved in; for example, as a citizen participating in the political process through voting.

parties   Persons involved in court actions or administrative proceedings; persons who enter contracts.

patents, copyrights, and trademarks   Species of intangible property rights, often referred to today as intellectual property.

pendency of the appeal   The period after an appeal is filed but before the appeal is adjudicated.

Pendleton Act   See *Civil Service Reform Act of 1883.*

per curiam opinion   An opinion rendered "by the court" as distinct from one attributed to one or more judges.

pervasively regulated businesses   Businesses and industries that are closely regulated by federal or state law; for example, those that dispense alcoholic beverages.

petitioner   A person who brings a petition before a court of law.

places of public accommodation   Businesses that open their doors to the general public.

plain meaning of statutory language   A rule of statutory construction that holds that when the language of a statute is plain its meaning must be determined from its language without aid of any extrinsic evidence.

plaintiff   The party initiating legal action; the complaining party.

pluralism   A social or political system in which diverse groups compete for status or power; the theory that the role of government is to serve as broker among competing interest groups.

police power   The power of government to legislate to protect public health, safety, welfare, and morality.

policy-making process   The governmental process by which public policy is produced. Key steps in the process include agenda setting, formulation of alternatives, adoption, implementation, and evaluation.

postagency action hearing   An evidentiary hearing held by an administrative agency after it has first taken action affecting a person's liberty or property interests.

postsuspension hearing   An evidentiary hearing held by an administrative agency after it has suspended a person's license. Commonly associated with suspension of a driver's license when a predetermination hearing has not been held.

power of contempt   The authority of a court of law to punish someone who insults the court or flouts its authority. See also *civil contempt, legislative contempt.*

power to control litigation   The Department of Justice (DOJ) headed by the attorney general controls federal litigation. The solicitor general represents the United States before the Supreme Court. The president appoints these officials to implement the president's constitutional mandate to "take Care that the Laws be faithfully executed."

power to investigate   Refers to the power of a legislative body to conduct hearings and subpoena witnesses in order to investigate an issue or area over which it has legislative authority.

power to regulate interstate commerce   Refers to the power of Congress, and to a lesser extent, the powers of state and local governments, to enact laws and regulations affecting commerce involving more than one state.

powers of appointment and removal   Vested typically in chief executives, this is the legal authority to designate and to remove a person from office.

precedent   A prior decision cited as authority controlling or influencing the outcome of a similar case.

preclearance of proposed rules   A key element of the president's oversight of federal agency rulemaking in which proposed rules are submitted to the Office of Management of Budget (OMB) for approval prior to the initiation of the rulemaking process.

predetermination hearing   An administrative agency hearing held prior to taking action that adversely affects a person's liberty or property interest.

preemption In constitutional law, the doctrine under which a field of public policy is brought by the U.S. Congress within the primary or exclusive control of the national government, thereby superseding inconsistent state or local laws or regulations.

prehearing conference A conference held prior to formal adjudication proceedings to determine issues to be tried, ascertain undisputed facts, and discuss prospects of settlement between an agency and parties involved.

prehearing processes Practices that occur prior to formal adjudication proceedings, for example, motions for consolidation of cases and other forms of relief; discovery proceedings; requests for compulsory process to obtain witnesses; requests for production of documents.

preliminary injunction An injunction issued pending a trial on the merits of the case.

preponderance of evidence Evidence that has greater weight than countervailing evidence.

preservation of error rule Requirement that a party make an objection to some administrative or judicial ruling order as a prerequisite to challenging such order or ruling in an appellate court.

presidential immunity The barrier against bringing a civil suit against the president for any of his official actions.

presumption (1) An inference drawn by reasoning; (2) A rule of law subject to rebuttal.

presumption of constitutionality The doctrine of constitutional law holding that laws are presumed to be constitutional with the burden of proof resting on the plaintiff to demonstrate otherwise.

presumption of correctness A legal assumption that action taken by a trial court or administrative agency is clothed with an inference of being correct.

pretermination hearing Hearing held by administrative agency before terminating a tenured employee.

prima facie At first glance; on the face of it. Referring to a point that will be considered true if uncontested or unrefuted.

primary jurisdiction doctrine Where a matter presented to a court in an independent lawsuit falls within the jurisdiction of an administrative agency, the court, as a matter of comity, should defer ruling on the issue until the agency has had an opportunity to resolve it.

Privacy Act Refers to Federal Privacy Act of 1974, which limits personal information in files of federal agencies; prohibits secret personnel records; and affords employees right to challenge accuracy of such information.

private legislative act A law enacted to compensate a person who has suffered a wrong at the hands of the government.

private property Property held by individuals or corporations, not by the public generally.

privilege In general, an activity in which a person may engage without interference. The term is often used interchangeably with "right" in American constitutional law, with reference to the Privileges and Immunities Clauses of Article IV and the Fourteenth Amendment of the U.S. Constitution.

privilege against self-incrimination A person's right under the Fifth Amendment to the U.S. Constitution not to be compelled to testify or otherwise incriminate himself or herself.

privileged communications Confidential communications that persons are not required to disclose in court proceedings.

privileges Rights extended to persons by virtue of law.

pro bono "For the good." Performing service without compensation.

pro forma Merely for the sake of form.

probable cause Knowledge of specific facts providing reasonable grounds for believing that unlawful activity is afoot.

procedural due process Set of procedures designed to ensure fairness in a judicial or administrative proceeding.

procedural legitimacy Popular acceptance of an institution based on the perception that it operates by valid procedures.

procedural regularity Processes and practices of a court or administrative agency that are conducted according to established norms that comport with due process of law.

procedural rules Rules that govern the practices and procedures of a court or administrative agency.

professional judgment standard The criterion for measuring conduct of a person in a learned profession or occupation that requires extensive training.

Progressive Era Movement during the early 1900s aimed at reforming government by eliminating fraud, corruption, and inefficiency.

prohibited personnel practices Refers to a lengthy itemization of practices prohibited by federal law for federal employees, for example, discrimination, deception, granting unlawful preferences, acts of nepotism, failure to take certain required actions, etc.

Prohibition Refers to the period between 1919 and 1933 in which the federal government banned the importation, production, and sale of alcoholic beverages.

prohibition, writ of A judicial order issued by a superior court directing a lower tribunal to cease acting in excess of its lawful jurisdiction.

property rights Refers to the bundle of rights that exist relative to private ownership and control of property.

protective order A court order protecting a person from whom discovery is sought prior to trial or agency hearing from annoyance, oppression, or undue expense in complying with demands of a party seeking discovery.

proximate cause The cause that directly produces an event or result; usually refers to the act nearest a given effect in a causal relationship. Sometimes referred to as the legal cause of injury or damage.

public defender A public official responsible for defending indigent persons charged with crimes.

public figures Persons who are in the public eye; persons who have achieved fame. If a public figure brings a lawsuit alleging defamation, the plaintiff (public figure) must prove that the defendant acted with actual malice in actions against the plaintiff.

public law General classification of law consisting of constitutional law, administrative law, international law, and criminal law.

public officials Persons who hold public office by virtue of election or appointment.

public policy Whatever government attempts to do about an issue or problem; principles that legislative bodies (and sometimes courts and agencies) determine to be of basic concern to society.

publicly traded corporations Corporations whose securities are traded in the public markets; for example, on a national stock exchange.

puffing Exaggerated, but not fraudulent, claims by a seller or sales person.

punitive damages A sum of money awarded to the plaintiff in a civil case as a means of punishing the defendant for wrongful conduct.

qua As; in the character or capacity of.

qualified immunity Immunity from liability that protects public officials for their actions unless they violate "clearly established statutory or constitutional rights of which a reasonable person would have known."

quash To vacate or annul.

quasi-judicial act (1) An adjudicative act performed by executive or administrative officials; (2) An act performed by a judge who is not acting in a judicial capacity.

quasi-judicial bodies Public boards of administrative officers who make factual determinations as a basis for their rulings.

quasi-judicial power Refers to the authority of certain regulatory or administrative agencies to make determinations with respect to the rights of private parties under their jurisdiction.

quasi-legislative Refers to agency actions such as rulemaking, which are neither wholly legislative nor wholly administrative in nature.

quasi-legislative power Generally refers to an administrative agency's authority to engage in rulemaking.

qui tam **action** Civil suit brought by a private party on behalf of the government against a party that has allegedly defrauded the government.

rational basis test The test of the validity of a statute inquiring whether it is rationally related to a legitimate government objective.

rationality (1) The quality of being reasonable; (2) The ability to make decisions based on logic and evidence, rather than emotion; (3) The ability to choose a course of action that is most likely to result in a desired outcome.

real evidence Refers to such maps, photographs, and other tangible items introduced into evidence.

real property Land and buildings permanently attached thereto.

reapportionment The redrawing of legislative district lines to make boundaries conform to population changes and thereby remedy any existing malapportionment.

reasonable accommodation Requirement under the Americans with Disabilities Act that employers take reasonable steps to accommodate employees with disabilities. Also refers to a First Amendment requirement that public employers generally attempt to accommodate reasonable demands by employees who desire to follow certain religious traditions.

reasonable expectation of privacy A person's reasonable expectation that his or her activities in a certain place are private; society's expectations with regard to whether activities in certain places are private.

recommended decision An initial decision issued by an Administrative Law Judge (ALJ) or an administrative hearing officer issued in formal agency adjudication.

recusal A decision of a judge to withdraw from a case, usually due to bias or personal interest in the controversy.

regulation A legally binding rule or order prescribed by a controlling authority. The term is generally used with respect to the rules promulgated by administrative and regulatory agencies.

regulatory agencies Governmental offices that are empowered by statutes to promulgate and enforce regulations within particular substantive areas.

regulatory capture A situation in which a regulatory agency is controlled by those interests it is supposed to regulate.

Regulatory Flexibility Act (RFA) An act enacted by Congress in 1980 to minimize the effects of agency regulations on small businesses and not-for-profit organizations. Requires federal agencies to file initial and final regulatory flexibility analyses to accompany notices of proposed rules and final rules where regulations have a significant impact on small businesses.

regulatory flexibility analysis An analysis made pursuant to the Regulatory Flexibility Act that seeks to minimize the economic effects of regulations on small businesses and assist them in compliance and reporting requirements.

regulatory policy Any policy that places restrictions on certain kinds of activities by individuals or corporations.

regulatory state Term used to describe the increasing role of government in the economic affairs of American citizens that has occurred since the Industrial Revolution.

regulatory taking Governmental regulations that result in a substantial diminishment in the value of an owner's property.

rehabilitation Restoring someone or something to its former status; a justification for punishment emphasizing reform rather than retribution.

Rehabilitation Act A federal law enacted in 1973 that prohibits discrimination against qualified individuals with disabilities who work in the federal government.

remand To send back, as from a higher court to a lower court, for the latter to take specified action in a case or to follow instructions or conduct proceedings designated by the higher court.

removal power The power of the president to remove officials in executive departments and agencies.

removal-for-cause Discharge of a public employee supported by a legitimate reason.

reply brief A brief submitted in response to an appellee's answer brief.

reporters Books containing judicial decisions and accompanying opinions.

representative government   A political system in which most policy decisions emanate from legislatures that represent the people, even if indirectly.

representative institutions   Governmental institutions whose members are chosen so as to reflect the interests of their constituencies.

republican form of government   A political system in which power is exercised by representative institutions that are limited by the rule of law.

res judicata   "A thing decided." A matter decided by a judgment, connoting the firmness and finality of the judgment as it affects the parties to the lawsuit. *Res judicata* has the general effect of bringing litigation on a contested point to an end.

res nova   "New thing." A new issue or case.

residential preferences   Policies affording residents of states or communities preferential treatment in public employment, admission to educational programs, or access to other governmental benefits.

resolution   A legislative act expressing the will of one or both houses of a legislature. Unlike a statute, a resolution has no enforcement clause.

respondeat superior   "Let the superior answer." The doctrine under which a principal may be held liable for the actions of an agent who acts in the scope of employment.

respondent   A person asked to respond to a lawsuit or writ.

restitution   The act of compensating someone for losses suffered.

restraining orders   Court orders prohibiting named persons from taking specified actions.

reverse   A higher court's decision to overturn the decision of a lower court.

reverse   To set aside a decision on appeal.

RICO Act   The Racketeer Influenced Corrupt Organizations Act, a key element of federal law addressing the problem of organized crime.

right   Anything to which a person has a just and valid claim.

right of confrontation   The right guaranteed by the Sixth Amendment to directly confront and to cross-examine witnesses for the opposing party in a criminal case.

right of cross-examination   A litigant's right to question a witness who has testified on behalf of the opposing party. Cross-examiners are typically allowed to pose leading questions to a witness related to matters testified by the witness on direct examination and to matters that might affect the witness's credibility.

right of privacy   Constitutional right to engage in intimate personal conduct or make fundamental life decisions without interference by the state.

right to appeal   Statutory right to appeal decisions of lower courts in certain circumstances.

right to counsel   (1) The right to retain an attorney to represent oneself in a legal proceeding; (2) the right of an indigent person to have counsel appointed to represent him or her in a criminal prosecution.

right to strike   The ability of employees to legally participate in an organized cessation of work with the objective of forcing an employer to meet wage and working condition demands.

right-to-sue letter   An Equal Employment Opportunity Commission (EEOC) document stating that an employee who has filed a complaint alleging unlawful discrimination has grounds to file a lawsuit.

right-to-work laws   State laws that prevent labor agreements from requiring all workers to join a union.

ripeness   Readiness for review by a court of law. An issue is "ripe for review" in the Supreme Court when a case presents adverse parties who have exhausted all other avenues of appeal.

rule of four   U.S. Supreme Court rule whereby the Court grants certiorari only on the agreement of at least four justices.

rule of law   The idea that law, not the discretion of officials, should govern public affairs. In popular usage, refers to the supremacy of law and the principle that all persons are equally subject to the law.

rulemaking The power of a court *or administrative agency* to promulgate rules; the process through which such rules are promulgated.

rulemaking authority Power of federal and state regulatory agencies to promulgate rules of general applicability over matters within the agency's jurisdiction.

rulemaking record A documentation of agency rulemaking proceedings, generally sought to support judicial review of agency action.

rules (1) Norms or principles established for conduct of administrative and judicial proceedings, for example, Federal Rules of Civil Procedure describe the required practices for litigating in federal courts; (2) Regulations promulgated by administrative agencies.

rules of evidence Rules that govern the introduction of evidence in courts. In administrative proceedings the rules of evidence are relaxed to allow relevant evidence; for example, hearsay that is excluded in judicial proceedings.

rules of practice Rules regulating the practice of law before courts and administrative agencies.

rules of procedure Rules promulgated by courts governing civil, criminal, and appellate procedure.

rules-based decision making Decision making according to objective rules rather than subjective motives, interests, or judgments.

sanction Penalty or other mechanism of enforcement.

scope of employment Activities that an employee is authorized to perform or that it is foreseeable an employee will engage in while carrying out the work of an employer. In military parlance, the term "line of duty" is generally synonymous with the term "scope of employment."

search and seizure Refers to the search for and/or seizure of contraband or other evidence of crimes or violations of regulations.

search warrant A court order authorizing a search of a specified area for a specified purpose.

Section 1983 action A federal lawsuit brought under 42 U.S. Code § 1983 to redress violations of civil and/or constitutional rights.

seditious speech Expression aimed at inciting insurrection or overthrow of the government.

seizure Action of police in taking possession or control of property or persons. See *administrative searches; administrative search warrants.*

selective incorporation Doctrine under which selected provisions comprising most of the Bill of Rights to the U.S. Constitution are deemed applicable to the states by way of the Fourteenth Amendment.

self-incrimination See *compulsory self-incrimination.*

separation of powers Constitutional assignment of legislative, executive, and judicial powers to different branches of government.

session laws (1) Laws enacted at a given session of a legislature; (2) A collection of the same.

set aside An affirmative action policy reserving a certain proportion of government contracts for minority business enterprises.

Seventh Amendment Provision of the Bill of Rights guaranteeing the right to a jury trial in civil suits at common law.

severability The doctrine under which courts will invalidate only the offending provision of a statute and allow the other provisions to remain in effect.

severability clause A clause that legislative bodies frequently include in a statute indicating that if any particular provision of the law is invalidated, the other provisions are to remain in effect.

sexual harassment Offensive interaction of a sexual nature in the workplace.

shadow government Term used to describe the numerous consultants, contractors, and grantees that government has come to rely upon for the delivery of services.

Sherman Antitrust Act of 1890 A federal statute prohibiting any contract, combination, or conspiracy in restraint of trade. The act is designed to protect and preserve a system of free and open competition. Its scope is broad and reaches individuals and entities in profit and nonprofit activities as well as local governments and educational institutions.

show cause   A court order requiring a party to appear and present a legal justification for a particular act or for failure to do a required act.

sine qua non   "Without which not." A necessary or indispensable condition or prerequisite.

Social Security   A federal program instituted by Congress in 1935 under which employers withhold a portion of their employees' wages, match these amounts, and transfer these sums to the government. Self-employed individuals also pay into the system. From these funds the government pays benefits to disabled persons, retirees, surviving spouses, and dependents.

social welfare legislation   Laws creating programs designed to promote the social welfare; for example, Social Security, Medicare, Medicaid, and Food Stamps.

sovereign immunity   A common law doctrine under which the sovereign may be sued only with its consent.

sovereign states   Refers to the idea that each of the states comprising the United States of America is a sovereign entity, i.e., it cannot be abolished by the national government and has the inherent right to establish and conduct its own government within federal constitutional parameters.

sovereignty   The right to rule; the legitimate authority of government.

special counsel, office of   An independent agency within the executive branch established to protect federal employees and job applicants from prohibited personnel practices, including retaliation for whistleblowing.

special exception   The grant by a zoning board of adjustment to allow a certain use in a zoning district under specified conditions.

special prosecutor   Also known as an "independent counsel," a prosecutor appointed specifically to investigate a particular episode and, if criminal activity is found, to prosecute those involved.

specific performance   A court-imposed requirement that a party perform obligations incurred under a contract.

Speech or Debate Clause   Provision of Article I, Section 6, of the U.S. Constitution protecting members of Congress from arrest or interference with their official duties.

spending power   The power of the legislature to spend public money for public purposes.

spoils system   A political term based on the old adage that "to the victor go the spoils." In practice, the award of contracts and jobs to supporters of a winning candidate.

spousal privilege   The right of a husband or wife not to be forced to give testimony against the other spouse in respect to confidential marital communications and to prevent one's spouse from giving such testimony.

stakeholders   Parties that stand to win or lose as a result of a policy decision.

standing   The right to initiate a legal action or challenge based on the fact that one has suffered or is likely to suffer a real and substantial injury.

stare decisis   "To stand by decided matters." The principle that past decisions should stand as precedents for future decisions. This principle, which stands for the proposition that precedents are binding on later decisions, is said to be followed less rigorously in constitutional law than in other branches of the law.

state constitution   The written charter upon which each of the fifty state governments is based.

state supreme court   The highest state court; however, in New York the supreme court refers to a court with trial and appellate divisions, and the highest state court is the Court of Appeals.

state's attorney   A state prosecutor.

statute   A generally applicable law enacted by a legislature.

statute of limitations   A law barring the commencement of a lawsuit or criminal prosecution.

statutory ambiguity   The condition in which a legislative provision contains terms of unclear or uncertain meaning.

statutory clarity   The condition in which a legislative provision contains terms of clear or obvious meaning.

statutory construction   The official interpretation of a statute rendered by an agency or court of law.

statutory directives   Legislative provisions directing public officials to perform certain acts.

statutory interpretation   See *statutory construction*.

statutory preclusion of judicial review Because the jurisdiction of the lower federal courts is dependent on federal legislation, Congress can enact a legislative act to preclude judicial review of certain agency actions altogether or under certain circumstances.

statutory waivers of sovereign immunity Acts of Congress and the state legislatures allowing plaintiffs to sue the federal and state governments, respectively, for damages.

stay   To postpone, hold off, or stop the execution of a judgment; to require that certain judicial or administrative actions not be taken pending further ruling.

stay of execution   An order suspending the enforcement of a judgment of a court. In criminal law, the postponement of a sentence to death.

strict scrutiny   The most demanding level of judicial review in cases involving alleged infringements of civil rights or liberties.

strike   A collective decision by workers to refuse to work in order to dramatize a grievance or force their employers to make some concession, usually as to wages, benefits, or working conditions.

subject matter jurisdiction   Courts' authority over certain subjects, e.g., bankruptcy, torts, criminal offenses.

subpoena   "Under penalty." A judicial order requiring a person to appear in court or before an administrative agency or legislative committee in connection with a designated proceeding.

subpoena *duces tecum*   "Under penalty you shall bring with you." A judicial order requiring a party to bring certain described records, papers, books, or documents to a court or agency.

substantial evidence   Information that reasonable minds accept as sufficient to support a rational conclusion.

substantial federal question   A significant legal question pertaining to the U.S. Constitution, a federal statute, treaty, regulation, or judicial interpretation of any of the foregoing.

substantive due process   Doctrine that due process clauses of the Fifth and Fourteenth Amendments to the United States Constitution or their counterparts in the state constitutions require legislation to be fair and reasonable in content as well as application.

substantive law   That part of the law that creates rights and proscribes wrongs and regulates the rights and duties of persons.

substantive rules   Rules relating to the substance of matters, as distinct from procedural rules.

summary judgment   A judicial decision rendered in favor of a moving party without a formal trial where the court finds there is no genuine issue of material fact as to a claim or defense of the opposing party. Federal Rules of Civil Procedure and the procedural rules of most state courts provide for this practice.

sunshine laws   Federal and state statutes that require specified public agencies to open their meetings to the public.

supervisory power   The power of the Supreme Court to supervise the lower federal courts; similar power is usually vested in the highest court of a state.

supply-side economics   Theory that holds that a reduction in government taxation will stimulate the economy so that government revenue will eventually increase, thus reducing deficits.

suppression doctrine   See *exclusionary rule*.

supra   "Above."

Supremacy Clause   Provision of Article VI of the U.S. Constitution making that document, and all federal legislation consistent with it, the "supreme law of the land."

surplus   The condition that occurs when government revenues exceed government spending in a given fiscal year.

suspect classification doctrine The doctrine that laws classifying people according to race, ethnicity, and religion are inherently suspect and subjected to strict judicial scrutiny.

suspension and revocation of licenses and permits The act of a regulatory authority in temporarily or permanently denying a licensee or permittee the right to continue to act under a license or permit issued by a government agency.

sustain To uphold.

taking Refers to government action taking private property or depriving owner the use and control thereof.

Takings Clause Provision of the Fifth Amendment to the United States Constitution limiting power of eminent domain to public uses and requiring that owners be justly compensated for property taken.

tariff A tax charged on products imported into a country.

Tax Court A tribunal established by Congress in 1924 to resolve disputes between taxpayers and the Internal Revenue Service.

tax exemptions Rules under which certain organizations or individuals are not required to pay certain taxes.

tax fraud False or deceptive conduct performed with the intent of violating revenue laws, especially the Internal Revenue Code.

taxing power The power of government to levy taxes on incomes, property, imports, transactions, etc.

taxpayer suits Lawsuits brought by taxpayers to challenge certain government actions. Taxpayer suits as such are prohibited in the federal courts in that one does not acquire standing merely by virtue of paying taxes to support policies of which one does not approve.

technocracy Government by technical experts.

Tenth Amendment The amendment to the Constitution found in the Bill of Rights reserving to the states powers not delegated to the federal government.

testimony Evidence given by a witness who has sworn to tell the truth.

think tanks Organizations that employ policy specialists, scientists, and lawyers to perform research on various topics and propose policy changes.

Title IX Refers to Title IX of the Education Amendments of 1972, which prohibits discrimination based on sex in education programs or activities that receive federal funding.

Title VII Refers to Title VII of the Civil Rights Act of 1964 which, as amended, prohibits employment discrimination on the basis of race, color, religion, sex, or national origin.

tort A wrong or injury other than a breach of contract for which the remedy is a civil suit for damages.

transcript A written record of a trial or hearing.

treaty A legally binding agreement between one or more countries. In the United States, treaties are negotiated by the president but must be ratified by the Senate.

trespass An unlawful interference with one's person or property.

trial A judicial proceeding held for the purpose of making factual and legal determinations.

trial by jury A trial in which the verdict is determined not by the court but by a jury of the defendant's peers in a criminal case or of the parties' peers in a civil case.

trial courts Courts whose primary function is the conduct of civil and/or criminal trials.

trial *de novo* "A new trial." Refers to trial court review of convictions for minor offenses by courts of limited jurisdiction by conducting a new trial instead of merely reviewing the record of the initial trial.

trial-type hearing An administrative hearing conducted along the lines of a judicial hearing where the parties are accorded such due process rights as the right to be represented by counsel, the right of counsel to make opening statements and closing arguments, the right to cross-examine opposing witnesses and to challenge the admissibility of evidence.

trial-type procedures Procedures used in formal agency rulemaking and/or adjudication which resemble a civil trial in a court of law.

tribunal A court of law or other agency empowered to adjudicate cases.

trustee A person entrusted to handle the affairs of another.

Tucker Act An act, originally enacted by Congress in 1887, which today vests jurisdiction in the Court of Federal Claims to adjudicate claims against the United States founded on the U.S. Constitution, acts of Congress, regulations of an executive department, or based on an express or implied contract with the United States. This includes actions against the United States for "takings" of property; for example, when Government condemns someone's land.

U.S. Civil Service Commission Agency established in 1883 to administer the federal civil service. Abolished in 1979, its functions were assigned to the newly created Merit System Protection Board, the Office of Personnel Management, and the Federal Labor Relations Authority.

ultra vires Beyond the scope of a prescribed authority.

unemployment compensation A federal program administered by state agencies and funded through taxes on employers that provides temporary payments to unemployed workers.

unfunded mandates Programs or policies that the federal government requires, but does not fund.

Unfunded Mandates Reform Act. Enacted in 1995, this act prohibits Congress from considering legislation containing new unfunded mandates without a cost statement produced by the Congressional Budget Office. It also requires federal agencies to conduct a cost-benefit analysis before adopting new rules that mandate expenditures by state and local governments.

uniform codes A collection of laws designed to be uniformly adopted by the various states. The Uniform Commercial Code (UCC) is a classic example of a uniform code of laws.

United States Attorneys Attorneys appointed by the president with consent of the U.S. Senate to prosecute federal crimes in a specific geographical area of the United States.

United States Code The systematic collection of all federal statutes currently in effect.

United States Code Annotated (U.S.C.A.) The systematic collection of all federal statutes currently in effect, supplemented by annotations that refer to court decisions interpreting provisions of the Code.

United States Courts of Appeals The intermediate appellate courts of appeals in the federal system that sit in geographical areas of the United States and in which panels of appellate judges hear appeals in civil and criminal cases primarily from the U.S. District Courts.

United States District Court The principal trial courts in the federal system that sit in ninety-four districts where usually one judge hears proceedings and trials in civil and criminal cases.

United States Sentencing Commission A federal body that promulgates sentencing guidelines for defendants convicted of federal crimes.

United States Statutes at Large Organized chronologically, this is the official collection of statutes enacted by Congress since 1879.

United States Supreme Court The highest court in the United States consisting of nine justices that has jurisdiction to review, by appeal or writ of certiorari, the decisions of lower federal courts and many decisions of the highest courts of each state.

USA PATRIOT Act Controversial legislation enacted by Congress and promptly signed into law by the president shortly after the terrorist attacks of 9-11-2001. The act expands the government's power to engage in surveillance and electronic eavesdropping, provides the federal government with new powers to prohibit money laundering and detain and remove foreign terrorists from the United States. The act also creates new crimes and penalties, and authorizes new practices for use against terrorists.

variance Deviation granted by a Board of Adjustment where because of the applicability of the zoning code as to a particular parcel of land enforcement of zoning regulations would impose an undue hardship on the property owner.

venire The group of citizens from whom a jury is chosen in a given case.

venue The location of a trial or hearing.

vested rights Rights acquired by the passage of time.

veterans' preferences Refers to policies under which veterans of military service are given preferential treatment in employment, educational admissions, or other government programs.

veto The power of a chief executive to block adoption of a law by refusing to sign the legislation.

Voting Rights Act of 1965 Landmark federal legislation protecting voters from racial discrimination.

waiver The intentional and voluntary relinquishment of a right, or conduct from which such relinquishment may be inferred.

waiver of sovereign immunity An act by Congress or a state legislature allowing the government to be sued in certain instances for actions by government officials and employees.

warrant A court order authorizing a search, seizure, or arrest.

warrant requirement The Fourth Amendment's "preference" that searches be based on warrants issued by judges or magistrates.

warrantless administrative searches Reasonable searches of premises by government officials to determine compliance with health and safety regulations.

warrantless inspections See *warrantless administrative searches.*

warrantless searches Searches conducted by police or other officials acting without search warrants.

warranty deed A deed from a grantor conveying an interest in real property to the grantee with various covenants including the grantor's warranty to defend the title to the property conveyed.

Ways and Means Committee Powerful committee of the U.S. House of Representatives responsible for drafting legislation affecting taxes and other revenue measures.

welfare state A term used to describe the role of modern governments in creating programs to assure social welfare.

Westfall Act Another name for the Federal Employees Liability Reform and Tort Compensation Act of 1988, which allows the Attorney General to certify that a federal employee who is a defendant in a tort suit was acting within the scope of his office or employment at the time of the alleged tort and that the federal government should be substituted as defendant.

whistleblower An individual working for either the government or a company under government contract who exposes corruption, violations of the law, and/or environmental abuses within the organization.

white–collar crime Various criminal offenses committed by persons in the upper socioeconomic strata of society, often in the course of the occupation or profession of such persons.

World Trade Organization (WTO) An international organization established by treaty to enforce trade agreements among states.

writ A court order requiring or prohibiting the performance of some specific action.

writ of certiorari See *certiorari, writ of.*

writ of habeas corpus See *habeas corpus, writ of.*

writ of mandamus See *mandamus, writ of.*

writ of prohibition See *prohibition, writ of.*

zoning Local laws regulating the use of land.

Table of Cases

Index